DATE DUE

			PRINTED IN U.S.A.

Literature Criticism from 1400 to 1800

Guide to Gale Literary Criticism Series

For criticism on	Consult these Gale series
Authors now living or who died after December 31, 1959	*CONTEMPORARY LITERARY CRITICISM (CLC)*
Authors who died between 1900 and 1959	*TWENTIETH-CENTURY LITERARY CRITICISM (TCLC)*
Authors who died between 1800 and 1899	*NINETEENTH-CENTURY LITERATURE CRITICISM (NCLC)*
Authors who died between 1400 and 1799	*LITERATURE CRITICISM FROM 1400 TO 1800 (LC)* *SHAKESPEAREAN CRITICISM (SC)*
Authors who died before 1400	*CLASSICAL AND MEDIEVAL LITERATURE CRITICISM (CMLC)*
Black writers of the past two hundred years	*BLACK LITERATURE CRITICISM (BLC)*
Authors of books for children and young adults	*CHILDREN'S LITERATURE REVIEW (CLR)*
Dramatists	*DRAMA CRITICISM (DC)*
Hispanic writers of the late nineteenth and twentieth centuries	*HISPANIC LITERATURE CRITICISM (HLC)*
Native North American writers and orators of the eighteenth, nineteenth, and twentieth centuries	*NATIVE NORTH AMERICAN LITERATURE (NNAL)*
Poets	*POETRY CRITICISM (PC)*
Short story writers	*SHORT STORY CRITICISM (SSC)*
Major authors from the Renaissance to the present	*WORLD LITERATURE CRITICISM, 1500 TO THE PRESENT (WLC)*

ISSN 0740-2880

Volume 39

Literature Criticism from 1400 to 1800

Critical Discussion of the Works
of Fifteenth-, Sixteenth-, Seventeenth-, and
Eighteenth-Century Novelists, Poets, Playwrights,
Philosophers, and Other Creative Writers

Jelena O. Krstović, Editor

GALE

DETROIT · NEW YORK · TORONTO · LONDON

This book is printed on acid-free paper that meets the minimum requirements of American National Standard for Information Sciences—Permanence Paper for Printed Library Materials, ANSI Z39.48-1984.

Library of Congress Catalog Card Number 94-29718
ISBN 0-7876-1248-0
ISSN 0740-2880
Printed in the United States of America

10 9 8 7 6 5 4 3 2 1

Contents

Preface   vii

Acknowledgments   xi

Preface

*L*iterature Criticism from 1400 to 1800 (*LC*) presents critical discussion of world authors of the fifteenth through eighteenth centuries. The literature of this period reflects a turbulent time of radical change that saw the rise of modern European drama, the birth of the novel and personal essay forms, the emergence of newspapers and periodicals, and major achievements in poetry and philosophy. Many of these historical forces continue to influence modern art and society. *LC,* therefore, provides valuable insight into the art, life, thought, and cultural transformations that took place during these centuries.

Scope of the Series

LC provides an introduction to the great poets, dramatists, novelists, essayists, and philosophers of the fifteenth through eighteenth centuries, and to the most significant interpretations of these authors' works. Because criticism of this literature spans nearly six hundred years, an overwhelming amount of scholarship confronts the student. *LC* organizes this material into volumes addressing specific historical and cultural topics, for example, "Literature of the Spanish Golden Age," or "Literature and the New World." Every attempt is made to reprint the most noteworthy, relevant, and educationally valuable essays available.

Readers should note that there is a separate Gale reference series devoted exclusively to Shakespearean studies. Although belonging properly to the period covered in *LC,* William Shakespeare has inspired such a tremendous and ever-growing corpus of secondary material that the editors have deemed it best to give his works extensive coverage in a separate series, *Shakespearean Criticism*.

Each author entry in *LC* presents a survey of critical response to a topic or an author's oeuvre. Early criticism is offered to indicate initial responses, later selections document any rise or decline in literary reputations, and retrospective analyses provide students with modern views. The size of each author entry is a relative reflection of the scope of criticism available in English. Every attempt has been made to identify and include the seminal essays on each author's work and to include recent commentary providing modern perspectives.

The need for *LC* among students and teachers of literature and history was suggested by the proven usefulness of Gale's *Contemporary Literary Criticism (CLC), Twentieth-Century Literary Criticism (TCLC),* and *Nineteenth-Century Literature Criticism (NCLC),* which excerpt criticism of works by nineteenth- and twentieth-century authors. There is no duplication of critical material in any of these literary criticism series. Major authors may appear more than once in one or more of the series because of the great quantity of critical material available and because of their relevance to a variety of thematic topics.

Thematic Approach

Beginning with Volume 12, the authors in each volume of *LC* are organized around such themes as specific literary or philosophical movements, writings surrounding important political and historical events, the philosophy and art associated with eras of cultural transformation, and the literature of specific social or ethnic groups. Each volume contains a topic entry providing a historical and literary overview, and several author entries which examine major representatives of the featured period.

Organization of the Book

Each entry consists of the following elements: author or thematic heading, introduction, list of principal works, annotated works of criticism (each preceded by a bibliographical citation), and a bibliography of further reading. Also, most author entries contain author portraits and other illustrations.

- The **Author Heading** consists of the author's name (the most commonly used form), followed by birth and death dates. (If an author wrote consistently under a pseudonym, the pseudonym is used in the author heading, with the real name given in parentheses on the first line of the biographical and critical introduction.) Also located here are any name variations under which an author wrote, including transliterated forms for authors whose native languages use nonroman alphabets. Uncertain birth or death dates are indicated by question marks. Topic entries are preceded by a **Thematic Heading,** which simply states the subject of the entry.

- The **Biographical and Critical Introduction** contains background information that concisely introduces the reader to the author or topic.

- Most *LC* author entries include **Portraits** of the author. Many entries also contain illustrations of materials pertinent to an author's career, including author holographs, title pages, letters, or representations of important people, places, and events in an author's life.

- The **List of Principal Works** is ordered chronologically, by date of first book publication, identifying the genre of each work. In the case of foreign authors whose works have been translated into English, the title and date (if available) of the first English-language edition are given in brackets following the foreign-language listing. Unless otherwise indicated, dramas are dated by first performance, not first publication.

- **Criticism** is arranged chronologically in each author entry to provide a useful perspective on changes in critical evaluation over time. For the purpose of easy identification, the critic's name and the date of first composition or publication of the critical work are given at the beginning of each piece of criticism. Unsigned criticism is preceded by the title of the source in which it appeared. All titles by the author featured in the critical entry are printed in boldface type. Publication information (such as publisher names and book prices) and some parenthetical numerical references (such as footnotes or page and line references to specific editions of works) have been occasionally deleted to provide smoother reading of the text. Footnotes that appear with previously published pieces of criticism are reprinted at the end of each essay or excerpt. In the case of excerpted criticism, only those footnotes that pertain to the excerpted text are included.

- Critical essays are prefaced by **Annotations** as an additional aid to students using *LC*. These explanatory notes provide information such as the importance of a work of criticism, the commentator's individual approach to literary criticism, and a brief summary of the reprinted essay. In some cases, these notes cross-reference the work of critics within the entry who agree or disagree with each other.

- A complete **Bibliographical Citation** of the original essay or book precedes each piece of criticism.

- An annotated bibliography of **Further Reading** appears at the end of each entry and suggests resources for additional study. In some cases, significant essays for which the editors could not obtain reprint rights are included here.

Cumulative Indexes

Each volume of *LC* includes a cumulative **Author Index** listing all the authors that have appeared in the following sources published by Gale: *Contemporary Literary Criticism, Twentieth-Century Literary Criticism, Nineteenth-Century Literature Criticism, Literature Criticism from 1400 to 1800,* and *Classical and Medieval Literature Criticism,* along with cross-references to the Gale series *Short Story Criticism, Poetry Criticism, Children's Literature Review, Authors in the News, Contemporary Authors, Contemporary Authors Autobiography Series, Contemporary Authors Bibliographical Series, Dictionary of Literary Biography, Concise Dictionary of Literary Biography, Something about the Author, Something about the Author Autobiography Series,* and *Yesterday's Authors of Books for Children.* Readers will welcome this cumulative author index as a useful tool for locating an author within the various series. The index, which includes authors' birth and death dates, is particularly valuable for those authors who are identified with a certain period but whose death dates cause them to be placed in another, or for those authors whose careers span two periods. For example, F. Scott Fitzgerald is found in *TCLC,* yet a writer often associated with him, Ernest Hemingway, is found in *CLC.*

Beginning with Volume 12, *LC* includes a cumulative **Topic Index** that lists all literary themes and topics treated in *LC, NCLC, TCLC,* and the *CLC* Yearbook. Each volume of *LC* also includes a cumulative **Nationality Index** in which authors' names are arranged alphabetically under their respective nationalities and followed by the numbers of the volumes in which they appear.

Each volume of *LC* also includes a cumulative **Title Index,** an alphabetical listing of all literary works discussed in the series. Each title listing includes the corresponding volume and page numbers where criticism may be located. Foreign-language titles that have been translated followed by the tiles of the translation—for example, *El ingenioso hidalgo Don Quixote de la Mancha (Don Quixote).* Page numbers following these translated titles refer to all pages on which any form of the titles, either foreign-language or translated, appear. Titles of novels, dramas, nonfiction books, and poetry, short story, or essays collections are printed in italics, while individual poems, short stories, and essays are printed in roman type within quotation marks.

A Note to the Reader

When writing papers, students who quote directly from any volume in the Literary Criticism Series may use the following general format to footnote reprinted criticism. The first example pertains to material drawn from periodicals, the second to material reprinted from books.

T. S. Eliot, "John Donne," *The Nation and the Athenaeum,* 33 (9 June 1923), 321-32; excerpted and reprinted in *Literature Criticism from 1400 to 1800,* Vol. 10, ed. James E. Person, Jr. (Detroit:

Gale Research, 1989), pp. 28-9.

Clara G. Stillman, *Samuel Butler: A Mid-Victorian Modern* (Viking Press, 1932); excerpted and reprinted in *Twentieth-Century Literary Criticism,* Vol. 33, ed. Paula Kepos (Detroit: Gale Research, 1989), pp. 43-5.

Suggestions Are Welcome

Since the series began, features have been added to *LC* in response to various suggestions, including a nationality index, a Literary Criticism Series topic index, and thematic organization of entries.

Readers who wish to suggest new features, themes or authors to appear in future volumes, or who have other suggestions or comments are cordially invited to write to the editor (fax: 313 961-6599).

Acknowledgments

The editors wish to thank the copyright holders of the excerpted criticism included in this volume and the permissions managers of many book and magazine publishing companies for assisting us in securing reproduction rights. We are also grateful to the staffs of the Detroit Public Library, the Library of Congress, the University of Detroit Mercy Library, Wayne State University Purdy/Kresge Library Complex, and the University of Michigan Libraries for making their resources available to us. Following is a list of the copyright holders who have granted us permission to reproduce material in this volume of *LC*. Every effort has been made to trace copyright, but if omissions have been made, please let us know.

COPYRIGHTED EXCERPTS IN *LC*, VOLUME 39, WERE REPRODUCED FROM THE FOLLOWING PERIODICALS:

A Review of English Literature, v.1, Reproduced by permission of the publisher.--*Bibliotheque D'Humanisme et Renaissance*, v. XXVI, 1964. Reproduced by permission.--*ELH*, v. 63, Fall, 1996 for "A Woman's Touch: Astrophil, Stella and 'Queen Vertue's Court,'" by Sally Minogue. Copyright (c) 1996 by The Johns Hopkins University Press. Reproduced by permission.--*English Literary Renaissance*, v. 17, Spring, 1987. Reproduced by permission.--*Renaissance Quarterly*, v. XLIII, Spring, 1990. Reproduced by permission.--*Studies in English Literature*, 1500-1900, v. 27,Winter, 1987. Copyright (c) 1987 William Marsh Rice University. Reproduced by permission of SEL Studies in English Literatrure 1500-1900 and the author.--*Studies in the Renaissance*, v. 5,1989. Reproduced by permission.--*The Yearbook of English Studies*: Colonial Imperial Themes Special Number, v. 13, 1983. Reproduced by permission.

COPYRIGHTED EXCERPTS IN LC, VOLUME 39, WERE REPRODUCED FROM THE FOLLOWING BOOKS:

Anderson, Judith. From "In liuing colours and right hew: The Queen of Spenser's Central Books" in *Poetic Traditions of the English Renaissance*. Edited by Maynard Mack and George DeForest Lord. Yale University Press. (c) 1982 by Yale University. All rights reserved. Reproduced by permission.--Brooke, Tucker. From *Essays on Shakespeare and Other Elizabethans*. Yale University Press, 1948. Copyright (c) 1948 by Yale University Press. All rights reserved. Reproduced by permission.--Cain, Thomas H. From *Praise in "The Faerie Queene."* University of Nebraska Press, 1978. Copyright (c) 1978 by the University of Nebraska Press. All rights reserved. Reproduced by permission.--Fienberg, Nona. From *Elizabeth, Her Poets, and the Creation of the Courtly Manner: A Study of Sir John Harrington, Sir Philip Sidney, and John Lyly*. Garland Publishing, Inc., 1988. Copyright (c) 1988 by Nona Fienberg. All rights reserved. Reproduced by permission.--Fisken, Beth Wynne. From *Silent But for the Word: Tudor Women as Patrons, Translators, and Writers of Religious Works*. Edited by Margaret Patterson Hannay. Copyright (c) 1985 by The Kent State University Press. All rights reserved. Reproduced by permission.--Fisken, Beth Wynne. From *The Renaissance Englishwoman in Print: Counterbalancing the Canon*. Edited by Anne M. Haselkorn and Betty S. Travitsky. The University of Massachusetts Press, 1990. Copyright (c) 1990 by The University of Massachusetts Press. All rights reserved. Reproduced by permission.--Greenblatt, Stephen J. From *Sir Walter Raleigh: The Renaissance Man and His Roles*. Yale University Press, 1973. Copyright (c) 1973 by Yale University Press. All rights reserved. Reproduced by permission of the author.--Hager, Alan. From *Dazzling Images: The Masks of Sir Philip Sidney*. Associated University Presses, 1991. Copyright (c) 1991 by Associated University Presses, Inc. All rights reserved. Reproduced by permission.--Hamilton, A. C. From *Sir Philip Sidney: A Study of His Life and Works*. Cambridge University Press, 1977. Copyright (c) 1977 by Cambridge University Press. Reproduced by permission of the publisher and the author.--Hammond, Gerald. From *Sir Walter Ralegh: Selected Writings*. Carcanet Press, 1984. Copyright (c) 1984 by Gerald Hammond .Reproduced by permission.--Hardison, Jr., O. B. From *The Enduring Monument: A Study of the Idea of Praise in Renaissance Literary Theory and Practice*. The University of North Carolina Press, 1962. Copyright (c) 1962, 1990 by The University of North Carolina Press. Reproduced by permission.--Herman, Peter C. From *Squitter-Wits and Muse-Haters*. Wayne State University Press, 1996. Copyright (c) 1996 by Wayne State

Age of Spenser

INTRODUCTION

The Age of Spenser in English literature refers to the latter half of the sixteenth century, a period that coincided with the reign of the last Tudor monarch Queen Elizabeth I, who brilliantly bound the destiny of England to the cause of her own success. Thus, a primary object of sixteenth-century English Renaissance writers—whose livelihood depended heavily upon literary patronage and the Court's favor—was the creation of a national literature befitting England's emerging status as a formidable world power and the implicit, and often explicit, celebration of the Queen herself. Considered the golden age of English history, Elizabeth's reign was an era of increased religious tolerance and relative peace until the war with Spain and the defeat of the Spanish Armada in 1588. During Elizabeth's tenure treasury coffers were replenished, shipping, trade, and commerce proliferated, and new roads were built that helped unify and connect the English population. Parliament also passed many reform laws touching currency, aid to the poor, agriculture, and industry. It was only in the last decade of Elizabeth's reign that England's fortunes soured and the country was again vexed by debt and increased internal strife. Yet her rule was primarily a time of peace, national unity, and affluence. This prosperity, coupled with Elizabeth's fervent patronage of the arts, nurtured the English Renaissance which peaked during her era. Virtually all fields flourished, including music, architecture, and painting, but especially literature, where important works appeared in the genres of drama, poetry, and prose. The latter included ecclesiastical tracts such as Richard Hooker's *Laws of Ecclesiastical Polity* (1593-97), literary criticism including Sir Philip Sidney's seminal treatise *The Defence of Poesie* (1595), and travel narratives by Sir Walter Raleigh, Richard Hakluyt, and others. Hakluyt's *Principal Navigations, Traffics, Voyages and Discoveries of the English Nation* (1589) both reflected and encouraged the English fascination with geography, exploration, and empire building.

The courts of Europe, with the Tudors being no exception, depended heavily upon the writings of others to serve as apologists and propagandists to shore up popular support. Those who wrote encomia to a ruler were frequently rewarded with land grants, franchises, and positions of influence within the court as rewards for their tributes and service. Elizabeth pru-

dently availed herself of this system. She had ascended the throne in 1558 upon the death of her half-sister, Mary, and ruled until her own death in 1603. Although she, too, was the daughter of Henry VIII, Mary had been raised in the staunch Catholic faith of her mother, Catherine of Aragon, and in her brief five-year reign had sought to undo her father's break from Rome and reestablish Catholicism as the official state religion. The daughter of Henry VIII and Anne Boleyn, Elizabeth had been raised a Protestant and, upon her ascension to the throne by an act of Parliament, she sought to reassert the primacy of the Church of England and establish her sovereignty over Rome. Her judicious course of pursuing a moderate form of Protestantism ameliorated religious strife and enabled her to surmount challenges from both dispossessed Catholics who never accepted the Anglican Church and from Puritans who felt her Protestant reforms too tepid. Without the security of a standing army to put down rebellions, Elizabeth relied upon her own formidable yet charming personality as a fortification against dissent. A gifted orator and poet in her own right, she was an active agent in creating a persona that garnered the loyal adulation of her subjects, inspiring cult-like worship even though she governed in a world where an illegitimate female monarch was normally an anathema.

No longer dominated by the vestiges of either Rome or feudal institutions, English writers in the Age of Spenser turned to classical humanism, modeling much of their work upon the poets and dramatists of Greek and Roman antiquity, especially Homer and Virgil. Sir Philip Sidney, a scholar, soldier and poet served as a premier literary patron, having championed Edmund Spenser's career from its beginning. While the English Renaissance yielded many notable poets, Spenser is considered the greatest and his reputation has endured. His contemporaries also regarded Spenser as the leading poet of his day. Spenser completed most of his writing in Ireland, where he held several political appointments in Cork. Spenser's genius was immediately heralded with the publication of *A Shepheardes Calender* (1579), a work comprised of twelve poems, one for each month of the year. But it is Spenser's *The Faerie Queene* (1590-96), a pastoral epic, that is his most famous work. Though Spenser originally intended *The Faerie Queene* to be composed of twelve eclogues, he published only six books before his death. Each of the six eclogues is an allegorical representation of the quest of an individual knight to achieve specific virtues such as charity, bravery, or chastity. Spenser composed *The Faerie Queene* in honor of Elizabeth I; Gloriana, Queen of Fairyland, represents Elizabeth Tudor in his poem. The nine-line stanza Spenser invented in the poem has become one of his enduring hallmarks and was soon employed by other poets. Although Elizabeth I did grant him a royal pension of fifty pounds a year after the publication of *The Faerie Queene*, she remained somewhat cool to Spenser. Some critics have suggested that his work may have been too subtle to have had the clear propaganda value the Queen desired. Other notable English Renaissance poetical achievements include Samuel Daniel's *Delia* (1592) and Michael Drayton's *Idea* (1593).

Perhaps even more than by poetry, the last decades of the sixteenth century are characterized by an abundance of superior literature produced by playwrights. Christopher Marlowe, whose works include *Tamburlaine the Great* (1587), *The Tragical History of Doctor Faustus* (c.1588), and *The Jew of Malta* (c. 1589), ranks as a preeminent dramatic genius and is credited with originating the blank verse meter later brilliantly employed by William Shakespeare. Shakespeare's plays, the centerpiece of this period in England, reflect the Renaissance preoccupation with both the potential and frailties of humankind. Another exemplary dramatist of the age is Ben Jonson, who modeled his work primarily upon Greek drama. Jonson's most important plays, however, were not published until after Elizabeth's death. Other notable English Renaissance plays include Thomas Kyd's *The Spanish Tragedy* (produced between 1584 and 1589) and John Lyly's *Euphues, the Anatomy of Wit* (1579). During the Age of Spenser the popular interest in drama increased significantly and by 1600 there were at least eight playhouses operating in London alone—the first permanent playhouses in western history.

The Age of Spenser remains an area of vital research and interest for modern literary critics. Recent scholarship of the era continues to examine how the literary patronage system created the abundance of writing that constitutes the English Renaissance. Much new feminist literary criticism focuses on iconography of Elizabeth I and the general treatment of women in Renaissance literary texts. Still other scholars study the contribution of literature during this period to the growth and development of English national identity as well as its role in supporting the notion of colonialism.

OVERVIEWS

H. A. Taine (essay date 1889)

SOURCE: "Book II: The Renaissance—The Pagan Renaissance," in *History of English Literature*, Henry Holt and Company, 1889, pp. 227-49.

[*Below, Taine attributes the flourishing of Renaissance thought and art in England to English peace and prosperity, the demise of feudalism, and the release from the domination of the Catholic Church. Taine argues that the spirit of cultural renewal pervaded all social strata and fostered artistic and literary interest in Greek and Roman culture.*]

For seventeen centuries a deep and sad thought had weighed upon the spirit of man, first to overwhelm it, then to exalt and to weaken it, never loosing its hold throughout this long space of time. It was the idea of the weakness and decay of the human race. Greek corruption, Roman oppression, and the dissolution of the ancient world, had given rise to it; it, in its turn, had produced a stoical resignation, an epicurean indifference, Alexandrian mysticism, and the Christian hope in the kingdom of God. "The world is evil and lost, let us escape by insensibility, amazement, ecstasy." Thus spoke the philosophers; and religion, coming after, announced that the end was near; "Prepare, for the kingdom of God is at hand." For a thousand years universal ruin incessantly drove still deeper into their hearts this gloomy thought; and when man in the feudal state raised himself, by sheer force of courage and muscles, from the depths of final imbecility and general misery, he discovered his thought and his work fettered by the crushing idea, which, forbidding a life of nature and worldly hopes, erected into ideals the obedience of the monk and the dreams of fanatics.

It grew ever worse and worse. For the natural result of such a conception, as of the miseries which engender it, and the discouragement which it gives rise to, is to do away with personal action, and to replace originality by submission. From the fourth century, gradually the dead letter was substituted for the living faith. Christians resigned themselves into the hands of the clergy, they into the hands of the Pope. Christian opinions were subordinated to theologians, and theologians to the Fathers. Christian faith was reduced to the accomplishment of works, and works to the accomplishment of ceremonies. Religion, fluid during the first centuries, was now congealed into a hard crystal, and the coarse contact of the barbarians had deposited upon its surface a layer of idolatry: theocracy and the Inquisition, the monopoly of the clergy and the prohibition of the Scriptures, the worship of relics and the sale of indulgences began to appear. In place of Christianity, the church; in place of a free creed, enforced orthodoxy; in place of moral fervour, fixed religious practices; in place of the heart and stirring thought, outward and mechanical discipline: such are the characteristics of the middle ages. Under this constraint thinking society had ceased to think; philosophy was turned into a text-book, and poetry into dotage; and mankind, slothful and crouching, delivering up their conscience and their conduct into the hands of their priests, seemed but as puppets, fit only for reciting a catechism and mumbling over beads. (See, at Bruges, the pictures of Hemling [fifteenth century]. No paintings enable us to understand so well the ecclesiastical piety of the middle-age, which was altogether like that of the Buddhists.)

At last invention makes another start; and it makes it by the efforts of the lay society, which rejected theocracy, kept the State free, and which presently discovered, or re-discovered, one after another, the industries, sciences, and arts. All was renewed; America and the Indies were added to the map of the world; the shape of the earth was ascertained, the system of the universe propounded, modern philology was inaugurated, the experimental sciences set on foot, art and literature shot forth like a harvest, religion was transformed: there was no province of human intelligence and action which was not refreshed and fertilised by this universal effort. It was so great, that it passed from the innovators to the laggards, and reformed Catholicism in the face of Protestantism which it formed. It seems as though men had suddenly opened their eyes and seen. In fact, they attain a new and superior kind of intelligence. It is the proper feature of this age, that men no longer make themselves masters of objects by bits, or isolated, or through scholastic or mechanical classifications, but as a whole, in general and complete views, with the eager grasp of a sympathetic spirit, which being placed before a vast object, penetrates it in all its parts, tries it in all its relations, appropriates and assimilates it, impresses upon itself its living and potent image, so life-like and so powerful, that it is fain to translate it into externals through a work of art or an action. An extraordinary warmth of soul, a superabundant and splendid imagination, reveries, visions, artists, believers, founders, creators,—that is what such a form of intellect produces; for to create we must have, as had Luther and Loyola, Michel Angelo and Shakspeare, an idea, not abstract, partial, and dry, but well defined, finished, sensible,—a true creation, which acts inwardly, and struggles to appear to the light. This was Europe's grand age, and the most notable epoch of human growth. To this day we live from its sap, we only carry on its pressure and efforts.

When human power is manifested so clearly and in such great works, it is no wonder if the ideal changes, and the old pagan idea reappears. It recurs, bringing with it the worship of beauty and vigour, first in Italy; for this, of all countries in Europe, is the most pagan, and the nearest to the ancient civilisation; thence in France and Spain, and Flanders,[1] and even in Germany; and finally in England. How is it propagated? What revolution of manners reunited mankind at this time, everywhere, under a sentiment which they had forgot-

ten for fifteen hundred years? Merely that their condition had improved, and they felt it. The idea ever expresses the actual situation, and the creatures of the imagination, like the conceptions of the mind, only manifest the state of society and the degree of its welfare; there is a fixed connection between what man admires and what he is. While misery overwhelms him, while the decadence is visible, and hope shut out, he is inclined to curse his life on earth, and seek consolation in another sphere. As soon as his sufferings are alleviated, his power made manifest, his prospects brightened, he begins once more to love the present life, to be self-confident, to love and praise energy, genius, all the effective faculties which labour to procure him happiness. About the twentieth year of Elizabeth's reign, the nobles gave up shield and two-handed sword for the rapier;[2] a little, almost imperceptible fact, yet vast, for it is like the change which sixty years ago, made us give up the sword at court, to leave us with our arms swinging about in our black coats. In fact, it was the close of feudal life, and the beginning of court-life, just as to-day court-life is at an end, and the democratic reign has begun. With the two-handed swords, heavy coats of mail, feudal keeps, private warfare, permanent disorder, all the scourges of the middle-age retired, and faded into the past. The English had done with the Wars of the Roses. They no longer ran the risk of being pillaged to-morrow for being rich, and hung the next day for being traitors; they have no further need to furbish up their armour, make alliances with powerful nations, lay in stores for the winter, gather together men-at-arms, scour the country to plunder and hang others.[3] The monarchy, in England as throughout Europe, establishes peace in the community,[4] and with peace appear the useful arts. Domestic comfort follows civil security; and man, better furnished in his home, better protected in his hamlet, takes pleasure in his life on earth, which he has changed and means to change.

Toward the close of the fifteenth century[5] the impetus was given; commerce and the woollen trade made a sudden advance, and such an enormous one that cornfields were changed into pasture-lands, "whereby the inhabitants of the said town (Manchester) have gotten and come into riches and wealthy livings,"[6] so that in 1553, 40,000 pieces of cloth were exported in English ships. It was already the England which we see to-day, a land of green meadows, intersected by hedgerows, crowded with cattle, and abounding in ships— a manufacturing opulent land, with a people of beef-eating toilers, who enrich it while they enrich themselves. They improved agriculture to such an extent, that in half-a-century the produce of an acre was doubled.[7] They grew so rich, that at the beginning of the reign of Charles I the Commons represented three times the wealth of the Upper House. The ruin of Antwerp by the Duke of Parma[8] sent to England "the third part of the merchants and manufacturers, who made silk, damask, stockings, taffetas, and serges." The defeat of the Armada and the decadence of Spain opened the seas to English merchants.[9] The toiling hive, who would dare, attempt, explore, act in unison, and always with profit, was about to reap its advantages and set out on its voyages, buzzing over the universe.

At the base and on the summit of society, in all ranks of life, in all grades of human condition, this new welfare became visible. In 1534, considering that the streets of London were "very noyous and foul, and in many places thereof very jeopardous to all people passing and repassing, as well on horseback as on foot," Henry VIII. began the paving of the city. New streets covered the open spaces where the young men used to run races and to wrestle. Every year the number of taverns, theatres, gambling rooms, bear-gardens, increased. Before the time of Elizabeth the country-houses of gentlemen were little more than straw-thatched cottages, plastered with the coarsest clay, lighted only by trellises. "Howbeit," says Harrison (1580), "such as be latelie builded are commonlie either of bricke or hard stone, or both; their roomes large and comelie, and houses of office further distant from their lodgings." The old wooden houses were covered with plaster, "which, beside the delectable whitenesse of the stuffe itselfe, is laied on so even and smoothlie, as nothing in my judgment can be done with more exactnesse."[10] This open admiration shows from what hovels they had escaped. Glass was at last employed for windows, and the bare walls were covered with hangings, on which visitors might see, with delight and astonishment, plants, animals, figures. They began to use stoves, and experienced the unwonted pleasure of being warm. Harrison notes three important changes which had taken place in the farmhouses of his time:

> "One is, the multitude of chimnies lately erected, whereas in their yoong daies there were not above two or three, if so manie, in most uplandishe townes of the realme. . . . The second is the great (although not generall), amendment of lodging, for our fathers (yea and we ourselves also) have lien full oft upon straw pallets, on rough mats covered onelie with a sheet, under coverlets made of dagswain, or hop-harlots, and a good round log under their heads, instead of a bolster or pillow. If it were so that the good man of the house, had within seven yeares after his marriage purchased a matteres or flockebed, and thereto a sacke of chaffe to rest his head upon, he thought himselfe to be as well lodged as the lord of the towne. . . . Pillowes (said they) were thought meet onelie for women in childbed. . . . The third thing is the exchange of vessell, as of treene platters into pewter, and wodden spoones into silver or tin; for so common was all sorts of treene stuff in old time, that a man should hardlie find four peeces of pewter (of which one was peradventure a salt) in a good farmers house."[11]

It is not possession, but acquisition, which gives men pleasure and sense of power; they observe sooner a small happiness, new to them, than a great happiness which is old. It is not when all is good, but when all is better, that they see the bright side of life, and are tempted to make a holiday of it. This is why at this period they did make a holiday of it, a splendid show, so like a picture that it fostered painting in Italy, so like a piece of acting, that it produced the drama in England. Now that the axe and sword of the civil wars had beaten down the independent nobility, and the abolition of the law of maintenance had destroyed the petty royalty of each great feudal baron, the lords quitted their sombre castles, battlemented fortresses, surrounded by stagnant water, pierced with narrow windows, a sort of stone breastplates of no use but to preserve the life of their master. They flock into new palaces, with vaulted roofs and turrets, covered with fantastic and manifold ornaments, adorned with terraces and vast staircases, with gardens, fountains, statues, such as were the palaces of Henry VIII. and Elizabeth, half Gothic and half Italian,[12] whose convenience, splendour, and symmetry announced already habits of society and the taste for pleasure. They came to court and abandoned their old manners; the four meals which scarcely sufficed their former voracity were reduced to two; gentlemen soon became refined, placing their glory in the elegance and singularity of their amusements and their clothes. They dressed magnificently in splendid materials, with the luxury of men who rustle silk and make gold sparkle for the first time: doublets of scarlet satin; cloaks of sable, costing a thousand ducats; velvet shoes, embroidered with gold and silver, covered with rosettes and ribbons; boots with falling tops, from whence hung a cloud of lace, embroidered with figures of birds, animals, constellations, flowers in silver, gold, or precious stones; ornamented shirts costing ten pounds a piece. "It is a common thing to put a thousand goats and a hundred oxen on a coat, and to carry a whole manor on one's back."[13] The costumes of the time were like shrines. When Elizabeth died, they found three thousand dresses in her wardrobe. Need we speak of the monstrous ruffs of the ladies, their puffed out dresses, their stomachers stiff with diamonds? As a singular sign of the times, the men were more changeable and more bedecked than they. Harrison says:

> Such is our mutabilitie, that to daie there is none to the Spanish guise, to morrow the French toies are most fine and delectable, yer long no such apparell as that which is after the high Alman fashion, by and by the Turkish maner is generallie best liked of, otherwise the Morisco gowns, the Barbarian sleeves . . . and the short French breeches. . . . And as these fashions are diverse, so likewise it is a world to see the costlinesse and the curiositie; the excesse and the vanitie; the pompe and the braverie; the change and the varietie; and finallie, the ficklenesse and the follie that is in all degrees.[14]

Folly, it may have been, but poetry likewise. There was something more than puppyism in this masquerade of splendid costume. The overflow of inner sentiment found this issue, as also in drama and poetry. It was an artistic spirit which induced it. There was an incredible outgrowth of living forms from their brains. They acted like their engravers, who give us in their frontispieces a prodigality of fruits, flowers, active figures, animals, gods, and pour out and confuse the whole treasure of nature in every corner of their paper. They must enjoy the beautiful; they would be happy through their eyes; they perceive in consequence naturally the relief and energy of forms. From the accession of Henry VIII. to the death of James I. we find nothing but tournaments, processions, public entries, masquerades. First come the royal banquets, coronation displays, large and noisy pleasures of Henry VIII. Wolsey entertains him

> In so gorgeous a sort and costlie maner, that it was an heaven to behold. There wanted no dames or damosels meet or apt to danse with the maskers, or to garnish the place for the time: then was there all kind of musike and harmonie, with fine voices both of men and children. On a time the king came suddenlie thither in a maske with a dozen maskers all in garments like sheepheards, made of fine cloth of gold, and crimosin sattin paned, . . . having sixteene torch-bearers. . . . In came a new banket before the king wherein were served two hundred diverse dishes, of costlie devises and subtilities. Thus passed they foorth the night with banketting, dansing, and other triumphs, to the great comfort of the king, and pleasant regard of the nobilitie there assembled.[15]

Count, if you can, the mythological entertainments, the theatrical receptions, the open-air operas played before Elizabeth, James, and their great lords.[16] At Kenilworth the pageants lasted ten days. There was everything; learned recreations, novelties, popular plays, sanguinary spectacles, coarse farces, juggling and feats of skill, allegories, mythologies, chivalric exhibitions, rustic and national commemorations. At the same time, in this universal outburst and sudden expanse, men become interested in themselves, find their life desirable, worthy of being represented and put on the stage complete; they play with it, delight in looking upon it, love its ups and downs, and make of it a work of art. The queen is received by a sibyl, then by giants of the time of Arthur, then by the Lady of the Lake, Sylvanus, Pomona, Ceres, and Bacchus, every divinity in turn presents her with the first fruits of his empire. Next day, a savage, dressed in moss and ivy, discourses before her with Echo in her praise. Thirteen bears are set fighting against dogs. An Italian acrobat performs wonderful feats before the whole assembly. A rustic marriage takes place before the queen, then a sort of comic fight amongst the peasants of Coventry, who represent the defeat of the Danes. As she is

returning from the chase, Triton, rising from the lake, prays her, in the name of Neptune, to deliver the enchanted lady, pursued by a cruel knight, *Syr Bruse sauns Pitee*. Presently the lady appears, surrounded by nymphs, followed close by Proteus, who is borne by an enormous dolphin. Concealed in the dolphin, a band of musicians with a chorus of ocean-deities, sing the praise of the powerful, beautiful, chaste queen of England.[17] You perceive that comedy is not confined to the theatre; the great of the realm and the queen herself become actors. The cravings of the imagination are so keen, that the court becomes a stage. Under James I., every year, on Twelfth-day, the queen, the chief ladies and nobles, played a piece called a Masque, a sort of allegory combined with dances, heightened in effect by decorations and costumes of great splendour, of which the mythological paintings of Rubens can alone give an idea:—

> The attire of the lords was from the antique Greek statues. On their heads they wore Persic crowns, that were with scrolls of gold plate turned outward, and wreathed about with a carnation and silver net-lawn. Their bodies were of carnation cloth of silver; to express the naked, in manner of the Greek thorax, girt under the breasts with a broad belt of cloth of gold, fastened with jewels; the mantles were of coloured silke; the first, sky-colour; the second, pearl-colour; the third, flame colour; the fourth, tawny. The ladies attire was of white cloth of silver, wrought with Juno's birds and fruits; a loose under garment, full gathered, of carnation, striped with silver, and parted with a golden zone; beneath that, another flowing garment, of watchet cloth of silver, laced with gold; their hair carelessly bound under the circle of a rare and rich coronet, adorned with all variety, and choice of jewels; from the top of which flowed a transparent veil, down to the ground. Their shoes were azure and gold, set with rubies and diamonds.[18]

I abridge the description, which is like a fairy tale. Fancy that all these costumes, this glitter of materials, this sparkling of diamonds, this splendour of nudities, was displayed daily at the marriage of the great, to the bold sounds of a pagan epithalamium. Think of the feasts which the Earl of Carlisle introduced, where was served first of all a table loaded with sumptuous viands, as high as a man could reach, in order to remove it presently, and replace it by another similar table. This prodigality of magnificence, these costly follies, this unbridling of the imagination, this intoxication of eye and ear, this comedy played by the lords of the realm, showed, like the pictures of Rubens, Jordaens, and their Flemish contemporaries, so open an appeal to the senses, so complete a return to nature, that our chilled and gloomy age is scarcely able to imagine it.[19]

To vent the feelings, to satisfy the heart and eyes, to set free boldly on all the roads of existence the pack of appetites and instincts, this was the craving which the manners of the time betrayed. It was "merry England," as they called it then. It was not yet stern and constrained. It expanded widely, freely, and rejoiced to find itself so expanded. No longer at court only was the drama found, but in the village. Strolling companies betook themselves thither, and the country folk supplied any deficiencies, when necessary. Shakspeare saw, before he depicted them, stupid fellows, carpenters, joiners, bellows-menders, play Pyramus and Thisbe, represent the lion roaring as gently as any sucking dove, and the wall, by stretching out their hands. Every holiday was a pageant, in which townspeople, workmen, and children bore their parts. They were actors by nature. When the soul is full and fresh, it does not express its ideas by reasonings; it plays and figures them; it mimics them; that is the true and original language, the children's tongue, the speech of artists, of invention, and of joy. It is in this manner they please themselves with songs and feasting, on all the symbolic holidays with which tradition has filled the year.[20] On the Sunday after Twelfth-night the labourers parade the streets, with their shirts over their coats, decked with ribbons, dragging a plough to the sound of music, and dancing a sword-dance; on another day they draw in a cart a figure made of ears of corn, with songs, flutes, and drums; on another, Father Christmas and his company; or else they enact the history of Robin Hood, the bold archer, around the May-pole, or the legend of Saint George and the Dragon. We might occupy half a volume in describing all these holidays, such as Harvest Home. All Saints, Martinmas, Sheepshearing, above all Christmas, which lasted twelve days, and sometimes six weeks. They eat and drink, junket, tumble about, kiss the girls, ring the bells, satiate themselves with noise: coarse drunken revels, in which man is an unbridled animal, and which are the incarnation of natural life. The Puritans made no mistake about that. Stubbes says:

> First, all the wilde heades of the parishe, conventing together, chuse them a ground capitaine of mischeef, whan they innoble with the title of my Lorde of Misserule, and hym they crown with great solemnitie, and adopt for their kyng. This kyng anoynted, chuseth for the twentie, fourtie, three score, or a hundred lustie guttes like to hymself to waite uppon his lordely maiestie. . . . Then have they their hobbie horses, dragons, and other antiques, together with their baudie pipers and thunderyng drommers, to strike up the devilles daunce withall: then marche these heathen companie towardes the churche and churche-yarde, their pipers pipyng, their drommers thonderyng, their stumppes dauncyng, their belles rynglyng, their handkercheefes swyngyng about their heades like madmen, their hobbie horses and other monsters skirmishyng amongest the throng; and in this sorte they goe to the churche (though the minister bee at praier or preachyng), dauncyng, and swingyng their handkercheefes

over their heades, in the churche, like devilles incarnate, with such a confused noise, that no man can heare his owne voice. Then the foolishe people they looke, they stare, they laugh, they fleere, and mount upon formes and pewes, to see these goodly pageauntes, solemnized in this sort. Then after this, aboute the churche they goe againe and againe, and so forthe into the churche-yarde, where they have commonly their sommer haules, their bowers, arbours, and banquettyng houses set up, wherein they feaste, banquet, and daunce all that daie, and peradventure all that night too. And thus these terrestriall furies spend the Sabbaoth daie! . . . An other sorte of fantasticall fooles bringe to these helhoundes (the Lorde of Misrule and his complices) some bread, some good ale, some newe cheese, some olde cheese, some custardes, some cakes, some flaunes, some tartes, some creame, some meate, some one thing, some an other.

He continues thus:

> Against Maie, every parishe, towne and village assemble themselves together, bothe men, women, and children, olde and yong, even all indifferently; they goe to the woodes where they spende all the night in pleasant pastymes, and in the mornyng they returne, bringing with them birch, bowes, and branches of trees, to deck their assemblies withall. But their cheefest iewell they bringe from thence is their Maie poole, whiche they bring home with great veneration, as thus: They have twenty or fourtie yoke of oxen, every ox havyng a sweete nosegaie of flowers tyed on the tippe of his hornes, and these oxen, drawe home this Maie poole (this stinckyng idoll rather) . . . and thus beyng reared up, they strawe the grounde aboute, binde greene boughes about it, sett up sommer haules, bowers, and arbours hard by it; and then fall they to banquet and feast, to leape and daunce aboute it, as the heathen people did at the dedication of their idolles. . . . Of a hundred maides goyng to the woode over night, there have scarcely the third parte returned home againe undefiled.[21]

"On Shrove Tuesday," says another,[22] "at the sound of a bell, the folk become insane, thousands at a time, and forget all decency and common sense. . . . It is to Satan and the devil that they pay homage and do sacrifice to in these abominable pleasures." It is in fact to nature, to the ancient Pan, to Freya, to Hertha, her sisters, to the old Teutonic deities who survived the middle-age. At this period, in the temporary decay of Christianity, and the sudden advance of corporal well-being, man adored himself, and there endured no life within him but that of paganism.

To sum up, observe the process of ideas at this time. A few sectarians, chiefly in the towns and of the people, clung gloomily to the Bible. But the court and the men of the world sought their teachers and their heroes from pagan Greece and Rome. About 1490[23] they began to read the classics; one after the other they translated them; it was soon the fashion to read them in the original. Queen Elizabeth, Jane Grey, the Duchess of Norfolk, the Countess of Arundel, and many other ladies, were conversant with Plato, Xenophon, and Cicero in the original, and appreciated them. Gradually, by an insensible change, men were raised to the level of the great and healthy minds who had freely handled ideas of all kinds fifteen centuries before. They comprehended not only their language, but their thought; they did not repeat lessons from, but held conversations with them; they were their equals, and found in them intellects as manly as their own. For they were not scholastic cavillers, miserable compilers, repulsive pedants, like the professors of jargon whom the middle-age had set over them, like gloomy Duns Scotus, whose leaves Henry VIII.'s Visitors scattered to the winds. They were gentlemen, statesmen, the most polished and best educated men in the world, who knew how to speak, and drew their ideas not from books, but from things, living ideas, and which entered of themselves into living souls. Across the train of hooded schoolmen and sordid cavillers the two adult and thinking ages were united, and the moderns, silencing the infantine or snuffling voices of the middle-age, condescended only to converse with the noble ancients. They accepted their gods, at least they understand them, and keep them by their side. In poems, festivals, on hangings, almost in all ceremonies, they appear, not restored by pedantry merely, but kept alive by sympathy, and endowed by the arts with a life as flourishing and almost as profound as that of their earliest birth. After the terrible night of the middle-age, and the dolorous legends of spirits and the damned, it was a delight to see again Olympus shining upon us from Greece; its heroic and beautiful deities once more ravishing the heart of men; they raised and instructed this young world by speaking to it the language of passion and genius; and this age of strong deeds, free sensuality, bold invention, had only to follow its own bent, in order to discover in them its masters and the eternal promoters of liberty and beauty.

Nearer still was another paganism, that of Italy; the more seductive because more modern, and because it circulates fresh sap in an ancient stock; the more attractive, because more sensuous and present, with its worship of force and genius, of pleasure and voluptuousness. The rigorists knew this well, and were shocked at it. Ascham writes:

> These bee the inchantementes of Circes, brought out of Italie to marre mens maners in England; much, by example of ill life, but more by preceptes of fonde bookes, of late translated out of Italian into English, sold in every shop in London. . . .

> There bee moe of these ungratious bookes set out in Printe wythin these fewe monethes, than have bene sene in England many score yeares before. . . . Than they have in more reverence the triumphes of Petrarche: than the Genesis of Moses: They make more account of Tullies offices, than S. Paules epistles: of a tale in Bocace than a storie of the Bible.[24]

In fact, at that time Italy clearly led in everything, and civilisation was to be drawn thence, as from its spring. What is this civilisation which is thus imposed on the whole of Europe, whence every science and every elegance comes, whose laws are obeyed in every court, in which Surrey, Sidney, Spenser, Shakespeare sought their models and their materials? It was pagan in its elements and its birth; in its language, which is but Latin, hardly changed; in its Latin traditions and recollections, which no gap has interrupted; in its constitution, whose old municipal life first led and absorbed the feudal life; in the genius of its race, in which energy and joy always abounded. More than a century before other nations,—from the time of Petrarch, Rienzi, Boccaccio,—the Italians began to recover the lost antiquity, to set free the manuscripts buried in the dungeons of France and Germany, to restore, interpret, comment upon, study the ancients, to make themselves Latin in heart and mind, to compose in prose and verse with the polish of Cicero and Virgil, to hold sprightly converse and intellectual pleasures as the ornament and the fairest flower of life.[25] They adopt not merely the externals of the life of the ancients, but its very essence, that is, preoccupation with the present life, forgetfulness of the future, the appeal to the senses, the renunciation of Christianity. "We must enjoy," sang their first poet, Lorenzo de Medici, in his pastorals and triumphal songs: "there is no certainty of tomorrow." In Pulci the mocking incredulity breaks out, the bold and sensual gaiety, all the audacity of the free-thinkers, who kicked aside in disgust the worn-out monkish frock of the middle age. It was he who, in a jesting poem, puts at the beginning of each canto a Hosanna, an In principio, or a sacred text from the mass-book.[26] When he had been inquiring what the soul was, and how it entered the body, he compared it to jam covered up in white bread quite hot. What would become of it in the other world? "Some people think they will there discover becafico's, plucked ortolans, excellent wine, good beds, and therefore they follow the monks, walking behind them. As for us, dear friend, we shall go into the black valley, where we shall hear no more Alleluias." If you wish for a more serious thinker, listen to the great patriot, the Thucydides of the age, Machiavelli, who, contrasting Christianity and paganism, says that the first places "supreme happiness in humility, abjection, contempt for human things, while the other makes the sovereign good consist in greatness of soul, force of body, and all the qualities which make men to be feared." Whereon he boldly concludes that Christianity teaches man "to support evils, and not to do great deeds;" he discovers in that inner weakness the cause of all oppressions; declares that "the wicked saw that they could tyrannise without fear over men, who, in order to get to paradise, were more disposed to suffer than to avenge injuries." Through such sayings, in spite of his constrained genuflexions, we can see which religion he prefers. The ideal to which all efforts were turning, on which all thoughts depended, and which completely raised this civilisation, was the strong and happy man, possessing all the powers to accomplish his wishes, and disposed to use them in pursuit of his happiness.

If you would see this idea in its grandest operation, you must seek it in the arts, such as Italy made them and carried throughout Europe, raising or transforming the national schools with such originality and vigour, that all art likely to survive is derived from hence, and the population of living figures with which they have covered our walls, denotes, like Gothic architecture or French tragedy, a unique epoch of human intelligence. The attenuated mediæval Christ—a miserable, distorted, and bleeding earth-worm; the pale and ugly Virgin—a poor old peasant woman, fainting beside the cross of her Son; ghastly martyrs, dried up with fasts, with entranced eyes; knotty-fingered saints with sunken chests,—all the touching or lamentable visions of the middle-age have vanished: the train of godheads which are now developed show nothing but flourishing frames, noble, regular features, and fine easy gestures; the names, the names only, are Christian. The new Jesus is a "crucified Jupiter," as Pulci called him; the Virgins which Raphael sketched naked, before covering them with garments,[27] are beautiful girls, quite earthly, related to the Fornarina. The saints which Michel Angelo arranges and contorts in heaven in his picture of the Last Judgment are an assembly of athletes, capable of fighting well and daring much. A martyrdom, like that of Saint Laurence, is a fine ceremony in which a beautiful young man, without clothing, lies amidst fifty men dressed and grouped as in an ancient gymnasium. Is there one of them who had macerated himself? Is there one who had thought with anguish and tears of the judgment of God, who had worn down and subdued his flesh, who had filled his heart with the sadness and sweetness of the gospel? They are too vigorous for that, they are in too robust health; their clothes fit them too well; they are too ready for prompt and energetic action. We might make of them strong soldiers or superb courtesans, admirable in a pageant or at a ball. So, all that the spectator accords to their halo of glory, is a bow or a sign of the cross; after which his eyes find pleasure in them; they are there simply for the enjoyment of the eyes. What the spectator feels at the sight of a Florentine Madonna, is the splendid creature, whose powerful body and fine growth bespeak her race and her vigour; the artist did not paint moral expression as now-

adays, the depth of a soul tortured and refined by three centuries of culture. They confine themselves to the body, to the extent even of speaking enthusiastically of the spinal column itself, "which is magnificent;" of the shoulder-blades, which in the movements of the arm "produce an admirable effect." "You will next draw the bone which is situated between the hips. It is very fine, and is called the sacrum."[28] The important point with them is to represent the nude well. Beauty with them is that of the complete skeleton, sinews which are linked together and tightened, the thighs which support the trunk, the strong chest breathing freely, the pliant neck. What a pleasure to be naked! How good it is in the full light to rejoice in a strong body, well-formed muscles, a spirited and bold soul! The splendid goddesses reappear in their primitive nudity, not dreaming that they are nude; you see from the tranquillity of their look, the simplicity of their expression, that they have always been thus, and that shame has not yet reached them. The soul's life is not here contrasted, as amongst us, with the body's life; the one is not so lowered and degraded, that we dare not show its actions and functions; they do not hide them; man does not dream of being all spirit. They rise, as of old, from the luminous sea, with their rearing steeds tossing up their manes, champing the bit, inhaling the briny savour, whilst their companions wind the sounding-shell; and the spectators,[29] accustomed to handle the sword, to combat naked with the dagger or double-handled blade, to ride on perilous roads, sympathise with the proud shape of the bended back, the effort of the arm about to strike, the long quiver of the muscles which, from neck to heel, swell out, to brace a man, or to throw him.

Notes

[1] Van Orley, Michel Coxcie, Franz Floris, the de Vos', the Sadelers Crispin de Pass, and the artists of Nuremberg.

[2] The first carriage was in 1564. It caused much astonishment. Some said that it was "a great sea-shell brought from China;" others, "that it was a temple in which cannibals worshipped the devil."

[3] For a picture of this state of things, see Fenn's *Paston Letters*.

[4] Louis XI. in France, Ferdinand and Isabella in Spain, Henry VII. in England. In Italy the feudal regime ended earlier, by the establishment of republics and principalities.

[5] 1488, Act of Parliament on Enclosures.

[6] *A Compendious Examination,* 1581, by William Strafford. Act of Parliament, 1541.

[7] Between 1377 and 1588 the increase was from two and a half to five millions.

[8] In 1585; Ludovic Guicciardini.

[9] Henry VIII. at the beginning of his reign had but one ship of war. Elizabeth sent out one hundred and fifty against the Armada. In 1553 was founded a company to trade with Russia. In 1578 Drake circumnavigated the globe. In 1600 the East India Company was founded.

[10] Nathan Drake, *Shakspeare and his Times,* 1817, i. v. 72 *et passim.*

[11] Nathan Drake, *Shakspeare and his Times,* i. v. 102.

[12] This was called the Tudor style. Under James I., in the hands of Inigo Jones, it became entirely Italian, approaching the antique.

[13] Burton, *Anatomy of Melancholy,* 12th ed. 1821. Stubbes, *Anatomie of Abuses,* ed. Turnbull, 1836.

[14] Nathan Drake, *Shakspeare and his Times,* ii. 6, 87.

[15] Holinshed (1586), 1808, 6 vols. iii. 763 *et passim.*

[16] Holinshed, iii., *Reign of Henry VIII. Elizabeth and James Frogresses,* by Nichols.

[17] Laneham's Entertainment at Killingworth Castle, 1575. Nichol's *Progresses,* vol. i. London 1788.

[18] Ben Jonson's works, ed. Gifford, 1816, 9 vols. *Masque of Hymen,* vol. vii. 76.

[19] Certain private letters also describe the court of Elizabeth as a place where there was little piety or practice of religion, and where all enormities reigned in the highest degree.

[20] Nathan Drake, *Shakspeare and his Times,* chap. v. and vi.

[21] Stubbes, *Anatomie of Abuses,* p. 168 *et passim.*

[22] Hentzner's *Travels in England* (Bentley's translation). He thought that the figure carried about in the Harvest Home represented Ceres.

[23] Warton, vol. ii. sect. 35. Before 1600 all the great poets were translated into English, and between 1550 and 1616 all the great historians of Greece and Rome. Lyly in 1500 first taught Greek in public.

[24] Ascham, *The Scholemaster* (1570), ed. Arber, 1870, first book, 78 *et passim.*

[25] Ma il vero e principal ornemento dell' animo in ciascuno penso io che siano le lettere, benchè i Franchesi solamente conoscano la nobilità dell'arme . . . et tutti i litterati tengon per vilissimi huomini. Castiglione, *il Cortegiano,* ed. 1585, p. 112.

[26] See Burchard (the Pope's Steward), account of the festival at which Lucretia Borgia was present. Letters of Aretinus, *Life of Cellini,* etc.

[27] See his sketches at Oxford, and those of Fra Bartolomeo at Florence. See also the Martyrdom of St. Laurence, by Baccio Bandinelli.

[28] Benvenuto Cellini, *Principles of the Art of Design.*

[29] *Life of Cellini.* Compare also these exercises which Castiglione prescribes for a well-educated man, in his *Cortegiano,* ed. 1585, p. 55:CAPeró voglio che il nostro cortegiano sia perfetto cavaliere d'ogni sella. . . . Et perchè degli Italiani è peculiar laude il cavalcare benè alla brida, il maneggiar con raggione massimamente cavalli aspri, il corre lance, il giostare, sia in questo de meglior Italiani. . . . Nel torneare, tener un passo, combattere una sbarra, sia buono tra il miglior francesi. . . . Nel giocare a canne, correr torri, lanciar haste e dardi, sia tra Spagnuoli eccellente. . . . Conveniente è ancor sapere saltare, e correre;. . . . ancor nobile exercitio il gioco di palla. . . . Non di minor laude estimo il voltegiar a cavallo."

Jeffrey L. Singman (essay date 1995)

SOURCE: "The Elizabethan World," in *Daily Life: Elizabethan England,* Greenwood Press, 1995, pp. 9-36.

[*In the excerpt below, Singman examines the roles of class, politics, and religion in shaping daily life in Elizabethan society.*]

Society

The population of England was probably over 3 million when Elizabeth came to the throne in 1558, and it grew to over 4 million by the time of her death in 1603. These figures represent roughly a tenth of the population of England today. This rapid growth meant that a large part of the population at any time were young people: it has been estimated that roughly a third were under the age of 15, a half under age 25. Population density was highest in the south and east, with the mountainous areas of the north and west more sparsely settled. The overwhelming majority lived in rural areas, although London was growing rapidly.

Not all of this population were ethnically or culturally English. Wales and western Cornwall were subject to the English crown, and were often counted as a part of England, yet they still spoke Welsh and Cornish—languages similar to each other but quite unintelligible to an Englishman. Ireland was also officially under English rule, although effective English control was limited to the eastern part of the country. The population of Ireland included Englishmen and English-speaking Irishmen in the east, with the remainder of the country inhabited by Gaelic-speaking Irishmen. Scotland was still an independent kingdom, although England and Scotland came to be under a single ruler when the Scottish king, James VI, inherited the English throne in 1603. Southern Scotland spoke its own dialect of English, whereas the northern and western parts of the country still spoke Scottish Gaelic, a close relative of Irish Gaelic.

Within England itself there was a significant population of foreign immigrants, typically Protestants who had fled the Continent because of wars or religious persecution. These immigrants came primarily from the Low Countries, Germany, and France, with a few from Spain and Italy. The proportion of foreigners was highest in London—perhaps close to 10% of the population. It was much lower in other areas, and there were few in the countryside. Finally, by this period the Romany, or gypsies, had come across the Channel to England. The gypsies were a culture largely to themselves; they had a language of their own and led wandering lives on the fringes of society. They did not generally assimilate to mainstream English society, although they had a significant impact on the culture of vagrancy and the underworld.[1]

Elizabethan society was in many ways still dominated by the feudal and manorial system inherited from the Middle Ages. During the Middle Ages, society and the economy had focused on people's relationship to land, a relationship of "holding" rather than owning. A landholder inherited the right to occupy and use a certain allotment of land—the landholding—under certain terms. Theoretically, all land actually belonged to the monarch, and was passed downwards in a hierarchical chain, each landholder providing service or payment to a landlord in exchange for the landholding. Landholdings were not owned outright, for they could not be freely bought or sold, and it was very difficult in the Middle Ages to acquire land by any means other than inheritance of a holding.

The upper ranks of society were supposed to pay for their land with military service. When their lord called upon them, they were expected to come to him fully equipped as mounted knights with a following of soldiers. This was the gentlemanly form of service, and those who owed military service were considered to be of gentle birth, as was everyone in their families. Gentle status went hand in hand with political influence, social privilege, and

cultural prestige. A gentleman's landholding would be large—a hundred acres or so was the lower end of the scale.

Part of a gentleman's landholding was demesne land, that is, land that he himself administered, hiring workers to cultivate it. The rest was rented out as landholdings to tenants (a word that means "holders"). This rental was likewise determined by inheritance: a landlord's tenants inherited the right to their landholdings, and paid for them according to the custom associated with the holding, typically a combination of labor service and rents in kind. The labor service was usually an obligation to spend a certain amount of time doing work for the landlord. The rents in kind were produce from the land—especially grain and livestock. Tenants who paid in labor or material rents were considered commoners. In fact, the label "commoner" applied to everyone who did not belong to the gentle class (except the clergy, who in the Middle Ages were considered a class by themselves).

This was the principle; it was of course much more complex in practice, and there had been some important changes since the height of medieval feudalism. By the end of the Middle Ages, labor rents and rents in kind had largely been replaced by money rents: people simply paid a certain amount of cash annually for their holding. When Henry VIII abolished the monasteries during the 1530s, a great deal of monastic land came onto the market; unlike traditional medieval holdings, this land could be freely bought or sold. Another major change was in the nature of gentlemen's landholdings. By the Elizabethan period, the armored knight and his followers were no longer very useful on the battlefield. Armies were now relying on professional soldiers instead, so the gentleman's responsibility for military service had become somewhat nominal.

However, the privileges of gentle birth persisted. The gentlemen of Elizabethan England still dominated government and society, and they were the effective owners of most of the land in the country. Whereas the medieval aristocrat had been defined by his military activities, the Elizabethans laid more emphasis on the other aspects of gentle birth. The classic Elizabethan definition of the gentleman is the formulation offered by Sir Thomas Smith in his treatise on English society, *De Republica Anglorum:*

> Who can live idly and without manual labor and will bear the port, charge, and countenance of a gentleman, he shall be called "master," for that is the title which men give to esquires and other gentlemen, and shall be taken for a gentleman.

As Smith suggests, the principal characteristic of the gentleman was that he could live handsomely without labor, which generally meant having enough land to live off the rents. Many people of gentlemanly birth held little or no land, but there were alternatives. Government service was considered an acceptable occupation for a gentleman, who might also supplement his income through commercial speculation. Military service, although no longer required, was still a gentlemanly occupation: the officers of Elizabeth's army and navy were invariably gentlemen. In addition, anyone with a university education or working in a profession (i.e., as a physician, lawyer, priest, etc.) was considered a gentleman.

The gentlemanly class was subdivided into its own hierarchy. At the top was the titled nobility, comprising around fifty noblemen and their families. Titles of nobility were inherited: the eldest son would receive the title of his father, and his siblings would be lords or gentlemen, ladies or gentlewomen, depending upon their father's actual rank. The Elizabethan titles of nobility were, in descending order, Duke, Marquis, Earl, Viscount, and Baron; the female equivalents were Duchess, Marchioness, Countess, Viscountess, and Baroness. Below these was the title of Knight, which was never inherited; it had to be received from the monarch or a designated military leader. Knighthood in the Middle Ages was supposed to be a military status, but by the Elizabethan period it had become a general mark of honor. There were probably about 300 to 500 knights in England at any given time.

At the bottom of the gentlemanly hierarchy were esquires (also called squires) and simple gentlemen. The distribution between the two was not always clear. In theory, an esquire was a gentleman who had knights in his ancestry, but he might also be a gentleman of especially prominent standing. Esquires and gentlemen together may have numbered some 16,000 at the end of Elizabeth's reign. Seventeenth-century estimates suggest that lords, knights, and esquires accounted for well under 1% of the population, and simple gentlemen for about 1%.

Special mention should be made of the clergy, who had once been considered a class of their own but were now more likely to be identified with the gentlemanly class. They were far fewer in number than they had been during the Middle Ages, especially since there were no longer any monks, friars, or nuns. However, they still enjoyed considerable prestige, and the church remained one of the best avenues by which a commoner might advance in society. Furthermore, the Catholic ban on clerical marriage had been lifted as part of the Protestant reformation, so it was now possible to be a clergyman and have a family as well. Among the clergy, archbishops and bishops were classed with the titled nobility and sat in the House of Lords. Below these were some 8,000 parish clergymen, as well as a smaller number of other church officials—notably deacons and archdeacons, who were responsible for church administration.[2]

Below the gentlemen in the manorial hierarchy were the landholding commoners. The most privileged, called freeholders, held their lands in perpetuity: their holdings were passed on from generation to generation with no change in terms. The rent charged for freehold lands had generally been fixed in the Middle Ages, and inflation had rendered the real cost of these holdings minimal. A freeholder was therefore in a very strong financial position, and was almost the effective owner of his landholding. Freeholders may have numbered around 100,000 in all.

Less fortunate than the freeholders were the leaseholders. Their tenancies were for fixed periods, sometimes as much as a lifetime, sometimes as little as a year. When the tenancy ended, it was usually renewed, but the landlord was able to change the terms of the lease: he might charge a higher rent from the tenant or his heir, or even terminate the lease altogether. At the very bottom among landholders were the copyholders, also called customary tenants or tenants at will. Their holdings were simply by custom, and the rent could be altered or the tenancy terminated at any time.

This does not mean that all such tenants were in constant danger of homelessness or impoverishment. Not all landlords were inclined to raise rents or evict tenants. There was a genuine belief in tradition and social stability, and many landlords were reluctant to engage in behavior that would so obviously disrupt the social system. Still, in an age of rising prices and intense economic pressures, there were strong incentives for landlords to make the most of their lands at whatever social cost. Many contemporaries complained about landlords who were either "racking" (increasing) rents or evicting tenants so they could use their lands more efficiently or even convert arable lands into pasture.

The nature of a tenant's holding was theoretically independent of its size, although the larger holdings were more likely to be held by freeholders, smaller ones by leaseholders or copyholders. Freeholders whose lands yielded revenues of at least 40 shillings a year were considered yeomen, a very respectable title for a commoner, that not only implied a fairly high degree of economic prosperity but also entitled the holder to vote in Parliamentary elections. A seventeenth-century estimate suggests that yeomen constituted about 15% of the total population of England; a sixteenth-century estimate numbers greater yeomen at around 10,000. A large landholding for a commoner would be some 50 to 100 acres. Lesser landholders were known as husbandmen, a term that might also be applied generally to anyone who worked his own landholding. The smallest landholders were called cottagers: these held only the cottage they lived in and perhaps a few acres of land. Their holdings were too small to support them, so they had to supplement their income by hiring themselves out as laborers.

The rural hierarchy was the most prominent in the Elizabethan world-view, but there also existed a fully developed and independent social structure in the towns. Towns had been established during the Middle Ages to encourage commerce. They were independent of the feudal hierarchy, owing allegiance directly to the monarch, and they enjoyed extensive privileges of self-government. They were semi-democratic, being in the control of the citizens (sometimes called burgesses). Citizenship in a town was a privilege restricted to male householders who were not dependent on others for their wages, typically craftsmen and tradesmen who had their own shop. Citizens may have numbered as many as a quarter to a half of the adult male population in any given town; a seventeenth-century estimate suggests that citizens constituted roughly 5% of the overall population. As the towns were self-governing, they relied heavily on their own population for filling public offices: perhaps 1 freeman in 4 or 5 held office at any given time.

Whereas the rural hierarchy was centered on agriculture, the urban hierarchy was based on trades and crafts. Each craft and trade had a hierarchy of its own, based on the medieval "guild" system. For example, all grocers in a given town would belong to a corporate body, governed by the master grocers, who would regulate the manner in which the trade was plied. Elizabethans usually called these bodies "companies," although today they are often referred to as guilds. A boy would begin in his teenage years as an apprentice to a master. After seven years he might finish his apprenticeship and become a journeyman; this meant he was free to sell his services in the craft or trade. Those who had adequate means or connections could ultimately become masters themselves, which meant that they could set up a business of their own and take on their own journeymen and apprentices. The citizenry of a town consisted primarily of its master tradesmen and craftsmen.

At the base of both the rural and urban hierarchies were he laborers and servants. In the country, there was need of shepherds, milkmaids, harvesters, and other hired hands; the towns required porters, water carriers, and other unskilled workers. In the country, paid labor sometimes went to cottagers, but increasingly it fell to a growing class of mobile and rootless laborers who followed the market in search of employment. Unskilled laborers in the city and hired workers in the country made up the bulk of the population—agricultural laborers alone represented a quarter to a third of the rural population. In addition, there was a small but increasing demand for labor in a few industries, notably coal and iron production. Such people were always at risk of slipping into the ranks of the vagrants and chronically unemployed.

A distinctive feature of Elizabethan society was the very high proportion of the population who were employed in service. Both rural and urban families hired servants: a quarter of the population may have been servants at any given time, and a third or more of households may have had servants. The relationship of servants to their employers in many ways resembled that of children to their parents. They were not just paid employees, but subordinate members of their employer's household who actually lived with the family. Servants might be in a better position than laborers, since service was often a temporary stage on the road to a better social position. For young people, service could be a means of accumulating money, making useful contacts, and acquiring polish in the ways of polite society. Even aristocratic youths might spend some time as pages, gentlemen-ushers, or ladies-in-waiting in a prestigious household. Between the ages of 20 and 24, some 80% of men and 50% of women were servants; two-thirds of boys and three-quarters of girls went away from home in service from just before puberty until marriage, or a period of about 10 years.

At the very base of the social hierarchy was a substantial and growing number of unemployed poor. The number of poor people unable to sustain themselves may have been 10% in the country and 20% in towns. The poor particularly included children, widows, abandoned wives, the elderly, and the infirm; but their ranks were increased by growing numbers of unemployed but able-bodied men displaced by economic transformations or returning home from service in the army or navy. There was also a significant community of permanent beggars and vagabonds, who may have numbered as many as 20,000. In combination with the gypsies, they were beginning to create an underworld culture of their own; in fact, the Elizabethans were both fascinated and horrified with their world of lawlessness, much as people today are intrigued by stories of the Mafia and of street gangs.

In response to growing concerns over the problems of poverty and vagrancy, Elizabeth's government began to take active steps to suppress vagrants while helping those who were genuinely unable to work. For some time there had been local provisions to deal with poverty, but under Elizabeth a body of legislation known as the Poor Laws established a national system for assisting the poor, acknowledging for the first time the existence of involuntary unemployment. The Poor Laws sought to solve the problem of poverty at the level of the parish. Parishioners were to pay money to a parish fund, which would be used to support those unable to support themselves. The able-bodied unemployed were to be given work, whereas those able-bodied people who shirked labor might be whipped or imprisoned. Vagrants from outside the parish were to be sent back to their own places of origin. The Poor Laws were a serious attempt to address a growing problem, but their effectiveness was limited. Poverty was an enormous national problem, and it was linked to an ever-increasing degree of geographic mobility. Under these circumstances, a parish-by-parish solution could only have a limited effect, and it was often difficult to ensure that parishes would enforce the laws effectively, especially given the expense of implementing them.

In addition to social class, the status of every Elizabethan was governed by whether they were male or female. In fact, gender was an even more determining factor: social class can be vague and flexible, but gender is obvious and permanent.

According to a proverb that was current in Elizabeth's day, England was "the Hell of Horses, the Purgatory of Servants, and the Paradise of Women." The phrase is highly revealing. On the one hand, it confirms the observations of contemporary visitors from the Continent who remarked that English women were particularly free and had substantial control over their own households. At the same time, it reminds us that women, like horses and servants, were expected to be in a position of subordination. The Elizabethan political theorist Sir Thomas Smith, in his *De Republica Anglorum,* offered this view of a woman's role in society:

> Women . . . nature hath made to keep home and to nourish their family and children, and not to meddle with matters abroad, nor to bear office in a city or commonwealth no more than children or infants.

Whereas a male child might have some expectation of moving to a position of relative social and economic independence at some point in his life, a girl would exchange subordination to her father for subordination to an employer or husband. Only in widowhood was a woman legally recognized as an independent individual. A widow took over as head of her husband's household; if he left her sufficient means to live on, she might do quite well, perhaps taking over his trade, and she would be free to remarry or not as she chose.

Yet the theory was rather harsher than the practice. Women played a very important role in the Elizabethan economy, a fact which must have enhanced their real status. They sometimes even served as churchwardens or manorial officials.[3] Even if husbands believed that God had placed them in authority over their wives, their power could not be exercised through sheer force, as recognized in Nicholas Breton's advice on how a husband should treat a wife:

> Cherish all good humors in her: let her lack no silk, crewel, thread, nor flax, to work on at her pleasure, force her to nothing, rather prettily chide her from her labor, but in any wise commend what she doeth: if she be learned and studious, persuade her to translation, it will keep her from idleness, and it is a cunning kind task: if she be unlearned, commend her to housewifery, and make much of her carefulness, and bid her servants take example at their mistress. . . . At table be merry to her, abroad be kind to her, always be loving to her, and never be bitter to her, for patient Griselda is dead long ago, and women are flesh and blood.[4]

Elizabethan England was truly a family-oriented society: the family constituted the basic unit not only of the society but of the economy as well. A household consisted not only of the nuclear family of father, mother, and children, but might also include employees, notably servants and apprentices. The mean household size was about 4 to 5, but it varied with social class. According to one seventeenth-century estimate, a typical lord's household would include some 40 people, a knight's 13, a squire's or gentleman's 10, a merchant's 6 to 8, a freeholder's 5 to 7, a tradesman's, craftsman's, or cottager's 3 to 4. It was unusual for relatives beyond the nuclear family to live within the household—one region that has been studied in detail shows this happening in only 6% of households, with only 2% including more than one married couple in the same household. This was less true in upper-class households, which were more likely to house additional relatives. Due to the high rate of mortality, single-parent families and stepparents were fairly common. In one village in 1599, a quarter of the children living at home had lost one parent.

It was through the family that the individual was connected to society: everyone was expected to be either a head of household or subject to one. Society was considered to consist not of individuals but of households, and in counting population it was customary only to reckon householders; wife, children, servants, and apprentices were subordinate to the householder. The family was also the typical unit of production—the family business was the rule rather than the exception.

In principle, Elizabethan society was a rigid and orderly hierarchy. Social and economic advancement of the individual were not priorities. People were expected to live within the social class of their parents, a man following his father's vocation or one comparable to it, a woman marrying a man of her father's status. Each person was supposed to fit into a stable social network, remaining in place to preserve the balance of the whole. For most people in Elizabethan England, this principle probably held true.

In practice things were not always so straightforward. Sometimes it was difficult to be entirely certain of a person's social status. Actual titles were easy to verify, as in the case of a nobleman, a knight, or a master craftsman. However, the distinction between an esquire and a gentleman, or between a gentleman and a yeoman, was not always so clear. A prosperous yeoman might hold as much land as a minor gentleman; by subletting it to tenants of his own, he could live off the rents and slip into the gentlemanly class. Successful burgesses often used their profits to purchase land and make themselves gentlemen. A woman might marry a man of significantly higher social station. William Shakespeare is one good example of Elizabethan social mobility: born the son of a glover in Stratford-upon-Avon, he returned from his successful theatrical career in London to live as a gentleman, the proud possessor of a coat-of-arms and the largest house in town. Conversely, a gentleman who acquired excessive debts might slide down the social scale, and we have already seen that landholders and laborers could sometimes find themselves without a livelihood.[5]

Government and the Law

The government of England centered on the figure of the monarch, who relied heavily on her Privy Council for the day-to-day running of the country. The monarch, and the Council acting in the monarch's name, had some power to issue decrees enforceable at law, but the exact extent of these powers was ill-defined. This constitutional ambiguity led to bloody results in the 1640s when King Charles and his Parliament came to civil war over the issue of the King's authority.

The most comprehensively powerful organ of government was the monarch sitting in Parliament: a bill passed by Parliament and assented to by the monarch was the highest legal authority in the land. Parliament was divided into two houses: the House of Lords, consisting of approximately 65 lay peers, 22 bishops, and the country's 2 archbishops (Canterbury and York); and the House of Commons, consisting of 2 representatives chosen from each of England's 39 shires, 2 from each of about 65 English cities and towns (with some exceptions, including London, which sent 4), as well as a single representative from each of 12 Welsh shires and 1 each from 12 Welsh towns, for a total of about 450 representatives. The exact means by which the representatives were chosen depended on the shire or town, but in the shires any holder of lands worth 40 shillings a year was entitled to vote.

In general, the institutions of Elizabethan government seem haphazard by modern standards. The basic unit of governmental organization in both town and country was the parish. Each parish had its own officials, such as a constable who was responsible for basic law enforcement, ale-conners who ensured that the laws regulating the quality of ale were observed, and churchwardens who were responsible for the state of

the parish church. In towns there were also scavengers who oversaw public sanitation.

The actual bureaucracy was small and woefully underfunded. This meant that the governmental apparatus required extensive participation by the citizenry. Great lords might serve in the Privy Council or in major offices of the state, army, or navy; local gentlemen were vital in administrating the individual shires; and even ordinary craftsmen, yeomen, and husbandmen might be called upon to serve in minor local offices of the village, town, or parish. At the same time, this kind of unpaid work was a cause of governmental corruption; men who had to spend considerable time and money on an unsalaried government office would frequently find other ways to make the post profitable.

The mechanisms for legal enforcement were quite complex. There were several legal institutions for trying a criminal case. It might be tried in one of several royal courts; it might fall under the jurisdiction of ecclesiastical courts; a minor matter might be handled summarily by a gentleman commissioned as a justice of the peace. Professional law enforcement did not exist—there was no actual police force, which meant that the various tasks associated with police work had to be done by other sorts of officers or not at all. At the local level, two important institutions were the town watch, responsible for patrolling the streets of the town at night, and the constable, the closest thing to a local policeman, although this was always a temporary and part-time office.

Capital offenses were treason, murder, and felony, of which the last included manslaughter, rape, sodomy, arson, witchcraft, burglary, robbery, and grand larceny (stealing of goods worth at least 12 pence). All these offenses carried a mandatory death sentence, for which reason juries were sometimes reluctant to convict. A man convicted of a capital crime might be pardoned by the crown, or in the case of a felony might pray "benefit of clergy." In the Middle Ages the clergy had been exempted from secular punishment for felony, an exemption that extended to any man who could prove he was literate. The custom was still in use in the late sixteenth century, but in slightly altered form: benefit of clergy could only be exercised once, at which time the convict would be branded on the thumb to mark that he had exercised this privilege. Benefit of clergy was not available to those convicted of the most serious felonies, such as burglary and robbery. In some instances, serious crimes might be punished by branding or loss of a body part such as a hand or ear.

In addition, there were diverse lesser crimes of the sort which that now be called misdemeanors. Punishments for such crimes might include fines, whipping, or imprisonment. In some cases the punishment might be confinement in the stocks or the pillory. The pillory was more unpleasant, as it confined both the head and hands, leaving the convict vulnerable to the abuse of passers-by. The stocks confined only the legs, and most of the time only one leg was confined.

Ecclesiastical courts might impose public penance, which would involve some form of public ritual in which the wrongdoer would publicly acknowledge his or her offense. It was difficult for the church courts to enforce their punishments against the truly recalcitrant. The ultimate sanction was excommunication, or exclusion from church services. This punishment theoretically excluded the wrongdoer from society, but in practice many people defied such sanctions—in fact, as many as 5% of the population may have lived excommunicate.[6]

Religion

To be a part of Elizabethan society was considered the same as being part of the church, and everyone in Elizabethan England was expected to receive basic religious instruction. By law, every parish minister was required to provide religious instruction on alternate Sundays and on all holy days; all children over age 6 were required to attend. In particular, every child was expected to memorize the Ten Commandments, the Articles of Belief (also called the Creed—the basic statement of Christian belief), and the Lord's Prayer. They were also to memorize the catechism, a series of questions and answers regarding Christian belief. Parents who failed to send their children to receive this instruction might be prosecuted in the church courts, and children who could not recite the catechism might be required to do penance.

Religion played a very different role in people's lives than it does today. There was no question of the separation of church and state. Only one church was legally permitted, the Church of England. To be a citizen of England was to be a part of its church, and the parish was the basic unit of political as well as religious organization. People were required to attend the church of the parish where they lived. Religion was not merely a personal matter, but a contentious social issue. Few people actually believed in freedom of worship: instead, they argued over what form the country's official religion should take.

During the Middle Ages, the countries of western Europe had been officially part of the Catholic Church. In the 1530s, soon after the first Protestant reformations on the Continent, Henry VIII of England found himself at odds with the Pope: he wanted a divorce from his first wife Catherine of Aragon, who had born him a daughter but no sons.

The Pope refused, and Henry withdrew England from the Catholic Church, placing the English church under the authority of the king.

Henry himself had no desire to make any significant changes in church teachings, but there was growing pressure in the country to follow the lead of the Continental Protestants such as Martin Luther; English Protestants were later heavily influenced by Jean Calvin, a French Protestant who established a rigidly Protestant state in Geneva. The differences between the ideas of Catholicism and those of Protestantism were complex, but many of them related to the contrast between concrete and intellectual approaches to religion. Catholicism tended to adhere to the concrete aspects of religion, such as religious ceremony, veneration of saints, and charitable deeds; the Catholic Church taught that such things had the power to bring people closer to God. Protestants generally rejected this idea and stressed a more abstract kind of religion: a person would not go to heaven by doing good deeds but by having faith in God, and the word of the Bible was to be taken as more important than traditional ceremonies. As one seventeenth-century author put it, "Calvin's religion was too lean, and the Catholic religion too fat, because the one had many ceremonies, the other none."

The English church moved only very slightly toward Protestantism in Henry's lifetime. During the brief reign of Henry's young son Edward VI, the government came to be dominated by more eager reformers and became a fully Protestant church. In 1553 Edward died, and his half-sister Mary came to the throne. Mary was the daughter of Henry VIII by his first wife, Catherine of Aragon. Mary was opposed to the changes that had begun with her father's divorce, and she brought England back into the Catholic Church. Her reign is remembered for the execution of some 300 Protestants, which is why she is known by the nickname Bloody Mary.

Mary died three years later, leaving her half-sister Elizabeth to inherit the throne. Elizabeth was the daughter of Henry VIII and his second wife, Anne Boleyn. She was not an ardent Protestant, but she was of Protestant leanings. Even more important, her claim to the throne depended on the independence of the English church. The Pope had never recognized Henry's divorce, so in Catholic eyes Elizabeth was the illegitimate child of an adulterous union and could not be queen. Elizabeth duly withdrew England from the Catholic Church once more.

The Elizabethan church was Protestant in its teachings but still retained conservative features inherited from Catholicism. For example, the number of saints' days was severely reduced, but they were not entirely eliminated; the garments worn by Elizabethan ministers were simpler than those of Catholic priests, but still more elaborate than the severe gowns of the Protestants of Geneva. The decoration of the church was more austere than in Catholic churches. However, an important feature that the church inherited from Catholicism was its administration by bishops and archbishops, who were ultimately subject to the Queen.

On the whole, Elizabeth was primarily concerned with her role as a queen: religion was important to her, as it concerned the social well-being of the nation, but she took a much more pragmatic and tolerant approach to religious matters than was common in Europe at the time. Her laws on religion insisted on outward conformity and obedience but did not meddle too deeply in people's actual beliefs. People were required, under pain of a fine, to attend church each Sunday. Public officials, teachers, and other persons of authority were required to take the Oath of Supremacy, which stated that the swearer upheld the official religion of England and the Queen as the supreme governor of the Church. Beyond this, there was comparatively little persecution of people for their religious beliefs, especially in comparison to the religious wars that were rocking the Continent at this time.

In fact, there were still quite a number of Catholics in England. They may have constituted some 5% of the population, and were especially numerous in the north. Elizabeth was inclined to let English Catholics believe as they pleased. To some degree, her policy of tolerance diminished from the late 1560s onwards, as international tensions between Protestants and Catholics increased. In 1568, Mary Stuart, the Queen of Scotland (known today as Mary Queen of Scots), fled her rebellious kingdom to become a prisoner in England. As the principal Catholic claimant to the English throne, Mary became a focus for Catholic plots. In 1569 there was an unsuccessful rebellion in the north, especially supported by Catholics. In 1570 the Pope issued a decree officially deposing Elizabeth from the crown. At this point it became very difficult to maintain loyalty both to the Catholic Church and to the Queen, and it was in this year that the Queen first began to execute Catholics for acts in support of the Pope and his policies. Tensions rose even further in the 1580s when the Pope sent Jesuit missionaries into England, with the intent of ministering to English Catholics and winning converts. The Jesuits were regarded as the worst sort of spies, and if caught they were subject to a protracted and agonizing execution.

Catholicism was not the only sort of church separatism. Many English Protestants felt that the Church of England had not gone far enough along the path of reform; they wanted a more fully Protestant church like those in Scotland, the Netherlands, and Geneva. They objected to even the minor degree of ritual re-

tained in the church. The continuing existence of bishops was a matter of especially heated controversy: many people wanted a "presbyterian" church government, run by assemblies of clergy and godly laymen, an idea that Elizabeth considered a threat to her royal authority. These extreme reformers came to be known as Precisians or Puritans.

Initially the reformers focused their efforts on reshaping the Church of England, but eventually some came to feel that if they wanted a truly pure church, they would have to form one of their own. Notable among these were the Brownists, forerunners of the Congregationalists, who formed small independent congregations for common worship. In the eyes of the government, such separatism was treasonous; it was ruthlessly suppressed, although it was later to play a major role in the founding of the early colonies in America.

By law, everyone was required to attend the morning service at their local parish church every Sunday. During the course of an Elizabethan church service, the parishioners would sing psalms and the priest would offer two biblical readings, one each from the Old and New Testaments, followed by the ceremony of communion and a sermon. The sermon was a major vehicle for public propaganda in both religious and political matters, and the priest was not allowed to preach a sermon of his own devising unless he had been specifically licensed to do so. Instead, the government published books of approved sermons that stressed religious conformity and political obedience, as well as the teachings of Christian doctrine.

Communion, the ceremony in which the parishioners received the sacred bread and wine, had always been a particularly important ritual in the Christian church. The Protestant Church of England taught that communion was a ceremony of commemoration, rather than the mystical transformation of bread and wine into the body and blood of Christ, as in the Catholic Church. In contrast with modern religious customs, people did not normally take communion every time they went to church, and the ceremony might even be omitted; it was only required on certain major holidays.

Most churches had been built in the Middle Ages, but the Protestant reformation brought about many important changes in the interior arrangement of the church. The Catholic crucifix above the altar was replaced by the royal coat-of-arms, and as stained-glass windows decayed they were replaced with plain ones. In Catholicism, the church was arranged so that the religious ceremonies, particularly that of communion, took place in a special holy space: the altar was located at the far east end, away from the parishioners, and was separated from them by a screen. The Protestants considered this arrangement superstitious; in an Elizabethan church the elaborate altar was exchanged for a simple communion table, which was placed in the center of the church right in front of the congregation, without any separation. Pews were in use by this time, but the church was equally likely to be outfitted with stools for the parishioners. Seating in church was sometimes a contentious issue, since a seat in front was considered a mark of high social rank. In some traditional communities, seats were assigned to particular landholdings, but in many places this system had broken down, and there was a great deal of jockeying for the most prestigious positions.

Religious observance did not stop at the church door. Elizabethan people lived in a society steeped in religion, so it was naturally a major part of their ordinary life. It was common for people to pray every morning and evening, and to say grace before and after meals. As literacy spread, more and more people were able to read the Bible; naturally, the next step was to discuss it and how it should be applied to the world around them. Even those who could not read were familiar with the contents of the Bible, since they heard readings from it every week in church. Another important book was John Foxe's *Book of Martyrs,* which told of the faithfulness of English Christians throughout history, with special emphasis on Protestants who had died under the persecutions of Bloody Mary. In a world where church and state were indivisibly linked, Protestantism was seen by many as a form of patriotism.

Yet in spite of earnest efforts at public religious education, atheism and irreligion were still present; doubtless, many people maintained religious uniformity only because of the severe sanctions against nonconformity. Contemporaries complained that it was "A matter very common to dispute whether there be a God or not." Some citizens were known to profane religious sacraments: on one occasion a goose and gander were married; on another a horse's head was baptized; on yet another an entire dead horse was brought to receive communion.

Side by side with the official teachings of the church was a continuing belief in magic. Many people still believed in supernatural creatures, particularly fairies; they used magical charms and recipes, and consulted people believed to have supernatural skills or powers, especially in matters such as illness, childbirth, loss of property, or love-longing. Witchcraft was accepted as real not only by simple folk but by the church and government—it was a crime punishable by death. Witchcraft accusations peaked in 1580s and 1590s, although they were never as numerous as they tend to be in the modern popular imagination. On the whole, superstition was more firmly entrenched in the country than in the city. . . .[7]

Notes

[1] On the population of England, see D. M. Palliser, *The Age of Elizabeth* (London: Longman, 1992), ch. 2.

For a contemporary atlas of England, see John Speed, *The Counties of Britain* [1616] (London: Pavillion, 1988).

[2] On the structure of the church see William Harrison, *Description of England* [1587] (Ithaca: Cornell University Press, 1968), Bk. 2, chs. 1-2; Palliser, ch. 11.

[3] On women, see C. C. Camden, *The Elizabethan Woman* (Houston: Elsevier Press, 1952).

[4] From *An Old Man's Lesson,* cited in Gamaliel Bradford, *Elizabethan Women* (Cambridge MA: Houghton Mifflin, 1936), 60.

[5] On the social structure in general, see Harrison, Bk. 2, ch. 5; Sir Thomas Smith, *The State of England, A.D. 1600 [De Republica Anglorum],* ed. F. J. Fisher. Camden Miscellany 3:52 (London: Offices of the Camden Society, 1936); Palliser, ch. 3; G. M. Trevelyan, *Illustrated English Social History* (Harmondsworth: Penguin, 1942), 243.

[6] On government, see Harrison, Bk. 2, chs. 8-11; Palliser, ch. 10; Arthur Underhill, "Law," in *Shakespeare's England* (Oxford: at the Clarendon Press, 1916), 1.381-412.

[7] On religious life and beliefs, see Harrison, Bk. 2, ch. 1; Michael MacDonald, "Science, Magic, and Folklore," in *William Shakespeare: His World, His Works, His Influence. Vol. 1: His World,* ed. John F. Andrews (New York: Scribner, 1985), 175-94; F. G. Emmison, *Elizabethan Life: Morals and the Church Courts* (Chelmsford: Essex County Council, 1973); Patrick Collinson, "The Church: Religion and Its Manifestations," in Andrews, 21-40; Keith Thomas, *Religion and the Decline of Magic* (New York: Scribner, 1971); Rev. Ronald Bayne, "Religion," in *Shakespeare's England,* 1.48-78. Another important source is *The Book of Common Prayer,* which laid out the format of public religious observances [*The Prayer-Book of Queen Elizabeth 1559* (London: Griffith, 1890)]. . . .

Edmund Gosse (essay date 1897)

SOURCE: "The Age of Elizabeth (1560-1620)," in *A Short History of Modern English Literature,* D. Appleton and Company, 1897, pp.73-128.

[*In the following excerpt, Gosse argues that the literature of the early Elizabethan period was inferior to, yet preparatory of, a golden age in poetry inaugurated with the publication of Edmund Spenser's* The Shepherd's Calender *in 1579.*]

The accession of Queen Elizabeth, in 1558, was immediately followed by such a quickening of the political, social, and religious life of England as makes a veritable epoch in history. In literature, too, we are in the habit of regarding the development and range of those "spacious" times as having been extraordinary. Ultimately, indeed, nothing that the world has seen has been more extraordinary, but this expansion of the national temperament did not by any means reach the sphere of letters at once. For the first twenty years of the Queen's reign English literature was apparently stationary in its character, unadorned by masterpieces, and oblivious of distinction in style. If we look more closely, however, we may see that these years, inactive although they seem, were years of valuable preparation, education, and whetting of the national appetite.

The sentiment of the early Tudors, in all things connected with the mind, had been narrow and opposed to the movements of Continental thought. But Elizabeth, although her vehement Protestantism might seem to cut her off from European sympathy, was in reality much more drawn to its intellectual manifestations than her predecessors had been. It would be more to the point, perhaps, to say that her subjects were drawn into the general life of the world more than theirs had been. Everywhere new emotions, a new order of thought, were abroad, and what had passed over Italy long before, and had seized France half a century earlier, now invaded England. With the death of Mary, the bondage of the Middle Ages was finally broken through; a rebellion against the ascetic life was successful; a reaction against exclusive attention to religious ideas set in, almost with violence, among men of a literary habit of mind. Calvinism, a new phase of the ascetic instinct, made a footing in England, but it advanced slowly, and allowed literature time to develop by the side of it. In short, there obtained, from wider knowledge of the material world, from slackening theological torment, from a larger commerce with mankind, a reassertion of human nature, a new pleasure in the contemplation of its joys, its passions, its physical constitution. It is to this altered outlook upon life and man that we owe the glories of Elizabethan literature.

But these glories were not able to display themselves at once. In the tradition of English writing, especially of English verse, everything was still primitive and feeble, uncertain and inconsistent. The lyrics of Wyatt and Surrey had given a suggestion of a path which poetry might take, but a pretty copy of verses here and there flashing in the midst of a sea of jingling prose, did not show that even the gentle lesson of *Tottel's Miscellany* had been practically learned. We have but to compare what was written in England in 1560 with the slightly earlier literature of Italy, or even of France, to see that this country still languished in a kind of barbarism. To contrast the madrigals and epigrams of Marot, which it is perfectly fair to com-

pare with work of the same class produced by the early Elizabethans, is to draw a parallel between the product of an accomplished and in his way perfectly modern master, and the stumblings of ignorant scholars, who, eager to learn, yet know not what they should be learning.

The best that can be said, indeed, of the early Elizabethans is, that they were conscious of their deficiencies, and that they spared no pains in groping after self-education. They avoided no labour which might help them to improve the English language, to make its vocabulary rich enough and its syntax supple enough for the designs they had before them. But it is very strange for us to observe how little their vigour was aided by intelligence or their activity by sureness of touch. Humanism came upon the nation, but in forms curiously foreign to the rest of Europe; it came in an almost infantine curiosity to become acquainted with the ideas of the ancient classics, without taking any trouble to reproduce the purity of their style or to preserve the integrity of their language. England was flooded with "translations" in prose and verse; it has become the fashion of late to find surprising merits in the former, but no one has yet been bold enough to champion the latter. Lovers of paradox may hold that Adlington (1566) is a picturesque writer on lines dimly suggested by Apuleius, or that Heliodorus is sufficiently recognisable in the "witty and pleasant" pages of Underdowne (1569). But in dealing with verse we are on firmer ground, and it may safely be asserted that viler trash, less representative of the original, less distinguished in language, less intelligent in intention, is not to be found in the literature of the world, than in the feeble, vague, and silly verse-translations from the classics which deformed the earlier years of Elizabeth's reign. Phaer (1558) would be the worst of all translators of Virgil were he not surpassed in that bad eminence by the maniac Stanyhurst (1582). As for the group of gentlemen who put Seneca into rhyme—the Newtons and Nevilles and Studleys and Nuces—they, in their own words, "linked lie, with jingling chains, on wailing Limbo shore," the complete mockery of every stray reader who comes across them. Arthur Golding, who paraphrased the *Metamorphoses* of Ovid (1565-67), was the best of this large class of verse-translators of the early part of the reign; he possessed no genius, indeed, but a certain limpidity and sweetness in narrative lifts him out of the "limbo" of the Jasper Heywoods and the Churchyards.

This labour of translating occupied a vast number of persons at the Universities and the Inns of Court, where, as we are told in 1559, "Minerva's men and finest wits do swarm." Much, possibly the majority of what was written, never reached the printing-press at all. More interesting, perhaps, but scarcely more meritorious than the work of the translators, were the attempts at original or imitative poetry. The earliest name is that of Barnabee Googe, whose most important poem, the *Cupido Conquered,* shows, like the *Temple de Cupido* of Marot (the comparison is cruel for Googe), a tendency to return to mediæval forms of allegory, and to the school of the *Roman de la Rose.* George Turbervile, a translator from Mantuan and Boccaccio, wrote so-called "songs and sonnets" (1567) of his own. The *Romeus and Juliet* of Arthur Broke has the interest of having certainly been enjoyed by Shakespeare. These and other minor poets of this experimental period were greatly hampered by their devotion to the tiresome couplet of alternate six and seven beats, a measure without a rival in its capacity for producing an effect at once childish and pedantic. But it is in the frequent and popular miscellanies of this age, and particularly in the *Paradise of Dainty Devises* (1576) and the *Gorgeous Gallery of Gallant Inventions* (1578), that the triviality and emptiness of early Elizabethan verse-style may be most conveniently studied. Poetry was in eager request during these years, but the performance was not ready to begin; the orchestra was tuning up.

One musician, indeed, there was who produced for a very short time a harmony which was both powerful and novel. The solitary poet of a high order between Dunbar and Spenser is THOMAS SACKVILLE, afterwards Lord Buckhurst and Earl of Dorset. Born in 1536, he went early to Oxford, and became locally celebrated for "sonnets sweetly sauced," which have entirely disappeared; we may conjecture that they were of the school of Wyatt. In 1561 there was played at Whitehall the "great mask" or tragedy of *Gorbuduc,* by Sackville and his friend Norton. Finally, the second or 1563 edition of the narrative miscellany called *A Mirror for Magistrates* contained two contributions, an "Induction" and a story of "Henry Stafford, Duke of Buckingham," from the pen of Sackville: it is supposed that these were written about 1560. In the latest of these compositions the poet, addressing himself by name, says that it was his purpose "the woeful fall of princes to describe" in future poems; but this he was prevented from doing by his absorption in political and public life. He rose to the highest offices in the state, living on until 1608, but is not known to have written another line of verse.

Sackville's poetical life, therefore, closed at about the same age as Keats's did; he is among "the inheritors of unfulfilled renown." His withdrawal from the practice of his art probably delayed the development of English literature by a quarter of a century, since of Sackville's potentiality of genius there can be no question. What he has left to us has a sombre magnificence, a stately fulness, absolutely without parallel in his own age. The poetlings around him were timid, crude, experimental, but Sackville writes like a young and inexperienced master perhaps, yet always like a master. He shows little or not at all the influence of Wyatt and Surrey, but with one hand he takes hold of the easy richness of Chaucer and with the other of the majesty of Dante, to whose *Inferno* the plan of his *Induction* is deeply indebted. In his turn, Sackville exercised no slight fascination over the richer, more elaborate and florid, but radically cognate fancy of Spenser; and even Shakespeare must have read and admired the sinister fragments of the Lord High Treasurer. Scarce an adjective here and there survives to show Sackville faintly touched by the tasteless heresies of his age. His poetry is not read, partly because of its monotony, partly because the subject-matter of it offers no present entertainment; but in the history of the evolution of style in our literature the place of Sackville must always be a prominent one.

It is to be noted, as a sign of the unhealthy condition of letters in this hectic age, that although it produced experiments in literature, it encouraged no literary men; that is to say, the interest in books was so faint and unsettled, that no one man was persuaded to give his life to the best literature, or any considerable portion of his life. The only exception may seem to be that of GEORGE GASCOIGNE, whose talent needed but to have equalled his ambition to reach the highest things. Unfortunately, his skill was mediocre, and though he introduced from Italy the prose comedy, the novel, and blank verse satire, and was the first translator of Greek tragedy and the earliest English critic—success in any one of which departments might have immortalised him—he was tame and trifling in them all. He was still writing actively when, in 1577, he died prematurely, at the age of forty. Nash, in the next generation, summed up the best that can be said for Gascoigne in describing him as one "who first beat the path to that perfection which our best poets have aspired to since his departure."

What has been said of the verse of the early Elizabethan period is in some measure true of its prose, with the exception that bad taste and positive error were less rampant because there was much less ambition to be brilliant and less curiosity in experiment. The prose of this period is not to be sharply distinguished from that of the earlier half of the century. It presents to us no name of a creator of style, like Cranmer, and no narrator with the vivacity of Cavendish. ROGER ASCHAM, who survived until 1568, was the leading writer of the age in English; his influence was strenuously opposed to the introduction of those French and Italian forces which would have softened and mellowed the harshness of the English tongue so beneficially, and he was all in favour of a crabbed imitation of Greek models, the true beauty of which, it is safe to say, no one in his day comprehended in the modern spirit. It is impossible to call Ascham an agreeable writer, and pure pedantry to insist upon his mastery of English. His efforts were all in an academic direction, and his suspicion of ornament was in diametric opposition to the instinct of the nation, as to be presently and in the great age abundantly revealed. Meanwhile to Ascham and his disciples the only thing needful seemed to be "to speak plainly and nakedly after the common sort of men in few words." North sacrificed, indeed, all distinction, but secured a merry species of vigour, in his paraphrase of Amyot's translation of Plutarch. A deserved popularity was won by Day's 1563 translation of the Latin of Foxe's so-called *Book of Martyrs* and by Holinshed's familiar *Chronicles,* of which Shakespeare made abundant use. In a sketch less hurried than this must be, the laborious compilations of Grafton and of Stow would demand an attention which we dare not give to them here. All these compositions were of value, but the progress of English prose is not apparent in any of them.

On no point of literary criticism have opinions differed more than as to the place of JOHN LYLY in the development of style. Extravagantly admired at the time of its original publication, ridiculed and forgotten for two centuries, the *Euphues* (1579-80) has recovered prestige only to have its claims to originality contested. It has been elaborately shown that Lyly owed his manner and system to the Spaniard Guevara, and his use of English to Lord Berners, while the very balance of his sentences has been attributed to imitation of the *Prayer-Book.* In all this there seems to me to be too much attention paid to detail; looking broadly at the early prose of Elizabeth's reign, it is surely impossible not to recognise that a new element of richness, of ornament, of harmony, an element by no means wholly admirable, but extremely noticeable, was introduced by Lyly; that, in short, the publication of *Euphues* burnishes and suddenly animates—with false lights and glisterings, if you will, but still animates—the humdrum aspect of English prose as Ascham and Wilson had left it. Splendour was to be one of the principal attributes of the Elizabethan age, and *Euphues* is the earliest prose book which shows any desire to be splendid.

It is a very tedious reading for us, this solemn romance of a young Athenian of the writer's own day, who visits Naples first and then England. But to the early admirers of *Euphues,* its analysis of emotion, its wire-drawn definitions of feeling, its high sententiousness, made it intensely attractive. Above all, it was a book for ladies; in an age severely academic and virile, this author turned to address women, lingeringly, lovingly, and he was rewarded as Richardson was two centuries later, and as M. Paul Bourget has been in our own day. Of the faults of *Euphues* enough and to spare is said in all compilations of criticism. Lyly's use of antithesis is always severely reproved, yet it broke up successfully the flat-footed dulness of his predecessors; his method of drawing images from fabulous zoology and botany is ridiculed, and deservedly, for it degenerates into a trick; yet it evidences a

lively fancy; his whole matter is sometimes styled "a piece of affectation and nonsense," yet that merely proves the critic to have never given close attention to the book he condemns. The way Lyly says things is constantly strained and sometimes absurd, but his substance is always noble, enlightened, and urbane, and his influence was unquestionably as civilising as it was extensive. As to his Euphuism, about which so much has been written, it was mainly a tub to catch a whale,—a surprising manner consciously employed to attract attention, like Carlylese. It had no lasting effects, fortunately, but for the time it certainly enlivened the languid triviality of the vernacular.

Of infinitely greater importance was the revolution effected in poetry, in the same eventful year 1579, by the publication of the *Shepherd's Calender* of EDMUND SPENSER. With this book we begin a new era; we stand on the threshold, not of a fashion or a period, but of the whole system of modern English poetry. The strange obscurity which broods over most of Elizabethan biography—where the poetry was everything and the poet little regarded—lifts but seldom from the life of Spenser. He may have been born in 1552; some translations of his from Petrarch and Joachim du Bellay, already showing the direction of his reading, were printed in 1569; from 1570 to 1576 he was at Cambridge, where he fell into a literary, but extremely tasteless and pedantic set of men, who, nevertheless, had the wit to perceive their friend's transcendent genius; and during three obscure years, while we lose sight of him, we gather that he was bewitched by the charming form and character of Sir Philip Sidney, his junior by two years. The influence of Sidney was not beneficial to Spenser, for that delightful person had accepted the heresy of the Cambridge wits, and was striving to bring about the "general surceasing and silence of bald rhymers," and the adoption in English of classic forms of rhymeless quantitative verse, entirely foreign to the genius of our prosody.

For a moment it seemed as though Spenser would succumb to the authority of Sidney's Areopagus, and waste his time and art on exercises in iambic trimeter. But at the end of 1579 came the anonymous publication of the *Shepherd's Calender,* and in the burst of applause which greeted these lyric pastorals, the danger passed. The book consisted of twelve eclogues, distantly modelled on those of Theocritus, and more closely upon Virgil and Mantuan; they were in rhymed measures of extreme variety, some of the old jingling kind, from which Spenser had not yet escaped, others of a brilliant novelty, conveying such a music as had yet been heard from no English lips. "June" is the most stately and imaginative of these eclogues, while in "May" and "September" we see how much the poet was still enslaved by the evil traditions of the century. The *Shepherd's Calender* is momentous in its ease and fluent melody, its novelty of form, and its delicate grace. Throughout England, with singular unanimity, "the new poet" was hailed with acclamation, for, as Sidney quaintly put it two years later, "an overfaint quietness" had "strewn the house for poets," and the whole nation was eager for song. Yet we must remember that the positive value of these artificial pastorals of 1579 might easily be, and sometimes has been, overrated.

Spenser now disappears from our sight again. We divine him employed in the public service in Ireland, associated there with Raleigh, and rewarded by the manor and castle of Kilcolman. We get vague glimpses of the composition, from 1580 onwards, of a great poem of chivalry, in which Spenser is encouraged by Raleigh, and in 1590 there are published the first three books of the *Faerie Queen*. From this time forth to the end of his brief life, Spenser is unchallenged as the greatest of the English poets, no less pre-eminent in non-dramatic verse among his glorious coevals than Shakespeare was presently to be in dramatic. He published in 1591 his *Complaints,* a collection of earlier poems; *Colin Clout's Come Home Again* in 1595, *Amoretti and Epithalamia* in the same year, three more books of the *Faerie Queen* and the *Four Hymns* in 1596. The close of his life was made wretched by the excesses of the Irish rebels, who burned Kilcolman in October 1598. Spenser, reduced to penury, fled to England, and died "for lack of bread" in London, on the 16th of January 1599.

It is by the *Faerie Queen* that Spenser holds his sovereign place among the foremost English poets. Taken without relation to its time, it is a miracle of sustained and extended beauty; but considered historically, it is nothing less than a portent. To find an example of British poetry of the highest class, Spenser had to search back to the Middle Ages, to Chaucer himself. So great was the change which two centuries had made in language, in prosody, in attitude to life, that Spenser could practically borrow from Chaucer little or nothing but a sentimental stimulus. The true precursors of his great poem were the Italian romances, and chiefly the *Orlando Furioso*. It is not to be questioned that the youth of Spenser had been utterly enthralled by the tranquil and harmonious imagination of Ariosto. In writing the chivalrous romance of the *Faerie Queen,* Spenser, although he boasted of his classical acquirements, was singularly little affected by Greek, or even Latin ideas. There was no more of Achilles than of Roland in his conception of a fighting hero. The greatest of all English poems of romantic adventure is steeped in the peculiar enchantment of the Celts. It often seems little more or less than a *mabinogi* extended and embroidered, a Celtic dream tempered with moral allegory and political allusion. Not in vain had Spenser for so many years inhabited that

"most beautiful and sweet country," the Island of Dreams and melancholy fantasy. Cradled in the richness of Italy, trained in the mistiness of Ireland, the genius of Spenser was enabled to give to English poetry exactly the qualities it most required. Into fields made stony and dusty with systematic pedantry it poured a warm and fertilising rain of romance.

The first three books of the *Faerie Queen* contain the most purely poetical series of pictures which English literature has to offer to us. Here the Italian influence is still preponderant; in the later books the Celtic spirit of dream carries the poet a little too far into the realms of indefinite fancy. A certain grandeur which sustains the three great cantos of Truth, Temperance, and Chastity fades away as we proceed. It would be, indeed, not difficult to find fault with much in the conduct of this extraordinary poem. The construction of it is loose and incoherent when we compare it with the epic grandeur of the masterpieces of Ariosto and Tasso. The heroine, Queen Gloriana, never once makes her appearance in her own poem, and this is absurd. That a wind of strange hurry and excitability seems to blow the poet along so fast that he has no time to consider his grammar, his rhymes, or even his continuity of ideas, but is obliged, if the profanity be permitted, to "faggot his fancies as they fall"—this is certainly no merit; while the constant flattery of Elizabeth has been to some fastidious spirits a stumbling-block.

But these are spots in the sun. The rich and voluptuous colour, the magical landscape, the marvellous melody, have fascinated young readers in every generation, and will charm the race till it decays. More than any other writer, save Keats, Spenser is interpenetrated with the passion of beauty. All things noble and comely appeal to him; no English poet has been so easy and yet so stately, so magnificent and yet so plaintive. He is pre-eminent for a virile sweetness, for the love and worship of woman, for a power of sustaining an impression of high spectacular splendour. What should constitute a gentleman, and in what a world a gentleman should breathe and move—these are his primary considerations. His long poem streams on with the panoply of a gorgeous masque, drawn through the resonant woodlands of fairyland, in all the majestic pomp of imitative knight-errantry. And then his music, his incomparable harmony of versification, the subtlety of that creation of his, the stanza which so proudly bears his name—the finest single invention in metre which can be traced home to any English poet! All these things combine to make the flower of Edmund Spenser's genius not the strongest nor the most brilliant, perhaps, but certainly the most delicately perfumed in the whole rich garden of English verse. . . .

LITERARY STYLE

William Rossky (essay date 1989)

SOURCE: "Imagination in the English Renaissance: Psychology and Poetic," in *Studies in the Renaissance*, Vol. V, 1989, pp. 49-73.

[*Below, Rossky discusses the Renaissance notion of the poet's proper use of imagination—that imaginative writing must be based upon accurate perceptions, but that controlled and disciplined artifice can actually aid the poet in reconstructing objective, real events.*]

Shakespeare couples lunatic, lover, and poet as 'of imagination all compact' (*Dream* v.i.7-8); Spenser finds that Phantastes' chamber is filled with 'leasings, tales, and lies' (*F.Q.* ii.ix.51.9) and that his eyes seem 'mad or foolish' (*F.Q.* ii.ix.52.7); Drayton speaks of the 'doting trumperie' of imagination;[1] when men's minds become 'inflamed', says Bacon, 'it is all done by stimulating the imagination till it becomes ungovernable, and not only sets reason at nought, but offers violence to it'.[2] These views of imagination and its activity, echoed in other important literature of the age of Elizabeth, hardly suggest a favorable view of the faculty assigned to the poet. The explanation of such derogatory views lies in the popular psychology of the period. This study therefore proposes, first, to examine the psychological account of the operation of imagination and thus to show not only the disrepute but the specific grounds of the disrepute of the faculty and, secondly, to indicate briefly how the particular grounds for disrepute influence the view of imagination expressed by poets and literary critics, are indeed converted into a justification of the poet's imagination.

The general view seems to be that the Elizabethan criticism, much of which is highly defensive of poetry, is evoked by the so-called 'Puritan' attack upon poetry. That the Puritan attack played a large part in eliciting the defenses is certain, but the condemnation is sometimes much less direct, and much less influential upon the criticism, than is sometimes thought. After all, much of the stock in trade of the attacks consisted of criticism of the morality of actors, of the opportunity for vice presented by the gathering of a theater audience, and even of the littering of the streets by playbills—to which arguments we do not find much direct response in the poetic. Examination reveals that the Elizabethan defenses of poetry do surely as much to overcome the disrepute of imaginative activity which is fostered by the popular[3] psychology as they do to meet the charges of the Puritan attack. But that Elizabethan criticism does this we can show only by presenting the particular grounds of disrepute to which the critics respond.

I

The technicalities, individual refinements, and variations among the psychologists describing imagination are beyond the scope of this study; for it is concerned to establish those characteristics which are common to most of the writers and which therefore are most apt to have been common knowledge among the fairly well-read men we may assume the Elizabethan critics to have been.

Always the imagination or fantasy[4] is seen as a power operating in a framework of other faculties and functions. In a definite hierarchical order of communication, knowledge travels from the so-called 'outer' senses (the five primary senses), to the 'inner' (Common Sense, Imagination and/or Fantasy, Sensible Reason, and Memory, which occupy cells in the brain), and thus to the highest rational, incorporeal powers (the Intellect or Wit or Understanding, and the Will). More specifically, the general course of communication runs from the perception of the outward senses to common sense, or directly to imagination, which unites the various reports of the senses into impressions that are in turn submitted to the examination of a rational power and then passed to memory which retains the impressions and reflects them back to the Imagination and Sensible Reason, should they turn to it to recall past incidents. Beyond these faculties and functions lies the overseeing and judging power of the highest Understanding, which in turn informs the Will.

Ultimately, then, all knowledge, thought, and action depend upon the transmission of data through a hierarchy of powers. And in this 'instrumental'[5] system, imagination is a key faculty; for, as Wright puts it, 'whatsoever we vnderstand, passeth by the gates of our imagination'.[6] Moreover, by imagination 'wee apprehend likenesse and shapes of things of perticulars receyued',[7] the 'formes of things',[8] and a sound, healthy imagination is one which reflects to higher powers only accurate images of reality, else, in the instrumental scheme, sound knowledge, proper thought and action become impossible. Therefore, imagination in its healthy reproductive capacity ought—like a mirror—to reflect accurate sensible impressions of the external world, and upon the need for such accuracy in the images of imagination the greatest stress is placed.

> Knowledges next organ is *Imagination*;
> A glasse, wherein the obiect of our Sense
> Ought to reflect true height, or declination,
> For vnderstandings cleare intelligence,

says Greville.[9] An 'obiect' must be 'made no greater nor lesse then it is in deed' (Bright, p. 86; see also pp. 78-79). The concern of the Elizabethan is that the imagination deliver accurate images. When it faces toward reason, Bacon expects imagination to have 'the print of Truth' (*Works*, III, 382).

If the report of the senses is accurately delivered, man's reactions are healthy and proportional; but if false reports are rendered, matters are 'otherwise taken then the obiect requireth' (Bright, p. 86); man's reasoning is good 'so farre as the naturall principles lead, or outward obiectes be sincerely taken, & truely reported to the minds consideration' (Bright, p. 73). But when fantasy reports 'mishapen obiects', the mind is off balance and reason is 'troden vnder foote'.[10] If fantasy is 'marred', says Sir John Davies, wit perceives everything falsely.[11] Indeed, as a consequence of the theory that it was the inaccurate report of imagination which misled reason, it was common opinion that injured minds—for example, those of idiots or madmen—could reason as well as those of ordinary men, but were misled by the faulty reporting of faulty imagination. Reason would be only as accurate as the images presented to it. As an instrument for correct reason, then, imagination should present accurate, mirror-like images.

Furthermore, since reason is conventionally described as the power which distinguishes good from evil, the ultimate result of inaccurate images of reality is immorality. Since the higher soul is itself incorruptible, the odium falls on the false images of fantasy:

> But if a frenzy do possess the brain;
> It so disturbs and blots the forms of things,
> As Phantasy proves altogether vain,
> And to the Wit, no true relation brings.
>
> Then doth the Wit admitting all for true,
> Build fond conclusions on those idle
>   grounds!
> Then doth it fly the Good, and Ill pursue!
> Believing all that this false spy propounds.
>
>   (Sir John Davies, p. 193)

Indeed, 'Some ascribe all vices to a false and corrupt imagination . . . deluding the soul with false shews and suppositions', declares Burton (p. 221).

Obviously, then, a good deal of the reputation of imagination depends upon the accuracy of its images; for if this most important instrument of the soul, container of all images and source of knowledge, is inaccurate, distorts reality, it betrays reason and thus immorality results. According to the psychologists, with inaccurate representations of reality we are little better off than—indeed we may be—madmen or idiots. Nevertheless, to the psychologist, imagination, in both passive and active operation, is, for the most part, notoriously fragile, highly inaccurate in its reproductions of life; thereby misleads the soul in general and reason

in particular; is, in short, as we shall now see, a most fallible and consequently disreputable faculty.

II

The widespread disrepute of imagination as a falsifying and misguiding faculty rested, even in its passive functions, upon many elements. A rather obvious one was its close tie to and dependence upon the senses, which had been condemned from classical through medieval times to the Renaissance, their disrepute dramatized in accounts of the conflict of the spirit with the animal flesh or philosophized in Platonic descriptions of the secondary and inadequate reality of sensory objects. This unfavorable view the psychologists continue, and to it they add. Wright's derogatory view of the senses as faculties which relate us to 'bruite beastes' (p. 7) is a usual one. Thus merely as a near neighbor of the senses in the instrumental scheme, imagination shares their general disrepute. 'For *Fantacie* becing neere the outward *Sences,* / Allures the *Soule* to loue things bodily,' says Davies of Hereford (*Works*, I, 9-10). The world's things, then, 'do, by fits, her [the soul's] Phantasy possess', agrees Sir John Davies (p. 186).

And for the psychologists, as might be expected, the senses are suspect not only because they are tied to the flesh and in their very nature corrupt, but also because they fail in providing that accurate picture of life which Elizabethan psychology demands for healthy functioning. Only before the fall of man, concludes Bright, did the outer senses 'perfectly and sincerely' present 'the condition of sensible things' (p. 122). It follows, then, as Greville has it, 'So must th'Imagination from the sense / Be misinformed' (*Poems and Dramas*, I, 157). Thus the fallibility of the senses, since they supply the images of imagination, affects the reliability and hence the reputation of imagination. Moreover, about the senses hangs the suggestion of immorality, in which fantasy, their neighbor, shares: imagination, like the senses, is attracted by things of the body.

But, according to the psychologists, the very nature of the imagination itself and its susceptibility to all sorts of influences produces monstrously deformed reflections of external reality in the mirror which it is supposed to be. Greville, after telling us, as does writer after writer, that imagination should function as a 'glasse', decries the lack of veracity in the distorted 'pictures' of *Imagination'* which are 'still too foule, or faire; / Not like the life in lineament, or ayre' (*Poems and Dramas*, I, 156). Despite the fact that it is the function of the faculty to present accurate pictures of reality, imagination makes 'vntrue reports' (DuLaurens, p. 74). 'Corrupt' is a favored adjective for the faculty.[12] 'Fonde and absurde imaginations' and 'apparitiōs and sights' (Lemnius, fol. 132ᵛ) are more often associated with imagination than the clear images required of sound and healthy imagination.

And the distortion of real objects when reflected in the imagination is the result of its own great fragility. The agencies which corrupt its images and thus upset its healthy functioning in the hierarchical organization are almost innumerable and practically inescapable. In fact, fantasy may operate 'as life is led, wel, or amisse' (Davies of Hereford, I, 8). Thus gluttony fills the head with 'fantasyes'.[13] A bad constitution will lead to the fantastic dreams of imagination (Lemnius, fols. 95^r, 113^r). Much always depends upon the impressionability of the brain, and to the lack of a proper degree of moisture for the impression of images are due, for example, the distorted imaginations of old age.

As has perhaps already been suggested, not only the distortion but also the disrepute of some of its agents helps to make imagination a disreputable faculty in the Elizabethan mind, and it soon becomes clear why Huarte remarks that 'the sciences which appertaine to the imaginatiue, are those, which such vtter as dote in their sicknesse, and not of those which appertaine to the vnderstanding, or to the memorie' (p. 63).[14] And as might be expected from Shakespeare's reference to lunatics, perhaps as frequent a disreputable relationship as any is that to madness; 'for', as Batman has it, 'by madnesse that is called *Mania,* principally ye imagination is hurt' (Bk. VII, chap. 6), while DuLaurens refers to the 'foolish and vaine imaginations' of 'franticke' men (p. 79). Indeed, so closely tied to imagination is the frenzy of madness that the prescription for madness is confinement of the patient to a room where there are no pictures to stimulate the imagination (Batman, Bk. VII, chap. 5; Boorde, *Dyetary,* p. 298), and hence, often, to a wholly dark room. It is this conventional association of idiocy and madness with fantasy that Spenser recognizes when he tells us that Phantastes 'mad or foolish seemd' (*F.Q.* II.ix.52.7). As a result of madness, of course, the images of imagination are distorted and the instrumental process is disturbed; for 'frenzy' mangles 'the forms of things' so that fantasy makes a false report to the understanding (Sir John Davies, p. 193).

Not only does the accepted association with madness cast further aspersion on the reputation of imagination and its images, but madness is frequently linked with the disease of melancholy and its distorted imagination. However, in its own right melancholy had a claim on the power to distort images of imagination, a claim easily as great as that of madness, since almost anything from diet (e.g., DuLaurens, p. 104; Lemnius, fol. 143^v) to sin (e.g., Bright, pp. 187-189; Burton, pp. 156, 176) could cause melancholy. And when we consider that melancholy was considered a disease and was itself tied to 'enuy, emulation, bitternesse, hatred, spyght, sorcery, fraude, subtlety, deceipte, treason,

sorrow, heauinesse, desperation, distrust, and last of all to a lam'table and shamefull end' (Lemnius, fol. 23^v), the relation between imagination and melancholy is clearly not to the advantage of imagination. And that association, with its consequent distortion of images, is almost inevitable: as Lemnius has it, 'No man but is subiect to Melancholy' (fol. 136^v).

Typical of the connection made between melancholy and imagination, with consequent disrepute for imagination from the distortion and resultant lack of veracity of images on the one hand and its bad associations on the other, is the comment of Lemnius, according to whom melancholy persons 'feeding theyr owne Phantasies' see 'that which was not so in deede' (fol. 150^r). Although some types of melancholy are said to encourage intellectual activity, by far the more frequent view is that of Nashe: 'And euen as slime and durt in a standing puddle, engender toads and frogs, and many other vnsightly creatures, so this slimie melancholy humor still still thickning as it stands still, engendreth many mishapen obiects in our imaginations' (*Terrors, Works,* III, 232-233). With all commentators, the result is similarly the distortion of images in imagination. For DuLaurens, the cold and black of melancholy affect 'principally the imagination, presenting vnto it continually blacke formes and strange visions' (p. 91). For Bright, the result is 'monsters, which nature neuer bred' (p. 106); and Burton says, 'that melancholy men and sick men, conceive so many phantastical visions, apparitions to themselves, and have such absurd suppositions . . . can be imputed to naught else but to a corrupt, false, and violent imagination' (p. 222).

Specifically, it is the fumes from the melancholy humors which, rising into the brain, do the distorting (Bright, p. 102). Thus, not only the fumes of melancholy, but those of other humors affect and distort fantasy. Any 'ill humours' may send 'confused ymaginations and vayne foolish visions' into the brain (Lemnius, fol. 95^r). For example, the fumes of choler, ascending to the brain, change 'stronglye the brayne and the vertue imaginatiue' (Batman, Bk. IV, chap. 10). resulting in 'phantasticall imaginations' (Lemnius, fol. 132^v). And when we consider the conventional view expressed by DuLaurens' statement that 'there is not one bodie in the whole world to be found of so equall a mixture, as that there is not some excesse in one of the foure qualities ouer and aboue the rest' (p. 169), so that the perfectly balanced combination of humors is impossible, we can see how deplorably little accuracy and integrity the imagination could be conceded.

But we are not done, for the passions also distort imagination: 'you may well see how the imagination putteth greene spectacles before the eyes of our witte, to make it see nothing but greene, that is, serving for the consideration of the Passion'; and thus 'a false imagination corrupteth the vnderstanding, making it beleeve that thinges are better than they are in very deede' (Wright, pp. 51, 52). Again there is no correspondence to external reality. Affections 'In fancy make us heare, feele, see impressions, / Such as out of our sense they doe not borrow' (Greville, *Poems and Dramas,* I, 157). It was inevitable, then, that the lover's imagination should be conventionally described as corrupted.

Even the occupations of men distort their imaginations, again making imagination 'deliuer thinges vnto the minde after an impure sort' and 'otherwise then they are indeed' (Bright, pp. 78-79; see also DuLaurens, p. 98). The Elizabethan had even to reckon with susceptibility to the influence of the devil who might imprint upon his imagination 'such things as neither men nor deuilles themselues can possibly perfourme' (LaPrimaudaye, p. 156). In view of the possibilities described, the chances for a healthy imagination, producing sound and accurate images, would seem, to an Elizabethan, rather remote.

Thus the 'sicknesse' of the imagination—tied to idiocy, old age, madness, and gluttony; susceptible to the vagaries of every constitution, the fumes of every humor, the influences of every occupation, producing visions impossible, 'monsters', images 'mishapen', 'fonde and absurde', 'confused'—in short, 'false'.

Hitherto we have considered imagination as acting rather passively so that its disrepute seems to stem chiefly from its very openness to influences which in turn make its testimony unreliable. In this role imagination seems perhaps abused as much as it abuses. But imagination is not merely passive. As Bacon puts it: 'Neither is the Imagination simply and only a messenger; but is invested with or at leastwise usurpeth no small authority in itself, besides the duty of the message' (*Works,* III, 382). Imagination receives and conveys images, but, as Huarte has it, it also devises 'some others of his own framing' (p. 79). The imagination 'taketh what pleaseth it, and addeth thereunto or diminisheth', says the translator of LaPrimaudaye (p. 155); and he speaks of the 'newe and monstrous things it forgeth and coyneth' (p. 156): the verbs as well as the adjectives are significant. So Bright finds that, under the influence of melancholy, the fantasy 'compoundeth, and forgeth disguised shapes', that it 'fayneth vnto the heart' terrible 'counterfet goblins' (pp. 103-104).[15] For Burton, fantasy not only receives objects and retains them for a while, but also has the power of 'making new of his own'; 'by comparison' to the objects provided by sense, he continues, fantasy 'feigns infinite others unto himself' (p. 139).

'Feign', 'forge', 'frame', 'coyn'—all are words for the active, in a sense creative, functioning of imagination. Although words like 'feigning' or 'forging', which

are particularly popular, suggest the improbability of the products of imagination, they also convey the building power of the faculty. And in this active functioning, of course, the possibility of a lack of correspondence to life—with consequent disrepute—becomes as pronounced as it can be; for imagination, left to its own devices, may make what it will, creating in almost absolute disregard of the images furnished by the senses and hence fashioning often the fondest impossibilities. A brief examination of this activity of the imagination—feigning—will make clearer the concept of the operation of imagination and explain why the active imagination might be accused of producing monsters and lies.

Although imagination feigns the unreal, for the Elizabethan psychologist pursuing his empirical approach, its unreal images are in a very tangible way still derived ultimately from impressions of real objects. Like all other images and almost everything in the mind, feigned images have their origin, through the senses, in the external world. Feigning, even at its wildest, is based ultimately on external reality, framing from it, and, sometimes, even according to it. Thus objects never seen are created upon the basis of 'perticulars receyued, though they bee absent: As when it seemeth that we see golden hils, either else when through the similitude of other hils we dreame of the hill Pernasus' (Batman, Bk. III, chap. II); without matter from life the 'fantasie can doe nothing', but with it can forge all sorts of impossibilities (LaPrimaudaye, p. 156). Thus it is that out of the images with which it is supplied fantasy may, as we have seen, feign 'new of his own' 'by comparison' with the forms of things which it has received. Consequently even the wildest dreams, products of imagination, are conventionally described as having their source in images from real life. Without 'Patterns' imagination cannot feign its 'things vnlikely' (Davies of Hereford, *Works,* I, 8).

But it is when we see how fantasy handles its raw material in the creation of its original images that their unreality is fully explained. Perhaps as a result of the belief in the concreteness and tangibility of the empirically perceived images, Elizabethan doctrine pictured imagination as almost literally cutting up its images into parts and then rejoining them into forms that never exist in the external world of nature. A centaur as an imaginary creation could result from cutting away the head of a horse and substituting the torso of a man. Imagination, 'being not tied to the laws of matter, may at pleasure join that which nature hath severed, and sever that which nature hath joined, and so make unlawful matches and divorces of things' (Bacon, *Works,* III, 343). Instead of merely receiving the images of external objects passively and conveying them whole to higher powers, imagination not only 'taketh what pleaseth it' but 'addeth thereunto or diminisheth, changeth and rechangeth, mingleth and vnmingleth, so that it cutteth asunder and seweth vp againe, as it listeth' (LaPrimaudaye, p. 155). For Huarte, 'this imagination hath force not onely to compound a fygure possible with another, but doth ioyne also (after the order of nature) those which, are vnpossible, and of them growes to shape mountains of gold, and calues that flie' (p. 132). 'The imagination', says DuLaurens, 'compoundeth and ioyneth together the formes of things, as of Golde and a mountaine, it maketh a golden mountaine' (p. 74). Thus it is that the imagination of man may 'faine . . . flying asses' (*ibid.*, p. 75).

When Bright, then, says 'compoundeth', he is using the word in an exact way. And so too when Davies of Hereford speaks of the faculty as crippling the whole and making whole the crippled, making and marring (*Works*, I, 8)—of *Fantacie, / Which doth so forme reforme, and it deformes, / As pleaseth hir fantasticke faculty* (*ibid.*, I, 7)—he has not only described the instability of imagination and the unreality of its products but given us an accurate account of the processes from which that unreality results.

In this way, then, the imagination 'forgeth disguised shapes'. As a result of such severing and compounding, the shapes of imagination must prove unreal, and it is the unreality of its products which is accented— as these very comments suggest. Not only does it 'reforme' but it also 'deformes' reality. Crippling or recreating life, it wrests from reality 'things vnlikely', joining, as Huarte put it, things 'which are vnpossible' to create its 'golden hils' or 'flying asses'. Almost invariably it is described as creating the disreputably incredible and false— 'terrible' and 'monstrous fictions' that do not depend at all upon 'externall occasiō', building 'fansies' that are 'vayne, false, and voide of ground' (Bright, pp. 102-103). Monsters, wild dreams, and chimerasC—'monstrous and prodigious things' (Burton, p. 140)—are traditionally its products. Speaking of the force of imagination 'in such as are awake', Burton exclaims: 'how many chimaeras, anticks, golden mountains, and castles in the air, do they build vnto themselves!' (p. 220) and finds that, through the vagaries of imagination, not only the sick but even the well may 'conceive . . . phantastical visions, apparitions to themselves' (p. 222). LaPrimaudaye emphasizes both the monstrous and distorted quality of fantasy's images: 'it is a wonder to see the inuentions it [fantasy] hath after some occasion is giuen it, and what new and monstrous things it forgeth and coyneth, by sundry imaginations arising of those images and similitudes, from whence it hath the first paterne' (p. 156). Out of such a background come Spenser's 'Infernall Hags, *Centaurs*, feendes, *Hippodames*' (*F.Q.* II.ix.50.8), which abound in Phantastes' chamber. This 'fayned fantasie' which misinforms reason is, for DuLaurens, 'vntrue', 'false' (p. 74), while for Scot the imaginations of some melancholy men conceive 'strange, incredible, and impossible things' (p. 30) making them 'beleeve they see, heare, and doo that, which never was nor shall be' (p. 38). As Spenser puts it, in a 'fayning fansie' occur 'Sights neuer seene' ('An Hymne in Honour of Love', lines 254-255) and 'such as in the world were neuer yit' (*F.Q.* II.ix.50.4). The giddy fantasy manufactures 'those things which neuer haue bin, shalbe, or can be', says LaPrimaudaye. 'For it staieth not in that which is shewed vnto it by the senses that serue it' (p. 155). Different as the connotations are, it is not very far from this and some of the preceding language to Sir Philip Sidney's description of poets who 'to imitate borrow nothing of what is, hath been, or shall be'.[16]

The power of fantasy actively to create monstrously distorted visions, lies about external reality, is, then, a cardinal tenet of Elizabethan psychology. These creations are called 'tales', 'fables', 'fictions', 'lyes', 'leasings'.[17] And although imagination feigns not only the grotesque or the monstrous but also the beautiful, not only 'flying asses' and chimeras but also 'golden hils' and 'castles in the air', all are incredible and therefore disreputable. The bias of the material in the psychological writings stands very heavily against this active function of the faculty.

And the lack of control over imagination is shown not only by the easy distortion of its images but by their unpredictable, accidental sequence. 'Now shee *Chimeraes*, then shee *Beauties* frame' (Davies of Hereford, *Works*, I, 8). Haphazardly imagination makes monsters one moment and castles in the air the next. In the Elizabethan psychology, the images of imagination are idly capricious, fleeting and inconstant, purposeless and insubstantial, succeeding each other, without control or order, in a restless procession. A faculty 'still in motion', creating 'toyes' (Davies of Hereford, *Works*, I, 8), its forming, reforming and deforming provide a quickly changing scenery for the mind. 'Pow'refull yet . . . most vnstaid', it 'resteth not' in its creation of 'visions vaine' (*ibid.*, I, 7), but remains forever busy; even in sleep 'A thousand dreams, phantastical and light, / With fluttering wings, do keep her still awake!' (Sir John Davies, p. 176; cf. also Scot, pp. 101-102 and Bright, p. 118). It is 'another *Proteus, or a Chameleon*' (Burton, p. 223). Speaking appropriately of the 'giddinesse of Fantasie', LaPrimaudaye's translator finds the faculty 'sudden, & so farre from stayednes, that euen in the time of sleep it hardly taketh any rest', being occupied in dreams of impossibilities (p. 155). It is for him a 'light and dangerous' faculty (p. 153). This is the background of thought that Spenser turns into metaphor when he tells us that Phantastes' chamber is filled with buzzing flies which represent 'idle thoughts and fantasies' (*F.Q.*II.ix.51.1-6), and appropriately Spenser describes Phantastes' wit as forever restless (*ibid.* II.ix.49.9).

There are, in the psychological views of the active, feigning imagination, hints of control and even of value. Some value in feigning is suggested by its creation of ideal beauties, and some control of feigning by 'paterne' is suggested in the view that a 'Pernasus' of imagination is created by 'similitude of other hils' or that images are created 'by comparison' to those from life. And, although references to this function are comparatively infrequent, the imagination feigns healthily when it conjures up images of future possibilities. In the balanced soul, comes often 'a great imagination to see what is to come' (Huarte, p. 240). Indeed, at times in a good sort of melancholy, says DuLaurens, the melancholy man can 'by the forwardness of his imagination . . . see that which must come to passe, as though it were present before him' (p. 98).

But an especially legitimate manifestation of the feigning power of imagination occurs when, feigning images which act as counters of thought, it invents, and thus aids in the discovery or creation of new and valuable matter. From the 'Fancie', says Davies of Hereford, come 'all maruellous *Inuentions*' and thus 'all *Artes and Sciences*' (*Works*, I, 6). Huarte speaks similarly of the 'inuention of arts' which results from the conjunction of understanding 'with the memorie, or with the imaginatiue' (p. 67) and declares that 'From a good imagination, spring all the Arts and Sciences, which consist in figure, correspondence, harmonie, and proportion', listing poetry, music, eloquence, medicine, mathematics, astrology, government, art of warfare, painting, drawing, reading, '& the engins and deuises which artificers make' (p. 103). It is this power of fantasy of which Puttenham is thinking when he declares that fantasy presents 'visions, whereby the inuentiue parte of the mynde is so much holpen, as without it no man could deuise any new or rare thing'.[18] Thus, although rarely treated at much length, imagination as inventor has a sound reputation. It is worth nothing that this reputable function of active imagination is presented at times, as in Huarte, as the result of co-öperation with the higher understanding. Thus, given purpose and direction, feigning is good imagination. Here feigning, even though an active function of imagination, is that good imagination which results for the psychologists from the control of reason.

Nevertheless, as we have seen, the weight of the material is against the faculty. It remains essentially a faculty tied to sense and disease, uncontrolled, easily distorted and distorting and hence lying, idle and purposeless, flighty and inconsistent, and therefore irrational and immoral in the instrumental scheme. Yet to these sources of disrepute must be added one more— its dangerous alliance with the emotions, and hence with action.

Conventionally it is imagination, and specifically its images, which stimulate emotion; and the very nature of the emotion, in the theory, depends upon the nature of the images. Even in his definition of passions, Wright, principal writer on the emotions, reveals how inextricably emotion and imagination are related; for a passion is 'a sensual motion of our appetitive facultie, through imagination of some good or ill thing' (p. 8). Indeed we 'cannot love, hate, feare, hope, &c. but that by imagination' (*ibid.*, p. 31). As he tells us in his chapter 'The manner how Passions are mooved', the objects of imagination are communicated to the heart— generally accepted as seat of the emotions[19]—which is thus aroused to irascible (avoiding) or concupiscible (desiring) reactions with, of course, subsequent appropriate action (Wright, p. 45).[20]

In the natural course of events, the process of arousing emotion outlined by the psychologists may be not only acceptable but necessary; for the avoiding and approaching reactions are natural responses to life, necessary to survival. However, reactions are proportional to the stimulus, the image in imagination. If that image is a true and accurate picture of the object, reactions are also proportional and desirable. 'Perturbations naturall', says Bright, arise 'vpon an outward accasion, if the bodie be well tempered, and faultles in his instruments, and the obiect made no greater nor lesse then it is in deed, and the hart, aunswer proportionally thereunto', but the 'vnnaturall' arise when external life is 'otherwise taken then the obiect requireth' (p. 86).[21] When an object is 'deliuered otherwise then it standeth in nature', then is 'the hart moued to a disorderly passion' (Bright, p. 93).

The emotions are not in themselves, then, evil, but the distorted pictures of imagination which are presented to the heart make them so: the distorted images create distorted, excessive emotions. Discussing such perturbations, Burton declares 'that the first step and fountain of all our grievances in this kind is a distorted imagination, which, misinforming the heart, causeth all these distemperatures, alteration and confusion, of spirits and humours'. And the distortion of emotions, he declares, takes place when 'to our imagination cometh, by the outward sense or memory, some object to be known . . . which he, misconceiving or amplifying, presently communicates to the heart, the seat of all affections' (p. 219). The forged 'shapes' and 'counterfet goblins, which the brayne dispossessed of right discerning, fayneth vnto the heart' stimulate irrational terror (Bright, pp. 103-104); the feigned 'monstrous fictions' delivered to the heart cause it to break out 'into that inordinate passion, against reason' (*ibid.*, p. 102). And the process may develop into a pernicious cycle; for after the distorted images produce inordinate passion against reason, the passion may in turn further distort the images of imagination, which again return to create further excesses in feeling and further mislead reason (Wright, p. 52). Thus if the 'obiect' is accurately presented to the heart, reactions are proportional and adequate; but if it is distorted, so are the passions, becoming ungovernable and defying reason.[22]

Ultimately, then, the result of the relation between imagination and emotion is again that 'the vnderstanding looking into the imagination, findeth nothing almost but the mother and nurse of his passion for consideration'; thus it is that the conjunction of imagination and passion puts 'greene spectacles before the eyes of our witte' so that it cannot make proper decisions (Wright, p. 51). Passion and imagination are in league against reason. Although, when accurate, images may lead to natural emotion and sound action, the familiar failure in the veracity of images once more upsets the healthy operation of the instrumental scheme, leading to irrational and hence immoral behavior. The association between imagination and emotion reflects, once more, little credit upon the imagination, and the insistent demand is, again, for the veracity of images and the rule of reason.

III

Such disrepute, then, creates a formidable problem for the adherents of poetry to which in the Renaissance the faculty imagination is assigned; and, in his defense of poetry, it is clearly to the disrepute of imagination that Sidney responds when he declares that poetic imagination 'is not wholie imaginatiue, as we are wont to say by them that build Castles in the ayre' (p. 157), and it is surely the psychological descriptions of imagination which lead Puttenham similarly to distinguish between the good phantasy of the poet and the bad phantasy of others and to defend 'despised' poets and poetry on the grounds that 'the phantasticall part of man (if it be not disordered) [is] a representer of the best, most comely and bewtifull images or apparances of things to the soule and according to their very truth. If otherwise, then doth it breede *Chimeres* & monsters in mans imaginations, & not onely in his imaginations, but also in all his ordinarie actions and life which ensues' (pp. 18-19). We turn them to showing how adherents of poetry and of imaginative activity respond to the grounds of disrepute and how, drawing in defense upon familiar Renaissance materials, they evolve, as a result, significant views of imaginative activity.

In the face of the disrepute the adherents of poetry even depend upon the psychological view, seem even to glory in the power to distort. Where, according to the psychology, imagination, severing and joining, feigns 'things which neuer haue bin, shalbe, or can be', 'castles in the air', 'golden mountains', incredible beauties or monsters, and what 'never was nor shall be', the poet's imagination similarly creates imaginary composites, 'formes such as neuer were in Nature, as the *Heroes, Demigods, Cyclops, Chimeras, Furies,* and

such like', a 'golden' world beyond the 'brasen' world of nature (Sidney, p. 156), beyond the 'bare *Was*' of history (*ibid.,* p. 168). The poet casts 'life in a more purer mold'.[23] Poetry makes 'thinges seeme better then they are by nature'.[24] The 'Bodie' of a poet's work is 'fictiue', and for his purposes the poet creates what seems even 'beyond Possibilitie to bring into Act'; scorning 'a Lord Maiors naked *Truth*', the poet's is a 'going beyond life'.[25] To mend men's minds, says Chapman, poets create 'shapes of Centaurs, Harpies, Lapithes' (*Poems,* pp. 22-23). Joining and severing, the poet creates 'things which in nature would never have come to pass'.[26]

Indeed the poetical view insists repeatedly that feigning is the very criterion of what is poetry. He who does not feign is a mere versifier or a historian and no poet; feigning is the poet's function and fiction his product:[27] 'hee is call'd a *Poet,* not hee which writeth in measure only; but that fayneth and formeth a fable'.[28] With Touchstone's punning verdict that 'the truest poetry is the most feigning' (*As You Like It* III.iii. 19-20), almost every poet and critic of the period would agree.

But, parallel though they may the psychological account, these very statements contain, of course, a distinction from the psychological view; for poet and critic, the poet's freedom to feign is a wonderful creative power which, unlike the psychologists, they exalt and in which they glory. In their very agreement with the psychologists lies a difference. The difference is emphasized, however, by their distinction between good use and abuse, between good and bad imagination. Poetic imagination is a good imagination. Poetic feigning is feigning with a difference. And the good imagination, which is the poetic, is good and reputable principally because it is controlled. Reacting against the current disrepute and drawing upon contemporary and classical thought, their poetic asserts the very controls demanded in the psychological view. The distortion of the poet's feigning is not haphazard, but deliberate and purposeful, moral and rational; his creations are, indeed, 'true' rather than false. His imaginative creation and its emotional effect are guided by the conscious purpose, ordering, reason, and morality of the writer to secure, in turn, directly or indirectly, rational and moral effects. It is, again, feigning with a difference. As we have seen Sidney put it, it is not the same imagination that builds 'Castles in the ayre': the 'figuring foorth good things', says Sidney, is to be distinguished from the infection of 'the fancie with vnworthy obiects' (p. 186).[29] It is necessary, as Puttenham indicates, to make 'difference betwixt termes'; it is the failure of the ignorant to make such a distinction that prompts them to term the poet's work '*phantasticall,* construing it to the worst side' (p. 18).[30] Poetic imagination is, by the addition of various controls, transformed—a far cry from the diseased imagination of the psychology. Poetic imagination is good imagination.

What then is the good imagination from which the bad is to be distinguished?

Basis for much of the disrepute of imagination in the psychological exposition is, we have seen, the lack of veracity in its content or product, its proneness to false and gross distortion of reality which misleads head and heart. But good imagination, insist the defenders of poetry, does not lie. Influenced by the complexly interacting emphases on plausibility and decorum found in contemporary and classical rhetoric and in classical literary criticism,[31] the defenders declare, almost unaminously although sometimes inconsistently, that the poet's, the good imagination does not lie, for it creates lifelike, verisimilar imitations of life which thus tell the truth about life. In this process the necessity for reasonable and plausible as well as vivid resemblance to real life requires the poet's control over feigning, yet leaves room for the poet's license to create more than exact reproductions. Though it is an exact reproduction of no specific external reality, the verisimilar imitation *seems* true; though the poet's images do go beyond life, they are nevertheless true since, as verisimilar imitations, they resemble life; are, therefore, probable and lifelike. The poet creates 'things like truth' (Chapman, dedication to *The Revenge of Bussy D'Ambois*), frames 'his example to that which is most reasonable' (Sidney, p. 168). Indeed, argues the defender, it is the exact copy of reality which, compared to the poet's, may be 'foolish' (*ibid.,* p. 170), whereas the poet's power to feign may create the greater 'likelihood' (*ibid.,* pp. 167, 168). His license to feign may, paradoxically, permit him to create a greater verisimilitude than is at times present in the odd reality of life itself. He is thus 'both a maker and a counterfaitor' (Puttenham, p. 3). By definition, the poet, for Ben Jonson, is a 'fainer' who 'writes things like the Truth' (*Discoveries,* p. 89). To a degree then, 'things like the Truth', the rhetorical and ancient critical principle of verisimilitude, reconciles the distortion of feigning with the demands of veracity. By adopting the bridle of verisimilitude, critic and poet at once preserve freedom for poetic imagination and avoid the disrepute of the traditionally false, ungoverned, distorting imagination. The poet's creations are still licensed and beyond life; yet, controlled by the doctrine of verisimilar imitation, they retain the veracity of being like life.

Not only does the emphasis on verisimilitude obviate the charges of falsehood, and thus, to a degree, of immorality, but, since the verisimilar is the plausible or 'reasonable', the doctrine also dissipates the aura of irrationality with which the psychological view surrounds imagination. Moreover, the control of feigning by the need to resemble life means that good imagination will not create in the volatile, haphazard fashion suggested by the psychology.

But it is even more in the familiar doctrine that the poet presents in his feigning a higher truth than the exact, arid literal truth of reality that the poetic defends the veracity of his imagination as well as its rationality and purposiveness. Of course merely by feigning ideal composites of a higher degree of good or beauty, of a world and being superior to this (even as the psychologist himself suggests that imagination may create beauties as well as monsters), the poet presents a higher truth. His golden world is a better world and hence a world of higher truth; his imagination creates 'the best, most comely and bewtifull images or apparances of things to the soule' (Puttenham, p. 19). But, fusing with Platonic and Aristotelian influences and the influence of medieval allegory, the rhetorical doctrine of presenting higher concepts and truths through their embodiment in the concrete furnishes the foundation for the poetic doctrine of the higher universal truth presented through the feigned image of poetry. The value of the example—particularly of the historical example—to communicate precepts is a commonplace of rhetoric. The very presentation of philosophical, especially moral, truth through he concrete example is familiar rhetorical doctrine. Thus in his *Arte of Rhetorique* (1560), Thomas Wilson even recommends the fictitious example, the fable, to teach 'weightie and graue matters'[32] and finds that 'brute beastes' provide excellent 'paterns and Images of diuers vertues' (p. 191). Taken up by the defenders of imaginative activity, these rhetorical dicta furnish perhaps the most popular defense: by his feigning, the poet illustrates virtues and thus teaches higher abstract truth by rhetorical example; indeed, because he feigns the concrete, the poet is superior to the philosopher in teaching higher truths. Like the orator, the poet 'coupleth the generall notion with the particular example' (Sidney, p. 164). By his power of feigning the poet thus becomes the 'right Popular Philosopher' (*ibid.,* p. 167), conveying higher truths which 'lye darke before the imaginatiue and iudging powre, if they bee not illuminated or figured foorth by the speaking picture of Poesie' (*ibid.,* p. 165). The literal truth is thus a 'barren truth' for Drayton (*Works,* II, 284), who regards his fictionalized historical lives, his *Legends,* as example teaching higher truth (*Works,* II, 382). So completely does this become the accepted version of the higher truth of poetry that Spenser, closely following Sidney, explains the intention of his allegory. *The Faerie Queene,* in these same rhetorical terms: 'So much more profitable and gratious is doctrine by ensample, then by rule' (*F.Q.,* 'A Letter of the Authors'). Poetry, therefore, is not 'phantastique, or meere fictiue; but the most material, and doctrinall illations of *Truth*' (Chapman, dedicatory epistle to *Odysseys, Poems,* p. 407). To illustrate the abstract virtue, the poet creates his fictive 'Bodie' and that conveys 'a Soule' (*ibid.*).

And it is not merely that the poet can do the job of the orator. 'Truth builds in Poets faining' (Chapman, dedicatory epistle to *Iliads, Poems,* p. 386): it is precisely the power of the poet's fantasy to feign images, to distort, that permits him to create the most valid image or example and to communicate his ideals most effectively. By his power to distort, the poet may present the most perfectly adapted image for the communication of truth because he can mold his images exactly to convey his concepts. Precisely because he is not captive to a literal truth, he may better convey a higher truth. Puttenham puts the position well when he tells us that 'a fained matter' is not only more pleasing but 'works no lesse good conclusions for example then the most true and veritable: but often times more, because the Poet hath the handling of them to fashion at his pleasure.' In one day the poet may feign not only more but 'more excellent examples' than 'ages' of history provide. And such feigning, he concludes, is 'for a maner of discipline and president of commendable life' (pp. 40-41). By his feigning, the poet can provide the 'perfect patterne' (Sidney, p. 168). In this power to distort lies the superiority of the poet to the historian who, because he cannot feign, is 'so tyed . . . to what is, to the particular truth of things, and not to the general reason of things, that hys example draweth no necessary consequence, and therefore a lesse fruitfull doctrine' (*Ibid.*, p. 164). The 'fained' Cyrus is 'more doctrinable' than the 'true' (*Ibid.*, p. 168). Even Bacon, who does not always regard poetry very seriously, argues that the poet's power to feign beyond the limiting 'nature of things' permits him to present 'a more ample greatness, a more exact goodness' than can be found in 'true history' (*Works,* III, 343). Thus the very distortion, the charge of lies, is turned to an argument for the truth of poetic imagination, and for the superior truth of poetic imagination.

Clearly, this view of the power of the poet to control his image-examples, in molding them to fit his purpose of higher truth, emphasizes, again, disciplined feigning. It is because his feigning is controlled that the poet's creation of what 'neuer was' becomes the very agency of his higher truth. The poet must exercise conscious control to mold his image appropriately. Such control is rational and deliberate, not a matter of haphazard feigning. And it is not merely that the actual feigning is a disciplined activity, but that the ultimate guide and control even to that discipline is the wisely perceived rational and moral truth of the poet. For that matter,

the very emphasis on use of the logical device of rhetorical example lends, further, an emphasis on the rational. Good feigning, a feigning which conveys higher truth and not 'lies', is controlled, rational.

But it is through the assimilated rhetorical doctrine of persuasion[33] by moving emotion that the Elizabethan critic and poet justify, not only feigning, but the admitted emotional power of the feigned image. It is true, as this article has already suggested, that the feigned poetic image which presents higher truth acts as rhetorical example and, like the feigned or true images recommended by the rhetorics, may act as logical argument addressed to the understanding and thus persuade to higher truth. The view of the feigned image as example emphasizes, however, instruction or explanation as strongly as, or more strongly than, persuasion. But persuasion, according to the rhetoricians, was accomplished not only by appealing to intellect, but by moving emotion. And more, meeting the charges that the orator immorally makes the worse appear the better reason and that he stirs inordinate passion against reason and morality, charges leveled from classical times, the rhetoricians emphasize that the persuasion, even when emotional, is persuasion to good. Thus Cicero praises the influence of the orator in curbing and rousing passions in good causes and for good results (*De Oratore* II.ix.35), and Quintilian approves of the definition of rhetoric as the power to persuade men to do what they should (II.xv.35; see also II.xvi.10).[34] And this end is to be achieved not only by appealing to intellect but by moving emotion—and often specifically by arousing proper concupiscible and irascible emotions: thus, for example, the figure *Paradigma,* which, significantly, may be feigned or true, has, according to Peacham, the power 'to perswade[,] moue, and enflame men with loue of vertue, and also to deterre them from vyce',[35] and the writer of the persuasive epistle stimulates 'loue to well doing' and 'hate vnto badnes', according to Angel Day.[36]

It is not even half a step from these familiar rhetorical dicta to the adaptation that the feigned images of vice and virtue in poetry persuade to good by stirring appropriate, desirable emotions—love (of virtue) and hatred (of vice). Poetry, poet and critic declare, *is* persuasion. For Puttenham, 'the Poets were also from the beginning the besf perswaders and their eloquence the first Rethoricke of the world' (p. 8). Further, the poet persuades to good, and is the best persuader to good.[37] Poetry 'doth intende the winning of the mind from wickednesse to vertue' (Sidney, p. 172); the poet's imitations 'moue men to take that goodnes in hande' (*ibid.,* p. 159). And it is precisely because his feigning stirs emotion most stronglyexactly because his feigned images of vice and virtue move more completely than exact copies of life, and can, under the wisdom of the poet, be molded to secure the proper moral emotional effect—that the poet is the best persuader to good.

That it is his feigning which is the source of the poet's power to persuade is clear. As we have just seen, it is the poet's 'imitations' that 'moue' men to goodness. It is 'fiction' which most persuades.[38] Persuasion is a matter not only of teaching but also of 'moouing to well doing', for 'moouing is of a higher degree then teaching' (Sidney, p. 171); and the 'moouing' is the effect of feigning. Whether 'a fayned example hath asmuch force to teach as a true example' Sidney regards as at least a question to be asked; but there is no possibility of dispute about which best moves men to good— 'for as for to mooue, it is cleere, sith the fayned may bee tuned to the highest key of passion' (p. 169). The very power to distort, to feign, leads to a more intense moving to virtue. Thus the poet's feigning moves and persuades to good, stirring 'passion' to the very goal of virtue which it is the end, even according to the psychology, of true and exact images to attain.

But not only does the poet 'tune' his feigned images to secure emotional response, but, more specifically, he molds his images to secure the proper, moral response. In order to move to good, therefore, the poet presents feigned images of vice and virtue that secure appropriate concupiscible and irascible reactions: 'If the Poet doe his part a-right, he will shew you in *Tantalus, Atreus,* and such like, nothing that is not to be shunned; in *Cyrus, Aeneas, Vlisses,* each thing to be followed; where the Historian, bound to tell things as things were, cannot be liberall (without hee will be poeticall) of a perfect patterne, but, as in *Alexander* or *Scipio* himselfe, shew dooings, some to be liked, some to be misliked. And then how will you discerne what to followe but by your owne discretion, which you had without reading *Quintus Curtius?*' (Sidney, p. 168). Thus the feigned, and consequently 'perfect', images have the advantage of eliciting, under the poet's control, the proper psychological response. If he presents vices as well as virtues, he does so that men may learn 'by loathing such vile vices'.[39] His 'natural fictions' or 'things like truth' provide 'excitation to virtue, and deflection from her contrary' (Chapman, dedication to *The Revenge of Bussy D'Ambois*).[40]

Thus the criticism of the excessive emotional power of the imaginative activity is defended by the doctrine of persuasion to good. The very distortion of feigning and its resultant emotional power become the very means of persuasion to good; feigning and emotional effect are not only permitted but demanded.

The defensive value of the doctrine derives in part, of course, from the very assimilation of a reputable activity, persuasion, from a reputable art; but this defense pictures the poet once more as in control of his materials and makes once more the distinction between good imagination and bad, between proper use and abuse. The poet 'tunes' his feigned image; he must 'doe his part a-right'. The emphasis is, as Harington puts it, on imaginative activity 'being rightly vsed' (in Smith, II, 209). The poet molds his products, disciplined by his understanding of morality and by his practical, moral end. Good imagination is, once more, controlled imagination as distinct from the uncontrolled described by the psychologists. Moreover, since the poet's feigning has ultimately the reputable, practical purpose of persuasion, the charges of lightness, insubstantiality, and idleness are weakened. Most importantly, of course, the doctrine combats the disrepute based on the charges of excessive emotion which frustrates reason and morality—and this it does on the very grounds of the psychologist. The poet moves emotion to good by arousing through his feigned images of vice and virtue proper concupiscible and irascible reactions. Thus the reader of poetry reacts even as psychologist or Puritan attacker would have him and 'willeth good things, and refuseth the contrarie' (Bright, p. 77), just as the exactly apprehended image of the 'offensiue or pleasaunt obiect' (*ibid.,* p. 93) should make the heart answer with proper responses, according to the psychologist. The feigned image is a calculated and selected agent for achieving the end of virtue.

Utilizing the very apparatus of psychology, agreeing with the psychologist concerning the power of the 'distorted' image to achieve heightened emotion, and, indeed, emphasizing it, poetic, through the assimilation of the rhetorical doctrine of persuasion, thus meets many of the charges against feigning. A far cry from the uncontrolled feigning of lunatic and melancholic that leads to the stirring of evil perturbations, the feigned image of poetry is the precisely controlled means of effective persuasion to good: it is the best example; it is the most effective mover.

Thus laboring to free the poetic imagination from the current disrepute of the faculty, Elizabethan poetic responds to the very bases of the disrepute. Although instrumental to the healthy operation of the soul, imagination, according to the psychology, is a faculty for the most part uncontrolled and immoral—a faculty forever distorting and lying, irrational, unstable, flitting and insubstantial, haphazardly making and marring, dangerously tied to emotions, feigning idly and purposelessly. And from the attempt to combat these grounds of disrepute through the adoption and adaptation of materials which were an absorbed part of every educated Elizabethan's background—materials often from the very psychology itself—there evolves a concept of poetic feigning: that poetic feigning is a glorious compounding of images beyond life, of distortions which are yet verisimilar imitations, expressing a truth to reality and yet a higher truth also, controlled by the practical purpose, the molding power and, in almost every aspect, by the reason and morality of the poet. Poetic imagination is disciplined imagination. Arising out of the natural interaction of important areas of thought, it becomes feigning with a difference: controlled feigning.

Notes

[1] Michael Drayton, *The Tragicall Legend of Robert, Duke of Normandy* (*The Works of Michael Drayton,* ed. J. William Hebel, Oxford, 1931-1941, I, 262).

[2] Francis Bacon, *Of the Dignity and Advancement of Learning* (*The Works of Francis Bacon,* ed. James Spedding et al., London, 1889-1892, IV, 406).

[3] The current psychology is a thread which weaves itself everywhere into the tissue of Elizabethan thought and influences views on subjects from education to witchcraft. The currency and influence of the contemporary psychology are suggested not only by the number of works published on the subject but by the number of editions through which most of these went. Significantly, in translating Guglielmo Grataroli, William Fulwood declares that the faculties of the brain have been so often 'scene in the bookes of many' that his discussion would be 'superfluous' (*Castel of Memorie* London, 1573, sig. B^v). The 'many' include of course a long line of earlier commentators stretching back to Aristotle (*De anima*). We expect the Elizabethan critic, then, to be aware of the psychology.

[4] Although in classical times the functions of imagination and fantasy were carefully distinguished on the bases of passive or active function, by Elizabethan times the distinctions had, for the most part, been lost and terms like 'phantasy', 'fantsie', even 'fancy', are used interchangeably with 'imagination'. Thus in his translation of Grataroli, Fulwood lists as the first faculty of the brain 'Fantasie (or immagination[)]' (sig. B^v). On a single page of *Mirum in Modum* John Davies of Hereford uses 'Imagination' and 'Fantasie' interchangeably (*The Complete Works of John Davies of Hereford,* ed. Rev. A. B. Grosart, Edinburgh, 1878, I, 6)—this despite his declaration that, unlike others, he will make 'distinction' (I, 7). Even though he lists them as separate faculties, Pierre de LaPrimaudaye concludes that he will 'vse these two names *Fantasie* and *Imagination* indifferently', since so many regard them as 'the same facultie and vertue of the soule', and still later uses the term 'fancie' as a synonym (*The Second Part of the French Academie,* tr. T. B., London, 1594, pp. 155, 157). See also Robert Burton, who discusses the *'Phantasy, or imagination'* (*The Anatomy of Melancholy,* ed. Floyd Dell and Paul Jordan-Smith, New York, 1938, p. 139) and uses 'fancy' as synonym (pp. 222, 223).

[5] See, for example, LaPrimaudaye, p. 149; Timothy Bright, *A Treatise of Melancholie,* printed by Thomas Vautrollier (London, 1586), pp. 77, 104; Levinus Lemnius, *The Touchstone of Complexions,* tr. Thomas Newton (London, 1581), fol. 14^r; Juan Huarte Navarro, *Examen de Ingenios,* tr. R. C., Esquire (London, 1594), p. 75.

[6] Thomas Wright, *The Passions of the Minde in Generall* (London, 1604), p. 51.

[7] Stephen Batman, *Batman vppon Bartholome* (London, 1582), Bk. III, chap, 11.

[8] André DuLaurens, *A Discourse of the Preservation of the Sight: of Melancholike diseases . . . of Old Age,* tr. Richard Surphlet (London, 1599), p. 8.

[9] Sir Fulke Greville, *A Treatie of Humane Learning* (*Poems and Dramas of Fulke Greville,* cd. Geoffrey Bullough, New York, 1945, I, 156).

[10] Thomas Nashe, *Terrors of the Night* (*The Complete Works of Thomas Nashe,* ed. Rev. A. B. Grosart, London and Aylesbury, 1883-1885, III, 233).

[11] *Nosce Teipsum,* in *An English Garner,* ed. Edward Arber (Birmingham, 1877-1896), v, 193. Subsequent references to Sir John Davies will be to *Nosce Teipsum* in Vol. v of Arber's text.

[12] See Burton, p. 222, and Reginald Scot, *The Discoverie of Witchcraft* (London, 1930), p. 33.

[13] Andrew Boorde, *Dyetary,* in *The First Boke of the Introduction of Knowledge and A . . . Dyetary of Health,* ed. F. J. Furnivall, Early English Text Society, Extra Series, No. 10 (London, 1870), p. 250; see also Batman, Bk. VI, chap. 27.

[14] Among such 'sciences' Huarte later lists poetry (p. 108).

[15] In the examples of distortion of images by vapors of melancholy humor, the imagination, as we have seen, seems passive. However, the imagination of the melancholy man is also often regarded as abnormally active and creative in its own right. The disrepute of the disease of melancholy, and, for that matter, of the other agents of distortion, follows imagination, of course, into its active operation.

[16] *An Apologie for Poetrie,* in *Elizabethan Critical Essays,* ed. G. Gregory Smith (London, 1904), 1, 159. (Subsequent references to Sir Philip Sidney will be to the *Apologie* in Vol. 1 of Smith's text.) From these quotations it is perhaps even not very far to William Wordsworth's 'The light that never was, on sea or

---

Van Dorsten on the nature of patronage in England:

The main object of patronage in the the first three decades of Elizabeth's reign was indeed not belles-lettres. Authors dedicated books in order to gain support for a cause or to draw attention to their loyalty and personal expertise in an attempt to imporove their own social position through 'preferment.' Both the works themselves and their dedicatory pages almost invariably stressed political, religious, or educational usefulness to Queen and country. Writers therefore tried to approach influential political figures with their dedications—the Earl of Leicester, for instgance, or even the Queen herself—rather than enlightened connoiseurs, if they existed. Books tended to be purposely propagandistic. No true humanist would raise an objection to this, for what use are the *bonae litterae* if they fail to serve the interests of the *res publica*?

Yet among these countless useful books, pamphlets, manuscript notes, and what not, items sometimes occur, even early in the reign of Elizabeth, that by any definition must be called literature, or attempts at literature. Often they serve a cause, but occasionally their principal service is to give pleasure to their dedicatees—their patrons, if that is the correct word. To appreciate them as they were intended to be appreciated one needs to bear in mind that they were generally written to suit a particular occasion and a known taste. The Elizabethans . . .wrote 'as often as not, for someone with whom they dined a few days ago.'

J. A. Van Dorsten, The Anglo-Dutch Renaissance, *edited by J. Van Den Berg and Alastair Hamilton, E. J. Brill, 1988.*

---

and, The consecration, and the Poet's dream' ('Elegiac Stanzas: Suggested by a Picture of Peele Castle in a Storm').

[17] Bright, pp. 102, 104; Nashe, *Terrors* (*Works,* III, 233); Spenser, *F.Q.* II.ix.51.9; Huarte, p. 118.

[18] George Puttenham, *The Arte of English Poesie,* ed. Gladys Doidge Willcock and Alice Walker (Cambridge, 1936), p. 19.

[19] See Ruth L. Anderson, *Elizabethan Psychology and Shakespeare's Plays* (Iowa City, 1927, University of Iowa Humanistic Studies, Vol. III, No. 4), p. 73.

[20] For parallel accounts, see also Sir John Davies, p. 177; Bright, p. 81; Burton, p. 224; and Huarte, p. 31.

[21] Bright does not make here the usual Elizabethan distinction, according to which perturbations are dis-

tinguished from other emotions as unruly and excessive.

[22] On the distortion of the images of fantasy by emotion see also Greville, *Treatie* (*Poems and Dramas,* I, 157), and *Caelica* (*Poems and Dramas,* I, 145); Burton, p. 221; Shakespeare, *Dream* v. I.21-22.

[23] Drayton, *The Tragicall Legend of Robert, Duke of Normandy* (*Works,* I, 285).

[24] Nicholas Ling, *Politeuphuia: Wits Common wealth* (London, 1598), fol. 52ʳ. Cf. also Puttenham, p. 304.

[25] George Chapman, dedicatory epistle to *Odysseys* (*The Poems of George Chapman,* de. Phyllis Brooks Bartlett, New York, 1941, p. 407).

[26] Bacon, *Of the Dignity . . . of Learning* (*Works,* IV, 292); see also *Description of the Intellectual Globe* (*Works,* V, 504). Cf. Shakespeare, *Dream* v.i.14-15.

[27] See Sidney, p. 160; *Francis Meres's Treatise 'Poetrie': A Critical Edition,* ed. Don Cameron Allen (Urbana, Ill., 1933, Univ. of Illinois Studies in Lang. and Lit. XVI), pp. 71, 73-74; Richard Mulcaster, *Positions,* ed. Robert H. Quick (London, 1888), p. 269; Sir John Harington, 'Preface to . . . *Orlando Furioso*' (*Elizabethan Critical Essays,* ed. G. Gregory Smith, London, 1904, II, 203, 204); Samuel Daniel, dedicatory epistle to *The Civill Wars* (*The Complete Works in Verse and Prose of Samuel Daniel,* ed. Rev. A. B. Grosart, London, 1885-1896, II, 6); Drayton, 'To . . . Henery Reynolds, Esquire, of Poets and Poesie, (*Works,* III, 229); John Marston, *Satires* (*The Works of John Marston,* ed. A. H. Bullen Boston, 1887, III, 283-284); Thomas Blundeville, *The True Order and Methode of Wryting and Reading Hystories* (London, 1574), sig. [E4]ᵛ.

[28] Ben Jonson, *Discoveries 1641; Conversations . . . 1619,* ed. G. B. Harrison (London, [1923]), p. 89.

[29] See also *Sir Fulke Greville's Life of Sir Philip Sidney* (Oxford, 1907), p. 223.

[30] Murray W. Bundy has already pointed out that by distinguishing men of good fantasy 'from mere *phantastici*' the Renaissance attempted to avoid the disrepute of the coupling, through imagination, of lunatics and poets ('Fracastoro and the Imagination', *Renaissance Studies in Honor of Hardin Craig,* ed. Baldwin Maxwell et al., Stanford Univ., 1941, p. 47).

[31] The contemporary rhetorics, for example, often inherit doctrines from classical literary criticism and return them to criticism in Elizabethan times, while the very classical literary criticism which influences later rhetoric and poetic is itself often based on ancient

rhetoric. See, for example, Donald L. Clark, *Rhetoric and Poetry in the Renaissance* (New York, 1922, Columbia Univ. Studies in Eng. and Comp. Lit.), pp. 80-81, and note also Clark, pp. 31-32, 42. The general influence of the contemporary rhetoric upon Elizabethans, their literature and criticism in particular, has been so frequently pointed out as to require no further examination in this study.

[32] Ed. G. H. Mair (Oxford, 1909), p. 198. See also Quintilian, *Institutio Oratoria* I.Pr.10-13, and particularly Bacon, *Of the Dignity . . . of Learning* (*Works*, IV, 456). For an account of the absorption of this rhetorical material by poetic, see Clark, pp. 138-161.

[33] The rhetorical origins of the poetic doctrine of persuasion have been recognized for some time. See, for example, Clark, pp. 136-137; Rosemond Tuve, 'Imagery and Logic: Ramus and Metaphysical Poetics', *JHI*, III (1942), 369; William Ringler, commentary on John Rainolds, *Oratio in Laudem Artis Poeticae,* tr. Walter Allen, Jr. (Princeton, 1940, Princeton Studies in Eng. No. 20), pp. 21-22, 61.

[34] On the superiority of emotional over merely intellectual appeal in persuasion, see Quintilian VI.ii.5.

[35] Henry Peacham, *The Garden of Eloquence* (London, [1577]), fol. Uij[v].

[36] *The English Secretary* (London, 1599), [I], 47.

[37] See Jonson, *Discoveries,* pp. 95-96; Puttenham, p. 196. For Jonson particularly, it is the poet's superiority in moving emotion which makes him preëminent.

[38] Puttenham, p. 196; Harington, in Smith (note 27 above), II, 204.

[39] William Webbe, *A Discourse of English Poetrie* (*Elizabethan Critical Essays,* ed. G. Gregory Smith, London, 1904, I, 251). See also Harington, in Smith, II, 209.

[40] See also Thomas Heywood, *An Apology for Actors (1612)* (New York, 1941), sig. C3, and Jonson, *Discoveries,* p. 42, for very parallel views on love-hate responses. How current this view was is suggested by Gower's listing of each of the principal characters at the end of *Pericles* (v.iii.85-98) as a 'figure' of vice or virtue. It is interesting to speculate on how much of this rhetorical purpose lay behind Shakespeare's histories and tragedies.

POETS AND THE CROWN

O. B. Hardison, Jr. (essay date 1962)

SOURCE: "Rhetoric, Poetics, and Theory of Praise," in *The Enduring Monument: A Study of the Idea of Praise in Renaissance Literary Theory and Practice,* The University of North Carolina Press, 1962, pp. 24-42.

[*Below, Hardison examines the influence of classical authors on sixteenth-century poets in terms of their praise of public figures and the shaping of their subjects' reputions through poetry.*]

. . . To trace all the ramifications of the theory of praise during the sixteenth century would be to write a small-scale history of Renaissance criticism. Therefore, the present survey makes no pretense of being complete. Its object is to sketch a few representative variations of the theory of praise and to demonstrate the continuity of this theory throughout the period.

The keynote of the period was struck by its most dazzling *uomo universale,* Lorenzo de'Medici, in a letter prefacing an anthology of Italian poetry which he prepared for Frederick of Aragon. Recalling Cicero's impassioned defense of literature in the *Pro Archia,* Lorenzo attributed the military and philosophical achievements of the ancients to the desire for the immortal fame conferred by the poet's praise. "Honor," he wrote, "is what provides nutriment for every art; nor are the minds of mortals inflamed to noble works by anything so much as glory."[42] To Lorenzo poets were "holy givers of praise" (*sacri laudatori*), and this note continued to dominate humanistic criticism. Indeed, in 1637, the last, and in some ways the noblest, humanist of them all, John Milton, would write, "Fame is the spur which the clear spirit doth raise . . . To scorn delights and live laborious days." That it was also for Milton "that last infirmity of noble mind" is simply a reminder of the precariousness of the humanistic compromise.

Corollary to the image of the poet as custodian of fame is the idea that the truest poetry is the poetry of praise. Critics who were sympathetic with the aims of the Florentine humanists commonly repeated this idea. Vida insisted that hymn and epic—praise of gods and heroes—surpassed all other forms of poetry, while Bernardino Daniello admitted that the philosopher-poet of his *Poetica* would often rise "like the melodious swan . . . from earth to heaven, carrying high the praises of another's virtue in sweet lyric song; or, excoriating vice . . . descend to the depths."[43] No critic of the period was destined to have more influence than Scaliger. In his *Poetics* he quite consciously invoked the Platonic-humanistic tradition to justify his high estimate of poetry: "Good fame is the reward of wise men. Thus Plato in the *Laws* made ill fame a punishment for crimes. And he says the same in the *Ion*. Poets make others what they are themselves. Thus by the art which makes them immortal they confer immortality on those whom they celebrate. So boasted Pindar; so sang Theocritus; and so say the rest."[44]

Sebastian Minturno was of the same generation and eclectic frame of mind as Scaliger. He too benefited from the "new criticism" generated by the rediscovery of Aristotle's *Poetics*. Even more than Scaliger, however, he sympathized with the ideals of the Florentine humanists. To him the basic poetic emotion is emulation (*aemulatio*), and emulation is the struggle to live up to the virtues of those who have been praised by the poets: " . . . emulation spurs good men to virtue that they may attain the praise and glory which they seek. . . . For those on whom poets or historians bestow the highest praise are indeed not without emulators."[45] At the end of the century, although the humanist tradition deteriorated, a few critics still defended it. Of these Tommaso Campanella is the most persuasive. In his *Poetics* he defends many lost causes—among them the cause of the poet-theologue—and he expresses special fondness for the poetry of praise: "If poetry is an art, it should have use in the republic . . . since it is concerned with the good rather than the truth for its own sake, it is an instrument of the legislator. Therefore it will praise good men and virtues and rebuke vice and evil men. Thus it will stabilize law and religion and pleasantly offer precepts to help the cause of the state and of amicable social relations."[46]

A more technical slant was given poetics by those critics who were concerned to reconcile it with rhetoric. Pontanus attempted to do this in the *Actius,* a dialogue on poetics composed at the end of the fifteenth century. The point of the dialogue is that both history and poetry rely on oratory. This observation leads Pontanus to many conclusions about both arts. One of the most interesting is that both are limited to two categories: "history and poetry both utilize the demonstrative [epideictic] category and also the deliberative, as is shown by their speeches and councils."[47] Again, both poetry and oratory "are forms of discourse . . . and they have praise in common, which is called the demonstrative genus, and also deliberations. . . ."[48] Since set speeches, councils and "deliberations" form only a small part of most poetic compositions, Pontanus' theory seems to emphasize epideictic rhetoric heavily. This is borne out by the remark that poetry favors "amplifications, digressions and variety"—an echo of the standard prescriptions for epideictic style.[49]

The revival of the *Poetics* naturally encouraged further discussion of praise and blame in literature. The Averroes paraphrase was a factor in this discussion, as may be demonstrated by references to Averroes in the commentaries. Partly because of the tradition encouraged by the paraphrase and partly because of the contents of the *Poetics,* all commentaries deal with praise and blame to some degree. Emphasis varies from Robortello and Castelvetro,[50] for whom epideictic concepts are secondary and enter chiefly in connection with the evolution of poetic genres, to Trissino, who referred frequently in the Aristotelian sections of his *Poetica* (Bks. V and VI, publ. 1562) to the theory of praise. Trissino's ideas are not new. His references to praise constitute a more sophisticated version of Averroes, supplemented by an acquaintance with literature which was both scholarly and practical, Trissino being a moderately successful poet.[51] The first poetry, we learn, was encomium and vituperation, from which arose the two basic 'genres' of poetry. Homer's *Iliad* and *Odyssey* were elaborations of encomium and the *Margites* of vituperation. Tragedy is the highest kind of praise, and comedy is a form of ridicule, treating vice which is not vile but merely ugly.[52] Lyric is halfway between these two forms: "such kinds of poem, that is, *canzoni, serventesi* and the rest, include both genres of poetry; that is, that of praise and admiration of better things, as in tragedy and heroic poetry, and that of execration and the blame of evil, as in comedy."[53] The result of the use of poetic devices is to create an "example, or an excellent idea, which men can imitate"—in other words, an idealized portrait.[54]

Praise continued to be discussed in connection with the *Poetics* as late as 1575. Alessandro Piccolomini's commentary, published in that year, begins with a fairly conventional attempt to place poetry among the sciences. Poetics, the art of poetry, is considered a technique (*techne*) and hence a part of the *Organon.* Its end (*fin*), however, is the improvement of mankind. This makes it a part of practical philosophy subject to the doctrines taught in ethics. In fact, "art would not be art if it did not hold some end in mind which serves and assists our lives."[55] Inevitably this leads back to the theory of praise: "While the species of poetry are diverse, they equally in their various kinds seek to bring utility and improvement to our life. By the imitation and praise of virtuous men we are inflamed and excited to virtue in order to become similar to those whose praises we heard. If we hear poetic imitation of the vices and crimes of the other sort and its expression is negative and in the form of blame, we immediately begin to be repelled and hate the vicious actions, far more excited by such imitations than by admonitions, no matter how well expressed."[56]

Many critics were unwilling to make the praise-blame formula as fundamental to poetics as it is for Piccolomini. Aristotle distinguished between six parts of drama—plot, character, diction, thought, spectacle, and melody (1450[a])—and this list was often used to organize discussions of poetry. When it was, only one of its six topics demanded treatment in terms of moral philosophy. This was character. Aristotle's term, *ethos,* and its Latin and Italian translations (*mores* and *costumi*) all point toward the ethical rather than psychological phase of character-portrayal. The way in which discussion of character led to discussion of praise is illustrated in Alessandro Lionardi's *Dialogue on Poetic Invention* (1554).[57] As the rhetorical term "invention" suggests, the dialogue is a self-conscious attempt to show how poetry and rhetoric (and history as well!) are related. As Lionardi approaches the topic of character his terminology becomes explicitly epideictic: "It is necessary that the poet know in what form and manner he ought to speak. . . . And he will take this perfection from the orator. If he treats characters or works either virtuous or vicious, he will have recourse to the demonstrative category of oratory, providing honors for virtues and dishonor for vice."[58] The extremely broad application of this principle is evident from Lionardi's list of "demonstrative" works. Among others he cites the *Symposium,* the funeral orations of Demosthenes and Plato, the *Cyropaedia* of Xenophon, and Petrarchy's lyrics.[59]

Many other critics approached character in the same way. Giraldi Cinthio, for example, maintained, "In respect to conduct (*costume*) the office of our poet is to praise virtuous actions and rebuke vices and make them hateful through terror and pity. . . ."[60] Here the theory of praise leads to a definition of catharsis as the purgation of the desire to sin which Cinthio confidently attributes to "the definition which Aristotle gives of tragedy."[61] A similar position is taken by Tasso. His statement of the case is interesting for two reasons. First, it recapitulates the history that we have been following in the present chapter. And second, it was written in answer to Castelvetro. In effect it is a re-affirmation of the Christian humanist tradition. Tasso believed that character is made exemplary in literature by the techniques of praise and blame. Being essentially an epic poet, he was particularly concerned with the fate of this form. He concluded his rebuttal of Castelvetro by declaring: ". . . without doubt Castelvetro erred when he said that praise was not appropriate to the heroic poet, for if the heroic poet celebrates heroic virtue he ought to raise it to the heavens with his praises. And Saint Basil says that Homer's *Iliad* is nothing other than the praise of virtue; and Averroes has the same opinion in his commentary on poetry; and Plutarch. . . . Therefore, leaving aside the followers of Castelvetro in their opinion, we will follow the opinion of Polybius, of Damascus, of Saint Basil, of Averroes, of Plutarch, and of Aristotle himself."[62]

Tasso's remarks merit, I believe, special consideration. They confirm the history of the theory of praise as it has been presented in the present chapter. Moreover they are not the idle speculations of an academic critic. They are the comments of one of the great poets of the age, and they are obviously made with feeling. Tasso was not only aware of the tradition of praise, he valued it highly. It is fair to suppose that the *Gerusalemme liberata* reflects his feeling.

If we turn briefly to English critics of the latter half of the sixteenth century we find the same opinions that were popular in Italy. Golding's translation of the *Metamorphoses* appeared in 1567 at the beginning of the golden age of English literature. Its quality has, perhaps, been overrated, but its influence was felt from the age of Marlowe to that of Milton. Golding was at some pains to justify Ovid in view of his dubious reputation. His first defense, given in the epistle to Leicester, is that Ovid's myths are profound allegories. Ovid has not one but four levels of meaning. Of these the first three are related to natural philosophy but the fourth is moral. Golding insists that Ovid's character portrayal consists of ". . . pitthye, apt, and pleyne / Instructions which import the prayse of virtues, and the blame / Of vices . . ." (ll. 64-66). Later, in the epistle to the reader, the point is restated in slightly more elaborate form: " . . . under feyned names of Goddes it was the Poets guyse / The vice and faults of all estates too taunt in covert wyse. / And likewise too extolle with prayse such things as doo deserve" (ll. 83-5).

Golding's remarks are elementary, but English critics were quick to improve their art by drawing on Italian sources. Both Spenser and Sidney were influenced by the theory of praise. George Puttenham, whose *Arte of English Poesie* appeared in 1589, based his classification of genres on praise and blame in the manner of such Italian critics as Trissino and Piccolomini: ". . . the chief and principall [type of poetry] is the laud, honour, and glory of the immortall gods . . . : secondly, the worthy gests of noble Princes, the memoriall and registry of all great fortunes, the praise of vertue, reproofe of vice, the instruction of moral doctrines, the revealing of sciences naturall & other profitable Arts, the redresse of boistrous & sturdie courages by perswasion, the consolation and repose of temperate myndes: finally the common solace of mankind in all his travails and cares of this transitorie life."[63] In this passage praise is the method of the "chief and principall" type, the hymn; and the second type is merely a paraphrase for encomium. In fact, Puttenham summarizes the standard rhetorical topics for encomium when he remarks in a later passage that princes and heroes were treated "by a second degree of laude: shewing their Princely genealogies and pedigrees, mariages, aliances, and such noble exploites, as they had done in th'affaires of peace and of warre. . . ."[64] Classical myths are considered as originally historical encomia.[65] And of poetry concerning the "inferiour sort" we learn that "inferiour persons with their inferiour vertues have a certaine inferiour praise. . . ."[66] Puttenham also discusses the poetry evolving from blame. In Chapters XIII through XVII of the *Arte of English Poesie,* satire, comedy and trag-

edy are grouped together as poetic types "repre-
hending vice."

Although it became unimportant in Italy, the theory
of praise persisted in England. Milton, for example,
commonly associated poetry and praise. The morning hymn of Adam and Eve in *Paradise Lost,* V, is
a Miltonic symphony on the theme of "Laudate
nomen." Milton thought of the elegiac poets that it
was "the chief glory of their wit, in that they were
ablest to judge, to praise, and . . . to love those high
perfections which under one or other name they took
to celebrate. . . ." And considering his own aspirations and talents he hoped, "with more love or virtue" to choose "the object of not unlike praises."[67]
The last we hear of the theory of praise in English
criticism is David Hume's offhand remark, "All polite
letters . . . inspire us with different sentiments, of
praise and blame."[68]

The theory of praise is one of the most persistent of
critical traditions. Originating in the Greek ideal of
paideia, receiving indirect—and doubtless uninten-
tional—support from Aristotle's *Poetics,* it achieved
the status of a system when combined with the technical lore of epideictic rhetoric. During the Middle
Ages its effects are evident in both practice and theory. It received particular emphasis in the paraphrase
of the *Poetics* by Averroes. It entered the Renaissance in two ways—first via late classical and medieval sources; and second via Averroes and such intermediary authors as Benvenuto da Imola and Salu-
tati. In the early sixteenth century the late classical
and medieval influences predominated. Later, Aristotle—and with him Averroes—became important. Finally there appeared eclectic critics who drew on the
humanistic tradition but were also well-schooled in
Aristotle. Minturno and Tasso are the best of these.
Their work summarized some of the most typical
ideas of Italian criticism at the moment of its decline
and transmitted them to northern Europe. The theory
of praise was transmitted in this way, and it continued to interest poets long after Italy had sunk into
the sterilities of Marinism and the banalities of the
Arcadia.

Notes

. . .[42] "Allo illustrissimo Signore Frederigo D'Aragona,"
in *Prosatori volgari del quattrocento,* ed. Claudio
Varese (Milan, n.d.), pp. 985-90. "L'onore è vera-
mente quello che porge a ciascuna arte nutrimento;
nè da altra cosa quanto dalla gloria sono gli animi de'
mortali alle preclare opere infiammati." (p. 985) Compare Cicero, *Pro Archia poeta,* 26: "Trahimur omnes
studio laudis et optimus quisque maxime gloria duca-
tur."

[43] Bernardino Daniello, *La poetica* (Venice, 1536), p.

19: "Hora non altrimenti che canore cigno, altro le
lode dell'altrui virtù portando, con soave canto, de
terra al cielo si leva. Hora il vitio biasmando, a basso
discende."

[44] Scaliger, *Poetices libri septem* (5th ed., 1617), I, iii:
"Sapientum namque praemium bona fama. Sic Plato in
suis Legibus, malam faman pro supplicio statuit mul-
tis. Quod antem dicit idem in Ione. Poetae hoc ipsum
quod ipsi sunt, alios quoque esse faciunt. Quare quibus artibus esse reddunt immortales, iisdem illos quoque
quos celebrant, consecrant immortalitati. Sic gloriatur
Pindarus: sic canit Theocritus: sic caeteri sunt secuti."

[45] Antonio Minturno, *De poeta* (Venice, 1559), p. 222:
"aemulatio probos ad studia virtutis hortatur, ut ad
quam laudem gloriamque contendunt, perveniant. . . .
Nam quos poetae, aut scriptores historiarum summis
laudibus efferunt, iis profecto non desunt aemulator-
es."

[46] Tommaso Campanella, *Poeticorum liber unus,* in
Opere, ed. Luigi Firpo (Milan, 1954), I, 908: "Si igitur
poetica ars est, habet usum in republica: igitur instru-
mentum est legislatoris, quoniam non circum vera per
se, sed circa bonum versatur. Igitur laudabit bonos et
virtutes; vitia detestabatur et pravos; hic legem et re-
ligionem stabiliet et cum voluptate propinabit praecep-
ta, quibus respublica et amicitiae servantur."

[47] Giovanni Pontano, *Actius,* in *Dialoghi,* ed. C. Pre-
vitera (Florence, 1943), p. 193: "utraque enim demon-
strativo versatur in genere, nec minus enim in deliber-
ativo, quod ipsum conciones indicant ac consilia."

[48] Ibid., p. 232: "uterque versatur in dicendo et . . .
utrisque communes sunt laudationes, quod demonstra-
tivum genus dicitur, tametsi et deliberationes quoque.
. . ."

[49] Ibid., p. 193: "utraque etiam gaudet amplificationi-
bus, digressionibus item ac varietate. . . ."

[50] See Francesco Robertello, *Explicationes* (Florence,
1548), p. 35; Lodovico Castelvetro, *Poetica d'Aristotele*
(Basel, 1576), pp. 76-80.

[51] Trissino wrote several tragedies of which *Sofonisba*
(1515) is probably best known, and an epic, *Italia
liberata dai Goti* See Bernardo Morsolin, *Giangiorgio
Trissino* (Florence, 1894).

[52] Giangiorgio Trissino, *Poetica,* in *Tutte le opere*
(Verona, 1729), II, 92-93.

[53] Ibid., p. 138: ". . . le Canzoni, e i Serventesi, e gli
altri, riceve . . . tutte i due generi de la Poesia, cioè
quello di laudare, et ammirare le cose migliori, come fa
Tragedia, e lo Eroico, e quello di dileggiare, e biasmare

le cattive, come fa la Commedia."

[54] Ibid., p. 118: "per lasciare uno exemplare, overo una idea eccellente, la quale gli uomini possono imitare."

[55] *Annotationi di M. Alessandro Piccolomini nel libro della poetica d'Aristotele* (Venice, 1575), 6ᵛ: "L'arte non sarebbe arte, se qualche fine non reguardasse, che servisse, & giovisse alla vita nostra."

[56] Ibid., 7ʳ: ". . . sì come diverse son [le spetie di Poesia] fra di loro spetie, così parimente in diversi modi cercan tutte di recar'utile, & giovamento alla vita nostra. posciachè con l'imitation degli huomini virtuosi, & con la spressione delle lodi loro, veniamo ad infiammarci, & ad escitarci alle virtù, per devenir simili a quelli, che celebrar'udiamo. se i vitii, & le sceleratezze dall'altra banda sentiamo con poetica imitation esprimere, & esprimando vilipendere, & vituperare, subito comminciamo a disporsi alla fuga, & all'odio delle vitiosa attioni; molto più incitati a questo da cotai imitationi, che da quanto si voglia efficace, & aperta particolari ammonitione."

[57] *Dialogi di Messer Alessandro Lionardi della inventione poetica, et insieme di quanto alla istoria et all'arte oratoria s'appartiene, et del modo di finger la favola* (Venice, 1554).

[58] Ibid., p. 24: "Egli è anco necessario poi, che il poeta sappia in che forma & in qual maniera dee parlare. . . . E cotal perfettione prendera dall'oratore. Perciochè se tratterà de persone o di opere virtuose o vitiose, recorrerà al genere oratorio dimostrativo, acquistandosi delle virtù honore, & de'vitii dishonore."

[59] Ibid., p. 25.

[60] Giraldi Cinthio, *Discorsi* (Venice, 1554), p. 59: "L'ufficio adunque del nostro Poeta, quanto ad indurre il costume, è lodare le attioni virtuose, et biasmare i vitii."

[61] Ibid., p. 58.

[62] Torquato Tasso, *Discorsi del poema eroico,* in *Prose diverse,* ed. Cesare Guasti (Florence, 1875), I, 165-66: ". . . i più magnifici [poeti] imitarono l'azioni più belle e de' più simili a loro; ma i più dimessi quelle de' più vili, componendo da prima villanie ed ingiurie, come gli altri laudi e celebrazioni . . . errò senza dubbio il Castelvetro quando egli disse, che al poeta eroico non si conveniva il lodare; perciò che se il poeta eroico celebra la virtù eroica, dee inalzarla con le lodi sino al cielo. Però san Basilio dice, che l'Iliade d'Omero altro non è che una lode della virtù; ed Averroe, sopra il comento della poesia, porta la medesima Sopinione; e Plutarco. . . . Ultimamente s'a l'istorico è lecito a lodare . . . molto più dovrebbe esser lecito al poeta.

Lasciando dunque i seguaci del Castelvetro nella loro opinione, or noi seguiam quella di Polibio, di Damascio, di san Basilio, d'Averroe, di Plutarco e d'Aristotele medesimo."

[63] George Puttenham, *The Arte of English Poesie,* in ECE, II, 25. I have used this edition for its convenience. The complete text of the *Arte* is available in the edition by G. D. Willcock and A. Walker (Cambridge, 1936).

[64] Ibid., II, 37.

[65] Ibid., II, 37.

[66] Ibid., II, 45.

[67] Milton, *An Apology . . . Against Smectymnuus,* in *Works,* ed. F. A. Patterson, *et al.* (N.Y., 1931-42), III, Pt. i, 302-3.

[68] *The English Philosophers from Bacon to Mill,* ed. E. A. Burtt (N.Y., 1946), p. 588.

Nona Fienberg (essay date 1988)

SOURCE: "Elizabeth, Her Poets, and The Creation of the Courtly Manner," in *Elizabeth, Her Poets, and the Creation of the Courtly Manner: A Study of Sir John Harrington, Sir Philip Sidney, and John Lyly,* Garland Publishing, Inc., 1988, pp. 1-43.

[*In the excerpt below, Fienberg discusses how the court poets (through verse) and Queen Elizabeth (through the rhetoric of her speeches) shaped their own public personas while exercising power and influence.*]

I.

The court's status as the center of cultural ambition and activity in the Renaissance expresses both the idealism and realism of the age. Many Renaissance writers depended upon the patronage of the court to secure financial, social, and political preferment. The court provided the setting poets needed in which to exercise their talents. These interests were frequently supplemented by the idealistic desire to show how learning and eloquence could serve the court. The humanist belief that learned men were necessary to create an ideal commonwealth nurtured an ideal of service to the court, and gave the court setting a new kind of significance. Princes sought out and supported poets because their writing cast an aura of cultured refinement on the court. The prince needed the poet to express his magnificence to both present and future audiences, and less ambitiously, to articulate his political position. Poets could write the prince out of difficult political situations, and into immortality.

At least, so went the poet's claims, and the princes' hopes. The power of these promises and expectations derived in part from the intellectual and educational tradition which both shared. In the waning years of Queen Elizabeth's reign both poets and prince were pupils of the humanists, who had been taught not only to value learning and eloquence, but to use their talents in the service of the common weal. Moreover, prince and poets shared a concern for the qualifications not only of those who served, but of whom they served. Sir Thomas Elyot concludes *The Governor* (1531) with a metaphorical expression of the humanist belief that the court should be the center of culture and virtue:

> The end of all doctrine and study is good counsel, whereunto as unto the principal point, which geometricians do call the centre, all doctrines (which by some authors be imagined in the form of a circle) do send their effects like unto equal lines, as it shall appear to them that will read the books of the noble Plato, . . . proving thereby that the conclusion and (as I might say) the perfection of them is in good counsel, being (as it were) his proper mansion or palace. . . .[1]

The court is finally the image of the center, an ideal vision of healing and perfection. It offers the possibility of virtue in action.

For the court of Queen Elizabeth in her mature years—which J. E. Neale calls the "waning years"—to project so aesthetically, psychologically, and politically satisfying an image required the combined efforts of Queen, nobles, and poets, a kind of collaboration among the disparate elements of this elite. Their common humanist education seemed to create a community of purpose. To Elyot's metaphor of centricity, we can add Roger Ascham's characterization in *The Schoolmaster* (1570) of young Elizabeth as the model for her subjects:

> It is your shame (I speak to you all, you young gentlemen of England) that one maid should go beyond you all in excellency of learning and knowledge of divers tongues. Point forth six of the best given gentlemen of this court, and all they together show not so much good will, spend not so many hours, daily, orderly, and constantly, for the increase of learning and knowledge as doth the Queen's Majesty herself. Yea, I believe that, beside her perfect readiness in Latin, Italian, French, and Spanish, she readeth here now at Windsor more Greek every day than some prebendary of this church doth read Latin in a whole week. And that which is most praiseworthy of all, within the walls of her privy chamber she hath obtained that excellency of learning, to understand, speak, and write, both wittily with head and fair with hand, as scarce one or two rare wits in both the universities have in many years reached unto. Amongst all the benefits that God

hath blessed me withal, next the knowledge of Christ's true religion, I count this the greatest: that it pleased God to call me to be one poor minister in setting forward these excellent gifts of learning in this most excellent prince. Whose only example if the rest of our nobility would follow, then might England be, for learning and wisdom in nobility, a spectacle to all the world beside.[2]

Written and circulated in manuscript early in Elizabeth's reign, Ascham's encomium helps to establish the useful convention that Elizabeth was an ideal audience for intellectual endeavor. Ascham lauds the "Queen's Majesty" to inspire a response in his audience, the young gentlemen of England, so that every learned gentleman could be construed as a tribute and compliment to Elizabeth's example of learning. But even more than praise of her learning, Ascham's paean is a humanist prayer. He compares Elizabeth to "some prebendary of this church," and likens his pedagogical mission to the blessing of "the knowledge of Christ's true religion." He imaginatively reconciles the secular and the sacred in the emblem of "this most excellent prince."

Celebration of the monarch is, however, only part of Ascham's purpose. He also admonishes his audience. Ascham's wish that the court should be "a spectacle to all the world beside" challenges the gentlemen to educate themselves and persuades the court to avail itself of the talents of an educated aristocracy. At a time when noblemen were discovering that blood and birth were no longer the sole criteria for qualification for government service, there were many to heed such humanist exhortations to education. In fact, the Queen herself reinforced the lesson that the proper sphere for learning was the court, when she echoed from her position of power the promise which humanists had made. In her visit to Cambridge in 1564, the Queen seemed to make the humanist goal her own, exhorting the scholars:

> Bear this one thing in mind, that no road is more adapted to win the good things of fortune, or the good will of your prince than the pursuit of good letters. . . .[3]

But although many learned men devoted their lives and fortunes to the fulfillment of that promise, their reward was often disillusionment and frustration.

Court poets, like the rest of Elizabethan society, had to learn that Elizabeth did not act directly in anything, least of all in matters of personal promotion. In *Leicester: Patron of Letters* (1955) Eleanor Rosenberg argues that Elizabeth delegated the responsibility of patronage to some of her nobles. They were to use their wealth and influence to control and direct public opinion by their patronage of men of learning. Rosenberg shows that patrons initially encouraged moral treatises, translations, and political propaganda—works with a patriotic, utilitarian justification. Only late in the reign were *belles lettres* encouraged. Patrons engaged writers in an effort which developed what E. C. Wilson called 'The Legend of Eliza,'[4] through which Elizabeth was able to use "an apotheosis of herself as an instrument of government."[5] By the later years of her reign she had succeeded in tying her subjects to her with highly emotional bonds. One of the roles through which Elizabeth ruled was that of the dean of the "little academe" called the court. Other roles which her poets created for her were essential not only to the literary life of Elizabethan England, but also to the public, political conduct of affairs. Elizabeth illustrates the uses of a flexible sense of selfhood in her various metamorphoses as Astraea, Cynthia, Eliza, Gloriana, Diana and Belphoebe. But her court poets ultimately confronted the disillusioning paradox that a figure who so well knew how to use the literary strategies and manner which her poets helped to create might merely receive their literary tributes, but not reward them financially or politically.

In the October Ecologue of *The Shepheardes Calendar* (1579), for example, Spenser uses the voices of Cuddie and Piers to articulate the disillusionment which this paradox created among Elizabethan poets:

> But ah *Mecoenas* is yclad in claye,
> And great *Augustus* long ygoe is dead:
> And all the worthies liggen wrapt in leade
> That matter made for Poets on to playe: . . .
>
> O pierless Poesye, where is then thy place?
> If nor in Princes pallace thou doe sitt:
> (And yet is Princes pallace the most fitt)
> Ne best of baser birth doth thee embrace.
> (p. 457, ll. 61-64)[6]

The strain of pastoral complaint is insistent in those poets of sufficient social standing and financial resources to aspire to a connection with the court. Spenser voices the disappointment which accompanied the conflict of real circumstances with great promises and expectations. The attractions of "Princes pallace" exceeded its ability or desire to meet the needs of its poets. Yet the same tension between ideal and real, promise and performance, expectation and betrayal, released the great creative energies of the age.

Elyot's conception of the court as a center provides a useful metaphor for the relationship to the court of the three poets with whom I shall be primarily concerned. Sir John Harington, Sir Philip Sidney and John Lyly shared the humanist education and tradition which inculcated a desire to serve the court's needs. All responded to the popular romance mode wherein the court served as a center of healing and perfection, a source of virtue in action. The life and work of the three poets can also, very generally, be seen to present ambivalent responses to the idea of a courtly center of power and action. The importance of the courtly center for their imagination and ambition is attested to by both the attraction and repulsion they express toward that setting. While Harington's letters from court regale the reader with the complexities of courtly intrigue, they nonetheless record his longing to return to his "oves and boves."[7] Sidney's letters to Hubert Languet test his friend's patience by referring to his desire to "relax without reluctance."[8] The letters of Lyly's Euphues speak of increasingly reclusive retreats.[9] The "place" and "matter" for their writing is the court. The pastoral nostalgia of all three, however, is not less sincere because it depends on the wit and sophistication of courtly society.

Each of my poets stood in a different relationship to the court which attracted and repelled him. The tension of their positions raises fundamental questions for the age about the role of the poet in society. Was the writer an amateur for whom literary excellence was a function of breeding and status? Was he a professional whose talent was a special calling in which he could serve the court and the nation, and for which he ought to be paid? Was he, as Ben Jonson claimed, a priest, a moral teacher and an educator? Or was he a morally questionable and socially unacceptable corrupter of society? Each of the writers in this study is concerned in his writing and his career to dignify his own role as poet. Each attempts to define his place in society by shaping an audience who will respond to his version of the courtly manner.

By the third generation of humanists, G. K. Hunter suggests that

> The Humanist ideal shrunk to that of 'the courtier' who was required, within a certain elegant and disdainful playfulness of manner (what Castiglione calls *sprezzatura*) to have some knowledge of classical authors. But the courtier was to use his learning as decoration, not as part of his belief.[10]

Hunter describes a setting which was conscious of itself as a community, an elite of learning. Many gentlemen hazarded fortunes old and new to attain membership in the courtly community. But it is difficult to define the qualifications for access to that coterie. Both Harington and Sidney wrote for the social class to which they belonged. Their confidence in addressing that community, whether in praise or blame, reflects both their awareness that they are speaking to social equals, and their responsibility to courtly decorum, which included an air of gentlemanly unconcern for professionalism. Their careers tended in two seemingly antithetical directions: both wrote crucial defenses for the age of poetry and poets, yet both intended their eloquence to prove their ability to serve the court in political posts. Although they sought the patronage of the court in the form of such rewards as monopolies and embassies, they disdained the public marketplace and were not subject to the demands of a relationship between employer and employee. While Harington sought favors directly from Elizabeth, Sidney himself patronized poets. Although John Lyly was a gentleman, he lacked the status and fortune of Harington and Sidney. Because the court commissioned his comedies, and because he was the first court poet to attempt to make writing a profession, Lyly's relationship to the court constituted a particularly precarious example of employer-employee relations. Lyly stood in his age as the exemplar of a new standard of ornate style which expresses his obligation to the court world. But his style also expresses his attempt to translate the courtly manner for an audience of outsiders.

In *John Lyly: The Humanist as Courtier* (1962), G. K. Hunter describes the importance of artifice in the Elizabethan court:

> Elizabeth and her establishment remained at the centre of the national consciousness throughout the "spacious days" we admire so much, and this would seem enigmatic if we were to suppose that the main national effort of the time was in the direction of freedom and naturalness. Its ritual was artificial to the last degree, despotic and repetitive. The sovereign was a painted idol rather than a person; the codes of manners it encouraged were exotic, Petrarchan and Italianate. Yet this artificial and insincere world had the power to harness the diverse energies of high and low alike. Its artifice does not seem to have cut off the sovereign from her people, but on the contrary seems to have focussed more clearly what they wanted to see—a manifestation of Divine Order on earth, and a guarantee of the meaning of secular energy, in terms which recalled the ritual of divine service.[11]

The erection of this fabric of national consciousness and the extent of its power was in part a product of the uneasy collaboration of Elizabeth, her nobles, and her poets. Court poets helped to "english" the Italianate, Petrarchan courtly mode. The fiction that the court was a closed, private, intimate circle, self-consciously imitative of the court of Urbino which Castiglione described in *The Courtier*, gave value to association with the court, sanctioned the economic neglect of poets, and heightened the glimpses that the public had of what was really a public effort and performance.

In fact, the artifice of Elizabeth's court can be most adequately understood in theatrical terms, as performance. It was a society of relentless mutual self-consciousness. In this heliocentric universe, with the sun-Queen at the center of awareness, the visibility of the Queen was as important as her subjects' knowledge of her observation. There is no relief from her gaze. If we feel in the writing of her poets the strain of such tyranny and such subjection, the oppression of being aware in the most personal and private acts of your life that you represent the presence and power of another, we feel also the concomitant satisfaction and security of the knowledge that the subject is a satellite in a stable universe. Through the control of role-playing, the participants in the courtly theater gave aesthetic form to their emotions. In this sense, courtly *sprezzatura,* for example, is a kind of play which belies the effort of living under surveillance: the real work of being a poet is masked in an attitude of playful disregard for intensity and professionalism.

Performance, then, becomes the key to survival in a court from which patronage and posts were not sufficiently forthcoming. In the effort to display his ability to fulfill a variety of roles, the courtier performed in the areas which Lawrence Stone describes in *The Crisis of the Aristocracy 1558-1641* (1967) as "the five overlapping cultural ideals, those of the man of war, the man of learning, the statesman, the polished cavalier, and the virtuoso."[12] The concept of performance includes the deliberate shaping of the self in relation to the courtly audience. In his article, "Exhibitionism and the Antitheatrical Prejudice," Jonas A. Barish discusses Castiglione's philosophical development of the "principle of display of self" in *The Courtier,* in which

> The ideal courtier, as sketched by the little academe at Urbino, has as one prime characteristic an unremitting awareness of being on view. It is proper that he seek occasions to exhibit himself, and that he do so with full consciousness of his audience.

Barish concludes that

> the further the courtier can go in the direction of legitimate self-display, the more fully he realizes himself, the more sharply he differentiates himself from the herd. Self-realization *is* self-differentiation.[13]

By playing a role, the courtier can explore the nature of his character and situation, and can discover new ethical, moral and social possibilities in the new circumstances of his role.

Stephen J. Greenblatt's *Sir Walter Ralegh: The Renaissance Man and His Roles* (1973) demonstrates how the life as well as the writing of a Renaissance man was a performance. By examining Ralegh in his historical and cultural setting, that of Elizabeth's court, Greenblatt reveals that Ralegh's commitment to his various roles is not mere pretense, but an authentic response to his place and time. He demonstrates that Ralegh's insistence on his personality in the *History of the World,* for example, is part of his conception of history:

> the writing of history entailed the full involvement of the individual, not the stifling of the personal and the subjective. Far from suppressing references to his own time, or even to his own career, Ralegh allows them full play, not inadvertently, not because he could not bring himself to write "objectively," but because such references are essential to his conception of history.[14]

Similarly, an understanding of the full involvement of the individual poet in the works of Harington, Lyly and Sidney will lead to a more complete understanding of the Renaissance poet's conception of his place in society.

When Greenblatt discusses how Ralegh's performance emerges from the Renaissance view of man and 'dramatic sense of life,' he places those views in the context of three traditions: the Augustinian, the Stoic, and that of the writers of the continental Renaissance. For the latter tradition, Thomas M. Greene's "The Flexibility of the Self in Renaissance Literature" (1968) examines the dramatic imagination in the Renaissance and the age's concern with the metamorphosis of the self. Using Pico della Mirandola's "Oration on the Dignity of Man" as his philosophical basis and Petrarch as his literary model, Greene explores the humanist ideal of "the fashioning of the pupil by the pedagogue." He argues that the humanist ideal was replaced by the ideal of "the reflexive fashioning of the individual's own mind and soul."[15] The poets with whom this study is primarily concerned explore both ideals. In the role of the pedagogue they praise and admonish apt pupils, and in various other roles, they dramatize the connection between making images of the self and attaining self-knowledge.

In their efforts to create ideal roles for themselves and for their audience, court poets used various strategies to create the sense of a poetry of address. In framing devices such as dedications, letters and prefaces, they attempted to create the illusion of intimacy, the fiction of a private communication. In epic poetry, and through manuscript circulation, for example, the poets reminded their audience of an older, oral tradition, when, they imagined, the poet was a singer of tales, and when the interaction of poet and audience was direct. Through such self-reflexive nostalgia for the world of oral poetry, court poets attempted to treat their audience as part of an extended family. But while they used dedications to claim membership in that family, they also, paradoxically, hoped that their appeal might win financial support, or a political appoint-

ment, or protection from censorship. Subject to brute economic and political necessity, they had to appeal to the nobility for support. But in order to win that support, they had to maintain the illusion that they were amateurs, playfully independent of harsh economic reality. In the tension between celebration and exhortation, court poets reveal the paradox inherent in the claim to membership in an elite community and the plea for financial support from that circle. While he celebrates the moral, cultural and social values of the members of his audience, the poet must also urge them to fulfill a vision of an ideal which includes patronage.

The form of presentation of court poets' works epitomizes the difficulty of this paradox. The poet does not speak privately, but for an audience, for some form of public approbation. But the aristocratic disdain for professionalism, an expression of courtly *sprezzatura,* attached a stigma to publication, as J. W. Saunders has documented in "The Stigma of Print."[16] By his very publication of his translation of *Orlando Furioso* in 1591, Harington branded himself an eccentric. In fact, Harington involved himself in minute and technical details of the printing and publication of his work. He considered it a portable expression of his personality and used it as a sort of social calling card with which to introduce himself to persons of note. Yet even in Harington's volume, the pleasure of reading derives in part from his insider's account of courtly fashion and personal claims to attention. It is appropriate that Harington is the courtier who challenged the stigma of print. He characteristically created situations where explicit formulation of the difficulty of being a courtier and court poet became necessary. Whether in his books, or in his diaries and letters, he is an articulate spokesman for the public nature of the private self in Elizabeth's court.

We need not, however, share the bias of the age against professionalism and publication, as does John F. Danby in *Elizabethan and Jacobean Poets* (1965). Although Danby does not recognize the court's need for its poets, he provides a valuable consideration of the poet's need for court patronage and connection. But because he shares the aristocratic disdain for professionalism, Danby neglects the social and political motives of the writers of the period. Danby claims, for example, that because Sidney did not publish his own work, he was writing for himself. Danby praises Sidney's "Ironia," a term which Fulke Greville uses in his biography, and describes Ironia as the "literary virtue of holding yourself above professionalism."[17] It is clear, however, that Sidney wrote not only for himself, but in order to gain a political post. Although he did not deign to publish his works, he manifests his concern for his role as poet and for his audience. Through manuscript circulation of the *Arcadia,* he maintained the illusion that he was an amateur and that his writing was a private, intimate mode of communication. The readers of his manuscript valued old ways, old secrecies, old intimacies, and enjoyed the luxury of entrance into an oral illusion. And Sidney worked to sustain the illusion of a poetry of address throughout his work.

While Harington and Sidney wrote for the few, Lyly wrote and published *Euphues,* which became a bestseller of the day, and also had a hand in the publication of his plays. Although a gentleman, Lyly attempted to make writing a profession, and to dignify that profession. While his plays were courtly entertainment, commissioned by the court, when published they presented to an increasingly literate middle class a picture of the court as they wanted to see it, and as the court wanted to see itself. Lyly trod a difficult path between his desire to gain acceptance as a learned gentleman of the court, and his need to make a living by his pen.

Besides such strategies of address as manuscript circulation, the court poets' intellectual heritage and social circumstances also taught them to use strategies of veiling, such as allegory, allusion and dramatic inductions. For the Elizabethan court poet, the wit of veiling responded to the neo-Platonic tradition. As court poets explored questions about the nature of truth, how to achieve and how to reveal it, they learned from neo-Platonists that immediate sensory perception may seem to reveal truth, while it really dazzles and deceives. In contrast, allegory and allusion may seem to disguise, but ultimately, through tests of perception, lead to truth. Through allegory, poets give value to the effort of reading, by creating complexities which will distinguish an elite readership. Just as they protected their poetry and their ideal selves from the vulgar multitude, so too did they protect their monarch. Their task of creating a mythology of Elizabeth involved similarly complex strategies. In this way, court poets' essential analogy between the forms they used to present their poetry, themselves and the Queen herself developed as they tested its implications. What began as a way to persuade Elizabeth that they were qualified for service in the court, became an argument that writing itself served as an essential form of action.

II.

Elizabeth's use of the roles her poets created for her, of the oratorical tradition in which she was educated, and of the literary strategies and devices of the courtly mode reveal her dependence on the assent of her people to the literary conventions of the age in order to maintain her sovereignty and to conduct her policy. From its early expression in Ascham's eulogy, the task Elizabeth set herself and her publicists was to enlarge her opportunities for virtuous action, and to provide a context for the virtue she found in calculated inaction. It was a task inevitably forced upon a

woman ruler. For much of the early part of Elizabeth's reign, many assumed that the only essential choice she faced was whom to marry. The Queen's determination to exercise her power demanded a certain education of her subjects. Such education was well suited to her court poets, to the "exotic, Petrarchan and Italianate" courtly manner, and to the popular romance mode.

In Elizabeth's carefully planned appearances, her progresses in and outside of London, she relied on the munificence of her nobles and subjects to pay poets to celebrate her in verse and drama. But she also wrote her own artful speeches to her subjects, most notably in Parliament. Just as a poet, by quoting his earlier successes, reminds his readers of the continuity of his career, Elizabeth quoted herself in her speeches. Her constant themes, as she reiterated them to Parliament and people throughout her reign, were her love for her people, her care for them, her willingness to sacrifice herself for them, and even more insistently their love for her—themes suited to the maternal and wifely roles she assumed in relation to her people. For the Queen as orator, such echoes served much the same function as the formulae of the oral epic poet. They were refrains adaptable to most occasions, and were available to elevate the material, and to comfort both speaker and audience with the familiarity of their ties. Like the epic poet, Elizabeth was herself a creator of myths and a maker of heroes. Out of the ritual repetition of her self-reflexive speeches came power. She was conscious of making of her reign a work of art. As the reign lengthened, such recurrent themes created a continuity between past and present, and served, moreover, as an echoing reminder to her subjects of their duty to reciprocate her love and responsibility.

For example, Elizabeth was fond of reminding her audience of the charming pastoral musing which John Foxe attributed to her in his account of her sufferings under Mary. Foxe's encomium of the new Protestant monarch and hero at the close of his tome formed a part of the popular Elizabethan mythology, and provided Elizabeth with the role of a pastoral maiden. Inspired, it seems, by his reading of romances, Foxe dramatizes a moment in the princess's "desolate" imprisonment at Woodstock:

> Whereupon no marvel if she, hearing upon a time, out of her garden at Woodstock a certain milkmaid singing pleasantly, wished herself to be a milkmaid as she was; saying that her case was better, and life more merry than was hers, in that state as she was.[18]

Like the courtly fashion for pastorals, the witty fancy draws attention to the sophistication of the dreamer.

In an address to the Parliament of 1576, which had begged her to settle the question of succession, Elizabeth exploited that pastoral nostalgia to remind her audience that she knew her responsibilities to her people. To their oft-repeated request that she marry, she apologized as she demurred:

> Though I must needs confess mine own mislike—so much to strive against the matter—as, if I were a milkmaid with a pail on my arm, whereby my private person might be little set by, I would not forsake that poor and single state to match with the greatest monarch.[19]

We might note parenthetically that Elizabeth was sufficiently pleased with the speech to send it to her godson, John Harington, then fifteen, admonishing him to study her words carefully, "Ponder them in thy hours of leisure—play with them till they enter thy understanding. . . . " She thus offered the youth a notable invitation to the courtly world and the courtly manner.

Elizabeth's strained relationship with Parliament expresses the age's conflicting conceptions of kingship and the responsibilities of articulate citizenship. While the Queen protected her prerogative, veiled the mysteries of imperial action, and retained the initiative for action, she faced a newly self-conscious group of articulate citizens, which was determined to advise and have a role in the initiation of action. In 1586, for example, when renewed discovery of Mary, Queen of Scots' plotting reawakened the popular clamor for Mary's life, Elizabeth sought Parliament's support for her caution. The long story of her reluctance to accede to the pressures of her council and Parliament to kill Mary documents her awareness of her visibility, of her place on the world's stage. In 1586, she addressed a deputation of Lords and Commons in her Withdrawing Chamber at Richmond, saying:

> we Princes, I tell you, are set on stages, in the sight and view of all the world duly observed. The eyes of many behold our actions; a spot is soon spied in our garments, a blemish quickly noted in our doings. It behoveth us, therefore, to be careful that our proceedings be just and honourable.[20]

In the same speech, Elizabeth conveyed her reluctance to be the agent of Mary Stuart's death, using her favorite play of wit and fancy:

> And if, even yet, now the matter is made but too apparent, I thought she truly would repent—as perhaps she would easily appear in outward show to do—and that for her none other would take the matter upon them; or that we were but as two milk-maids, with pails upon our arms; or that there were no more dependency upon us, but mine own life were only in danger, and not the whole estate of your religion and well doings; I protest—

wherein you may believe me, for although I may have many vices, I hope I have not accustomed my tongue to be an instrument of untruth—I would most willingly pardon and remit this offence.[21]

By involving her audience in the pleasure of the juxtaposition of sophistication and simplicity, she temporarily dissipates a cruel political reality into a pastoral fancy. But she does so only to return her audience to the real world, where all remember that the "if" is contrary to fact.

Elizabeth employs the vigor of her speeches to Parliament to mask the passivity of her political stance. In order to maintain her role as the merciful Virgin Queen, she wished, in this crisis, events to act upon her. Her speech to Parliament on November 24, 1586, again mulling over the dangers of Mary, is full of difficult structures, and uses a persona both maidenly modest and princely learned. Initially, she seems to brood to herself, and to allow the Parliament access to a personal meditation. She grants that liberty, however, in a most calculated, controlled manner, just as the sonneteer permits the public to enter a private world, but shaped carefully into public, conventional form:

> Full grievous is the way whose going on and end breeds cumber for the hire of a laborious journey. I have strived more this day than ever in my life whether I should speak or use silence. If I speak and not complain, I shall dissemble; if I hold my peace, your labour taken were full vain.

> For me to make my moan were strange and rare, for I suppose you shall find few that, for their own particular, will cumber you with such a care. Yet such, I protest, hath been my greedy desire and hungry will that of your consultation might have fallen out some other means to work my safety, joined with your assurance, than that for which you have become so earnest suitors, as I protest I must needs use complaint—though not of you, but unto you, and of the cause. . . .[22]

Elizabeth's slow, solemn exordium, suitable to the gravity of the occasion, establishes the heroic character both of her ordeal and of her effort to express it. Through the subtle shift of the "cumber" or burden from her own shoulders in the first sentence, to the "cumber" of her audience's responsibility for her well-being in the fourth sentence, she reminds her audience of their role in the problem both share. Speaking, as she says, to "earnest suitors," she deliberately confuses the language of legal complaint and of love complaint. By playing on the familiar Petrarchan analogy between the power of love and the power of sovereignty, Elizabeth implicates her audience in the intimacy of her revelations about "my moan," and "my greedy desire and hungry will." The tension of Elizabeth's exordium derives from the difficulty of giving public form to a private pain. While majestic assertions of her oratorical dilemma suggest her confidence in her role and in her public presentation of a "particular" cause, the very "strange" and "rare" quality of her dramatic situation creates a decorous wonder at the lifting of the veil from imperial mysteries.

Although the language and deliberately ambiguous stance of the speaker echo the Petrarchan tradition, Elizabeth's strategy differs significantly from the Petrarchan lover's. In a more direct response to the Petrarchan tradition, in Spenser's *Amoretti,* Sonnet XLIII, the speaker's repeated rhetorical questions similarly involve his reader in the process of creating an adequate role:

> Shall I then silent be or shall I speake?
> And if I speake, her wrath renew I shall:
> and if I silent be, my heart will breake,
> or choked be with overflowing gall.
> What tyranny is this both my hart to thrall,
> and eke my toung with proud restraint to tie?
> that nether I may speake nor thinke at all,
> but like a stupid stock in silence die.
> Yet I my hart with silence secretly
> will teach to speake, and my just cause to plead:
> and eke mine eies with meeke humility,
> loue learned letters to her eyes to read.
> Which her deep wit, that true harts though can spel,
> will soone conceiue, and learne to construe well.
>
> (p. 596)

Like Elizabeth, Spenser struggles to translate powerful emotion into rational, ordered form, by drawing witty, self-conscious attention to such effort. The sonneteer, like the monarch, debates whether to speak or to remain silent. He too forces himself to plead his "just cause." But he must, in so doing, redefine his rhetoric, and reshape the role of his lover, through a mutual process of education. Spenser assumes the part of the humanist pedagogue leading an apt pupil.

The speaker of Spenser's sonnet will teach his heart to speak "with silence secretly." The adverb "secretly," emphatically ending the first line of the sestet, wittily resolves the conundrum posed in the octave. The *O.E.D.* tells us that "secretly" can mean "in an inaudible voice," thus silent. It can also mean "with a hidden meaning," such as would require "deep wit" to "spel" or decipher.[23] Through his exploration of the problems of communication, Spenser determines to write in a style which only an initiated one, that one solely his beloved, can understand. The mystery of his language of love rivals the mystery of the *arcana imperii*.

Through the analogy between a love and the relationship of judge and plaintiff, between tyrant and subject, Spenser confronts the power of his beloved. Like the tyrant, she can reward or punish, wound or heal. If the "wrath of the prince is death," what, to the poet, is the "wrath" of his beloved? He will, therefore, speak through allegory or metaphor, to retain the essential mystery and exclusiveness of his heart's thought. By promising to mirror the mystery of the love in the mystery of his style, Spenser alters the usually passive role of his beloved. Instead, he offers her the more active role of initiate and witty reader.

Elizabeth, on the other hand, uses her mysterious style to justify her own inaction, while simultaneously declining to sanction any Parliamentary action. By means of the difficult opening of her speech, Elizabeth seeks to confuse part of her audience and to impress them with the complexity of her position. After she introduces the metaphor of life's journey and characterizes herself as a pilgrim on the "way," she quickly assumes a more courtly role. Elizabeth's speech, like Spenser's sonnet, blends intimacy and formality. It tempers entreaty with praise. The conclusion allows Elizabeth the liberty *not* to do what Parliament has requested, but she characteristically effects that delicate extrication using the signature Petrarchan device of oxymoron:

> And as for your petition: your judgment I condemn not, neither do I mistake your reasons, but pray you to accept my thankfulness, excuse my doubtfulness, and take in good part my answer-answerless. . . . Therefore, if I should say, I would not do what you request, it might peradventure be more than I thought; and to say I would do it might perhaps breed peril of that you labour to preserve, being more than in your own wisdoms and discretions would seem convenient, circumstances of place and time being duly considered.[24]

As though she were responding to a lover's complaint of "restless rest" or "living death," she gives an "answer-answerless." In a masterly form of evasion, she returns Parliament's expressions of frustrated will to them. Although she strives to maintain the illusion that they have a role in her decision, the infinitive verb forms of "excuse," "take," and "accept" all describe a passive stance. When they labor, it is "to preserve." In this way, Elizabeth advances the illusion of intimacy only to make her true distance the more attractive, and her legal language the more decorous for a woman ruler. In a remarkable demonstration of the flexibility of her self, Elizabeth transforms a Laura *loquens* into a judicial Deborah or Astraea. The Queen serves notice that she will not allow an insistent Commons to play upon her. She will retain the heart of her mystery.

The juxtaposition of the speech and the sonnet illuminates the way art and life, and public and private selves interact in the age. The analogy between the role of the lover and the sovereign reveals the persistence, the use, and the truth of the real fiction of mutual love and concern with which Elizabeth ruled. It reveals, moreover, the way the language through which she exercised her power made the wielding of that power more acceptable to her male audience. Just as Elizabeth distanced her style from clear, plain speech, so she distanced herself from her audience by discovering the political uses of the courtly manner.

Finally, as the Queen allowed events to shape themselves, her mystery remained inviolate. According to the historian Conyers Read, Lord Burghley, not Elizabeth, took the decisive step towards the execution of Mary. Burghley's despair that the Queen would never assume responsibility for the act, combined with his conviction that she wished the act done, led him to what Read calls the most "heroic" choice of his career.[25] Surely that heroic role was one which Elizabeth most willingly relinquished.

The Queen knew, approved of and supervised the speech's publication in England and abroad, and in several languages, including Latin. But Elizabeth employed her strategy of indirection in this publication, as in her relationship with the poets who created worlds for her. Young Robert Cecil, Burghley's son and aspiring successor, published the speech, feigning apologies for the inadequacy of his text.[26]

The power of print both challenged and threatened Elizabeth. She condemned the Puritan firebrand and Parliament man, Peter Wentworth, to live out his days in the Tower for the indecorous manner in which he chastised his sovereign in *A Pithie Exhortation to her Majesty*. Yet he neither presented the tract to her, nor published it, but merely gave it to several men to read—one of whom found its contents sufficiently alarming to report the author.

The public response to the Queen's proposed marriage to the Duke of Alençon, and his visit to her court in the spring of 1579 reveals a variety of manners of addressing the Queen, and elucidates some complexities of the role of the articulate citizen in the affairs of the commonwealth. The Duke of Alençon intended his visit to secure a marriage contract. He left England that fall, however, with little more than Elizabeth's promise to try to win her subjects' trust in such a marriage. Her claim to act only with her people's good will is itself significant, but all realized that the proposed marriage to a French Catholic would severely divide the country. Some historians have argued that Elizabeth, at 46, did not really intend to marry Alençon, and that the pretended courtship allowed her to play her best game in foreign affairs. But the risk which

articulate men of the court and country took in addressing the issue attests to their real fear that the Queen would marry. In addition, their response demonstrates their welcome of an opportunity to test their eloquence in public affairs.

Among the writers for the Protestant opposition, Sir Philip Sidney, Edmund Spenser, and John Stubbs all paid for their boldness in addressing courtly issues.[27] Sidney temporarily retreated from the Queen's displeasure about his "Letter to Queen Elizabeth" to his estate at Wilton. Edmund Spenser's post in Ireland may have provided an expeditious way to remove the uncomfortable presence of the author of the puzzling *Mother Hubberds Tale*. For John Stubbs, a writer with neither courtly connections nor courtly aspirations, the publication of *The Discovery of a Gaping Gulf* occasioned one of the great dramatic scaffold scenes of the age, and stirred the imagination of the whole country. Queen Elizabeth could hardly have expected that punishing Stubbs would silence the Puritan opposition which he aroused and inflamed. She may not, however, have anticipated the sensation of which the Spanish ambassador, Bernardino de Mendoza, wrote:

> As the proclamation was only dated two days before its promulgation (which was carried out with great ceremony) people are attaching a good deal of importance to it, and are saying that it was advisable to cut short the sensation caused by the book, in order to effect the marriage.[28]

He mistook the motive, but he seems not to have exaggerated the sensation the book aroused, a sensation exacerbated by the spectacle of Stubbs' punishment. He was tried and sentenced to have his right hand cut off. On the scaffold, he protested his loyalty "duty and affection toward her Majesty," and bade his audience to pray for him, "because, when so many veins of blood are opened, it is uncertain how they may be stayed and what will be the event thereof." Camden records the bravado of his performance:

> Stubbs, having his right hand cut off, put off his hat with his left and said with a loud voice, 'God save the Queen.'

Camden records too the response of Stubbs' audience:

> The multitude standing about was altogether silent, either out of horror of this new and unwonted punishment, or out of pity towards the man, being of most honest and unblameable report, or else out of hatred of the marriage, which most men presaged would be the overthrow of religion. (p. xxxv)

The career of the hero of this theatrical experience, which evoked the tragic emotions of "horror" and "pity," had just begun. He later became a member of Parliament, and was hired by Lord Burghley to write a response to Catholic polemics.

The Queen condemned the book in her proclamation of September 29, 1579 because of the image it presented of her. She protested the tract's inflammatory premise that she needed to be taught to care for her country. Further, she feared that the book would arouse an ideologically motivated public. Beyond condemning Stubbs' presumption in writing about courtly affairs, she deplored the presumption he taught and preached to his audience:

> offering to every most meanest person of judgment, by these kind of popular libels, authority to argue and determine in every blind corner at their several wills of the affairs of public estate, a thing most pernicious in any estate. (p. xxxvi)

The very "popularity" of the book threatens her Queenly role, and her conception of the hieratic nature of the monarchy.

The very "lewd and seditious" style which offended the Queen moved Stubbs' audience. Neither writer nor audience accepted the decorum of the courtly mode. Stubbs designed his title to startle:

> *The Discovery of a Gaping Gulf Whereinto England is Like to Be Swallowed by an other French marriage, if the Lord forbid not the banes, by Letting her Majestie see the sin and punishment thereof.* (p. 152)

A metaphorical voyage of discovery turns readily into an announcement of an impending apocalypse. From the role of intrepid explorer and hero of epic adventures, Stubbs develops the voice of the prophet, tearing away the veil from hidden truth, and finding doom. His rhetoric ranges from the homely:

> This is but Reynard's flattering of our kingly bird and well-natured Chanticleer in his good sweet voice and fair feathers, (p. 75)

to the horrific:

> if they went up to the knuckles in French blood, they will up to the elbow in English blood. (p. 40)

He interweaves references to "the massacring marriage," reviving memories of the Saint Bartholomew Day Massacre only seven years earlier, wallowing in a vision of a national Black Mass:

> From these men that have eaten the people of God as bread, have been fleshed in murdering of multitudes, and drunk the blood of noblemen,

why should any good manner stay a good loving subject from fearing the same dangers and cruelties from the same men to our queen? And so, a wretched confusion in this land if for the sins thereof she should come in their fingers to be a doleful bride in their bloody chambers, which God for his Christ's sake prevent. Amen. (p. 40)

In a theatrical vision, he portrays Elizabeth as the tempted everyman, or youthful prince of morality tradition, exhorting:

> stop your Majesty's ears against these sorcerers and their enchanting counsels, which seek to stay this happy course of yours and to provoke God's anger against you, pray against these dangerous tempters and temptations, and know assuredly, to your comfort, that all the faithful of God pray for you, and when you are in your secret closet of prayer they join with you in spirit. (p. 40)

Although such prying into the secret closet of princes would hardly gratify his Queen, Stubbs does not really expect his exclamations to move her directly. Rather, by simplifying issues, and creating vivid, if hysterical, images of terror, he aroused popular Protestant opinion and offered a political stance to the multitude.

Stubbs knew the risk of his boldness. At the close of his pamphlet he drew attention to his readiness to martyr himself for his cause. He must address the issue, "though it should cost me my life" (p. 85). Although he suffered mutilation, not death, he prepared his audience to appreciate the significance of his witness. Stubbs played upon the fears of the emerging middle class: fears of change, of disorder, of loss of livelihood, of the overthrow of established religion. By presenting an image of confusion to those who had much to gain from a continuance of the *status guo,* he aroused their involvement in government affairs.

Sidney's *Letter to Queen Elizabeth* was, like Stubbs' tract, ideologically motivated, but the courtier addressed a different audience. In his first, careful words, he announces his primary audience:

> Most feared and beloved, most sweet and gracious Sovereign: to seek out excuses of this my boldness, and to arm the acknowledging of a fault with reasons for it, might better show I knew I did amiss, than any whit diminish the attempt; especially in your judgment, who is able lively to discern into the nature of the thing done. (p. 46)

Like Stubbs, Sidney recognizes the risk in addressing the Queen on a matter of such intimacy. But like the Petrarchan lover, Sidney gracefully sugars "this my boldness" with praise for his Sovereign's sweetness and discernment. He must speak to relieve "the overflowing of my mind" and the "deep wellspring of most loyal affection." Sidney's responsibility to his secondary audience, that of the fellow nobles among whom his manuscript letter circulated, demanded that he allay their scruples about influencing public policy. In this way, like Stubbs' tract, Sidney's letter intrudes into the *arcana imperii*. But while both take great liberty, the form and circumstances of the two are significantly different. The position of nobleman allowed the use of learning and eloquence to advise the Queen. Stubbs played, in contrast, the self-appointed role of the Puritan prophet and martyr. While Stubbs published his tirade and caused a public sensation, Sidney circulated his letter in manuscript among the court circle. While Stubbs presented the Queen as a misguided victim, Sidney created a present ideal and a heroic future in which Elizabeth could play out the role of careful, loving monarch.

In a strategy with double-edged effect, Sidney employs the Queen's own words to buttress his arguments. Although Elizabeth often quoted herself, and might be flattered to hear her own arguments quoted with approval, she may not have enjoyed hearing the witty use to which Sidney puts them. Using what rhetoricians call an *argumentum ex concessis,* Sidney says:

> Often have I heard you with protestation say, 'No private pleasure nor self affection could lead you unto it.' But if it be both unprofitable for your kingdom and unpleasant to you, certainly it were a dear purchase of repentance. (p. 46)

At the next stage of his argument, Sidney marshalls elaborate metaphors, *sententiae,* and historical precedent apparently to support the Queen's contentions, but he then deflates them by the more artificial metaphors and maxims which follow:

> Now resteth to consider what be the motions of this sudden change, as I have heard you in most sweet words deliver: fear of standing alone in respect of foreign dealings, and in home respects, doubt of contempt. Truly, as standing alone with good foresight both of peace-government, and war-defence, is the honourablest thing that can be to a well established monarchy, those buildings being ever most strongly durable which, leaning to no other, remain firm upon their own foundations: so yet in the particularities of your estate presently, I will not altogether deny that a true Masinissa were very fit to countermine the enterprises of mighty Carthage. But how this general truth can be applied unto Monsieur, in truth I perceive not. (p. 51)

A geometrical metaphor, followed by precisely measured comparison of interests conveys the impossibility of reconciling "Monsieur's desires and yours":

> how they should meet in public matters I think no oracle can tell: for as the geometricians say that parallels, because they maintain diverse lines, can never join, so truly, who have in the beginning contrary principles, to bring forth one doctrine, must be some miracle. He of the Romish religion, and if he be a man, must needs have that man-like disposition to desire that all men be of his mind: you the erector and defender of the contrary, and the only sun that dazzleth their eyes; he French, and desiring to make France great: your Majesty English, and desiring nothing less than that France should grow great. . . . (p. 51)

In the two passages, Sidney plays wittily on the meaning of "truth." He disarms his readers, confusing them initially about where the truth resides. His first "truly" leads readers to expect him to corroborate the Queen's "sweet words." Instead, the *sententia* illustrates the truth that England should stand strongly alone. Further, Sidney's grudging concessions fail to resolve the paradox of a "true Masinissa," a figure known for his betrayal of his upbringing. When we reach the dismissive reference to "Monsieur," we know that the relation between "this general truth" and Monsieur's suit is very faint and insubstantial. It is finally reassuring to enter a realm of mathematical certainty, in which parallel lines "truly" can never join. Sidney's confident presentation of the true relationship between France and England afforded him the role of spokesman for the truth. But he assumed that role not through direct assertion, but through indirection, wit and sophistication.

In Sidney's peroration, he urges Elizabeth to use propaganda to promulgate the image of the ideal he celebrates:

> Against contempt at home, if there be any, which I will never believe, let your excellent virtues of piety, justice and liberality daily, if it be possible, more and more shine. Let some such particular actions be found out (which is easy, as I think, to be done) by which you may gratify all the hearts of your people. Let those in whom you find trust, and to whom you have committed trust in your weighty affairs, be held up in the eyes of your subjects. Lastly, doing as you do, you shall be as you be: the example of princes, the ornament of this age, the comfort of the afflicted, the delight of your people, the most excellent fruit of all your progenitors, and the perfect mirror to your posterity. (pp. 56-57)

His advice, like the fact of writing the letter, encourages employment for an educated aristocracy, and enhances their importance in the court. His closing sentence unfolds an image of the ideal in a prophetic vision of the future as a continuation of the ideal present. For the moment, Sidney suspends the doubts and fears of "contempt at home" which introduced the need for propaganda, as he provides a model of how poets can create an image of the ideal, in the poise between admonishment and eulogy.

Through the formality and careful balances of Sidney's letter, he acknowledges his responsibility to his fellow Protestant nobles. His sophisticated, witty letter defines a new measure of activity in courtly affairs. Sidney wrote for Leicester's party, served the interests of aggressive Protestants throughout his life, and presented an ideologically controlled version of the self-interest of his class. In contrast, the third respondent to the Alençon crisis, Edmund Spenser also followed Leicester's career, but he sought the patronage of the famous Maecenas, and was not the family member of a powerful faction. Still, Spenser shares some of Sidney's self-assurance and wit. His *Mother Hubberds Tale* evinces his confidence that his select audience would enjoy the challenge of filling in suggestive hints with real persons and events.

Spenser too addresses a courtly audience from an ideologically motivated perspective, but his choice of form, a *prosopopoia,* an allegorical beast fable in simple couplets, protects him from immediate risk. The self-effacing sub-title, *Mother Hubberds Tale,* like the frame's disclaimer, protests the poem's innocuousness:

> No Muses aide me needes heretoo to call;
> Base is the style, and matter meane withall.
> (11. 43-44)

Similarly, in the dedication to the 1591 publication, Spenser declares that his is merely a tale of "honest mirth":

> Simple is the device, and the composition meane, yet carrieth some delight, even the rather because of the simplicitie and meannesse thus personated.
> (p. 495)

Although many would recognize that he protests too much, Spenser both protects himself from prosecution and reflects his real position as an outsider. Unlike Stubbs' and Sidney's direct advocacy of action, Spenser's allegory influences action through moral teaching. He neither addresses nor advises the Queen, but plays the satirist, who speaks from outside the circle of power. Yet he knows the courtly world well enough to ridicule the abuse of power and position he sees there. Unlike the allegory in Spenser's *The Shepheardes Calendar* or in *The Faerie Queene,* the *Prosopopoia* has no commentary or guide for the readers. Perhaps the clear danger of the issue he questioned dictated the mysterious form.

The poem's form also attests to the particular taste of his coterie of readers, who enjoy the political relevance of the allegory. Where Stubbs made fleeting reference to "Reynard's flattering of our kingly bird and well-natured Chanticleer" (p. 75), Spenser uses the Reynard tradition to structure his satire. In a device particularly suited to the intimacies of Elizabeth's court, where the Queen playfully dubbed her favorites with animal nicknames, Spenser ridicules Alençon's emissary, Simier, as her ape, and Alençon himself as the fox:

> So well they shifted, that the Ape anon
> Himselfe had cloathed like a Gentleman,
> And the slie Foxe, as like to be his groome,
> That to the Court in seemly sort they come.
> Were the fond Ape himselfe uprearing hy
> Upon his tiptoes, stalketh stately by,
> As if he were some great *Magnifico,*
> And boldlie doth amongst the boldest go.
> (11. 659-665)

Spenser echoes the image later in the fable, when the Ape steals the Lyon's ornaments of kingship:

> Upon his tiptoes nicely he up went,
> For making noyse, and still his eare he lent
> To euerie sound, that vnder heauen blew,
> Now went, now stept, now crept, now backward drew,
> That it good sport had been him to haue eyde. . . .
> (11. 1009-1013)

A beast on tiptoe, in garments like a gentleman images disorder in the chain of being. But as he mocks the deceitful performance of the Ape in the court, Spenser also suggests the complicity of the courtiers in accepting so false a performance as true. Spenser makes his moral more explicit as he turns from a description of the Ape as a false poet to a celebration of the true poet, usually understood to be a portrait of Sidney:

> For he is practiz'd well in policie,
> And thereto doth his Courting most applie:
> To learne the enterdeale of Princes strange,
> To marke th'intent of Counsells, and the change
> Of states, and eke of priuate men somewhile,
> Supplanted by fine falshood and faire guile;
> Of all the which he gathereth, what is fit
> T'enrich the storehouse of his powerfull wit,
> Which through wise speaches, and graue conference
> He daylie eekes, and brings to excellence.
> Such is the rightfull Courtier in his kinde:. . .
> (11. 783-793)

Like Sidney, Spenser advocates the public use of the virtues of a learned courtier.

But Spenser's treatment of the political issue differs from Sidney's in that the poem can aso stand independent of its particular occasion. Although Spenser's poem circulated in manuscript, as did Sidney's letter, it was not published until 1591, eleven years later. By that time, the Alençon issue was quite dead, but the interest in the *Tale* remained. Thus, the "mystery" of the fable serves to protect the author at the time of the crisis, and to maintain its value subsequently. By indulging the Renaissance taste for obscurity, Spenser could write a tale which addressed immediate political emergencies without endangering himself, and which transcended its occasion to stand as a moral fable of enduring value.

Although Stubbs, Sidney and Spenser wrote in very different styles, each writer contributed to the same process of social change. They all sought to redefine the role of the articulate man in government affairs, and to test the bounds of acceptable speech to a monarch. Like the parliamentarians, who tried concurrently to extend their privileges of "liberty of speech," the literate men expected, through their eloquence, either to win a direct role in courtly affairs, or to influence those who filled such a role.

The ambivalence of court poets' relation to the court echoes Parliament's adoring yet contumacious attitude toward Elizabeth. Both reflect an age which saw the growth in strength of the Tudor monarchy in uneasy simultaneity with the emergence of an informed, literate, and ideologically motivated public. Through their writing and their speeches, they participated in a process of social change which reevaluated the very nature of the sovereignty they hailed. For a time, Elizabeth herself held those conflicting forces in suspension, by means of the various roles, conventions and metaphors through which she exercised her power. But just as court poets learned to define their own role increasingly clearly, so they also learned to redefine the role of their monarch.

Notes

[1] Sir Thomas Elyot, *The Book named The Governor,* ed. S. E. Lehmberg (London: Dent, 1962), p. 238.

[2] Roger Ascham, *The Schoolmaster,* ed. Lawrence V. Ryan (Ithaca, New York: Cornell University Press, 1951), p. 56.

[3] George P. Rice, *The Public Speaking of Queen Elizabeth* (New York: Columbia University Press, 1951), p. 72.

[4] E. C. Wilson, *England's Eliza* (Cambridge, Mass.: Harvard University Press, 1939).

[5] Eleanor Rosenberg, *Leicester: Patron of Letters* (New York: Columbia University Press, 1955), p. 7.

[6] Edmund Spenser, *Poetical Works,* ed. J. C. Smith and E. de Selincourt (London: Oxford University Press, 1912). All references to Edmund Spenser's works are taken from this edition. Page or line numbers will appear in parentheses after the quotation.

[7] Norman Egbert McClure, *The Letters and Epigrams of Sir John Harington* (Philadelphia: University of Pennsylvania Press, 1930), p. 29.

[8] Neil Rudenstine, *Sidney's Poetic Development* (Cambridge, Mass.: Harvard University Press, 1967), p. 7.

[9] R. Warwick Bond, ed., *The Complete Works of John Lyly* (Cambridge: Harvard University Press, 1962).

[10] G. K. Hunter, *John Lyly: The Humanist as Courtier* (Cambridge: Harvard University Press, 1962).

[11] Ibid., p. 7.

[12] Laurence Stone, *The Crisis of the Aristocracy: 1558-1641,* abridged edition (Oxford: Oxford University Press, 1967), p. 313.

[13] Jonas A. Barish, "Exhibitionism and the Anti-Theatrical Prejudice," in *ELH,* 36, March, 1969, p. 12.

[14] Stephen J. Greenblatt, *Sir Walter Ralegh: The Renaissance Man and His Roles* (New Haven: Yale University Press, 1973), p. 137.

[15] Thomas M. Greene, "The Flexibility of the Self in Renaissance Literature," in *The Disciplines of Criticism,* ed. Peter Demetz et al. (New Haven: Yale University Press, 1968), p. 252.

[16] J. W. Saunders, "The Stigma of Print," in *Essays in Criticism* 1, 1951, pp. 139-164.

[17] John F. Danby, *Elizabethan and Jacobean Poets: Studies in Sidney, Shakespeare, Beaumont and Fletcher* (London: Faber and Faber, 1965), p. 33.

[18] John Foxe, *The Acts and Monuments of John Foxe,* ed. the Rev. Stephen Reed Cattley (London: Seeley and Burnside, 1839), vol. VIII, p. 619.

[19] J. E. Neale, *Elizabeth I and Her Parliaments: 1559-1581* (New York: W. W. Norton and Co. Inc., 1958, 1966), p. 366.

[20] Ibid., p. 119.

[21] Ibid., p. 117.

[22] Ibid., p. 126.

[23] *OED*, pp. 356-359. The listing of "secret" provides the range of meanings required by this context. In the listing of "secretly," 1 b and 3 are quoted.

[24] Neale, p. 129.

[25] Conyers Read, *Lord Burghley and Queen Elizabeth* (New York: Alfred A. Knopf, 1960), p. 369.

[26] Neale, p. 130.

[27] Katherine Duncan-Jones and J. A. Van Dorsten, ed., *Miscellaneous Prose of Sir Philip Sidney* (Oxford: Clarendon Press, 1973), pp. 34-35. All references to Sir Philip Sidney's *Letter* are taken from this edition. Page numbers will appear in parentheses after the quotation. For an argument that Sidney's letter did not anger the Queen, and had no connection to his retreat at Wilton, see Van Dorsten's Introduction to the Letter in this edition.

[28] Lloyd E. Berry, ed., *John Stubbs' Gaping Gulf with Letters and Other Relevant Documents* (Charlottesville: The University Press of Virginia, 1968), p. xxvii. All references to John Stubbs are taken from this edition. Page numbers will appear in parentheses after the quotation.

John N. King (essay date 1990)

SOURCE: "Queen Elizabeth I: Representations of the Virgin Queen," in *Renaissance Quarterly*, Vol. XLIII, No. 1, Spring, 1990, pp. 30-74.

[*Below, King discusses the "Cult of the Virgin Queen" Elizabeth in art and literature, noting that this iconography reflects her virginity as a source of personal independence and political power.*]

It is commonly acknowledged that although Elizabeth I vowed herself to a life of perpetual virginity, she entered into a symbolic marriage with England as her husband.[1] In this way she could receive the adulation of her subjects as the universal object of a Petrarchan religion of love, one that pervaded ballads, pageants, and dramatic entertainments. Scholars claim that she was able to convert her unprecedented weakness as a celibate queen into a powerful propagandistic claim that she sacrificed personal interests in the name of public service. Her maidenly chastity was therefore interpreted not as a sign of political or social deficiency, but rather as a paradoxical symbol of the power of a woman who survived to govern despite illegitimization, subordination of female to male in the order of primogeniture, patriarchy, and masculine supremacy, and who remained unwed at a time when official sermons favored marriage and attacked the monastic vow of celibacy and veneration of the Virgin Mary. It

seems, then, that from the accession of Elizabeth in 1558, at the age of twenty-five, celebration of her virginity was a synchronic phenomenon noticeable in works of literature and art that flattered her as a new Judith or Deborah, Eliza Triumphans, Astraea, Cynthia, or even Venus-Virgo.

A lively scholarly discourse has grown up in support of the proposition that the cult of Elizabeth as a virgin queen was produced by political, social, and cultural forces. It is undeniable that Elizabeth's retention of virginity constituted "a political act"[2] and that the celebration of her remoteness from erotic love played an important role during her reign. Elkin Wilson articulates the modern consensus that "from 1558 to 1603 the virgin queen of England was the object of a love not dissimilar in quality from that which for centuries had warmed English hearts that looked to the virgin Queen of Heaven for all grace." Frances Yates concurs that the "virginity of the queen was used as a powerful political weapon all through her reign."[3] Yates's influential views and those of her student, Roy Strong, attribute the secularization of Mariological imagery in Elizabethan iconography to the revolutionary political and social impact of the Protestant Reformation.[4] Stephen Greenblatt modifies this picture by emphasizing the role of cultural forces not under the control of the individual in the fashioning of an Elizabethan image imposed from above as an imperialistic device by an authoritarian state.[5] Louis Adrian Montrose qualifies Greenblatt's ideas concerning the hegemonic formulation of an authorized queenly image, under royal authority, by examining the alternative possibility that Elizabethan subjects could fashion, indeed subvert, the official royal image. According to Montrose, "such fashioning and such manipulation were reciprocal" processes engaging the efforts of the queen and her government from above and Elizabethan subjects from below.[6] The tendency of Yates and Strong to emphasize the classicization of the queen's image as Astraea or Cynthia has undergone qualification in recent work that charts the fundamental importance in Elizabethan iconography of scriptural and medieval formulas that had been employed in literary and artistic praise of both the Protestant Tudors, Henry VIII and Edward VI, *and* their Catholic successor, Mary I.[7]

Little scrutiny has been given to the widespread assumption that Elizabeth I set in motion her cultic celebration by means of esoteric literary and artistic symbolism when she made a youthful vow to remain a virgin. The corollary view that her own action generated a public image that remained intact throughout the rest of her reign has gained many adherents. Louis Montrose thus concludes that from the beginning of the queen's reign "she was already formulating the discourse by which she would continue to turn the political liability of her gender to advantage for nearly half a century." Affirming that the queen "defended her maidenly freedom and royal prerogative against . . . patriarchal expectations," he claims that she legitimated "her desire for autonomy among men by invoking a higher patriarchal authority . . . of her heavenly father, the ultimate ground of her sovereignty." Montrose gathers together such chronologically disparate works as the "April" eclogue in Edmund Spenser's *Shepheardes Calender* (1579), the *Armada Portrait* (ca. 1588), Spenser's 1590 *Faerie Queene,* and William Camden's *Historie of . . . Elizabeth, Late Queene of England* (1630) as timeless reflections of Elizabeth's perpetuation of "her maidenhood in a cult of virginity."[8]

A diachronic review of contemporary manuscripts, printed books, and artistic works indicates that instead of a continuous and timeless phenomenon, Elizabethan iconography was closely tied to the life history of the monarch and to political events of her reign. Few scholars have pinpointed the shift from Elizabeth's early praise as a nubile virgin to her late adulation as a perpetual virgin, who remains ever youthful and attractive, during the course of the 1579-83 marriage negotiations between the queen and the final suitor for her hand in marriage, François, duc Alençon (later duc d'Anjou).[9] The identification of separate phases of Elizabethan culture makes it possible to reassess the internalization of the queen's image in some major works of Elizabethan literature and art. Spenser's "April" eclogue exemplifies this shift because its publication during the heat of the Alençon controversy marks it as a borderline text that enhances the queen's standing as a princess eligible for marriage at the same time that it praises her in a manner that may be read as an appeal to remain unmarried. When the poet came to portray Elizabeth in *The Faerie Queene* (1590-96), however, Belphoebe personified her virginity as a permanent state.

The Origins of a Myth

Modern scholarship has transmitted a frequently cited report by William Camden that supports the widespread view that the queen chose a life of perpetual virginity. He indicates that at the outset of her reign Elizabeth rejected advice that she settle the succession by marrying and bearing an heir to the throne. She spoke in response to a 1559 petition from the House of Commons urging her to choose a husband on the ground that "nothing can be more repugnant to the common good, than to see a Princesse, who by marriage may preserve the Common-wealth in peace, to leade a single life, like a Vestal Nunne."[10] According to the tradition established by Elizabeth's first historian, this speech provided the earliest sign that the queen would flout patriarchal convention through a deliberate decision to remain unwed:

> And therefore it is, that I have made choyce of this kinde of life, which is most free, and agreeable

for such humane affaires as may tend to his [God's] service . . . and this is that I thought, then that I was a private person. But when the publique charge of governing the Kingdome came upon mee, it seemed unto mee an inconsiderate folly, to draw upon my selfe the cares which might proceede of marriage. To conclude, I am already bound unto an Husband, which is the Kingdome of England. . . . (And therwithall, stretching out her hand, shee shewed them the Ring with which she was given in marriage, and inaugurated to her Kingdome, in expresse and solemne terms.) And reproch mee so no more, (quoth shee) that I have no children: for every one of you, and as many are English, are my Children. . . . Lastly, this may be sufficient, both for my memorie, and honour of my Name, if when I have expired my last breath, this may be inscribed upon my Tombe:

> Here lyes interr'd ELIZABETH,
> A virgin pure untill her Death.[11]

The youthful queen's "prophecy" was borne out at the approach of her death, according to Camden, when she ordered that the "Ring, wherewith shee had beene joyned as it were in marriage to her kingdome at her inauguration, and she had never after taken off, to be filed off from her finger, for that it was so growne into the flesh, that it could not be drawne off." This action "was taken as a sad presage" of the coming dissolution of her "marriage with her kingdome."[12]

Camden's account provides every indication that Elizabeth skillfully manipulated political language and imagery by adapting a patriarchal vocabulary whereby kings governed as "fathers" of their people and as "husbands" of the country.[13] She was known to style herself as the virgin mother of her people. Accounts based on Camden's interpretation argue that Elizabeth's invocation of divine authority as an external and universal source of power supported her effort to validate royal sovereignty and to deny its limitation by male subjects.[14] Louis Montrose therefore concludes that she refused "to enact the female paradigm desired by . . . [her] advisors: to become the medium through which power, authority, and legitimacy are passed between generations of men."[15]

As appealing as Camden's view may be, it begs quite a few questions. The absence of the queen's reported epitaph upon her tomb need not be too troublesome, because James I established her naturalistic funerary monument at Westminster Abbey in 1606 as a counterpart to the flattering memorial that vindicates his own mother, Mary, Queen of Scots.[16] But what about the analogy that Camden draws between the queen's marriage to England as her husband and the tradition that nuns are betrothed to Christ the Bridegroom? Is it a simple coincidence? How authoritative is Camden's historical testimony, which appeared in print more than half a century after the events described and midway through her successor's reign? Did the queen actually speak the words that her first historian attributes to her?

Scholars have tended to accept at face value Camden's declaration that he has inaugurated a historiographical method that makes unprejudiced use of manuscript "monuments." In actual fact, it is difficult to track down his sources because he omits citations. His use of Tacitus as the model for compiling a work in the annals format might suggest the need for caution in assessing his "objectivity," because of the Roman author's commitment to moralizing history, his habit of silently harmonizing conflicting sources, and his invention of speeches in a rhetoric appropriate to the character and style of historical personages. Camden himself acknowledges that he views Tacitus as a model for moralized exemplary history because the Roman author declares that the "principall office" of compiling annals "is to take care, that Vertue be not obscured, and by the relation of evill words or deeds, to propose the feare of infamie, with posteritie." Camden informs the reader that his testimony is drawn from the archives of his patron, William Cecil, Lord Burghley, who, shortly before his death, "willed me to compile a *Historie of Q. Elizabeths* Raigne from the beginning." Camden acknowledges the manifest point that Cecil's goal of providing "for the propagation of the Queenes honour"[17] was not disinterested, because a flattering view of the queen would necessarily reflect glory on the man who served as her chief minister throughout four decades.

The preservation of a transcript of the queen's speech among the Cecil papers makes it possible to assess Camden's accuracy.[18] Examination of the Cecil manuscript reveals an entirely new set of problems, however, because Camden (or an unnamed intermediary) falsified the contemporary record of the queen's speech.[19] This falsification offers one indication that Camden transmits a hagiographical account that may be less accurate as a portrayal of the Tudor queen than it is of Jacobean patronage and politics. After all, the historian admits that he turned away from this project in dismay at its arduous nature until James I returned him to the task. The concluding section of the present essay explains how the *Annales* came to enshrine a posthumous myth of Elizabeth as a perpetual virgin, one that has passed into modern scholarship through many retellings. Camden's version of events provides a Jacobean representation of Elizabeth as a virgin queen, one that followed in sequence upon her earlier celebration, first as a marriageable maiden, and second as a mythically youthful object of courtly desire. An awareness of the anachronistic processes at work in the first history of Elizabeth's reign throws light on these earlier phases of Elizabethan iconography and demonstrates how the entire Gloriana cult

was defined by the practicalities of Elizabethan *and Jacobean* politics. Differentiation among the different "cults" of the Virgin Queen demonstrates how the royal image was fashioned dynamically by Elizabeth and her government from above, and by her apologists and suppliants from below.

The "Cult" of the Marriageable Virgin

Within months of her accession to the throne, Elizabeth acknowledged to a parliamentary delegation the desirability of marriage. The transcript of "The Ansuere of th[e] Quenes highnes to th[e] peticion proponed [i.e., set forth] unto hir by th[e] Lower howse Concerning[e] hir mariage" in MS Lansdowne 94 contains a version of her 10 February 1559 address that differs in many respects from the Camden variation. In all likelihood this very clean copy was transcribed at the behest of Cecil or someone close to the man who served as chief secretary of state throughout most of the queen's reign. Cecil's collected papers provide what may be the most complete and reliable contemporary account of Elizabethan state events. Because neither MS Lansdowne 94 nor the profuse contemporary documentary record refers to a queenly vow to remain a chaste virgin married to her realm, one may presume that this promise is a later addition. The absence of contemporary reference to the regal display of the coronation ring suggests that this historionic gesture is an apocryphal embellishment, one possibly modeled on the custom that nuns wear rings commemorating their vow of celibacy and wedding to Christ.[20] The version of the speech that Camden attributes to the parliamentary delegation establishes an iconographical link between the alleged unacceptability of Elizabeth's behavior and that of a "Vestal Nunne," but this reference is absent from contemporary Elizabethan documents for this Parliament.[21]

The manuscript version of the queen's speech records no vow of perpetual virginity; indeed, any such vow would have violated the official disapproval of all vows, including that of celibacy, by the Church of England, of which Elizabeth served as Supreme Governor. The locus classicus for this position is in the third section of the homily "Of Good Works" in the first *Book of Homilies,* which was preached in English churches at royal command. Elizabeth's speech testifies that at the outset of her reign she fashioned a public identity not upon a vow of celibacy but upon her well-known preference for an unmarried life. She does promise, however, that if God wills that she marry, her choice of a husband would benefit the public interest. An underlying reason for this idealized commitment to a vocation of religious and political service may reflect the practical reality that her supremacy as head of state would not necessarily extend to the headship of her own family were she to marry. Although the law of inheritance made her an exception to the rule of masculine supremacy in her public capacity as queen, husbands were the legal heads of families. Her acknowledgement that she "can not so certenlie determyne" the actions of any potential husband may be grounded on the precedent of the marriage of her sister, Mary, to Philip of Spain, which demonstrated that even though a treaty and parliamentary act might preserve a married queen's political authority, they had no necessary effect on her husband's actions.[22] Furthermore, she voices the realistic fear that as a mother she would be unable to guarantee that her offspring might not "growe out of kynde [i.e., behave in an unfilial fashion?], and become perhappe ungracious." The conditional nature of her promise that she *would* be content, *should* she remain unmarried, to have on her tomb the inscription "that a Queen having raigned such a tyme, lyved and dyed a virgin" is lost sight of in Camden's hindsight view of this epitaph as a self-fulfilling prophecy. Words that she spoke in 1559 might have undergone embellishment in an oral tradition that resulted in the legendary account in Camden's *Annales*. According to the Cecil transcript, these are the words that were read on the queen's behalf by a member of the House of Commons:

> I may saye unto yow, that from my yeares of understanding syth I first had consideracion of my self to be borne a servitor of almightie god I happelie chose this kynde of life in w[hi]ch I yet lyve. w[hi]ch I assure yow for myne owne p[ar]te hath hitherto contented my self and I trust hath bene moost acceptable to god. . . . Nevertheles, if any of yow be in suspect, that whensoever it may please god to enclyne my harte to an other kynd of Life. Ye may well assure yo[u]r selves my meaninge not to doe or determyne anie thinge, wh[e]arw[i]th the Realme may or shall have iuste cause to be dyscontented. . . . I will never in that matter conclud[e] any thing that shalbe preiudiciall to the realme. ffor the weale, good & safetie whereof *I will never shune* to spend my life. And whomsoev[e]r my *chaunce* shalbe to light apon I trust he shalbe as carefull for the realme and yow I will not saie as my self because I can not so certenlie determyne of any other. *but at the least wayes, by my good will and desire, he shalbe suche as shalbe as carefull for the preservacion of the realme and yow as my self.* And albeit, it might please almightie god to contynew me still in this mynde, to lyve out of the state of mariage, yet it is not to be feared, but he will so worke in my harte, And in yo[u]r wisdomes as good provision by his healpe may be made in convenient tyme wherby the realme shal not remayne destitute of an heir th[a]t may be fitt [to] governe and peraventure more beneficiall to the realme then such ofspring as may come of me. ffor although I be never so carefull of yo[u]r well doinge and mynd ever so to be, yet may my issue growe out of kynde, and become perhappe ungracious. And in the end this shalbe for me sufficient that a marble stone shall de[cl]ar[e],

[t]h[at a] Q[ueen h]a[v]ing ra[i]gne[d such] a tyme[, l]y[ved and] dyed a virgin.[23]

During the 1560s and 1570s virtually everyone assumed that Elizabeth would marry, including the queen herself, if her statements are to be accepted at face value. Regardless whether she genuinely desired to wed, her marriageability was an essential element of her youthful image. The diplomatic utility of her eligibility and the many proposals she received argue against the premise that she had taken a public vow of celibacy; indeed, her portraits were sent abroad in 1567, 1571-74, and 1578-81 in connection with marriage negotiations.[24] Although she had no want of suitors, each one had personal or political liabilities. Thus a renewal of the English marital alliance with Spain through marriage to her sister's widower, Philip II, was never seriously entertained. Her well-known refusal to wed a man she had never met may have reflected the disastrous influence of the flattering portraits that were made for use during the negotiations leading up to the marriage of Henry VIII and Anne of Cleves. Elizabeth's declaration in a letter of 25 February 1560 to Eric, King of Sweden, that she was determined "not to marry an absent husband"[25] surely reflects her memory of the ill effect of the prolonged absenteeism of Philip of Spain during her sister's reign; this objection implies the corollary fear that a married queen must depart with her husband "out of her own native country and sweet soil of England."[26] Archduke Charles of Austria offered the best possibility for a diplomatically successful marriage, but his Catholicism and Hapsburg lineage represented stumbling blocks for the English who regarded the queen as the nation's only hope for preserving political independence and the Protestant settlement in religion. Elizabeth's interest in Robert Dudley, Master of the Queen's Horse (later Earl of Leicester), incurred no opposition on religious or nationalistic grounds, but the queen refused to marry her own subject. Furthermore, he was a married man who made domestic political enemies. The death of his wife in 1560 under mysterious circumstances dashed any real hope that the queen might achieve a true love match.[27]

During an age of early menopause and a high rate of death in childbed, Elizabeth's advancement into her fourth decade fueled anxiety that the House of Tudor would die with the queen.[28] Her own statements indicate that during her thirties and forties she fashioned a public identity as an unmarried ruler who is eligible, indeed eager, for marriage to a politically *appropriate* husband. Elizabeth's reply to a 1563 petition from her second parliament therefore argued that she was no less capable of childbirth than Saint Elizabeth, to whom God sent offspring despite her advanced years (Lk. 1:5-25).[29] Even though she may have been the saint's namesake, this scriptural comparison was not distinctively Elizabethan because apologists for Mary Tudor used the same precedent to declare that providential intervention would produce a royal heir when she was close to forty, a very old age for bearing children during the sixteenth century.[30]

Continuing agitation in favor of a royal marriage caused Elizabeth to go on record for a third time on 5 November 1566 in response to a petition from her second parliament that she marry and settle the succession. This reply follows along the lines of the first, except that the queen explicitly vows to marry despite her personal inclination toward a celibate life. Her elaboration that the sole reason for marriage is her wish to bear children acknowledges the political expediency of producing heirs to perpetuate her dynasty; it accords further with the orthodox view that the chief purpose of wedlock is "the procreation of children."[31] Once again the queen acknowledges the political difficulties attendant upon this issue, this time mentioning the probability that the most earnest proponents of marriage are those most likely to object to her choice of a husband. At the same time, she takes strenuous exception to the expression of doubt concerning the sincerity of her intention to take a husband. In actual fact, neither the privy council nor parliament ever agreed on the appropriateness of any of the queen's many suitors. In her promise to marry and in her awareness of the problematic nature of her choice, the speech accords with the queen's actions during the 1560s and 1570s. According to a contemporary manuscript, these are the words that she delivered in 1566 to a delegation made up of thirty members from each of the two houses:

> I dyd send theym aunswere by my counseyle I wolde marrye (althowghe of myne own dysposycion I was not enclyned thereunto), but that was not accepted nor credyted, althowghe spoken by theyre Prynce. And yet I usede so many wordes that I coulde saye no more. And were yt not nowe I had spoken those wordes, I wold never speke theyme ageyne. I wyll never breke the worde of a prynce spoken in publyke place, for my honour sake. And therefore I saye ageyn, I wyll marrye as sone as I can convenyentlye, yf God take not hym awaye with whom I mynde to marrye, or my self, or els sum othere great lette happen. I can saye no more except the partie were presente. And I hope to have chylderne, otherwyse I wolde never marrie. . . . But theye (I thynke) that movythe the same wylbe as redy to myslyke hym with whom I shall marrie as theye are nowe to move yt, and then yt wyll apere they nothynge mente yt. I thowght theye wold have byn rathere redye to have geven me thankes then to have made anye newe requeste for the same. There hathe byn some that have or [i.e., ere] thys sayde unto me they never requyred more then that theye myght ones here me saye I wold marrie. Well, there was never so

great a treason but myght be coveryde undere as fayre a pretence.[32]

Political concerns of the kind stated by the queen shaped the representation of her virginity in the iconography of the first half of her reign. Maidenly chastity was a necessary attribute of her claim to be a legitimate and marriageable queen. The straightforward virginity symbolism of Elizabeth's early images differs from the esoteric iconography of the virgin goddessC— Cynthia or Venus-Virgo—that emerged in the 1580s and flowered during her final decade. The *Coronation Portrait* in which the queen wears the regalia of investiture typifies the early phase, as do related miniatures by Nicholas Hilliard (ca. 1600). Although the portrait was painted on a panel close to the time of her death (ca. 1600-10), its depiction of the queen's youthful features is modeled on a lost original painted ca. 1559. Her facial appearance is in line with the anachronistic "mask of youth" characteristic of her last years. Possibly this portrait was used as a funerary image. It is noteworthy that Elizabeth's long hair flows down onto her shoulders in the style of an intact virgin.[33]

Because of the close ties between the English establishment and the Inns of the Court, where many members of the royal court, privy council, and parliament received their legal education, it was a natural move to dramatize questions concerning royal marriage and succession in revels and entertainments staged by lawyers. Although a royal proclamation of 16 May 1559 forbade discussion of religion and politics in the popular drama, dramatic performances at the royal court and the Inns of the Courts were excluded from the prohibition. *Gorboduc* is a case in point, because Thomas Norton, a prominent member of the House of Commons, and Thomas Sackville, later Earl of Dorset, designed the play to reflect upon the dangers attendant upon a realm where the royal succession remains unsettled. Although the work was written for only a single production at the Inner Temple on Epiphany, 6 January 1562, the work was revived before Elizabeth at Whitehall Palace twelve days later. Along with other revels and entertainments during this season, it takes a position critical of the queen on the controversial political issues of royal marriage and succession.[34]

Modern scholarship associates the moon goddess Diana (or Cynthia) with the praise of Elizabeth's chastity.[35] Although many iconographical variations of the classical protectress of virginity and hunting were identified with the queen's maiden state during her last decades, they were conspicuously absent from her early literary and artistic praise. It was not until the 1580s and 1590s that the "moon cult" of Elizabeth as a perpetually virgin goddess emerged and took root after the failure of her last effort at marriage.[36] Entertainments designed during the 1560s lauded her instead as Pallas Athena because Cynthia's "sylvan chastity seemed inimical to the perpetuation of the English body politic."[37] Wisdom and political virtue were the divine virtues attributed to the marriageable queen, but the virginity of the patron goddess of ancient Athens received little if any emphasis. It is Athena rather than Cynthia who appears in what Roy Strong identifies as "the earliest of the allegorical paintings of Elizabeth," *Queen Elizabeth and the Three Goddesses,* the 1569 variation of the Judgment of Paris in which she not only takes the place of the Greek hero, but also outranks Venus, Juno, and Athena.[38] In place of the golden apple that Paris awarded to Venus, however, Elizabeth retains her own coronation orb. The verse inscription specifies that Elizabeth exceeds Juno in political power, Athena in wisdom, and Venus in beauty.

During the 1560s the widespread concern for the chaste perpetuation of the Tudor dynasty made it appropriate to avoid—or suppress—praise of Elizabeth as Diana or Cynthia in Inns of the Court masques. The goddess of virginity received unflattering treatment in several performances that were staged prior to the third parliamentary petition concerning marriage and succession. Although Cynthia appeared in a 12 February 1566 wedding masque at Lincoln's Inn, she was not a figure for the queen; rather than honoring virginity, the masquing lawyers paid homage at the altar of Hymen, the ancient god of wedlock. At a second wedding celebration at Lincoln's Inn on 1 July 1566, Elizabeth herself attended a masque in which Diana was implicated in criticism of the queen for her failure to marry. Thomas Pound, the author and presented, delivered to Elizabeth the censure that he received from Juno, goddess of marriage, for his own failure to wed. He quotes Juno thus:

> for wedlocke I lyke best
>   it is the honorablest state
>   it passethe all the rest
> my Jove saithe she doth knowe this ioye
>   this bodye is his owne
> And what swete use I haue of his
>   to men may not be knowen.

If the serio-comic treatment of Diana is directed at the queen, it cannot be taken as complimentary praise. Marie Axton comments that the slighting comments on the overly robust and florid figure of Diana betray no hint of the "lineaments of the elegant huntress of later Elizabethan verse." The ultimate irony involves Diana's resignation at the "loss of her nymph"—Frances Radcliffe, the betrothed of Thomas Mildmay—and acceptance of the necessity that maidens will become wives.[39]

The claims of Diana were subordinated to those of Juno, protectress of married women and, in the guise of Lucina, goddess of wedlock and childbirth, as late as 1575 in a series of outdoor masques and entertainments designed by George Gascoigne and others for the queen's visit to Kenilworth Castle, the Warwickshire seat of Robert Dudley, Earl of Leicester. Although he was her chief favorite and the English subject most likely to win her in marriage, in all likelihood he had already abandoned genuine hope for the success of his suit.[40] The scripts were published under Gascoigne's name in the following year as *The Princely Pleasures at Kenelworth Castle.* These celebrations are notable for the infusion of classical gods and goddesses into the nativist frame of Arthurian romance, because a series of mythological deities including Neptune and Proteus pay homage to the queen after an opening tableau in which the Lady of the Lake greets Elizabeth as the greatest of British sovereigns since the death of King Arthur.

Although the rescue of the Lady of the Lake from attempted rape by Sir Bruce associates "Cynthia, the Ladie of the Sea," with Elizabeth as a maiden queen,[41] her dedication to virginity is not presented as a permanently desirable state. The messenger Triton announces the appeal of his lord, Neptune, that Elizabeth fulfill Merlin's prophecy that the Lady of the Lake must remain hidden beneath the waters of her pool "Except a worthier maide than she, / her cause do take in hand." Neptune had "envyroned hir with waves" in defense of her virginity. The return of the queen from hunting manifests the transcendent power of chastity in a manner sufficient "to make sir *Bruse* withdrawe his forces." Gender conflict is a real issue in this water masque; after all, the queen forges a "naval" alliance with a maiden in distress in order to exercise sovereignty over the militaristic personification of masculine desire. The permanent victory of maidenly chastity is not foreseen, however, as the ideal outcome of Elizabeth's romantic career. Triton's speech instead poses the unresolved question of whether the queen should marry: "Howe then can *Diane, Junos* force, / and sharpe assaults abyde?" The possibility that this maidenly victory would be transitory had already been suggested by a display of fireworks that advertised Leicester's devotion to the queen by appearing to pass beneath the waves only to "rise and mount out of the water againe, and burne very furiously untill they were utterlie consumed." This spectacle was analogous to the gifts Elizabeth had received as tokens of Leicester's "true love." Verses delivered by "one clad like a Savage man," a hirsute personification of masculine desire, advertised a potential victory over the "watery" power of feminine virginity:

> What meant the fierie flames,
>   which through the waves so flue?
> Can no colde answers quench desire?
>   is that experience true?

The feminine voice of Echo supplied the answer: "True."[42]

The planned involvement of Diana and her nymphs in one of the entertainments was appropriate to this royal hunting holiday in a woodland setting. Although Gascoigne claims in the printed text that his masque of Diana and Zabeta was cancelled because of "lack of opportunitie and seasonable weather," it seems more likely that the performance was cancelled because of the queen's distaste for its advocacy that she choose a husband and marry. The printed text records Diana's efforts to relocate "one of her best beloved Nimphes," who was reputed to have gone over into the company of Juno "neere seventeene yeares past." This explicit reference to the 1558 accession of the queen identifies her not with Diana but with the lost nymph, whose name, Zabeta, is an obvious truncation of Elizabeth. Diana recalls that prior to her coronation chaste Zabeta, whom she terms a "peereles Queene" famous for "prudence" and "pollicie," had followed her for "twentie yeeres or more." As the emissary of all-knowing Jove, Mercury acknowledges the problem that although Juno has tried for sixteen years to win Zabeta over to marriage through the proposals of the greatest kings that "this our age foorth brings," she has continuously refused to yield. Diana's joy that the nymph has taken a "constant vowe, / of chaste unspotted life" is premature, however. As the messenger of Juno, Iris, the rainbow goddess, would have crossed over the fictional line between mythological romance and dynastic politics by directly addressing Queen Elizabeth with Juno's appeal to marry:

> A world of wealth at wil,
>   you hencefoorth shall enjoy
> In wedded state, and therewithall,
>   holde up from great annoy
> The staffe of your estate:
>   O Queene, O worthy Queene,
> Yet never wight felt perfect blis,
>   but such as wedded beene.

Although Elizabeth never saw this performance, the text does record an encouragement to marry that Gascoigne prepared under the patronage of the most powerful man in England. Diana had not yet won the place that she would occupy during the last phase of the Elizabethan age as an unambiguous figure for a queen resigned to die a virgin.[43]

Widespread public concern about royal marriage may be noted in civic pageantry devised for the queen's entry into Norwich, the second city in the realm, during her summer progress of 1578. Thomas Churchyard's "Shew of Chastitie" modifies the iconography of Petrarch's *Trionfi* by identifying Elizabeth with Dame Chastity in an encounter in which the latter dethrones Cupid, the patron of erotic love, and takes his place in a triumphal pageant cart. In the company of her attendant maidens, Modesty, Temperance, Good Exercise, and Shamefastness, Dame Chastity confers Cupid's bow and arrows upon the queen because she has "chosen the best life," presumably one of celibacy.

She further explains her action, stating that "since none coulde wounde hir highesse hart, it was meete . . . that she should do with *CUPIDs* bow and arrowes what she pleased."[44] This appeal is delicately ambiguous, however, because the queen might play either her own Cupid, by choosing a suitable husband,[45] or the archer Diana, by continuing her unmarried life. It should be noted that this performance was designed on behalf of the Lord Mayor and aldermen of the corporation of Norwich, which was a notorious hotbed of radical Protestant sentiment. The initiation of a new round of marriage negotiations during the following year suggests that this performance lodged oblique advice that the queen consider only suitors of suitable religious faith.

The last great flurry of excitement over Elizabeth's professed desire to marry began in 1579, when Alençon arrived in England to court her during the final interval when she was still remotely capable of bearing an heir. The queen's taking of the initiative late in the wooing suggests that she had every intention of wedding the duke, despite her personal distaste for marriage and despite the opposition of powerful Protestant lords on the privy council who believed that the choice of a husband who was both an heir to a foreign throne and a Catholic would threaten England's religious settlement and its political autonomy.[46] Her own letters specify that the chief stumbling block to marriage was the Catholicism of the younger brother of the king of France. At the height of the controversy over the proposed match, she wrote that she wished to wed should he modify his "public exercise of the Roman Religion."[47]

Spenser's *Shepheardes Calender* evokes the political milieu of the Alençon courtship. The assumption that the queen remained eligible and interested in marriage well into her forties underlies the inclusion of a transparent allusion to the earl of Leicester in the "October" eclogue. Piers's appeal that Cuddie devote himself to epic poetry includes an aside on the queen's love for the great noble that seems to nominate him as a candidate for her hand in marriage:

> Whither thou list in fayre *Elisa* rest,
> Or if thee please in bigger notes to sing,
> Advaunce the worthy whome shee loveth
>   best,
> That first the white beare to the stake did
>   bring.
>
>   (ll. 45-47)[48]

The prominence of this allusion to the Dudley device of the staked bear places Spenser in the camp of the Protestant progressives who opposed the Alençon match, even though Leicester's secret marriage during the previous year excluded him as a potential mate for the queen.[49] Further indication of the poet's interest in this topic is provided by the presumable composition of part of *Mother Hubberds Tale* at about this time, given the likely satire directed against Alençon and his agent, Jean de Simier, in the form of the Ape. The connection of that poem to the *Calender* may be noted in Spenser's 1591 description of the *Tale* as a work "composed in the raw conceipt of my youth" and in its affinity with the satirical mode of his ecclesiastical eclogues.[50]

The appearance of the *Calender* during the immediate aftermath of the political explosion triggered by the publication of the most notorious appeal that Elizabeth spurn a foreign marriage, John Stubbs's *Discoverie of a Gaping Gulf whereinto England is like to be Swallowed by an other French mariage* (August 1579), may account for Spenser's last-minute alteration of the *Calender's* dedication from Leicester to his nephew, Sir Philip Sidney.[51] Whereas the queen's anger over the appearance of this tract gave the earl every reason to distance himself from the anti-Alençon faction, Sidney went on record against the French marital alliance in a letter that he sent directly to the queen.

Even though the writings of Stubbs and Sidney document the existence of broadly-based opposition to the Alençon match, they never argue against the desirability of marriage as such; indeed, they assume that Elizabeth will marry and bear children. The fact that no one adopts the rhetorical strategy of reminding the queen of a 1559 vow to live out her life like a celibate nun wedded to England provides yet another proof that Camden (or an unknown intermediary) invented that apocryphal story. Sidney presumably wrote his letter "Touching Her Marriage with Monsieur" after the appearance of Stubbs's *Discoverie of a Gaping Gulf* because he often follows the tract in argument and phraseology; manuscript copies of his letter were in circulation at about the time that Spenser's *Calender* went to press in late 1579. Although Sidney ennumerates Alençon's liabilities both as a foreigner and as a Roman Catholic, he nevertheless assumes that the queen will choose a more appropriate husband and bear children who will be "the perfect mirror to your posterity."[52] According to tradition, Sidney withdrew to his sister's estate to escape the queen's wrath.[53] Sidney's unpublished advice incurred no punishment, but Stubbs suffered the penalty of the loss of his right hand for publically challenging the queen's prerogative concerning her potential marriage.

Unlike Sidney, who remains discreetly silent about the queen's age and vulnerability to fatal complications in a pregnancy, Stubbs explicitly raises the danger of death in childbirth. His acknowledgment of the queen's real age and mortality lacks Sidney's courtly delicacy: "If it may please her Majesty to call her faithfulest wise physicians and to adjure them by their conscience towards God, their loyalty to her, and faith to the whole land to say their knowledge simply . . . how

exceedingly dangerous they find it by their learning for Her Majesty at these years to have her first child, yea, how fearful the expectation of death is to mother and child; I fear to say what will be their answer." Stubbs's witty reference to "her natural body" as "her very self or self self, as I may say" suggests mockery of the legal fiction of the queen's "two bodies." Furthermore, his use of bestial imagery to compare the proposed marital union to "contrary couplings together . . . [like] the uneven yoking together of the clean ox to the unclean ass" could only draw the queen's wrath.[54] By lodging strictures based upon biblical injunctions against "unnatural" acts (Dt. 22:10), Stubbs evokes the widespread association between Roman Catholicism and sexual uncleanliness; Protestants widely assumed that devotion to Roman "idolatry" constituted "spiritual fornication" (Rev. 2:14, 17:2). Prejudice of this kind flared up against French Catholics after the St. Bartholomew Massacre (1572).

If it was not until after the failure of this last effort at marriage, one third of the way through Elizabeth's reign, that the patriotic cult of an unmarried virgin queen who would remain ever wedded to her nation took hold in officially-sponsored propaganda, in poetry of praise generated outside of the royal court, and in the popular imagination, how are we to interpret the celebration of Eliza as the "flowre of Virgins" and "a mayden Queene" in Spenser's "April" eclogue (ll. 48, 57)? It is important to note that Hobbinol sings the lay to Eliza in the place of Colin Clout, who no longer sings this song of praise. The absence of Colin, Spenser's pastoral surrogate, distances the poet from this blason. Eliza's portrait obviously fuses classical mythology and Christian iconography associated with yet another virgin queen, Mary:

> For shee is *Syrinx* daughter without spotte,
> Which *Pan* the shepheards God of her
>   begot:
>   So sprong her grace
>   Of heavenly race,
> No mortall blemishe may her blotte.
>
> (ll. 50-54)

The "argument" explains that the eclogue "is purposely intended to the honor and prayse of our most gracious sovereigne, Queene Elizabeth," just as Eliza's company of virgins (nymphs, muses, graces, and shepherds' daughters) idealizes the sociology of the privy chamber, where the queen surrounded herself with attendant maidens whom she watched over like a jealous mother. The naturalistic representation of Eliza in the eclogue's woodcut illustration is devoid of the esoteric symbolism often found in Elizabeth's later portraits, although muses playing upon their musical instruments do attend her.

Even though this eclogue was "a seminal work in creating the image of the Virgin Queen,"[55] a French marriage was still regarded as a distinct possibility, indeed a threat, in the eyes of Protestant progressives, until *after* the entry of the *Calender* in the Stationers' Register on 5 December 1579. The "April" eclogue's floral imagery indicates that Eliza is the "goddess of love and procreation as well as goddess of chastity and virginity."[56] Spenser alludes to the Ovidian account that Syrinx preserved her virginity when her flight from Pan, the Arcadian fertility god, resulted in her transformation into a reed-bed (*Meta.* ll. 688-712). In a paradoxical rewriting of the classical myth, Syrinx fails to evade Pan; indeed, she conceives of Eliza by means of an insemination vaguely aligned with the virgin birth of Christ. Nevertheless, the Mariological tag "without spotte" refers to Eliza's virginity, not that of her mother, and she clearly derives her "heavenly race" from her father. We should not look for tight one-to-one correspondences because Spenser situates this eclogue within a complicated symbolic matrix. After all, it is ultimately the poet who makes Eliza spotless because the progeny of Syrinx are songs.[57] E. K.'s gloss on line 50 recognizes Spenser's synthesis of Christian and classical imagery by noting that Christ "is the verye Pan and god of Shepheardes."[58] The comment that Pan also refers to "the most famous and victorious King, her highnesse Father, late of worthy memorye K. Henry the eyght" reflects the icononographical inconsistency of Colin Clout's song.

What E. K. leaves unstated is more significant historically than his explanation of the Pan reference, because Syrinx must refer to Anne Boleyn, the mother of the queen who was executed on grounds of adultery during Elizabeth's infancy. Soon after Anne's death and Henry's remarriage to Jane Seymour in 1536, Princess Elizabeth was declared illegitimate in order to clear the way for the accession of the male heir expected of her father's third wife. When Elizabeth acceded to the throne long after her father's death, she did so as the bastardized daughter for whose sake her father had rejected papal authority. The recovery of personal and political legitimacy was therefore always a matter of concern to the queen, whose legalism disconcerted her counselors and parliament when it extended even to defense of the claim of Mary, Queen of Scots, "as heir presumptive to the Tudor throne."[59] The emphasis of the "April" eclogue on Eliza's purity runs counter to long-standing Catholic allegations concerning Elizabeth's bastardy.[60]

The witty mythologization of Elizabeth's birth constitutes a flattering rewriting of the historical record, one that glosses over the chronic succession crisis that England had experienced because of her inability and that of her entire dynasty to perpetuate a sturdy line of male—or female—heirs to the throne. Colin Clout's blason declares:

> *Pan* may be proud, that ever he begot
> such a Bellibone,

> And *Syrinx* rejoyse, that ever was her lot
> to beare such an one.
>
> (ll. 91-94)

According to this view, both Henry VIII and Anne Boleyn could take satisfaction for having produced such a splendid heir to the throne. Poetic diction suggests further that Elizabeth may yet continue the Tudor line if the choice of words is aligned with Perigot's love-smitten praise of "the bouncing Bellibone" in the "August" eclogue, whose green skirt and floral crown are clearly appropriate to a nubile maiden (ll. 61-112). Although the "April" eclogue's mythic view of dynastic history crumbles under a literal interpretation, it succeeds on a figurative level due to the syncretic combination of pagan myth with a trope of scriptural pastoral (the Good Shepherd), whereby both father *and daughter* receive homage as Christlike monarchs. It is debatable, however, whether celebration of a king deeply implicated in dynastic chaos is appropriate to a poem dedicated to praising Queen Elizabeth.

The delicate ambiguity of Spenser's praise of queenly virginity may be noted in the "April" eclogue's very early comparison of Elizabeth to Cynthia, goddess of the moon, in her guise as Phoebe, the twin sister of Phoebus Apollo: "Tell me, have ye seene her angelick face, / Like *Phoebe* fayre?" (ll. 64-65). This astronomical figure highlights the political power of the queen's femininity when Eliza outshines the sun-god, Phoebus, who "blusht" in amazement "to see another Sunne belowe" (l. 77). This imagery is androgynous because Elizabeth's lunar qualities as both a woman and a queen are overlaid with the solar symbolism that iconographical tradition accorded to kings as males. The singer identifies Eliza's moonlike qualities with the queen's dominant aspect:

> Shew thy selfe *Cynthia* with thy silver
> rayes,
>   and be not abasht:
> When shee the beames of her beauty
> displayes,
>   O how art thou dasht?
>
> (ll. 82-85)

Having introduced this complicated astronomical conceit, Spenser ostentatiously denies its appropriateness to queenly iconography by employing *occupatio,* a rhetorical device that emphasizes something by seeming to omit it: "But I will not match her with *Latonaes* seede, / Such follie great sorow to *Niobe* did breede" (ll. 86-87). Having introduced the possibility of lauding Eliza as a new Cynthia, the singer immediately retreats from that simile in a manner that is inconsistent with an interpretation of Elizabeth's virginity as a permanent condition.

Spenser's homage to Eliza as a virgin queen is poised at a liminal moment in the development of Elizabethan iconography. He shares Sidney's realization that ambiguity is the appropriate posture for one to assume in praising or advising a queen whose own image and desires are ambiguous. The "April" eclogue enhances the queen's standing as an eligible woman at virtually the last moment when she is still remotely capable of marriage and child-bearing, on the one hand, but it praises her in a manner that may be understood as an appeal that she retain her unwedded state, on the other hand. Colin's blason praises a marriageable queen who is on the verge of a decision to remain unmarried. Virgilian emblems spoken by Thenot and Hobbinol highlight the transitional standing of Colin's lay to Eliza. E. K. interprets them as words spoken "in the person of Aeneas to his mother Venus, appearing to him in the likenesse of one of Dianaes damosells: being there most divinely set forth." Although these words, "O quam te memorem virgo?" and "O dea certe" ("By what name should I call thee, O maiden?" and "O goddess surely!"), were to become famous as a "prophetic" compliment to the perpetual innocence of Elizabeth as Venus-Virgo, the *Calender*'s publication during the marriage controversy creates a delicate ambiguity about whether the phrase emphasizes Elizabeth's virginity, her potential maternity, or both qualities. The Graces who appear in the eclogue may accompany Venus (or Athena, or the muses), but not Diana. The potential fusion of chastity and erotic love afforded by this early application of the Venus-Virgo figure would soon be forgotten.[61]

The eclogue's involvement with questions of dynastic politics and succession is made manifest by E. K.'s interpretation of Colin's description of Eliza's cheeks, where the "Redde rose medled with the White yfere" (l. 68), as a figure for "the uniting of the two principall houses of Lancaster and of Yorke: by whose longe discord and deadly debate, this realm many yeares was sore traveiled, and almost cleane decayed. Til the famous Henry the seventh, of the line of Lancaster, taking to wife the most vertuous Princesse Elisabeth, daughter to the fourth Edward of the house of Yorke, begat the most royal Henry the eyght aforesayde, in whom was the firste union of the Whyte Rose and the Redde." This gloss corresponds to a wellknown dynastic image, the Tudor rose arbor designed for the title page of a work published soon after the *Calender,* the first edition of John Stow's *Chronicles of England, from Brute unto this present yeare of Christ 1580.* This figure is modeled ultimately upon the Tree of Jesse, the genealogy of Jesus as the scion of the royal House of David, which was reapplied during the Middle Ages in praise of Christian kings. The Tree of Jesse had already undergone adaptation for purposes of dynastic praise in the title page border for Edward Halle's *Unyon of the twoo noble and illustre famelies of Lancastre and Yorke* (1550), in which Henry VIII occupies the place of honor as a Christlike king. The Stow border constitutes a reconfiguration of a conventional dynastic image in which the marriage of Henry VII and "Elizabeth daughter to Kinge Edward the fourth" unites the houses of York and Lancaster in the form of their second son and heir.[62] Interpretation of the Stow title page is ambiguous, however, like that of the "April" eclogue. Would Elizabeth be the last bud upon the rose arbor? Or, flanked by sterile offshoots, Edward VI and Mary I, is she still capable of perpetuating her line? The liminality of both of these "texts" disappears in a poem attributed to the queen, "On Monsieur's Departure," that employs Petrarchan vocabulary to lament the dashing of her hope to marry when Alençon made his final departure from England in 1582:

> I grieve and dare not show my discontent,
> I love and yet am forced to seem to hate,
> I do, yet dare not say I ever meant,
> I seem stark mute but inwardly do prate.
>   I am and not, I freeze and yet am burned,
>   Since from myself another self is turned.[63]

The Cult of the Virgin Goddess

Emerging during the tortuous negotiations that marked the last phase of the Alençon courtship (1579-83), the best-known face of the Elizabethan image made it possible to argue for the first time that by reigning as England's perpetually virgin queen, Elizabeth could escape the political compromises necessitated by the marriages of her kindred monarchs, Mary I and Mary, Queen of Scots. After the danger of foreign Catholic entanglement had subsided, progressive Protestants could acclaim "this virgin queen with all the greater enthusiasm, and her virginity became a symbol of national independence." That this change coincided with increased emphasis on classical mythology in royalist panegyrics may be noted in Thomas Blenerhasset's *A Revelation of the True Minerva* (1582) and George Peele's *The Araygnement of Paris* (1584), a "pastorall" performed before Queen Elizabeth by the children of the Chapel Royal.[64]

This iconographical shift is clearly evident in royal portraiture, which begins to incorporate esoteric virginity symbols into arcane allegories that may be impenetrable to casual observers. Thus the mundane utensil held by the queen in the "Sieve" portraits (1579-83) celebrates her standing as a latter-day Vestal Virgin, whose maiden state is essential to the imperialistic program proposed by John Dee. Roy Strong concludes that these paintings "must be seen as statements against the [Alençon] marriage by means of a deliberate intensification of the mystique of chastity as an attribute essential to the success of her rule."[65] In the *Ermine Portrait* (1585), the queen captivates the ermine of chastity, which stands transfixed without a tether but with a royal crown about its neck. After Isaac Oliver's disastrous experiment with naturalistic portraiture of the queen as an aging woman (ca. 1592), authorized images shifted to the anachronistic "Mask of Youth" that appears in paintings of the queen until her death. It may be noted in the convoluted *Rainbow Portrait* (ca. 1600-03), which depicts the preternaturally youthful queen with the shoulder-length hair of a marriageable virgin.[66]

Praise of Elizabeth as Cynthia (or Diana, or Belphoebe, or any one of a number of other variants) became indelibly imprinted during the last half of the reign. Marie Axton notes that as the queen "grew older and hope for offspring faded, Diana or Cynthia as a public image found reluctant acceptance."[67] Unlike the *Princely Pleasures at Kenelworth Castle* and the "April" eclogue, in which unambiguous praise of Zabeta or Eliza as Cynthia had not yet won a place, the emergence of the queenly moon-cult typifies the increasing Petrarchism and Platonism of royal circles, where courtiers paid homage to Elizabeth as an ever-youthful yet unapproachable object of desire.[68] The cult originated in Giordano Bruno's praise of Elizabeth during his mid-1580s residence in England, according to Roy Strong, who concludes that it "must have become public" by the end of the decade. Her status as "Cynthia, Queen of Seas and Lands" further alludes to John Dee's claim for England's status as an imperialistic military and naval power, which was voiced with increased stridency following the destruction of the Spanish Armada. Thus jeweled crescent moons symbolic of Diana appear in the queen's hair in miniatures by Nicholas Hilliard (ca. 1586-1603) and at the apex of the headpiece in the *Rainbow Portrait*.[69] The queen actually appears as crescent-crowned Diana in a portrait in which she bears bow and arrows and holds the tether of a hunting dog.[70]

The apotheosis of the queen as Cynthia was complete by the time that boy actors from St. Paul's School performed John Lyly's *Endimion: The Man in the Moone* at the royal court on Candlemas 1588. Her cult image is clearly apparent in a fiction showing (paradoxically) her love for a mortal. Although it cannot be proved that this elaborate play contains a detailed program of topical allegory, queenly symbolism differentiates between the celestial state of the moon goddess and the mortality of her subjects, who are associated with Tellus (the earth). The goddess herself is significantly absent during the first two acts, which dramatize the condition of the lovesick shepherd, Endimion. Eumenides explains that his companion's desire is incapable of satisfaction because "there was never any so peevish to imagin the Moone eyther capable of affection, or shape of a Mistris: for as impossible it is to make love fit to her humor which no man knoweth, as a coate to her forme, which continueth not in one bignesse whilst she is measuring."[71] (Her inconstancy and variable form refer to the waxing and waning of the moon.) Although this viewpoint might seem critical of the unending virginity of the queen, the play "apotheosizes a queen for whom marriage is unthinkable," and whose courtiers may now direct toward her "harmonious, platonic affection without rivalry for special favor."[72] One critic concludes that Endimion's adoration dramatizes the "proper worship of the ideal courtier for his monarch." Cynthia's manifestation of truth, justice, mercy, and peace in the concluding act, after her kiss releases Endimion from the enchantment of sleep, accords with the attribution of all virtue to the queen in her later iconography.[73] The goddess herself proclaims that this mythic act of noblesse oblige manifests virginal innocence, in accordance with her own comment that "my mouth hath beene heere tofore as untouched as my thoughts" (5.1.20-21). The direct appeal for royal favor in the epilogue makes explicit the identification between the queen as a member of the audience and the boy playing her role as the moon goddess: "but if your Highnes vouchsafe with your favorable beames to glaunce upon us, we shall not only stoope, but with all humilitie, lay both our handes and heartes at your Majesties feete."

The place of Sir Walter Ralegh as a major disseminator of the moon-cult may be noted in his nocturnal portrait (1588),[74] which depicts the ability of feminine Luna to govern the male. The device of the crescent moon in the upper left corner compliments the queen as the goddess controlling Ralegh's tides in a nautical conceit that presumably refers to the importance of his own maritime skills in advancing Elizabethan imperialism. This symbolic image defines the courtier's relationship to the queen as Cynthia, who in turn gave him the punning nickname of "Water." His wearing Elizabeth's colors of black and white affiliates him with the Virgin Queen as a nighttime figure who is ever alluring and changeable, but the motto *Amor et Virtute* reaffirms the innocent chastity of his love. Several years later, Ralegh lamented the loss of the intimate and protected relationship that he once enjoyed as the queen's favorite in "The 11th: and last booke of the Ocean to Scinthia" (ca. 1592): "What stormes so great but Cinthias beames apeased? / What rage so feirce that love could not allay?"[75] George Chapman's celebration of the cult of the Moon Queen in *The Shadow of Night* (1594), which includes his "Hymnus in Noctem" and "Hymnus in Cynthiam," is aligned with Ralegh's views and those of their originators, John Dee and Giordano Bruno. The ascendancy of the powerful Elizabethan moon over the European sun through the grand conceit of a solar eclipse may allude in particular to the outcome of the Alençon courtship a decade earlier. Surely it lodges a general claim to English imperialistic triumph late in the queen's reign:

> Then set thy Christall, and Imperiall throne,
> (Girt in thy chast, and never-loosing zone)
> Gainst Europs Sunne directly opposit,

And give him darknesse, that doth threat
   thy light.[76]

The Faerie Queene's dedicatory "Letter to Ralegh" (23 January 1589/90) declares that Spenser models the name Belphoebe on "your owne excellent conceipt of Cynthia, (Phoebe and Cynthia being both names of Diana)." When the narrator praises Elizabeth as the enshrinement of chastity at the outset of the "Legend of Chastity," he indicates that the most perfect representation of the queen's image, "in living colours, and right hew," is to be found in the "sweet verse" of Ralegh, "In which a gracious servant pictured / His *Cynthia,* his heavens fairest light" (3.proem.4). Spenser presumably refers to a lost section of the fragmentary manuscript of *Ocean to Cynthia* that predated Ralegh's disgrace.

The androgynous conceit that fuses solar and lunar qualities in the "April" eclogue is akin to some queenly images in the *Faerie Queene,* where the concealment of Una's brilliant whiteness beneath a "black stole" (1.1.4) suggests a lunar image that is a witty variation of the figure of the Woman Clothed with the Sun, who has "the moon . . . under her feet" (Rev. 12:1). Una wears Elizabeth's personal colors of black and white in the manner of Ralegh's nocturnal portrait. The subordination of the masculine sun to the feminine moon in Britomart's dream at Isis Church raises the intriguing possibility that Elizabeth's crescent moon imagery may derive from Isis as well as Cynthia. In Britomart's vision the Crocodile, that is Osiris or the sun, submits as a consort to Isis, who "doth the Moone portend." The "rich Mitres shaped like the Moone" worn by the priests of Isis correspond to the moon devices that appear in the queen's portraiture during her last decade (5.7.4). The Egyptian fertility goddess shares the queen's androgynous nature, and the history of her search for the dead Osiris, whom Typhon had dismembered, makes her look like a type for Elizabeth in her restless quest for a spouse. Although Isis recovers the rest of her husband's body, she never finds his phallus, a lost member that forever eludes her.[77]

Belphoebe personifies Elizabeth's private capacity as a woman according to the "Letter to Ralegh." Her portrayal is problematic, however, because it tends to identify chastity with perpetual virginity, even though Spenser characteristically associates that virtue with the consummation of love in marriage. Belphoebe's status as the elder sister of Amoret, the twin who is destined for marriage to Scudamour, might appear to elevate the celibate life above wedded love in the mythic account of their birth, but Amoret participates equally in their virgin birth by Chrysogone:[78] "Pure and unspotted from all loathly crime, / That is ingenerate in fleshly slime" (3.6.3). It looks as if Spenser has cleaved the virginal and fertile sides of Eliza into two charac-

ters, one remote and divine and the other approachable and worldly. The anomalous aspect of Belphoebe's virginity invites the reader, almost automatically, to equate her unmarried state with that of Elizabeth, whose private capacity as woman rather than queen is "fashioned" in the chaste huntress (3.proem.5). Nevertheless, the queenly nubility of Britomart and Gloriana makes it difficult to accept Belphoebe as any *more* representative of Elizabeth than those other queenly figures or to assimilate the huntress into an unequivocal sanction of Elizabeth's status as a virgin queen. Indeed, the "paradoxical doubleness" of the huntress combines attributes of Venus and Diana in a complicated symbolic depiction of the queen.[79]

Although Belphoebe is a strong woman who conquers enemies and hunts, Spenser passes her over to make the female knight, Britomart, his chief personification of chastity. Her commitment to heterosexual love contrasts sharply with Belphoebe's celibacy. While the "martiall Mayd" (3.2.9) matches Belphoebe's militance in defending her virginity against an inappropriate suit like that of Malecasta, that she is destined to marry Artegall is never in question. This "Magnificke Virgin" is clearly labeled as a type for Elizabeth by her name ("martial Britoness"), by her dream at Isis Church, and by the maidenliness and chastity that she shares with the queen. As a member of the blood royal and Tudor ancestress, she shares many of the queen's attributes. Like Elizabeth, she is the heir to a "Crowne" and a giver of "royall gifts of gold and silver wrought" (5.7.21-24). When Britomart removes her helmet, the reader learns that she wears her hair long in the manner of a marriageable virgin, a style similar to the one that Elizabeth maintained as an aged queen according to the *Rainbow Portrait* (fig. 4). The presence of this symbolic detail indicates that the knight's appearance is analogous to the "Mask of Youth" found in so many other portraits made during Elizabeth's last decade of life:

> Her golden locks, that were in tramels gay
> Upbounden, did them selves adowne
>   display,
>   And raught unto her heeles; like sunny
>   beames,
>   That in a cloud their light did long time
>   stay,
>   That vapour vaded, shew their golden
>   gleames,
> And through the persant aire shoote forth
>   their azure streames.
>
>   (3.9.20)

The Jacobean Apotheosis

The advent of James I cast Elizabethan fashion into eclipse at court. The new regal style reverted to traditional masculine models for praising kings and downplayed the commitment to militant Protestantism which ideologues had attached without warrant to a queen whose own inclinations lay in the direction of pacifism and noncontroversial religion. At the same time, patriarchal theory of royal absolutism underwent enhancement. Spenser's death during the last years of the late queen's reign created a "vacancy" in the unofficial position of laureate poet, which the Catholic convert Ben Jonson filled when he rose to ascendancy as a prominent celebrator of the Jacobean royal image; he had never achieved the place he desired under the old regime. Johnson felt an aversion to the political and millennial fervor that marked the last years of Elizabeth. Even before the end of her reign, his "demotion" of the queen to the status of an arbitrator of comic action in *Every Man Out of his Humour* (acted in 1599) could have been taken as an insult to her honor, and he openly mocked the cult of the Faerie Queene in *The Alchemist* (acted in 1610).[80]

Nevertheless, sentimental idealization of the late queen began soon after her death. James's early years on the throne were welcomed in the public theater by plays that praised Elizabeth as a Protestant heroine and contrasted the disastrous events of the reign of Mary I with the mythic "golden age" that followed. It may be that emphasis upon the errors of the Marian government constituted oblique advice to the new king to observe precedents established under Elizabeth rather than to follow the example of Mary I or his own mother, Mary Queen of Scots. Typical of this concern is *The Famous History of Sir Thomas Wyat* (1607), a collaborative composition by Thomas Dekker and John Webster that was performed in the early years of the new reign. In contrast to an idealized line of Protestant succession extending from Henry VIII through Edward VI and even Lady Jane Grey, the regime of Mary I as a "catholicke Queene" and her husband Philip, the "forraine Prince" (sigs. A4ᵛ, E3), is dramatized as a historical anomaly immediately preceding the advent of Elizabeth. Explicit historical analogies may be drawn between historical antecedents found in the play and Jacobean events, for example the parallel between Mary's marriage to the Spanish heir and the proposed wedding between Prince Henry Frederick and Anne, Princess of Spain.[81]

The two parts of Thomas Heywood's *If You Know Not Me, You Know No Bodie: Or, The Troubles of Queene Elizabeth* (1605) have a far broader historical scope because they dramatize events from the "tragic" fall from favor of Princess Elizabeth after her brother's death until the Spanish Armada. Acted in 1604, the first part resembles a Protestant saint's legend by sentimentalizing Elizabeth's suffering during her sister's reign, when suspicion of complicity with antigovernment plotters threatened the young princess with execution. Her own testimony during imprisonment takes on the quasi-prophetic cast that would become

famous through Camden's *Annales:* "If I miscarry in this enterprise, and ask you why, / A Virgine and a Martyr both I dy" (*If You Know,* ll. 341-42). The play follows a tragicomic trajectory by dramatizing Elizabeth's survival of a series of perils that culminate in imprisonment at the Tower of London, where one scene dramatizes a by now legendary instance of perseverance through the keeping of her own counsel. The pious princess inscribes into her Bible an epigram that had long since won a place of honor in Foxe's "Book of Martyrs": "Much suspected by me, nothing prov'd can be, / *Finis quoth Elizabeth* the prisoner" (ll. 1036-37).[82] The first part of the play closes at the same point where Foxe concludes his hagiographical celebration of the accession of Elizabeth as an example of providential intervention on behalf of the English nation. It dramatizes Elizabeth's self-presentation as an evangelical queen (ll. 1578-98) by recapitulating an actual event during her entry into London on the eve of her coronation, when she kissed a Bible as an endorsement of the popular reading of the scriptures in the vernacular.[83] Heywood's sequel traces events of Elizabeth's reign leading up to the climax of patriotic fervor that greeted England's "providential" deliverance from the Spanish Armada. This nationalistic "triumph" could be applied adversely to James I and his policies because the self-styled heroism of Sir Francis Drake and the Elizabethan seadogs served as a blunt argument in favor of the militantly imperialistic and anti-Spanish foreign policy that the new king was reluctant to espouse. The outset of his reign was instead marked by the establishment of the 1604 peace treaty that ended two decades of hostility toward Spain.[84]

Jacobean politics provided a motive for the anachronistic revival of the cult of Elizabeth as a model ruler whose perpetual virginity symbolized political integrity, Protestant ideology, and a militantly interventionist policy against Spain. Because these values were increasingly found wanting at the court of England's Scottish king, Protestant militants praised the late queen in order to attack Jacobean pacifism. In the aftermath of the Gunpowder Plot, Thomas Dekker's *Whore of Babylon* (acted ca. 1606-07) fused Spenserian allegory with the well-known scene from Elizabeth's coronation pageantry when newly awakened Truth, the daughter of Time, presents the Faery Queen with a Bible symbolic of Protestant evangelical truth. The kissing of the scriptures by this unambiguous type for Queen Elizabeth precedes the idealized triumph of the Reformation when Roman clergy are expelled from the realm.[85] Dekker led the way in developing the Spenserian revival that was to flower after the 1610 assassination of the French king, Henri IV. Although Spenser was not himself a Puritan, his poetry appealed to the moral sensibility of Puritans and other progressive Protestants who increasingly opposed James I. When the king frustrated expectations that he would ally England with the German Protestant princedoms against the Hapsburg empire, Prince Henry Frederick served as a magnet for the apocalyptic fervor and militant hopes of radical Protestants. It seemed clear that a return to a political style approaching Elizabethan "majesty" must await the accession of James's militantly Protestant heir.[86]

Although these hopes were dashed by the untimely death of the Prince of Wales in 1612, it may be no accident that an aura of fervent expectation surrounds the birth of Elizabeth Tudor in Shakespeare's roughly contemporaneous *Henry VIII* (ca. 1612-13). The play may be associated with the 14 February 1613 wedding of the late prince's sister, Elizabeth Stuart, to Frederick, Elector Palatine, who occupied a prominent place in the leadership of Protestant Germany. Protestant zeal imbues Archbishop Cranmer's prediction of the infant's future greatness as England's Virgin Queen in a retrospective prophecy of the kind found in Camden's *Annales:*

> She shall be, to the happiness of England,
> An aged princess; many days shall see her,
> And yet no day without a deed to crown it.
> Would I had known more! but she must die,
> She must, the saints must have her; yet a
>   virgin,
> A most unspotted lily shall she pass
> To th' ground, and all the world shall mourn
>   her.
>
> (5.4.56-62)

This play differs, nevertheless, in an important respect from the works of disaffected authors who felt alienated from the royal court. Cranmer's "prophecy" is more accurate than the radical efforts to rewrite history by transforming Elizabeth's pacifism and noncontroversial religion into precedents for a militantly Protestant foreign policy. It flatters James I as a peaceable monarch who is not only the legal heir of "the maiden phoenix" (5.4.40), but also her spiritual progeny:

> Who from the sacred ashes of her honor
> Shall star-like rise as great in fame as she
>   was,
> And so stand fix'd. Peace, plenty, love,
>   truth, terror,
> That were the servants to this chosen
>   infant,
> Shall then be his, and like a vine grow to
>   him.
>
> (5.4.45-50)

This hindsight prophecy accords with the policies of a king who attempted to balance a pro-Spanish foreign policy and a marital alliance with Protestant Germany.

William Camden completed the original Latin text of

the *Annales of the Famous Empresse Elizabeth* against the backdrop of Jacobean patronage and politics. After abandoning work on Cecil's papers in 1598, he restarted the project in 1608 at the behest of James I. The historian went along with the vetting that his manuscript received at the hands of the king or his confidant, Henry Howard, Earl of Northampton, to the extent of providing the sympathetic account of Mary, Queen of Scots, that her son desired. Camden also rewrote the historical record by vindicating James against charges that he accepted his mother's execution with little protest or grief. Because the king's interest in the chronicling of Elizabethan events dried up after Mary's death and his own exculpation, royal command blocked publication of the last installment, which treated events following her trial and execution. Although Camden completed this section in 1617, the posthumous publication of *Tomus alter annalium rerum Anglicarum, et Hibernicarum, sive pars quarta* was held off until 1627, after the king's death.

Although James's wishes channeled Camden's handling of Scottish affairs and Mary's imprisonment, the author's distaste for Jacobean extravagance, political corruption, and the king's conciliatory foreign policy colors his extravagantly partisan account of the previous reign. Christopher Haigh observes that the "virtues and successes of Elizabeth were therefore defined by the flaws and omissions of James, and Camden wrote a commentary on the rule of James in the guise of a history of the rule of Elizabeth."[87] An English translation of books 1-3 of the *Annales* (1625) was entered into the Stationers' Register in March 1624, soon after the furor aroused by the unsuccessful proposal that Charles, Prince of Wales, marry the Infanta of Spain.[88]

Because the generations that had grown into adulthood under Elizabeth had dwindled and accurate memories of her reign had dimmed, Camden provided a very influential record of Elizabethan public events, one that still dominates most twentieth-century accounts of Elizabethan history and culture.[89] The elaborately symbolic title page of the 1625 *Annales* highlights the hagiographical nature of Camden's text. Its woodcut border portrays events that shaped the heroic myth of an Elizabethan "golden age" of imperialistic triumph: Sir Francis Drake's circumnavigation of the globe in 1577-79, his 1587 attack on Cadiz, the defeat of the Spanish Armada in 1588, the earl of Cumberland's 1591 raid on San Juan de Puerto Rico, and the 1596 Cadiz expedition of the earl of Essex. Inset portrayals of naval scenes illustrate these events along with stentorian captions like "ALBIONS COMFORT, IBERIAS TERROR. The famous overthrow of the Spanish Navie the 30th yeare of the Q[ueen] R[egnant]." The Tudor rose and the queen's motto of "Semper Eadem," along with its symbolic equivalent of the reborn Phoenix rising from its own ashes, crown the title page. The accom-

panying frontispiece incorporates the famous Elizabethan devices of the jeweled crescent moon and the fan
into its portrayal of the queen's apotheosis. The attendant cherub confers a celestial crown with the sun,
moon, and stars of the Woman Clothed with the Sun
above an inscription proclaiming that Elizabeth, "that
famous Queene," still lives. The verses printed boldly
on the flyleaf rise to a crescendo that makes it clear
that Elizabeth was, in every respect, the antithesis of
James I. Stridently patriotic hyperbole of this kind
shaped the posthumous representation of Elizabeth as
the triumphant Virgin Queen of modern reputation:

> By this Good Princes never dye,
> Death but refines their MAJESTY:
> For in this Maiden-Queene Story,
> Admire and view Englands Glory,
> Beauties Mapp, DIANAS Mirror:
> Who built up Truth, banisht Error.
> In whose blest raign true Gospels light
> Shines in spight of all Romish might:
> Foes with undaunted mind Reject,
> France friended, Netherland protect,
> POPE exiled, SPAINES Armado
> Confounded with their Bravado.
> here read the days when britan ground
> With blessings all was compast round.

Notes

* This essay was prepared with the support of a National
Endowment for the Humanities Senior Residential Fel-
lowship at the Folger Shakespeare Library and a Roger
C. Schmutz research grant from Bates College. I have
profited from conversations with Andrew Gurr, Patricia
Harris, Peter Lake, Peter Lindenbaum, Jeanne Roberts,
Lois Schwoerer, and other readers and staff members at
the Folger Library. James Bednarz has offered helpful
advice, and William Watterson has provided good counsel back in Maine. An initial version of this essay was
written before publication of Roy Strong, *Gloriana: The
Portraits of Queen Elizabeth I* (1987), rev. ed. of *Portraits of Queen Elizabeth I* (Oxford, 1963). My text has
been revised in light of Strong's findings.

¹ See Elkin Wilson, *England's Eliza* (Cambridge, MA,
1939), 217.

² Maureen Quilligan, *Milton's Spenser: The Politics of
Reading* (Ithaca, NY, 1983), 213.

³ Wilson, 215; Yates, *Astraea: The Imperial Theme in
the Sixteenth Century* (London-Boston, 1975), 86-87.

⁴ Yates, *Astraea*, 34-36, 78-79; Strong, *The Cult of
Elizabeth: Elizabethan Portraiture and Pageantry*
(1977), 16. Robin H. Wells applies the Yates-Strong
thesis in *Spenser's "Faerie Queene" and the Cult of
Elizabeth* (London-Totowa, NJ, 1983).

⁵ Greenblatt, *Renaissance Self-Fashioning: From More
to Shakespeare* (Chicago, 1980), 166-68.

⁶ Montrose, "The Elizabethan Subject and the Spenserian Text," in *Literary Theory / Renaissance Texts,*
ed. Patricia Parker and David Quint (Baltimore, 1986),
318.

⁷ See John N. King, *Tudor Royal Iconography: Literature and Art in an Age of Religious Crisis* (Princeton, NJ, 1989), 182-266.

⁸ Montrose, 309-10, 314-15, 321-28, 335 n. 16.

⁹ David Norbrook, *Poetry and Politics in the English
Renaissance* (London, 1984), 83-84; Strong, 1987, 41-
42, 96-97. See also Marie Axton, *The Queen's Two
Bodies: Drama and the Elizabethan Succession* (London, 1977), 60.

¹⁰ Camden, *Annales: The True and Royall History of
the Famous Empresse Elizabeth, Queene of England,
France, and Ireland, etc. True Faith's Defendresse of
Divine Renowne and Happy Memory* (1625), bk. 1,
26, trans. from *Annales rerum Anglicarum et Hibernicarum, regnante Elizabeth* (1615).

¹¹ Ibid., 27-29.

¹² Idem, *The Historie of the Most Renowned and Victorious Princesse Elizabeth, Late Queene of England,*
trans. R. N[orton]. (London, 1630), 222. This edition
contains the account of the last half of the reign in bk.
4 of Camden's *Annales*, which had been published
posthumously in 1627 as *Tomus alter annalium rerum
Anglicarum, et Hibernicarum*. The concluding section
of the present essay explains why *Annales rerum Anglicarum et Hibernicarum* and the English translation
of 1625 end after Camden's account of the trial and
execution of Mary, Queen of Scots.

¹³ See Axton, 133-34.

¹⁴ See Wilson, 6 (note) and 61; Lacey Baldwin Smith,
Elizabeth Tudor: Portrait of a Queen (Boston, 1975),
120, 122; Axton, 38-39. Compare the aligned use of
Camden's testimony in Leonard Tennenhouse, *Power
on Display: The Politics of Shakespeare's Genres* (London, 1986), 22. Although Yates claims that "from the
very beginning of her reign the Virgo-Astraea symbol
was used of Elizabeth," I have discovered no examples between 1558 and 1569. Yates, 59, cites the
unverified testimony of Camden's *Remains* (1674) that
the figure was in use "'in the beginning of her late
Majesties Reign.'"

¹⁵ Montrose, 310.

¹⁶ J[odocus] C[rull], *The Antiquities of St. Peters, or*

the Abbey Church of Westminster (London, 1711), 93; Edward Brayley, *The History and Antiquities of the Abbey Church of St. Peter, Westminster,* vol. 1 (London, 1818), pt. 2, 65.

[17] Camden, 1625, sigs. [b7-8].

[18] British Library, MS Lansdowne 94, fol. 29. Transcribed in T. E. Hartley, ed., *Proceedings in the Parliaments of Elizabeth I* (Leicester, 1981), 1:44-45; the textual introduction lists many contemporary manuscript and printed copies.

[19] George P. Rice, Jr., transcribes both versions of the queen's speech in *The Public Speaking of Queen Elizabeth: Selections from Her Official Addresses* (New York, 1951), with the undocumented claim that the Camden variation represents a "second, much shorter, and obviously superior version" (114-18). With rare skepticism, John E. Neale acknowledges Camden's version of the queen's address in *Elizabeth I and Her Parliaments,* vol. 1 (London, 1953), 47 n. 3, where he remarks: "I know of no text from which he could have made it, and it does not correspond with the Queen's description. I have therefore ignored it." On the contrary, Louis Montrose, 309, makes the unsubstantiated claim that the Camden transcript is drawn from "official records."

[20] See Herbert Thurston, in *The Catholic Encyclopedia,* vol. 13 (New York, 1912), 60, s. v. "Rings." The wedding ring was also attributed to St. Catherine, whose cult had a strong following in medieval England, as the bride of Christ.

[21] Camden, 1625, bk. 1, 26. What appears to be the earliest printed account of the parliamentary petition and the queen's answer is in *Grafton's Abridgement of the Chronicles of Englande,* 3d ed. (London, 1570), sigs. Z3ᵛ-4ᵛ. Richard Grafton, who sat as a member of several parliaments, claims to provide an eyewitness account, "as nere as I could beare the same away," of the queen's address to the parliamentary delegation at Whitehall Palace. Holinshed's *Chronicles* and the second edition of John Stow's *Annales* (1592) agree almost completely with MS Lansdowne 94, fol. 29, and Grafton. John Nichols provides the same speech in *Progresses and Public Processions of Queen Elizabeth,* vol. 1 (London, 1823), 63-65. Neale quotes extensive extracts; 1953, 47-50.

[22] See Neale, *Queen Elizabeth* (London, 1934), 82; and Mortimer Levine, "The Place of Women in Tudor Government," in *Tudor Rule and Revolution: Essays for G. R. Elton from his American Friends,* ed. D. J. Guth and J. W. McKenna (Cambridge, 1982), 109-11off. For the queen's statement in a 1571 letter to Sir Francis Walsingham that the treaty governing Mary I's marriage provides a binding precedent for a mar-

riage that she herself might undertake, see *The Letters of Queen Elizabeth,* ed. and trans. G. B. Harrison (London, 1935), 98.

[23] MS Lansdowne 94, fol. 29. Italics have been added to emphasize the only significant variants in the printed transcript. The line that is fragmentary due to the folding of the sheet of paper has been restored by reference to Grafton, sig. Z3ᵛ-4ᵛ, which records these words: "that a marble stone shall declare that a Queene, having reygned suche a tyme, lived and dyed a virgin." It reads "as a good mother of my country, I will never shonne" for "I will never shune." The substitution of "choyse" for "chaunce" may be attributed to Grafton's misreading (or that of the typesetter) of the secretary hand in which the original manuscript was copied. The omission of the sentence, "but . . . selfe," could have resulted from an error of an amanuensis or compositor. Grafton's quotation of a queenly desire to be "a good mother of my country" may record a phrase actually used by Elizabeth.

[24] Strong, 1987, 22-24.

[25] Elizabeth I, 1935, 31.

[26] John Stubbs, *John Stubb's "Gaping Gulf" with Letters and Other Relevant Documents,* ed. Lloyd E. Berry (Charlottesville, 1968), 49.

[27] Neale provides a useful account of the "marriage problem" even though he minimizes the queen's commitment to wedlock (1934, 76-90). See also Smith, 118-25. From the age of fifteen, Elizabeth's letters record her awareness of the political complications of courtship and marriage (Elizabeth I, 1935, 9-11). Axton, 11-25, considers the succession debate in light of the Elizabethan adaptation of the theory of the king's two bodies.

[28] Forty was the average age at menopause according to Lawrence Stone, *The Family, Sex and Marriage in England 1500-1800* (New York, 1977), 63 and n. 48.

[29] Neale, 1953, 110. Minutes in the queen's own hand concerning her reply to Parliament are preserved in MS Landsdowne 94, fol. 30.

[30] King, 216.

[31] John E Booty, ed., *The Book of Common Prayer 1559; The Elizabethan Prayer Book* (Charlottesville, 1976), 290.

[32] From a copy of the speech in Cambridge University Library MS Gg.iii.34, fols. 208-12; transcribed in Hartley, 145-49. A fragment of the draft in the queen's own hand, with an endorsement by Cecil, is preserved in Public Record Office, State Papers Domestic, Eliz-

abeth 41/5. Modernized texts are in Elizabeth I, 1951, 77-81; and Neale, 1953, 146-50.

33 London, National Portrait Gallery, no. 5175. See Strong, 1987, 41, 125-28, 147, 163-64, 178, and fig. 157.

34 Axton, 38-41; David Bevington, *Tudor Drama and Politics: A Critical Approach to Topical Meaning* (Cambridge, MA, 1968), 141-47.

35 See Wilson, chaps. 5 and 7; and Yates, 29, 76.

36 Strong pinpoints the origins of the Diana and Cynthia compliments in panegyrics that Giordano Bruno addressed to Elizabeth in 1584-85 (1987, 125-26).

37 Axton, 48.

38 Strong, 1987, 65 and figs. 52-53.

39 Axton, 47-53. Quotation follows her transcription from masque texts in Bodleian Library, MS Rawlinson poet. 108, fols. 24-37. She also cites Emilia's transient devotion to Diana in another 1566 masque witnessed by Elizabeth, Richard Edwards' *Palamon and Arcite*.

40 David Norbrook, "Panegyric of the Monarch and Its Social Context under Elizabeth I and James I," unpub. diss., Oxford University, 1978, 46.

41 Wilson, 274, 277-78.

42 Gascoigne, *Complete Works,* ed. John W. Cunliffe, vol. 2 (Cambridge, 1910), 95-97, 99, 102-103.

43 Ibid., 106, 109, 114-15, 117, 120. See Axton, 63-65.

44 Churchyard, *A Discourse of the Queenes Majesties Entertainement in Suffolk and Norffolk* (1578), sig. D1ᵛ. See David M. Bergeron, *English Civic Pageantry, 1558-1642* (Columbia, SC, 1971), 41-42.

45 Ellen M. Caldwell, "John Lyly's *Gallathea:* A New Rhetoric of Love for the Virgin Queen," *English Literary Renaissance* 17 (1987): 28.

46 Wallace T. MacCaffrey, *Queen Elizabeth and the Making of Policy, 1572-1588* (Princeton, NJ, 1981), 254-66. On the prolific literature in opposition to the Alençon match, see Doris Adler, "Imaginary Toads in Real Gardens," *English Literary Renaissance* 11 (1981):235-60.

47 Elizabeth I, 1935, 136. In 1581 Walsingham counseled that if she meant to marry, she should make haste (ibid., 149). Articles that Alençon proposed on 16 June 1579 for governing the marriage were anno-

tated with Elizabeth's replies on the following day (MS Lansdowne 94, fols. 58-60). For Cecil's "satisfaction," scriptural and legal precedents were compiled to support an affirmative answer to the question of "Whether a Protestant may marye with a Papyste" (MS Lansdowne 94, fols. 62-69).

48 Spenserian references are to *The Works of Edmund Spenser: A Variorum Edition,* ed. Edwin A. Greenlaw, C. G. Osgood, F. M. Padelford, et al. (Baltimore, 1932-57), 10 vols. in 11.

49 Norbrook, 1984, 86-87.

50 Edwin A. Greenlaw, *Studies in Spenser's Historical Allegory* (Baltimore, 1932), 119; Spenser, Vol. 7, Pt. 2, 105.

51 William A. Ringler, Jr., "Spenser, Shakespeare, Honor, and Worship," *Renaissance News* 14 (1961):159-61. The dedication was changed from Dudley to Sidney after E. K. dated his epistle to Gabriel Harvey on 10 April 1579, by which time Spenser's composition must have been virtually complete.

52 *Miscellaneous Prose of Sir Philip Sidney,* ed. Katherine Duncan-Jones and Jan Van Dorsten (Oxford, 1973), 57, ll. 7-8. Cecil preserved an anonymous letter written close in time to Sidney's composition that reviews the problem and urges the queen to marry (MS Lansdowne 94, fols. 70-71).

53 Andrew Weiner, *Sir Philip Sidney and the Poetics of Protestantism: A Study of Contexts* (Minneapolis, 1978), 22. Duncan-Jones and Van Dorsten challenge this view in Sidney, 34-37.

54 Stubbs, 9, 51, 68.

55 Norbrook, 1984, 84.

56 Patrick Cullen, *Spenser, Marvell, and Renaissance Pastoral* (Cambridge, MA, 1970), 116. Anne Lake Prescott has commented to me that Eliza's scarlet attire is appropriate to a "mayden Queene" (l. 57) who remains marriageable.

57 Thomas H. Cain, *Praise in "The Faerie Queen"* (Lincoln, NE, 1978), 16-17; David Lee Miller, *The Poem's Two Bodies: The Poetics of the 1590 "Faerie Queene"* (Princeton, NJ, 1988), 95, 238. See also n. 78 below.

58 On the Christianization of Pan, see D. C. Allen, *Mysteriously Meant: The Rediscovery of Pagan Symbolism and Allegorical Interpretation in the Renaissance* (Baltimore, 1970), 245-46.

59 Smith, 64-65. See also Norman L. Jones, "Eliza-

beth's First Year: The Conception and Birth of the Elizabethan Political World," in Christopher Haigh, ed., *The Reign of Elizabeth I* (London, 1984), 28.

[60] Norbrook, 1984, 85.

[61] *Aeneid,* 1. 327-28, in Virgil, *Eclogues, Georgics, and Aeneid,* vol. 1, ed. and trans. H. Rushton Fairclough (Cambridge, MA, 1940); *Variorum,* 7, pt. 1, 41, 45, 287-88. According to Virgil, Venus appears as a nymph, possibly a votaress of Diana. On a contemporary application of the Venus-Virgo figure to Elizabeth, see King, 259, 261.

[62] See Michael O'Connell, *Mirror and Veil: The Historical Dimension of Spenser's "Faerie Queene"* (Chapel Hill, 1977), 6-7.

[63] *The Poems of Queen Elizabeth I,* ed. Leicester Bradner (Providence, RI, 1964), 5. He expresses doubt concerning the accuracy of this attribution (xiii), but see Caldwell, 22 n. I.

[64] Norbrook, 1978, 58.

[65] Strong, 1987, 94-99, 107.

[66] Ibid., 112-14, 130-33, 142-47; Yates, 215. Louis Montrose, 315, proposes that the presence of a virgin-knot in the *Armada Portrait* (ca. 1588) "suggests a causal relationship between her sanctified chastity and the providential destruction of the Spanish Catholic invaders" without exploring the alternative possibility that this jeweled bow is no more than a straightforward symbol of the kind that appears throughout Elizabeth's pre- and post-Armada portraiture. His daring view is based upon analogy to his interpretation of Henry VIII's codpiece in the Holbein cartoon of *Henry VIII with Henry VII,* which argues for the presence of political symbolism in "the king's phallic self-assertion" (312-14). Here again, Montrose neglects the alternative possibility that this appendage is no more than an item of conventional attire. Codpieces appear with some frequency in portraits of Renaissance royalty, nobility, and commoners.

[67] Axton, 60.

[68] Leonard Forster notes that it is after the failure of the Alençon negotiations that "the icon of Elizabeth as Laura begins to take shape" in *The Icy Fire: Five Studies in European Petrarchism* (Cambridge, 1969), 135.

[69] Strong, 1987, 91-93, 124-27, 146-50. For an opposed view that the Cynthia cult predated the Alençon courtship, see Ray Waddington, *The Mind's Empire: Myth and Form in George Chapman's Narrative Poems* (Baltimore, 1974), 78-79.

[70] Lawrence G. Holland, *Catalogue of the Pictures at Hatfield House* (privately printed, 1891), no. 51, attributed to Cornelius (or Henrik) Vroom and cited, 36, in an inventory of 1611 as "a portrait of her late majesty." Ill. Mandell Creighton, *Queen Elizabeth* (Edinburgh, 1896), facing 76.

[71] *The Complete Works of John Lyly,* ed. R. Warwick Bond (Oxford, 1902), 1.1.19-23.

[72] Bevington, 178-81.

[73] Peter Saccio, *The Court Comedies of John Lyly: A Study in Allegorical Dramaturgy* (Princeton, NJ, 1969), 173-77, 184-85. See also G. K. Hunter, *John Lyly: The Humanist as Courtier* (London, 1962), 184-93, 237-41.

[74] Strong, 1987, 127, fig. 135.

[75] *The Poems of Sir Walter Ralegh,* ed. Agnes M. C. Latham (London, 1951), 29, ll. 118-19.

[76] "Hymnus in Cynthiam," *The Poems of George Chapman,* ed. Phyllis Bartlett (New York, 1941), ll. 116-119. See Yates, 76-77; and Waddington, 73-74.

[77] *Plutarch's Moralia,* ed. and trans. Frank C. Babbitt (Cambridge, MA, 1969), 5:358.18, 365.36, 371-72.51. I am indebted to William Watterson concerning the importance of the Isis imagery.

[78] See Thomas P. Roche, *The Kindly Flame: A Study of the Third and Fourth Books of Spenser's "Faerie Queene"* (Princeton, NJ, 1964), 103. In an otherwise astute analysis, David Lee Miller identifies the births of Belphoebe and Amoret, and before them Eliza, as types of the Immaculate Conception (95, 235-36, 238-40). Surely the allusion is to the virgin birth of Christ rather than to the Immaculate Conception whereby St. Anne bore the Virgin Mary. Furthermore, it is debatable whether the explicit comments that Pan "begot" (i.e., procreated) Eliza define a virginal conception ("April," ll. 51, 91). See n. 57 above, and related text.

[79] O'Connell, 100-103. On some of the cautiously negative touches in Spenser's portrayal of Belphoebe or Elizabeth, see Judith H. Anderson, "'In living colours and right hew': The Queen of Spenser's Central Books," in *Poetic Traditions of the English Renaissance,* ed. Maynard Mack and George deForest Lord (New Haven, 1982), 47-66; and Miller, 6, 100, 233, and passim.

[80] Richard Helgerson, *Self-Crowned Laureates: Spenser, Jonson, Milton and the Literary System* (Berkeley and Los Angeles, 1983), 104; Norbrook, 1984, 175-77.

[81] See Judith Doolin Spikes, "The Jacobean History Play and the Myth of the Elect Nation," *Renaissance Drama* 8 (1977):117-49.

[82] Ed. Madeleine Doran, Malone Society Reprints (Oxford, 1935), 2 vols. According to Foxe's *Actes and Monuments* (1563), 1714, Princess Elizabeth wrote this epigram with a diamond upon a window when she was under house arrest at Woodstock. The works of Foxe and his fellow ideologue, John Bale, were widely used as dramatic models after Elizabeth's death, according to Spikes, 120-25, 135-37. It is important to remember that because the "Book of Martyrs" stops short immediately following Elizabeth's accession, Foxe's idealized account of Princess Elizabeth *molded* rather than reflected her queenly image.

[83] King, 229.

[84] Christopher Hill, *The Century of Revolution, 1603-1714,* rev. ed. (London, 1980), 6-7.

[85] King, 228-31.

[86] Norbrook, 1984, 195, 202-204. For further discussion of the strategy of idealizing Elizabeth in order to blame James I and praise Prince Henry, see Graham Parry, *The Golden Age Restor'd: The Culture of the Stuart Court, 1603-42* (Manchester, 1981), 72-74, 82-83; and Simon Shepherd, *Amazons and Warrior Women: Varieties of Feminism in Seventeenth-Century Drama* (New York, 1981), 124-25, 128-31.

[87] Haigh, 9.

[88] On the theatrical controversy generated by the proposed marital alliance with Spain, see Jerzy Limon, *Dangerous Matter: English Drama and Politics, 1623/24* (Cambridge, 1986), 98-129; and Annabel Patterson, *Censorship and Interpretation: The Conditions of Writing and Reading in Early Modern England* (Madison, WI, 1984), 75-79.

[89] Haigh, 6-11. See also Hugh Trevor-Roper, *Queen Elizabeth's First Historian: William Camden and the Beginnings of English "Civil History"* (London, 1971), 11, 16-17, 19; and Kevin Sharpe, "The Foundation of the Chairs of History at Oxford and Cambridge: An Episode in Jacobean Politics," *History of the Universities* 2 (1982):127-52.

FURTHER READING

Bassnett, Susan. "The Faerie Queen." In *Elizabeth I: A Feminist Perspective*, pp. 52-66. Oxford: Berg Publishers, 1988.

    Discusses Elizabeth I's roles as both a spectator and a performer in music and poetry. Focuses on how she crafted a public persona suitable for wielding power in an era of emerging modern nation-states.

Bell, Ilona. "Elizabeth I, Always Her Own Free Woman." In *Political Rhetoric, Power, and Renaissance Women*, edited by Carole Levin and Patricia A. Sullivan, pp. 57-82. Albany: State University Press of New York, 1995.

    Argues that Elizabeth I was an early feminist who used the marriage question to her advantage to maintain personal and political power. The article also challenges traditionally held assumptions about the Queen's commitment to chastity.

Buxton, John. "The Tradition of Patronage." In his *Sir Philip Sidney and the English Renaissance,* pp. 1-32. London: MacMillan, 1966.

    Discusses the role of patrons, especially Sir Philip Sidney, in cultivating literary talent and how, in championing famous writers, patrons became immortalized as well.

Craig, Hardin. "The Universal Nature of Things." In his *The Enchanted Glass: The Elizabethan Mind in Literature,* pp.1-31. Oxford: Basil Blackwell, 1960.

    Analyzes how the dominance of Aristotelian and neo-Platonic interpretations of the nature of the universe helped shape the cosmology of Renaissance thinkers.

Jordan, Constance. "Woman and Natural Law." In her *Renaissance Feminism: Literary Texts and Political Models*, pp. 65-133. Ithaca: Cornell University Press, 1990.

    Contains a section examining sixteenth-century texts that deflated natural law arguments and claimed women's unsuitability for leadership roles.

Javitch, Daniel. "Chapter III." In *Poetry and Courtliness in Renaissance England*, pp. 76-106. Princeton: Princeton University Press, 1978.

    An important essay in which Javitch discusses the stylistic devices used by Elizabethan court poets.

Rowse, A. L. "The Elizabethan Discovery of England." In his *The England of Elizabeth: The Structure of Society*, pp. 31-65. London: MacMillan and Co., 1950.

    Overview of British Renaissance historiography with emphasis on sixteenth-century interest in geography, county surveys, narrative histories; also includes a discussion of Shakespeare's works as celebrating the triumph of Tudor England.

Sharpe, J. A. "Culture, Popular and Elite." In his *Early Modern England: A Social History 1550-1760*, pp. 280-301. London: Edward Arnold, 1987.

    Overview of popular culture in England from the mid-sixteenth to the mid-eighteenth centuries that examines the role of literary patronage, the development of an elite culture, and the evolution of a consumer-driven mass culture.

Tillyard, E. M. W. *The English Renaissance: Fact or Fiction?* London: The Hogarth Press, 1960, 103 p.

> Discussion of how sixteenth-century English Renaissance thought departed from its Medieval antecedents.

Van Dorsten, J. A. "Literary Patronage in Elizabethan England: The Early Phase." In his *The Anglo-Dutch Renaissance: Seven Essays*, pp.58-71. Leiden: E. J. Brill, 1988.

> Examines the role of patrons in the early Elizabethan period, suggesting that most relationships were mutually beneficial; also focuses on writers as propagandists, with discussion of Sydney as the first patron of the new poetry.

Yates, Frances A. "Queen Elizabeth as Astraea." In her *Astraea: The Imperial Theme in the Sixteenth Century*, pp. 29-87. London: Routledge & Kegan Paul, 1975.

> Discusses how Elizabethan apologists drew upon mythological symbols to justify the Queen's rule and place in English history and to show how her break from Rome was the legitimate restoration of a previous golden age.

Sir Walter Raleigh

1554-1618

(Also spelled Ralegh.) English courtier, poet, and prose writer.

The following entry contains critical essays focusing on Raleigh's role in the Age of Spenser. For further information on Raleigh, see *LC*, Vol. 31.

INTRODUCTION

Few of Queen Elizabeth I's courtiers symbolized the Elizabethan era so comprehensively as Sir Walter Raleigh. His flamboyant personal style, adventurous spirit, outspoken political views, and wide-ranging ambition epitomize the Renaissance ideals of exploration and learning. A man of action, Raleigh is also recognized as a highly accomplished literary stylist and craftsman in both verse and prose. His *The History of the World* (1614), an unfinished chronicle undertaken while he was imprisoned, was a standard reference in England and the American colonies for a century after its publication and influenced political and religious thought throughout the seventeenth century. His poem *The Ocean to Cynthia* (1592?), undiscovered until the 1870s, confirmed in modern times the poetic ability praised by his contemporaries, among them his friend Edmund Spenser. Some critics have also compared Raleigh's poetry with that of John Donne and Philip Sidney and have discovered that it in some ways anticipates the seventeeth-century metaphysical style.

Biographical Information

Raleigh was born c. 1554 in Hayes, Devonshire, England, into a family of moderate prosperity. (The family name has been spelled in various ways including Raleigh and Ralegh both in Raleigh's own time and later; scholars now agree that the most authentic spelling is most likely "Ralegh.") Although not of the nobility, Raleigh's family had ties to Elizabeth's court through marriage. Raleigh's early education is not documented, but his lifelong anti-Catholic stance, while in keeping with Elizabeth's policies, is attributed to a strict Protestant upbringing. As a very young man Raleigh was in France during the civil wars, where he fought for the Huguenot forces. Upon his return to England, Raleigh studied at Oriel College, Oxford, from 1572 to 1574. He left without taking a degree and enrolled in one of the four Inns of Court, which, according to biographer Steven May, were social clubs as well as law schools, "and thus the proper address-

es for gentlemen in search of patronage and career openings at court or in the state at large." Raleigh's earliest poetry, a series of commendatory verses for George Gascoigne's *The Steele Glas* (1576), dates from this period. In 1578 Raleigh took part in his half-brother Sir Humphrey Gilbert's expedition on the ship *Falcon* in search of the Northwest Passage. The journey was derailed by privateering and piracy; the *Falcon* was defeated by the Spanish off Cape Verde, giving Raleigh his first naval military experience. In 1580 Raleigh was appointed head of an infantry company in the Irish Wars and quickly distinguished himself in battle. Upon his return to England in 1581, Raleigh's military successes, including the capture of important enemy documents (as well as support from his influential patrons), led to his meteoric rise in Elizabeth's favor. Legend has it that Raleigh first caught the Queen's attention by covering a muddy patch in her path with his cloak, but, more likely, it was his knowledge of Irish affairs, his eloquence and learning, and his high recommendations from other important courtiers that quickly established Raleigh as a favorite of the Queen.

For the next two decades, Raleigh held a position of power and prestige in the political life of England. Elizabeth granted him many important posts and privileges, including the patent for licensing wine sales, a monopoly that brought Raleigh much wealth and influence. In 1584 he was elected to Parliament, and in 1587 he gained official standing in Court as captain of the Queen's Guard, an important post for its intimate access to the Queen. Raleigh was one of the first to realize that England's hope for domination over Spain lay in the establishment of a lucrative colonial empire. He sponsored England's first voyages to the New World, sending colonists to Virginia in 1585 and 1587, and he popularized his efforts in England through the introduction of tobacco to court circles. Although the colonists of 1585 came home safely aboard Francis Drake's ship, the later colonists from Roanoke mysteriously disappeared. Raleigh never abandoned the lost colony and continued to send rescue ships to Virginia as late as 1602. These efforts at exploration were interrupted by the threat from the Spanish Armada in 1588. Although Raleigh's role in Spain's defeat was apparently conducted from shore, the warship he designed for the campaign was chosen as the flagship for the great battle. In 1589 a minor rift with Elizabeth, caused by mounting rivalry between several of her privileged courtiers, led Raleigh to travel to Ireland, where he formed a close friendship with Spenser, who was at that time serving a political post in Cork. Philip Sidney, Spenser, Edward Dyer, and several other friends formed a literary club, the "Areopagus." Immediately recognizing the significance of Spenser's *Faerie Queene*, Raleigh brought Spenser back to court to present the work to Elizabeth. In addition, Raleigh wrote several dedicatory sonnets to the work. During his period of greatest influence, Raleigh wrote and published prose pieces on important political questions and historical events, including treatises on war, essays on England's relations with Spain, and an account of the 1596 battle with the Spanish at Cadiz. Raleigh probably wrote most of his verse during this time, all of which was privately circulated, reflecting his relationship as a privileged courtier and suitor to the Queen.

Raleigh's confident, often swaggering court persona and his many successes over his rivals led to conflicts with other powerful courtiers, among them the Earl of Essex. Due to these rivalries, Raleigh's position in Elizabeth's favor began to erode in the late 1580s and early 1590s, culminating in the revelation in 1592 of Raleigh's secret marriage to Elizabeth Throckmorton, an attendant of the Queen. The couple were immediately imprisoned in the Tower of London, and Raleigh expressed his sense of loss and anger about the incident in his most important surviving poem, *The Ocean to Cynthia*. By 1593 the Queen's need for Raleigh's services to halt Spanish piracy led to his release from the Tower. He returned to Parliament and eventually regained his post as captain of the Guard, although the intimate royal access he had once enjoyed was never fully restored. In an attempt to gain royal favor as well as to satisfy his restless spirit, Raleigh undertook an expedition to Guiana, publishing an account of the wealth and potential of the area in 1596. Upon the Queen's death in 1603, Raleigh's fortunes became increasingly precarious. King James I distrusted Raleigh because of his role in Essex's execution and because of their conflicting views towards Spain and Catholicism. Acrimony between the two led to a charge of conspiracy against Raleigh involving Spain and James I. Although Raleigh conducted himself with characteristic wit and aplomb during his defense, the outcome of his trial was a foregone conclusion for political reasons. Raleigh was imprisoned in the Tower for treason in 1603. He spent most of the rest of his life there and it was for him a very productive intellectual time. Raleigh pursued his interests in politics, geography, religion, and philosophy and produced several influential prose works, including his ambitious *The History of the World*. Written as a tribute to his patron, Prince Henry, the incomplete work, which was published in 1614, contained influential passages on the danger of incompetent rulers. In an attempt to restore his court status, Raleigh convinced the King to release him from prison for a return expedition to Guiana in 1617, to obtain the riches he failed to find on his first voyage. The expedition was a failure, resulting in the death of his son and the humiliation of his forces. Upon his return, Raleigh wrote an "Apology" for his second Guiana trip and attempted to flee to France, but he was intercepted, arrested, and informed of his imminent execution. Raleigh was beheaded for treason on October 29, 1618, displaying at his death a courage, calm, and fortitude that earned him immediate martyrdom among his contemporaries and summed up his extraordinary career for subsequent generations.

Major Works

Raleigh's two great surviving works, *The Ocean to Cynthia* and *The History of the World*, attest to his status as the embodiment of the quintessential Renaissance gentleman scholar, learned and ambitious. Raleigh followed the Elizabethan courtly convention of privately circulating his poetry. Because of this circumstance, much of his poetry was lost, and his renown as a writer was limited to the *History* until the discovery of four fragments of *The Ocean to Cynthia* in 1870 in Lord Salisbury's library at Hatfield. Spenser provided scholars with evidence of the existence of Raleigh's long Cynthia poem in his *Colin Clouts Come Home Againe* (1595), a recollection of his first meeting with Raleigh in Ireland in which he refers to the poem, and again in a reference to the work in the *Faerie Queene*. The Hatfield fragments are entitled "The 21th: and last booke of the Ocean to Scinthia" and "The end of the 22 Boock, entreatinge of Sorrow." The former is over five-hundred lines, while the latter breaks off after twenty lines. The enigmatic titles of the fragments led scholars to believe that an immense and ambitious epic poem in twenty-two parts had once existed. However, recent scholarship has doubted the existence of such a work, crediting Raleigh with using the titles to suggest an epic scope to please the Queen. As is true of all Raleigh's court poetry, *The Ocean to Cynthia* is addressed to the Queen and reflects his standing in her favor at the time. There is evidence that Raleigh and Elizabeth exchanged original poetry as a means of communication and as a method of enhancing the perpetual courtship the Queen demanded from her courtiers. Poems dating from Raleigh's early days at court are written in the Petrarchan mode, from the point of view of an adoring lover, to which the Queen sometimes responded with verses of her own. It is not surprising, then, that poetry was the method Raleigh chose in his attempt to appease the Queen after her discovery of his secret marriage; *The Ocean to Cynthia* is also an expression of frustration and anger at Raleigh's imprisonment, a courtier's plea of mercy to his Queen, a rejected suitor's plea to his object of love. Among his prose works, Raleigh's Guiana essays, his several discourses on Parliament on relations with Spain, and his essay offering worldly advice to his son (1603-05) were most influential. However, the popularity of *The History of the World* overshadowed Raleigh's other literary accomplishments for nearly a century after its publication (the book went through twice as many editions in the seventeenth century as the collected works of either Spenser or Shakespeare). Characteristically ambitious in scope, the work was intended to cover all of history from the Creation to his own time, but the work was never finished, breaking off after the second century B.C. Although discredited after the seventeenth century, the work endured as a standard text for a hundred years after its publication and is thought to be among the first attempts at a comprehensive worldwide historical study. In addition, the *History*, which expressed Raleigh's confirmed belief in the Christian doctrine of providence, did much to dispel the notion that he was an atheist, a rumor that had been spread by his enemies. The "Preface" to the work, also referred to as "A Premonition to Princes," was celebrated for its lucid warning against the danger of tyrants. The *History*'s closing paragraph—beginning "O eloquent, just, and mighty Death!"—is still regarded as a superb example of Raleigh's ability to blend his learning and craftsmanship into expressive, enduring poetic constructions.

Critical Reception

Prior to the discovery of the Hatfield fragments, scholars were preoccupied with establishing a definitive body of work that could be directly attributed to Raleigh.

Poems in several different anthologies were wrongly identified as Raleigh's. It is only in the twentieth century that controversies surrounding authorship have begun to settle. Raleigh's poetry and prose writings in general have been viewed primarily as examples of Elizabethan patronage literature, with an emphasis on the works' relationship to Elizabeth, James I, and Prince Henry. Critics have also studied Raleigh's philosophical and poetic impact on Spenser and the *Faerie Queene*. Late-twentieth-century critics have examined Raleigh's contribution to Elizabethan literary form apart from the traditional client-patron model, focusing on the language and structure of his works both as prime examples of the literature of his time and as precursors to later trends. Critics have also argued over the relative completeness of his *History* and *The Ocean to Cynthia* and the effectiveness of the works as independent texts. The study of Raleigh's important writings, particularly his complex *The Ocean to Cynthia*, is ongoing as scholars continue to be challenged to identify and interpret Raleigh's works. His life, too, still generates interest for, as Philip Edwards has remarked, "By his capacity for excellence in so very many spheres, as courtier, soldier, historian, poet, scientist, explorer, administrator, he . . . is a living example of the belief of his age that a man should develop all his potentialities and realise his whole personality."

PRINCIPAL WORKS

A Report of the Truth of the Fight about the Iles of Acores, this last Sommer. Betwixt the Reuenge, one of her Maiesties Shippes, And an Armada of the King of Spaine (essay) 1591

The Ocean to Cynthia (poetry) 1592?

The Discoverie of the Large, Rich and Bewtiful Empire of Guiana (travel essay) 1596

*A Relation of Cadiz Action, in the Year 1596 (essay) 1596

Of a War with Spain and our Protecting the Netherlands (essay) 1602

**Sir Walter Raleighs Instrvctions to his Sonne and to Posterity (prose) 1603-05

The History of the World (history) 1614

***The Prerogative of Parliaments in England (essay) 1615

Sir Walter Raleigh's Sceptick (essay) 1651

Three Discourses of Sir Walter Ralegh (prose) 1702

The Works of Sir Walter Ralegh. 2 vols. (essays, letters, and poetry) 1751

The Works of Sir Walter Ralegh. 8 vols. (essays, letters, and poetry) 1829

The Poems of Sir Walter Ralegh (poetry) 1929

*First published in 1628.

**First published in 1632.

***First published in 1700.

CRITICISM

Tucker Brooke (lecture date 1938)

SOURCE: "Sir Walter Ralegh as Poet and Philosopher," in *Essays on Shakespeare and Other Elizabethans*, Yale University Press, 1948, pp. 121-44.

[*In the following excerpt, which is drawn from a lecture originally delivered in 1938, Brooke discusses Raleigh's poetry and prose, as well as his personality and career, as products of Elizabethan romanticism.*]

When Sir Walter Ralegh was beheaded, October 29, 1618, there died the last of the Elizabethan romanticists. He outlived his age, and came in the end to suffer by the defects of the very virtues which had made him great.

He has a vast deal in common with each of his romantic colleagues, Sidney, Spenser, and Marlowe. He shares Sidney's courtly brilliance and chivalry, Spenser's political imagination, and Marlowe's luminous independence of mind. He is more like each of the three than any of them was like another. He had been acquainted with them all: with Sidney at the intriguing court, with Spenser in Irish solitudes, with Marlowe at the Mermaid, or wherever else in London speculative and daring thought ran freest. Of the four, Ralegh is the least perfect in his literary work and in his life. In the elements of greatness he was hardly inferior to the greatest of them, but these elements did not so mix in him as to make him the consummate man and artist that Sidney, that Spenser, and even Marlowe each had been.

For this very reason there is a profit in studying Ralegh's mind. The forces of Elizabethan romanticism are seen in him not fused, but in divergence, not in harmony, but in conflict. Ralegh's imagination destroyed nearly as much as it created. It is easier in his case than in Sidney's, Spenser's, or Marlowe's to analyze, and—if one has the heart for it—to dissect.

He began his poetic career with entire appropriateness. While sojourning at the Middle Temple he wrote a commendatory poem[1] on *The Steel Glass* of George Gascoigne, the soldier poet who had his portrait painted bowing the knee before Queen Elizabeth, with a quill pen in his ear, a lance in one hand, and a book in the other, and who adopted as his motto: *Tam Marti quam Mercurio*. No one in England might more properly have succeeded to Gascoigne's motto than Ralegh. Mars and Mercury were ever contending for his allegiance.

Ralegh's poetry is less romantic than his prose. The one had its chief inspiration in the emulation and re-

pinings of his life at court; the other on the battlefield or voyage of discovery, or in his prison cell. There is in the poetry more of his mind, which was fierce, swift and restless as a bird of prey; in his prose there is more of his grave and steadfast heart.

His poems are intensely interesting and characteristic—though not characteristic of the whole man. They are unsurpassed in their own peculiar way, but the best of them have little in common with the work of Ralegh's great romantic brethren. They are highly poignant, often bitter or defiant, savoring more of fierce insight than of ordered meditation. They are rich in epigram and very clever in conceit, and they have a tang that makes them unforgettable. They reveal, as Sir Edmund Chambers has said,[2] a "fundamental brainwork, a power of concentrated phrasing, which was only too rare among his contemporaries"—except, one might add, that junior contemporary, John Donne, whose intuitive lyric strangenesses (but *not* his "not keeping of accent") Ralegh seems often to be preluding. **"The Lie"** is a bewildering series of rapier thrusts:

> Say to the court, it glows
>   And shines like rotten wood;
> Say to the church, it shows
>   What's good, and doth no good:
> If church and court reply,
> Then give them both the lie. . . .
>
> Tell men of high condition,
>   That manage the estate,
> Their purpose is ambition,
>   Their practice only hate.
> And if they once reply,
> Then give them all the lie. . . .
>
> Tell fortune of her blindness;
>   Tell nature of decay;
> Tell friendship of unkindness;
>   Tell justice of delay:
> And if they will reply,
> Then give them all the lie.[3]

The epitaph on Leicester is cool assassination of the dead man's memory:

> Here lies the noble warrior that never
>   blunted sword;
> Here lies the noble courtier that never kept
>   his word;
> Here lies his excellency that governed all
>   the state;
> Here lies the Lord of Leicester that all the
>   world did hate.[4]

Equally biting, but in nobler key, is the famous passage said (however fancifully) to have been written the night before his death and found in his Bible:

Even such is time, that takes in trust
   Our youth, our joys, and all we have,
And pays us but with age and dust;
   Who, in the dark and silent grave,
When we have wandered all our ways,
Shuts up the story of our days;
But from this earth, this grave, this dust,
My God shall raise me up, I trust![5]

Very applicable to Ralegh's poems are the words of Shelley:

Our sincerest laughter
With some pain is fraught:
Our sweetest songs are those that tell of
   saddest thought.

Like Othello, he did "agnize a natural and prompt alacrity" he found in hardness. He is often gayest (if the word can ever be used of him) when contemplating the mortal dissolution which so constantly overhung him. There is an unforgettable combination of defiance and mystic fervor in his romantic poem, **"Sir Walter Ralegh's Pilgrimage"**:

Give me my scallop-shell of quiet,
   My staff of faith to walk upon,
My scrip of joy, immortal diet,
   My bottle of salvation,
My gown of glory, hope's true gage;
And thus I'll take my pilgrimage. . . .

Blood must be my body's balmer;
   No other balm will there be given
Whilst my soul, like a white palmer,
   Travels to the land of heaven;
Over the silver mountains,
Where spring the nectar fountains:
   And there I'll kiss
   The bowl of bliss;
And drink mine everlasting fill
Upon every milken hill.
My soul will be a-dry before;
But after, it will ne'er thirst more. . . .

Then by the happy blissful way
   More peaceful pilgrims I shall see,
That have shook off their gowns of clay,
   And go apparelled fresh like me.
     I'll bring them first
     To slake their thirst
And taste of nectar suckets,
     At those clear wells
     Where sweetness dwells,
Drawn up by saints in crystal buckets.[6]

Even in his love songs there is a note of scornful dubiety; and his address to his beloved son does not

mask the grinning death's head that Ralegh saw behind all the masques and mummeries of the world:

Three things there be that prosper all apace,
   And flourish while they grow asunder far;
But on a day, they meet all in one place,
   And when they meet, they one another
     mar.
And they be these; the Wood, the Weed,
   the Wag:
The Wood is that which makes the gallows
   tree;
The Weed is that which strings the
   hangman's bag;
The Wag, my pretty knave, betokens thee.
Now mark, dear boy—while these assemble
   not,
Green springs the tree, hemp grows, the wag
   is wild;
But when they meet, it makes the timber rot,
It frets the halter, and it chokes the child.[7]

Three of Ralegh's happiest poems were inspired by his three friends, Sidney, Spenser, and Marlowe. The reply to Marlowe's song of the Passionate Shepherd, which achieved a popularity almost equal to that of the original, comes as near to lightheartedness as anything that Sir Walter wrote. It declares, indeed, the impracticality of Marlowe's pure romance, but pays a real and wistful tribute to its loveliness:

If all the world and love were young,
And truth in every shepherd's tongue,
These pretty pleasures might me move
To live with thee and be thy love.
But time drives flocks from field to fold,
When rivers rage and rocks grow cold; . . .
The flowers do fade, and wanton fields
To wayward winter reckoning yields. . . .

But could youth last, and love still breed;
Had joys no date, nor age no need;
Then those delights my mind might move
To live with thee and be thy love.[8]

Ralegh's epitaph on Sidney is worthily characteristic of the author. It lacks the emotional warmth of Spenser's praise of Sidney, but it speaks of him nobly, as only one high and soldierly spirit could speak of another. "A king gave thee thy name," says Ralegh; "a kingly mind,—That God thee gave." "Kent thy birthdays, and Oxford held thy youth. . . . "

Whence to sharp wars sweet honour did
   thee call,
Thy country's love, religion, and thy
   friends;
Of worthy men the marks, the lives, and
   ends,

And her defence, for whom we labour all. . . .

What hath he lost that such great grace
hath won?
Young years for endless years, and hope
unsure
Of fortune's gifts for wealth that still shall
dure:
O happy race, with so great praises run![9]

Ralegh's sonnet in praise of Spenser's great poem, which he calls **"A Vision upon this Conceit of The Fairy Queen,"** is (out of hundreds) the most adequate contemporary tribute to that work, and is itself one of the great sonnets of the language:

Methought I saw the grave where Laura lay,
Within that temple where the vestal flame
Was wont to burn: and, passing by that
way,
To see that buried dust of living fame,
Whose tomb fair Love and fairer Virtue kept,
All suddenly I saw the Fairy Queen,
At whose approach the soul of Petrarch
wept;
And from thenceforth those graces were not
seen,
For they this Queen attended; in whose
stead
Oblivion laid him down on Laura's
hearse. . . .   [10]

Evidently (as others have pointed out) Milton was indebted to this sonnet when he wrote the great one which begins, "Methought I saw my late-espoused saint." And it gives one a high pleasure to know, from the other, more personal, sonnet that Ralegh appended to the one from which I have just quoted, that this poet—sometimes so like Donne in voice and thought—appreciated the incomparableness of *The Fairy Queen.* "Of me," says Ralegh to Spenser,

no lines are lov'd, nor letters are of
price,
Of all which speak our English tongue, but
those of thy device.[11]

This is a requital, not altogether insufficient, for the many testimonials which Spenser has left of his gratitude for Ralegh's friendship and his admiration of his genius; for Spenser's dedicatory sonnet to Ralegh, and his inscribing of the important explanatory letter, "expounding his whole intention in the course of" *The Fairy Queen* "to the Right noble, and valorous, Sir Walter Raleigh knight"; for the winning picture of the Shepherd of the Ocean in "Colin Clout's Come Home Again" and the allegorical warning of Clarion in "Muiopotmos"; for the stirring and pathetic scenes in which the squire Timias mirrors the loyal chivalry of Sir

Walter, and finally for the modest and appreciative stanzas, prefatory to the third book of *The Fairy Queen,* in which Spenser praises Ralegh's poetical tribute to Queen Elizabeth at the expense of his own:

How then shall I, Apprentice of the skill,
That whylome in diuinest wits did raine,
Presume so high to stretch mine humble
quill?

. . . . .

But if in liuing colours, and right hew,
Your selfe you couet to see pictured,
Who can it doe more liuely, or more trew,
Then that sweet verse, with Nectar
sprinkeled,
In which a gracious seruant pictured
His *Cynthia,* his heauens fairest light?
That with his melting sweetnesse rauished,
And with the wonder of her beames bright,
My senses lulled are in slomber of delight
But let that same delitious Poet lend
A little leaue vnto a rustick Muse. . . .

Ralegh's **Cynthia,** his one long poem, we do not really possess. It was never printed, and, as Sir Edmund Chambers reminds us, "was already lost by the middle of the seventeenth century." We can only conjecture, as Sir Edmund does: "You can guess at the theme, with its fine central image of the mistress swaying the hopes and fears of the lover, as the moon sways the ebb and flow of the tides. The lover is both shepherd and mariner; the moon now rides remote and inaccessible among the cloud drifts; now descends to hang like a golden lamp upon the treetops as in that serene Latmian night, when Diana came down to sleep with Endymion. We do not know what Ralegh made of it; we should gladly know. Spenser tells us that it was the music of 'the summer's nightingale.'"[12]

All that we do possess is an addendum of 550 lines, which somehow fell into Cecil's fingers and came to light when Hatfield House was gone over. It is not likely that this fragment, composed in profound despair, represents favorably the merits of the earlier work. It is a cloudy and somber performance, but touched with grandeur and deep feeling. The poet now writes "the thoughts of passed times," which

like flames of hell
Kindled afresh within my memory
The many dear achievements that befell
In those prime years and infancy of love
Which to describe were but to die in
writing.[13]

He recalls the thrilling uncertainties of his service of Elizabeth in the days when he set out

To seek new worlds for gold, for praise, for
    glory,
    To try desire, to try love sever'd far.
When I was gone, she sent her memory,
    More strong than were ten thousand ships
    of war.[14]

In words that remember Spenser he describes the
queen's anger:

A queen she was to me, no more Belphebe;
    A lion then, no more a milkwhite dove;
A prisoner in her breast I could not be,
    She did untie the gentle chains of
    love. . . .

It's now an idle labour and a tale
    Told out of time, that dulls the hearer's
    ears,
A merchandise whereof there is no sale.[15]

Mordantly he pictures his present forlorn state:

But as a body violently slain
    Retaineth warmth although the spirit be
    gone,
And by a power in nature moves again,
    Till it be laid below the fatal stone. . . .

So my forsaken heart, my wither'd mind,
    Widow of all the joys it once posses'd,
My hopes clean out of sight, with forced
    wind
    To kingdoms strange, to lands far off,
    address'd,
Alone, forsaken, friendless on the shore,
    With many wounds, with death's cold
    pangs embrac'd,
Writes in the dust, as one that could no
    more,
    Whom love, and time, and fortune, had
    defac'd.[16]

In the following stanzas he seems even to prophesy
the *History of the World* and the circumstances in
which it was written:

As if, when after Phoebus is descended,
    And leaves a light much like the past
    day's dawning,
And, every toil and labour wholly ended,
    Each living creature draweth to his resting,
We should begin by such a parting light
    To write the story of all ages past,
And end the same before th' approaching
    night.[17]

Defiant, volatile, darkly imaginative and jauntily reck-
less, Ralegh as he is manifested in these poems was
indeed a man after Queen Elizabeth's heart. The reasons for the immense fascination he exerted and the
deadly enmities he provoked are equally apparent. His
poems as a whole are radically different from any
others in English literature: they can hardly be forgotten by anyone who reads them. In a sense they are
superficial; they usually show the surface and not the
depths of his personality, but their superficiality is
impressive and oddly sinister. It is the froth that rises
where unplumbed waters break on adamant.

The breadth and depth of Ralegh's genius are best
revealed in his prose, into which he put more of his
heart and soul than went into his brilliant verse—and
which alone he intended for the English nation and for
posterity. The difference is worth repeating; it is the
difference between the bagpipe and the organ. Ralegh
was a daring and accomplished master of both. The
one is dashing, shrill, and provocative; the other of a
sonorous dignity which few English writers have
equaled. One famous sentence of Ralegh's stands in
all good anthologies as the *ne plus ultra* of prose
eloquence, matchable with the best of Sir Thomas
Browne or De Quincey:

O eloquent, just, and mighty Death! whom none
could advise, thou hast persuaded; what none
hath dared, thou hast done; and whom all the
world hath flattered, thou only hast cast out of
the world and despised: thou hast drawn together
all the far-stretched greatness, all the pride,
cruelty, and ambition of man, and covered it all
over with these two narrow words, *Hic jacet!*[18]

This is the rich and solemn melody to which is set
nearly all of Ralegh's formal prose. In his letters we
find often the more superficial fierceness habitual to
the poems. Here, for example, is Elizabeth's discredited wooer, writing from prison in 1592 to Sir Robert
Cecil:

My heart was never broken till this day, that I
heard the Queen goes away so far off,—whom I
have followed so many years with so great love
and desire, in so many journeys, and am now left
behind her, in a dark prison all alone. . . . I that
was wont to behold her riding like Alexander,
hunting like Diana, walking like Venus, the gentle
wind blowing her fair hair about her pure cheeks,
like a nymph; sometime sitting in the shade like a
Goddess; sometime singing like an angel; sometime
playing like Orpheus. Behold the sorrow of this
world! Once amiss hath bereaved me of all.[19]

And here is the practiced and deadly courtier, giving
the *coup de grâce* to his fallen rival, Essex (again to
Cecil, in 1600):

SIR,—I am not wise enough to give you advice,
but if you take it for a good counsel to relent

towards this tyrant, you will repent it when it shall be too late. His malice is fixed and will not evaporate by any your mild courses. For he will ascribe the alteration to her Majesty's pusillanimity and not to your good nature. . . . Lose not your advantage; if you do I read your destiny.[20]

This is Ralegh the opportunist and the realist. It is Ralegh as his enemies saw him at court, the man of whom Coke could venture to say "Thou hast a Spanish heart, and thyself art a spider of Hell."

What the gypsy palmists say of the lines of the two hands might be said of the two sides of Ralegh's work. One shows the spirit with which he was born, and which never ceased to be fundamental in him—a high romantic spirit. The other shows what he made himself when under the influence of courtly feud and self-seeking. The lower voice sounds often in what he wrote on impulse without view to publication. We hear the higher voice when he looks beyond the court and writes consciously for posterity. Prose is then his language, and he speaks a noble tongue. His greatest prose writings—the *History of the World,* the *Discovery of Guiana,* and the *Last Fight of the Revenge*—are splendid monuments of his romantic spirit. They show him to have been a deeply original thinker and moralist, a glorious patriot, and an enthusiastic amateur of the marvels of life.

As a moral philosopher Ralegh is highly impressive. Witness his dignified and subtle reasoning against the contemporary code of the duello—the practice of dueling over the giving of the lie:

> But now for "the lie" itself, as it made the subject of all our deadly quarrels in effect; to it I say that whosoever giveth another man the lie, when it is manifest that he hath lied, doth him no wrong at all; neither ought it to be more heinously taken than to tell him he hath broken any promise which he hath otherwise made. . . . On the other side, he that gives any man the lie, when he himself knows that he, to whom it is given, hath not lied, doth therein give the lie directly to himself. And what cause have I, if I say that the sun shines when it doth shine, and that another fellow tells me I lie for it's midnight, to prosecute such an one to death for making himself a foolish ruffian and a liar in his own knowledge?[21]

The Preface to the *History of the World* contains a praise of history worthy of comparison with Sidney's praise of poetry:

> True it is, that among many other benefits, for which it hath been honored; in this one it triumpheth over all humane knowledge, That it hath given us life in our understanding, since the world itself had life and beginning, even to this day; yea, it hath triumphed over time, which besides it nothing but eternity hath triumphed over: for it hath carried our knowledge over the vast and devouring space of many thousands of years, and given so far and piercing eyes to our mind that we plainly behold living now, as if we had lived then, that great World, *Magni Dei sapiens opus,* the wise work (saith Hermes) of a great God, as it was then, when but new to itself.[22]

With an august eloquence rarely more impressively employed Ralegh points the great moral which he derives from the course of human history: the folly of ruthless ambition, the fallacy of the principle that might makes right.

> For who hath not observed [he asks] what labor, practice, peril, bloodshed, and cruelty the Kings and Princes of the world have undergone, exercised, taken on them, and committed, to make themselves and their issues masters of the world? And yet hath Babylon, Persia, Egypt, Syria, Macedon, Carthage, Rome, and the rest no fruit, flower, grass, nor leaf springing upon the face of the earth of those seeds. No, their very roots and ruines do hardly remain.[23]

In a brilliant survey of English history, he shows how the wages of sin has been death in the cases of Henry I, Edward II, Richard II, Henry IV, Henry VI, Richard III, and finally Henry VIII:

> Now for King Henry the Eight. If all the pictures and patterns of a merciless prince were lost in the world, they might all again be painted to the life out of the story of this king. For how many servants did he advance in haste (but for what virtue no man could suspect), and with the change of his fancy ruined again, no man knowing for what offence? To how many others of more desert gave he abundant flowers from whence to gather honey, and in the end of harvest burnt them in the hive? How many wives did he cut off and cast off, as his fancy and affection changed? How many princes of the blood . . . with a world of others of all degrees . . . did he execute! . . . What laws and wills did he devise, to establish this kingdom in his own issues! using his sharpest weapons to cut off and cut down those branches which sprang from the same root that himself did. And in the end (notwithstanding these his so many irreligious provisions) it pleased God to take away all his own, without increase; though for themselves in their several kinds all princes of eminent virtue.[24]

The *History of the World* is no more food for the rapid reader than John Ruskin's *Modern Painters* is; but one can hardly dip for as much as half an hour into its amber translucences without bringing up an idea or an image that will haunt the imagination. The eleventh section of the first chapter deals with one of the main hinges on which Elizabethan thinking turned: "Of Fate; and that the Stars have great influence: and that their operations may diversely be prevented or furthered."

> And if we cannot deny [so Ralegh reasons] but that God hath given virtues to springs and fountains, to cold earth, to plants and stones, minerals, and to the excremental parts of the basest living creatures, why should we rob the beautiful stars of their working powers? For seeing they are many in number, and of eminent beauty and magnitude, we may not think that in the treasury of His wisdom, who is infinite, there can be wanting (even for every star) a peculiar virtue and operation, as every herb, plant, fruit, and flower adorning the face of the earth hath the like. For as these were not created to beautify the earth alone, and to cover and shadow her dusty face, but otherwise for the use of man and beast, to feed them and cure them; so were not those uncountable glorious bodies set in the firmament to no other end than to adorn it, but for instruments and organs of His divine providence, so far as it hath pleased His just will to determine.[25]

Yet, though the stars above us may in some sense be held to govern our conditions (as Kent says in *Lear*), it is only by working through our own weaknesses; for, says Ralegh, "that either the stars or the sun have any power over the minds of men immediately, it is absurd to think," and "he that contendeth against those enforcements may easily master or resist them."[26] And, as ever, he vitalizes and illumines his conclusion by a daring poetic simile, to the aptness and profundity of which a deep pathos is added when one remembers that the man writing was at the time the king's prisoner.

> Lastly, we ought all to know that God created the stars, as He did the rest of the Universal, whose influences may be called His reserved and unwritten laws. But let us consider how they bind: even as the laws of men do; for although the kings and princes of the world have by their laws decreed that a thief and a murderer shall suffer death; and though their ordinances are daily by judges and magistrates (the stars of kings) executed accordingly, yet these laws do not deprive kings of their natural or religious compassion, or bind them without prerogative to such a severe execution, as that there should be nothing left of liberty to judgment, power, or conscience: the law in his own nature being no other than a deaf tyrant. But seeing that it is otherwise, and that princes (who ought to imitate God in all they can) do sometimes, for causes to themselves known, and by mediation, pardon offences both against others and themselves, it were then impious to take that power and liberty

from God Himself which His substitutes enjoy, God being mercy, goodness, and charity itself.[27]

Ralegh's patriotism was bred in his bone and ripened by his experience. For him it was no personal passion simply. The incomparable superiority of English soldiers and sailors, manners and morals, and government were in his view incontrovertible facts to whose truth he had been witness infinite times on land and sea. The Englishman who did not prefer his own country to all others sinned not merely against duty and right feeling. For Ralegh he stood convicted of brutish stupidity as well. There must be little in English prose which compares for controlled passion with the account which he published in 1591 of the last fight of his cousin, Sir Richard Grenville: *A Report of the Truth of the Fight about the Isles of Azores, this last summer, betwixt the Revenge, one of her Majesties Ships, and an Armada of the King of Spain*.

It would be almost an impertinence to dwell long upon this work. The whirligig of history has given its truth and its sentiment a renewed validity during the present century. Not only is it one of the best examples of patriotic narrative; it is also a masterpiece of farseeing political philosophy. Ralegh's arraignment of what we should now call the spirit of Pan-Hispanianism—of Spanish diplomacy and propaganda, Spanish ambition for world dominion, and Spanish atrocities—said the last word on these subjects in the sixteenth century. Three hundred and twenty-five years later, with a change of adjective which no reader could fail to make, it became again luminous and decisive. . . .

The great task of Elizabethan romanticism was to expand the world in which men live—the world of the senses and the world of the spirit. Imagination and courage are the striking qualities of the four chief leaders of the movement. In these qualities Ralegh was certainly not the least. The fortunes of his life register the rise and decline of the Elizabethan spirit, for of Ralegh is true the precise converse of Macaulay's famous estimate of Bacon: "Whom the wise Queen Elizabeth distrusted and the foolish King James honored and advanced."

Notes

[1] Printed in A. M. C. Latham, *The Poems of Sir Walter Ralegh* (1929), p. 27. The text of Ralegh's poems is peculiarly uncertain. The passages quoted in this essay generally, but not invariably, follow Miss Latham's readings.

[2] "The Disenchantment of the Elizabethans," in *Sir Thomas Wyatt and Some Collected Studies,* 1933.

[3] Latham, *op. cit.,* pp. 45-47.

[4] *Ibid.,* p. 114.

[5] *Ibid.,* p. 64.

[6] *Ibid.,* p. 43.

[7] *Ibid.,* p. 102.

[8] *Ibid.,* p. 40.

[9] *Ibid.,* pp. 32-34.

[10] *Ibid.,* p. 30.

[11] *Ibid.,* p. 31.

[12] Chambers, *op. cit.,* p. 196.

[13] Lines 166-170 (Latham, *op. cit.,* pp. 82, 83).

[14] Lines 61-64.

[15] Lines 327-330, 357-359.

[16] Lines 73-76, 85-92.

[17] Lines 97-103.

[18] *History of the World* (1614), p. 669. This sentence, the last but one in the book, should be read in connection with the paragraph that precedes it.

[19] *Ralegh's Letters,* ed. E. Edwards (1868), p. 51.

[20] *Ibid.,* p. 222.

[21] *History of the World,* p. 468 (Bk. V, Ch. 3, Sec. 17.2).

[22] *Ibid.,* Preface, sig. A2.

[23] *Ibid.,* sig. A2 verso.

[24] *Ibid.,* sig. A4ᵛ, A5.

[25] *Ibid.,* p. 12.

[26] *Ibid.,* p. 13.

[27] *Ibid.,* p. 14.

Ernest A. Strathmann (essay date 1951)

SOURCE: "The Judicious Historian," in *Sir Walter Ralegh: A Study in Elizabethan Skepticism,* Columbia University Press, 1951, pp. 254-75.

[*In the following excerpt, Strathmann examines the considerable fluctuations in Ralegh's reputation dur-*ing his lifetime and on into the twentieth century, focusing on the History *and Ralegh's alleged atheism.*]

> *Informations are often false, records not always true, and notorious actions commonly insufficient to discover the passions which did set them first on foot.* (***History,*** *II, xxi, 6*)

The chronicle of Ralegh's fame and disrepute, in Chapter II, stops with his imprisonment for treason in 1603, although a number of later allusions have been cited for their bearing upon specific problems in the interpretation of his writings. Some further samplings of opinion about him, especially in the century after his death, will be helpful both in concluding this survey of his thought and influence and in evaluating recent theories about his association with a "School of Night." After 1603 popular feeling against him subsided, or perhaps it would be more accurate to say that his unpopularity waned into neglect; and after his death admiration for his achievements outran memories of partisan strife.

I

The change in Ralegh's reputation is epitomized in the contrast between the harsh accusations of the judge who sentenced him in 1603 and the temperate words of his judge in 1618: "Your faith hath heretofore been questioned, but I am satisfied you are a good Christian, for your book, which is an admirable work, doth testify as much."[1] The "damnable fiend of hell, / Mischievous Machiavel" of the early libels is permitted to say, balladwise:

> A Christian true I die:
> Papistry I defy,
> Nor never atheist I
>   as is reported.[2]

The unfair trial in 1603; the loss of oppressive powers which, in their exercise, had made Ralegh hated; his ***History;*** his speech upon the scaffold; the course of events which raised him, the anti-Spanish victim of a Stuart king, to a kind of martyrdom: all tended to soften gossip into legend, bitter conflicts into conflicting evidence. Not that imprisonment and execution killed all enmities: to the day of his death he suffered an opposition ranging from the indifference of a changed Court to active hostility; after his death, his integrity was challenged in the pamphlets of Stukeley and Bacon;[3] and in the next generation his son, Carew, sought to retrieve his losses in name and property.

The importance of the ***History*** in offsetting the old charges of atheism derives from the high esteem in which that work was held in the seventeenth century, when it went through twice as many editions as the collected works of either Spenser or Shakespeare. Naturally enough, Ralegh's exploits at Court and in the field figure prominently in histories and memoirs, sometimes with unfriendly comment; but his fame in the century following his death encompasses all his varied interests and activities without disproportionate emphasis upon his political career. He was credited with a statesman's wisdom; his miscellaneous writings were sought after and frequently published; his name was often invoked in opposition to Spain; even his experiments, and most notably his "cordial," were held in respect for a generation or two. But dominating all, and in a sense including all, was *The History of the World,* with its religious orthodoxy, its moral philosophy, and its frequent digression into commentary on affairs of state. In a book on history which served as a text at Cambridge until the beginning of the eighteenth century, the scholar Diggory Whear[4] praised Ralegh for his "universal history"; the soldier Oliver Cromwell[5] commended the *History* to his son; the churchman Edward Stillingfleet[6] quoted it on the Flood; the antiquary Sir William Dugdale[7] could not "better express or account for" the origin of government "than in the words of Sir Walter Ralegh"; and the philosopher John Locke[8] recommended the work for "general history."

These representative judgments in the seventeenth century are not without parallels in the eighteenth, perhaps with greater emphasis on the style of the *History.* One of the most extravagant encomiums is from the pen of Henry Felton:

> Sir Walter Ralegh's *History of the World* is a work of so vast a compass, such endless variety, that no genius but one adventurous as his own durst have undertaken that great design. I do not apprehend any great difficulty in collecting and commonplacing an universal history from the whole body of historians; that is nothing but mechanic labor. But to digest the several authors in his mind, to take in all their majesty, strength, and beauty, to raise the spirit of meaner historians, and to equal all the excellencies of the best, is Sir Walter's peculiar praise. His style is the most perfect, the happiest, and most beautiful of the age he wrote in; majestic, clear, and manly; and he appears everywhere so superior, rather than unequal, to his subject that the spirit of Rome and Athens seems to be breathed into his work. . . . If he had attempted the history of his own country, or his own times, he would have excelled even Livy and Thucydides; and the annals of Queen Elizabeth by his pen, without diminishing from the serious, judicious Camden, had been the brightest glory of her reign, and would have transmitted his history as the standard of our language even to the present age.[9]

Of the writers before 1650, only King Charles I, in Felton's judgment, is comparable in his style to Sidney, Bilson, Hooker, or Ralegh. Tempering this fulsome praise, Samuel Johnson considers Ralegh's *History* "deservedly celebrated for the labor of his researches and the elegance of his style," but concludes that "he has produced an historical dissertation, but seldom risen to the majesty of history."[10] The opinions of Felton and Johnson must stand here for many. In the course of the eighteenth century, Ralegh's *History* lost the immediacy in content and method that it had for the preceding age, and some pertinent comments reflecting the change have already been cited.[11]

Not even the *History,* thus commended and read, cut off entirely the memory of his reputation as a freethinker. When the provincial inquiry at Cerne Abbas had been long forgotten in the scandals of the court of James I, when even Father Parsons' widely published *Responsio* had been buried under an avalanche of new controversial pamphlets, the tradition of Ralegh's "atheism" remained alive. References to it in the seventeenth century illustrate further the three principal definitions of "atheism" by which I have examined Ralegh's works in Chapters IV to VI. Thus Ralegh's alleged denial of God becomes an instrument to puff a translation of a book written by Leonard Lessius "against atheists and politicians of these days."[12] The translator, A. B., entitles his work *Ralegh His Ghost,* and in prefatory remarks by "The Apparition to His Friend" allows the ghost of Ralegh to reject "a foul and most unjust aspersion upon me for my presumed denial of a Deity," to appeal to his "friend's" recollection of his praise of Lessius, and to call for a translation of this "proof of the being of a Deity." With an unghostly concern for the book trade, the prefatory spirit further charges, "Let the title bear my name, that so the readers may acknowledge it as done by my solicitation." The translator, in his preface to the reader, blandly acknowledges his fiction as a device to attract readers:

> I have feigned the occasion hereof to be an apparition of Sir Walter Ralegh's ghost to a living friend of his, entreating him to translate the same. My reason of using this fiction is because it is well known that Sir Walter was a man of great natural parts, and yet was suspected of the most foul and execrable crime of atheism. How truly, God and himself only know; though I must think the best of him, and the rather in regard of that most excellent and learned description of God which himself setteth down in the first lines of his history or chronicle.

> Now, in regard of his eminency in the world when he was alive, I am the more easily persuaded that the very name of him (by way of this feigned apparition, and the like answerable title of the translation) may beget in many an earnest desire of perusing this book. . . .

The device, says A. B., wrongs no one, not Sir Walter "since I do vindicate and free him from the former blot as presuming him to be innocent of the suspected crime." The Preface, of course, has no independent value, either as a "vindication" of Ralegh or as a confirmation of the old charges. The clumsy trick is worth citing only as an indication of the drawing power of Ralegh's name, of the lingering record of his "atheism," and of the influence of the *History* in countering that tradition.

An association between "atheism" and misconduct is made by an early biographer, John Shirley. Aware of the charges against Ralegh but ignorant of any formal record of them, Shirley seeks an explanation in his hero's misdeeds.

> [Ralegh] was seized with the idle court-disease of love, the unfortunate occasion of the worst action of his whole life. For in the year 1595, I find him under a cloud, banished the court, and his mistress' favor withdrawn, for devirginating a maid of honor. But why for this one action he should lie under the imputation of an atheist, and from a single crime get the denomination of a debauch, is the logic of none but the vulgar.[13]

By this logic, writes Shirley, other favorites—Leicester, Cecil, and Essex—merit the same titles; "neither ever was it accounted any great crime in the orb of courts." A direct connection between Ralegh's alleged offense and his reputation as an atheist is pure guesswork on Shirley's part. What is interesting about his explanation is that he is living in a religious and moral climate enough like that of the Elizabethans to accept wrongdoing as a possible definition of "atheism."

A third allusion to Ralegh's atheism links it with his independence in philosophy. This one, from the pen of Francis Osborne, is also muddled in its facts but clear in intent.

> Sir Walter Ralegh was the first (as I have heard) that ventured to tack about, and sail aloof from the beaten tract of the Schools: who upon the discovery of so apparent an error as a torrid zone intended to proceed in an inquisition after more solid truths, till the mediation of some whose livelihood lay in hammering shrines for this superannuated study possessed Queen Elizabeth that such doctrine was against God no less than her father's honor, whose faith (if he owed any) was grounded upon school-divinity. Whereupon she chid him, who was (by his own confession) ever after branded with the title of an atheist, though a known asserter of God and providence.[14]

Bacon and Selden, Osborne continues, suffered a like imputation. With all its distortions and ambiguities, Osborne's statement contains one significant idea: that Ralegh's "atheism" was somehow associated with his

hostility to scholasticism, a hostility which we have seen in action in the debate with Ironside.

There is little profit in following through the eighteenth and nineteenth centuries the commentary upon Ralegh as a "free-thinker." Two of these later comments, however, are noteworthy as showing how the passage of time had obscured certain Elizabethan concepts. The first, by the philosopher Dugald Stewart writing "Of the Fundamental Laws of Human Belief," concerns the skeptical passage from Ralegh's Preface which I have discussed at length in Chapter VII. The significant point about Stewart's remark is a slip in quotation which transforms Ralegh into a thoroughgoing rationalist.

> It has been observed to me very lately by a learned and ingenious friend, that in one of the phrases which I have proposed to substitute for the *common sense* of Buffier and Reid, I have been anticipated, two hundred years ago, by Sir Walter Ralegh. "Where natural reason hath built anything so strong against itself, as the same reason can hardly assail it, much less batter it down; the same, in every question of nature and infinite [*sic*] power, may be approved for a *fundamental law of human knowledge.*" (Preface to Ralegh's *History of the World.*) The coincidence, in point of *expression*, is not a little curious, but is much less wonderful than the coincidence of the *thought* with the soundest logical conclusions of the eighteenth century. The very eloquent and philosophical passage which immediately follows the above sentence is not less worthy of attention.[15]

Had Ralegh actually written "in every question of nature and *in*finite power" he would have contradicted himself on almost every page of his *History*. For Stewart, of course, this is merely an aside of small consequence to his own work, and he may have taken his quotation at second hand; but the unconscious reversal of Ralegh's meaning highlights the difference in philosophy between the sixteenth century and the Age of Reason. Elsewhere, Stewart approves the linking of the names of Bacon and Ralegh, in terms that are flattering but free from gross error.

> Both of them owed to the force of their own minds their emancipation from the fetters of the school; both were eminently distinguished above their contemporaries by the originality and enlargement of their philosophical views; and both divide, with the venerable Hooker, the glory of exemplifying to their yet unpolished countrymen the richness, variety, and grace which might be lent to the English idiom by the hand of a master.[16]

The second comment, by Matthew Arnold, also bears upon the quality of Ralegh's thought, with no advantage to the Elizabethan. Where Henry Felton had detected the "spirit of Rome and Athens" in the *History* and considered Ralegh, had he but written of his own times, capable of excelling even Livy and Thucydides, Arnold uses the *History* to demonstrate why Thucydides is more "modern" than Ralegh. He compares the two on "the manifestation of a critical spirit, the endeavor after a rational arrangement and appreciation of the facts." Thucydides chooses his subject for its meaningfulness and undertakes to present it in perspective. Here Arnold quotes a few lines from the opening of Ralegh's discussion of the terrestrial paradise, as an example of woolgathering in content and method.

> Which is the ancient here, and which is the modern? Which uses the language of an intelligent man of our own days? which a language wholly obsolete and unfamiliar to us? Which has rational appreciation and control of his facts? which wanders among them helplessly and without a clue? Is it our countryman, or is it the Greek? And the language of Ralegh affords a fair sample of the critical power, of the point of view, possessed by the majority of intelligent men of his day; as the language of Thucydides affords us a fair sample of the critical power of the majority of intelligent men in the age of Pericles.[17]

The passage which Arnold quotes from the *History* serves his purpose well. That it does not represent fully either Ralegh or his book, or that Arnold could have found passages comparable to what he admires in Thucydides, is beside the point. Even allowing for Arnold's strict doctrine on what is "classic," we have here a clear indication that the part of the *History* which was once much admired has become obsolete, something to be dismissed by others than David Hume as "rabbinical learning."

This selection of widely dispersed comments on Ralegh and the quality and independence of his thinking emphasizes the need, if we would understand him, of reading his works in their Elizabethan setting. The judgments of his seventeenth-century readers, even when marked by errors in fact or bias in politics, show at least an understanding of his "language." Later changes in philosophy, religion, and language carry with them inevitable changes in emphasis and construction; in time the reputation for freethought and independence that was once a liability to Ralegh becomes his praise—but with equal dangers of distortion. In most of the biographies down to the late nineteenth century, references to Ralegh's "atheism" are brushed aside, sometimes lightly (as belied by the evidence) and sometimes indignantly. In the studies of the past half century there has been a tendency to accept the Elizabethan charges against him as evidence, at the least, of broad views in religion. The discovery and publication of the testimony at Cerne

Abbas accelerated this trend and led to the elaboration of theories about a "School of Night," to which we must now turn.

II

Arguments for the existence in the sixteenth century of a "School of Night," a coterie interested in esoteric studies, begin with the topical possibilities of Shakespeare's play, *Love's Labour's Lost*. A prime target for banter in that play is the ease with which nobles sworn to intellectual pursuits are distracted by an embassy of fair ladies. To Berowne's description of his lady, "No face is fair that is not full so black," the King replies:

> O paradox, Blacke is the badge of Hell,
> The hue of dungions, and the Schoole of night:
> And beauties crest becomes the heauens well.[18]

About the time of the first performance of *Love's Labour's Lost* appeared George Chapman's *The Shadow of Night* (1594), two abstract and obscure poems exalting the studious, careful approach to learning:

> No pen can anything eternal write
> That is not steeped in humour of the Night.[19]

In a dedication to Matthew Royden, Chapman laments the neglect of learning, with one note of optimism:

> But I stay this spleen when I remember, my good Matthew, how joyfully oftentimes you reported unto me that most ingenious Derby, deep-searching Northumberland, and skill-embracing heir of Hunsdon had most profitably entertained learning in themselves, to the vital warmth of freezing science and to the admirable luster of their true nobility. . . .

Comparing these lines and their contexts, Mr. Arthur Acheson,[20] early in the present century, developed the thesis that *Love's Labour's Lost* and *The Shadow of Night* are antagonistic. Later elaborations of this theory, notably by the editors of the "New Cambridge Shakespeare," make Matthew Royden, the three noblemen praised by Chapman, and Chapman himself the nucleus of the "School of Night," devoted to the serious study of the arts and sciences.[21] The next step is to unite with them the "School of Atheism," charged to Ralegh's leadership by the Jesuit Parsons. Northumberland, mentioned by Chapman, was Ralegh's friend, and, as we have already seen, Harriot and Marlowe have been brought, the latter by inference, into Ralegh's group.[22] The study of astronomy, the philosophical doubt, the air of aloofness and superiority attributed to these men have led to the identification of

Ralegh's "School of Atheism" with the "School of Night" to which Shakespeare presumably refers. Other tenets ascribed to the group are a devotion to art for art's sake, a conviction of the need for deep study to accomplish anything worth while, and an affectation of the vague symbolism of Night and the presiding deity Cynthia. The Elizabethan charge of atheism against them has been variously construed—rarely in its strict modern meaning, more commonly as implying unorthodox opinions and religious liberalism.

Opposed to the "School of Night," according to the theory, is another coterie, in which the chief figures are Shakespeare, his patron Southampton, and his patron's friend, Essex. These gentlemen profess to scorn the laborious nocturnal way of study, and their philosophy is summed up in Berowne's excuses for the sudden renunciation of academic retirement by the King and his three courtiers:

> Never durst poet touch a pen to write,
> Until his ink were temp'red with Love's
>   sighs; . . .
> From women's eyes this doctrine I derive:
> They sparkle still the right Promethean fire;
> They are the books, the arts, the academes,
> That show, contain, and nourish all the
>   world. . . . [23]

Earlier Berowne had objected to the studious retirement in these words:

> Small have continual plodders ever won,
> Save base authority from others' books. [24]

In the opposition of the two groups, say those who argue for the existence of the "School of Night," lies part of the meaning of *Love's Labour's Lost*.

This theorizing has done much to color Ralegh studies, simply by postulating for him an intellectual and temperamental outlook that derives more from his assumed associations than from anything he said or wrote. Some writers have accepted these postulates as established and have based their interpretations upon them. Miss M. C. Bradbrook[25] has used the theory as a convenient point of reference for the discussion of Ralegh, Marlowe, Chapman, and, finally, Shakespeare's satirical allusions. Miss Frances A. Yates,[26] however, broadens the field to find in *Love's Labour's Lost* references to a number of literary rivalries (for example, John Florio and John Eliot, Gabriel Harvey and Thomas Nashe, Shakespeare and Chapman), allusions to the marital difficulties of Ralegh's friend, Northumberland, and even a defense of Sidney's "Stella." . . .

. . . I find little agreement between the doctrines credited to the "School of Night" and the opinions of Ralegh that can be derived from his own speeches or writings. The doctrines of the "School," as variously described by proponents of the theory, imply more radical departures from orthodox religious thought than I have been able to find in Ralegh. He had a driving curiosity, abetted by an impulsiveness of temperament, which led him to seek knowledge where he could find it; but these very qualities make him a poor candidate for a coterie. In his studies he commonly sought practical ends: improved navigation; better ships; a more effective cure-all in physic; success in politics; a stronger empire—and personal power. When he is meditative and speculative, as he often is and in the grand manner, he keeps within the limits of a serious, even somber, ethic and an orthodox religion.

The fundamental difficulty of the "School of Night" theory, of course, goes back to Shakespeare's text. Those who propound the theory find an allusion in *Love's Labour's Lost* and develop to the utmost the topical possibilities of that play, with the result that, as in most studies of Elizabethan topical allusions, identifications abound and conflict. I find no personal allusion in the King's scoffing rejection of Berowne's praise of his "black" lady, and I believe that other evidence for a "School" has been applied too selectively to be convincing. The great value of studies of the "School of Night" has been the light they have thrown upon some literary relationships and theories in the flourishing last decade of the sixteenth century. That value remains even when we abandon attempts to organize these impermanent and often casual associations into formally opposed coteries, and to discover in Shakespeare's play topical allusions of a subtlety one would be surprised to meet in Elizabethan literature.

III

Clearly, three and a half centuries have witnessed wide fluctuations in opinion about Ralegh. He has appeared posthumously in even more roles than he attempted in his tempestuous lifetime, and his reputation has changed as near-contemporaries who shared his intellectual background yielded to writers who judged him by different standards. With such diverse and even flatly contradictory estimates before us, simple caution enjoins a recollection of the premises and major themes of this study before we attempt to draw from it any general conclusions. The most severe limitation upon the available evidence is that we know so little about Ralegh's youth, and the little we know about his early years concerns almost entirely his active, not his contemplative, life. Keeping in mind the problems of evidence set forth in Chapter I, we must be content to base our conclusions on our knowledge of Ralegh in his thirties and of his life thereafter.

In brief, Ralegh's reputation as an "atheist" is traceable in large part to the Catholic polemics against him, especially Parsons' widely circulated attack, and to the casual usage of "atheist" in moral censure. Whatever the cause of the reputation, Ralegh's arrogance and unpopularity did nothing to abate it, although his trial and imprisonment paradoxically won him a reprieve in the court of public opinion. Yet sober accounts of his table talk, by such competent reporters as the Reverend Ralph Ironside and Sir John Harington, in no wise support the charge of "atheism" against him; and his conversations on religious topics, as reported, are consistent with the orthodoxy of his published writings. Only by reading his remarks or his writings out of their Elizabethan setting, or by underestimating the place of natural theology in Elizabethan religious thought, is it possible to discern in Ralegh, so far as we know him, any signs of radical departure from the dominant religious beliefs of his time and country. By finding in his works sober answers to Elizabethan questions designed to ferret out dangerous opinions, and by matching with his statements passages from works of known orthodoxy, I have attempted to restore Raleigh's opinions on religion to their sixteenth-century context. In ethics, as we have seen, it is another story: in action, and to some extent in thought, Ralegh perhaps earned the epithet "Machiavellian," one of the many Elizabethan synonyms for "Atheist." Although his excursions in natural philosophy may have deepened popular distrust of his orthodoxy, where science conflicted with religion Ralegh chose religion, notably in his painstaking attempts to harmonize chronology and Scripture.

The key to Ralegh's skepticism and to its utility is his exception from dogmatic principles of "every question of nature and finite power." If skepticism about the powers of human reason is invoked at all in religious discussion, it is in defense of faith. Ralegh's attack on Aristotelian principles could be construed as heretical only if those principles were wrongly identified (as they were in some minds) with the essentials of Christian belief—what Ralegh sometimes called our "saving faith." As I have suggested, some such misunderstanding may have arisen from the debate with Ironside. But in the realm of second causes Ralegh is indeed a "free" thinker. Once we rid ourselves of the notion that his philosophical skepticism applies to religion, or that his theology is in advance of his time, we can see Ralegh more clearly as an influential worker in a transitional period.

Ralegh's boldest statement of the skeptical position, his attack on the "principles" in the Preface to the *History,* is of ancient lineage. It is possible to trace his ideas, both directly and indirectly, to the skeptics of Greece and Rome, and to distinguish in them a partiality for the Academics, who were willing to reason from probabilities, rather than for the uncompromising position of the Pyrrhonists. Thoroughgoing Pyrrhonism is found only in his fragmentary translation from

Sextus Empiricus and in some sentences of the Preface, there worked into the framework of a philosophy intended to produce results by investigation of second causes. The distinction is significant in its effects: as one historian of philosophy has pointed out, Pyrrhonism strictly and consistently followed was sterile, though it could be the prelude to "freedom of conscience and rational criticism and the absolute right of scientific thought."

> The Skeptics, however, reaped none of the benefits of their own system. They remained, as it were, always on the threshold of possible progress. With the keys to great discoveries in their hands, the doors of philosophical and scientific advancement were for ever closed to them by limitations of their own system. The inherent weakness of Pyrrhonism lay in its psychological inconsistency and its negative character. I think that we may safely say that Pyrrhonism was the most consistent system of Skepticism ever offered to the world, and yet it proves most decidedly that complete Skepticism is psychologically impossible.[36]

From such frustration Ralegh was happily free, both by temperament and by philosophy. It would be an exaggeration to trace his respect for reason and his acceptance of probability directly to the formal philosophy of the Academy; the connection is interesting largely because it places his thought in historical perspective. In practice Ralegh belongs with those men, conspicuous in times of transition, for whom skepticism is a highway, not a dwelling place. Skepticism serves chiefly for the criticism of dogma, and if the criticism is effective the discredited ideas are superseded by new beliefs.[37] In this practical function the popular forms of skepticism are akin to the more strictly defined modes of philosophical criticism.

Hence the importance of such amateurs as Ralegh in the history of ideas. Sir Francis Bacon wrote to his uncle Lord Burghley, in the famous letter of 1592 which takes all knowledge as his province for reform, that he sought a "place of any reasonable countenance" because it "doth bring commandment of more wits than a man's own." By his own high place in the last decades of the sixteenth century, Ralegh secured just this command of other "wits" and exercised the command by patronage of men of science—or worked as a partner through his own studies in natural philosophy and navigation. The universal appeal of his ***History*** extended his "command" posthumously and won for Ralegh a respectful hearing in the seventeenth century.

As I indicated at the beginning of my study, it would be misleading to generalize about an age from the intensive study of one man, however representative he may have been. Professor Lynn Thorndike's observations concerning the careers of Lucilio Vanini and Francesco Sanchez rightly emphasize the subtle gradations of belief and disbelief which may be found in individuals.

> These two cases lend support to the point which we have made more than once: that there is no regular correlation or variation in inverse ratio between theology and science, skepticism and the occult, or science and superstition. In one's man's mind they made one combination: in another, another.[38]

Keeping in mind this salutary caution, we may yet find in the varied passages from other writers cited by way of parallel to Ralegh's remarks some indication of the extent to which his thought is in harmony with that of his contemporaries. He is throughout more a spokesman than an innovator. His moral philosophy and his religion are deeply rooted in the past, and he shows no inclination to uproot the ancient growth, although he is willing to prune some superfluous branches of Biblical exegesis. He shares some of the superstitions and credulities of his age. But in the new world opening before him, literally in the lands across the sea and figuratively in the science of his day, he seeks, with his fellows, the opportunity for free exploration, unhampered by the "fables of principles." Certain beliefs remain inviolate: the truth of Scripture, the primacy of wisdom over knowledge, of goodness over intellect. Ralegh is neither the Elizabethan "atheist" (save perhaps in the broad implications of ethical criticism) nor the freethinker of twentieth-century fame, but a leader in that energetic company who did not find religious faith a barrier to philosophical and scientific speculations. There are many echelons in the progress of human thought: Ralegh's company was not the vanguard, though some seventeenth-century writers assigned him that post; yet it constituted a body of support without which a vanguard is lost in premature action.

Notes

[1] David Jardine, *Criminal Trials,* 2 vols. (London, 1832-35), I, 501.

[2] "Sir Walter Ralegh His Lamentation," from a Huntington Library photostat of the unique original copy in the Pepysian Collection, Magdalene College, Cambridge. In 1918 the ballad was twice reprinted (once with an accompanying reproduction) in connection with the Ralegh Tercentenary Commemoration.

[3] Quoted above, chap. iv.

[4] *De ratione et methodo legendi historias dissertatio* (Oxford, 1625); 1st ed., 1623. In the 1625 edition the praise of Ralegh's *History* is in a marginal note (sig.

F3ʳ). In the expanded 1637 edition, the comment is incorporated in the text (p. 45) and includes praise of Ralegh as well as of his book.

[5] Charles H. Firth, "Sir Walter Raleigh's *History of the World,*" *Proceedings of the British Academy,* VIII (1918), 15.

[6] See above, chap. vi.

[7] *Origines juridiciales,* 3d ed. (1680); quoted by William Oldys, *The British Librarian* (1738), p. 169.

[8] "Some Thoughts Concerning Reading and Study for a Gentleman," *Works,* 9 vols. (London, 1824), II, 409.

[9] *A Dissertation on Reading the Classics and Forming a Just Style,* 2d ed. (London, 1715), pp. 245-48.

[10] *The Rambler,* No. 122, Saturday, May 18, 1751; in *Works,* 16 vols. (New York, 1903), III, 66. Johnson's subject is the difficulty of writing narrative prose and the deficiencies of the British as historians.

[11] See above, chap. vi, "Of the Deluge."

[12] *Ralegh His Ghost. Or a Feigned Apparition of Sir Walter Ralegh to a Friend of His, for the Translating into English the Book of Leonard Lessius (That Most Learned Man) Entitled "De Providentia Numinis et Animi Immortalitate"* . . . Translated by A. B. ([St. Omer], 1631).

[13] *Life,* 8 vo. ed. (London, 1677), pp. 36-37. See above, chap. i, note 1.

[14] *A Miscellany of Sundry Essays, Paradoxes, and Problematical Discourses* (London, 1659), Preface, sig. (a) 2. Quoted in part by J. Beau, "La Religion de Sir Walter Ralegh," *Revue Anglo-Americaine,* XI (1934), 410-22. Ralegh appears as a skeptic in an anecdote (too late in origin to have any value) which illustrates the untrustworthiness of eyewitness accounts. See T. N. Brushfield, *Bibliography of Sir Walter Ralegh* (Exeter, England, 1908), No. 171 and the references there cited.

[15] *Collected Works,* ed. Sir William Hamilton, 11 vols. (Edinburgh, 1854-60), III, 376. Stewart's references to Ralegh have been quoted in part by Macvey Napier, "The Life and Writings of Sir Walter Raleigh," *Edinburgh Review,* CXLIII (1840), 67, 96.

[16] "Dissertation Exhibiting the Progress of Metaphysical, Ethical, and Political Philosophy, Part I," *Works,* ed. Hamilton, I, 78.

[17] "On the Modern Element in Literature," *The New Eclectic Magazine,* V (July, 1869), 54-55. Arnold's

comment on Ralegh has been quoted in part by Charles H. Firth, *op. cit.*

[18] Quoted with the spelling and punctuation of the 1598 Quarto, sig. F2ʳ; IV, iii, 254-56, in the conventional numbering of the lines.

[19] "Hymnus in Noctem," lines 376-77.

[20] *Shakespeare and the Rival Poet* (New York, 1902).

[21] *Love's Labour's Lost,* ed. Sir Arthur Quiller-Couch and John Dover Wilson (Cambridge, 1923), pp. xviii-xxxiv, 97-130, and notes on IV, iii, 250-52. Cf. *Willobie His Avisa,* ed. G. B. Harrison (London, 1926), pp. 181-231; and G. B. Harrison, *An Elizabethan Journal, 1591-1594* (New York, 1929), Appendix I (b), "Topical Allusions."

[22] See above, chap. ii.

[23] IV, iii, 346-53. In this quotation and the next I follow the text of *The Complete Plays and Poems of William Shakespeare,* ed. W. A. Neilson and C. J. Hill (Cambridge, Mass., 1942).

[24] I, i, 86-87.

[25] *The School of Night* (Cambridge, England, 1936).

[26] *A Study of "Love's Labour's Lost"* (Cambridge, England, 1936). . . .

[36] Mary Mills Patrick, *Sextus Empiricus and Greek Scepticism* (Cambridge, England, 1899), pp. 96-97.

[37] *Ibid.*

[38] *A History of Magic and Experimental Science,* VI (New York, 1941), 572.

Philip Edwards (essay date 1953)

SOURCE: "The Renaissance Imagination," in *Sir Walter Ralegh,* Longmans, Green and Co., 1953, pp. 46-71.

[*In the following excerpt, Edwards explains why he considers Raleigh the embodiment of the chief characteristics of the Renaissance, primarily discussing Raleigh's interest in science and the arts and his religious beliefs.*]

We have grown rather shy of using the term 'Renaissance': as we know more, it becomes increasingly hard to say *when* it was or *what* it was. I use the word to define that long period of overlap between the medieval and the modern worlds: a period for which the thirteenth century is hardly too early a beginning or the eighteenth too late a close, when new values, our values, began to contest the old; a period whose commonest quality is tension, in which two ages, one dying and one being born, strive for mastery. The tension is in religion, philosophy, morals, politics, economic and social structure. The peculiar vigour that we recognise in the period in both literature and action derives, perhaps, from this very tension: a safe sleep is impossible when all assumptions and traditions are challenged; either the old ways must be explained and defended or the new ways must be fought for. The period in England when the tension between old and new is at its peak, and most stirred men's minds, is of course, the late Elizabethan and the Stuart period; Shakespeare's tragedies, the growth of nonconformity, *The Advancement of Learning,* the colonising of America, the Civil War and *Paradise Lost,* are all witnesses of the clash of meeting currents.

It is hard to think of any one person who better embodies the various elements, the conflicts and contradictions of old beliefs and new attitudes, who better sums up in himself the inimitable imagination of this period of stress that we call the Renaissance in England, than Sir Walter Ralegh. He is the ideal Renaissance case-history.

The Compleat Gentleman

His very versatility points to the ideal of the age that the courtier or 'compleat gentleman' should strive to fulfil all the functions open to a man, should live with the whole of his being and not just a part of it. It was not enough for a man to be a statesman, or a poet, or an expert in the history of his country, or a soldier; he must try to unite the practical, the active, the artistic, the intellectual ways of living within his own life. In his *Mother Hubberds Tale* Spenser describes the perfect courtier (to fashion whom, he wrote his *Faerie Queene*), who desires to serve his Prince with honour, and can do so

> Whether for armes and warlike amenaunce
> Or else for wise and civill governaunce,

who delights as much in exercising his body as feeding his mind or entertaining himself with music; one for whom there is no greater pleasure than

>   wise discourse
> Of Natures workes, of heavens continuall
>   course,
> Of forreine lands, of people different,
> Of kingdomes change, of divers
>   gouvernment.

That the ideal was more than mere talk is obvious if one thinks of men like Sir Philip Sidney, a pattern of Christian behaviour, a highly skilled poet and critic, interested in the new science, and an example of service to his country in peace and war. That Ralegh was considerably less than a model of Christian behaviour and that he was never officially a statesman, goes without saying. But by his capacity for excellence in so very many spheres, as courtier, soldier, historian, poet, scientist, explorer, administrator, he too is a living example of the belief of his age that a man should develop all his potentialities and realise his whole personality.

He was, first, very closely identified with the intellectual life of his times: he sought knowledge as zealously as he sought position and honour. It was, of course, much easier in his day for a man whose life was largely spent in business and active matters to acquire a real proficiency in all branches of learning because the extent of human knowledge was so much smaller than it is now. Nevertheless, supreme energy was needed to become more than a mere dabbler in the various arts and sciences, and that Ralegh had this energy is clear from the early accounts. 'He was an indefatigable reader, whether by sea or land', said Naunton, and David Lloyd tells us that 'five hours he slept, four he read, two he discoursed, allowing the rest to his business and necessities. . . . So contemplative he was, that you would think he was not active: so active that you would say he was not prudent—a great soldier, and yet an excellent courtier; an accomplished gallant and yet a bookish man.' At his trial, when questioned about his possession of a suspicious writing, by one Snagge, which Cobham had borrowed from his library, he protested that there was no book published in those days, when he was a young man, that he did not buy. In the Tower, he took more true comfort in those prison-companions, his books, 'than ever he took of his courtly companions in his chiefest bravery', according to Sir John Harrington.[1]

Interest in the past was one of the significant intellectual developments of the Renaissance; it is associated with the growth both of science and of nationalism—science, in the sense that man begins to be curious about himself, sees himself as an object for empirical study and begins to question his own development from early times; nationalism, in the sense that a people's awareness of themselves as a nation made them inquisitive about their background. There will be much to say in a later chapter of Ralegh's efforts as an historian. His *History of the World* is one of the major achievements of his life. He gave years to the work, and the patience and pains and thought expended in tackling the many formidable difficulties are not to be made light of. In its time, his *History* was a great and original contribution to the study of man and it still expounds, to an age which has outgrown Ralegh's methods of research, an important philosophy and outlook on life. That this philosophy is largely a medieval philosophy at once

reminds us of the strange blending of the old and the new in this typical Renaissance man.

The new spirit of scientific historical enquiry found expression in England in the formation of the Society of Antiquaries, probably about the year 1580. All too little is known about the Society, but the seriousness of the group can be measured by the terms of their application to the Queen to become formally incorporated as a royal historical society, with a library; this society and library would have a national responsibility for collecting and preserving records and matters of general historical interest. It is not certain whether Ralegh was an official member of this very select group, but he was closely associated with several of its fellows (who included Camden, Lancelot Andrewes, Lambard and Stowe). There exists an interesting letter of Ralegh's, written from the Tower to Sir Robert Cotton, a guiding spirit of the society, giving a list of books and manuscripts relating to British antiquities that Ralegh wished to borrow. John Hooker and Richard Carew were other antiquaries with whom Ralegh was in intimate association.

Ralegh's close connexions with the scientific movements of his day are extremely important, but as they bring up the whole general problem of his intellectual attitude, they must be left for later discussion.

Ralegh's preoccupation with the world of learning can be seen in the delight he had in being surrounded by scholars. His patronage of the mathematician Thomas Harriot brings him as much credit, almost, as anything else in his life. His lieutenant and assistant, Keymis, had been a Fellow of Balliol; his interests extended from the writing of Latin verse to geography and mathematics. One John Talbot shared Ralegh's imprisonment for eleven years and went on the last Guiana expedition with him, to win only a brief epitaph that Ralegh scribbled in his journal: ' . . . my honest friend, an excellent general scholar, and as faithful and true man as lived'.

Turning now to Ralegh's interest in the arts, we find that here he is indeed at the centre of the life of his time. Music and painting he encouraged with his purse, and in poetry there is the wealth that it is a chief part of this book's purpose to discuss. Ralegh was deservedly one of the most admired of the court-poets and, as we should expect, he was in some way associated with three of the four major poets of his time, Spenser, Marlowe and Jonson, as well as lesser figures from an earlier period, like Gascoigne and Churchyard. Ralegh's associations with Shakespeare have naturally been explored by some who have been determined that the exploration should not be unfruitful: but there is no real evidence of any association. . . .

Ralegh's most important poetic fellowships were with those gifted amateurs at court whose work so enriches Elizabethan literature. In Henry VIII's reign, Wyatt and Surrey had set a high standard for court poetry. George Puttenham, in his *Art of English Poesie,* described their successors:

> And in Her Majesty's time that now is, are sprung up another crew of courtly makers, noblemen and gentlemen of Her Majesty's own servants, who have written excellently well, as it would appear if their doings could be found out and made public with the rest, of which number is first that noble gentleman, Edward, Earl of Oxford, Thomas, Lord of Buckhurst (when he was young), Henry Lord Paget, Sir Philip Sidney, Sir Walter Ralegh, Master Edward Dyer, Master Fulke Greville, Gascoigne, Breton, Turberville and a great many other learned gentlemen, whose names I do not omit for envy, but to avoid tediousness, and who have deserved no little commendation.

These courtly poets, as Puttenham's words indicate, gave little thought to publishing their works. Their poems were not written for unknown men who bought books and read them in their scattered homes. They wrote for their own circle in court; poems were passed round in manuscript and then thought of no more. Written for particular occasions and for a particular group, written without an eye to fame among a wide public or among after-generations, this verse is yet often the freshest and finest of the age. Like the popular dramatist, the courtier-poet effaced himself as a personality and took no particular care to prolong the life of his art. Though this attitude is in many ways admirable, it has left a heritage of problems to the modern scholar. Much court-poetry has not survived, and the authorship of what has been (almost by accident) preserved is often very uncertain. A typical perplexity is the difficulty of disentangling the poems of Sir Arthur Gorges (Ralegh's close friend and captain of his flagship in the Islands Voyage) from Ralegh's own.

The extent of Ralegh's verse-writing is very difficult to assess. Much that he wrote has been lost, and no-one can say how much, or whether what we have represents his best work. At every turn there is the problem of authorship: poems which are indisputably Ralegh's are very scarce; works are given to him on the slender evidence of initials in printed anthologies or ascriptions in manuscript collections and commonplace books—or on the dangerous logic of style. There is hardly a poem where the true text can be confidently established: most poems appear in widely different versions in different manuscripts. (Luckily, we have the long poem of **The Ocean to Cynthia** in Ralegh's own handwriting, and here these problems do not arise.)

Aubrey held that Ralegh 'was sometimes a poet: not often', but the sureness of style and discipline of craftsmanship in the majority of poems which are fairly

certainly his would seem to argue that Ralegh was very much more than an occasional versifier. Miss Latham well says that to a man like Ralegh, poetry was 'as natural as breathing'; his first poem which can be dated was written when he was twenty-four, and on the night before his death (so goes the tradition) he composed his own epitaph in verse: all his life, Ralegh was a poet. He was not, of course, a poet in the dedicated sense like the English Romantics, nor was he a man for whom poetry was the only means of expressing his imagination; he was a poet because his age encouraged him, as a courtier and gentleman, to write verse, because the circles in which he moved provided an attentive audience with sensibility like his own, and because his own genius continually found occasions needing the comment of poetry, which his talents could most ably supply.

If, to these wide interests of Ralegh, we add his achievements in so many directions in the world of action, we see how his versatility not only reflects the Renaissance ideal of courtly behaviour, but shows how he shares the life of his age in all its variety.

The Spirit of the Age

It remains to look at Ralegh as the embodiment of his age at deeper levels of the spirit. We may well begin with his intense and individualistic ambition, which is a Renaissance theme if there ever was one. The modern American belief in the virtue and necessity of 'getting to the top' has as its illustrious ancestor the spirit that drove those Elizabethans who were not born to great place and wealth to exercise their whole beings in the colourful attainment of them. Tamburlaine the Great may or may not have been an object of admiration to the Elizabethans, but, as Marlowe presents him, he is certainly the incarnation of an Elizabethan spirit of self-assertion, which the modern world must also recognise as its own. Ralegh possessed this spirit of self-assertion to the full; in a way, his whole life is a record of striving for money, position and power for himself. But immediately we find the Renaissance paradox. **The History of the World** is unceasing in its condemnation of personal ambition, that 'eldest and most monstrous vice', synonymous with Pride, the first of the seven deadly sins. Ralegh's attitude to the struggle of nations shows exactly the same paradox as his attitude to the struggle of individuals: in his writings, he condemns the strife of nations for mastery as mere viciousness and greed, yet in his life he is an ardent nationalist, believing wholeheartedly in the greatness of his nation and the need for England to exalt herself among other nations by crushing her rivals, particularly Spain.

This paradox between words and deeds shows lack of logic and consistency, but no more hypocrisy than the age itself must answer for. For the notion that the unprincipled struggle for power in both nations and individuals was evil, was something the age inherited from the Middle Ages and was very deeply embedded in its thinking. But the world of ideas was lagging behind the world of action. The static medieval age was over; 'progress' had begun, and progress demanded self-assertion. Ralegh seems unaware of the discrepancy between the two ideals, but he reflects the tension of his age in sanctioning in his active career the ambition which he denounced as selfishness and self-aggrandisement when he reflected on it *sub specie aeternatis.*

The age's paradoxes and ambiguities are reflected very clearly in Ralegh's colonial ambitions. What was he trying to achieve? What spirit led him on? There are a dozen answers, cynical or romantic in varying degrees, all perhaps partly true and no one wholly true. Ralegh was out for personal profit and power; he was the instrument of the laws of economic development, ushering in the period of imperialist expansion; he was a symbol of the awakening mind of man, seeking to explore the globe and extend mastery over nature; he was a conscious exponent of nationalism; he was the embodiment of the Elizabethan spirit of adventure. Ralegh himself, as he wrote his **History of the World,** was often perplexed to account for the leading motives of men in bringing about some important action. Had he understood how subtle and tangled his own motives were, and of necessity were, as the spearhead of Elizabethan imperialism, he might have worried less about choosing a single, dominant motive inspiring the behaviour of others.

Atheism and Science

Ralegh's religious views were in his own day, and have remained ever since, the subject of a babel of ill-founded gossip. His 'atheism' was as much a matter of course as his pride, in popular judgment. The Jesuit controversialist, Robert Parsons, made in 1592 the famous attack on Sir Walter Ralegh's 'School of Atheism', 'wherein both Moses and Our Saviour, the Old and New Testament are jested at, and the scholars taught among other things to spell God backward.' In 1594, a commission which met at Cerne Abbas to investigate allegations of godlessness and heretical opinions in Dorset heard alarming stories about Ralegh. The Rev. Nicholas Jeffries had 'heard by report of divers that Sir Walter Ralegh and his retinue are generally suspected of atheism' and had also heard that Harriot had been before the Lords of the Council for denying the resurrection of the body. The minister of Gillingham could not remember who told him, but he had heard that Ralegh's man Harriot had brought the Godhead into question. The curate of Motcombe knew the general report that Ralegh could reason against the omnipotence of God. The Reverend Ralph Ironside had a longer tale to tell, and, what is more, a tale not

based on hearsay, but his evidence must be considered later. In 1603, at his trial, Ralegh was a 'damnable atheist' to Coke, and Popham would not repeat the 'heathenish, blasphemous, atheistical and profane opinions' which the world taxed Ralegh with holding and which Christian ears could not endure to hear.

Well after Ralegh's death, the 'scandal of atheism' still clung to his name. Aubrey had heard the stories, and had come to the conclusion that, rather than an atheist, Ralegh was a non-Christian Deist—a position taught to him by Harriot. In the present century, a new and ingenious story has emerged: the story of the 'School of Night'. According to this, the School of Atheism was a society of satanists, including literary figures, Marlowe, Chapman and Roydon; noblemen, the Earls of Derby and Northumberland; scholars, Harriot, Keymis and Walter Warner. This esoteric society dedicated itself to the arcane and occult in art and science, and its members were distinguished for holding in common very 'advanced' and 'progressive' views on religion and politics. Opposed to it was a group owing allegiance to Essex and Southampton, the spokesman of which was Shakespeare, whose *Love's Labour's Lost* was the group's manifesto and an attack on Ralegh's society. Much has been written about this society,[2] but I have never been persuaded that the 'School of Night' ever existed in reality; the evidence adduced to support the theory has to my mind been convincingly discredited by two American scholars, P. H. Kocher and E. A. Strathmann.[3]

Professor Strathmann has, indeed, earned the gratitude of all interested in Ralegh and the Elizabethan intellectual climate for his very patient and thorough examination of Ralegh's religious views. He is able to show that, however the pregnant and versatile term 'atheist' might have been intended to apply to Ralegh, his expressed opinions everywhere clear him of the charge. Sometimes, of course, 'atheist' is simply used as a term of abuse. Parsons' charges are shown to be part of a Catholic campaign to discredit Elizabeth's counsellors and favourites and to have no value as evidence. If Ralegh *had* been an atheist or a violent heretic or a Deist or a pagan or an agnostic, the whole argument of this chapter would crumble, for he would cease to represent his very religious and orthodox age. But no one who has paid careful attention to Ralegh's own words can have doubt that he was a sincere and fundamentally orthodox Christian.

It is easy enough to see why Ralegh and orthodox religious feeling have never seemed to go together. He was associated with the *avant-garde* of the scientific movement which eventually broke down the medieval Christian attitude of mind and, secondly, his haughtiness of manner, determination to question things, lack of restraint in expressing his opinions, would often obscure from his contemporaries his genuine and profound piety. Let us look at some of the cross-currents in Ralegh's faith, and first, his connexions with science.

Science was still a suspect occupation in Ralegh's day—an impious prying into the secrets of Creation, an arrogant presumption and a seeking for a power that God did not intend man to have. Chapter Eleven of the first book of Ralegh's *History of the World* contains a very interesting and spirited defence of 'lawful magic'; it makes a separation of that knowledge of the secrets of nature which can be considered not only legitimate but laudable, from the black and devilish arts of the Faustian kind: a defence, in fact, of the fundamental piety of proper scientific investigation. 'The third kind of magic,' he says, for example, 'containeth the whole philosophy of nature; not the brabblings of the Aristotelians, but that which bringeth to light the inmost virtues and draweth them out of nature's hidden bosom to human use.' God had given hidden properties to His Creation, and it is a right and necessary endeavour of man to investigate these virtues and apply them for 'the help and comfort of mankind'.

This justification of science as a means of ministering to the needs of mankind is characteristic of the age, and is reminiscent of Francis Bacon's approach. Actually, science was identified in the sixteenth century with practical needs: 'pure' investigation was not very interesting to a man like Ralegh. The union of mathematics and astronomy with the practical needs of navigation is a classic example of how knowledge and its application went hand in hand. John Dee and Thomas Harriot were the greatest of the sixteenth-century scientists in England, and with both of them Ralegh associated for the main purpose of aiding discovery and exploration. Ralegh (and others like him) financed and encouraged these men; the work they did in solving the kind of problems he set them really marks the beginning of the co-operative scientific activity in England that culminated in the founding of the Royal Society at the Restoration. . . . Hakluyt was one who learned from Dee, and he very clearly recognises the association of research with practical needs in his dedication to Ralegh of Peter Martyr's *Decades of the New World* (1587):

> Since you clearly saw that skill in the arts of navigation, the chief glory of an insular nation, would obtain its greatest splendour among us by the firm support of the mathematical sciences, you have trained up and supported now a long time, with a most liberal salary, Thomas Harriot, a young man well versed in those studies, in order that you might acquire in your spare hours by his instruction a knowledge of those noble sciences, and your own numerous sea-captains might unite profitable theory with practice.

Harriot worked with Ralegh in many capacities over a number of years. He was sent to Virginia, and he returned with a very fine account of the country (printed in Hakluyt), his survey ranging from Indian religious customs to the potentialities for agriculture. It is important to understand just what care Ralegh took, as in this instance, to make sure that all his expeditions should be fully scientific explorations. With the men and means at his disposal, he had as much concern in this matter as the organisers of a modern polar expedition have. His own *Discovery of Guiana* is spoken of highly as a 'geographical classic' by the great authority on Tudor geography, Professor E. G. R. Taylor. We have to remember that men whose heads grow beneath their shoulders are but one mistaken report in an account that shows Ralegh's great interest in and capacity for studying 'human' and physical geography. As in *The History of the World,* we cannot fail to be aware of Ralegh's absorption in the awakening sciences of man: in, for example, what we should call ethnography, anthropology and comparative religion.

Shipbuilding may seem a far cry from astronomy, but there is no drawing a hard and fast line between where research ended and its application to voyages of discovery began. . . . Ralegh was noted for his experiments and innovations in shipbuilding, and for the money he spent on them. The *Bark Ralegh,* the *Ark Ralegh* (sold to the Crown in 1592) and the *Roebuck* were famous ships, and Howard, who used the *Ark Ralegh* as his flagship against the Armada called it 'the oddest ship in the world, and the best for all conditions'. . . .

There is no doubt at all that the scientific spirit, which Ralegh certainly shared, proved in the long run incompatible with the Christian modes of thought that inspired St. Augustine and Dante. The expense of time in measuring the phenomena of the visible world seemed a profitless activity to men who considered the purpose of existence to be the union of the soul with its creator. . . . Modern scientific man seeks a different kind of knowledge from medieval religious man, and seeks it by different means. He seeks to know, not God, but the material world, in order that he may have power over the material world; faith, conscience and reason are not his instruments, but observation and experiment. There is a fundamental disagreement of attitude here; there was another disagreement which seems more superficial, but it was almost more important because more obvious: the fact that the results of the new scientific enquiry often seemed to deny the account of the world and human history given in the Bible.

Francis Bacon is perfectly aware that the new directions he wishes human thought to take are incompatible with traditional religious thought, and God holds an equivocal place in *The Advancement of Learning;*

Bacon is not very much interested in knowledge that cannot be proved by experiment and put to the use of relieving man's physical estate. Sir Thomas Browne, on the other hand, is passionately concerned to preserve belief, and struggles hard to reconcile what are often, for him, the opposed teachings of faith and scientific enquiry. In Ralegh's work it is remarkable not to find either Bacon's avoidance or Browne's reconciliation. The core of his belief, which is that of the medieval Christian, is most surprisingly free from the kind of questionings and conflicts that one would have expected in one who did enthusiastically foster the new science. It is not stupidity or intellectual short-sightedness that produces this effect. Ralegh knows he has to make a choice, and traditional thinking is what he chooses. His religious faith is primary with him: God and the word of God are for him mightier things than the questionings of the human mind. Scientific knowledge may be used, as it is in *The History of the World,* to provide confirmation of the truth of the miracles and mysteries of the Christian faith; where human knowledge provides disturbingly different answers from those taught in the Bible and by the Church, it must be rejected, since it is arrogance for man to pit his petty mind against the received word of God. Ralegh does not reject scientific enquiry out of hand any more than he blindly and unquestioningly accepts his faith, but the point that must be made here is that his acquaintance with science has convinced him of the limitations of human knowledge; has taught him not arrogance, but humility. He turns to accept as fundamental a knowledge which he considers to derive from a higher source than the enquiries of the human mind.

. . .

Ralegh's Religion

Ralegh's real devotion and belief in God are clear in every section of his *History*. He is not a theologian, but he expresses with power and often with great beauty the traditional medieval view of God and man that found its last great expression in *Paradise Lost*. How his belief that man exists only for union with God in eternity informs his vision of human history will be discussed in Chapter Four. Here we may comment specifically on his expression of the Renaissance tradition of Christian humanism.

Belief in the existence of God, holds Ralegh, is a reasonable thing, even if faith did not teach us. 'As all the rivers in the world, though they have divers risings and divers runnings, though they sometimes hide themselves for a while underground and seem to be lost in sea-like lakes, do at last find and fall into the great ocean; so after all the searches that human capacity hath, and after all philosophical contemplation and curiosity, in the necessity of this Infinite Power, all the reason of man ends and dissolves itself.' But reason is only 'the beginning of knowledge', or it can

only confirm what comes from a higher source. Nothing is more mistaken than to perpetuate, as some scholars do, Aubrey's error that Ralegh was a Deist. The nature and purpose of God can only be known in so far as they are revealed through Christ, and though this revelation is everywhere reasonable, 'they grow mad with reason' who endeavour to pursue their inquisition into the essence of God by their own efforts. 'But by his own Word, and by this visible world, is God perceived of men.'

That there is no knowledge of God or of the purpose of life save what is revealed in Scripture, but that the knowledge so gained is not antagonistic to 'natural' thinking, but is indeed everywhere acclaimed and assented to by man's reason, is a typical Christian humanist position—a position which enabled the humanists to fortify the scriptures by the teachings of the pagan writers of ancient Greece and Rome. But we must watch the two uses of the word 'reason'. As I have been using or quoting it, it means 'reasoning power'. But there is also the humanistic 'right reason', which Professor Douglas Bush describes as not an instrument of inquiry, or simply the religious conscience, but 'a kind of rational and philosophic conscience which distinguishes man from the beasts and links man with man and with God'. It is implanted in man to enable him to perceive the law of God. So Ralegh uses the term 'reason' in his discourse on laws (*History of the World,* Book II, Ch. 4) which leans heavily on Augustine and Aquinas. 'To love God, by whom we are, and to do the same right unto all men which we desire should be done unto us, is an effect of the purest reason, in whose highest turrets the quiet of conscience hath made her resting-place and habitation.' Worship of God is human and natural and reasonable; man is made able to receive the knowledge of the law of God. This is the essence of Ralegh's acceptance of Christian humanism. 'As the north-star is the most fixed director of the seaman to his desired port, so is the law of God the guide and conductor of all in general to the haven of eternal life.'

Ralegh accepts without question the fall of man: that God created man for eternal life in union with Himself, that He granted him reason, to be able to know Him and love Him, and free-will to be able to love Him willingly; that man denied the dictate of his reason, disobeyed God and rejected union. But God of His mercy left the light of right reason burning within man, to be attended to by those with eyes to see and ears to hear, and granted the possibility of salvation even to those who had erred and disobeyed. Almost any chapter of the *History* could be quoted to show how Ralegh believes that the fall of man is continually repeated, that man will sin and deny God in setting before himself objectives in this world which deny the fundamental truth that man is formed only for eternal life. Ralegh is constantly persuading man to reject the magnets of the world and to seek God again. Book I, Chapter Two contains this passage, for example:

> Though nature, according to common understanding, have made us capable by the power of reason, and apt enough, to receive this image of God's goodness which the sensual souls of beasts cannot perceive, yet were that aptitude natural more inclinable to follow and embrace the false and dureless pleasures of this stage-play world than to become the shadow of God, by walking after him; had not the exceeding workmanship of God's wisdom and the liberality of his mercy formed eyes to our souls as to our bodies, which, piercing through the impurity of our flesh, behold the highest heavens, and thence bring Knowledge and Object to the mind and soul, to contemplate the ever-during glory and termless joy prepared for those which retain the image and similitude of their Creator, preserving undefiled and unrent the garment of the new man, which after the image of God is created in righteousness and holiness, as saith St Paul.

It is a strange misreading of Ralegh to suppose that he could believe in God as he did, and believe in the possibility of salvation, without accepting the fact of the Incarnation and the redemption of man through Christ. It is perfectly true that there is little debate in Ralegh's writings on the mystery of the Atonement. He seems to have a temperamental reluctance to explore the doctrine. But to accept a doctrine is not necessarily to dwell upon it. Christ is everywhere 'our Saviour'; there are many specific and devout references to redemption, and even where these are absent, his references to salvation *must* imply Christian doctrine. Most telling of all are his recorded utterances just before his death: Ralegh was not a man for death-bed repentances or one who would avow beliefs he did not hold in order to placate priests. The Dean of Westminster, who attended him in prison, was perfectly satisfied by his speaking 'very Christianly'. Ralegh received the Eucharist on the morning of his execution, and is reported to have said on the scaffold: 'I die in the faith professed by the Church of England. I hope to be saved and have my sins washed away by the precious blood and merits of our saviour Christ.'

Thus the man who stands at the threshold of the modern world in his enthusiasm for the discoveries of modern science and their application can still hold fast to the faith that, though it was central in the formulated beliefs of his age, was rapidly ceasing to be a reality in the lives of men. The conflict between the concept of the world as a divine harmony, the happiness of man depending on his aspiring to play his part in that harmony, and the concept of the world as a material entity to be measured and controlled by man, is the fundamental conflict of the Renaissance. Had Ralegh lived 50 years later he would not have been able to tuck science into a predominantly religious world-view so conveniently as he does; perhaps, like Milton, he would have had to reject scientific inquiry altogether.

Another way of expressing the Renaissance conflict is to say that it is a conflict between the notion of man as dependent on God and the notion of man as self-sufficient. In these terms we can see how Ralegh manages to find room in himself for both sides of the conflict at almost every turn. Religion and science, humility and pride, desire for wealth and contempt for the world, these can coexist within him as they coexisted in his age. Just as he touches Elizabethan life at every point, so he owns all its contradictions. Active and meditative, tolerant and intolerant, bellicose and pacific, romantic and cynical, humane and cruel, Ralegh *is* the Elizabethan world.

Notes

[1] In the extremely interesting notebook recently identified as Ralegh's by Mr. W. F. Oakeshott (see *The Times*, 29 November 1952, and below, pp. 101 and 147), Ralegh has set about making a catalogue of books. They may well be those he had with him in the Tower; most of them would be useful to an historian. The general books range from 'A treatis of specters' to "Opera Petrarchæ', 'Cassanion de gigantibus' to 'Essays French', 'Laurentius præservation of health' to 'Cardanus de subtilitate'; Copernicus, Machiavelli, Pico della Mirandola, Hakluyt and Camden are represented.

[2] e.g. M. C. Bradbrook, *The School of Night* (1936).

[3] *Christopher Marlowe* (1946), pp. 7-18; *Sir Walter Ralegh: A Study of Elizabethan Scepticism* (1951), pp. 262-271.

Works Cited

Ernest A. Strathmann, *Sir Walter Ralegh, a Study in Elizabethan Skepticism* (1951). . . .

R. W. Battenhouse, *Marlowe's Tamburlaine* (1941) (see pp. 50-68).

G. T. Buckley, *Atheism in the English Renaissance* (1932).

G. B. Harrison (editor), *Willobie his Avisa* (1594) (1926).

F. R. Johnson, *Astronomical Thought in Renaissance England* (1937).

F. R. Johnson, 'Gresham College: Precursor of the Royal Society', *Journal of the History of Ideas*, i (1940).

P. H. Kocher, *Christopher Marlowe* (1946).

E. G. R. Taylor, *Tudor Geography, 1485-1583* (1930) and *Late Tudor and Early Stuart Geography, 1583-1650* (1934).

I. A. Shapiro, 'The Mermaid Club', *Modern Language Review*, xlv (January 1950); see also P. Simpson, *ibid.,* xlvi (January 1951).

Peter Ure (essay date 1960)

SOURCE: "The Poetry of Sir Walter Ralegh," in *A Review of English Literature*, Vol. 1, No. 3, July, 1960, pp. 19-29.

[*In the following essay, Ure contrasts Raleigh's poetry with that of Spenser and emphasizes that, as both a literary artist and man, Raleigh left an ambiguous impression.*]

When Sir Walter Ralegh paid a visit to Edmund Spenser in the autumn of 1589, a few months after Spenser had acquired his castle and estate near Cork, he was a man who had already created his own legend. He was perhaps the most brilliant figure at the brilliant court, hated and courted for his pride and power, already a sea-captain, an empire-builder, and an Irish landowner. Spenser has left us an idealised account of their poetical intercourse in *Colin Clouts Come Home Again*. They read each other's poems. Spenser had the first three books of *The Faerie Queene* to show, and Ralegh had a portion of a long poem which he was writing in praise of Queen Elizabeth. The two poets travelled back to England together across Ralegh's domain, the wide wilderness of waters that was the Shepherd of Ocean's element. But in little over a year Spenser was back at Kilcolman, having lost many illusions about his aptitude for court-favour; and Ralegh's career, in the many years that remained to him, was to take on an increasingly ghastly aspect until the shameful moment, twenty-eight years later, when King James cut off his head to please the Spanish Ambassador.

The episode at Spenser's Irish castle and its poetical interludes are perhaps the pleasantest glimpses we have of Ralegh, although the scarlet thread of his political ambition runs through even that. It would be easy to draw false inferences from the episode. Both men were old acquaintances, both were conscious proponents of the English Protestant Renaissance; both were engaged on ambitious poems dedicated to and in large measure about their sovereign, and both were hoping by such means to advance their fortunes in the state. Yet, if we set their poetry side by side, what strikes us is not the likeness but the difference. Ralegh must have been as fully aware as anybody else alive in his time that he

was living in the Age of Spenser. But he was not a Spenserian. It is not simply that *The Faerie Queene* demands a lifetime's study, while you can, if you wish, read through all Ralegh's poems in an afternoon—there are not more than forty in the canon, and all of them, except for the five hundred lines of *Cynthia* (his poem to the Queen, or, rather, what survives of it), are quite short. The differences go deeper than that.

Writing poems to and about the court and the Queen is often the compositional centre in the work of both men. But Spenser, although he touched the fringes of preferment and hoped to enjoy more of it, writes essentially as an outsider. Because of this, he was able to see the brilliant and perilous working of power as a whole. In *The Faerie Queene* he was able to convey a sense of the court as only a part of the nation, a sense of the existence of the nation itself. When he addresses the Queen, the tone is distant, humble and yet proud. He is the inspired Bard of England speaking to England's Sovereign, and both are servants of something greater than themselves. 'Queen of Love', 'Prince of Peace', he calls her, 'Great lady of the greatest isle':

> Dread Soverayne Goddesse, that doest
> highest sit
>   In seate of judgement, in th'Almightie's
>   stead,
>   And with magnificke might and wondrous
>   wit
>   Doest to thy people righteous doome
>   aread,
>   That furthest Nations filles with awfull
>   dread . . .[1]

But the court is Ralegh's own ground, and, when it proves to be a quicksand, the poems that reject it have a note of personal feeling which is not present when Spenser writes of his retirement from it. Ralegh's note can be one of savage disassociation—his own world has betrayed him and that is hard to bear—as in the obsessive rhythms and brutal anaphora of **'The Lie'**:

> Say to the Court it glowes
>   and shines like rotten wood,
> Say to the Church it showes
>   whats good, and doth no good.
> If Church and Court reply,
>   then give them both the lie.
>
> Tell men of high condition,
>   that mannage the estate,
> Their purpose is ambition,
>   their practise onely hate:
> And if they once reply,
>   then give them all the lie.

This theme of the rejection of the court is a traditional one. It is used by Sidney in his 'Disprayse of the Courtly Life', and many poems on the subject will be found in *Tottel's Miscellany* and the other anthologies that preceded the work of the major Elizabethan poets. But in **'The Lie'** it has a personal force that is a long way from a merely theoretical contempt of the world epitomized by the court. And what is savagery in this poem can be transformed in Ralegh's other poems into a throbbing clamour of personal regret and sadness of spirit, as though Ralegh could not see further than his own disappointments. We know from his prose-writings that in actuality he could see much further. As a man, he had as keen a sense of the nation and of the world beyond it as Spenser; but he keeps all that out of his poems. Therefore his great poem of disappointment, the five hundred lines of **Cynthia**, Ralegh's counterpart to *The Faerie Queene,* is a very private poem. When Ralegh addressed his sovereign, the convention which he adopted is quite different from the one employed by Spenser. Spenser plays the role of the vassal-bard, Ralegh that of the rejected lover. The analogy between the courtier out of favour and the dismissed lover is pressed home until it becomes a sharp lament over a waste land and a wasted life:

> From fruitfull trees I gather withred leaves
> And glean the broken eares with misers
>   hands,
> Who sometyme did injoy the waighty
>   sheaves
> I seeke faire floures amidd the brinish sand.

The praise of Elizabeth with which the poem is charged has this personal note too. Of the two ways in which Elizabethan poets were most accustomed to celebrate the Queen, as a sovereign divinity or as a virtuous mistress, Ralegh naturally chose the latter. It is what we would expect of an insider. Spenser himself made the point in the induction to the third book of *The Faerie Queene.* There he tells the Queen that, with his humble quill, he is only writing at a distance from her living colours; if she wishes to see herself rightly pictured in her true beauty, let her turn to Ralegh.

Ralegh's own compliment to Spenser is also interesting. It occurs in the form of a sonnet printed in 1590 in commendation of the first three Books of *The Faerie Queene.* But it is interesting not so much because it conveys Ralegh's opinion of that great work as because of its own magnificence. It is one of the best of Ralegh's poems, and one of the greatest of Elizabethan sonnets:

> Methought I saw the grave, where *Laura*
>   lay,
> Within that Temple, where the vestall flame
> Was wont to burne, and passing by that
> way,
> To see that buried dust of living fame,
> Whose tombe faire love, and fairer vertue
>   kept,
> All suddeinly I saw the Faery Queene:
> At whose approch the soule of *Petrarke*
>   wept,
> And from thenceforth those graces were not
>   seene.
> For they this Queene attended, in whose
>   steed
> Oblivion laid him downe on *Lauras* herse:
> Hereat the hardest stones were seene to
>   bleed,
> And grones of buried ghostes the hevens
>   did perse.
>   Where *Homers* spright did tremble all for
>   griefe,
>   And curst th' accesse of that celestiall
>   theife.

In some ways, this sonnet might be by a contemporary of Wyatt and Surrey; in others, it belongs very much to the era of Sidney and Shakespeare. Ralegh has taken the ancient *topos* of the great new poet outdistancing and outshining the classical giants. For its time, its diction is a little old-fashioned—the *groaning ghosts* and *bleeding stones* take us back to *Tottel's Miscellany*. But, on the other hand, the ordering of the sentences, the wonderful planning of the sonnet as a whole (a feature on which Sir Edmund Chambers remarked) are signs of the new flowering of poetry in the 1580's and 1590's. Yet, magnificent though the sonnet is, it is also puzzling. It celebrates the appearance of a great new work of art, yet it has a tragic rather than a joyous air. Jonson, who used the same *topos* when he praised Shakespeare in the First Folio, was able to impart an air of jollity, of bell-ringing, fireworks, and water-music to the occasion. That is much nearer the note we expect when a theme of this kind is handled. Ralegh's welcome to Spenser is, by contrast, very dark. He seems more moved to pity by the fate of the displaced poets than pleased because a new one has outclassed them. His sonnet is constructed so that all the force of feeling gathers into the sestet, on Petrarch's weeping soul, and on 'Oblivion laid him down on *Lauras* herse': a magnificent conceit, but too grim and ghastly for the occasion, as though Michelangelo's 'Night' had suddenly been glimpsed at the heart of the revel. And by the two concluding lines we are irresistibly reminded of that grand thief Satan climbing up into God's fold in the third Book of *Paradise Lost*. Indeed, it has long seemed likely that Milton did borrow from this sonnet when he wrote his own sonnet 'Methought I saw my late espoused saint'; but Milton's sonnet is concerned with his vision of his dead wife, and the tragic tone is fitting.

There is, therefore, a faint air of miscalculation about Ralegh's poem, of emotion in excess of its object, of a man being more serious than he really intends to be. It is probably foolish to suggest that there was something in the commonplace of the displaced poet that went too near to Ralegh's heart. For displaced poet did he too easily read displaced courtier? However this may be, it is true that the tragic note, the note of fear and betrayal, which seems to make such an indecorous intrusion on this gay occasion, is recurrent in Ralegh's extant verse. We can observe this tone—one might almost call it an obsession—at work in such a poem as **'Nature that washt her hands in milke'**. In this poem it has the effect of producing a new, sombre, and fearful poem out of the old shell of what was originally a gay and pretty one. The poetic toy suddenly turns into a weeping funeral verse, and we see the skull beneath the skin. Ralegh describes in the first stanzas how nature took snow and silk at love's behest and made from them a fair but heartless girl. With that pretty fancy, such as it is, the poem might well have seemed complete. But then Time comes on the scene:

> But Time which nature doth despise,
>   And rudely gives her love the lye,
> Makes hope a foole, and sorrow wise,
>   His hands doth neither wash, nor dry,
> But being made of steele and rust,
> Turnes snow, and silke, and milke to dust.
>
> The Light, the Belly, lipps and breath,
>   He dimms, discolours, and destroyes,
> With those he feedes, but fills not death,
>   Which sometimes were the foode of
>   Joyes;
> Yea Time doth dull each lively witt,
> And dryes all wantonnes with it.
>
> Oh cruell Time which takes in trust
>   Our youth, our Joyes and all we have,
> And payes us but with age and dust,
>   Who in the darke and silent grave
> When we have wandred all our wayes
> Shutts up the story of our dayes.

There is no question here of emotion in excess of the object, or inappropriate to it, and we have come a long way from Spenser. Spenser was often plangent about the ruins of Time, but he had none of this shrinking horror, and for him, in the end, Time itself was only an aspect of revolving change.

It is tempting, indeed, to take these stanzas as an index of Ralegh's modernity as compared with Spenser's antiquity. Was Spenser unable to sound this note because of his share in the large-eyed innocence of an earlier, golden world; because he was a man who died before the Elizabethan adventure ran aground in the

shallows of Jacobean disappointment and anti-climax? In these three stanzas, it might be argued, there is reflected the true voice of Jacobean feeling, of Hamlet by the graveside, of Vindice and the poisoned skull in *The Revenger's Tragedy*, all that melancholy and malcontentism which is supposed to have invaded literature at the turn of the century. **'Nature that washt her hands in milke'** could be used as a handy symbol of the transition from Elizabethan to Jacobean, the delicate art of its first portion and the disgusted disrelish of the second straddling the two worlds of *The Faerie Queene* and *Hamlet*. Other evidence for Ralegh's transitional status could be brought into court in the form of his most celebrated poem, the **'Nymph's Reply to the Shepherd'** (if it is indeed by Ralegh— we have only Izaak Walton's word for it). Christopher Marlowe's song, to which Ralegh's poem is an answer, 'Come live with me and be my love', is the perfection of pastoral innocence, of uncorrupted and uncourtly pleasure. The reply said to have been devised by Ralegh is another of his savage reminders of mutability, an utter refusal to dream:

> Thy gownes, thy shoes, thy beds of Roses,
> Thy cap, thy kirtle, and thy posies,
> Soone breake, soone wither, soone
>   forgotten:
> In follie ripe, in reason rotten.

Here, perhaps, Jacobean disillusion deliberately flouts the Elizabethan hope.

Yet the argument would be a very weak one. What we are listening to, in the last three stanzas of **'Nature that washt her hands in milke'** or in the **'Nymph's Reply',** is not Jacobean disaccord. It is an altogether older note: an echo of the sententious mournfulness of the 1570's. The anthologies of that period, which are the chief repositories of such verse as has survived from the earlier years of Elizabeth Tudor, are full of poems which contemplate the ghastliness of the grave, the swiftness of time's passage, or the vanity of youthful love. 'My youthfull partes be played', they never tire of saying, 'And I must learne to die':[2]

> To earth the stout, the prowd, the ritch
>   shall yeeld,
> The weake, the meeke, the poore, shall
>   shrowded lye
> In dampish mould, the stout with Speare
>   and Sheeld
> Cannot defend himselfe when hee shall dye.[3]

Or:

> Hope for no immortalitie, for welth will
>   weare away,
> As we may learne by every yeare, yea
>   howres of every day . . .

The rage of stormes done make all colde
    which somer had made so warm
Wherefore let no man put his trust in that
    that will decay,
For slipper welth will not continue, pleasure
    will weare away.
For when that we have lost our lyfe, & lye
    under a stone,
What are we then, we are but earth, then is
    our pleasure gon.[4]

Spenser, too, can write like this, but it is not what we chiefly remember about him. He moved away from gazing at the ruins of Time, finding the Heavenly Jerusalem more interesting. Another glance at the contrast between Ralegh and Spenser will strengthen the argument that Ralegh is more affected by post-medieval melancholy than by Jacobean disillusion. It is a true generalisation about Spenser to say that he is one of the great pioneers of the rich, splendid, and decorated style, despite his many qualities of sageness and sobriety. Ralegh, although he, too, has touches of gold, mainly practises the plainer style, the sententiousness and lack of adornment characteristic of Spenser's predecessors. The contrasting ways in which each poet mourned in verse the death of their mutual friend, the great Sir Philip Sidney, illustrate this. Spenser adopts the creamy elegance of the pastoral guise; Sidney becomes Astrophel the shepherd boy:

For he could pipe and daunce and caroll
    sweet,
Emongst the shepheards in their shearing
    feast:
As Somers larke that with her song doth
    greet
The dawning day forth comming from the
    East.
And layes of love he also could compose,
Thrise happie she, whom he to praise did
    chose.[5]

Untimely slain while hunting the boar, like Adonis, Astrophel too is transformed into a flower. Spenser marries Ovidian legend with Christian fancy, for in another part of the poem the dead soldier's soul lies in paradise on beds of lilies, roses, and violets, 'like a newborne babe'. This is Spenser's way.

Ralegh's is very different. Critics have noticed how each stanza of his sixty-line poem on the death of Sidney reads like something carved on stone. The lines are plain, stern, lapidary. They use their big, uncompromising words without concealment or reservation, words such as *virtue* or *honour,* names such as *England* or *Flanders*; it is not Astrophel who is being laid to rest but 'the right Honorable Sir Philip Sidney, Knight, Lord Governor of Flushing':

Backe to the campe, by thee that day was
    brought,
First thine owne death, and after thy long
    fame;
Teares to the soldiers, the proud Castilians
    shame;
Vertue exprest, and honor truly taught.

What hath he lost, that such great grace
    hath woon,
Yong yeeres, for endles yeeres, and hope
    unsure
Of fortunes gifts, for wealth that still shall
    dure,
Oh happie race with so great praises run.

England doth hold thy lims that bred the
    same,
Flaunders thy valure where it last was tried,
The Campe thy sorrow where thy bodie
    died,
Thy friends, thy want; the world, thy
    vertues fame.

This note of marble gravity is common enough in Ralegh's extant poetry for it to be safely regarded as characteristic of him. We meet it again, for example, in **'The Advice',** a strange poem, ostensibly a warning to a virgin to beware of those who would betray her. But it resembles the sonnet to Spenser in its excess of strength and tragic sound. It is almost as though half the poet's mind was on power, not love; on the betrayed statesman as much as on the betrayed girl. This ambiguity is characteristic of Ralegh, and ambiguities of one kind or another must torment every judgement of Ralegh's poetry as of his personality.

The ambiguities, indeed, deserve the final emphasis. Ralegh's greatest poem is **'The Passionate Man's Pilgrimage supposed to be written by one at the point of death'.** It is his greatest poem, but his least characteristic. So uncharacteristic is it that his authorship of it has often been questioned, although it has as good authority for being admitted to the canon as many others. Much of what has been said here about Ralegh is denied by this poem. **'The Passionate Man's Pilgrimage'** is a vision of death and judgement, but it is not one of a stern or mournful kind. The heaven that the poet imagines is a florid and baroque place of nectar fountains and milky hills, diamond ceilings and bowers of pearl. As well as its wealth of golden imagery, it is charged with a combination of humble joy and metaphysical wit which is found nowhere else in Ralegh. Its vision of the judgement of the soul marvellously combines the continued witty image with the heartfelt prayer. It speaks of

heavens bribeless hall
Where no corrupted voices brall,

No Conscience molten into gold,
Nor forg'd accusers bought and sold,
No cause deferd, nor vaine spent Journey,
For there Christ is the Kings Atturney:
Who pleades for all without degrees,
And he hath Angells, but no fees.

When the grand twelve million Jury
Of our sinnes and sinfull fury,
Gainst our soules blacke verdicts give,
Christ pleads his death, and then we live,
Be thou my speaker taintless pleader,
Unblotted Lawer, true proceeder,
Thou movest salvation even for almes:
Not with a bribed Lawyers palmes.

If this is Ralegh, it is a Ralegh whom Spenser never knew. And by a strange irony, it is a Spenserian Ralegh, which turns upside down the usual contrast between the two poets. In this poem Ralegh draws close to Spenser in his vision of heaven (which resembles the Red Cross Knight's vision of the Heavenly Jerusalem in the first Book of *The Faerie Queene*) and in the *allegoria* of the soul-as-pilgrim, which is emblematised in the Spenserian manner.

To consider Ralegh's poetry, therefore, is to conclude upon an enigma. He was thoroughly enigmatic to his contemporaries, and since his death he has had a dozen incompatible reputations. The Shepherd of Ocean who piped so pleasantly to Spenser in his dark little Irish tower was to Sir Edward Coke a damnable atheist, a traitor with a Spanish heart.

Ralegh doth time bestride,
He sits 'twixt wind and tide,
Yet up hill he cannot ride
For all his bloody pride.
He seeks taxes in the tin,
He polls the poor to the skin,
Yet he swears 'tis no sin.
   Lord, for thy pity![6]

The mischievous Machiavel of the anonymous rhyme-ster[7] was the same man as the liberal historian and champion of liberty devoutly admired by the seventeenth-century parliamentarians. The grotesque lover whom Shakespeare may have caricatured him as in the person of Don Armado in *Love's Labour's Lost* is the paragon of Elizabethan gallantry who used to figure in the school history-books. But one reputation is increasingly firm: he ranks ever better amongst the minor poets of his time and was lucky in his muse, if in nothing else.

Notes

[1] *Faerie Queene*, V. Prologue, II.

[2] H. E. Rollins ed. *A Gorgeous Gallery of Gallant*

Inventions (1578), (Cambridge, Mass.), 1926, p. 44.

[3] *Ibid.*, p. 99.

[4] H. E. Rollins, ed. *Tottel's Miscellany* (1557-8), (Cambridge, Mass.), 1928, I, 153

[5] *Astrophel*, ll. 31-6.

[6] Quoted E. Thompson, *Sir Walter Ralegh*, 1955, p. 151.

[7] *Poetical Miscellanies*, ed. Halliwell (Percy Society, 1845), pp. 13-14.

Stephen J. Greenblatt (essay date 1973)

SOURCE: "Ralegh and the Dramatic Sense of Life," in *Sir Walter Ralegh: The Renaissance Man and His Roles*, Yale University Press, 1973, pp. 22-56.

[*In the following excerpt, Greenblatt traces the origins of Raleigh's histrionic conception of himself and of his surroundings, a worldview that, according to the critic, manifested itself in Raleigh's writings in both deeply pessimistic and highly optimistic appraisals of humankind's ability to control their destiny.*]

What is our life? A play of passion

At his execution, as at other crucial moments of his life, Ralegh displayed the talents of a great actor. Again and again we see him performing a brilliant part in what he called "this stage-play world" [*History of the World*, London, 1614 (hereafter referred to as *H.W.*), II, ii, 2, p. 27], reciting his splendid lines, twisting facts for dramatic effect, passionately justifying his actions, and transforming personal crises into the universal struggle of *virtù* and *fortuna*. Emotions are exaggerated, alternatives are sharpened, moods are dramatized. Ralegh's letters, like his actions, reveal a man for whom self-dramatization was a primary response to crisis:

I only desire thatt I may be stayd no on[e] houre from all the extremetye that ether lawe or presedent can avowe. And, if that be to[o] litle, would God it weare withall concluded that I might feed the lions, as I go by, to save labor. [Edward Edwards, *The Life of Sir Walter Ralegh . . . Together with His Letters*, London, 1868 (hereafter referred to as *Letters*), p. 54]

I am sure, if I weare a Turke I could not be worss dealt withall then I am by them, who have dun nothinge for Her Majesties sake butt rackt mee yeven asunder. [*Letters*, p. 97]

[A]nd yeven so, only gasing [gazing] for a wynde

to carrye mee to my destiny, I humblie take my leve. [*Letters*, p. 107]

[Y]our Majesty havinge left mee, I am left all alone in the worlde, and am sorry that ever I was att all. [*Letters*, p. 259]

Name, bloud, gentillety or estate, I have none; no, not so mich as a beeing; no, not so mich as *vita plantae*. I have only a penetent sowle, in a body of iron, which moveth towards the loadstone of Death. [*Letters*, p. 296]

For my own tyme, good my Lord, consider that it cannot be calde a life, but only misery drawn out and spoone into a long thride, without all hope of other end then Death shall provide for mee; who, without the healp of kings or frinds, will deliver mee out of prison. [*Letters*, p. 313][1]

The letters display an intense histrionic sensibility constantly striving for a moving presentation of the self. Even at their most personal and emotional, there is little that seems to reach back into the tangled inner world of the suffering individual: the reader is asked to pity and to admire, but not to inquire too deeply. Ralegh's letters are miniature stages on which to perform, spaces to be filled with grand—usually tragic—gestures. There are moments of inadvertent comedy and self-parody: "So I leve to trouble yow at this time, being become like a fish cast on dry land, gasping for breath, with lame leggs and lamer loonges" (*Letters*, p. 51). But at their best, the self-dramatizations have none of this clumsy and anxious groping after effect. Rather, they take simple words and images and infuse them with unexpected power. Perhaps the finest of such moments occurs in what Ralegh thought would be his farewell to his wife, the letter he wrote on the eve of his expected execution in 1603:

I cannot wright much. God knowes howe hardlie I stole this tyme, when all sleep; and it is tyme to separate my thoughts from the world. Begg my dead body, which living was denyed you; and either lay itt att Sherborne if the land continue, or in Exiter church, by my father and mother. I can wright noe more. Tyme and Death call me awaye. [*Letters*, p. 287][2]

The final words seem to place us for a moment at the close of a morality play where the hero, severed from the world and all of its concerns, is at last literally called away by Time and Death.

At times, Ralegh succumbs to the dangers of the histrionic sensibility: self-indulgence, self-pity, posturing. For example, when the aging queen discovered his secret marriage and imprisoned him in the Tower, Ralegh sent an account of his sorrows to Robert Cecil in the hope that Cecil would show it to the queen. The excuse for this effusion is the "bills for the Gards' coats, which are to be made now for the Prograsse":

My heart was never broken till this day, that I hear the Queen goes away so far of[f],—whom I have followed so many years with so great love and desire, in so many journeys, and am now left behind her, in a dark prison all alone. While she was yet nire at hand, that I might hear of her once in two or three dayes, my sorrows were the less: but even now my heart is cast into the depth of all misery. I that was wont to behold her riding like *Alexander*, hunting like *Diana*, walking like *Venus*, the gentle wind blowing her fair hair about her pure cheeks, like a nymph; sometime siting in the shade like a Goddess; sometime singing like an angell; sometime playing like *Orpheus*. Behold the sorrow of this world! Once amiss, hath bereaved me of all. O Glory, that only shineth in misfortune, what is becum of thy assurance? All wounds have skares, but that of fantasie; all affections their relenting, but that of womankind. Who is the judge of friendship, but adversity? or when is grace witnessed, but in offences? There were no divinety, but by reason of compassion; for revenges are brutish and mortall. All those times past,—the loves, the sythes, the sorrows, the desires, can they not way down one frail misfortune? Cannot one dropp of gall be hidden in so great heaps of sweetness? I may then conclude, *Spes et fortuna, valete*. She is gone, in whom I trusted, and of me hath not one thought of mercy, nor any respect of that that was. Do with me now, therefore, what you list. I am more weary of life then they are desirous I should perish; which if it had been for her, as it is by her, I had been too happily born. [*Letters*, pp. 51-52]

The anguish is genuine enough, for the imprisonment of 1592 had shaken Ralegh to the core, but the voice is false. The letter unintentionally calls attention to exactly what it should conceal: the distance between role and reality, the passionate lover and the calculating courtier, the elusive nymph and the spinsterish queen. As a failure of the histrionic sensibility, it evokes those epithets—"exhibitionist," "stagey," "melodramatic," "theatrical," etc.—which embody the age-old prejudice against the theater.[3] The problem, however, is not theatricalism itself, but the clumsiness of these particular gestures and the inappropriateness of this particular stage. In Ralegh's poetry of the period, the same emotions receive more convincing expression:

My boddy in the walls captived
Feels not the wounds of spigh*t*ful envy,
Butt my thralde mind, of liberty deprived,
Fast fettered in her auntient memory,
Douth nought beholde butt sorrowes diinge face;
Such prison earst was so delightfull
As it desirde no other dwellinge place,

Bu*tt* tymes effects, and destin*ies* dispightfull
Have changed both my keeper and my fare,
Loves fire, and bewt*ies* light I then had
    store,
Butt now close keipt, as captives wounted
    are,
That food, that heat, that light I finde no
    more,
    Dyspaire bolts up my dores, and I alone
    Speake to dead walls, butt thos heare not
        my mone.[4]

The feelings here are those expressed in the letter, but the uneasiness, the confusion, and the falseness have fallen away. In the letter, Ralegh had tried to use the language and cadence of lyric poetry and had sounded forced and insincere. Now, in lyric poetry itself, he found a coherent and effective dramatic role. The courtly lovers of scores of poems from the time of Wyatt and Surrey had expressed exactly the tangle of emotions, the love, despair, and resentment, which Ralegh was trying to convey.

This correspondence between life and art was not accidental. In his relationship with the middle-aged queen, Ralegh had cast himself in the part of a passionate lover pursuing a remote and beautiful lady. That fantasy was all but shattered by the queen's discovery of the secret marriage. Imprisoned in the Tower, Ralegh attempted to recreate the poetic illusion, now as the faithful lover cruelly mistreated by his mistress. In his sonnet, role and reality, the literary type and the actual situation, spill over into each other. The woman in whose "auntient memory" the poet is imprisoned has actually put him in prison. The poem enables Ralegh to reenter the realm from which his disgrace had driven him, that zone at the boundary of fiction and truth in which he chose to exist.[5]

Ralegh's adoption of the conventional *persona* of a rejected lover in "My boddy in the walls captived" corresponds to the self-dramatization in his letters and the role-playing in actual scenes of his life. He seems to have had what I should like to call a "dramatic sense of life": a histrionic life-style and, with this, a consciousness of the universe and of the self shaped in theatrical terms. It is not surprising that for Ralegh, as for so many of his contemporaries, the theater was a central metaphor for man's life:[6]

What is our life? a play of passion.
Our mirth the musicke of division,
Our mothers wombes the tyring houses be,
Where we are drest for this short Comedy,
Heaven the Judicious sharpe spectator is,
That sits and markes still who doth act
    amisse,
Our graves that hide us from the searching

Sun,
Are like drawne curtaynes when the play is
    done,
Thus march we playing to our latest rest,
Onely we dye in earnest, that's no Jest.
            [Poems, pp. 51-52][7]

Ralegh's epigram, probably written during his thirteen-year imprisonment in the Tower, weaves back and forth between a sense of the triviality of life and a feeling of anxiety in the face of death and God's judgment. Man's actions have no more dignity or permanence than the hollow gestures of an actor, yet they will be judged severely by a searching critic. . . .

For Ralegh, life is a brief, uneasy comedy, while death is the only reality. He confronts this somber thought with a kind of jauntiness and courage, but beneath the wit of the epigram there lurks the bitterness of Macbeth's image of man as a poor player who struts and frets his hour upon the stage and then is heard no more.

Ralegh uses the play metaphor again and again in his works, almost always with undertones of disillusionment. Birth is merely the player's entrance onto the tawdry stage; rank and title are but a false show of power like a player's costume; man's vaunted freedom is no more than the illusory spontaneity of an actor, reciting the lines assigned to him. Like Shakespeare, Ralegh sees Richard III as the epitome of the actor in history:

> To *Edward* the fourth succeeded *Richard* the Third, the greatest Maister in mischeife of all that fore-went him: who although, for the necessity of his Tragedie, hee had more parts to play, and more to performe in his owne person, then all the rest; yet hee so well fitted every affection that playd with him, as if each of them had but acted his owne interest. [*H. W.,* Preface, sig. A4ᵛ]

Two distinct notions of "playing" are at work here in the figure of Richard. On the one hand, there is the subtle and treacherous Richard, playing a great variety of roles that both mask and further his villainy. The evil king so cunningly manipulates the fears and ambitions of men like Hastings and Buckingham ("so well fitted every affection") that they become mere instruments of his own designs, extensions of his own will to power ("as if each of them had but acted his owne interest"). But set against this kind of playing is the notion of Richard and his accomplices as unwitting actors in a tragedy. All of Richard's schemes were ultimately "for the necessity of his Tragedie"; Richard used those "that playd with him." He could dissemble brilliantly, but he never understood that he was an actor in a play not of his own making, and appropriately his fate was to become "a spectacle":

And what successe had *Richard* himselfe after all these mischefes and Murders, policies, and counter-policies to Christian religion: and after such time, as with a most mercilesse hand hee had pressed out the breath of his Nephews and Naturall Lords; other than the prosperity of so short a life, as it tooke end, ere himselfe could well looke over and discerne it? the great outcrie of innocent bloud, obtayning at GODS hands the effusion of his; who became a spectacle of shame and dishonor, both to his friends and enem[ie]s. [*H. W.,* Pref., sig. B1ʳ]

The whole course of English (and European) history as Ralegh presents it in the Preface to **The History of the World** shows this pattern of the false presumption of men and the "secret and unsearchable judgment" of God (*H.W.,* Pref., sig. A3ᵛ). Those who have the most confidence in their power to shape their destiny are always brought the lowest:

Oh by what plots, by what forswearings, betrayings, oppressions, imprisonments, tortures, poysonings, and under what reasons of State, and politique subteltie, have these forenamed Kings, both strangers, and of our owne Nation, pulled the vengeance of GOD upon themselves, upon theirs and upon their prudent ministers! [*H.W.,* Pref., sig. C2ʳ]

There are a very few wise men who strive to make themselves the willing instruments of God's plan, and thereby attain a measure of happiness, but they too come to dust in the end. The proper attitude toward this "stage-play world," Ralegh suggests, is a bitter resignation to the vicissitudes of fortune and a harsh contempt for man's pretensions to greatness:

For seeing God, who is the Author of all our tragedies, hath written out for us, and appointed us all the parts we are to play: and hath not, in their distribution, beene partiall to the most mighty Princes of the world; That gave unto *Darius* the part of the greatest Emperour, and the part of the most miserable begger, a begger beginning water of an Enemie, to quench the great drought of death; That appointed *Bajazet* to play the *Grand Signior* of the *Turkes* in the morning, and in the same day the *footstoole* of *Tamerlane* . . . : why should other men, who are but [as] the least wormes, complaine of wrongs? Certainly there is no other account to be made of this ridiculous world, than to resolve, That the change of fortune on the great Theater, is but as the change of garments on the lesse. For when on the one and the other, every man weares but his owne skin; the Players are all alike. . . . For seeing Death, in the end of the Play, takes from all whatsoever Fortune or Force takes from any one: it were a foolish madnes in the shipwracke of worldly things, where all sinks but the Sorrow, to save it. [*H.W.,* Pref., sigs. DIᵛ - D2ʳ][9]

Two rather different attitudes are mingled in this pessimistic vision of the world as stage. One evokes the tragic figures of history, men who had experienced what Marlowe's Tamburlaine calls the "sweet fruition of an earthly crown" only to lose everything; the other likens such stupendous changes of fortune to an actor's change of costume. One looks to God, "the author of all our tragedies," who shows us by the spectacle of the misfortune of mighty princes the insignificance of our own troubles; the other looks to Death, the great leveler, who shows us the miserable quality of all mortal beings in the shipwreck of worldly things. One sees life as a tragedy; the other as a bitter comedy. Finally, one sees man as a tragic hero; the other as a miserable player tricked out, like Shakespeare's great rebel York in *3 Henry VI,* with a paper crown.

This ambivalent vision of life and the play metaphor by which it is expressed are rooted in medieval thought. John of Salisbury, the learned and influential bishop of Chartres, entitles a chapter of the *Policraticus* (1159), "De mundana comedia, vel tragedia." Comedy or tragedy—it does not really matter which term is used provided we agree that all the world's a stage:

[T]he end of all things is tragic, or if the name of comedy be preferred I offer no objection, provided that we are agreed that, as Petronius remarks, almost all the world is playing a part. . . . It is surprising how nearly coextensive with the world is the stage on which this endless, marvelous, incomparable tragedy, or if you will comedy, can be played; its area is in fact that of the whole world.[10]

Like Ralegh, John of Salisbury points to sudden and violent changes of fortune in the lives of the great to show that all the men and women are merely players:

The different periods of time take on the character of shifts of scene. The individuals become subordinate to the acts as the play of mocking fortune unfolds itself in them; for what else can it be that invests at one moment some unknown upstart with wide flung power and raises him to a throne and again hurls another born to the purple from his imperial height down into chains, dooms him to captivity, and casts him forth into extreme misery? Or, and this is his usual fate, stains the blades of ignoble men or even vile slaves with the blood not merely of rulers but of princes.[11]

But the bishop of Chartres finds consolation for the human condition in contemplation of a merciful and loving God and in trust that Paradise awaits the just man beyond the grave.[12] For Ralegh, there is no such consolation; his God is stern, the heavens are "high, far-off, and unsearchable" (*H.W.,* Pref., sig. C2ᵛ), and death is an undiscovered country from whose bourn no traveler returns.

Deep pessimism, linked with the dramatic sense of life, is central to *The History of the World* and to much of Ralegh's poetry as well. The play metaphor was a conventional vehicle for such pessimism. It had been used for centuries to suggest the limitations of man's life on earth, its transience, its unreality, its lack of freedom, the instability of its greatness. Yet, paradoxically, the actual effects of the dramatic sense in Ralegh's life seem bound up with an intense optimism about the possibilities of human achievement and a belief in man's power to control his destiny. In the final scenes of his life, for example, Ralegh's role-playing (when it was not simply, like the feigned illness, a device to gain time) was an assertion of human dignity. At a moment when circumstances conspired to reduce him to total impotence, his theatrical self-possession acted out the integrity and even the freedom of the individual. And, of course, this is only the extreme example. At those other moments of his life when we most sense the histrionic sensibility, as in the assault on Cadiz, the 1603 treason trial, and the two voyages to Guiana, Ralegh's theatrical heroism similarly affirmed the power of the human will over fortune.

The dramatic sense of life as self-affirmation and the vision of life as no more real than a play may both be traced ultimately to the writings of the Stoics. Seneca, for example, following Epictetus, at once exposes the vanity of human greatness—

> None of those whom you behold clad in purple is happy, any more than one of those actors upon whom the play bestows a sceptre and a cloak while on the stage; they strut their hour before a crowded house, with swelling port and buskined foot; but when once they make their exit the foot-gear is removed and they return to their proper stature—

and asserts the necessity of performing well in whatever part you have been assigned—

> It is with life as it is with a play—it matters not how long the action is spun out, but how good the acting is.[13]

In Ralegh's life and art, however, one finds not the realization of a single tradition but a struggle between opposing forces. On the one hand, the play metaphor as an image of life's limitations reaches back to medieval theologians like John of Salisbury, to Fathers of the Church like St. John Chrysostom and St. Augustine, and to a diverse array of classical authors. Behind all of these is most probably the Book of Job with its dark picture of human fortunes manipulated and marked by God.[14] Ralegh's self-assertive theatricality, on the other hand, has its intellectual origins in those Renaissance writers who saw in man's mimetic ability a

token of his power to transform nature and fashion his own identity. The belief in this power, which goes far beyond anything conceived by the Stoics, had a profound effect upon Ralegh. . . .

Behind Ralegh's dramatic sense of life, I have suggested, were two contradictory traditions, one that likened life to a play to express the emptiness and unreality of man's earthbound existence, the other that saw in playing an image of man's power to fashion the self. A major source of the fascination and complexity of Ralegh's career is that neither of these deeply antagonistic views of human nature and destiny could gain a decisive ascendancy; indeed, they needed and fed upon one another. At one moment Ralegh writes of the vanity of mortal endeavors in this stage-play world, at the next he is sailing to Guiana to discover El Dorado and found an empire; at one moment he likens man to a player to suggest the hollowness of human existence, at the next he deliberately plays a part to affirm human dignity. And in several extraordinary instances during his long career—in *Ocean to Cynthia,* in *The History of the World,* and in the final scenes of his life—both traditions seem inseparably bound up in the same words and actions.

To understand the complex relation between these two traditions and, still more, to grasp their simultaneous expression, we must consider another manifestation of the dramatic sense of life in late sixteenth- and early seventeenth-century England, the theater itself. Elizabethan public theaters like the Globe were, by a symbolism inherent in their very structure, models of the world. As scholars have observed, they represented emblematically the hierarchical order of the universe, as conceived by late-medieval thought.[33] Still more significant, I suggest, is their *ambivalence* as emblems. They may imply that life is no more real than a play, that "the great globe itself" will dissolve like their own wood and plaster and leave not a rack behind. But they may also point to the immense, godlike power of human creativity which can range through all the elements and fashion wonderful images of the universe. For certain optimistic humanists, the capacity to create a mirror of nature, a model of the world, is almost equivalent to the Creation itself. Thus Marsilio Ficino shows boundless admiration for the model-making power displayed in Archimedes' spheres of brass:

> Since man has observed the order of the heavens, when they move, whither they proceed and with what measures, and what they produce, who could deny that man possesses as it were almost the same genius as the Author of the heavens? And who could deny that man could somehow also make the heavens, could he only obtain the instruments and the heavenly material, since even now he makes them, though of a different material, but still with a very similar order?[34]

Ficino relates this creative genius in man to his power of self-transformation. Like Pico and Vives, whom he strongly influenced, he celebrates the soul as a kind of supreme actor capable of playing all parts: "Does not the soul try to become everything just as God is everything?"

The implied connection between such models—emblems of man's power to understand and control his world—and the theater was often made explicit in the Renaissance. According to Thomas Heywood, for example, in the "little compass" of Caesar's theater "were comprehended the perfect modell of the firmament, the whole frame of the heavens, with all grounds of Astronomicall conjecture."[35] Likewise, an imaginary stage described in the "English Wagner Book" of 1594 manages to squeeze within its limits practically the whole universe: the firmament above, "often spotted with golden teares which men callen Stars," "the whole Imperiall Army of the faire heavenly inhabitaunts," the king's high throne, a splendid castle, a battlefield, even a hell-mouth.[36]

The theater then is a vivid and powerful model of heaven, earth, and hell, including all the creatures who inhabit these regions, a model more admirable and complex even than Archimedes' spheres. It may retain its ageold suggestions of human emptiness, it may represent a static, closed world-order, but at the same time it may be both symbol and proof of those qualities which make man "a great miracle, a living creature worthy of reverence and adoration."[37]

The dramatists of the age—and, as we might expect, Shakespeare above all—made full use of the ambivalence of the theater and of the dramatic sense of life. In Hamlet's famous description of his melancholy state, for example, the play metaphor evokes precisely those contradictory poles of belief which we have seen at work in Ralegh:

> I have of late—but wherefore I know not—lost all my mirth, forgone all custom of exercises; and indeed, it goes so heavily with my disposition that this goodly frame, the earth, seems to me a sterile promontory; this most excellent canopy, the air, look you, this brave o'er hanging firmament, this majestical roof fretted with golden fire—why, it appeareth no other thing to me than a foul and pestilent congregation of vapors. What a piece of work is a man! how noble in reason! how infinite in faculties! in form and moving how express and admirable! in action how like an angel! in apprehension how like a god! the beauty of the world, the paragon of animals! And yet to me what is this quintessence of dust? [II, ii, 307-22]

The terms Hamlet uses for the world are also technical terms for the various parts of the theater.[38] "Goodly frame," "most excellent canopy," "majestical roof"—

the theater is the symbol for all that is splendid and reassuring in the universe, just as the power of acting helps to define the greatness of man. But at the same time the theater darkly suggests the illusory quality of life, the element of artifice and feigning, the final insubstantiality of an existence which ends in dust.

We get even closer to Ralegh's special kind of theatricalism in *Othello*, so close indeed that it is worth pausing to examine the way the idea of man as actor is explored in the play. Iago is the epitome of the actor as hypocrite and dissembler. As he tells Roderigo, he is one of those

> Who, trimm'd in forms and visages of duty,
> Keep yet their hearts attending on
>   themselves;
> And, throwing but shows of service on their
>   lords,
> Do well thrive by them, and when they have
>   lin'd their coats,
> Do themselves homage. . . .
>
> Heaven is my judge, not I for love and
>   duty,
> But seeming so, for my peculiar end;
> For when my outward action doth
>   demonstrate
> The native act and figure of my heart
> In compliment extern, 'tis not long after
> But I will wear my heart upon my sleeve
> For daws to peck at. I am not what I am.
>   [I, i, 50-54, 59-65]

"Forms," "visages," "shows," "seeming," "outward," "extern"—this is the language of the man who has adopted a role in order to hide his true identity. But in Iago's final phrase Shakespeare contrives to suggest a disturbing meaning that somehow goes beyond the contrast of role and reality. We expect Iago to say "I am not what I seem," asserting at least a hidden identity, but his actual words imply a sinister and terrifying emptiness, an absence of being that is outside the pale of human logic and experience. They are a cosmic negation, a mockery of God's words to Moses at the burning bush: "I AM THAT I AM" (Exodus 3 : 14).

"Acting" in the Iago sense leads to a terrible, almost unthinkable annihilation of being. Each time Iago lowers his voice to speak in soliloquy or in confidence to Roderigo, we expect the mask to be stripped away for a moment and the true face, however hideous, to show forth. But always we are disappointed. One mask is removed to reveal what is patently only another mask beneath it. At the end, when the deception has been exposed and the role can no longer be played, Iago ceases to have any human identity at all—he becomes a creature without words, voluntarily abjuring that which distinguishes man from beasts:

Demand me nothing. What you know, you
know.
From this time forth I never will speak word.

[V, ii, 303-04]

Set against Iago, of course, is Desdemona, who is, by
total contrast, all being, the embodiment of pure love
and beauty. There is in Desdemona no hint of the
theatrical, of self-dramatization. Instead, she is characterized by a wonderful, simple frankness:

That I did love the Moor to live with him,
My downright violence, and storm of
fortunes,
May trumpet to the world.

[I, iii, 249-51]

This simplicity is not only an assertion of all that Iago
seeks to negate, but, in its absence of theatricality, a
contrast to Othello's romantic self-dramatization:

Othello. It gives me wonder great as my
content
To see you here before me. O my soul's
joy!
If after every tempest come such calms,
May the winds blow till they have
waken'd death!
And let the labouring bark climb hills of
seas
Olympus-high, and duck again as low
As hell's from heaven! If it were now to
die,
'Twere now to be most happy; for I fear
My soul hath her content so absolute
That not another comfort like to this
Succeeds in unknown fate.

Desdemona.   The
heavens forbid
But that our loves and comforts should
increase
Even as our days do grow!

[II, i, 185-97]

Othello stands between Iago and Desdemona; he is
neither a hypocrite nor a man of radical simplicity, but
an actor in the more complex and subtle sense of
which we have spoken. He is an alien who, by his
valor and energy, has carved out a role in a hostile
world, and he has a powerful sense of the identity he
has fashioned. His is by no means the self-consciousness of a Hamlet—of all Shakespeare's tragic heroes,
Othello is the least aware of the complexities of his
own character—but rather a feeling for his role and a
mastery of self-manifestation. Almost his first words
recall his services to the Signiory which have earned
for him his place in Venice. When Iago counsels him

to hide from Desdemona's angry father, Othello replies with a full and serene awareness of himself and
the part he must play:

Not I. I must be found.
My parts, my title, and my perfect soul
Shall manifest me rightly.

[I, ii, 30-32]

The sense of role becomes even clearer when Othello
grandly prevents a fight between his followers and
those of Brabantio:

Were it my cue to fight, I should have
known it
Without a prompter.

[I, ii, 83-84]

And we hear the Othello voice, rich with a sense of
its own dignity, in his acceptance of the commission
to fight the Turks:

The tyrant Custom, most grave senators,
Hath made the flinty and steel couch of war
My thrice-driven bed of down. I do agnize
A natural and prompt alacrity
I find in hardness; and do undertake
These present wars against the Ottomites.

[I, iii, 230-35]

Here is that phenomenon we have had occasion to
note in Ralegh: the full commitment of the self to a
role which is yet recognizable as a role. . . .

As in *Othello,* so in many of his plays Shakespeare
explores what happens when a man's identity, fashioned by himself or by society, or most commonly by
both together, is stripped away, discarded, or rendered useless. He was fascinated, it appears, by characters—Richard II, Brutus, Lear, Coriolanus, Othello,
Timon—who seem to have a deep sense of self as
role-player and who, consequently, suffer most terribly when these roles—king, noble Roman, hero, patron—are shattered. The pressures that led Castiglione
and Machiavelli to create the ideal courtier and the
perfect prince as models of the artificial self are profoundly felt in Shakespeare's plays. But where the
former sought in their works to teach men to relieve
those pressures by fashioning the self as a work of
art, Shakespeare constantly looks face to face at un-
accommodated man, stripped of all his roles.

If man's greatness and dignity are deeply allied to his
power to commit himself to a role and thereby transform his own nature, the villainy of Iago, the dissembler, the man totally without commitment, is the ultimate villainy. As they were intrigued by those who
were wedded to their roles, Shakespeare and his con-

temporaries were also fascinated, frightened, and repelled by the cold players, the clever manipulators of
the self as mask and the world as stage prop. In their
fundamental hollowness, in the disintegration and annihilation of the self which inevitably results from their
hypocrisy, these characters are the negation of the
optimistic vision of man as actor. Iago's terrible refusal to speak, Richard III's nightmare vision of his
murderous self-hatred, the Jew of Malta's inability to
free himself from the habit of dissembling and treachery even when he has triumphed over all his enemies,
Flamineo's death "in a mist"—these are images of
human emptiness which reflect the darkest aspect of
the dramatic sense of life.

At work in the Elizabethan and Jacobean theater was
the same dialectic that manifested itself so powerfully
in Ralegh's life and writings. Indeed, the theater of the
age, like *The Courtier* and *The Prince,* most probably
contributed indirectly to the development of his dramatic sensibility. But there was a more direct contemporary source. At the very heart of Ralegh's society,
at the symbolic center of England and quite literally at
the center of power and glory, there was a figure who
perfectly embodied the idea of the individual as an
actor totally and irreversibly committed to a role: Elizabeth I. The English court was truly, in Ralegh's
phrase, "the great theater," with the queen as playwright, director, and leading performer. Both by temperament and intellect she understood, as no one before or since, the latent drama in kingship and exploited it to the fullest. "We princes," she told a deputation
of Lords and Commons in 1586, "are set on stages in
the sight and view of all the world duly observed."[39]

The queen's power was linked in a quite technical
sense with the assumption of a fictional role: her reign
witnessed the first major elaboration of the mystical
legal fiction of "the King's Two Bodies." When she
ascended the throne, according to the crown lawyers,
her very being was altered; in her mortal "Body natural" was incarnated the immortal and infallible "Body
politic." Her body of flesh would age and die, but the
body politic, as Plowden wrote, "is not subject to
Passions as the other is, nor to Death, for as to this
Body the King never dies." Her visible being was a
hieroglyphic of the timeless corporate being with its
absolute perfection, just as, in Coke's phrase, "a king's
crown was a hieroglyphic of the laws."[40] She was a
living emblem of the immutable within Time, a fiction
of permanence.

Even without this elaborate doctrine, of course, kingship always involves fictions, theatricalism, and even
mystification. The notion of "the King's Two Bodies"
may, however, have heightened Elizabeth's conscious
sense of her identity as at least in part a *persona ficta*
and of her world as a theater. She believed deeply—
virtually to the point of religious conviction[41]—in dis-

play, ceremony, and decorum, the whole theatrical
apparatus of royal power. Her gorgeous clothes, the
complex code of manners and the calculated descents
into familiarity, the poetic tributes she received and the
poetry she herself wrote, the portraits and medals she
allowed to circulate like religious icons or the images
of the Roman emperors, the nicknames she imposed
upon her courtiers—all were profoundly theatrical and
all contributed to the fashioning of what was perhaps
the single greatest dramatic creation of the period: the
queen herself.

This was the fashioning of the self as a work of art
on the grandest scale, and, as Machiavelli understood,
the primary reward was quite simply survival. For,
when she assumed the throne in 1558, Elizabeth's
position was by no means secure. Not only was her
title in itself subject to question, but her sex was a
profound hindrance, especially because England had
just undergone an exceedingly unhappy period of female rule. With consummate skill she managed to turn
this dangerous obstacle into a triumphant advantage—
and one key to her success was the brilliant employment of all that was most "artificial" in kingship.

In the official progresses and pageants, everything was
calculated to enhance her metamorphosis into an almost magical being, a creature of infinite beauty, wisdom, and power.[42] But even her ordinary public appearances could be wonderfully impressive. Bishop
Goodman recalled in later years having seen the queen
emerge from council on a December evening in 1588:

> This wrought such an impression upon us, *for
> shows and pageants are ever best seen by
> torchlight,* that all the way long we did nothing
> but talk of what an admirable queen she was, and
> how we would adventure our lives to do her
> service.[43]

Goodman was anything but a cynic; yet, in recollection at least, he could see the royal appearance as a
performance calculated to arouse precisely the emotions that he felt. And a performance it was. The
queen's words to the crowd on that occasion—"You
may well have a greater prince, but you shall never
have a more loving prince"—were repeated with variations throughout her reign. They were part of a stock
of such phrases upon which she was able to draw
when need arose. Her famous "Golden Speech" of
1601 was little more than a particularly felicitous combination of these refrains—there is scarcely a phrase
in it that she had not used again and again.

The whole public character was formed very early,
then played and replayed with few changes for the
next forty years. Already in her formal procession
through the City on the day before her coronation, the
keynotes were sounded. "If a man should say well,"

wrote one observer, "he could not better tearme the citie of London that time, than a stage wherein was shewed the wonderfull spectacle, of a noble hearted princesse toward her most loving people, & the peoples exceding comfort in beholding so worthy a soveraign." Where her sister Mary had been silent and aloof at her accession, Elizabeth bestowed her gratitude and affection on all. "I wil be as good unto you," she assured her well-wishers, "as ever quene was to her people. . . . And perswade your selves, that for the safetie and quietnes of you all, I will not spare, if nede be to spend my blood." . . .[44]

The artificial world which had this supreme actress at its center was Ralegh's world during his years of happiness, fortune, and influence. The self-dramatizing that was the essence of the court deeply influenced his life, coloring not only his relations with the queen but his entire personality. His theatricalism in the crucial scenes of his life, his sense of himself as an actor in a living theater, his capacity truly to believe in the role he played though it was in many of its elements an evident fabrication, his self-manifestation in poetry and prose are all profoundly related to the example and effect of the remarkable woman on the throne of England.

Ralegh must have been deeply sensitive and responsive, in a way surpassing mere calculation, to the personality of the queen. For from the autumn of 1582 when he came to the court until his crisis and imprisonment (arising from the queen's discovery of his secret marriage) in the summer of 1592, he held on to the slippery position of favorite in a dangerous, envious, and constantly shifting court. Essex had the backing of his powerful and distinguished family as well as a body of supporters who came more and more to resemble a constituency or even a kingdom within the kingdom. But while Ralegh's vigorous West-country kinsmen helped him get an introduction to the court, he was alone for most of his career. There were temporary alliances—the most notable with Robert Cecil who later contrived to turn King James against him—but no true friends in high places, and, far from having any popular support, he was described (in May 1587) as "the best hated man of the world, in Court, city, and country."[47] It is difficult to fix precisely the source of this hatred—his descent from gentry and not nobility, the extremely profitable monopolies he received at the queen's hand, the simple fact of the queen's favor. Perhaps the best explanation is Aubrey's: "he was damnably proud."[48] Ralegh's extraordinary haughtiness is noted by a wide range of contemporary commentators, from the nameless political correspondent of Lord Burghley—

> his pride is intolerable, without regard for any, as the world knows

to Ralegh's virulent enemy, Lord Henry Howard—

> Rawlie, that in pride exceedeth all men alive. . . .
> the greatest Lucifer that hath lived in our age

to Ralegh's uneasy ally, the Earl of Northumberland—

> I know him insolent, extremely heated, a man that desires to seem to be able to sway all men's courses

to the balladmaker—

> Ralegh doth time bestride:
> He sits 'twixt wind and tide:
> Yet uphill he cannot ride,
> For all his bloody pride.[49]

The very qualities which won for him his place as a royal favorite—his "brilliance," his desire to master others, the gorgeous clothes he wore, his forwardness, in short, his life-style—inspired passionate resentment, fear, and hatred both in the court and in the world at large. And though Elizabeth herself was fascinated and attracted by him and made him Captain of the Guard so that he would be near her at all times, she too appears to have thought him in some way dangerous or unstable. Of her favorites over the years, only Ralegh was never appointed to the Privy Council. Apart from the tragic folly of her infatuation for Essex, the queen preferred more stable and prosaic men for her councillors.

Without a power-base of any kind, then, Ralegh was totally dependent upon the queen. All his powers of intellect and imagination, all his immense energies—and he could, we are assured by Robert Cecil, "toil terribly"[50]—were focused upon this relationship. Spenser's portrayal of the intense, almost hysterical anguish of Timias when he is abandoned in anger by Belphoebe need not be a poetic exaggeration—the queen's favor was everything to Ralegh. More than anyone of stature in the court, Ralegh was committed in his whole being to that strange, artificial, dangerous, and dreamlike world presided over by Gloriana, the world of adulation so intense that it still has power to shock us.[51]

Abbreviations

Discoverie: Sir Walter Ralegh, *The Discoverie of the Large, Rich, and Bewtiful Empyre of Guiana . . .* (London, 1596). Edited by V. T. Harlow. London, 1928.

Harlow: V. T. Harlow. *Ralegh's Last Voyage*. London, 1932.

H.W.: Sir Walter Ralegh. *The History of the World*.

London, 1614. Citations are to book, chapter, section, part (where indicated in the text), and page. The 1614 edition is paged 1 to 651 for Books I-II and 1 to 776 for Books III-V.

Letters: Edward Edwards. *The Life of Sir Walter Ralegh . . . Together with His Letters.* London, 1868. Volume 2.

Poems: *The Poems of Sir Walter Ralegh.* Edited by A. M. C. Latham. London, 1951.

Notes

[1] Cf. also from the same letter (to Robert Cecil, 1604): "And while I know that the best of men are but the spoyles of Tyme and certayne images wherwith childish Fortune useth to play,—kisse them to-day and break them to-morrow,—and therfore can lament in my sealf but a common destiney, yet the pitifull estate of thos who ar altogether healpless, and who dayly wound my sowle with the memory of their miseries, force mee, in dispight of all resolvedness, bothe to bewayle them and labor for them" (*Letters,* p. 312).

[2] It is touching that fifteen years later, when Ralegh was really brought to execution, Lady Ralegh echoed a phrase from this letter: "The Lordes have geven me his ded boddi, thought [*sic*] they denied me his life" (*Letters,* p. 413).

[3] Cf. Jonas A. Barish, "The Antitheatrical Prejudice," *Critical Quarterly* 8 (1969): 329.

[4] [*The Poems of Sir Walter Ralegh*, edited by A. M. C. Latham. London, 1951 (hereafter reffered to as *Poems*.)], p. 24 1. 1-25. The poem appears in Ralegh's own handwriting in MS Hatfield (Cecil Papers, 144) along with "If Synthia be a Queene, a princes, and supreame," "The 21th: and last booke of the Ocean to Scinthia," and "The end of the bookes, of the Oceans love to Scinthia, and the beginninge of the 22 Boock, entreatinge of Sorrow." An attempt to assign a much later date to this group of poems has recently been made by Katherine Duncan-Jones in "The Date of Ralegh's '21th: and Last Booke of the Ocean to Scinthia,'" *Review of English Studies,* new series 21, 82 (1970): 143-58. It is extremely difficult to imagine that the cruel mistress of these poems is dead.

[5] Robin Grove has suggested that "My boddy in the walls captived" reveals a disparity between style and feeling: "Even as he complains of his fettered mind, 'of liberty deprived,' he is writing a sonnet where his skill denies his complaint. To write in this way, however, necessitates a transformation of personal feeling into conventional attitudes, of real distress into 'destinies dispightful'. . . . If the sonnet is, ostensibly, the conventional plaint of the displaced courtier or reject-

ed lover, its real action is to judge the worthiness of the life that sustains these conventions" ("Ralegh's Courteous Art," *Melbourne Critical Review,* 7 [1964]: 107). Grove has, I think, misunderstood Ralegh's use of convention. Ralegh is not trapped in the conventional role but rather embraces it: for him literary convention is not an artificial mold imposed on real feelings struggling to emerge but a means of fashioning and manipulating the self. There may, however, be a criticism of the courtly life buried—perhaps unconsciously—in the poem: "Such prison earst was so delightfull" suggests that the relationship was a prison even when the poet's "keeper" was his love. The poet has been locked away all along; only now with the loss of those things that made captivity seem delightful, he feels himself "close keipt."

[6] Cf. Anne Righter, *Shakespeare and the Idea of the Play* (London, Penguin Books edition, 1967), p. 76: "In sermons and song-books, chronicles and popular pamphlets, Elizabethans were constantly being reminded of the fact that life tends to imitate the theatre. Comparisons between the world and the stage were so common as to become, in many instances, almost automatic, an unconscious trick of speech. . . . The play metaphor was for Elizabethans an inescapable expression, a means of fixing the essential quality of the age."

[7] "Jest" in this context suggests not only a trifling joke but an "amusing or entertaining performance: a pageant, masque, masquerade, or the like" (*O.E.D.*). For a useful survey of the background of the play metaphor, see Jean Jacquot, "'Le Théâtre du Monde'," *Revue de Littérature Comparée,* 31 (1957): 341-72. Jacquot emphasizes the continuity of the major themes: "le rôle de l'humanisme a principalement résidé dans sa transmission et sa diffusion" (p. 371). For a study emphasizing the special preoccupations of the Renaissance, see Richard Bernheimer, "Theatrum Mundi," *Art Bulletin,* 38 (1956): 225-47.

Ralegh's epigram is highly conventional in form as well as content. Cf., for example, epigram by Richard Barnfield (1574-1627):

Mans life is well compared to a feast,
Furnisht with choice of all Varietie:
To it comes Tyme; and as a bidden guest
Hee sets him downe, in Pompe and
　　Majestie;
The three-folde Age of Man, the Waiters
　　bee.
　　Then with an earthen voyder (made of
　　clay)
　　Comes Death, & takes the table clean
　　away.
[*Complete Poems,* ed. A. B. Grosart (London,
　　　　　　1876), p. 194.] . . .

[9] I have followed the 1829 edition of Ralegh's *Works* in emending the original "of the least wormes" to "as the least wormes."

[10] John of Salisbury, *Frivolities of Courtiers and Footprints of Philosophers,* trans. Joseph B. Pike (Minneapolis, 1938), 175-76. The reference to Petronius is to *Satiricon* 80 (Cambridge, Mass., Loeb edition, 1930): 160.

[11] *Frivolities,* 172-73. Perhaps *tyrannorum,* which Pike translates as "rulers," should, in this context, be read as "tyrants"—"non modo tyrannorum sed et principum" (*Policraticus,* ed. Clemens C. I. Webb [Oxford, 1909], 1: 192).

[12] "None the less those departing hence have been kindly dealt with in that they are not taken from this drama of fortune to be cast into exterior darkness, where there shall be weeping and gnashing of teeth. . . . Kindly have they been dealt with in that they await their Elysian Fields, which the sun of justice illuminates with his light" (*Frivolities,* 176-77). John even goes so far as to affirm that the world has its own Elysian Fields, "stretching away with the broadness of good souls to whom it has been granted by the Father of lights to devote their entire energy to the knowledge and love of good" (p. 177).

[13] Epistles LXXVI and LXXVII, in Seneca, *Epistulae Morales,* trans. R. M. Gummere (Cambridge, Mass., Loeb edition, 1962), 2: 165, 181.

[14] Job and Ecclesiastes seem to have been Ralegh's favorite books of the Bible. *The History of the World* closes with a passage from Job: "besides many other discouragements, perswading my silence; it hath pleased GOD to take that glorious *Prince* out of the world, to whom they [the volumes of the *History*] were directed; whose unspeakable and never enough lamented losse, hath taught me to say with JOB, *Versa est in Luctum Cithara mea, & Organum meum in vocem flentium.*" . . .

[33] See George R. Kernodle, *From Art to Theatre* (Chicago, 1944), pp. 130-53; Francis Fergusson, *The Idea of a Theater* (Princeton, 1949), pp. 116 ff.; Alvin B. Kernan, "Hamlet and the Nature of Drama," in *Report of the 13th Yale Conference on the Teaching of English* (New Haven, 1967), p. 3. For a somewhat different view of the symbolism of the theater, see Frances A. Yates, *Theatre of the World* (London, 1969), p. 189; Bernheimer, "Theatrum Mundi," on Camillo's magic theater.

[34] *Platonic Theology,* trans. Josephine I. Burroughs, in *JHI* 5 (April 1944): 235. See Paul Oskar Kristeller, *The Philosophy of Marsilio Ficino* (New York, 1943), pp. 92-100, 407-10.

The fascinated interest in models continued throughout the Renaissance. See, for example, the admiration in *The Faerie Queene* for Merlin's wonderful mirror: "Forthy it round and hollow shaped was / Like to the world it selfe, and seemd a world of glas" (III, ii, 19). Georges Poulet, in *The Metamorphoses of the Circle* (English trans., Baltimore, 1966), notes the importance of models in seventeenth-century consciousness (p. 17).

[35] *An Apology for Actors* (1612), ed. Richard H. Perkinson (New York, 1941), sig. D3^r.

[36] Quoted in E. K. Chambers, *The Elizabethan Stage* (Oxford, 1923), 3 : 72. See also Serlio's "Trattato Sopra le Scene," in Chambers, vol. 4, esp. pp. 355-56.

[37] *Platonic Theology,* p. 236. Ficino quotes a saying ascribed to Hermes Trismegistus. Cf. Pico, *Oration,* in *Renaissance Philosophy of Man,* ed. Cassirer, *et al.* p. 223.

[38] Cf. Kernan, "Hamlet and the Nature of Drama," p. 5. All quotations of Shakespeare are from *Works,* ed. George Lyman Kittredge (Boston, 1936).

[39] Quoted in J. E. Neale, *Elizabeth I and her Parliaments, 1584-1601* (London, 1965), 2: 119. Subsequent citations are in the text as "Neale." "She is a Princess," the French ambassador remarked of Elizabeth, "who can act any part she pleases" (quoted in J. E. Neale, *Queen Elizabeth I* [New York, Anchor Books edition, 1957], p. 263). Cf. Francis Osborne, *Historical Memoires on the Reigns of Queen Elizabeth, and King James* (London, 1673, first published in 1658), pt. 2: "Her sex did bear out many impertinences in her words and actions, as *her making Latine Speeches in the Universities,* and professing her self in public *a Muse,* then thought something too Theatrical for a Virgin Prince. . . . " (p. 441).

[40] Plowden and Coke quoted in Ernst H. Kantorowicz, *The King's Two Bodies* (Princeton, 1957), p. 13. Cf. Righter, *Shakespeare and the Idea of the Play,* pp. 113-16; G. K. Hunter, *John Lyly* (London, 1962), p. 7.

[41] Witness, in the Vestarian Controversy, her staunch support, against the opposition of most of her advisers, for the old ecclesiastical ornaments and clothing.

[42] See John Nichols, *The Progresses and Public Processions of Queen Elizabeth,* 3 vols. (London, 1823); David M. Bergeron, *English Civic Pageantry, 1558-1642* (London, 1971); Frances A. Yates, "Queen Elizabeth as Astraea," *JWCI* 10 (1947): 27-82, and "Elizabethan Chivalry: The Romance of the Accession Day Tilts," *JWCI* 20 (1957): 4-25; Roy C. Strong, "The

Popular Celebration of the Accession Day of Queen Elizabeth I," *JWCI* 21 (1958): 86-103.

[43] Godfrey Goodman, Bishop of Gloucester, *The Court of King James the First* (London, 1839), p. 163 (italics mine). Perhaps the phrase "ordinary public appearance" is misleading here—we would do well to remember that in 1588 any royal appearance before a crowd was a courageous act, as there was great and justified fear of assassination attempts.

[44] *The Quenes majesties passage through the citie of London to westminster the day before her coronacion* [1559], ed. James M. Osborn (New Haven, 1960), pp. 28, 46. On Queen Mary's accession, see *The Chronicle of Queen Jane and of Two Years of Queen Mary,* ed. John Nichols, Camden Society, 48 (1850): 14— "The queenes grace stayed at Allgate-streete before the stage wheare the poore children stood, and hard an oration that one of them made, but she sayd nothinge to them." . . .

[47] Sir Anthony Bagot, quoted in Edward Thompson, *Sir Walter Ralegh* (New Haven, 1936), p. 33.

[48] John Aubrey, *Brief Lives,* ed. O. L. Dick (London, 1950), p. 254.

[49] All quoted in Thompson, pp. 34, 176-77, 187, 164. Cf. John Clapham, "Certain Observations Concerning the Life and Reign of Queen Elizabeth" [1603], ed. E. P. Read and Conyers Read, *Elizabeth of England* (Philadelphia, 1951), p. 93: Ralegh "was a man of a very bold spirit and of a quick conceit, in adversity not altogether dejected; insolent in prosperity and ungrateful to such as had supplied his wants in his first and mean estate. He was commonly noted for using of bitter scoffs and reproachful taunts which bred him much dislike. He was so far from affecting popularity, as he seemed to take a pride in being hated of the people, either for that he thought it a point of policy, of else that he scorned the approbation of the multitude."

[50] Quoted in Edward Edwards, *Life,* 1:154.

[51] There are a few brief and guarded moments of detachment verging on cynicism—as when he writes in a letter to his "Cussen George" that "The Queen thincks that George Carew longes to see her; and therefore see her" (*Letters,* pp. 42-43)—but on the whole, Ralegh seems to have taken the cult of Elizabeth with complete seriousness.

John Racin (essay date 1974)

SOURCE: "The Historian and His Appropriate Subject Matter," in *Sir Walter Ralegh as Historian: An Anal-*

ysis of "The History of the World," Institut für Englische Sprache, 1974, pp. 43-76.

[*In the following excerpt from his book-length study of Raleigh's* History, *Racin elucidates Raleigh's concept of truth in historiography and his understanding of his role as a historian.*]

The historian's *raison d'être* for Ralegh was the search for truth. We see in the **History** his laborious efforts to establish the historicity of the past, a task which required a carefully wrought synthesis of authority, reason, conjecture, and personal experience. For Ralegh only the Scriptures were beyond doubt, but all other evidence must be tested by "nature," "reason," and "time." Even the early Church Fathers were not exempt from close scrutiny and criticism. In his study of the possible physical sites of Paradise, he noted: "And it is true, that many of the Fathers were farre wide from the vnderstanding of [Paradise]. I speake it not, that I myselfe dare presume to censure them, for I reuerence both their learning and their pietie, and yet not bound to follow them any further, then they are guided by truth: for they were men; *Et hommus est errare.*" (pp. 33-34 [Page numbers from the **History** cited throughout the essay are from the 1614 edition.]) He made frequent claims of objectivity, of exclusive pursuit of truth, of placing "no valuation [on] the opinions of men, conducted by their own fancies: be they ancient or moderne. Neither haue I any end herein, private, or publicke, other than the discouery of truth. For as the partialitie of man to himselfe hath disguised all things: so the factious and hireling historians of all Ages (especially of these latter times) haue by their many volumes of vntrue reports left Honour without a Monument, and Vertue without Memorie . . . . " (pp. 177-78) Relative to the monumental religious and political conflict of his period, Roman catholicism versus Protestantism, he affirmed that he would not oppose an opinion "because commonly those of the *Romish* Religion labour to vphold it," nor favor it "because many notable men of the *Protestant* writers have approued it," but would be guided by the "truth itselfe." (p. 227)

Of course, adherence to "truth" was a Renaissance commonplace on historiography. The historical pyrrhonism seen in Cornelius Agrippa's *De incertitudine et vanitate scientiarum declamatio* (1530) and to a greater degree in Charles de la Ruelle's *Succintz adversaires* (1567) had little influence in England. History, for Agrippa, " . . . being a thing that above all things promises Order, Fidelity, Coherence, and Truth, is yet defective in every one; For Historians are at such variance among themselves, delivering several Tales of one and the same Story, that it is impossible but that most of them must be the greatest Lyers in the World."[1] For Ruelle, to know the past is impossible, and if it were possible, such knowledge would be useless:

Reste a examiner l'autre partie, Rapport du Passe. La verite duquel est totalement incertaine; et bien qu'elle fust certaine, seroit meantmoins de nul usage et proffit: et ne rien sinon inutilement et frustoirement contenter une vaine et plus que puerile curiosite.[2]

Sir Philip Sidney would not have welcomed such support for his attack on historians in the *Apologie* (1595). Whereas Sidney's attack raised issues of considerable importance, he nevertheless granted that historians present "truth," even though limited to the particularity of "a foolish world." Samuel Daniel, perhaps the harshest English critic of historiography, stated in his *Defense of Ryme* (1603) that "reading an Historye . . . dooth no otherwise acquaint vs with the true Substance of Circumstances, than a superficiall Carde dooth the Seaman with a Coast neuer seene which alwayes prooues other to the eye than the imagination fore cast it."[3] John Clapham, in calling for a new historiography, one devoted to "Truth in her nakednesse," (*The Historie of England* [1602], Sig. A3ᵛ) attempted to meet the charges of those who "will not sticke to call in question the truth of all Histories, affirming them to be vaine and fabulous." He granted that "it is impossible for any man (though neuer so great a louer of truth) to relate truely all particular matters of circumstance" but argued that the salient facts of circumstance are accurate and that if historiography were discarded: " . . . we should depriue the world of a very great portion of humane learning." (Sig. Bʳ⁻ᵛ)

Although it was generally agreed in the 16th and 17th centuries that the historian's proper subject matter was truth, the nature of that truth was the source of much controversy. The fullest and perhaps most influential account of historiography in the 16th century was Jean Bodin's *Methodus ad facilem historiarum cognitionem,* which first appeared in 1566 and went through thirteen editions up to 1650.[4] In his first chapter Bodin distinguished between three kinds of history: human, natural, and divine. Human history, restricted to the acts of man in society, concerns the probable, distinguishes between the base and honorable, leads to prudence, and is the arbiter of human life (*humanae vitae moderatricem*). Natural history, restricted to the hidden causes in nature, concerns the inevitable, distinguishes between the true and false, leads to knowledge, and is the revealer of all things (*rerum omnium inventricem*). Divine history records the power of God and immortal souls, distinguishes between piety and impiety, produces faith, and is the destroyer of vice (*vitiorum expultricem*). Bodin then assigned divine history to the theologian, natural history to the philosopher, and human history and its governing laws to the historian. These categories (suggestive of Bacon's) were unthinkable to Ralegh. He assumed all three roles.

Ralegh as Theologian

As "theologian" Ralegh was concerned with the effects of Divine Will acting in time. The visible world, properly understood, is "the vnderstood language of the Almightie, vouchsafed to all his creatures, whose Hieroglyphical Characters, are the vnnumbered Starres, the Sunne, and Moone, written on these large volumes of the firmament: written also on the earth and seas, by the letters of all those liuing creatures, and plants, which inhabit and reside therein." All this men perceive "in their reasonable soules." (p. 2) Reading God's "large volumes" within His Creation provides the historian with a major source of his subject matter. In addition, he has God's Scripture, which has "a singular prerogatiue aboue all that haue been written by the most sufficient of meerly humane authors: it setteth downe expresly the true, and first causes of all that happened." (p. 536) The acts of Providence recorded in the Old Testament establish the precedents by which all succeeding ages may be understood and judged:

> And as in those times the causes were exprest, why it pleased God to punish both Kings and their People: the same being both before, and at the instant deliuered by Prophets; so the same iust God who liueth and gouerneth all thinges for euer, doeth in these our times giue victorie, courage, and discourage, raise, and throw downe Kinges, Estates, Cities, and Nations, for the same offences which were committed of old, and are committed in the present: for which reason in these and other the afflictions of *Israel,* alwaies the causes are set downe, that they might bee as precedents to succeeding ages. (pp. 508-509)

When confronted by catastrophes, men err to seek explanations in second causes alone. Such causes may properly be investigated by the historian "as long as hee had forborne to derogate from the first causes, by ascribing to the second more than was due." (p. 538) Though all in nature and in man is mutable: "the judgements of GOD are foreuer vnchangeable; neither is he wearied by the long process of time, and won to giue his blessing in one age, to that which he cursed in another." (Sig. A3)

Thus the historian properly concerns himself with the emanations of an eternal God of Being, whose every act in time is germane to His purpose. However, the historian must impose some practical limitations on his subject matter:

> To repeat GODS judgements in particular, vpon those of all degrees, which haue plaied with his mercies; would require a volume apart: for the *Sea* of examples hath no bottome. The markes, set on priuate men, are with their bodies cast into the earth; and their fortunes, written only in the memories of those that liued with them: so as they who succeed, and haue not seene the fall of

others, doe not feare their owne faults. GODS judgments vpon the greater and greatest, haue beene left to posterity; first, by those happy hands which the Holy Ghost hath guided; and secondly, by their vertue, who haue gathered the acts and ends of men, mighty and remarkeable in the world. (Sig. A2ᵛ)

Thus God's judgments upon "the greater and the greatest" constitute the historian's proper subject matter. Enlightened by reason (reason grasps the existence of Providence) and by faith (some providential acts transcend rational analysis), men may gather out of the past "a policy no lesse wise than eternall." (*Ibid.*)

For Ralegh, Providence is the unifying power which, in man's efforts to cope with pluralistic human experience, not only justifies historiography, but also provides the criteria by which all events must be judged. The historian is the interpreter of God's will; and as he ranges over Old Testament history and that of the Persians, Greeks, Carthaginians, Romans, and the modern states of Spain, France, and England, the historian, armed with Old Testament precedents, an eternally stable moral order, and his proper formal methods, becomes comparable to God pronouncing His judgments on the follies and crimes of men, the "greater and the greatest." King James had good reason to be astonished and angered by the audacity of his prisoner, one "civilly dead."

Comparable attitudes toward history as a series of God's judgments upon mankind were not uncommon in the 16th and 17th Centuries, as, for example, in John Sleidan's *De Quatuor Summis Imperiis* (1556, Englished in 1563), Philip Melanchthon's *Chronicon Carionis* (1558), Thomas Beard's *The Theatre of Gods Ivdgements* (1597), Richard Knolles' *Historie of the Turkes* (1603), Anthony Munday's *Briefe Chronicle* (1611), Sir Henry Spelman's *The History and Fate of Sacrilege* (1632), Archbishop James Ussher's *Annales Veteris Testamenti* (1650), and Jacques-Benigne Bossuet's *Discours sur l'histoire universelle* (1681).

However, such attitudes were far outweighed by political, scientific, and theological forces which turned the historian away from the first cause to a greater concern with second causes, not to mention the renewed interest in classical learning, part of which involved the historiography of Thucydides, Polybius, Livy, and, of course, Cicero. Influenced by such classical models, the practice, theories, and subsequent influence of such figures as Giovanio Pontano, *Actius de Numeris Poeticis: & lege Historiae* (1507), Estienne Pasquier, *Les Recherches de la France* (1560, and ten augmented editions to 1611), Francesco Guicciardini, *The Historie of . . . the Warres of Italie* (Englished in 1579), Machiavelli, *The Florentine Historie* (Englished in 1585), William Camden, *Rerum*

Anglicarum et Hibernicarum annales regnante Elizabetha (1615, 1625), and Sir Francis Bacon, *The Historie of the Raigne of King Henry the Seuenth* (1622), carried the day for second-cause historiography. Moreover, the danger of detecting God's will in (or absent from) the political and religious struggles was all too clear. The *Anglica Historia* (1534) of Polydore Vergil, who demonstrated the inaccuracies of Geoffrey of Monmouth (the stuff from which the Tudor Myth was shaped) and thus undermined the argument that the Tudor assumption of power was providential, suffered almost total eclipse and earned him the reputation (shared by William Parnus) of having exhibited "lying tongues, enuyous detraction, malicious slaunders, reproachfull and venomous language, wilfull ignorance, dogged enuie, and canckered mindes. . . ."[5]

In addition, the growing interest in exploration, in the discoveries of science, in man's power to control and exploit his environment turned man's attention more to nature, to second causes. On the other hand, the resurgence of a reforming pietism which signalized the unworthy, fallen state of man carried with it the suggestion that human explanations of Divine Will could only be impious distortions.

As is well known, Bacon directed his efforts toward justifying greater attention to second causes (the formal and material causes of nature) rather than to the first cause (the efficient and final causes). In the *Advancement of Learning* (1605), he described the "History of Providence" as containing "that excellent correspondence which is between God's revealed will and his secret will; which though it be so obscure as for the most part it is not legible to the natural man; no, nor many times to those that behold it from the tabernacle," yet it may have value in warning "mere sensual persons" to heed God's judgments.[6] His warning of providential historiography's necessary obscurantism, his restriction of its value to "mere sensual persons" are far less embracing than his claims for second cause historiography. Edmund Bolton complained in 1618 that "Christian Authors, while for their ease they shuffled up the reasons of events, in briefly referring all causes immediately to the Will of God, have generally neglected to inform their Readers in the ordinary means of Carriage in human Affairs, and thereby singularly maimed their Narrations."[7] By the time Ralegh's ***History*** was published, such attitudes towards providential historiography had filtered down to the level of secondary figures such as Richard Brathwait, who argued in 1614 against its practice:

> Yet in making use of this especiall Branch of History: *Explanation of the discovery of causes,* I will limit and restraine it to an assertaine bound.
>
> We must not search causes above their Natures; there may be many hidden and concealed reasons, which to enquire after were unlawfull; much less

to wade into the secret conventions of that sacred Power, from whom all visible and apparent causes borrow their light.

What we may gather by authentick relation, or probable imagination, may without prejudice, or errour, be produced. As for supernaturall causes, the more we sound them, the more we sound into the shallownesse of our owne judgements; never farther from apprehending them, than when we seeme to apprehend them.[8]

Ralegh, however, who was quite familiar with such strictures, having read of "the Lawes of Historie, and of the Kindes" taught by that "excellent learned Gentleman *Sir Francis Bacon*" (Sig. E3ᵛ), had full confidence in his ability to "wade into the secret conventions of that sacred Power." Nevertheless, he did argue for limitations to providential historiography stemming from two sources: man's nature and God's. The historian may detect the effects of Providence; "yet the manner and first operation of [God's] diuine power cannot bee conceiued by any minde, or spirit, compassed with a mortall body." (p. 6) Man's reason may know that Providence exists, that it operates in history, that "God worketh by Angels, by the Sunne, by the Starres, by Nature, or infused properties, and by men, as by seuerall organs, several effects; all second causes whatsoeuer being but instruments, conduits, and pipes, which carry and disperse what they haue receiued from the head and fountaine of the Vniuersall." (p. 13) However, "of the manner how God worketh in them, or they in or with each other, which the Heathen Philosophers, and those that follow them, haue taken on them to teach: I say there is not any one among them, nor any one among vs, that could euer yet conceiue it, or expresse it, euer enrich his owne vnderstanding with any certaine truth. . . . " (*Ibid.*)

It would be misleading to isolate such passages in the **History** in order to support an argument for Ralegh's skepticism (as some critics have done); for he is simply reflecting the negative theology tradition long indigenous to Christianity, the *si comprehendis, non est Deus* of St. Augustine, what Josef Pieper has described as a corrective against Greek rationalism within the Christian tradition.[9] This negative theology tradition, given its greatest authority by Dionysius the Areopagite, the friend of St. Paul, appears even in the writings of the supreme "rationalist" of the Middle Ages, St. Thomas Aquinas. St. Thomas, dedicated to elucidating the legitimate claims of reason, nevertheless believed that "God is honoured by silence—not because we cannot say or understand anything about Him, but because we know that we are incapable of comprehending Him." (*De trinitate*, 2, 1 *ad* 6) In *Quaestiones disputatae de potentia Dei* he wrote: "This is the extreme of human knowledge of God: to know that we do not know God." (7, 5 *ad* 14)

For Ralegh, to inquire "of the essence of God, of his power, of his Art, and by what meane He created the world: Or of his secret iudgment, and the causes; is not an effect of Reason . . . but they grow mad with reason that inquire after it." (Sig. E3) Historiography is the most exalted (albeit difficult) human art, it presents universal truth, it records the acts of God; yet it can not discover the precise workings of divine formal causes. This position is not strange to Renaissance historiography, to say nothing of theology. James Amyot indicated that the historian is "but as a register to set downe the judgements and definitive sentences of Gods Court," and even though some of these sentences can be understood by man's "weake naturall reason," others "goe according to Gods infinite power and incomprehensible wisedom, above and against all discourse of mans understanding. . . . "[10]

Qua "theologian," Ralegh recorded the acts of God's will, taking a grim satisfaction in describing the destruction of impiety and vice by divine vengeance. At the same time, he was keenly aware of the fact that divine will is ultimately unfathomable. For example, in "explaining" the cause of Creation, he concluded: "there was no other cause preceding then [God's] owne will"; (p. 27) *i. e.*, at the point where human knowledge must stop, man can only say that God's will wills.

Ralegh as Philosopher

In the role of "philosopher," proceeding as he said by reason, Ralegh sought to prove the certainty of Creation *ex nihilo* and to refute the "necessitarianism" implicit in Aristotle's eternal world. In addition, acting within the province of Bodin's philosopher, he offered exhaustive definitions and analyses of nature, man, law (divine, natural, and human), government, magic (what we would term experimental and applied science), etc.

It is not easy to determine why Ralegh felt it necessary to preface his **History** with a long, difficult argument for Creation and an impassioned refutation of Aristotle's eternal world. Of course, the issue at stake was most crucial: *the very possibility of providential historiography*, an issue he well recognized:

The examples of diuine prouidence, euery where found (the first diuine Histories being nothing else but a continuation of such examples) haue perswaded me to fetch my beginning from the beginning of all things; to wit, Creation. For though these two glorious actions of the Almightie be so neare, and (as it were) linked together, that the one necessarily implyeth the other: Creation, inferring Prouidence: (for what Father forsaketh the child that he hath begotten?) and Prouidence presupposing Creation. . . . (Sig. D2)

Previously, of course, the importance of the doctrine of Creation *ex nihilo* had been recognized, and detailed arguments in its favor had been presented by Tertullian, *Adversus Hermogenem* (*ca.* 220), Lactantius, *Divinae Institutiones* (304-11), II, ix, and by St. Augustine, *Civitas Dei* (413-26), XI, i-xxiii. The doctrine was pressed with considerable vigor in the Middle Ages. Writers such as St. Anselm, Richard of St. Victor, St. Bonaventure, Alexander of Hales, Robert Grosseteste, Roger Bacon, and Richard Middleton held that Creation *ex nihilo* was demonstrable by reason; and others such as St. Thomas and his school held that it was not, but accepted it on faith, as did St. Augustine.[11] Siger of Braband in his *De Aeternitate Mundi* (*ca.* 1270), following Aristotle, argued for an eternal world, but his thesis was condemned by the Church in 1277.

Recognizing the importance of the controversy for the Christian views on God's power versus necessitarianism, linear time versus cyclical time, the definitions of nature and man as creature or creator, we still may ask why the controversy should be revived or continued in the 16th and 17th centuries, especially since to my knowledge no serious efforts were made to argue against Creation *ex nihilo,* unless the continuing or growing authority of Plato (Creation of eternal duration) or of Aristotle still encouraged efforts at refutation. It is true that George Hakewill, whose main target was Godfrey Goodman's *The Fall of Man* (1616) but included Ralegh's *History,* argued for cyclical time in attempting to refute the idea of universal decay: "There is (it seemes) both in wits and Arts, as in all things besides, a kinde of circular progresse: they have their birth, their growth, their flourishing, their failing, and within a while after their resurrection, and reflourishing again." (*An Apologie Or Declaration of the Power and Providence of God in the World,* 1627. I used the much augmented 3rd edition [1635], p. 259.)

But his is a lonely voice when seen in the context of the many arguments for Creation *ex nihilo* and linear time (proved either by reason or faith) in the works of Melanchthon, *Loci Communes* (1538), Fol. 28ᵛ-32; Calvin, *Commentaries* [on] . . . *Genesis* (1539); Steuchus Eugubinus, *De Perenni Philosophia Libri* X (1540, an influential work, reprinted in 1542, 1577, 1578, and 1591), pp. 337-57 of the 1542 edition; Bodin, *Methodus* (1566), Ch. VII; Sir Edward Dyer, *The Prayse of Nothing* (1585), Sig. B-B2ᵛ; Louis Le Roy, *Of the Interchangeable Course . . . in the Whole World* (Englished in 1594), Fol. 33-36; Guillaume Du Bartas, *The First Day of the Worldes Creation* (Englished in 1595); Henry Cuffe, *The Differences of the Ages of Mans Life* (1600); Pierre de la Primaudaye, *The Third Volume of the French Academie* (1613), I, ii; Geoffrey Goodman, *The Fall of Man* (1616); and of Ralegh, the Preface to the *History* (Sig. D2-E3). Of these, the arguments of Steuchus Eugubinus (cited by Ra-

legh as a main source), Bodin, and La Primaudaye (whose works he possessed)[12] were the most influential on Ralegh's discussion, as well as those by Lactantius and St. Augustine. However, unlike many of his authorities, Ralegh grounded his argument for Creation on "Naturall reason" not on Christian faith, although the Scriptures offered, he felt, infallible proof. Thus his providential historiography did not owe its being to faith; rather, the very possibility of its existence was established, with great effort, through "Naturall reason."

Ralegh selected Aristotle as his chief target: "I shall neuer be perswaded that GOD hath shut vp all light of Learning within the Lantorne of *Aristotles* braines." The concept of Creation in time is "too weighty a work for *Aristotles* rotten ground to beare vp"; even so, "that the necessitie of infinite power, and the worlds beginning, and the impossibility of the contrary euen in the iudgement of Naturall reason, wherein hee beleeued, had not better informed him; it is greatly to bee mar[u]ailed at." (Sig. D2ʳ⁻ᵛ) Even though Ralegh's anti-Aristotelianism was mainly due to his recognition that Creation *ex nihilo* was the *sine qua non* of providential historiography, in addition, Ralegh possessed a strong empiricist strain, a desire to ground theory in experience, a distrust of the contemplative reason of the scholastics, who "spinne into small threds, with subtile distinctions, many times the plainenesse, and sinceritie of the Scriptures: their wits being like that strong water, that eateth through and dissolueth the purest gold." (p. 23) Ralegh distrusted that "reason" which is "more subtile in distinguishing vpon the parts of doctrine already laid downe," than in discovering "any thing hidden, either in Philosophie or Diuinity. . . . " (p. 9) "That these and these bee the causes of these and these effects, Time hath taught vs; and not reason: and so hath experience, without Art. The Cheese-wife knoweth it as well as the Philosopher, that sowre Runnet doth coagulate her milke into a curde." (Sig. D2ᵛ)

Ralegh's arguments for Creation reveal a surprisingly sound grasp of the central conflict: God's freedom versus "Greek necessitarianism." His solution was based on a definition of a "voluntarist" God.

The problem of God's freedom as opposed to Greek necessitarianism is the subject of a penetrating discussion by Josef Pieper. (*Scholasticism,* Ch. XI) Pieper examined the necessitarianism (the principle of *rationes necessariae*) in St. Anselm's argument that human souls would replace the fallen angels because no other possible source for replacement existed. (*Cur Deus homo,* I, 16) Pieper asks:

> Under what assumption (aside from the revelation of truth assumed by faith) can Anselm's line of argument lay claim to validity? The answer must

be: Under the dual assumption that—first—everything which God does must be rational; and that—secondly—man, or more precisely, the believing man, for his part can recognize and prove this rationality.

> This idea of Anselm's, however, leads us almost immediately to a further idea: that God is acting under necessity and cannot help acting in a certain way—namely, to do in every case what is most rational; and hence, that in each case the rationality of what He does can be intelligible to reason of (believing) man. . . . (*Scholasticism*, pp. 137-38)

The idea that God must necessarily act in certain rational ways, as Etienne Gilson has shown,[13] was an inheritance of Aristotle's thought which, through the influence of Avicenna and Averroës, shaped the nature of scholastic philosophy before the condemnations of 1277. This rationalism, for example, permeates the thought of Siger of Brabant, many of whose theses, such as "God by necessity brings forth everything that proceeds directly from Him," were among the 219 propositions condemned by Bishop Tempier of Paris. The bishops at Paris and Oxford involved in the 1277 and 1286 condemnations were reacting against what they felt was the dangerous rationalism of some of the scholastics, St. Thomas included. Among the condemned theses, incidentally, was the proposition that Creation *ex nihilo* is impossible, that matter existed eternally.

Ralegh cited this proposition, that the world was created *ex materia praeexistente,* and answered that if eternal matter existed, either it fitted itself to God (which is impossible since things without sense can not adapt to the workman's will) or that God accommodated himself to matter (which is untenable since it implies that God's will is limited by natural necessity). (Sig. D3ᵛ) Further, he took Aristotle's proposition that *"A sufficient and effectuall cause being granted, an answerable effect thereof is also granted,"* i. e., since God (the cause) is eternal, the world (the effect) must also be eternal and answered:

> But what a strang mockerie is this in so great a Maister, to confesse a sufficient and effectuall cause of the world, (to wit an almighty GOD) in his Antecedent; and the same GOD to be a GOD restrained in his conclusion; to make GOD free in power, and bound in will; able to effect, vnable to determine; able to make all things, and yet vnable to make choyce of the time when? For this were impiously to resolue of GOD, as of naturall necessitie; which hath neither choice, nor will, nor vnderstanding; which cannot but work matter being present; as fire, to burne things combustible. (Sig. D4ᵛ)

His answer, a stinging denunciation of the *rationes necessariae* principle, argues God's freedom in a way suggestive of the voluntarism defended by Duns Scotus approximately three hundred years earlier. Pieper writes:

> The watchword "freedom," which I said characterized Duns Scotus, refers above all to the freedom of *God.* This may seem to us a purely theological thesis, but we will think otherwise as soon as we see the conclusion which Duns Scotus quickly draws from this: Because God is absolutely free, everything that He does and effects has the character of nonnecessity, of being in a particular sense "accidental" (contingent). This applies both to God's creative work, and therefore to Creation itself, and to the events included within the history of Salvation. . . . In a word: there are no "necessary reasons" for the work of God. (*Scholasticism*, p. 140)

Similarly, Ralegh would not tolerate any suggestion that God's will can be restricted. If God is bound by rational necessity and if man is sufficiently rational, the historian could fathom even the formal causes of history. Such restrictions involve an "impietie monstrous"; they confuse God with nature:

> For it is God, that only desposeth of all things according to his owne will; and madeth of one Earth, *Vessels of honor and dishonor.* It is Nature that can dispose of nothing, but according to the will of the matter wherein it worketh. It is God, that commandeth all: It is Nature that is obedient to all. It is God that doth good vnto all, knowing and louing the good he doth: It is Nature, that secondarily doth also good, but it neither knoweth nor loueth the good it doth. It is God, that hath all things in himselfe: Nature, nothing in it selfe. It is God, which is the Father, and hath begotten all things: It is Nature, which is begotten by all thinges; in which it liueth and laboureth; for by it selfe it existeth not. (Sig. E2ᵛ)

It seems clear that for Ralegh the ultimate ground of reality is the absolutely free will of God. In this sense he is a voluntarist, and in subsequent pages, we shall see that he is a voluntarist in other senses as well.

Ralegh as Historian

By the time the **History** was published, providential historiography was out of favor. The Renaissance humanist view, reflecting classical and Florentine influences, settled on human acts and causation as the historian's proper subject matter (as we have seen in Bodin), under which religious, political, military, and even geographical influences were treated. Writing in 1553, Roger Ascham summarized the humanist position (I quote in part):

First point was, to write nothing false: next, to be bold to say any truth; whereby is avoided two great faults, flattery and hatred: for which two points Ceasar is read to his great praise, and Jovius the Italian to his just reproach. Then to mark diligently the causes, counsels, acts, and issues in all great attempts: and in causes, what is just or unjust; in counsels, what is proposed wisely or rashly; in acts, what is done courageously or faintly; and of every issue, to note some general lesson of wisdom and wariness, for like matters in time to come; wherein Polybius in Greek, and Philip Comines in French, have done the duties of wise and worthy writers. Diligence also must be used in keeping truly the order of time; and describing lively, both the site of places and nature of persons, not only for the outward shape of the body, but also for the inward disposition of the mind. . . . [14]

Ascham's historical "truth," the *consilia, dicta, and facta* of human affairs, and just as important, the "inward disposition of the mind," differs profoundly from Ralegh's. Ascham said nothing of Providence.

A fuller and more systematic account of classical or humanist historiography is Francisco Patricio's, whose precepts, together with those of Accontio Tridentio, were translated by Thomas Blundeville in 1574. After having restricted the subject of histories to politics, Patricio continued: "Euery deed that man doth, springeth eyther of some outwarde cause, as of force, or fortune, (which properlye ought not to be referred to man:) or else of some inward cause belonging to man: of which causes there be two, that is, reason and appetite. Of reason springeth counsell and election, if affaires of the lyfe, which not being letted, do cause deedes to ensue. Of appetite doe spryng, passions of the mynde, which also doe cause men to attempt enterprises."[15] Thus Patricio played down the importance of "outwarde" causes (under which Providence as well as "fortune" must necessarily be placed) in the interests of an intensive analysis of "inward" causes. The historian must "consider well the cause that mooued the doer to enterprise the deed, & to declare the same accordingly. And note here, that by the cause, I meane the ende. For the matter whereon the doer worketh, is the deede of peace, of warre, or of sidicion. And the shape or forme thereof, is the meanes and maner of doing, which the doer vseth therein. And the cause efficient is the doer himselfe. Affections also haue a fynall cause, as the ende of wrath, is reuenge: of loue, the fruition of the thing beloued: and of mercy, the ende is helpe and comforte." (*The true order*, p. 156)

Patricio then discussed each cause separately. Amplification of the efficient cause, the "doer," is character analysis. The material cause is the act itself, the formal is the means used to carry out the act, and the final cause is its purpose. Patricio thus felt that he had

systematically provided the historian with all the tools needed for his craft. The role of Providence was ignored, for if admitted, it could only result in mystery or contingency intruding upon history's ordered patterns. Ralegh discovered a number of ordered patterns in history also, but these were created by God's will. But the humanists limited historiography (as Bodin stated) to "the activities of men only," activities "which spring from plans, sayings, and deeds of men, when volition leads the way. For will power is the mistress of human activity, whether it follows reason or the lower faculty of the soul, in seeking and avoiding things." (*Method*, p. 29)

Ralegh, in handling Greek and Roman history, confined himself mainly to the motives, counsels, acts, and issues of human events and also placed great importance on the "inward disposition of the mind." He was well aware, as he stated, of the "Lawes of Historie, and of the Kindes." For Ralegh, however, a historiography confined to human causes, counsels, and acts was severely deficient, not only because it ignored Providence, but also because it assumed that reason could explain everything human. Apply reason, apply Aristotle's four causes to human affairs, Patricio intimated, and understanding will follow. This optimism Ralegh did not share. Just as he resisted the principle of *rationes necessariae* applied to God's nature, he resisted analogous application to man's. In Parts III and IV of this study we shall see that Ralegh's treatment of man acting in history is by no means consistent, that he utilized the assumptions and methods from conflicting traditions, but for now it is enough to show that almost invariably Ralegh displayed a deep pessimism about the vagaries, the perversity of human nature, a pessimism derived from his study of history and reinforced by his wide experience.

In one of his darker passages, he came close to stating that any generalizing science or art of human nature is impossible:

> But such is the Multiplying and extensiue vertue of dead Earth, and of that breath-giuing life which GOD, hath cast vpon Slime and Dust: as that among those that were, of whom we reade and heare, and among those that are, whom we see and conuerse with; euery one hath receiued a seuerall picture of face, and euerie one a diuerse picture of minde; euery one a forme apart, euery one a fancy and cogitation differing: there being nothing wherein Nature so much triumpheth, as in dissimilitude. (Sig. A^v)

Even though this triumph in dissimilitude would render impossible an accurate history of human mind and volition, nevertheless, Ralegh felt, man's acts sometimes do offer clues for determining thoughts and motives, despite the masks created by craft, fear, and love of the world:

And though it hath pleased GOD, to reserue the Art of reading mens thoughts to himselfe: yet, as the fruit tels the name of the Tree; so doe the outward workes of men (so farre as their cogitations are acted) giue vs whereof to guesse at the rest. Nay, it were not hard to expresse the one by the other, very neare the life: did not craft in many, feare in the most, and the worlds loue in all, teach euery capacity, according to the compasse it hath, to qualifie and maske ouer their inward deformities for a time. (Sig. A2)

To make even more difficult the historian's task, at times matters of great consequence are grounded in such "pettie trifles" that "no Historian would either thinke vpon, or could well search out." (p. 537) At other times the difficulties attending the study of human causation are insurmountable, *"For the heart of man is unsearchable."* [italics mine] Such is the craft of princes that even when closely observed by "those many eyes which prie both into them, and into such as liue around them; yet sometimes either by their owne close temper, or by some subtill miste, they conceale the trueth from all reports." (p. 536)

Ralegh's awareness of diversity, close tempers, subtle mists, and unsearchable hearts was an important factor in preventing him from becoming Bodin's historian of human mind and volition. He did not share Ascham's nor Patricio's confidence about discovering the "inward disposition of the mind," no matter how rigorous the methods applied. For Ralegh, rational motives were easiest to determine, the irrational more difficult, the trifling virtually impossible. Then too must come the realization, when the limits of human knowledge are reached, that the heart of man is unsearchable. At this point, the historian can show only that the human will wills itself; he writes a history of revelation rather than one of motivation.

It seems clear that Ralegh's conception of the historian synthesized and transcended Bodin's theology-philosophy-history division of historiography. Not only did he resist Bodin's tripartite fragmentation, he also tried to establish the rational grounds of providential historiography, while attempting to maintain faith's superordinate position. He recognized the legitimate claims for reason in historiography; he also recognized the dangers of claiming too much for it in relation both to Providence and to mankind.

History, Philosophy, and Poetry

A commonly used procedure in the Renaissance was to compare history with philosophy and poetry. Each art had its advocates for supremacy, and a brief summary of the familiar positions of Sir Philip Sidney, who championed poetry, of James Amyot who argued for historiography, and of Sir Francis Bacon, who gave the primacy to philosophy, will help us define

further Ralegh's position on "truth" and historiography. As we shall see, Ralegh differed with all three, perhaps most markedly with Sidney.

Sidney argued three positions with which Ralegh totally disagreed: that poetry presents universals, while history does not; that historical events contain no clue to divine retributive justice, to the operations of Providence; that the poet is a "creator," analogous to God.

Sidney in his *Apologie for Poetry* (written *ca.* 1580 and separately published in two 1595 editions) attacked historiography on grounds that denied the very *raison d'être* of Ralegh's providential historiography. In the *Apologie,* of course, Sidney was responding to the arguments against poetry launched by the Puritan reformers.[16] One thrust of their attack echoed Plato's view that the poet is thrice removed from truth, that he merely imitates an imitation of a universal. The second, also based on Plato's authority, accused poets of stimulating the passions rather than addressing reason, of pandering to the inferior sensible soul. Thus the poet cannot properly teach. He can only give pleasure, and the habit of pleasure becomes vicious and degrading.

Sidney met the first charge by arguing that far from being thrice removed from truth, poetry offers "perfect pictures," a coupling of particular and universal truths. In meeting the second charge, he recognized that poetry delights or gives pleasure, but saw these delightful qualities as necessary virtues to "move" man to overcome his "infected will" in order to embrace truth. The rational apprehension of truth and virtue is by itself insufficient. The poet delights in order "to move men to take that goodness in hand which without delight they would fly as from a stranger."[17] The poet not only shows the way, "but giveth so sweet a prospect unto the way as will entice any man to enter it. . . . " (p. 38) The poet's feigned example is superior to the historian's literal truth because, although both may teach, the former is far superior in moving power because it "may be tuned to the highest key of passion." (p. 33) The poet's moving power also makes him superior to the philosopher:

> For suppose it be granted (that which I suppose with great reason may be denied) that the philosopher, in respect of his methodical pro-ceeding, teach more perfectly than the poet: yet do I think that no man is so much *philophilosophos* as to compare the philosopher in moving with the poet. And that moving is of a higher degree than teaching, it may be this appear: that it is well nigh the cause and the effect of teaching. For who will be taught if he be not moved with desire to be taught . . . ? (pp. 36-37)

Of equal importance in proving the poet's superiority is his special relationship with truth. For Sidney, as guides to truth the philosopher and historian proceed "the one by precept, the other by example. But both, not having both, do both halt." (pp. 26-27) The philosopher, "setting down with thorny argument the bare rule, is so hard of utterance and so misty to be conceived, that one that hath no other guide but him shall wade in him until he be old before he shall find sufficient cause to be honest. For his knowledge standeth so much upon the abstract and general that happy is that man who may understand him, and more happy that can apply what he doth understand." (*Ibid.*)

On the other hand, the "peerless poet," in presenting a "perfect picture," "coupleth the general notion with the particular example." (*Ibid.*) The perfect picture can strike, pierce, and possess the rational soul of man far more effectively than can the philosopher's "wordish description."

Having banished the philosopher to a pseudo-platonic limbo of misty abstractions, which lack moving power, Sidney banished the historian to a foolish world of isolated particulars, which lack teaching power. The historian, "wanting the precept, is so tied, not to what should be but to what is, to the particular truth of things and not to the general reason of things, that his example draweth no necessary consequence, and therefore a less fruitful doctrine." (*Ibid.*) Sidney, as Robert Flint noted of Aristotle, assumed "that history treats only of the particular, multiple, and isolated,—that it is devoid of unity and unconcerned with the universal."[18] Sidney, unlike Ralegh, precluded any possibility of a philosophy of history; he made impossible the providential frame of reference basic to Ralegh's conception of history.

Sidney anticipated the objection that if the poet is superior to the philosopher because the former presents "images" of matter, the historian must be superior to the poet because the historian presents "images of true matters, such as indeed were done." (p. 31) He saw this characteristic of historiography as evidence for its inferiority to poetry. He granted that a truly described act is better than one falsely described, but the important question went beyond literal truth. Rather it concerned "for your own use and learning, whether it be better to have it set down as it should be or as it was. . . ." (pp. 31-32) For the sake of the "perfect pattern," Sidney concluded that the *should be* is far better than the *was*. The past can never be a logical basis for present and future action, as if "because it rained yesterday therefore it should rain today." (p. 33) At best the historian can only come to a "conjectured likelihood" on appropriate present and future policies. Ralegh's position, of course, is diametrically opposed, for men may gather out of the past "a policy no lesse wise than eternall," an assertion which presupposes an eternal, providentially enforced moral frame of reference.

Further, for Sidney, since the historian is tied to the *was*, he labors under the burden of "being captived to the truth of a foolish world." Therefore, instead of presenting examples of virtue rewarded and vice punished, the historian is "many times a terror from well doing and an encouragement to unbridled wickedness." (p. 35) Unlike Ralegh, for Sidney the historian's subject matter is not informed with divine justice; it is not the "vnderstood language of the Almightie." Rather, controlled by second causes, it is a place where the wicked may triumph and the virtuous suffer defeat.

Finally, summarizing the history of poets, Sidney concludes by claiming for poets a power superior to nature's, a power to make "things either better than nature bringeth forth, or quite anew, forms such as never were in nature. . . ." (p. 14) As M. H. Abrams has shown,[19] Sidney is one of the first English writers to claim that the poet "lifted up with the vigor of his own invention," may "create" other worlds (heterocosms) which contain higher truths than nature's world. The claim is a daring one, for previously such power had been exclusively reserved for the God of Creation *ex nihilo.*

The references to poetry in the **History** are brief and scattered; yet they show that Ralegh would most emphatically deny Sidney's argument that the poet's work improves on literal reality. Ralegh defined poetry (along with Bacon) as "feigned" or "imagined" history, and very clearly *qua* historian he distrusted the "feigned" and "imaginations." Of course, enough of Ralegh's poetry has survived to prove him an accomplished poet;[20] however, in the **History** the most he granted to poetry is the possibility that those readers "as can either interpret [the poets'] fables, or separate them from the naked trueth, shall finde matter in *Poems,* not vnworthy to bee regarded of Historians." (p. 451)

When Ralegh searched such "fables" for their "naked trueth," the results are devasting to poetry. In his discussion of "poeticall inuentions," the stories of Aeneas, the early kings of Alba, the founding of Rome, the relations between gods and men in early Greek and Roman history, he gave them brutally literal interpretations, a portion of which follows: "*Aeneas* was a bastard and begotten vpon some faire Harlot, called for her beautie *Venus,* and was therefore the child of lust, which is *Venus. Romulus* was nurst by a Wolfe, which was *Lupa,* or *Lupina,* for the Curtesans in those daies were called Wolfes. . . ." (p. 589) Despite the fact that the "*Græcian* Historians and Poets, imbroder and intermixe the tales of auncient times, with a world of fictions and fabulous discourses," (p. 434) their works may be useful when handled very cautiously: "But as a skilfull and learned *Chymist* can as well by separation of visible elements draw helpfull medicines out of poyson, as poyson out of the most healthfull hearbs and plants (all things hauing in themselues both life and death) so, contrarie to the purposes and hopes of the Heathen, may those which seeke after God and Truth finde out euery where, and in all the ancient Poets and Philosophers, the Story of the first Age. . . . " (p. 84) Ralegh nowhere even hints that the poet's invention is analogous to God's creation. Such "Poeticall addition" may "beautify," but it cannot enhance "meere Historicall truth." (p. 28)

Of the differences between Sidney and Ralegh, the most significant concern Sidney's separation of universal and particular truths and their coupling in poetry, and Sidney's limitation of the historian to second cause particularity in the world; rather, Ralegh saw the world and its inhabitants as part of God's "poem," created *ex nihilo,* and the historian as explicator of that poem.

James Amyot, whose preface to Plutarch's *Lives* was included in North's translation (1579 and seven editions to 1631), reflects the rhetorico-literary tradition of historiography. Historiography should not merely inform; it must *move* as well, and thus is a species of oratory. This tradition, its main classical authorities being Cicero and Quintilian, is expressed in Caxton's "Prohemye" to the *Polychronicon* (1482): "And also yf the terryble feyned Fables of Poetes haue moche styred and moeued men to pyte / and conseruynge of Justyce How moche more is to be supposed/ that Historye assertryce of veryte / and as moder of alle philosophye/ moeuynge our maners to vertue. . . . "[21] In the preface to his popular translation of Froissart (1523), Lord Berners argued that history "exciteth, moveth, and stirreth" men to seek fame through noble deeds, "and it prohibiteth reprovable persons to do mischievous deeds, for fear of infamy and shame."[22] In 1614 Brathwait offered identical arguments for history, whose examples are "a moving kinde of perswasion for imitation of goodnesse; and aversion from whatsoever is evill" (*Survey of History,* pp. 351-52) and beget "a manly spirit" in the pursuit of fame. (p. 20) Amyot's argument for history's superiority to philosophy and poetry was based on their relative powers to profit, delight, and move: "these things [history] doth with much greater grace, efficacy, and speede, than the bookes of moral Philosophie doe: forasmuch as examples are of more force to move and instruct, than are the arguments and proofes of reason, or their precise precepts, bicause examples be the very formes of our deedes, and accompanied with all circumstance." (*Lives,* I, p. xvi) Both history and philosophy present truth, but history teaches more effectively since its examples move and instruct, whereas the books of moral philosophy "doe seeme somewhat harshe to divers delicate wits, that can not tary long upon them." (*Ibid.,* p. xiii)

He also attacked poetry: "The reading of bookes [of poetry] which bring but a vaine and unprofitable plea-sure to the Reader, is justly misliked of wise and grave men." (*Ibid.*) History is superior because "it doth things with greater weight and gravity, than the inventions and devices of the Poets: bicause it helpeth not it selfe with any other thing than with the plaine truth, wheras Poetry doth commonly inrich things by commending them above the starres and their deserving, bicause the chiefe intent thereof is to delight." (*Ibid.,* p. xix) History presents truth, poetry feigns; history profits, poetry brings vain and idle pleasure. If we derive pleasure from hearing an old man recite true stories from his experience, "how much more we be ravished with delight and wondring, to behold the state of mankind, and the true successe of things, which antiquitie hath and doth bring forth from the beginning of the world. . . . " (*Ibid.,* pp. xxii-xxiii) Thus Amyot justified historiography as did Sidney poetry, that it profits, delights, and moves.

The justification of historiography in terms of its ravishing, delightful, or moving powers went unmentioned by Ralegh. Indeed (as we shall see in Part V), he despaired of its possible good effects, a conclusion quite unrelated to the historical pyrrhonism of Agrippa and Ruelle, and which took nothing from his arguments for historiography's revelation of truth. He simply denied that it "moves" as Amyot claimed. Ralegh referred to the Horatian formula of profit and delight only once in the entire *History,* and that in a reference to poetry. He cautioned that poetry yielded "small profit to those which are delighted ouermuch." (p. 451) Throughout the *History,* as he judged the actions and characters of various historical figures, he harshly condemned those whose reason was dethroned by passion. He strongly advocated the habit of rational control, an advocacy which supports his silence on claims such as Amyot's. Although Ralegh's view of history differed very radically from that of Thomas Hobbes (as we might expect), on this issue they would have agreed. Hobbes in the preface to his translation of Thucydides (1629) emphatically rejected the argument that historiography must please or delight. He too claimed to be concerned only with "truth" or profit. (Sig. A3)

Bacon based his distinctions between the relative value of philosophy, history, and poetry on faculty psychology: "I adopt that division of human learning which corresponds to the three faculties of the understanding. Its parts therefore are three: History, Poesy, and Philosophy. History is referred to the Memory; Poesy to the Imagination; Philosophy to the Reason."[23] Basic to all learning is history, which "is properly concerned with individuals; the impressions whereof are the first and most ancient guests of the human mind, and are as the primary materials of knowledge." (*Ibid.*)

These "images of individuals" provide the mind with exercise and with "sport." "For as all knowledge is the exercise and work of the mind, so poesy may be regarded as its sport. In philosophy the mind is bound to things; in poesy it is released from that bond, and wanders forth, and feigns what it pleases. . . ." (*Ibid.*) Poetry, or "feigned history," unlike "true history," can give some "shadow of satisfaction to the mind of man in those points wherein the nature of things doth deny it." (*Works*, p. 88) The poet can feign events agreeable to the merits of virtue and vice (as Sidney argued for different reasons) and can bring the outcome of events more in accord with retribution and with "revealed providence." The historian, however, bound as he is to the "nature of things," cannot depict the roles of retributive justice and revealed providence (Bacon's assumption here, of course, strikes at the roots of Ralegh's historiography). Poetry submits the "shews of things to the desires of the mind; whereas reason doth buckle and bow the mind unto the nature of things." (*Ibid.*)

Poetry then brings only a "shadow of satisfaction." Man's unpredictable and lawless imagination produces it. It is unrelated to truth because "being not tied to the laws of matter, [it] may at pleasure join that which nature hath severed, and sever that which nature hath joined, and so make unlawful matches and divorces of things. . . ." (*Works*, p. 87) In this way Bacon discredited poetry.

History, however, concerns the "primary material of knowledge," and as such is the basis for philosophy, which "digests" the particulars of history into "general notions." (*Works*, p. 677) As a discipline, history has no way of discovering universals, but simply serves as a repository for particulars, similar to a receptive but passive memory which lacks any active principle through which universals may be reached. In his account of natural history Bacon describes its necessary yet subordinate role: "Natural history . . . is in its use two-fold. For it is used either for the sake of the knowledge of the particular things which it contains, or as the primary material of philosophy and the stuff and subject matter of true induction." (*Works*, p. 403)

Whereas Ralegh and Bacon generally agreed on poetry's deficiencies and on truth as the proper subject matter of both history and philosophy, they differed profoundly on truth's nature. For Bacon, philosophy working with history's particulars could aspire to secular or "scientific" universals; historiography could not. For Ralegh, God's universal imperatives were intelligible within the particular. Bacon's universals, available to the highest reach of human reason, were surpassed wholly by the truths of faith, the legitimate province of what he termed "Divine Theology." These truths were supported only by divine authority: "We are obliged to believe the word of God, though our reason be shocked at it. For if we should believe only such things as are agreeable to our reason, we assent to the

matter, and not to the author. And therefore, the more absurd and incredible any divine mystery is the greater honor we do to God in believing it; and so much the more noble the victory of faith." (*Ibid.*, p. 666)

Bacon's separation of reason and faith duplicated Siger of Brabant's double truth doctrine: that which is true by faith need not be true by reason, that which is true by reason need not be true by faith. As we have seen, Ralegh was keenly aware of reason's limitations in its searching out the motives of God and man. Yet Bacon's adaptation of Tertullian's *Certum est quia impossibile est* (whether ironic or not) was rejected by Ralegh. In discussing the celestial spheres, he concluded:

> and what vse there should be of this icye, or cristalline, or waterie heauen, I conceiue not, except it be to moderate and temper the heat, which the *Primum mobile* would otherwise gather and increase: though in very truth, in stead of this helpe, it would adde an vnmeasurable greatnesse of circle, whereby by the swiftnesse of that first Moueable would exceede all possibilitie of beleefe. *Sed nemo tenetur ad impossibilia, but no man ought to be held to impossibilities;* and faith it selfe (which surmounteth the heighth of all humane reason) hath for a forcible conducter the word of truth, which also may be called *lumen omnis rationis, & intellectus, the light of all reason and understanding.* (p. 12)

Thus Ralegh still clung to an essential element of Christian rationalism as exemplified by St. Thomas Aquinas and Richard Hooker: the necessary synthesis of faith and reason in all areas of human learning. This element accounts for his resistence to the many forces working for the fragmentation of learning. It is evidenced by his use of "naturall reason" to justify providential historiography, by his claiming for the historian what Bodin claimed for the theologian, philosopher, and historian, what Sidney claimed for the poet, and far more than what Bacon claimed for the philosopher and historian combined. In this, the tides were turned strongly against him. Despite the important differences in the theories of such as Bodin, Amyot, Patricio, Sidney, Bacon, and others, they agreed on the limitation of historiography to second causes; and Amyot, Sidney, Bacon, and many others endlessly elaborated on the generic differences between history, philosophy, and theology. Ralegh denied all these views. Parenthetically, it should be added that the readers of the *History* who isolate its providential elements for praise (or blame) are not seeing it whole, and those who admire the classical or humanist elements misread it also.

Such was the magnitude of Ralegh's historical vision, such was his confidence and audacity, that he took all human knowledge as his province, knowledge which included glimpses of the eternal. Fulfillment of this vision was denied him, but this should not detract from what he set out to do. Of course, in terms of the development of thought within the late Renaissance, the battle was lost even before he took the field. As we shall see, he was unsuccessful in fighting it even on his own grounds, the **History** itself.

Textual Note

I have used the 1614 edition of the *History* for my citations, an edition superior to all others, including the recently reprinted Oxford 1829 edition. The scholarly convention has been to cite the *History* by Book, Chapter, section, sub-section, and also by page; and thus a citation could read I, VII, x, 10, p. 123, a cumbersome method suggestive of wearing both belt and suspenders. Books I-II of the 1614 folio volume are paginated 1-651, and Books III-V, 1-776. Therefore, for the sake of simplicity and with no loss of accuracy, I refer to both paginations by page number, *italicizing* the second series. References to the *History's* Preface are by signation.

Notes

[1] *The Vanity of Arts and Sciences,* trans. by Ja. Sanford (London, 1684), p. 27. The passage closes in the 1537 Latin edition: "*Vt impossible fit, plurimos illoru non esse mendacissimos.*" Sig. B5[v]. For an excellent summary of 16th century historical pyrrhonism, see Julian H. Franklin's *Jean Bodin and the Sixteenth-Century Revolution in the Methodology of Law and History* (New York, 1963), pp. 89-102.

[2] Quoted from John L. Brown, *The Methodus ad Facilem Historiarum Cogitionem of Jean Bodin* (Washington, D. C., 1939), p. 164.

[3] *Ancient Critical Essays,* II, p. 206.

[4] See the Introduction to Beatrice Reynolds' translation *Method for the Easy Comprehension of History by John Bodin* (New York, 1945), p. x.

[5] Thomas Churchyard, "To the Reader," *The Worthiness of Wales,* reprinted from the 1587 edition (Manchester, 1876), Sig. A2[v].

[6] *The Philosophical Works of Francis Bacon,* reprinted from the texts and translations with the notes and prefaces of Ellis and Spedding, ed. by John M. Robertson (London, 1905), pp. 86-87.

[7] *Hypercritica, Ancient Critical Essays,* II, p. 255.

[8] *A Survey of History: or a Nursery for Gentry* (London, 1638), p. 267. First printed as *The Scholler's*

Medley, or, An Intermixt Discourse Upon Historical and Poetical Relations (London, 1614).

[9] *Scholasticism,* trans. by Richard and Clara Winston (New York, 1960). See Ch. III.

[10] "Amiot to the Reader," *The Lives of the Noble Grecians and Romanes . . . Translated out of Greeke into French by James Amyot . . . and . . . into Englishe by Thomas North 1579.* 8 vols. (Oxford, 1928), I, p. xxi.

[11] The bibliography on Creation is extensive. Very useful are Etienne Gilson, "Creation," *The Christian Philosophy of St. Thomas Aquinas* (New York, 1956), pp. 147-59; H. Pinard, "Creation," *Dictionnaire de Theologie Catholique,* III, col. 2034-2201; and *St Thomas Aquinas Siger of Brabant St. Bonaventure On the Eternity of the World,* trans. by C. Vollert, L. H. Kendzierski, and P. M. Byrne (Milwaukee, Wis., 1964).

[12] Walter F. Oakeshott, "Sir Walter Ralegh's Library," *The Library,* XXIII, No. 4 (1968), 301.

[13] *The History of Christian Philosophy in the Middle Ages* (New York, 1955), p. 409.

[14] Prefixed to *A Report and Discourse of the Affairs and State of Germany, The Whole Works of Roger Ascham,* ed. by J. A. Giles, 3 vols. in 4 (London, 1864), III, pp. 5-6.

[15] *The true order and methode of Wryting and reading Hystories, according to the precepts of Francisco Patricio, and Accontio Tridentino,* ed. by Hugh G. Dick, *HLQ,* III (1940), 156.

[16] For a very thorough discussion of the *Apology* see the "Introduction" to *An Apology for Poetry,* ed. by Geoffrey Shepherd (London, 1965), pp. 1-91.

[17] I quote from Forrest G. Robinson's edition, *An Apology for Poetry* (New York, 1970), p. 20. This edition is the first to incorporate the readings from the recently discovered Norwich MS of the *Apology.*

[18] This is part of Robert Flint's characterization of Aristotle's views on history, *History of the Philosophy of History* (New York, 1894), pp. 145-46. Aristotle discussed history in the *Poetics,* Ch. 9.

[19] *The Mirror and the Lamp* (Oxford, 1953). See his chapter "The Poem as Heterocosm."

[20] C.S. Lewis sees Ralegh as a poet "among the belated writers of Drab. . . . The truth is that Ralegh has no style of his own; he is an amateur, blown this way and that . . . by his reading." *English Literature in the Sixteenth Century Excluding Drama* (Oxford,

1954), p. 519. For a convincing refutation of Lewis' views see Yvor Winters' review of Lewis' work, "English Literature in the Sixteenth Century," *The Function of Criticism* (Denver, 1957), pp. 191-200. Winters sees Ralegh as one of the great lyric poets of the Renaissance.

[21] W. J. B. Crotch, *The Prologues and Epilogues of William Caxton, EETS,* Original Series, n. 176 (London, 1928), p. 65.

[22] *The Chronicles of Jean Froissart: In Sir Lord Berner's Translation,* ed. by Gillian and William Anderson (Carbondale, Ill., 1962), p. 2.

[23] *A Description of the Intellectual Globe (ca.* 1612), *The Philosophical Works,* p. 677.

Gerald Hammond (essay date 1984)

SOURCE: An Introduction to *Sir Walter Ralegh: Selected Writings,* Carcanet Press, 1984, pp. 7-20.

[*In the following introduction to his edition of Ralegh's selected works, Hammond underscores the essentially pessimistic tone of Raleigh's writings and describes the stylistic features of his poetry and prose.*]

Sir Walter Ralegh was a bad walker and did not know Hebrew.[1] These two readily admitted deficiencies apart, it is difficult to think of any other large limitations to his achievement or ambition. He was soldier, scholar, horseman, and much else: father of the idea of the British Empire; chemist and alchemist; patron of poets, and yet a fine enough poet himself to rival any he patronized; prize courtier of England's greatest monarch, but a hero of the republican generation after his death; introducer of the potato to Ireland and tobacco to England; a founder of modern historical writing; explorer; ship-designer; naval and military strategist; quack doctor; notorious atheist, but the last great asserter of God's providential pattern of history; the most hated man in England after Essex's downfall, but the most loved after his own. The list could go on and on, and any selection from his writings can hardly fail to lay open to us the extraordinary energy of the man.

Yet the prevailing tone of virtually everything Ralegh wrote is of disappointment and defeat. His favourite line of his own poetry seems to have been 'Of all which past, the sorrow only stays'; and his favourite image, of life as a play acted out on a stage, is usually tragic, and if comic, only sardonically so. In the Preface to his *History of the World* he describes men as 'Comedians in religion', but God as 'the author of all our tragedies', setting his plays on the 'great Theatre' where 'the change of fortune . . . is but as the change of garments on the less'.

Here is the clue to what makes Ralegh's writing, whether verse or prose, so enthralling: the collision of an energetic and strenuous mind with a nature which gravitated towards resignation and endurance, as if the entire combustible world burnt on and on in the one small room, rather than flaring up for a brief instant of time. This is true of even the two most vigorous pieces of prose reproduced here, the narrative of the last fight of the *Revenge* and Ralegh's account of his voyage to Guiana. Both are, in their ways, propaganda pieces: the one to turn a defeat into a kind of victory, the other to persuade the Queen and the gentlemen of England to sink their money into a colonial adventure. But both emerge as tales of endurance. The time scales are different, the ***Revenge*** spanning only hours, while ***Guiana*** takes up months, but for both Grenville and Ralegh the test is ultimately the same—the need to continue, whatever the opposition of men or elements. The terms I use here are almost Miltonic, and rightly so, for Ralegh's influence on Milton should not be underestimated; but still Ralegh avoids the heroic fortitude which Milton gives Samson or Adam. Grenville emerges from the ***Revenge*** narrative as a bungler, not really the heroic figure which Tennyson fashioned out of Ralegh's account. A brave bungler, perhaps, but the cause of the worst loss the English navy had experienced. In ***Guiana*** likewise, we do not have to read too far between the lines to perceive Ralegh's own failure in the expedition, and the sense that it gradually delivers up of a failed enterprise which never will generate support from the monarch or the merchants.

Still, it is Ralegh the poet I ought to consider first, for there have been, both in his day, and in this century, strong claims for Ralegh's achievement in verse. Among his contemporaries George Puttenham[2] found the vein of Ralegh's 'dittie and amorous Ode' to be 'most loftie, insolent, and passionate', and for Edmund Spenser[3] he was 'the sommers Nightingale' whose verse ravished with 'melting sweetness'. The twentieth-century view of Ralegh is that while he may be too limited to be considered a great poet, his achievement is too substantial for him not to be thought a major one. To cite two poet-critics, Yvor Winters[4] described him as 'a far more serious poet than Sidney and Spenser', and Donald Davie[5] 'a greatly endowed and greatly scrupulous poet'.

To begin, though, I ought to emphasize that any claims for Ralegh's poetic stature are inevitably based on shaky foundations. We simply cannot be sure that half of the poems commonly attributed to him are actually his; and strong and frequent attempts are made to deny him some of his best known poems, such as **'The passionate man's pilgrimage'** or **'The nymph's reply to the shepherd'**. Ralegh the poet is, in effect, a composite figure. At the centre are a few poems which are undoubtedly his. Then come layers of accretions, perhaps attracted to him because they fit his tone or circumstances, or perhaps really his. And there is too the chance, in a poet who shunned the 'stigma of print', that some of his best work has disappeared. Not the least, it is possible, if unlikely, that twenty books of *The Ocean to Cynthia* have been lost.

Nonetheless, from those poems which are certainly his we can gather a strong impression of Ralegh's fascinatingly grim poetic personality. Peter Ure, in a brief but fine survey of Ralegh's poetry,[6] drew attention to one of the sonnets which he wrote to herald Spenser's *Faerie Queene,* where instead of a poem of welcome and praise, we find 'all the force of feeling gathering into the sestet', in a vision of tears, regret, and oblivion. Equally distinctive is another dedicatory sonnet which Ralegh wrote nearly a quarter of a century later. It is **'To the Translator of Lucan',** prefixed to Sir Arthur Gorges' translation of Lucan's *Pharsalia.* If Milton recalled the opening line of the *Faerie Queene* sonnet when he wrote his most personal sonnet, 'Methought I saw My Late Espoused Saint', it is not inconceivable that this sonnet praising Gorges' translation should have pointed the way towards the sterner tone of Milton's republican sonnets. This is fitting, for Lucan was the poet of *libertas* and *res publica,* and had earlier been translated in part by Marlowe, a radical spirit often linked with Ralegh. Now Ralegh's sonnet stamps Gorges' translation with the prophecy that Lucan's fate—execution by being forced to commit suicide—may well be Gorges' own; but the parallel to Ralegh himself, the prisoner in the Tower, is, of course, much the closer. In Miltonic fashion the sonnet's lines are brought to the point of buckling by the strenuous syntax they are required to carry:

> For this thou hast been bruised: but yet
> those scars
> Do beautify no less than those wounds do
> Received in just and in religious wars,
> Though thou hast bled by both, and bear'st
> them too.
> Change not. To change thy fortune 'tis too
> late . . .

And given the strength of these two sonnets, we might reasonably find support for Ralegh's authorship of the sonnet **'To his Son',** a poem which appears only in manuscript versions. Its opening picks up the tone of the riddles in the Book of Proverbs: 'Three things there be that prosper up apace / And flourish . . .' recalling 'There be three things that order well their going: yea, four are comely in going' (Prov. 30:29, Geneva version); but the poem develops into a grim account of the coming together of the wood, the weed, and the wag. 'Grim', incidentally, is Agnes Latham's[7] word for this sonnet, although she opposes its being read tragically, as if it were a 'painful poem'. Still, behind this sonnet lies the poet's grasp of the mystery

of riddles: that to fail to solve them means death. Ralegh gives the solution to this one in two lines of characteristically epigrammatic force, at the close of the third quatrain:

> But when they meet, it makes the timber rot,
> It frets the halter, and it chokes the child.

Describing Ralegh as characteristically epigrammatic may seem strange, however, when one considers the long, sprawling poem (or fragment) in Ralegh's own hand, *The Ocean to Cynthia.* Here endurance is stretched to the limits of mental agony, in a poem so undisciplined that it mocks the attempts of commentators to explicate it. The image which is most often used to describe it is of tides of passion. In this sense only does it fulfil the promise of its title, for there is little in its imagery or theme to explain the ocean-moon (Cynthia) reference. But possibly much of its oddness lies in its being, in all its length, the stuff of epigrams, for frequently the wave of passion breaks on an epigrammatic line:

> Joys under dust that never live again (4)

> The broken monuments of my great desires
> (14)

> Woes without date, discomforts without end
> (20)

> Whom love defends, what fortune
> overthrows? (52)

> And worlds of thoughts described by one
> last sithing (96)

> Of all which past, the sorrow only stays
> (123)

Not single lines only, but whole passages are hammered out in the concise, pithy manner of the epigram, as in the remarkable lines towards the end, which follow the sudden appearance of Hero and Leander (487-96):

> On Sestos' shore, Leander's late resort,
> Hero hath left no lamp to guide her love—
> Thou lookest for light in vain, and storms
> arise:
> She sleeps thy death, that erst thy danger
> sithed.
> Strive then no more, bow down thy weary
> eyes—
> Eyes which to all these woes thy heart have
> guided.
> She is gone, she is lost, she is found, she
> is ever fair:
> Sorrow draws weakly, where love draws not

too.
    Woe's cries sound nothing but only in
        love's ear:
    Do then by dying what life cannot do.

The result is curious, as if every word were loaded with passion and meaningful reference, but with little or no sense of continuity, or even progression—only the constant drive toward the epigram.

In his finished poems Ralegh uses this drive toward the epigram to create some of his most powerful effects. It appears first in the **'Epitaph'** upon Sir Philip Sidney, where the stately dignity of the poem's first half gives way to a greater intensity of expression, as if the lines were now being asked to contain double the meaning:

    Tears to the soldiers, the proud Castilian's
        shame,
    Virtue expressed, and honour truly taught.

                                        (39-40)

The aim of poems changes too, so that **'Nature, that washed her hands in milk'** moves from being a conceited love poem to a plain meditation on time and death. And Ralegh's Shakespearean readiness to employ such great generalizations makes his answer to Marlowe's 'Passionate shepherd' poem so much more moving than any of its rivals. It opens in parody, but suddenly gains emotional depth at the beginning of the second stanza, on the lines 'Time drives the flocks from field to fold, / When rivers rage, and rocks grow cold', where the images expand through night, winter, and death, to the death of the whole planet.

Another source of the power of Ralegh's poetry comes from his being the one major late Elizabethan poet who had absorbed and retained the style of earlier poets like Wyatt and Gascoigne. 'Plain' was the word which came to be used to describe this style, but it now seems too vague to describe usefully the curious rhythms of Wyatt and the heavily literal language of Gascoigne. Again, it is Peter Ure who makes this point most tellingly: that what we might fancy to be Ralegh's precocious anticipation of Jacobean cynicism is, more truly, a distinctive belatedness, a real inheritance from those earlier poets and Tottel's *Miscellany*. Indeed, the first poem in this selection, a tribute to Gascoigne, reads very much like something out of the *Miscellany;* and one would not need to be too uncharitable to describe it as a poor poem, halting and inflexible, if not actually clumsy. But in retrospect it deserves the pride of place it has, as a young poet's (Ralegh was twenty-three when he wrote it) declaration that one cannot please all, and ought therefore to aim to please the worthiest audience only. The poem opens with great emphasis, and

develops towards a Wyatt-like image of the slippery slope of achievement:

    Sweet were the sauce would please each
        kind of taste;
    The life likewise were pure that never
        swerved; . . .

    For whoso reaps renown above the rest
    With heaps of hate shall surely be
        oppressed.

                                        (1-2, 11-12).

One can see how this young poet will later write a poem as vehement as **'The lie'**. While Gascoigne was praised for having had the nerve to censure abuses which range 'from prince to poor, from high estate to low', **'The lie'** not only censures all, but challenges them too, with the certain knowledge that to speak such truth 'deserves no less than stabbing'. In this poem Ralegh finds the ideal fusion of inflexible form and starkly literal content: the rhythms are jagged, pretence of grammatical logic dissolves, all imagery is discarded, and even words are finally dismissed by the brutal acknowledgement that the only truthful human intercourse is with a dagger (67-78):

    Tell faith it's fled the City,
        Tell how the country erreth,
    Tell manhood shakes off pity,
        Tell virtue least preferreth;
    And if they do reply,
        Spare not to give the lie.

    So when thou hast, as I
        Commanded thee, done blabbing,
    Although to give the lie
        Deserves no less than stabbing,
    Stab at thee he that will,
        No stab thy soul can kill.

Again, giving the lie is a matter not of heroism, but of fortitude—similar in kind to the pilgrimages of the two poems of resolution, **'The passionate man's pilgrimage'** and **'As you came from the holy land'**.

Whatever our qualifications about the authorship of Ralegh's poems, we need have none about his prose. There used to be some doubt, based on a remark of Ben Jonson's,[8] about the degree to which he might have had help in writing the *History of the World,* but it is generally accepted now that the work is almost entirely Ralegh's own. And to clear away any doubts one might have about Ralegh as a prose stylist, there are already the splendid examples of *A Report of the Truth of the Fight About the Isles of Azores . . . Betwixt the Revenge . . . and an Armada of the King of Spain* (1591) and *The Discovery of the Large, Rich and Beautiful Empire of Guiana* (1596).

Despite its being his first piece of published prose, the *Revenge* shows Ralegh's total control over his material. The centre of the narrative, the battle itself, is made memorable by the economy with which he describes the hopelessness of the *Revenge*'s situation:

> . . . Unto ours there remained no comfort at all, no hope, no supply either of ships, men, or weapons; the masts all beaten overboard, all her tackle cut asunder, her upper work altogether razed, and in effect evened she was with the water, but the very foundation or bottom of a ship, nothing being left over head either for flight or defence.

But Ralegh does not allow the action to overwhelm his account, and for all its heroism and adventure, the sense it leaves with us is of the coolness, even percipience, of its narrator. There are key sentences, early on, where he makes it clear that not even the most well-disposed judge can excuse Grenville for his foolhardiness:

> But Sir *Richard* utterly refused to turn from the enemy, alleging that he would rather choose to die, than to dishonour himself, his country, and her Majesty's ship, persuading his company that he would pass through the two Squadrons, in despite of them: and enforce those of *Seville* to give him way. Which he performed upon diverse of the foremost, who as the Mariners term it, sprang their luff, and fell under the lee of the *Revenge*. But the other course had been the better, and might right well have been answered in so great an impossibility of prevailing. Notwithstanding out of the greatness of his mind, he could not be persuaded.

This idea, that outstanding bravery most often leads to disaster becomes a common theme of the *History of the World*. Here it should already make the reader question the positive quality which he might normally attribute to 'greatness of mind'. The final part of the *Revenge* is written very much in the detached, judging tone of the *History*, too, as Ralegh carefully analyses the inevitable consequences for any Englishman who could be persuaded to betray himself to the Spaniards. Just as Grenville stands for all the great-hearted fools of history, so is Maurice of Desmond, the seducer towards Spain, who contrived in three years to lose all that his family had spent three centuries building up, the model for all traitors. The lesson is one of *realpolitik:* 'But what man can be so blockishly ignorant ever to expect place or honour from a foreign king, having no other argument or persuasion than his own disloyalty?'

In the *Discovery of Guiana* Ralegh is no longer merely a narrator, but the chief participant too. The result is one of the finest pieces of Elizabethan prose, for it has all the narrative control of the *Revenge,* but with the advantage that one is, all the time, inside the head of the ever inquisitive Ralegh, seeing the land through his eyes. There are some marvellous perceptions too—not least of natural phenomena, like the oysters on trees, or the sudden unexpected paradise which they encounter after hours of arduous travel

> . . . here we beheld plains of twenty mile in length, the grasses short and green, and in divers parts groves of trees by themselves, as if they had been by all the art and labour in the world so made of purpose: and still as we rowed, the Deer came down feeding by the water's side, as if they had been used to a keeper's call.

Most interesting of all are the people who inhabit the country: the canny Berrio, Spanish Butcher, but elegant gentleman too; an old Indian guide who comes as close to an execution as he could possibly get, as he spins out excuses as to why the settlement he promised has not yet been reached; a beautiful native woman who reminds Ralegh of a certain lady back in England; and his own men also, not individualized, but suffering along with him heat, hunger, torrential rain, near shipwreck—but not one of whom, Ralegh rightly boasts, failed to return safe and sound. And at the edge of the narrative there are figures reported to Ralegh, but which he can only imagine: the Amazons, and the Ewaipanoma who have their eyes in their shoulders and their mouths in the middle of their breasts. Imagined places haunt the narrative as well: most of all, El Dorado and the gold mines which fed it, and which Ralegh's imagination never lost grip of, even as he mouldered in the Tower.

It may well be that the *Discovery* was too well written—so evocative that the hard-headed Elizabethans preferred to treat it as a good yarn rather than as a map of England's colonial future. Richard Hakluyt,[9] for instance, included it in his *Voyages,* but it also seems probable that he was instrumental in advising men like Robert Cecil against any further involvement. Its influence was literary, not economic. No Contractation house was set up in London, but some of the exotic lists of places in *Paradise Lost* drew their inspiration from it (and perhaps Othello's anthropophagi too). Its main target, Elizabeth herself, remained unimpressed. Ralegh had lost her favour after his affair and marriage with Elizabeth Throckmorton, and not even the engaging reference to her as *Ezrabeta Cassipuna Acarewana,* a true Amazonian queen, could win her round. No investment was made in Guiana, and English explorations there gradually petered out.

Ezrabeta Cassipuna Acarewana is only one in a long list of descriptions which Ralegh made of Elizabeth. Most of them occur in the poetry—Cynthia, Diana, the Queen whose memory was 'more strong than were ten thousand ships of war'—and there is the remarkable letter where he pictures her as 'hunting like Diana, walking like Venus'. But Ralegh's most poignant description came soon after her death, while on trial for his life: 'and instead of a Lady whom Time had surprised . . .'. Instead of that lady there was now 'an active King', whose activity centred most on the removal of Ralegh. The trial was a moral defeat for James; so much so that it saved Ralegh from execution, but condemned him, instead, to thirteen years in the Tower. One consequence of this imprisonment was the desperate attempt to salvage all on a final voyage to Guiana . . . ; another was the *History of the World*.

In many senses Ralegh had been preparing to write the *History* all his life, not least in the omnivorous reading which he engaged in, even while at sea. At odd points in the poetry, also, one comes across the embryo of an historical imagination, as in the *Ocean to Cynthia*:

> We should begin by such a parting light
> To write the story of all ages past,
> And end the same before th' approaching night.
> Such is again the labour of my mind,
> Whose shroud, by sorrow woven now to end,
> Hath seen that ever-shining sun declined
> So many years that so could not descend . . .

> (101-7)

There is, too, the cool analysis of power in **'The lie'**. Then, towards the end of the *Revenge*, Ralegh shows his early readiness to see the workings of Providence in the rise and fall of nations, as he comments on God's judgment of the Spanish abuse of power: 'Thus it hath pleased God to fight for us, and to defend the justice of our cause, against the ambitious and bloody pretences of the Spaniards, who seeking to devour all nations, are themselves devoured'. Most of all, Ralegh had experience of power and the people who wield it. He had seen, and possibly aided, Essex's overthrow, and had himself been the victim of the arbitrary abuse of power by both Elizabeth and James. So although the *History* takes care to emphasize a providential pattern to history, the 'first cause' of things, it spends most of its strength delineating the arbitrariness of second causes, usually rulers and their flatterers.

There are heroic figures in the *History,* but they come few and far between. One, perhaps, is Hannibal, but his heroism derives in part from his not having total power. Ralegh makes a powerful case for the causes of Hannibal's failure lying with the Carthaginian power-brokers who would not let him have the money and materials he needed. The one indisputable hero is Epaminondas,[10] eulogized by Ralegh in the only un-

qualified paean of praise in the *History*. This, by implication, is what all other princes have fallen short of:

> So died *Epaminondas,* the worthiest man that ever was bred in that Nation of *Greece,* and hardly to be matched in any Age or Country: for he equalled all others in the several virtues, which in each of them were singular. His Justice, and Sincerity, his Temperance, Wisdom, and high Magnanimity, were no way inferior to his Military virtue; in every part whereof he so excelled, that he could not properly be called a Wary, a Valiant, a Politic, a Bountiful, or an Industrious, and a Provident Captain; all these Titles, and many other, being due unto him, which with his notable Discipline, and good Conduct, made a perfect composition of an Heroic General. Neither was his private Conversation unanswerable to those high parts, which gave him praise abroad. For he was Grave, and yet very Affable and Courteous; resolute in public business, but in his own particular easy, and of much mildness; a lover of his People, bearing with men's infirmities, witty and pleasant in speech, far from insolence, Master of his own affections, and furnished with all qualities that might win and keep love. To these Graces were added great ability of body, much Eloquence, and very deep knowledge in all parts of Philosophy and Learning, wherewith his mind being enlightened, rested not in the sweetness of Contemplation, but brake forth into such effects as gave unto *Thebes,* which had evermore been an underling, a dreadful reputation among all people adjoining, and the highest command in *Greece.*

The magisterial style of this passage is typical of the whole *History,* but it is more often used for scorn and contempt than for praise. A succession of princes strut through the pages, only to be brought dramatically low: Jezebel eaten by the dogs; Nebuchadnezzar eating grass; Xerxes forced to flee back to Asia leaving a shattered army of millions; Darius reduced to a chained captive in a cart; and Perseus 'beholding to the courtesy of his enemies for a wretched life'.

But the *History* is no mere *Mirror for Magistrates*. Ralegh's aim is less to educate men in the way the wheel of fortune turns than to show the invariably terrible effects of power. Under its pressure men always choose to do the wrong thing. In the hands of a succession of English and European monarchs, as the Preface shows, it led to ambition for more power, miscalculation, and retribution. Apart from Epaminondas, and a few like him, the actual *History* itself presents an unremitting analysis of the tyranny of rulers. No wonder that James I condemned it for being 'too saucy in censuring princes', and no wonder either that it became a prime text for the regicides of the next generation; Oliver Cromwell,[11] for instance, recommended it to his son to 'recreate' himself with 'Sir

Walter Ralegh's History: it's a body of History, and will add much more to your understanding than fragments of story'.

Another regicide who read it carefully was John Milton. The *History's* influence has been traced through *Paradise Lost,* but there are signs, too, that for the young Milton it was a formative work. At twenty-one he included in his 'Nativity Ode' the image of the silencing of the pagan deities at Christ's coming

> The oracles are dumb,
> No voice or hideous hum
>   Runs through the archèd roof in words
>   deceiving.
> Apollo from his shrine
> Can no more divine,
>   With hollow shriek the steep of Delphos
>   leaving.
> No nightly trance, or breathèd spell,
> Inspires the pale-eyed priest from the
>   prophetic cell.

The idea is a commonplace, but one which Ralegh repeatedly turns to in the opening book of the *History,* and often in terms which seem very close to Milton's

> . . . There are none now in *Phoenicia,* that lament the death of *Adonis;* nor any in *Libya, Creta, Thessalia,* or elsewhere, that can ask counsel or help from *Jupiter.* The great god *Pan* hath broken his pipes, *Apollo's* Priests are become speechless. . . .

It is worth emphasizing that Milton was probably most interested in those parts of the *History* which are the least attractive to a modern taste. It is a massive work, and to choose extracts from it as I have done is certainly to misrepresent it. Ralegh's developing, cumulative picture of man's history is lost in reducing it to a series of purple passages. Also, in a selection such as this, the choice of extracts is governed more by a literary than an historical bias. In the first two books Ralegh uses the Bible as his yardstick, both for chronology and for the recounting of what happened. Whole sections are given over to his attempts to make biblical chronology consistent and to fit it into what was known of the rest of the world's history during that period. Such speculations seem arid now, and they were the kind of thing which drew down Matthew Arnold's[12] scorn on the whole enterprise—but they helped set a pattern of parallelism between the biblical and the pagan, which probably had a greater influence upon *Paradise Lost*[13] than any of the specific passages to which commentators have drawn our attention.

In this selection the emphasis falls on two other elements of the *History:* Ralegh's digressions and his narrative skill. The two are really elements of the same thing, as Ralegh explains in the defence of his digressionary style which he gives in the Preface, in a striking anticipation of modern narrative theory:

> For seeing we digress in all the ways of our lives: yea seeing the life of man is nothing else but digression; I may the better be excused in writing their lives and actions. I am not altogether ignorant in the Laws of *History,* and of the *Kinds.*

This principle of digression runs through the entire *History.* Sometimes whole sections explore such matters as whether the Roman or the English soldier were the better, or the strategy of defending 'hard passages'. Then there are digressions at the lower levels of paragraph and sentence, where we see the love of the sententious and epigrammatic which marks the poetry, as in this passage from Book V, where Ralegh sums up the character of Dionysius. It moves outward, from discussion of the specific man, to generalized comment on all flatterers:

> When he had reigned eight and thirty years, he died: some say, in his bed, peaceably; which is the most likely, though others report it otherwise. A cruel man he was, and a faithless; a great Poet, but a foolish one. He entertained *Plato* a while, but afterward, for speaking against his tyranny, he gave order to have him slain, or sold for a slave. For he could endure no man, that flattered him not beyond measure. His Parasites therefore styled his cruelty, *The hate of evil men;* and his lawless slaughters, *The ornaments and effects of his justice.* True it is, that flatterers are a kind of vermin, which poison all the Princes of the World; and yet they prosper better, than the worthiest and valiantest men do: And I wonder not at it; for it is a world; and as our *Saviour Christ* hath told us, *The world will love her own.* (chap. 1:4)

Flattery brings out the best in Ralegh's prose. Too 'damnable proud', in Aubrey's words, to consider himself ever to have been a flatterer, he must have looked mordantly upon the hangers-on at the Stuart court. Such types pop up again and again in the *History*—as in the description of Darius as one 'who had been accustomed to nothing so much as to his own praises, and to nothing so little as to hear truth', or the sardonic generalizations in the opening chapter of Book I:

> For whosoever shall tell any great man or Magistrate, that he is not just, the General of an Army, that he is not valiant, and great Ladies that they are not fair, shall never be made a Counsellor, a Captain, or a Courtier.

Another idea which Ralegh returns to eloquently is the unpredictability of history, the complete uncertainty we must have for the perpetuation of any state of affairs, prosperous or otherwise. In a telling phrase from the Preface he describes the fortunate and the wretched, the two extreme states of human existence, as both being 'so tied by God to the very instant, and both so subject to interchange'. This becomes a dominant theme of the *History:* part of the reciprocal process whereby the children of an oppressor become the victims of the children of their father's victims. And in one fine digression the uncertainty of things is tied firmly to Ralegh's disgust at flattery:

> All, or the most, have a vain desire of ability to do evil without control: which is a dangerous temptation unto the performance. God, who best can judge what is expedient, hath granted such power to very few: among whom also, very few there are, that use it not to their own hurt. For who sees not, that a Prince, by racking his Sovereign authority to the utmost extent, enableth (besides the danger of his own person) some one of his own sons or nephews to root up all his progeny? Shall not many excellent Princes, notwithstanding their brotherhood, or other nearness in blood, be driven to flatter the Wife, the Minion, or perhaps the Harlot, that governs one, the most unworthy of his whole house, yet reigning over all?

As these extracts show, it is possible to praise Ralegh's style at the level of single sentences, even phrases. He writes, for example, of the greatest men who, 'to be made greater, could lose the sense of other men's sorrow and subjection'. He defines peace 'between ambitious Princes, and States' as 'a kind of breathing'; and pithily traces the workings of Providence in the epigram that 'where God hath a purpose to destroy, wise men grow short lived'. Sometimes, as befits his prophetic role, he moves from the historian's register to the biblical prophet's 'The vanities of men beguile their vain contrivers, and the prosperity of the wicked, is the way leading to their destruction . . .'. Other times he introduces eloquent images into his prose, as in the ambiguous rats (hostile readers or literal rats in the Tower?) who gnaw his papers in the Preface; or, from elsewhere in the Preface, time as a 'consuming disease'; Opinion travelling the world 'without a passport'; Ralegh himself being 'on the ground already' and therefore having 'not far to fall'; or the prospect for the writer of modern histories, that by following truth 'too near the heels, it may happily strike out his teeth'. Flattery also gets an idiomatic image, when Ralegh denies that he is one of those who 'flatter the world between the bed and the grave'. Occasionally the literal sense of what he says is so disturbing that one flinches from it and gives it the distance of an image, as in the digressionary paragraph where he describes the degeneration of mankind (my italics):

> . . . we have now greater Giants, for vice and injustice, than the World had in those days, for

bodily strength; for cottages, and houses of clay and timber, we have raised Palaces of stone; we carve them, we paint them, and adorn them with gold; insomuch as men are rather known by their houses, than their houses by them; we are fallen from two dishes, to two hundred; from water, to wine and drunkenness; from the covering of our bodies with the skins of beasts, not only to silk and gold, but *to the very skins of men.*

These, however, are the individual felicities of Ralegh's style. Most of the extracts here, especially from Books III-V, show his skill in telling sustained narratives—in particular, of battles, and of the fall of tyrants. Greater matters are narrated too, but at a length too great to be demonstrated in any selection: the rise and fall of whole nations, for instance. The pattern is, in its particulars, cyclical. Rome starts and ends with a shepherd's crook (although the *History* itself only gets as far as 168 BC); Macedon begins and ends in obscurity. Great rulers, like Caesar and Alexander, are reduced to 'troublers of the world', agents of decline rather than progress:

> *Caesar,* and *Alexander,* have unmade and slain, each of them, more than a million of men: but they made none, nor left none behind them. Such is the error of Man's judgment, in valuing things according to common opinion.

But the *History* as a whole, in its general view, is apocalyptic; summed up in a theatrical image which Ralegh uses early in Book I, when he writes of 'the long day of mankind drawing fast towards an evening, and the world's Tragedy and time near at an end'. Over the whole lies the shadow of death, both Prince Henry's, and Ralegh's own. Seldom can a great work have come into the world with a preface which begins so bleakly, with Ralegh picturing himself as one wounded by fortune and time, disabled, defective, aching, uncured, and tried by the fire of adversity. Through the five books he expands this vision to cover the whole of mankind, whose history is one long tale of endurance, ending with the phrase 'here lies'. The *History of the World* deserves to be set near *King Lear* as one of the English Renaissance's powerfully negative visions of the state of man on 'this stage-play world'[14].

Notes

[1] Ralegh describes himself as a 'very ill footman' in the *Discovery of Guiana,* and apologizes for his lack of Hebrew knowledge towards the end of the Preface to the *History of the World.*

[2] In *The Arte of English Poesie* (1589), Bk I, ch. 31.

[3] The quotations come from a sonnet Spenser wrote

'To the right honourable and valorous knight, Sir Walter Ralegh', and from the introduction to Book III of *The Faerie Queene*.

[4] In *Forms of Discovery* (New York, 1967), p. 23.

[5] In *Elizabethan Poetry,* ed. J. R. Brown and B. Harris (London, 1960), p. 89.

[6] In 'The Poetry of Ralegh', *Rev. Eng. Lit.,* I (1960), p. 19.

[7] In her *Muses Library* edition of the poems (London, 1951), p. 140.

[8] Drummond reported Jonson as having claimed that he had written a draft of the Punic war narrative which Ralegh 'altered and set in his book'.

[9] See George Bruner Parks, *Richard Hakluyt and the English Voyages* (New York, 1928), pp. 138-9.

[10] A Theban general who died fighting the Spartans in 362 BC.

[11] See *The Letters and Speeches of Oliver Cromwell,* ed. S. C. Lomas (New York, 1904), vol. 2, p. 54.

[12] In Arnold's inaugural lecture at Oxford he contrasted Thucydides' introduction to the *Peloponnesian War* with Ralegh's *History,* entirely to the latter's detriment.

[13] For an account of Ralegh's influence on Milton, see George Wesley Whiting, *Milton's Literary Milieu* (New York, 1964), pp. 15-35.

[14] Ralegh's own phrase, in the *History,* I, 2:2.

Robert E. Stillman (essay date 1987)

SOURCE: "'Words cannot knytt': Language and Desire in Ralegh's *The Ocean to Cynthia,*" in *Studies in English Literature, 1500-1900,* Vol. 27, No. 1, Winter, 1987, pp. 35-51.

[*In the following essay, Stillman emphasizes the connection in* The Ocean to Cynthia *between Raleigh's loss of Elizabeth I's favor and the inadequacy of language—specifically, the symbolic mode formerly used by Raleigh to represent the Queen's cultic status as a beloved deity—to express his suffering.*]

Every mode of thought is bestowed on us, like a gift, with some new principle of symbolic expression. It has a logical development, which is simply the exploitation of all the uses to which that symbolism lends itself; and when these uses are exhausted, the mental activity in question has found its limit. Either it serves its purpose and becomes truistic, like our orientation in 'Euclidean space' or our appreciation of objects and their accidents (on the pattern of language structure significantly called 'logic'); or it is superseded by some more powerful symbolic mode which opens new avenues of thought.[1]

Susanne Langer supplies in this passage a model for analyzing the transformation of one symbolic mode to another. Her account of the exhaustion of older symbols and their replacement by new, more powerful means of symbolizing experience presents a clearly optimistic paradigm for cultural change. Symbols that no longer work make room for symbols that work better; knowledge advances; culture marches on. Langer provides one version of the old story. It is a version that offers, nonetheless, a useful if unexpected introduction to Ralegh's poetic practice in **"The 21th: and last booke of the Ocean to Scinthia"**. For Ralegh, too, has a strong interest in the exhaustion of the symbolic order (to use Langer's terms) or in what Ralegh himself might otherwise describe as "fancy's tragedy," the discovery that the mythology surrounding a queen whom one worships is mere mystification and that time leads all things to decay, including love and language.

The Ocean to Cynthia is an extended complaint for the loss of Queen Elizabeth's favors. Ralegh writes as a courtier in disgrace, whether on account of his secret marriage to Elizabeth Throckmorton or some other indiscretion, and in apparent hope of a return to favor.[2] The subject of the poem is the frustration of desire. In losing Elizabeth, Ralegh makes clear, he has been subjected to multiple losses that the uniformly elegaic tone of the complaint renders nearly equivalent in importance. He has been deprived of a love that deserved requiting, of a well-merited place at court, and of a near-religious faith in what can only be called the cultic status of the Queen. Cynthia assumes a special kind of importance in ***The Ocean*** because of the significance attached to Elizabeth as the reigning deity of a national cult. It is useful to remember that the Queen was the center of a symbolic order whose existence helped to consolidate and perpetuate the power of the Tudor state. Virgin Queen, heavenly Venus, triumphant Diana, returned Astraea—these are only a few of the roles that Elizabeth played in a national mythology providing aesthetic, religious, and philosophical legitimacy to her sovereignty. The coherence of what used to be called the Elizabethan world picture was founded upon the order of symbols surrounding the Queen.[3]

It is useful to remember the Queen's cultic status because Ralegh reminds us repeatedly in ***The Ocean*** that he had been instrumental in its creation. Like so many other poets, he had once celebrated Elizabeth as "natures wonder, Vertues choyse," "Th'Idea remayning of thos golden ages."[4] As Shepherd of the Ocean, Ralegh gives every indication that he believed in his symbolism, that the Queen and the cultic images surrounding her were one. The loss of her love changed all that, however, depriving him of everything that he had formerly valued in those symbols, and more disastrous still, of the capacity to believe in the validity of the symbols themselves and the activity of mind which produced them. After his loss, Ralegh writes, "A Queen shee was to mee, no more Belphebe" (327). She has been demythologized. The once-loving cult goddess descends from benefactress to tormentor, from a sustaining symbol to one more especially painful part of his fragmented reality. Even the golden-age symbolism that Ralegh had earlier applied to Elizabeth is now dismissed as a deceitful fiction that "worthless worlds but play onn stages" (350).

Ralegh's poem, then, represents as a personal tragedy exactly that process of symbolic exhaustion that Langer describes at the level of cultural change. His complaint is more than a courtier's lament for the loss of a queen's favors, amorous or professional. The loss that Ralegh has suffered—or so he represents it—is the exhaustion of a whole order of symbolism upon whose existence his status at court, his identity, and the coherence of his world depended. Elizabeth had been more than his beloved or his sovereign. She was the repository of all that was valuable in the world. The striking disproportion between the event reported—a courtier's loss of his queen's favors, and the terms in which it is represented—the demise of the symbolic order, is responsible for much of the poem's extraordinary melodrama and, strangely, for much of its conceptual interest.

The Ocean to Cynthia emerges, then, from the absence created by the now exhausted order of symbols with which Ralegh had once surrounded the Queen. His poem is an extended attempt to discover what Langer might call "some more powerful symbolic mode" to replace the older order of discarded symbolism. This does not mean that we can read Ralegh's lament with Langer's optimism about the ease with which one more effective form of symbolism replaces another. There is nothing easy about the task that Ralegh undertakes; his failure is sufficient proof of that. Ralegh does not discover in *The Ocean to Cynthia* the more powerful symbols for which he is in search. The strange ebb and flow of the poem's fragmented imagery does not finally rescue from love, time, and fortune, the poet's primary antagonists, any values of transcendent importance. But Ralegh's poem does explore the reasons for his failure, for the insufficiency of all modes of symbolizing, and this clarification is significant both in itself and for an un-

derstanding of attitudes toward language in Elizabethan culture as a whole.

When Ralegh comments upon his art in *The Ocean to Cynthia,* he compares his labors, significantly enough, to those of a historian. Overwhelmed by the enormity of his loss and the impossibility of fully measuring its extent, Ralegh describes his poetic task as if it were an attempt "when after Phebus is dessended . . . To write the story of all ages past / And end the same before th'aprochinge night" (97, 102-103). (We think ahead, inevitably, to his unfinished *History of the World.*) His analogy is telling. Ralegh looks to history with its parade of mutability for an understanding of his own decline, and he represents his decline as if it were a microcosmic version of the decay of the world. In good pastoral fashion, the complex is incorporated into the simple. The analogy is typical of Ralegh as a self-aggrandizing effort to lend pathos to his sufferings, and it is certainly characteristic of the Ralegh who has come to dominate contemporary critical thinking; Greenblatt has written a fine study of the courtier's lifelong devotion to theatrical self-presentation.[5] Ralegh's urge for self-aggrandizement is apparent, but the form in which that urge finds expression, as the poet bemoans the frustration of his desires, remains puzzling and problematic. Why do complaints about frustrated desire appear so frequently in *The Ocean to Cynthia* in conjunction with laments about the inadequacies and failures of language? How does an event so personal (the loss of love) come to be associated with an issue so seemingly abstract (linguistic adequacy)? When Ralegh draws the analogy between his attempt to write the story of his fall and an effort to record all history on a single evening before the world's decay, he comments not just about the extent of his desires, but about the failures of writing. His poem is not so much unfinished as unfinishable, since in Ralegh's view language lacks the resources to allow him adequately to express the greatness of his loss. When he complains that he "Writes in the dust as onn that could no more" (91), he laments the ineffectuality and impermanence of words. Words fail to satisfy desire, since mutability rules both love and language; the connection among these terms needs further exploration.

Ralegh is only one among many Renaissance writers who lament mutability's sway over language.[6] The increased historical awareness and philological sophistication of the Renaissance brought with it a greater consciousness of linguistic change, but without the intellectual structures with which to interpret change in language as something other than decadence or decay, the new learning also carried a new sense of linguistic crisis. Because words change form and meaning, because they lose currency over time, they cannot be trusted. Abraham Fraunce echoes Horace when he writes "Woordes are lyke leaves . . . : leaves spring before Summer, and fall before Winter; and the same inconstancy is in words."[7] When William Drummond illustrates "The Instabilitie of Mortall Glorie," "what wee write to keepe our Name" takes its place alongside triumphant arches and proud obelisks destined to be "made the sport of Dayes."[8] At the end of his *Defence of Ryme,* Samuel Daniel warns his contemporaries against importing foreign words into English, only to conclude in near-desperation: "But this is but a Character of that perpetuall revolution which wee see to be in all things that never remaine the same, and we must heerein be content to submit our selves to the law of time, which in few yeeres will make al that, for which we now contend, *Nothing*."[9] Castiglione notes that all words in the course of time "come to their end, because at the last both wee and whatsoever is ours, are mortall."[10] There is real sadness here over the decay of words, but clearly much of that sadness derives from what words stand for; so often in the Renaissance the mutability of language comes to represent synecdochally human mortality and sometimes even the decay of the world.

In this context, Ralegh's lament for the decline of language and the world's decay becomes more comprehensible as the expression of a larger cultural crisis, but the sadness of his lament derives, as we have seen, from something more specific than a consciousness of mutability. The failure of language is intimately linked in **The Ocean to Cynthia** to the frustration of desire. There is an important cultural context for this linkage as well. Ralegh's dark pastoral takes its place among a large body of English Renaissance poems in which an erotic occasion provides the context for direct and pointed complaints about linguistic inadequacies. An obscure but fascinating pastoral lyric incorporated into *England's Helicon* (1600), Edmund Bolton's "Theorello. A Shepherd's Idillion," provides a paradigm for these complaints. The lyric dramatizes the love of Theorello (a rather intellectual-sounding shepherd) for Cosma (the world) as an allegory of the poet's effort to seduce nature into satisfying his desires. This is pastoral turned metaphysics. The poet woos nature as a lover woos his mistress. As the lover seduces his beloved by flattery, so the poet pays tribute to the beauties of a divinely inspired cosmos by naming them aright: "Yet hath the world no better name than she: [Bolton puns] / And then the world, no better thing can be."[11] However, the desire to fix words properly is frustrated by the fact that "names her beauty show not" (31). Language is not adequate to the task of naming the world correctly. Bolton's frustration over the failure of words finds expression in Theorello's unsatisfied and unsatisfiable desire for Cosma.

The same connection between frustrated desire and the inadequacies of language is repeatedly employed by Sidney in *The Old Arcadia* as a warning against the dangers of the impassioned imagination. When Phili-

sides, a lovesick shepherd exiled from court, bemoans the loss of Mira's favors in the second eclogues, he sings an echo poem that reflects upon the causes of his frustrations:

> But when I first did fall, what brought most
> fall to my heart?
> Art.
> Art? What can be that art which thou dost
> mean
> by thy speech?
> Speech.
> What be the fruits of speaking art? What
> grows by the words?
> Words.
> O much more than words: those words
> served more to me bless.
> Less.[12]

Nature contradicts the logic of passion. What Sidney comically portrays in these lines is the consternation of the romantically idealizing poet upon discovering that his words, far from satisfying his desires, have actually compounded his sufferings. Words deceive, the sarcastic nymph reminds Philisides. They load the mind with corrupt and insatiable passions that turn men into fools. Sidney is inclined to treat comically the failures of language and the frustrations of desire that are for John Donne (to cite one more example) primary sources of tragedy. In the disintegrating universe that Donne describes in *The First Anniversary,* the death of a loved woman, Elizabeth Drury, is made symbolic of a lost cosmic coherence; nature is out of joint, fragmented, and that fragmentation is identified in the poem with the failure of language to contain experience and observation, to build causeways over the abyss. Elizabeth is the world's "name," now fatally divorced from it. Donne addresses his decaying world:

> thou art speechlesse growne.
> Thou hast forgot thy name, thou hadst;
> thou wast
> Nothing but she, and her thou hast o'rpast.
> . . .
>
> Her name defin'd thee, gave thee forme and
> frame,
> And thou forgetst to celebrate thy name.[13]

He, too, laments the mutability of the world as a matter of mutable words. In Donne, as in Sidney, Bolton, and Ralegh, the loss of a desired woman is connected with the failure of language. I do not mean to suggest that the theme of desire and the inadequacy of language is in any sense unique to the texts in question. Desire and the failure of words to serve that desire haunt Sidney's Astrophil as he attempts to make Stella "pity the tale of me," just as the persona of Shakespeare's *Sonnets* must struggle against "all-oblivious enmity" to secure his love and language against the ravages of time. The subject is one of broad cultural importance in late Elizabethan and Jacobean society, and it remains so throughout the seventeenth century. When midway through the century, John Webster envisions the creation of a universal language to make words adequate tools for expressing things, he makes the revealing argument that the discovery of this new Adamic language would serve *"to marry the world, that is, fitly and duly to join and connex agents to their patients, masculines to faeminines, superious [sic] to inferiours, Caelestials to Terrestials, that thereby nature may act out her hidden and latent power."*[14] A perfect language is the fulfillment of desire: it is the marriage of man to nature.

In an effort to account for the persistence with which language and desire are "married" in these works, it is useful to remember that they appear in the context of a Renaissance critical tradition which acknowledges, at times in surprisingly current terms, the force of that connection. Joachim Du Bellay's *Defence and Illustration of the French Language* begins, as an explanation of the diversity of languages, with a telling rationalization of the myth of Babel:

> If nature . . . had given to men a common will or consent, besides the innumerable commodities which would thereby have resulted, human inconstancy would not have needed to forge for itself so many manners of speaking. Which diversity and confusion can rightly be called the Tower of Babel. For languages are not born of themselves after the fashion of herbs, roots, or trees: . . . all their virtue is born in the desire and will of mortals. That (it seems to me) is a great reason why one should not thus praise one language and blame the other; since they all come from a single source and origin, that is from the caprice of men.[15]

Language springs from the restlessness of human desire; it is a product of what Sidney would call will, not wit. Du Bellay's insistence upon the origins of language in desire is less commonplace in Renaissance criticism than an emphasis upon speech as the expression of human reason, but it is scarcely idiosyncratic; this passage follows closely one in Speroni. In any case, Du Bellay's insistence is significant because it helps to clarify the poetic practice of Sidney, Donne, and most important for my purposes, of Ralegh. For if language is a function of desire, whether that entails in a poetic context the seduction of a queen or the wooing of a shepherdess, then the frustration of desire presents a natural occasion for a lament over the inadequacy of words. The Renaissance critical tradition brings more clarity to Ralegh's poetic practice, even as it suggests by means of the very terms it highlights—language and desire—that

Ralegh's poetry can usefully be understood in light of contemporary critical theory.

"Language is an operational superstructure on an erotic base": Norman O. Brown's formula has become axiomatic in much contemporary criticism for the analysis of discursive practices.[16] For semioticians like Barthes and Kristeva, "there is no other primary *significatum* in literary works than a certain desire: to write is a mode of Eros";[17] for neo-Freudians like Ricoeur and Lacan, speech is demand, and the desire that motivates demand is both the cause and "perpetual effect of symbolic articulation."[18] The connection between language and desire that is thematized so frequently and explicitly in Renaissance poetic texts occupies in these contemporary critical schools the central place in investigating not just all literary, but all linguistic acts. In light of such criticism, texts like those of Sidney, Donne, and Ralegh acquire particular interest because they are self-conscious explorations of the dynamic that semiotics and psychoanalysis locate at the foundations of discourse. In turn, a theoretical perspective of this kind—and I am thinking particularly of Ricoeur's—provides an intellectual framework in which to analyze how these texts function.

In Ricoeur's words, "what makes desire speak [is] namely, the *absence* inherent in instincts and the connection between lost objects and symbolization" (p. 503n.).[19] Language is an effort to recover or to compensate for what has been given up in the past; its function is determined etiologically by its origins in the individual's development. In some of the most influential pages from *Beyond the Pleasure Principle,* Freud locates the genesis of signs in a child's game of *"fort"* ["gone"] *"da"* ["there"]. In the absence of the mother, the child whom Freud observes devises a simple game by which he makes his toys disappear and reappear. His playing reenacts the mother's departure as a necessary preliminary to the pleasure of her return, and in this way he compensates himself for the "renunciation of the instinctual satisfaction which he had made in allowing his mother to go away without protesting."[20] What this game defines is the institution of signs, which are universally a giving up of what Ricoeur calls "brute presence and an intending of presence in absence" (p. 385).

The child's game functions, it is important to recognize, not as a passive response to loss, but as an active effort to achieve mastery over privation. A similar function has been claimed, at times usefully it seems to me, for the more sophisticated games of art. Ralegh's lament in **The Ocean to Cynthia** for the loss of Queen Elizabeth's favors is suffused with familiar pastoral nostalgia for a golden age of requited love; at the same time, the poem strives to achieve mastery over that loss (as I will show) by the creation of new, more powerful symbols to replace the now exhausted order of symbolism surrounding the Queen. *The Ocean to Cynthia* can be read, then, as an elaborate game of *"fort-da,"* with some crucial differences. Ralegh's "game" endlessly reenacts in memory the painful loss of love, but it concludes not with the restoration of the Queen's favors, a goal deemed hopeless, or even with the creation of more powerful, sustaining symbols, a task specifically abandoned, but with a sobering awareness of the inevitability of frustrated desire and linguistic failure. In the process of bringing the unconscious toward consciousness, of making explicit the interconnection between desire and language, the poet can *reflect* upon what the child can only *enact*. In this way, as Norman O. Brown writes, "consciousness in the artistic use of language is subversive of its own instrument" (p. 73). Language, the instrument of desire, functions to unmask the futility both of itself and the master who drives it. This is art in the service of the reality, not the pleasure principle—or so it seems.

Language is replete with mystifications: "In and through man desires advance masked" (Ricoeur, p. 162). This is a point worth making here, because before Ralegh is too quickly enlisted as a servant of the reality principle (after all, this is a courtier who devoted a lifetime to the pursuit of visionary projects), it is important to recognize that his desperation over the fate of love and language can itself be interpreted as simply one more function of desire. The very act of writing is a continued demand for royal favors, favors that are the object of Ralegh's erotic and political aims. His desire for Elizabeth's love is both a sexual desire and a desire for the power that she represents, though his rhetoric so closely associates the two that it seems impossible to distinguish between them. The difficulty in making that distinction works, of course, to Ralegh's advantage, since it allows him to negotiate under cover of a plea for love what is also a ploy for power. When Ralegh points at the opening of his poem to "The broken monuments of [his] great desires," he both reflects upon the frustration of desire in preparation for an analysis of its hopelessness and manifests desire in the hope of being restored to favor. These are indeed great desires, and they lead to great contradictions. The construction of Ralegh's poem is governed by the unresolvable tension between a wish to expose the futility of passion and an urge to find satisfaction for it, whether in substitute symbols or in the favors of the Queen.

In the attempt to clarify how an event so personal (frustrated love) comes to be associated with an issue so seemingly abstract (linguistic adequacy), I have invoked several large contexts in which to situate *The Ocean to Cynthia:* a network of poems in the English Renaissance in which the failure of desire is explicitly associated with linguistic inadequacies; a sixteenth-century critical tradition that posits the origins of lan-

guage in desire; and contemporary psychoanalytic theory that represents all discourse as an operation motivated by eros to recover or to compensate for what has been lost in the past. These contexts in turn should now help to shed light on how desire speaks in and through *The Ocean to Cynthia* as Ralegh struggles with his problems of symbolic expression.

"The 21th: and last booke of the Ocean to Scinthia" begins in a sea of confusion. As Ralegh struggles to make sense out of his loss, the reader struggles with him, astonished, even overawed, by his capacity to endure emotional agony. For all of the poem's pastoral trappings, this speaker intones against fate with a distinctly heroic voice. Who can believe, while reading, that there could have been twenty previous books like this one? (And who, if the truth be told, is not slightly relieved at having been spared them?) Ralegh dates his loss from "when first my fancy erred" (3). "Fancy" is an important word in the poem and needs clarification here. In the faculty psychology that Renaissance writers inherited from the classical tradition, the term has a specific and clearly defined meaning; it is the mind's ability to represent images to itself in the absence of sense perception.[21] As neutral and unambiguous as such a description might appear, fancy is a mental faculty loaded with equivocal moral potential. A recognition of the faculty's ambiguity is apparent in Sidney's *Apology for Poetry*. Sidney writes: "Man's wit may make poesy (which should be *eikastike*, which some learned have defined, figuring forth good things) to be *phantastike*, which doth contrariwise infect the fancy with unworthy objects."[22] The kind of infection that concerns Sidney, as well as many of his contemporaries, is the seduction of the fancy by desire. If the good painter portrays "Judith killing Holofernes, David fighting with Goliath," the artist controlled by fantasy "please[s] an ill-pleased eye with wanton show of better hidden matters" (Sidney, pp. 59-60). It is desire's complicity with the imagination that makes art vulnerable to criticism, a point that Bacon later enforces in an extremist argument about poetry and the dangers of fancy. Poetry operates, Bacon writes, "by submitting the shows of things to the desires of the mind."[23] Given this cultural background, and the repeated association of desire and "fancy" in Renaissance critical theory, Ralegh's use of the word in *The Ocean* becomes more comprehensible; fancy refers in his poem to the imagination and those passions inextricably connected with it. The term provides a ready vehicle for relating the poet's desires to the image-making faculty by which he attempts to satisfy those desires.

Ralegh's effort to date his loss from "when first my fancy erred" is less an attempt to explain his error than it is to find some fixed point in time from which he can make meaningful divisions in his experience. (How did his fancy err? He fails to say.) As Ralegh drives a wedge between his past and his present, isolating the "happy then" of his courtship of Elizabeth from the woes that he suffers now, he strives to rescue from that "golden age" something of value for his present (31). Time, however, is a more difficult antagonist than Ralegh anticipates. In the wild ebb and flow of the poem's imagery, past and present refuse to remain separate, as every attempt to idealize the "happy then" of Elizabeth's love ends in frustration. If she is remembered as "The seat of joyes, and loves abundance," Ralegh is unable to forget the "great worlds of woes" that he endured under her sovereignty (44, 50). (Petrarchan metaphor has a terrifying literalness for a courtier in love with his queen.) Cynthia not only "apeesed," she "wounded"; she not only "gave," she "tooke" (56). If Ralegh recalls "The honor of her love," he is also reminded that her love forced him "to leve great honors thought" (57, 65). His sorrows did not begin with fancy's error. They were present all along. Nothing illustrates this point better than the swift transition which takes place between Ralegh's praise of the "force" which her "angellike aparance had / To master distance, tyme, or crueltye" (112-13), and his bitter recognition that:

> Twelve yeares intire I wasted in this warr,
> Twelve yeares of my most happy younger dayes,
> Butt I in them, and they now wasted ar,
> Of all which past the sorrow only stayes.
>
> (120-23)

What lends this illustration such power is that Ralegh makes us aware in the very next line ("So wrate I once"), that these verses are themselves the product of his earlier years, the flotsam and jetsam cast ashore by some previous agonizing undulations of the ocean. No small part of Ralegh's tragedy consists, then, in the fact that his experience has been far less discontinuous than he would like to believe. The sorrows of his past are a piece with those of his present. To date his woes from "when first my fancy erred" is simply to make another error in fancy since the past contains no golden age from which value can be rescued for the present.

The further that Ralegh extends our awareness of the sorrows which he endured in the past, the clearer it becomes both to himself and to us that his love for Cynthia was doomed from the first to frustration. As he recalls a queen "Whose Love outflew the fastest fliinge tyme" (182), Ralegh confronts the symbolism of Elizabeth's cult in its most idealizing form. He remembers admiring her as

> A springe of bewties which tyme ripeth not
> Tyme that butt workes onn frayle mortallety,
> A sweetness which woes wronges outwipeth not,
> Whom love hath chose for his devinnitye.
>
> (185-88)

Even as Ralegh gives, he takes away; he has acquired one of his sovereign's tricks. Time does not ripen Cynthia's beauties. But if Cynthia's beauties are unripe, are they also imperfect? Some doubt is cast upon her store of "frayle mortallety." More telling still is the evidence which Ralegh marshalls from "strong reason" (173) to undermine her status outside of time. The mythology of Elizabeth's cult is subjected to historical critique as the poet holds before his eyes

> The Images, and formes of worlds past
> Teachinge the cause why all thos flames that rize
> From formes externall, cann no longer last,
>
> Then that thos seeminge bewties hold in pryme
> Loves ground, his essence, and his emperye,
> All slaves to age, and vassalls unto tyme
> Of which repentance writes the tragedye.
>
> (174-80)

Mutability rules both world and self. A queen's love will decay just as certainly as her empire. History and suffering replace an exhausted mythology, as the poetic argument turns from exalting Cynthia's love above time to acknowledging time's power over her, to identifying, finally and tragically, her love with the power of time itself. As mutable as the moon, the Queen is a heavenly body whose absence has blighted his mental landscape:

> But as the feildes clothed with leves and floures
> The bancks of roses smellinge pretious sweet
> Have but ther bewties date, and tymely hores,
> And then defast by winters cold, and sleet,
>
> So farr as neather frute nor forme of floure
> Stayes for a wittnes what such branches bare,
> Butt as tyme gave, tyme did agayne devoure
> And chandge our risinge joy to fallinge care;
>
> So of affection which our youth presented,
> When shee that from the soonn reves poure and light
> Did but decline her beames as discontented
> Convertinge sweetest dayes to saddest night.
>
> (241-52)

Ralegh's is a dark pastoralism. By associating Cynthia's love with the order of nature's decay, he im-

parts a strong sense of inevitability to his sufferings. It is the nature of a moon to change. The
Queen has come to embody devouring time itself.

Ralegh's love was doomed to frustration, it is important to recognize, more because of the way in
which he conceived the Queen than because of any
attributes that she in fact possessed. Fancy's error
plays a greater role in his tragedy than either the
poet or the reader at first suspects. For what becomes increasingly evident as the poem proceeds is
that the Cynthia at whose feet Ralegh worshipped is
a construct of his own imagination. She is, as he
tells us, "my object, and invention," a "princely
forme, my fancies adamande" (37, 41). As one more
especially ardent devotee of her cult, Ralegh transformed an imperfect, time-bound Elizabeth into
Cynthia, a symbol of transcending perfections, thereby setting "the stage of fancies tragedye" (144).
History is raised to mythology with drastic consequences. For as Ralegh makes plain, "thos marvelous perfections" which he bestowed upon the Queen
became "The parents of my sorrow and my envy"
(193-94). His fancy—the imagination driven by desire—gave her a symbolic significance too weighty
to bear, and with her inevitable collapse from the
timeless Cynthia to the mutable Elizabeth, Ralegh
found himself in love with a fiction of his own
creation, tormented by the loss of an ideal which
had no existence outside of his imagination. He laments his "Unlastinge passion, soune outworne consayte / Whereon I built, and onn so dureless trust!"
(295-96). Once more Ralegh associates the frustration of his desires with linguistic failure. In the midst
of his loss, he rejects not only the exhausted symbols with which he had once surrounded the Queen,
as he again and again disables their idealizing significance, but the very principle that had generated
them. Fancy errs in attributing transcendent value
to the persons and objects of a time-bound world.

Fancy's error produces fancy's tragedy; this is the
blunt logic at the heart of *The Ocean to Cynthia*.
There is no single consequence of his fall from the
Queen's favor that Ralegh details more painstaking-
ly than the effects of that fall upon his imagination.
In the "happy then" of Cynthia's love, his thoughts
had been "confinde" (or so he hoped) by a central
object for his inventions (32). With her loss, the
floodgates of his imagination burst open, inundating
the fancy with a sea of chaotic images. As Ralegh
writes, "Then furious madness wher trew reason
lackt / Wrate what it would, and scurgde myne
owne consayte" (145-46). No small part of the poet's
loss is his weakened ability to repair it. His images
no longer cohere. In an attempt to discover some
new center in which to confine his fancy, Ralegh
undertakes an important change of direction midway through his complaint.

Cynthia has already been demythologized as "A
Queen . . . , no more Belphebe"; her influence over
the poet has been identified with time's devouring
power. In her place, Ralegh attempts to substitute a
new symbolic order whose center is the transcendent power of his own love. It is no longer Cynthia
who survives time, but the poet's adoration of her,
as Ralegh exclaims in a new, more assertive tone of
voice: "My love is not of tyme, or bound to date"
(301). Ralegh here follows the near-obligatory pattern of the Petrarchan poet, who, denied the possibility of erotic satisfaction in his mistress because
of her loss or death, seeks fulfillment in the substitute gratifications of poetic composition. It is well
to remember, however, that the fulfillment he seeks
goes beyond what is typical of the Petrarchan writer in the self-consciousness of Ralegh's search for
a new set of sustaining symbols to replace those
that have been exhausted. Almost immediately, as if
hesitating to take the leap, he retreats from his new-
found theme into increasingly somber laments for
the loss of Cynthia and increasingly bitter attacks
upon the golden-world mythology which he had once
applied to her. His past praises for the Queen seem
"now an Idell labor, and a tale / Tolde out of tyme
that dulls the heerers eares; / A marchandise whereof ther is no sale" (357-59). In the midst of tragic
posturing that looks ahead to Macbeth's, the poet
complains once more that the old symbols have lost
their value, metaphysical and professional. In full
awareness of this fact, Ralegh returns to his new
theme with an increased decisiveness. Once again,
he exalts his love as a power "Too great and stron-
ge for tymes Jawes to devour" (383). But now,
instead of retreating into laments or remonstrations,
Ralegh proceeds to attribute to his love qualities
which he had formerly reserved for the Queen. As
he had once done for Cynthia, he exalts his passion
above "age" and "natures overthrow," "honors bay-
te" and "worlds fame" (401, 406). What he praises
is an "essentiall love, of no frayle parts cumpound-
ed" (410). As a new center of imaginative and
emotional coherence, "Thes thoughts, knitt up by
fayth, shall ever last, / Thes, tyme assayes, butt
never can untye" (391-92). Ralegh's metaphor is
important. The faith of his essential love provides a
tool for "knitting" together the broken threads of
the old symbolic order.

In the flux of the Ocean's mental turmoil, new confidence quickly gives way to new despair. The very
memory of his essential love creates "a relapps of
passion" (414), as the poet is driven back into his
consuming woe. In search of a cure for his "minds
long deseas" (421), Ralegh stumbles upon one of
The Ocean's greatest ironies. His long pursuit to
rescue something of value from time itself appears
exhausted, as he turns to his single most powerful
antagonist for the mental relief that he is unable to

discover elsewhere: "Externall fancy tyme alone re-curethe / All whose effects do weare away with ease" (422-23). Fancy is now time's patient, not its conqueror. Ralegh appears permanently trapped in history, with no sustaining mythology to turn to. It is precisely this understanding, one suspects, that motivates the poet's final desperate attempt to exalt his love above time. All the stops are pulled out, as Ralegh likens his love to a first principle of nature, as a cosmic power equally fundamental to his being, "As water to the fyshe, to men as ayre, / As heat to fier, as light unto the soonn" (434-35). Love is the new "Center" of his imaginative life, the new prime "mover" of his being (442, 455). A timeless abstraction seems somehow more secure as the foundation for a sustaining order of symbols than the time-bound Elizabeth.

Security, however, is not one of the strong points of Ralegh's world. With the recognition that love has destroyed the "better part" (461) of his being, he abandons any further attempt to discover a fixed order of transcendent values. Ralegh rejects as merely one more error of mythmaking fancy the effort to idealize his own love.

> But what of thos, or thes, or what of
>   ought
> Of that which was, or that which is, to
>   treat?
> What I possess is butt the same I sought;
> My love was falce, my labors weare
>   desayte.
>
> (462-65)

The complete flatness of his diction is a measure of his frustration, but how do we allow our understanding of his emotional state to guide our interpretation of the final line? Is Ralegh convinced that his love was false, or is he mimicking Cynthia's estimation of its value?

The very fact that he allows us to pose such questions, without caring to resolve them, indicates the hopelessness of his condition. For it simply no longer matters whether his love was true or false. All that now concerns Ralegh is that he has been victimized, partially by love, partially by time, and partially by his own fancy. He understands, at last, that "Words cannot knytt, or waylings make a new" (481). Trapped in a time-bound landscape, amidst the outworn conceits of a disabled symbolic order and the imagery of a natural world that itself perpetually decays, the poet has available to him no linguistic resources for discovering symbols of transcendent value.

Notes

1 Susanne K. Langer, *Philosophy in a New Key: A Study in the Symbolism of Reason, Rite, and Art* (Cambridge, Mass.: Harvard Univ. Press, 1960), p. 201.

2 For studies of the biographical circumstances surrounding the poem's composition, see Katherine Duncan-Jones, "The Date of Ralegh's, '21th: and Last booke of the Ocean to Scinthia'," *RES,* n.s. 21 (1970): 143-58; Philip Edwards, *Sir Walter Ralegh* (London: Longmans, Green, 1953), pp. 90-96; Stephen Greenblatt, *Sir Walter Ralegh: The Renaissance Man and His Roles* (New Haven and London: Yale Univ. Press, 1973), pp. 59-98; Pierre Lefranc, *Sir Walter Ralegh, écrivain* (Paris: Librairie Armand Colin, 1968), pp. 99-132.

3 Two recent informative studies of Elizabeth's cult are Helen Cooper's *Pastoral: Medieval into Renaissance* (Totowa, N.J.: Rowman and Littlefield, 1977), pp. 193-213, and Louis Adrian Montrose's "'Eliza, Queene of Shepheardes,' and the Pastoral of Power," *ELR* 10 (1980): 153-82.

4 *The Poems of Sir Walter Ralegh,* ed. Agnes M. C. Latham (Cambridge, Mass.: Harvard Univ. Press, 1951), pp. 25-43, lines 344, 348. All further citations from *The Ocean* are documented in the text by line number.

5 Greenblatt's arguments (pp. 76-98) are cogent and often persuasive, but they do not reckon with Ralegh's equally important concerns with the Queen's symbolic status and with the nature of symbolic expression. See also Donald Davie, "A Reading of *The Ocean's Love to Cynthia,*" in *Elizabethan Poetry* (New York: St. Martin's Press, 1960), Stratford-upon-Avon Studies 2, pp. 71-90; Michael L. Johnson, "Some Problems of Unity in Sir Walter Ralegh's *The Ocean's Love to Cynthia,*" *SEL* 14 (1974): 17-30; and A. D. Cousins, "The Coming of Mannerism: The Later Ralegh and the Early Donne," *ELR* 9 (1979): 86-107.

6 See also Thomas M. Greene, *The Light in Troy: Imitation and Discovery in Renaissance Poetry* (New Haven and London: Yale Univ. Press, 1982), pp. 4-27; and Jane Donawerth, *Shakespeare and the Sixteenth-Century Study of Language* (Urbana and Chicago: Univ. of Illinois Press, 1984), pp. 13-55.

7 Abraham Fraunce, *The Lawier's Logicke* (London: W. How for T. Newman and T. Gribbin, 1588), *STC* 11345, sig. 2ʳ.

8 *William Drummond of Hawthornden: Poems and Prose,* ed. Robert H. Macdonald (Edinburgh: Scottish Academic Press, 1976), p. 88.

9 Samuel Daniel, *A Defence of Ryme in Poems and A Defence of Ryme,* ed. Arthur Colby Sprague (Cambridge, Mass.: Harvard Univ. Press, 1930), p. 158.

[10] Baldassare Castiglione, *The Book of the Courtier,* trans. Sir Thomas Hoby (London: J. M. Dent; New York: E. P. Dutton, 1928), p. 60.

[11] *England's Helicon, 1600, 1614,* ed. Hyder E. Rollins, 2 vols. (Cambridge, Mass.: Harvard Univ. Press, 1935), 1:9, lines 32-33.

[12] Sir Philip Sidney, *The Countess of Pembrokes Arcadia* (The Old Arcadia), ed. Jean Robertson (Oxford: Clarendon Press, 1973), p. 161.

[13] *The First Anniversarie* in *The Complete Poetry of John Donne,* ed. John T. Shawcross (Garden City, N.Y.: Anchor Books, 1967), lines 30-32, 37-38.

[14] John Webster, *Academiarum Examen, or the Examination of Academies* in Allen G. Debus, *Science and Education in the Seventeenth Century: The Webster-Ward Debate* (London: Macdonald; New York: American Elsevier, 1970), p. 152.

[15] Joachim Du Bellay, *The Defence and Illustration of the French Language,* trans. Gladys M. Turquet (London: J. M. Dent, 1939), p. 21.

[16] Norman O. Brown, *Life Against Death. The Psychoanalytical Meaning of History* (Middletown, Conn.: Wesleyan Univ. Press, 1959), p. 69.

[17] Roland Barthes, *Critical Essays,* trans. Richard Howard (Evanston: Northwestern Univ. Press, 1972), p. xvi.

[18] Jacques Lacan, *Écrits: A Selection,* trans. Alan Sheridan (New York: W. W. Norton, 1977), p. viii.

[19] Paul Ricoeur, *Freud and Philosophy: An Essay on Interpretation,* trans. Denis Savage (New Haven and London: Yale Univ. Press, 1970), p. 503n.

[20] Sigmund Freud, *Beyond the Pleasure Principle,* trans. James Strachey (New York: Bantam Books, 1967), p. 34.

[21] For an excellent discussion of imagination in Renaissance critical theory, see John Guillory, *Poetic Authority: Spenser, Milton, and Literary History* (New York: Columbia Univ. Press, 1983), pp. 1-22.

[22] Sir Philip Sidney, *An Apology for Poetry,* ed. Forrest G. Robinson (Indianapolis: Bobbs-Merrill, 1970), p. 59.

[23] Sir Francis Bacon, *The Advancement of Learning* in *The Works of Francis Bacon,* ed. James Spedding et al, 14 vols. (New York: Garrett Press, 1870), 2:343.

FURTHER READING

Bibliography

Armitage, Christopher M., ed. *Sir Walter Ralegh: An Annotated Bibliography.* Chapel Hill: University of North Carolina Press, 1987, 236 p.

A bibliography of primary and secondary sources divided into seven sections: 1) Published Works Written by or Attributed to Raleigh; 2) Raleigh in Biography; 3) Raleigh in England, Ireland, and Europe; 4) Raleigh in the Americas; 5) Raleigh in Literary History and Criticism; 6) Raleigh in Literature, Music, the Visual Arts, and Books for Children; and 7) Raleigh in Bibliography.

Biography

May, Steven W. *Sir Walter Ralegh.* Edited by Arthur F. Kinney. Boston: Twayne Publishers, 1989, 164 p.

A study of Raleigh as a man and a poet that, according to the editor, "provides at last an authoritative canon of Sir Walter Ralegh's work, a brief but definitive biography of Ralegh's puzzling and controversial life, and a fresh review of all his literary, historical, and occasional prose and poetry."

Oakeshott, Walter. *The Queen and the Poet.* London: Faber and Faber, 1960, 232 p.

A study of Raleigh divided into two parts, the first of which is devoted to a discussion of Raleigh's relationship with Elizabeth I, and the second of which reprints Raleigh's poems that are associated with the Queen.

Rowse, A. L. *Ralegh and the Throckmortons.* London: Macmillan & Co., 1962, 347 p.

A biography that focuses entirely on Ralegh's personal life, his family, and the family he married into, the Throckmortons.

Criticism

Bradbrook, M. C. *The School of Night: A Study in the Literary Relationships of Sir Walter Ralegh.* Cambridge, England: Cambridge University Press, 1936, 189 p.

Examines Raleigh's involvement in the "School of Night," an esoteric group of writers, scholars, and nobles in England known for their atheism and their progressive views on religion and politics.

Edwards, Philip, ed. "The Last Voyage of Sir Walter Ralegh,

1617-1618." In *Last Voyages: Cavendish, Hudson, Ralegh, the Original Narratives*, pp. 175-252. Oxford, England: Clarendon Press, 1988.

> An account of Raleigh's second trip to Guiana, told largely through his own writings, including a journal and letters.

Firth, Sir Charles. "Sir Walter Raleigh's *History of the World.*" In *Essays, Historical & Literary*, pp. 34-60. Oxford, England: Clarendon Press, 1938.

> Considers Raleigh's *History* in relation to the development of historical writing in England and describes contemporary response to it.

Fussner, F. Smith. "Sir Walter Ralegh and Universal History." In *The Historical Revolution: English Historical Writing and Thought, 1580-1640*, pp. 191-210. New York: Columbia University Press, 1962.

> Argues that Raleigh's *History* comes closer than any other literary work to defining the character of early seventeenth-century historical thought. Fussner discusses, among other topics, Raleigh's providential view of history, his approaches to sacred and profane history, and his handling of the problems of evidence and proof.

Grove, Robin. "Ralegh's Courteous Art." *The Melbourne Critical Review* 7 (1964): 104-13.

> Considers most of Raleigh's poetry stylized and conventional, but finds that in a few verses, such as "The Nimphs Reply to the Sheepherd" and "To His Love When He Had Obtained Her," he successfully integrates form and feeling.

Horner, Joyce. "The Large Landscape: A Study of Certain Images in Ralegh." *Essays in Criticism* V, No. 3 (July 1955): 197-213.

> Discusses sea and earth imagery in *The Ocean to Cynthia* and Raleigh's prose works.

Skelton, R. A. "Ralegh as a Geographer." *The Virginia Magazine of History and Biography* 71, No. 2 (April 1963): 131-49.

> Deals with the geographical aspects of Raleigh's writings, both intellectual and practical, discussing his work as a patron and creator of maps and other geographical records.

Stephen, Harry L. "The Trial of Sir Walter Raleigh." In *Transactions of the Royal Historical Society,* fourth series, Vol. II, pp. 172-87. London: Offices of the Royal Historical Society, 1919.

> Considers the evidence and the legal procedures followed in the treason case against Raleigh in 1603.

Tennenhouse, Leonard. "Sir Walter Ralegh and the Literature of Clientage." In *Patronage in the Renaissance,* edited by Guy Fitch Lytle and Stephen Orgel, pp. 235-58. Princeton, N. J.: Princeton University Press, 1981.

> Views Raleigh's poetry and prose in terms of the system of patronage, focusing on the contrast between the economic and social realities of patronage and the cultural myth suggesting that Queen Elizabeth I's favor could be won through composing literature complimentary to her.

Additional coverage of Raleigh's life and career is contained in the following source published by Gale Research: *Literature Criticism from 1400 to 1800*, Vol. 31.

Mary Sidney

1561-1621

(Full name Mary Sidney Herbert, Countess of Pembroke.) English poet, translator, and editor.

The following entry contains critical essays on Sidney's role in the Age of Spenser. For further information on Sidney, see *LC*, Vol. 19.

INTRODUCTION

A prominent figure in literary circles in the Age of Spenser, Sidney is best known for her verse translations of biblical psalms, a project begun in conjunction with her brother, Sir Philip Sidney, and completed by her after his death. Although psalm translations were common during the Renaissance, the Sidneian psalms are considered poetically superior to other versions because of the energetic rhythms and diverse stanzaic forms skillfully chosen to mirror the content of each psalm. Critics have also praised Sidney's psalm translations for their emotional power and personal tone, and they are widely viewed as a major contribution to Elizabethan poetry.

Biography

Sidney was born at Tickenhall, Worcestershire, to a renowned and powerful family; the marriage of her parents, Mary Dudley and Henry Sidney, had united two prominent families in what was known as the Dudley/Sidney alliance. In an England often torn by religious conflict, the union of ruling-class, Protestant families created a major political force. Mary Sidney's maternal grandfather, John Dudley, Duke of Northumberland, had been executed in 1553 for his part in the attempt to put the Protestant Lady Jane Grey on the throne in place of the Catholic Mary Tudor. When the Protestant Queen Elizabeth replaced Queen Mary, Sidney's parents became central figures at court, where her father served as Lord President Council of the Marches of Wales and Lord Governor of Ireland, and her mother as lady-in-waiting to the Queen.

Mary Sidney received an education at home that exceeded the learning usually available to Elizabethan women; she studied literature, religion, science, and several languages. She went to court at the age of thirteen and in 1577 married Henry Herbert, second Earl of Pembroke, who—thirty years her senior—had also been involved in the Lady Jane Grey affair. Like

many aristocratic unions of the age, their marriage was a pre-arranged political alliance; it also apparently proved a happy match for Sidney. After her marriage, her home at Wilton House, Pembroke's ancestral estate, became the most important literary center outside Elizabeth's court and sponsored the work of such prominent writers as Edmund Spenser and Fulke Greville. With her brother Philip, one of the most renowned and respected writers of the time, Sidney used Wilton House to cultivate and patronize the Sidney Circle, a group of literary figures praised for their theological learning as well as their artistic talents. John Aubrey described her as "the greatest Patroness of witt and learning of any Lady of her time." Sidney also pursued her own work at this time, primarily undertaking translations. Initially, she collaborated with her brother on English translations of biblical psalms. After his death in 1586— perhaps the most tragic event of her life—she continued the work alone and ultimately produced a volume greatly acclaimed by readers then and since. After her husband's death in 1601 Sidney was less active in public life, and her sons, William and Philip, continued the tradition of patronage she had established at Wilton House. She died of smallpox in 1621.

Major Works

In the sixteenth century even the most well-educated of women were not encouraged to produce original verse. Propriety restricted Mary Sidney to translations and editorial work. Her efforts from 1592 and 1593 typify the kind of writing befitting a woman of her rank: translations of Philippe de Mornay's essay *Discours de la vie et de la mort* (1576), Robert Garnier's play *Marc-Antoine* (1579), and Petrarch's poem *Trionfo della Morte* (1353?). Her major work, however, are the *Psalms* that she began with her brother and completed before the end of the century. Because of the considerable skill and innovation that these translations demonstrate, critics have come to treat them as tantamount to original compositions and as a vital contribution to the development of English literature. Approximately forty of the poems were in initial translations begun before her brother's death; Sidney revised these further and undertook the translation of approximately another one hundred on her own. Although she consulted numerous French, Latin, and English versions of the psalms, her work is based primarily on a Protestant French psalter of 1562 by Clément Marot and Théodore de Bèze and relies heavily on the commentary of John Calvin. Her work was relatively complete in 1599, when she presented a copy to Queen Elizabeth, but critic Gary Waller has speculated that she continued to revise for at least another decade. While Philip's psalms focus on the subject matter from a position of detached examination, his sister's convey an intense involvement with the psalmist and an intimate expression of piety. Using conversational syntax and powerful images drawn from her own experiences, Sidney created a personal tone in her psalms which subtly reinforces her concept of religion as a deeply felt connection with God. Critics have also noted that Sidney's translations represent a major stylistic advancement over earlier versions, stressing in particular her use of one hundred sixty-four stanzaic forms and ninety-four metrical patterns to match her structure to the content of her sources. Such an attempt to unify form and content had never before been undertaken by psalm versifiers.

In addition to editing Philip's *The Countess of Pembrokes Arcadia* (1593) and *Astrophel and Stella* (1598), Sidney wrote "The Doleful Lay of Clorinda," which was published in *Colin Clouts Come Home Againe* (1595), a collection of elegies for Philip edited by Edmund Spenser, and a pastoral poem for Elizabeth entitled "A Dialogue Between Two Shepheards, Thenot and Piers, in Praise of Astraea." She also composed two dedicatory poems for the *Psalms*, one addressed to her brother and the other to the Queen. In "To the Angell Spirit of Sir Philip Sidney" Sidney praised her brother not only for his nobility of character, but also for his dedication to the cause of Protestantism. In "Even Now that Care which on thy Crown attends," a conventional adulatory poem for Elizabeth, Sidney combines praise for the Queen with a strong political message, equating Elizabeth with the biblical King David and implying that it is her duty to protect and further the cause of Protestant Christianity.

Critical Reception

Though intended for private devotion, the *Psalms* were distributed beyond the Sidney Circle, and contemporary poets referred to them frequently. John Donne's poem "Upon the translations of the Psalms by Sir Philip Sidney, and the Countess of Pembroke his sister" expresses the admiration and respect the Sidneian psalms generated among her peers. During her life, however, the psalm translations were thought to be primarily the work of her brother and her own contribution was largely overlooked. Most praise directed to Sidney emphasized her role as patroness: Spenser addressed her as "most Honourable and bountifull Ladie . . . to whome I acknowledge my selfe bounden, by manie singular fauours and great graces," and Samuel Daniel praised her as "the happie and iudiciall Patronesse of the Muses." Critics speculate that perhaps Sidney's humility prevented her contemporaries from identifying her more closely with the *Psalms*; her signature, "Sister of that Incomparable Sidney," emphasizes her relation and debt to Philip rather than pride in her own achievements. Consequently, her reputation as a poet has languished for centuries; in the introduction to his 1977 edition of her poetry, Waller refers to Sidney as "this too long neglected Elizabethan poet."

An 1823 edition of the *Psalms* spawned only a brief revival of interest in her work. Although A. B. Grosart acknowledged in his 1873 edition of Philip's poems that Sidney's work was "infinitely in advance of her brother's in thought, epithet and melody," hers were not published until 1963 in a collection edited by J. C. A. Rathmell. Since that time critics have acknowledged Sidney's importance as a bridge between traditional psalm translators and religious lyric poets; some even suggest that seventeenth-century poets used her psalms as a model for their own work. More recently, her work has generated interest among feminist scholars who have reclaimed her as vital to the development of both women's literature and English verse as a whole. Critics often explain the emotional urgency of Sidney's psalms in the context of Renaissance restrictions on women's writing; although translations of religious material were permitted, women were not expected to articulate any personal commentary. The exclusion of women from other forms of discourse forced Sidney to express herself through the voice of the psalmist, and the distinctive style and poetic force of her psalms originate in this sense of personal commitment. Examining her work in the context of Renaissance conventions that generally silenced women, these critics have praised her personal self-assertion and poetic skill.

Long overshadowed by her brother's reputation, Sidney is now recognized for her contribution to the development of religious poetry, and she is currently recognized as one of the first important English women poets. Her psalms are considered the most significant precursor to the prodigious production of religious verse in the seventeenth century, as well as the finest example of that genre from the Elizabethan era.

PRINCIPAL WORKS

Antonius: A Tragedie [translator] (drama) 1592

A Discourse of Life and Death [translator] (essay) 1592

The Countess of Pembrokes Arcadia [editor] (poetry) 1593

The Triumph of Death [translator] (poetry) 1593; published in journal *PMLA,* 1912

"The Doleful Lay of Clorinda" (poem) 1595; published in *Colin Clouts Come Home Againe,* edited by Edmund Spenser

Astrophel and Stella [editor] (poetry) 1598

The Psalms of Sir Philip Sidney and the Countess of Pembroke (poetry) 1599

"A Dialogue Between Two Shepheards, Thenot and Piers, in Praise of Astraea" (poem) 1602

The Triumph of Death and Other Unpublished and Uncollected Poems by Mary Sidney, Countess of Pembroke (1561-1621) (poetry) 1977

CRITICISM

Frances Berkeley Young (essay date 1912)

SOURCE: "Lady Pembroke as Editor, Translator, and Author," in *Mary Sidney: Countess of Pembroke,* Long Acre, 1912 , pp. 123-49.

[In the following excerpt, Young conducts a brief review of both Sidney's career and the scholarship that had unearthed her manuscripts and significance by the early twentieth century.]

Any survey of Lady Pembroke's literary work should naturally begin with her brother's novel, 'Arcadia,' and her connection with that work. The permanent form in which that famous romance has come down to us is a form determined in great part by Lady Pembroke, to

whom the book itself is dedicated. As is well known, she—after her brother's death—acted as editor for the second edition of 'Arcadia.' Although critics in the past have attributed portions of the novel itself to her pen, it seems certain now that she contributed practically nothing original to the story. Since Mr. Bertram Dobell's recent discovery of three new early manuscripts of 'Arcadia,'[1] he has thrown so much light on what Lady Pembroke's part of the work actually was, that I can do no more than summarise his conclusions. First, however, I shall sketch the known facts concerning the composition and first publication of the romance.

It has been generally supposed that Sir Philip Sidney began to write 'Arcadia' during his prolonged stay at Wilton in 1580. That he may have begun it a year or so earlier, however, is of course entirely possible. The earliest mention of it at present known is that occurring in Thomas Howell's 'Devises' (1581), a collection of short miscellaneous poems, dedicated to the Countess of Pembroke, and containing the following lines, 'Written to a most excellent Booke, full of rare inuention.'[2] 'Arcadia' was not printed till 1590, but Howell had doubtless seen it in manuscript at Wilton.

> Goe learned booke, and unto Pallas sing,
> Thy pleasant tunes that sweetely sounde to hie
> For Pan to reache, though Zoylus thee doth
>   sting,
> And lowre at they lawde, set nought thereby.
>   Thy makers Muse in spight of enuies
>   chinne,
>   For wise deuise, deserued praise shall winne.

> Who views thee well, and notes thy course
>   aright,
> And syftes eche sence that couched is in thee:
> Must needes extoll the minde that did thee
>   dight,
> And wishe the Muse might neuer weary bee.
>   From whence doth flowe such pithe in filed
>   phrase,
>   As worthiest witte may ioy on thee to gase.

> How much they erre, thy rare euent bewrayes,
> That stretch their skill the Fates to ouerthrow:
> And how mans wisedome here in vaine seekes
>   wayes,
> To shun high powers that sway our states
>   below.
>   Against whose rule, although we striue to
>   runne,
>   What Ioue foresets, no humaine force may
>   shunne.

> But all to long, thou hidste so perfite worke,
> Seest not desyre, how faine she seekes to
>   finde:

Thy light but lost, if thou in darknesse lurke?
Then shewe thy selfe and seeme no more
    unkinde.
  Unfolde thy fruite, and spread thy maysters
  praise,
  Whose prime of youth, graue deeds of age
  displaies.

Go choyce conceits, Mineruas Mirrour bright,
With Rubies ritch yfret, wrought by the wise:
Purfled with Pearle, and decked with delight,
Where pleasure with profite, both in their
    guise.
  Discourse of Louers, and such as folde
  sheepe,
  Whose sawes well mixed, shrowds misteries
  deepe.

Goe yet I say with speede thy charge delyuer,
Thou needst not blushe, nor feare the foyle of
    blame:
The worthy Countesse see thou follow euer,
Tyll Fates doe fayle, maintaine her Noble
    name.
  Attend her wyll, if she vouchsafe to call,
  Stoope to her state, downe flat before her
  fall.

And euer thanke thou him, that fyrst such
    fruite did frame,
By whome thy prayse shall liue, to thy
    immortall fame.

The internal references here are indubitable, and the fourth stanza, which urges that the author of the romance should allow it a wider circulation, is especially interesting.

Mr. Bertram Dobell thinks that by 1580 or 1581, Sidney had entirely completed the original first draft of the romance. In support of this opinion he recalls to us the sentence in the dedication to Lady Pembroke, 'Now, it is done onely for you, onely to you.' Such an opinion is certainly borne out also by the poem of Howell's, quoted above.

I shall now summarise Mr. Dobell's conclusions:

Sidney died October 17, 1586. During his life-time, many copies of *Arcadia* in its first form had been circulated in manuscript; and immediately after his death, one of the printers or publishers of the time attempted to bring out an edition, which would have been printed from one of these manuscripts. We learn this by a letter written by Fulke Greville, Lord Brooke, in November, 1586, to Sir Francis Walsingham, Sidney's father-in-law.[3]

'S[r], this day, one Ponsonby, a booke bynder in Poles Churchyard came to me and told me that ther was one in hand to print S[r] Philip Sydney's old arcadia, asking me yf it were done with your honors consent, or any other of his frendes? I told him, to my knowledge, no: then he aduised me to giue warninge of it, either to the archbishope or doctor Cosen, who haue, as he says, a copy to peruse to that end.

S[r] I am loth to renew his memory vnto you, but yeat in this I must presume; for I haue sent my lady, your daughter, at her request, a correction of that old one, done 4 or 5 years sinse, which he left in trust with me, whereof ther is no more copies, and fitter to be printed then the first, which is so common: notwithstanding euen that to be amended by a direction sett downe vnder his own hand, how and why; so as in many respects, especially the care of printing of it, is to be don with more deliberation.'

From the above passages, it is clear that there was an 'old Arcadia' which was common in manuscript form; that the author had been engaged, perhaps some time, in revising it; and that he left it in the hands of one of his most intimate friends, with particular directions as to how it was to be dealt with. It is also clear on what account, and in what manner, the publication of the original version of the romance was prevented.

This William Ponsonby, who thus stopped the publication of an unauthorized edition, was really a responsible publisher who probably hoped in this way to obtain the privilege of publishing an authorized edition. Somewhat less than two years later, as appears from an entry for August 23, 1588, in the Stationers' Register,[4] Ponsonby was authorized to publish the romance; but it was not until 1590 that the work was offered for sale.

The *Arcadia,* as published by Ponsonby in 1590, seems to have been superintended and possibly edited by Lord Brooke. He was perhaps the overseer of the print, who made the division into chapters;[5] and his own manuscript copy of the romance was probably the one printed from.[6]

Although this first edition breaks off in the middle of Book III, and is therefore less complete than later editions, Mr. Dobell considers its text quite as authoritative as that of the folio edition of 1593, which was published under the direction of the Countess of Pembroke.

In this second edition of 1593 the division into chapters and the explanatory headings which had appeared in Lord Brooke's edition were omitted. It is clear that the 1590 edition had not been authorised by Lady Pembroke, as is shown by the 'Address to the reader,' by 'H. S.,'[7] which appears in the folio of 1593.

The disfigured face, gentle Reader, wherewith this worke not long since appeared to the common view, moued that noble Lady to whose Honour it was consecreated, to whose protection it was committed, to take in hand the wiping away of those spottes wherewith the beauties thereof were unworthely blemished. But as often repairing a ruinous house, the mending of some old part occasioneth the making of some new; so here her honourable labor begun in correcting the faults, ended in supplying the defects; by the view of what was ill done, guided to the consideration of what was not done. Which part with what aduise entered into, with what accesse it hath been passed through, most by her doing, all by her directing, if they may be intreated not to define, which are unfurnisht of means to discerne, the rest it is hoped will fauorably censure. But this they shall for their better satisfaction understand, that though they find not here what might be expected, they may find neuerthelesse as much as was intended, the conclusion, not the perfection of Arcadia, and that no further than the Authors owne writings or known determinations could direct. . . . But howeuer it is, it is now by more than one interest the Countesse of Pembrokes Arcadia, done as it was, for her, as it is, by her. Neither shall these paines bee the last (if no unexpected accident cut off her determination) which the euerlasting loue of her excellent brother will make her consecrate to his memory.

The sentence 'But . . . though they find not here what might be expected, they may find neuerthelesse as much as was intended, the conclusion, not the perfection of Arcadia,' certainly seems to bear out Mr. Dobell's conclusions, as they will be presently explained.

I shall now summarise Mr. Dobell's account of the three new manuscripts of 'Arcadia' that were discovered by him, and his conclusions, from these manuscripts, as to the nature of Lady Pembroke's editorship. He names and describes them as follows:

(1) The 'Clifford' copy. (So-called from name on title-page.)

Complete. Large quarto. c. 400 pp. Text good. Contains in addition, at end, 'Dyuers and Sondry Sonetts' Cabout 25 in number. These give many variants from the printed versions, and also one hitherto-unprinted poem.

(2) The 'Ashburnham' copy.

First leaf gone; no title, in consequence.

(3) The 'Phillips' copy.

This one, instead of the usual title, has 'A Treatis made by Sir Phillip Sydney, Knyght, of certeyn accidents in Arcadia, made in the year 1580, and

emparted to some few of his friends in his lyfe tyme, and to more since his unfortunate deceasse.

Of these three Mr. Dobell considers the 'Clifford' MS. most valuable. It and 'Ashburnham' were sold by him to Messrs. Dodd, Mead & Co., and have now passed into the hands of an American collector. The 'Phillips' MS. was, in 1909, still in Mr. Dobell's possession.

In Mr. Dobell's opinion, these three manuscripts represent the very earliest version of 'Arcadia.' This was, apparently, much more complete and coherent, as to the story, than were Sidney's later revisions. From the 'juvenility of style,' Mr. Dobell thinks that this earliest version might have been begun as early as 1578, though it was probably not finished before 1580. Sidney's revisions at the time of his death had got no further than the middle of the third book, as exemplified by Lord Brooke's copy, and probably also by one in the possession of Lady Pembroke. When the Countess undertook the second edition, then, she naturally resorted to the first draft to see how this might be utilised in completing the romance. Several stories, new in the revised edition but unfinished there, are unavoidably left unfinished. But the romance as a whole is completed by a part of the third book, and all of the fourth and fifth books of the original or early version.

Except for a sentence now and then, or a negligible change in phrasing, the work seems to be entirely that of Sir Philip Sidney. Lady Pembroke *added* practically nothing; it seems, however, that she *left out* some things of value.

An extremely interesting study is yet to be made of the changes and insertions which Sidney himself made in revising his first draft. However, these do not concern our immediate subject. But Mr. Dobell points out two significant omissions made by Lady Pembroke, in adding the conclusion from the original draft.

(1) In these new manuscripts Sidney, as *Philisides,* gives a short account of his life, education, hopes, and disappointed love.[8] Mr. Dobell considers this passage frankly autobiographical, and believes this to be the reason why Lady Pembroke omitted it.

(2) In the manuscripts occurs also a rather sensual description of Musidorus' feelings during his elopement with Pamela. This is omitted from the printed versionCan omission that Mr. Dobell considers to be characteristic of a woman's feeling for what was, and what was not, suitable to the rest of the story.

The conclusion of the whole matter seems to be that whatever Lady Pembroke may or may not have contributed to the book while her brother was actually writing it at Wilton, she performed her editorial duty honestly and conscientiously. She evidently added no more than she could help; left out only those things that she deemed too personal to be printed; and employed not merely the simplest, but also the only possible means of completing the story.[9]

Lady Pembroke's principal literary activity seems to have been in translation. Of the original compositions attributed to her, only two poems have survived, and of one of these her authorship is not absolutely certain. Probably much of her work was lost, or—as Miss Luce suggests[10]—printed anonymously in some of the poetical miscellanies of the day. Gabriel Harvey, in 'Pierce's Supererogation,'[11] says of her:

> And what if she can publish more works in a moneth than Nash hath published in his whole life; or the pregnantest of our inspired Heliconists can equall?

However doubtful this may be, as evidence, it is hard to believe that a woman of so much evident literary ability and living in an age when poetic expression was not only the fashion, but a matter of course, did not do a greater amount of original composition than we now find remaining.

Of the two poems, one is an elegy, and the other a pastoral dialogue in honour of the Queen. The latter, **'Astrea,'** was first published in Davison's 'Poetical Rhapsody,' in 1602,[12] under the title, **'A Dialogue between two shepheards, Thenot and Piers, in praise of Astrea, made by the excellent Lady, the Lady Mary, Countess of Pembroke, at the Queenes Maiesties being at her home at—, Anno 15—.'** There seems to be no record of any such visit of the Queen at Wilton. Possibly the poem was written in anticipation of some projected visit, and the date and place left blank to be filled in later.

The other poem, probably but not certainly written by Lady Pembroke, is an elegy on the death of her brother Philip. It was first published in Spenser's 'Astrophel,' which appeared as an appendix to 'Colin Clouts Come Home Againe,' in 1595.[13] The elegy itself has no date, but Spenser's prefatory epistle to 'Colin Clout' is dated 'From my house at Kilcolman, the 27 of December, 1591'; the elegy, then, probably belongs within the five years after Philip Sidney's death, in 1586. This poem is usually printed with the title, **'The Doleful Lay of Clorinda,'** from the name given by Spenser to the sister of Astrophel. In the group of poems that constitute 'Astrophel,' Spenser introduces Clorinda's elegy as follows:

> And first his sister that Clorinda hight,
> That gentlest shepherdess that liues this day,
> And most resembling both in shape and
>   spright
> Her brother deare, began this doleful lay,
> Which lest I marre the sweetnesse of the

vearse,
> In sort as she it sung I will rehearse.

It is rather hard for a modern reader to appreciate the 'sweetnesse of the vearse,' but the implication of Lady Pembroke's authorship is sufficiently clear. In neither of these poems is the literary merit remarkable.

Those translations by Lady Pembroke that still survive are **'The Tragedie of Antonie,'** and **'A Discourse of Life and Death,'** from the French; **'The Psalms of David,'** done in conjunction with her brother Philip, and said to have been translated by Lady Pembroke from the original Hebrew; and **'The Triumphe of death,'** a rendering of Petrarch's 'Trionfo della Morte.' I shall take these up in what seems to be their chronological order.

Lady Pembroke's and her brother's joint translation of the Psalter is usually supposed to have been begun in 1580, during Philip Sidney's long stay at Wilton; it was finished by Lady Pembroke after her brother's death. It seems to have circulated in many manuscript copies during her lifetime, and . . . was enthusiastically praised by other writers of her day. Dr. John Donne wrote a poem in praise of this translation, and Dr. Thomas Moffatt, in his 'Silkewormes and their Flies' (1599) begs her to

> Vouchsafe a while to lay thy taske aside;
> Let Petrarke sleep, giue rest to Sacred Writte:
> Or bowe or string will breake, if euer tied,
> Some little pawse aideth the quickest witte:

The reader will remember, in Aubrey's description of the contents of the library at Wilton, his mention of 'a translation of the whole book of Psalmes in English verse, by Sir Philip Sydney, writt curiously, and bound in crimson velvet and gilt; it is now lost.' Many of these copies, partial or complete, must have met a like fate. Of the surviving manuscripts, one is in the library at Penshurst; one in the library of Trinity College, Cambridge; two are in the Bodleian, and two in the British Museum. This translation of the Psalter has—strangely enough, in view of its authorship—been published only once, by Robert Triphook, in 1823[14]. The manuscript from which Triphook's version was printed is that now at Penshurst, whither it passed after the Bright sale. Triphook, in his preface, describes it as follows:

> The manuscript from which it [the present version] has been printed is in folio, copied from the original by John Davies of Hereford (writing master to Prince Henry); himself a poet of no mean attainments, and a contemporary of Sir Philip Sidney. It exhibits a beautiful specimen of the calligraphy of the time. The first letters of every line are in gold ink, and it comprises specimens of all the hands in use, more particularly the Italian, then much in fashion at court.

From the pains bestowed it is by no means improbable that it was written for the Prince.

Under Triphook's direction this manuscript was collated with one of the copies now in the Bodleian (Rawlinson, poet. 25). The version thus achieved is a beautiful one, and probably the most accurate one now possible.

The Bodleian copy thus employed has an especially interesting history. It is a small folio with no title-page (vii + 157 leaves), and the handwriting is that of Dr. Samuel Woodford (1636-1700), who tells us that he copied it from an older and imperfect manuscript then in his possession. This older manuscript, it is presumed, was written under the direction of Sir Philip Sidney himself, for it had corrections and alterations in Sidney's own hand. Dr. Woodford, with great pains and care, has copied all of these corrections, as well as the text itself. On the first leaf he has written:

> The originall Copy is by mee, given me by my Brother Mr. John Woodford, who bought it among other broken books to putt up Coffee pouder as I remember.

At the end of Psalm 43 he notes:

> In the margin [i.e. of the original MS.] hitherto Sir Philip Sidney. Ita testor Sam. Woodforde, who for Sir Philip Sidney's sake, and to preserve such a remaine of him undertook this tiresome task of transcribing—1694/5.

The psalms which were lost from the original 'broken book' are from 88 to verse 2 of 102, both inclusive, and from **Psalm 131** to the end.

That Lady Pembroke was the translator of **Psalms 44-150** is presumed from various contemporary references,[15] from Woodford's note 'hitherto Sir Philip Sidney,' from the title-pages of the Penshurst MS. and the other Bodleian MS. (Rawlinson, poet. 24), and from the seven psalms accredited to Lady Pembroke in Sir John Harington's 'Nugae Antiquae.'[16] Also, in a letter from Fulke Greville to Sir Francis Walsingham,[17] November 1586, he mentions, among other literary remains of Sidney, 'about 40 of the psalms.'

In these **Psalms**, Lady Pembroke's ability as a translator is admirably shown. The consensus of critical opinion seems to be that her part shows more literary merit than her brother's, especially in the skill and ingenuity of the versification. Her stanzas vary from four to twelve lines, and exhibit a wonderful variety of rime schemes. One of the most interesting translations is that of **Ps. 55.** It has six stanzas, each composed of four triplets, with the rime-scheme abc—cba: acb—bca. Through seventy-two lines, thus, there are only

three riming words. Many of these psalms have also an admirable musical movement—for example, **Ps. 44,** the first one by Lady Pembroke:

> Lorde, our fathers true relation
>   Often made, hath made us knowe
> How thy power, on each occasion,
>   Thou of old, for them did showe.[18]

Lady Pembroke's translation of Du Plessis Mornay's 'Le Excellent Discours de la Vie et de la Mort' is signed 'The 13. of May 1590. At Wilton.'[19] Philippe Du Plessis Mornay (1549-1623) was a most prominent member of the Protestant party in France at the close of the sixteenth century. When in the summer of 1577 he was sent to England to ask aid of Elizabeth for the French Protestant cause, he and Philip Sidney, first known to each other through Hubert Languet, on the continent, became intimate friends. In June 1578 Du Plessis Mornay returned to England, bringing his wife with him, and Sidney stood godfather for their infant daughter.[20] Four or five years later Sidney undertook a translation of 'De Veritate Christiana,' a treatise written by his friend Du Plessis Mornay. As he was too busy to complete the task, however, he intrusted it to a scribe, Arthur Golding. The latter finished the undertaking, and published, in 1587, 'A Worke concerning the Truenesse of the Christian Religion.'[21] It may have been in accordance with some plan prearranged with her brother, that Lady Pembroke undertook the translation of another of Du Plessis Mornay's essays.

This essay by Du Plessis Mornay was originally prefixed to his translation of selections from certain letters and essays of Seneca. The book was first written in 1575,[22] and first translated into English in 1577, by Edward Aggas.[23] Lady Pembroke's version was first printed, together with her **'Tragedie of Antonie,'** in 1592.[24] I give two parallel passages, from the French and the English, to show the character of the translation. [See original for French, which has been deleted here].

> A Discourse of Life and Death, Written in French by *Ph. Mornay. Sieur du Plessis Marly*[25]

> It seemes to mee strange and a thing much to be marueiled, that the laborer to repose himselfe hasteneth as it were the course of the Sunne: that the Mariner rowes with all force to attayne the porte, and with a ioyfull crye salutes the descryed land: that the traueiler is neuer quiet nor content till he be at the ende of his voyage: and that wee in the meane while tied in this world to a perpetuall taske, tossed with continualle tempest, tyred with a rough and combersome way, cannot yet see the ende of our labour but with griefe, nor behold our porte but with teares, nor approch our home and quiet abode but with horrour and trembling. This life is but a *Penelopes* web, wherein we are alwayes doing and

undoing: a sea open to all windes, which sometime within, sometime without neuer cease to torment us: a weary iorney through extreame heates, and coldes, ouer high mountaynes, steepe rockes, and theeuish deserts. And so we terme it in weauing at this web, in rowing at this oare, in passing [A 2 *verso*] this miserable way. Yet loe when death comes to ende our worke, when she stretcheth out her armes to pull us into the porte, when after so many dangerous passages, and lothsome lodgings she would conduct us to our true home and resting place: in steede of reioycing at the ende of our labour, of taking comfort at the sight of our land, of singing at the approch of our happie mansion, we would faine, (who would beleeue it?) retake our worke in hand, we would againe hoise saile to the winde, and willinglie undertake our iourney anew. No more then remember we our paines, our shipwracks and dangers are forgotten: we feare no more the trauailes nor the theeues. Contrarywise, we apprehende death as an extreame payne, we doubt it as a rocke, we flye it as a theefe.[26]

To ende, we ought neither to hate this life for the toiles therein, for it is slouth and cowardise: nor loue it for the delights, which is follie and vanitie: but serue us of it, to serue God in it, who after it shall place us in true quietnesse, and replenish us with pleasures whiche shall neuer more perish. Neyther ought we to flye death, for it is childish to feare it; and in flieng from it, wee meete it. Much lesse to seeke it, for that is temeritie: nor euery one that would die, can die. As much despaire in the one, as cowardise in the other: in neither any kinde of magnanimitie. It is enough that we constantly and continually waite for her comming, that shee may neuer finde us unprovided. For as there is nothing more certaine then death, so is there nothing more uncertaine then the houre of death, knowen onlie to God, the onlie Author of life and death, to whom wee all ought endeuour both to liue and die. (*Die to liue, Liue to die*)[27]

From the point of view of literary history and literary influences, however, by far the most important work of Lady Pembroke was her translation of **'Marc Antonie,'**[28] a French tragedy on the Senecan model, by Robert Garnier (1534-1590). This was first published in 1592, with the translation from Du Plessis Mornay. A second edition appeared in 1595. I quote and summarise the bibliographical and critical account of this play from Miss Alice Luce's admirable reprint.[29]

The title-page of the edition of 1595 reads:

The Tragedie of Antonie

Doone into English by the Countesse of Pembroke

(Vignette)

Imprinted at London for William Ponsonby

1595

The copy in the British Museum is an unpaged quarto, well printed, with a woodcut border about each page.

In the Bodleian are two copies of **'Antonie.'**[30] One is an octavo, the title-page of which agrees with that of the 1595 edition quoted above, except that the name Sidney (Mary) is inserted before the Countess of Pembroke, and that the imprint is 'London, by P.S. for Will Ponsonby, 1595.'

There is another edition, a quarto, in which a manuscript title in ink has been supplied in place of the lost original. The date 1595 written hereupon is known by comparing the book with other existing copies of the same edition. The only date printed anywhere in this copy is in the inscription at the end: 'At Ramsburie, 26 of November, 1590.'

Lady Pembroke's *Antonie* is the first of that series of pure Seneca plays which appeared in the last decade of Elizabeth's reign, and which indicate the continuous revolt in higher literary circles against the overwhelming progress of the English romantic drama. We shall see that it afterwards became the model of the only two plays in English literature which are written wholly in the style of the French Senecan drama. . . .

The translation reproduces very faithfully the content of the original. . . . It follows in general the verse order of the original, but in the choruses, where the translator is hampered by rime, the rendering is much freer, and the order of the verse often much transposed, as in the chorus at the end of Act II. . . .

The verse of the French original, except in the choruses, is the Alexandrine, the verses riming in pairs. . . . Lady Pembroke translates these Alexandrines into English blank verse. She has followed the text of the original so closely that the English verse is often rough, and the inverted sentences sometimes give a strained effect to the measures; but if we consider that 'Marlowe's mighty line,' though it had existed in a few plays for thirty years, first became the property of the English public in *Tamburlaine,* printed 1590, we must admit that she uses the new metre with a very considerable degree of skill. Kyd, who probably was a protégé of Lady Pembroke's,[31] had already written in this metre and may have encouraged her to attempt the measure which he had already used so skilfully. . . .

Lady Pembroke's command of form and metre, which has already been noticed in connection with her translation of the psalms, is shown in her rendering of the choral lyrics. By far the most skilful part of her translation of *Antonie* is in these choruses.[32] . . .

That *Antonie* must have been a popular play in certain circles is shown by the fact that it reached two editions within three years.

Kyd's translation of Garnier's 'Cornélie' (1594-5) and Daniel's tragedies 'Cleopatra' (1594) and 'Philotas' (1605) will be referred to in the next chapter. The dedication to Daniel's 'Cleopatra'[2] shows that it was undoubtedly written at Lady Pembroke's suggestion:

> Lo. here the labours which she did impose
> Whose influence did predominate my muse;
> The starre of wonder my desires first chose,
> To guide their travels in the course I use; . . .

> I who (contented with a humble song)
> Made music to myself that pleased me best,
> And only told of Delia and her wrong,
> And prais'd her eyes, and plain'd mine own unrest—
> (A text from which my muse had not digresst)
> Madam, had not thy well-graced Antonie,
> (Who all alone hauing remained long)
> Wanted his Cleopatras company.

'The Triumphe of death translated out of Italian by the Countesse of Pembroke' is a poetical rendering of Petrarch's 'Trionfo della Morte.' A copy of this translation survives among the Petyt MSS.[33] at the Library of the Inner Temple in London. The manuscript is accompanied by a letter (copied in the same hand) from Sir John Harington to Lucy, Countess of Bedford. The letter is dated 29 December, 1600, hence it seems reasonable to suppose that the translation had been completed some years previous, as manuscript copies were in circulation in 1600. The popularity of Petrarch was great at this period. In Roger Ascham's 'Scholemaster' we are told that

> Then they [the Englishe men Italianated] haue in more reuerence the *Triumphes* of Petrarch then the *Genesis* of Moses.[34]

And Lady Pembroke's interest in Petrarch is shown by the lines already quoted from Moffatt's 'Silkewormes' (1599):

> Let Petrarke sleep, give rest to Sacred Writte.

This hitherto unpublished translation, which is an interesting and attractive one, is printed in this volume, Appendix A. It renders the original faithfully, and reproduces with great success the *terza rima* of

Petrarch's poem. It is the only translation (ancient or modern) of the 'Trionfo della Morte' that keeps the *terza rima* of its Italian original.

The general result of this survey of Lady Pembroke's literary work is to show her a conscientious editor, a verse writer of average ability, and a translator of great merit. That she enjoyed translating is evident, both from the fact that she did it well, and because the major part of her work seems to have consisted of translation. It is of course perfectly possible that new works from her hand may yet be discovered. As has already been suggested, she must have written more than has come down to us. But at any rate, enough remains to show her an interesting, if not a significant or important figure among the greater literary personages of her great time.

Notes

[1] Dobell, Bertram: *New Light upon Sir Philip Sidney's 'Arcadia,' Quarterly Review,* July 1909, London (vol. 211, pp. 74-100). . . .

[2] Howell's *Devises,* 1581, p. 44. Reprinted by Clarendon Press, 1906. Introd. by Walter Raleigh.

[3] *State Papers,* 1586.

[4] 'William ponsonby. Receaued of him for a booke of Sir Philip Sidneys makinge intitled *Arcadia:* aucthorised under the Archbishop of Canterbury hand.' Edward Arber: *Transcript of the Registers of the Company of Stationers of London, 1554-1640 A.D.,* vol. 2, fol. 231 *b,* 'August 23ᵈ, 1588.'

[5] See Dr. Oskar Sommer's facsimile reprint of *Arcadia* (edition of 1590). London: Kegan Paul, Trench, Trübner and Co. 1891.

[6] This is strongly supported by a passage in the dedication of a manuscript translation of part of Montemayor's *Diana,* by Thomas Wilson, in which the translator, addressing Lord Brooke, speaks of *Arcadia,* 'wᶜʰ by yor noble vertue the world so hapily enioyes.' W. W. Greg, *Pastoral Poetry and Pastoral Drama* (London, 1906), p. 148.

[7] The identity of 'H. S.' is apparently determined by the following passage from Aubrey (*Brief Lives,* ed. cit. vol. I, art. *Mary Herbert*):

> Mr. Henry Sanford was the earle's secretary, a good scholar and poet, and who did penne part of the *Arcadia* dedicated to her (as appeares by the preface). He haz a preface before it with the two letters of his name.

[8] This passage occurs (in the MSS.) in the *Fourth*

Eclogue, i.e. between the fourth and fifth books. In the edition of 1590 the eclogues (which in the MSS. are inserted between each book and the next) are omitted.

Mr. Dobell, it seems to me, reads too much actual confession into this passage. What Sidney says about 'Mira' (supposedly Penelope Devereux), for example, is surely very conventional in form.

[9] For a complete collation of the edition of 1593 with that of 1590, see Dr. Oskar Sommer's introduction to his invaluable facsimile reprint of the quarto of 1590. This introduction contains also a bibliography of the different editions of *Arcadia,* from 1590 to the present time.

An interesting business detail concerning *Arcadia* may be found in one of Rowland Whyte's letters to Sir Robert Sidney. R. Whyte writes from *Strand Bridge,* September 1, 1599:

> The *Arcadia* is newly printed in *Scotland,* according to the best Edition; which will make them good cheepe; but is very hurtful to Pownsonby, who held them at a very high rate: he must sell as others doe, or they will lye upon his hands. Collins, *op. cit. supra,* vol. 2, p. 119.

[10] *Op. cit. supra,* p. 22.

[11] See chap. v. p. 170.

[12] Also in 1611 edition of *Poetical Rhapsody,* p. 23, reprinted later in Nichols' *Progresses of Queen Elizabeth,* vol. 3, p. 529.

[13] *Vide* the note to *Astrophel* in the Cambridge edition of Spenser, edited by R. E. Neil Dodge, Boston, 1908, p. 699. . . .

[14] The / Psalmes of David / translated into / divers and sundry kindes of Verse / More rare and excellent / for the / Method and Varietie / than ever yet hath been done in English. / Begun by / the noble and learned gent. / Sir Philip Sidney, Knt., / and finished by / the right honorable / the Countess of Pembroke / his sister / Now first printed from / a copy of the Original Manuscript / Transcribed by John Davies of Hereford / in the reign of James the first. 1823.

[15] See *Mouffet* and *Donne* in chap. v. of this book.

[16] 2nd edit. of 1792, nos. 51, 69, 104, 112, 117, 120, 137. (Park's later edition of the *Nugae* omits them all but 112 and 137, (vol. 2, p. 407)). MS. copies of three of these psalms—51, 104, and 137—exist also in the Library of the Inner Temple, London: *Petyt MSS.* 538, 43i. ff. 284-286. They are accompanied by a copy of a letter from Sir John Harington presenting them to

Lucy, Countess of Bedford. The letter is dated December 29, 1600. In it the writer speaks of Lady Pembroke as 'that Excellent Countesse, and in Poesie the mirrois of our age.' These copies present variant readings from the same psalms printed in Sir John Harington's *Nugae Antiquae.* See Appendix A for a further account of this MS.

[17] *State Papers,* November 1586.

[18] Besides those psalms printed in *Nugae Antiquae,* extracts of varying length have appeared in Daniel's *Poetical Works,* 1739, vol. I, p. 256; in *The Guardian,* no. 18; in Bishop Butler's *Sidneiana* (Roxburghe Club, 1837); in Zouch's *Memoirs of Sir Philip Sidney* (two psalms, printed, but incorrectly, at the end); in Ruskin's *Rock Honeycomb;* and in *A Cabinet of Gems* (1892) by Dr. George Macdonald. A modern reprint of Triphook's version would doubtless be a useful and acceptable work.

[19] From the unique copy in the British Museum. (E. 3 *recto.*) See Bibliography for complete notice.

[20] H. R. Fox Bourne, *Sir Philip Sidney,* ed. cit. *supra,* p. 138. See also *Memoires de Madame de Mornay,* ed. Mme. de Witt (Paris, 1868), vol. I, p. 120.

[21] Fox Bourne, *ut supra,* p. 275.

[22] *Memoires of Mad. de Mornay,* ed. cit. *supra,* vol. I, p. 89.

[23] *The Defence of Death,* by E(dward) A(ggas), London, 1577, (Cop. in Brit. Mus.)

[24] See pp. 144 *et seq.*

[25] *Excellent Discours de la Vie et de la Mort,* par Phillipes de Mornay, Seigneur du Plessis Marlin, Gentilhomme François, Rochelle, 1581. . . .

[26] *Op. cit. supra,* p. 140. (A2, *recto and verso.*). . .

[27] E. 2, *verso,* E. 3, *recto.*

[28] First acted and published in Paris, 1578. Second edition, 1585. The latter text is the one used by Lady Pembroke. . . .

[29] The Countess of Pembroke's *Antonie,* ed. with introd. by Alice Luce, Weimar, 1897, pt. ii. pp. 31-120 *passim.*

[30] Malone, 208.

[31] Herrig's *Archiv, XC,* pp. 190-91, art. by J. Schick.

[32] In the *Dict. Nat. Biog.* the choruses are incorrectly

called Lady Pembroke's original compositions: 'adding choral lyrics of her own.' . . .

[33] 538, 43, i. ff. 286-289.

[34] *The Scholemaster,* London, 1570, reprinted in *Cambridge English Classics, The English Works of Roger Ascham,* ed. W. A. Wright (Cambridge, 1904), p. 232.

G. F. Waller (essay date 1977)

SOURCE: "Introduction: The Life and Milieu of Mary Sidney, Countess of Pembroke," in *Elizabethan & Renaissance Studies*, Institut fur Englische Sprache und Literatur Universitat Salzburg, 1977, pp. 1-65.

[*In the following introduction to his edition of Sidney's poetry, Waller presents an extensive survey of Sidney's work with a short biography. His careful attention to each of her major works and extant manuscripts includes speculations about the history of each and about her growth as a poet.*]

The Life and Milieu of Mary Sidney, Countess of Pembroke

> UNDERNEATH this sable herse
> Lies the subject of all verse:
> Sidney's sister, Pembroke's mother:
> Death, ere thou has slain another,
> Fair, and learn'd, and good as she,
> Time shall throw a dart at thee.[1]

Thus William Browne, in one of the Jacobean age's most famous epitaphs, and his praise of Mary Sidney, Countess of Pembroke (1561-1621) is echoed by many contemporary poets. For Spenser, she was "*Urania,* sister unto Astrofell, / In whose brave mynd, as in a golden cofer, / All heavenly gifts and riches locked are"; Samuel Daniel praises her for preserving literature "from those hidious Beastes, oblivion and Barbarisme." Almost a century later, John Aubrey commented that in the Countess' time, "Wilton House was like a College," and the Countess herself "was the greatest Patronesse of witt and learning of any Lady in her time."[2] Subsequent biographers eulogized her as the age's greatest blue-stocking, but paid token, if polite, attention to her writings.

Our knowledge of her life is based on a relative wealth of documentation unearthed by students of her brother. Mary Sidney was born, in 1561, into a family relatively new to the Tudor governing class, rising in its fortunes but anxious about its past traditions and its all too evident present penury. She spent her childhood in the family homes at Ludlow and Penshurst; while her brother was sent in 1564 to Shrewsbury School, she was tutored at home, acquiring a love for literature, a

fluency in English composition, French, Italian, and probably Latin and Greek. In 1575, she joined her mother as one of the ladies-in-waiting in Elizabeth's court. The first public record of her appearance in court occurs in Gascoigne's account of the ceremonial welcome to the Queen and her ladies to Woodstock in 1575 where she was told, in the somewhat laboured words of a welcoming verse:

> Ths yonge in yeares, yet olde in wit
> A gest dew to your race,
> If you hold on as you begine,
> Who ist youle not deface?[3]

The accolades were, fortunately, to increase in poetical merit as she grew older.

By 1575-6, there was talk at court about a marriage between Mary and the middle-aged Henry Earl of Pembroke. Despite some financial embarrassment to Sir Henry Sidney regarding her dowry, the marriage took place on April 22, 1577 and the new Countess of Pembroke henceforth lived at the Herbert family home at Wilton. The Earl was himself a collector of note as well as a patron of drama and literature and no doubt encouraged his young wife to set up what became the most important literary centre outside Elizabeth's court—what Aubrey called the "College" of Wilton. Between 1577 and his death in 1586, Philip Sidney spent long portions of time at Wilton, or at nearby Ivychurch, also part of the Pembroke estates, and it was there that the Countess gathered the poets and men of letters who were to develop and continue Sidney's hopes for Elizabethan literature. From the late 1580s, especially, as the Countess herself took over her dead brother's vocation, Wilton did indeed become like a college or academy: writers such as Greville, Spenser, Daniel, Drayton, Breton, Fraunce and Watson gathered there. She and her Circle provided the means by which the spirit and influence of the Sidneian revolution in literature were mediated to late Elizabethan and Jacobean literature.

There is little evidence to suggest that the Countess' own writings were commenced before her brother's death: it seems, on the contrary, that the literary experimentations, translations and other writings she completed were directly inspired by his example and dedicated to his memory. In May 1590, she completed her translation of Philippe de Mornay's *Discours de la Vie et de la Mort,* and about the same time, a translation of Robert Garnier's *Marc-Antoine.* Both works were first published in 1592. Around 1590, too, she completed the translation of Petrarch's *Trionfo della Morte,* while the handful of extant lyrics seem also to date from this time. Her major literary achievement was, however, the ***Psalms,*** a task she took up from among Sidney's manuscripts and which was largely, though not completely, finished by 1599. As well, she was engaged in presenting adequate editions of Sidney's worksCthe *Arcadia* appeared in 1593, the *Defence* in 1595, and a collected edition of his writings, including the corrected text of *Astrophel and Stella,* in 1598.

Her literary activity grew out of her active interest in patronage. As John Buxton suggests, but for the work of the Countess and her brother the work of many Elizabethan poets would have been rendered negligible.[4] On his return from his European grand tour in the 1570s, Sidney had looked at the state of English letters and seen that while a vigorous cultural tradition flourished in France, the low Countries and Italy, English literature had seemed to stagnate, and he set about enquiring "why England the Mother of excellent mindes should be growne so hard a stepmother to *Poets*. . . . "[5] The beginnings of his attempts to advance English letters coincide with his sister's marriage, and while it would be foolish to suggest that the family single-handedly changed the face of Elizabethan literature, without the Sidneys and Wilton House, the literature of the 1580s and 1590s would have been much drabber and less exciting.

The Sidney's patronage operated not primarily through financial support or by providing employment but by means of hospitality and active encouragement. The accolades to the brother and sister constantly emphasize their example and encouragement: they knew, in Nashe's words, "what belonged to" scholars, poets and musicians.[6] The initial results of the Sidney's efforts were, perhaps, of varying quality. They can be seen in the experiments, from the late 1570s, with quantitative verse, but gradually the movement broadened to include Petrarchist love-poetry, treatises, romances, religious verse, drama. Above all, the Sidneys provided a continuous if informal organization. Although scholars have long doubted the existence of the "aeropagus" Spenser and Harvey seem to refer to in their correspondence of 1579-1580, the idea cannot be entirely dismissedCthe there is strong, if indirect, evidence for some kind of rudimentary organization. Certainly what John Buxton calls "the endeavour of Sidney and his friends . . . to remedy the want of desert which they acknowledged in contemporary poetry"[7] could not have taken place in isolated studies: the obvious parallels amongst the works of, say, Philip and Robert Sidney, Greville, Spenser, Dyer and, later, Spenser, Greville, Breton, Fraunce, Daniel and the Countess herself are too numerous to suggest anything other than close and constant conference and competition.

It is one of the more delightful contributions made by domesticity to English literature that the marriage of Mary Sidney provided such a diverse group with a common bond. In informal and unsystematic ways the Sidneys provided in their family homes for the varied interests of their friends and protégés. Where in Italy or France, Renaissance culture was centered on towns

and salons, on Urbino or in Baif's *académie,* in England "we think not of cities but of houses" and "almost always deep in the country."[8] There are, indeed, constant references in records and letters to a persistent path between the court and Wilton from 1578 onwards. As James Osborn puts it, Sidney and his Circle set out "to free English poetry from its 'balde Rymers' and succeeded in doing so. The golden phase of Elizabethan poetry grew out of these sessions."[9]

After 1586, it seems the Countess herself took a singularly active part. Contemporary references start to mention her writing, not merely her patronage. Like the ladies Elizabetta Gonzago or Emilia Pia, or Marguerite, Queen of Navarre, the Countess provided inspiration, hospitality and most especially, a working example. She was to Barnabe Barnes the "Great Favourer of *Phoebus* offspring," and herself one "in whom, even *Phoebus* is most flourishing!" Nashe writes that the "fayre sister of Phoebus" surpasses even "the Lesbian Sappho with her lirick Harpe."[10] A host of similar tributes can be collected: many poets flourishing in the 1590s wrote in her praiseCand their applause does ·ot just express the commonplace gratitude for favours received but constantly emphasizes the Countess' own literary talents.

In considering the interests that unite the Countess' Circle in the 1580s and 1590s, it is difficult to find any explicit programme for political, religious or even cultural reforms, although in Greville's treatises or Breton's poems, something systematic, almost a political platform, is certainly implied. What unites the Sidney Circle is rather a spirit of a particular kind and interest to students of late Elizabethan culture: what I have elsewhere called, in a series of studies of their works, a "matching of contraries." The Sidneian spirit combines diverse intellectual worlds that separately would seem to fly apart. They were courtiers and so imbued with the fashionable, diverse ideas of courtly philosophers like Castiglione or Guazzo; they had more esoteric philosophical interests in neo-Platonism and Hermetic philosophies. But they were also pious, Calvinistic Christians, and the spirit of the Countess' "little court," to use Breton's phrase, is as much tempered by Calvin as by Castiglione. Breton, in fact, has two lengthy discussions of the atmosphere of Wilton which are especially revealing. In *Wits Trenchmour* (1597), he writes:

> . . . under heaven it was my greatest happiness . . . to light into the courtlike house of a right worthy honourable Lady. . . . Her house beeing in a maner a kinde of little Court, her Lorde in place of no meane command, her person no lesse than worthily and honourablie attended . . . where first, God daily served, religion trulie preached, all quarrels avoyded, peace carefully preserved, swearing not heard of, where truth was easilie beleeved, a table fully furnished, a house richly garnished, honor kindly

entertained, vertue highly esteemed, service well rewarded, and the poore blessedly relieved.

Implied in Breton's praise is, of course, a comparison with the ideal court of Castiglione's Urbino—and in the dedication to the Countess of *The Pilgrimage to Paradise* (1593), Breton does in fact make the comparison explicit:

> Right noble Lady, whose rare vertues, the wise no lesse honour, then the learned admire, and the honest serve . . . who hath redde of the Duchesse of Urbina, maie saie, the Italians wrote wel: but who knowes the Countesse of Penbrooke, I think hath cause to write better.[11]

Yet the distinction between Urbino and Wilton is clear, and indeed is typical of the adaptions made by Elizabethan England to the ideal of the court and civil behaviour. The English reading of Castiglione and his followers is, as Daniel Javitch and others have shown, consistently moralized.[12] In the *Cortegiano,* religion, for instance, is just one subject of polite discourse: theology and personal piety are largely ignored, demanding as they would a singularity of intensity and commitment that would clash with the urbane and gentile refinement of the court. But the Countess of Pembroke's "little court" is constantly praised for its piety and theological learning. In 1623 Walter Sweeper, a conforming but puritanically inclined theologian, dedicated to the Countess' two sons *A Briefe Treatise declaring the True Noble-man, and the Base Worldling.* After praising the recently deceased Countess, to whom he had hoped to dedicate the work, Sweeper goes on to define the nature of true nobility and courtesy which, he claims, he first learnt at Wilton:

> I gained the greatest part of my little learning through my acquaintance with your honorable fathers house and family . . . your famous Wilton house, like a little Universitie . . . had in it that learned Phisitian and skilfull Mathematician M. Doctor *Moffet* . . . great *Hugh Sanford,* learned in all arts, sciences, knowledge human and divine. . . . Never noble house had successively deeper divines. . . . In this noble House [Bishop] *Babington* rules of pietie and honestie swayed, swearing was banished; yea the housekeepers and inferiour servants well knew and practised the grounds of Religion.[13]

The remainder of the work is less directly relevant but it goes on to advocate a view of the courtier that is essentially in agreement with Breton's praise of the Countess thirty years earlierCone based on the Christian life and disdainful of mere earthly honours or titles. Courtliness and piety—Castiglione, we might say, and Calvin. The spirit of the Countess' Circle, and her own writings, is essentially such a matching of contraries.

Wilton's religious tone is reflected in its literary influences. Breton himself wrote religious verse; Fraunce,

Lok, Greville, all devotional poets of some skill, were closely linked with Wilton and the "little court." As well, the Wilton Circle reflected more diverse intellectual interests. Along with the strain of piety and theology, it seems to have been deeply interested in that rich and suggestive variety of speculative thought that starts to attract, irritate and inspire English writers in the late 1580s and 1590s. A significant date is the visit of Giordano Bruno to England in 1583-85. Bruno was in close contact with Sidney, Greville, Gwinne, and FlorioCand there are distinct signs of his influence upon these and other writers of the same generation, including Spenser, Fraunce, Daniel, Donne and Shakespeare. The confrontation between Bruno's emphasis on man's imaginative autonomy, his belief in the radical freedom of the will and the Protestant emphasis upon man's limitations and sinfulness, is a point of intellectual tension that proved to be fundamentally creative in the literature of the time. What appear to be intellectual contraries may become, in the zodiac of the poet's wit, a thing of strange beauty. The tension is summed up by a passage in Sidney's *Defence,* where he isolated each element in a phrase—on the one hand, man's "erected wit," on the other, his "infected wil."[14] In the Countess' writing, the same tension can be seen in the very scope of her writings—the religious drive in her ***Psalms*** and the translation of de Mornay; the courtly-romantic strain in the Petrarch; the fusing of courtliness and piety in the elegy on her brother, her pastoral dialogue and her poem to the Queen, and the mixture of romantic idealization and moralization in her portrayal of Cleopatra in ***Antonie.***

The Countess' writing career seems to have been confined largely to the years between her brother's death in 1586 and that of her husband in 1601. Some of her writings may have perished in a fire at Wilton of 1648 that destroyed, among other things, many of the family papers, but the Countess seems to have retired very much from the public arena in the last twenty years of her life. She died, after an attack of the smallpox, in 1621, and was buried in the family grave in Salisbury Cathedral where, today, a plaque bearing the text of Browne's epitaph commemorates her.

The literary career of the Countess seems almost certainly to have been confined to the period 1586-1611. A list of her extant writings, with approximate dates, is as follows:

c. 1586   ***Psalms*** commenced.

c. 1588   **"The Dolefull Lay of Chlorinda."**

1590   ***A Discourse of Life and Death*** (published 1592, reprinted 1595, 1600, 1607).

1592   ***Antonie*** published (reprinted 1595).

1593   Edited *The Countesse of Pembrokes*

Arcadia.

c. 1593 **The Triumph of Death**.

1595 *The Defence of Poesie* published by Ponsonby.

1598 Edited *Astrophel and Stella;* the authorized edition of Sidney's works issued.

1599 Poems of dedication to Sidney and the Queen.

1599 Presentation Copy of **Psalms** prepared for the Queen.

c. 1599 **"A Pastorall Dialogue betweene two Shepherds."**

c. 1611 Probable terminal date of final extant revisions to the **Psalms** (MSS *G M:* Trinity College, Cambridge G.3.16 and the Huntington Library HM. 117). . . .

The Triumph of Death

The Countess' translation of the *Trionfo* is found in the Petyt MSS in the Library of the Inner Temple. One of the manuscripts (538.43.1) contains an interesting miscellany including a letter from Sir John Harington to Lucy Countess of Bedford, which praises Mary Sidney as "in Poesie the mirror of our Age," and alludes to three of her Psalms which he copied out and sent to the Countess of Bedford. In the same collection, in the same scribal hand, is the **Triumph of Death,** ascribed in both the title and at the poem's end to the Countess of Pembroke. It is obviously the poem referred to by Thomas Churchyard in *Wits Conceit* (1593) and Thomas Moffat's *The Silkewormes and Other Flies* (1599), where similar allusions are made to the Countess' translating Petrarch. It lay unpublished until 1912 when Frances Berkeley Young printed it in two formsCas appendix to her biography of the Countess, and as an article in *PMLA*. The work has been increasingly discussed by scholars, who have invariably quoted from one or the other of these printings; however, nobody, it would seem, either compared Young's two versions or checked them against the original. In fact, the version in her book excludes, without comment, lines 118-141 of chapter One of the text; the version in *PMLA* restores these missing lines, but includes many minor errors and a number of quite serious major errors of transcriptionCall within 363 lines of verse. The present edition is offered as the first full and accurate text of the Countess' poem, and is printed by the kind permission of the Masters of the Bench of the Inner Temple.

Petrarch's *Trionfi* was probably the most influential poem of the Renaissance. Written during Petrarch's period of exile in the 1340s and 1350s, it was first published in 1470. Thereafter the work went into numerous editions, either singly or as part of collected editions of Petrarch's *Rime*. Building upon the precedents of Dante (in the *Purgatorio XXIX*) and Boccaccio (the *Amora Visione*), Petrarch's work is a series of dream visions portraying the successive triumphs of Love, Chastity, Death, Fame, Time and Eternity. The *Trionfo della Morte* itself describes a vision in which the poet meets a group of ladies who have witnessed the death of Laura which is then movingly evoked. The second *capitolo* of the work consists of a moving depiction of Laura who confesses her long, faithful but only now acknowledged love for the poet.

The work seems to have been widely read and highly regarded in sixteenth-century England. Ascham, among others, commented on its greatness, even bewailing that Englishmen revered the *Trionfi* above Genesis. It was first translated in the 1540s, by Henry Parker, Lord Morley, in a laboured, wordy and metrically erratic version published in 1554; a second complete translation, even more clumsy, was made by William Fowler in 1587-88. Different parts of the work were translated by various court poets, including Queen Elizabeth; Mary Sidney may have completed more than the one *Trionfo* extant, but there is no evidence for her having done so.

While, as Robert Coogan comments, all Elizabethan readers would have enjoyed the poem's idealization of the chaste yet passionate love between Laura and the poet,[15] nevertheless the subject of this particular *Trionfo* must have appealed in a peculiarly personal way to the Countess. The work reflects, we might fairly speculate, her own deeply idealized love for her brother, the impossibility of its sexual consummation and the realization that his inspiration of her own writing could be the only real and lasting fruit of her love. If the Countess did translate only the one part of the poem, her choice is especially significant.

It is difficult to pin down the exact text the Countess would have used among the many editions of Petrarch's work which were available in England by the late sixteenth century. Morley's translation was probably based on the text published in Venice in 1544, *Il Petrarca con l'espositione di Alessandrio Vellutello*. In preparing this edition, I have consulted this and a number of standard Renaissance and modern texts of Petrarch's work.

The most outstanding feature of the Countess' translation is the way she reproduces the original's stanzaic pattern. Petrarch's poem is in terza rima, where the middle line of one stanza rhymes with the outer lines of the next tercet: aba, bcb, cdc, etc. Here each *terzina* is rendered by an English equivalent and yet an admirable idiomatic fluency is maintained. The 11-syllable line is compressed into English iambic decasyllables and she demonstrates an acute ear for the movement and tone of both the English poetical line and that of her original and a consistent grasp of the high emotional level of Petrarch's poem. Her version is also remarkably succinct. By contrast with Morley's, which clumsily expands the original by half its length again, her version is never wordy, and usually vastly superior poetically. She certainly seems to have known Morley's version for there are occasions when she is misled by his translation into omitting a phrase. Where Petrarch reads "Le belle donne intorno al casto letto / Triste diceano . . ." and Morley has " . . . sayde they that were present there . . ." the Countess of Pembroke's version reads " . . . in mourneful plight / the Ladies saide" (I. 147-148).[16] Actual errors of translation, however, occur infrequently: she does not see "altri so che n'avrà più di me doglia" refers to Petrarch himself and so renders the line "this charge of woe on others will recoyle" (I. 52) and she misreads "avei" in II.128-129:

> Questo mi taccio; pur quel dolce nodo
> Mi piacque assai ch'ntorno al cor avei;

> I saie not, now, of this, right faine I am,
> Those cheines that tyde my eart well lyked
>   me.

Where Petrarch writes that Death is fierce and relentless only to the deaf and blind—

> Io son colei che sì importuna e fera
> Chiamata son da voi, e sorda e cieca;
> Gente a cui si fa notte inanzi sera

the Countess attributes, though not perhaps inappropriately, the deafness and blindness to Death itself:

> Loe, I am shee, so fierce, importunate,
> And deafe, and blinde, entytled oft by yow,
> yow, whom with night ere evening I awate.
>   (I.37-39)

Similarly, Petrarch speaks of Laura as being without a peer, "che fu nel mondo una," which is translated by the rather flat "who in the world was one" (I.51). Where the poem depicts the poet trying to escape the fact of his aging, the Countess evidently misunderstands and reverses the meaning, rendering "e debito all' etate" as "to my yeares was due" (I.139).

However, unlike Morley, the Countess is generally true to both word and spirit. Where Petrarch celebrates the glorious array of Laura's attendants, Morley's version is much more pedestrian:

> Petrarch: Poche eran, perchè rara è vera
>   gloria;

> Ma ciascuna per sè parea ben
>   degna
> Di poema chiarissimo e d'istoria.

> Morley: Vertuous glory is rath and ever
>   shall.
>   But those that were present in
>   that place
>   Eche one by them selves (A
>   playne case)
>   Semed well worthy of laude to
>   reherse
>   Of Poete or Oratour in prose or
> verse.

> Pembroke: A few, for nature makes true
>   glorie rare,
>   But eache alone (so eache alone
>   did shine)
>   Claym'd whole Historian's, whole
>   Poete's care
>   (I.16-18)

Similarly much more moving is the Countess' rendition of Petrarch's evocation of Death's ruthlessness in saying the "cose eccelse":

> Così del mondo, il più bel fiore
>   scelse;
> Non già per odio, ma per
>   dimostrasi
> Più chiaramente nelle cose eccelse.

> Morley: And so the fayrest flower that ever
>   was
>   She dyd roote up (Alas, I say,
>   Alas!)
>   No for no hate that she to her
>   then hadde,
>   But in heaven for to make her
>   spirit gladde.

> Pembroke: So cropt the flower, of all this
>   world most faire,
>   To shewe upon the excellentest
>   thing
>   Hir supreme force, And for no
>   hate she bare.
>   (I.115-117)

Besides the Countess' version, Morley's rhetoric is empty and trite.

At the poem's great moments of idealized passion and elevated suffering, the Countess is especially impressive. The opening, with its delicate light vowels and stately movement is typical of her interpretation of the poem as a courtly pilgrimage, an allegorical revelation of the power of passion before the threat of death:

That gallant Ladie, gloriouslie bright,
    The statelie piller once of worthinesse,
    And now a little dust, a naked spright:
Turn'd from hir warres a ioyefull
    Conqueresse:
    Hir warres, where she had foyl'd the mightie
    foe,
    whose wylie strategems the world distresse,
And foyl'd him, not with sword, with speare
    or bowe,
    But with chaste heart, faire visage, upright
    thought,
    wise speache, which did with honor linked
    goe:

                                        (I.1-9)

The last terzina here is notable for the way the Countess brings a refreshing specificness to what in Petrarch's original is a mere generic term:

Non con altr'arme che col cor pudico,
E d'un bel viso e de' pensieri schivi
D'un parlar saggio e d'onestate amico.

The grim description of Death, "stealing on with unexpected wound," the praise of Laura, her voice "repleate with Angell-lyke delight," (I.44, 150) and the sombre, formal tone of the conclusion all stand out as superbly evoked, in image and tone, the more remarkable because of the tightness of form. Where the Countess does expand images or phrases, she consistently makes her original more concrete. "In Petrarch's original," it has been suggested in, perhaps, something of an overstatement, "despite its eloquence and nobility, one feels at times that the language is a little vague, a little stylized. The poetic tool seems to have become a shade worn and blunted. Lady Pembroke seems to refurbish it and give it a new edge. . . ."[17] She certainly uses vigorously active verbs and constantly ringing epithets: "con onor" becomes "a ioyefull conqueresse" (I.4), "non con altr' arme" is expanded to "not with sword, with spear or bow" (I.7). The emotions evoked are strong and passionate, and the poem's style is appropriately elevated and energetic. If we contrast the Countess' poem with the original, an immediate difference in tone is striking. A more dynamic opposition is set up between Laura and Death in the Countess' version. Petrarch subordinates his characters to the abstractions which they represent, giving them little dialogue—even Laura is "not so much a woman as the essence of virtuous love," while, as R. N. Watkins puts it, Petrarch himself "appears as an interested but not as an interesting spectator; he sees and applauds, he hardly moves, inquires, or responds."[18] By contrast, the dramatic nature of the encounter between the poet and the spirit of his dead mistress is stressed by the Countess. The tone is modulated carefully throughout: Petrarch in the first chapter is quiet and sorrowful, narrating the events, resignedly anticipating his own death. Laura's attitude to Death has the serenity of transcendence, accepting Death's homage to her uniqueness, but willing to undergo the penalty of her mortality. In chapter Two, however, the tone changes. As Petrarch encounters Laura in his dream, the poem becomes a dialogue between lovers, the tone more dramatic and less expository. Laura becomes a complex composite figure—the religious ideal, certainly, but as well what by the late sixteenth century had developed into the familiar Petrarchan mistress of love-poetry. Laura's brightness threatens that of the sun, eclipsing the darkness of Death—both are familiar compliments to the Petrarchan mistress. The second chapter rises to an impressive culmination in Laura's farewell to the poet (II. 184-190)—a parting which, it might be speculated, echoed something of the Countess' own feelings for her brother, a subject which will be touched on in discussing the poems she wrote in his memory:

Ladie (quoth I) your words most sweetlie
    kinde
Have easie made, what euer erst I bare,
But what is left of yow to liue behinde.
Therefore to know this, my onelie care,
If sloe or swift shall com our meeting-daye.
She parting saide, As my coniectures are,
Thow without me long time on earth shalt
    staie

                                        (II.184-190)

"The Triumph of Death" is by the highest poetical standards, a remarkable piece of work. It makes its readers wish that the Countess of Pembroke had not, seemingly, obeyed Moffat's petition to let Petrarch rest—although, perhaps a little wistfully one observes that the probable lapse of time between her finishing the work (*c.* 1593) and his remark (1599) might suggest that she did in fact complete more of the *Trionfi.* No trace of any other *Triumphs* has survived—indeed it is only because someone, presumably Harington, happened to have had the work copied, that it survived at all. It stands as one of her most successful productions with its rhythmical subtlety, concrete evocation and technical mastery not merely adding up to a fine translation but to a remarkable literary achievement.

The Psalms

It was not until the 1960s that a reasonably accurate account of the historical and intrinsic importance of the Countess of Pembroke's psalms was made. In 1962, William A. Ringler Jr. published an account of the fourteen then-known manuscripts of the Sidney Psalms; in 1963 J. C. A. Rathmell published an edition of the Psalms from one of the manuscripts, that at Penshurst Place. Since then, fifteenth and sixteenth manuscripts have been located, and research on textual and literary matters has been carried out by a number of scholars. In what follows, I offer a summary of the present state of our understanding of the text of the Sidney Psalms, and some brief indications of their literary importance, focussing on those psalms here printed for the first time. . . .

Except for Manuscript B, a transcript made by Bishop Samuel Woodford in 1694-95, all the . . . manuscripts date from *c.* 1595-1630. They exist in a clearly defined relationship, which is almost unique in the Elizabethan canon for its fullness and clarity, and for the amount of information revealed or implied about the poet's habits of composition. Many of the manuscript variants are not simply scribal inaccuracies but represent distinct phases of authorial revision. The Countess was, as Ringler put it, in a term we should qualify somewhat, "an inveterate tinkerer"[19] with her text. In preparing his edition of Sidney's 43 psalms, Ringler was concerned with restoring Sidney's original revision and so removed the Countess' later revisions. Rathmell, on the other hand, aimed to print an emended version of Manuscript A, the Penshurst text, and so was concerned with what he presented as the Countess' final revisions—although, as I shall show, certain of the manuscript variants do in fact somewhat call in doubt the finality of the versions in A. Certainly, between Sidney's versions and the Countess' latest revisions lie a great many variants and independent or parallel versions, all making up a rich and fascinating story of nothing less than the growth of the Countess of Pembroke's literary vocation and poetical skills. The printing of the Psalms in this edition will help to make this process clear.

A full collation of the 16 manuscripts shows that there are three distinct kinds of variant—scribal errors and alterations, and both minor and major authorial variants. Collation also reveals, as both Rathmell and Ringler showed, that the Countess had two working copies, one presumably at Wilton, the other probably at the family's London residence, Baynard's Castle. The London copy seems to have contained independent revisions which were occasionally transferred back to the original at Wilton. The London copy is also the source of manuscripts containing still further independent versions: it would be in London where the Psalms would naturally find an audience outside the Countess' immediate Circle at Wilton and where requests for copies would be most numerous. Most of the extant manuscripts are therefore derived from the London copy.

The two working copies will, following Rathmell's *sigla,* be designated as B^{0-1-2} (from which at a late stage of revision [B^2] was derived A, B, J, and part of F), and X, which was itself derived from an earlier stage of revision in B (B^1). As initially reconstructed by Rathmell, B^1 first gave rise, through a conjectural copy Z, to K and through another conjectural intermediary, Y, to F (Psalms 1-26) and I. Another line of descent

goes from Z to the London working copy X. From X is derived a set of closely related manuscripts C D G1 E H L G M, sometimes through conjectural intermediaries.

Rathmell used A, the Penshurst text, as his copy-text, and together with J, it is the most important source for establishing the Countess' final versions of most of his Psalms. However, the most important manuscripts for the purpose of the present edition are B and the two closely related manuscripts G and M. B, Ringler's copy-text, is undoubtedly the most perplexing of all the extent manuscripts. It was copied by Woodford from a manuscript, which must have been a late stage of the Countess' revision of Sidney's original text. It had probably been sold, like A and the other books and manuscripts at Wilton, by the fifth Earl. It was transcribed with some 200 errors and rather modernized spelling and punctuation in 1694-95. The original, as is revealed by the corrections to A, must have been much written over by interlineations, strike-outs and marginal additions. These consisted of successive layers of the Countess' revisions, especially a number of early versions which were later abandoned ("expung'd" is Woodford's constant remark) and many minor revisions. Many of the later versions seemed to have been inserted into his copy-text on loose sheets and were lost by the time he made his transcription. Woodford selected what seemed to be the Countess' final intentions and, as well, noted the rejected readings. He copied his original with reasonable care, but could have saved himself and later editors a great deal of labor if instead of undertaking his "tiresome task of transcribing"[20] the original, he had merely folded it up and preserved it. In its unrevised state, his copy-text was clearly the Countess' text inherited by the Countess from her brother, much worked over, at a stage before her then-final 1599 revisions were made.

Associated with B, and used by Ringler to collaborate some of its readings, is K. It was, as Ringler showed, derived from the Countess' Wilton manuscript before the London working-copy was established. But as well, it records a number of important readings not found in B that were evidently added by the Countess herself to K; these were afterwards transmitted to X and a number of the manuscripts derived from it. Through scribal corruption and the occasional authorial intervention, many were progressively lost, but tracing the process of their transmission and disappearance helps us to show precisely the order in which the manuscripts in X were copied. Many of K's variants are recorded in G1, for instance, and are gradually lost through the series of intermediaries which gave rise to L, E, and H.

Manuscript G, now at Trinity College, Cambridge, was prepared for publication in the mid-seventeenth century, and for the student of the Countess' Psalms along with the close-related manuscript M is certainly the most important of the manuscripts in X. It contains unique endings to **Psalms 25, 31,** and **42,** and rhymed versions of **Psalms 120** to **127,** against versions in quantitative meters in all other manuscripts except M, now in the Huntington Library. For reasons I shall advance below, these and other minor variants suggest that these manuscripts, or at least the common intermediary between them and X (Rathmell's conjectural manuscript S) have some claims to containing the very last revisions prepared by the CountessCafter the completion of A, which was made for presentation to the Queen in 1599, and possibly as late as 1611 as there are occasions when the Countess appears to be guided by the King James version of the Bible in her revisions.

The revisions recorded in B represent the Countess' early experiments, the hesitant products of a writer feeling her way. Sidney probably left the Countess a fairly clean copy of his first 43 Psalms. In the stemma above, B^0 represents the text as Sidney left it; it survives only through Woodford's transcript, and was probably a scribal copy rather than a holograph since some of the typical Sidneian spellings occasionally show through.

When B and the manuscripts derived from B^1 and B^2 are examined to ascertain the Countess' method of working, however, an important difference presents itself. The manuscripts reveal a process of constant alteration and experimentation which adds up to nothing less than a poet's self-education. The Countess' very inexperience as a poet, her initial relatively unsophisticated handling of poetic form, make the relationship between her psalms and her originals less predictable and thus, in a sense, more open to development. Eventually, as she grows in confidence and competence, her versions are frequently deliberately more independent than her brother's. Where Sidney shows a workmanlike facility to keep to the logical and metaphorical structure of his original, the Countess' Psalms never maintain a constant distance from her text. She continues in her brother's footsteps in her fertility of technical experimentation, but she takes various paths away from strict translation, and develops a poetic voice very different from his—at times narrower but, usually, more intense, certainly more formally inventive, and more adept at extending the metaphorical structure of the psalm or re-creating the original into surprising Elizabethan life. To study the Countess' revisions is to be given a fascinating if often conjectural insight into the way this earnest, dedicated Elizabethan lady realized and cultivated her poetic talents. Her rewritings of her brother's psalms suggest that she used them initially as the basis for her own poetic experiments, feeling her way amongst his varied metrical patterns, and gradually developing a style and tone of her own.

To support these assertions, I shall now turn to the manuscripts themselves. The disappearance of the orig-

inal of Woodford's copy is, of course, the most frustrating factor in the reconstruction of the manuscript revisions. Woodford noted that "the Originall Copy is by me Given me by my Brother Mr. John Woodford who bought it among other broken books to putt up Coffee pouder. . . . " Dr. Bent Juel-Jensen, the owner of J, suggests that the original was still in existence in the possession of the Woodford family some 30 years ago, and although it has never been turned up in the family papers, there are hopes that it might have survived. Nevertheless, by means of B—after collating the other manuscripts to trace Woodford's emendations and errors—we can trace the sequence of the Countess' revisions through A, K, and the manuscripts in X. It seems that the Countess permitted copies to be made, usually from her London working-copy; sometimes she supplied quite new versions for these transcripts, made for friends, court acquaintances and admirers such as Harington. The reliability of these manuscripts varies: G1 E H L N are, for instance, more affected by scribal corruption than C D O G M, partly reflecting the number of intermediaries involved in the line of transmission.

Sidney presumably left his manuscript of the Psalms, the original of the Countess' Wilton working-copy, with her. She seems to have mulled over her brother's manuscript, altering his text not merely from perversity but through a constant desire to practice the rudiments of verse construction and, eventually, to bring what was obviously an unfinished manuscript entrusted to her to a stage of fuller completion. She was, for instance, obviously dissatisfied with Sidney's awkward phrasing at certain points, and removes the irregular stanzas at the conclusion of seven of his psalms. Thus she alters Sidney's aberrant 6-line concluding stanza to **Psalm 31** as follows:

> Then love the lord all ye that feel his grace
> Who pares the proud, preserves the faith full
>   race
>   Be strong in hope his strength shall you
>   supply.
>
> > (**31** A.64-66)

This version was transcribed as her then final thoughts in the 1599 presentation volume, and is preserved in A J F. Some time later, however, when she was still engaged in supervising transcriptions from the London text, the Countess obviously felt that the compression was too extreme. She restored the first part of Sidney's original conclusion, and then made two closely related versions of the final lines which are preserved in G and M, which are probably the latest authorially supervised transcriptions to be made.

It would seem probable that she continued to revise in this way even after having completed the bulk of her work on the psalms, since certain of the revisions in X appear to have been made later than when A reached its final state. Thus Sidney's conclusion to Psalm 42 is left unchanged in A B F J and K, versions derived from the Wilton text, and they also appear in O and D, which were perhaps among the earliest manuscripts transcribed from X, the London working-copy. Four subsequent revisions of the lines, however, then appear in X—one in C, one shared by E H L N, and others in G and M. Unquestionably, the enormous number of revisions which the Countess made to her brother's text, largely although not fully recorded by Ringler in his edition, betray a mind unable to leave the text alone, but more importantly they also show the Countess feeling for the appropriate form, the exact word, measuring the way sentiment attaches to or contrasts with rhythmical and metrical expectation. The degree to which, first, the Countess had to struggle with poetic composition, and, second, the extent to which her verse matured, is clearly seen when her own early versions are considered. The occasional over-regularity, the tentative probings for greater intellectual definiteness—indeed all the revisions she constantly imposed on her brother's text—must have increasingly given her confidence as she commenced her own independent translations. What were something probably close to her first versions of the remaining 107 psalms were recorded in Woodford's original, and his transcription, once it has been purged of his errors and alterations, is most valuable in tracing her development in poetical competence. B records (and I print below) early versions of 22 Psalms: **44, 46, 50, 53, 58, 60, 62, 63, 64, 68, 69, 70, 71, 75, 80, 85, 86, 105, 108, 117, 199**ghsw, and **122**. As well, where Woodford's copy-text included both the early and revised versions (evidently on loose leaves), he marginally noted the readings of many early drafts. **Psalm 49** is amended in virtually every line and so for the purpose of this edition, its original version has been assembled from B and printed (**Psalms 61, 72, 110** and **118** are also heavily revised, but not so extensively as to virtually constitute a version substantively different from that in A). Woodford made a number of speculative remarks to account for the Countess' dissatisfaction with her first attempts. Thus he writes on **Psalm 46**: "I suppose this Psalm may be crosst because of the conclusion or last staffes not answering the rest being shorter by four verses as in the former Psalms above, which are therefore corrected." At **48. 9-10**, he writes "the two last verses are putt in the margin instead of these expunged," and then adds a revision from the manuscripts in X:

> Ev'ry pallace yt enfouldeth
> God for surest refuge howldeth
>
> (**48** C.9-10)

From such variants we can, incidentally, learn something further about Woodford's copy-text. Because he included in the main body of his text some revisions found elsewhere only in X and not in I or K, his orig-

inal was presumably still being worked on at the same time as X, the Countess' London copy. There seem to have been when she chose to transfer fairly minute particulars from one copy to the other, a surmise born out by similar evidence elsewhere. That Woodford does not, however, include all the variants in X suggests again that the Countess revised particular transcripts made from the London copy on an individual, rather random basis and did not transfer all such variants.

The high number of heavily revised versions among the first third of the Countess' psalms (16 heavily revised or abandoned versions in the first 36) might suggest what would be logical, that she started where her brother left off. Certainly, the first version of **44** is very different from the later one. But some of the early psalms were barely or hardly revised: **51** (A) one of the best in the collection, is a magnificently controlled poem, displaying a sophisticated handling of technique and tone that is vastly superior to the early versions of **50**, the psalm before. There exists no early version of **51**, which might suggest that the Countess at first, at least, adopted a quite random order of proceeding. **Psalms 46** and **61** in MS B are also probably among the earliest attempts by the Countess since they show the "imperfect" endings favored by Sidney which she later revised.

From those Psalms with early versions recorded in B, we do get a fascinating insight into the Countess' methods of poetic composition. **50,** for instance, is a psalm where relatively minor changes only were made to B[1]; the variants Woodford records amount to a first sketch competent enough to build upon rather than a distinct early, later abandoned, version. **50** (B) is a relatively clumsily constructed draft in 12-line stanzas, with an irregular rhyme scheme which looks as if it might eventually have developed into double sixains, rhyming aabbc ddeec. **50** (A) by contrast is a tightly constructed poem in an 8-line tetrameter stanzas rhyming ababcdcd. It is also a finely wrought piece, with the opening theophany evoked in strongly dramatic terms:

> The mightie god, the ever-living lord,
>   all nations from the earthes uttermost
>   confines
> summoneth by his pursevant, his worde,
>   and out of beauties beautie, Sion shines.
> God comes, hee comes, with eare and tongue
>   restor'd:
>   his garde huge stormes, hott flames his
>   usshers goe:
> and called their appearance to record,
>   Heav'n hasteth from above, earth from
>   below.
>
> (**50** A.1-8)

The balanced phrases, the repetition in 11.4-5, and the sonorous dramatic note make the opening stanza reminiscent of a herald's formal announcement of a monarch's decree. By contrast, **50** (B) stumbles weakly, and is barely held together; the comparison shows how in working over her material the Countess, did, however, see exactly where she needed to improve the opening:

> The ever living God the mighty Lord
> Hath send abroad his pursevant his Word
> To all the Earth, to which in circling race
> Rising or falling sun doth shew his Face
> Beauty of Beautys Sion is the place
> 　Which he will beautify by his appearing
> God comes, becomes and will not silent stay
> Consuming Flames shall usher him the way
> A guard of storms about him shall attend
> Then by his voice he for the Earth shall send.
>
> 　　　　　　　　　　**(50** B.1-10)

The contrast is a revealing one. The diction has been heightened where appropriate and made more concrete and there has been a dramatic syntactical tightening. The flaccid monosyllables of 11.3-4 in the earlier draft are replaced by the clashing climaxes of the final version. The weak attempt at philosophical underlining of line 7 ("God comes, becomes and will not silent stay") emerges as a dramatic metaphor of urgency—AGod comes, he comes, with eare and tongue restor'd"—and the summoning of the Earth and Heavens is similarly rendered more dramatically and urgently, by compressing and breaking up the lines.

Other revisions show a similar sureness of touch. The original version of the **Psalm**'s verse 12 (**50** A.25-28) has none of the revisions' vigorous movement and finely wrought scorn which in the early draft is mere petulence:

> If I hungry that I hungry were
> Since earth is mine, and all that earth doth
> 　beare
> I would not tell it thee to begg thy meate
> 　　　　　　　**(50** B.31-33)

Similarly, the energetic conclusion of the later poem with its especially fine note of threat—

> in vaine to others for release you flie,
> if once on you I griping fingers sett
> 　　　　　　　　　　(A. 59-60)

is only a hint in the original:

> Mark this I say, least if with griping hand
> I once lay hold of you, none may withstand
> My matchlesse might, nor loose the pinching
> 　hand . . .
>
> 　　　　　　　　　　(B. 63-65)

The value of Woodford's transcription is clearly seen in such poems: **50** (B) is an early draft worked over by an apprentice poetic mind groping for the desired tone and image, but sufficiently promising to be used as the basis for later versions. So the Countess' final achievements can be better realized when we see the mechanics of the process of revision so clearly revealed.

The difference in quality seen in the two closely related versions of **50** is also observable in **Psalm 44**. B's version is in 12 8-line stanzas, well constructed, the advanced stage of competence suggesting that the Countess' habit was to give early attention to stanzaic and metrical form. Each stanza is carefully shaped into a pattern of 76968687 syllables, mainly in pentameters and using a high proportion of feminine rhyme. In the revised version, however, she tightens the rhyme scheme to ababbcbc, making a more succinct and rounded form. Particular details are, as well, constantly changed. The opening lines are reworked with a simpler diction and a more dramatic movement. B reads:

> Our fathers Lord by hearing
> 　Have made us understand . . .

The revision rewords the lines thus, breaking up the monotonous movement and simplifying the diction:

> Lorde, our fathers true relation
> 　often made, hath made us known . . .

Similarly, the contrast between the pagans and the Lord's chosen at the end of the opening stanza is made more emphatic and clear. Early in her work on the psalm the Countess saw the force of extending the original verse's barely hinted metaphor of planting and growth, and B reads:

> How rooting nations, them thy hand
> 　Did plant and planted nourish
> The stock prophane did leafeless grow
> 　The faithfull branch did flourish
>
> 　　　　　　　　　　**(44** B.5-8)

The revision irons out the confused syntax, compresses the clumsy wordiness, and reinforces the metaphor:

> . . . the Pagan foe
> rooting hence, thie folke implanting,
> 　leaveless made that braunch to grow,
> 　this to spring, noe verdure wanting.
>
> 　　　　　　　　　　**(44** A.5-8)

A process of constant tightening and variation can be seen throughout: the flaccid "Their sword did not procure them/ Possession of the land" (B.9-10) becomes "Never could their sword procure them / Conquest of the promist land" (A.9-10); by constantly shifting the caesura, tightening the rhymes and making the vocabulary more concrete and specific, the poem becomes more dramatic and taut. The original opening quatrain of each stanza, rhymed abac, gains much more force becoming abab as in the fine sixth stanza:

> Right as sheepe to be devowred,
>   helplesse heere wee lie alone:
> scatteringlie by thee out-powred,
>   slaves to dwell with lordes unknown.
> Sold wee are, but silver none
>   told for us: by thee soe prised
> as for nought to bee forgone,
>   gracelesse, worthlesse, wile, despised.
>
>   (**44** A.41-48)

By comparison with the original, this stanza has an impressive force, achieving the carefully worked for simplicity that becomes the characteristic mark of the Countess' mature style. The final lines in particular have been consciously shaped for greater clarity and force:

> As sheep to be devoured
>   Thou hast us left alone
> Thou scattringly hast us out poured
>   Among our heathnish foes
> Thou sellst us but coin hast none
>   Thy folk thou hast prised
> As things from whence no profit growes
>   Base, worthless, vile, despis'd.
>
>   (**44** B.41-48)

Another psalm where B shows how the original can be viewed as a first draft rather than an independent version is **69**. The final poem is a magnificently evoked and sustained cry of anguish, with an especially fine opening stanza:

> Troublous seas my soule surround:
>   save, O God, my sinking soul,
> sinking, where it feeles noe ground,
>   in this gulph, this whirling hoale.
> Waiting and, with ernest eying,
> calling God with bootlesse crying:
> dymn and dry in me are found
> eye to see, and throat to sound.
>
>   (**69** A.1-8)

Through the brooding movement of the opening, the almost surrealistic, and original, image of the "whirling hoale," and the mounting cry of the last 4 lines, the poem opens with an impressive evocation of fear. The earlier version contains the possibilities of this achievement, although it is much clumsier:

> Save me O God, O save my drowning soul
> For fast I stick in depth of muddy hole
>   When I no footing find:
> Now, now, into the watry gulfs I fall

> And with the streame I go,
> Hoarse is my throat, so long I cry and call
> So long look for my God, that dymn nay
>   blind
> Mine eyes with looking grow.
>
>   (**69** B.1-8)

The process of revision is fairly clear. The number of syllables has been reduced, the diction sharpened; line 4 has been entirely reworked, and the overall tension greatly increased. The most consistent revisions seem to have been toward simplification of vocabulary. The opening of the third stanza in B reads:

> O mighty Lord, let not discountnant be
> By my occasion such as trust in thee
>
>   (**69** B.17-18)

Reducing the line length, simplifying the vocabulary makes the final version much more effective:

> Mighty Lord, lett not my case
> blank the rest that hope on thee
>
>   (**69** A.17-18)

Examples could be multiplied throughout the poem.

Psalms 44 and **69** are examples where the original is close enough to the final version to be regarded merely as a first draft. The Countess obviously saw the possibilities inherent in her first attempts, and used them as the basis of later more competent versions. With other psalms, the resemblances are much more distant. In these cases, the versions in B indicate that the Countess made virtually new starts. 46 B, for instance, has relatively few points where any close relationship can be traced except through the common original. It is clearly a draft that was largely abandoned because of its sheer inadequacy as a poem. It certainly reads like a poet's typical early experiment, with an incomplete final stanza, a number of very clumsy rhymes, and much verbal padding:

> Our hope is God, God is our stay
>   A shield to keep us sound
>   Still ready to be found
> When troubles would our minds dismay
>
> When albeit the Earth quake all
>   And highest hills do fall
>   Into the deepest deep
> Yet still we will us fearlesse keep.
>
>   (**46** B.1-8)

The revised version not only shows a much less singsong movement and a tighter rhyme scheme; it is entirely more personal and dramatic:

> God gives us strength, and keepes us sounde,

a present helpe when dangers call;
then feare not wee, lett quake the grounde,
    and into seas let mountaines fall,
    yea soe lett seas withall,
        in watry hills arise
    as mail the earthlie hills appall,
        With dread and dashing cries.

(46 A.1-8)

There are some lines where the Countess obviously used material from her early version, but it is fairly clear that in this case, she recognized the general ineptitude of her first draft and started entirely anew. Similarly, with **Psalm 58,** the Countess used a quite different stanza form in revision, and as well as constantly generally strengthened the concreteness and simplicity of the diction, reducing the poem's length by almost a third.

Many of the early versions recorded in B are therefore valuable for tracing the development of the Countess' poetic maturation, although there are occasional early lines or stanzas which are superior to their later equivalents. In general, however, there is a marked technical maturity: tighter stanzaic patterns (as in **60**), a greater sense of meditative depth (as in **63**), and above all a cultivated and muscular simplicity, and a firmer sense of metaphor (as in **80,** A.16-32; cf. **80,** B.29-56) Woodford's transcription, even with his original tantalizingly missing, is a document of first rate importance in understanding the Countess' psalms.

So far as the other MSS are concerned, K contains a large number of small authorial revisions, some of which it shares with the manuscripts in X, suggesting that it reflects changes made at a relatively early stage and retained in the London text. It includes the original versions, found also in B and the manuscripts in X, of **119**ghsw, a version of **75** found also only in B I N, and as well a number of distinct variants, some shared with C, D, N or G1. I corroborates many of B's early versions and preserves a version of **89** which almost certainly would have been found in B had Woodford's copy-text not been damaged. It also includes a unique version of **Psalm 113,** "you that the life of servants doe professe," in 20 eleven-syllable lines in couplets, employing a high proportion (60%) of feminine rhymes. Despite a great deal of textual corruption, I is therefore an especially interesting MS for reconstructing the Countess' writing habits.

Among the most interesting versions the Countess made in X is the sequence of **Psalms 120-127,** recorded in G and M, and printed below. It seems that if A records the Countess' apparently final versions of the psalms, these and probably some of the other unique variants in G and M are exceptions, and were composed later. In the 1599 copy, **Psalms 120-127** are in quantitative metres, and an early version of **Psalm 122,** preserved in B I G1 E H L, is also a quantitative experiment. Similarly, **89** I is another such experiment and, indeed, one of the age's finest attempts at employing classical versification in English. But **Psalms 120-127** in G M are in rhymed verse, suggesting that the Countess eventually saw the folly of these neo-classical experiments. A J F B I K O D N G1 C E H L N preserve the quantitative versions; only G and M have the rhymed versions. By the end of the century, most Elizabethan poets had abandoned the quantitative experiment. Daniel's *Defence of Rhyme,* dedicated to the Countess' elder son, William the third Earl, was published in 1603, and it is possible that the Countess herself was aware of his arguments. As well, there are echoes of the King James version, as in the opening of **Psalm 122.** The wording here is slightly different from that of the Geneva version and may suggest that these versions of **Psalms 120-127** were written after the Countess had read the new Authorized version.[21] G and M have, therefore, on these grounds, some claim to representing the Countess' final thoughts, at least in **Psalms 120-127.**

The Psalms as Poetry

Even in the Countess' early experiments, we can see something of the struggle which eventually produced the best collection of post-Reformation religious verse in English before Herbert's *The Temple.* In the first place, as a participant in the technical revolution initiated by her brother, the Countess was clearly determined that the Psalms should be translated into an appropriate variety of metrical and stanzaic forms. In her complete collection, and not counting Sidney's original 43 psalms or psalms to which she made only minor revisions, there are 164 distinct stanzaic patterns, with only one repeated (122 G M, 126 G M), and 94 quite distinct metrical patterns. As well, the choice of a particular stanzaic form often determined that the Countess' version moved significantly away from her original. One instance is the acrostic Psalm 117, where the manuscripts reveal something of the habits of thought that went into the poem's making. The first draft, recorded in B, shows how she devised her initial letters to form the words PRAIS THE LORD, and then wrestled with the rest of the lines, arriving first at a rough rhyme-scheme of abcbaccdcedf and the mere draft of a poem:

Praise, prayse the Lord, All that of lowest
    sphere
Reside on any side
All you I say
In countrys scattered wide
Se in your joyes Jehovas prayse appeare
That worthily your songs display
His worth whose every way
Exceeding grace
Layd upon us doth overlay

Our greatest force; whose promise ever true
Restrained within no space
Decayes not, he needs it not renew.

(117 B)

From such rough beginnings, the Countess realized the essence of an acrostic poem—neatness of execution and pithiness of statement, with the meaning reflecting the formal patterning. In her subsequent revision, she reduced the length of line, worked out an appropriately brief utterance and a simple rhyme-scheme of ababcd-cdefef:

Praise him that ay
remaines the same:
all tongues display
Jehovas fame.
sing all that share
this earthly ball:
his mercies are
expos'd to all.
Like as the word
once he doth give,
rold in record,
doth tyme outlyve.

(117 A)

Comparing her final version with the Biblical original, it is very difficult to find any connection except in the most general sense: both are hymns of praise, but there is no more specific relationship.

Ten of the Countess' psalms (**120-127** A, **89** I K, **122** B I G1 E H L) were written in quantitative metres. They are part of a widespread Elizabethan attempt to adapt classical forms to the vernacular, and in composing these psalms the Countess seems to have been guided by her brother's practice of bringing the rhythmical regularity as close as possible to native stresses. Two of her poems are modelled upon poems from the *Arcadia* (**121** A on O A 33, and **122** B I G1 E H L on O A 34). **Psalm 120** A, in asclepiads, combines the regular pattern of O A 32 with the irregular stressing typical of classical models. . . .

It is, however, written in alcaic stanzas, and thus has three contrasting types of line, which lends a degree of variety to the poem. **121** is in phaleuciacs . . . ; both versions of **122** in asclepiads; **123,** in elegiac pentameters starting with short stressed syllables and ending with disyllables. **124** is in iambics, although the Countess typically varies the stress to bring the poem's movement closer to vernacular rhythms. **125** is in sapphics; **126,** as Woodford, who scanned it incorrectly, was perhaps aware, in somewhat irregular asclepiads, achieving greater poetic flexibility at the expense of strict regularity. **126** I is in the same metre. Of all the quantitative poems, **89** I, in hexameters, is the most successful, combining quantitative strictness with rhyth-

mical intensity, using a high proportion of accentual spondees to create appropriately strong rhythms. It has some especially fine passages evoking God's majesty—for instance the almost Miltonic description of the angel's humbling themselves before God:

Who can among th' exalted train of glorious
  angells
Like to Iehoua be found? All him, with an
  awfull obeisance
Terrible acknowledge, of flock affrighted
  about him—
Thow, commander of hosts, indeed most
  mighty Iehoua,
Seest not a match in powr . . .

(16-20)

Unusually for such a long poem, the Countess keeps up the appropriate tone of ringing exaltation—and while in general her quantitative experiments are earnest failures, **89** I K is "the most successful Elizabethan attempt to naturalize the hexameter,"[22] and certainly is comparable in quality with Fraunce's poems.

The relevance of the quantitative poems to a discussion of the Countess' poetic independence is primarily in the demands made on her translation by the strict regularity of the form. Something of the way she worked can be grasped by comparing the rhymed versions of **120-127** recorded in Manuscripts G and M. **Psalm 125** G M stays close to the original in its imagery, stanzas two and three, for instance:

For as the Hills which Salem round
  Encompasseth: so God his flock
About doth stand, and still is found
  Their refuge sure, theire force and rocke.

The imagery is closely based on the original, the versification competent if rather ordinary. The version in sapphics, by contrast, makes certain formal demands upon the Countess so that she is forced to move significantly away from the Psalm's original metaphors. The result is a far more autonomous poetic structure:

As Salem braveth with her hilly bullwarkes
roundly enforted: soe the great Jehova
closeth his servantes, as a hilly bulwark
  ever abiding;
Though Tirantes hard yoke with a heavy
  pressure
wring just the shoulders: but a while it
  holdeth
lest the best minded by too hard abusing
  bend to abuses.

The Countess' technical virtuosity is, then, important and remarkable for her time; with few models, certainly in English, she extends the technical range of English versification, and may well have contributed to the formal revolution popularly associated with Donne and Herbert over the next 40 years or so. As Rathmell observes, in her Psalms we can see how the Countess "*meditated* on the text before her, and the force of her version derives from her sense of personal involvement . . . it is her capacity to appreciate the underlying meaning that vivifies her poems."[23] Usually, if not exclusively, it is the "underlying meaning" that the Countess is concerned to evoke in her Psalms.

The spirit in which she approached the **Psalms** is clearly revealed by the many changes she made as she developed her poetical skills in successive manuscript revisions. Even in the earliest versions, those recorded in the Woodford manuscript (B), she can be seen habitually reaching for the underlying tone of the psalm and then seeking to embody it in appropriate Elizabethan modes of thought and image. One early example of her meditational independence can be seen in two stanzas in the early draft of **Psalm 62,** for which she had only the barest hint in the original text:

> Your trustfull faith, O all your people plight
> To God, to God your hearts uncloathed show
> And God your help your only refuge know
> For who possesse this earth in Adams right
> Are all so vain, that if to weights they go
> Ev'n vanity for weight will fall more low.

> Look in good ground your confidence you
>   sow,
> Be skilfull husbands, chuse your seed aright.
> Think not to have good harvest of your slight
> Nor of your ravin many sheaves to mowe
> Nay tho with fruits your barnes be throughly
>   dight
> Yet on such sand build not your best delight.

> **(62, B. 32-43)**

Obviously the passage required some drastic revisions in its syntax and coherence, but even at this early stage the Countess' determination to express her original's sense through a telling metaphor can be seen. The imagery of planting and harvesting, although appropriate to the context, is nowhere hinted at in her sources. In fact, the revised version in A omits most of these original additions to the Psalm—the Countess' second thoughts were not always best.

A useful comparison may be made among the three very different versions of **Psalm 122**: one found in A J F K C D O N, a second in B I G1 E H L (both in asclepiads) and the third in G M (a rhymed version, in 6 six-line ababcc stanzas). Despite their common original, each poem develops independently, with related but distinctive imagery and variations in tone and movement. The opening will serve as an example. The Geneva Bible version of verses 1-3 reads:

> [1]I rejoyced, when they said to me, We wil go
>   into the house of the Lord.

> [2]Our fete shal stand in thy gates, o Jerusalem.

> [3]Jerusalem *is* buylded as a citie, that is
>   compact together in it self.

In the early version in asclepiads found in B I G1 E H L these verses are somewhat awkwardly expressed, as the Countess attempts to master the demands of quantitative verse:

> O what lively delight, O what a jollity
> This news unto me brought newly delivered
> That Gods house ruined should be re-edifyd
> And that shortly we should every man enter
>   it.

> O now thy galerys, lovely Jerusalem
> Thy gates shall be my rest; now at unorderd
> Nor wide scatred as erst, but very citty-like
> All commond in one shall be Jerusalem.

> (1-8)

The version prepared for the presentation copy to the Queen uses five lines only, and has a slightly different emphasis:

> O fame most joyfull! O joy most lovly
>   delightfull!
> Loe, I do heare Godds temple, as erst, soe
>   again be frequented,
> And we within thy proches againe glad-
>   wonted abiding,
> Lovly Salem shall find: thou Citty rebuilt as a
>   Citty,
> Late disperst, but now united in absolute
>   order.

> (1-5)

When the final version (G M) was written, and the quantitative experiments abandoned, the Countess uses two leisurely hymn-like stanzas:

> Right gladd was I in heart and mind
>   When as I heard the people saie
> With one assent so well inclind
>   To serue thee, Lord, and to him praie
>   Come let us to his Temple goe,
>   And there our seruice to him showe.

> Within thy gates (O cittie faire)
>   Ierusalem wee will abide,
> Since wee to thee have made repaire
>   Our feete from thee shall never slide

For thou in Union, peace and Loue
Art now establist from aboue.

(1-12)

Clearly, what we have are three separate poems, with a similar subject and tone, but with few precise hints of a common original. Indeed, with the quantitative versions, the exigencies of form are such that it is possible only in the most general terms to relate the Countess' poems to the original Psalm. With the relatively easier demands of the rhymed stanzas, the G M version is more easily established as being derived directly from the Psalm. But in no sense does the Countess appear to be concerned with literal accuracy of translation. In fact, two of the three versions give different interpretations to the third verse of the Psalm. The Countess speaks of Zion being "rebuilt" (**122 A**), "re-edifyd" (**122 B**) suggesting the speaker is overjoyed at returning to a city, rebuilt on former ruins. None of the translations, glosses or commentaries suggest such an interpretation, but it certainly underlines the mood of rejoicing. The "wee to thee have made repaire" of **122 G M**, simply means "return," a sense also found in Sidney's Psalm 9.5, and here the Countess returns to the Psalm's accustomed reading.

What the psalms in this edition offer, then, above all, is a chance to see an Elizabethan poet through the process of revision discovering the means of writing sophisticated and moving verse. None of the psalms printed here are, therefore, among the Countess' best. Their interest lies largely in the way they help us to trace the growth of her poetical skills—and, often, the mechanics of a poet's development may be seen best in his least finished works. For her best psalms, we should turn, perhaps, to the Penshurst Manuscript [A], printed by Rathmell—to her magnificent versions, say, of **Psalms 51, 88, 90, 130,** or **148** which are among the high points of religious verse of the age. We can see then how her Psalms helped to mark a new direction for post-Reformation poetry in England. As a patroness she directed others to the possibilities of writing religious verse in English as fine as that she saw across the Channel; but she was, even more importantly, a practitioner—ambitious, uneven, sometimes brilliant—and her poems stand at their best as some of the finest contributions to a tradition of religious verse she helped to initiate. The psalms printed here should help us trace the mechanics of her poetical education.

Miscellaneous Poems and the Dedicatory Poems to the Psalms

Prefacing manuscript J of the Sidney Psalms, and presumably once existing in the incomplete manuscript A from which J was copied, are two poems by the Countess, a dedicatory poem to the Queen in 12 8-line stanzas, and a 13 stanza, 91-line poem signed at the end

"By the Sister of that Incomparable Sidney," and entitled **"To the Angell spirit of the most excellent Sir Phillip Sidney."** The poem to the Queen, **"Even now that Care wch on thy Crowne attends,"** has never been discussed before the present study, while the only easily accessible printed version of **"To the Angell spirit . . ."** exists in Ringler's edition of Sidney. In the 1623 edition of the works of Samuel Daniel, however, appeared the text of a poem similarly entitled **"To the Angell Spirit of the most excellent, Sʳ. Phillip Sidney";** it was reprinted by Grosart in his collected edition of Daniel and until the version in J was brought to light, Daniel's authorship was unquestioned.[24] J proves that the version attributed to Daniel was clearly an early draft which somehow found its way into Daniel's papers before being revised by the Countess for inclusion in the presentation volume of the *Psalms*. In 1962, Dr. B. E. Juel-Jensen, the owner of J printed a limited, private edition of the two poems in his manuscript. They are printed here from J with his most generous permission.

"Even now that Care . . ." is dated 1600 on folio iiⁱᵛ of J, but the date has been corrected in another hand (perhaps that of the Countess herself) to 1599. It is written in 12 8-line stanzas in iambic pentameters rhyming ababbdbd, a demanding stanzaic form that she uses in **Psalm 104,** one of her more successful longer poems of celebration. The form is confidently handled; the poem is clearly structured and rises at time to moving heights of passion—particularly when the Countess recalls her dead brother. Generally the poem combines the qualities of the *encomium,* a poem, according to Puttenham's description, which honours "the persons of great Princes," with the elegy of lamentation of the "death, the irrecoverable losse, death, the dolefull departure" of her brother.[25] Typically, the Countess modifies what is essentially a public form into a more private meditation. The first two stanzas thus stress the unworthiness of such a gift to lay before the transcendent majesty of the Queen yet, the poet asserts, " . . . dare I so, as humblenes may dare / cherish some hope they shall acceptance finde . . ." (9-10).

The following four stanzas go on to suggest, however, that the psalms are offered not just as "Postes of Dutie and Goodwill," but are as well a gift with peculiar personal poignancy:

. . . once in two, now in one Subject goe,
the poorer left, the richer reft awaye:
Who better might (O might ah word of woe,)
haue giv'n for mee what I for him defraye.

(21-24)

Stanzas seven and eight return to the praise of Elizabeth, the centre and epitome of England's glory and the inspirer of its poets:

For in our worke what bring wee but thine
   owne?
What English is, by many names is thine.
There humble Lawrells in thy shadowes
   growne
To garland others woorld, themselves repine.
Thy brest the Cabinet, thy seat the shrine,
Where Muses hang their vowed memories . . .

               (41-46)

The final four stanzas go on to extend the complement to the Queen. "A King should onely to a Queene bee sent" (53), and hence David's Psalms are an appropriate gift. As well, the Psalms prophetically anticipate Elizabeth's own reign:

And who sees ought, but sees how justly
   square
his haughtie Ditties to thy glorious daies?

               (58-59)

Elizabeth as the second David was a favourite notion of Elizabethan Protestant propagandists. The Countess dwells briefly on the parallels between King David and the Queen, and the poem culminates in a wish that

. . . shee may (farre past hir living Peeres
And Rivall still to Iudas Faithfull King)
In more than hee and more triumphant yeares,
Sing what God doth, and doo What men may
   sing.

               (93-96)

A great deal of what is typical of the Countess' poetry is found in this poem: a high degree of metrical competence, a fine sense of structure, good control of decorous tone, a varied syntactical movement, marred occasionally by strained idioms or syntax. As well, there are hints of the intellectual dialectic which I have found throughout her work and the Sidney Circle as a whole. The praise of the Queen, like that in the pastoral dialogue with which I shall deal below, mounts to an assertion of her near-supernatural powers:

Thus hand in hand with him thy glories
   walke:
but who can trace them where alone they goe?
Of thee two hemispheres on honor talke,
and lands and seas thy Trophees iointly
   showe.
The very windes did on thy partie blowe,
and rocks in armes thy foe men eft defie . . .

               (73-78)

Not only the royal servant of the Lord, she is the glory of the world, waited on by the Creation itself, which (the reference to the Armada is unmistakable) lends her aid against her enemies. Then, a more sceptical voice intervenes, tempering such praise:

But soft my muse, Thy pitch is earthly lowe;
forbeare this heau'n, where onely Eagles flie.

               (79-80)

On the public level, the poem is competent if somewhat commonplace. It is particularly interesting, however, for the way the encomium to Elizabeth is interrupted by four stanzas of particular passion on the subject of Sidney. Although such personal asides were a well established part of elegaic poems, the *digressio* here is as unusual in its way as that in Milton's *Lycidas*. The fourth stanza, especially, has an urgency and depth of personal feeling unusual for the kind of poem **"Even now that care . . ."** purports to be:

How can I name whom sighing sighes extend,
and not unstopp my teares eternall spring?
but hee did warpe, I weau'd this webb to end;
the stuffe not ours, our worke no curious
   thing,
Wherein yet well wee thought the Psalmist
   King
Now English denizend, though Hebrue borne,
woold to thy musicke undispleased sing,
Oft having worse, without repining worne.

               (25-32)

The depth and extent of the Countess' devotion to her brother's memory makes this poem of dedication to the Queen a tribute to Sidney.

Its companion poem, **"To the Angell Spirit . . ."** intensifies in an even more interesting way our awareness of the Countess' love for and debt to her brother. If, as seems certain, the version printed by Samuel Daniel's brother in Daniel's collected works of 1623 is an early draft of the Countess' poem, then once again we can watch the process of the Countess' revisions. The early version (Dn) has two rather syntactically confused stanzas between stanzas three and four of the version in J, and it lacks any versions of the later stanzas eight, ten, and twelve. The version in J has 13 7-line stanzas rhyming abbacca, in regular lines of 10 syllables, mainly pentameters. The stanza form resembles those of the Countess' **Psalms 63** and **106,** except that the rhyme scheme is somewhat tighter. Although the stanza pattern of the earlier version is the same it is much more loosely executed, as one would expect from an early draft.

To set the two versions side-by-side is to reinforce the observations made earlier on the Countess' revisions of the Psalms. As well as the substantial additions and deletions, virtually every line is altered in accidentals. Sometimes phrases or words are shifted from lines nearby, usually the meaning is tightened or made more succinct. Thus "Made only thine, and no more else must weare" (Dn, 73) becomes "well are they borne, no title else shall beare" (J.87); "Thine by his owne, and what is done of mine . . ." (Dn, 3) becomes the more evocative "First rais'de by thy blest hand, and what is mine . . ." (J.3). A similar advance in both force and meaning is gained from changing "Nor can enough, though justly here contrould" (Dn, 42) to "Nor can enough in world of words unfold" (J.28).

The revised version, too, is a much more personal work; in fact its strength arises from its tone of peculiarly sincere and personal grief for Sidney, expressed in evocative and moving tones of gratitude for his love and inspiration. Indeed, it is as if the Countess had no other motive for writing than to express her private grief and dedication:

> And sithe it hath no further scope to goe,
>   nor other purpose but to honor thee,
>   Thee in thy workes where all the Graces
>   bee,
> As little streames with all their all doe flowe
>   to their great sea, due tribute's gratefull fee:
>   so press my thoughts my burthened
>   thoughtes in mee,
> To pay the debt of Infinits I owe
>
>   (29-35)

One special revision the Countess made which intensifies this note of love is found in the second stanza. Dn's version reflects the Sidney Circle's constant concern with the patriotic duty of enhancing literary standards and, rather pompously, praises English as a fit language for a translation of the Psalms:

> That Israels King may daygne his owne
>   transform'd
> In substance no, but superficiall tire:
> And English guis'd in some sort may aspire
> To better grace thee what the vulgar form'd:
> His Sacred Tones, age after age admire.
> Nations grow great in pride, and pure desire
> So to excell in holy rites perform'd.
>
>   (Dn, 9-15)

In J, however, the stanza is significantly changed. The tone becomes less stentorian, a more personal note intrudes, as the lines become more concerned with the inexactitude of the Countess' work beside her brothers':

> . . . those high Tons, so in themselues
>   adorn'd,
> which Angells sing in their coelestiall Quire,
> and of all tongues with soule and uoice
>   admire
> Theise sacred Hymnes thy Kinglie Prophet
>   form'd.
>
>   (11-14)

Looked at in the context of the many poetic laments written for Sidney, the poem compares favourably with the majority of those written after Sidney's death, with the obvious exception of Spenser's *"Astrophel."* It is, of course, not strictly an elegy in the classical sense, although the Elizabethan's understanding of "elegy" varied greatly. It fits what Puttenham calls a "poeticall lamentation," even though Puttenham himself links the elegy with love plaints. Commenting on the confusion of genres in Elizabethan poetic theory, Howard C. Cole notes that "love is surely a fundamental part of that often lamentable human condition. Our more restricted sense of this kind as fit only to mourn and praise the dead had not yet evolved . . . from the elegy [and] the Elizabethan reader expected a certain mood and tone, but no special subject."[26] Hence the variety of Elizabethan elegies: some of Spenser's *Amoretti* as well as his *Astrophel* would be accurately described as elegaic by strict Renaissance criteria.

But rather than being judged strictly by generic terms, the Countess' poem is most usefully seen in terms of her own life and writings. Her mixture of dedication, mourning, and deep love again turns a public poem into an intensely, perhaps even morbidly, interesting and moving poem. Expanding on and echoing the personal digression in the preceding poem to the Queen, it is in fact addressed solely to her brother's "Angell spirit":

> To thee pure sprite, to thee alone's addrest
>   this coupled work, by double int'rest thine
>
>   (1-2)

It is intended as a private dedication of the completed work on the Psalms to Sidney and as an apology for what she feels to be the inferiority of her part:

> First rais'de by thy blest hand, and what is
>   mine
> inspir'd by thee, thy secrett power imprest.
>   So dar'd my Muse with thine it self c
>   combine,
>   as mortall stuffe with that which is diuine
>
>   (3-6)

The conventional note of praise that a generation of fellow-poets gave to Sidney is in the Countess' poem intensely personalized and indeed, acquires a strangely rapturous tone. Sidney is her poetic inspiration—"what is mine / inspir'd by thee, thy secrett power imprest" (3-4)—and, as well, the conventional "Phoenix," the "Matchlesse Muse," his example, like his person, exceeding "Nature's store" (8, 23, 36). The poem relates in more formal elegaic style how he died with so many unfulfilled achievements:

> Immortall Monuments of thy faire fame,
>   though not compleat, nor in the reach of
>   thought,

howe on that passing peece time would have
  wrought
Had Heau'n so spar'd the life of life to frame
  the rest? But ah! such losse hath this world
  ought
can equall it? or which like greevance
  brought?
Yet there will live thy euer praised name.

(71-77)

Sidney the Phoenix, the Muse, the ever-praised Name: however passionately expressed, such terms are conventional enough. Typically, too, the Countess' neo-Platonic tendencies are seen in the transcendent terms she chooses to praise her brother. He becomes, in heaven, the very embodiment of divine Grace, whom even to approach is "presumption too too bold" (25):

Thy Angell's soule with highest Angells
  plac't
There blessed sings enjoying heav'n delights
  thy Maker's praise: as farr from earthy tast
  as here thy workes so worthilie embrac't
By all of worth . . .

(59-63)

Furthermore, it is, the poem goes on, for him alone that the Countess has been stirred to discover her own talents and complete the **Psalms**. In this passage, the reader notes something of unusual interest. We are encountering not merely the conventional admiration of Sidney "by all of worth," but something more personal and disturbing:

Oh! when to this Accompt, this cast upp
  Summe,
    this Reckoning made, this Audit of my woe,
I call my thoughts, whence so strange
  passions flowe;
Howe workes my hart, my senses striken
  dumbe?
    that would thee more, then euer hart could
    showe,
  and all too short who knewe thee best doth
  knowe
There liues no witt that my thy praise become.

(43-49)

Especially in the context of the Countess' other poems on her brother—and her evident dedication of her life to his ideals—such a stanza provokes more than usually intense speculation. The tone of adulation might well have provoked comments like those from Ben Jonson upon Donne's *Anniversary* poems as "profane and full of blasphemies . . . if it had been written of the Virgin Mary it has been something." To such a remark the Countess might well have replied, in her Thenot vein, that she too was describing the Idea of Sidney—and gone on to add, like Donne, "not as he

was." But for the pious Countess, this praise of her brother has a peculiarly personal ring, underlined by the strangely worded note of intense intimacy in a line which was not found in the earlier version, " . . . my thought, whence so strange passions flowe" (46). It is as if in revision what has been implied throughout this poem, its companion piece and, indeed, her whole career as a poet is now being made explicit. It is as if a veil is being lifted very briefly, unwillingly, even unconsciously. Her love for her brother passes even her own understanding. With caution, we may recall Aubrey's speculation that "there was so great love between [Sidney] and his faire sister that I have heard old Gentlemen say that they lay together . . ."[27] Although scandalously unfounded on any public fact, Aubrey's gossip may vaguely point to something real, to the degree of intensity of feeling between Philip and Mary, especially on the side of the Countess. Without trying to turn the Countess of Pembroke into an Elizabethan Dorothy Wordsworth, there is no doubt that the deepest emotional commitment of her life was to her brother, both before and especially after his death. All the evidence of her writings suggests that Sidney's person, example and ideals were at the centre of her life, and while any further speculation about the relationship takes the scholar into the perils of historical psychoanalysis, nevertheless it is important for our understanding of the Countess to realize that the feelings she retained for her brother were, for a sister, remarkable in their strength. Here in this second, personal poem dedicating her life's literary work, we see revealed feelings that could perhaps only be revealed in a few lines of verse, years after their subject was dead.

Less certainly but probably the Countess' is the so-called **"Dolefull Lay of Clorinda."** Sometime in the 1590s—a later scribe adds the date 1594—the Countess wrote to Sir Edward Wotton:

Cossen Wotton[:] the first message this paper shall deliuer is my best saluta*f*on and euer welwishinge to yr self[:] from that wonted good affec*f*on still continued doe acknowledge yow worthy of the same regarde wherein yow are asseured to rest for suche hath bin your merit not onlie towards my self but in memory of that loue to him wch held you a deere and speciall frende of his (who was to me as you knowe) [.] I must and doe and euer will doe you this right[.] wch downe[,] the next is that these maie redeeme a certaine Idle passion which longe since I left in your hands onlie being desyrous to reuiew what the Image could be of those sadd tymes. . . . [28]

The Countess' reference to the "certaine Idle passion," is not only reminiscent of the appropriate *sprezzatura* that a refined courtly lady would have towards her own writing, but an echo of Sidney's own remark on the *Arcadia* that it was an "idle work . . . fitter to be swept away than worn to any other purpose."[29] The remark obviously refers to a poem associated with "those sadd tymes" surrounding the death of Sidney. It is doubtful, if the letter does date from 1594, that the "passion" is **"To the Angell spirit . . ."** which seems to have been written in the later years of the decade, after the Psalms had been completed and collected for the presentation copy to the Queen. It refers, instead, to a poem written specifically on the death of Sidney, which is probably the so-called **"Dolefull Lay of Clorinda,"** first published along with Spenser's "Astrophel" and other elegies by Ralegh, Royden, Dyer and Bryskett in *Colin Clouts Come Home Again* (1595).

The 1595 Quarto of *Colin Clout,* which has been used as the copy-text and collated with later editions, is dedicated as a whole to Ralegh, and contains the title-piece, followed by "Astrophel, / A Pastoral Elegie upon / the death of the most Noble and valorvs / Knight, Sir Philip Sidney." It is dedicated to the Countess of Essex, Sidney's widow. "Astrophel" is followed by what is now usually known as **"The Dolefull Lay of Clorinda,"** an untitled poem, clearly separated from "Astrophel" by a tailpiece on sig. F4ᵛ, a headpiece of a band of type-ornaments on sig. G1ʳ, a three-quarter blank page on sig. F4ᵛ, and an ornamental initial capital letter at the start of the new poem. It is linked with "Astrophel" by 6 lines of explanatory verse and with the following elegy, by Bryskett, with 12 lines on sig. G3ʳ. The title-page of the collection of elegies mentions no authors or editor, but "Astrophel" is clearly Spenser's, and it seems probable that he collected the other elegies, briefly introducing the others in the body of the work in the link passages at "Astrophel" (211-216), and that following the lay of Clorinda (107-108).

Did the Countess of Pembroke write the "dolefull lay"? Spenser certainly seems to state this quite explicitly:

> But first his sister that Clorinda hight,
> The gentlest shepheardesse that lives this day
> And most resembling both in shape and
>   spright
> Her brother deare, began this dolefull lay . . .
>   (211-214)

Doubts about the attribution might seem unnecessary, and the Countess' authorship was in fact unchallenged until Ernest de Selincourt asserted in his Oxford Standard Authors edition of Spenser (1908) that the poem was Spenser's. He suggested briefly that the Lay showed "the peculiarly Spenserian effects of rhythm and melody" and that since it was "not a separate work . . . it is more natural . . . to believe that Spenser wrote it in her name."[30] In 1920, Percy W. Long similarly argued for Spenser's authorship, pointing out likenesses between the Lay and the August and November Eclogues in *The Shepheards Calender.* He concentrated in particular upon stanzaic and metrical similarities,

arguing somewhat simply that in all three poems, the second line of the stanza usually ends in a colon.[31]

Following Long's arguments, Charles G. Osgood and H. D. Rix further analysed the rhetorical structure of the Lay, arguing for its characteristically Spenserian effects.[32] Few scholars bothered to challenge their ascription and for want of a champion, the Countess might have lain unrescued. However, in 1935, in the first fully detailed review of the evidence, W. G. Friedrich came to the conclusion that the Lay was almost certainly written by the Countess. He pointed out that the "Spenserian" effects on which former arguments were based are common to a number of Elizabethan poets, that the sixain is equally common, and that Long's argument about colons at the end of the stanza's second line is "absurd in the light of what we know about Elizabethan punctuation."[33] Moreover, as he wryly indicated, some of the Lay's careless or strained lines are hardly up to Spenser's standard of competence, and for Spenser to attempt deliberately to write less polished verse in order to pass it off as the Countess' would have been an insult to both of them.[34]

More positively, there is in fact sound evidence for the Countess' authorship. The Lay is clearly separated by three quarters of a page of blank space from "Astrophel"; the running title of Spenser's elegy is discontinued; there are ornamental head and end pieces to the Lay and an ornamental initial capital letter to mark the poem's beginning—all of which suggest specific authoritative instructions to or inferences by the printer. As well, there is a distinct difference in quality between the two poems and a vital difference in tone. The Lay approximates closely to a formal Greek elegy, while "Astrophel" is a narrative lyric suggestive of the Homeric hymns. Moreover, not only, as Friedrich showed, do the "Spenserian" tone and ornamentation of the Lay include features common to a host of Elizabethan pastoral elegies, but there are definite verbal links with the Countess' own **"To the Angell spirit. . . . "** The Lay reads:

> But that immortall spirit, which was deckt
> With all the dowries of celestiall grace:
> By soueraine choyce from th'hevenly quires
>   select,
> And lineally deriu'd from Angels race . . .
>   (61-64)

The echoes of **"To the Angell spirit . . ."** with its emphasis on "Thy Angells soule with highest Angells plac't" (59) are evident and constitute internal evidence at least as strong as anything offered in support of Spenser. Finally, there is the definite ascription of the Lay to Sidney's sister in the introductory verses, already quoted. Elsewhere, in "The Ruines of Time," Spenser writes:

Then will I sing: but who can better sing
Than thine owne sister, peerles Ladie bright,
Which to thee sings with deep harts
    sorrowing,
Sorrowing tempered with deare delight.
That her to heare I feele my feeble spright
Robbed of sense, and ravished with joy,
O sad joy made of mourning and anoy.[35]

"The preponderance of evidence," as Friedrich sums up, "is certainly in favor of the Countess of Pembroke's authorship."[36] The poem would take its place naturally within a memorial volume edited by Spenser, in cooperation with William Ponsonby, who had something like the unofficial status of the Sidney family publisher. The Countess was probably consulted about the collection; her letter to Wotton mentioning the "certaine Idle passion" may refer to a request for a copy of her poem to be returned so it might be included in the volume.

We have some hints as to the poem's date. While most of the elegies to Sidney appeared in or about 1587, "Astrophel" itself was probably not written until 1590 or 1591. Spenser's apologies for not publicly bewailing Sidney's death appeared in the dedicatory epistle to *The Ruines of Time* (1591) addressed to the Countess herself. He speaks there of friends' complaints "that I haue not shewed anie thankefull remembraunce towards him,"[37] although it may be the epistle had been written some time before the work's publication, perhaps shortly after Spenser's return from Ireland late in 1589. However, in the lines from *The Ruines of Time* already quoted, he speaks of the Countess singing *her* poem: " . . . with deep harts sorrowing, / Sorrowing tempered with deare delight," and the probable inference is that by 1589-1591, the "dolefull lay" was in existence; Friedrich in fact speculates, although without real evidence, that the Countess may, like so many others, have written it in 1587, the year of Sidney's funeral.[38] The authorship of the **"Lay"** can probably never be finally settled by the external evidence available: but what there is points to the traditional and (it should be added) authoritatively Spenserian attribution to the Countess.

I turn now to the poem itself. The **"Lay"** is written, carefully but not always competently, within the originally Greek elegiac tradition of Theocritus, Biron, Virgil's *Bucolics* and a number of Renaissance French and Italian elegists. The major features of the tradition are carefully inserted into the poem—the mourning for the dead shepherd by all nature (25-28), the complaint against the heavens for allowing such a tragedy (7-12), the address to fellow shepherds (37-42), the change from mourning to consolation caused by the reassurance of the dead shepherd's immortality (69-90). But as in **"To the Angell spirit . . ."** the Countess brings to the commonplaces of the tradition a note of deeply personal grief:

Great losse to all that ever him did see,
Great losse to all, but greatest losse to mee.

(35-36)

There are lines strongly reminiscent of the reference to Sidney in **"To the Angell Spirit . . . ,"** again suggesting a similarity of tone and intention between the two poems. He is "that immortall spirit" (61) in the **"Lay,"** just as "thy Angell's soule" is "with highest Angells plac't" (**"To the Angell Spirit,"** 59). As I suggested, such conventional neo-Platonic terminology is constantly given an extra intensity by the Countess' personal grief. Although her argument is somewhat tangled syntactically in this poem, the sense can be made out reasonably clearly. Sidney's mortal body, she asserts, is only a reflection of his departed soul, and yet it too is but a shadow, passing quickly through its earthly existence, back to its origin "lineally deriv'd from Angels race" (64). Spenser has a similarly worded passage in "Daphnaida" (211-217), but the closest parallel here is clearly the Countess' other poem to her brother.

So far as its quality is concerned, the **"Lay"** is a mixture of personal intensity, solid metrical competence, and much flatness and not a little padding. After the smooth, mellifluous melancholy of "Astrophel" it reads like the work of a competent amateur—although it does compare favourably with the other elegies in the volume. Typically, it is carefully structured, moving from two initial complaints to the heavens and men to the personal:

Then to my selfe will I my sorrow mourne,
Sith none aliue like sorrowful remaines . . .

(19-20)

Then follows a series of *apostrophes*: Nature is called on to mourn, the shepherds are exhorted to cease their singing and abandon their garlands, death itself is assailed, until a final note of reassurance is reached in the vision of immortality.

The structure is clear, if conventional; the execution is somewhat wooden, a careful exercise in rhetoric, moving from the *dubitatio* of the first stanza to the *expeditio* of stanza four. The most important rhetorical scheme is the *allegoria* of Sidney as a flower in stanzas five to seven, which is couched in terms again reminiscent of **"To the Angell spirit. . . ."** The final flourish, too, is an echo of the later poem—an *apostrophe* which is an appropriate mixture of the personal and the conventional:

But liue thou there still happie, happie spirit,
And giue us leave thee here thus to lament:
Not thee that doest thy heauens ioy inherit,
But our owne selues that here in dole are
    drent.

Thus do we weep and waile, and wear our
    eies,
Mourning in others, our owne miseries.

                 (91-96)

Unquestionably the Countess' work is a modest pastoral poem entitled "**A Dialogve between two shepheards,** *Thenot* **and** *Piers,* **in Praise of** *Astrea.*" It was first published in Francis Davison's *A Poetical Rhapsody,* which first appeared in 1602, with subsequent editions in 1608, 1611, and 1621. The 1602 edition has been used as the copy-text for this edition and collated with the later printings of the work. The miscellany includes verses from a collection of poets including Campion, Sidney, Wotton and Spenser. The "**Dialogue**" is ascribed to the Countess, and subtitled in the first edition "Made by the excellent Lady, the Lady Mary Countess of Pembroke, at the Queen Majesty's being at her house at ######, Anno 15##." Nothing is known of such a visit to Wilton, although manuscript A of the Psalms was obviously prepared as a presentation copy to the Queen for such a visit. Most likely, a visit was planned, and the "**Dialogue**" composed in anticipation of the event, which never took place.

The "Astrea" of the poem is, of course, Elizabeth the righteous virgin, and the poem is one of a host of similar commonplace tributes to Elizabeth, but it is more interesting than most. Conventionally, the two shepherds, Thenot and Piers, compete with each other to sing Astrea's praises. Thenot's celebration is courtly in tone and neo-Platonic in its philosophic implications, with the divinity of Astrea being apprehended by her subjects through natural and cosmic phenomena. She is "a field in flowery robe arrayed," the "heauenly light that guides the day"; she "sees with wisdom's sight" and "works by virtue's might" (38, 43, 19, 20). Virtue and wisdom are not just represented by her but embodied in her—they "iontly both do stay in her." By seeing and meditating on Astrea's beauty, man may attain to truth. "Let us therefore," argues Bembo, "bend all our force and thoughtes of soule to this most holy light, that sheweth the way which leadeth to heaven . . . let us climbe up the staires, which at the lowermost steppe have the shadowe of sensuall beauty, to the high mansion place where the heavenly, amiable and right beautie dwelleth, which lyeth in the innermost secretes of God. . . ."[39]

Piers, on the other hand, is characterized as a conscientious, indeed iconoclastic, Protestant, who voices the doctrine so stressed by Calvinists of the absolute transcendence of the divine and the inability of man's unaided mind to attain to genuine truth. He warns against fallen man's tendency to self-deceptiveness, and clearly echoes the Platonic rejection of poetry as untrustworthy:

Thou needst the truth but plainly tell,
Which much I doubt thou canst not well,
    Thou art so oft a lier.

Not only is the corrupt human mind unable to reach any truth, but plain speaking without the distorting intervention of the fancy is stressed. To each of Thenot's claims, Piers' response is firmly in the Protestant tradition which rejects any metaphorical means of describing the Divinity, until the confrontation is summed up in the final verse:

Then.   Then *Piers* of friendship tell me why,
       My meaning true, my words should ly,
         And striue in uain to raise her?

Piers.   Words from conceit do only rise;
       Above conceit her honour flies;
         But silence, nought can praise her.

Words cannot embody the ineffability of the divine. Although Piers' final rejection means that a greater compliment is thereby paid to Astrea/Elizabeth, it is not unimportant that it is the Calvinist suspicion of the mind's ability to apprehend truth which has the last word.

The poem's verbal texture regrettably does not match its intellectual aspirations. It is merely a charming minor piece, and can be called no more than competent, as if the Countess was over-captivated by the ideological contrast she was developing and somewhat neglectful of its metaphorical impact. It is, however, typically well-constructed. It is written in sixains, 10 stanzas rhyming aabccb, and the movement of the lines is often appropriately forceful. The structure, too, is clear and logically developed: Elizabeth is progressively praised in terms of the whole creation, the earth itself, wisdom and virtue, goodness, joys and riches, the seasons, the divine light, the generative creativity of the universe, and finally the power of the transforming human imagination seen in poetry itself. As each compliment mounts to the height of the poet's erected wit, Piers' answering qualification is appropriately formulated. The poem's effect is, however, often spoiled by a rather unidiomatic syntax—especially in the breathlessly tumbling syllables of Piers' replies, which are perhaps designed to convey the cryptic plainness of the Protestant. The Countess was probably striving to echo in miniature the sparse, tortured lines of a poet like Greville whose scepticism about the power of poetry is rather like that of Piers, just as Thenot recalls the aspiring wit of the poet of Sidney's *Defence,* or the "clear spirits" of Greville's Caelica.[40]

The poems [in my volume], therefore, offer the modern student the opportunity to assess her place within late Elizabethan poetry. Her more famous brother Philip has long been served well by editors and commentators; her other brother Robert's poetry has recently been discovered and editorial and critical work is now commencing upon his poetry. Their equally deserving sister, the Countess of Pembroke, occupies an important place within the Sidney family's attempts to give a firm basis to the Elizabethan poetical revolution and along with J. C. A. Rathmell's edition of the Penshurst text of the Psalms, the present edition should help to bring out the substantial merits of this too long neglected Elizabethan poet.

Notes

[1] *Poems of William Browne of Tavistock,* ed. George Goodwin (London, n.d.), II, p. 294.

[2] See Edmund Spenser, "Colin Clout," ll. 487-491; Aubrey's *Brief Lives,* ed. O. L. Dick (Harmondsworth, 1962), pp. 219-221; Samuel Daniel, *Delia* (London, 1592), Dedication; John Aubrey, *The Natural History of Wiltshire,* ed. John Britton (London, 1847), p. 86.

[3] J. W. Cunliffe, "The Queens Majesties Entertainment at Woodstocke," *PMLA,* XXVI (1911), 100.

[4] *John Buxton, Sir Philip Sidney and the English Renaissance* (London, 1954), p. 3.

[5] Sir Philip Sidney, *Works,* ed. Albert Feuillerat (Cambridge, 1961), III, p. 35.

[6] Thomas Nashe, *Pierce Pennilesse,* in *Works,* ed. E. D. McKerrow (London, 1958), I, p. 139.

[7] Buxton, *Sidney,* p. 12.

[8] *Ibid.,* p. 236.

[9] James O. Osborn, *Young Philip Sidney* (Cambridge, Mass., 1972), p. 5.

[10] Barnabe Barnes, *Poems,* ed. E. Arber, *An English Garner,* V (London, 1895), p. 485; Thomas Nashe, preface to *Astrophel and Stella* (London, 1591).

[11] Nicholas Breton, *Wits Trenchmour* (London, 1593), pp. 18-20: *A Pilgrimage to Paradise* (Oxford, 1592), Dedication.

[12] See Daniel Javitch, "The Philosopher of the Court: a French Satire Misunderstood," *CL,* XXIII (1971), 97-124.

[13] Walter Sweeper, *A Brief Treatise declaring the True Noble-man, and the Base Worldling* (London, 1623), sigs A3ʳ-A4ᵛ.

[14] Sidney, *Works,* III, pp. 8-9.

[15] Robert Coogan, "Petrarch's *Trionfi* and the Renaissance," *SP,* LXVII (1970), 306.

[16] Quotations from Morley's translation are taken from the edition of D. D. Carnecelli (Cambridge, Mass., 1971).

[17] D. G. Rees, "Petrarch's 'Trionfo della Morte' in English," *Italian Studies,* VII (1952), 86-87.

[18] Renee Neu Watkins, "Petrarch and the Black Death: From Fear to Monuments," *SRen,* XXIX (1972), 222.

[19] Ringler, p. 502.

[20] Bodleian MS Rawlinson poet. 25, fol. 131ᵛ.

[21] Other possible echoes of the Authorized Version are given in Noel J. Kinnamon, "Melle de Petra: The Sources and the Form of the Sidneian Psalms," Diss. University of North Carolina 1976, p. 168.

[22] Derek Attridge, *Well-Weighed Syllables* (Cambridge, 1976), p. 205.

[23] J. C. A. Rathmell (ed.), *The Psalms of Sir Philip Sidney and the Countess of Pembroke* (New York, 1963), p. xx.

[24] Quotations from Daniel's version are taken from *The Complete Works in Verse and Prose of Samuel Daniel,* ed. A. B. Grosart (London, 1885), I, 267-269.

[25] *Elizabethan Critical Essays,* ed. G. Gregory Smith (London, 1908), II, 49-50.

[26] *Elizabethan Critical Essays,* II, p. 49; Howard C. Cole, *A Quest of Inquirie* (New York, 1973), p. 285.

[27] *Ben Jonson,* ed. C. H. Herford and Percy Simpson (London, 1928), I, p. 133; John Aubrey, *Brief Lives,* ed. O. L. Dick (Harmondsworth, 1962), p. 220.

[28] F. B. Young, *Mary Sidney Countess of Pembroke* (London, 1912), p. 56.

[29] Sir Philip Sidney, *Works,* ed. Albert Feuillerat (Cambridge, 1912), I, p. 3; *The Countess of Pembrokes Arcadia: the Old Arcadia,* ed. Jean Robertson (Oxford, 1974), p. 3.

[30] Edmund Spenser, *Poetical Works,* ed. E. de Selincourt (Oxford, 1908), p. xxxv.

[31] Percy W. Long, "Spenseriana: the Lay of Clorinda," *MLN,* XXI (1916), 79-82.

[32] H. D. Rix, "Spenser's Rhetoric and the 'Doleful Lay'," *MLN,* LIII (1938), 261-265; Charles G. Osgood,

"The Doleful Lay of Clorinda," *MLN,* XXXV (1920), 90-96.

[33] "The Astrophel Elegies," Diss. Johns Hopkins 1934, 15.

[34] *Ibid.,* 25.

[35] "The Ruines of Time," ll. 316-322, Spenser, *Minor Poems,* ed. Ernest de Selincourt (Oxford, 1912), p. 137.

[36] Friedrich, 25.

[37] "The Ruines of Time," Dedication, *Minor Poems,* p. 126.

[38] Friedrich, 45.

[39] Baldesar Castiglione, *The Boke of the Courtier,* trans. Sir Thomas Hoby, introd. W. H. D. Rouse (London, 1928), pp. 268-269.

[40] Fulke Greville, *Caelica,* LXXX.

Hannay on Sidney's position as a patron:

At Wilton, Ivychurch, Ramsbury, Barnards Castle, or Ludlow, the Countess of Pembroke held a position analogous to that of a medieval lady of the castle . . . . Married to a powerful older man in a match arranged for political or property considerations, the lady was surrounded by young men, either unmarried or separated from their families. These young men wrote verses courting the lady as *midons,* a word used interchangeably as "master" or "mistress." Although their intent appeared to be romantic, glorifying the beauty and virtue of the lady while bewailing her coldness to them, the real intent of these young troubadours was usually political. Jostling for positions in the service of the lord, they served the lady in order to attract the attention of the husband. . . . The lady herself may have been quite blind to the political dimensions of the extravagant praise showered on her, but if she lost her socioeconomic position, she lost her troubadours. This is exactly waht happened to Mary Sidney, who was celebrated by poets until the death of her husband. . . .

Margaret P. Hannay, Philip's Phoenix: Mary Sidney, Countess of Pembroke, *Oxford University Press, 1990.*

Pearl Hogrefe (essay date 1977)

SOURCE: "Mary Sidney Herbert: Countess of Pembroke," in *Women of Action in Tudor England: Nine*

Biographical Sketches, Iowa State University Press, 1977, pp. 103-35.

[*In the excerpt that follows, Hogrefe reconstructs Sidney's centrality as a patron in the world of Elizabethan letters by examining a selection of the many dedications that leading writers of the day composed for her.*]

Mary Sidney Herbert was perhaps the most self-effacing of the [prominent women in Tudor England]. She devoted her energy to helping others; her influence did not have breadth, but within her area of influence she was unusually effective. She was not actively concerned with extravagant entertaining, political affairs, exerting an influence at court, or promoting religious views in others though she was a devout woman herself. Her contribution was the encouragement of literature, not as a goddess inspiring writers from a throne above, but as a human being offering them a home at Wilton House (her chief residence during her married life) with chances to discuss problems and learn literary forms. Men of science were also longtime residents there; some of the latter may have been brought in by her husband, but it seems evident that both writers and scientists were welcomed by husband and wife. It is said that she made Wilton House into a college or a "little university," and we need not depend upon John Aubrey for the evidence.

She contributed to literature in other ways. She encouraged her brother Sir Philip Sidney to write and to begin his *Arcadia* in a period when he needed an outlet. After his early death she edited and published his works. She did literary work of her own, including translations from Italian and French, and she transformed more than a hundred of the Psalms into Elizabethan lyrics. Perhaps she was the only woman of the period with poetic talent—though the evidence is mainly in her work with the Psalms. Either she wrote no other poems or they were never published under her name. She seemed content to remain "Sidney's sister, Pembroke's mother." She was also remarkable in her personalityC—generous, desirous of helping many people, courteous, and gracious. As others said, she was fair, good, learned, and wise. Perhaps she deserves even more recognition than she has received.

. . . . .

Mary Sidney Herbert, Countess of Pembroke, made an important contribution to the literary life of her period when (with the support of her husband) she developed Wilton House as an intellectual and literary center. It seems impossible to find out how and when she began this service. It may have been a gradual evolution, or she may have thought of the plan after the death of her brother to help her adjust to the loss and to honor his memory. She received dedications before 1586, such as the one from Thomas Howell in 1581 and the one from Gervase Babington in 1583. But neither suggested that she had helped his literary development, and the work of Babington was theological; so far as we know it did not include poems, plays, or other secular work. But Howell had by some means discovered that she had an urge to help many people. Writers who dedicated work to her because they lived and studied at Wilton House usually dated their work in 1588 and later. Though these statements do not prove that she opened Wilton House to other writers because of her brother's death, they do suggest the interesting possibility.

The earliest available statement about Wilton House as a place where writers learned their craft is that of Samuel Daniel, who probably became a resident there about 1590. He made the statement in 1603 when he dedicated his own work, *A Defense of Rhyme,* to Mary's son William, then Earl of Pembroke, and was explaining how he began to use rhyme:

> Having been first encouraged or framed thereunto by your most worthy and honorable mother, receiving the first notion for the formal ordering of those compositions at Wilton, which I must ever acknowledge to have been my best school, and thereof always am to hold a feeling and grateful memory.

Another contemporary, Walter Sweeper, made the most reliable and definite statement of all about the activities at Wilton House when he published his *Brief Treatise* in 1622. He described Thomas Moffett as a physician, his own worthy friend, and one of the "distinguished guests" that had made Wilton House "a little university." His statement is broad enough to cover scientists and literary men of all kinds and the interests of both Mary Herbert and her husband. From other sources we learn that Moffett had studied medicine in Basel, became a member of the College of Physicians in England, was a pioneer in chemical medicine and in entomology, though his *Insectorum . . . theatrum* was not published for some years after his death. One might suppose that the Earl of Pembroke persuaded him to come to Wilton House because he wished to have a resident physician; but if so, Moffett soon became concerned with other interests of the family. At the end of 1592 he was writing *Nobilis,* a life of Sir Philip Sidney intended to inspire to virtue the older son William—though it seems doubtful whether he completely succeeded in that aim! At the close he added, "At Wilton, the Calends of January . . . 1593." He gave the biography in manuscript to William Herbert as a New Year's gift, and it remained in that form until 1940. In it Moffett paid a rare compliment to William's mother when he discussed the reactions of Sir Philip not long before his death in 1586. Sidney could have borne the news of his parents' death, Moffett thought, if he had received no other bad news; but it

was reported to him also that his sister was mortally ill—"such a sister . . . as no Englishman, for aught I know, had ever possessed before."

In 1599 Thomas Moffett dedicated *The Silkworms and their Flies* to Mary Herbert, using a three-stanza poem for the purpose and characterizing her as a noble nurse of learning and a renowned patron. He began:

> Vouchsafe a while to lay thy task aside:
> Let Petrarch sleep; give rest to sacred writ;
> Or bow or string will break if ever tied.
> Some little pause aideth the quickest wit.

In the third stanza he begged her, humorously or seriously, to give aid to his subjects:

> I sing of little worms and tender flies,
> Creeping along or basking on the ground.
> Grace't once with thy heavenly-humane eyes,
> Which never yet on meanest scholar frowned . . .
> Deign thou but breathe a spark or little flame
> Of liking, to enlife for aye the same.

Though Moffett published his work in 1599, it is not possible to deduce with certainty that Mary Herbert was translating Petrarch and working on the Psalms in that exact year; probably the dedication was written about that time or a little earlier. Neither is it possible to assert with no shadow of doubt that Thomas Moffett, physician and entomologist, turned poet because of his association with her, but it seems likely.

When the Earl of Pembroke made his will about 1601, he left Moffett an annuity of a hundred pounds, twenty pounds a year for a livery gown, and an additional sum for medicines if he continued to act as a physician for members of the family. Aubrey stated, without citing evidence, that Moffett spent his last years at Bulbridge, a manor house owned by Pembroke. After the earl's death in 1601, Moffett survived him till 1604.

Years later, John Aubrey was following the lead of informed contemporaries Sweeper and Daniel; and thus his statements, taken with a grain or two of salt, may deserve consideration:

> In her time Wilton House was like a college, there were so many learned and ingenious persons. She was the greatest patroness of wit and learning of any lady in her time. She was a great chemist and spent yearly a great deal in that study. She kept for her laborator in the house Adrian Gilbert . . . halfbrother to Sir Walter Raleigh, who was a great chemist in those days. . . . She also gave an honorable yearly pension to Dr. Moffett. . . . Also one . . . Boston, a good chemist . . . and she would have kept him but he would have all the gold to himself and so died, I think, in a gaol.

While other direct evidence is lacking for Mary Herbert's interest in chemistry, indirect evidence is available because her brother studied it. In *Nobilis,* Moffett said of him: "Astrology alone . . . he could never be so far misled as to taste, even with the tip of his tongue." But "with Dee as teacher and with Dyer as companion, he learned chemistry. . . ." John Dee also recorded in his *Diary* two visits of Philip Sidney to himself—on January 16, 1577, with Leicester and Dyer; and on June 15, 1583, when a Polish prince came to honor Dee and was attended by Sidney, Lord Russell, and others. Mary Herbert may have provided a "laborator" and equipment for her brother years earlier, and she may have become interested in the science herself.

Aubrey also records that Mary Herbert brought together at Wilton House "a noble library of books." It has also been said that they included books of history and polity as well as the chief Italian poets. These statements all seem reasonable; they are in part supported by her literary interests, her translations from Petrarch, and perhaps by the interest of Abraham Fraunce in Tasso. Later, the books were dispersed, and one might be tempted to point a finger of suspicion at Philip Herbert, who inherited the title in 1630 from his brother William. But instead, the great fire of 1647 at Wilton House may have consumed the books; for it destroyed all the structure except the east front and most of the contents of the building.

Writers who were helped by Mary Herbert and lived for a time at Wilton House included Gervase Babington, Nicholas Breton, Samuel Daniel (whose comment was mentioned earlier), and Abraham Fraunce.

In 1583 Gervase Babington dedicated to her *A Brief Conference betwixt Man's Frailty and Faith.* He had been sent from Cambridge as a tutor, he may have been a chaplain first, and he became a friend of the whole family. His works, published after his death in 1615, carried a dedication to the sons, but he praised the lady mother and also the father for the way he had governed the family.

Nicholas Breton's dedications, like many others, expressed friendship, personal attachment, and gratitude. In 1592 he addressed her in *The Pilgrimage of Paradise Joined with the Countess of Pembroke's Love.* Her noble virtues, he said, "the wise no less honor than the learned admire, and the honest serve." He likened her to the Duchess of Urbino, describing himself as "your poor unworthy named poet, who by the indiscretion of his youth, the malice of envy, and the disgrace of ingratitude, had utterly perished (had not the hand of your honor revived the heart of humility)." He felt sure that "the judgment of the wise and the tongues of the learned" would clear him of any suspicion of flattery. In the second part

of his work he emphasized the idea that the real love of the countess was heaven with eternal life.

Breton was almost certainly speaking of Wilton House in *Wit's Trenchmour,* 1597, in his comparison of the home of a lady to a little court with "God daily served, religion truly preached, all quarrels avoided, peace carefully preserved, swearing not heard of, where truth was easily believed, a table fully furnished, a house richly garnished, honor kindly entertained, virtue highly esteemed, service well rewarded, and the poor blessedly relieved."

In 1597 and in 1601 Breton addressed other brief dedications to Mary Herbert. In *A Divine Poem,* 1601, he again characterized her as one whom "the wise admire, the learned follow, the virtuous love, and the honest serve." He closed by saying "in all humble thankfulness for your bountiful undeserved goodness, praying for your eternal happiness, I take my leave." About this time Pembroke died and his wife ceased to be the real mistress of Wilton House; though Breton lived till about 1626, his connections with Mary Herbert apparently ended.

Samuel Daniel, who went to Wilton House as a tutor for William, possibly about 1590, became a protégé and dedicated a number of works to the countess. In 1592 an edition of his sonnets, *Delia,* had a prose dedication to her, and a second edition adding an ode and *The Complaint of Rosamond* repeated the dedication. He said in part, "I desire only to be graced by the countenance of your protection, whom the fortune of our time hath made the happy and judicial patroness of the Muses. . . ." A 1594 edition carried also a dedicatory sonnet to her. When he published his tragedy *Cleopatra* in 1594, he prefaced it with a long dedicatory poem beginning, "Lo, here the labour which she did impose"; he added that her "well-graced **Antonie**" had long remained alone, desiring the company of his *Cleopatra.* In his introductory fourteen-stanza poem he predicted that she would be known for her work on the Psalms after Wilton House had been leveled to the ground; this dedication was repeated in an edition of 1623, *The Whole Works . . . in Poetry.*

Daniel dedicated to Mary Herbert a prose work also, *The First Four Books of the Civil War between the Two Houses of Lancaster and York,* concluding his remarks by stating that he had been revived by her goodness, held himself ever bound to her and her noble family, and would labor to do them honor and service. His expression of gratitude to Mary Herbert for training him in the use of rhyme, with his admission that Wilton had been his "best school," was mentioned earlier.

Abraham Fraunce was aided by several members of the Sidney-Herbert families, including the countess. He attended Shrewsbury School, but some years after Philip Sidney had been a pupil there, and apparently with Sidney's help, he entered St. John's College, Cambridge, where he resided for perhaps five years. Called to the bar at Gray's Inn, he practiced in the court of the Marches of Wales, doubtless with the help of the Sidneys. After the death of Sir Philip, he came under the patronage of Sidney's sister and thus dedicated most or all of his poetic work to her. As he was one of those who tried to use classical meters in English verse, his poems are in hexameters. They seem awkward and unreadable today, but his contemporaries placed a high value on his work.

Though Fraunce lived until 1633, his poetic work was published about 1587 to 1592, apparently about the time when he was being assisted by Mary Herbert. His dedications to her began in 1587 with *the Lamentations of Amintas for the Death of Phyllis,* a work he described as "paraphrastically translated out of Latin into English hexameters." At this time he said, "Mine afflicted mind and crased [diseased, infirm] body, together with other external calamities have wrought sorrowful and lamentable effects in me that for this whole year I have wholly given over myself to mournful meditations." Then he continued to give reasons for making his translations and for using the meter he had chosen. In 1588 he addressed to her his *Arcadian Rhetoric* signing his Latin lines, "Your honor's most affectionate, Abraham Fraunce." In 1591 he dedicated *The Countess of Pembroke's Emanuel* "To the right excellent and most honorable Lady, The Lady Mary, Countess of Pembroke," closing with the same phrasing. Also in 1591 he published *The Countess of Pembroke's Ivychurch* . . . and in 1592 *The Third Part of the Countess of Pembroke's Ivychurch entitled Amintas Dale,* again dedicating to her.

The Earl of Pembroke, having succeeded Sir Henry Sidney in the government of Wales, recommended Fraunce to Lord Burghley for appointment as queen's solicitor in the Court of the Marches, but he was not given the position. Sometime in the early 1590s Fraunce entered the service of the Earl of Bridgewater. The reason for his leaving Wilton House remains uncertain.

In addition to the preceding comments concerning activities at Wilton House, Mary Herbert received an amazing number of other tributes to her writing or her personality. Some were informal comments within articles not devoted to her exclusively, and one was in a letter; others were formal dedications. They were usually in restrained language, not romantic flattery; they have a way of seeming sincere; instead of soliciting future favors, they convey affectionate gratitude for what she had already done. Exceptions, perhaps, were Nathaniel Baxter and Robert Newton. In 1606 Baxter (Philip Sidney's tutor in Greek twenty-five years or

more earlier and known to him as Tergaster) dedicated to her *Philip Sidney's Ouranis,* with metrical addresses to other members of the Sidney and Herbert families. And in 1620, Newton, author of *The Countess of Montgomery's Eusebiae,* referred to Susan de Vere Herbert in his title; but on his title page he named Mary Herbert first and added names of others connected with the family. Possibly Baxter and Newton hoped for rewards. In some instances we do not know why an author (for example, Thomas Morley, who published *Canzonets,* songs for three voices, in 1593) chose to address his restrained dedication to Mary Herbert.

Interesting comments that were not formal dedications include those by Thomas Nashe, Gabriel Harvey, Francis Meres, and Sir John Harington as well as a poem by Sir Benjamin Rudier on her picture. Nashe's comment appeared in the first edition of *Astrophel and Stella,* in a prefatory article with the title "Somewhat to Read by them that List" and was signed by him. His wording is not typical of the tributes to her, but it illustrates comment within an article. He spoke of the many goodly branches that overshadow grief at the loss of Philip Sidney: "amongst the which, fair sister of Phoebus and eloquent secretary of the Muses, most rare Countess of Pembroke, thou are not to be omitted; whom arts do adore as a second Minerva and our poets extol as the patroness of their invention; for in thee the Lesbian Sappha with her lyric harp is disgraced. . . . Learning, wisdom, beauty, and all other ornaments of nobility whatsoever, seek to approve themselves in thy sight and get a further seal of felicity from the smiles of thy favor."

For once, Nashe seemed to realize that his rhetoric was getting out of control, for after a one-line Latin quotation he said, "I fear I shall be counted a mercenary flatterer for mixing my thoughts with such figurative admiration, but general report that surpasseth my praise condemneth my rhetoric of dullness for so cold a commendation."

Gabriel Harvey praised her in *Pierce's Supererogation* in 1593. He said, "though the furious tragedy **Antonius** be a bloody chair of estate, yet the divine **Discourse of Life and Death** is a restorative electuary of gems." He did not expressly name her, he added, "not because I do not honor her with my heart, but because I would not dishonor her with my pen, whom I admire and cannot blazon enough."

Francis Meres, in *Palladis Tamia* in 1598, described her as "learned . . . liberal unto poets; and besides, she is a most delicate poet. . . ." He may have seen manuscript copies of some of her Psalms, or perhaps she wrote other poems that were never published with her name attached. Sir John Harington, writing to Lucy, Countess of Bedford, December 19, 1600, sent her "the divine and truly divine translation of three of David's

Psalms done by that excellent countess, and in poesy, the mirrois [sic] of our age." He tactfully added that she and the countess he was addressing were alike in blood and degree and were not unlike in appearance and those gifts of the mind that clothe the nobility with virtue. Harington also wrote an epigram on women named Mary, beginning with his wife and ending with Mary Herbert.

Sir Benjamin Rudier, who may never have known her personally but was an associate of her son William, entitled a poem "On the Countess of Pembroke's Picture." His poem appeared in the 1660 edition of poems by William Herbert and also some by Rudier.

> Here (though the lustre of her youth be spent)
> Are curious steps to see where beauty went;
> And for the wonders in her mind that dwell
> It lies not in the power of pens to tell.
> But could she but bequeath them when she
>   dies,
> She might enrich her sex by legacies.

Among others who paid tribute to Mary Herbert, but not in formal dedications, were Charles Fitzgeoffrey in *Affaniae* in 1601 and Sir John Stradling in *Epigrammatum* in 1607; each devoted to her an epigram in a collection of them. William Smith, probably in the late sixteenth century, wrote a poem as a tribute to her; and he added poems to make a "posie" of flowers from her "devoted servant" to the "right noble, honorable, and the singular good lady, the Countess of Pembroke." His "posie," still in manuscript, was noted by Frances B. Young in the British Museum. Daniel Rogers, poet, diplomat, and man of scholarly tastes, addressed lines to her picture before his death in 1591; but his poem is not available.

John Taylor included her as the subject of sonnet five in a series of sonnets, *The Needle's Excellency.* The date of his first edition is unknown, but in speaking of her he used the past tense. His sonnet to her began:

> A pattern and a patroness she was
> Of virtuous industry and studious learning.

It ended:

> She wrought so well in needlework that she
> Nor yet her work shall ere forgotten be.

William Browne (1591-1643), who lived at Wilton House presumably when her older son was master there, wrote an elegy on Mary Sidney Herbert some time after her death if the first line is a literal statement: "Time hath a long course run since thou wert clay." Though Browne was praised by such contemporaries as John Davies of Hereford and Ben Jonson, his elegy is a long, pedestrian poem. Reading it impels one to-

ward accepting Ben Jonson as the more probable author of the well-known epitaph—the most beautiful poem written about her.

From the formal dedications to Mary Herbert a few will be selected for brief discussion. Others are listed in *The Index of Dedications* by Franklin B. Williams, Jr. The earliest was *Devices* in 1581 by Thomas Howell, appearing when she was nineteen or twenty years old, the year after the birth of her first child. Howell mentioned her desire to benefit many people, her virtuous life, rare wisdom, honorable courtesy, and sweet behavior. Similar qualities were often mentioned in future comments on her, not because others copied Howell, it seems, but because they observed her.

John Davies of Hereford honored Mary Herbert in several different publications. In *Microcosmos* in 1603 he added, at the close of his volume, poems addressed to leaders of Scotland and England, several poems addressed to other members of the Herbert family, and one addressed jointly to Mary Herbert and her daughter Anne. In *Other Essays* Davies published two sonnets honoring "the right noble and well-accomplished lady, the Dowager Countess of Pembroke." In the first of the two he wrote:

> If aught be fair or right in me, it is
> Not mine but thine, whose worth possesseth
>   me;
> If I be all amiss, I all assign
> To shame and sorrow, sith no part is thine.

Davies also addressed three women in *The Muses' Sacrifice* in 1612 as "the most noble and no less deservedly renowned ladies, as well darlings as patronesses of the Muses, Lucy, Countess of Bedford, Mary, Countess-Dowager of Pembroke, and Elizabeth Lady Carey (wife of Sir Henry Carey), glories of women." He added pages of quatrains for "the heavenly three."

Other outstanding writers praised and thanked Mary Herbert. When Edmund Spenser published the first three books of the *Faerie Queene* in 1590, he directed to her one of the seventeen sonnets at the close of the work; the memory of her brother, he said, commanded him to worship that "goodly image in her face," but she embellished the resemblance with her own special virtues. In 1591 when he dedicated to her "The Ruins of Time" in *Complaints,* he admitted that he was bound to her "by many singular favors and great graces." In his elegiac poem for her brother, *Astrophel,* he complimented her as the sister Clorinda, "The gentlest shepherdess that lives this day." He also included what he called her doleful lay, though he probably wrote that part of the poem himself. However, he dedicated the whole poem to Sidney's widow, who had become the Countess of Essex. Again in *Colin Clout's Come Home Again,* Spenser praised Mary Herbert as Urania, the sister of Astrophel, for her brave mind with its heavenly graces and "in her sex more wonderful and rare."

John Donne joined those who valued the literary work of the countess when he wrote his poem "Upon the Translation of the Psalms by Sir Philip Sidney and the Countess of Pembroke, his Sister." He mentioned the poor versions used in churches and in England and the better ones used in private homes and on the Continent. He concluded:

> So though some may, some have some Psalms
> translate
> We thy Sydnean Psalms shall celebrate.

Perhaps no one was better fitted than John Donne, clergyman and poet, to comment on versions of the Psalms.

It may be safe to conclude that no other woman in Renaissance England was praised as often, as sincerely, and by as many people for qualities she possessed and for both personality and literary work as Mary Herbert, Countess of Pembroke.

Mary Herbert also persuaded her brother Sir Philip to begin his writing—and that was a service to literature. The time was 1580. He felt himself exiled from the court because he had written the defense of his father's work in Ireland, had refused to humble himself to Oxford after the quarrel at the tennis court, and had worded and signed the letter with the objections of important Englishmen to their queen's marriage to Alençon. His plans for the future had failed to interest the queen. She had not rewarded Sir Henry Sidney for his service. Sir Philip must have known of other difficulties that were leading up to the frank letter his father wrote Walsingham in 1583, when the question of Philip's marriage to Walsingham's daughter came up. In that letter Sir Henry explained his lack of money. He spoke of his losses years earlier on his first trip to Ireland—losses of all his "household stuff and utensils," his wife's clothing and jewels, and many horses with "stable stuff." In 1583, he told Walsingham, he was 5,000 [pounds] in debt and worse off by 30,000 [pounds] than he had been at the death of Edward VI.

So from about 1578 to 1580, Sir Philip Sidney brooded over his own and his father's problems. In a letter to Hubert Languet, March 1, 1578, he described his attitude, which doubtless had a mixture of melancholy: he accused himself of slothfulness, of avoiding self-examination, of inability to write, and of playing the stoic, adding that he would become a cynic unless Languet reclaimed him. One biographer, M. W. Wallace, said of him at this period, "Always inclined to melancholy, he now felt utterly depressed by Elizabeth's failure to show any adequate appreciation of his father's services or to be really interested in his own

plans." Wallace added, "Sidney's inaction and consequent gloom are reflected in all we hear of him."

It seems almost certain that in 1580 Mary Herbert would have known the main facts about the queen's neglect of her father, even if her father and brother tried to conceal the difficulty in paying her portion—as they might well have done. It seems equally certain in 1580 when her brother was spending weeks of time at Wilton House, that she would discover the chief reasons for his melancholy and his absence from court. And it seems safe to conclude that she shared her brother's concern. Few records if any suggest that Mary Herbert, though she was Countess of Pembroke, attended court while Elizabeth was queen. When her husband paid a visit to court in 1595, Rowland Whyte reported to Robert Sidney that the queen treated him very well "at his departure" and sent "my lady your sister a jewel." His report carries a faint suggestion, at least, that the earl's visit was unusual. Perhaps we need no stories from gossips to explain the absence of Mary Herbert from the court of Elizabeth but only need facts about the Sidneys and the queen. It is a matter of record that Mary Herbert and her daughter made appearances at court after James came to the throne.

It also seems evident that in 1580 Mary Herbert would wish to divert her brother from his melancholy. That the *Arcadia* was written or mostly written in those weeks or months at Wilton House is generally accepted as fact, and when Philip Sidney dedicated the work to his sister he explained her influence on its composition:

> But you desired me to do it, and your desire, to my heart, is an absolute commandment. Now it is done, only for you, only to you: if you keep it to yourself or to such friend who will weigh errors in the balance of good will. . . . For indeed, for severer eyes it is not, being but a trifle, and that triflingly handled. Your best self can best witness the manner, being done in loose sheets of paper, most of it in your presence, the rest by sheets sent unto you as fast as they were done. . . . And so you will continue to love the writer, who doth exceedingly love you, and most heartily prays that you may long live to be a principal ornament to the Sidney family.

Eventually Mary Herbert assumed the task of editing and publishing all her brother's literary work after his death. Though her establishment of Wilton House as a center for literature touched many lives, her publication of her brother's prose and poetry gave the world in satisfactory form the work of a greater writer than any she had aided at Wilton House. Recalling that the first edition of *Arcadia* had been unfinished and that the early edition of *Astrophel and Stella,* issued without her help, was filled with errors, one might safely conclude that she did much for his reputation and performed a service for the world. Perhaps her supervision of his work for publication was her greatest service to literature.

The first work by her brother that she guided through the press was *Arcadia*. In 1588, two years after the death of Sir Philip Sidney, it was entered in the Stationers Register for publication. One day Ponsonby, a responsible bookbinder, came to Fulke Greville, who had been an intimate friend of Sidney, to warn him that someone meant to bring out the older version of the work and to ask if this was being done with the consent of Walsingham or other friends. Greville then sent Sidney's widow, at her request, a corrected copy, "fitter to be printed than the first, which is so common," and even it was "to be amended by a direction set down in his own hand." Sidney had started revising the work, but his revision seems not to have progressed beyond the middle of the third book. As a result, Ponsonby published a first edition in 1590, probably with the help of Greville, possibly with some of Greville's editing and his chapter divisions. But the work broke off within Chapter III.

Another edition, called the authorized one, was published in 1593 under the direction of Sidney's sister. The "Address to the Reader" with it was signed H. S., no doubt indicating Henry Sanford, a long-time secretary to the Earl of Pembroke, acting for Mary Herbert. The writer of the address said that "the disfigured face" with which the work had been published earlier had "moved that noble lady to whose honor it was consecrated, to whose protection it was committed, to take in hand the wiping away of those spots wherewith the beauties thereof were unworthily blemished." Readers should also understand "that though they find not here what might be expected, they may find nevertheless as much as was intended, the conclusion, not the perfection of *Arcadia*, and that no further than the author's own writings or known determinations could direct. . . . But . . . it is now by more than one interest the Countess of Pembroke's *Arcadia*, done as it was for her, as it is, by her."

Probably Mary Herbert acted as honestly as she could in issuing the authorized edition. As Sidney's revision had not progressed beyond the middle of the third book, she left unfinished several stories that he had added in the rewriting. She completed the third book and added the fourth and fifth books from the earlier version. If she left out chapter divisions that had appeared in the first edition, she probably believed them to be the work of Fulke Greville.

In 1591, five years after Sidney's death, Mary Herbert came to the rescue of *Astrophel and Stella*. It had been published "from a circulating manuscript by Thomas Newman, who later in the same year printed a second version (altered in some 350 places) based on a manuscript either supplied or approved by the Sidney fam-

ily." According to Jack Stillinger, Lord Burghley ordered the first edition confiscated, presumably at the request of the family or of Mary Herbert. The earlier version is full of garbled phrases or misprints. In sonnet 31 the moon climbs the sky with a *mean* face instead of a *wan* face; in sonnet 39 sleep is addressed as the *bathing* place, not the *baiting* place of wit; and in sonnet 102 a line reads "How doth the color fade of those vermillion *eyes*," instead of *dyes*. Though there may be a question about the exact date of the second edition, whether it was also in 1591 or a little later, there is no doubt about its comparative value. Again, for this corrected edition, we are indebted to Mary Herbert.

In 1595 two editions of *The Defense of Poesy* were published. One, issued by Ponsonby, was apparently edited with care and was described as "the first authorized edition." Again the person responsible was undoubtedly Sidney's sister. In 1598 another volume of his work came from the press. It contained *Arcadia*, with Sidney's dedication to his sister and the address to the reader signed by H. S.; certain poems called sonnets that had not been published before; *The Defense of Poesy;* the *Astrophel and Stella* sonnets in their final form; and a minor work *The Lady of the May*, earlier presented to the queen at Wanstead. All these works in a final authorized form we owe to the Countess of Pembroke. It is a large debt.

The literary production of Mary Herbert consisted entirely of translations, one work published with her name, the **"Dialogue between Two Shepherds in Praise of Astrea,"** being a mere trifle. Even her versions of the Psalms, which she made into individual Elizabethan poems, were translations in the strict sense, since she made every effort to express the original thought. Also all her own literary work, so far as we know, was done within a period of fifteen years after the death of her parents and her brother. All of it, excepting some of the Psalms, dealt with death. If Sir Philip Sidney had lived for a normal length of time, would Mary Herbert ever have done any literary work, either editing and publishing or translating from the French and Italian? It is an interesting idea, even if it must remain a speculation.

She signed her translation of Mornay, *A Discourse of Life and Death,* on May 13, 1590, at Wilton. She signed her *Antonius,* a translation of *Marc Antonie* by Robert Garnier, November 26, 1590, at Ramsbury. The two were published in 1592 in one volume with one title page. Though we do not know when she began the work, translations such as these are not usually done in haste. She may have planned and started translating or at least mulling over the work soon after she heard of her brother's death. The Mornay especially may have developed from her personal struggle to adjust to the accidental death of a man so young, gifted, and beloved as her brother had been. Philip Sidney and Mornay had become close friends. They met first on the Continent through Hubert Languet. In 1577 when Mornay came to England to ask help from Queen Elizabeth for the French Protestants, an intimate friendship developed between the two men. When Mornay returned in 1578 for a longer stay, bringing his family, Sidney stood as godfather for his son. It is highly probable that Sidney's sister also became acquainted with the Mornay family. About this time Sidney began to translate another work by Mornay, *De veritate Christiana;* but being busy, he asked a scribe, Arthur Golding, to finish it. In 1587 the scribe published it as *A Work concerning the Trueness of the Christian Religion.* While Mary Herbert was translating *A Discourse of Life and Death,* it was possible for her to recall memories of a time when her brother was alive and to find consolation for her loss in Mornay's ideas, since the essay developed both Stoical and Christian philosophies about the acceptance of death. Her translation began:

> It seems to me strange . . . that the laborer to repose himself hasteneth as it were the course of the sun, that the mariner rows with all force to attain the port . . . and that we in the mean while, tied in this world by a perpetual task, tossed with continual tempest . . . cannot yet see the end of our labour but with grief, nor behold our port but with tears, nor approach our home and quiet abode but with horror and trembling.

Toward the close of her translation she said:

> To end, we ought neither to hate this life for the toils therein, for it is sloth and cowardice, nor love it for the delights, which is folly and vanity, but serve us of it, to serve God in it, who after it shall place us in true quietness. . . . It is enough that we constantly and continually wait for her [death's] coming, that she may never find us unprovided. . . .

Mary Herbert's *Antonius,* signed in the same year and published with the translation of Mornay, was probably not chosen for the same personal reason; it dealt with death, but in a quite different way. It may have grown from an interest in classical drama, and it came early in a series of Senecan dramas translated in the 1590s. Thus it was important in the reaction of intellectuals against romantic drama, a reaction that Philip Sidney had possibly furthered by his discussion in *A Defense of Poesy.* Samuel Daniel, following her in 1594 with his *Cleopatra,* clearly indicated that he was translating it at her suggestion; in 1605 he wrote *Philotas* on the same Senecan principles. By 1594 Thomas Kyd had translated *Cornelia,* another tragedy by Robert Garnier, signing his dedication to the Countess of Sussex as T. K. He had promised to put Garnier's *Portia* into English, it is said, but if so, apparently his

death in 1594 prevented him. Though he followed the Senecan tradition in the plays that are mentioned here and perhaps in an early version of *Hamlet,* no available evidence indicates that he came under the personal influence of the Countess of Pembroke.

Mary Herbert also translated the first and second chapters of Petrarch's *Trionfo della Morte* as **The Triumph of Death**. Though she was reproducing the ideas the original author had expressed, at least she chose the material. The only definite date connected with her work is 1599, when Thomas Moffett, dedicating to her *The Silkworms and their Flies,* asked her to "Let Petrarch sleep, give rest to sacred writ." In the first chapter of her English version death appears as a woman in black, ready to destroy youth and beauty, and with innumerable victims in the past—civilized nations, barbarians, people in every period of history; popes, kings, and emperors, forced to leave behind them all the honors they had struggled to gain in this world, with even their names forgotten. Thus the ideas are personal and universal; they resemble those in *A Discourse of Life and Death.* Again, the material may have been chosen by the translator in an effort to temper her own losses. Unlike other early translators of the *Trionfo,* she used the difficult terza rima; and though Frances B. Young admits that her phrases were sometimes obscure, she adds that the countess was faithful to the thought of the original.

Evidence that Mary Herbert had poetic talent depends largely upon her translation or poetic recreating of the Psalms. It is generally agreed that her brother's work included only forty-three Psalms, and that she changed the other hundred and seven into Elizabethan poems. He may have begun his work at any time after 1580; he probably finished by 1585 when he went to the Low Countries. She may have settled to serious work on them about 1587 or 1588 (there is no definite evidence); she must have made real progress by 1594 when Samuel Daniel praised her work, predicting that it would outlast Wilton House. She probably completed them about 1599 or 1600, judging partly from Moffett's mention about 1599 and partly from the statement that she sent the queen a complete manuscript with a dedication in 1599. Also J. C. A. Rathmell, the recent editor of the Psalms, estimates that she had begun her work by 1593 and had completed it before 1600. Though the Psalms were passed about in manuscript, were known to John Donne, and may have influenced George Herbert's *Temple,* they did not appear in print until 1823; the modern edition with the excellent introduction by Rathmell was published in 1963.

During the reign of Elizabeth, Psalms were versified and issued for use in churches because both Anglicans and Puritans approved them. By 1562 *The Whole Book of Psalms* had been published, and one hundred fifty editions eventually appeared. But they were utilitarian versions. The Psalms of the Sidneys, as Rathmell said, were literature; they had "energy, intensity, and emotional piquancy"; they emphasized an allegorical significance and used a variety of forms, adapting the form to the emotion of a particular Psalm. They resulted from an effort to use all the resources of the Elizabethan lyric; and both the Sidneys, Rathmell concluded, tried to create for each one "a unique combination of stanza pattern and rhyme scheme" adapted to the individual Psalm.

Neither of the Sidneys, according to Rathmell, knew Hebrew; and though Philip knew Greek well enough to read it easily without a translation, neither needed Greek for work on the Psalms. They compared versions in the psalter of the Prayer Book with the two current English versions of the Bible (the Geneva Bible of 1560 and the Bishops' Bible of 1568). They also used the elaborate commentaries on the Psalms; those of Beza had been translated into English by Gilby and those of Calvin by Golding. Mary Herbert especially often expanded an image because the commentaries gave her the right to do so. Of course the *Vulgate* was available, but Rathmell did not mention it; and they would probably not have considered using the version authorized by the Catholic church. However, they may have read Beza in French. In Rathmell's opinion, the work that "most obviously served as a model to the Sidneys is the French psalter of 1562," a collection based on fifty Psalms that Clement Marot composed between 1532 and 1543 and that Beza completed at Geneva in 1562.

Informed critics express the view that the work of Mary Herbert with the Psalms was superior to that of her brother. In the nineteenth century A. B. Grosart had said that the Psalms she created are "infinitely in advance of her brother's in thought, epithet, and melody." Quoting him, Rathmell added that "they demand to be considered not only in the context of Elizabethan psalmody, but as significant and attractive poems in their own right." Again he said, "The Countess has, in a devotional sense, mediated on the text before her, and the force of her version derives from her sense of personal involvement; she has taken into account Calvin's interpretation of the verse, and it is her capacity to appreciate underlying meaning that vivified her lines." Quoting from *The Poetry of Meditation* by Louis L. Martz, Rathmell agreed with his statement that the work of the Sidneys was "the attempt to bring the art of the Elizabethan lyric into the service of psalmody, and to perform this in such a way that it makes the psalm an intimate, personal cry of the soul to God." The comment, he added, "applies . . . with even greater force to the Psalms of the Countess of Pembroke."

Mary Sidney Herbert, Countess of Pembroke, one may conclude, should be remembered for her gracious, generous personality, her services to other writers, including her brother, and her own poetic talent. Perhaps she deserved the epitaph written for her by either William Browne or Ben Jonson:

> Underneath this sable hearse
> Lies the subject: of all verse,
> Sidney's sister, Pembroke's mother.
> Death, ere thou hast slain another,
> Fair, and learned, and good as she,
> Time shall throw a dart at thee.

Notes and Sources

These abbreviations are used in the Notes and Sources:

AHR American Historical Review

BM British Museum

Cal. Pat. Rolls, Hen. VII Calendar of Patent Rolls, Henry VII, or Edward VI, or Elizabeth

Cal. S. P. Dom. Ser. Calendar State Papers, Domestic Series, or Foreign, or Spanish, or Venetian

DNB Dictionary of National Biography

EETS Early English Text Society

Econ. H.R. Economic History Review

EHR English Historical Review

Hist. MS. Comm. Historical Manuscripts Commission

HLQ Huntington Library Quarterly

JEGP Journal of English and Germanic Philology

Letters and Papers or L. and P. Letters and Papers, Foreign and Domestic of . . . Henry VIII

PCC Prerogative Court of Canterbury

PRO Public Record Office

STC Short-Title Catalogue of Books . . . 1475-1649, ed. A. W. Pollard and G. R. Redgrave

Trans. R. H. Soc. Transactions of the Royal Historical Society

Aubrey, John. *Brief Lives,* ed. O. L. Dick. London, 1949. Wilton House "like a college," 138-39.

Babington, Gervase, *The workes . . . STC 1077.*

Beza, Theodore. *The Psalmes of David,* transl. A. Gilby, 1580. Material available to the Sidneys. *STC* 2033.

Breton, Nicholas. *The Works.* Edinburgh, 1879. Chertsey Worthies' Library. "Wits Trenchmour," the house of a lady, II, 18-19. Breton's other titles, see *STC*.

Browne, William. *The Poems.* London, 1894. "An Elegy on the Countess Dowager of Pembroke," II, 248-55.

Cal. Carew MSS, 1575-1588, ed. John Brewer and George Bullen. London, 1868. Letter of Henry Sidney to Walsingham, no. 501, 334-60. (Source: PRO Dom. Eliz. clix, no. 1, fol. 38).

Cal. Pat. Rolls, Edw, VI. London, 1925, 1926. Grants to Henry Sidney, III, 174; V. 1, 7, 60, 201, 242.

Cal. S. P., Dom. Ser., 1547-1580. Lady Mary Sidney's plea against title, I, 442; queen's offer to take daughter Mary at court, 494. Henry Sidney's 1583 letter to Walsingham, II, 98-99.

Cal. S. P., Spanish, 1558-1567. Lady Mary Sidney as queen's intermediary, I, 95, 96, 98-100, 105, 107, 109, 112-13, 115-16. Mendoza's report on a loss of lodging at court, II, 682; meeting at Pembroke's house of those opposed to queen's marriage, 693.

Calvin, John. *The Psalmes of David . . . ,* with J. Calvin's commentaries, transl. A. Golding, 1571. Material available to the Sidneys. *STC* 4395.

Collins, Arthur. *Letters and Memorials of State.* London, 1746. Vol. I, *Memoirs of the Sidneys.* Gratitude of Duchess of Northumberland to Spanish, 33, 34; Henry Sidney's work in Ireland and Wales, 82-93; births, also marriage of Mary, 96-97; Leicester's payment on Mary's portion, 97; quarrel between Philip Sidney and Oxford, 101; Sir Philip's will, 109-13. Vol. I, *Letters and Memorials of State,* Henry Sidney's letter to a twelve-year-old son, 8; his letter to Burghley about his penury, 43; letter to Leicester about Mary's marriage, 88; Sir Philip Sidney's praise of his mother, 247; her letters to Mollineux on lodgings at court, 271, 272; illnesses often attended by Dr. Goodrich, I, 363, 372; II, 120, 123, 124, 128.

Complete Peerage, ed. Vicary Gibbs et al. London, 1910-1959.

Daniel, Samuel. *The Complete Works.* London, Aylesbury, 1885-1896. For works mentioned here, dedications are reproduced. See also *STC*.

————. *A Panegyrike . . . A Defence of Rhyme.* 1603. *STC* 6259.

Davies, John of Hereford. For titles and dates, see *STC*.

Dee, John. *The Private Diary,* Camden Society, Vol. XIX, 1842. Visits of Philip Sidney to Dee, 2, 20.

Fraunce, Abraham. *Amyntas, with Translation of the Lamentations,* ed. F. M. Dickey. Chicago, 1967. Dedication to countess, 8. For other titles by Fraunce, see *STC*.

Gentleman's Magazine, Vol. XXIV (1845). Three articles, "Lady Mary Sidney and her Writings," by H. T. R[oach], 129-36, 254-59, 364-70.

Goss, Charles W. F. *Crosby Hall.* London, 1908. Lease by countess, 89.

Halle, Edward. *Chronicle. The Union of the . . . Two Families. . . .* ed. Grafton. 1550. Additions by Sidneys, on blank pages between Edward IV and V, and Henry VII and VIII. Folger Shakespeare Library copy 2, *STC* 12721.

Harington, Sir John. *The Letters and Epigrams,* ed. N. E. McClure. Philadelphia, 1930. His letter praising Psalms of the countess, 87; epigram on women named Mary, 310.

Harvey, Gabriel. *Pierce's Supererogation.* London, 1815. His tribute, 89.

Herbert, Mary. *A Discourse of Life and Death* (by Mornay) and *Antonius,* transl. Countess of Pembroke. 1592. *STC* 18138.

Jayne, Sears. *Library Catalogues of the English Renaissance.* Berkeley, Los Angeles, 1956. Gift by William Herbert of Greek manuscripts to Bodleian, no. 1629.

Languet, Hubert. See Pears.

Luce, Alice. *The Countess of Pembroke's Antonie.* Weimar, 1897. General background.

Lysons, Daniel. *Magna Britannia. . . .* London, 1806. Mansion in Ampthill Park, I, 96.

Moffett, Thomas. *Nobilis,* ed. V. B. Heltzel and Hoyt Hudson. San Marino, Calif., 1940. Sidney's attitudes to astrology and chemistry, 75, 119; comment on Mary Herbert, 85.

Nichols, John. *The Progresses . . . of Queen Elizabeth.* London, 1823. Details on "Astrea," III, 529-31.

CCC. *The Progresses . . . of King James the First.* London, 1828. I, 195, 327, 513; II, 99.

Osborn, James M. *Young Philip Sidney, 1572-1577.* New Haven, London, 1972. Contrast in Dudleys and Sidneys, 5-6; Philip Sidney's knowledge of Greek 89; meeting of anti-Alençon group at Baynard's Castle, 503; Sidney's rejection of astrology, App. 1.

Pears, S. A. *The Correspondence of Sir Philip Sidney and Hubert Languet.* London, 1845. Mood of Sidney in March 1578, 143-45.

Pembroke, Countess of. *A Discourse of Life and Death . . . Antonius, a Tragedie.* 1592. STC 18138.

Pembroke, William, Earl of, and Sir Benjamin Rudier. *Poems,* ed. John Donne the Younger. London, 1660. Rudier's poem on countess, 26.

Rathmell, J. C. A. *The Psalms of Sir Philip Sidney and the Countess of Pembroke.* Garden City, N.Y., 1963. Introduction, xi-xxxii; quotations, xvii, xx, xxi.

Sidney, Sir Philip. *Astrophel and Stella,* 1st ed. 1591. Film Acc. 366. 1, B. M. 22536. Used at Folger Shakespeare Library. For other works of Sidney, see *STC.*

Stillinger, Jack. "The Biographical Problem of *Astrophel and Stella.*" *JEGP,* LIX(1960), 617-39. First ed., 619.

Sweeper, Walter. *A Briefe Treatise.* . . . 1622. STC 23526. Original not available.

Taylor, John. *The Needle's Excellency,* 10th ed. 1634. STC 23776.

Victoria History. . . . *Co. of Bedford.* London, 1912. Houghton House, Ampthill Park, III, 289-90.

Wallace, M. W. *The Life of Sir Philip Sidney.* Cambridge, 1915. Education and ability of Lady Mary Sidney, 17, 20; cause (about 1578-1580) of Philip Sidney's mood, 197-200, 226.

Williams, Franklin B., Jr. *Index of Dedications . . . in English Books before 1641.* London, 1962. Dedications to Mary Herbert, Countess of Pembroke.

Williamson, George C. *Lady Anne Clifford.* Kendall, 1922. Her view of Philip Herbert, 183.

Young, Frances B. *Mary Sidney, Countess of Pembroke.* London, 1912. Letters to Sussex about lodgings at court, 16-20; will of Henry Herbert (PCC 39 Woodhall, 1601) and his wife's dower, 77-82; death and burial of Mary Herbert, 117; reprint of her translation from Petrarch, 209-18.

Beth Wynne Fisken (essay date 1985)

SOURCE: "Mary Sidney's Psalmes: Education and Wisdom," in *Silent But for the Word: Tudor Women as Patrons, Translators, and Writers of Religious Works*, edited by Margaret Patterson Hannay, The Kent State University Press, 1985, pp. 166-83.

[*In the following in-depth study of Sidney's Psalms, Fisken argues that, as a translator Sidney both respected the conventions of her era, which demanded self-effacement, and exceeded them with her poetic innovation.*]

Mary Sidney's verse translations of the Psalms began as an education in how to write poetry and ended in a search for wisdom. Through close work with her brother Philip's translations as well as painstaking revision of her own efforts, she slowly gained the confidence to develop an individual style which stressed the immediacy of God's power and presence and dramatized the quandary of the psalmist seeking God's grace in adversity. Eventually Sidney's growing confidence in her work encouraged her to develop original patterns of imagery, reflecting her public experiences as lady-in-waiting at court and manager of her husband's estate as well as her individual perceptions as a woman and a mother. In doing so, she transformed her verse translations into independent poems and exercises in private meditation, teaching herself not only how to write poetry, but ultimately, how to speak to God.

Mary Sidney's process of composition revealed her dedication to the classical ideal of the education of a poet. As Gary Waller has demonstrated in his study of the extant manuscripts of her psalms, she began by revising her brother Philip Sidney's versions of Psalms 1 to 43, and then undertook the rest of the psalms, working between two copy-texts and constantly reworking and revising, at times arriving at varying independent versions of the same psalm. This process of composition, begun sometime after her brother's death in 1586, continued steadily until 1599, when the presentation copy was readied for a projected visit from Queen Elizabeth. Mary Sidney learned first from imitating a master, her brother, and then through perseverance and laborious revision, she discovered her own style. Certainly the dazzling variety of stanzaic forms and metrical patterns she experimented with constituted a course in the discipline of suiting sound to sense that led to a technical mastery of poetic forms.[1]

The Sidneian psalms, with their inventive structure and extended imagery, were a significant departure from the unadorned literalism which was found in, for example, the prose paraphrases of the Book of Common Prayer and the Geneva Bible, or in the simple metrical psalms in common measure of the Sternhold-Hopkins psalter, a literalism which was deemed necessary for the congregational use of psalms as communal expressions of Christian devotion. Rather, the Sidneian psalms addressed a parallel tradition of reading and reciting the psalms in solitary, meditative sessions, examining the relationship between the individual spirit and God. Certainly, Mary Sidney's choice of the Psalms as the basis for her poetic endeavors reflects her intense commitment to this introspective Protestant tradition which stressed the role of the psalms as meditative paradigms; yet perhaps it also reveals a shrewd understanding on her part that religious translations were a sanctioned form of intellectual exercise for noblewomen of her time, Queen Elizabeth herself having tried her hand at them. Writing without models of serious, committed women poets for her to emulate, Mary Sidney erected her version of the Psalms on the foundations of her brother's work, plumb with the religious practices and social conventions of her time. Thus, by doubly buttressing her work, she was gradually able to build sufficient self-confidence to develop a poetic voice that would fully express the richness of her interior spiritual life.

Although Mary Sidney's poetic efforts were nourished in the security of the socially accepted forms of her time which sanctioned modest displays of scholarly attainment when subordinated to pious endeavors, she soon surpassed the conventional boundaries of mere ladylike accomplishment. Her scholarship was thorough; she consulted many available sources such as the Prayer Book Psalter to Coverdale's Great Bible of 1539, the Geneva Bible of 1560, the Bishops' Bible of 1568, and the Marot-Bèze psalter of 1562, as well as Golding's translation of Calvin's commentaries and Gilby's version of de Bèze. Mary Sidney was a learned and sensitive exegete, seeking to dramatize the predicament of the psalmist and through her reconstruction of the psalmist's voice to establish her own relationship to the spiritual issues of her time, defining her views by selecting or rejecting the glosses offered by others and then adding comparisons and elaborations unique to her. In these verse translations she discarded the literalism of her previous translations of Garnier's *Antonie* and Mornay's *Discours* in favor of a mixture of translation and interpretation which allowed for additions based on personal reflection and experience. This freer translation made her psalms exercises in the classical mode of imitation, in which Sidney strove to reconstruct the style and matter of the original within a context that would carry weight and meaning, first for her contemporary society, and ultimately, for herself as an individual. As such, her psalms are grounded in the Protestant tradition which stressed the application of the Scriptures to the situation of the individual. The psalms were interpreted simultaneously as the "emotional history of all the faithful, and . . . the particular spiritual autobiography of every particular Christian." Hence, by reworking them, Mary Sidney sought to become a "correlative type," a new David forging "a new work in the same spirit, under the impress of the same emotions."[2] Yet, for her, it was equally important that the meaning of the originals be adhered to

faithfully, because to do otherwise would be to set one's own work above that of God—the very antithesis of wisdom. To personalize the meaning of the Psalms without distorting it was a delicate and demanding task, requiring both judgment and sensitivity to tone and connotation.

The Psalms were a particularly appropriate choice for models in poetic composition, as Philip Sidney himself urged in his "Defence of Poesie." The best English scholars of that time recognized that the Hebrew originals were themselves remarkable poems, and they deplored the lack of an English hymnal the equal of the French Marot-Bèze psalter at reconstructing the beauty of the originals. The complex voice of the psalmist, David's "often and free chaunging of persons," as Philip Sidney described it in his "Defence,"[3] contributed to the immediacy and intensity of the psalms as dramatizations of the conflicts of the spirit wrestling with itself in search of God. Consequently, the Psalms were thought to be a Bible in miniature, a searching "Anatomy of all the partes of the Soule," revealing "all the greefes, sorowes, feares, doutes, hopes, cares, anguishes, and finally all the trubblesome motions wherewith mennes mindes are woont to be turmoyled."[4] Therefore, the psalmist's voice subsumes all our individual voices and private concerns, and as a result, the voice of the translator becomes our voice and "translates" our hopes and desires into his or her expression of David's petitions and prayers. Not only was Mary Sidney as translator of the Psalms encouraged by her material to speak in many voices, but also to speak in her own voice when her voice was congruent with the meaning of the text. The translator, as well as the reader in private meditation, is continually urged to apply the psalms to his or her own situation for the full revelation of their meaning.[5] Not only did her material challenge Sidney to stretch her poetic repertoire to dramatize the psalmist's many personations, but also it ultimately threw her back on herself, to develop the confidence to find a poetic equivalent for her own small, personal voice, "my self, my seely self in me."[6]

By examining some of the revisions Mary Sidney made when reworking and condensing the final stanzas of seven of her brother's psalms, we can see how specific exercises in versification led to the eventual development of a style independent of her brother's influence, reflecting her own ideas, tastes, and experiences. By setting herself the task of condensing and tightening her brother's stanzas, Mary Sidney taught herself how to sharpen an image by eliminating superfluous expressions and how to dramatize rather than explain. For example, at the end of **Psalm 26,** she changed "That hand whose strength should help of bribes is full"[7] to "With right hands stain'd with gifts," permitting us to supply the moral connotations of "right hands." She chose to emphasize the force of the speaker's righteousness reflected in his carriage, his physical pride in standing erect and walking a straight path, in her revision of

> But in integrity
> My stepps shall guided be,
> Then me redeem Lord then be mercifull,
> Even truth that for me sayes
> My foot on justice stayes,
> And tongue is prest to publish out thy prayse
>
> (ll. 34-39),

to:

> But while I walk in my unspotted waies,
> Redeeme and show mee grace,
> So I in publique place,
> Sett on plaine ground, will thee Jehovah
> praise.
>
> (ll. 33-36)

Everyday routine is luminous with signs of grace if we only know how to see them. Mary Sidney's emphasis on action rather than abstraction, her speaker's foot "sett on plaine ground" rather than "on justice stayes," make the present material sphere seem laden with spiritual significance without the need for extrapolation.

This commitment to the palpable and perceptible objects and events of the daily routine defines the essence of the meditative self "that speaks constantly in the presence of the supernatural, that feels the hand of the supernatural upon himself and upon all created things."[8] There is urgent drama in every hour of the day, as the human spirit struggles to sustain its belief in God's grace; and it was the desolation of the soul, cut off from God and crying for a sign of forgiveness, that most engaged Mary Sidney as a writer.

In fact, throughout her *Psalmes,* Mary Sidney tended to view affirmations of grace as precious gifts—awarded only after intense grappling and soul searching—which are in imminent danger of loss because of the incapacity to sustain faith through testing and ordeal. It is the intimate relationship between the supplicant spirit and God which is the focus of her psalms and which is italicized by her style. God as portrayed by her psalmist's prophetic voice is familiar and plainspoken, often brusque and impatient with human foibles:

> Bragg not you braggardes, you your saucy
> horne
> Lift not, lewd mates: no more with heav'ns
> scorne
> Daunce on in wordes your old repyning
> measure.
>
> **(Ps. 75, ll. 10-12)**

Yet, Mary Sidney's God is ever-present at the psalmist's elbow, available to comfort as well as to discipline, and in the following memorable passage from **Psalm 50,** both voices are counterpointed:

> Invoke my name, to me erect thy cries,
> Thy praying plaints, when sorow stopps thy
> waie,
> I will undoe the knott that anguish tyes,
> And thou at peace shalt glorifie my name:
> Mildly the good, God schooleth in this wise,
> But this sharpe check doth to the godlesse
> frame:
>
> How fitts it thee my statutes to report?
> And of my covenant in thy talk to prate
> Hating to live in right reformed sort,
> And leaving in neglect what I relate?
>
> (ll. 35-44)

In this dramatic monologue Sidney transformed the spare assurance of the original—"And call upon me in the time of trouble: so will I hear thee, and thou shalt praise me"[9]—into an active, sympathetic engagement with the tortured spirit of the petitioner: "I will undoe the knott that anguish tyes." The God imaged in these psalms penetrates the recesses of our souls and speaks to us in our own language to make us understand His will.

Mary Sidney not only personalized and dramatized the psalmist's relationship with God but also the internal conflicts of her speaker and, by extension, of all of us. She favored a complicated, conversational syntax studded with questions, exclamations, interruptions, and parenthetical interjections to dramatize her speaker's fits and starts of anxiety, despair, and renewed hope. At times this syntax underlines the speaker's bitterness when estranged from God and His healing grace:

> Shall buried mouthes thy mercies tell?
> Dust and decay
> Thy truth display?
> And shall thy workes of mark
> Shine in the dreadfull dark?
> Thy Justice where oblivions dwell?
>
> **(Ps. 88, ll. 50-54)**

These headlong, tumbling questions measure the psalmist's loss of self-possession, the extent to which he is obsessed with his own suffering and self-importance, unable to wait for or even hear an answer to his complaints. At other times the speaker realizes that he has lost control and chastises himself for presumption: "What speake I? O lett me heare / What he speakes for speake he will" **(Ps. 85, ll. 21-22).** Often the speaker's exclamations underscore the intensity of his pleas for pardon and renewed favor: "Ah! cast me not from thee: take not againe / Thy breathing grace! againe thy comfort send me" (**Ps. 51,** ll. 33-34). In **Psalm 62** Sidney paralleled the gradual change in her speaker's attitude from provisional to total faith in his capacity to withstand all trials, by repeating the line, "Remove I may not, move I may (l. 4), with some crucial syntactical changes: "Remove? O no: not move I may" (l. 20).

Mary Sidney's use of vigorous, colloquial language to personalize God's voice and emphasize His nearness recreates before the reader's eye the spiritual drama of the psalmist in relation to the God who raises and crushes him. An illusion of spontaneity is sustained by her conversational syntax which depicts the conflicts of a mind "quailed in mind-combats manifold" (**Ps. 94,** l. 35), continually revising and reassessing, despairing and then disciplining itself, channeling its frustrated energies into new petitions and assertions of faith. These techniques define Mary Sidney's style—both what she chose to preserve and stress from her sources and models and how she chose to do so.

Not only does a characteristic style emerge from examination of Mary Sidney's versions of the psalms, but it is also possible to sketch an outline of her personality, temperament, tastes, and interests, particularly in those passages in which she permitted herself greater freedom to develop or elaborate on her text, as the voice of the psalmist became distinctively her own. **Psalm 45,** an epithalamium on the marriage of Solomon, is one of the most striking examples of this fusion of translation with personal experience. In it, she drew on her own brief career as lady-in-waiting, during which she witnessed Elizabeth's progress to Kenilworth and the ceremonial welcome to the queen and attendant ladies at Woodstock. Despite the suggestions of Calvin and de Bèze that the lavish pomp and ceremony of this psalm should be contemplated in light of its allegorical significance as the prefiguration of Christ's union with the Church, Sidney chose to elaborate on the pageantry of the original as visual demonstration of the king's power and authority, unrolling the scene as if it were occurring before her eyes during her own timeCone of the most effective ways to achieve a composition of place to dramatize and enliven her material.[10] In her hands **Psalm 45** became an exposition of the divine rights of monarchs as well as the duties that these rights entailed, and she emphasized in it a chain of prerogatives and obligations issuing from God to king to his new queen and the members of his court.

> The king is beyond other men, a reflection of
>   God on earth:
> Fairer art thou than sonnes of mortall race:
>   Because high God hath blessed thee for ay,
> Thie lipps, as springs, doe flowe with
>   speaking grace.
>
>   (ll. 6-8)

Sidney stressed the trappings of power in **Psalm 45,** not just for their magnificence, but because they are resonant symbols in a ceremony revealing the links between God and monarch. The sceptre held in the right hand is an emblem or "ensigne of thie kingly might, / To righteousness is linckt with such a band, / That righteous hand still holds thie Sceptre right" (ll. 22-24). Therefore, it is a constant reminder that the king must dispense justice as well as inspire awe and fear. The formulaic repetition of "righteous" and "righteousness" transforms this psalm into an invocation to God to make this ideal representation of the monarchy a reality on earth. Likewise, with her counterpoised repetition of "terror" and "mortall," emphasizing the two spheres linked in the image of the monarch, Sidney created an awesome incantation of power and majesty:

> Soe that right hande of thine shall teaching
>   tell
> Such things to thee, as well maie terror bring,
>   And terror such, as never erst befell
> To mortall mindes at sight of mortall king.
>
>   (ll. 13-16)

This focus on the king's terrifying power might reflect the underlying insecurity of the Sidney's fortunes at Elizabeth's court. Mary Sidney's father was overworked as Lord President of Wales and Governor and Lord Deputy of Ireland and consistently underpaid with insufficient allowance for his public expenses. The family was often in financial difficulty, to the extent that Henry Sidney was forced to refuse a peerage as too expensive without an accompanying pension or land grant. Philip, of course, was in brief disfavor with Elizabeth for formally protesting her marriage to the Duc d'Alençon and d'Anjou, as was her brother, Robert, for marrying Barbara Gamage over the queen's objections. Lurking always in the Sidney's minds, perhaps, was an uneasiness born out of the past complicity of the families of both Mary Sidney's husband and her mother in the abortive attempt to place Lady Jane Grey on the throne, a history that would make them doubly vulnerable to Elizabeth's whims.

When Mary Sidney describes in **Psalm 45** the position of the royal women in the king's cortege, who "By honoring thee of thee doe honor hold" (l. 34), she gives us a brief glimpse of the dependency of these women on the monarch's good will. Similarly, in a vignette sketching the situation of the queen's maids-of-honor, who "shall on her attend / With such, to whome more favoure shall assigne / In nearer place their happie daies to spend" (ll. 54-56), we are permitted a glance backstage at the politics and ambition governing the hierarchy of court life. As Mary Sidney knew, however, there could be unfortunate consequences to being a queen's favorite. Her mother's devotion in nursing Elizabeth through her bout with smallpox ruined her own appearance and health. At times, also, there was simply not enough "favour" to go around at court, as was attested to by her mother's frequent petitions for less cramped quarters with adequate heating. In this psalm, there are no overt references to the potentially unpleasant consequences attendant on the subordinate position of these women, but certainly the repeated emphasis on the terror inspired by the monarch was rooted in the experiences of Mary Sidney and her family.

Sidney's verse paraphrase of **Psalm 45** is a rich tapestry of interwoven privilege and obligation, as the rights and duties of the king, the noblewomen of the court, and the maids-of-honor are carefully outlined. It is the queen, however, whom the psalmist wishes to instruct by explaining her position, the homage due her by the court and other nations, as well as her corresponding duty to leave behind memories of her family and home to concentrate on producing an heir to guarantee the perpetuation of the hierarchy. Sidney's advice to the queen on how to maintain her husband's love, for example, is practical and unromantic. She should remember that:

> Soe in the king, thie king, a deere delight
> Thie beautie shall both breed, and bredd, maintaine:
> For onlie hee on thee hath lordlie right,
> Him onlie thou with awe must entertaine.
>
> (ll. 41-44)

Beauty, fidelity, and the proper demeanor of awe are the queen's calling cards; appearance and subordination are all. This perspective on marriage recalls the Mary Sidney who conformed to the expectations of her family and the court by marrying, when she was but fifteen years old, Henry Herbert, the second Earl of Pembroke, a man twenty-five years her elder. Yet there is an ambiguity in these lines which suggests a more intimate link between the king and his new bride. If her beauty breeds in him a "deere delight," the syntax of these lines makes it equally possible to read them as saying that it is his delight in her that nourishes her beauty, a beauty based on internal contentment rather than external show. As such, the delight is mutual and reciprocal, and the gold in the "fasshion Arte divine" she wears under her clothes becomes a metaphor for the rare wealth and beauty of her soul.

There is, indeed, an "Arte divine" which fashions **Psalm 45**. The color and magnificence of the pageantry of the original psalm is captured so well that the procession seems to advance slowly before the reader; however, Mary Sidney was always careful to place the pomp and material splendor within the perspective of God's decrees, as but symbols of His righteousness and the ordination of His monarch over earth. This monarch's rule, reflective of God's justice, is nevertheless a rule over fallible humans, and as such requires a constant show of strength to instill a terror which then makes possible "justice, truth, and meekness." There is a tough-minded political pragmatism informing Sidney's elaboration of the following lines from the Book of Common Prayer: "Thy arrows are very sharp, and the people shall be subdued unto thee: even in the midst among the King's enemies" (p. 105). Her version of these lines gives a Machiavellian slant on how to maintain power:

> Sharpe are thie shaftes to cleave their hartes in twaine
> Whose heads do cast thy Conquestes to withstand
> Good cause to make the meaner people faine
> With willing hartes to undergoe thie hand.
>
> (ll. 17-20)

Here is revealed an aristocratic contempt for the people's capacity for political judgment; if the masses are to be content, "with willing hartes" to be ruled, it can only be as a result of a grim demonstration of power. Sidney knew that the enemies of the state, when subjected to its will, always "frown in heart" although "they fawn in sight" (**Ps. 66,** l. 8).

Sidney's version of **Psalm 45** is one of her most inspired imitations, as well as one of her most independent. Her emphasis is on the problem of power, how to reconcile God's mandate with the realities of an imperfect earth. She herself was no stranger to the difficulty of distinguishing between the use and abuse of power. As a result of her husband's poor health in the mid-1590s, Mary Sidney gradually undertook more and more responsibility for the management of his estate. For example, in a letter written August 3, 1602, to Sir Robert Cecil, she enclosed an exasperated, yet thoroughly practical assessment of the appropriate punishment suited to the different behavior of two rebellious bailiffs:

> Now for this sedisious beggerly wretche whom it pleasd yow to bring downe under my mercy & now seemes most penetent, I must confess it were no conquest to his utter ruein & yet thinke it not fitt to take his present submission to retorne him to be disposed of according to yr will, if please yow in regard of his missery to be released of his imprisonment. The other his barbarus demeanur hath bin so odious & therein so obstinate as this hand may in no reason consent to become any meane for his release till by a more thorow fealing of his fowle offence others lykewise will be better tought by his smart. . . . [11]

The blunt self-assurance of her statement, her stern invective, reminiscent of the scornful voice of the prophet in her *Psalmes,* demonstrate a show of power essential for a woman in her position. These lines reveal an experienced pragmatism. She remains suspicious of the seeming penitence of the first prisoner, but the appearance of reform is sufficient for her purposes. Rather, it is the obstinate unregeneracy of the second prisoner that is most threatening to peace and discipline because it poses a potentially dangerous example for others.

If publicly Mary Sidney was a tough-minded pragmatist, a firm supporter of the divine right of monarchs and the aristocratic traditions of government, we must remember that privately Mary Sidney chose to live at Wilton, in retirement from the court. Certainly she knew firsthand the sordid opportunism and factionalism that defined life at court, and it would seem that she chose to withdraw from the arena, arranging her life at Wilton so she could use her hospitality and influence to attract the fine minds of her society and through them affect the literature of her age. It was not just weariness and intellectual ambition that motivated her retirement from court, however. The privacy of her life at Wilton enabled the concentrated meditation that prepares the soul for the "searching sight" of God: "Search me, my God, and prove my hart, / Examyne me, and try my thought" (**Ps. 139,** ll. 85-86). The discipline of private prayer and meditation, far from the distractions and intrigues of court life, schools the soul to submit itself as naturally and unself-consciously as a child to God's examination.

One facet of this private Mary Sidney shines through in her images of birth and child care. This comparison did not originate with her, of course,[12] but Sidney invested a unique tenderness in her use of it which renders those sections of the *Psalmes* softly luminous. She never forgot the reality of the experience behind the comparison. Even in the midst of a long passage calling for the destruction of David's enemies, her tone of relentless indignation is momentarily softened by the pathos of her stillbirth comparison:

> So make them melt as the dishowsed snaile
> Or as the Embrio, whose vitall band
> Breakes er it holdes and formlesse eyes do
>   faile
> To see the sun, though brought to lightfull
>   land.
>
>   (Ps. 58, ll. 22-25)

The specific details of "vitall band" and "formlesse eyes," as well as the beautifully alliterative "lightfull land" in the explorer image, were added by Sidney to heighten the tragedy of a baby brought senseless out of the womb. As the only one of three daughters to survive past childhood, and as a mother who lost her own daughter, Katherine, at the age of three, it was perhaps impossible for her to exploit such a metaphor merely as a display of wit.

Similarly, there is an authenticity in her amplification of the standard image of God as a merciful father in **Psalm 103**: "Yea like as a father pitieth his own children: even so is the Lord merciful unto them that fear him" (BCP, p. 243). The father she envisions is fond of His refractory child:

> And looke how much
>   The neerly touching touch
> The father feeles towards his sonne most
>   deare,
>   Affects his hart,
>   At Ev'ry froward part
>   Plaid by his child:
>   Soe mercifull, soe mild,
> Is he to them that beare him awfull feare.
>
>   (ll. 57-64)

The charming and clever polyptoton, "touching touch," has an incantatory, yearning quality, capturing the tug of parental love by conjuring the image of a father holding out his arms to a toddling child.

In **Psalm 139,** in one of Mary Sidney's strongest, most arresting stanzas, the development of the fetus is used as an image of the conflation of spiritual and physical growth. The theme of the psalm is God's absolute knowledge of men and women. Stanza after stanza reveals yet another layer of God's penetrating understanding until the very formation of the body in the womb is laid bare to His scrutiny:

> Thou, how my back was beam-wise laid,
>   And raftring of my ribbs, dost know:
>   Know'st ev'ry point
>   Of bone and joynt,
>   How to this whole these partes did grow,
> In brave embrod'ry faire araid,
>   Though wrought in shopp both dark and
>   low.
>
>   (ll. 50-56)

The image of the embroidery wrought in a dark shop came from suggestions made in the commentaries of Calvin and de Bèze, but the taut, tortured extension of "back was beam-wise laid" and "raftring of my ribbs" was original to Sidney. Calvin mused upon the "inconceivable skill which appears in the formation of the human body,"[13] inspiring Sidney to reenact the stress and strain of growth. The images are ambiguous in that they suggest both the expanding pressure on the ribs and back of the mother, as well as the developing fetus. Her choice of the embroidery comparison suggests the texture of sinew and muscle, the woven skin that covers and knits "ev'ry point / of bone and joynt." The "inconceivable skill," the miraculous workings of God on earth, are described in terms of a painful distension of body and spirit, naked before God's scrutiny.

Mary Sidney's version in **Psalm 51** of the psalmist's meditation on his own conception centers around the repetition of the word "cherish," chosen from Calvin's commentary. She then added a gloss from de Bèze found in *Chrestiennes Méditations* (1582)[14] in order to capture the spiritual dilemma posed by parenthood:

> My mother, loe! when I began to be,
>   Conceaving me, with me did sinne
>   conceave:
> And as with living heate she cherisht me,
>   Corruption did like cherishing receave.
>
>   (ll. 15-18)

Here the standard declaration of original sin voiced in the Book of Common Prayer, "Behold, I was shapen in wickedness: and in sin hath my mother conceived me" (p. 119), is transformed into a striking portrait of frustrated maternal energy that is not only helpless to save the child from sin, but actually generates the child's fate. The instinctive animalism of "living heate" emphasizes our sensual origins, while the alliterative connection between "conceave," "corruption," and "cherishing" underlines the irony that this physical bond between mother and child reflects the spiritual peril that is our birthright from conception.

Perhaps it was Mary Sidney's commitment to a poetry which sought to reconcile our imperfect origins with our spiritual aspirations that led her to develop a style juxtaposing a sweet lyricism celebrating the inexhaustible bounty of nature with a plain realism reminding us of our mortal roots. She gives the commonplace figure of Mother Earth some new twists:

> Earthe, greate with yong, her longing doth not
>   lose,
> The hopfull ploughman hopeth not in
>   vayne. . .
> All things in breef, that life in life maintaine,
> From Earths old bowells fresh and yongly
>   growes.
>
>   **(Ps. 104,** ll. 43-48)

The image of the earth as an aging mother, once again pregnant, underscores the miraculous renewal of spring and suggests the potential for regeneration in all of us. In **Psalm 65** she chose her words carefully to convey the exuberant vitality, as well as the barren and withered source of that new life which only God can quicken. The antithetic "buried seed" and "yelding grave" epitomize the resurrection of the land:

> Thy eie from heav'n this land beholdeth,
>   Such fruitfull dewes down on it rayning,
> That, storehowse-like her lap enfoldeth
>   Assured hope of plowmans gayning.

> Thy flowing streames her drought doe temper
>   so,
> That buried seed through yelding grave doth
>   grow.
>
>   (ll. 31-36)

This cycle of birth and death can be made explicit, as in the above example, or can be merely suggested: "Even then shall swell / His blossoms fatt and faire, / When aged rinde the stock shall beare" (**Ps. 92,** ll. 40-42). Here the opposition of "fatt and faire" prepares the reader for the "aged rinde" that generates the flower. Similarly, in the description of Jehovah, "By whom the rayne from cloudes to dropp assign'd / Supples the clodds of sommer-scorched fields" (**Ps. 147,** ll. 25-26), the blunt force of "clodds" and the ominous threat of "scorched" attest to the glory of God who causes this dead land to be fertile, and yet serve as reminders that this soft abundance is ephemeral. The ample wisdom of these counterpoised images reflects, perhaps, Mary Sidney's hard-earned ability to come to terms with private sorrow. While writing these psalms, she was looking back on the deaths of her daughter, father, mother, and brothers Philip and Thomas, as well as working through the progressive decline of her husband's health—losses which were counterbalanced by the births of her children. By alternating sweetly alliterative language with the plain and vulgar diction of "fatt," "aged rinde," "bowells," "grave," and "clodds," Sidney played one vocabulary off the other to reveal the inseparability of life from death, natural beauty from aged and gnarled roots.

Throughout her *Psalmes* Mary Sidney contrasted the foolish pretensions of earthly endeavors with the wise paradoxes of heavenly wisdom. This theme is developed most clearly in her legal and business metaphors which were undoubtedly inspired by direct experience in managing her husband's estate. In her handling of this strain of imagery, the practical knowledge of the public woman was reinterpreted in light of the wisdom gleaned from private meditation, usually to emphasize the inadequacy of a merely legalistic point of view. Her comparisons continually remind us that this is how affairs are conducted on an imperfect earth, rather than in heaven. God's covenant with us is referred to as a "league" in which the land of Canaan is promised "in fee," yet we are reminded that the limited scope implied by such contractual arrangements cannot encompass the omnipotence and omnipresence of God:

> The daies bright guide, the nightes pale
>   governesse
> Shall claime no longer lease of their enduring:
>   Whome I behold as heav'nly wittnesses
> In tearmlesse turnes, my tearmlesse truth
>   assuring.
>
>   **(Ps. 89,** ll. 93-96)

"Tearmlesse" refers to both timelessness as well as freedom from restrictive legal and financial conditions. Day and night serve not as earthly witnesses to a testament of our inevitable decay, but rather as "heav'nly wittnesses" of the eternal glory of God. A lease, of course, cannot designate "tearmlesse truth," and all our contracts and stipulations only demonstrate our foolish distrust that would make conditions with that which must be unconditional.

Mary Sidney employed a major strain of antithetical repetition throughout her translation of the **Psalms** which contrasts the limitations of human understanding with the infinite power and wisdom of God: "O Lord, whose grace no limits comprehend; / Sweet Lord, whose mercies stand from measure free" (**Ps. 51,** ll. 1-2). Human arrogance "would in boundes that boundless pow'r contain" (**Ps. 78,** l. 128), but God always reminds us that "speciall bonds have bound" us (**Ps. 145,** l. 32), that we have a clearly defined position with accompanying duties outlined in the universal plan:

> All formed, framed, founded so,
> Till ages uttmost date
> They place retaine, they order know,
> They keepe their first estate.
>   (**Ps. 148,** ll. 21-24)

The emphatic resonance of Sidney's alliteration and parallel syntax, as well as the legal, political, and class connotations of estate, would seem to suggest a confining rigor to God's arrangements on earth, but that is true only from the human perspective narrowed by a mind accustomed to operating in terms of leases and contracts. The best indication of God's grace is the free acceptance of His will; the faithful soul does not feel straitened but rather chooses freely to occupy the ordained place: "Who uncontrol'd / Sure league with him doe hold, / And doe his lawes not only understand" (*Ps. 103,* ll. 78-80). Once again legal imagery is used ironically to reveal its own limitations; the only genuine league is that which is "uncontrol'd." This pattern of imagery urges us to learn the distinctions between an earthly contract and our covenant with God. The one is null and void upon our death, at which time we lose all that we vainly sought to preserve as our own under its protection. The other is eternal and our only security against oblivion.

Throughout Mary Sidney's *Psalmes,* therefore, we find a sophisticated use of sacred paradox that attempts to illuminate the unknowable and yet maintain the integrity of God's mystery, to emphasize both the potential and the limit of human knowledge. Sidney chose her comparisons carefully to remind us that the soft abundance of our world can scorch and shrivel in a moment, that it is wrung from withered bowels, that the cherishing animal warmth of our mother's womb incubates the seeds of our sinfulness, and that our terms,

contracts, and leases but reflect our powerlessness and the transitory nature of all earthly goods and arrangements. These paradoxes underline the folly of all human attachments and measure the vast distance between earth and heaven.

This distance is bridged in a handful of Mary Sidney's psalms where we find the peace and serenity, the simple, hopeful confidence of the soul in concert with the universe. These psalms are distinguished by a simple eloquence that is at once subdued and ecstatic:

> Looke how the sunne, soe shall his name
>   remayne;
>   As that in light, so this in glory one:
> All glories that, at this all lights shall stayne:
>   Nor that shall faile, nor this be overthrowne.
>   The dwellers all
>   Of earthly ball
> In hym shall hold them blest:
>   As one that is
>   Of perfect blisse
> A patterne to the rest.
>   (**Ps. 72,** ll. 71-80)

The preponderance of one-syllable words joined with the lack of qualifiers ("earthly" and "perfect" are counterpoised as the only two descriptive adjectives) create an aura in which single words are able to convey absolute meaning, reflecting the oneness of the divine spirit. There is no need here for the involved syntax, the paradoxes and wordplay that usually characterize Mary Sidney's writing. Such displays of wit are inappropriate and unnecessary in those rare moments when faith is spontaneous rather than labored. In such moments the infused state of contemplation which reveals the "single viewe of the eternall veritye"[15] supersedes the self-conscious, analytic process of meditation, as wordplay and extended comparisons can only measure the extent to which we approximate rather than know the ways of God. In this transcendent phase, reliance on the mere "Wisdom of Words" obscures the stunning simplicity of the "Word of Wisdom."[16]

It is Mary Sidney's commitment to "the wandering voices of the fallen world,"[17] however, which marks her greatest poetic achievement. Her best passages dramatize the dilemma of her speaker, who represents all of us, sinking in an apprehension of unworthiness, yet calling for a renewal of special favor from God. Her psalms are centered in the world as we know it; God speaks to us in our own words, but too often we do not hear and our pleas to Him are confused and troubled. The very effort we make to understand God's will marks our failure to do so, since such understanding must come simply and naturally without effort. Education can be inimical to wisdom and obscure the unitive way to special grace, blinding the restless spirit to the correspondences underlying diversity, the essential rightness of the way things are. However, Mary Sidney's dedication to her verse translations of the Psalms is a testimony to her faith in human effort in general and in our capacity for self-education in particular. During her many years working with the psalms, she taught herself both how to write poetry and how to speak to God. In fact, it is her insistence on the validity of applying to the psalms knowledge and understanding gained from study and personal experience that makes them exemplary models for private meditation. In the fusion of Mary Sidney's voice with that of the psalmist, the process of education and the purpose of wisdom coincide. Wisdom is gained neither by the suppression of individual energy and intelligence, nor by a vainglorious display of these qualities, but rather by an abiding appreciation that God's spirit works through individual talent which reflects the capacity of all humankind.

Notes

[1] For a complete discussion of Mary Sidney's manuscripts, as well as speculation that she revised some psalms as late as 1611, after publication of the King James Version, see Gary F. Waller, *Mary Sidney, Countess of Pembroke: A Critical Study of Her Writings and Literary Milieu* (Salzburg: Univ. of Salzburg, 1979), pp. 152-78. For further discussion of the variety of stanzaic and metrical forms in Mary Sidney's *Psalmes,* see pp. 190-203.

[2] Barbara K. Lewalski, *Protestant Poetics and the Seventeenth-Century Religious Lyric* (Princeton: Princeton Univ. Press, 1979), pp. 234, 245. See, in particular, her discussion of the Sidneian psalms as "re-revelations."

[3] Philip Sidney, "Defence of Poesie," in *The Prose Works of Sir Philip Sidney,* ed. Albert Feuillerat (Cambridge: Cambridge Univ. Press, 1962), III, 7.

[4] Jean Calvin, *Psalmes of David and Others,* trans. Arthur Golding (London, 1571). David was assumed to prefigure Christ and to be dimly aware of his antecedent role. As such he spoke in the person of Christ as well as himself, and ultimately, as a representative voice for the congregation of the Church.

[5] For detailed discussion of the multiple voices of the psalmist, as well as the conflation of translator with psalmist, see Lewalski, pp. 39-53 and 231-50.

[6] Mary Sidney, "Psalm 104," in *The Psalms of Sir Philip Sidney and the Countess of Pembroke,* ed. J. C. A. Rathmell (New York: New York Univ. Press, 1963), p. 244, l. 101. All other references to Mary Sidney's psalms will come from this edition and will be indicated in the text by psalm and line numbers.

[7] Philip Sidney, "Psalm 26," in *The Poems of Sir Philip Sidney,* ed. William A. Ringler, Jr. (Oxford: Clarendon Press, 1962), l. 33. All other references to Philip Sidney's psalms will come from this edition and will be indicated by psalm and line numbers in the text.

[8] Louis Martz, *Poetry of Meditation* (New Haven: Yale Univ. Press, 1954), p. 324.

[9] Miles Coverdale, ed., *The Prayer Book Version from the Great Bible 1539-41,* in *Our Prayer Book Psalter,* ed. Ernest Clapton (London: Society for Promoting Christian Knowledge, 1934), p. 117. All other references to this version of the psalms will come from this edition and will be indicated by page number and the abbreviation BCP for Book of Common Prayer in the text.

[10] A technique of concrete visualization of a scene to enable extended meditation on its significance. See Martz, pp. 27-30.

[11] Salisbury MSS, Cecil Papers, holograph, as quoted in Frances Berkeley Young, *Mary Sidney: Countess of Pembroke* (London: David Nutt, 1912), p. 97.

[12] For example, Philip Sidney used it in his dedication included in the 1590 *Arcadia,* in which he referred to his work as "a baby I could well find in my harte, to cast out in some desert of forgetfulness" and a fetus that "if it had not ben in some way delivered, would have growen a monster." Feuillerat, I, 3.

[13] Jean Calvin, *Commentary on the Book of Psalms,* trans. Rev. James Anderson (Edinburgh, 1846), V, 215.

[14] Text estab. by Mario Richter (Geneva: Droz, 1964), p. 74. "Deslors mon Dieu, que ceste povre creature fut conceue, la corruption y estoit attachee: deslors, di-je, que ma mere m'ayant conceu m'eschauffa en son ventre, le vice y estoit au dedans de moy comme las racine . . ." Also, trans. I. Stubbs (London: Chirstopher Barker, 1582).

[15] Luis de la Puente, *Meditations upon the Mysteries of our Holie Faith. . .,* trans. John Heigham (St. Omer, 1619), I, 29, as quoted in Martz, p. 16.

[16] These terms were used to distinguish the Anglican style of preaching with its emphasis on wit, classical allusions, and extended comparisons, from the Puritan style, which concentrated on the Scriptures without elaboration.

[17] David Kalstone, Introd., *The Selected Poetry and Prose of Sidney* (New York: Signet, 1970), p. xxx. Although Kalstone is referring to the flexibility of Philip Sidney's poetic voice in *Astrophel and Stella,* these words also apply to Mary Sidney's *Psalmes* which dramatize the same sort of perplexed, divided sensibil-

ity on the part of the religious soul seeking union with God as that oof the lover portrayed in *Astrophel and Stella.*

Beth Wynne Fisken (essay date 1990)

SOURCE: "To the Angell Spirit. . . Mary Sidney's Entry into the World of Words," in *The Renaissance Englishwoman in Print: Counterbalancing the Canon,* edited by Anne M. Haselkorn and Betty S. Travitsky, The University of Massachusetts Press, 1990, pp. 263-75.

[*In the following essay, Fisken discerns a strain of subversiveness in "To the Angell Spirit," which she describes as "the disjunction between Mary Sidney's internalized definitions of her role as a woman and her burgeoning ambition as a writer."*]

"To the Angell spirit . . ." is one of just four known original poems by Mary Sidney.[1] The bulk of her writing fell within the parameters of translation and religious paraphrase which were considered culturally acceptable literary activities for women during her time. However, her verse-paraphrases of Psalms 44-150, which completed a project initially conceived and begun by her brother Philip Sidney would be more rightly termed "imitations" in the classical sense, as they surpass the literalism of her translations of Robert Garnier's *Antonie* and Philippe de Mornay's *Discourse of Life and Death.* In Mary Sidney's verse-translations of the Psalms, she conflated the voice of the psalmist with her own by adding original comparisons and elaborations which reconstructed the matter of the Psalms in a style and context that would illuminate the issues of her contemporary society as well as have personal application to her own spiritual welfare. For her imagery she drew from her public experiences as a woman of responsibility, influence, and power (first as daughter to Henry Sidney, lord deputy of Ireland, and as a youthful lady-in-waiting at Elizabeth's court, and then as wife to the earl of Pembroke). She also drew upon her private perceptions as a woman and a mother to transform her paraphrases of the Psalms into individual exercises in meditation.[2]

Nevertheless, in these verse-translations of the Psalms, despite the inventiveness of portions of her writing, Mary Sidney was still working within the limits of literary ambition observed by such scholarly predecessors as Margaret Beaufort, Margaret Roper and Mary Bassett, Anna (Cooke) Bacon and Elizabeth (Cooke) Russell, and Queens Mary Tudor and Elizabeth, who undertook religious translations, as well as Queen Catherine Parr and Anne Wheathill, who wrote original prayers and meditations.[3] Even the more liberal sixteenth-century humanist attitudes toward women's aspirations as scholars and writers (exemplified in

Richard Hyrde's popular translation of Juan Luis Vives's conduct book, *The Instruction of a Christian Woman*) recommended private classical and religious instruction to keep women occupied and focused on the chaste and virtuous life, but cautioned women not to undertake any public displays of learning (including original writing) because their supposed innate moral instability might lead others astray. A woman was encouraged, rather, to copy the moral sentiments of male writers or perhaps to translate such passages from English to Latin, but not to add to or evaluate what she wrote.[4] Such a plan of exercises would inevitably lead women to internalize these prescribed limits and restrict themselves to translation of male religious writing as the appropriate outlet for their learning. As Mary Ellen Lamb explains, to do otherwise "was to risk the charge, perhaps even by their own consciences, of being foolish, indiscreet, vain, and even irreligious, all attributes of loose women" (115).

To go beyond these tacit and internalized boundaries to write original verse on nonreligious subjects, to enter the lists of declared poets, had been attempted by few women previous to Mary Sidney.[5] It is scarcely surprising, then, that her four known original poems were rooted in what Margaret Hannay calls "the usual feminine genres of dedications and epitaphs" (149), which emphasized her temporal subordination to Elizabeth and her creative and emotional obligation to the memory of her brother Philip. To dare to write poetry at all was an act of unprecedented boldness that could only be excused by the guise of humility necessitated by the conventions of her subject matter.

Of these four poems, her finest and most ambitious effort was **"To the Angell spirit of the most excellent Sir Phillip Sidney,"** an elegiac lament dedicated to her brother's memory, which was appended to a scribal manuscript of their verse-translations of the Psalms. As Margaret Hannay suggests, the conjunction of this poem with the admonitory dedication, "To the Thrice Sacred Queen Elizabeth," contained a strong partisan religious and political statement concealed under the conventional humility *topos,* both poems contributing to an ongoing campaign, the canonization of Philip Sidney as a type of martyred Protestant saint. In this way, Mary Sidney covertly reminded the queen (without directly challenging or criticizing her) of the central role she should play in the establishment of Protestantism in Europe as well as in England (149-65). Yet this poem also simultaneously reveals and conceals Mary Sidney's intense personal ambitions as a poet as well as these public aspirations as a political mediator. That such ambition is not shown directly but rather is deflected by the conventional stances of apology and humility is a reflection of her internalization of cultural strictures against women speaking and writing in public modes, which were assumed to be, morally, exclusively masculine domains. As such, **"To the**

Angell spirit . . ." is quietly subversive on a private as well as a public level.

As Mary Ellen Lamb describes them, epitaphs generally "provided non-threatening outlets for their author's learning and poetic skills" (120) because they reinforced the writer's central womanly functions of devotion and dependence as defined by her culture. In *The Triumph of Death* Gary Waller has described **"To the Angell spirit . . ."** as an intensely personal expression of grief, in particular focusing on Mary Sidney's exaggerated Neoplatonic terms of praise, agitated syntax, and the use of the cryptic phrase "strange passions" as indications of her neurotic attachment to her brother's memory (50-53). Indeed, all of Mary Sidney's literary endeavor centered on her brother's example, whether it was editing his work, translating a play in the classical tradition he approved, penning a translation of a work by de Mornay, his personal friend (perhaps as a companion piece to his own incomplete translation, *Of the Trewnes of the Christian Religion*), finishing his verse-translations of the Psalms, or composing poetry in his memory.[6] Since Mary Sidney's writing was a daunting act of courage for a woman of her time, however, it is readily understandable why she would anchor her efforts in her brother's example; as Waller himself points out, she had available in the successive stages of her brother's work a literary model from which she could teach herself how to write. By first editing Philip's works and translating those of others and by then revising the final irregular stanzas of some of Philip's psalms, Mary Sidney taught herself the art of composition and the discipline of revision (as is apparent in her own heavily emended manuscripts), which eventually enabled her to develop the skill to experiment with an astonishing variety of stanzaic and metrical forms as well as the self-confidence to create a poetic voice distinct from that of her brother. Perhaps, in part, the fervent devotion voiced in **"To the Angell spirit . . ."** is a reaction to the combination of gratitude and discomfort she felt at having used his example to find her own means of expression. It is not surprising that in this ambitious poem, which resembles the best passages of her *Psalmes,* Mary Sidney found it necessary to camouflage the assertiveness of her style with the self-abnegation of her subject matter. That her theme of humility and dedication to her brother's memory seems overstated is a measure, perhaps, of the giddiness she felt at the height of her own aspiration, the shame at her own "presumption too too bold," and her sincere and intense gratitude for her brother's model of excellence that enabled her to write as herself.[7] Although this bold and elaborately constructed tribute focused on her artistic and emotional dependence on her brother, in the act of writing it she most completely realized her independence from his influence. In **"To the Angell spirit . . ."** the disjunction between Mary Sidney's internalized definitions of her role as a woman and her burgeoning ambitions as a writer is most apparent.

This disjunction between the assertiveness of her form and the humility of her tone is most evident in Mary Sidney's audacious breach in stanzaic integrity between stanzas 5 and 6:

> And sithe it hath no further scope to goe,
>   nor other purpose but to honor thee,
>   Thee in thy workes where all the Graces bee,
> As little streames with all their all doe flowe
>   to their great sea, due tribute's gratefull fee:
>   so press my thoughts my burthened thoughtes in mee,
> To pay the debt of Infinits I owe
>
> To thy great worth; exceeding Nature's store,
>   wonder of men, sole borne perfection's kinde,
>   Phoenix thou wert, so rare thy fairest minde
> Heav'nly adorned . . .
>
>   (Ll. 29-39)

This stanzaic rupture reenacts the bold leap of her imagination in an attempt to fuse her efforts with her brother's divine inspiration to complete his work and thereby honor his memory. However, this break in stanza only serves to underscore her central theme of humility as it records her failure to scale the wall of "Infinits." She is left mourning in the mutable world of debts and burdens, unable to either achieve or adequately express even a dim reflection of her brother's worth, "sole borne perfection's kinde." Piling superlative upon superlative does not adequately convey her wonder, as the subsequent defensive insistence that these epithets are not exaggerated indicates:

> . . . Earth justlye might adore,
>   where truthfull praise in highest glorie shin'de:
>   For there alone was praise to truth confin'de;
> And where but there, to live for evermore?
>
>   (Ll. 39-42)

Her separation from her brother is absolute and irrevocable and she is left groping in the darkness of her own grief and failure: "Where thou art fixt among thy fellow lights: / my day put out, my life in darkenes cast" (ll. 57-58).

This daring breach of stanzaic integrity as well as the use of stellar imagery in this poem prefigured Ben Jonson's Pindaric ode to Cary and Morison, in which he separated his name between two stanzas to demonstrate his own attempt to re-create "that full joy" known by Morison, who "leap'd the present age, / Possest with holy rage, / To see that bright eternall Day."[8] Jonson also used astronomical metaphors to describe the division between the two friends:

> In this bright *Asterisme:*
> Where it were friendships schisme,
> (Were not his *Lucius* long with us to tarry)
> To separate these twi-
> Lights, the *Dioscuri;*
> And keepe the one halfe from his *Harry*
> But fate doth so alternate the designe,
> Whilst that in heav'n, this light on earth must
>   shine.
>
> (Ll. 89-96)

The brief separation of "twi- / Lights" repeats the major break between *"Ben / Jonson"* (ll. 84-85), reinforcing the theme of "friendships schisme." Stellar imagery in elegiac verse was not uncommon during Mary Sidney's time. In fact, those who eulogized her also included this strain of imagery, perhaps in emulation of her tribute to her brother, as is seen in this example from the "Extra Sonnets of Henry Lok":

> Whereby you equall honor do attain,
> To that extinguisht lamp of heavenly light,
> Who now no doubt doth shine midst angels
>   bright,
> While your faire starre makes clear our
>   darkened sky.[9]

Although this type of imagery was not original, Ben Jonson and Mary Sidney were allied in their sophisticated development of variations on the conventions. Mary Sidney tested one vocabulary against another; she was alternately awkward and eloquent, simple and ornate, in an attempt to bridge earth and heaven, much as Jonson's style was, at turns, joking and poignant, proverbial and obscure. That Jonson was familiar with Mary Sidney's verse-paraphrases of the Psalms is demonstrated by the fact that he reminded Drummond of Hawthornden that some of them were written by Philip. Whether he knew or was influenced by **"To the Angell spirit . . ."** remains an intriguing but unanswered question.

If during the early portion of her career Mary Sidney used her brother's writing as a model for her revisions, it is clear from a comparison of an earlier version of **"To the Angell spirit . . ."** with the final one that she used the example of her own ***Psalmes*** to help her improve that piece. Gradually during the process of writing her ***Psalmes,*** she developed a distinctive style that mirrored the internal conflicts of the psalmist, the fits and starts of anxiety, despair, and renewed hope, the successive stages of doubt and reaffirmation. In order to capture the intensity of the speaker's dilemma, she used a complicated conversational syntax, studded with questions, interruptions, parenthetical interjections and exclamations. (**Psalm 51**, 34-35; **Psalm 62**, 19-20; **Psalm 85**, 212-13; and **Psalm 102**, 34-36 are just a few striking examples of this characteristic syntax.) To generate a similar illusion of spontaneity in **"To the Angell spirit . . ."** she added parenthetical interjections to stanzas 4 and 8 when she revised. In stanza 4 the change from "Behold! O that thou were now to behold, / This finisht long perfections part begun" (ll. 36-37)[10] to "Yet here behold (oh wert thou to behold!) / this finish't now, thy matchlesse Muse begunne" (ll. 22-23) strengthens the overall rhetorical strategy of the poem which is conceived as a direct address to her dead brother, both as a commemoration of his genius and as an apology for her contributions. She seems to be thinking out loud, visualizing her brother standing before her, and as a result the poem seems less formal, more sincerely personal and immediate. In stanza 8, with the addition of "Truth I invoke (who scorne else where to move / or here in ought my blood should partialize)" (ll. 50-51), the illusion created is that of the speaker correcting herself, anxious to speak the truth as well as invoke it. She changed stanza 11 which originally read:

> Had divers so spar'd that life (but life) to
>   frame
> The rest: alas such losse the world hath
>   nought
> Can equall it, nor O more grievance brought
> Yet what remaines must ever crowne thy
>   name
>
> (Ll. 67-70)

to:

> Had Heav'n so spar'd the life of life to frame
>   the rest? But ah! such losse hath this world
>   ought
> can equall it? or which like greevance
>   brought?
> Yet there will live thy ever praised name.
>
> (Ll. 74-77)

Her alteration of syntax to the exclamatory and interrogative modes recreates her agitation at the memory of her brother's death. The return to the declarative mode in the last line serves as a reconfirmation of her faith in the immortality of his fame, enabling her to regain self-possession.

In addition to these changes in syntax, Mary Sidney's other revisions demonstrate an increased self-confidence as a poet, a new willingness to take risks with more elaborate imagery, as is seen in her extension of the comparison of Philip's works with "goodly buildings" that become "Immortall Monuments" of his fame (ll. 64-75) and the baroque comparison of the ink in which her psalms are written with the "bleeding veines of never dying love," the lines of verse becoming "wounding lynes of smart / sadd Characters indeed of simple love" (ll. 80-82). Her experience with patterns of alliteration in her *Psalmes* enabled her to conceive the felicitous phrase: "Nor can enough in world of words unfold" (l. 28).

Although this "world of words" is a fallen one, inadequate to express the "strange passions" of her heart, her "sences striken dumbe" (ll. 45-46), still it has seized her imagination. It was her brother who first gave her the key to unlock that masculine world:

> To thee pure sprite, to thee alone's addres't
>> this coupled worke, by double int'rest thine:
>> First rais'de by thy blest hand, and what is
>> mine
> inspird by thee, thy secrett power imprest.
>> (Ll. 1-4)

And it is her gratitude for the possibility of the poem itself that joins with her grief to fuel the intensity of her praise, a praise that will foster his fame, just as his example nurtured her as the maker of that praise.

The interlocking rhyme scheme employed within the stanzas composed of seven iambic pentameter lines seems admirably suited to the subject matter of the poem. Each stanza has only two end rhymes, one of which forms double couplets in lines 2 and 3 and lines 5 and 6, mirroring the joint undertaking of Mary and Philip in their verse-translations of the psalms:

> this coupled worke, by double int'rest thine:
> First rais'de by thy blest hand, and what is
> mine
>> (Ll. 2-3)

and Mary's avowal of absolute devotion to her brother:

> if love and zeale such error ill-become
> 'tis zealous love, Love which hath never done.
>> (Ll. 26-27)

The other rhyme is delayed and separated by these couplets, however, occupying lines 1, 4, and 7 of the stanza, reflecting the ultimate separation of the two:

> I can no more: Deare Soule I take my leave;
>> Sorrowe still strives, would mount thy
>> highest sphere
>> presuming so just cause might meet thee
>> there,
> Oh happie chaunge! could I so take my leave.
>> (Ll. 88-91)

The return to the exact rhyme "leave" after the couplet resembles the tolling of a bell, recalling Mary from her futile attempt at spiritual reunion with her brother. There

is a pivotal irony to the word "leave," as it represents both her farewell to Philip and her anticipated death that will enable her to rejoin him eventually.

In combination with her interlocking rhyme, Mary Sidney constructed a latticework of interlacing allegiances throughout the poem. Her acknowledgment of her brother's inspiration is expressed in words traditionally reserved for God:

> So dar'd my Muse with thine it selfe
> combine,
>> as mortall stuffe with that which is divine,
> Thy lightning beames give lustre to the rest.
>> (Ll. 5-7)

Just as her brother was both a creation and a reflection of God's perfect will, so her brother's poetry was analogous to divine creation: "Thee in thy workes where all the Graces bee." Therefore, in paying tribute to her brother she was also paying tribute to her God because Philip embodied his "Maker's praise" (stanzas 5, 9). Likewise, the ambition that fired the two of them to write their *Psalmes* was not arrogant, but worshipful, sanctioned by God:

> That heaven's King may daigne his owne
> transform'd
>> in substance no, but superficiall tire
>> by thee put on; to praise, not to aspire
> To, those high Tons, so in themselves
> adorn'd,
>> which Angells sing in their caelestiall Quire.
>> (Ll. 8-12)[11]

The uneasy defensiveness of these lines has a double origin. First, Mary Sidney must clear herself from the charge of blasphemy for daring to undertake this sacred task of paraphrasing the Psalms, despite Paul's injunction: "But I suffer not a woman to teach, nor to usurp authority over the man, but to be in silence."[12] Not only did Mary Sidney choose not to be silent (although she limited her public voice to passing her manuscript around among a select audience rather than publishing it to reach a larger one), but she also chose to speak on a level with her brother. Therefore, second, she must defend herself not only from being thought presumptuous for translating the Psalms, but also for finishing her brother's work:

> Pardon (oh blest soule) presumption too too
> bold:
>> if love and zeale such error ill-become
>> 'tis zealous love, Love which hath never
>> done,
> Nor can enough in world of words unfold.
>> (Ll. 25-28)

To escape such criticism she fashioned an elaborate Chinese box of obligations, placing herself as the last, the smallest, and the least significant in the series. Mary Sidney was inspired by her brother, who emulated David, "thy Kinglie Prophet," in re-creating the "high Tons . . . which Angells sing in their caelestiall Quire" in praise of "heaven's King" (ll. 14, 11, 8). The traditional religious hierarchy in which the woman takes the lowest seat is invoked in this poem to recreate a lineage of poetic inspiration with Mary Sidney the apologetic inheritor. Her confirmation of subordination and inferiority, however, is also a statement of affirmation and poetic purpose. As a woman she must sit at the end of the footstool when worshipping her God, but still she is claiming her place in this "world of words."

Two disparate vocabularies jostle each other in this poem, the mundane terminology of business and the ornate manner of the miraculous. The contrast between these two levels of diction measures the distance between Mary Sidney imprisoned on an imperfect earth and her brother enshrined in heaven. What was hers was loaned, "imprest" by him and by "double int'rest" his (ll. 2, 4). She owed him "due tribute's grateful fee," a "debt of Infinits," and she was left bereft and counting " . . . this cast upp Summe, / This Reckoning made, this Audit of my woe" (ll. 33, 35, 43-44). Underscoring this language of calculation are constant reminders of incompletion that refer to her contributions: "this half maim'd peece," "the rest but peec't," "in ought my blood should partialize," "passing peece," and "meanest part" (ll. 18, 24, 51, 73, 84). By contrast, her brother was a "Phoenix," a "wonder" beyond "Nature's store" (l. 36), and upon weeping for him, "not eie but hart teares fall" (l. 20), a baroque religious metaphor that emphasizes once again the conjunction of her "zealous love" for both Philip and her God—her mentor on earth and her Master in heaven. This contrast between worldly incompletion and spiritual perfection is deepened by an oscillation in the poem between awkward, convoluted questions and qualifications (as previously noted in stanzas 4, 7, 8, and 11) and simple, eloquent grief: "sadd characters indeed of simple love." This contrast in tone reflects Mary Sidney's insecurity, yearning to be worthy of Philip's "perfection," yet impeded by her own "mortall stuffe," her inadequacy before the "secrett power" of the universe (ll. 4-6), terms that apply equally to her spiritual condition and her poetic aspirations.

Although Mary Sidney ended **"To the Angell spirit . . ."** with a confession of her failure to achieve union with her brother in either spirit or creative endeavor, the achievement of the poem itself belies the humble and discouraged tone of its final stanzas. Through her writing Mary Sidney forged a bond with her brother that his death could not sever, and through that writing she gave meaning and purpose to her life after his death, dedicating herself to continuing his political Protestantism as well as his poetic idealism by finishing his verse-translations of the Psalms. Yet, the crowning result of her labor was the formation of a style uniquely her own, first seen in her paraphrases of the Psalms and most evident in this tribute to her brother's memory. If the theme of **"To the Angell spirit . . ."** is her unworthiness, the style in which that unworthiness is expressed is an affirmation of both her ambition and her talent. She paid to her brother "the debt of Infinits I owe," but by following him, learned to find her own way. The legacy he left her was not only his memory and his work, but the inspiration that impelled *her* to work as well, and the justification for her to do so; in honoring him she created herself. The irreconcilable separation between her spirit and his, bemoaned at the end of **"To the Angell spirit . . . ,"** made possible the achievement of that poem.

Notes

[1] "To the Angell spirit of the most excellent Sir Philip Sidney" is appended to J, a copy of A, the Penshurst manuscript of the Sidney *Psalmes,* which was transcribed by John Davies of Hereford. J is in the possession of Dr. B. E. Juel-Jensen and is dated 1599. The other poems are "The Dolefull Lay of Clorinda," c. 1588, first published in *Colin Clouts Come Home Again* (1595); "A Dialogue between two shepheards, Thenot and Piers, in praise of Astrea," c. 1599, published in Francis Davison's *Poetical Rhapsody,* 1602; and "Even now that Care," dated 1599, also appended to this copy of the Penshurst manuscript. See Gary F. Waller, *The Triumph of Death,* 10, 44-64. Although I disagree with Coburn Freer's assessment of Mary Sidney's poetic ability, I am indebted for the title of my essay to his "Countess of Pembroke in a World of Words."

[2] Mary Ellen Lamb, in "The Art of Dying," makes a case for the "intellectual self-assertion" of Mary Sidney's translations of Mornay's *Discours,* Garnier's *Antonie,* and Petrarch's *Triumph of Death,* contrasting Sidney's ambitious scholarship with these works' underlying theme of passive womanly heroism expressed through stoical "self-effacement."

See also my essay, "Mary Sidney's *Psalmes:* Education and Wisdom," which discusses Sidney's formation of an original poetic style through her verse-translations of the Psalms.

[3] See Travitsky for a history of women writers before Mary Sidney.

[4] See Wayne; see also Lamb, "The Cooke Sisters," and Kelso for further discussion of the education of women in the sixteenth century.

[5] Anne, Jane, and Margaret Seymour had written Latin distichs commemorating the death of Margaret of Navarre, pub. 1550. Isabella Whitney had published

The Copy of a Letter . . . to her unconstant Lover (1567) and *A Sweet Nosegay* (1573). Elizabeth Cooke Hoby had written several epitaphs in Latin, Greek, and English for both of her husbands, as well as for her brother, sister, son, and daughter. Katherine Cooke Killegrew wrote a Latin epitaph in preparation for her own death. Mildred Cooke Cecil's daughter, Anne, published four epitaphs on the death of her son in 1584.

[6] Mary Sidney edited both his *Arcadia* and *Astrophil and Stella* after her brother's death. Her dual translation of *Antonie*, a faithful rendition of Robert Garnier's *Marc Antoine,* and of *A Discourse of Life and Death,* taken from the original by Philippe de Mornay, was published in 1592. She wrote and revised her verse-translations of the Psalms from the time of her brother's death in 1586 until 1599, when the presentation copy was readied for a projected visit from Queen Elizabeth.

[7] Line 25. All references from the final version of "To the Angell spirit . . ." will come from J .C . A. Rathmell, ed., *The Psalms of Sir Philip Sidney and the Countess of Pembroke,* xxxv-xxxviii.

[8] Ben Jonson, "To the Immortall Memorie, and Friendship of That Noble Paire, Sir Lucius Cary, and Sir H. Morison," in *The Complete Poetry of Ben Jonson,* ed. William B. Hunter, Jr. (New York: Norton, 1963), 226 (ll. 87, 79-81). All other references will come from this edition.

[9] Quoted in Young 193.

[10] These lines come from stanza 6 in the early version of "To the Angell spirit . . ." that was mistakenly published in the collected works of Samuel Daniel in 1623 and is reproduced in Waller's *Triumph of Death,* 190-92. All references to the earlier version of this poem will come from this source.

[11] The metaphor of Sidney as an angel in a "caelestiall Quire" is, of course, borrowed from her own, earlier, "Dolefull Lay of Clorinda," ll. 61-64.

[12] I Timothy 2:11-12 (King James version).

Works Consulted

Bornstein, Diane. "The Style of the Countess of Pembroke's Translation of Philippe de Mornay's *Discours de la Vie et de la Mort.*" In Hannay, *Silent But for the Word,* 126-34. Discusses the graceful concision and metaphorical additions of Mary Sidney's translation.

Fisken, Beth Wynne. "Mary Sidney's Psalmes: Education and Wisdom." In Hannay, *Silent But for the Word,* 166-83. Discusses the verse-paraphrases of the Psalms

as meditative exercises in self-education, poetic and spiritual, for which Mary Sidney drew upon her own experiences in her expanded metaphors and applications.

Freer, Coburn. "The Countess of Pembroke in a World of Words." *Style* 5, no. 1 (1971): 37-56. Some valuable commentary on Mary Sidney's characteristic style in her verse-translations of the Psalms, although Freer's general characterization of her poetic voice as "narrow" seems unwarranted.

Hannay, Margaret P. "'Doo What Men May Sing': Mary Sidney and the Tradition of Admonitory Dedication." In Hannay, *Silent But for the Word,* 151-65. A convincing argument demonstrating that "Even now that Care" and "To the Angell spirit . . . ," the two dedicatory poems appended to the 1599 Juel-Jensen manuscript of the Sidnean Psalter, couple a lament for Philip Sidney with a disguised political recommendation to Queen Elizabeth that she further his dedication to the Protestant cause in Europe.

———. ed. *Silent But for the Word: Tudor Women as Patrons, Translators, and Writers of Religious Works.* Kent, Ohio: Kent State University Press, 1985. This collection of essays explores the contributions of Renaissance women to the dissemination of partisan religious works, as well as the ways in which these women subtly changed their texts to reflect personal and political perspectives.

Kelso, Ruth. *Doctrine for the Lady of the Renaissance.* 1956. Reprint. Urbana: University of Illinois Press, 1978. Discusses Renaissance ideals and recommendations for the proper education and conduct defining the role of the "lady."

Lamb, Mary Ellen. "The Art of Dying." In *Women in the Middle Ages and the Renaissance,* edited by Mary Beth Rose, 207-26. Syracuse: Syracuse University Press, 1986. Hypothesizes that Mary Sidney's choice of works to translate presents a model of stoic self-denial consistent with patriarchal values but at odds with Sidney's own aggressive scholarship.

———. "The Cooke Sisters: Attitudes toward Learned Women in the Renaissance." In Hannay, *Silent But for the Word,* 107-25. Discusses how the Cooke sisters' internalization of patriarchal strictures led them to limit their work to religious translations, personal letters, and epitaphs.

Rathmell, J. C. A., ed. *The Psalms of Sir Philip Sidney and the Countess of Pembroke.* New York: New York University Press, 1963. The standard text of the final versions of the Sidneian psalter, which is introduced by a ground-breaking essay on the style of Mary Sidney's verse-translations of Psalms 44 through 150.

Travitsky, Betty, ed. *The Paradise of Women: Writings by Englishwomen of the Renaissance*. Westport, Conn.: Greenwood Press, 1981. An anthology of Renaissance women's writing with biographical and critical introductions to individual writers.

Waller, G. F. *Mary Sidney, Countess of Pembroke: A Critical Study of Her Writings and Milieu*. Salzburg: Salzburg University Press, 1979. The first full-length biographical-critical study of Mary Sidney since Frances Young's.

———. "The Text and Ms. Variants of the Countess of Pembroke's Psalms." *Review of English Studies* 26 (1975):6-18. A valuable reconstruction of Mary Sidney's process of self-education as a poet through analysis of her revisions.

———. "'This Matching of Contraries': Calvinism and Courtly Philosophy in the Sidney Psalms." *English Studies* 55, no. 1 (1974): 22-31. Contrasts two themes, Calvinism and courtly Neoplatonism, in the style of the Sidney psalter.

———, ed. *The Triumph of Death and Other Unpublished and Uncollected Poems by Mary Sidney, Countess of Pembroke (1561-1621)*. Salzburg: Salzburg University Press, 1977. Includes previously unpublished variant versions of some of the psalms, as well as an earlier version of "To the Angell spirit. . . ."

Wayne, Valerie. "Some Sad Sentence: Vives' *Instruction of a Christian Woman*." In Hannay, *Silent But for the Word*, 15-29. Discusses the restrictive influence of Juan Luis Vives' popular conduct book on Renaissance women's intellectual lives.

Young, Frances Campbell. *Mary Sidney, Countess of Pembroke*. London: David Nutt, 1912. The first biographical study of Mary Sidney's life, works and influence as a patron. Includes several of Sidney's letters as well as *The Triumph of Death* as an appendix.

FURTHER READING

Bornstein, Diane. "Introduction." In *The Countess of Pembroke's Translation of Philippe de Mornay's "Discourse of Life and Death,"* edited by Diane Bornstein, pp. 1-24. Detroit: Michigan Consortium for Medieval and Early Modern Studies, 1983.

Traces the personal and historical circumstances in which Sidney translated de Mornay's work and

contends that "her changes even improved the original."

Brennan, Michael. *Literary Patronage in the English Renaissance: The Pembroke Family*. London: Routledge, 1988, 251 p.

A comprehensive survey of the patronage system focusing on the Pembrokes' literary influence.

Buxton, John. "The Countess of Pembroke." In his *Sir Philip Sidney and the English Renaissance*, pp. 173-204. New York: St. Martin's Press, 1954.

In the context of Philip Sidney's significance, Buxton narrates Mary Sidney's extensive work as her brother's posthumous editor and as a patron of letters.

Costello, Louisa Stuart. "Mary Sidney, Countess of Pembroke." In her *Memoirs of Eminent Englishwomen*, Vol. I, pp. 334-69. London: Richard Bentley, 1844.

Discusses Sidney's family and particularly her relationship with Philip.

Hannay, Margaret P. "'Princes You as Men Dy': Genevan Advice to Monarchs in the *Psalmes* of Mary Sidney." *Literary Renaissance* 19, No. 1 (Winter, 1989): 22-41.

Looks at Sidney's Psalms in the context of religious and political, as well as literary, history, contending that she embedded a very concrete and pointed commentary for the Queen in her translations.

———. *Philip's Phoenix: Mary Sidney, Countess of Pembroke*. New York and Oxford: Oxford University Press, 1990, 317 p.

Comprehensive biography by a leading Sidney scholar which takes into account the late-twentieth-century revision of Sidney's reputation, treating her as an important artist and scholar in her own right.

———. "'This Moses and This Miriam': The Countess of Pembroke's Role in the Legend of Sir Philip Sidney." In *Sir Philip Sidney's Achievements*, edited by M. J. B. Allen et al., pp. 217-26. New York: AMS Press, 1990.

Shows that Mary Sidney assumed her brother's mantle at his death, taking over his work as literary patron and as champion of the family reputation.

Lamb, Mary Ellen. "The Countess of Pembroke's Patronage." *English Literary Renaissance* 12, No. 2 (Spring 1982): 162-79.

Claims that Sidney's patronage has been greatly exaggerated and criticizes the "second-rate nature of much of the writing" produced at Wilton.

Martin, Randall. "Mary (Sidney) Herbert, Countess of Pembroke (1561-1621): Introduction." In *Women Writers in Renaissance England*, edited by Randall Martin, pp. 311-15. London and New York: Longman, 1997.

Provides a brief introduction to examples of Sidney's work, emphasizing the traits of the poetic voice that she developed.

Todd, Richard. "'So Well Attyr'd Abroad': A Background to the Sidney-Pembroke Psalter and Its Implications for the Seventeenth-Century Religious Lyric." *Texas Studies in Literature and Language* 29, No. 1 (Spring 1987): 74-93.

Delineates the place of the *Psalms* in their literary context and their impact on the ensuing development of English religious verse.

Additional coverage of Sidney's life and career is contained in the following source published by Gale Research: *Literature Criticism from 1400 to 1800*, **Vol. 19.**

Sir Philip Sidney

1554-1586

English poet, prose writer, essayist, and playwright.

The following entry contains critical essays focusing on Sidney's role in the Age of Spenser. For further information on Sidney, see *LC,* Vol. 19.

INTRODUCTION

Regarded by many scholars as the consummate Renaissance man, Sidney was a prominent and highly influential literary figure, scholar, and courtier of the Elizabethan period. Almost legendary in his own lifetime, Sidney is remembered today for the romance *The Countesse of Pembrokes Arcadia* (1590), the most recognized work of English prose fiction of the sixteenth century; for *Astrophel and Stella* (1591), the first sonnet sequence in English; and for *The Defence of Poesie* (1595), which is, in Arthur F. Kinney's words, "the first (and still most important) statement of English poetics."

Biographical Information

Born in Kent to aristocratic parents—Sir Henry Sidney, the Lord Deputy of Ireland, and Mary Dudley, sister of the Earl of Leicester—Sidney received the financial, social, and educational privileges of the English nobility and was trained as a statesman. In 1564 he entered the Shrewsbury School on the same day as Fulke Greville, who became his lifelong friend and later gained renown as a scholar and Sidney's biographer. Sidney matriculated at Christ's Church, Oxford, in 1568, where he studied grammar, rhetoric, and religion. He left three years later without taking a degree, possibly due to an outbreak of plague that forced the university to close temporarily. Sidney continued his education with a "Grand Tour" of continental Europe, learning about politics, languages, music, astronomy, geography, and the military. During this time he became acquainted with some of the most prominent European statesmen, scholars, and artists; he also became friends with the humanist scholar Hubert Languet, with whom he spent a winter in Germany. Sidney's correspondence with Languet is a valuable source of information about Sidney's life and career. Languet's censure of Catholicism and his espousal of Protestantism, as well as his attempts to encourage Queen Elizabeth I to further this cause in England, are believed to have strongly influenced Sidney's religious and political convictions. After further travels, including through Hungary, Italy, and Poland,

Sidney returned to England in 1575, where he promptly established himself as one of the Queen's courtiers. Although he pursued literary interests, associating with such prominent writers as Greville, Edward Dyer, and Edmund Spenser, Sidney's chief ambition was to embark on a career in public service. Aside from acquiring some minor appointments, he was never given an opportunity to prove himself as a statesman. Critics speculate that his diplomatic career was deliberately discouraged by Elizabeth, whose policy of caution in handling domestic and religious matters conflicted with Sidney's ardent support of Protestantism. In 1578 Sidney wrote and performed in, along with the Queen herself, an "entertainment," or pageant, entitled *The Lady of May*. He also began writing the first version of *Arcadia*. After writing a letter towards the end of 1579 which urged the Queen not to enter into a planned marriage with the Roman Catholic Duke of Anjou, heir to the French throne, Sidney found himself in strained relations with Elizabeth. Denied court duties, Sidney lived at the estate of his sister Mary Sidney Herbert, the Countess of Pembroke, and occupied himself with writing: probably in 1580 he completed the *Old Arcadia,* and began *The Defence of Poesie;* he began *Astrophel and Stella* around 1581. Also in 1581 Sidney took part in a performance for the Queen of the "entertainment" *The Four Foster Children of Desire,* which scholars believe was at least partially written by Sidney. In 1583 Sidney was knighted so that he might complete an assignment for the Queen. Sidney began a major revision of the *Arcadia* in 1584 and in the following year began work on a verse translation of the psalms, which was later finished by his sister. In 1585 he was appointed governor of Flushing, an area comprising present-day Belgium and the Netherlands, where the English were involved in the Dutch revolt against Spain. In 1586 he participated in a raid on a Spanish convoy at Zutphen in the Netherlands. Struck on the leg by a musket ball, Sidney developed gangrene and died a few weeks later, just one month short of his thirty-second birthday. His death was marked with a lavish, ceremonial state funeral at St. Paul's cathedral in London.

Major Works

All of Sidney's major works were published posthumously, although many of them circulated among friends and relatives in handwritten copies. Although Sidney died before completing the *Arcadia* and requested on his deathbed that his manuscripts be burned, an edition, now referred to as the *New Arcadia,* was published in 1590 containing the revised chapters. Drawing on elements of Italian pastoral romance and Greek prose epic, the plot of the *Arcadia* concerns two princes who embark on a quest for love in the land of Arcadia, fall in love with two daughters of the Arcadian king, and eventually, after a series of mistaken identities and misunderstandings, marry the princesses. Elaborately plotted with a nonchronological structure, interspersed with poetry, and characterized by extensive alliteration, similes, paradoxes, and rhetorical devices, the *Arcadia* is artificial, extravagant, and difficult to read by modern standards. A printing of a composite *Arcadia* was made in 1593, comprising Books I-III of the *New Arcadia* and Books III-V of the *Old Arcadia.* In 1909 Bertam Dobell announced that he had discovered original manuscripts of the *Arcadia,* including one of the *Old Arcadia* which Sidney had presented to his sister. This *Old Arcadia,* a relatively straightforward, unadorned, and much shorter version than the *Arcadia*s published previously, was included in *The Complete Works* in 1926. *Astrophel and Stella,* regarded by many critics as Sidney's masterpiece, was published in 1591. Its 108 sonnets comprise a sequence which tells the story of Astrophel (also called Astrophil), his passion for Stella, her conditioned acceptance of his advances and, finally, his plea to be released from his obligation to her. *An Apologie for Poetrie* was published by Henry Olney without authorization early in 1595. William Ponson-

by, who had registered *The Defence of Poesie* late in 1594, gained all of Olney's copies. *The Defence of Poesie* responds to Stephen Gosson's *School of Abuse* (1579), which charges that modern poetry exerts an immoral influence on society by presenting lies as truths and instilling unnatural desires in its readers. Sidney answered Gosson's invective by asserting that the poet provides a product of his imagination which does not pretend to literal fact and therefore cannot present lies. Sidney declares that the purpose of poetry is to instruct and delight.

Critical Reception

Memoirs of Sidney began almost at once upon his death. Spenser wrote an elegy entitled "Astrophel" and Edmund Molyneux wrote of him in Holinshed's *Chronicles,* published in 1587. Greville's hagiographic biography even made use of spurious stories to further Sidney's reputation. Various critics contend that the creativity and concern for literary detail intrinsic to Sidney's prose style in the *New Arcadia* were valuable innovations which encouraged experimentation and greater attention to craftsmanship among Renaissance writers. *Astrophel and Stella* popularized the sonnet sequence form and inspired many other poets. In a seminal study of Sidney's poetry, Theodore Spencer cited his "direct and forceful simplicity, his eloquent rhetoric, his emotional depth and truth, [and] his control of movement, both within the single line and throughout the poem as a whole" as innovations to poetic form which exerted a profound impact on subsequent poets. C. S. Lewis wrote that *Astrophel and Stella* "towers above everything that had been done in poetry . . . since Chaucer died," and that "the fourth [sonnet] alone, with its hurried and (as it were) whispered metre, its inimitable refrain, its perfect selection of images, is enough to raise Sidney above all his contemporaries." More recently Ronald Levao has asserted that despite evidence of faulty logic, the *Defence of Poesie* is "one of the most daring documents of Renaissance criticism." Although he has been widely respected and read for centuries, Sidney's popularity has suffered a setback in modern times, leading Duncan-Jones to observe that Sidney is "the least-read of the major Elizabethans."

PRINCIPAL WORKS

The Lady of May (drama) 1578

The Four Foster Children of Desire (drama) 1581
The Countesse of Pembrokes Arcadia [*New Arcadia*] (prose) 1590
Astrophel and Stella (poetry) 1591
The Countesse of Pembrokes Arcadia [composite *Arcadia*] (prose) 1593

The Defence of Poesie [also published as *An Apologie for Poetrie*] (essay) 1595
Certaine Sonets (poetry) 1598
The Psalms of David (with Mary Sidney Herbert) [translator] (poetry) 1823
The Correspondence of Sir Philip Sidney and Hubert Languet (letters) 1845
The Complete Works of Sir Philip Sidney. 4 vols. (poetry, essays, letters) 1912-26
The Countesse of Pembrokes Arcadia [*Old Arcadia*] (prose) 1926

CRITICISM

Kenneth Muir (essay date 1960)

SOURCE: "Sidney and Political Pastoral," in *Sir Philip Sidney*, Longmans, Green & Co., 1984, pp. 91-108.

[*In the following excerpt from an essay written in 1960, Muir discusses contemporary and modern opinions of the* Arcadia *and Sidney's purpose in writing and rewriting the work.*]

The Countess of Pembroke's *Arcadia* is the only English masterpiece which has been allowed to go out of print. It has never been included in a popular series of classics and one must conclude that it is read now only by scholars. It has, indeed, a reputation for tediousness. Mr. T. S. Eliot, though writing in defence of the Countess of Pembroke's circle, dismissed *Arcadia* as 'a monument of dullness'; Mr. F. L. Lucas called it 'a rigmarole of affected coxcombry and china shepherdesses'; Virginia Woolf described her reactions as 'half dreaming, half yawning'; and dullness is the one fault which the general reader neither can nor should forgive. Yet for three generations the book was read by everyone interested in literature, and there were thirteen editions between 1590 and 1674. Its popularity was partly due, like that of Rupert Brooke's poetry, to the legend attaching to the author; but it was perused by dramatists in search of plots—with Shakespeare at their head—by those who loved romances and by those who liked their moral lessons presented in a delightful form, by Charles I and by John Milton who spoke of it as a 'vain, amatorious poem' while conceding its worth and wit.

If, therefore, the modern reader finds it tedious, it may be because he comes to it with the wrong expectations. The development of the novel during the last two hundred and fifty years has conditioned our views of what prose fiction should be: we look for a plot embodying a theme, for subtle characterisation, for criticism of society, and usually for realism. But Sidney was not attempting to write a novel; his book is set in an imaginary past; his characters are much less vital than those of the best Elizabethan and Jacobean dramatists; and his story is wildly improbable. We are bound to be disappointed if we ask of his masterpiece what it makes no attempt to provide.

Arcadia has been published in three versions. The short version, not published until 1926, was written first. Sidney described it in the dedication as 'this idle work of mine, telling his sister, the Countess, that it was not intended for publication:

> being but a trifle, and that triflingly handled. Your dear self can best witness the manner, being done in loose sheets of paper, most of it in your presence, the rest, by sheets, sent unto you, as fast as they were done.

This version (the Old *Arcadia*, as it is called) is in five books or acts. In his last years Sidney began expanding and rewriting the book, and he had got half way through the third book, without making any use of the original third book, when he died or when he departed to take up his post as Governor of Flushing. The first two books in the revised form are twice as long as in the old *Arcadia*. This second version, divided into chapters probably by Fulke Greville, was published in 1590. Three years later, the Countess of Pembroke published the third version which consists of the 1590 version, without Greville's aids to the reader, but with the addition of the unexpanded concluding books. Some of the alterations in these books were apparently made by Sidney himself, or in accordance with his intentions by his sister; for others she may have been wholly responsible. Sidney had expressed a wish that the manuscript should be destroyed, partly no doubt because the revision was incomplete.

The old *Arcadia* is a straightforward romance, with the events in approximately chronological order.[1] In the new *Arcadia* Sidney remodelled the book under the influence of the *Æthiopian History* of Heliodorus and the *Diana* of Jorge de Montemayor. He deliberately upset the chronological sequence of events, interspersing the main plot with others. We know from *The Defence of Poesie* that Sidney regarded both Xenophon's *Cyropaedia* and Heliodorus' *Æthiopian History* as 'absolute heroical poems', notwithstanding the fact that they were written in prose; and he rewrote *Arcadia* to convert it into a poem, mingling the heroic and the pastoral as Montemayor had done. Even in the old *Arcadia* Sidney had followed Montemayor's example in interspersing verses in a predominantly prose narrative.

Some critics have argued that Sidney spoiled the original *Arcadia* by his attempt to improve it. They admit the extraordinary ingenuity of the revised version, the 'marvellous involution and complexity' (as Dr. S. L.

Wolff calls it), a kind of jug-saw puzzle in which every piece is essential to the grand design of the whole; but they suggest that the book is made impossibly difficult by its complicated structure, that no one at a first reading can follow the various strands in the pattern, and that, as Hazlitt put it, it is 'one of the greatest monuments of the abuse of intellectual power on record'. It has even been maintained that the style of the first version, less highly wrought than that of the revision, is for that very reason without the excessive ornament and preciosity which makes Sidney's later prose so difficult to read, and so unhappy a model.

Elizabethan reading habits were different from ours, and there is no evidence that Sidney's contemporaries found *Arcadia* unnecessarily complicated. That all would not be clear at a first reading is surely irrelevant to an estimate of the book's success. It would be re-read and discussed, digested and savoured, and the very complications would be a source of added pleasure. The modern reader, if he wishes to appreciate the book, cannot skim through it as he would through a recent bestseller. He must be prepared to read it more as he would a narrative poem or Joyce's *Ulysses*. Nor, I think, can it be seriously maintained that the style of the old *Arcadia* is superior to that of the new. Although as early as 1588 Abraham Fraunce had used a manuscript of the old *Arcadia* to provide examples of figures of speech for his *Arcadian Rhetorike,* its style is rough and unpolished compared with that of the new *Arcadia*. Many passages, it is true, Sidney used again with only slight modifications; but others he polished and refined, and many of the finest passages in the revised version are completely new.

A typical comparison may be made of the passages in the two versions describing Pyrocles after he has been lectured by Musidorus for falling in love with Philoclea:

> These words spoken vehemently and proceeding from so dearly an esteemed friend as Musidorus did so pierce poor Pyrocles that his blushing cheeks did witness with him he rather could not help, than did not know his fault. Yet, desirous by degrees to bring his friend to a gentler consideration of him, and beginning with two or three broken sighs, answered to this purpose.

> Pyrocles' mind was all this while so fixed upon another devotion, that he no more attentively marked his friend's discourse than the child that hath leave to play marks the last part of his lesson; or the diligent pilot in a dangerous tempest doth attend the unskillful words of a passenger: yet the very sound having imprinted the general point of his speech in his heart, pierced without any mislike of so dearly an esteemed friend, and desirous by degrees to bring him to a gentler

consideration of him, with a shamefast look (witnessing he rather could not help, than did not know his fault) answered him to this purpose.

The revised version is superior in several ways. Sidney has obviously improved the structure of the prose; he has added two useful psychological touches to the character of Pyrocles; and he has inserted two similes and a metaphor. These might be regarded as supererogatory in prose fiction, but they are desirable ornaments in an heroic poem which the new *Arcadia* was intended to be.

How much Sidney's style was admired by his contemporaries can be seen not merely from numerous references to it, but from the way it was imitated. Greene, for example, who had written in a euphuistic style in the 'eighties, adopted the Aracadian style for his two best romances, *Menaphon* and *Pandosto*. Sidney himself had complained of the artificiality and monotony of euphuism, and his own style employs a much wider range of rhetorical figures, and avoids the exaggerated use of antithesis and alliteration, as well as the absurd similes, which make *Euphues* so tedious. His own similes and metaphors, though frequently far-fetched, are never mechanical. He speaks, for example, of blood mingling with the sea in these terms: 'their blood had (as it were) filled the wrinkles of the sea's visage'. He describes a tree reflected in a stream: 'It seemed she looked into it and dressed her green locks by that running river.' He writes of 'beds of flowers, which being under the trees, the trees were to them a pavilion, and they to the trees a mosaical floor'. He speaks of a storm as winter's child, 'so extreme and foul a storm, that never any winter (I think) brought forth a fouler child'. Instead of saying that Queen Helen spoke, he says: 'But when her breath (aweary to be closed up in woe) broke the prison of her fair lips.'

A longer passage, describing Pamela at her embroidery, has been condemned for absurdity:

> For the flowers she had wrought carried such life in them that the cunningest painter might have learned of her needle: which with so pretty a manner made his careers to and fro through the cloth, as if the needle itself would have been loth to have gone fromward such a mistress, but that it hoped to return thenceward very quickly again: the cloth looking with many eyes upon her, and lovingly embracing the wounds she gave it: the sheers also were at hand to behead the silk that was grown too short. And if at any time she put her mouth to bite it off, it seemed, that where she had been long in making of a rose with her hand, she would in an instant make roses with her lips.
> . . .

The reader who does not enjoy this bravura piece is

unlikely to appreciate *Arcadia* as a whole, for it is not only delightful in itself but it helps to create the total impression of one of the two heroines. Dr. G. K. Hunter has rightly observed that Sidney's similes are not, on the whole, concerned to make things more plain or even more vivid, but by comparing the less artificial to the more artificial to stress the importance, the complexity, the significance, of the world described. Each individual incident, every gesture, one might almost say, becomes universalised.

Hoskins, in his *Directions for Speech and Style,* written but not published in 1599, used *Arcadia* as his storehouse for figures of rhetoric; and, in commenting on the way Sidney 'shunned usual phrases', he explained that 'this of purpose did he write to keep his style from baseness'. Virginia Woolf even suggested that 'often the realism and vigour of the verse comes with a shock after the drowsy languor of the prose'. But although Sidney was careful to keep his style from baseness in the heroic parts of *Arcadia*, he did this from a sense of literary decorum, as can be seen from the straightforward and direct prose he uses in passages of comic relief. In the heroic parts he was aiming at what Minturno advocated, 'magnificent and sumptuous pomp of incidents and language'.

This sumptuous pomp is not mainly a matter of vocabulary, though Sidney is fond of hyphenated epithets, but of using all the resources of rhetoric. Two of the commonest figures in *Arcadia* are antonomasia and periphrasis. Philoclea, for example, is called 'the ornament of the Earth, the model of Heaven, the triumph of Nature, the light of Beauty, Queen of love'; and, instead of saying that the lambs bleated for their dams, Sidney tells us that 'the pretty lambs with bleating oratory craved the dam's comfort'. Hoskins gives several examples of this figure. Sidney calls a thresher 'one of Ceres' servants' and instead of 'his name was known to high and low' he writes absurdly: 'No prince could pretend height nor beggar lowness to bar him from the sounds thereof.'

Many of the rhetorical figures consist of the repetition of words in different ways, the playing with them, and the departure from their natural order. Sometimes Sidney will end a sentence with a word taken from the beginning:

> The thoughts are but overflowings of the mind, and the tongue is but a servant of the thoughts.

> In shame there is no comfort, but to be beyond all bounds of shame.

At other times the word is repeated in the middle of the sentence, and in the following example the figure is underlined by alliteration:

> That sight increased their compassion, and their compassion called up their care.

Sometimes Sidney interrupts a sentence with a parenthesis, reinforcing the meaning, or correcting it (i.e. epanorthosis):

> In Thessalia I say there was (well I may say there was) a Prince.

Sometimes he uses oxymoron, as in the phrase 'humane inhumanity'; and sometimes he plays with the meanings of words, as in the description of 'a ship, or rather the carcass of the ship, or rather some few bones of the carcass'.

These are only a few typical examples of the scores of different figures used by Sidney. The Arcadian style depends, not as euphuism does on comparatively few overworked figures, but on the intensive use of a wide variety of figures, so that there is no danger of the reader becoming tired of any particular one. It is a restless, brilliant, self-conscious prose, continually calling attention to itself as much as to the thing described, and, it must be admitted, becoming intolerably affected in the hands of imitators without Sidney's comprehensive intelligence and without his high purpose.[2]

There are two qualities of Sidney's prose which have been appreciated by those who have been unable to enjoy its more obviously Elizabethan characteristics—its descriptive power and its rhythms. There had been great works of prose before the *Arcadia*, but Sidney was the first English writer to construct long and finely-articulated sentences with a conscious but varied prose rhythm, the first, perhaps, to spend as much pains on the composition of prose as others spent on verse. On every page there are touches of beauty, visual and descriptive beauty and beauty of rhythm, often combined, as in the justly famous conclusion to a long sentence describing Arcadia:

> Here a shepherd's boy piping, as though he should never be old: there a young shepherdess knitting, and withal singing, and it seemed that her voice comforted her hands to work, and her hands kept time to her voice's music.

Another example, put into the mouth of the villainous Cecropia, has the same combination of qualities:

> Have you ever seen a pure rosewater kept in a crystal glass; how fine it looks, how sweet it smells, while that beautiful glass imprisons it? Break the prison, and let the water take his own course, doth it not embrace dust, and lose all his former sweetness and fairness? Truly so are we, if we have not the stay, rather than the restraint, of crystalline marriage.

Sidney's art, however, was a means to an end. We have seen how he maintained that the function of poetry was to teach delightfully. Although some critics have supposed that Sidney taught by means of allegory, it is clear that apart from a few allegorical touches, he avoided the method of his friend, Spenser. What he was seeking to do was to create an imaginary world in which human actions and passions could be displayed, freed from the accidentals of the real world. The golden world created by the poet was, moreover, more beautiful than the brazen world in which we live. Nature, he tells us:

> never set forth the earth in so rich tapestry as diverse poets have done, neither with so pleasant rivers, fruitful trees, sweet-smelling flowers, nor whatsoever else may make the too much loved earth more lovely: her world is brazen, the poets only deliver a golden.

The poet's method is to teach indirectly by means of his story:

> He cometh to you with words set in delightful proportion . . . and with a tale forsooth he cometh unto you, with a tale which holdeth children from play and old men from the chimney-corner; and pretending no more, doth intend the winning of the mind from wickedness to virtue.

Like the ideal actor of whom Hamlet speaks, Sidney's purpose was 'to show virtue his own feature, scorn her own image, and the very age and body of the time his form and pressure'.

In some ways the old *Arcadia* is more directly didactic than the new. Sidney cut out the narrator's moralising, often transferring it to one or other of the characters in the story. The debates, as Professor Myrick shows, 'have been subordinated to the action, and the aphorisms have been half concealed in dramatic narration'. The teaching is to be found mainly in the examples of human beings, good and bad, in their actions and words. As Hoskins points out, 'Men are described excellently in *Arcadia* . . . But he that will truly set down a man in a figured story must first learn truly to set down an humour, a passion, a virtue, a vice, and therein keeping decent proportion add but names and knit together the accidents and encounters'. Hoskins adds that 'the perfect expressing of all qualities is learned out of Aristotle's ten books of moral philosophy' and that 'the understanding of Aristotle's *Rhetoric* is the directest means of skill to describe, to move, to appease, or to prevent any motion whatsoever; whereunto whosoever can fit his speech shall be truly eloquent'. It is significant that Sidney had translated the first two books of *Rhetoric,* which are concerned with the tasks of persuasion, an analysis of human motives and emotions, and a list of the various

lines of argument available to different kinds of speaker. Hoskins' views are supported by Greville who tells us that Sidney's

> purpose was to limn out such exact pictures of every posture in the mind, that any man being forced, in the strains of this life, to pass through any straits or latitudes of good or ill fortune, might (as in a glass) see how to set a good countenance upon all the discountenances of adversity, and a stay upon the exorbitant smilings of chance.

Although it was natural for Hoskins, writing on rhetoric, and for Greville, who in his old age sought in Sidney's works for the qualities he aimed at in his own and who was belabouring in his account of Sidney the decadence of a later age, to stress the moral purpose of *Arcadia*, they undoubtedly understood Sidney's intentions: but it would be wrong to suppose that the characters in *Arcadia* are mere *exempla,* or that they are all plainly black or white. Cecropia has no redeeming characteristics, and Philanax and Pamela appear to be wholly admirable; but between these extremes there are many characters, weak and amiable, vain and brave, sinful but not vicious, who together provide a representative pageant of human nature. Basilius may be condemned for his foolishness, his credulity and his attempted adultery, Gynecia may be held up as a bad example of passion usurping the place of reason, Amphialus may be a deluded egotist, but no one could pretend that these characters are wholly evil. The characters are revealed in their actions and the reader is always guided in his response to what they do and say.

Even the heroes, Pyrocles and Musidorus, are not depicted as perfect; but it is interesting to notice that Sidney removed two flaws in their characters in the process of revision. In the old *Arcadia*, at the end of Book 3, the love of Pyrocles and Philoclea is consummated before matrimony. Sidney may well have felt, or have come to feel, that it was dangerous to depict Pyrocles succumbing to this temptation, especially as the author's comment is not disapproving:

> He gives me occasion to leave him in so happy a plight, lest my pen might seem to grudge at the due bliss of these poor lovers, whose loyalty had but small respite of their fiery agonies.

Musidorus, with less excuse, is so overcome by the beauty of Pamela as she lies asleep that he determines to ravish her, when he is prevented by the timely arrival of some bandits. Musidorus is an unlikely ravisher, and Sidney may have felt that the incident would make Musidorus's final happiness undeserved. There is no reason to suppose that the Countess of Pembroke was responsible for altering these two passages;

but, if she did, the alterations were probably in accordance with Sidney's known wishes.

Sidney's teaching in *Arcadia* covers the whole range of private and public morality, We see the operations of lust, pride, ambition, anger and egotism, no less than those of love, friendship, courtesy and valour. We see the evils of superstition, tyranny and anarchy, as well as the value of magnanimity, justice and good counsel. We see how rebellion is caused by bad government, how courtesy and injustice, love and egotism can be embodied in a single character. Sidney was providing, among other things, a lesson to his aristocratic readers on their duties to the state as well as on questions of private behaviour. He shows the dangers of a weak monarchy and of factious nobles; he shows the evils of 'policy'; and, on a different plane, he exemplifies the workings of divine providence.

Nor does he convey these lessons merely by the presentation of appropriate incidents and the depicting of different types of character: scattered through *Arcadia* there are orations, letters, and set speeches which further illustrate his points. Early in the first book, for example, we are given a letter written by Philanax to Basilius, urging him to follow wisdom and virtue, and to ignore the oracle. Pyrocles, disguised as Zelmane, makes a 'pacificatory oration' to the mutinous Arcadians. Pamela is given a prayer which Charles I borrowed for his private devotions. The evil Cecropia is given three powerful speeches, one tempting Philoclea to marriage (III. 5), one similarly addressed to Pamela (III. 10), and one addressed to her son, urging him to rape Philoclea (III. 17). It can be seen from the extract from the second of these quoted above, that Sidney was quite prepared to give the devil his due, as Milton was to give some of his best poetry to Comus and Satan. In the second speech Cecropia is endeavouring to combat Pamela's appeals to conscience by undermining her religion with Lucretian arguments:

> Dear niece, or rather, dear daughter (if my affection and wish might prevail therein) how much doth it increase (trow you?) the earnest desire I have of this blessed match, to see these virtues of yours knit fast with such zeal of devotion, indeed the best bond, which the most politic wits have found, to hold man's wit in well doing? For, as children must first by fear be induced to know that, which after (when they do know) they are most glad of: so are these bugbears of opinions brought by great clerks into the world, to serve as shewels to keep them from those faults, whereto else the vanity of the world and weakness of senses might pull them. But in you (niece) whose excellency is such, as it need not to be held up by the staff of vulgar opinions, I would not you should love virtue servilely, for fear of I know not what, which you see not: but even for the good effects of virtue which you see. Fear, and indeed, foolish fear and fearful ignorance, was the first inventor

of those conceits. . . . Be wise, and that wisdom shall be a God unto thee; be contented, and that is thy heaven: for else to think that those powers (if there be any such) above, are moved either by the eloquence of our prayers, or in a chafe by the folly of our actions, carries as much reason as if flies should think, that men take great care which of them hums sweetest, and which of them flies nimblest.

Such a speech displays not merely Sidney's usual eloquence but his capacity to put himself in the place of characters with whom he could have had little sympathy. It could be said of him, to adapt Keats's remark, that he had as much delight in depicting a Cecropia as a Pamela.

It is true, in a sense, as Virginia Woolf said, that 'in the *Arcadia*, as in some luminous globe, all the seeds of English fiction lie latent'. Although, as we have seen, *Arcadia* is essentially an heroic poem rather than a novel, we can find in it foreshadowings of later novels. It was not an accident that Richardson christened his first heroine Pamela, though Sidney's Pamela is closer in character to Clarissa. But we do Sidney an injustice if we treat him as a forerunner, an imperfect experimenter in a form of literature which was yet to be invented. *Arcadia* is, indeed, closer to Elizabethan drama than to any kind of novel, and closer still, in spite of his avoidance of allegory, to *The Faerie Queene*. Unfinished though it is, *Arcadia* is incomparably the greatest Elizabethan prose work, the greatest precisely because it was conceived as a poem. Peter Heylyn said it was:

> a book which besides its excellent language, rare contrivances, and delectable stories, hath in it all the strains of Poesy, comprehendeth the universal art of speaking, and to them which can discern, and will observe, notable rules for demeanour both private and public.

Notes

[1] For those who have not yet read the book the following summary of the old *Arcadia* may be helpful:— Basilius, terrified by an oracle, prophesying disgrace and disaster to his family, abdicates for the year to which the prophecy refers. The two heroes, Pyrocles and Musidorus, fall in love with Philoclea and Pamela, the two daughters of Basilius. Pyrocles disguises himself as a woman, and Musidorus as a shepherd. Both Basilius and Gynecia, his wife, fall in love with Pyrocles, Gynecia having penetrated his disguise; but he tricks them both so that they share a bed with each other instead of with him, thus fulfilling part of the prophecy. Pyrocles and Musidorus are accused of seducing the princesses and of conspiring with Gynecia to murder Basilius who, having taken a love-potion

intended for Pyrocles, appears to be dead. The heroes are about to be executed when Basilius revives: they are thus enabled to marry the princesses.

In the new *Arcadia* many other plots are interwoven with that of the original book: e.g. the story of Argalus and Parthenia, the story of the King of Paphlagonia and his two sons (used by Shakespeare for the underplot of *King Lear*), and the intrigues of Cecropia to obtain the throne for her son, Amphialus, and her cruel treatment of Philoclea and Pamela.

Sidney was confusing in his choice of names. Daiphantus is the name assumed by Pyrocles as well as a name given to Zelmane, the daughter of Plexirtus, and Zelmane is also a name used by Pyrocles.

[2] Shakespeare seems to have been influenced by Sidney's style in the prose of *King Lear,* I. ii (presumably because he had been reading *Arcadia* for the Gloucester scenes); but his most notable exercise in the Arcadian style, reading like a parody of it, and put into the mouth of an anonymous courtier, is in *The Winter's Tale,* V. ii. 'They seem'd almost, with staring on one another, to tear the cases of their eyes; there was speech in their dumbness, language in their very gesture; they looked as they had heard of a world ransom'd, or one destroy'd. A notable passion of wonder appeared in them; but the wisest beholder that knew no more but seeing could not say if th'importance were joy or sorrow—but in the extremity of the one it must needs be.'

F. J. Levy (essay date 1964)

SOURCE: "Sir Philip Sidney and the Idea of History," in *Bibliotheque D' Humanisme et Renaissance*, Vol. XXVI, 1964, pp. 608-17.

[*In the following essay, Levy discusses why Sidney believed poetry superior to history as a teacher of morality.*]

Sometime around the end of the sixteenth century a change took place in the reasons men gave for writing history. The nature of the change is obvious to anyone who has compared the works of Sir John Hayward or the *Annals* of William Camden with the writing of Hall or Holinshed, let alone with the *Mirror for Magistrates.* To put the matter crudely, early in the century history was a branch of moral philosophy, later a branch of politics.[1] During this crucial period, few Englishmen wrote on the theory of history at all; and of those who did, the most profound was probably Sir Philip Sidney, who touched on history only secondarily in his *Defense of Poesy,* but who, we know, was strongly interested in history and who was a friend of at least one of the important historians of the day.

Thus, even though we know that Sidney's *Defense* concerned itself with history only as a side issue, the views expressed in the essay were of importance, especially when they are held against a background of a great paucity of other material.

What was the older view? History and poetry together had been considered branches of rhetoric because of their persuasive powers, and it was agreed that each might entertain; but it was incomparably more important that they could teach morality and, because of this, both were frequently thought of as a branch of moral philosophy. Hubert Languet, in a letter to Sidney, had stressed the importance of history, "by which more than anything else men's judgements are shaped," but in his classification history followed in order of importance salvation and "that branch of moral philosophy which treats of justice and injustice."[2] The moral lessons of history could and should be taught to every man, but most especially to princes and magistrates. It was the fact that Sidney was invariably considered one of the latter which explains Languet's concern that he master history; and Sidney himself seems to have felt the same. The idea of history as a teacher of morality was already very old in Sidney's time. John Lydgate had made some use of it, as had William Baldwin and the other authors of the *Mirror for Magistrates* and as, too, had Sackville and Norton in *Gorboduc,* a play which Sidney praised.[3] The *Mirror* serves as a convenient illustration of the doctrine of "with howe greuous plages vices are punished," and the whole is addressed to the nobility of the realm and all others in office, "for here as in a loking glas, you shall see (if any vice be in you) howe the like hath bene punished in other heretofore, whereby admonished, I trust it will be a good occasion to move you to the soner amendment. This is the chiefest ende, whye it is set furth . . ."[4]

Not that there are not difficulties. The authors of the *Mirror* are never altogether sure whether to blame Fortune or the individual malefactor, though in the end Fortune does seem to get the palm. But, as George Cavendish made clear in another classic statement of the doctrine, Fortune is usually abetted by him whom she would whirl about. Nor is this all. Alas, virtue is often defeated and vice successful. The preface to the *Mirror* puts the issue very clearly:

> And although you shall finde in it, that sum haue for their vertue been enuied and murdered, yet cease not you to be vertuous, but do your offices to the vttermost: punish sinne boldly, both in your selues and other, so shall God (whose lieutenauntes you are) eyther so mayntayne you, that no malice shall preuayle, or if it do, it shal be for your good, and to your eternall glory both here and in heaven, which I beseche God you may couet and attayne. Amen.[5]

Within the context of the *Mirror,* this is just permissible: although in contradiction to the statement that the punishment of vice would be demonstrated, it is compatible with the theory that a malevolent Fortune bears sway.

With their dual purpose of exposing the fickleness of Fortune and revealing the plagues which follow vice, the authors of the *Mirror* had now to attack the historical material which constituted their subject matter. No one could expect that they would engage in full-scale research; it was enough that the obvious chroniclers—Fabyan, Hall—should be consulted. What if these disagreed? Here trouble set in again. When the matter of Lord Grey's parentage came up, just such a disagreement occurred, and the authors of the prologue to the tale grew wroth. Such a disagreement was a great hindrance to truth, they said, and the fault lay with the nobility, who had been too neglectful to collect all their documents. It was they who should have written a full and true chronicle. But the *Mirror* itself was a didactic book, and since research was out of the question, they will follow Hall in matters which are doubtful. "And where we seme to swarve from hys reasons and causes of dyuers doynges, there we gather vpon coniecture such thinges as seeme most probable, *or at the least most convenient for the furderaunce of our purpose.*"[6] So much for historical accuracy.

Much may be excused a poem, however historical and didactic. Yet the attitude of the authors of the *Mirror,* both in terms of underlying purpose and of attitude toward accuracy, can easily be duplicated. Even Camden, surely the most conscientious of all the Tudor historians, omitted detailed description of some few events because elaboration would not be conducive to morality.[7] And Samuel Daniel—the poet turned historian—tells us that "the Computation of Times is not of so great moment, figures are easily mistaken, the 10. of July, and the 6. of August, with a yeare over or under, makes not a man the wiser in the businesse then done, which is onely that he desires."[8] History with an ulterior purpose of this sort led inevitably to bad history.

The best summary of the older Tudor attitude is extant in a work which was not English but French, and which was naturalized only immediately before Sidney set about writing his *Defense.* Bishop Amyot's preface to the readers of his Plutarch points out that history was to be commended because it combined profit and delight, and because it always taught moral lessons, and political, "for it is a certaine rule and instruction, which by examples past, teacheth us to judge of thinges present, and to foresee things to come: so as we may know what to like of, and what to follow, what to mislike, and what to eschew."[9] No success is possible without the study of history, for it gives examples and precepts. Moreover history-writing itself is part of the mechanism by which good is rewarded and evil punished, because the evil are deterred by "the reproch of everlasting infamie," while the good are spurred on by the thought of "immortall praise and glorye."[10] Granted that the study of history cannot alone make a wise magistrate or an able captain: nature, art and practice are all necessary, and history can only aid the second. But, in Amyot, the old difficulty recurs: the historian must not show hatred or favor, but he must be a man of "good judgement to discerne what is to be sayd, and what is to be left unsayd, and what would do more harm to have it declared, than do good to have it reproved or condemned."[11] It was the historian's task do serve the commonweal, and to act "as a register to set downe the judgements and definitive sentences of Gods Court."[12] If history is thus useful, and delightful, to ordinary men, how much more is it for great princes and kings! And so Amyot goes on, quite naturally, to praise Plutarch.

All the old contradictions arise here. If, as Amyot says, God's judgments are inscrutable, what business has the historian to omit matters? If one is to learn from history's examples the differences between good actions and bad, successful actions and unsuccessful, what right has the historian to choose some events as more suitable than others? Worse yet, if everything is determined by Providence—for Amyot eschews Fortune—how can man profit at all? This is no place to discuss the intricacies of the problem of free will, but it is as well to point out that the issue itself was much involved in the Elizabethan discussions of the usefulness of history.

Sidney was perfectly aware of these obstacles in the path of the moralist-historian. Whether we can take everything in his ***Defense of Poesy*** *au pied de la lettre* is perhaps arguable, for he certainly overstated his case—just as Amyot had overstated his own case against the poet. But that is not to say that we can believe nothing of what Sidney says. A few of the points he scores off the historian are obvious enough: feigned orations, already condemned by Bodin, are in the realm of fiction as is the "passionate describing of passions" and fiction belongs to the poets.[13] His chief attack on the historians, however, has to do with their claim to teach morality. In the realm of virtue, the poet should reign supreme, and to defend his title, Sidney attacked the pretences of the historian and the lawyer and the moral philosopher. The lawyer is easily disposed of; but the historian and the moral philosopher—figures of fun, both of them—attack each other so lustily that the poet must needs be called in as moderator, and in the end the judge awards himself the prize. For the original disputants are too successful in pointing out each other's weaknesses, and the poet realizes that while one has the precept and the other the example, neither has both together. The philosopher is too abstruse, and "happy is that man who may understand him," while the poet's wisdom is "food for the tenderest stomachs, the poet is indeed the right popular philosopher."[14] On the other hand, the historian's particularities are, in themselves, meaningless. But, it may be argued, at least the historian is concerned with truth, not with abstractions or feigned tales. Insofar as the question is one of truth and falsehood, there is no argument; "but if the question be for your own use and learning, whether it be better to have it set down as it should be, or as it was," then surely the feigned Cyrus in Xenophon is "more doctrinable" than the true Cyrus in Justin.[15]

> And whereas a man may say, though in universal consideration of doctrine the poet prevaileth, yet that the historian, in his saying such a thing was done, doth warrant a man more in that he shall follow, the answer is manifest: that if he stand upon that *was*—as if he should argue, because it rained yesterday, therefore it should rain today— then indeed it hath some advantage to a gross conceit. But if he know an example only informs a conjectured likelihood, and so go by reason, the poet doth so far exceed him, as he is to frame his example to that which is most reasonable, be it in warlike, politic, or private matters; where the historian in his bare *was* hath many times that which we call fortune to overrule the best wisdom. Many times he must tell events whereof he can yield no cause; and, if he do, it must be poetically.[16]

Here Sidney went too far. In his zeal, he attacked not only the historian's claim to make reasonable generalizations, which is fair enough, but also the claim that we can learn something from events, a theory which depends on the repetition of the events themselves, or at least on the innate sameness of human beings. The poet must claim something similar if he is to teach. Moreover, the remark concerning Fortune, while shrewd enough, was just as applicable to tragic poets who, instead, were praised for teaching "the uncertainty of this world, and upon how weak foundations gilden roofs are builded."[17]

Sidney had still another demonstration of his theory that poetry taught morality more successfully than history, and on this occasion he turned history's best weapon against it. Everyone agreed that history was possessed of the realm of the true, poetry of that of the feigned. As we have seen, Sidney had disposed of the idea earlier to his own satisfaction by showing that history's "truth" was meaningless; now, he returned again to the distinction, with the purpose of demonstrating that poetry's invention was more useful than history's truth. For poetry, unlike history, can make virtue triumph always, can indeed make "Fortune her well-waiting handmaid."[18] The historian can do no such thing, for "history, being captivated to the truth of a

foolish world, is many times a terror from well doing, and an encouragement to unbridled wickedness."[19] Thus, history's one great advantage is turned against it. Not that Sidney believed everything which can be found in history books. In his thorough fashion he had assaulted both the historians and their sources with a mixture of shrewd sense and mocking raillery. And so it was that the historian was removed from his ancient position as a moral arbiter.

If anything, Sidney was too thorough. His treatise provokes a smile quite as readily as it does a nod of agreement, and the rhetorical exaggeration is frequently carried to such an extreme that we know it to be a pose. There is, in short, the danger that we have been engaged in dissecting a soufflé with a dull axe. And so we have. Yet even this admission is insufficient to make one believe that Sidney was not occasionally serious, even when discussing that comic figure the historian. Two other points, however, also give one pause. It is a truism that much of the *Defense* is borrowed from the Italians; Sidney's ideas of history may be among the borrowings. What is worse, Sidney seems to contradict much of the argument of the *Defense* in a letter written to his brother not much more than a year before he wrote his treatise. Even if both these arguments be granted, it does not necessarily prove that the reasoning in the *Defense* is invalid, nor even that Sidney did not himself believe it. Still, it is worth our while to examine the two points.

Professor Weinberg, in his study of the sixteenth century Italian theorists, has told us that the connection of history and poetry to moral philosophy came late; much the same point is made by Professor Beatrice Reynolds in her analysis of a group of sixteenth century texts on the art of history.[20] The implication is that the theory Sidney attacked was a relatively recent one. To an extent this is true. But it is clear that the connection of history and moral philosophy is a good deal older than that: one finds it, for instance, in some of the fifteenth century treatises on education, and it is implicit in much late medieval writing. In fact, the connection between rhetoric and history was a relatively recent one, having come about through the increased interest in Cicero and Quintilian. The great change that Professor Weinberg finds is, it seems to me, a return to an older idea; and in England, Ciceronianism had never penetrated vernacular history-writing at all. The most that may be said is that the connection was once again fashionable at the time that Sidney wrote, not that it was new.[21] Once the connection between history (or poetry) and morality is granted, it is relatively easy to establish the superiority of poetry. The prime advantage of history—truth—becomes of little account, and the single-mindedness of poetry is its greatest asset. Indeed that single-mindedness was included in the very definitions: history is an account of the actions of many men, poetry that of a single action of one man. Naturally, the poet had an easier time inculcating virtue; and the fact that he had to regard truth as only secondary helped still further. History was diffuse, inarticulate; poetry went straight to the point.[22] Obviously, both arts had a good deal in common: the connection to rhetoric was still valid (everyone assumed that history, because persuasive in some sense, should be well-written); both are narrative arts (epic poetry is meant here); both use historical data; and so on.

It was generally considered—at least by the theorists of poetics—that the two arts had a common purpose as well: "both seek to teach, to delight, to move, and to bring profit; history especially seeks utility."[23] But another view of the utility of history was gradually evolving: history was to teach men how to behave, not necessarily in terms of morality, but in terms of politics. At this point, the disadvantages of the historian suddenly became advantages. An art which described the actions of many men was closer to reality than one which described a great action by one man. An art which showed that the virtuous are often punished, and that the wicked as often flourished, while not moral, was at least a description of the world as it is. For the embryo politician, history was a much more useful study than poetry. One mark of this new history was an interest in the causes of events, as much as in the events themselves. To a purely moral historian, causes, while interesting, were not of great importance; to a political historian, they were essential. Although the whole idea of political history was not new, it may be said to have become effectively established through the writings of Machiavelli and Guicciardini, and by the 1580's this view of the utility of history had become of considerable importance.

It is now possible to understand Sidney's famous letter to his brother more clearly. The recommendation of history there began with a definition: "a story, he is nothing but a narration of thinges done, with the beginings, cawses, and appendences therof," and to understand so much, an exact knowledge of chronology was essential.[24] In more detailed and constructive histories, such as those of Herodotus and Thucydides, "yow have principally to note the examples of vertue or vice, with their good or evell successes, the establishments or ruines of great Estates, with the cawses, the tyme and circumstances of the lawes they write of, the entrings, and endings of warrs, and therin the stratagems against the enimy . . . ; and thus much as a very Historiographer."[25] Sidney was unable to resist pointing out that the historian borrowed much of his plumage from the poet. "The last poynt which tendes to teach profite is of a Discourser, which name I give to who soever speakes, *non simpliciter de facto, sed de qualitatibus et circumstantiis facti . . .*" and then Sidney went on to show how the historian at times partook of the nature of a divine, a natural philoso-

pher, a lawyer and especially a moral philosopher.[26] But Sidney ended with a method of learning the historian's analysis of "politick matters",[27] and the repetition of that idea of history, throughout the relevant parts of the letter, shows clearly enough where his own interests lay.

There is nothing in the letter which contradicts the *Defense*. Since Sidney, in his treatise, had never gone to the extreme of suggesting that history is utterly useless as a moral teacher—individual episodes might be useful, even if the body of history were not—it is no surprise to find that point alluded to in the letter. He had not, to be sure, made out much of a case for the historian as a master of politics in the *Defense*, but then defending the historian was no part of his business there, and he had not altogether excluded the notion. The *Defense* emphasized the negative argument, the letter the positive, and the only sort of history for which those arguments hold is the political sort which we have been describing. That there is, nonetheless, exaggeration in the *Defense* is undeniable; but the amount of exaggeration is not such as to invalidate the suggestion that Sidney meant what he said.

It thus becomes clear that Sidney looked on history as being useful only insofar as it gave specific instruction to men of action. If history did teach morality at all, it did so accidentally, and poetry could do the job much more satisfactorily. But poetry could not teach a magistrate how to behave politically; poetry might inculcate in the magistrate the view that one action was morally right and another morally wrong, but it could not teach him to make a good political choice between a number of possible actions, all of which might be equivalent morally. That task belonged to history.

If this statement of Sidney's views on history is correct, we have in the *Defense* the best critical argument on the subject written in Tudor England. Only Sidney really understood the peculiar predicament into which authors such as Baldwin and AmyotCand a myriad of othersChad worked themselves. The analysis argues a knowledge of historical writing of some depth. Precisely what Sidney had read is open to question: of the major sixteenth century writers, only Thomas More (*Richard III*), Machiavelli (*The Prince*) and Jean Bodin come readily to mind. To be sure, Sidney mentioned the great Greek and Roman writers, and the chronographers Lanquet and Melanchthon, but the extent of his reading in them is doubtful. Nonetheless, Languet, so early as 1577, mentioned that Sidney had an inclination to history and had made great progress in it.[28] Moreover, Sidney was acquainted with Camden and Hakluyt, and knew Daniel Rogers, the poet, diplomat and historian manqué, rather well. He was interested in George Buchanan's historical work, and was opposed to the foolishness of the "Brute" legend.[29]

Furthermore, his own writings show a grasp of the subject: the treatise on Ireland backed a Machiavellian maxim by a suggested use of the history of that country, a knowledge which Sidney surely had[30]; the argument against the Queen's marriage used historical examples to prove a generalization about alliances. Even the jesting at Humphrey Lhuyd's little book on early Britain got matters exactly right: it was Lhuyd's cavalier treatment of etymology which made the volume almost useless.[31] Sidney's comments on history are not, then, merely the converse of his judgments on poetry.

The importance of all this in the history of historical writing lies in its timing. A mild sort of revolution was occurring in the art of history, a revolution occasioned by the evident failure of the older form of moral history to produce any great works. Moreover, a revolution was needed in poetics as well and, because the two subjects had been so long connected, the two revolutions were bound to interact. Sidney solved the problem of history by ejecting the subject from the realm of moral philosophy, and by leaving moral philosophy—as a practical subject—to the poets. Whether his resolution—or this part of his resolution—of the problem of poetry was that which finally produced the "Elizabethan" age, others can judge better than the present author. But his resolution of the historical problem was, surely, of importance. His fellow-scholar and friend, William Camden, the best historian of the time, when it came to explaining his motives for writing put the matter of circumstances—of reasons and causes—first; it is not that the moral purpose of history is altogether omitted, but that what had once occupied the first place was now relegated to a subordinate position, and it is this relegation which made possible Camden's work, and Hayward's, and Bacon's.

Notes

[1] On this, F. S. FUSSNER, *The Historical Revolution* (London, 1962), and my "The Elizabethan Revolution in Historiography," *History,* 4 (Meridian Books, 1961), 27-52. There is also a great deal of information in E. M. W. TILLYARD, *Shakespeare's History Plays* (London, 1944), and in the works of Lily B. CAMPBELL, especially *Shakespeare's "Histories", Mirrors of Elizabethan Policy* (San Marino, 1947).

[2] *The Correspondence of Philip Sidney and Hubert Languet,* ed. W. A. Bradley (Boston, 1912), 30.

[3] See Willard FARNHAM, *The Medieval Heritage of Elizabethan Tragedy* (Oxford, 1956).

[4] *The Mirror for Magistrates,* ed. Lily B. Campbell (Cambridge, 1938), 62 (reproduction of title page of 1559), 65-6.

[5%] *Ibid.,* 67.

[6] *Ibid.,* 267; the italics are mine.

[7] William CAMDEN, *The History of the . . . Princess Elizabeth* [*Annales*] (London, 1675), 235.

[8] Samuel DANIEL, *The Collection of the History of England,* rev. ed. (London, 1634), A4r.

[9] PLUTARCH, *Lives of the Noble Grecians and Romanes,* trans. Sir Thomas North, ed. G. Wyndham (London: Tudor Translations, 1895), "Amiot to the Readers," I, 10.

[10] *Ibid.,* 11.

[11] *Ibid.,* 15.

[12] *Ibid.,* 15.

[13] Sir Philip SIDNEY, *The Defense of Poesie,* in *Literary Criticism, Plato to Dryden,* ed. A. H. Gilbert (Detroit, 1962), 409. I use this as the most convenient good edition, though Gilbert modernizes the spelling.

[14] *Ibid.,* 420, 423.

[15] *Ibid.,* 423.

[16] *Ibid.,* 424.

[17] *Ibid.,* 432.

[18] *Ibid.,* 425.

[19] *Ibid.,* 425-6.

[20] Bernard WEINBERG, *A History of Literary Criticism in the Renaissance,* 2 vols. (Chicago, 1961), I, 30; Beatrice Reynolds, "Shifting Currents in Historical Criticsm", *Journal of the History of Ideas,* XIV, No. 4 (Oct. 1953), 477-8.

[21] Perhaps it would be most accurate to say that the moral and rhetorical theories of history had coexisted ever since the time of the ancients, and that the issue at any given moment was which of the two was predominant.

[22] Again, of course, the point is over-stated. Characters who are either all black or all white are difficult to believe in, and Sidney, when it came to writing his own epic, did sometimes modify the extremes. At least, he seems to have allowed the innocent to suffer: just the sort of thing that happened in history and should not in poetry. See J. F. Danby, *Poets on Fortune's Hill* (London, 1952), 52.

[23] Weinberg I. 41, summarizing Dionigi Atanagi.

[24] *The Complete Works of Sir Philip Sidney,* ed. A. Feuillerat, 4 vols. (Cambridge, 1922-6), III, 130.

[25] *Ibid.,* 130-1.

[26] *Ibid.,* 131.

[27] *Ibid.,* 132.

[28] *The Correspondence of Philip Sidney and Hubert Languet, loc. cit.*

[29] Sidney, Camden and Hakluyt were at Oxford together; the first two shared the historian, Thomas Cooper, as tutor. For Rogers' connection to Sidney, and the connection of both to George Buchanan, J. E. Phillips, "George Buchanan and the Sidney Circle," *Huntington Library Quarterly,* XII, No. 1 (Nov. 1948), 23-55, and J. A. van Dorsten, *Poets, Patrons, and Professors* (Leiden, 1962).

[30] SIDNEY, *Complete Works,* III, 49-50; Sidney refers to the same maxim (attributed by him to Machiavelli) in the *Correspondence of Philip Sidney and Hubert Languet,* 60.

[31] *The Correspondence of Philip Sidney and Hubert Languet,* 38-40.

Richard A. Lanham (essay date 1965)

SOURCE: "Sidney the Narrator," in *The Old Arcadia,* Yale University Press, 1965, pp. 318-31.

[In the following excerpt, Lanham explores the complex, shifting, and sometimes ambiguous narration of the Old Arcadia.*]*

An age that cherishes the memory of Henry James can hardly be expected to allow Sidney the narrator to escape unscathed. The spectacle of an author frankly telling a tale *in propria persona,* commenting on it as it flows from his pen in asides to his "Dear Ladies," obviously regulating the unfolding of the narrative, makes the modern reader as uncomfortable as James felt in the loquacious I've-got-no-secrets company of Trollope. Sidney seems in many places to give the show away, to tell us twice over how we should feel. Myrick comments: "In the original version, where Sidney so often disregards the principles of the *Defence,* he frequently drops his role of 'maker' and comments upon the story."[1] But, as we have seen, the "message" of the Old *Arcadia* may not be quite so obvious, the reader's response not so clearly predictable, as has formerly been thought. It is logical, then, to seek in Sidney as narrator a figure more

complex than the chatty, brotherly, facile moralizer he at first seems to be.

The narrator of the Old *Arcadia* is ostensibly Philip Sidney—no *persona* is involved. He tells the tale to his sister and her friends. If he were writing today he would probably eliminate all his parenthetical assertions and simply report, or seem to report, what happened. There would be no asides to his "Dear Ladies." The mask of "maker" would never slip from his face. Not having our advantages, he lets it slip so often it is difficult to tell when it is up and when down. He seems not to have taken a great deal of care to keep the two roles separate, not to have acknowledged, in fact, any fundamental separation at all. "Maker" and "Commentator" is a misleading dichotomy for the Old *Arcadia.* Instead, we might distinguish first a narrator who is essentially a reporter, who describes the scenes to his "Dear Ladies" as if he were watching a play. His principal function at times seems to be that of a man changing a play into a prose romance. Scenery, pose, gesture, expression, all are given through his "comment." In this way, his interruptions could be said to heighten the dramatic vividness, not to detract from it. This kind of comment Myrick would presumably construe as legitimately belonging to the "maker." But the narrator also annotates, both implicitly and explicitly, what he describes. He is omniscient, he has seen the play before. He has also written, produced, and directed it. He even plays a part in it. In none of these roles is he less of a "maker" than in any other, and the "product" results from the complex interaction of these roles upon one another, not from any single one.

To be more explicit: we have first the basic story of the princes' adventures in Arcadia, in which Love pursues its inevitable triumph. The narrator simply describes this. He is powerless to change it, though he clearly would like to at certain points. He sympathizes with the characters much as he would had they been created by somebody else. But he knows what is going to happen, and try as he does to put a good face on some of the dastardly deeds, he cannot change the fundamental facts. Even when he becomes bored with their speeches he cannot shorten them: at one point when Basilius is reopening his heart to Cleophila he remarks on Basilius' discourse, "with many other suche hony wordes, which my penn growes allmoste weary to sett downe" (168). This is simply to say that Sidney, once he has made his initial assumption, that his characters are violently in love, does not interfere with the events which he—as "maker" and "commentator" and "actor"—sees as inevitably following from this assumption. The consequences of passion are in no way softened. There is only one exception to this, the happy ending. (It is a vital exception, of course.) But by not otherwise softening the effects of passion, Sidney avoids the very thing to which James so objected in Trollope: the author's confession that he could make things turn out differently if he wanted to. The narrator's comments and regrets have precisely the opposite effect here; they emphasize the inevitability of the "Pilgrimmage of Passion" passing before us. Sidney at one point even says he is simply retelling what is contained in official records: "And doubt yow not, fayre Ladyes, there wanted no questioning how thinges had passed, but bycause I will have the thanckes my self, yt shall bee I yow shall heare yt of, And thus the Auncyent Recordes of *Arcadia* say, yt fell owte" (47). Too much ought not to be made of this mythical authority, for it is not seriously or repeatedly introduced, but it does indicate that Sidney intended to place himself in the role of an omniscient narrator reporting a story whose main events are unalterable. Occasionally he rearranges speeches uttered in haste or emotion. He gives in full the text of songs which only run rapidly through the mind of his characters: "But doo not thincke (Fayre Ladyes) his thoughtes had suche Leysure as to ronne over so longe a Ditty: The onely generall fancy of yt came into his mynde fixed upon the sence of the sweet Subject [Philoclea]" (226). But he does not change any of the essentials of the story or radically alter the character of his personages.

The narrator also comments on the action being played out before him. Sometimes Sidney is a modest narrator: "In what Case pore *Gynecia* was, when shee knewe the voyce and felt the body of her husband? Fayre Ladyes, yt ys better to knowe by imaginacyon, then experyence?" (214). Occasionally he seems personal, almost autobiographical, as when Pyrocles and Philoclea are tucked in bed at the end of Book III: "Hee gives mee occasyon to leave hym in so happy a plighte, least my Penn mighte seeme to grudge, at the due Blisse of these pore Lovers, whose Loyalty had but smalle respite of theyre fyery Agonyes" (227). At other times, he seems to be the impersonal mouthpiece of conventional wisdom. The first sentence of Book IV, "The Everlasting Justice" etc., is one of innumerable examples. The Old *Arcadia* is larded with sententiae, many of them voiced by this speaker of conventional wisdom. They are part of the romance in a way that such speculations as the one quoted, about Gynecia's disappointment at finding her lover become her husband, are not. They supply a moral framework within which the action can be judged. Critics have, of course, objected to this. Aristotle's dictum that "the poet should speak as little as possible in his own person for it is not this that makes him an imitator."[2] developed into the modern preference for "showing" over "telling," has caused the Old *Arcadia* to be ranked beneath the New because in the Old the second method allegedly predominates over the first. Muir writes, for example: "In some ways the old *Arcadia* is more directly didactic than the new. Sidney cut out the narrator's moralizing, often transferring it to one or other of the

characters in the story."[3] Yet the moral orientation which the narrator provides is essential to the reader's evaluation of the action. The narrator performs, in fact, the function Aristotle looked for from the chorus.[4]

Not all of the narrator's moralizings are the expected opinions. The beginning sentence of Book IV, though conventional, is still in its context surprising and strong; . . . it colors the whole of our reading of the book which follows. It is misleading to view these as pointless asides of a garrulous narrator. This difference between the narrative poses does not lend itself to absolute demonstration but will, I am confident, become obvious with a close reading. The important point to be made is that sometimes Sidney stands distanced from the narrator or, to put it another way, his comments upon the action are often so general or traditional as to be rather part of the narrative than personal asides. It is a mistake to make out a complete distinction between the "real" Sidney and "Sidney the narrator," for the distance between them frequently changes. But there are differences between the two nevertheless. Sidney's tongue is more fully in his cheek at some times than at others.

The first Pyrocles-Musidorus scene, for example, shows a narrator who describes its humor without betraying an understanding of it. He is careful to make the comedy clear for us but he does not acknowledge it openly or seem even to be aware of it. He goes on, much in the manner of one of Swift's narrators, being precise about details and oblivious to larger issues. When Pyrocles, in the midst of his passionate confession to his friend of his noble love for Philoclea, reveals his real motive in a moment of heat, the narrator reports it without emphasis along with the praises of heavenly love which have preceded it: "And thus gently, yow may, yf yt please yow, thincke of mee, neyther doubte yow, because I werre a womans apparell, I will bee the more womannish, since I assure yow (for all my apparell) there ys no thing I desyer more, then fully to proove my self a man, in this enterpryse" (19-20). There can be little doubt that Sidney placed this here as a parenthetical ironic comment on the extravagant language Pyrocles uses to describe his love, but the narrator is specifically made blind to it. At other times, his perception of the comedy is partial, and deliberately understated. He is closer to the author but not coincident with him, as when Musidorus reverses his stand against Pyrocles' falling in love: "*Pyrocles* harte was not so oppressed with the twoo mighty passions of Love & unkyndenes, but, that yt yeelded to some myrthe at this Comaundement of *Musidorus,* that hee shoulde love *Philoclea*" (22). Another example leaves us in doubt as to how widely the narrator is willing to be caught smiling. In the midst of the suicide debate which follows the seduction, Pyrocles pretends to agree to Philoclea's demand that he stay alive in order to humor her:

"*Pyrocles* who had that for a Lawe unto hym not to leave Philoclea in any thinge unsatisfyed, allthoughe hee still remayned in his former purpose, and knewe the tyme woulde growe shorte for yt" (275). When Dorus, questioned in Book I about his desires for employment, replies (so that he can remain close to Pamela) that his mind is "wholly sett up on pastorall affaires" (49) the ironic dismissal of the pastoral element is passed on by a tongue-in-cheek narrator without comment. Such a dismissal of what at least purports to be the central concern of the story—pastoral affairs—is likely to escape a modern reader but presupposes, one must think, a considerable meeting of minds between Sidney and his anticipated audience. Otherwise such persistent ironic shorthand simply would not succeed.

Sometimes Sidney comments wryly on his characters in asides which take the reader fully into his confidence. He describes Pyrocles' awakening after his night with Philoclea: "But, so yt was yt *Pyrocles* awaked, grudging in hym self, that sleepe (though very shorte) had robbed hym, of any parte of those his highest Contentmentes" (269). He is even more obvious in his reflections on his clowns, as when Dametas is hastening on to his buried treasure:

> Many tymes hee cursed his horses want of Consideratyon that in so ymportunate a Matter woulde make no greater speede, many tymes hee wisshed hym self the back of an Asse to help to carry away his newe soughte Riches: An unfortunate wissher, for yf hee had aswell wisshed the hedd, yt had beene graunted hym, at lengthe, beeyng come to the Tree whiche hee hoped shoulde beare so golden Ackornes.
>
> [177]

Sometimes the mockery is made more indirect by being put into the mouth of the character: Mopsa, for example, after she has been told about the wishing tree by Dorus, "Conjured hym by all her precyous Loves, that shee mighte have the first possession of the wisshing Tree, assuring hym, that for the enjoyng of her hee shoulde never neede to Clyme farr" (184).

The moral is sometimes explicitly drawn, sometimes left entirely up to the reader. In the fifth book, for example, Philanax goes to meet Euarchus, who has paused just inside the boundary to make clear his peaceful intent. Philanax finds the great King "taking his Rest under a Tree, with no more affected pompes, then as a Man that knewe (howe so ever hee was exalted) the beginning & ende of his Body was earthe" (331). The moral is unmistakable: privilege does not extend beyond the grave, better not abuse it on this side. Then on the next page we read:

> These Rightly wyse and temperate Consideracyons mooved *Euarchus,* to take his Laboursome

Journey to see whether by his authority hee might drawe *Basilius* from this burying him self alyve, and to returne ageane to employ his oulde yeares in doyng good, the onely happy action of mans lyfe: Neyther was hee withoute a Consideracyon in hym self to provyde the Mariage of *Basilius* twoo Daughters, for his Sonne and Nephewe ageanst theyre returne. The tedyus expectation of which joyned with the feare of theyre miscarrying (having beene long withoute hearing any newes from them) made hym the willinger to ease that parte of Melancholy with chaunging ye objectes of his wearyed sences. [332-33]

The full context is given to demonstrate how unobtrusively this tremendously ironic and important fact—that the two princes and princesses would have been married anyway—is offered to the reader. The really important moral is not drawn at all, is almost hidden in fact.

Even these few examples show that the narrator does not remain at a fixed distance either from his characters or from his audience. This easily confuses the modern reader, who soon learns that such a narrator cannot be trusted. We cannot follow his lead always, and cannot feel sure that we are understanding the moral orientation of the romance.

This untrustworthy narrator is one of the real difficulties of the romance. The narrator accepts Euarchus as the all-wise king and moralizes, as we have just seen, on his countless evidences of wisdom and probity. Yet the same narrator also seems to be in full sympathy with the heroic seductions carried out by the princes. His praise of them is too frequent throughout the romance to need documentation. The reader is bound to think his attitude inconsistent; in the first half of the romance he is all for love, in the second all for justice.[5] It is tempting to postulate a narrator quite separate from Sidney, a *persona* who accepts the tale uncritically as a pastoral romance of serious, intentional, noble sentiment, and to place Sidney the author outside him altogether. We could then introduce Sidney into the romance with Euarchus and the inconsistency would be solved. But this postulation ignores the many instances of Sidney in propria persona. It fails to notice, also, the instances in which the narrator seems to see further than Euarchus does. The narrator comments, for example, on the irony of Euarchus' sitting in judgment on his son and nephew: "In suche shadowe or rather pit of Darckenes the wormish mankynde lives that neyther they knowe howe to foresee nor what to feare; and are but lyke Tennys balles tossed by the Rackett of the higher powers" (358). The opposite position—that Sidney is frank and frankly himself at all times—is as easy to refute.

The reader can never lay his hand on a constant rule, applicable to all situations. He must read carefully, of course, but even then the author's attitude toward his creation remains often puzzling, sometimes frankly ambiguous. Sidney is always getting up from his seat in the audience, climbing on stage to act a scene, turning to comment on it in an aside, arranging his characters in specific poses and facial expressions, and then going back to his seat for the next scene. Much as we would like him to stay put, he will not. This movement makes the romance much harder to interpret, but it also offers the possibility of an ultimate meaning a little more bracing than the predigested Tudor political philosophy and overcooked Petrarchan passions which are usually given as its raison d'être. For these various roles affect one another in interesting combinations. The basic action laid down by Sidney the "maker" proceeds from a single action—Basilius' withdrawal—without outside help. The narrator makes the traditional observations, often so obvious that they cause a good deal of irritation, but neglects to comment on facts he relates which are of great interest to the careful reader of the primary, unchangeable story. Immediately the two kinds of "morals," the obvious ones drawn by the narrator and those implicit in the logic of the plot, begin to be compared in the reader's mind. Sidney the "maker" begins to question the adequacy of traditional wisdom about his chosen subject of love.

The unreliable narrator introduces several difficulties of interpretation. First of all, the comedy is weakened, for we are not always sure when to laugh or how hard. L. C. Potts has written that "the first requisite of a comic narrative is that it should be precise; the finest shades of character should stand revealed, and the situation must be clear."[6] Sidney is sometimes imprecise. Potts also sensibly points out that all comic narrators moralize, that comic illumination is part of the role. Sidney's fault is perhaps not intrusion but maladroit intrusion. More generally, the ambiguous narrator is at the root of the confusion as to how seriously the romance is to be taken. Doubtless it is true, as Wayne C. Booth has recently said, that "It is only by distinguishing between the author and his implied image that we can avoid pointless and unverifiable talk about such qualities as 'sincerity' or 'seriousness' in the author."[7] But what do we do if we cannot distinguish between them? The thesis of Booth's brilliant book, that an author ought not to allow this confusion to occur, may be correct but hardly helps in deciding when author and "implied image" coincide and when they do not. The presence of an undependable narrator means that the romance lacks a completely reliable control, for no other character is adequate to this function. This lack is not acute when the narrator's traditional moralization is sufficient for interpretation of the events he describes, but when his comments move us in one direction and the logic of events the opposite way, the reader is bewildered. This bewilderment may, of course, be intended[8] but if

we suspect it to arise from inadvertent shifts of narratorial distance and posture we shall be seriously disoriented in the world of Arcadia.

Such disorientation has not been felt by many of Sidney's commentators. The license of romance has operated to excuse Sidney the narrator from anything like a consistent moral scrutiny of his own tale. This moralistic point of view, it will be immediately objected, simply does not apply to a romance. A modern reader must do as the Elizabethans did and accept the superficial moral with gusto. He must read for the rhetoric. He should not make rhetorical mouthpieces into moral beings; he should not seek out subtleties where they do not exist. But if they do exist? They obtrude themselves on any reader who is willing to credit Sidney with a moral judgment beyond the kindergarten level.

The didacticism of the Old *Arcadia* has been commonly misunderstood because the dialectic nature of the romance has been overlooked. The teller's ambivalent character has been ignored. Speeches have been quoted to prove that Sidney believed this or that, and a following speech which presents the opposite case has been ignored, or dismissed—if it disagreed with the commentator's theory—as token opposition erected only to be demolished. Sidney was, obviously, often more convinced by one side than by the other, but the contest, both in his own mind and in the romance, is not so one-sided as conventional moralists on the prowl for examples of virtue often proclaim. There are no easy answers to Gynecia's outcries, for example, no ready solutions for Cupid's blindness. The affirmative statement never wholly cancels out the negative one preceding it. The first stays in mind to color and add depth to the second. The proposed resolution of the two opposing forces of the romance, reason and passion, is Christian marriage. But circumstances combined to make Sidney see it as a not wholly harmonious synthesis, a sometimes inadequate compromise with passion. He clearly indicates this in the irresistible force of passion which leads up to the near-catastrophe a happy ending so narrowly averts. The proper moral is drawn, but in the teeth of contradictory evidence. We are meant to "take" the moral solution, but with the remembrance of the forces with which it must contend fresh in mind.

Sidney's fondness for dialectic in his literary practice has been obscured, as I see it, by ignoring the great sophistication of his attitude toward rhetoric. That the Old *Arcadia* uses rhetoric is common knowledge. That it is also *about* the use of rhetoric seems to me equally important. We might go so far as to say that, obliquely at least, the Old *Arcadia* addresses itself to the main point of defense in the *Defence* that rhetoric (or poetry—the two are almost synonymous in this case) is a neutral weapon, lending itself alike to good uses and bad. Cleophila/Pyrocles, for example, calms the rebel mob with the same arts she/he uses in trying to excite the mob to desert Euarchus and rally to the two princesses. Gynecia uses the same language to express her anguish as her husband does to voice his ludicrous infatuation. The many instances of ironic qualification of the speeches, which together create the tension between speech and action, show Sidney aware of the opportunity for deception that rhetorical training offered. The constant conflict in *Astrophil and Stella* between the direct language of real passion and the feast of cold compliment with which literature in his time set it out recurs repeatedly in the Old *Arcadia*. Most often it is not Sidney but one of his characters who employs the arts of rhetoric, and the reader watches it in the devil's work as often as not. The reader is not fooled. He is specifically intended to remain undeceived.

The *Defence* reveals how closely poetry and rhetoric were linked in Sidney's mind. Sidney's literary method in the Old *Arcadia* (and in *Astrophil and Stella* too) is, however, diametrically opposed to the rhetorical. It is dialectical through and through. The reader watches rhetoric persuade others while Sidney aims to persuade him through dialectic. A little reflection shows the informing traits of the romance to be clearly dialectical. Zandvoort has remarked Sidney's fondness for analyzing a proposition into two opposite points of view.[9] Many of the rhetorical "occasions" are in fact disputations or debates. The soliloquies present, for the most part, a character arguing with himself or with the universe. The fundamental organizing principle of the eclogues is a division into two opposing camps, on both trivia and large issues. In its largest sense, the romance may be fairly described as a dialectic between reason and passion, in which each side, through an often-changing personification, uses all the devices of rhetoric to prevail over the other. Thus rhetoric, as widely as Sidney uses it, is always kept at a safe distance. Its flowers are—as it were—always smelled by somebody else. It is in this sense that the Old *Arcadia* is about rhetoric, about its abuses and, to be fair, its beauties as well.

Sidney must have felt he could rely on his original small, sophisticated audience properly to separate narrator and rhetorical excess. He could depend on their personal knowledge of himself to supply the needed control. He did not have to write it in. It may well be that the shifting in the New of some narrative comment to characters in the romance, which has been called an evidence of Sidney's growth as a storyteller, is actually an attempt to provide direction for the needs of a larger and anonymous audience.

A sense of the original audience excuses us from thinking that the asides to his "Fayre Ladyes" crash the barriers of fictional form. For the Old *Arcadia* is not a pastoral romance pure and simple, but rather a pastoral romance told by a brother to his sister. The recurrent references to his audience and to himself remind the reader of the larger context of the romance—that it is from an aristocratic brother to an aristocratic sister, that it is to be read with the lightness of touch not to be looked for in an adolescent's whole-hearted absorption in Sir Walter Scott. The reader often feels himself in the place of the fair ladies, at a third remove from what is happening in Arcadia. The asides are still another attempt by Sidney to indicate the spirit in which we are to read.

The sense of a particular audience is part of the romance. The introductory letter should be accepted to this extent at least—a general, heterogeneous audience was not envisaged. Rather we should picture a Wilton fireside. The comedy is immeasurably improved when the work is read aloud. It might be as well to think of it as something like closet drama. Set speeches or a rapid exchange of repartee were probably given dramatic heightening, perhaps divided into parts, during the reading. The songs would almost certainly have been sung. Although delivery is often the subdivision of rhetoric most briefly dealt with by writers on the subject, it is always stressed, often with poetry as an example of the advantages it offers. Aristotle, for example, comments in *Rhetorica*:

> This [the proper method of delivery] is a thing that affects the success of a speech greatly; but hitherto the subject has been neglected. Indeed, it was long before it found a way into the arts of tragic drama and epic recitation: at first poets acted their tragedies themselves. It is plain that delivery has just as much to do with oratory as with poetry.[10]

Unquestionably, a reader or group of readers would have heightened the comedy, just as they would have reinforced the psychology of each scene by the gestures Sidney describes.

Youthful Sidney has been taken to task by Zandvoort as a clumsy, immature storyteller,[11] and even those who praise the narrative technique of the Old do so because it is so simple and straightforward. Actually it is neither clumsy nor straightforward. The plot, as we have shown, is artful to a fault. The manner of telling may in the last analysis be equally so. If we call Sidney clumsy because he overworks the phrase "as yow shall shortly heare,"[12] while ignoring, for example, the great skill with which he interweaves narration and speech, we shall distort both his skill at the time of writing the Old and his rationale in the revision. His narrative style has obvious faults—witness the cliffhanger stratagem. But denied the grace of these warhorses, who would be saved? There are easier ways to tell a love story if that is all one wants to do. That was *not* all Sidney wanted to do. He was concerned to make clear his complex—perhaps contradictory—feelings about that love story, or more precisely that kind of love story. I suggest that this concern prompted him to develop a complex use of the narratorial pose which English prose fiction had not up to that time possessed.

The Sidney one imagines as author of the Old *Arcadia* emerges as less a plaster saint than is usually thought. He becomes, though, a shrewder author. For the dialectical approach is far superior to the rhetorical for an imaginative work. An intelligent reader is never insulted by an author's moralization if he is informed of the desperate paradox it attempts to solve. The author becomes the preacher only when he sets up his tray of simple solutions for the problems endemic to mankind. The genuinely persuasive part of his work states the paradox, not its solution. Sidney clearly saw this as an artist, if he did not always admit to it as a man. His romance is not simply a rhetorical statement of the good old truths, though there are enough of them in it. Rather it shows how perilous a life those truths have in a world "by love possessed." The Old *Arcadia* is a dramatic statement of the fundamentally paradoxical relation between passion on the one hand and a livable public and private order on the other. For Sidney knew that though the rhetorician can never admit to doubt, the poet—if he is wise—will never pretend to certainty.

Notes

[1] *Sidney as Literary Craftsman*, p. 243.

[2] *Aristotle's Theory of Poetry and Fine Art*, trans. S. H. Butcher (4th ed. London, 1920), p. 93.

[3] "Sidney," p. 21.

[4] If the narrator is in some way a chorus, Sidney has an Aristotelian shield: "The Chorus too should be regarded as one of the actors; it should be an integral part of the whole, and share in the action" (Butcher, p. 69).

[5] This problem has been discussed apropos of the *Arcadia* by Kenneth T. Rowe, and a verdict of fundamental inconsistency brought in ("Romantic Love and Parental Authority in Sidney's Arcadia," University of Michigan, *Contributions in Modern Philology*, No. 4 [April 1947], p. 16). There, of course, the problem is easier to solve. The inconsistency results from the grafting together of two fragments of fundamentally different intent. In the Old, the remedy comes harder. Here the reader does seem to be clubbed from behind by a surprise ending à la Herman Wouk.

[6] *Comedy* (London, n.d.), p. 67.

[7] *The Rhetoric of Fiction* (Chicago, 1961), p. 75.

[8] See below, Chapter 6, for a discussion of this.

[9] *Sidney's Arcadia*, p. 172.

[10] 3. 1403 b.

[11] *Sidney's Arcadia*, pp. 67 and passim.

[12] Ibid., p. 84.

J. G. Nichols (essay date 1974)

SOURCE: "A Feeling Skill," in *The Poetry of Sir Philip Sidney: An Interpretation in the Context of His Life and Times*, Liverpool University Press, 1974, pp. 136-54.

[*In the following excerpt, Nichols analyzes several sonnets from* Astrophil and Stella *and contends that they demonstrate that Sidney was a master of meter and a precise, imaginative poet.*]

One of the fascinations of any sonnet-sequence is the pull between our inclination to read each sonnet as a self-contained poem and our knowledge that it is also part of a larger whole. To revert to the metaphor of *Astrophil and Stella* as a play—each sonnet has its own distinctive personality, and this personality interacts with the personalities of the other sonnets. Such a comment as this is particularly relevant to *Astrophil and Stella*: 'Every sonnet is a compressed drama, and every sonnet-sequence is a greater drama built up of such dramatic moments.'[1] Since I have discussed some sonnets, or parts of them, with reference to the main question of how we should read the drama as a whole, I shall in this chapter discuss in a little detail some of the 'dramatic moments'. I shall choose among those which seem to me to be most successful and (a further indication of the generally high standard maintained in the sequence) they will be sonnets which I have more or less neglected up to now.

The dramatic qualities of individual sonnets are evident even in comparatively small matters of technique. The frequent contrast between an elaborate tissue of figures and a simple, often colloquial, diction[2] is dramatic. The beginning of the first sonnet is typical:

> Loving in truth, and faine in verse my love
> to show,
> That the deare She might take some
> pleasure of my paine:
> Pleasure might cause her reade, reading
> might make her know,
> Knowledge might pitie winne, and pitie
> grace obtaine,

I sought fit words to paint the blackest
  face of woe . . .[3]

Here we may notice the use of alliteration, personification, and metaphor, all combined in the main figure
of climax (a more complex figure than appears from
these few lines, since this climax is only one of several in the poem all leading up to the main climax at
the end); and we may notice too the simplicity of the
diction in contrast to the complexity of the figures.
This contrast is one reason why the poems in *Astrophil and Stella* seem so often to be both highly wrought
and artless at the same time. The ending of the second
sonnet may look at first like simplicity itself; certainly
the diction is simple:

  . . . And now employ the remnant of my
    wit,
  To make my selfe beleeve, that all is well,
  While with a feeling skill I paint my hell.[4]

If we wished for an instance of a 'natural style', the
concluding couplet might well come to mind; but on
a careful reading we are bound to become aware of
the artifice which has gone into its making, if only
when we notice that the full rhyme of 'well' and 'hell'
is combined with half-rhymes made by 'all' and 'skill'.[5]
These half-rhymes have the effect of muting what
would otherwise be a strong rhyme at the ends of the
lines; the statement 'all is well', strong in itself, is
qualified by the preceding 'To make my selfe beleeve';
and the last line is slowed down by the parenthetical
'with a feeling skill': these details work against the
natural tendency of the couplet to seem self-confident.
We gather what Astrophil means by 'the remnant of
my wit', and we are glad to find that 'the remnant' is
sufficient to ensure the adequate expression of his
plight.

As with diction and figures, so with metre. Any writer
of poetry in English is, and any reader of poetry in
English ought to be, aware of the constant tug between the regular pattern of the metre and the variations caused by the speech-stress, the stress demanded by the sense and tone of the lines.[6] Many things go
to make up the total effect which we call 'rhythm';
but this dramatic conflict of stresses is arguably the
most important. It is part of the tension there always
is between a poem as a sort of ritual celebration, a
well-proportioned artefact, and a poem as something
that seems the natural, inevitable expression of human
notions and feelings. These lines, for instance, are
perfectly metrical, and to that extent are formal and
even ritualistic:

  It is most true, that eyes are form'd to serve
  The inward light: and that the heav'nly part
  Ought to be king, from whose rules who do
    swerve,

Rebels to Nature, strive for their owne
  smart.[7]

The inversion of the first foot in the third line, where
'Ought' takes a stress instead of 'to', is an example
of a practice very common in English verse, a practice which we may call 'allowable' in the sense that it
is something poets may do while still preserving the
feel of a metrical pattern. It is worth mentioning,
however, that such devices, now part of any poet's
equipment, were not always so obvious: Sidney's
metrical skill has some historical importance. One need
only read Gascoigne to notice a difference:[8]

  My woorthy Lord, I pray you wonder not,
  To see your woodman shoote so ofte awrie,
  Nor that he stands amased like a sot,
  And lets the harmlesse deare (unhurt) go
    by.[9]

These are not lines which I would wish to denigrate,
and there are signs of something metrically very interesting at the beginning of the third line; but Gascoigne's regularity is comparatively uncomplicated, with
the metrical and speech stresses tending to coincide,
and this is evidence of a lack of certainty about metre
which is noticeable generally in English poets before
Sidney and Spenser. However, Sidney's historical
importance, as one of the first to exploit fully a quality
of English verse which now seems obvious, is not
what I am mainly concerned with here. It is the subtly
dramatic use he makes of it which matters. He could,
of course, have ensured a stress on 'Ought' by placing it in a position where it would take a metrical
stress. But, by stressing it in conflict with the metrical
pattern, he stresses it more;[10] this is important in a
poem whose theme is the distinction between what
ought to be and what is; the extra weight on 'Ought'
is a hint of what to expect later in the poem, what is
stated directly in the very last line:

  True, and yet true that I must *Stella* love.[11]

Such metrical dexterity is normal in *Astrophil and
Stella*.

To say that some of the sonnets in *Astrophil and
Stella* are better than others is only to say what might
safely be hazarded by someone who had never read
the sequence. I shall concentrate on some of Sidney's
successes, partly because the proportion of them is
very high, and partly because, with such a fine poet,
effort is better spent in attempting to appreciate the
subtlety of his effects than in picking out faults. Nevertheless, it would be misleading to imply that the
writing in *Astrophil and Stella* is faultless:

  There is so much careless writing in *Astrophel
  and Stella* that malicious quotation could easily

make it appear a failure. Sidney can hiss like a serpent ('Sweet swelling lips well maist thou swell'), gobble like a turkey ('Moddels such be wood globes'), and quack like a duck ('But God wot, wot not what they mean').[12]

The main point here is sound, and the examples given speak (or 'hiss' or 'gobble') for themselves. But some caution is necessary. Certainly the last words Lewis quotes do 'quack like a duck'; but it is arguable that they are meant to: in their context, where the tone is one of mock-solemnity,[13] their ludicrous sound is dramatically appropriate:

> Some do I hear of Poets' furie tell,
> But (God wot) wot not what they meane by
>   it:
> And this I swear by blackest brooke of hell,
> I am no pick-purse of another's wit.[14]

Similarly, the tongue-twisting nature of a line worse than any quoted by Lewis may be a way of stressing the difficulties faced by 'Reason', who is addressed in the poem:

> Why shouldst thou toyle our thornie soile
>   to till?[15]

In contrast, it is easy to pick out harmonious lines:

> And in her eyes of arrowes infinit.[16]

> No lovely *Paris* made thy *Hellen* his . . .[17]

> O do not let thy Temple be destroyd.[18]

In general, however, it is not mellifluence which we can expect, so much as a dramatic appropriateness of the sound and rhythm:

> Vertue awake, Beautie but beautie is,
> I may, I must, I can, I will, I do
> Leave following that, which it is gaine to
>   misse.
> Let her go. Soft, but here she comes. Go to,
> Unkind, I love you not: O me, that eye
> Doth make my heart give to my tongue
>   the lie.[19]

Another problem in *Astrophil and Stella* is the frequent inversion of word-order. Often this is justified by the emphasis it gives (we still use inversion in speech for this effect):

> His mother deare *Cupid* offended late . . .[20]

At other times it helps to give that sense of formality, even ritual, which all poetry must have, and which is particularly needed on some occasions:
> Muses, I oft invoked your holy ayde,

> With choisest flowers my speech to
>   engarland so;
> That it, despisde in true but naked shew,
> Might winne some grace in your sweet skill
>   arraid.[21]

Sometimes, I must admit, it is simply a nuisance,[22] it seems to be only a way (convenient to Sidney, but not to his reader) of coping with the demands of rhyme or metre:

> Who hath the voyce, which soule from
>   sences sunders,
> Whose force but yours the bolts of beautie
>   thunders?
> To you, to you, all song of praise is due:
> Only with you not miracles are wonders.[23]

The inversions in the first and second lines are rhetorically justified, since they throw the weight of emphasis on the powerful verbs 'sunders' and 'thunders'; the inversion in the third line also puts the emphasis where it is needed, on 'To you, to you'; but there seems to be an inversion in the fourth line caused by the demands of metre and possibly by the need for a rhyme, and it results in an unfortunate ambiguity. The line may mean 'Only with you miracles are not wonders';[24] it may mean 'Only with you wonders are not miracles';[25] or it may mean 'Only with you things that are not miracles are wonders'. The last is possibly the strongest and most appropriate sense, and it does not involve an inversion. It does, however, involve a rather strange form of expression, and our doubt as to the meaning of the line is a weakness in the poem. On the other hand, there are occasions when inversion results in a fruitful ambiguity.[26]

In reading any poem in *Astrophil and Stella* we must be alive to all sorts of ingenuity. I do not mean that we should look for any possible meaning a word could have: Sidney's ambiguities are normally precise and their presence is indicated by the context within which the various meanings co-operate. The play on 'touch' in Sonnet 9 is a case in point;[27] meanings are multiplied, but in a lucid, if difficult, way, and the meanings are not such as to cancel each other out: Sidney is sure of his touch. I do not think that Sidney ever intends us to go off at a tangent to pursue any possible meanings his words may have; he wants us to be alive to the mutually supporting meanings which the context suggests. A line from one of the *Certain Sonnets* may illustrate the point; the poem is about desire:

> Thou blind man's marke, thou foole's selfe
>   chosen snare . . .[28]

The meaning of 'marke' here is 'target';[29] but one critic, after recognizing this, says: 'But desire is the blind man's mark also because it marks him, like the patch over his eyes."[30] The difficulty is that the notions of 'target' and 'sign' are mutually exclusive: I do not think that anyone can read both meanings at once. One might just as well argue that 'marke' suggests a sum of money, and so desire is the sole wealth of one who cannot see what other wealth there is, and so on, and so on. If Sidney had wanted the ambiguity which Hoffman suggests, he would have shown he wanted it, and also fitted the extra meaning into the poem so that it worked with, and not against, the obvious one: many poems demonstrate his ability to do this.

Sonnet 39, 'Come sleepe, ô sleepe, the certaine knot of peace',[31] has (very appropriately for a poem addressed to sleep) an almost hypnotic effect:

> Come sleepe, ô sleepe, the certaine knot of
>   peace,
> The baiting place of wit, the balme of woe,
> The poore man's wealth, the prisoner's
>   release,
> Th'indifferent Judge betweene the high and
>   low;
>   With shield of proofe shield me from out
>   the prease
> Of those fierce darts, dispaire at me doth
>   throw:
> O make me in those civill warres to cease;
> I will good tribute pay if thou do so.

Even the smallest details of the sound here are beautifully controlled:

> The nice variation of vowel sounds; the subtle alliteration of p, l, s, in the octave, binding the lines and quatrains together, yet interrupted in the sixth line (because of its content) by the hard dentals; the cross-alliteration in the second line (bwbw): these are some of the indications of the poet's craftsmanship.[32]

These details are supported by conscious rhetoric on a larger scale: the second and third lines both contain a pair of metaphors for sleep, and so are balanced within themselves and with each other, and they are rounded off by a fourth line made up of only one metaphor.[33] This does not exhaust the artistry of the first four lines. The second and third lines are balanced not only in the way I have just mentioned. They are also related in a sort of syllabic chiasmus, since line 2 is made up of six syllables plus four syllables, and line 3 of four syllables plus six syllables. There is also a grammatical contrast, in the different forms used to show possession, between the two lines. The casual, throw-away manner of the eighth line is surprising in its context and contrasts dramatically with the stateliness of the poem's opening,[34] a stateliness to which the rhetorical complexity I have described con-

tributes. The poem reaches a preliminary climax in this eighth line with its promise of tribute; the line also creates further suspense, since we are waiting to hear what the tribute will be;[35] the main climax comes, as so often, at the very end of the poem, when we are told that the greatest tribute offered is '*Stella's* image'.

The first eight lines are mainly an assembly of images used to build up an idea of the nature and desirability of sleep, and the last six lines balance them with a catalogue of the various kinds of tribute offered:

> Take thou of me smooth pillowes,
>   sweetest bed,
> A chamber deafe to noise, and blind to
>   light:
> A rosie garland, and a wearie hed:
> And if these things, as being thine by right,
>   Move not thy heavy grace, thou shalt in
>   me,
>   Livelier then else-where, *Stella's* image
>   see.

The adjective in 'sweetest bed' may seem rather vague and weak, until we remember that this word was often used of scents; probably the reference is to scented sheets.[36] With its touch of formality, 'rosie garland' contrasts with the homeliness of 'smooth pillowes'. The garland is not merely decorative; it is emblematic of silence and secrecy, as in the proverbial phrase '*sub rosa*';[37] and the origin of this emblem is appropriately recalled in this poem on love and sleep; the rose was dedicated to the god of silence, Harpocrates, by Cupid in return for help in Venus' intrigues.[38] Vanna Gentili has pointed out[39] the subtlety in the apparently simple phrase 'thy heavy grace'. This is both a form of address to sleep and also a reference to the favour hoped for from sleep. In addition, the word 'grace' can denote a quality, and the adjective 'heavy', by its unexpectedness, suggests this further sense: we usually think of gracefulness as something light and delicate. The adjective 'heavy' is unexpected, and yet it is clearly accurate: sleep's 'grace', whether as a polite form of address, or as a favour, or as a quality, must be 'heavy' because of the torpor associated with sleep.

All these details are controlled by the main strategy of the poem, a strategy of which Sidney is very fond.[40] We expect the poem to be about Stella, but it is only in the last line that the poem is explicitly brought round to her. All the previous poems of the sequence, and particularly the one immediately preceding,[41] and hints in this poem itself (the 'civill warres'[42] and the 'rosie garland') have led us to expect this ending, which still comes as a surprise, largely I think because of the shock of the word 'Livelier' in a poem so evocative of sleep. The last line draws together various strands in the poem: it satisfies us by taking us where we thought we must be going—to Stella; it answers the question which everything has tacitly encouraged us to ask—Why is he awake? and it brings the offers of tribute to a climax, and so compliments Stella.

Sonnet 39, while perhaps more musical than most, is still in a manner familiar from many other sonnets in **Astrophil and Stella**; but Sonnet 103, 'O happie Tems, that didst my *Stella* beare',[43] comes as something of a surprise. It is comparatively undramatic, lacking conflict[44] except for the simple 'faire disgrace' of Stella's dishevelment, and rather reminiscent of the more stately and straightforward sonnets of Spenser's *Amoretti*.[45] The poem is pictorial, in a special way:

> O happie Tems, that didst my *Stella* beare,
> I saw thy selfe with many a smiling line
> Upon thy cheerefull face, joye's livery
> weare:
> While those faire planets on thy streames
> did shine.

This is a picture in the sense in which Sidney uses the word in his **Apology**: 'Poesy therefore is an art of imitation, for so Aristotle termeth it in his word *mimesis,* that is to say, a representing, counterfeiting, or figuring forth—to speak metaphorically, a speaking picture—with this end, to teach and delight.'[46] Sidney makes it clear he does not mean anything like what we call a photographic representation; this is particularly obvious in his comparison of his 'right poets' with a painter who paints qualities like 'the constant though lamenting look of Lucretia, when she punished in herself another's fault; wherein he painteth not Lucretia whom he never saw, but painteth the outward beauty of such a virtue'.[47] This poem is 'a speaking picture' of Astrophil's joy; and the half-comic unreality of his addressing a river,[48] and his cheerful attribution to the river of his own joy, are appropriate to his mood.

The inversion in line 5, 'The bote for joy could not to daunce forbeare', is a means of representing rhythmically the movement of the boat which is itself mentioned only because it is a picture of joy. The 'wanton winds' which twine themselves in Stella's hair are also mentioned not for the sake of naturalistic description but as a means of embodying Astrophil's own feelings. The winds are not at first visualized at all sharply:

> . . . While wanton winds with beauties so
> devine
> Ravisht, staid not, till in her golden haire
> They did themselves (ô sweetest prison)
> twine.

When we are encouraged to visualize them, immediately afterwards, it is as emblematic figures:

> And faine those *Aeols'* youthes there
> would their stay
> Have made, but forst by Nature still to flie,
> First did with puffing kisse those lockes
> display . . .

They bring to mind the representation of the winds in Botticelli's *Birth of Venus,* and one cannot help wondering whether Sidney had seen this painting.[49] Botticelli has a pair of '*Aeols'* youthes' puffing their cheeks to blow Venus' hair into charming disorder as she floats to land on a shell, and there is a joyful, spring-like quality, and 'a lucid elegance'[50] in both works. If, as has been suggested, the painting shows 'the dual nature of love, both sensuous and chaste',[51] then that is a further similarity to the poem where Stella is ashamed to be 'discheveld' and yet still worthy of the highest honour:

> . . . She so discheveld, blusht; from window
> I
> With sight thereof cride out; ô faire
> disgrace,
> Let honor' selfe to thee graunt highest
> place.

Of course the Thames, however 'happie', makes a background very different from the stylized and unspecified sea of the *Birth of Venus*. In the poem the situation is mythologized in a contemporary setting. The same thing happens, with a comic effect, in Sonnet 20, 'Flie, fly, my friends, I have my death wound; fly'.[52] Astrophil announces his death at the hands of a footpad; while enjoying the view he has been shot from the ambush of a 'darke bush' by a 'bloudie bullet'; he is ending up as many Elizabethans must have done. But the footpad has started his career young, he is a 'murthring boy', and turns out in fact to be Astrophil's usual antagonist Cupid, completely identified near the end of the poem by 'the glistring of his dart'. The change from 'bullet' to 'dart' is, I think, intentional: the modern and the obsolescent are mingled[53] so that we have strongly presented to us both the sense of a particular situation and the universal significance of that situation. Although I think it is intentional, I am still not quite happy about this mixture; however, it is a relief to be sure that 'bullet' can here be taken in its modern sense of a small missile,[54] and that we do not have to imagine a footpad firing cannon-balls.

The comic effect of the poem comes mainly from the disproportion between its theme—Astrophil has been looked at by Stella—and the imagery used to convey this.[55] Details in the poem support this effect of comedy, and the poem is a good instance of witty compliment, all the more complimentary for being witty. The 'darke bush' in which Cupid lies in wait is Stella's black eyes, and

Poore passenger, passe now thereby I did,
And staid pleasd with the prospect of the
place,
While that black hue from me the bad guest
hid . . .

Astrophil's blissful ignorance just before he is hit is that of the clown moving into position for the custard-pie, and the inversion of word-order in the first line, 'Poore passenger, passe now thereby I did,' gives just the impression of pomposity needed for the coming disaster to seem most funny. None of this is to deny that the ending of the poem seems serious:

. . . straight I saw motions of lightning'
grace,
And then descried the glistring of his dart:
But ere I could flie thence, it pierc'd my
heart.

The poem is intended seriously enough in one sense, as a compliment.

As I have already suggested,[56] a compliment is all the more effective when it is offered by one who is patently intelligent and witty. Sonnet 59, 'Deare, why make you more of a dog then me?'[57] comes to a climax in Astrophil's acceptance of all the demands of love, even if they include the loss of that very wit which the poem has demonstrated to be so fertile and subtle:[58]

Alas, if you grant only such delight
To witlesse things, then *Love* I hope
(since wit
Becomes a clog) will soone ease me of it.

This is partly a last fling in the attempt to strike some response from Stella, and partly a veiled threat to her that the compliments may stop. The poem as a whole is a series of highly ingenious arguments to prove that Astrophil is—and this is the most comic thing of all—worth more than a dog. We have therefore the dramatic paradox that Astrophil is ludicrous in his humility and admirable for his wit. The arguments are not only consistently clever, but also subtly varied in their emotional impact. Astrophil can be ardent:

Deare, why make you more of a dog then
me?
If he do love, I burne, I burne in love . . .

Much of the effect here comes from the contrast in the rhythm of the lines: the first is only just metrical, and it plods along with but one slight break (after the first word), while the second has a heavily emphasized metre, moves quickly, and is broken twice so that the effect is of sudden, sharp, deeply felt excla-

mations. Almost immediately afterwards Astrophil adopts a coaxing tone:

If he be faire, yet but a dog can be.

The implication here is that Astrophil is suggesting what any reasonable person would see to be true. In the very next line the tone changes to one of scorn:

Litle he is, so litle worth is he . . .

Yet in one way the scorn rebounds on Astrophil, who is reduced to being scornful of a dog. The comparison of a lover to a dog was a poetical commonplace;[59] the effectiveness of it in this poem does not lie only in the 'turn of wit at the end',[60] fine though this is, but in the striking of a number of different right tones; the comparison is never given any more seriousness than it can bear. Once again we have a comic poem intended seriously, as a compliment.

Sonnet 75, 'Of all the kings that ever here did raigne',[61] is one of those poems which begin apparently far away from Stella, only to reach her at the very end. Many of the effects in *Astrophil and Stella* are repeated, but usually with some variation. This poem reaches Stella only implicitly: it is an oblique indication of Astrophil's own attitude to Stella when Edward IV is praised because he

durst prove
To lose his Crowne, rather then faile his
Love.

The poem is deliberately shocking. It catalogues praiseworthy qualities, especially military skill and statesmanship, which it says Edward possessed, so that he seems an outstanding example of 'virtue',[62] and then it disparages these qualities:

Of all the kings that ever here did raigne,
Edward named fourth, as first in praise I
name,
Not for his faire outside, nor well lined
braine,
Although lesse gifts impe feathers oft on
Fame,
Nor that he could young-wise, wise-valiant
frame
His Sire's revenge, joyn'd with a kingdome's
gaine:
And gain'd by *Mars,* could yet mad *Mars*
so tame,
That Ballance weigh'd what sword did late
obtaine,
Nor that he made the Flouredeluce so
fraid,
Though strongly hedg'd of bloudy Lyon's
pawes,

That wittie *Lewis* to him a tribute paid.
Nor this, nor that, nor any such small cause
　. . .

These lines show Sidney's characteristic weaknesses as well as some of his strengths. The sound of the fourth line is not very satisfactory: it would be an exaggeration to call it cacophonous, but it is undistinguished in sound except for the f's and s's, which make it rather hard to read. In contrast the seventh line has a powerful sound which reinforces the sense:

And gain'd by *Mars,* could yet mad *Mars*
　so tame . . .

The alliteration on m draws attention to Mars and to the change in the attitude to war which the adjective 'mad' brings about. The verbs 'gain'd' and 'tame' are placed so as to stand out and contrast with each other. The structure of the line is itself an example of the wise subordination of means to ends for which Edward is said to be famous. There is a similar strength in this line:

That Ballance weigh'd what sword did late
　obtaine . . .

The line is thoughtfully poised, with 'Ballance' against 'sword' and 'weigh'd' against 'obtaine', in imitation of the consideration in Edward's mind.

There are other faults in the sound of the poem. The first eight lines are rhymed ABABBABA; but the similarity of the nasals in all the rhyme-words causes much of the distinction between the A-rhymes and the B-rhymes to be lost, so that we have the impression of an unsuccessful attempt at monorhyme. In contrast to this, the strategy of the poem is highly successful: discussion of a historical figure is brought to bear on Astrophil's personal situation, while this discussion has also its own value as political comment. Further, the poem is rather more shocking than I have so far shown. It is not simply that Edward is praised for his love rather than his statesmanship: most of the poem is devoted to stressing the statesmanship of a king who was more renowned for unscrupulous political manoeuvring and self-indulgence.[63]

There is, if anything, an even more patent sophistry in Sonnet 63, 'O Grammer rules, ô now your vertues show',[64] where Astrophil seizes on Stella's twice saying no to him to argue

That in one speech two Negatives affirme.

Even if we read the poem with modern usage in mind, it is clear that Astrophil is indulging in sophistry, since Stella's intention was obvious; but in Sidney's day, when the double negative was a customary form of

emphasis, without an affirmative effect, then the sophistry would be even greater, since Astrophil's 'Grammer rules' are those of Latin and not of English.[65] It would be a misreading to object that, since the argument is false, Stella would be unlikely to be persuaded by it. Seduction by sophistry is not the intention. The whole point of the poem lies in the fact, obvious although never stated directly, that Astrophil is trying to persuade himself of the opposite of what Stella meant. The 'high triumphing' of the poem is only on the surface, a cover for an underlying sadness. Astrophil knows that he is trying to deceive himself: he admits that Stella said no twice 'Least once should not be heard.' We have again the paradox that Astrophil seems ridiculous in his attempted self-deception and also masterful and in command of the situation because of the wit which reveals he knows where he stands. If there is an epithalamic suggestion in the shout of triumph *'Io Pean',*[66] then this is a further touch of wit: there can be no question of a marriage between Stella and Astrophil whose intentions are far less honourable.

Sonnet 69, 'O joy, too high for my low stile to show',[67] is another poem in which apparent joy partly conceals real sadness. Stella has now given her heart to Astrophil, but on a condition that detracts from much of the pleasure of this: he must take a 'vertuous course'. The shout of triumph in Sonnet 63, *'Io Pean'*, is subtly recalled here:

I, I, ô I may say, that she is mine.[68]

This shows once more how the poems gain when read together, and it stresses what a careful reading the poems require. The effect is important—Astrophil is shown in artistic command of a situation he finds distressing—and yet it may easily go unnoticed. It practically disappears from a modernized text:

I, I, oh I may say that she is mine.[69]

Like the sonnet on Edward IV, this poem uses political ideas for the expression of love, and, although the expression of love is the dominant intention, the political ideas are also interesting in their own right:

. . . though she give but thus conditionly
This realme of blisse, while vertuous course
　I take,
No kings be crown'd but they some
　covenants make.

Sonnet 69 is addressed to a friend 'that oft saw through all maskes my wo', and the mask in that poem is the political image. An earlier sonnet uses a different mask, one often employed in *Astrophil and Stella*, that of literary discussion:

Stella oft sees the verie face of wo
    Painted in my beclowded stormie face:
    But cannot skill to pitie my disgrace,
Not though thereof the cause her selfe she
    know:
Yet hearing late a fable, which did show
    Of Lovers never knowne, a grievous case,
    Pitie thereof gate in her breast such place
That, from that sea deriv'd, teares' spring
    did flow.
    Alas, if Fancy drawne by imag'd things,
Though false, yet with free scope more
    grace doth breed
Then servant's wracke, where new doubts
    honor brings;
Then thinke my deare, that you in me do
    reed
    Of Lover's ruine some sad Tragedie:
I am not I, pitie the tale of me.[70]

Some incidental felicities may be mentioned briefly. The ambiguity in the fourth line is justified[71] because both possible meanings are relevant: 'even though she herself knows what the cause of my woe is', and 'even though she knows that she herself is the cause of my woe'.[72] Line 11 contains a similar relevant ambiguity in 'where new doubts honor brings'. 'Doubts' means 'qualms' or 'scruples'.[73] The primary sense is that Stella's sense of honour, her chastity, makes her all the more scrupulous in the face of Astrophil's distress. There is also a secondary meaning, or implication, that the scruples bring her honour; and this meaning is critical of her, since her honour depends on Astrophil's distress. The wit and playfulness of the poem's ending should not be lost,[74] particularly since, when Astrophil says 'I am not I', we are led to consider who he might be, and his literary ideas here are exactly those of Sir Philip Sidney.

The sonnet is both a complaint of Stella's cruelty and a piece of critical theory. It has been argued that, although the literary discussion is proposed as a means of discussing the love situation, the emphasis in this poem is such as to make the love situation really a way of talking about literature.[75] I should not wish to go quite so far: the manifest absurdity of the suggestion in the last line makes me think that the love situation is as important here as elsewhere in the sequence. As in other sonnets,[76] Astrophil manages to cover both subjects at once. The literary theory involved is that poetry may move us when reality does not. In his *Apology* Sidney puts it like this:[77]

. . . how much it can move, Plutarch yieldeth a notable testimony of the abominable tyrant Alexander Phraeus, from whose eyes a tragedy, well made and represented, drew abundance of tears, who without all pity had murdered infinite numbers, and some of his own blood; so as he

that was not ashamed to make matters for tragedies, yet could not resist the sweet violence of a tragedy.[78]

There is, in the sonnet, a comic disproportion between the 'sad Tragedie' of which Astrophil says he wants Stella to think and its analogue in Astrophil's real life (which, to complicate matters further, is an artistic creation itself): the tone of the last three lines is such as to preclude our taking the 'Tragedie' too seriously. As so often, passion disappears behind the ingenuity which makes the poem a compliment.

In that poem Astrophil is, as usual, very conscious of the part he has chosen to play. This typically Elizabethan zest in the role of the moment continually makes it hard, if not impossible, for us to assess the exact nature of Astrophil's love (not to mention Sidney's feelings which were presumably involved somehow) in any other terms than those which the poems use. I think it helps, however, to suggest that Astrophil would have appreciated what Yeats meant when he said:

O what am I that I should not seem
For the song's sake a fool?[79]

Sidney certainly saw no reason why he should not make Astrophil seem a fool and at the same time a skilled artist, and both for the song's sake. Astrophil's sophistication (a reflection of course of the sophistication of his creator) must be matched by a sophisticated reading. A sophisticated reading demands a constant awareness of the poems as artefacts, human fabrications which could have been different. One of the greatest pleasures of Sidney's poetic masterpiece is missed if we are not always alive, not only to the effects created, but also to the ways in which they are created. This kind of response, which Sidney could expect of his contemporary audience,[80] is the kind of response which Spenser encourages us to give to the picture of Leda in the House of Busyrane:

O wondrous skill, and sweet wit of the man,
That her in daffadillies sleeping made . . .[81]

However we look at it, *Astrophil and Stella* presents us with paradoxes. Astrophil talks much of his misery, and yet his conversation is a joy to listen to; the poems are witty, elaborately wrought, and sometimes enigmatic, and all while Astrophil protests his plainness and simplicity; the tone is aristocratic and masterful, perhaps most when Astrophil mentions his utter subjection to Stella; and line after line reads like 'a moment's thought'[82] in the very instant of betraying, or even flaunting, its conscious artistry. *Astrophil and Stella* was written for an audience that saw, not mere affectation as opposed to something vaguely called 'sincerity', but a fine regard for the dignity of man in the careful choice of armour made by Amphialus in the *New Arcadia*:

> . . . he furnished him selfe for the fight: but not in his wonted furniture. For now (as if he would turne his inside outwarde) he would needes appeare all in blacke; his decking both for him selfe, and horse, being cut out into the fashion of very ragges: yet all so dainty, joyned together with pretious stones, as it was a brave raggednesse, and a riche povertie: and so cunningly had a workeman followed his humour in his armour, that he had given it a rustie shewe, and yet so, as any man might perceive was by arte, and not negligence; carying at one instant a disgraced handsomnesse, and a new oldnes.[83]

Notes

[1] F.T. Prince. "The Sonnet from Wyatt to Shakespeare," *Elizabethan Poetry* (Stratford-upon-Avon Studies 2), J.R. Brown and Bernard Harris, eds., 1960, p. 20.

[2] Robertson, 'Sir Philip Sidney and his Poetry', p. 128.

[3] W. A. Ringler, ed. *The Poems of Sir Philip Sidney*. 1962 p. 165.

[4] *A.S.* 2, ibid., p. 166.

[5] N. L. Rudenstine. *Sidney's Poetic Development*. 1967 p. 192.

[6] There is an interesting discussion of this matter in Martin Halpern, 'On the Two Chief Metrical Modes in English', *P.M.L.A.* lxxvii (1962), 177-86.

[7] *A.S.* 5, Ringler, p. 167.

[8] Thompson, *The Founding of English Metre,* p. 152.

[9] Gascoigne, ed. cit., 'Gascoignes woodmanship', i, 348.

[10] Thompson, *The Founding of English Metre,* p. 151.

[11] *A.S.* 5, Ringler, p. 167.

[12] Lewis, *English Literature in the Sixteenth Century,* 329.

[13] See above, pp. 19-20.

[14] *A.S.* 74, Ringler, p. 204.

[15] *A.S.* 10, ibid., p. 169.

[16] *A.S.* 17, ibid., p. 173.

[17] *A.S.* 33, ibid., p. 181.

[18] *A.S.* 40, ibid., p. 185.

[19] *A.S.* 47, ibid., p. 188.

[20] *A.S.* 17, ibid., p. 173.

[21] *A.S.* 55, ibid., p. 192.

[22] See above, p. 68, on *C.S.* 5.

[23] Song 1, lines 29-32, Ringler, p. 197.

[24] Ibid., p. 479.

[25] Vanna Gentili, ed. *Sir Philip Sidney: Astrophil and Stella.* 1965 p. 367.

[26] See below, p. 151.

[27] See above, pp. 5-6.

[28] *C.S.* 31, Ringler, p. 161.

[29] Ibid., p. 434.

[30] Hoffman, 'Sidney's *Thou blind man's mark*', *Explicator,* viii (1949-50), Article 29.

[31] Ringler, p. 184.

[32] Muir, *Sir Philip Sidney,* p. 34.

[33] Buxton, *Elizabethan Taste,* p. 284.

[34] Ibid., p. 285.

[35] Ibid., p. 284.

[36] Ibid., pp. 284-5.

[37] Ibid., p. 285.

[38] Ringler, p. 473.

[39] Gentili, p. 312.

[40] See above, pp. 116, 132-3.

[41] *A.S.* 38, Ringler, p. 183.

[42] See above, p. 117.

[43] Ringler, p. 232.

[44] Gentili, p. 489.

[45] Spenser, p. 561.

[46] Geoffrey shepherd, ed. *An Apology for Poetry*. 1965, p. 101.

[47] Shepherd, p. 102.

[48] See above, p. 132.

[49] Gentili, p. 489.

[50] Wind, *Pagan Mysteries in the Renaissance,* 1967, p. 132.

[51] Ibid., p. 131.

[52] Ringler, p. 174.

[53] Gentili, p. 260.

[54] Ibid., p. 261.

[55] See above, p. 134, on *A.S.* 48.

[56] Above, p. 134.

[57] Ringler, p. 194.

[58] Gentili, p. 355; Kalstone, p. 160.

[59] Ringler, pp. 477-8.

[60] Ibid., p. 478.

[61] Ibid., p. 204.

[62] See above, pp. 75-6.

[63] Ringler, p. 481.

[64] Ibid., p. 196.

[65] Ibid., p. 478.

[66] R.B. Young. 'English Petrarke: A Study of Sidney's *Astrophel and Stella*', *Three Studies in the Renaissance: Sidney, Jonson, Milton*. 1958, p. 61; but see Ringler, p. 478. The use of 'io Paean' was not restricted to marriage celebrations, and for them a more precise exclamation was 'io Hymen' (see Spenser's *Epithalamion,* line 140, Spenser, p. 581). Nevertheless, we can easily see that 'io Hymen' would have been obviously unfitting in this context, whereas *'Io Pean'* may well contain an ironic hint of marriage.

[67] Ringler, p. 200.

[68] Young, p. 63; Evans, op. cit., p. 104: 'There is superb irony in the way Sidney makes Astrophil's ex-ultant cry suggest the Io, Io of the traditional marriage song, at the moment when he is protesting the purely spiritual nature of his love.'

[69] Craik, op. cit., p. 59.

[70] *A.S.* 45, Ringler, p. 187.

[71] But see ibid., p. 474.

[72] Ibid., pp. 474-5; Gentili, p. 326.

[73] Ibid.

[74] Myrick, op. cit., p. 312.

[75] Gentili, pp. 324-5.

[76] e.g., *A.S.* 15, Ringler, p. 172.

[77] The relation between this poem and the *Apology* is stressed in T. B. Stroup, 'The "Speaking Picture" Realised: Sidney's 45th Sonnet', *P.Q.* xxix (1950), 440-2.

[78] Shepherd, p. 118.

[79] Yeats, 'A Prayer for Old Age', op. cit., p. 326.

[80] See above, pp. 24-5.

[81] *F.Q.* III.xi.32, Spenser, p. 203.

[82] Yeats, 'Adam's Curse', op. cit., p. 88.

[83] Feuillerat, ed. cit., i, 454.

A. C. Hamilton (essay date 1977)

SOURCE: "Sidney in Life, Legend, and in His Works," in *Sir Philip Sidney: A Study of His Life and Works,* Cambridge University Press, 1977, pp. 107-22.

[*In the following excerpt, Hamilton discusses Sidney's noble background, frustrated political career, and legendary reputation.*]

'Some are born great, some achieve greatness, and some have greatness thrust upon them': the aphorisms are used by Maria, in *Twelfth Night,* to gull Malvolio. To the Renaissance mind, an aspiration to greatness is overweening in a pompous major-domo. He is mocked by greatness when his actions prove him to be only a great fool. Yet the aspiration itself, the intense desire for worldly honour and fame, 'that last infirmity of noble mind', marks most men of the time. In particular, it marks Sir Philip Sidney. Because he was born great, great expectations were held for him throughout his life; after his death, his reputation for personal greatness helped to establish the legend that he was the ideal Renaissance gentleman. Like Malvolio, however, he has been mocked by greatness: the legend thrust upon him has prevented any understanding of the life he actually lived by placing a barrier between his life and works, and between both and the modern reader.

Sidney was born great. He was the eldest son of a family distinguished on his father's side for several generations by personal service to English kings. This lineage was acknowledged by the French king when he elevated him to a Gentleman Ordinary, 'considerans combien est grande la maison de Sydenay en Angleterre'.[1] He was even more distinguished on his mother's side. His father told him to remember 'the noble blood you are descended of by your mother's side; and think that only by virtuous life and good action you may be an ornament to that illustrious family'.[2] Later Sidney boasted that 'though in all truth I may justly affirm that I am by my father's side of ancient and always well esteemed and well matched gentry, yet I do acknowledge, I say, that my chiefest honour is to be a Dudley'.[3] Such great birth, particularly as he was for much of his life the prospective heir of his rich—and childless—uncles, the earls of Leicester and Warwick, gave great hope for advancement, as Hubert Languet, his chief mentor and tutor, indicated to the ambassador of Poland during Sidney's tour of Europe:

> His father is the Viceroy of Ireland, with whom, I am told, scarcely anyone among the nobility of England can compare in *virtus* and military experience.
>
> His mother is a sister of the Earl of Warwick and of Robert the Earl of Leicester, the most favoured at Court: since neither has children, this gentleman [i.e. Sidney] will probably be their heir.
>
> His father's sister is married to the Earl of Sussex. . . . His mother's sister is the wife of the Earl of Huntingdon, who is related to the Royal family.
>
> Neither nobleman has any sons: so that on this one person they have placed their hopes, and him they have decided to advance to honour after his return.[4]

Sidney's own recognition of his position is suggested by his emblem, *'Spero'*.[5] For few in that age were prospects through high birth more dazzling.

Yet Sidney was not born great enough. His mother's family was tainted by treason. His great-grandfather was executed by Henry VIII for extortion; the year before he was born, his grandfather, John Dudley, Duke of Northumberland, was executed for treason;

and in the year that he was born, his uncle, Guilford, was also executed for treason. Although Sidney boasted 'I am a Dudley in blood', he did so in the course of defending his uncle, the Earl of Leicester, against the anonymous libel that 'from his ancestors, this Lord receiveth neither honour nor honesty, but only succession of treason and infamy'.[6] He could excuse the fall of his family only on grounds that it was high enough to fall:

> Our house received such an overthrow, and [as?] hath none else in England done; so I will not seek to wash away that dishonour with other honourable tears. I would this island were not so full of such examples; and I think, indeed, this writer, if he were known, might in conscience clear his ancestors of any such disgraces. They were too low in the mud to be so thunderstricken.[7]

Sidney's mixed pride in his ancestors, and his recognition that he must act himself, is nicely registered in the motto which he wore under his arms: *Vix ea nostra voco* (I hardly dare call our ancestors' deeds our own).[8]

But worse than this, his father's family was blighted by poverty. The Sidney family was, as he admits, 'so youngly a fortuned family':[9] it was, in fact, impoverished, and became increasingly so. The family place at Penshurst was granted to his grandfather only two years before Sidney was born, and his father always lacked the means to maintain his state. Sir Henry's lengthy service to the Queen—he was thrice Lord Deputy Governor of Ireland besides being Lord President of the Marches of Wales—was rewarded only by new service which left him deeper in debt. He was forced to refuse a barony because he could not afford to maintain the rank. As a result, Sidney more than most experienced the special crisis of the Elizabethan aristocracy: being forced to attend court, courtiers so neglected their own affairs that they became increasingly dependent on the Queen for their support.[10] Fulke Greville records how for him—and it would be the same for Sidney—the Queen's actions 'fell heavy in crossing a young man's ends', and how she 'made me live in her court a spectacle of disfavour, too long as I conceived'.[11] For reasons of her own, she withheld her favours from the Sidney family, forcing them to beg, usually in vain, for the means to live. As a consequence, Sidney was in debt all his life; and not only did he die bankrupt, but left such debt that his father-in-law, in discharging it, became bankrupt.

The promise of Sidney's birth proved to be only disappointing. If Leicester had married the Queen, if Warwick had left him his wealth, if the Queen had favoured him: but none of these things happened. Leicester married instead the widow of the Earl of Essex, and their son, born in 1581, became heir to the family fortunes. At the next tilt-day, according to

Camden, Sidney wore the impresa thus dashed through, to show his hope therein was dashed'.[12] Although Leicester's son died three years later, Sidney's two rich uncles outlived him. The Queen never favoured him, and knighted him only because the Prince of Orange, who was to receive the Order of the Garter, named him his proxy, an office that protocol required should bear a title. Two minor events reveal his position at court. When the Queen granted him stipends from lands confiscated from Roman Catholics, he protested: 'I think my fortune very hard that my reward must be built upon other men's punishments';[13] then he accepted the gift. When the Earl of Oxford called him a 'puppy' during a quarrel on a tennis court, Sidney challenged him to a duel, but the Queen forced him to withdraw, laying before him 'the difference in degree between Earls and Gentlemen; the respect inferiors ought [owed] to their superiors'.[14] All his life Sidney lived only on the fringe of the establishment and under the shadow of greatness.

Sidney was expected to achieve greatness through public service, as his father recognized when he advised his sons 'that if they meant to live in order, they should ever behold whose sons, and seldom think whose nephews, they were'.[15] Sir Henry spent his life in public service, fulfilling what Malcolm Wallace describes as his 'engrossing conviction that only in disinterested service for prince and country could a man find a worthy end toward the achieving of which he could bend the whole of his energies'.[16] Sidney was expected to follow his father's example. He was groomed for public service first by his education at Shrewsbury School and Christ Church, Oxford, and then by an extended continental tour from 1572-5. By the end of that tour, he was poised to play a major role in England's affairs. In 1576, the dying Essex said of him: 'he is so wise, so virtuous and godly; and if he go on in the course he hath begun, he will be as famous and worthy a gentleman as ever England bred'.[17] His youth—he was only 22—was bright with promise. Yet all his effort to achieve greatness came to little: apart from one embassy in 1577, he was not employed by the Queen in any important office until the year of his death. His life had a promising beginning and an heroic end, but no middle in public service. A recent biographer, Roger Howell, quite rightly concludes that the central event of Sidney's career was his death.[18] The explanation of his failure—if any is needed for a man who died in his thirty-first year—is simply that 'his short life and private fortune were . . . no proper stages to act any greatness of good or evil upon'.[19]

Sidney had greatness thrust upon him by his death. The circumstances which led to his death, the death itself, and the national orgy of grief on the occasion of his extravagant funeral in London four months later, promoted the legend that he embodied all the val-

ues cherished by the age: the ideal man, the perfect knight and pattern of the courtier, the mirror of princes and 'the world's delight'.[20]

In the previous year, by forcing the Queen's hand, Sidney initiated the sequence of events which led to his death. Frustrated at his failure to be appointed to the English expeditionary force to Holland, he was determined to accompany Drake to Virginia. Before he could sail, the Queen forbade him to leave, and promised to appoint him Governor of Flushing and General of the Horse. His appointment was confirmed on 9 November 1585, and he arrived in the Netherlands later that month. For the next nine months he was engaged in preparing the defences for the coming war against Spain. After waiting almost a decade to serve his country, at last he was given his great opportunity. As governor of Flushing, he could embody Sir Thomas Elyot's governor, that ideal of civic humanism expressed in Erasmus's claim that 'there is no better way to gain the favor of God, than by showing yourself a beneficial prince for your people'.[21] In leading a successful assault against the city of Axel, he was able to display himself as the ideal captain. As Stow records, Sidney addressed his men before the assault with an oration that 'did so link the minds of the people, that they desired rather to die in that service, than to live in the contrary'.[22] In the assault, not one English soldier was lost while all the defenders were massacred. George Whetstone, who may have served under Sidney, records that 'he always was a special favourer of soldiers'.[23] Then on 22 September in a minor skirmish at Zutphen against some Spanish forces, he was mortally wounded because he had discarded his leg-armour when he saw a fellow-knight not wearing his. Fulke Greville's account of what followed is too well known to be omitted:

> The horse he rode upon . . . forced him to foresake the field, but not his back, as the noblest and fittest bier to carry a martial commander to his grave. In which sad progress, passing along by the rest of the army . . . and being thirsty with excess of bleeding, he called for drink, which was presently brought him; but as he was putting the bottle to his mouth, he saw a poor soldier carried along, who had eaten his last at the same feast, ghastly casting up his eyes at the bottle. Which Sir Philip perceiving, took it from his head, before he drank, and delivered it to the poor man, with these words, 'Thy necessity is yet greater than mine'. And when he had pledged this poor soldier, he was presently carried to Arnheim.[24]

Sidney's failure to wear leg-armour displays the conspicuous bravery, or bravado, of the Renaissance courtier. That act is closely related to his act of offering water to the soldier. A gesture which is flamboyant in not caring for himself has its counterpart in caring for another. Both acts are private, yet become fully public in that they display ideals of personal and social behaviour.

The twenty-five days between being wounded at Zutphen and dying of gangrene poisoning at Arnheim allowed Sidney to act out his death in a fitting manner. While his preparations for death enact the ritual of holy dying expected of any Christian, some details are personal. He asked that a song which he entitled 'La cuisse rompue' (The Broken Thigh) be set to music and played to him; but he also asked that his **Arcadia** be burned, for 'he then discovered, not only the imperfection, but vanity of these shadows'.[25] He repented what his closest friend, Fulke Greville, terms obliquely 'the secret sins of his own heart', which an attending chaplain, George Gifford, spells out as the final vanity which Sidney feared would prevent his salvation: 'a vanity wherein I had taken delight, whereof I had not rid myself. It was my Lady Rich. But I rid myself of it, and presently my joy and comfort returned.'[26] Greville records also that Sidney asked 'the opinion of the ancient heathen touching the immortality of the soul; first, to see what true knowledge she retains of her own essence, out of the light of herself; then to parallel with it the most pregnant authorities of the Old, and New Testament, as supernatural revelations, sealed up from our flesh, for the divine light of faith to reveal, and work by'.[27] Orthodoxy allowed that knowledge of the soul's immortality was attainable by natural reason, and the concern to fuse reason and revelation is characteristic of most men of the age; but what seems deeply personal is Sidney's concern, surprising at this late hour, with what reason alone may reveal and how it may lead to faith. Interest in what reason may discover of Christian truth had led to his translating De Mornay's *De la verité de la religion Chrestienne;*[28] and interest in reason working apart from faith may have encouraged him to use the classical Arcadia as the setting for his prose fiction: his characters debate moral virtue, and even answer atheism, without the support of revelation. His concern with man as a rational being shows why his writings remain profoundly secular despite his strongly religious nature.

The basis of the Sidney legend was laid during his life by the great expectations held out for him: for example, in Essex's dying prophecy cited above, that he 'will be as famous and worthy a gentleman as ever England bred', and in his father's eloquent judgment, which seems sincere, when he advised his son Robert to 'imitate his [Sidney's] virtues, exercises, studies, and actions; he is a rare ornament of this age, the very formular that all welldisposed young gentlemen of our court do form also their manners and life by. In truth, I speak it without flattery of him, or of myself, he hath the most rare virtues that ever I found in any man.'[29] While Sidney aroused some envy, praise of him by his contemporaries was almost uniformly extravagant, even by Renaissance standards. Later, when the Elizabethan age was idealized, as it was by Daniel, for example, Sidney became its exemplar.[30] It is surprising to learn that the legend continued in later centuries. In *Adonais,* Shelley writes: 'Sidney, as he fought / And as he fell and as he lived and loved / Sublimely mild, a Spirit without spot'.[31] The legend survives even today, for example, in Yeats's poem, 'In memory of Major Robert Gregory'. Sidney's best biographer, Malcolm Wallace, tries his best to be impartial by listing his faults:

> He was foolishly extravagant in the spending of money, and was sometimes forced to seek to improve his financial position by means which were at least not dignified. He was somewhat arrogant and hot-headed. He was inclined to be egotistical. . . . To us there appears something strangely simple in Sidney's attitude toward most of life's problems. It is scarcely possible that he had been seriously touched by the philosophic and scientific stirrings of his time. His religious beliefs were as simple as those of a little child. None of the daring speculations of Bruno or the scepticism of the intellectuals of his day finds utterance in his writings. His only religious doubts had to do with his failure to be obedient to the God who was his heavenly Father. His political creed could hardly have been more simple. The enemies of England and of Protestantism were his enemies.

Yet he allows that 'no one can have familiarized himself with the details of Sidney's life without realizing what a large measure of truth there is in the popular conception of his character'.[32]

The legend may strike us simply as a legend, one that may be challenged by Sidney's own argument in the **Defence** for placing the poet's image of an ideal man above the work of Nature: 'Nature never set forth . . . so excellent a man every way.' One may wonder if there is any conflict between the life and the legend. Katherine Duncan-Jones refers to the gap 'which is often to be found between the magnificence of his personality and reputation, and the prosaic or even sordid facts of his life'.[33] Yet nothing that we know reveals any clash in Sidney himself between 'reality' and the ideal: there is no man apart from the legend, no face under the mask. From the beginning he seems to have lived a fully public life, which he sought to shape into an ideal of virtue expressed in public service. From all that we know, he dedicated his life to fulfil what was expected of him by his family and friends. As a result, his life satisfies Milton's dictum that the poet 'ought himself to be a true poem, that is, a composition, and pattern of the best and honourablest things, not presuming to sing high praises of heroic men, or famous cities unless he have in himself the experience and the practice of all that which is praiseworthy'.[34] If there is no man *behind* the legend, there is a man *in* it—one who tried to live as he ought, and succeeded.

The problem about the legend is not only that it overwhelms Sidney's life as known from his biography, but also that it all but ignores his life as a writer. Outside his circle of close friends, few of his contemporaries knew enough to praise him as a poet. One is Scipio Gentili:

> Others admire in you, Philip Sidney, the splendour of your birth—your genius in your childhood, capable of all philosophy—your honourable embassy undertaken in your youth, and . . . the exhibition of your personal valour and prowess in the public spectacles and equestrian exercises, in your manhood: let others admire all these qualities. I not only admire, but I love and venerate you, because you regard poetry so much as to excel in it.[35]

No contemporary, except Greville, seems to have suspected that Sidney would achieve greatness through his literary works. Since his works were not published during his lifetime, except by the circulation of manuscripts among close friends, he remained largely unknown as a writer.

More letters to Sidney, and by him—165 and 117 respectively, by Osborn's count—survive than for any other writer of his age; yet none reveals any plans for writing or comments even indirectly upon what he had written. For the poetry there is only one reference in a letter to a friend urging him to sing his songs; for the prose fiction, the promise in a letter to his brother to send him his 'toyful book' and the reported deathbed wish to have the *Arcadia* burned. As a consequence, none of his works may be dated with certainty, and even their titles are confused.[36] Only when it is known that he was not busy at court may one infer that he was free to write. He seems to have lived two separate lives: a known life as a Renaissance courtier seeking political office, and a private life as a poet. Accordingly, the standard biography by Malcolm William Wallace treats Sidney's writings separately, and so does the most recent biography by Roger Howell. James M. Osborn's extended study of *Young Philip Sidney 1572-1577* provides only one fact directly relevant to Sidney as a writer, a passing reference to his songs.

That the legend and known facts of Sidney's life all but ignore him as a writer is astonishing when one considers what he achieved in his writings simply in terms of comprehensiveness and orginality, and the commitment which that achievement demanded of him.

When Sidney began writing in the late 1570s or early 1580s, the English literary scene was barren. As he notes in the *Defence of poetry,* apart from a few works of worth such as Surrey's lyrics and Spenser's *Shepherd's Calendar,* a wasteland stretched back to Chaucer. Of Chaucer he wonders 'whether to marvel more, either that he in that misty time could see so clearly, or that we in this clear age go so stumblingly after him'. One may infer what he intended to do about this lamentable state from what he did, that is, by his literary criticism, writings, and influence, create a Renaissance of English literature. He was seen as the leader of such a Renaissance by Daniel in an address to Sidney's sister in 1594:

> Now when so many pens (like spears) are charg'd,
> To chase away this tyrant of the north;
> Gross Barbarism, whose power grown far enlarg'd
> Was lately by thy valiant brother's worth
> First found, encountered, and provoked forth:
> Whose onset made the rest audacious,
> Whereby they likewise have so well discharg'd,
> Upon that hideous beast encroaching thus.

When *Astrophel and Stella* appeared in 1591, Nashe heralded it as a work which ushers in the golden age: '*Tempus adest plausus; aurea pompa venit:* so ends the scene of idiots, and enter Astrophel in pomp', and Thomas Newman, who published the first edition, called it a work 'wherein the excellence of sweet poesy is concluded'.[37] Ringler concludes that 'no previous English poet, from Old English to Tudor times, even approached Sidney in the variety and complexity of metrical forms that he used'.[38] Henry Olney, the first editor of the *Defence of poetry*, refers to 'excellent poesy, so created by this *Apology*'.[39] Finally, the *Arcadia* is the first work of original prose fiction in our language, the first prose work of European stature in English, and one in which, as Virginia Woolf saw, 'as in some luminous globe, all the seeds of English fiction lie latent'.[40] Through these three works Sidney became the seminal writer of the Elizabethan age: *Astrophel and Stella* initiated the Petrarchan sonnet cycle in English as a literary form, the *Defence* provided the critical basis for Elizabethan literature, and the *Arcadia* promoted first a school of Arcadian fiction and later, through Richardson's *Pamela,* the English novel. At a time when the English literary scene was barren, and it was necessary to demonstrate that the English language was, as he claimed in the *Defence*, 'indeed capable of any excellent exercising of it', Sidney appeared as the one right man at the right time. Through his critical insight and literary craftsmanship, he pointed to what should be done and showed how it could be done.

To achieve such originality in poetry, literary criticism, and prose fiction, Sidney read widely and thoroughly in earlier literature. As sources of his poetry, Ringler cites Ovid, Virgil, Horace, Petrarch, Sannazaro, Montemayor and his continuators, and Tottel's *Songs and Sonnets*.[41] As sources of the *Defence*, Shepherd cites Scaliger, Elyot, Agrippa, Landino, Horace, Plato, and Aristotle, and adds Sidney's wider reading in humanist writing: 'he read in Petrarch, Boccaccio, Tasso, Mantuan, Pontanus, Sannazaro, Erasmus, More, Ascham, Ramus, Bembo, Patrizi, Bodin, Buchanan, Ronsard, du Bartas. He knew the old Roman poets, historians, moralists, and dramatists well. Certain books and authors were particularly congenial to him: Plutarch notably, and the Bible; also Xenophon, Virgil, and Seneca.'[42] While the sources of the *Arcadia* are few—chiefly Sannazaro, Montemayor, *Amadis of Gaul,* and Heliodorus—they reveal that Sidney drew comprehensively upon what earlier literature could provide as models in the classical, medieval, and modern periods. Further, he thoroughly assimilated his reading so that each of his writings is a well-wrought artifact, uniquely his own, and characterized by an original argument and careful, deliberate structure. Even in size these works are considerable, particularly *Astrophel and Stella* with its 108 sonnets and II songs, and the *Arcadia* with its 180,000 words in its first version (later expanded to more than 230,000 words) interlaced with over 70 poems either set within the prose or organized into the eclogues that conclude the separate books. Yet the biography of Sidney provides almost no record of this labour.

One might conclude that Sidney's works are unrelated to his life and to the age in which he lived. Ringler notes that his poetry 'is remarkable for what he did not write about':

> He was a courtier, but except for some passages in *The Lady of May* he never wrote in praise of the Queen. He was sincerely religious, but he never wrote a poem of personal devotion. He placed a high value upon friendship, but except for his **'Two Pastorals'** and a single mention of Languet he never wrote a commendatory or memorial poem for a real person. The major interest of his life was politics, but only once did he deal with problems of government, and then under the veil of a beast fable. Except for *Astrophil and Stella* his verse was neither official nor personal and dealt almost entirely with imagined situations.[43]

One may add that he chose to write a defence of poetry, which he himself refers to as 'this ink-wasting toy of mine', while his friends wrote political and religious tracts in defence of liberty and the Protestant faith, and that the setting of his *Arcadia*, which he refers to as 'a trifle, and that triflingly handled', is classical Greece rather than one which could have

easy allegorical reference to contemporary England. According to Coleridge's distinction, Sidney would seem to be the kind of impersonal poet, like Shakespeare, who leaves no trace of himself in his works, and not the personal poet, like Milton, who may be found in every line that he writes.

Yet Sidney's presence dominates all his works. In the *Old Arcadia*, he inserts himself into the story as the character Philisides; and as narrator everywhere controls and directs the reader's response. *Astrophel and Stella* centres upon Astrophel, whom no reader may fail to associate with Sidney. The argument of the *Defence* is persuasive chiefly because of Sidney's persuasive voice. The ideals treated in the *New Arcadia* are Sidney's as well as those of his class and age. While his writings are never personal in the sense of treating the stuff of biography—courtly gossip, quarrels, rumours of appointments, or whatever is simply personal—they are always centrally concerned with the business of a man (and that man is Sidney) living at a certain moment and place in human history. Equally his writings are never impersonal in the sense of treating man or mankind: they are dominated by the presence of an individual man responding to the immediate pressures of his life and times.

I see a close and significant relationship between Sidney and his writings, and between both and his age. That relationship is not direct: the writings do not reveal his actual life—whatever that may have been like; instead, his life provides the setting, occasion, or point of departure for what he writes. While the personal is included in all that he writes, it is transcended. He was not a Romantic poet for whom poetry could record the spontaneous overflow of emotions. He is never personal, as Spenser is, and could never begin a poem, as Spenser does, with the line, 'Lo I the man, whose Muse whilom did mask'—not even with Virgil's authority. On the other hand, in reading Sidney one never reaches the point as one soon does with Spenser, where the writer's life and times become irrelevant. If one could strip the mask from Sidney's *persona*, most likely one would uncover another mask, and another under that. The reason, I suspect, is that from his birth he began to live the legend confirmed by his death; and, to adapt Keats's phrase, his works are comments on it. By his own nature, as well as by nurture, education, and the urging of his friends, he shaped his life into an image of virtue. Or to adapt his own words in the *Defence*, his essential life is not recorded in what is, but rather in 'what may be and should be'. He lived on the level of art; or, as he might say, he lived by rules of decorum which required him to fulfil the promise of his birth and place in society.

As a result of the kind of life that he lived, his life and works are closely related to his age. In retrospect, it seems inevitable that of all those who attended Elizabeth's court, he should be singled out as the ideal Renaissance gentleman, the one alone who may be awarded the praise given the young Hamlet: 'the courtier's, soldier's, scholar's, eye, tongue, sword; / Th' expectancy and rose of the fair state, / The glass of fashion and the mould of form, / Th' observ'd of all observers'. As with his life, his works have become the norm by which we may understand the nature of the English literary Renaissance. Accordingly, Richard B. Young interprets Sidney as the English Petrarch; C. S. Lewis sees the *Arcadia* as a kind of touchstone or work of distillation that 'gathers up what a whole generation wanted to say'; and Shepherd notes of the *Defence* that Sidney's 'articulations are moments of European self-consciousness'.[44] One reason why his life is so closely related to his age is that his mind was receptive to ideas, comprehensive in scope, and constantly eclectic and assimilative. By virtue of his birth, position, promise of political power, and apparently great personal charm, he was sought out by the chief men of his day: there was no movement in politics, philosophy, or religion to which he was not exposed. One may say of all his writings what Shepherd says of the *Defence*, that the more it is studied, 'the more astonishing appears Sidney's sensitivity to contemporary intellectual development, in the arts, in religion, in politics, and in science'.[45] The movements in current thought to which he was exposed did not lead him to endorse any personal or independent position, in part because he sought instead a synthesis in which opposing points of view were balanced; in part because he had a unifying, rather than a unified, sensibility; and in chief part because of an introspective nature which separated him from the world even while he was deeply engaged in it. Greville, who knew him best, understood this Christian position of being in the world yet not of it:

> . . . When Sir Philip found this, and many other of his large and sincere resolutions imprisoned within the plights of their fortunes, that mixed good and evil together unequally; and withal discerned how the idlecensuring faction at home had won ground of the active adventurers abroad; then did this double depression both of things and men lift up his active spirit into an universal prospect of time, states, and things: and in them made him consider what possibility there was for him, that had no delight to rest idle at home, of repropounding some other foreign enterprise, probable and fit to invite that excellent Princess's mind and moderate government to take hold of. The placing of his thoughts upon which high pinnacle laid the present map of the Christian world underneath him.[46]

One consequence was that while Sidney led a fully public life, one in which he always played a role on the public stage, and his writings respond fully to the pressures of his time, his life and writings are not submerged by the age. Both remain highly individual. In Geoffrey Whitney's *A choice of emblems* (1586), the emblem addressed to Sidney is entirely fitting: it shows a plumed horseman on a prancing war-horse, with the motto: *non locus virum, sed vir locum ornat*. Another consequence is that Sidney gained the perspective of the poet, of one not being subject to nature but 'having all . . . under the authority of his pen'.[47] While the world 'mixed good and evil together unequally', he was free to assume the poet's task of separating them, what Jonson aptly describes as the 'proper embattling' of the virtues and vices.[48]

. . . Sidney's life is closely related to his works, and both to the age, [and] I may illustrate it briefly here by tracing his use of a common motif: life as a prison which tests man's worth. The motif is based on the religious view that the soul is imprisoned by the body, as in the Psalmist's cry, 'Bring my soul out of prison.' For Sidney, that view would be confirmed on the secular level by his own confined life, largely spent waiting impatiently, and finally in despair, for some public appointment. The image of man's body or mind confined in a dungeon is found throughout his poetry, as in Pyrocles's lament in the *Old Arcadia*:

> . . . the stormy rage of passions dark
> (Of passions dark, made dark by beauty's light)
> With rebel force hath closed in dungeon dark
> My mind ere now led forth by reason's light.
>
> (179-80)

The testing of man's worth by imprisonment provides the climax to that work: when Pyrocles and Musidorus are imprisoned and then sentenced to death, they fully reveal their virtue.[49] So, too, at the end of *Astrophel and Stella*: even when his life as the lover of the star is reduced to a 'dungeon dark', he rejoices in his love, and thereby proves himself to be one 'loving in truth'. At the climax to the *New Arcadia*, the two princesses, Philoclea and Pamela, manifest their virtue when they are imprisoned in Amphialus's castle. Behind all these works is the view, implicit in Sidney's poetic theory, that man's virtue is tested by the confines of life, and the faith that virtue makes man free.

'Our erected wit maketh us know what perfection is, and yet our infected will keepeth us from reaching unto it': this observation in the *Defence*[50] may serve as an epigraph to Sidney's life and works. Central to his thought is an awareness of the gulf between man's life as it is and as it should be. In his poetry and prose he shows how reality falls short of the ideal, and in the *Defence* he justifies the work of the poet on the grounds that it may best move the reader's 'infected will' to embrace the perfection which he knows by his 'erected wit'. His phrases, 'erected wit' and 'infected will' suggest generally the central secular and religious movements of the age, which H. J. C. Grierson identifies as its cross-currents, and specifically the two traditional views of man's nature, the one optimistic as it affirms man's perfectibility and the other pessimistic as it affirms his corruption.[51] The former is associated with the neo-Platonists, such as Pico della Mirandola whose *Oration on Human Dignity* allows man freedom so to fashion himself that he may become at one with Godhead itself. This view of human nature tends to ignore original sin, manifest in the 'infected will', and allows man to depend in some measure upon himself, upon good works apart from grace. The latter is associated with the Calvinists who stress man's radical imperfection in his fallen state: since man is deprived of his original perfection and depraved through sin, his will is so infected that he must depend entirely upon God's grace.

As a humanist, Sidney acknowledges man's 'erected wit': he believes with Erasmus that man may be shaped through education—*homines non nascuntur, sed finguntur*. As a Protestant, he notes man's 'infected will': the doctrine of the Fall provides the basis of his religious beliefs. His careful balancing of the two phrases reveals him to be a Christian humanist who believes that man is radically imperfect, but stresses the possibility of his regeneration. Douglas Bush's comment on the confidence in the goodness and greatness of man among the chief writers of the Renaissance applies, above all, to Sidney: 'that confidence was one element in Christian humanism, but it was kept in check by a religious sense of man's littleness and sinful frailty. . . . With a simultaneous double vision they see man as both a god and a beast. That double vision is, to be sure, the mark of the greatest writers of all ages, especially the ancients; but the Christian religion intensified the paradox by exalting man's sense of his divinity and deepening his sense of bestiality.'[52] In this double view of man, the secular and religious need not conflict: the end of learning is not to rival God but, in Milton's words, 'to repair the ruins of our first parents'.[53] Sidney would agree with Milton's complaint in *Tetrachordon* that 'nothing nowadays is more degenerately forgotten than the true dignity of man, almost in every respect'.[54] Yet his full awareness of man's 'true dignity' is based upon his full acceptance of the doctrine of man's 'infected will'. While he was receptive to the most radical intellectual currents of his time, he 'made the religion he professed the firm basis of his life'.[55] As a result, his writings reveal the central conflicts in his age between the Renaissance and the Reformation. Since they treat man's life comprehensively in relation both to his own nature and to his society, Sidney deserves his legend as the representative Elizabethan—representative, that is, of the age at its best.

ABBREVIATIONS FOR SIDNEY'S WORKS

AS *Astrophel and Stella*
CS *Certain sonnets*
LM *The Lady of May*
NA *New Arcadia*
OA *Old Arcadia*

REFERENCES FOR EDITIONS OF SIDNEY'S WORKS

Feuillerat *The complete works of Sir Philip Sidney*, ed Albert Feuillerat. Cambridge 1912-26. Volumes cited: I. *NA;* II. 1593 *Arcadia;* III. Correspondence

Levy *The correspondence of Sir Philip Sidney and Hubert Languet, 1573-1576*, tr. and ed Charles Samuel Levy, unpub. doctoral diss. Cornell 1962

Pears *The correspondence of Sir Philip Sidney and Hubert Languet*, tr. Steuart A. Pears. 1845

Prose Miscellaneous prose of Sir Philip Sidney, ed Katherine Duncan-Jones and Jan von Dorsten. Oxford 1973. Prose cited: *Defence of the Earl of Leicester; A defence of poetry; Discourse on Irish affairs; LM; A letter written . . . to Queen Elizabeth;* George Gifford, *The manner of Sir Philip Sidney's death*

Ringler *The poems of Sir Philip Sidney*, ed William A. Ringler, jr. Oxford 1962

Robertson Sir Philip Sidney, *The Countess of Pembroke's Arcadia* (The *Old Arcadia*), ed Jean Robertson. Oxford 1973

Shepherd Sir Philip Sidney, *An apology for poetry*, ed Geoffrey Shepherd. 1965

ABBREVIATIONS FOR JOURNALS

CBEL *Cambridge Bibliography of English Literature*
CL *Comparative Literature*
ELH *Journal of English Literary History*
ELN *English Language Notes*
ELR *English Literary Renaissance*
ES *English Studies*
HLQ *Huntington Library Quarterly*
JEGP *Journal of English and Germanic Philology*
JWCI *Journal of the Warburg and Courtauld Institutes*
MLQ *Modern Language Quarterly*
MLR *Modern Language Review*
MP *Modern Philology*
PLL *Papers on Language and Literature*
PQ *Philological Quarterly*
RES *Review of English Studies*
RQ *Renaissance Quarterly*
SEL *Studies in English Literature*
SP *Studies in Philology*

TSLL Texas Studies in Literature and Language

Notes

[1] James M. Osborn, *Young Philip Sidney, 1572-1577* (New Haven 1972) 54.

[2] Malcolm William Wallace, *The life of Sir Philip Sidney* (Cambridge 1915) 69.

[3] *Defence of the Earl of Leicester,* in *Miscellaneous prose of Sir Philip Sidney,* ed Katherine Duncan-Jones and Jan van Dorsten (Oxford 1973) 134.

[4] Osborn 246.

[5] George Whetstone, *Sir Philip Sidney: his honourable life, his valiant death and true virtues* (1587) B₃ʳ.

[6] *The copy of a letter* [*Leicester's commonwealth*] (1584) 196.

[7] *Prose* 139.

[8] The motto is Ulysses's reproof to Ajax who claims that he deserves Achilles's arms because of the deeds of his ancestors (Ovid, *Metamorphoses* xiii 141). Like Spenser's Red Cross Knight, Sidney wears borrowed armour for which he must prove himself worthy. On his keen interest in *imprese,* see Katherine Duncan-Jones, 'Sidney's personal *imprese*', *JWCI* 33 (1970) 321-4.

[9] *The complete works of Sir Philip Sidney,* ed Albert Feuillerat (Cambridge 1912-26) III 139.

[10] See Lawrence Stone, *The crisis of the aristocracy 1558-1641* (Oxford 1965) 385. He notes (403) that 'by the 1580s the key to advancement lay at the Court'.

[11] Sir Fulke Greville, *Life of Sir Philip Sidney* etc. (1652), ed Nowell Smith (Oxford 1907) 146, 148. The work was written between 1610 and 1614; see Joan Rees, *Fulke Greville, Lord Brooke* (1971) 25.

[12] William Camden, *Remains concerning Britain* (1605) 174.

[13] Feuillerat III 140.

[14] Greville 67-8.

[15] Noted Edmund Molyneux, in Holinshed, *Chronicles* (1587) 1550.

[16] Wallace 71.

[17] Wallace 169.

[18] Roger Howell, *Sir Philip Sidney, the Shepherd Knight* (1968) 5. Virgil B. Heltzel and Hoyt H. Hudson, ed and tr. *Nobilis* [1589] by Thomas Moffet (San Marino 1940) xxiii, note that 'all of the early writers upon Sidney laid as much stress upon his death as upon his life', for they felt that his death 'was as great and as full of significance as his life—that, indeed, the end crowned the work'.

[19] Greville 41.

[20] Sir Walter Raleigh, 'Epitaph upon the right honourable Sir Philip Sidney', in Spenser, *Minor poems,* ed Ernest de Sélincourt (Oxford 1910) 366. Unfortunately, the elegies on Sidney must be heavily discounted because they compete in fulsome praise. Sidney's reputation and influence have been traced by W. H. Bond, unpub. diss. (Harvard 1941) and his emerging legend by R. S. Esplin, unpub. diss. (Utah 1970). See also Jan van Dorsten, *Poets, patrons, and professors: Sir Philip Sidney, Daniel Rogers, and the Leiden humanists* (1962) 152-66 and Appendix I.

[21] Desiderius Erasmus, *The education of a Christian prince,* tr. Lester K. Born (New York 1936) 154. On the humanist emphasis upon public service, see John M. Major, *Sir Thomas Elyot and Renaissance humanism* (Lincoln, Neb. 1964). Wallace 373 notes that the Burgomaster and Council of Flushing esteemed Sidney an ideal governor.

[22] John Stow, *The annals of England* (1592) 1245.

[23] *Sir Philip Sidney* B₂ᵛ.

[24] Greville 129-30.

[25] Greville 138, 16. In *The Ruins of Time* 594-5 Spenser records that Sidney, 'most sweetly sung the prophecy / Of his own death in doleful elegy'.

[26] Greville 135. George Gifford, 'The manner of Sir Philip Sidney's death', in *Prose* 169.

[27] Greville 137. On Sidney's interest in 'the opinion of the ancient heathen', see D. P. Walker, *The ancient theology* (1972) 132-63.

[28] Chapter 15 is entitled 'That the immortality of the soul hath been taught by the philosophers of old time'.

[29] Arthur Collins, *Letters and memorials of state* (1746) I 246. Greville 6 records that he heard Sir Henry call his son *lumen familiae suae.*

[30] Epistle to *The tragedy of Philotas* (1605) 77-87. Cf. Gabriel Harvey, *Pierce's supererogation* (1593), *Elizabethan critical essays,* ed G. Gregory Smith (Oxford 1904) II 260: 'England, since it was England, never bred more honourable minds, more adventurous hearts,

more valorous hands, or more excellent wits, than of late.' See Harry Levin, *The myth of the golden age in the Renaissance* (New York 1969).

[31] Shelley, *Adonais* (1821) XLV 5-7.

[32] Wallace 401, 400. Richard A. Lanham, 'Sidney: the ornament of his age', *Southern Review* (Adelaide) 2 (1967) 319-40, seeks to debunk the legend but all he is able to suggest is that the idealistic Sidney was not cunning enough in political matters.

[33] *Prose* 143.

[34] *Apology for Smectymnus, Complete prose works,* ed D. M. Wolfe *et al.* (New Haven 1953-. The Yale edn) I 890. Cf. Jonson, Preface to *Volpone, Works,* ed C. H. Herford, P. and E. M. Simpson (Oxford 1925-52) V 17: 'the impossibility of any man's being the good poet, without first being a good man'.

[35] Scipio Gentili, Dedication to *The assembly of Plato* (1584); cited Thomas Zouch, *Memoirs of the life and writings of Sir Philip Sidney* (York 1808-9) 308. The few contemporary references are noted by William A. Ringler, jr, ed, *The poems of Sir Philip Sidney* (Oxford 1962) lxi-lxii, and by John Buxton, *Sir Philip Sidney and the English Renaissance* (1954) chap. 5. Especially noteworthy is Geoffrey Whitney's praise of Sidney's 'vein in verse' as Surrey's successor: 'More sweet than honey, was the style, that from his pen did flow, / Wherewith, in youth he us'd to banish idle fits; / That now, his works of endless fame delight the worthy wits. / No halting verse he writes, but matcheth former times, / No Cherillus he can abide, nor poet's patched rhymes' (*A choice of emblems,* Leiden 1586, 196-7). Whitney adds that Sidney refused his praise, saying that it belonged to Dyer. See Dorsten, *Poets* 137-8. Dorsten 62-7 adds a poem by Daniel Rogers, dated 14 January 1579, in praise of Sidney as a poet: 'when your [poetic] passion seizes our arts, then how abundant are the streams in which your wit flows forth'. See also Dorsten, 'Gruterus and Sidney's *Arcadia*', *RES* 16 (1965) 174-7.

[36] His first work, *The Lady of May,* remained untitled until 1725. His *Defence of poetry* was published in 1595 in two independent editions, one entitled *The defence of poesy* and the other *An apology for poetry.* The *Arcadia* has appeared in three separate texts: an original version (called the *Old Arcadia*) in 1926, a revised but incomplete version (called the *New Arcadia*) in 1590, and a composite version (the *New Arcadia* completed by the *Old*) in 1593. To compound confusion, *Astrophel and Stella,* which appeared twice in 1591 in pirated editions, has been re-entitled *Astrophil and Stella* in Ringler's edition. I prefer the spelling 'Astrophel' for the sake of assonance, as I note in *ELH* 36 (1969) 60: for the sake of the Greek root and

the play upon Philip, 'Astrophil' by itself may be allowed, as Ringler 458 argues, following Mona Wilson in her edition of the poem (London 1931, xvi-xvii); but the only spelling when coupled with Stella can be 'Astrophel'. No one can *say* 'Astrophil and Stella'.

[37] Thomas Nashe, 'Preface to *Astrophel and Stella*', *Works,* ed R. B. McKerrow (1904-10) iii 329; Ringler 542.

[38] Ringler lviii.

[39] *Prose* 186.

[40] Virginia Woolf, *The second common reader* (New York 1932) 48. Buxton 135 writes: 'the *Arcadia* was probably the first literary work of any kind to be translated from English into either French or Italian. Truly Sidney had set English on the way to become one of the chief literatures of Europe.'

[41] Ringler xxxvi.

[42] Sir Philip Sidney, *An apology for poetry,* ed Geoffrey Shepherd (1965) 9.

[43] Ringler li.

[44] Richard B. Young, *English Petrarke: a study of Sidney's 'Astrophel and Stella'* (New Haven 1958); C. S. Lewis, *English literature in the sixteenth century* (Oxford 1954) 339; Shepherd II.

[45] Shepherd II. Robert Kimbrough, *Sir Philip Sidney* (New York 1971) Preface, claims that 'the life of Sidney and the nature of his art must be studied together'.

[46] Greville 77-8.

[47] *Defence* 89.

[48] *Discoveries, Works* VIII 595.

[49] As source of the prison scene, Walter R. Davis, *A map of Arcadia: Sidney's romance in its tradition* (New Haven 1965) 63, cites Duplessis-Mornay's *Trueness of the Christian religion* (1587) 246, part of which Sidney translated: 'And therefore we ought surely to say that this mind or reason ought not to be ever in prison . . . as man is prepared in his mother's womb to be brought forth into the world, so is he also after a sort prepared in this body and in this world to live in another world.'

[50] *Defence* 79.

[51] H. J. C. Grierson, *Cross currents in English literature of the seventeenth century* (1929). For the general

background to the two views of man's nature, see Theodore Spencer, *Shakespeare and the nature of man* (Cambridge, Mass. 1942) and Thomas Greene, 'The flexibility of the self in Renaissance literature', *The disciplines of criticism,* ed Peter Demetz *et al.* (New Haven 1968) 241-64. G. F. Waller, ' "This matching of contraries": Bruno, Calvin and the Sidney circle', *Neophilologus* 56 (1972) 331-43, discusses the intellectual tension in Sidney between the Magical tradition of Bruno and the Calvinist tradition.

[52] Douglas Bush, *English literature in the earlier seventeenth century 1600-1660* (Oxford 1962) 37. To illustrate Bush's point briefly: when Sidney refers in the *Defence* to the mind 'not enclosed within the narrow warrant of her [Nature's] gifts, but freely ranging', he suggests his affinity with Pico, who urges: 'let us fly beyond the chambers of the world to the chamber nearest the most lofty divinity' (*On the dignity of man,* tr. C. G. Wallis, New York 1965, 7). Yet he is careful to add that man's mind ranges 'only within the zodiac of his own wit'. Similarly, when he writes that learning may 'lift up the mind from the dungeon of the body to the enjoying his own divine essence', he would seem to endorse Bruno's sonnet on the soul: 'I spread proud pinions to the wind, and contemn the world, and further my way toward heaven' (*The heroic frenzies,* tr. P. E. Memmo, jr, Chapel Hill 1966, 118). Yet he has already noted that man's soul is 'degenerate' and may be drawn only 'to as high a perfection' as it 'can be capable of', which may not prove very high.

[53] *Of education, Complete prose works* II 366-7.

[54] *Tetrachordon, Complete prose works* II 587.

[55] Greville 35.

Thomas P. Roche, Jr. (essay date 1982)

SOURCE: "Astrophil and Stella: A Radical Reading," in *Spenser Studies: A Renaissance Poetry Annual* III, University of Pittsburg Press Vol. III, 1982, pp. 139-91.

[*In the following excerpt, Roche contends that Sidney meant Astrophil to represent a negative example, someone who "must end in despair because he never learns from his experience."*]

Sidney's **Astrophil and Stella**, although the third English sequence in order of publication, holds pride of place as the most influential of the English sequences. Its author was a young nobleman who died a hero's death in 1586; its heroine a beautiful lady of the court. The story of Astrophil's love for Stella, as told in the poem, was well known through circulated manuscripts before it appeared posthumously in 1591 in a pirated edition by Thomas Newman and in 1598 in an edition authorized by Sidney's sister, the countess of Pembroke, which contained 108 sonnets among which were interspersed eleven songs.[1] The appreciation of Sidney's achievement over that of his predecessors is clearly announced by his first critic, Thomas Nashe, in the preface to the 1591 edition:

> *Tempus adest plausus aurea pompa venit,* so ends the Sceane of Idiots, and enter *Astrophel* in pompe. Gentlemen that haue seene a thousand lines of folly, drawne forth *ex vno puncto impudentiae,* & two famous Mountaines to goe to the conception of one Mouse, that haue had your eares deafned with the eccho of Fames brazen towres, when only they haue been toucht with a leaden pen, that haue seene *Pan* sitting in his bower of delights, & a number of *Midasses* to admire his miserable horne pipes, let not your surfeted sight, new come frō such puppet play, think scorne to turn aside into this Theater of pleasure.[2]

Nashe's prediction proved true, for not only did **Astrophil and Stella** become a quarry for pickpockets of others' wits but also its 108 sonnets became a symbol to other poets of Sidney's achievement, through which they paid him the compliment of using 108 as a structural device in their own poetry.[3] Spenser's elegy for Sidney, *Astrophel,* to which is added the *Doleful Lay of Clorinda* (presumed by some to be the work of the Countess of Pembroke) contains 216 lines (2 x 108) and the *Lay* 108. Mute tribute is also paid by the 108 poems of the anonymous *Alcilia* (1595) and of Alexander Craig's *Amorous Songs, Sonnets, and Elegies* (1606), some of which are addressed to Lady Penelope Rich, Sidney's Stella. The 109 poems of *Caelica* with their numerous borrowings from Sidney may also be an acknowledgment of praise from Fulke Greville, Sidney's closest friend. Of such emulative influence there can be no question; the excellence of Sidney's wit guaranteed that, as Nashe foresaw.

What is surprising is that a story of such moral bleakness should have found such welcome from the moral Elizabethans. Again, Nashe's description is instructive, for his theater of pleasure offers

> a paper stage streud with pearle, an artificial heau'n to ouershadow the faire frame, & christal wals to encounter your curious eyes, whiles the tragicommody of loue is performed by starlight. The chiefe Actor here is *Melpomene,* whose dusky robes dipt in the ynke of teares, as yet seeme to drop when I view them neere. The argument cruell chastitie, the Prologue hope, the Epilogue dispaire, *videte queso et linguis animisque fauete.*

The accuracy of Nashe's description is attested to by the fact that most later critics use it as the starting point of their own critiques of Sidney. Few critics cite the equally instructive dedication by Thomas Newman, who like Nashe appreciates Sidney's achievement in "the famous deuice of *Astrophel and Stella,* which carrying the generall commendation of all men of iudgement, and being reported to be one of the rarest things that euer any Englishman set abroach," but he nevertheless worries that "the Argument perhaps may seeme too light for your graue viewe" (i.e., the view of Frauncis Flower, to whom it is dedicated). Both Newman and Nashe give unqualified praise to the excellence of the poetry, but Newman's concern for the possible lightness of the argument in the grave view of Mr. Flower should alert us to the discrepancy between Sidney's excellence and his argument, a discrepancy implicit in Nashe's description. His "Theater of pleasure" is nothing more or less than a "paper stage . . . , an artificial heau'n to ouershadow the faire frame" in which "the tragicomedy of loue is performed by starlight. . . . The argument cruell chastitie, the Prologue hope, the Epilogue dispaire." Sidney's rival creation is filled with shadows and false lights and ends in the darkness of despair, facts that have not deterred modern critics from finding cause to praise Astrophil's pursuit of desire. But to the Elizabethans who firmly believed that "all the world's a stage," the pleasures of such theaters lay in their just imitation of nature to teach true morality. As Sidney himself writes in the *Defense of Poetry*:

> that imitation whereof *Poetrie* is, hath the most conveniencie to nature of al other: insomuch that as *Aristotle* saith, those things which in themselves are horrible, as cruel battailes, unnatural monsters, are made in poeticall imitation delightful. Truly I have knowne men, that even with reading *Amadis de gaule* which God knoweth, wanteth much of a perfect *Poesie,* have found their hearts moved to the exercise of courtesie, liberalitie, and especially courage.[4]

Poetry teaches the lessons of morality, but we must ask then what kind of morality Astrophil's despair teaches. It teaches us about a man pursuing a married woman for whom he has conceived a passion, "Not at first sight," a man who steals a kiss from her while she is asleep, worrying all the while about her anger and later chiding himself for not being more adventurous (Song II), a man who frankly propositions her despite her gentle, "No, no, no, no, my dear, let be" (Song IV), and then churlishly vilifies her because she has not given in (Song V), a man who once more tries rather gawkily to seduce her (Song VIII), is again repulsed and retires into pastoral exile (Song IX), only too soon to be found under her window still refusing to accept her refusal until she sends him packing (Song XI) to the despair of the final sonnets. In a theater this would be viewed as morally reprehensible behavior in spite of the fact that the majority of modern critics

feel a necessity to praise Astrophil's actions because he is, after all, driven by love. The poetic success of Astrophil's failure to win Stella has captivated these critics into believing that we should follow his lamentations and praise of Stella with total sympathy for his endeavors. These lenient modern assessments of Astrophil, it seems to me, miss the point of Sidney's poem. I think that Sidney wanted us to be delighted by Astrophil's wit and to be instructed by the image of a man whose reason gives way to his will and whose hopeful desires finally lead him into despair.[5] Astrophil is not a hero, and he is not a hero precisely because he succumbs to wholeheartedly to the pursuit of his desires. He teaches morality by negative example. The vacancy at the heart of Sidney's poem proclaims in chorus with all the other English sequences: Go, and do not likewise.

The most explicit statement of the virtues of negative example is the advice of the anonymous "gentleman friend" Philaretes to the author of *Alcilia:*

> In perusing your Loving Folly, and your Declining from it; I do behold Reason conquering Passion. The infirmity of loving argueth you are a man; the firmness thereof, discovereth a good wit and the best nature: and the falling from it, true virtue. Beauty was always of force to mislead the wisest; and men of greatest perfection have had no power to resist Love. The best are accompanied with vices, to exercise their virtues; whose glory shineth brightest in resisting motives of pleasure, and in subduing affections. . . . Yet herein it appeareth you have made good use of Reason; that being heretofore lost in youthful vanity, have now, by timely discretion, found yourself!

> Let me entreat you to suffer these your Passionate Sonnets to be published! which may, peradventure, make others, possessed with the like Humour of Loving, to follow your example, in leaving; and move other *Alcilias* (if there be any) to embrace deserving love, while they may.[6]

Interpreting the sonnets as negative example makes sense of Newman's hesitation about the lightness of Sidney's argument and places Nashe's description in a context that shows that accurate description does not necessarily imply approbation or praise. The "paper stage" betrays the lack of a firmer foundation; the "artificial heau'n" does "ouershadow the faire frame" of God's intended creation; the "tragicomedy of loue is performed by starlight" only for lack of better light. The argument is "*cruell* chastitie" only because that chastity will not respond to Astrophil's desires. Sidney, as I hope to prove, is using Astrophil's journey from hope to despair as a fictional device for the analysis of human desire in Christian terms.

Most commentators on Sidney find an irresistible impulse to draw into *Astrophil and Stella* the final two sonnets of *Certain Sonnets*, "Thou blindman's mark" and "Leave me, O Love, which reachest but to dust."[7] The impulse is entirely understandable not only because those two sonnets analyze the inadequacies of human desire within a context that accounts for the inadequacy but also because the ending of *Astrophil and Stella*, if read as a justification or glorification of Astrophil's actions, is grievously inconclusive and uninstructive. Those two explicitly Christian poems cry out to be included unless one sees that beneath the witty surface of Astrophil's lamentations and selfish demands lies the old battle of the "erected wit" and the "infected will" that as Sidney assures us in the *Defense of Poetry* continues to deprive us of the golden world that was once ours by right. Nevertheless, it would be a great mistake to include those two poems in the sequence. They show a repentance and a knowledge of desire that Astrophil never achieves. The brilliance of Sidney's negative example is that he realized that Astrophil must end in despair because he never learns from his experience. We the readers are meant to supply the Christian context that will make sense of the insufficiencies of Astrophil's insights into his predicament.

The title itself should give us some hint of the disjunction that is Sidney's subject: *Astrophil and Stella*, Most sonnet sequences, if titled, use only the name of the lady, the presumed subject and object of the poetry. Sidney uses a copulative title, one part derived from Greek and one from Latin, announcing even before we start to read a disjunction, minor but perhaps significant. Even disallowing the etymological disjunction, inspection reveals a disunity in the title, a doubleness, a duplicity. Two names are joined by a grammatical copula, which we accept out of hand as a unity, which it will not become. We are so used to accepting the unity of a Romeo and Juliet that we forget that the true coupling is the full title: *The Tragedy of Romeo and Juliet*. Misfortune and not love is their final union, and that is the reason we still read their story. Astrophil and Stella are separate from the moment the title is read, and if we stop to think even for a moment about the title, what possible union is there for a star-lover and a star? Petrarch makes his Laura into a false sun; Scève creates a false moon (Délie); but neither one uses as the major name of his loved one a name from another order of nature. I do not know how common the name Stella was for women in the sixteenth century, but surely Sidney is indicating in his choice of names a being of a different order, distant, unattainable, and reflected, a light that does not illuminate, that leaves us in the dark, a light that is shared and shown by thousands of other Stellas, which goes far to dispute the uniqueness of Astrophil's claims for his Stella.

The ambiguity of the title is carefully demonstrated inthe sequence. The tragicomedy of love performed by starlight is inadequately lighted. Stella's eyes, "nature's chiefest work," are black, "that sweete blacke which vailes the heav'nly eye" (sonnet 20). Astrophil's starlit stage is dark and perilous. His theatre is of the mind "that sought fit words to paint the blackest face of woe" (sonnet 1). The face can be none other than his own face, his own rejected desires. Astrophil, in calling for "some fresh and fruitfull showers upon my sunne-burn'd braine" (sonnet 1), is sounding a retreat from the light of common day, a retreat that will engulf him in the blackness of his own mind as figured by the blackness of Stella's eyes. Who ever heard of black stars before the discovery of black holes?[8]

The metaphor of blackness expands under Astrophil's preoccupations. He reaches out to the common sunlit world he has rejected to find the metaphors to describe the blackness he now recognizes as his world:

> I call it praise to suffer Tyrannie:
> And now employ the remnant of my wit,
>   To make my selfe beleeve, that all is well,
>   While with a feeling skill I paint my hell.
> (Sonnet 2)

His painting of the scenery of his starlit world draws upon the common Christian opposition of heaven and hell, but no lover has ever thought that a denial of what he considers heaven is anything else but a hell. By sonnet 86 he has transferred the responsibility for his fate to Stella:

> Use something else to chast'n me withall,
>   Then those blest eyes, where all my hopes
>   do dwell,
>   No doome should make one's heav'n
>   become his hell. . . .

Astrophil at this point is playing a more skillfully feeling game in drawing in other common words from Christian eschatology. "Doome" carries a heavy overtone of Christian damnation, of judgment against the speaker, but in point of fact, the "doome" is nothing more than Stella's judgment of his love suit, which has turned his heaven into his hell. Astrophil has inverted every image he uses. Black has replaced light. Heaven is Stella's submission to him; Hell is her refusal of her grace. Astrophil exploits every ambiguity of common Christian imagery to paint his own case in the most salutary light, which he calls in sonnet 1 "the blackest face of woe." In every way he uses spiritual meanings for physical ends:

> So while thy beautie drawes the heart to

love,
As fast thy Vertue bends that love to
good:
'But ah,' Desire still cries, 'give me some
food.'

(Sonnet 71)

These lines are the mid-lines of the entire sequence, a
point to which I shall return in the last section of this
essay. At this point we need only say that Astrophil is
painting most skillfully but only feelingly, that is, self-
ishly.

This simple technique of inversion is evident even in
the light imagery used to describe Stella. The single
star that Stella's name implies becomes by sonnet 7
two black stars, her eyes, which Astrophil would have
us believe to be Nature's "chiefe worke." By sonnet
68 Stella has become "the onely Planet of my light, /
Light of my life, and life of my desire," and by sonnet
76 his star has been metamorphosed into his sun: "But
now appeares my day, / The onely light of joy, the
onely warmth of *Love*." By the end of the sequence
his sun is only memory because of Stella's absence
from him (sonnets 88, 89, 91, 96, 97, 98).

But soone as thought of thee breeds my
delight,
And my yong soule flutters to thee his
nest,
Most rude dispaire my daily unbidden
guest,[10]
Clips streight my wings, streight wraps me
in his night,
And makes me then bow downe my head,
and   say,
Ah what doth *Phoebus'* gold that wretch
availe,
Whom iron doores do keepe from use of
day?

(Sonnet 108)

The imagery of light associated with Stella's eyes is,
to say the least, contradictory: "When Sun is hid, can
starres such beames display?" (sonnet 88). The contradiction is intended by Sidney to alert us to the confusion of Astrophil's apprehension, climaxed most explicitly in sonnet 89, the only sonnet in the sequence
to employ just two rhymes:

Now that of absence the most irksome
night,
With darkest shade doth overcome my
day;
Since *Stella's* eyes, wont to give me my
day,
Leaving my Hemisphere, leave me in night,
Each day seemes long, and longs for long-
staid night,

The night as tedious, wooes th'approch of
day;
Tired with the dusty toiles of busie day,
Languisht with horrors of the silent night
Suffering the evils both of the day and
night,
While no night is more darke then is my
day,
Nor no day hath lesse quiet then my night:
With such bad mixture of my night and
day,
That living thus in blackest winter night,
I feele the flames of hottest sommer day.

Every possible inversion of day and night is wrung out
of this infernal litany of the lover's despair. The literary sources of this inversion of day and night is Vergil,
Aeneid, 4.522-32 and more directly Petrarch's *Canzo-
niere* 22, but Sidney complicates the issue by having
Astrophil confuse both inner and outer day and night.
They have become all one to him, and from this point
on the sequence is shrouded in darkness both physical
and moral.

The permutations of Stella's light-giving qualities in
these later sonnets is anticipated in an earlier block of
poems (31-40), which also describe the lover's night
world. Sonnet 32, the central sonnet of the first unbroken block of sonnets (1-63), about which I shall
speak later, is an invocation to Morpheus, which will
require some elucidation because of its importance to
Astrophil's predicament. Morpheus, the son of Som-
nus, god of sleep, is most elaborately described in
Ovid's story of Ceyx and Alcyon (*Metamorphoses,*
11.591 ff.). He is the god who appears to dreamers in
human shape, and it is he who appears to the grieving
Ceyx to inform her of her husband's death. Ovid
describes him:

At pater e populo natorum mille suorum
excitat artificem simulatoremque figurae
Morphea: non illo quisquam sollertius alter
exprimit incessus vultumque sonumque
loquendi;
adicit et vestes et consuetissima cuique
verba.

(633-38)

[But the father rouses Morpheus from the throng
of his thousand sons, a cunning imitator of the
human form. No other is more skilled than he is
representing the gait, the features, and the speech
of men, the clothing also and the accustomed
words of each he represents.][11]

Ovid emphasizes the artifice of the verisimilitude. Sidney undoubtedly knew the Ovidian story because he
imitates lines 623-26 in sonnet 39, but he would also
have known Chaucer's use of Ovid's story in *The*

Book of the Duchess where the ambivalence of this beneficent dissimulator is more apparent. We should also recall that Spenser has Archimago send to the house of Morpheus to fetch him evil spirits to deceive Una and Red Crosse (*FQ* I.ii.36-44). Thus, an invocation to Morpheus should not be read as a simple request for sleep:

> *Morpheus,* the lively sonne of deadly
> sleepe,
>   Witnesse of life to them that living die:
>   A Prophet oft, and oft an historie,
> A Poet eke, as humours fly or creepe,
> Since thou in me so sure a power doest
> keepe,
>   That never I with clos'd-up sense do lie,
>   But by thy worke my *Stella* I descrie,
> Teaching blind eyes both how to smile and
> weepe.

Morpheus' power over Astrophil is that he is the bringer of Stella's image, but it should be observed that even Astrophil is aware of the artifice. I am not so sure that Astrophil is aware of the double edge of those "blind eyes" or of the earlier "Witnesse of life to them that living die." Sidney's invocation of Morpheus introduces a note of the hellish nature of Astrophil's infatuation. He has closed out every consideration of the waking world. In sonnet 30 he enumerates the great political problems of his time and concludes:

> These questions busie wits to me do frame;
>   I, cumbred with good maners, answer do,
>   But know not how, for still I thinke of
> you.

In sonnet 31 he projects his wretched plight onto the moon ("With how sad steps, o Moone, thou climb'st the skies") before succumbing to the blandishments of Morpheus in the sonnet under discussion. Astrophil is busy enclosing himself in the night of his own desires under the dubious patronage of Morpheus.

The complex of metaphors I have been describing derives ultimately from a common Christian metaphor, most forcefully stated in Romans 13. 10-14 (Geneva version):

> Loue doeth not euil to his neighbour: therefore is loue ye fulfilling of the law.

> And that considering the season, that it is now time that we shulde arise from slepe: for now is our saluation nerer, then when we beleued it.

> The night is past, & the day is at hand: let vs therefore cast away the workes of darkenes, and let vs put on the armour of light,

> So that we walke honestly, as in the day: not in glotonie, and dronkennes, neither in chambering and wantonnes, nor in strife and enuying.

Paul's injunction to put on the new man of spirituality and to put away the old man of bondage to sin, couched here in metaphors of light and dark, sleep and waking, is picked up again in 1 Thessalonians 5.5-6: "Ye are all the children of light, and the children of the day: we are not of the night neither of darknes. Therefore let vs not slepe as do other, but let vs watch and be sober." The Genevan gloss to these lines is instructive: "Here slepe is taken for contempt of saluation, when men continewe in sinnes, and wil not awake to godlinesse." "Watch" is glossed: "And not be ouercome with the cares of the world." Astrophil's concerns throughout the sequence lock him up in his "sleep of the senses" and prevent his seeing that worship of the idol he himself has created has imprisoned him in his hellish night. Sidney's brilliant inversion of traditional imagery cries out for the Christian context, which finally does give meaning to Astrophil's negative example of what a lover should be.

Notes

[1] The 1591 edition, first quarto, contains 107 sonnets (37, the sonnet punning on Lord Rich's name, omitted) and ten songs (XI omitted). The order of the poems is different in that 55 and 56 are reversed, and the ten songs appear as a block at the end of the sonnets. The many verbal differences are cited in William A. Ringler, Jr., ed., *The Poems of Sir Philip Sidney* (Oxford: Oxford University Press, 1962), to which edition all further citations of the poems are made. Ringler's excellent discussion of the textual history of the poems is on pp. 447-57.

[2] Thomas Nashe, preface to *Syr P. S. His Astrophel and Stella* (1591; rpt. Menston-Scolar Press, 1970), Sig A.3.

[3] Alastair Fowler, *Triumphal Forms* (Cambridge: Cambridge University Press, 1970), 175-76. . . .

[4] *The Prose Works of Sir Philip Sidney,* ed. Albert Feuillerat (Cambridge: Cambridge University Press, 1912-1926), vol. 3, p. 20.

[5] For example, Leonora Leet Brodwin, "The Structure of 'Astrophel and Stella,'" *MP* 67 (1969), 25-40, in a very perceptive study leaves Astrophil in a thoroughly untenable situation: "In the first section [1-35], Astrophel sought a virtuous resolution of the conflict between *ideal reason* and desire caused by a love which had no hope of reciprocation. In the second section [36-86], Astrophel's internal struggle is displaced by the 'new warre' of *external* struggle with Stella following upon her unexpected show of favor to him.

This wrecks the *virtuous* resolution toward which he had struggled so painfully in the first section and leaves him in the third section [87-108], with no *moral* armor against the unrelieved despair *caused* by Stella's final rejection of his love" (p. 27, emphasis added). I do not accept the *virtue* of Astrophil's dilemma. With Anne Romayne Howe, "Astrophil and Stella: Why and How?" *SP* 61 (1964), 150-69, I can recognize much poetic talent in Astrophil but no virtue. I do not want to restructure the sequence as she would, nor do I want to divide the persona of Astrophil into pure and impure persuasion as does Richard A. Lanham, "*Astrophil and Stella:* Pure and Impure Persuasion," *ELR* 2 (1972), 100-15. James J. Scanlon, "Sidney's Astrophil and Stella: 'See what it is to love' Sensually!" *SEL* 16 (1976), 65-74, is closer to the points I want to make, but I would like to trace Sidney's use of sonnet themes back to pre-Bembo sources, since Neoplatonism tends to becloud the basic Christian issues at stake. A reading closer to mine is Alan Sinfield, "Astrophil's Self-Deception," *EIC* 28 (1978), 3-17.

⁶ *Some Longer Elizabethan Poems*, ed. A. H. Bullen (Westminster: Archibald Constable, 1903), pp. 321-22. Alexander Craig, another follower of Sidney, makes the same point: *"So haue I in middest of my modest Affections, committed to the Presse my vnchast Loue to Lais, that contraries by contraries, and Vertue by Vice, more cleerely may shine"* ("To the Reader," *Amorose Songes, Sonets, and Elegies* [1606], Glasgow: Hunterian Club Publications, No. 5 [1873], p. 11). The basic critical issue is whether one achieves the moral purpose of literature by writing strict doctrine or by slyly using ironic techniques while implying the opposite. The most ancient and common version of the issue is whether Ovid was a lewd or a moral poet. In recent scholarship the problem has been debated on the meaning of Andreas Capellanus's *De amore*. See D. W. Robertson, Jr., "The Subject of the *De amore* of Andreas Capellanus," *MP* 50 (1953), 145-61. An interesting example of the problem, roughly contemporaneous with Sidney, is Robert Greene's *Vision* in which the supposedly dying author reflects on his own literary practice and has both Chaucer and Gower tell a tale on how to drive out jealousy, Chaucer taking the ironic, witty route and Gower taking the straightforward moral route. Greene describes the business of the true writer not "in painting out a goddesse, but in setting out the praises of God; not in discovering of beauty, but in discovering of virtues, not in laying out the platforms of love, nor in telling the deep passions of fancy, but in perswading men to honest and honorable actions, which are the steps that lead to true and perfect felicity." (*Life and Works of Robert Greene, MA,* ed. A. B. Grosart, 15 vols. [1881-1886], vol. 12, p. 189). The further irony of Greene, very lively, writing about his death and repentance, deserves

further study.

⁷ For example, see David Kalstone, *Sidney's Poetry, Contexts and Interpretations* (Cambridge, Mass.: Harvard University Press, 1965), p. 178.

⁸ For a different interpretation of the star imagery, see Ruth Stevenson, "The Influence of Astrophil's Star," *TSL* 17 (1972), 45-57. . . .

¹⁰ The phrase "daily unbidden guest" seems to me to foreshadow Milton's "worthy bidden guest" of *Lycidas* 118, derived from Matthew 22:8: "Truely the wedding is prepared but they which were bidden were not worthie."

¹¹ Text and translation from Loeb edition, ed. and trans. Frank Justus Miller. . . .

David Norbrook (essay date 1984)

SOURCE: "Sidney and Political Pastoral," in *Poetry and Politics in the English Renaissance*, Routledge & Kegan Paul,1984, pp. 91-108.

[*In the following excerpt, Norbrook discusses Sidney's pastoral writings, emphasizing that Sidney imbued them with his political thought.*]

Spenser dedicated *The Shepheardes Calender* to Sir Philip Sidney, a man who was acclaimed by his contemporaries as the ideal courtier, the embodiment of chivalric magnanimity and gracefulness of speech. It was especially appropriate to dedicate a pastoral work to him because Sidney himself assumed the persona of the 'shepherd knight' in tournaments at court and was the author of pastoral poetry.¹ Sidney had helped to introduce the new courtly forms of pastoral to England. He was well acquainted with Sannazaro's *Arcadia* and admired the Italian poet's gift of verbal harmony and courtly metrical virtuosity and purity of diction.² In 1578 or 1579 he wrote a pastoral entertainment, **The Lady of May**, which helped to inaugurate the cult of Elizabeth as a pastoral goddess. The relative merits of the May Lady's two suitors, a shepherd and a forester, were debated and at the end Elizabeth was praised as the true Lady of May. Sidney became so closely associated with pastoral verse that after his death in 1586 one elegist, George Whetstone, assumed that he had written *The Shepheardes Calender,* which had appeared anonymously.³ In his **Defence of Poetry** Sidney had praised Spenser's eclogues but he had also found fault with them for being insufficiently courtly: he disliked Spenser's use of the old rugged pastoral diction, and his own pastoral verse is much more polished and courtly in metre and diction than Spenser's poetry.⁴ Sidney was very conscious of his kinship with some prominent noble families and would have regarded it as beneath him to put his poetry on public sale as Spenser had done. Sidney is a courtier rather than a prophet.

Sidney's major pastoral work, the *Arcadia*, borrows its title from Sannazaro and has much in common with the atmosphere of Italian courtly pastoral. Sidney tells how two heroic princes, Musidorus and Pyrocles, arrive in Arcadia in disguise and fall in love with Pamela and Philoclea, the daughters of Duke Basilius. The princes have to disguise themselves to woo the princesses, for their father, trying to escape the effects of a threatening oracle, has retired to the country and put aside official business. Basilius delights in this abandonment of the active for the contemplative life, and takes pleasure in the joys of the countryside and in particular in pastoral entertainments. Monarchy, we are told, benefits the arts: nothing lifted up the shepherds' poetry 'to so high a key as the presence of their own duke'.[5] Between the books or acts of the *Old Arcadia* there are singing-contests which provide Sidney with an opportunity of displaying his own virtuosity as a poet. The leisure of Arcadia permits a high degree of metrical and stylistic experimentation, and most of the Arcadian poems adopt complex verse forms.

Sidney emphasises the link between social rank and poetic skill: the very shepherds of Arcadia are socially superior to their counterparts elsewhere, but when they engage in singing contests with the princes they are outdone. Thus in the 'first eclogues' (pp. 58-64) the shepherd Lalus challenges Musidorus to sing of his loved one, initiating the contest in a very difficult verse form ('terza rima' with triple rhymes); Musidorus effortlessly meets every metrical challenge Lalus sets him while at the same time producing a more complex and intellectual kind of poetry, abstract and philosophical where Lalus's language is concrete and rustic. The whole exercise reveals Sidney's mastery of Italian verse forms, which he uses with an ease and grace that no previous English poet had achieved.[6] Sidney also experiments with imitations of classical metres. Humanists throughout Europe had made similar experiments, the product not of mere pedantry but of the belief that the ancient Greeks had achieved a uniquely harmonious balance between words and music in their lyric poetry, and that if poetry imitating classical metres were set to the new 'monodic' music it might be possible to regain this powerful and quasi-magical harmony.[7] In the Arcadia these experiments are given to the princes alone: they require an erudition beyond the abilities of the vulgar.

The *Old Arcadia* describes an aristocratic society in which love is the main preoccupation and in which contemplation is valued more than action. This is the kind of society celebrated by Castiglione and other defenders of court life. The state has become a work

of art: strife and disagreement have been banished and the monarch's presence instils harmony. But having aroused certain expectations by the title *Arcadia* and the courtly atmosphere, Sidney proceeds to subvert them. It appears that the duke's attempt to turn his life into a work of art is precisely the problem: by delighting in pastoral poetry in the charmed seclusion of his rural retreat he has neglected more important political issues. Sidney has produced a critique of irresponsible absolutism by means of a critique of courtly poetic forms. The reader of courtly romance would normally expect a relaxed, associative structure without clear formal principles; the *Old Arcadia* is a masterpiece of controlled plotting. The pastoral interludes are enclosed within a main plot that is tightly and ingeniously constructed on the model of classical drama rather than the rambling romances in which so many aristocratic readers delighted. Sidney was one of the first English writers to have made a careful study of Aristotle's *Poetics,* which had been rediscovered only in the late fifteenth century but was already becoming extremely influential in Italy as the basis of neoclassical poetics. In its later developments neoclassicism became an intellectually authoritarian movement, binding the writer's freedom with rigid rules and prescriptions; and it is often regarded as having authoritarian political implications. It is true that the dominance of neoclassical theory in Italy and France coincided with periods of political absolutism.[8] Italian neoclassical drama tended to combine rigid formal unity with relatively bland and courtly subject-matter. But Sidney was aware of more radical currents in classical studies. One of the few contemporary writers he singled out for commendation in *The Defence of Poetry* was the Scottish poet George Buchanan, whose Neo-Latin plays reflected his radical views. Bale had praised him as a Protestant martyr in his *Summarium* but in fact he had escaped to the Continent and had returned to Scotland in the 1560s.[9] In 1567 he had supported the Protestant coup d'état that overthrew Mary Stuart, and had written a theoretical justification of the episode in his treatise 'De jure regni'. Sidney and his circle were interested in Buchanan as much for his politics as for his poetry: at the height of the crisis over the French match Sidney's friend Daniel Rogers arranged to have the 'De jure regni' surreptitiously printed in England, and he also encouraged him to complete his *History of Scotland* which was a vindication of the people's right to overthrow tyrants. Another friend of Sidney's[10] arranged the English publication of Buchanan's *Baptistes,* a play which portrayed the grim fate reserved for the prophet who dared to speak truths that went against the interests of the establishment: in 1643 the House of Commons ordered a translation of this work as part of the campaign to justify their rebellion.[11] Like many Protestant intellectuals, Buchanan wavered in his attitude to the people. Truth had sometimes been preserved amongst the common people when the established church had been irredeemably corrupt, but on the other hand the masses were more likely than the educated to believe in superstitions and to resist new ideas. 'For the most part', he complained, 'the people like to stick to old ways and customs, and are opposed to change.'[12] They preferred fantastic plays which portrayed impossibly idealised princes to neo-classical drama in much the same way that they preferred religious rituals and processions to the pure word of God. But the drama Buchanan most loved, that of classical Greece, had been produced in a democracy. He had translated some plays of Euripides—whose critical, rationalistic outlook was to make him Milton's favourite dramatist. Sidney may have been working on the **Defence of Poetry** during the controversy over the French match, and he may have been thinking of Buchanan's plays when he wrote that tragedy 'makes kings fear to be tyrants'.[13] Sidney defended poetry on fundamentally didactic grounds, arguing that it was superior to philosophy and history in moving people to action. His type of the pedantic enemy to poetry was not the Puritan—he shared the puritans' hostility to the French match, and indeed to much popular theatre—but the philosopher; he was reviving the old quarrel between philosophy and rhetoric.

There is, however, a certain tension in the **Defence** between humanist didacticism and a rather more courtly view of poetry. Sidney's conception of the poem as a 'golden world', more richly adorned than anything to be found in nature, recalls the increasing escapism of sixteenth-century Italian court culture, the search for ideal aristocratic utopias which would transcend political crisis.[14] But Sidney's argument is not just that the 'golden world' is more beautiful than the natural world but also that, as Aristotle had put it, poetry is more philosophical than history because less dependent on contingent facts. The poetic world is a model whose very autonomy, its freedom from subjection to empirical fact, allows a detachment from traditional ideas and the free exploration of alternatives. The detached and critical cast of mind that enabled Sidney to conceive of the work of art as a 'world' was the same kind of capacity that produced the concept of the 'commonwealth' as a complex entity independent of the person of the ruler. In the **Defence** Sidney draws a distinction between different kinds of poetic idealisation. Some writers, like Xenophon and Virgil, create a portrait of the ideal prince (a genre which was, of course, especially popular with courtiers). But, Sidney continues, it is also possible to feign 'a whole commonwealth, as the way of Sir Thomas More's *Utopia*'.[15] In praising not the communist ideas but the 'way' of the *Utopia* Sidney was presumably referring to More's ability to see all the evils of society as closely interrelated rather than remaining content with moral denunciations of particular 'abuses'. In the **Arcadia** Sidney presents not just an idealised prince but a whole commonwealth. At first the focus seems to be limited, as is customary in courtly romance, to

the prince and his followers. But when a group of rebels unexpectedly storm his retreat Basilius is made to remember that a commonwealth is made up of more people than just the prince, that his personal well-being is not necessarily identical with the well-being of his subjects. Towards the end of the work the neighbouring monarch Euarchus arrives to remind Basilius of the need to join a Grecian alliance against the Roman threat: this episode recalls the Leicester circle's frustration at the queen's reluctance to join an anti-Habsburg alliance. Basilius's retreat is a sign of effeminacy, a fact symbolised by his falling in love with Pyrocles in his female disguise. The Leicester circle felt that Elizabeth lacked the firm decisiveness that might have been shown by a male ruler. Sidney hints that a monarchy may not necessarily be the best form of government for consulting the interests of all: under Basilius's rule 'public matters had ever been privately governed', and we are told that this is 'a notable example how great dissipations monarchal governments are subject unto' (p. 320). Sidney's 'feigned commonwealth' of Arcadia is not just a timeless idyll but a state with a complex economy and social structure. Sidney takes considerable pains to give historical verisimilitude to the setting in classical Greece: his feigned commonwealth must be made politically accurate. Sidney has politicised Italian courtly romance, enclosing it within a carefully organised humanist framework.[16]

The princes as well as Basilius have allowed private interests to interfere with public responsibilities. On their way to visit Pyrocles's father Euarchus, they are so enchanted by the princesses' beauty that they resolve to adopt disguises in order to enter their presence. Because they are disguised, not only does Euarchus worry about their fate but their friend Plangus, who is searching for them to tell them that the virtuous queen Erona is in danger and needs their help, is unable to find them. His despairing story is told during the first eclogues, and a bitter lament by him is sung in the second eclogues. The princes decide that they have time enough to save Erona, but this sub-plot darkens the work's atmosphere. Their own poems, in which they declare their love to the princesses, give a sense of confinement, almost claustrophobia: they are forced to disguise their identities and cannot speak their passion openly. Their attempt to win the princesses without their father's consent leads to political chaos: they abduct the princesses, while Basilius, in love with Pyrocles, and Gynecia, in love with Musidorus, engage in a series of devious manoeuvres which end in the duke's drinking a sleeping-potion and being feared dead. The princes are put on trial for abducting and raping the princesses and for murdering Basilius. Though they adopt their best courtly garb to gain the crowd's sympathy, the laws of Arcadia strongly reject the aristocratic double standard of sexual conduct and Euarchus, who has arrived in search of the princes and has been appointed regent, decides that the laws must sentence them to cruel deaths. Only a twist of the plot, the belated revival of the duke who has not after all been poisoned, saves the princes from their fate. Basilius arbitrarily sets aside the laws which condemned them, for though they have been innocent of trying to murder him the law still prescribes death for seducing and kidnapping princesses.

The *Old Arcadia* thus subverts the expectations aroused by its title and subjects the Italian courtly ideals of retirement, contemplation and love, to severe Protestant humanist scrutiny. It reflects the ambivalence with which the Leicester circle viewed Italian culture. In the *Defence of Poetry* Sidney argued that English literature was underdeveloped, that it had not yet acquired the rhetorical skill of classical literature, and his poetic practice shows that he felt he had nothing to learn from the mid-century 'gospelling' poets or indeed from much previous English poetry. He found the best models in Romance languages amongst the Italians. But Sidney always judged cultural issues in their political context, and he did not admire current tendencies in Italian politics. Greville was speaking for the Leicester circle when he later declared that Italy's 'excellent temper of spirits, earth, and aire' had 'long been smothered and mowed down by the differing Tyrannies of *Spain,* and *Rome*'.[17] Languet warned Sidney that the Italians' 'spirits are broken by long servitude', and that 'nothing is more harmful to the intellects of free men' than the 'arts' of courtly flattery, 'which soften their manly virtue and prepare their spirits for servility'.[18] On Languet's advice Sidney confined his visit to Italy to Venice, a republic that jealously defended its political traditions. He admired Contarini's description of the laws of Venice, which was to become a key text for seventeenth-century republicans, and advised his brother Robert to study the Venetian constitution. He considered all other Italian regimes to be too servile and oligarchical.[19] The *Old Arcadia* reflects the radical humanist's suspicion of the aestheticisation of politics, of the tendency of princes to compensate their subjects for the loss of liberty by spectacles and courtly festivities. Sidney certainly did not think of Elizabeth as a tyrant, and he wrote a pastoral masque for her himself. But *The Lady of May* is relatively muted in its praise of the queen. Sidney may have intended the queen to favour the forester, whose active life would contrast with the pacific and contemplative existence of the shepherd and might be taken to symbolise the more active foreign policy favoured by the Leicester circle. This allegorical interpretation is debatable; what is notable, however, is that both forester and shepherd criticise the life of the court with its 'servile flattery' and futile wooing of an evasive royal mistress. The only poem Sidney wrote in praise of Queen Elizabeth, which prefaces the masque, declares that 'your face hurts oft' even though 'still it doth delight'.[20] Like *The Lady*

of May, the *Old Arcadia* combines courtly pastoral with a detached and critical view of monarchy.

At one point, indeed, Sidney abandons the newer, Italianate pastoral idiom and writes an eclogue under the traditional rugged persona of the plain-speaking, anticourtly shepherd. Between the third and the fourth books, at a crucial point in the work's structure, Sidney includes a long beast fable. The poem is a classic exposition of the radical Protestant fear of the growing power of absolute rulers. It tells how at one time the beasts were represented by a few aristocratic senators, but the baser beasts stupidly made suit to Jove:

> With neighing, bleing, braying, and barking,
> Roaring, and howling, for to have a king.

Jove warns them that kings will become tyrants, but the beasts are obdurate and even yield up their right to freedom of speech in their eagerness to be ruled by a monarch. The new king—Man in the allegory—begins his reign by provoking dissension in the aristocracy and wiping them out. At first the people are delighted to have lost their noble oppressors, but they learn by bitter experience that the aristocracy at least acted as a buffer between themselves and the tyrant, who now proceeds to enslave them. The people are urged, ominously if vaguely, to 'know your strengths' (p. 259). Significantly, this is the one part of the *Arcadia* where Sidney reverts to the self-consciously archaic diction of mid-century prophetic poetry. The reciter of the poem, 'Philisides', explains that he learned it from a shepherd on Ister Bank: this is a reference to Hubert Languet, the Huguenot intellectual who was Sidney's lifelong mentor and correspondent. Languet was closely involved with international Protestant politics: he helped to draft the *Apology* with which William of Orange justified his rebellion against Philip II. Languet's friend Philippe Duplessis-Mornay was probably the author of one of the most eloquent Huguenot justifications of resistance against tyranny, the *Vindiciae contra tyrannos*. The sixteenth-century theorists of resistance were not democrats: they argued that only men of rank and property had the right to resist tyranny, otherwise there would be social chaos. Sidney's Ister Bank eclogue reflects the view of these aristocratic radicals that only a strong nobility could safeguard liberty. It is possible to trace a clear line of succession, both in intellectual and familial kinship, from Sidney and his circle down to the classical republicans of the Commonwealth in the 1650s—down to Sir Philip's greatnephew Algernon Sidney.[21]

There can be little doubt that Sidney's close contacts with radical political thinkers contributed to the queen's suspicion of her young nephew. Despite his image as the ideal courtier, Sidney was not on particularly good terms with Elizabeth, who was reluctant to entrust him with important diplomatic or military duties. Even the knighthood by which he is known to posterity was conferred on him only late in his short life to enable him to carry out a minor diplomatic ceremony. The queen knew that on the Continent Sidney was regarded as an important political figure because of his family connections with the Earl of Leicester: it was not inconceivable that he might become a candidate for the throne. Negotiations began at one time for a marriage between Sidney and the sister of William of Orange: this project, if followed through, would have brought him to the centre of European Protestant politics. Elizabeth did not want this brilliant young man to have ideas above his station. The fact that he was in contact with foreign radicals does not, of course, mean that he endorsed all their ideas. He would probably have agreed with Harvey that because he was living in Smith's commonwealth rather than More's Utopia he had to adjust himself to political realities. What concerned him was to make sure that the monarchy did not step beyond the bounds traditionally allotted to it.[22]

Sidney's political caution was intensified by an element of social fear. His generation had been deeply affected by the upheavals of 1549: Leicester as a young man had ridden with his father the Protector to crush the revels. Aristocratic privilege was liable to threats from below as well as from above. Sidney completely lacks the interest of earlier generations in the social problems caused by economic changes such as enclosures: the *Arcadia* itself was, according to legend, written in a park which had been made by enclosing a whole village and evicting the tenants, and where Sidney could enjoy leisure and contemplation.[23] Many members of Leicester's circle were essentially nouveaux riches, despite the archaising feudal costumes they wore at court tournaments. Sir Henry Lee, who aided Leicester in devising entertainments for the queen and appeared as the Queen's champion in Accession Day tilts, 'belonged to the new school of landowners, for whom landowning was a business'.[24] A great sheep-farmer, he owed much of his wealth to enclosures. His relations with his tenants were not particularly paternalistic. He gained a licence from the queen to make the many serfs remaining on his lands pay large sums to buy their liberty: if they refused he had the right to seize their lands.[25] His activities as a landlord helped to provoke an uprising in Oxfordshire in 1596. Sidney was acutely conscious that members of old landed families looked down on his own more modest ancestry. The Earl of Oxford, a Catholic supporter of the French match, engaged in an extremely public quarrel with Sidney in 1579 in which he cast scorn on his lowly origins. To Oxford Sidney was an upstart with dangerous political ideas; his antagonist responded by stiffly insisting on his own and Leicester's good breeding. Hence his insistence on the immense gulf between himself and Spenser the professional poet—the distance was not quite as great as he might have liked.

Sidney's aristocratic consciousness thus affects his political outlook in complex ways: if it makes him sympathise with noble rebels against tyrannous monarchs, it also instils considerable social caution. This caution tempers his severe judgment of the princes for their neglect of their duty. Some critics have argued that Sidney means the princes to be found wanting by a rigorous Calvinist standard of morality, that the *Arcadia* is, in the sexual sense, a puritan work.[26] There is certainly a tension in the *Old Arcadia* between sensualism and morality. The reader is constantly put in the position of princes as they watch with relish an attractive female body: Philoclea's garment, says the appreciative narrator, was light enough 'to have made a very restrained imagination have thought what was under it' (p. 37). But having aroused such imaginations, Sidney seems to quell them at the end by showing the disastrous consequences of the princes' self-indulgence. Though Sidney later revised the *Old Arcadia* to mitigate their guilt in abducting the princesses, in the original version they are undoubtedly guilty of this offence and the sentence of death is, though harsh, definitely legal. By the standards of the conduct of the heroes in many sixteenth-century romances, however, their behaviour has not been particularly heinous.[27] The aristocratic 'double standard' tolerated strong sexuality in young noblemen if not young women: in *Astrophel and Stella* Sidney enters sympathetically into the predicament of a courtier who wants to seduce a married lady.

Why, then, did Sidney submit his heroes to such rigorous judgments? The trial scene indicates the keen interest of Sidney and his circle in legal issues: in composing the prosecution and defence speeches Sidney draws heavily on Cicero's account of legal rhetoric in 'De Inventione'. The relationship of the law to sexual morality was in fact being debated in the 1570s: the Puritans were campaigning for stricter laws against sexual misconduct, drawing their precedents not only from the Old Testament but also from the laws of Greece and Rome. The Puritans did not go so far as the Arcadians in wanting to punish fornication by death, but they did want the death penalty for adultery. Such rigour was not easily compatible, however, with the traditionally more indulgent aristocratic attitude to sexual misconduct. In 1593 a proposal to have men as well as women whipped for adultery was rejected 'for fear, the penalty might chance upon gentlemen or men of quality'.[28] Pyrocles asks Philanax not to be too 'precise' in his judgment (p. 267): the word 'precise' was often applied to Puritans, and the topical controversy may have influenced Sidney's presentation of the issues. Shakespeare was to explore similar questions in his presentation of 'the precise Angelo' in *Measure for Measure*.[29] Like Shakespeare, Sidney dramatises a conflict between law and equity. Euarchus is renowned for his equity, but he announces at the outset that he will set aside all considerations other than the letter of the law of Arcadia. He does this because only the prince is empowered to dispense equity, and as a mere outsider called in by the Arcadians to exercise judgment he is extremely anxious not to do anything that might imply that he wants to usurp the ducal authority. Sixteenth-century legal theory indeed normally associated equity with the monarch, who was empowered in special cases to overrule the letter of the law. In England, equity was especially associated with prerogative courts like the Star Chamber.[30] More generally, equity was associated by political theorists with aristocratic societies which were governed by distributive rather than commutative justice: in democracies the narrow letter of the law prevailed and all citizens were treated alike irrespective of circumstances, while in an aristocracy or monarchy there was more latitude for equity. Sidney clearly expects his readers to feel the injustice of treating noble and magnanimous princes in the same way as anyone else: where Puritanism seems to have democratic tendencies, he fears it. And what resolves the conflict is the revival of the duke, who alone is able to dispense equity and to pardon the princes. But many critics have found this ending unsatisfactorily perfunctory: the pardoning seems to partake more of 'blatant favouritism' than of equity.[31] Sidney tried to remedy this defect in revision, but it is an interesting index of the social and political tensions that affected his writing.

Without the monarch, the status of the nobility would be threatened. The plot of the *Arcadia* ultimately points this moral. The harmony of the landscape can be disturbed without warning by an armed uprising, the country houses that adorn the Arcadian countryside abruptly become islands in a 'violent flood' of rebellious 'clowns' carried 'they themselves knew not whither' (123). The social focus in Sidney's 'feigned commonwealth' is much narrower than in More's. Sidney does not view the social order as a naturally harmonious, organically ordered body but as a precarious union of warring elements: once the duke has withdrawn from political life the state becomes 'like a falling steeple, the parts whereof . . . were well, but the whole mass ruinous' (p. 320). In the revised *Arcadia* Sidney expands on the social motives of the rebels in order to show how contradictory they are: the peasants 'would have the Gentlemen destroied', the citizens 'would but have them refourmed', while the richer burgesses look down on both groups.[32] The Leicester circle had supported the Dutch rebels against Philip II, but William of Orange had been careful to emphasise that this was a rebellion with strong feudal precedents and with aristocratic leaders. When he took command in the Netherlands Leicester sided strongly with the Calvinist party because the more liberal Protestant party was led by mere merchants. He recommended that[33]

> only the nobility of the land or other learned persons, well versed in matters of state should be

appointed to the country's councils. . . . True, there are many good and trusty merchants whose services one might use, but nonetheless they will always seek profit for themselves.

Leicester wanted to impose a firm and efficient central government on the different states of the Netherlands. A seventeenth-century Dutch historian feared that had Sidney lived he would have 'used his industry, valour, and ability in undermining liberty'.[34] The ambivalence with which the Sidney circle viewed rebellion emerges especially clearly in the opening sections of the *New Arcadia*, in which Musidorus finds himself involved in a class war 'betweene the gentlemen and the peasants' in Laconia: but elsewhere the Helots are viewed as not just the common people but a whole nation who have been oppressed by foreign overlords—like the Dutch in their struggle against Philip II.[35] The ambiguity is left unresolved; the episode indicates Sidney's anxiety about the difficulty of distinguishing between controlled aristocratic uprisings and social revolutions. Sidney is also aware that not all aristocratic uprisings serve the good of the state as a whole or even of all members of their own class: on Basilius's death the selfish Timautus gains the support of 'most part of the nobility' for a scheme to seize the queen and the princesses and thus effectively hold power, but Timautus's aims are purely selfish and he wants power for himself rather than his class. And there are problems in more constitutional forms of aristocratic government. Some Arcadians want to establish 'the Lacedemonian government of few chosen senators' on Basilius's death (p. 320): this would clearly be an aristocratic republic on the Venetian model. Others even call for a democratic republic. But only 'the discoursing sort of men' favour such radical changes, which are 'a matter more in imagination than practice' (p. 321). The more active politicians are well aware that a republic, however attractive it might be in theory, could never take root in a country that 'knew no government without a prince'.

Though the *Old Arcadia* reflects the Sidney circle's suspicion of monarchs who try to turn political life into a theatre, substituting spectacle and pageantry for proper political debate, the work also reveals the importance of ceremony in maintaining social order. Sidney sometimes seems closer to Puttenham than to Languet. The wise king Euarchus stage-manages the trial of the princes effectively, clothing himself in black and sitting in the ducal judgment-seat, 'for Euarchus did wisely consider the people to be naturally taken with exterior shows far more than with inward consideration of the material points . . . in these pompous ceremonies he well knew a secret of government much to consist' (*OA*, p. 375). The princes try to manipulate the power of the imagination, dressing themselves in their most spectacular clothes in order to arouse the people's sympathy. This is clearly a dishonest attempt to disguise their failings; but they have earlier used precisely the same technique to save Basilius from the rebels. Pyrocles, still in his female disguise, climbs into the very judgment-seat in which Euarchus is later to sit, and harangues the crowd in a speech that appeals to their imagination more than their reason: necessarily so, since a fully honest and rational explanation of why he was there would make him emerge in an unfavourable light and confirm the Arcadians' suspicion that their prince is irresponsibly allowing himself to be led astray by a foreigner. He peppers his speech with rhetorical questions, which are, as the rhetorician John Hoskins pointed out, 'very fit for a speech to many and indiscreet hearers, and therefore much used in Pirocles's oration to the seditious multitude'.[36] He reinforces his points by means of striking gestures, which display a 'sweet magnanimity' (or, in another manuscript, 'sweet imagination' (*OA*, p. 131), and these gestures 'gave . . . a way unto her speach through the rugged wildernesse of their imaginations'.[37] In their pursuit of their loved ones the princes use somewhat Machiavellian strategies of pursuit and disguise: Musidorus callously exploits the low-born Mopsa in order to gain access to Pamela by this 'policy' (*OA*, p. 102), while Pyrocles is said to display a 'dangerous cunning'. But their skill in disguise is politically useful: Pyrocles plans to outwit the Helots by disguising soldiers as peasants so that the rebels will admit them to their town under the impression that they sympathise with their class war. Sidney argued in the ***Defence of Poetry*** that literature was more exemplary than history because it distributed rewards and punishments justly, but many critics have found the treatment of the princes at the end more indulgent than just. But Sidney may not always have thought as moralistically as he tried to do in the ***Defence of Poetry***. He is known to have translated the first two books of Aristotle's *Rhetoric,* a work which takes a cynically pragmatic view of the best means of influencing an audience, notably different from the more moralistic conceptions of rhetoric and political virtue found in Cicero or Quintilian. John Hoskins makes an interesting comment about Sidney's processes of composition:[38]

> The perfect expressing of all qualities is learned out of Aristotle's ten books of moral philosophy; but because, as Machiavel saith, perfect virtue or perfect vice is not seen in our time, which altogether is humorous and spurting, therefore the understanding of Aristotle's *Rhetoric* is the directest means of skill to describe, to move, to appease, or to prevent any motion whatsoever.

Sidney, says Hoskins, had learned this lesson. The *Arcadia* can be seen as the product of Machiavellian rhetoric rather than moral philosophy.

Sidney seems to have decided that the first version of

the *Arcadia* was not didactic enough, for soon after it was completed he began to revise it, making the conduct of the princes less devious and more exemplary. These revisions became more and more elaborate until they overshadowed the original narrative. The revised version of the *Arcadia* became a heroic romance, a celebration of Protestant magnanimity. Sidney added lengthy descriptions of chivalric combats. Humanists in the earlier sixteenth century had ridiculed romance with its glorifications of meaningless combats and adulterous loves; but Sidney tries to give romance political significance and a clear, coherent structure. Pyrocles and Musidorus do battle with political evils rather than mythical beasts: when they do meet some giants, Sidney adds the demystifying comment that they are really only 'two brothers of huge both greatnesse & force'.[39] The princes roam through Asia Minor righting wrongs and deposing tyrants, their sympathies going to 'the yong men of the bravest minds' who 'cried with lowde voice, Libertie'.[40] The political scenes seem to indicate Sidney's endorsement of the Huguenot theory of limited rebellion, though, as has been seen in the case of the Helot episode, there are hesitations and ambiguities.[41] Sidney is trying to synthesise the aristocratic cult of honour with humanist and Protestant didacticism, to produce a work that men like Languet or Buchanan could respect on political as well as literary grounds.[42]

But the attempt is not a complete success. The revisions are not fully integrated with the original framework. The heroic deeds of Pyrocles and Musidorus are recounted in extensive flashbacks: the princes are in fact telling the princesses of their heroic deeds in order to make their wooing more effective. The rhetorical end of these narratives may be didactic as far as the reader is concerned but it is meant to be erotic to the princesses. At the start of Book III the plot takes a new turn and the princesses are abducted, not by the princes but by the tormented aristocrat Amphialus. The centre of interest now passes to the princesses and Pyrocles and Musidorus play a relatively subordinate part from now on. Basilius comes to rescue the princesses but the siege becomes a frustrating stalemate. Amphialus tries to justify his resistance to Basilius by using some of the commonplaces of Calvinist theories of rebellion, but his motives are essentially personal and selfish, springing from a romantic obsession rather than a political objective. In analysing Amphialus's conduct, and throughout the romance, Sidney oscillates between sophisticated humanist political discourse and the clichés of chivalric romance. Battle is confined to a series of single combats, which can be described in terms borrowed from courtly tilts rather than in the language of sixteenth-century military science. The knights dress up in fantastic and colourful costumes; the field of battle becomes a 'blooddy Teniscourt' in which 'the game of death' is played; blood becomes a caparison 'decking' Philautus's armour.[43] Violent action is blocked and displaced into spectacle; Amphialus stages a grisly mock-execution of Pamela in front of Philoclea, a sadistic 'Tragedie'.[44] The princesses are kidnapped after they have been lured into a grove on the premise of being shown pastoral 'devises'. The captivity scenes reflect Sidney's growing interest in inner spiritual qualities which make external pomp and ceremony seem emptily theatrical.

But Sidney's essentially courtly style did not offer a suitable vehicle for exploring inner states and the result is normally somewhat clumsy and external. Art is persistently associated with violence in the revised *Arcadia*. Sidney extended his portrayal of the defeat of the rebels in Book II, including a scene in which a 'poor painter' who had tried to portray the battle has both his hands chopped off. Spectacular representations of massacres were, it may be noted, in vogue in European courts of the sixteenth century, but Sidney seems exceptional in the sadistic comedy he tried to extract from scenes like that of the painter 'well skilled in wounds, but with never a hand to performe his skill'.[45] In another episode an evil king writes the sonnets of his love in the blood of his subjects and tunes them in their cries.[46] The grotesque juxtapositions of warfare and courtly spectacle grow more and more insistent in the later part of the revised *Arcadia*. Sidney broke off the revision before he had reached the end of the third book, possibly because he realised that the work's serious religious and political concerns, and its increasing inwardness, were becoming incompatible with the courtly framework.

The later parts of the *Arcadia* reveal a tendency which, as will be seen, becomes increasingly explicit in the later writings of Spenser and of Sidney's closest friend, Fulke Greville: the imagery of courtly ceremonial is associated with violence and imprisonment rather than delight. The claustrophobic atmosphere reflects Sidney's frustration at enforced inactivity. It has often been noted that the tournaments in the *Arcadia* are modelled on the joustings held at Queen Elizabeth's court; in Book II he portrays 'Philisides' in the costume of the Shepherd Knight which he had himself adopted at court, and pays tribute to Queen Helen of Corinth, who bears a resemblance to Queen Elizabeth. But the specific compliment to Elizabeth is in fact remarkably brief, in comparison with the tendency of many Elizabethan romance-writers to drop into praise of Elizabeth at the slightest provocation. The political connotations of tournaments were complex. In the Middle Ages tournaments had often been viewed with suspicion by the monarchy because they tended to foment rivalry and dissension amongst the nobility. While the aristocrats tended to stress the practical function of tournaments, monarchs anxious to discipline their often anarchic desire for personal honour preferred to turn them into spectacles, displays of

courtly elegance rather than military valour.[47] The Tudor monarchs had been anxious to curb the military power of the aristocracy, and this process was effectively completed by Elizabeth when she crushed the last major Catholic uprising in 1570-1. After the Northern Rising the tilts held to commemorate the queen's Accession Day acquired a strongly Protestant colouring, and the Leicester circle were enthusiastic participants. For the old Catholic nobility the cult of aristocratic honour was associated with the old religion, but the Leicester circle saw themselves as Protestant noblemen with a firm commitment to the monarchy. There were still tensions, however: they were anxious to serve the queen on the battlefield, whereas Elizabeth was reluctant to spend money on warfare. The 'Vindiciae contra tyrannos' gave an eloquent warning against the danger that monarchs would aestheticise politics, would turn real privileges into empty spectacle:[48]

> You speak of peers, notables, and officials of the crown, while I see nothing but fading names and archaic costumes like the ones they wear in tragedies. I see scarcely any remnant of ancient authority and liberty. . . . Let electors, palatine, peers, and the other notables not assume that they were created and ordained merely to appear at coronations and dress up in splendid uniforms of olden times, as though they were actors in an ancient masque playing the parts of a Roland, Oliver, Renaldo or any other great hero for a day, or as though they were staging a scene from King Arthur and the Knights of the Round Table . . . and that when the crowd has gone and Calliope has said farewell, they have played their parts in full.

Sidney participated in tournaments in order to testify his loyalty, but he was more and more eager to turn tiltyard fictions into military reality. There was an element of bitter irony in his chosen persona of the 'shepherd knight': he was forced to spend his time in peaceful, contemplative pursuits because he was forbidden the opportunity to put his ideals into action. His New Year's gift to the queen in 1581 concentrated the political ambivalence of the Arcadia into a striking symbol: it was a jewel-encrusted whip.

In his last years Sidney seems to have turned to more explicitly Protestant literary forms: he translated parts of Duplessis-Mornay's *Of the Truth of the Christian Religion* and the *Divine Weeks and Works* of the Huguenot poet Du Bartas. His chance to serve the queen in action did not come until 1585, when Elizabeth at last gave way to circumstances—after the assassination of William of Orange, the Spanish had been gaining ground against the rebels—and allowed Leicester to lead an expedition to the Netherlands. The expedition became a Protestant crusade; the queen nearly revoked Leicester's appointment when she realised the radicalism of many of the followers he had chosen.

When they arrived in the Netherlands Leicester and his allies angered the queen by seeming to go beyond their instructions. Certainly Sidney, in moments of Protestant enthusiasm, came to see the expedition as a crusade in which religious considerations were ultimately more important than service of the queen: she was 'but a means whom God useth . . . I am faithfully persuaded that if she shold withdraw her self other springes woold ryse to help this action'.[49] But Leicester's campaign was a failure, marred by tensions analogous to those which prevented Sidney from completing the *Arcadia*. Leicester and his supporters complained that they did not receive enough backing from England: their religious zeal made them rather suspect to conservatives at home. On the other hand, their military effectiveness may have been diminished by the fact that they were much more experienced in symbolic conflicts in the tiltyard than in real warfare. Fulke Greville's account of Sidney's death was almost certainly much distorted by hindsight but it does capture something of the atmosphere that surrounded the expedition; Sidney, he says, removed a crucial part of his armour so that he would not be better protected than his peers, and was thus unprotected from his fatal wound.[50] Aristocratic role and godly self formed a perfect union only in what Sidney had called 'the game of death'.

Notes

[1] New evidence about connections between Sidney's poems and his appearances in tournaments is provided by Peter Beal, 'Poems by Sir Philip Sidney: the Ottley Manuscript' *Library,* 5th series, 33 (1978), pp. 284-95.

[2] On the influence of Sannazaro see David Kalstone, *Sidney's Poetry: Contexts and Interpretations,* Cambridge, Mass., 1965, pp. 9-39.

[3] George Whetstone, *Sir Philip Sidney, his honorable Life, his valiant Death and true Vertues,* London, 1587, sig. B2v.

[4] *The Defence of Poetry* in *Miscellaneous Prose,* p. 112.

[5] *The Countess of Pembroke's Arcadia (The Old Arcadia),* ed. Jean Robertson, Oxford, 1973, p. 56. References in the text are to this edition.

[6] John Thompson, *The Founding of English Metre,* London, 1961, pp. 139-55.

[7] John Hollander, *The Untuning of the Sky: Ideas of Music in English Poetry 1500-1700,* New York, 1970, pp. 141-3; Frances A. Yates, *The French Academies of the Sixteenth Century,* London, 1947, pp. 36ff.

[8] Vernon A. Hall, *Renaissance Literary Criticism: A Study of its Social Content,* New York, 1945.

[9] I.D. McFarlane, *Buchanan,* London, 1981, p. 77; on the possible influence of Bale's John the Baptist play on Buchanan see pp. 381-2.

[10] James E. Phillips, 'George Buchanan and the Sidney Circle' *HLO,* 12 (1948-9), pp. 23-55.

[11] McFarlane, *Buchanan,* pp. 391-2.

[12] Quoted by Williamson, *Scottish National Consciousness in the Age of James VI,* p. 113.

[13] Sidney, *Miscellaneous Prose,* p. 68.

[14] Martines, *Power and Imagination,* pp. 452ff.

[15] Sidney, *Miscellaneous Prose,* p. 86.

[16] In his excellent study *Sir Philip Sidney: Rebellion in Arcadia,* Hassocks, 1979, Richard C. McCoy gives a much fuller study of the critical issues involved than is possible here.

[17] Greville, *Life of Sidney,* p. 104.

[18] Quoted by McCoy, p. 16.

[19] Sidney, *Complete Works,* ed. A. Feuillerat, 4 vols, Cambridge, 1912-26, III, p. 127.

[20] A.C. Hamilton, *Sir Philip Sidney: A Study of his Life and Works,* Cambridge, 1977, pp. 25-6; *Miscellaneous Prose,* p. 22.

[21] Blair Worden, 'Classical Republicanism and the Puritan Revolution' in *History and Imagination: Essays in Honour of Hugh Trevor-Roper,* ed. Hugh Lloyd-Jones et al., London, 1981, pp. 185-90.

[22] On the possible influence of Smith on Sidney see Ernest W. Talbert, *The Problem of Order: Elizabethan Political Commonplaces and an Example of Shakespeare's Art,* Chapel Hill, 1962, pp. 89-97.

[23] Noted by R.H. Tawney, *The Agrarian Problem in the Sixteenth Century,* London, 1912, p. 194.

[24] *D.N.B., Sir Henry Lee.*

[25] E.K. Chambers, *Sir Henry Lee,* Oxford, 1936, pp. 43-6, 92-3, 165-8. Yates, *Astraea,* pp. 89-108, discusses Lee's career in terms of an 'imaginative refeudalisation' of European culture.

[26] Franco Marenco, *Arcadia Puritana,* Bari, 1968; An-

drew D. Weiner, *Sir Philip Sidney and the Poetics of Protestantism,* Minneapolis, 1978. An interest in representations of female beauty was, of course, far from unknown amongst Puritans: it is interesting to study the passages from the *Arcadia* transcribed by the American Puritan Seaborn Cotton (S.E. Morrison, 'The Reverend Seaborn Cotton's Commonplace Book' *Publications of the Colonial Society of Massachussetts,* 32 (1937), p. 323).

27 John J. O'Connor, *Amadis de Gaule and its Influence on Elizabethan Literature,* New Brunswick, 1970, pp. 204-5, notes that most English adaptations of Contiental romances adopt a stricter sexual morality.

28 Keith Thomas, 'The Puritans and Adultery: The Act of 1650 Reconsidered', in *Puritans and Revolutionaries: Essays in Seventeenth-century History presented to Christopher Hill,* ed. Donald H. Pennington and Keith Thomas, Oxford, 1978, p. 267.

29 D.J. McGinn, 'The Precise Angelo', in *J.Q. Adams Memorial Studies,* ed. J.G. McManaway et al., Washington, 1948, pp. 129-40.

30 Frank Kermode, *The Faerie Queene Books I and V,* in *Shakespeare, Spenser, Donne,* London, 1971, pp. 50-2. On the Sidney circle's interest in equity, see Woudhuysen, *Leicester's Literary Patronage,* pp. 70-4.

31 McCoy, p. 136.

32 Sidney, *Works,* I, 315 (*New Arcadia,* Book II, chapter 26).

33 Quoted by Jan Albert Dop, *Eliza's Knights: Soldiers, Poets, and Puritans in the Netherlands, 1572-1586,* Alblasserdam, 1981, p. 164.

34 J.A. van Dorsten, *Poets, Patrons and Professors: Sir Philip Sidney, Daniel Rogers and the Leiden Humanists,* Leiden and London, 1962, p. 167.

35 Sidney, *Works,* I, 14 (*New Arcadia,* pp. 1, 2).

36 John Hoskins, *Directions for Speech and Style,* ed. Hoyt H. Hudson, Princeton, 1935, p. 33.

37 Sidney, *Works,* I, 318 (*New Arcadia,* II, p. 26).

38 *Directions for Speech and Style,* p. 41.

39 *Works,* I, 204 (*New Arcadia,* II, p. 9).

40 *Works,* I, 200 (*New Arcadia,* II, p. 8).

41 M. Bergbusch, 'Rebellion in the *New Arcadia,*' *PQ,* 53 (1974), pp. 29-41.

42 On the Protestantisation of the cult of honour in relation to Sidney see James, *English Politics and the Concept of Honour,* pp. 68-74.

43 *Works,* I, pp. 390, 456 (*New Arcadia,* III, pp. 8, 18).

44 *Works,* I, p. 476 (*New Arcadia,* III, p. 21).

45 *Works,* I, p. 313 (*New Arcadia,* II, p. 25).

46 *Works,* I, p. 233 (*New Arcadia,* II, p. 13).

47 Richard Barber, *The Knight and Chivalry* London, 1970, pp. 293ff.

48 Julian H. Franklin, *Constitutionalism and Resistance in the Sixteenth Century,* New York, 1969, pp. 167, 191-2.

49 *Works,* III, p. 166.

50 Greville, *Life of Sidney,* pp. 128-30.

Ronald Levao (essay date 1985)

SOURCE: "Sidney's Feigned Apology," in *Renaissance Minds and Their Fictions: Cusanus, Sidney, Shakespeare,* University of California Press, 1985, pp. 134-56.

[*In the following excerpt, Levao examines some of the difficulties and paradoxes in Sidney's* An Apology for Poetry.]

Any attempt to discuss Sidney's theory of poetic fictions proves to be something of a paradox, since *An Apology for Poetry* opens with a warning not to take theories too seriously. There Sidney compares himself to his master in horsemanship, John Pietro Pugliano, who, not content to teach his young students the practical side of his profession, "sought to enrich [their] minds with the contemplations therein." So mighty does his art appear, thanks to the light of self-love, that "if I had not been a piece of a logician before I came to him, I think he would have persuaded me to have wished myself a horse" (p. 95).[1] Following his master, Sidney opens with a theoretical justification of his own vocation, poetry, but with such a precedent, the reader may wonder if Sidney will persuade him to wish himself a poem (which is, in fact, where Sidney's Astrophil ends up in Sonnet 45 of *Astrophil and Stella*).

The paradoxical opening of the *Apology* sets the tone for the rest of the work, which is filled with contradictions and shifts of emphasis. Its studied carelessness and playfulness are in marked contrast to the intense engagement of a Minturno or a Tasso, yet it is through these gestures that Sidney makes his most suggestive critical probings. What those probings reveal can be maddeningly elusive. Readers have often mistaken his intellectual affinities because of the oblique and self-conscious way in which he echoes traditional philosophical and critical attitudes, or have felt compelled to sketch in the lines of coherence they assume must underlie the argument. The result has been a series of alternative maps to Sidney's many fascinations: the nature of poetic invention and imitation, of moving through delight, of the distinction between legitimate and illegitimate fictions. These issues were indeed important to Sidney and became increasingly so over the short course of his poetic career. A closer look at his performances both here and in his other major works, however, reveals no single theoretical affinity or formulation, but rather an effort to come to terms with the deepest tensions of Renaissance poetics, as well as Sidney's kinship with the most penetrating and original thought of his time.

The Fore-Conceit

Sidney's purpose seems familiar enough: to justify poetic fictions against the charge that they are unreal and irresponsible fantasies. For the sake of clarity, I begin by dividing my examination into two parts, following the line drawn by Sidney's own argument:

> Any understanding knoweth the skill of the artificer standeth in that *Idea* or fore-conceit of the work, and not in the work itself. And that the poet hath that *Idea* is manifest, by delivering them forth in such excellency as he hath imagined them. Which delivering forth also is not wholly imaginative, as we are wont to say by them that build castles in the air; but so far substantially it worketh, not only to make a Cyrus, which had been but a particular excellency as Nature might have done, but to bestow a Cyrus upon the world to make many Cyruses, if they will learn aright why and how that maker made him. (p. 101)

What is striking about this defense of poetic invention is that Sidney seeks to justify poetry by turning toward the two extremes it mediates, first to its source in the poet's "Idea" and then to the moral effect it has on the reader's world; it becomes a conduit of the ideal into the actual. To understand how Sidney puts his argument together, we must take a closer look at these two extremes and their relations.

First, what is the Idea, or "fore-conceit"? Modern critics often point to it as an example of Renaissance Neoplatonism and/or Augustinianism. Sidney's poet sets his mind on the Ideas beyond phenomenal appearance; the consequent poetic image "proliferates meanings which the discursive reason cannot hope to encompass."[2]

The *Apology* does entertain echoes of Neoplatonism, or at least the claims Neoplatonism had made possible. After reviewing the arts of man and deciding that all follow the "works of nature" as their object, Sidney follows Landino and Scaliger in setting the poet apart as a free creator:

> Only the poet, disdaining to be tied to any such subjection, lifted up with the vigour of his own invention, doth grow in effect into another nature, in making things either better than Nature bringeth forth, or, quite anew, forms such as never were in Nature, as the Heroes, Demigods, Cyclops, Chimeras, Furies, and such like: so as he goeth hand in hand with Nature, not enclosed within the narrow warrant of her gifts, but freely ranging only within the zodiac of his own wit.

> Nature never set forth the earth in so rich tapestry as divers poets have done; neither with pleasant rivers, fruitful sweet-smelling flowers, nor whatsoever else may make the too much loved earth more lovely. Her world is brazen, the poets only deliver a golden. (p. 100)

The motive for connecting this golden world to Platonic Ideas, or to Augustinian illumination that grants "an apprehension of the reality of things," is succinctly stated by Panofsky in his discussion of the sixteenth-century revival of Neoplatonism:

> The Idea was reinvested with its apriori and metaphysical character . . . the autocratic human mind, now conscious of its own spontaneity, believed that it could maintain this spontaneity in the face of sensory experience only by legitimizing the former *sub specie divinitatis;* the dignity of genius, now explicitly recognized and emphasized is justified by its origin in God.[3]

Italian critics, as we have seen, often turned to such justifications, and Sidney seems to need them as well. Like the Neoplatonists before him, he praises the poet as a creator "freely ranging only within the zodiac of his own wit," independent of nature and of any given subject matter. The poet does not derive "conceit out of a matter, but maketh matter for a conceit" (p. 120). In the *Apology*, however, Sidney tends to regard the protection the Platonic-Augustinian argument would afford as part of a voice that he self-consciously affects, and a voice he asks us to think about critically.

Sidney's discussion of poetic inspiration, for example, is deliberately tangled and ambivalent. He starts by examining the Roman term for poet, *vates:* he translates this "heavenly" title as "diviner, forseer, or prophet" and says that the Romans attributed the power of prophecy to Virgil. Sidney then gives us two contradictory reactions to this information. First he condemns the Romans for their "vain and godless superstition" (p. 98), and then he tells us they were "altogether not without ground." He softens his criticisms because "that same exquisite observing of number and measure in words, and that high flying liberty of conceit proper to the poet, did seem to have some divine force in it" (p. 99). The poet, then, is not really inspired; his heavenly and divine nature is at best metaphorical. It is an illusion, but an understandable one, basd on verbal artifice and the "high flying liberty of conceit." The irony is clear: inspiration is not the *cause* of the poet's conceit but the *effect* that the conceit has on the reader.[4]

Where Sidney does mention poets who were truly inspired by God (David, Solomon, et al.), he is careful to set them apart from "right poets," his subject.[5] He makes so many motions in distinguishing these right poets from philosophical and historical poets (those who follow a "proposed subject" instead of their own "invention") that another distinction is easily missed.[6] It can, however, be deduced easily enough, and it is equally important to his argument. Sidney is interested in a poetic grounded in the human mind, and inspiration would compromise its autonomy. As Sidney tells us later, Plato in his *Ion* "attributeth unto Poesy more than myself do, namely, to be a very inspiring of a divine force, far above man's wit" (p. 130).

Sidney's use of metaphysics can be deceptive. Though he uses its terms to praise the poet's creativity, he then dismisses them before they can compromise the mind's autonomy. The same pattern recurs immediately after the *vates* discussion, when Sidney turns to the word *poet*: "It cometh of this word *poiein*, which is 'to make.'" Sidney's use of Greek etymology, like Landino's, serves as an occasion to honor the poet, and Sidney follows with the previously quoted celebration of poetry's golden world and the poet's creation of a new nature. Sidney then defends his claims:

> Neither let it be deemed too saucy a comparison to balance the highest point of man's wit with the efficacy of Nature; but rather give right honour to the heavenly Maker of that maker, who having made man to His own likeness, set him beyond and over all the works of that second nature: which in nothing he showeth so much as in Poetry, when with the force of a divine breath he bringeth things forth far surpassing her doings, with no small argument to the incredulous of that first accursed fall of Adam: since our erected wit maketh us know what perfection is, and yet our infected will keepeth us from reaching unto it. (p. 101)

Man's position is a gift of God, and he is fitted into a hierarchical series of makers, beginning with God, who surpasses him, and concluding with nature, which he surpasses. But if the gift explains man's capacity, it does not control his use of it, nor bind it to the fixed order of things. After his ironic reading of the super-

stitious *vates* argument, Sidney invokes the poet's "divine breath" with a self-conscious sense of its status as metaphor, referring to man's own efforts as he brings forth his own creations, echoing only obliquely Scaliger's claim that man "transforms himself into a second deity."[7]

Nor is there a clear graduation from the mind's operations to a transcendental source. Sidney's "highest point of man's wit" is *not* a mystical *apex mentis* directly sparked by the divine. It is the faculty that creates fictions, the faculty that creates another nature and so reveals our divinity to ourselves. In order to demonstrate "erected wit," we must be "lifted up with the vigour of [our] own invention" (p. 100). We know our Ideas, not by tracing them back to an eternal Logos, but by making them "manifest, by delivering them forth in such excellency as [we have] imagined them" (p. 101).

Furthermore, the above quotation on the hierarchy of makers is a defense of one possible metaphor—an attempt to show that it is not "too saucy." After his magnificent praise of the erected wit, Sidney tells us that "these arguments will by few be understood, and by fewer granted. Thus much (I hope) will be given me, that the Greeks with some probability of reason gave him the name above all names of learning" (p. 101). He pulls us up with a reminder that the passage is something of an indulgence, a voice he has assumed in order to sound out certain attractive, if abstruse, arguments. He is not concerned with proving their validity, and he neither affirms nor denies them to those who will not grant them. He is satisfied, rather, with showing that the Greek name displays "some probability of reason." Indeed, the argument for the poet as maker is not so much a justification of the wit as a demonstration of it. It is a bold "comparison," which, according to Aristotle and Renaissance rhetoricians, is a prime way of exhibiting wit.[8]

Sidney's discussion of the fore-conceit, or Idea, then, may remind us of Neoplatonic art theory, but its orientation is closer to Cusanus's art of conjecture. The mind's highest capacity, like Cusanus's *intellectus,* may suggest an intuitive leap to a higher unity, but it always return us to the mind's active fashioning. The metaphysical terms of the **Apology**, like the elaborate schemata of *De coniecturis,* must be pictured as lying within, rather than outside of, the sphere of human making.

Many Cyruses

If the poet is "lifted up with the vigour of his own invention," so, too, is the reader. Poetry, as its humanist defenders often tell us, is the best teacher, the "first light-giver to ignorance," and the first study to show us the "pleasure in the exercises of the mind" (pp. 96, 98). The separation of the Idea from a fixed ontology, moreover, makes poetry a special kind of exercise. In a fascinating article, A. E. Malloch argues that, for Sidney, it is only in poetry that reason finds an object properly proportioned to its capacities. But Malloch sees this in a Thomist light: the fallen world is deficient, whereas poetry's golden world reveals a "fullness of being" that fully actualizes the act of cognition.[9] I would argue, on the contrary, that the poetic object is best proportioned to our reason because that object is a projection of our reason. Jacopo Mazzoni made this very argument in Italy only a few years after the *Apology* was written. The object of poetic imitation is one that is consciously framed to fit the poet's intellectual needs.[10]

The more autonomous the poet's Idea becomes, however, the more insistent the need to attach it to something outside itself. And if a metaphysical foundation is problematic, then a practical and ethical application becomes all-important. The function of poetry is to reform the will, as well as to perfect the wit, since "no learning is so good as that which teacheth and moveth to virtue" (p. 123). Using a suggestive pun, Sidney writes: "The poet . . . doth draw the mind more effectually than any other art doth" (p. 115). The poet both depicts the mind and leads it to action. And this brings us to the second part of Sidney's theory, that poetry is justified not only by the brilliance of the Idea but by the way it works in the world, bestowing a "Cyrus upon the world to make many Cyruses."

Sidney echoes the rhetorical interpretation of poetry, and following Minturno's transference of Cicero's "teach, delight, and move" from the orator to the poet, he writes that poets "imitate both to delight and teach: and delight to move men to take that goodness in hand" (p. 103). Poetry's rhetorical address to the reader, however, is shaped by Sidney's radical conception of the poet's Idea, and the result is a discussion of didacticism that brings to the surface the intrinsic difficulties of such justifications.

Sidney approaches this discussion by pretending to moderate a dispute between the educative claims of philosophy and history, only to carry the prize away for poetry. A philosopher claims that by teaching what virtue is, his discipline makes clear "how it extendeth itself out of the limits of a man's own little world to the government of families, and maintaining of public societies" (p. 105). Sidney objects that the philosopher never extends himself. He is trapped within the closed world of his fellow philosophers: "The philosopher teacheth, but he teacheth obscurely, so as the learned only can understand him; that is to say, he teacheth them that are already taught" (p. 109). Sidney later parodies the circularity of such discourse: "Nay truly, learned men have learnedly thought that where once

reason hath so much overmastered passion as that the mind hath a free desire to do well, the inward light each mind hath in itself is as good as a philosopher's book; seeing in nature we know it is well to do well" (p. 113). The learned learnedly discuss how it is well to do well, but their terms only point to themselves: "Happy is that man who may understand him, and more happy that can apply what he doth understand" (p. 107). The same charge reappears indirectly, if a bit more cruelly, during a later discussion of love: "Some of my masters the philosophers spent a good deal of their lamp-oil in setting forth the excellency of it" (p. 125). Lamp oil, Sidney suggests, is all a philosopher usually "spends" in love. The philosopher fails in teaching and seduction because his definitions "lie dark before the imaginative and judging power, if they be not illuminated or figured forth by the speaking picture of poesy" (p. 107).

If philosophy gives us reason devoid of external application, history poses an opposite extreme, for it is circumscribed by the world of experience, one devoid of any perceivable rationality. The historian is "bound to tell things as things were" and "cannot be liberal . . . of a perfect pattern" (p. 110):

> The historian, being captived to the truth of a foolish world, is many times a terror from well-doing, and an encouragement to unbridled wickedness.

> For see we not valiant Miltiades rot in his fetters? the just Phocion and the accomplished Socrates put to death like traitors? the cruel Severus live prosperously? (pp. 111-12)

Not only is the historian's world one of moral chaos, but history, in recording it, lacks logical coherence. His example "draweth no necessary consequence," and so he follows the logic of "because it rained yesterday, therefore it should rain to-day" (pp. 107, 110). The historian cannot understand the nature of examples and how the mind uses them,

> but if he know an example only informs a conjectured likelihood, and so go by reason, the poet doth so far exceed him as he is to frame his example to the which is most reasonable . . . where the historian in his bare *was* . . . must tell events whereof he can yield no cause; or, if he do, it must be poetical. (p. 110)

The poet knows that the mind must work through conjectures, that examples can lead only to "a conjectured likelihood." Thus the poet is freed from imitating things as they have been, the "bare *was*," and may concentrate, instead, on the modes of understanding themselves, the lines of connection or consequence the mind attempts to draw in making sense out of the world. His examples are framed according "to that which is most reasonable," rather than any external *res*. It is of small importance that the historian can boast that he brings us "images of true matters, such as indeed were done, and not such as fantastically or falsely may be suggested to have been done" (p. 109), for he knows better "how this world goeth than how his own wit runneth" (p. 105). The poet, by contrast, having no law but wit, can frame examples into purified types of moral ideals: "If the poet do his part aright, he will show you in Tantalus, Atreus, and such like, nothing that is not to be shunned; in Cyrus, Aeneas, Ulysses, each thing to be followed" (p. 110).

The argument, as Sidney notes, is based on Aristotle: poetry is more philosophical than history because it deals "with *Katholou* . . . the universal consideration" (p. 109). Italian critics often fortified Aristotle's universal by associating it with Platonic exemplars, and it is sometimes suggested that Sidney follows their lead. The golden reshaping of the world, like the "Idea" argument, does echo Neoplatonic claims. Ficino writes, for example: "What, then, does the intellect seek if not to transform all things into itself by depicting all things in the intellect according to the nature of the intellect? . . . the universe, in a certain manner, should become intellect"[11] But again, Sidney both appeals to metaphysical claims and refuses their protection. After his ridiculing of philosophers, we cannot leap so adroitly to fixed and timeless exemplars. Nor did Aristotle, as Sidney's cagey circularity suggests: Aristotle's "reason . . . is most full of reason." A closer philosophical analogue to Sidney's "universal consideration" is the Cusan conjecture. The latter, as we have seen, is the mind's response to the unknowable, whether the hidden God or a world without apprehensible quiddities and fixed points; the mind turns to its purest forms of thought, usually mathematics, and projects them outward in a display of its own fecundity. Sidney's "highest point of man's wit" may not produce mathematical forms, but its poetic fictions fulfill a parallel function: the poet's wit is lifted up with the vigor of its own invention.[12] The poet faces a brazen world of moral disorder, which snares the historian in its senselessness, but delivers back a golden world, another nature structured by his mind.

Sidney's justification for such invention is not ontological authority but didactic efficacy. If we look back to the Idea/Cyrus passage, we can see how insistently Sidney attempts to join his golden world and didacticism in a bond of dialectical necessity. The poet's fiction, his delivering of the Idea, is "not wholly imaginative, as we are wont to say by them that build castles in the air; but so far substantially it worketh, not only to make a Cyrus, which had been but a particular excellency as Nature might have done, but to bestow a Cyrus upon the world, to make many Cyruses" (p. 101). Moreover, the poet's effect on the

world is as important to the poet as it is to the world he affects. It is the only way he can grant substance to his creations, the only way he can be sure they are not a sign of his estrangement. Like Danielle Barbaro and others, Sidney cautions that eloquent fantasies must be carefully directed to prevent the teacher of the many from becoming the frenzied and solitary builder of "castles in the air."[13]

At crucial junctures in the *Apology*, where Sidney would have found a metaphysical argument most useful, we find, instead, claims for didactic efficacy. Forrest Robinson, in keeping with his argument that the poet has access to absolute patterns, suggests that the fore-conceit is a preverbal mental diagram, which, because of its participation in absolute truth, serves as a universal frame to insure a uniform response in all readers.[14] But when Sidney comes to discuss how this frame works, he tells us simply that when readers of poesy are "looking for fiction, they shall use the narration but as an imaginative ground-plot of a profitable invention" (p. 124). Sidney does not claim that there is any true or universal Idea embodied by, or hidden in, the ground-plot. "Invention" carries its full ambiguity here,[15] and we cannot tell whether the reader comes upon a preestablished meaning or fashions his own, any more than we can be certain that one man's conjectures in Cusanus's universe are the same as another's. All we know is that the "invention" ought to be "profitable." We are not guaranteed a fixed unity between speaker and hearer; the most interpretation can aim for is some ethical utility.

A similar development appears in the icastic/fantastic opposition, so important for Renaissance criticism. As William Rossky has shown, the fear of imaginative distortion was a powerful theme in Renaissance England, and English texts are filled with admonitions to control the imagination.[16] In George Puttenham's *Arte of English Poesie* (1589), a sophisticated understanding of the contingency of cultural norms is chastened by the demand that the mind be fitted to objective truth. Puttenham warns against the "evill and vicious disposition of the braine," which can distort the judgment with "busie and disordered phantasies." Our concepts can become like "false glasses and shew thinges otherwise than they be in deede." Despite his earlier echoes of Sidney that the poet "contrives out of his owne braine" without "any foreine copie or example," Puttenham insists that the orderly imagination must represent things "according to their very truth. If otherwise, then doth it breede Chimeres and monsters in mans imaginations and not only in his imaginations but also in his ordinarie actions and life which ensues." The useful life must be "illuminated with the brightest irradiations of knowledge and of the veritie and due proportion of things."[17]

Sidney, by contrast, avoids such Augustinian metaphysics. More decisively committed to poetic feigning, he welcomes the mind's ability to create such new forms "as never were in Nature, as the Heroes, Demigods, Cyclops, Chimeras, Furies" (p. 100). For him, the icastic/fantastic dichotomy is not an issue of metaphysics but of ethics: "For I will not deny but that man's wit may make Poesy, which should be *eikastike,* which some learned have defined, 'figuring forth good things,' to be *phantastike,* which doth contrariwise infect the fancy with unworthy objects" (p. 125). There is no question here of approximating an image to an external model, of a faithful likeness being opposed to a mere semblance. For Sidney, as for Mazzoni (who places the fantastic over the icastic), this approximation has become too restrictive. But instead of reversing the distinction, Sidney redefines it: "good" and "unworthy" are purely ethical. Thomas Wright was to warn his English audience in 1605 that the distorted imagination "putteth greene spectacles before the eyes of the witte, to make it see nothing but greene."[18] But for Sidney, as for Cusanus, one can never take away the spectacles. All cognition implies some filtering or refraction; we can only hope to control the lenses we use.

But what is the basis of this control? Sidney admits that man's wit can produce irresponsible poetry, and hopes by this admission to answer those who see poetry as a corrupting influence: we should "not say that Poetry abuseth man's wit, but that man's wit abuseth Poetry" (p. 125). Shifting the blame closes one problem, but it opens a larger one. For poetry depends on the wit, it is born in the fore-conceit, and the poet follows no law but wit. Without a direct argument of inspiration or illumination, how can we be sure the light-giving poet himself has the proper light? What is the foundation for his claims? Some critics, borrowing from the rhetorical tradition, argue that the good poet must also be a good man, but this only begs the question.

Sidney's double justification—through the fore-conceit and through didacticism—proves to be doubly problematic. Both are traditionally founded on metaphysics, but Sidney wants to justify poetry without recourse to such support. The poetic "Idea" points to perfection by pointing back to itself; like Cusanus's conjectures, it justifies itself by repeating the act of creation. The other side of the argument, the attempt to translate poetic effects into moral ones, is pursued with perhaps even greater urgency. Sidney would very much like to present poetry as an instrument of the moral, active life, but the very process of making the argument exposes its gaps; indeed, it appears to face a dilemma similar to that of the Idea. Wimsatt alerts us to the problem:

> Sidney, like most of those who have maintained that poetry is (and ought to be) moral, has not been able to resolve an ambiguity of the word

ought as used in the formula. Is this a poetic "ought," or is it in fact only a moral "ought"? In the second sense, "ought to be moral" is a tautology—since moral is what all our works ought to be.[19]

The easiest way out for Sidney would have been to repeat Boccaccio's claims for the unity of poetry and theology, or to claim some metaphysical universal at work, as did many who propped up their interpretation of Aristotle's "ought" as a moral term. As Sidney's argument stands, it verges on telling us that poetry ought to be what it ought to be, and like the moral philosophers he parodies, Sidney finds his terms pointing back to themselves.

The Poet Nothing Affirms

One of the reasons there is such difficulty on both sides of the justification is the paradoxical nature of the poetic fictions that lie between them. Unlike some rhetorical critics who argue that the poet derives true conclusions from false elements, Sidney tells us that the poet

> nothing affirms, and therefore never lieth. For, as I take it, to lie is to affirm that to be true which is false; so as the other artists, and especially the historian, affirming many things can, in the cloudy knowledge of mankind, hardly escape from many lies. But the poet (as I said before) never affirmeth. The poet never maketh any circles about your imagination to conjure you to believe for true what he writes. (pp. 123-24)

Insisting on the fictional nature of poetry, Sidney argues that its essential feature is the poet's "feigning," "not rhyming and versing" (p. 103).[20] Poetry inhabits a special realm of discourse, one that, like Mazzoni's idols, eludes the strict laws of verification. While Sidney's claim is not unique in the Renaissance, the route by which he arrives at his claim, and the consequences he draws from it, have an important effect on the way we read the *Apology* as a whole and lead us to a more general sense of what all discourse implies for Sidney.

As he explores conventional categories and their limits, Sidney's procedure again resembles that of Cusanus, who is forever testing the coincidence of opposites by attempting to reconcile curvature and straightness, potentiality and actuality. Cusanus also submits personifications of competing cultural ideals—the philosopher and the humanist orator—to the scrutiny of the conjecturing *idiota,* a craftsman who creates forms that never were in nature. Sidney does not deal with the same kinds of puzzles, but his poetic fictions are likewise the result of a coincidence of opposites. The poet fuses the two extremes of the philosopher and the historian as he "coupleth the general notion with the particular example." Poetry is clearly *not* an Aristotelian mean between them, as some Italian theorists reckoned it on a scale of abstractions.[21] Sidney includes both extremes within the synthesis, which gives rise to a distinct mode of discourse, one that he claims surpasses the limits of its rivals. It is, in a sense, more abstract than metaphysics, because it is completely free from nature, unlike the "metaphysic, though it be in the second and abstract notions, and therefore be counted supernatural, yet doth he indeed build upon the depth of Nature" (p. 100). At the same time, it is more concrete than history, since its speaking pictures and shining images are able to instruct and move men immediately.

Neither Sidney nor Cusanus argues for the final sufficiency of conjecture or fiction, but both suggest that all human attempts to make sense out of the world must deal with the conditions of human apprehension. Cusanus tells us in *De docta ignorantia* that previous philosophers erred in their understanding of the nature of things because of their adherence to the illusion that their systems precisely represented some fixed structure. The doctrine of learned ignorance does not free men from the dilemma of representation but brings them to recognize its inevitability, allowing them to manipulate it consciously. The conjectural art, then, becomes a way of rejecting the constraints of both affirmative and negative ways. Sidney continually suggests such paradoxes; indeed, having released the "right poet" from the burden of affirming, he drives the paradox even further than does Cusanus. Poetry is only a special instance of the fictionality that pervades all discourse. The most casual observation shows that other disciplines use fictions to enhance their effectiveness: lawyers use such fictitious names as "John a Stile" and "John a Noakes" in their cases for the sake of making "their picture the more lively," and chess players call a piece of wood a bishop. So, too, historians, despite their claims of truthfulness, still give "many particularities of battles, which no man could affirm" and invent "long orations," which historical figures never pronounced (p. 97).

In a profounder sense, any attempt at rational communication leads to fiction making. Our only choice is whether or not to acknowledge the pretense. So the historian is described as "loaden with old mouse-eaten records, authorising himself (for the most part) upon other histories, whose greatest authorities are built upon the notable foundation of hearsay." Any art that purports to rest on the foundation of external verities finds that its support quickly disintegrates. Even those who go beyond books to nature find themselves in this vertiginous plight: "There is no art delivered to mankind that hath not the works of Nature for his principal object, without which they could not consist, and on which they so depend, as they become actors and players, as it were, of what Nature will have set forth" (pp. 99-100). They pretend to "follow nature" but find themselves on a stage, their words turned into players' lines, their deeds transformed into mere theatrics.

A.C. Hamilton has argued that Sidney's paradox is borrowed from Agrippa's skeptical attack on the vanity of human studies.[22] However much we attribute to Agrippa's influence, whether on the basis of his mocking tone or of his argument that nothing can be affirmed, it is clear that Sidney carries the skeptical argument to its conclusion, that our only access to reality is through fiction and conjecture. As Montaigne writes: "Have I not seen this divine saying in Plato, that Nature is nothing but an aenigmaticall poesie? As a man might say, an overshadowed and darke picture, inter-shining with an infinit varietie of false lights, to exercise our conjecture . . . philosophy is nothing else but a sophisticated poesie."[23] Sidney would object, however, that the only real "poesie" is poetic making itself. It is the greatest of the arts because it is the only one to realize that it is not anchored to a fixed and objective truth. Like Cusanus, Sidney does not let this realization force him back to a passive fideism: the poet recognizes the necessity of conjecture and so boldly sets about inventing his own.

This claim inevitably doubles back to affect the status of the *Apology*. If the only choice is between those who naively entertain fictions and those who act their own, then Sidney, as the speaker of the *Apology*, makes it clear that he thinks of himself as one of the latter.

At the beginning of the *Apology*, Sidney tells us that he is following the example of John Pietro Pugliano, the master horseman and self-promoter, and that in order to defend his own craft, poetry, he needs "to bring some more available proofs." He is alluding to Aristotle's definition of rhetoric as the "faculty of observing in any given case, the available means of persuasion," and so is signaling us that he is about to adopt the role of rhetorician. Kenneth Myrick's book on Sidney helps us to see how self-conscious an actor Sidney is, as he closely models his work after the "judicial oration in behalf of an accused client." Furthermore, Sidney seems to remind us continually of the role he is playing. As Myrick demonstrates, Sidney not only follows the seven-part form of an oration as he found it described by Thomas Wilson but does so in elaborate detail, following the recommended subject matter and style for each section and even marking the transitions between them with conspicuous phrases.[24]

This is a fitting role for Sidney, considering the highly rhetorical role he imagines for poetry. But the paradox thickens when we realize that Sidney is playing not only the rhetorician but the poet as well. He tells us at the start that he has slipped into the title of poet, and he often demonstrates the appropriateness of that title in the *Apology*. After describing poetry as "feigning notable images of virtues, vices, or what else," Sidney proceeds to feign notable images of the poet's competitors, including the moral philosophers, whom he envisions approaching him "with a sullen gravity," and the historian, staggering under a load of mouse-eaten records. Before they have a chance to speak, Sidney gives us a notable image of them as hypocrites and buffoons and, in the process, characterizes himself as one who acts out his own theories.

Sidney leads us to recognize his arguments for his craft as examples of his craft by showing us that they are in the same realm of discourse, the realm of feigned images and self-conscious conjectures. I have already mentioned the discussion of the poet as maker as a kind of conjecture. Later, during a crucial argument with those who claim that fictions are mere day-dreams or toys, Sidney counters, "If to a slight conjecture a conjecture may be opposed, truly it may seem, that as by him [Homer] their learned men took almost their first light of knowledge, so their active men received their first motions of courage" (p. 127).

There are, of course, advantages to adopting this role. Sidney can demonstrate the persuasive force of poetry even as he describes it. And by treating his arguments as conjectures, he can arrange a variety of them without strict regard for consistency. He presents us with "something for everyone," aiming different claims at different readers, hoping that all will find something to serve as "an imaginative ground-plot of a profitable invention." We often find, in fact, running counter to what I have described as the central theory, the testing of more conservative possibilities, aimed at those who may be unhappy with the more daring claims for the poet's creativity. We can see this, for example, in the notion of poetic "fitness."[25]

Early in the *Apology*, when praising the poet's creativity, Sidney argues for the peculiar "reverse adequation" found in critics such as Mazzoni. The mind does not fit its concepts to externals but, rather, invents forms to fit its own faculties. Poets are like painters, who, "having no law but wit, bestow that in colours upon you which is fittest for the eye to see" (p. 102). If verse is used in poetry, so much the better, because of the "fitness it hath for memory" (p. 122). But later, when discussing stage productions, Sidney moves far away from the freedom of Mazzoni's idols and closer to the unimaginative literalness of Castelvetro. Unity of place is essential because no audience could believe a rapid change of location. Playwrights are attacked for being too "liberal" with time as well. There must be a correspondence between the imitation and the action imitated.

The play should be "fitted to the time it set forth" (p. 134).

These reversals are not restricted to specific questions of dramaturgy. At one moment the poets are free of the works of nature, not enclosed by its "narrow warrant"; at another, they must rely on the "force truth hath in nature," and their proper effects are endangered if the matter is "disproportioned to ourselves and nature" (p. 136). We may even suspect that Sidney is allowing himself to act out his own ambivalence about the poet's "high flying liberty of conceit." Late in the *Apology*, Sidney tells us that "the highest-flying wit [must] have a Daedalus to guide him," and that this Daedalus has three wings, "Art, Imitation, and Exercise": "Exercise indeed we do, but that very fore-backwardly: for where we should exercise to know, we exercise as having known; and so is our brain delivered of much matter which never was begotten by knowledge" (p. 133). Sidney more strictly regulates the poet with a firmer objective orientation. The next sentence, in fact, complains, "For there being two principal parts—matter to be expressed by words and words to express the matter—in neither we use Art or Imitation rightly" (p. 133). Sidney does not openly contradict his earlier idealistic claim that the poet "bringeth his own stuff, and doth not learn a conceit out of a matter, but maketh matter for a conceit" (p. 120), but he is clearly suggesting a safer *res/verba* distinction, as used by the Horatian critics to direct poetry outward.[26]

Sidney can take these liberties because of the manifestly conjectural nature of the *Apology*.[27] But his retreat to more conservative themes does not solve his dilemmas; rather, their conjectural status serves only to remind us of those dilemmas. The claim that poetry neither affirms nor denies may not be unique in the Renaissance, but the suggestion that one's own defense of poetry follows the same pattern forces into question the very possibility of making such a defense.

Sidney's theory requires that he take an affirmative stand somewhere, that he find some first premise from which to deduce his conclusions. Sidney himself makes this need explicit by reducing his argument to a syllogism:

> If it be, as I affirm, that no learning is so good as that which teacheth and moveth to virtue, and that none can both teach and move thereto so much as Poetry, then is the conclusion manifest that ink and paper cannot be to a more profitable purpose employed. (p. 123)

Sidney makes this statement just after he has given a lesson in logic to the poet-haters, laughing at their argument that "doth (as they say) but *petere princip-*

ium" (p. 123). But immediately after his own argument, he undermines the clause on which the entire syllogism rests, "I affirm." For it is here that he chooses to place the already-quoted passage on how the poet "never affirmeth," unlike the others who, "affirming many things, can, in the cloudy knowledge of mankind, hardly escape from many lies" (p. 124). Even as he points out the logical mistakes of his opponents, Sidney seems to be deliberately committing his own, making *any* first premise impossible and so exposing himself to an inevitable infinite regress. To put the matter more simply, if the best the mind can accomplish is conjecture, then its justification is also a conjecture.

Sidney reminds us of this problem in the *peroratio,* or conclusion:

> I conjure you all that have had the evil luck to read this ink-wasting toy of mine, . . . to believe, with Aristotle, that they were the ancient treasurers of the Grecians' divinity; to believe, with Bembus, that they were first bringers-in of all civility; to believe, with Scaliger, that no philosopher's precepts can sooner make you an honest man than the reading of Virgil; to believe, with Clauserus, the translator of Cornutus, that it pleased the heavenly Deity, by Hesiod and Homer, under the veil of fables, to give us all knowledge, Logic, Rhetoric, Philosophy natural and moral, and *quid non?;* to believe, with me, that there are many mysteries contained in Poetry, which of purpose were written darkly, lest by profane wits it should be abused; to believe, with Landino, that they are so beloved of the gods that whatsoever they write proceeds of divine fury; lastly, to believe themselves, when they tell you they will make you immortal by their verses. (pp. 141-42)

The facetious tone is unmistakable from opening self-deprecation to insistence that we believe the love poet's favorite seduction line. But we also find a summary listing of nearly all the arguments made in the *Apology,* now paraded without distinction. We are conjured to believe arguments that Sidney has made essential—namely, for poetry as a civilizing force and for its didactic efficacy—as well as those he has rejected, such as Landino's claims for poetry as an emanation of divine fury, and those he has deliberately minimized or ignored, such as the view of poetry as a veil of allegory or as a mystery for the initiated. All are brought out like actors at the end of a play, taking their bows.

Sidney cannot expect that his readers will believe so many conflicting points of view, and the lack of distinction among them hurts their credibility. Even his insistence that we do believe them, when he "conjure[s us] . . . to believe," is a selfparody, teasing us with

verbal echoes of a previous denial: "The poet never maketh any circles about your imagination, to conjure you to believe for true what he writes."

Myrick, who gives an excellent survey of Sidney's rhetorical strategies, argues that this kind of playfulness adds to the *Apology*'s persuasiveness. It is a sign of Sidney's *sprezzatura,* a "courtly grace which conceals a sober purpose."[28] Sidney does praise the courtier who finds a style "fittest to nature" and who "doth according to art, though not by art," and contrasts him to the pedant who uses "art to show art, and not to hide art" (p. 139). But Sidney is not that courtier. Little is hidden by the style of the *Apology*. His adopted role is announced as an adopted role, and nearly all his persuasive tricks and witty anecdotes are relished as persuasive tricks and demonstrations of wit. We rarely lose sight of the self-conscious fashioning of the *Apology* and cannot forget that Sidney is, in Myrick's terms, a "literary craftsman" constructing a "literary artifact."

It would be tempting to conclude that the *Apology* acts out its own argument, that the work itself moves us through images and fictions while praising the power of poetry to move us through images and fictions. But if this were so, there would be no real argument to act out, only a fiction that neither affirms nor denies, taking as its subject still other fictions. The *Apology* requires another *Apology* to justify it, and so on without end. What the *Apology* does act out are the tensions characteristic of the most adventurous Renaissance thought, whether they appear in the texts of an Elizabethan courtier, an Italian critic, or a German philosopher.

Sidney's friend Hubert Languet had little patience with such protracted ambiguities, and Sidney enjoyed teasing him about it. In his correspondence with the older humanist, Sidney praises the joys of mental exercise: "I am never less a prey to melancholy than when I am earnestly applying the feeble powers of my mind to some high and difficult object."[29] Languet approves of his enthusiasm, but warns him not to spend too much time on studies that do not lead directly to a life of action. He recommends Cicero's letters "not only for the beauty of the Latin but also for the very important matter they contain."[30] But he is guarded about those who practice a double-translation method, turning Latin into a modern language and then closing the book to translate it back again. This exercise in style is considered useful by some, but it smacks too much of what Languet later calls "literary leisure." Sidney responds:

> I intend to follow your advice about composition, thus: I shall first take one of Cicero's letters and turn it into French; then from French into English, and so once more by a sort of perpetual motion

... it shall come round into Latin again. Perhaps, too, I shall improve myself in Italian by the same exercise.[31]

Like Languet, Sidney wants to direct his learning outward, to energize the will through the wit. As a prospective man of action, Sidney endorses the teleology of mental effort: "It is not *gnosis* but *praxis* must be the fruit." That such a transition can be made is confidently, even aggressively, proclaimed in the ***Apology***. But for Sidney, there always seems to be another game to be played by the wit, yet another circuit to be made by its self-circling energies, before it can make that transition.[32]

Notes

[1] All quotations are from *An Apology for Poetry,* ed. and introd. Geoffrey Shepherd (1956; reprint, London: Thomas Nelson and Sons, 1973). Page numbers are cited in text.

[2] Walter Davis, *Idea and Act in Elizabethan Fiction* (Princeton: Princeton University Press, 1969), p. 37. For Sidney as a Renaissance Neoplatonist, see in addition to Davis (chapter 2): F. Michael Krouse, "Plato and Sidney's *Defense of Poesie,*" *Comparative Literature* 6 (1954): 138-47; John P. McIntyre, S.J., "Sidney's 'Golden World,'" *Comparative Literature* 14 (1962): 356-65; and William Wimsatt and Cleanth Brooks, *Literary Criticism: A Short History* (New York: Knopf, 1957), p. 174. For a view of Sidney in dialogue with the original Plato, see Irene Samuel, "The Influence of Plato on Sidney's *Defense of Poesie,*" *Modern Language Quarterly* 1 (1940): 383-91. Besides the obvious metaphorical difference, Augustinian illumination is different from Platonic inspiration; the former deals with the general nature of cognition, the latter with a special poetic gift. But both fulfill similar functions in Renaissance poetics. The argument for Sidney's Augustinianism usually relies on the evidence of Mornay and Hoskins's hierarchy of inner "words," leading to the divine Logos. See *Apology,* ed. Shepherd, pp. 59, 157-58 n.; *An Apology for Poetry,* ed. and introd. Forrest G. Robinson (Indianapolis: Bobbs-Merrill, 1970), p. 17, n. 63; and Forrest G. Robinson, *The Shape of Things Known: Sidney's Apology in Its Philosophical Tradition* (Cambridge, Mass.: Harvard University Press, 1972), chapter 3.

[3] Erwin Panofsky, *Idea: A Concept in Art Theory,* trans. Joseph Peake (New York: Harper and Row, 1968), pp. 91-92.

[4] The disenchantment with, or distancing from, arguments for poetic inspiration in the later Renaissance has often been noted. See, for example, Baxter Hathaway on Fracastoro, *The Age of Criticism: The Late Renaissance in Italy* (1962; reprint, Westport, Conn.:

Greenwood Press, 1972), pp. 405-6; Robert Durling, *The Figure of the Poet in Renaissance Epic* (Cambridge, Mass.: Harvard University Press, 1965), pp. 199-200, where Tasso's yearning for inspiration and his view of poetry as "rationalistic, autonomous *techné*" are found to be in conflict; and Richard Willis's effort to rationalize inspiration: poets behave "as if ... roused by the divine breath, they seem to be transported," cited and discussed in J. V. H. Atkins, *English Literary Criticism:. The Renascence* (1947; reprint, New York: Barnes and Noble, 1968), pp. 109-10.

[5] See A. C. Hamilton, "Sidney's Idea of the 'Right Poet,'" *Comparative Literature* 9 (Winter 1957): 51-59.

[6] This silence is part of Sidney's rhetorical strategy. He wants us to be able to say, as does John Buxton, that "Sidney describes the poet as a combination of vates, divinely inspired seer, and poet, or maker" (*Sir Philip Sidney and the English Renaissance* [London: Macmillan, 1954]. p. 4). But Sidney is careful to leave us enough evidence to deduce a more precise set of theoretical distinctions.

[7] A useful survey of attitudes toward the poet as "maker" appears in S. K. Heninger, *Touches of Sweet Harmony* (San Marino, Calif.: Huntington Library, 1974), pp. 287-324. Sidney echoes the further analogy of human creativity to the divine, but he is oblique about the matter, compared not only to Cusanus, Ficino, and Scaliger, but also to other English apologists of the verbal arts, who, despite their caution, still invoke the analogy more directly. Thomas Wilson calls the eloquent man "halfe a GOD," in the preface to *The Arte of Rhetorique* (1553), ed. G. H. Mair from the 1560 edition (Oxford: Clarendon Press, 1909); Thomas Lodge alludes with favor to the ancient praise of Homer as *Humanus deus* in his *Defence of Poetry* (1579), in *Elizabethan Critical Essays,* ed. G. Gregory Smith (Oxford: Clarendon Press, 1904), 1:64. Sidney's indirectness cannot be accounted for in terms of religious scruples without also explaining why the pious Wilson did not share the same reluctance when he went halfway to asserting an equivalence. I suspect that Sidney is intrigued by the trope's claims for creativity, but views its ontological complacency with suspicion. Compare also George Puttenham's opening chapter, where after comparing God to a poet, he turns the analogy around, but only with a metaphorical dodge and a lower-case plural: "Poets thus to be conceived ... be (by maner of speech) as creating gods" (*The Arte of English Poesie,* ed. Gladys Doidge Willcock and Alice Walker [1936; reprint, Cambridge: Cambridge University Press, 1970], p. 4).

[8] William G. Crane, *Wit and Rhetoric in the Renaissance* (New York: Columbia University Press, 1937),

p. 14. There are, to be sure, religious themes sounded in the passage, from the exhortation to give "right honour to the heavenly Maker" to the mention of "that first accursed fall of Adam." But these references are keyed to rhetorical ends; the emphasis in the *Apology* is on man as the maker of images, not man as the image made. Acknowledgment of the Fall and the infected will does not draw the discussion into the orbit of theology—although diverging claims have been made for it as an indication of Sidney's Calvinism, Thomism, or semi-Pelagianism—so much as it advertises the way poetry can grant an argumentative edge over the "incredulous." If poetic fictions now seem, oddly enough, to assume the function of Anselm's "necessary reasons" in disputing with hypothetical unbelievers, that impression is only momentary. For we soon discover that the passage on the hierarchy of makers, despite multiple echoes of Genesis, is not an explication of faith; still less is it an objective account of the vertical structure of being.

[9] A. E. Malloch, "'Architectonic' Knowledge and Sidney's *Apologie*," *English Literary History* 20 (1953): 181-85.

[10] See discussion in chapter 4.

[11] Ficino, "Five Questions Concerning the Mind," in *Renaissance Philosophy of Man*, ed. Ernst Cassirer et al. (Chicago: University of Chicago Press, 1948), pp. 201-2. For an argument that Sidney's notion of poetic feigning may have been influenced by Ficino, see Cornell March Dowlin, "Sidney's Two Definitions of Poetry," *Modern Language Quarterly* 3 (1942): 579.

[12] Sidney appears nonetheless to have been intrigued by geometry as a form of intellectual mastery and self-mastery. Languet admits its usefulness, but is concerned that it will exhaust Sidney's intellect and health. Sidney answers by including geometry as one of the "high and difficult objects" that free him from melancholy (*The Correspondence of Sir Philip Sidney and Hubert Languet*, ed. and trans. Steuart Pears [London: William Pickering, 1845], pp. 28-29). Alastair Fowler's numerological analyses of Sidney's poems are of some interest in this regard, although I do not share his sense of Sidney's Neoplatonic grounding; see Fowler's *Triumphal Forms* (Cambridge: Cambridge University Press, 1970), pp. 174-80, and *Conceitful Thought* (Edinburgh: Edinburgh University Press, 1975), pp. 38-58.

[13] Hathaway, *Age of Criticism*, p. 332.

[14] Robinson, *The Shape of Things Known*, p. 118.

[15] See Murray Wright Bundy. "'Invention' and 'Imagination' in the Renaissance," *Journal of English and Germanic Philology* 29 (1930): 535-45, and Baxter

Hathaway, *Marvels and Commonplaces: Renaissance Literary Criticism* (New York: Random House, 1968), pp. 56, 121.

[16] William Rossky, "Imagination in the English Renaissance: Psychology and Poetic," *Studies in the Renaissance* 5 (1958): 49-73.

[17] *Arte of English Poesie*, p. 19. Compare Puttenham's discussion of figurative speech as abuse and trespass: the "iudges *Areopagites*" forbade figurative speeches as "meere illusions to the minde" (p. 154). But see also the excellent discussion of Puttenham's pluralistic attitude toward rhetoric and illusionism in Lawrence Manley, *Convention: 1500-1750* (Cambridge, Mass.: Harvard University Press, 1980), pp. 176-88.

[18] Quoted by Rossky, "Imagination in the English Renaissance," p. 56.

[19] Wimsatt and Brooks, *Literary Criticism*, p. 171.

[20] For arguments that his radical insistence on the poet's free feigning sets Sidney apart from such Italian sources as Scaliger and Minturno, see Cornell March Dowlin, "Sidney and Other Men's Thought," *Review of English Studies* 20, no. 80 (1944): 257-71, and Hamilton, "Sidney's Idea of the 'Right Poet.'"

[21] Bernard Weinberg, *A History of Literary Criticism in the Italian Renaissance* (Chicago: University of Chicago Press, 1961), 1:31. By contrast, Jacob Bronowski has noted that in the *Apology* poetry appears to be straining in two directions at once, toward liberated ideality and a forced application to the concrete (*The Poet's Defence* [Cambridge: Cambridge University Press, 1939], pp. 39-56).

[22] A. C. Hamilton, "Sidney and Agrippa," *Review of English Studies* 7, no. 26 (1956): 151-57. Similar claims are made in Hamilton's book on Spenser, cited in note 2.

[23] Montaigne, *Essays*, trans. John Florio (London: J. M. Dent and Sons, 1938), 2: 244-45.

[24] Kenneth Myrick, *Sir Philip Sidney as a Literary Craftsman* (1935; reprint, Lincoln: University of Nebraska Press, 1965), pp. 53-55.

[25] There are several recent discussions of the disjunctions in Sidney's argument, sometimes refining the older question of the relative importance of Aristotelianism and Platonism for the *Apology*. See Michael Murrin, *The Veil of Allegory* (Chicago: University of Chicago Press, 1969), pp. 184-89 for Sidney's witty and unclassifiable conflation of metaphysical and Neoclassical views, and O. B. Hardison, Jr., "The Two Voices of Sidney's *Apology for Poetry*," *English Lit-*

erary *Renaissance* 2 (Winter 1972): 83-99 for a possible shift in attitude by Sidney. "The *Apology* . . . was written in two phases. . . . Before a thorough revision was possible Sidney died (leaving the *Apology*) incompletely harmonized," Hardison writes (p. 98). For Sidney's eclecticism as a conscious rhetorical design, see Virginia Riley Hyman, "Sidney's Definition of Poetry," *Studies in English Literature* 10 (Winter 1970): 49-62, on Sidney as strategically selecting from his tradition; Catherine Barnes, "The Hidden Persuader: The Complex Speaking Voice of Sidney's *Defence of Poetry*," *PMLA* 96 (May 1971): 422-27, for the work's "'poetic' intricacy" (p. 426); and Margaret W. Ferguson, *Trials of Desire: Renaissance Defenses of Poetry* (New Haven: Yale University Press, 1983), chapter 4.

[26] See chapter 4, note 46, above. See also Philip's advice to his brother to avoid "Ciceronianisme the cheife abuse of Oxford, *Quidum verba sectantur, res ipsas negligunt*" (*The Prose Works of Sir Philip Sidney,* ed. Albert Feuillerat [1912; reprint, Cambridge: Cambridge University Press, 1962], 3: 132).

[27] Compare Cusanus's liberties in *De coniecturis,* where he sketches out a schematic World Soul and hierarchical cosmos after questioning them in *De docta ignorantia,* discussed in chapter 2.

[28] Myrick, *Sidney as Literary Craftsman,* p. 298.

[29] *Correspondence of Sidney and Languet,* ed. and trans. Pears, p. 29.

[30] Ibid., p. 20.

[31] Ibid., p. 23.

[32] Some of the discussion concerning this argument's first published version suggests the need for more specific clarification. I am not arguing that Sidney regards morality as ultimately divorced from ontology, or that he denies the final goodness of God's creation, but rather that he regards reliance upon such absolutes to justify human activities such as fiction making to be epistemologically untenable.

ABBREVIATIONS

Apology Sir Philip Sidney, *An Apology for Poetry*
AS Sir Philip Sidney, *Astrophil and Stella*
De con. Nicholas of Cusa, *De coniecturis*
DDI Nicholas of Cusa, *De docta ignorantia*
GGN Gammer Gurton's Needle
NA Sir Philip Sidney, *New Arcadia*
OA Sir Philip Sidney, *Old Arcadia*
PL Patrologia latina, ed. J. P. Migne

Schmitt *Sancti Anselmi opera omnia,* ed. F. S. Schmitt
ST St. Thomas Aquinas, *Summa theologica*

Maureen Quilligan (essay date 1988)

SOURCE: "Sidney and His Queen," in *The Historical Renaissance: New Essays on Tudor and Stuart Literature and Culture,* edited by Heather Dubrow and Richard Strier, The University of Chicago Press, 1988, pp. 171-96.

[*In the following excerpt, Quilligan explores Sidney's ambitions, career, and concern with his image, in the context of the Elizabethan court.*]

. . . In pursuit of chivalric bravado, if not victory for the Dutch rebels, during a skirmish with Spanish troops, Sidney took off his thigh armor before charging the enemy and received the bullet that, entering at the knee and shattering the thigh bone, left the festering wound from which he soon died at the age of thirty-one.[20] Before narrating the story of Sidney's tragic end in 1586, two years before the defeat of the Armada, [Sir Fulke] Greville outlines a map of his hero's imperial imagination in two chapters that encompass a remarkable analysis of the possible strategies open to England in what should have been, according to Greville's account of Sidney's thought, a concerted and strategic war with Spain. After canvassing all the political interconnections between such disparate parts of the map as Poland and the Ottoman Empire (Sidney's imperial politics are global), he settled, so Greville records, on taking the war with Spain to the New World. Sidney's intention was to plant England's empire on the mainland of America, thereby draining England of the excess population that threatened its stability while increasing trade, and hemming in Philip of Spain by cutting off his supply lines from the New World. On Greville's testimony, it would appear that the foundations of the British Empire were laid in Sir Philip Sidney's prophetic imagination.

Specifically, Sidney intended to revive the hazardous enterprise of "Planting upon the Main of America" (p. 117), a "new intended Plantation, not like an Assylum for fugitives . . . but as an Emporium for the confluence of all Nations that love, or profess any kinde of vertue, or Commerce" (pp. 118-19). [Page numbers refer to Greville's *The Life of Sir Philip Sidney* (London: Henry Seile, 1652).] The word "plant" takes on a special character in Greville's text, serving as a link in his narrative and contrasting the real politics of courtship, which Greville exposes in his analysis of his own, less heroically ideal life, with the heroic politics of his dead friend. Himself a much more successful courtier to Elizabeth than Sir Philip had been, Greville explains how his own success came to be: "I finding the specious fires of youth to prove far more scorching than glorious, called my second thoughts to counsell, and in that Map clearly discerning action and honor to fly with more wings than one; and that it was sufficient for the plant to grow where his Sovereigns hand had planted it; I found reason to contract my thoughts from those larger, but wandring horizons of the world abroad, and bound my prospect within the safe limits of duty, in such homes services, as were acceptable to my Sovereign" (p. 149). Greville would not plant America, but be a homegrown plant well-watered by his sovereign's hand. With his tragic death Sidney escaped such sad and resigned restrictions and sailed into history the most renowned member of his generation, as well as the most popular Elizabethan poet throughout the next century.[21] In this assessment of his and his friend's lives, Greville reverses our usual sense of success and failure in court careers. Judged by the terms of the day, Greville was far more successful because he had been chosen by Elizabeth, whereby, in Sidney's own admission, the queen was always "apt . . . to interpret everything to my disadvantage" ([*The Prose Works of Sir Philip Sidney,* ed. Albert Feuillerat, 4 vols. (Cambridge: Cambridge University Press, 1969)] 3:167); Greville, however, chooses to deprecate himself in relation to Sidney, who was not chosen and who could therefore remain independent, glorious, and heroic. For his own strategic purposes under James, Greville reverses the usual standard for evaluating a courtier's success: Sidney is to be judged not by what he accomplished, but by what he could have done, had his prince chosen him to do it.[22]

It may have been the same strategic purpose that inspired Greville to suppress any mention of Sidney's sonnet sequence—the work through which we of this century have best known him.[23] Greville gives a full list of all of Sidney's other texts, stressing in particular Sidney's politically motivated translation of the Psalms and analyzing his didactic procedures in the revised *Arcadia*. Of course, his suppression of *Astrophil and Stella*—which had spawned innumerable copies, and indeed, on which he himself modeled his own sonnet cycle *Caelica*—may have been due simply to the cycle's precipitous drop from fashion after the death of Elizabeth. And here too Greville shows his sensitivity to strategies. If courtly compliment to a putative female reader had been fashionable at Elizabeth's court, it was distinctly not so under James, who had, not surprisingly, no taste for the form.[24] Accordingly, although the sequence had been published in 1591, Greville neglects to include it in the oeuvre, possibly because it no longer had a recognizable political function.[25] Its intense and circumscribed efflorescence allows us, however, to consider possible analogies in political function among four "court" episodes: a challenge on a tennis court, a conflictual conversation between a sovereign and subject at court, the contextualizing courting negotiations for a mar

riage match, and a Petrarchan sequence that displays the maneuverings of an attempted erotic seduction, that is, a "courtship." Yet before going on to consider Astrophil's peculiarly Elizabethan politics, we need to ask, what does the reduplication of language in all these various kinds of "courtships" have to say about the relations between language and social practice in Elizabethan England?

In another of his arguments, Bourdieu points to the defensive blindness of structural linguistics about the social context of the object it academically constructs. If language were as polysemous as linguistics would have it, "speech would be," according to Bourdieu, "an endless series of puns."[26] Bourdieu objects to an artificial arena for language, an academic treatment of polysemy which specifically "breaks the organic relation between competence and the field"; such puns "are ungraspable in practice because production is always embedded in a field of reception. . . . One can only speak of the different meanings of a word so long as one bears in mind that their juxtaposition in the simultaneity of learned discourse (the page of the dictionary) is a scholarly artifact and that they never exist simultaneously in practice"—except, as Bourdieu allows, in actual puns (those produced for reception in the field). What such an interesting quarrel with contemporary linguistics points up is that the language of earlier eras was not so highly regulated as it is now and that, lacking dictionaries as we think of them and obviously in love with wordplay (if we are to trust Spenser's practice and Shakespeare's representations of courtly chat), the Elizabethan era is a most interesting one for attending to the practical possibilities of wordplay in the social field. Not only were there no dictionaries in Elizabeth's era, save for books giving English equivalents of Latin words (or other foreign languages) and definitions of technical (or "hard") words, there were also no rules by which to censure the pun as transgressive. The simultaneity of meaning that marks a pun may not have been so odd and out of the ordinary then as now.[27] What this means for a reading of sixteenth-century language is that not only must we attend to the polysemy of its texts—the punning potential of a word whose meaning would probably have been heard and seen by Elizabethan ears and eyes much more readily than by our far differently trained organs of perception—but that we must also attempt to hear the *social* resonance of wordplay as well. The simultaneity of meaning in a pun might provide a social as well as a verbal or poetic strategy. Read in these terms, the sonnet sequence Sidney wrote becomes a social practice that addresses relations of real power and does so through the most ostensibly textual of verbal manipulations: the pun.

In his edition of Sidney's poetry, after reviewing the fascinating biographical and political context of *Astrophil and Stella*, William Ringler summarizes,

When we compare the known facts of Sidney's life during the years 1581-82 with the sonnets, we are immediately struck with how much of his biography he left out of his poems. He tells us nothing about the disappointment of his hopes in being superseded as the Earl of Leicester's heir, nothing about his trip to Antwerp, nothing about his dominating interest in politics and international affairs . . . and most significant, nothing about his activities in opposition to the proposed marriage of the Duke of Anjou and the Queen. The sonnets concern courtship, and yet they do not contain a single hint of the attempts being made at the time he was writing to marry him to Stella's sister, Dorothy Devereux, or of his own interest in the same time in Frances Walsingham.[28]

In fact, Sidney did ultimately marry Frances Walsingham, and she, after his death, married the earl of Essex, the brother of Penelope Devereux—that is, of Stella. Prior to his marriage, Sidney had been disinherited by the birth of son to his uncle the earl of Leicester and his uncle's new wife, the countess of Essex-Cthat is, Penelope/Stella's mother. Sidney had been expecting to inherit from his uncle should Leicester die childless. It had been in part the cachet of being Leicester's heir—that is, heir to Elizabeth's most powerful favorite—that had made Sidney so welcome on the Continent, where Dutch and German princes wanted to marry him to their daughters.

Arthur Marotti has pointedly stressed the immediate historical context of Sidney's authorship of the sequence: "when Sidney wrote the sonnets (or gathered them into a sequence), he was and *he was known as* a politically, economically and socially disappointed young man."[29] According to Marotti, "love is not love" in **Astrophil and Stella** but rather Sidney's attempted reorganization of his humiliating experience as a failed courtier: the sequence "wittily converts the language of ambition into the language of love" (p. 402). The problem, as Marotti sees it, was that a private courtship finally provides "no compensation for sociopolitical defeat," especially because the sequence merely stages "a painful repetition of the experience in another mode" (p. 405). In this interpretation, Sidney is no more successful as a lover than he was as a courtier: ultimately he is denied his lady's favor.

What such an otherwise brilliant rereading of the sequence as Marotti's leaves out are the strategic possibilities open to Sidney upon his decision to write a *Petrarchan* sequence. A paradoxical strategy of sexual domination is one of the more intriguing interests of Petrarchan poetry; as Ann Jones and Peter Stallybrass summarize it, "although the lover depicts himself as humble suitor to a dominating lady, he actually performs an act of public mastery, demonstrating his virtuosity in the practice of a masculine convention."[30] Thus, while the language of love into which Sidney

translates his political frustrations was perfect for the problem, it was not, as they point out, unpolitical to begin with: "the inequality of the servant . . . to his master . . . , the inequality of the subordinated sex . . . to the dominant sex. . . . The blurring of these two discourses is the method by which Astrophil can continue to maneuver without too blunt a naming of unequal positions. He is concerned, indeed, not so much to alter the categories as to manipulate them so as to redistribute power" (p. 60). The overt plot of the sequence in which Stella denies Astrophil any final fulfillment (although the eighth song allows us to guess at more) may repeat Sidney's public defeat in politics, but, by the same token, it is the author's total control over Stella as a (silent) character in his plot which enacts his masculine, social mastery. Such a redistribution of power is at issue in any sonnet sequence (as in any honor challenge). What makes Sidney's sequence different is the remarkable historical specificity with which it attempts this distribution.

The signal point of interconnection between poetic text and cultural context is that Sidney distinctly identifies Stella as Penelope Devereux. He does so, moreover, by punning on her *husband*'s name. To do so is to name Stella specifically in terms of the traffic in women, a procedure that may have carried for Sidney the complicated history of Penelope Devereux's involvement in that quite circumscribed traffic, since she had once earlier been named as a possible bride for him. The certainty of this historical identification makes Sidney's sequence unique: while—*pace* A. L. Rowse—we will never know who Shakespeare's Dark Lady is, or resolve doubts about Rosalind and Elizabeth Boyle in the *Amoretti,* or at this late date discover the identity of Laura, we do know, absolutely, that Stella is Lady Rich.[31] If we pause for a moment to ask why the identification is through her husband's name rather than her own, we can see how the word "Rich" and the meanings it sustains in the sonnets not only names for Sidney his various sociopolitical failures, it offers a strategy for revaluing them. One could imagine a whole series of poems that might have identified Penelope Devereux in other ways just as certainly—to take only one possibility, in terms of her mythically resonant name, Penelope. Having previously named himself Philisides (Philip Sidney) in the character of the Arcadian poet, Sidney here signals a similar identification by the name Astrophil, which is properly spelled with the "i," for it takes a syllable from "Philip." What is, after all, in a name?

Is Stella Lady Rich because Penelope Devereux was the daughter of the woman whose giving birth to a son impoverished (disenriched) Sidney? Is she Lady Rich because her married name is the word for what Sidney thereby lost? Or is it that, by ironizing the name, Sidney avails himself of a poetic strategy that will allow him to claim his title as an autonomous author of his individual destiny, revaluing and enriching his career in his own terms?

> Towards Aurora's Court a Nymph doth
>   dwell,
>   Rich in all beauties which man's eye can
>   see:
>
>   . . . . .
>
> Rich in the treasure of deserv'd renowne,
> Rich in the riches of a royall hart,
> Rich in those gifts which give th'eternall
>   crowne;
> Who though most rich in these and everie
>   part,
> Which make the patents of true worldly
>   blisse,
> Hath no misfortune, but that Rich she is.
>   (Sonnet 37)

The notion of richness contained in Stella's real, historical name, offers Sidney not merely the chance to identify her (and therefore to indicate the dynastic disappointment her mother's bearing a son to his uncle had caused him) but also the chance to query the issue of value itself, as Elizabethan society understood it to work in various social discourses. Stella is "rich" in courtly reputation (achieved value), in her virtually royal nobility of character (class, or ascribed value), in religious spirituality (eternal crowns are better than earthly); she also has "patents," that is, monopolies, on the market in "true worldly bliss." Her only misfortune is that she is married to a dolt.[32] The dolt's name, however, allows Sidney to redefine his own poverty: "now long needy Fame / Doth even grow *rich,* naming my Stellas name" (Sonnet 35). How such a private revaluation of his sense of himself—no longer a defamed courtier, but a poet famously inspired by loveCwill affect that public career becomes an issue in the poems themselves.

> "Art not asham'd to publish thy disease?"
> Nay, that may breed my fame, it is so rare:
> "But will not wise men thinke thy words
>   fond ware?"
> Then be they close, and so none shall
>   displease.
> "What idler thing, then speake and not be
>   hard?"
> What harder thing then smart, and not to
>   speake?
>   (Sonnet 34)

Sidney's worry about publication here not only alerts us to the problematic position Petrarchan writing occupied at the time Sidney wrote (it would be thought fond ware), but it also makes clear that the privileged audience for the sonnets is not Stella herself, but the "wise men" who would probably find the poems fool-ish. Not to be heard by them, it appears, is not to be heard at all. The sonnets were in fact kept close, circulated to only the smallest coterie of readers, apparently kept closer than Sidney's other poetry.[33] So it would appear that Sidney held to his decision not to publish; hence any argument that would claim that Sidney expected to make up for his dynastic disappointments and answer the court's murmurings specifically about his ambition (which he denies in sonnets 23, 27, and 30) by stunning them with his exquisitely displayed folly in love is certainly not one that would work for Sidney in his lifetime. In order for him to achieve a display of "public mastery," as Jones and Stallybrass suggest, the poems need to have become public—as, of course, they did after his death. The first audience for the poems was, apparently, only his immediate family, in fact those who would have been most disappointed by his failures and to whom a palliative set of excuses might have been most welcome. Indeed, he may never have intended to publish—that is to circulate in any way—***Astrophil and Stella.*** (His brother Robert gave few clues as to the existence of his own poems, which were not published until 1984 from a single autograph manuscript.[34]) However, it is helpful, in evaluating just how useful a strategy the sequence could have been in Sidney's overall career, to remember that he did not live to implement it. He died accidentally only four years after he wrote it. It is therefore a bit hasty to dismiss the sequence as actual social strategy because it made no difference in Sidney's life. As imaginary poetic (and potentially social) strategy it does indeed stage a recuperation of competitive authority among court wits and poetasters and manages a nostalgic recapture of class rank.

Note, for example, that Sidney's address in Sonnet 37, in which he names Stella as Penelope Rich, is "Listen Lordings with good eare to me / For of my life I must a riddle tell." Doubtless an allusion to Chaucer's even then archaic oral stance, such an address asserts the high old, aristocratic rank Sidney ascribes to his poems by way of their imagined audience. Aurora's court, where Sidney enthrones Stella, is like the more valued courts of old. There such lordings are interpreters, as well, who will figure the riddle of the name; sympathetic readers unlike, presumably, the censorious auditors of a present-day court.

Other subjects of address (his fellow poets) are not necessarily high in birth rank, but, as poets, Astrophil can lecture them on the value of their own poetic endeavors. If speaking and not being "hard" is less hard than not speaking, speaking and being heard by an imaginary audience who will be daunted by the value of one's speech is remarkably easy.

> How falles it them, that with so smooth an
>   ease
> My thoughts I speake, and what I speake

doth flow
In verse, and that my verse best wits doth
    please?
Guess we the cause: "What, is it thus?" Fie
    no:
"Or so?" Much lesse: "How then?" Sure
    thus it is:
My lips are sweet inspired, with Stella's
    kisse.

(Sonnet 74)

In imagining the circulation of his poems, Sidney imagines his own socially recognized mastery. As a textual battleground, the poems compete not only with Spenser, Greville, Dyer, Sidney's own brother Robert, or prior court poets in the English tradition such as Wyatt and Surrey, who had used Petrarch's mode for similar court-serving ends; his rivals extend to all the male Continental practitioners of the sequence. That Oxford was known as a versifier might have some immediate significance; so too, Elizabeth was known to try her hand at poetry. Because Sidney's sequence specifically concerned an adulterous and unidealized passion (as Petrarch's did not), it would have made a commanding scandal in Elizabeth's court. That it was not addressed to the queen, in the midst of a prevailing fashion for courtly compliment of her, may have been its most pointed aggression against her central authority. He would not play politics by her rules but would turn her Petrarchan forms to his own purposes.[35]

Sidney makes a bid for poetic fame by denying such poetic ambition, just as he denies his political ambition: "Stella thinke not that I by verse seeke fame, / Who seeke, who hope, who love, who live but thee"; in this poem, he eschews as well a specific Petrarchan prominence indicated by the pun on Laura/laurel: "Nor so ambitious am I, as to frame / A nest for my yong praise in Lawrell tree." Sidney abjures the very name of poet: "In truth I sweare, I wish not there should be / Graved in mine Epitaph a Poet's name" (Sonnet 90). The name with which he consistently ends his poems is hers, Stella. And she, of course, is—so the historical identification says—more than a mere sign of his poetic fame, as Petrarch's pun on Laura/laurel implies. Unlike other mistresses of that tradition, Stella is real and identified, and Astrophil insists that his passion is no mere motive for verse making. Stella thus is not merely the sign of his poetic originality and authority, but of Sidney's problematical historical situation. He turns his Petrarchan abasement into authority, manipulating a character, Stella, who allows him to woo, conquer, and be rejected, and, by his manipulation of that rejection, discursively to control his own recent misfortunes in his career. His Petrarchan abasement changes his rank, from a vulgarity the muses would never visit ("Muses scorne with vulgar braines to dwell") to a private ease of nobility predicated on a kiss; it grants him, if only in his text, the power to

make her say what he wants her to, as in the refrain to the fourth song:

Take me to thee, and thee to me.
"No, no, no, no, my Deare, let be."

Wo to me, and do you sweare
Me to hate? But I forbeare,
Cursed be my destines all,
That brought me so high to fall:
Soone with my death I will please thee.
"No, no, no, no my Deare, let be."

Such a strategy turns traditional abasement into one kind of authority, in the process fulfilling the demands Sidney made on his countrymen in the *Apology*, to write as if they really were in love.[36]

Paying tribute, in humble manner though not in matter, to the imperative of erotic desire, Sidney obliquely claims his own political importance. Thus in Sonnet 30, he lists all the thorny diplomatic problems facing the Elizabethan ruling elite: will the Ottoman Empire make another attack on Christian Europe, what of Polish-Russian relations, what will happen in the French wars of religion, how will the prince of Orange's rebellion fare in the Netherlands, how will the Irish rebels take recent victories by his father, what will Scotland do? "These questions busie wits to me do frame; / I, cumbred with good maners, answer do, / But know not how, for still I think of you" (Sonnet 30). As Marotti acutely notes, this is the first time that Stella is directly addressed in the sequence (p. 401). The poem puts her (and privacy) directly in contrast to, and superior in value to, the affairs of court and state that her very important lover finds cumbering his public life. In opting for a different kind of courtship, private erotic suitorship, Sidney chooses a different kind of fame. Hereby rewriting his political frustrations, imposed from above by a queen jealous of the prerogatives he as a courtier had very insistently resisted, Sidney claims that the choice not to be a famous statesman was his own. His strategy here, to make his lack of preferment look like his own choice, by shifting the place of conflict away from the real court into his own psychic battles with honor and duty and desire, has certain costs. It is enslavement not to a queen—as Greville chose, letting himself be planted where his sovereign's hand would place him— but enslavement to Stella, a nineteen-year-old wife of a courtly cipher, whose name played ironically on the riches Sidney had, in any case, already lost.

What was Stella like? Greville consistently calls Sidney the "unattended Cassandra of his age," and—if we understand the underlying politics of the sequence as a subtle resistance to the queen—we may note that Sidney's selection of Penelope Rich for his Stella was not only punningly appropriate to his predicament, it was in time to prove itself prophetically so. Years later, Penelope Devereux was evidently very instrumental in her brother, the earl of Essex's, uprising against Elizabeth. At his interrogation, Essex rather ungallantly blamed his sister for helping to instigate his attack on the queen: "my sister . . . did continually urge me on with telling me how all my friends and followers thought me a coward, & that I had lost all my valour. . . . She must be looked to, for she had a proud spirit."[37] At the time of his uprising, Essex was married to Frances Walsingham, Sidney's widow. Brother of the woman for whom Sidney had famously written he'd given up all, husband to Sidney's wife—Robert Devereux, earl of Essex, may not have done what he did because he inherited Sidney's intransigence along with his wife and sword (which Sidney had willed him). But Essex can stand as emblem of the resistance potentially present in the dynastic faction (cemented by the traffic in women) for whom Sidney had earlier been spokesman. Penelope Devereux is without doubt Astrophil's Stella. She is also without doubt the only woman we know to have urged her brother to rebel against Queen Elizabeth.

At age eighteen, of course, recently departed from a virtuous upbringing at her home with the Huntingtons and married to a rich heir the same year that Elizabeth contemplated marrying the duke of Anjou, Sidney's Penelope Devereux Rich would not have been, when Sidney wrote, the rebel to all propriety and authority she turned out to be. However, only two years after Sidney's death, some six years after the sequence was written, she took up at age twenty-six with a veteran of Zutphen, Sir Charles Blount, with whom she had a total of five illegitimate children.[38] She also showed herself more loyal to Sidney's brother Robert than her own brother was and risked censure to aid him.[39] It is, of course, dangerous to judge how well *Astrophil and Stella* may have served Sidney by how favorably Penelope Rich received its identification with her and how little she apparently paid for any of her own transgressions against honor or authority.[40] Sidney, for his part, counted up his costs:

> My youth doth waste, my knowledge brings
>   forth toyes,
> My wit doth strive those passions to
>   defend,
> Which for reward spoile it with vaine
>   annoyes.
> I see my course to lose my selfe doth bend:
>   I see and yet no greater sorrow take,
>   Then that I lose no more for Stella's sake.
>   (Sonnet 18)

Sidney died bankrupt and in debt; not until the very end of his life did he regain that heritage of service to the crown which his father and uncle had enjoyed. In the meantime, the knowledge he had, he spent on toys

like the *Arcadia* and *Astrophil and Stella*. Sonnet 18 implies that, like some glorious Anthony, he is happy to destroy himself, a world well-lost for love. But he also confesses that he wished he had more to lose. He desires not only Stella but also all the riches, fame, and achievement he would happily throw away for her.

To see that, in such ambiguous balanced couplets as this last, Sidney manages to have it both ways is to see the overall strategy of the sequence. If he never, as Greville confessed, "was Magistrate, nor possessed of any fit stage for eminence to act upon," and even if his life was short and his fortunes private, yet there are—as Greville hopes—"lines to be drawn, not Astronomicall, or imaginary, but reall lineaments . . . out of which nature often sparkleth brighter rayes in some, than ordinarily appear in the ripeness of others" (pp. 38-41). If Sir Philip Sidney was denied his stage not only by the queen's abiding mistrust but by his early death, he yet left the lines in which he claims he authored his own ruined career. While Greville obviously felt the sequence needed to be suppressed, preferring an unpreferred statesman to a preeminent poet, Sidney's own legend for himself told a different story. Of course, he did not die of passion, or of Petrarchan poetics. He died, in fact, of Protestant politicsCand his own, not the queen's (the same Protestant politics that would harry James, and behead Charles). If we have to work this hard to retrieve that simple fact about his life, our difficulty is testimony to how thoroughly Sidney's self-creation as poet-lover has prevailed over Greville's legend of soldier-statesman. We need to read the politics back into the poetry not only to see that the politics are indeed embedded there but also to perceive how well Sidney's strategy of mystification succeeded. While it is not true that he threw over a blossoming career as courtier/statesman to become a love-struck poet, it *is* true that he did not succeed at winning either of his ladies' favor, neither Stella's or the queen's, because he refused to play by their rules of "tyran honor."

For finally, the poems are filled with the strategies of such a rich authority that to challenge that authority and give its author, as he did Oxford, the lie, risks making the critic too much of a cynic. If puppies are begotten by dogs, and children by men, it is useful to realize that poets still author, if not the entirety of their political lives, then at least the most powerful legends about them.[41]

Notes

. . .[20] Sidney placed such Protestant politics, his "love of the caws" [cause], as he put it, above his desire to please the queen, to be safe, rich, and graced by her favor. In a most revealing letter, Sidney confesses to his father-in-law that his radical Protestant activism, his very self, is more important to him than her favor. Elizabeth was perhaps very wise when she refused to reward such lack of devotion.

> I had before cast my court of dang[er] want and disgrace, and before God Sir it is trew [that] in my hart the love of the caws doth so far over-ballance them all that with Gods grace thei shall never make me weery of my resolution. If her Majesty wear the fowntain I woold fear considiring what I daily fynd that we shold wax dry, but she is but a means whom God useth and I know not whether I am deceaved but I am faithfully persuaded that if she shold with draw her self other springes woold ryse to help this action. For me thinkes I see the great work indeed in hand, against the abusers of the world, wherein it is not greater fault to have confidence in mans power, then it is to hastily to despair of God work. I think a wyse and constant man ought never to greev whyle he doth plai as a man mai sai his own part truly though othgers be out but if him self leav his hild becaws other marriners will be ydle he will hardli forgive him self this own fault. For me I can not promise of my own cource no nor of the my[   ] because I know there is a hyer power that must uphold me or els I shall fall, but certainly I trust, I shall not by other mens wantes be drawn from my self. . . . I understand I am called very ambitious and prowd at home, but certainly if thei knew my hart thei woold not altogether so judge me. (*Works* 3: 166-67)

21 Sidney's works went through nine editions in the next century, while Spenser had only three editions and Shakespeare four; of them all, only Sidney was translated into foreign languages, including French, German, Dutch, and Italian. See Ringler, *Poems of Sir Philip Sidney,* p. 440.

22 Ronald A. Rebholz, *The Life of Fulke Greville, First Lord Brooke* (Oxford: Clarendon Press, 1971), pp. 211-16, discusses Greville's "self-centered" account and argues that he depresses his worth to elevate Sidney's and with it his own in relation to the age of James.

23 The recent publication of the two versions of the *Arcadia* in accessible paperback format may change our sense of Sidney's achievement from poetry to proseCa distinction, of course, he held to be moot.

24 Jonathan Goldberg, *James I and the Politics of Literature* (Baltimore: Johns Hopkins University Press, 1983), pp. 23-24, traces James's own anti-Petrarchan poets and contrasts James and Elizabeth's styles of self-presentation.

25 See Tennenhouse, *Power on Display,* p. 34, and Louis A. Montrose, "Of Gentlemen and Shepherds: The Politics of Elizabethan Pastoral Forms," *ELH* 50

(1983): 441-48, for comment on the political function Petrarchism had during the reign of Elizabeth.

26 Pierre Bourdieu, "The Economics of Linguistics Exchanges," tr. Richard Nice, *Social Science Information* 16 (1977): 545-68.

27 I am indebted to Margreta DeGrazia for suggesting the possible ordinariness of the pun to me. In "Prelexical Possibilities in Shakespeare's Language," a paper delivered to the Shakespeare Association of America, March 1985, DeGrazia specifically argues that none of the rhetorical figures that name wordplay of various sorts (syllepsis, antanaclasis, paranomasia, significatio, traductio) describe what we postdictionary readers and speakers identify as a pun—that is, two separate words that are spelled and spoken identically. Sixteenth-century logic maunals do discuss the homonym but define it as "one word that signifieth diverse things," a very different sense from ours; as DeGrazia puts it "what a prelexical age considers one word, a postlexical age considers two or more words." According to the *OED,* the term "pun" was first used in 1660.

28 Ringler, *Poems of Sir Philip Sidney,* p. 447.

29 Arthur F. Marotti, "'Love Is Not Love': Elizabethan Sonnet Sequences and the Social Order, *ELH* (1982): 396-428; hereafter cited in the text.

30 Ann Rosalind Jones and Peter Stallybrass, "The Politics of *Astrophil and Stella,*" *SEL* 24 (1984): 53-68. See also Nancy J. Vickers, "Diana Described: Scattered Woman and Scattered Rhyme," *Critical Inquiry* 8 (Winter 1981): 265-79.

31 For a discussion of Laura's uncertain identity, see Robert M. Durling, *Petrarch's Lyric Poems: The Rime Sparse and Other Lyrics* (Cambridge: Harvard University Press, 1976), p. iv.

32 A dependent of his wife's powerful brother the earl of Essex, Rich acquiesced in his wife's later long-term liaison with Sir Charles Blount, yet he did not remain loyal to Essex's followers when the earl was executed for treason. As Ringler puts it, "he was zealous in religion and affected the air of a Puritan, but like Malvolio he was more of a 'time-pleaser' than anything else" (*Poems of Sir Philip Sidney,* p. 445).

33 Marotti, "Elizabethan Sonnet Sequences," p. 406. Poems from the sequence do not appear in contemporaries' manuscript collections until after Sidney's death, while other poems of his come into these miscellanies earlier. Ringler notes that Sir John Harington copied eight poems by Sidney into his collection. He himself first copied "Certain Sonnets 3" (on fol. 34), and then Song 10 from *Astrophil and Stella* (on fol. 36ᵛ). As

Ringler notes, Harington apparently did not know that Stella was Lady Rich at the time he first copied the poem, because he headed it "Sr Philip Syd: to the bewty of the worlde"; subsequently, he copied *Astrophil and Stella*, Sonnet 1 (on fol. 155) and headed the poem "Sonnets of Sr Philip Sydneys vppon to ye Lady Ritch." It is fascinating to see Harington hesitate in his designation of Penelope Devereux's relationship to the first poem. Is she its subject ("upon") or its addressee ("to")? Harington's confusion about how to state the relationship of the real, historical Stella to the poem (which does not, in fact, address her) nicely demonstrates the unstable position of the female with respect to the male poet of the Petrarchan tradition, an instability just as problematic for sixteenth-century as for later readers.

34 P. J. Croft, *The Poems of Robert Sidney* (Oxford: Clarendon Press, 1984).

35 Sir Walter Ralegh owed his later prominence as favorite to his cultivation of the cult of Elizabeth; his fragmentary "Cynthia" may stand as testimony to his sense (however disproved) that direct address in poetry could win back the queen's favor. Sidney addressed no poem to Elizabeth, save for *The Lady of May*.

36 Sidney's actual marriage to Sir Francis Walsingham's daughter Frances (when Sidney was age thirty and she sixteen) does not seem to have been based on love, for it obeyed all the tenets of a patriarchal match, save one: Queen Elizabeth, official patriarch of her society, was not notified. When the queen objected that she had not been asked her approval of this signal traffic in women, Walsingham explained that, the principals being of such low birth, he had not thought it necessary to obtain her permission. The maneuver is so like the suppression of Elizabeth's remarks about the choice of a husband for the Lady of May, one cannot help but wonder if the source was the same. Once again the hierarchy can be manipulated from below.

37 Ringler, *Poems of Sir Philip Sidney*, p. 443.

38 Interspersed between the first two children Penelope Devereux bore Blount was the birth of the final child she had with Lord Rich (in all, she bore the two men ten children). She was accepted by both the courts of Elizabeth and James as Blount's official mistress until the two illicitly got married after her divorce from Rich in 1605. Only after they were married were she and Blount ostracized. William Laud, who performed the ceremony and later became archbishop, kept the wedding anniversary, according to Ringler, as a day of penance (*Poems of Sir Philip Sidney*, pp. 445-46).

39 Both Lady Rich and Frances Walsingham helped Robert Sidney during his period of political unpopular-ity when even Essex had dropped his support; see Croft, *Poems of Robert Sidney*, p. 83. Walsingham's father also had a hand in arranging Robert's marriage against Elizabeth's express wishes (pp. 70-71).

40 Until Penelope married Blount, she never suffered any punishments, either for her adulterous liaison or for her loyal support of her brother or of Robert Sidney. Marrying only to legitimate their children (as Blount had himself succeeded to an earldom), she was punished for this transgression only; no more than Elizabeth could she bestow herself where she might wish.

41 I am grateful to Richard Strier for this final formulation as well as for other suggestions, clarifications, and corrections.

Richard C. McCoy (essay date 1989)

SOURCE: "Sir Philip Sidney: The Shepherd Knight," in *The Rites of Knighthood: The Literature and Politics of Elizabethan Chivalry*, University of California Press, 1989, pp. 55-78.

[*In the following excerpt, McCoy examines the courtly politics of* The Four Foster Children of Desire, *an "entertainment" staged by Sidney for Queen Elizabeth.*]

Sir Philip Sidney was the son of Robert Dudley's sister, and the Earl of Leicester was a powerful influence on his nephew's brief career. Philip's father, Sir Henry Sidney, saw the Dudley connection as the family's greatest distinction, urging him, "Remember, my son, the noble blood you are descended of by your mother's side."[1] When drawing up their own pedigree, the Sidneys employed their distinguished relative's herald, Robert Cooke, who obliged them with characteristic creativity. Cooke began by preparing a bogus genealogical roll tracing the descent of a fictive William de Sydney down to the fourteenth century, which he in turn used as "evidence" for the genealogy he presented as his own—the initial forgery "written on a narrow strip of parchment, which is in a very brittle state. The discoloured appearance of the parchment and the character of the handwriting suggest an attempt to feign antiquity for the Roll; which must have in fact been written little before 1580."[2] Cooke's forgery apparently worked, flattering as it was to the Sidneys' ancestral pride.

Philip's own ancestral pride was particularly fierce, and he was aroused to almost fanatical anger by the slanders leveled against his uncle in *Leicester's Commonwealth*, a book combining reportage on factional maneuvers at court with expert character assassination of the Earl of Leicester. *Leicester's Commonwealth* was published anonymously in Paris in 1584, and Elizabeth's government tried to suppress the book in England, but its circulation in manuscript did grave and lasting damage to Robert Dudley, darkening his reputation even to the present day.[3] He was accused of murder, treason, adultery, and atheism, among other heinous crimes, but the attack most galling to Sidney was aimed at Dudley's lack of long-standing nobility. According to *Leicester's Commonwealth,* Dudley's father was a "buck of the first head," or the first noble of his line, and Leicester himself had aroused the hatred of the "ancient nobility" by his efforts to supplant them.[4] Stung by this slur on "my dead ancestors,"[5] Sidney wrote a *Defence of the Earl of Leicester,* a tract he apparently planned to publish. Taking his father's admonition to heart, Sidney declares, "I am a Dudley in blood, that Duke's daughter's son, and do acknowledge, though in all truth I may justly affirm that I am by my father's side of ancient and always well esteemed and well matched gentry, yet I do acknowledge, I say, that my chiefest honour is to be a Dudley, and truly am glad to have cause to set forth the nobility of that blood whereof I am descended, which, but upon so just cause, without vain glory could not have been uttered: since no man but this fellow of invincible shamelessness would ever have called so palpable a matter in question."[6] Relying in part on the pedigree Robert Cooke prepared for Leicester in 1583, Sidney traces the Dudleys' descent from such venerable families as the Beauchamps, the Talbots, and the Grays.[7] The *Defence of the Earl of Leicester* concludes with a dramatic but futile chivalric gesture. The impassioned defender of family honor challenges his anonymous adversary to a duel within three months' time: "But to thee I say: thou therein liest in thy throat, which I will be ready to justify upon thee in any place of Europe, where thou wilt assign me a free place of coming, as within three months after the publishing hereof I may understand thy mind."[8] Sidney's vehemence abated, and cooler heads evidently prevailed; the *Defence of the Earl of Leicester* was never published, the challenge never promulgated, and the identity of the author of *Leicester's Commonwealth* never revealed.[9]

Some of Sidney's earliest writings were also linked to the Earl of Leicester, and these too met with a dubious reception. The *Lady of May* was a masque devised to entertain the Queen during a visit to Leicester's estate at Wanstead in 1578. The masque concerned that perennial subject of Leicester's entertainments, the marriage question, but here the topic may have figured Leicester's martial rather than marital ambitions. In this case, the Queen was asked to choose between two suitors for the May Lady's hand—a virile and active forester, and a cautious and passive shepherd. Sidney seems to favor the exuberant forester, Therion, and the final song celebrates the triumph of the forest god, Silvanus, over Pan.[10] In 1578 Leicester and his faction were promoting an activist foreign policy

by urging military intervention in the Netherlands.[11] Elizabeth found such a course too risky, and her choice of the prudent shepherd may have been a deliberate rebuff to Leicester and his nephew.

Sidney subsequently tried to address the Queen more directly on the subject of marriage, and he met with no more success. In 1579 it appeared that Elizabeth might finally accept the Duke of Alençon, younger brother to the King of France, as a husband. Good Protestants were horrified and their views of the marriage were publicized in a tract entitled "The Discovery of a Gaping Gulf whereunto England is like to be swallowed by another French marriage, if the Lord forbid not the banns by letting her Majesty see the sin and Punishment thereof." The author, John Stubbs, and his printer had their right hands cut off as punishment. Sidney boldly entered the controversy with a letter addressed "To Queen Elizabeth, Touching her Marriage with Monsieur." He probably also served as his uncle's spokesman on this occasion, but his own aversion to Alençon and his mother, Catherine de Médicis, were rooted in the latter's role in the Saint Bartholomew's Day Massacre, an event Sidney witnessed during his first visit to the Continent. His distrust of this "Frenchman, and a Papist . . . the son of the Jezebel of our age," was already deeply ingrained.[12] In his letter Sidney declares his "unfeigned love" for the Queen, but he warns her that her subjects' love was always conditional: "Virtue and justice are the only bands of the people's love. And as for that point, many princes have lost their crowns, whose own children were manifest successors."[13] It is an extraordinary threat, one that could hardly endear the author to the Queen. Sidney's politesse and higher status may have spared him the fate of John Stubbs, but almost all advice on marriage was offensive to the Queen.[14]

Shortly after he wrote the letter, Sidney confronted the Queen directly in an extraordinary showdown on the rights of subjects—rights he asserted by resorting to "the rites of knighthood." A quarrel with the Earl of Oxford over the use of a tennis court led to a formal challenge to a duel. The Privy Council intervened to block it, but Sidney insisted on following through, so the Queen herself interceded. Elizabeth sought to put him in his place, according to Sir Fulke Greville. In the latter's admiring account of this event, the Queen tries to remind Sidney of "the difference between earls and gentlemen; the respect inferiors ought to their superiors," but Sidney retorts "that place was never intended for privilege to wrong."[15] Greville declared that Sidney established here "a latitude for subjects to reserve native and legal freedom by paying humble tribute in manner, though not in matter, to them." In his own life, however, he was both more tractable and more successful in his relations with the monarch; indeed, for himself, he finally doubted "whether there be any latitude left—more than humble obedience—in these nice cases between duty and selfness in a sovereign's service."[16] Sidney also had to yield to his sovereign's authority and forgo the duel, and shortly afterward he withdrew to his sister's estate at Wilton.

In 1581 Sidney tried a somewhat different approach to courtly politics, now that he was determined to play more strictly by its rules. His New Year's gift to the Queen was a diamond-studded whip, the perfect token of courtly discourse. Instead of straightforward exhortation, he employs a device as ambiguous as Dudley's impresa shield, subtly suggesting both submission and resentment. He resumed an active public life as a member of Parliament and a frequent performer in court spectacle, participating in three tournaments and two marriage pageants. The grandest of these was *The Four Foster Children of Desire*, an entertainment combining tilting with an allegorical assault on "The Fortress of Perfect Beauty," the gallery housing the Queen. The four challengers, or "foster children," were the Earl of Arundel, Lord Windsor, Sir Fulke Greville, and Sir Philip Sidney. Sidney was the challengers' standard bearer because his men wore the "poesie, or sentence" justifying their assault, and the dramatic idea behind the tournament was probably his.[17] In organizing this spectacular chivalric fete, Sidney was following his uncle's lead. His magnificent entry is described in an account of the tournament published shortly afterward:

> Then proceeded M. Philip Sidney, in very sumptuous maner, with armor part blewe, & the rest gilt & engraven, with foure spare horses, having caparisons and furniture veri riche & costly, as some of cloth of gold embroidred with pearle, and some embrodred with gold and silver feathers, very richly & cunningly wrought, he had foure pages that rode on his four spare horses, who had cassock coats & venetian hose al of cloth of silver, layd with gold lace, & hats of the same with golde bands, and white fethers, and each one a paire of white buskins. Then had he a thirtie gentlemen and yeomen, & foure trumpetters, who were all in cassocke coats and venetian hose of yellow velvet, laid with silver lace, yellowe velvet caps with silver bands and white fethers, and every one a paire of white buskins. And they had uppon their coates, a scrowle or bande of silver, which came scarfewise over the shoulder, and so downe under the arme, with this poesie, or sentence written upon it, both before and behinde, Sic nos non nobis.[18]

Sidney's entry, with its four trumpeters, a page, and a liveried entourage of thirty, seems as extravagantly selfaggrandizing, and the siege as aggressive, as any of his uncle's performances. Nevertheless, their styles are significantly different.

The Four Foster Children of Desire addresses the issue of marriage more subtly and deferentially than

Sidney's earlier works. The show begins with a comically innocuous attack on the Queen's gallery by a wooden and canvas "Rowling trench" (***FFC***, p. 68). Musicians concealed within this contraption "cunningly conveyed divers kinde of most excellent musicke against the castle of Beauty" (p. 69). After the "trench or Mounte of earth was mooved as nere the Queenes Majestie as might be" (p. 71), two of Sidney's songs were sung, the first by a boy imploring the Queen to "Yeelde, Yeelde, o Yeelde" and the second by another, representing the defenders, defying their assault.[19] Afterward, "two Canons were shott off, the one with sweet powder, and the other with sweete water, very odoriferous and pleasaunt, and the noyse of the shooting was very excellent consent of mellodie within the Mounte: And after that, was store of prettie scaling ladders, and the footemen threwe Flowers and such fancies against the walles, with all such devices as might seeme fit shot for Desire" (pp. 72-73). The device evokes the symbolically erotic associations of siege warfare as well as earlier Tudor pageants of Beauty and Desire, including Henry VIII's masque of "Ardent Desire," in which Anne Boleyn made her debut, and Dudley's Christmas revels at the beginning of Elizabeth's reign. In both of these earlier shows, however, the siege was successful, and the masque concluded with a dance uniting the lady with the triumphant knight. In **The Four Foster Children of Desire** the challengers' aggression is muted, and their siege fails. The Fortress of Perfect Beauty proves "Impregnable" (p. 82), and they graciously concede defeat.

The position of the foster children is ambiguous from the beginning. They are, first of all, plaintive children rather than domineering suitors, and they desire only to be fostered, or nursed. This figure is one of Sidney's most striking, first appearing in **Certain Sonnet** 6, where Desire is a baby crying for pap, and beauty is a nurse whose care fails to satisfy. The figure is reworked in **Astrophil and Stella** 71, where "Desire still cries give me some food" and fails to obtain it. In both instances Desire is more helpless than aggressive. The foster children are also virtuously submissive, although their adversaries do not understand this. The Queen's defenders compare her to the sun and accuse the foster children of seeking their own gain in their assault on her castle: "Sir Knights, if in besieging the sunne, ye understood what you had undertaken, ye would not destroye a common blessing for a private benefit" (***FFC***, p. 75). The defenders urge them to "desist, sithe it is impossible to resist, content your selves with the sunnes indifferent succor" (p. 75). They do in fact desist, showing themselves capable of the altruism demanded of the true lover in **Astrophil and Stella** 61:

> That who indeed infelt affection beares,
>   So captives to his Saint both soule and
>   sence,

That wholly hers, all selfnesse he forbeares,
Thence his desires he learnes, his live's
    course thence.

However, they have announced their virtuous self-denial from the tournament's start. The "poesie, or sentence" worn by Sidney's entourage declares "Sic nos non nobis": "we [do or act] thus not for ourselves" (**FFC**, p. 70).

The righteous pathos of the challengers is one of the central points of the complex allegory of *The Four Foster Children of Desire*. At one level, the challengers' surrender can be seen as a tactful apology for the presumptuous interference in the Queen's marriage choice by Sidney and Leicester. At the same time, the tournament, which was devised for the entertainment of the French ambassadors, slyly denies the Queen to Alençon and every other suitor now that Leicester is out of the running, for Alençon must also content himself "with the sun's indifferent succor."[20] Finally, the allegory delicately hints at the political constraints on the Queen. She has no choice regarding a husband because "when Beawtie yeeldeth once to desire, then can she never vaunt to be desired again" (p. 80). Desire persists only as long as it is unrequited. By the middle of Elizabeth's reign the familiar romantic paradox had acquired an inescapable political significance for her as she rejected the last serious candidate for her hand.

Running through all these compliments is an undertone of resentment felt by those who cry futilely for succor. Patronage is the issue figured by this metaphor of fosterage. Sir Robert Naunton uses the same metaphor to describe the demands of the Earl of Essex, saying he "drew in fast like a child sucking on a uberous breast."[21] Uberous, linked to udder, means rich, full, and abundant, but in practice, Elizabeth seldom proved especially "uberous" to those dependent on her. Sir Francis Bacon remarks instead on "her wonderful art in keeping servants in satisfaction, and yet in appetite"; elsewhere he says that she "allows of amorous admiration but prohibits desire."[22] *The Four Foster Children of Desire* dramatizes this tantalizing situation, showing how its victims are pathetically "weake in Fortune"; they clamor for their "desired patrimonie" (**FFC**, p. 66) as well as maternal nurture, but what they receive is meager. Perfect Beauty "yeeldes continuall foode to all her foes, and though they feede not fat therewith, yet must they either feede theron or fast" (p. 79). The resentments intimated in *Certain Sonnet* 22, Sidney's only poem explicitly praising the Queen, resurface here: Elizabeth's admirers are in thrall to a lady "On whome all love, in whom no love is plaste."

The Four Foster Children of Desire consciously enacts the chivalric compromise. The participants declare "their most humble hearted submission" (**FFC**, p. 83), but their prowess in the tiltyard still "give[s] such true proofes of their valler, as at least shal make their desires more noble" (p. 68). Moreover, the tournament resolves the conflict between the Queen and her subjects since the latter apologize for interfering in the French marriage suit while righteously denying the Queen to all suitors. Finally, its allegory is a small masterpiece of what Louis Montrose calls "celebration and insinuation," one that simultaneously compliments and criticizes the Queen.[23] The impresa's insistence on the challengers' selflessness and the broader intimations of the Queen's cruel indifference are as slyly ambiguous as the diamond-studded whip. Less overtly hostile than the tournament depicted in Christopher Marlowe's *Edward II*, *The Four Foster Children of Desire* also masks its aggressions behind obsequious speeches. In Marlowe's play the King easily grasps the significance of the contestants' impresas, asking, "Can you in words make showe of amitie, / And in your shields display your rancorous minds?"[24] If the Queen discerned any comparable rancor behind Sidney's "show of amitie," she let it pass on this occasion.

Because it went so smoothly, *The Four Foster Children of Desire* was, in one sense, Sidney's most successful courtly performance. Nevertheless, it still did not produce the desired results, revealing the practical limits of "the rites of knighthood." Sidney returned to court in 1581, hoping to secure profitable employment, but he only met with further disappointments. The first occurred sometime before June when Lettice Knollys gave birth to a son. Prior to this event Sidney had been Leicester's sole heir, but he now found himself supplanted. Sidney could still dramatize his loss of a "desired patrimony" in the tiltyard by riding in a tournament with the device, "~~SPERAVI~~, thus dashed through to shew his hope therein was dashed."[25] However, by the end of the year his frustrations became harder to accept as he found himself entangled in a "comber of debtes."[26] He had followed his uncle's lead by staging *The Four Foster Children of Desire*, but Leicester's relationship to the Queen was harder to emulate. Sidney's frustration with his mentor is evident in a letter written to Leicester late in 1581: "Well my Lord your Lordeshippe made me a courtier do you think of it as seemes best unto you."[27] By year's end, according to Wallace, Sidney withdrew again from court and "remained at Wilton for Christmas, and the fact that he did not present a New Year's gift to the Queen, and that his name does not appear in the lists of challengers or defenders in the great royal tournament of January 1st which was held in honour of the Duke D'Alençon, makes it probable that he extended his visit into the New Year."[28] Following the activities of the previous year, this seems like a conspicuous absence.

Sidney's attitude toward the court at this point is just as ambiguous as his movements. Fifteen eighty-two is the year he composed *Astrophil and Stella*, and these sonnets are often seen as a turning away from the "busie wits" at court.[29] Arthur Marotti argues that the sequence is directed to a coterie audience that provides "an imaginative and social retreat more hospitable" than the court.[30] Annabel Patterson sees evidence of a growing alienation from court in the *New Arcadia*, whose revisions suggest a "loss of confidence in indirect or covert discourse, or in messages accommodated to the forms of Elizabethan courtship."[31] A. C. Hamilton traces Sidney's disillusionment with the court back to an earlier stage, contending that "by 1579 Sidney was becoming more estranged from the court, imaginatively if not physically," because of his failure to find employment. In Hamilton's view, all Sidney's serious writing from the *Old Arcadia* onward is the work of "a poet writing privately, apart from the court even while he belongs to it. From 1580 until the final year of his life, the pattern is more definite: his essential life took place in his writings, however outwardly busy he may have been in affairs at court."[32]

There is certainly ample evidence of hostility toward the court in all of Sidney's works, but the movement of his mind in both his literature and his life is not one of progressive disillusion but continual oscillation. The pastoral havens of literature beckon, but the court proves inescapable for him. In the first eclogues of the *Old Arcadia*, Musidorus sings:

> that better it is to be private
> In sorrows torments, then, tyed to the
>   pompes of a pallace,
> Nurse inwarde maladyes, which have not
>   scope to be
>   breath'd out.

At this point in the work, the hero has assumed his pastoral disguise and prefers to "disburden a passion / . . . by the helpe of an outcrye: / Not limited to a whispringe note, the Lament of a Courtier."[33] Sidney may have felt this way as well, but he still chose to take a prominent role in *The Four Foster Children of Desire*, one of the reign's grandest "pompes" shortly afterward, adapting his complaints there to the "whispringe note, the Lament of a Courtier."

Sidney's disaffection resurfaces in "**Two Pastorals**," written after 1581. The first is a celebration of true friendship with Fulke Greville and Edward Dyer, and the second, a frankly stated "Disprayse of a Courtly Life." The speaker of the "Disprayse" begins by describing his escape from the oppressive heat of the sun into a pleasant, flourishing wood:

> Walking in bright *Phoebus'* blaze
> Where with heate oppreste I was,

> I got to a shady wood,
> Where greene leaves did newly bud.
> And of grasse was plenty dwelling,
> Deckt with pyde flowers sweetely smelling.[34]

Elizabeth had been identified with the sun in *The Four Foster Children of Desire*, and here the speaker is "oppreste" by the blazing heat and light of courtly life. The "shady wood" of pastoral provides partial relief for another courtier, one who turns out to be a thinly disguised version of Sidney:

> In this wood a man I met,
> On lamenting wholy set:
> Rewing change of wonted state,
> Whence he was transformed late,
> Once to Shepheard's God retayning,
> Now in servile Court remayning.

The man laments his "change" from a retainer of the "Shepheard's God," Pan, and his return to the "servile Court." In the treacherous world of the court he cannot share his sufferings with anyone, and he finds solace only in pastoral solitude, venting his griefs to "a senceless tree." The shepherd misses his "old mates" who spent their time "never striving, but in loving," and he complains that he is poorly equipped for the competition and conflict of court life.

Sidney then distinguishes between the true love he feels for his friends and the deceptive "art of Love" required at court, insisting that he also lacks the skill needed for such an art:

> Therefore shepheardes wanting skill,
> Can Love's duties best fulfill:
> Since they know not how to faine,
> Nor with Love to cloake Disdaine,
> Like the wiser sorte, whose learning,
> Hides their inward will of harming.

The most repellent feature of the court was its enforcement of a code in which Love is used "to cloake Disdaine." Yet despite his aversion to such pretense, he is still "in servile court remaining."

Sidney's evident disillusion with "the rites of knighthood" is manifest in a poem recently discovered by Peter Beal and attributed to Sidney. It precedes two other poems linked to the occasion of the Accession Day tilt in the Ottley manuscript, and its references to the event are detailed and depressing:

> Waynd from the hope wch made affection
>   glad
> to show it self in himnes of delight
> yet highly pleased wth thos conceipts I had
> made me in deserts grow a desert knighte
> that synce no new impression shuld take

mee

vnto myne old I might the freer bee
Ocasion deare the nurse or hand of hope
by ecchoes sound made knowne yor enitry
    daye
Affection fond to take his former scope:
Make me of ioye tread on this comonwaye
Myne armor barke & mosse of faded tree
My speares wild poles my end to love and
    see.

The verses were "inclosed in a tree sealed with a grene leaf," addressed "to her that is mrs of men, . . . & Sainte of the sabaoth," and accompanied by an impresa of a "tree, the one half springing ye othr half dying & this word *hoc ordine fata.* Such be ye corse of Heavens."[35] The poem's metaphoric links to *The Four Foster Children of Desire* are especially interesting. In its description of a knight who is weaned from hope, it pursues the themes of nurturing and frustration, hope and despair. In the earlier tilt the "long haples, now hopeful fostered children of Desire" charged into the lists despite the efforts of their "dry nurse Dispaier [who] indevered to waine them from it" (*FFC*, p. 67). In the poem Despair has almost triumphed, depriving the event of the high-spirited ardor that "made affection glad / to show itself" in the annual tournament. The speaker is still "pleasd wth those conceipts I had [that] made me in deserts grow a desert knight." In his desolate, solipsistic contemplation, cut off from "new impression," he resembles Philisides in the *Old Arcadia*, who also sings "in those desert places."[36]

Hope and affection still persist, with affection still "fond to take his former scope"; but the double meaning of "fond" suggests the foolishness of this return to an old rut. Line 10 gives lip service to the knight's "ioye" while subverting this impression with a tone of weary resignation. The same line repeats the verb *make* for the fourth time, reinforcing the sense of pervasive coercion and passivity. The decision to "tread on this comon waye" hardly conveys any pleasure in the quest. This Accession Day tilt presents the image of a crowded treadmill, and the tone of weary, helpless resignation is confirmed by an impresa of a half-dead tree and the motto *hoc ordine fata.*

Hope and affection are only kept alive by the "nurse" Occasion rather than Desire. Occasion is, in one sense, the poem's central topic, the cause and opportunity for public celebration and performance, summoning the speaker from the "deserts" of private reflection. Nevertheless, as the melancholy tone of the poem indicates, such occasions must have seemed increasingly inadequate. Greville writes that Sidney "never was magistrate, nor possessed of any fit stage for eminence to act upon."[37] That the tiltyard at Whitehall provided the only public stage, the only alternative to

pastoral withdrawal, for so much of his career must have grated on Sidney at various points. Nevertheless, for all his melancholy posing, he kept coming back to the tiltyard. His impresa shield of 1584 displayed a buoyantly optimistic motto, countering the gloom of "Waynd from the hope" as well as the bitter complaint that his uncle had "made me a courtier." In the 1584 tournament, instead of complaining that his activities or identity were "made" by another, he resolutely declared, "*Inveniam viam aut faciam*—I will make or find a way."[38] Sidney decided in his *Apology for Poetry* that the poet's most "high and incomparable" title was "maker," and he remained determined to make his own way in life as well as literature.[39]

In Sidney's literature it becomes obvious that his melancholy pose was an integral part of his chivalric persona and style. Like the attraction to pastoral withdrawal, this attitude was incorporated into his tiltyard devices and chivalric fiction, complicating and enriching them. Instead of opposing the conventions of Elizabethan chivalry, these postures were part of the chivalric repertoire. In the *Old Arcadia* Sidney's fictional persona, Philisides, is a sorrowful lover and stranger shepherd, whose thoughts are supposedly far from "courtly pomps" (*OA*, p. 335), but in the *"New" Arcadia* he returns as a shepherd knight to join in the annual Iberian tilts devised to celebrate the royal wedding anniversary:

> The time of the maryinge that Queene was every year, by the extreame love of her husband & the serviceable love of the Courtiers, made notable by some publike honours, which indeede (as it were) proclaymed to the worlde, how deare she was to the people. Among other, none was either more gratefull to the beholders, or more noble in it selfe, than justs, both with sword and launce, mainteined for a seven-night together: wherein that Nation dooth so excell, bothe for comelines and hablenes, that from neighbour-countreis they ordinarily com, some to strive, some to learne, and some to behold.[40]

Philisides's entry into the lists is a paradoxical display of pastoral magnificence. He is announced

> with bagpipes in steed of trumpets; a shepheards boy before him for a Page, and by him a dosen apparelled like shepherds for the fashion, though rich in stuffe, who caried his launces, which though strong to give a launcely blow indeed, yet so were they couloured with hooks neere the mourn, that they pretily represented shephooks. His own furniture was drest over with wooll, so enriched with Jewels artificially placed, that one would have thought it a mariage between the lowest and the highest. His *Impresa* was a sheepe marked with pitch, with this word *Spotted to be knowne.* And because I may tell you out his conceipt (though that were not done, till the running for that time

was ended) before the Ladies departed from the windowes, among them there was one (they say) that was the Star, wherby his course was only directed. (*NA*, pp. 284-285)

Philisides jousts against the expert Lelius, "who was knowne to be second to none in the perfection of that Art" and who magnanimously lets his youthful adversary win (p. 285). Frances Yates and others have noted the clear references to Elizabeth's Accession Day tilts as well as the more specific allusion to an actual combat with Sir Henry Lee.[41]

Despite his own and his characters' supposed estrangement from "courtly pomps," Sidney's fiction remains firmly bound by their supposedly superficial splendors. His description of the Iberian jousts and similar events incorporates the customs and practices of contemporary tournaments in loving and expert detail.[42] At the same time, the corruption of the Iberian court makes its annual festivities a hypocritical sham. The marriage the tournaments celebrate has allowed the Queen, Andromana, to dupe her uxorious, sybaritic husband and seize control of the kingdom. Having first seduced the King's son, Plangus, the wicked Andromana then banishes him and replaces him as heir to the throne with her own son, Palladius. When the two heroes of the *New Arcadia*, Pyrocles and Musidorus, arrive in her kingdom, she attempts to seduce them and imprisons them for resisting. They are released during the Iberian jousts where they join her son, Palladius, and help him win the day's prize. When the honorable Palladius tries to help the heroes escape, he is killed by the troops Andromana sends to pursue them, and Andromana, overcome by grief and shame, kills herself. As David Norbrook has remarked, "the imagery of courtly ceremonial is associated with violence and imprisonment rather than delight" in the *New Arcadia*, giving the work what he calls an oddly "claustrophobic atmosphere."[43] Feelings of claustrophobia suffuse the episodes of Book II, as the protagonists' martial prowess and chivalric heroism prove increasingly ineffective. The adventures of Pyrocles and Musidorus culminate in a chaotic sea battle, which is terrifyingly claustral: "For the narrownesse of the place, the darkenesse of the time, and the uncertainty in such a tumult how to know friends from foes, made the rage of swordes rather guide, then be guided by their maisters" (*NA*, p. 305).

Book III initially promises to break free of this narrative impasse. The book focuses primarily on the war between King Basilius and the rebel Amphialus, and their struggle has a serious and unsettling political significance. The "justification" of his rebellion published by Amphialus draws heavily on Huguenot theories of the subaltern magistrate, theories Sidney would have known through his acquaintance with François Hot-

man's *Franco-Gallia* and with the *Vindiciae Contra Tyrannos,* presumably written by his friend Philippe de Mornay. Both works oppose to the potentially tyrannical powers of the crown the constitutional authority of the nobility, setting forth its right to legitimate resistance.[44] Amphialus also argues that responsibility for the country should be shared by the ruling classes: "The care whereof did kindly apperteine to those, who being subalterne magistrates and officers of the crowne, were to be employed as from the Prince, so for the people" (*NA*, p. 372). This responsibility requires that "the weale publicke was more to be regarded, then any person, or magistrate that thereunto was ordeined" (p. 372). Thus, "the duetie which is owed to the countrie, goes beyond all other dueties" (p. 371), superseding older loyalties to the monarch. Such rational abstraction subverts and demystifies traditional bonds, such as "all tender respects of kinred" and "long-helde opinions," because these are simply oppressive deceits, "rather builded upon a secreate of government, then any ground of truth" (p. 371).

Having established these general principles, Amphialus applies them to the political crisis in Arcadia. Because Basilius has "given over al care of government" and neglects the "good estate of so many thousands," the country founders in a "dangerous case" (*NA*, p. 372). He proposes to restore order by taking control himself, a move justified by claims of blood as well as political necessity: Amphialus is "descended of the Royall race, and next heire male" (p. 372). The duly appointed regent, Philanax, is denigrated as "a man neither in birth comparable to many, nor for his corrupt, prowde, and partiall dealing, liked of any" (p. 372). The inconsistencies of the theory begin to show at this point, as Amphialus's "justification" tries to have it both ways, alternately denying and asserting traditional standards of legitimacy. Such inconsistencies were inherent in assertions of the rights of subaltern magistrates, whose radical and revolutionary impulses were muted by a desire to preserve their place in the social hierarchy. Yet for all its logical weaknesses, Amphialus's justification of rebellion has a disturbing polemical power rarely matched in Elizabethan literature.

Amphialus's preparations for battle also show a strategic clarity and intelligence uncommon in chivalric romance:

> Then omitted he nothing of defence, as wel simple defence, as that which did defend by offending, fitting instruments of mischiefe to places, whence the mischiefe might be most liberally bestowed. Nether was his smallest care victuals, as wel for the providing that which should suffice both in store & goodnesse, as in well preserving it, and wary distributing it, both in quantitie, and qualitie; spending that first which would keepe lest. (*NA*, p. 373)

Once the battle begins, Amphialus is carried away by its excitement; but while the protagonist loses his sense of its larger ends, the author does not, at least not immediately. Sidney assigns a more practical perspective to an "olde Governour" of Amphialus and allows him to interrupt the action. The older authority breaks up a fight between his former charge and a Black Knight, wounding the latter warrior and killing his horse: "Amphialus cried to him, that he dishonoured him: You say well (answered the olde Knight) to stande now like a private souldier, setting your credite upon particular fighting, while you may see Basilius with all his hoste, is getting betweene you and your towne" (p. 393). The old governor rebukes him once again when Amphialus accepts another opponent's challenge to single combat, one whose motto is, "The glorie, not the pray" (p. 416). This irresponsible subordination of practical to chivalric ends is condemned by the seasoned veteran who accuses Amphialus of seeking "rather . . . the glorie of a private fighter, then of a wise Generall" (p. 414). The harsh and ugly violence of the opening scenes of the war seems to confirm Sidney's agreement with the old governor's point of view because he deliberately strips away the glorious facade of chivalry:

> For at the first, though it were terrible, yet Terror was deckt so bravelie with rich furniture, guilte swords, shining armours, pleasant pensils, that the eye with delight had scarce leasure to be afraide: But now all universally defiled with dust, bloud, broken armours, mangled bodies, tooke away the maske, and sette foorth Horror in his own horrible manner. (p. 392)

Nevertheless, despite these initial glimmers of critical insight, the *New Arcadia* remains bound by the conventions of chivalric romance. The old governor soon disappears from the narrative, and Amphialus can blithely ignore his admonitions. Oblivious to the requirements of supply, fortification, and military command, Amphialus concentrates instead on the decorations of his horse and armor in his efforts to impress his beloved. The war itself shrinks to a series of single combats, most involving Amphialus, and it regains the chivalric glamor lost in the first battle. In Sidney's eyes, combat presents a beautiful spectacle even when its outcome is painfully tragic. Amphialus easily defeats the "knight of the Tombe," only to discover that he has slain the lady, Parthenia. The wife of a knight killed in a previous encounter, she yearns only to join her husband in death, and she dies thanking Amphialus for this "service" (*NA*, p. 447). Amphialus is overwhelmed by feelings of "grief, compassion, & shame," but Sidney's description of the corpse is oddly exquisite:

> her necke, a necke indeed of Alablaster, displaying the wounde, which with most daintie blood laboured to drowne his owne beauties; so as here

was a river of purest redde, there an Iland of perfittest white, each giving lustre to the other; with the sweete countenance (God-knowes) full of an unaffected languishing: though these thinges to a grosly conceaving sense might seeme disgraces; yet indeed were they but apparailing beautie in a new fashion, which all looked-upon thorough the spectacles of pittie, did ever encrease the lynes of her naturall fairenes. (p. 447)

The cruel marks of her injuries might shock or horrify "a grosly conceaving sense," but the discerning esthete sees that they only make the victim more beautiful. Such chivalric equanimity imposes an elegant order on the dreadful mayhem of warfare, allowing its adherents to die a "beautiful" death, but it tends to lose sight of the larger purpose of war in its focus on the individual warrior and his encounters. Amphialus's struggle forfeits its strategic coherence as it degenerates into a string of self-contained, inconsequential contests.

The political aims professed in Amphialus's "justification" are similarly blurred. Despite its inconsistencies, that statement made claims for the nobility's subaltern authority that were truly revolutionary. However, responsibility for these unorthodox ideas is exclusively assigned to Amphialus's wicked mother, Cecropia, who finally dies for her role in kidnapping the princesses. The son's actual motives turn out to be entirely romantic. Like the heroes, Pyrocles and Musidorus, he also loves one of the daughters of King Basilius, but he resorts to open war rather than subterfuge to free them from their father's control. Moreover, his love is unrequited, driving him to ever more desperate measures. Amphialus's hopeless passion wins the sympathy of his harshest enemies, including the regent, Philanax, who says that his "fault passed is excusable, in that Love perswaded, and youth was persuaded" (*NA*, p. 401). His love for Philoclea inflames and then mollifies his aggression, "making all his authoritie to be but a footestoole to Humbleness" (p. 370). Romantic pathos finally supplants rebellious ambition. Enraged and grieved by the discovery of his mother's abuse of their captives, including his beloved Philoclea, Amphialus tries to kill himself and fails, presenting a "pittiful spectacle, where the conquest was the conquerors overthrow" (p. 494).

Caught between conflicting impulses of aggression and self-destruction, Amphialus is a typical Sidney hero. Pyrocles, the main protagonist of the *New Arcadia*, also oscillates between defiance of authority and resignation to the defeat of his desire. Toward the end of the *New Arcadia* he too bungles his attempt at suicide, his resistance to Basilius's authority overwhelmed by romantic pathos, but his last scene is more heroic than Amphialus's. At the end he rises to do battle with one last foe. Sidney's description of their struggle breaks off in mid-sentence, leaving the *New Arcadia* unfinished.

In several senses Sidney resembles his heroes, and the end of his book resembles his own. Sir Philip shared his characters' youthful energy, passionate activism, and high ideals. He was as determined as they were "to imploy those gifts esteemed rare in them to the good of mankind" (*NA*, p. 206), but when he did so, he too found himself entangled in intractable difficulties and conflicts with authority. As a result, many of his undertakings, including his last, resembled his heroes' adventures, which were "not so notable for any great effect they perfourmed, yet worthy to be remembered for the unused examples therein" (p. 206). Finally, both stories, Sidney's and the *New Arcadia's*, are cut off in the middle with stirring scenes of chivalric heroism, their larger contradictions remaining unresolved.

Sidney's "desyre for the beeing busied in a thing of som serviseable experience" grew increasingly urgent after the disappointments of 1581.[45] He attempted various projects, including joining Drake's voyage to the New World, but, as Fulke Greville says, "Sir Philip found this and many other of his large and sincere resolutions imprisoned within the plights of their fortunes that mixed good and evil together unequally."[46] The Netherlands expedition seemed the answer to his prayers since he could finally take his rightful place as a military commander in the sacred struggle against Spain, confident in the righteousness and ultimate triumph of the Protestant cause: "For me thinkes I see the great work indeed in hand, against the abusers of the world, wherein it is no greater fault to have confidence in mans power, then it is to hastily to despair of Gods work." Sidney's problems with the Queen persisted since she was apt "to interpret everything to my disadvantage," and he was eager to deny her suspicions on a particular point: "I understand I am called very ambitious and prowd at home, but certainly if thei knew my ha[rt] thei woold not altogether so judg me."[47] Throughout his life Sidney was hobbled by an inability to acknowledge his own ambitions.

Once in the Netherlands, Sidney proved to be a responsible and effective general, paying close attention to matters of finance and supply, discipline and tactics. Greville's description of his capture of Axel praises him accordingly:

> For instance, how like a soldier did he behave himself, first, in contriving, then in executing, the surprise of Axel, where he revived that ancient and severe discipline of order and silence in their march, and after their entrance into the town, placed a band of choice soldiers to make a stand in the market-place, for security to the rest that were forced to wander up and down by direction

of commanders, and, when the service was done, rewarded that obedience of discipline in every one liberally out of his own purse.[48]

His father's secretary, Edmund Molyneux, asserted that

> his advice for the service intended at Gravelin (dissenting in opinion from others, who were thought the most expert capteins and best renowned and sorted souldiours) gave such a sufficient proofe of his excellent wit, policie, and ripe iudgement, as onelie act and counsell, with the losse of a verie few of his companie, wrought all their safeties, which otherwise by treacherie had been most likelie to have beene intrapped.[49]

Sidney also became increasingly critical of his uncle's inept leadership and vainglorious shows, though his criticisms were necessarily muted. In a letter to the Earl of Leicester, he caustically recounted the "news in Roterdam, . . . that your band is of very hansome men, but meerly and unarmed spending monei and tyme to no purpos."[50] Later in the campaign he noted flaws in the overall strategy, complaining that instead of fortifying the "principal sea places" they already held, "we do still make camps and streight again mar them for want of meanes, and so lose our monei to no purpos." That same day he wrote Walsingham another guarded, but gloomy, assessment of their situation: "We are now four monthes behynd a thing unsupportable in this place. To complain of my Lord of Lester you know I mai not but . . . I did never think our nation had been so apt to go to the Enemy as I fynd them."[51]

The skirmish at Zutphen, where Sidney received his fatal wound, provided an escape from these increasingly depressing strategic concerns. When the fog around the English camp lifted to reveal a large Spanish convoy, the English charged. Amidst the frustrations and delays of a prolonged siege campaign, the chance for hand-to-hand combat proved irresistible; the skirmish at Zutphen was, as Simon Adams says, a kind of "military catharsis."[52] The Earl of Leicester's report of the event and of his nephew's injuries betrays his own mixed feelings regarding the clash between the demands of honor and military discipline: "There was too many indeed at this skirmish of the better sort, but I was offended when I knew it, but could not fetch them back: but since they have all so well escaped (save my dear nephew), I would not for ten thousand pounds but they had been there since they have all won that honour they have."[53] Even the general entrusted with the responsibilities of command affirms the supremacy of honor. George Whetstone's poetic tribute renders the contradictions of Sidney's death even more poignant. Sir Philip's friend and mentor, Hubert Languet, had presciently warned him that "a man who falls at an early age cannot have done much for his country,"[54] and Whetstone's fallen Sidney laments his "inability to do my Countrey good":

> my service is but greene
> My yeares are young, and brought forth
>   Leaves of late.
> The blomes were faire, but yet no fruit is
>   seene,
> I studied have to benefit the state
> To execute I am forbid by fate.[55]

Yet Whetstone, a professional soldier who also fought at Zutphen, still concludes, as Leicester had, that the "lasting fame" secured by this exploit justifies the loss of Sidney's life.

Later accounts of Sidney's final battle become more romantically chivalric, adding legendary incidents of bravery and altruism. Fulke Greville's *Dedication* is the most powerfully hagiographic. In his version Sidney is wounded in the thigh because "the marshal of the camp [was] lightly armed," and Sidney's "unspotted emulation of his heart to venture without any inequality made him cast off his cuisses."[56] After he is shot, Sidney yields his cup of water to a dying foot soldier, uttering the immortal words, "Thy need is greater than mine."[57] Thomas Moffet says Sidney failed to arm himself adequately because he was hurrying to rescue a friend when he was slain by "a brigand's hand craftily hidden in a ditch."[58] He employs a trope of Renaissance chivalric romance extending from Ariosto's attack on gunpowder to Cervantes's lament that "a base and cowardly hand . . . [can] take the life of a brave knight."[59]

In many of these tributes the chivalric heroism of Sidney's death explicitly mutes the contradictions of his life, the clash between his own autonomy and ambition and his deference to the Queen. One writer says he died "of manly woundes receiued in seruice of his Prince . . . in the open fielde, in Martiall Maner, the honorablest death that could be desired, and best beseeming a Christian Knight, whereby he hath worthely wonne to him selfe immortal fame among the godly." From this point of view Sidney's life acquires a happy unity, reconciling heroic virility and dutiful obedience, activism and contemplation, as he passes smoothly "from the companie of the muses to the campe of Mars . . . to followe the affayres of Chivalrie."[60] Fulke Greville's account of his friend's life is far more sophisticated, but it still imposes a balance between ambition and duty that is too pat. In Greville's biography Sidney's life finally presents an "exact image of quiet and action (happily united in him, and seldom well divided in any)."[61] In such elegiac tributes the chivalric compromise is imposed on the once volatile conflicts of Sidney's brief life. The "exact image of quiet and action" is, to some extent, a death mask of

his own devising, an image perfectly embodied by the figure of "the Shepherd Knight." His fascination with the ceremonial surface of "the rites of knighthood" and his guilt about his own deeper ambitions kept him bound by that image in life and death.

After Sidney's death the figure of the Shepherd Knight endured in popular memory, celebrated in chivalric verse and ceremony. In a ballad by John Phillips, Sidney is recalled as a vapidly contented courtier:

> In Marshall feates I settled my delight,
> The stately steede I did bestride with ioy,
> At tilt and turney oft I tried my might,
> In these exploits I never felt annoy.[62]

In the 1590 Accession Day tilt Sir Henry Lee, the Lelius of the *New Arcadia*, retired as the Queen's champion in a ceremony conducted with great solemnity. To his successor, the Earl of Cumberland, he bequeathed a collection of his own tilt devices and poems from Sidney's *Old Arcadia*, a text Frances Yates calls "the scriptures of the perfect knight of Protestant chivalry." Sidney's posthumous image exemplifies the ironies of what Stephen Greenblatt calls "Renaissance self-fashioning," a process that often drastically diminishes "human autonomy in the construction of identity."[63]

Yet even here, at Lee's retirement tilt, a dissonant note intrudes. In George Peele's *Polyhymnia,* a versified record of the 1590 Accession Day tilt, the entry of the Earl of Essex is at least as dramatic as anyone else's. He appears "Yclad in mightie Armes of mourners hue" in honor of Sir Philip Sidney, "whose successor he / In Love and Armes had ever vowed to be."[64] According to Roy Strong, Essex would have been chosen as the Queen's champion had not his marriage to Frances Walsingham, Sidney's widow, come to light.[65] Instead of playing down the offense, Essex defiantly flaunts it, proclaiming his allegiance to Sidney and his new wife. In doing so, Essex sought to upstage the new champion by establishing a line of chivalric succession worthier and more heroic than that bequeathed by Lee and formally declaring himself its heir. As we shall see, the Earl of Essex claimed and exploited the Sidney legend for his own purposes, reawakening some of the contradictions behind it and transforming the "exact image of quiet and action" into a "dangerous image."

Notes

[1] Malcolm William Wallace, *The Life of Sir Philip Sidney* (Cambridge: Cambridge University Press, 1915), p. 69.

[2] *HMC, De L'Isle and Dudley,* ed. C. L. Kingsford (London: HMSO, 1925), 1:304.

[3] See D. C. Peck's introduction to *Leicester's Commonwealth,* showing its influence on more respectable histories such as Camden's, Naunton's, Ashmole's, and others (p. 45).

[4] *Leicester's Commonwealth,* pp. 80, 174.

[5] Sidney, *Defence of the Earl of Leicester,* in *Miscellaneous Prose,* p. 140.

[6] Ibid., p. 134.

[7] Ibid., p. 135. Cooke's genealogy also includes, in addition to Guy of Warwick, these same families as in Dudley's family tree (Dudley Papers, Longleat, MS 149b).

[8] Sidney, *Defence of the Earl of Leicester,* p. 140.

[9] Peck argues that the author was not Robert Parsons, as is generally assumed, but Charles Arundel, with the assistance of others in the Catholic court party (*Leicester's Commonwealth,* p. 25-32).

[10] Sidney, *The Lady of May,* in *Miscellaneous Prose,* pp. 30-31.

[11] William Ringler discusses the connection between military aid to the Dutch and the *Lady of May* in his edition of *The Poems of Sir Philip Sidney* (1962; Oxford: Clarendon Press, 1967), p. 362.

[12] "A Letter Written by Sir Philip Sidney to Queen Elizabeth, Touching Her Marriage with Monsieur," in *Miscellaneous Prose,* p. 48.

[13] Ibid., pp. 46, 54.

[14] In her introduction to this letter in *Miscellaneous Prose* Katherine Duncan-Jones insists on the tact and intelligence of Sidney's letter and accurately notes the lack of evidence for his "banishment" from court (pp. 35-36). I find her contention that the letter "may have given little or no offence" (p. 36) less persuasive. Elizabeth raged at her Privy Council for addressing the subject, and Sidney's marginal status at court would only have made his advice seem more presumptuous rather than less.

[15] Greville, *Prose Works,* pp. 40-41.

[16] Ibid., p. 41, 87.

[17] Ephim G. Fogel argues that Sidney is probably the author of most of the challengers' speeches, in "A Possible Addition to the Sidney Canon," *Modern Language Notes* 75 (1960): 389-394.

[18] Sidney, *The Four Foster Children of Desire,* in *Entertainments for Elizabeth I* (Totawa, N.J.: Brewer, Rowman, and Littlefield, 1980), ed. Jean Wilson, p. 70; hereafter cited in the text.

[19] These are included by Ringler as "Poems possibly by Sidney" 4 and 5, in Sidney, *Poems,* pp. 345-346.

[20] See Norman Council, "*O Dea Certe*: The Allegory of the Fortress of Perfect Beauty," *Huntington Library Quarterly* 39 (1976): 334.

[21] Naunton, *Fragmenta Regalia,* p. 75. See also Arthur Marotti's discussion of desire as a trope for ambition, and grace as a trope for patronage, in "Love Is Not Love:' Elizabethan Sonnet Sequences and the Social Order," *ELH* 49 (1982): 396-428.

[22] Bacon, "Discourse in Praise of the Queen," in *Works,* ed. James Spedding, Robert Leslie Ellis, and Douglas Denon Heath (1857-1874; New York: Garrett Press, 1968), 8:139, and "In Felicem Memoriam Elizabethae," in *Works,* 6:317.

[23] Louis Adrian Montrose, "Celebration and Insinuation: Sir Philip Sidney and the Motives of Elizabethan Courtship," *Renaissance Drama,* n.s., 8 (1977): 3-35.

[24] Christopher Marlowe, *Edward II,* II.ii.34-35, in *The Complete Works of Christopher Marlowe,* ed. Fredson Bowers (1973; Cambridge University Press, 1981), p. 39.

[25] Camden, *Remaines* (1605), p. 174, cited by Ringler in Sidney, *Poems,* p. 441.

[26] "Correspondence," November 13, 1581, in *The Prose Works of Sir Philip Sidney,* ed. Albert Feuillerat (1912; Cambridge: Cambridge University Press, 1969), 3:138.

[27] Ibid., December 28, 1581, p. 140.

[28] Wallace, *Life of Sir Philip Sidney,* p. 273.

[29] Sidney, *Astrophil and Stella* 30, in *Poems,* p. 180.

[30] Marotti, "Love Is Not Love," p. 406. At the same time, Marotti contends that Sidney continues to address courtly issues of patronage and ambition throughout the sequence.

[31] Annabel Patterson, *Censorship and Interpretation* (Madison: University of Wisconsin Press, 1984), p. 41.

[32] A. C. Hamilton, *Sir Philip Sidney: A Study of His Life and Works* (Cambridge: Cambridge University Press, 1977), pp. 21, 17.

[33] Sidney, *Poems,* p. 35.

[34] Ibid., pp. 262-264. Ringler dates them after 1581 (p. 498); they were published in 1602.

[35] Peter Beal, "Poems by Sir Philip Sidney: The Ottley Manuscript," *The Library* 33 (1978): 284-295. Beal proposes both 1577 and 1583 as possible dates of composition since Elizabeth's Accession Day fell on a Sunday, the "sabaoth" referred to in the dedication; but there is no record of Sidney jousting in 1583.

[36] Sir Philip Sidney, *The Countess of Pembroke's Arcadia (The Old Arcadia)*, ed. Jean Robertson (Oxford: Clarendon Press, 1973), p. 159; hereafter cited in the text.

[37] Greville, *Prose Works*, p. 38.

[38] Emma Marshall Denkinger, "The *Impresa* Portrait of Sir Philip Sidney in the National Portrait Gallery," *PMLA* 47 (1932): 17.

[39] Sidney, *Apology for Poetry*, p. 99.

[40] Sidney, *The "New" Arcadia* (1590), in *Prose Works*, 1:282-283; hereafter cited in the text.

[41] Yates, *Astraea*, pp. 88-90.

[42] See Malcolm Parkinson, "Sidney's Portrayal of Mounted Combat with Lances," in *Spenser Studies* (New York: AMS Press, 1984), 5:231-251.

[43] David Norbrook, *Poetry and Politics in the English Renaissance* (London: Routledge & Kegan Paul, 1984), p. 106.

[44] For a discussion of the influence of Huguenot theories of the subaltern magistrate on Sidney's thought, see William D. Briggs, "Political Ideas in Sidney's *Arcadia*," *Studies in Philology* 28 (1931): 137-161, and my own *Sir Philip Sidney: Rebellion in Arcadia* (New Brunswick, N.J.: Rutgers University Press, 1979), pp. 8-11, 183-186. In *Faire Bitts: Sir Philip Sidney and Renaissance Political Theory* (Pittsburgh: Duquesne University Press, 1984) Martin N. Raitiere attributes the *Vindiciae* to Hubert Languet, Sidney's friend and mentor (pp. 113-141), and he concludes that Sidney repudiates the radicalism of the work (pp. 103-110). For a more comprehensive account of Huguenot theory, see J. W. Allen, *A History of Political Thought in the Sixteenth Century* (1928; London: Methuen, 1957), pp. 302-331, and Walzer, *Revolution of the Saints*, pp. 74-87. The major documents are included in Julian Franklin, ed., *Constitutionalism and Resistance in the Sixteenth Century*.

[45] Sidney, "Correspondence," January 27, 1583, in *Prose Works*, 3:143.

[46] Greville, *Prose Works*, p. 46.

[47] Sidney, "Correspondence," March 24, 1586, in *Prose Works*, 3:166, 167.

[48] Greville, *Prose Works*, p. 72.

[49] Edmund Molyneux, "Memoir," in Holinshed, *Chronicles*, p. 1552. See also John Gouws's commentary on Greville's *Dedication* in Greville, *Prose Works*, pp. 212-213.

[50] Sidney, "Correspondence," February 12, 1586, in *Prose Works*, 3:160.

[51] Ibid., August 14, 1586, 3:179, 180.

[52] Simon Adams, "The Military Campaign of 1586," paper presented at the International Conference on Sir Philip Sidney, Leiden, The Netherlands, September 2-4, 1986. The Netherlands war was, as J. R. Hale says, "largely a war of sieges." See J. R. Hale, *The Art of War and Renaissance England* (Washington, D.C.: Folger Press, 1961), p. 26.

[53] *CSP, Foreign*, Elizabeth (1586-1587), ed. Sophie Crawford Lomas and Allen B. Hinds (London: HMSO, 1927), 21(ii): 165.

[54] *The Correspondence of Sir Philip Sidney and Hubert Languet*, trans. Stuart A. Pears (London, 1845), p. 137.

[55] George Whetstone, *Sir Philip Sidney, his valiant death, and true vertues* (1586), sig. C 1v.

[56] Greville, *Prose Works*, p. 76. Sir John Smythe contends, on the other hand, that Sidney charged without leg armor because he was one of the "new fantasied men of war . . . [who] despise and scorn our ancient arming of ourselves both on horseback and on foot, saying that we armed ourselves in times past with too much armor," in his *Certain Discourses Military*, ed. J. R. Hale (Ithaca: Cornell University Press, 1964), p. 42.

[57] Greville, *Prose Works*, p. 77

[58] Thomas Moffet, *Nobilis or A View of the Life and Death Of a Sidney (and Lessus Lugubris)*, trans. Virgil B. Heltzel and Hoyt H. Hudson (San Marino, Calif: Huntington Library Press, 1940), pp. 90, 93.

[59] Ludovico Ariosto, *Orlando Furioso*, trans. Barbara Reynolds (1975; Harmondsworth, England: Penguin, 1977), pp. 350-351, and Miguel de Cervantes, *Don Quixote*, trans. J. M. Cohen (1950; Harmondsworth, England: Penguin, 1978), p. 344.

[60] Arthur Golding, "Epistle Dedicatorie," in Philippe de Mornay, *A Woorke Concerning the Trewenesse of the Christian Religion* (London, 1587), pp. 3*v, 4*r.

[61] Greville, *Prose Works,* p. 89. Compare Greville's claim that "in the whole course of his life he did so constantly balance ambition with safe precepts of divine and moral duty as no pretence whatsoever could have enticed that gentleman to break through the circle of a good patriot" (p. 75).

[62] John Phillips, *The Life and Death of Sir Philip Sidney* (London, 1587), sig. B 2v.

[63] Yates, *Astraea,* p. 103; Greenblatt, *Renaissance Self-Fashioning,* p. 256.

[64] Peele, *Polyhymnia* (1590), in *Works,* 1:235-236.

[65] Strong, *Cult of Elizabeth,* p. 140.

Arthur F. Kinney (essay date 1990)

SOURCE: "Puritans Versus Royalists: Sir Philip Sidney's Rhetoric at the Court of Elizabeth I," in *Sir Philip Sidney's Achievements*, M. J. B. Allen, Dominic Baker-Smith, Arthur F. Kinney, with Margaret M. Sullivan, AMS Press, 1990, pp. 42-56.

[*In the following excerpt, Kinney discusses Sidney's political statements, both masked and explicit, and his bids for authority in Queen Elizabeth's court.*]

One of the few encounters between Sir Philip Sidney and Elizabeth I that is documented in some detail is his appearance before her at Whitehall in 1581 during the performance of a court spectacle called *The Four Foster Children of Desire*. He is the third foster child to appear, following the earl of Arundel and Lord Windsor and preceding his friend Fulke Greville, and his striking appearance suggests the central role he means to play at court:

> Then proceeded M. Philip Sidney, in very sumptuous maner, with armor part blewe, & the rest gilt & engraven, with foure spare horses, having caparisons and furniture veri riche & costly, as some of cloth of gold embroidred with pearle, and some embrodred with gold and silver feathers, very richly & cunningly wrought, he had foure pages that rode on his four spare horses, who had cassock coats & venetian hose al of cloth of silver, layd with gold lace, & hats of the same with golde bands, and white fethers, and eache one a paire of white buskins. Then had he a thirtie gentlemen & yeomen, & foure trumpetters, who were all in cassocke coats and venetian hose of yellow velvet, laid with silver lace, yellowe velvet caps with silver bands and

white fethers, and every one a paire of white buskins. And they had upon their coates, a scrowle or bande of silver, which came scarfe wise over the shoulder, and so downe under the arme, with this poesie, or sentence written upon it, both before and behind, Sic nos non nobis ["so are we not out own"].[1]

But this is no typical royal entertainment; it is, rather, a highly charged political occasion. The pageant, with its colorful costumes, elaborate mechanisms, and splendid displays, is meant deliberately to resemble, and so to mock, the kind of pageantry associated with the Catholic French court of Catherine de Medici and Henri II. And the plot, such as it is, means to suggest, through the metaphor of the four *foster* children—that is, not English-born children—the blatant, self-aggrandizing desire of the duke of Alençon. This son of Catherine and Henri is even now laying siege to the queen of England, portrayed here as the Fortress of Perfect Beauty. The "message" of the two-day tournament, according to its modern editor Jean Wilson, "is clear. The Four Foster Children realize that they have overreached themselves, that Perfect Beauty is unattainable, that Desire by its nature cannot have what it desires, and, yielding to the queen, withdraw from the contest. The significance of this would not be lost on the French audience" then visiting the queen at Whitehall.[2] But we should add that the queen herself would not miss the significance of the fact that the whole entertainment was modeled after an Accession Day Tilt. And the fundamental message that it encodes is that the forces embodied in the "foster children," in those state visitors from France who have come to press for Elizabeth's hand in marriage to Alençon, will, if successful, undermine such celebrations as are held on Accession Day—celebrations that mark the majesty, and legitimacy, of Elizabeth I.

By 1581, even without the aid of rhetoric—for this show had what the Tudors called a "plot," but not a script—Sidney was using an art form to make a political statement on behalf of the Puritan faction of Elizabeth I's Privy Council. For those of us considerably removed in time from the court factions at Whitehall this statement may, at first, be lost. But it was surely a strong one at the time, when the knights in the play, dressed as the French courtiers who were also present, made their charges on the queen. And its political content is perfectly in keeping with the rest of Sidney's writings up to that time. According to Katherine Duncan-Jones, "Sidney's first literary work," *The Lady of May*—another royal performance, the masque having been acted before the queen at Wanstead in 1578 or 1579—is also an encoded statement. While the debate between the shepherd Espilus, representing the country life, and the forester Therion, representing the active and ambitious life, putatively involves their suing for the hand of a young woman, what it really represents are Sidney's two means of suing for the queen's favor. And when the queen is asked to choose one of the suitors at the end of the masque, she is in fact completing a tacit negotiation with Sidney, which the conditions of the performance make it impossible for her to avoid.[4]

At the same time that Sidney was writing the occasional and particular *Lady of May*, he was also writing his more theoretical *Defence of Poetry*.[5] It begins with a delightful anecdote mocking Stephen Gosson who, in his *Schoole of Abuse* (1579), had said that good horsemen were truly loyal subjects. So Sidney opens by recalling a teacher of good horsemanship with whom he had studied in Italy, John Pietro Pugliano. Sidney tells us Pietro had argued that

> no earthly thing bred such wonder to a prince as to be a good horseman—skill of government was but a *pedanteria* in comparison. Then would he add certain praises, by telling what a peerless beast the horse was, the only serviceable courtier without flattery, the beast of most beauty, faithfulness, courage, and such more, that if I had not been a piece of a logician before I came to him, I think he would have persuaded me to have wished myself a horse.[6]

It is a courtly flourish, this joke, but it also has its serious side. Courtiers are dismissed as flatterers, but the attributes Pugliano denied them, in comparison to the horse—service, beauty, faith, and courage—are just the attributes that will later in the *Defence* be awarded to the poet: he who practices what Sidney himself calls, modestly and misleadingly, "my unelected vocation."[7] He then proceeds to note that the true poet is not merely a maker, as the Greeks have it, but also a seer, as the Romans have it, "a diviner . . . or prophet, as by his conjoined words *vaticinium* and *vaticinari* is manifest: so heavenly a title did that excellent people bestow upon this heart-ravishing knowledge" (p. 76). The Elizabethan poet, like the biblical poet David, can thus invent *prosopopoeias,* fictions that envision holy truths, so that those readers "that with quiet judgements will look a little deeper, . . . shall find the end and working of it such as, being rightly applied, deserveth not to be scourged out of the Church of God" (p. 77). If we read the *Defence* closely, we find that it is a political document as well as a poetics; it is designed to enable the poet, to give him an unassailable position of power and authority. By teaching virtuous knowledge in the strongest and most permanent way, by encouraging readers to exercise virtue so as to know it—for that, Sidney says, is the true end of poetry—the poet becomes the moral leader, even the moral arbiter, of all men and women. On the one hand Sidney, as a poet, enfranchises himself by giving the "right poet" a central political role and access to rulers; on the other hand, the poet gains

this authority on the grounds and by the means of a morality that forwards the claims of the Puritan faction at court.

Royalist rhetoric and Puritan rhetoric are thus made indivisible. They supply, in their beauty and their faith, and through Sidney's own courageous use of them, the kind of courtly service without flattery that he set out to praise, *pace* Pugliano, in the exordium. Lest we forget either this potentially enormous power or Sidney's skill as a courtly rhetorician, he reminds us of both in closing:

> I conjure you all that have had the evil luck to read this ink-wasting toy of mine, even in the name of the nine Muses, no more to scorn the sacred mysteries of poesy; no more to laugh at the name of poets, as though they were the next inheritors to fools; no more to jest at the reverent title of a rhymer; but to believe, with Aristotle, that they were the ancient treasurers of the Grecians' divinity; to believe, with Bembus, that they were the first bringers-in of all civility; to believe, with Scaliger, that no philosopher's precepts can sooner make you an honest man than the reading of Virgil; to believe, with Clauserus, the translator of Cornutus, that it pleased the heavenly Deity, by Hesiod and Homer, under the veil of fables, to give us all knowledge, logic, rhetoric, philosophy natural and moral, and *quid non?;* to believe, with me, that there are many mysteries contained in poetry, which of purpose were written darkly, lest by profane wits it should be abused; to believe, with Landino, that they are so beloved of the gods that whatsoever they write proceeds of a divine fury; lastly, to believe themselves, when they tell you they will make you immortal by their verses. (pp. 121-22)

What a bold bid for authority this is: it does no less than threaten the queen with being forgotten, and robbing herself of immortality, if she does not take care to insure her memory with the aid of a poet—a poet like Sidney who, unwinding these allusions, suggests with the subtlety of a courtly poet that *he* can be the Vergil to her Augustus! It is all performed, of course, under the poetic fancy of conjuring, and the "conjurors" Sidney names are the authorities for the very civilization that Elizabeth I was fostering.

We must again see a double edge in the very last sentence of the *Defence*, which poses, wittily and seriously, as a "curse": "thus much curse I must send you, in the behalf of all poets, that while you live, you live in love, and never get favour for lacking skill of a sonnet; and, when you die, your memory die from the earth for want of an epitaph" (p. 121). "Thus much curse I must send you," he writes, not as a wicked man, but rather "in the behalf of all poets": "that while you live, you live in love"—pointing to the queen's own chief metaphor for her relationship to her people—"and never get favour for lacking skill of a sonnet"—such as those that Sidney himself had been writing, in *Astrophil and Stella*. And these sonnets, widely circulated about Elizabeth's court, mocked the rhetoric of courtly love that was used in political negotiations with the queen by showing how it represented a relationship both artificial and self-defeating. No ruler—indeed, no privy councillor—could mistake the latent meaning of Sidney's "curse," especially taking it in conjunction with the courtly criticism of the equally encoded *Astrophil and Stella*.

But at the same time that Sidney was participating in the production of such encoded statements, enfranchising both his own authority and Puritan morality under the guise of elegance, learning, and wit, he was also making explicit political statements. According to Katherine Duncan-Jones and the late Jan van Dorsten, coeditors of Sidney's *Miscellaneous Prose*, the composition of the *Defence of Poetry* (ca. winter 1579-80, pp. 62-63) was bracketed between *A Letter to Queen Elizabeth* (ca. November or December 1579, p. 34) and that of the *Defence of Leicester* ("probably written some time before the summer of 1585," p. 124). The earl in question was Robert Dudley, who as Elizabeth's favorite was the most powerful single figure on her Privy Council, as well as one of the uncles to whom Sidney was heir.

The first of these writings, *A Letter Written by Sir Philip Sidney to Queen Elizabeth, Touching Her Marriage with Monsieur*, starts with the customary compliment, but even in the first sentence begins to turn toward giving the *writer* authority, largely through the meaning both on the surface of, and concealed within, the rhetoric: "Most feared and beloved, most sweet and gracious Sovereign: to seek out excuses of this my boldness, and to arm the acknowledging of a fault with the reasons for it, might better show I knew I did amiss, than any whit diminish the attempt; especially in your judgement, who is able lively to discern into the nature of the thing done" (p. 46). But the letter, which follows closely the arguments then being made by another privy councillor, Sir Francis Walsingham, who was with Leicester a coleader of the Puritan faction (and later Sidney's father-in-law), becomes even more blunt in urging the Puritan opposition to the queen's proposed marriage with Aleçon. Sidney goes on to suggest that the match threatens the health of both Elizabeth's body and the body politic: "Hazardous indeed, were it for nothing but the altering of a well maintained and well approved trade. For as in bodies natural any sudden change is not without peril, so in this body politic, whereof you are the only head, it is so much the more, as there are more humours to receive a hurtful impression" (p. 47). Not only does the queen have no need of a husband for, married to England, all of its people are her children,

but she also risks losing the love of those children—and perhaps England as well—should she choose to go through with this proposed marriage to a member of the tyrannical (and Catholic) French royal family. On the topic of the ostensible reason for the match, Elizabeth's desire to produce a child to inherit the English throne, Sidney is pragmatically, even bluntly, honest: "Virtue and justice are the only bands of the people's love. And as for that point, many princes have lost their crowns, whose own children were manifest successors; and some that had their own children used as instruments of their ruin. Not that I deny the bliss of children, but only mean to show religion and equity to be of themselves sufficient stays" (p. 54). Religion and equity as the chief values, by which Sidney clearly means the Puritanism for which he, Walsingham, and Leicester all stood, is the subject he returns to in the letter's strong and memorable conclusion:

> I do with most humble heart say unto your Majesty that, laying aside this dangerous help, for your standing alone, you must take it as a singular honour God hath done unto you, to be indeed the only protector of his church. And yet in worldly respects your kingdom is very sufficient so to do, if you make that religion upon which you stand to carry the only strength, and have abroad those who still maintain the same cause: who as long as they may be kept from utter falling, your Majesty is sure enough from your mightiest enemies. (p. 56)

Even in the more plainspoken defense of his uncle, the earl of Leicester, apparently written for publication (editor's introduction, p. 124), Sidney has at times the rhetorical wit and flourish of the courtier. He has been tracing, in an age enamored of genealogies and in reply to an attack on Leicester's (and therefore Sidney's own) background and breeding, the Dudley genealogy in some detail, when he pauses to comment on other great men who have been subjected to scandalmongers like his opponent:

> A railing writer extant against Octavius Augustus saith his grandfather was a silversmith; another Italian, against Hugh Capet, though with most absurd falsehood, saith his father was a butcher. Of divers of the best houses of England there have been such foolish dreams, that one was a farrier's son, another a shoemaker's, another a milliner's, another a fiddler's: foolish lies, and by any that ever tasted any antiquities, known to be so. Yet those houses had luck to meet with honester railers, for they were not left fatherless clean; they descended from somebody; but we, as if we were Deucalion's brood new made out of stones, have left us no ancestors from whence we are come. (p. 138)

Despite his humor, Sidney saw the attack on Dudley, widely printed and circulated, as his contemporaries did: as a defamation "full of the most vile reproaches which a wit used to wicked and filthy thoughts can imagine" (p. 129); and he answers in kind. It is noteworthy that he once more uses, in defense of his uncle, the cause of right religion: the true Protestant religion for which Leicester has stood champion against incursions such as this one, written, Sidney suggests, by an anonymous recusant impostor. "And which is more base," he says, angrily and directly,

> (if anything can be more base than a defamatory libeller) he counterfeits himself in all the treatise a Protestant, when any man which with half an eye may easily see he is of the other party; which filthy dissimulation if few honest men of that religion will use to the helping of themselves, of how many carats of honesty is this man, that useth it, as much as his poor power can, to the harm of another? . . . evident enough it is to any man that reads it what poison he means to her Majesty, in how golden a cup soever he dress it. (p. 130)

The abuse of true religion leads to the abuse of language and the abuse of politics. The three are, for Sidney, indivisible. Religion and equity lead to good government, to wise behavior, and to right poetry. This poetry his progenitor, the psalmist David, set as a model, so that Sidney, among others, could realize their proper conjunction in his own day: at Wilton, at White-hall, even in distant Zutphen and Arnhem.

In thus openly defending Leicester, Sidney was also openly aligning himself with the increasingly radical and aggressive Puritan faction, which had members both at Elizabeth's court and on her Privy Council. We must not forget that even if the queen showed an ascertainable fondness for Leicester, she did not extend the same affection to other Puritans. And Leicester, according to Lawrence Stone,

> has been described as "the keystone of the whole edifice of Elizabethan Puritanism." As the leader of the moderate Puritan group in the Privy Council, he could block moves to persecute his protégés, and could get them out of prison; he could see that their books passed the censor, and as Chancellor of the University he could find them jobs at Oxford. In 1564 he is said to have stopped the Privy Council from authorizing Parker's Advertisements. He was the patron not only of Field and Cartwright, but also of scholars and educators like Laurence Humphrey, the Puritan President of Magdalen College at Oxford, and William Fulke, the Puritan Master of Pembroke Hall at Cambridge.[8]

Leicester was also the primary patron of Rowland Hall, printer of the Geneva Bible; and it was no accident that Arthur Golding dedicated to Leicester his translations of Calvin and Mornay. Wallace T. Mac-

Caffrey adds that "from 1572 onwards Leicester became increasingly drawn away from domestic Protestantism to the larger international concerns of the reformed religion. More and more he was consumed by the ambition to play a grand role on this international stage. Most immediately he pressed Elizabeth to intervene in the Low Countries."[9] Walsingham too, since his days as a Marian exile in Geneva, had been an exceptionally strong advocate of international Puritan activities.

Catholic aggression remained, for Puritan leaders, a near and present danger. The repression of the new religion by the old, beginning with the St. Bartholomew's Day Massacre (1572), which Sidney witnessed (James M. Osborn suggests Sidney may even have been forced to make the rounds, inspecting the Huguenot dead, with the duke of Nevers),[10] must have looked very much like the kind of tyranny practiced by evil leaders that Sidney would record in his grandest political poem, the *Arcadia*. Tyranny had been a subject for Sidney ever since he took up the study of Aristotle's *Politics* while at Christ Church, Oxford. Jan van Dorsten, to give one example of Sidney's continuing interest in the subject, notes "a slightly erratic quotation" concerning tyranny, from Seneca's *Oedipus,* that appears in both the *Defence* and *Certain Sonnets*. He adds that this "powerful summary of tyranny's self-destructiveness appears to have been very much in Sidney's mind—presumably in the months when he was doomed to be 'idly' looking on 'our Neighbours' fires,' discussing poetry and politics and writing the *Arcadia*" (introduction to *Defence*, p. 60). And he had much to think about, much of it in his own country. The queen had mounted a serious campaign against Puritans, following the *Admonition to Parliament* in 1570; by 1573 she had passed a royal proclamation ordering the suppression of all "contentious sects and disquietness," and then appointed "special commissions to ensure compliance."[11] In the meantime, William Cecil, the principal secretary, began his own campaign against the Catholics, with such pamphlets as *The English Roman Life* (1580), *The Execution of Justice* (1581), and the *Declaration of the Favourable Dealing* (1584). As for Parliament, in 1581 it passed two severe acts: making persons found teaching the Roman Supremacy guilty of treason, for which the penalty was death, and persons aiding them guilty of misprision, or concealing the knowledge of treason. In 1583 Whitgift, a known anti-Puritan newly appointed to the see of Canterbury, issued a set of articles enforcing laws on recusancy, forbidding authorized preaching by laymen, and—here was the catchCrefusing ordination to anyone without title of benefice. By 1586 even the Star Chamber was at work, tightening the control of all printing presses. And Jesuits were relentlessly hunted down, as in the wellknown case of Edmund Campion.

Such increasing restriction on the part of the Tudor monarchy must have reminded Sidney of the tyranny he had witnessed, at the age of eighteen, while on his Grand Tour: most probably, the religious tyranny in France under the Guises. And the danger of these restrictions must have been given added force by Sidney's awareness of Leicester's increasing anxiety regarding the Spanish threat to the cherished liberty of Protestants in the Low Countries. Everywhere, consciences seemed to be bent or threatened by the political wills of rulers. As a direct consequence, the revised *Arcadia*, surely begun by 1584, examines in detail many forms of moral and physical repression: in the acts of Erona, Andromana, and Artaxia (all, like Elizabeth, women), as well as in those of male characters like Plexirtus, or Anaxius and his brothers, Zoilus and Lycurgus. Sidney seems desirous, too, of showing how characters who are potentially more sympathetic—such as Gynecia, who falls passionately in love, or Cecropia, who feels betrayed by her brother-in-law Basilius and is protective of her son Amphialus—can easily fall into evil thoughts and actions in a world in which the tyranny of the passions seems much more human than impersonal political tyranny. But tyranny is not only ugly, it is contagious. We can measure with some accuracy Sidney's concern for and despair over tyranny when, even in the original *Arcadia*, through the patently transparent character of Philisides, he tells the story of mankind as an allegory about the origins of tyranny. In a study centered on this allegorical poem, Martin N. Raitiere, citing the Geneva version of 1 Sam. 8:11-18, relates Sidney's fable to God's warning to an apostate Israel:

> This shall be the maner of the king that shall reigne over you: he will take your sonnes, and appoint them to his charets, and to be his horsemen. . . . He will also take your daughters. . . . And he will take your fields, and your vineyards, and your best olive trees . . . the chief of your yong men, and your asses, and put them to his work. He will take the tenth of your sheep, and ye shall be his servants. And ye shall cry out at that day, because of your king, whome ye have chosen you, and the Lord will not heare you at that day.[12]

Calvin made much of this text in his gloss to the Geneva Bible, used throughout England by the Puritans. Sidney, in addition to this Calvinist concern with man's original apostasy, discusses two more forms of it: abandonment of responsibility, in his discussion of Basilius's surrender of the throne in book 1 of the *Old Arcadia*, and, later, mob rule, in Zelmane's address to the rebellious mob in the revised *Arcadia* (2.25). But it is tyranny on which Sidney centers his narrative. And he ends it with an exploration of the subtlest, and so the most attractive and dangerous, form of all: Euarchus's absolute application of Arcadian law in the great trial scene of book 5.

It is, in fact, in this matter of law that Sidney's firm advocacy of liberty and Puritanism comes through most strongly, for here he realized the joint concerns of religion and equity most completely and profoundly. We have paid too little attention to the fact that the *Arcadia* was written during a period of strong conflicts in England: not only between Catholics and Protestants, but also between courts of chancery and courts of common law, as they vied for judicial supremacy. Chancery, on occasion, even overturned judgments by courts of common law, albeit illegally; and such reversals were becoming more and more frequent in Sidney's day. From what must have seemed like time immemorial, common law had upheld the monarchy. It rested on two key principles: strict adherence to precedent and the uniform enforcement of the letter of the law. Over centuries, unyielding reliance on precedent gave to common law a stability that guaranteed consistent enactment of institutional and monarchical policies, for judges feared that any exception or deviation would result either in contradiction or in an ambiguity that would undermine the very validity of the law. Regardless of circumstances, judges applied—imposed might be a better word—a law with equal definition and force. As Sir William Holdsworth has it: "Narrow-minded judges, quibbling and overapprehensive, gradually surrounded each action with a mass of requirements of form. Each common law action had its own precedents, and the judges refused to admit a case was good in law if it did not rigorously meet the construction of the writ and the conditions laid down by precedent."[13] In sharp contrast, chancery supported the individual application of the law and the individual determination of justice by closely examining surrounding, even mitigating, circumstances. It invoked a new legal term—equity—which caused the strictness of traditional justice to be tempered by mercy. In fact, according to William Harrison in his *Description of England* (1587), the Court of Chancery came to be popularly called the "Court of Conscience."[14] The term was not unapt: the Court of Chancery, unlike courts of common law, had decidedly Christian roots, going back to the ecclesiastical appointments to the lord chancellorship first made by Henry III in the thirteenth century. The custom was interrupted in 1532 when Wolsey, as archbishop, appointed the secular statesman Thomas More to the position; but the ecclesiastical tradition was so strong that it continued to operate well into Sidney's day and beyond, into that of the longer-lived Francis Bacon. Chancery's jurisdiction, in fact, was at first little more than the power to intervene in cases of royal interest, when the harshness of the law necessitated the employment of equity to favor the crown; but over the centuries, chancery came to be thought of—however accurately—as an arm of justice affiliated with the church. By the time of the *Arcadia* chancery had become, by natural extension, the means by which Puritans insisted on individual legal justice compatible with and congruent to the individual consciences that they, but not the Catholics, proclaimed to be the foundation of religion.

The natural and progressively active collusion between chancery and Puritanism that I have been suggesting is anticipated very early indeed in a humanist dialogue, Christopher St. German's *Doctor and Student* (1523, 1530). In part an apology for English law, it was printed, partly in Latin and partly in English, "for the profyte of the multytude."[15] St. German introduced the word "conscience" into the English legal vocabulary, as that divine spark "in the midst of every reasonable soul, as a light whereby he may discern and know what he ought to do, and what he ought not to do."[16] The conscience, as popularly defined, was thus a kind of shorthand for equity itself, as is clear in the following definition from St. German:

> Equytye is a [ryghtwysenes] that consideryth all the pertyculer cyrcumstaunces of the dede the whiche also is temperyd with the swetnes of mercye.... And the wyse man sayth: be not ouer moch ryghtwyse for the extreme ryghtwysenes is extreme wronge (as who sayth yf thou take all that the wordes of the law gyueth the thou shalte somtyme do agaynst the lawe).[17]

In time, St. German's treatise was supplanted by *The Commentaries, or Reports of Edmund Plowden* (1571 et seq.), and a work subsequently written by Edward Hake, *EPIEIKEIA: A Dialogue on Equity in Three Parts,* which states that "in the said highe Courte the decrees . . . sholde be deryued upon Conscience, even the conscience of the judge there, directed with all good circumstances of facts, which shoulde be ever-more accompanied with comiseration and pitye."[18] Hake further notes, in the same preface "To the Reader," that "No more can the wordes of the lawe without *Equity* to dyrecte yt to the righte sense thereof be said to be the lawe then the bodye of a man withoute reason to directe yt in the actions of a man maye be said to be a man."[19] In this way, equity *fulfilled* the body and practice of common law and was made analogous to Calvin's notion that the New Testament fulfilled the meaning and prophecies of the Old (*Institutes,* 4.8.7). So popular, as an analogy to the concept of Christian mercy, did the legal notion of equity become—it is almost a commonplace by the time of Spenser's Mercilla and Shakespeare's Portia—that as the case loads in chancery increased to staggering numbers (by the time of Sir Francis Bacon, sixteen thousand cases were pending at one time), the Court of Requests also began to take up cases alleged to involve equity.

Through Elizabethan law and the various Tudor courts, then, English leaders of the Protestant cause—men like Leicester, Walsingham, and Sidney himself—founded a hierarchy of conscience. In fact, this hierarchy

directly challenged the traditional one that, through concepts like the absolute law of the monarchy, gave Elizabeth I her authority. This potential conflict, this contest between the equity of chancery and the precedents of common law, is the constant (and efficient) cause of the *Arcadia.* There Euarchus attempts to harmonize wise thought and just action through his enforcement of common law—an enforcement of both the precedents and the strict rules that were based on them—in Arcadia. But such judgment misses the mark because Euarchus takes apparent truths, such as the death of Basilius and the guilt of Pyrocles and Musidorus, as facts. Thus, in actuality he is neither wise nor just. When he is confronted with mitigating circumstances, like his blood relationship to the two young men, he is able to draw on neither the pliability characteristic of Basilius, which would allow for a change of heart and mind, nor the rigid stability of Philanax, which, by the time of the trial, has already grown tyrannical in tone and untruthful in statement. Sidney has set up the terms of his fiction, then, so that they coincide precisely with issues raised in the debate between the relative merits of common law and chancery. The equity that chancery advocated, which Euarchus will not hear of, supports the claims of Pyrocles, Musidorus, Pamela, Philoclea, and—though she refuses to make any—Gynecia. It also accommodates all of the facts—not simply the apparent facts—of *Arcadia*'s book 5. Equity admits flexibility and change, but it does not deny justice and stability. Equity also was, after all, what the Netherlands seemed to be struggling for; what Sidney's uncle, Leicester, would advocate; what his father, Sir Henry Sidney, argued for as the best means of establishing plantations in Ireland; and what Sidney's own youthful talent for negotiation and diplomacy, as honed during his Grand Tour, seemed to make him eminently qualified to practice.

Indeed, Sidney seems to have spent enormous time and energy rewriting, revising, and re-seeing the *Arcadia* because he perceived undeveloped potential in the materials of the fifth book of the *Old Arcadia.* We have testimony that this change of intention was substantial and important. After Sidney's unexpected death at Arnhem in 1586, Greville sent forth what Victor Skretkowicz calls "an urgent plea to Walsingham [as Sidney's executor] to prevent publication of the romantic though well polished 'old' *Arcadia* and to substitute for it 'a correction of that old one don 4 or 5 years since wch he left in trust wth me wherof ther is no more copies, & fitter to be printed then the first wch is so comon.'"[20] Sidney's sister Mary, Countess of Pembroke, agreed to publish the revised version and, as far as we can tell, destroyed what copies she could of the original. What she published, with great but justifiable pride, was the "new" *Arcadia,* which is in many decisive ways a very different work from the "old." The revisions Sidney made do not talk about "uncertainty," to which no man can respond adequately, as the first *Arcadia* did, but about "disfigurement," to which a man *can* respond. "Disfigured minds" follow from "disfigured" bodies and their perspectives. From the modified ideal of Kalander's home (doubtless based on Penshurst, which links Sir Henry Sidney with Kalander rather than with Euarchus, as was once thought) to the war with the Helots and the long "captivity episode" in book 3, the "new" *Arcadia* traces the motives and actions of men and women who are thwarted in their plans or desires. Some of them, in turn, thwart the plans and desires of others, while the worst among them set out to rid the world of opposition with vengeance.

Even the "disfigurement" of the heroes, who are posing as a shepherd and an Amazon, is no longer simply a condition of the plot but now also a consequence of their short-sightedness. They betray their stations and themselves to achieve their desires yet, by the time we get to book 5, it is clear that their actual stations and selves would have more than brought them what they sought had they been patient. But the outer "disfigurement" of a Musidorus or Pyrocles and the temporarily misplaced passions of a Gynecia or Mopsa show the fallibility and foolishness of a "tyrannical" lack of restraint, rather than the criminal intentions or evil instincts of the true tyrant. They are curable: obviously so, compared to the parade of tyrants in the revised book 2, or even to the unscrupulous behavior of Cecropia and Amphialus in the revised book 3. Nancy Lindheim sees Sidney's revisions not simply as an amplification, but as a rethinking, what she also calls a "re-vision," or "something substantially new."[21] In the "new" *Arcadia* the Phrygian citizens, supported by Musidorus, revolt against "chiefe instruments of Tyrannie" (2.9), and the prince himself demonstrates what Richard C. McCoy calls "sophisticated political insights and principles."[22] In other episodes added to book 2, the blind king of Paphlagonia, also symbolically disfigured, misjudges his two sons; Plangus misjudges Erona; and Pyrocles misjudges Dido. In book 3, Cecropia misjudges Amphialus, while the "Knight of the Tomb," the "disfigured" Parthenia, is recognized by no one until her death. But all of these "uncertainties" also involve some sort of tyranny, some deeply felt need for equity. Alongside such "uncertainties," which persisted unchecked in the "old" *Arcadia*, Sidney's revision places the trust of the heroes and the faith of Pamela: things that, if not strictly speaking "certain," suggest something more stable than "uncertainties." These new qualities look forward to a denouement already conceived as the fifth book of the "old" *Arcadia*.

There are other additions too: Pamela's theology is now decidedly Calvinistic; Philoclea's character is changed, to increase the emphasis on the importance of self-knowledge. Even Basilius's emotional and un-restrained decision to besiege the castle of Amphialus—despite Kalander's counseling withdrawal while Philanax argues that the king should, in politic fashion, seem ready to serve Amphialus by offering him a pardon—suggests a kind of humanity that might have instructed Euarchus, if he only could have known of it. Basilius's decision, it will be remembered, is quickly revoked when Cecropia threatens to harm Zelmane and the princesses: Basilius acts out of love, rather than law, and the reader can sympathize with his feelings even knowing that Cecropia intends to kill one of the princesses despite their father's capitulation. Human feelings, or "passions," are just what Euarchus lacks, as Sidney tells us: "The beholders . . . most of them, examining the matter by their own passions, thought Euarchus (as often extraordinary excellencies, not being rightly conceived, do rather offend than please) an obstinate-hearted man, and such a one, who being pitiless, his dominion must needs be insupportable" (p. 414). Such a position opposes the one that Zelmane sets forth in advising the rebels, and that Pamela uses in confronting Cecropia, in the revised text of the *Arcadia*. Thus, the resolution of the *Arcadia*, as worked out in the original book 5, is reinforced by and anticipated in the revisions of the earlier books. The old book 5 still fits in with the revisions, if a bit disjointedly; Sidney did not feel constrained to complete the revision because, in a very real sense, he already had.

But what he had also done, of course, was to show by example—by the pregnant images of life, as Greville puts it—how the virtuous knowledge taught by the *Arcadia* might lead directly to a virtuous exercise of that knowledge: As the *Arcadia* realizes in practice the theory of Sidney's *Defence of Poetry*, as chancery realizes in its use of equity the deep structures and original purposes of common law, so Sidney seems to have felt compelled to practice both the precepts of virtuous knowledge and the principle of equity in his own life. He did so for the sake of the Protestant cause, by following Leicester to the Low Countries to champion the Puritans against the invasion of the Catholic Spaniards. But by then his writing, thinking, actions, and politics had become a thing so compact that to mention one of them seems to be to mention them all. The steadiness of his spirit, when defending the Dutch he so admired, seems never to have flagged, not even during the black days of March 1586, when he wrote to Walsingham from Flanders,

> I receav dyvers letters from yow, full of the discomfort which I see and am sorry to see that yow daily meet with at home, and I think such is the goodwil it pleaseth yow to bear me that my part of the trouble is somthing that troubles yow, but I beseech yow le[t] it not. I had before cast my count of dang[er] want and disgrace, and before God Sir it is trew [that] in my hart the love of the caws doth so far overballance them all that

with Gods grace thei shall never make me weery of my resolution. If her Majesty wear the fowntain I woold fear considering what I daily fynd that we shold wax dry, but she is but a means whom God useth and I know not whether I am deceaved but I am faithfully persuaded that if she shold withdraw her self other springes woold ryse to help this action.[23]

His last recorded words too, after the wound at Zutphen took a turn for the worse at Arnhem, bring together naturally and succinctly all his concerns—politics, religion, mercy or equity, and poetry: "Love my memory, cherish my friends; their faith to me may assure you that they are honest. But above all govern your will and affections by the will and word of your Creator."[24] This sentiment recalls old Languet, the shepherd of the first *Arcadia* who taught that the true harmony of spirit is "To have a feeling taste of him that sits / Beyond the heav'n, far more beyond our wits" (*OA*, p. 255). Poetry and politics, burned to a luster in the alchemy of a faith that transcended courtly rhetoric and even his death, became, perhaps, Sidney's greatest legacy.

Notes

[1] *The Four Foster Children of Desire: 1581,* ed. Jean Wilson in *Entertainments for Elizabeth I* (Woodbridge, Eng., 1980), 70.

[2] Ibid., 61.

[3] Introduction to *The Lady of May* in *Miscellaneous Prose of Sir Philip Sidney,* ed. Katherine Duncan-Jones and Jan van Dorsten (Oxford, 1973), 17.

[4] The definitive discussion of the political implications of *The Lady of May* is in Stephen Orgel's *The Jonsonian Masque* (Cambridge, Mass., 1965), 44-57.

[5] For an argument that supports dating the *Defence* as early as late autumn or early winter 1579/80, see my "Parody and Its Implications in Sidney's *Defence of Poesie,*" *Studies in English Literature* 12 (1972): 1-19.

[6] *A Defence of Poetry,* in *Miscellaneous Prose,* 73. All further references to Sidney's prose works, cited parenthetically by page number in the text, are to this edition, except the following: for the "old" *Arcadia,* references are to *The Countess of Pembroke's Arcadia (The Old Arcadia),* ed. Jean Robertson (Oxford, 1973); for the "new" or revised *Arcadia,* references are to *The Countess of Pembroke's Arcadia,* ed. Maurice Evans (Harmondsworth, Eng., 1977); for Sidney's letters, see n. 23 below.

[7] The context of Sidney's remark is worth quoting in full:

If Pugliano's strong affection and weak arguments [about horsemanship] will not satisfy you, I will give you a nearer example of myself, who (I know not by what mischance) in these my not old years and idlest times having slipped into the title of a poet, am provoked to say something unto you in the defence of that my unelected vocation, which if I handle with more good will than good reasons, bear with me, since the scholar is to be pardoned that followeth the steps of his master. (*Miscellaneous Prose,* 73)

[8] Lawrence Stone, *The Crisis of the Aristocracy, 1558-1641,* abridged ed. (New York, 1967), 340-41.

[9] Wallace T. MacCaffrey, *Queen Elizabeth and the Making of Policy, 1572-1588* (Princeton, 1981), 440.

[10] James M. Osborn, *Young Philip Sidney, 1572-1577* (New Haven, 1972), 70.

[11] D. M. Loades, *Politics and the Nation, 1450-1600: Obedience, Resistance and Public Order* (1974; repr. London, 1979), 292.

[12] Martin N. Raitiere, *Faire Bitts: Sir Philip Sidney and Renaissance Political Theory* (Pittsburgh, 1984), 74.

[13] Sir William Holdsworth, *A History of English Law* (Boston, 1922), 2:326.

[14] William Harrison, *Description of England,* ed. Georges Edelen (Ithaca, N.Y., 1968), 70.

[15] Christopher St. German, *Doctor and Student,* ed. T. F. T. Plucknett and J. L. Barton, Selden Society (London, 1974), 177.

[16] Quoted in Stuart E. Prall, "The Development of Equity in Tudor England," *American Journal of Legal History* 8 (1964): 4.

[17] St. German, *Doctor and Student,* 95-97.

[18] Edward Hake, *EPIEIKEIA: A Dialogue on Equity in Three Parts,* ed. D. E. C. Yale, Yale Law Library Publication 13 (New Haven, 1953), 2.

[19] Hake, *EPIEIKEIA,* 12.

[20] Victor Skretkowicz, "Building Sidney's Reputation: Texts and Editors of the *Arcadia,*" in *Sir Philip Sidney: 1586 and the Creation of a Legend,* ed. Jan van Dorsten, Dominic Baker-Smith, and Arthur F. Kinney (Leiden, 1986), 116.

[21] Nancy Lindheim, *The Structures of Sidney's "Arcadia"* (Toronto, 1982), 133.

[22] Richard C. McCoy, *Sir Philip Sidney: Rebellion in Arcadia* (New Brunswick, N.J., 1979), 140.

[23] Letter 89 in *The Prose Works of Sir Philip Sidney,* ed. Albert Feuillerat (1912; repr. Cambridge, 1963), 3:166.

[24] Quoted in Malcolm W. Wallace, *The Life of Sir Philip Sidney* (Cambridge, 1915), 388.

Alan Hager (essay date 1991)

SOURCE: "Sidney's Official Indirection," in *Dazzling Images: The Masks of Sir Philip Sidney*, Associated University Presses, 1991, pp. 41-6.

[*In the following excerpt, Hager considers Sidney's choice of words in his famous letter to the Queen, and contends that the advice may not have met with her disapproval.*]

. . . Advice to the Queen (1579)

In Sidney's most serious political moment, when his uncle, Robert Dudley, the Earl of Leicester, apparently had him write a public letter to pressure the queen to terminate negotiations for marriage with the Duc d'Alençon—**"A Letter to Queen Elizabeth Touching Her Marriage With Monsieur"**—Sidney's witty and courtly—though pedantic—persona sets up distinctions and then undercuts them, most noticeably in his description of the French duke's personality. For example, his smooth "voice" juxtaposes d'Alençon's imagination as well as his personal education as prods to incite aspiration to power, but then undercuts the whole concept of such a desire: "he, both by his own fancy and by his youthful governors embracing all ambitious hopes, having Alexander's image in his head, but perchance ill painted" (52.19). In miniature this ironic procedure is a kind of rug-pulling. The reader is made to expect, by a courtly voice controlling rather majestic language, an observation about those hopes and the antithetical function of inherent imaginings as opposed to princely training—the reader is enticed onto the rug by splendid words—but then his expectations are overturned by an ironic aside about blurred portraits of Alexander and intellectual dullness.

A similar ironic undercutting, containing a reference to Ajax's huge shield in Homer, appears at the end of the letter: "And if he grow king, his defence will be like Ajax' shield, which weighed down rather than defended those that bore it" (56.30). Here the notion of unwieldy and unbearable weight undercuts the notion of kingship and lively national defense. Thus, although the work as a whole remains politely indirect about supposed flaws in the character, health, and person of d'Alençon, verbal irony delivered by

our letterwriting persona pictures Monsieur as an ambitious lightweight.

Sidney balances his ironic attacks on Elizabeth's suitor with equally subtle hyperbolic images of the queen as a virtually unapproachable object of erotic worship. Undoubtedly a frank letter by contemporary standards, Sidney's letter to the queen resembles more a poem of warning and eulogy, like Spenser's "April" or "November" in *The Shepheardes Calender* or Ralegh's *The Ocean to Cynthia,* because, while it is apparently candid and even intimate, it conveys its message poetically by means of indirection, by metaphor and complex words. If Sidney had tended to fashion a debile picture of d'Alençon by means of understatement, he opposed it to an idolatrous picture of the queen. Thus, in the words of his courtly persona, the proposed match could only have appeared faintly absurd.

The number of manuscript versions of Sidney's letter, one showing up in a seventeenth-century commonplace book under the category of "Advice,"[41] attests, I think, to attention given to the form as well as to the content of the work. Besides taking a negative stance in a real or imagined marriage crisis and a positive one on the queen's rule, the letter becomes a model of tactful indirection. Lack of tact was to cost John Stubbs his right hand in the controversy following his *The Discovery of Gaping Gap* (1579) on the unsuitability of the French king's brother. That so many versions of Sidney's work exist may even indicate the queen's approval of its circulation. Elizabeth was wise to recognize two opposing views of every major administrative problemCsuch as the disposition of Mary, Queen of Scots, or the founding of a Protestant League, or her marriageCin order to appear to be choosing among pieces of advice rather than generating public policy on her own. If some policy failed she could shift some of its blame from her by favoring its opponents. In this case, she received a letter from Sir Thomas Cecil favoring and one from Sidney opposing the match, and neither writer seems to have suffered for it.[42] Which view she came to favor is unclear, because she "tabled," in a sense, d'Alençon's proposal, after accepting it.

The wide distribution of Sidney's letter, however, creates an interesting problem for the editor at a crucial moment. At the end of an elaborate argument about the political worth of such a match, notably concerning its unlikelihood of bringing together factions in England, the recent Oxford edition reads: "So that if neither fear, nor desire, be such in him as are to bind any public fastness, it may be said that the only fortress of this your marriage is of his private affection: a thing too incident to your person, without laying it up in such ivy knots" (53.3). As if Sidney's final reservation confused his editors, many variants of the final words of this passage exist,[43] the more plausible ones having "slight knots" for "ivy knots." "Slight," however, as Duncan-Jones has pointed out,[44] seems to be a gloss on what ivy suggests metaphorically. Sidney constructs this letter around several familiar metaphors, of disease in the human and the body politic, the sun and the homonymous son as metaphor for kingship as well as lineage in reference to the need for a male heir, eyes that dazzle through love and authority, and the metaphor of the ship of state on turbulent seas. Here "ivy" seems more like Sidney, as does, "laying up," an archaic phrase for "twisting yarn to form a strand,"[45] rather than the more clear "tying up," an occasional variant.

In these words, Sidney's persona sets up the political disadvantages of Monsieur antithetically. As the groom he could neither bind up the English factions through common fear nor common desire. Then Sidney's persona suddenly introduces the question of "private affection," tacking on the final phrase "without laying it up in such ivy knots." "Ivy knots," placed at the very end of the sentence suggests that d'Alençon's private feeling, even a marriage based on that feeling, is far too slight, delicate, untyable, breakable. The ivy knot metaphor, echoing the denial of his power "to bind any public fastness," suggests a light person. If d'Alençon seems less than ordinary, however, what an extraordinary picture Sidney the courtier-letter-writer gives of the queen in this citation. Like the unapproachable Laura of the Petrarchan sonnets, men's love is a trophy, something she enjoys from too many people—"too incident to your person"—to make it worthwhile to add the duke's, especially by the restrictive bond of marriage contract ("knot").

Clearly Sidney intends this public letter of advice to picture the queen as that remote love object, attractive, awe-inspiring for the courtier, youthful and beautiful certainly, as well as unquestionably fertile, although the queen was forty-six years old at that time. To promote such a hyperbolic image of the queen, Sidney adopts the mask of the courtier-lover, proposing to make "the true vowed sacrifice of unfeigned love" (46.13) in an epistle "only for your eyes," though secrecy could hardly have been his intention. He considers "the perfections of your body and mind" (53.9). He likens slander of the queen to "blasphemy" (55.32). Finally he suggests on successive occasions that the happiness of having children must constitute the truly "blissful" excuse for marrying. Since, however, the question of looking for an heir and controlling factions in England were crucial to the argument of the letter, Sidney gradually allows the concept of producing children to vanish by expansion into a metaphor for engendering loyal subjects. When offspring is first mentioned, Sidney's persona speaks of "the bliss of children: which, I confess, were a most unspeakable comfort" (51.7). Here, we think strictly in terms of the joys of immediate family.

When he next mentions children, Sidney places them in the equivocal political light of possibly indifferent, fickle or estranged successors to the crown, returning to the bliss of having them only as an afterthought or concession: "Virtue and justice are the only bands of the people's love. And as for that point, many princes have lost their crowns, whose own children were manifest successors; and some that had their own children used as instruments of their ruin. Not that I deny the bliss of children." (54.27). Direct offspring do not tie up the bands of people's love. Good citizens are the true progeny of "virtue and justice." As Sidney the courtier has boldly stated early in this letter, "your inward force (for as for your treasures, indeed the sinews of your crown, your Majesty doth best and only know) consisteth in your subjects" (47.16).

The final word in the piece, the complex word "posterity," however, expands into the concept of "blood lineage," children and children's children, "simply those people who follow you in England," and also "loyal subjects and children of loyal subjects" who make England a stable commonwealth or state free from civil war between religious factions. The idea of the queen bearing children thus gradually dissolves in favor of rearing the good children of loyal subjects. The letter ends, "Lastly, doing as you do, you shall be as you be: the example of princes, the ornament of this age, the comfort of the afflicted, the delight of your people, the most excellent fruit of all your progenitors, and the perfect mirror to your posterity" (57.4). Landing squarely on "posterity" is part of a strategy to move the queen—and Sidney's many other readers—from contemplation of actual offspring to the contemplation of all subjects, from peasant to courtier, as the queen's metaphoric children. Subjects are children. The word "posterity," even in the context of "progenitors," suggests the political progeny of Elizabethan England as well as actual sons and daughters. "Posterity" thus informs the work as a whole. It forces us to go back and understand Sidney's cryptic remark that he has a choice of successor already, probably in Scotland, but that son of Mary Queen of Scots is, in his opinion, a good subject, although not a direct offspring, and not, oddly, the offspring of a loyal subject. Eliza must become the mirror to all her subjects and future generations of subjects. The final word of the whole piece sends us back through the whole argument to recollect that thought.

Irony can be defined in terms of the power of ending, the power of delaying final interpretation until the last word is out, a word, perhaps, that forces the reader back to the very beginning of a text. Here "posterity" forces us to reconsider Sidney's courtly voice's reiterated concept that the queen's power chiefly resides in her loyal subjects. Of course, Sidney, the courtly adviser, has, on a dangerous subject, said the right thing. He was not exactly a flatterer because an inflated idea of the queen, for various reasons, was considered by him and some of his friends sound public policy. Like the towering statues of a physically short Caesar Augustus, the idea of Eliza the goddess of rule and of love seemed an expedient piece of propaganda after a century of political disturbance.

Traditionally, Sidney was thought to have fallen out of favor with the queen in part because of this letter. It was even thought to have contributed to his purported "rustication"—his being sent away from court to the country, in his case, largely to Wilton. Having reexamined the evidence, Duncan-Jones asserted that, as in the case of Cecil's letter, "there is no evidence that any disfavor followed the advice."[46]

Like any prince, Machiavellian in the best sense of the word, as we have seen, the queen encouraged promulgation of opposing views of future decisions, as long as they were polite, so that she could appear to be selecting between sets of loyal advisers rather than operating according to a headstrong and possibly fallible monarchic "will and pleasure," the claim that sometimes marred her father's public image. Sidney himself writes Leicester from Clarindon within a year of the composition of the letter—perhaps at the height of its circulation—that he is much missed at court but would be a "very unpleasant company keeper"[47] because of a heavy cold which has taken away his voice. He remarks that he is "so full of the cold as one can not heere me speake: which is the cawse keepes me yet from the courte since my only service is speeche and that is stopped."

That Sidney's "only service is speeche" may indicate that he would like bolder service, a common complaint among Elizabeth's courtiers, but the queen was wise to keep her best speakers at home, and Sidney contributed to that maneuver as propagandist. As in the case of the Augustan artists, Elizabeth's poets, kept at home—or guiltily away from home—did her the greatest service among her contemporaries and her posterity. Sidney's and others' words in their perrenial appeal, did her image the ultimate propagandistic favor. Sidney's works, however, were preserved because he had more to say, in this case, his development of the paradox of progeny. He dismisses with gentle irony the direct progeny "of the Jezebel of our age" (48.6), the son of Catherine de Medici, and he opposes the notion of possibly ungrateful children with that of the good subject.

Notes

. . . [41] See *Miscellaneous Prose,* p. 39.

[42] Ibid., p. 36.

[43] Ibid., pp. 42-43. [Katherine] Duncan-Jones uses this passage to highlight the "manuscript tradition" (42).

[44] Ibid., p. 43.

[45] Ibid. Duncan-Jones quotes *OED.*

[46] Ibid., p. 36. For a contrary position, see King, "Queen Elizabeth I," p. 50.

[47] Feuillerat, vol. 3, p. 129. . . .

Sally Minogue (essay date 1996)

SOURCE: "A Woman's Touch: Astrophil, Stella and 'Queen Vertue's Court,'" in *ELH* Vol. 63, No. 3, Fall, 1996, pp. 550-70.

[*In the following excerpt, Minogue discusses what Sidney's Sonnets 9 and 83 reveal about the complex relationship between the poet and Queen Elizabeth.*]

When Sidney, in 1581, presented to his Queen the New Year's gift of a jewel in the shape of a diamond-bedecked whip, how did she take it? Not, we presume, lying down, since in this relationship it had already been made clear to Sidney who had the whip-hand. To be in a position to exchange New Year's gifts with the Queen was itself a mark of favor (one used by Steven May as a means of confirming who was an actual courtier to Elizabeth rather than a court hanger-on).[1] Sidney was in that position in both 1580 and 1581; but those dates punctuate a period when at least some commentators see him as having been banished from Court because of pressing too strongly the case against Elizabeth's possible marriage to Alençon.[2] Given that in 1579 John Stubbs had had his writing hand amputated for an over-fierce public attack on the Alençon suit (a medievally brutish form of retributive censorship), Sidney must have known when he was preparing the Alençon letter that his favored position was at the very least at risk, if not his own person; at that point he clearly thought the risk worth taking.[3] The long period of rustication which followed the delivery of the letter (according to most authorities, late in 1579), was perhaps signalled by his being pushed down to the very end of the New Year's gift rolls in 1580, and it evidently led him to reflect more fully on the Queen's authority.[4] Sidney's 1581 gift looks like a sign of his recognition of Elizabeth's absolute power over him, a witty, coded self-abasement, an acceptance that such power was the necessary accompaniment of a royal favor which he was pleased to have, against the odds, sustained or retrieved.[5] The teasing nature of such a gift does however imply a closeness of relationship with Elizabeth not typically attributed to Sidney; its symbolic nature is in keeping with the fashion of the time, but there is a self-conscious and personal dimension which does fit with what we know of Sidney's wit.[6] Here I shall look at two of the sonnets from *Astrophil and Stella*, 9 and 83, and suggest a reading of them as poetic versions of the jewelled whip, dramatizing both the public monarch-courtier relationship between Elizabeth and Sidney and a possible private relationship where at least the rhetoric of sexual subjection is used at once playfully and not-so-playfully. In sonnet 9, I will suggest, Sidney prostrates himself; in sonnet 83, he gives the Queen a speaking part and foretells his own possible political fate. The diamond sparkle of his wit, somewhat darker in the second poem, does not disguise, indeed it deliberately highlights, that he is under the whip.

Of particular interest to me in these readings is that, even while they seem to fall in with some of the current patterns of Renaissance criticism, they also cut against new orthodoxies insofar as they place Elizabeth as a woman firmly at the center of Sidney's poetic practice, and they also posit a Sidney showing signs through these sonnets of the frustration which resulted from his required submissiveness, a frustration which seems to have hardened later into positive dissent. My argument is conducted in terms not of discourse, but of materiality; it is realist and empiricist; in this I seek to add my voice to those which are now beginning to question the politics of new historicism. M. D. Jardine has convincingly demonstrated the potentially politically reactionary nature of certain versions of new historicism, arguing that:

> it is now more important than ever that critics on the left argue strenuously for the presence of competing sets of values and practices, before human struggle to overthrow systems which kept them from power is removed from our record of the past.[7]

While I recognize the ironies involved in attempting to answer this call by emphasizing the radical dimension of a period of monarchy, and identifying the "human struggle to overthrow systems which kept them from power" in the sullen dissent of at least a sort of aristocrat, I nonetheless believe it important to describe and identify correctly the contributions to change made by a female sovereign on the one hand, and by the courtier-poet who had perhaps the greatest influence on the English poetic tradition on the other.

The various historical, critical, and (new and old) historical-critical accounts of Sidney's relationship with Elizabeth during the crucial period 1580-82, and of the writing (and reading) of Sidney's sonnet sequence *Astrophil and Stella*, contain tensions, uncertainties, and flat contradictions which may be more than the product of the problematic nature of historical inquiry. Sidney's relationship with his Queen seems itself to have been shot through with like ambiguities. While

some argue that Wilton was an alternative Court and center of culture, it may also be seen as his retreat in times of disfavor. Sidney may be seen as powerless except for his potential inheritances from his uncles, or as having a sense of aristocratic and cultural power and position sufficient to allow him to forfeit royal patronage in favor of being himself a patron. As far as the poems themselves were concerned, there is no clear agreement about whether *Astrophil and Stella* circulated amongst the Court elite, or was private to Sidney himself, and so without an audience until after his death (and so no agreement about whether Elizabeth might have read any of the sonnets, and so whether they can now be read as contemporary appeals to Elizabeth's favor). With some of these issues it is impossible to determine what was the case, though this has not stopped critics from doing so, usually without cognizance that there might be a question mark.[8] For new historicists of the post-structuralist camp, the question mark has been elevated into the signifier *sine qua non;*[9] while new historicists of the cultural materialist stamp allow a little more room for maneuver, and indeed a little more room for actual history, though for most of them the dominant ideology is still in the end dominant, leaving no real possibility of change in the existing power relations.[10]

I shall argue that, while Sidney was himself torn between various ways of seeing and presenting himself, between early 1580 and at least the end of 1581, he recognized the need for submission to the Queen before all else.[11] He spends most of 1580 at Wilton, languishing in the Queen's disfavor; in a letter to Leicester in the August of 1580 he laments his loss of voice with the Queen, while also bemoaning his poverty; he submits with the New Year's gift in 1581; around July of that year he loses the heirdom to Leicester through the birth of Leicester's direct heir; in November of that year Penelope Rich marries and Alençon arrives again to pursue his suit, linking the defeat of Sidney's personal and political hopes; arguably, in the November Accession Day tilts, he appears wearing the crossed-through SPERAVI, signalling his public awareness of his lost hopes; and finally in late 1581 he is offered the prospect of some money from Elizabeth, but through a problematic avenue, the income from the forfeited goods of Papists—and still no position. This looks, presented thus baldly, like a very public and also a very private humiliation—shortly after which he probably begins writing *Astrophil and Stella*. The sonnets I shall examine reflect the bitternesses and tensions Sidney had experienced, but also reflect the inevitability of submission. In the light of the historical circumstances it is difficult to deny the presence of England's brightest female star behind the Stella to whom Sidney subjects himself in this sequence. Yet ultimately, the way in which he spent the last few years of his life, and the manner of his death, suggest that he kicked against the Queen's supremacy, knowingly at the cost of his ambition and, as it happened, his life. Writing was one alternative form of power for him: the courtly love format which he uses so flexibly enabled him to express the complexity of his submission to a monarch who was also a woman, and gave him the imaginative control as author to compensate for the political control he lacked as courtier. At the same time, in at least the poems I shall examine, Elizabeth is accorded her actual identity as a fleshly woman, through sometimes explicitly sexual language, and this I see as extending rather than diminishing her power.

There is ample evidence in sonnet 9 of reference to someone more powerful, and indeed richer, than the supposed model of Stella, Penelope Rich. The first and third words of the sonnet are "Queen" and "court," and they sandwich the personified "Vertue," which we can read explicitly as Elizabeth's virginity, raised into something larger than itself (as indeed by this time it was, her childbearing capacities weighing clearly upon her advisers', and others', attitudes to the proposed match with Alençon), or as a more generalized goodness or good, which here might be construed ethically or politically. Elizabeth had to be "good"; but she was also good for her country. "Which *some* call Stella's face" seems deliberately to distance the author from those "some" (suggesting he has in mind another, Elizabeth). The cold images of virginity which multiply—alabaster, pearl, marble, "without touch"Cmix paradoxically with the images of elaborate riches. The gold, porphir, and "locke of pearl" are precious petrifications of parts of the body (hair, lips, teeth). The Grace which "sometimes comes forth" from the pearl-locked mouth is that all too unreliable monarch's favor. Sidney/Astrophil, for all his power as writer of these lines, is indeed a "poore I" in comparison. He is touched (emotionally, sexually, persnally) by a woman, but without actually being touched; and though himself touched (affected), cannot touch back (physically, as well as in terms of influence).

If Sidney were writing only to Penelope Rich, or to some fictional Stella, or in a generalized way to a poetically conventional woman, it could be said that the element of power which the woman in the poem has over him would be outweighed both by his power as writer of the poetic fiction, and by the particular way in which in this poem the fleshliness of the woman is turned into stone and she is withdrawn even from the humanizing power of touch. One is reminded of Midas. But if it is Elizabeth who is addressed here, it is Astrophil who is petrified rather than Stella. The valuable metal and stone cease to be emblems; they are rather the natural accoutrements of a female monarch. That is not to say that they are not also used emblematically; but they are used by Sidney with a nice sense of the ironic interplay between what they actually are and what, poetically and politically, they

represent. The alabaster, gold, porphyry and marble might be the materials which actually *are* part of "Queen Vertue's court," with her privy chamber locked away behind those rich, promising porches, impenetrable except to her favorites. She can look out of its windows, but they may not look in, without her permission. There are a number of interesting references to windows in the documentary evidence surrounding Elizabeth; certainly Essex's 1591 letter to Elizabeth comes to mind, where he says that "no cause but a great action of your own may draw me out of your sight, for the two windows of your privy chamber shall be the poles of my sphere".[12]

Immediately one sees the sexual reading available here, as one can also in sonnet 9; both are made possible only because Elizabeth was a woman, and moreover one who used her sexual powers as part of her royal ones. But the sexual reading is interdependent with that in which access to the royal person means power, and where denial of that access renders the supplicant powerless. Essex is at the time of writing still in favor, indeed in touch; but even so his letter goes on to imagine a time when favor might be denied, and to predict his unwavering, indeed requisite, subjection in such a case. Sidney does not need to imagine it: the queen "without touch doth touch".

That Sidney's is the first sonnet sequence in English is often remarked, as is its influence, post-publication, on English poetry. The connection of such love poetry with political patronage is now seen as almost as well established, to the point where we are asked to recognize that "'love is not love'" in Elizabethan "love" poetry.[13] Elizabeth's profound influence on court culture goes without saying. There are a number of interpretations of Sidney's sonnets which put these factors together and offer "patronage" readings of the poems, or of the sequence as a whole. But I want to suggest that sonnet 9 is not just a patronage—or more properly, clientageC—poem, it is also, and first, a love poem. For if love is not love in such poems, what is? Patronage readings such as Marotti's, and John Barrell's of Shakespeare's sonnets, attempt, as they would have it, to foreground a particular sense of "love" and to thereby privilege a political reading; but in their actual practice they render the foregrounded reading as somehow free-floating, disconnected from what would once have been called the primary sense and reading.[14] Yet the very notion of foregrounding or privileging a sense depends on some concept of hierarchy in the first place, a hierarchy thus being displaced. Indeed Barrell makes this clear:

> I have tried to defamiliarise the word—to specify out of all of its possible and various and compound meanings one which most clearly represents it as a part of the discourse of patronage, and most

clearly removes it from the meanings we most readily attach to the word today.[15]

"Defamiliarise" and "the meanings we most readily attach" clearly suggest a commonly recognized primary meaning, though of course Barrell would argue that this is historically and culturally specific. But can we really be so confident that there was no similar sense of "love" in the sixteenth century? Is it not the case that the coded client/patron appeals are dependent on a prior understanding of the common use of the word "love"? If Marotti, Barrell, and many others who take the same critical line, are suggesting that sixteenth-century readers, unlike late twentieth-century readers (excluding literary critics), of these poems would see the patronage reading as primary, on the surface of the poem, then any notion of a code disappears. If we preserve the notion of a code—one which seems to be inherent in discussions of Renaissance culture, old and new historicist alike—then we have to see the metaphorical or hidden sense of the poem, and of the word "love," as dependent upon a prior sense.[16]

What that sense is I and all my contemporary readers are familiar with; Sidney also seems to have been familiar with it, when he remarks disparagingly of English "love" poetry:

> But truly many of such writings as come under the banner of unresistible love, if I were a mistress, would never persuade me they were in love: so coldly they apply fiery speeches.[17]

As this makes clear, the rhetoric of love was no guarantee of the actuality or the sincerity of the emotion; but that it was that emotion which was in question does not itself seem to be questioned by Sidney here. Jonathan Crewe reads Marotti as seeing the code of love rhetoric as being a sort of Elizabethan courtier back-slang, but back-slang is itself dependent on awareness of generally accepted meanings, since it works by reversing them.[18] With a word as important and extensive in its senses as "love," it looks as though even those in on the code might—indeed must—have sustained some usage of the word "love" in its non-patronage sense.[19]

The interpretation of the import of the word "love" in Elizabethan poetry is made less rather than more complicated by the fact that the chief patron of the period was a woman. Marotti recognizes early in his argument that Elizabeth's unmarried state, and therefore, *a fortiori,* her being biologically a woman, "preserved her symbolic *and real* value in both domestic and international transactions."[20] However, he is reluctant to see the amorous language "specifically encouraged" by her in her courtiers' addresses to her as anything other than a metaphorizing of "ambition and vicissitudes."[21] Yet we know that Elizabeth numbered

amongst those courtiers a succession of men, ambiguously termed her "favorites", whose relations with her are marked by an intimacy of access and of language. Is there no distinction between the amorous language they use, and that used as a formal code? Marotti appears to think not, since he cites Essex's vocabulary in that mode as showing that "he utilized the same politically-invested language of love" as Sir Christopher Hatton's.[22] Yet Marotti pours contempt on Hatton's fulsome writing to her "in the idiom of a Petrarchan lover separated from his mistress," suggesting that his are "fanciful words for an astute politician."[23] Well, if Marotti is right, they are far from fanciful if what they actually express is encoded ambition; but Marotti's own words here give the lie to his thesis for his seeing Hatton's Petrarchan rhetoric as fanciful shows that the rhetoric at least depends on a prior reading, of love as—well, love. Marotti's apparent embarrassment arises from words which, even if they are metaphorical, still inescapably hold their primary meaning, And his embarrassment, echoed elsewhere in various historians' and critics' patent discomfort at the thought of an ageing Elizabeth flirting, if even in a coded way, with her young men, betrays an anxiety about seeing Elizabeth as a sexual being at all. Wallace MacCaffrey, for example, nudges coyly:

> On the lips of Dudley and Hatton, contemporaries of the queen, the language of knightly homage, the conventional praise of feminine beauty, tripped forth lightly, but when the devotee was a young man of twenty and the lady had rounded fifty, the fiction was harder to sustain.[24]

Crewe, writing from a very different perspective, and trying to hide his prejudices behind an arch knowingness, nonetheless falls into the same stereotyping, sympathizing with "the painful indecorum of [Sidney's] having to court, for obviously political reasons, an ugly old rich woman, becoming the Miss Havisham of the English world by the 1580s."[25] MacCaffrey's very recent account doesn't even allow Elizabeth a personal response from her equals in age; and neither male interpreter can stomach the possibility that a younger man could have feelings towards a considerably older woman which were other than self-interested.

The haste to read the amorous addresses to Elizabeth as expressive of *exclusively* political desire effectively robs her of her power as a woman. Not surprisingly it has taken a woman, Philippa Berry, to show the process whereby Renaissance scholars were able

> to displace the fundamental problem of the queen's gender. Perceived as both more and less than a woman, because a woman supposedly purged of sexual desire, she is either asserted or implied to

reinforce rather than disturb the political and religious hierarchies of the patriarchy.[26]

Berry is arguing from a feminist perspective, and her interest at this stage of her argument is in revealing the way in which Elizabeth's relations with other women have thus been left out of account by Renaissance scholarship; but her closely argued view that Elizabeth's presence on the English throne "was a radical event" also allows us the freedom to give Elizabeth's sexuality a key place in her monarchy.[27] This in no way, in my view, weakens her power and its radical nature, but rather adds to those. It is quite evident from the length and nature of Elizabeth's reign, and in particular her manipulation of her (supposed) chastity, that she used, and was not used by, her sexual powers as part of her political powers. But to argue therefore that her sexual feelings and the sexual feelings of others about her never themselves came into play is reductive and unrealistic.

Elizabeth's own writings are inevitably short of evidence on this matter; she was an ever-cautious monarch. The tender intimacy of address which marks her correspondence with those she favored has an air of vulnerability which perhaps derives from its very disparity with her position, but it is counter-balanced by her fury when she was displeased. The only work we have of hers which seems to speak imaginatively of love is "I grieve and dare not show my discontent," generally seen as expressing her state of conflict on the failure of the Alençon suit.[28] Though it draws on some of the standard images and paradoxes of the love poetry of the time, it is impressive in its honesty in declaring feelings intended to be hidden by a public behavior that is itself revealed as a sham in the poem. There is a rhythmic shift in the second stanza, where the second and fourth lines adopt an eleventh syllable to produce an ending which in these circumstances of authorship it is perhaps not derogatory to call feminine. The unsettling produced by this small shift (regularity is restored in the final stanza) and the desire for an improbable escape from the ever-present "care" expressed in the wistful "Some gentler passion slide into my mind" again suggest a vulnerability which is particularly moving given the authorship. Since Elizabeth precisely addresses the conflict between personal feeling and public behavior here, her use of "love" would seem to be apolitical, since it is contrasted with "seem to hate," the latter which she is "forced" to do by the needs of the political situation. (The suggestion that the poem was actually addressed to the errant Essex would carry the same reading, though in that case the grief would seem more personal and more credible.)[29]

But if Elizabeth herself is unable to be more explicit than this rather generalized poem about her personal emotions and desires (and the frankness is even so

such that it is difficult to imagine what if any, audience she had in mind, other than herself), those who addressed her, in however coded a form, could be very explicit. If we accept the possibility that the Queen might have been central to Sidney's imagination when he composed some of the ***Astrophil and Stella*** sonnets (as Marotti's argument entails, and which Crewe sees almost as an old hat cover story to protect the real imaginative inspiration of the poems, Sidney's sister Mary Herbert), those poems which admit of a clearly sexual reading, among others, are particularly interesting.[30] Firstly, they show that at least the erotic sense of "love" is in play as well as a politically metaphorizing sense of it, and that therefore that sense of "love" can co-exist with its own metaphor. Such a double reading is hardly surprising in Renaissance poetry (and certainly not in Sidney's poetry, which yields many examples of what Daniel Traister calls his "ambidexterity"), yet it is one which those who want to insist that "love is not love" want to deny.[31] Secondly, these poems specifically associate this eroticism with Elizabeth in a way that is not just "ostensible" (Marotti's word) or "hollow" (Crewe in summarizing Marotti and other new historicists).[32] To return to sonnet 9, and to the word "touch"; it is used four times, three of them in the same line, as though the repetitions of the word could replace the missing actuality. From the myriad senses of "touch" available to Sidney, "magnet" is that most often used in the reading of his complex metaphor; but it seems more likely that he is referring to touchpowder, with himself as the straw about to be ignited. This reading fits with the use of "touch" as a euphemism for sexual contact, and accords with the excitability of the writing in the latter part of the poem.[33] It would be in keeping with the highly paradoxical nature of the whole poem and of the image of the woman's blowing both hot and cold that the sense of "touch" as touchstone, index of value, both materially and morally, is invoked. Does not this mixture of apparently contradictory meanings exactly fit the Elizabeth who drew suitors and favorites with the promise of her chastity (the promise being that they would be victorious over it) and kept them desiring while she remained desirable? There is of course a bitter side to such a relationship, and that is hinted at but not fully expressed in the self-denigrating images ("nothing such," "poore I," "straw"); and it is difficult not to be reminded of Freud's toothed vagina in the image of the door of red porphyry which is locked with pearl. But the somewhat unpleasant combination of sensuality and petrification, the sense of inflamedness with no mutual conflagration, is perhaps retrieved by the author's complete obeisance in the poem. He admires, desires, accepts; for it is the "Queene" who is at the head of the poem, and he, the "straw," at its, and her, foot.

If we move to sonnet 83 we see Sidney's bitterness much more fully in playCand as many commentators have noted, Sidney tends to "play" when he is most serious. Sonnet 83 has received relatively little attention, and where it has, the notion that the poem is addressed to Penelope Rich's sparrow "Philip" seems to be generally accepted. In fact much more noticeable is the self-referential element involved through the use of the name "Philip" and the playful diminutive "Sir Phip."[34] As soon as one sees the poem as therefore an address to the self, either from the self, or in the persona and voice of another, it becomes extremely interesting. For here the author's view of himself is overt, in a way seldom allowed in this most layered of sonnet sequences. In a letter to his uncle Leicester in 1580, during the period of his rustication, Sidney comments bitterly on the fact that if he returns to court, necessarily therefore in finery, the queen will assume from his silk doublet that all is well with him; he argues that anyway he has a cold and has lost his voice, "which is the only cawse keeps me from court since my only service is speech and that is stopped."[35] I am not the only one to see the double meanings here; but while Sidney was then writing in a position where he may still have had hope of regaining his queen's favor, as he seems whole-heartedly to have set out to do in his ironic submissiveness from the beginning to the end of 1581, sonnet 83 is likely to have been written from a position of hopelessness. The stopping of speech is here envisaged both in the comparing himself to a dumb creature, the sparrow, and in, finally, the threat of his neck being wrung. The sexual echoes of "billing" and indeed of "speech" itself reverberate here. My suggestion is that here Sidney is dramatizing Elizabeth's role in the sequence and in his own life by allowing her characteristic voice and view to speak in the poem. Sidney above all others would enjoy the irony of controlling the speech of his sovereign, at the very point when his voice can least be heard. The control is entirely literary—even to the point of again placing himself as the victim at the end of the poem, but here a victim not just of desire but of that final power of the monarch, the power of life and death.

A sort of ghastly wit pervades the poem, accompanying a sense of threat. One has encountered that sense of threat before, in Elizabeth's poems and letters, just as one has encountered those sometimes sinisterly playful *tendresses* and diminutives. It is impossible to establish Sidney's direct knowledge of those texts, but it is certain that he was fully acquainted with Elizabeth's style. The familiarity of "Good brother Philip" and "sir Phip" recalls "My Wat" of Elizabeth's "Ah silly pug" (which phrase itself finds an echo in "your silly selfe" in sonnet 83), and the tone of both poems is remarkably similar, characterized most clearly by affectionate impatience. (Accepting that May is right in pinning Elizabeth's poem to Ralegh to 1587, I am not attributing a direct influence, but noting the similarity of tone and language which suggests Sidney's

knowledge of Elizabeth and ability to coin her style.)[36] Sidney's poem has the sharper edge, however; while Elizabeth's is offering reassurance after a quarrel, sonnet 83 promises a quick despatch after a period of indulgence. The final line of both poems recalls a much earlier poem of Elizabeth's, "The doubt of future foes," where, after expressing uncertainty and vulnerability of the same kind, and in the same formal antitheses, as found in "On Monsieur's Departure," she issues a clear and shockingly graphic warning to her enemies in the final couplet:

> Our rusty sword with rest, shall first his
>   edge employ
> To poll their tops that seek such change
>   and gape for joy.[37]

The crudity of "poll their tops" (the words and the threat) and the horrid ambiguity of "gape for joy" (which suggests the foolish gaping to a future different from that provided by Elizabeth, equivalent to the physical gaping of the mouth in the polled head) leave us in no doubt about the monarch's acceptance of necessary responsibility in executing her enemies where necessary. We are reminded of the bloody retribution to Stubbs. Sidney needed no reminding, and his sonnet 83 seems to reflect literarily what he might have feared his fate to be literally. Perhaps the setting it down in words might have absolved him of his fear; and perhaps he was aware of Elizabeth's view, explicit in the poem to Ralegh, "The less afraid the better shalt thou speed."

It is interesting to consider the possibility that Elizabeth read sonnet 83, and that Sidney wrote it knowing she might read it. If so, it is a daring expression of knowledge of the sovereign, while remaining a document of utter submission in its self-knowledge and its awareness of impotence. Add to this the erotic dimension of the poem (fully explicated by Traister who takes the "sparrow" reading) and it strikes as an act at once of arrogant folly and of self-abasement. If we do/can read the poem as expressing Elizabeth's view (filtered through Sidney's) of her relations with the courtier-poet, even as it wields a monarch's power ("Lest off your neck be wrung") it also suggests at least a period of remarkable indulgence. The octet refers to a period of considerable intimacy ("I was content you should in favor creep") dependent on the author's recognition of his position ("While craftily you seemed your cut to keepe"); there is even the suggestion of sexual intimacy ("oft suffered you to sleep In Lilies' nest, where love's self lies along"— and "love" here can be taken in both ways, sexual and political). But the sestet, following the convention, signals an abrupt change of tone: "What, doth high place ambitious thoughts augment? Is sawcinesse reward of curtesie?". Elizabeth was notoriously furious with those who overstepped the bounds of their favor;

and this might be a direct reference to Sidney's injudicious letter advising avoidance of the marriage to Alençon. True impatience cuts through in "Cannot such grace your silly selfe content, But you must needs with those lips billing be?". This is the tone of one who knows the value of "grace" to one who is still caught up with "billing." Of course, all billing would cease, sexual, poetic, political, or otherwise, if the threat of the final line were carried out.

In mid-1581, the birth of a baby ended at least part of Sidney's aristocratic hopes, and later that year Alençon was back in England, his suit still encouraged by Elizabeth. Both events must have underlined Sidney's sense of his own impotence, where once he had promised to be so potent. His humiliation, partly at his own hands, culminated in December 1581 with his havering over accepting monies from the Queen (which he had begged) issuing from the revenues of the forfeited estates of recusant Catholics. Conscience, poverty and self-aggrandizement jostle on the page, and these letters do not make entirely comfortable reading.[38] Yet in 1582 Sidney was at work on a different sort of writing, cheerfully dramatizing pursuit and self-abasement in *Astrophil and Stella*. Sonnet 83 can be seen as the literary equivalent of Sidney's appearing. perhaps at the 1581 November Accession Day tilts, with his insignia SPERAVI crossed through.[39] That public and theatrical self-irony, probably in front of Alençon, whose presence would further underscore his crossed-through hopes, personal and political, somehow turned a humiliation into a victory. *Astrophil and Stella* seems to me to do the same, telling a story of vicissitude and despair with a wit and poetic bravado which have given it a lasting glamor. That the fate Sidney made for himself, turning away from a slow death by submission to what no doubt seemed an endless one by septicaemia, was translated from its squalid reality into a glorious story is a final, literary, irony he would have, grimly, enjoyed. But his touchy Queen had the last political word, delaying his grandiose funeral to a time when it suited her (to distract the public from the execution of Mary Queen of Scots)—and then refusing to pay the expenses. In the meantime, *Astrophil and Stella* retains *its* power as a canonized work, but one which is falsified if we do not see the breadth and complication of Sidney's relationship with Elizabeth as reflected in it. That Elizabeth was a source—*the* source—of cash and status is part of his poetic self-abasement, as I have tried to argue in the discussion of sonnet 9; but the sense of his personal engagement with his feelings about her, and of his submissiveness to her, are most clearly expressed in the sexual dimension of the sequence, as I have argued in discussing sonnet 83. Anger about both is central to the passion of the sequence.

To argue that "love is not love" in Elizabethan sonnet sequences, and specifically in Sidney's, is to deny the power of Elizabeth's being a woman, and thus the radical nature of her period of power. It is also to deny her influence *as a woman* on some of the major literary productions of the era. Finally it is to deny Sidney his many-levelled self-awareness in at least some poems in the sequence. The best we can do as critics and as readers of history is to see the complex picture as fully as possible, given that we cannot possibly recoup a full understanding of what the contemporary history of Sidney and Elizabeth was. To insist that "love is not love" is to falsify that complexity, just as surely as it would be to insist that love is *only* love; it is one of the powers of literary production that, in the case of *Astrophil and Stella,* both may be true.

Notes

[1] Steven May, *The Elizabethan Courtier Poets: The Poems and Their Contexts* (Columbia: Univ. of Missouri Press, 1991), 22. May uses presence on the New Year gift rolls as a necessary rather than a sufficient condition for courtier status.

[2] Dorothy Connell, *Sir Philip Sidney: The Maker's Mind* (Oxford: Clarendon Press, 1977), 107; F. J. Levy, "Sidney Reconsidered," in *Essential Articles for the Study of Sir Philip Sidney,* ed. Arthur F. Kinney (Hamden, CT: Shoe String Press, 1986), 5; for a counter-view see May, 98.

[3] On Stubbs, see *John Stubbs's "Gaping Gulf" with Letters and Other Relevant Documents,* ed. Lloyd E. Berry (Charlottesville: Univ. Press of Virginia, 1968).

[4] Katherine Duncan-Jones interprets this push to the end of the gift rolls as a possible sign of disapproval, *Sir Philip Sidney* (London: Penguin, 1991), 169, quoting *Progresses of Queen Elizabeth,* ed. J. G. Nichols, 1823.

[5] William Ringler interprets it as signalling submission specifically over the Alençon suit (*The Poems of Sir Philip Sidney,* ed. William A. Ringler Jr. [Oxford: Clarendon Press, 1962], 440). Duncan-Jones interprets it as a sign of a more extensive submission, as I do, and she provides convincing evidence of this, 192-93. Neither commentator sees the more intimate, perhaps sexual, element in the representative gift which I am here suggesting. All references to *Astrophil and Stella* are from Ringler's edition.

[6] See Alan Hager, "The Exemplary Mirage: Fabrication of Sir Philip Sidney's Biographical Image and the Sidney Reader," in Kinney, especially 23-24, for an interesting analysis of Sidney's "reflexive irony." See also Duncan-Jones's description of "his readiness to quip even in the most stressful circumstances" (290).

[7] M. D. Jardine, "New Historicism for Old: New Con-

servatism for Old?: The Politics of Patronage in the Renaissance," *The Yearbook of English Studies* 21 (1991), 293-94.

[8] Even the question of circulation, which might seem to be answerable by reference to historical record, attracts contradictory, confident, assertions. See Ringler, and May who follows him, for the view that the sonnets were entirely private to Sidney; most other critics adopt the generalized view of a small elite manuscript circulation. Others again would see the question as irrelevant. There is no direct evidence of circulation prior to the 1591 publication.

[9] For example, Gary F. Waller, "The Rewriting of Petrarch: Sidney and the Languages of Sixteenth-Century Poetry," in *Sir Philip Sidney and the Interpretation of Renaissance Culture,* ed. Gary F. Waller and Michael D. Moore (London: Croom Helm, 1984).

[10] For example, Laura Stevenson, *Praise and Paradox: Merchants and Craftsmen in Elizabethan Popular Literature* (Cambridge: Cambridge Univ. Press. 1984).

[11] Levy provides a persuasive account of Sidney as torn between allegiance to God and allegiance to the Queen.

[12] *Lives and Letters of the Devereux,* ed. Walter B. Devereux. 2 vols. (London: John Murray, 1857), 1: 249-50.

[13] Arthur Marotti, "'Love is not Love': Elizabethan Sonnet Sequences and the Social Order," *ELH* 49 (1982): 396-428.

[14] John Barrell, *Poetry, Language and Politics* (Manchester: Manchester Univ. Press, 1988), 18-43.

[15] Barrell, 23-24.

[16] See Jonathan Crewe, *Hidden Designs: The Critical Profession and Renaissance Literature* (London: Methuen, 1986), 76-88, for an interesting and amusing discussion of the levels of "encryption" in Sidney's sonnets.

[17] From *The Defence of Poesy, in Miscellaneous Prose of Sir Philip Sidney,* ed. Katherine Duncan-Jones and J. van Dorsten (Oxford: Oxford Univ. Press, 1973), 117.

[18] Crewe, 76.

[19] See Quentin Skinner, "Meaning and Understanding in the History of Ideas." *History and Theory* 8 (1969): 3-53, for an authoritative account of the falsifications produced in the historical analysis of texts by anachronistically attributing concepts to authors; ironically,

the new historicists who started out by issuing similar caveats have ended by falling into the very trap they warned against. Skinner places a premium on establishing authorial intention, whilst reminding us of the problems involved in doing so. David Norbrook, *Poetry and Politics in the English Renaissance* (London: Routledge and Kegan Paul, 1984), notes the reluctance of materialist and post-structuralist critics to acknowledge any role for intention, and warns that "to ignore the intention is effectively to depoliticise" (8).

[20] Marotti, 398; italics in original.

[21] Marotti, 398.

[22] Marotti, 398.

[23] Marotti, 398, 399.

[24] Wallace MacCaffrey, *Elizabeth I* (London: Edward Arnold, 1993), 396.

[25] Crewe, 80.

[26] Philippa Berry, *Of Chastity and Power: Elizabethan Literature and the Unmarried Queen* (London: Routledge, 1989), 65.

[27] Berry, 61.

[28] In *Elizabeth I,* ed. Lacey Baldwin Smith (St. Louis: Forum Press, 1980), 57-58.

[29] Suggested in a footnote to the poem, *The Norton Anthology of English Literature,* 6th edition, ed. M. H. Abrams, 2 vols. (London: Norton, 1993), 1:998.

[30] Alan Sinfield, "Sexual Puns in *Astrophil and Stella."* *Essays in Criticism* 24 (1974), has argued convincingly for the presence of sexual puns throughout Sidney's sonnet sequence, and notes that "sexual *double entendre* is an important feature of Sidney's verbal skill" (6).

[31] Daniel Traister, "Sidney's Purposeful Humor: *Astrophil and Stella* 59 and 83." *ELH* 49 (1982), 751.

[32] Marotti, 406; Crewe, 75.

[33] Sinfield notes this euphemistic reading, 346-47.

[34] Duncan-Jones mentions this self-referential reading, 242.

[35] *The Prose Works of Sir Philip Sidney,* ed. Albert Feuillerat, 4 vols. (Cambridge: Cambridge Univ. Press, 1962), 3:129.

[36] For the text of Elizabeth's poem and May's dating

discussion see May, 317-19.

[37] *The New Oxford Book of Sixteenth Century Verse,* ed. Emrys Jones (Oxford: Oxford Univ. Press, 1991), 183-84.

[38] See especially the letters of December, 1581, to Sir Christopher Hatton and to the Earl of Leicester respectively, in Feuillerat, 139 and 140.

[39] Duncan-Jones argues effectively for this date, though she also mentions counter-arguments, 194-95 and 218.

Peter C. Herman (essay date 1996)

SOURCE: "When Is a Defense Not a Defense? Sidney's Paradoxiacal *Apology for Poetry,*" in *Squitter-Wits and Muse-Haters,* Wayne State University Press, 1996, pp. 61-94.

[*In the following excerpt, Herman reconsiders the* Apology for Poetry *and its stance regarding poetry's superiority to history in the light of two of Sidney's letters.*]

. . .*"Do as I Say, Not as I Do": Sidney's Letters and the Apology*

On May 22, 1580, a few months after he (probably) completed the *Apology* and at approximately the same time that he was also occupied by the *Arcadia* and *Astrophil and Stella,* Sidney answered a request from his friend, Edward Denny, for a list of books that an educated man should read.[25] On October 18, 1580, Sidney wrote a similar, though less formal letter to his brother Robert that deals with the same issues.[26]

Taking the Denny letter first, the key difference between the Denny letter and the *Apology* is that *Sidney excludes poetry entirely from his list.* Even though in the *Apology* Sidney strenuously argues that poetry teaches virtue better than any other discipline, Sidney recommends no poetry whatsoever to his friend. Homer and Vergil, Petrarch and Sannazaro, Chaucer, Gower, Dante, *Amadis de Gaul,* the *Mirrour For Magistrates,* and the Earl of Surrey's lyrics, even the Arthurian legends, all are conspicuously absent.

Even further, Sidney transfers to philosophy and to history precisely those qualities which in the *Apology* assured poetry's superiority to its competitors. Sidney commences his letter by dividing the pursuit of knowledge into two parts: "the one as concerninge our selves, the other an outward application of our selves" (538). For spiritual knowledge, Sidney recommends that Denny read the Bible and "some parts of morall philosophy" (538), especially Aristotle's "*Ethickes.*" Recognizing that Aristotle (then as now) "is something

darke and hath need of a Logicall examination" (538), Sidney directs his friend to Cicero's *De Officiis* and to some of Plutarch's discourses.[27] Although Sidney clearly approves of Plutarch, his passion for Cicero is such that he ranks him (not Vergil or Homer) second only to the Bible: "But let Tully be for that mater your foundation, next to the foundation of foundations, and wisdome of wisdomes, I mean the holy scripture" (539). This evaluation of Cicero and Plutarch radically differs from his dismissal of philosophy in the *Apology* as "hard of utterance and . . . misty to be conceived" (27) and of philosophers as: "coming towards me with a sullen gravity, as though they could not abide vice by daylight, rudely clothed for to witness outwardly their contempt of outward things, with books in their hands against glory, whereto they set their names, sophistically speaking against subtlety" (23-24).

The divergences between these texts can be partially (but only partially) resolved through Sidney's implicit distinction in the Denny letter between the moral philosophy of antiquity and their scholastic followers ("these men casting largesse as they go of definitions, divisions, and distinctions" [24]). He mentions the former, but not the latter. Even so, Sidney declines to make this distinction in the *Apology.* Furthermore, even though Sidney claims in his defense that Alexander "received more bravery of mind by the pattern of Achilles than by hearing the definition of fortitude" (61), Sidney urges his friend—a soldier—to read Aristotle's *Ethics,* Cicero's *De Officiis,* and Plutarch's discourses for images of "what [it] is to be truly iuste, truly vallyant, rightly temperate, & rightly friendly, with their annexed quallityes and contraryes" (538), not the *Odyssey,* the *Illiad,* or the *Aeneid.*

In the next section, Sidney prescribes the books appropriate for "the trade of our lives," and since his friend has chosen the military life, Sidney recommends that he read books "that profess the arte [of soldiery], & in historyes" (539), that is, "Langeai in french, and Machievall in Italian" (539), but he quickly breaks off discussion since, as he freely admits, he has very little expertise in this area: "Of [other books] I will say noe further, for I am witness of myne owne ignoraunce" (539). The latter category commands more of Sidney's attention, and his bibliography stretches from antiquity to the Renaissance:

> [Y]ou shoold begin with Philip Melanchthons Chronolgy, so to Justine, then to Herodotus, Thucidides, Xenophon, Diodorus Siculus, Quintus Curtius, Polybius, Lyvy, Dionisius, Salust, Ca'sar, Dion, Tacitus, & then the Emperours lyves, gathered together in a volume by Henricus Stephanus. Then to take Zonaras, & Nicetas, for the Greek parts, & Procopius; and from thence to fall lower, to the particular chronicles of eche country, as Paulus Aemilius for France, Polidore

for Englande, and soe of the rest. But because this might seeme too longe, though in deed not soe longe, as a man woold thinke, my councell to you is even to being with our english Cronicle, sett out by Hollinshead; which you shoold reed thorow till you came to Edwarde the thirdes lyfe, then to take Froyssart. After him Anguetard of Monstrelett, written in old frenche, after him Philip de Commines, & then Guicciardin who reach almost to our tyme. And these will serve your turne for historicall matters. (539)

Sidney's treatment of history in this passage departs in two important ways from the *Apology*. First, in the *Apology* Sidney undermines the authority of historians by asserting that they rely "upon other histories, whose greatest authorities are built upon the notable foundation of hearsay" (24); but in the Denny letter no trace remains of these doubts over the historians' ability to accurately recover the past. Quite the opposite, for Sidney urges Denny to read military handbooks and history along-side each other because the *gnosis* of the former complements the *praxis* of the latter: "The first [military manuals] shewes what should be done, the other [histories] *what hath bene done*" (539; my emphasis). Works on military science and philosophy may have replaced poetry as sources of images depicting ideal behavior, but the ideal must be balanced with reality, and for that Denny must turn to history.

Regardless of Sidney's deconstruction of the historians' claim to firm grounding, he argues throughout the *Apology* that the historian is bound "not to what should be but to what is" (27). But in the Denny letter, the historian combines accurate reports of past events with idealized patterns of behavior: "[the Greek and Roman historians] were the wisest, and fullest of excellent examples, both of discipline & strategems" (539). This sentence, on which Sidney does not dwell, effectively collapses poetry into history, for the historian now provides models of good behavior as well as preserves the past. In a sense, poetry does not have to be mentioned because Sidney has so redefined history that it almost *becomes* poetry insofar as it teaches virtue, presents models, and gives helpful hints on military strategy. Significantly, this is exactly how Sidney characterizes Homer in the *Apology* (6, 62, 88). There are only two differences between Sidney's description of history in the Denny letter and his description of poetry in the *Apology*. First, the historian does not delight his reader; second, the historian does not create "forms such as never were in nature" (14). But given the practical bent of Sidney's letter, these are negligible qualities next to the historian's ability to combine factual detail with idealized portraiture.

The omission of poetry from the list of recommended subjects might be explained by assuming that Sidney, like a good orator, considered the nature of his audience before launching into his argument, and conse-

quently tailored his list to fit Denny's specific needs. In other words, the Denny letter does not represent an ideal program of study (which presumably would include poetry), but a curtailed list meant to have no application to anyone other than Edward Denny. This view receives some support from Sidney's admission towards the beginning of his letter that "one thinge is fitte to be knowne by a scoller that will reed in the schools and an other by Ned Denny" (538), and that "thinge" happens to be soldiery, not poetry. Therefore, one might assume that Sidney recommends what Denny needs to know, not what Denny ought to know.

If, however, we choose to privilege the *Apology* as more representative of Sidney's "true" feelings towards literature, then we must confront the fact that Sidney himself discredits this explanation. He lavishes scorn upon the notion that soldiers do not need to read Homer, calling it "the ordinary doctrine of ignorance" (61). Active men "took their first motions of courage" from the poets, and as proof he gives the example of Alexander, "the phoenix of warlike princes": "This Alexander left his schoolmaster, living Aristotle, behind him, but took dead Homer with him. He put the philosopher Callistenes to death for his seeming philosophical, indeed mutinous, stubborness; but the chief thing he ever was heard to wish for was that Homer had been alive" (61).

Even though Sidney states that "poetry is the companion of the camps" (61), when someone *from* the camps asks for aid in "directinge [his] studyes" (537), Sidney declines to mention poetry. Even further, he recommends philosophy to his soldier friend, which contradicts his assertion that "the quiddety of *ens* and *prima materia* will hardly agree with a corselet" and that Alexander "well found he received more bravery of mind by the pattern of Achilles than by hearing the definition of fortitude" (61).

Equally important, by omitting poetry Sidney contradicts the advice of such highly influential writer/pedagogues as Castiglione, Sir Thomas Elyot, and Roger Ascham. All three concerned themselves with investigating, in Elyot's words, "the order of learning apt for a gentleman" such as Denny, and all three insist upon the centrality of poetry.[28] In addition, the letter of advice about education constituted an important sub-genre of humanist discourse. Rabelais, Ariosto, and Montaigne wrote one, and in each case the author includes poetry among the disciplines essential to a gentleman's education.[29]

Consequently, poetry's absence in the Denny letter makes it a highly unconventional document, and we should not try to blunt its significance by either assuming that Denny need not have read Homer or Vergil or that Sidney merely adapted his advice to fit his audience. All Renaissance pedagogues would have disagreed with poetry's omission, and we need to attend to the disparity between the Denny letter and the *Apology*, not explain it away or diminish its significance.

Sidney does not make clear if his younger brother Robert asked for advice or, as older siblings often do, he spontaneously offered his advice on which disciplines best "teach profit."[30] Whatever its origin, the resulting letter (dated 18 October 1580) generally follows the same outlines as the Denny letter, although with some significant modifications.[31] Perhaps assuming that Robert already recognized the importance of the Bible, Sidney begins with history, recommending Jean Bodin "for the method of writing history" (219). Sidney gives the "chronologies of Melanchthon, Tarchagnota, Languet, and such others" as examples of "narrations of things done" (220), and he suggests that Robert read the ancient histories chronologically: "Xenophon to follow Thucydides, so doth Thucydides follow Herodotus, and Diodorus Siculus follow Xenophon; so generally do the Roman stories follow the Greek, and the particular stories of present monarchies follow the Roman" (220).

Sidney also strongly recommends that Robert attend to the "discoursers," whom he defines as anyone who writes "non simpliciter de facto, sed de qualitatibus et circumstantiis facti" (221)—not simply of the facts (i.e, the historians?), but of the qualities and circumstances of the fact. Sidney gives as examples the divine, "in telling his opinion and reasons in religion"; the lawyer, in "in showing the causes and benefits of laws"; and the "natural philosopher," "in setting down the causes of any strange thing."

As in the Denny letter, Sidney stresses that he particularly wants Robert to read the works of the "moral philosopher" in all his varieties: "either in the ethic part, when he sets forth virtues or vices, and the natures of passions, or in the politic, when he doth (as he often doth) meddle sententiously with matters of estate" (221).

The philosophers, not the poets, provide ideal models of actions (although Sidney does not specify, we may assume that he has in mind Aristotle and Cicero). Sidney's theoretical treatment of historians similarly follows the Denny letter, not the *Apology*. Sidney grants that the historian can reproduce the past accurately and, perhaps more importantly, it is the historian, not the poet, who provides ideal models for emulation, "examples of virtue and vice, with their good or evil successes": "the establishment or ruins of great estates, with the causes, the time, and the circumstances of the laws then written of, the enterings and endings of wars, and therein, the stratagems against the enemy, and the discipline upon the soldier, and thus much as a very historiographer" (220).

Nonetheless, Sidney's treatment of history differs subtly from the other two texts. In the Denny letter, Sidney collapses poetry into history, and in the *Apology*, he rigorously insists upon the boundary separating poetry from history. The historian, tied "not to what should be but to what is" (27), cannot but include the good with the bad: "But as in Alexander or Scipio himself, show doings, some to be liked, some to be misliked" (32-33). Sidney grants that occasionally the historian "must tell events whereof he can yield no cause," but when this happens, he ceases to be an historian and becomes "poetical" (32, 33). In neither text does Sidney admit the possibility of any middle ground.

Sidney allows precisely this excluded option in the letter to Robert. He admits poetry's existence, which he does not do in the Denny letter, and he grants history much greater leeway in adapting the *method* of poetry (feigning) without actually becoming poetry than he does in the *Apology*:

> Besides this, the historian makes himself a discourser for profit, and an orator, yea a poet, sometimes for ornament. An orator, in making excellent orations "e re nata," which are to be marked, but marked with the note of rhetorical remembrances: a poet, in painting forth the effects, the motions, the whisperings of the people, which though in disputation one might say were true, yet who will mark them well, shall find them taste of a poetical vein, and that kind are gallantly to be marked: for though perchance they were not so, yet it is enough they might be so. (220-21)

One could say that Sidney so valorizes those parts written in "the poetical vein" that they become the most valuable feature of history, thus coming very close to his statement in the *Apology* that "the best of the historian is subject to the poet" (34). Nonetheless, poetry is still subordinate to history, for if Sidney allows the historian to use "poetry" in order to teach virtue more effectively, he also says that the historian becomes an orator at other times. Although Sidney proposes an interdisciplinary approach in this passage, there is no doubt that history remains the preeminent science; poetry is a tool, not an equal partner. And so, Sidney does not recommend that Robert follow Alexander and read Homer. Using the example that Sidney gives in the *Apology*, this letter recommends that Robert spend his time reading Herodotus, not Xenophon, the fate of Zopyrus' nose notwithstanding. Even so, Sidney's theory of history in the Robert letter constitutes a compromise position between the unqualified denial of poetry in the Denny letter and the unqualified praise of poetry in the *Apology*.

The gulf between the *Apology* and the letters demonstrates that the *Apology* does not constitute an unambiguous, public statement of Sidney's poetics, but rather one statement among three, and which one we decide to privilege will reveal much about *our* preferences.[32] If, however, we give each text equal weight, not assuming that the *Apology* represents Sidney's "true" feelings, then Sidney's unsureness of poetry's place in the public and the private spheres becomes clearer. The *Apology*, we should remember, was not written for public consumption, but for a coterie audience, which Sidney knew was largely, but not exclusively, sympathetic towards literature. As for the letters, such texts were by convention semi-public documents (indeed the Denny letter survived only because a student copied it out as an exercise). Privately, Sidney allowed himself, however problematically, to defend poetry. But for public consumption, Sidney either ignores poetry altogether or subordinates it to a more respectable discipline. To borrow Greenblatt's terms, it would appear that Sidney wrote his letters with an eye towards fashioning and maintaining his *public* self, and as we know from Moffett's adjustments to Sidney's literary career, a sympathy for poetry did not jibe with maintaining an image as the leader of international Protestantism.

Notes

. . . [25] Sir Edward Denny (1547-99) led a highly successful career as a soldier-courtier. All we know of his education is that Denny attended Merton College, Oxford, but his military career is more fully documented. He accompanied the Earl of Essex to Ireland in 1573, went on a number of highly profitable privateering ventures between 1577 and 1578, and toward the end of 1588 accompanied his cousins Sir Humphrey Gilbert and Sir Walter Raleigh on their unsuccessful expedition to the New World. Denny and Sidney probably had known each other for some time before 1580, when Denny participated in a tournament officiated by Queen Elizabeth in which he and two other companions-at-arms, Philip, Earl of Arundel and Sir William Drurie, held the field against all challengers, including the Earl of Oxford, Edward de Vere, and Sir Philip Sidney. That same year Denny, upon the recommendation of Sir Philip's father, Sir Henry Sidney, who called him "my deere friend," accompanied Lord Grey de Wilton (his secretary was Edmund Spenser) on his mission to Ireland, where he distinguished himself in a number of military engagements. After Ireland, Denny and Sidney's friendship continued to thrive. In a 1581 letter to Walsingham, Denny calls Sidney "the most worthy young man in the world." Elizabeth frequently employed Denny as a private messenger, and for his distinguished service over the years she knighted him in 1588. Denny died in 1599, and his epitaphs depict a man who exemplified the Elizabethan ideal of a courtier: "religious, wise, just, liberall, right valiant, most active, learning friende, prides foe, kindly, lovinge, mutch beloved, was honoured wth y^t dignitie of knighthood by due deserte in ye field." A poem inscribed on a pillar next to his tomb sums up his life thus: "A courtier in the chamber, / A soldier in the fielde / Whose tongue could neuer flatter / Whose heart could neuer yield."

Did Denny follow Sidney's advice? Probably not, as he would have been too busy with the sordid details of fighting. Denny's sense of warfare was very much grounded in the traditions of chivalry, and he quickly became disillusioned with the Irish campaign. He complained that he had to fight in "boggs, gllimmes, and woods, as in my opinion it might better fit mastives than brave gentlemen that desier to win honour." The above information is summarized from H. L. L. Denny, "Biography of Sir Edward Denny," *East Herts Archaeological Society: Transactions* 2 (1902-1904): 248-49.

[26] Sidney's letter to Denny remained unknown to twentieth-century critics until a Renaissance transcript of it turned up at a 1971 auction at Sotheby's (London). Later that year, *English Literary Renaissance* reprinted a portion of the letter in holograph (*ELR* 2 [1971]) with an introduction by John Buxton. In *Young Philip Sidney: 1572-1577,* James M. Osborn reprints the entire letter. All further references to the Denny letter are to Osborn's edition and cited parenthetically in the text. Although these letters have been known for some years, their relationship to Sidney's poetics has escaped scrutiny. Elizabeth Story Donno ("Old Mouse-Eaten Records: History in Sidney's *Apology,*" in *Sir Philip Sidney: An Anthology of Modern Criticism,* ed. Dennis Kay [Oxford: Clarendon Press, 1987], 149-50) and Dorothy Connell (*Sir Philip Sidney: The Maker's Mind*) mention the Denny letter, and Katherine Duncan-Jones gives an extended summary of it in *Sir Philip Sidney: Courtier Poet* (New Haven and London: Yale University Press, 1991), 171-74. No one, however, mentions the discrepancies between the letter and the *Apology*.

[27] Sidney's choices are as follows: "of Refreining anger, of curiosity, of the Tranquility of the minde, of the Flatterer, & the friende, [and] of Morall vertew" (539).

[28] Elyot calls Homer "a fountain" from which proceeds "all eloquence and learning." Because the *Iliad* presents the best examples of both political and military behavior, "there is no lesson for a young gentleman to be compared with Homer," and Elyot gives the *Aeneid* similar praise (*The Book Named the Governor,* ed. S. E. Lehmberg [New York: Everyman's Library, 1966], 30). Ascham also deems Homer "learned" and "divine." He has "so much learning in all kind of sciences as, by the judgement of Quintillian, he deserveth so high a praise that no man yet deserved to sit in the second degree beneath him" (Roger Ascham, *The Schoolmaster,* ed. Lawrence V. Ryan [Ithaca: Folger

Shakespeare Library, 1967], 54-55. Castiglione has Count Ludovico pepper his talk with brief encomia of poets ancient and contemporary, and his declaration that courtiers should also be poets is famous: "Let [the ideal courtier] be versed in the poets, as well as in the orators and historians, and let him be practiced also in writing verse and prose" (*The Book of the Courtier,* trans. Charles Singleton [New York: Anchor Books, 1959], 70). He should not only emulate Alexander's respect for Homer's art, but, like Unico Aretino, be prepared to recite a "spontaneous" sonnet so accomplished that his audience wonders if he composed it the night before.

[29] As Claudio Guillén reminds us, "the letter may be regarded as one of the classical genres that are cultivated again or resurrected during the Renaissance" ("Notes toward the Study of the Renaissance Letter," *Renaissance Genres: Essays on Theory, History, and Interpretation [Harvard English Studies 14 (1986)],* 71). Rabelais, for example, "copies" Gargantua's letter to Pantagruel advising his son to become "a veritable abyss of learning," and Ariosto, in his sixth satire, a verse-epistle addressed to Pietro Bembo, details the humanist program of study he wants his son to follow. Montaigne casts the essay "Of the Education of Children" as a letter to the Comtesse de Gurson advising her upon the education of her progeny.

[30] Robert Sidney's life more or less followed the same path as his brother's. The younger Sidney even wrote poetry, although his competent verse does not compare to the splendors of *Astrophil and Stella.* Like Denny, Robert Sidney was a soldier (he served in the same Dutch campaign that proved fatal to his brother) and, like his older brother, Robert served his queen as a relatively high-level diplomat. In the face of the Spanish threat, Elizabeth sent Robert to Scotland in 1588 in order to secure James's loyalty as well as to "back the queen out of some intemperate promises" committed by William Asheby," of awarding James' an English duchy with accompanying revenues, five thousand pounds, and a force of fifty gentleman, one hundred foot, and one hundred horse to be maintained at the queen's expense. Not only did Robert Sidney succeed at nullifying Asheby's promises while still ensuring James's loyalty, he did so while earning James's affections" (Millicent V. Hay, *The Life of Robert Sidney* [Washington, DC: Folger Shakespeare Library, Associated University Press, 1984], 61-69).

[31] All references to Sidney's letter to Robert are from *The Correspondence of Philip Sidney and Hubert Languet,* ed. William A. Bradley (Boston: Merrymount Press, 1912), 219-25.

[32] For proponents of this view, see Neil Rudenstine, *Sidney's Poetic Development* (Cambridge; Harvard University Press, 1967), 51-52; A. C. Hamilton, *Sir*

Philip Sidney: A Study of His Life and Works (Cambridge: Cambridge University Press, 1977), 107-9; and Forrest G. Robinson, "Introduction," xxiii. . . .

FURTHER READING

Bibliography

Stump, Donald V., et al. *An Annotated Bibliography of Texts and Criticism.* Old Tappan, NJ: Hall Reference (Macmillan), 1994, 864 p.

Comprehensive reference source.

Biography

Boas, Frederick S. *Sir Philip Sidney: Representative Elizabethan—His Life and Writings.* London: Staples Press, 1955, 204 p.

Highly regarded, comprehensive study that also includes criticism of Sidney's works.

Duncan-Jones, Katherine. *Sir Philip Sidney: Courtier Poet.* New Haven: Yale University Press, 1991, 350 p.

Challenges hagiographical reports of Sidney and offers connections between his life and his writings.

Greville, Fulke. *Life of the Renowned Sir Philip Sidney.* 1652. Reprint. Delmar, N.Y.: Scholars' Facsimiles and Reprints, 1984, 255 p.

Contemporaneous and reverential work which helped to create Sidney's legendary status.

Osborn, James M. *Young Philip Sidney, Fifteen Seventy-Two to Fifteen Seventy-Seven.* Ann Arbor, Mi.: Books on Demand, 1972, 591 p.

Scholarly work that includes many letters and records.

Wallace, Malcolm William. *The Life of Sir Philip Sidney.* 1915. Reprint. New York: Octagon Books, 1967, 428 p.

Called "unsurpassed" by Duncan-Jones, includes significant, previously unpublished details on Sidney's childhood.

Criticism

Connell, Dorothy. *Sir Philip Sidney: The Maker's Mind.* Oxford: Clarendon Press, 1977, 163 p.

Examines Sidney's notions of love, poetry, and play.

Craft, William. *Labyrinth of Desire: Invention and Culture in the Work of Sir Philip Sidney.* Newark, N.J.: University of Delaware Press, 1994, 163 p.

Examines Sidney in the context of his Protestant, humanist, Tudor culture.

Doherty, M. J. *The Mistress-Knowledge: Sir Philip Sidney's "Defence of Poesie" and Literary Architectonics in the English Renaissance.* Nashville, Tenn.: Vanderbilt

University Press, 1991, 372 p.

    Discusses the idea of universal knowledge within the context of the English Renaissance, and why Sidney found poetry to be the best means of approaching it.

Haber, Judith. "Pastime and Passion: The Impasse in the *Old Arcadia*." In *Pastoral and the Poetics of Self-Contradiction: Theocritus to Marvell*, pp. 53-97. Cambridge: Cambridge University Press, 1994.

    Analyzes the *Old Arcadia* and explains why Sidney found problems with the structure of the pastoral romance.

Hager, Alan. "The Exemplary Mirage: Fabrication of Sir Philip Sidney's Biographical Image and the Sidney Reader." In *Sir Philip Sidney: An Anthology of Modern Criticism*, edited by Dennis Kay, pp. 45-59. Oxford: Clarendon Press, 1987.

    Argues that the idealistic, popular image of Sidney interferes with our appreciation of him.

Hardison, O. B., Jr. "The Two Voices of Sidney's *Apology for Poetry*." *English Literary Renaissance* 2, No. 1 (Winter 1972): 83-99.

    Examines Sidney's proofs for the excellency of poetry in the *Apology* and contends that the last section cannot be reconciled with the main body of the work.

Kalstone, David. *Sidney's Poetry: Contexts and Interpretation*. Cambridge: Harvard University Press, 1965, 195 p.

    Close examination of the poetry of *Arcadia* and *Astrophel and Stella*.

Kinney, Arthur F., ed. *Essential Articles for the Study of Sir Philip Sidney*. Hamden, Conn.: Archon Books, 1986, 458 p.

    Compilation of important non-textual and non-technical papers.

————. "Sir Philip Sidney and the Uses of History." In *The Historical Renaissance: New Essays on Tudor and Stuart Literature and Culture,* edited by Heather Dubrow and Richard Strier, pp. 293-314. Chicago: University of Chicago Press, 1988.

    Discusses how Sidney's poetry reflected his belief in the reading of history as instruction on how to live.

————. *Sidney in Retrospect: Selections from English Literary Renaissance*. Amherst: The University of Massachusetts Press, 1988, 273 p.

    Wide range of notable scholarly articles.

McCoy, Richard C. *Sir Philip Sidney: Rebellion in Arcadia*. New Brunswick, N.J.: Rutgers University Press, 1979, 230 p.

    Examines *Astrophil and Stella* and the two *Arcadias*, focusing on how the works relate to Elizabethan politics.

Raitiere, Martin N. *Faire Bitts: Sir Philip Sidney and Renaissance Political Theory*. Pittsburgh: Duquesne University Press, 1984, 154 p.

    Study of Sidney's political orientation that argues that Sidney's politics have generally been misconstrued.

Rudenstine, Neil L. *Sidney's Poetic Development*. Cambridge: Harvard University Press, 1967, 313 p.

    Examination of Sidney's style and technique that argues that there is continuity, consistency, and unity in all of his works.

Thompson, John. "Sir Philip Sidney." In his *The Founding of English Metre,* pp. 139-55. New York: Columbia University Press, 1961.

    Study of the "perfection" of Sidney's metre.

Wilson, Jean. *Entertainments for Elizabeth I*. Totowa, N.J.: Rowman and Littlefield, 1980, 179 p.

    Includes description and study of Sidney's *The Four Foster Children of Desire*.

Additional coverage of Sidney's life and career is contained in the following source published by Gale Research: *Literature Criticism from 1400 to 1800,* Vol. 19.

Edmund Spenser

1552?-1599

English poet and essayist.

The following entry contains critical essays on Sidney's role in his own time. For further information on Spenser, see *LC,* Vol. 5.

INTRODUCTION

Spenser is known as "the poet's poet" for his delight in the pure artistry of his craft: his pictorial imagery, sensuous description, and linguistic richness combine to establish him as one of the greatest of English poets. His work has earned the approbation and respect of some of the most illustrious names in poetry: John Milton spoke of "our sage and serious poet, Spencer"; John Dryden acknowledged him as his "master" in poetry; James Thomson referred to him as "fancy's pleasing son"; John Keats characterized him as "Elfin Poet"; and William Wordsworth envisioned "Sweet Spenser, moving through his clouded heaven / With the moon's beauty and the moon's soft pace. . . ." Such praise refers primarily to Spenser's epic allegorical poem *The Faerie Queene* (1590-96), which, though unfinished, is indisputably a masterwork of English literature. In this poem of chivalric romance and adventure, Spenser created a poetic world which has captured the imaginations of centuries of readers and a complex allegory which continues to fascinate critics.

Biographical Information

Spenser was born into a tailor's household in London. His early schooling took place at the Merchant Taylors' Free School, where he received an education considered quite progressive by the standards of the day. He studied a humanist curriculum that included the study of English language and literature—an unusual innovation at the time. In 1569 Spenser entered Pembroke College, Cambridge, receiving his bachelor's degree in 1573 and his master's in 1576. Upon finishing his education, Spenser was determined to be a poet, but, as a "gentleman by education only" he needed to work to support himself. In 1578 he served as Secretary to the Bishop of Rochester and in 1579 went to work for the Earl of Leicester. The latter position brought him into proximity of the court of Queen Elizabeth I, where he met Philip Sidney and others. In Renaissance England, the court was the center of social life and power and poetry was one means by which courtiers gained recognition and promotion. While

Spenser was friends with some established courtiers, he was never part of the court himself. His social distance from the court elite was exacerbated by geographical distance when he was sent to Ireland in 1580; some biographers have regarded this as a benign transfer, but others have interpreted it as punishment for critical ideas expressed in the poem "Mother Hubberd's Tale," which was privately circulated in 1579, but was not published until 1591 in *Complaints: Containing Sundrie Small Poemes of the Worlds Vanitie.* In any case, Spenser became secretary to Lord Grey de Wilton, and took up residence in Ireland, where a series of increasingly important positions and the acquisition of land kept him for nearly twenty years. A turning point in his career came in 1589, when he spent one more year at court under the patronage of his friend Walter Raleigh, who helped him publish the first books of *The Faerie Queene* in 1590. In 1594 Spenser married Elizabeth Boyle; their courtship and marriage are immortalized in Spenser's sonnet sequence, the *Amoretti,* and his wedding ode, the "Epithalamion" (1595). In 1598 political unrest in Ireland forced Spenser and his family to flee the country; his Irish estate, Kilcomen Castle, was destroyed in Tyrone's Rebellion. They went to London, where Spenser died soon after. He is buried in Poets' Corner, Westminster Abbey. At his burial the leading poets of the day gathered in a ceremony to toss commendatory verses into his tomb.

Major Works

By all accounts, Spenser's most important work is *The Faerie Queene*, a narrative epic of legends and romance, purportedly medieval in conception but actually more closely related to the sixteenth-century Italian romantic epic, particularly Ludovico Ariosto's *Orlando furioso* (1532) and Torquato Tasso's *Gerusalemme liberata* (1581). Like these works, *The Faerie Queene* is a series of chivalrous adventures, replete with tales of knightly honor, damsels in distress, and evil forces to be conquered. Spenser conceived of *The Faerie Queene* on an ambitious scale, outlining his design in a letter to Raleigh which appeared as a prefix to the first three published books of the poem. His intent was to write twelve books, each featuring a central hero or heroine representing one of twelve virtues. Spenser died before he could complete his task; as it stands, *The Faerie Queene* consists of six books and a fragment of a seventh, commonly referred to as the "Cantos of Mutabilitie." Spenser planned his poem as a "continued Allegory, or darke conceit," and critics agree that the pervasive allegory of *The Faerie Queene* is one of its most remarkable aspects. The allegory works principally on two levels—moral and political—although subsidiary spiritual, historical, and personal allegories have also been studied. The moral allegory is the most consistent as well as the most clear and accessible. The political allegory is the more obscure for the modern reader given the political complexities of the Elizabethan court. There is no doubt that the poem was written both to represent a model of gentlemanly *virtu* and to pay tribute to Queen Elizabeth. While Spenser was never more than a marginal figure in the world of the court, he certainly sought favor and notice there, and *The Faerie Queene* was a major project to that end. At the same time, his distance from the inner circles of the court allowed him to be more critical and ambivalent, especially in the later books of the epic. After 1590 most of his close associates in the court were dead or out of favor and so his connection to the court was especially weak by the time the later books of *The Faerie Queen* were published in 1596. The value of the allegory has been a contested issue for critics. While many have noted that a reader's lack of knowledge of the allegorical aspects does not prevent enjoyment of the poem, others insist that an understanding of the allegory is essential to a true appreciation of the work. Some maintain that, in either case, the allegory is cumbersome and unappealing; moreover, it is inconsistent and the narrative in places disjointed and careless as well. With regard to the poetry, critics are virtually unanimous in praising the originality and freshness of Spenser's technical style. Perhaps most striking in *The Faerie Queene* is Spenser's metrical innovation, which has come to be called the Spenserian stanza. Composed of eight iambic pentameters and a final alexandrine, the stanza has the rhyme scheme ABABBCBCC. Spenser's choice of meter is appropriate and the sonorous, stately rhythm helps to establish the dreamlike ambiance of the poem. Other aspects of Spenser's style complement the overall impression the poem creates: repeated alliteration and assonance contribute to the fluidity and grace that characterize *The Faerie Queene*'s romantic milieu. To heighten the sense of old-fashioned quaintness and to emphasize the poem's claim to legendary stature, Spenser adopted a quasi-medieval diction. To a liberal application of archaic words and phrases he added English adaptations of foreign words as well as a few ancient-sounding neologisms. Crowning all is Spenser's unique orthography, whereby he was able to make even the simplest words appear interestingly archaic. Compared with the magnitude of his achievement in *The Faerie Queene*, all of Spenser's other work is minor, though it shows a considerable range and diversity. *The Shepheardes Calender: Conteyning Twelve Æglogues Proportionable to the Twelve Monethes* (1579) is a series of twelve eclogues, one for each month of the year, written in the pastoral tradition. In *The Shepheardes Calender* and in *Colin Clouts Come Home Againe* (1595), a later poem in which Spenser resurrected many of the themes and characters of the *Calender*, Spenser revealed his attitudes toward art, pastoral idealism, and the sociopolitical world of the Elizabethan court. Spenser's sequence of love sonnets, the *Amoretti*, is fairly conventional in conception, based on the Petrarchan tradition. Yet where the Petrarchan sonnet ends in death or unfulfilled longing, Spenser's *Amoretti* quite remarkably ends with union. The "Epithalamion," an ode celebrating his marriage, is generally thought by modern critics to be Spenser's best work, with the sole exception of *The Faerie Queene*. Spenser's most notable prose piece is his *A View of the State of Ireland, Written Dialogue-wise, betweene Eudoxus and Irenæus* (1633), an essay describing and approving the harsh English policies of subjection in sixteenth-century Ireland.

Critical Reception

From the sixteenth century to the twentieth, Spenser's work has maintained a place of distinction in English literature. His masterpiece, *The Faerie Queene*, was very favorably received upon its publication and has remained popular ever since. However, since it is a work that elicits strong reactions, the poem has also had its detractors. Its length and complexity have daunted many readers; Francis Thompson has stated flatly that *The Faerie Queene* "is in truth a poem no man can read through save as a duty, and in a series of arduous campaigns (so to speak)." But most critics have focused on the lushness of *The Faerie Queene* as its most admirable aspect; Edward Dowden in 1910 described the poem as "a labyrinth of beauty, a forest of old romance in which it is possible to lose oneself more irrecoverably amid the tangled luxury of loveliness than elsewhere in English poetry." Spenser's series of twelve eclogues, *The Shepheardes Calender,* was also praised by early critics, among them Sidney, to whom it was dedicated. In his *The Defence of Poesie* (1595) Sidney remarked that Spenser "hath much Poetrie in his Eglogues; indede worthy the reading, if I be not deceived." He disapproved, however, of Spenser's "framing . . . his stile to an old rustick language." The enthusiastic praise accorded *The Shepheardes Calender* has waned in recent times and the poem is now accorded minor status. Nonetheless, Spenser's importance and his impact on the development of English poetry have been judged incalculable. He was not only a notable figure in his own time, but proved a profound influence on subsequent generations of English poets, earning a firm and permanent place in the tradition of English letters. He is still considered by many scholars the greatest nondramatic English poet of the Renaissance. Much of the criticism of his work has concentrated on its allegorical aspects and on Spenser's role as a stylistic innovator. Still, each generation of critics finds new aspects of his work to examine. In recent years attention has turned to analyses of the handling of gender (especially as it comments on Queen Elizabeth) in his works and to the historical and cultural context that makes his alllegory so rich.

PRINCIPAL WORKS

"Epigrams" and "Sonets" [translator] (poetry) 1569; published in *A Theatre for Worldlings*

The Shepheardes Calender: Conteyning Twelve Æglogues Proportionable to the Twelve Monethes (poetry) 1579

**Three Proper, and Wittie, Familiar Letters Lately Passed between Two Universitie Men: Touching the Earthquake in Aprill Last and Our English Reformed Versifying* (letters) 1580

***The Faerie Queene, Disposed into Twelve Bookes Fashioning XII Morall Vertues* [Books I-III] (poetry) 1590

Complaints: Containing Sundrie Small Poemes of the Worlds Vanitie (poetry) 1591

Amoretti and Epithalamion (poetry) 1595

Colin Clouts Come Home Againe (poetry) 1595

****The Faerie Queene, Disposed into Twelve Bookes Fashioning XII Morall Vertues: The Second Part of The Faerie Queene, Containing the Fourth, Fifth,*

and Sixth Bookes (poetry) 1596

Fowre Hymnes (poetry) 1596

Prothalamion; or a Spousall Verse (poetry) 1596

*****A View of the State of Ireland, Written Dialoguewise, betweene Eudoxus and Irenœus* (essay) 1633

The Complete Works in Verse and Prose of Edmund Spenser. 10 vols. (poetry, essay, and letters) 1882-84

*This work includes letters written by Gabriel Harvey

**This work was not published in its entirety until 1609, when the "Two Cantos of Mutabilitie" were added.

***This work includes a revision of the earlier *The Faerie Queene, Disposed into Twelve Bookes Fashioning XII Morall Vertues* [Books I-III].

****This work was written between1595 and 1597.

CRITICISM

H. A. Taine (essay date 1889)

SOURCE: "The Pagan Renaissance" in "The Renaissance," Book II of *History of English Literature,* Henry Holt and Company, 1889, pp. 289-321.

[*In the following excerpt from his survey of English literature, Taine gives an overview of Spenser and* The Faerie Queene *in the context of the English Renaissance.*]

Spenser belonged to an ancient family, allied to great houses; was a friend of Sidney and Raleigh, the two most accomplished knights of the age—a knight himself, at least in heart; who had found in his connections, his friendships, his studies, his life, everything calculated to lead him to ideal poetry. We find him at Cambridge, where he imbues himself with the noblest ancient philosophies; in a northern country, where he passes through a deep and unfortunate passion; at Penshurst, in the castle and in the society where the *Arcadia* was produced; with Sidney, in whom survived entire the romantic poetry and heroic generosity of the feudal spirit; at court, where all the splendours of a disciplined and gorgeous chivalry were gathered about the throne; finally, at Kilcolman, on the borders of a beautiful lake, in a lonely castle, from which the view embraced an amphitheatre of mountains, and the half of Ireland. Poor on the other hand,[1] not fit for court, and though favoured by the queen, unable to obtain from his patrons anything but inferior employment; in the end, wearied of solicitations, and banished to his dangerous property in Ireland, whence a rebellion expelled him, after his house and child had been burned; he died three months later, of misery and a broken heart.[2] Expectations and rebuffs, many sorrows and many dreams, some few joys, and a sudden and frightful calamity, a small fortune and a premature end; this indeed was a poet's life. But the heart within was the true poet—from it all proceeded; circumstances furnished the subject only; he transformed them more than they him; he received less than he gave. Philosophy and landscapes, ceremonies and ornaments, splendours of the country and the court, on all which he painted or thought, he impressed his inward nobleness. Above all, his was a soul captivated by sublime and chaste beauty, eminently platonic; one of these lofty and refined souls most charming of all, who, born in the lap of nature, draw thence their sustenance, but soar higher, enter the regions of mysticism, and mount instinctively in order to expand on the confines of a loftier world. Spenser leads us to Milton, and thence to Puritanism, as Plato to Virgil, and thence to Christianity. Sensuous beauty is perfect in both, but their main worship is for moral beauty. He appeals to the Muses:

> Revele to me the sacred noursery
> Of vertue, which with you doth there remaine,
> Where it in silver bowre does hidden ly
> From view of men and wicked worlds
>   disdaine!

He encourages his knight when he sees him droop. He is wroth when he sees him attacked. He rejoices in his justice, temperance, courtesy. He introduces in the beginning of a song, long stanzas in honour of friendship and justice. He pauses, after relating a lovely instance of chastity, to exhort women to modesty. He pours out the wealth of his respect and tenderness at the feet of his heroines. If any coarse man insults them, he calls to their aid nature and the gods. Never does he bring them on his stage without adorning their name with splendid eulogy. He has an adoration for beauty worthy of Dante and Plotinus. And this, because he never considers it a mere harmony of colour and form, but an emanation of unique, heavenly, imperishable beauty, which no mortal eye can see, and which is the masterpiece of the great Author of the worlds.[3] Bodies only render it visible; it does not live in them; charm and attraction are not in things, but in the immortal idea which shines through them:

> For that same goodly hew of white and red,
> With which the cheekes are sprinckled, shall
>   decay,
> And those sweete rosy leaves, so fairly spred
> Upon the lips, shall fade and fall away
> To that they were, even to corrupted clay:
> That golden wyre, those sparckling stars so
>   bright,
> Shall turne to dust, and lose their goodly
>   light.
> But that faire lampe, from whose celestiall ray
> That light proceedes, which kindleth lovers
>   fire,

> Shall never be extinguisht nor decay;
> But, when the vitall spirits doe expyre,
> Upon her native planet shall retyre;
> For it is heavenly borne, and cannot die,
> Being a parcell of the purest skie.[4]

In presence of this ideal of beauty, love is transformed:

> For Love is lord of Truth and Loialtie,
> Lifting himself out of the lowly dust,
> On golden plumes up to the purest skie,
> Above the reach of loathly sinfull lust,
> Whose base affect through cowardly distrust
> Of his weake wings dare not to heaven fly,
> But like a moldwarpe in the earth doth ly.[5]

Love such as this contains all that is good, and fine, and noble. It is the prime source of life, and the eternal soul of things. It is this love which, pacifying the primitive discord, has created the harmony of the spheres, and maintains this glorious universe. It dwells in God, and is God Himself, come down in bodily form to regenerate the tottering world and save the human race; around and within animated beings, when our eyes can pierce outward appearances, we behold it as a living light, penetrating and embracing every creature. We touch here the sublime sharp summit where the world of mind and the world of sense unite; where man, gathering with both hands the loveliest flowers of either, feels himself at the same time a pagan and a Christian.

So much, as a testimony to his heart. But he was also a poet, that is, pre-eminently a creator and a dreamer, and that most naturally, instinctively, unceasingly. We might go on for ever describing this inward condition of all great artists; there would still remain much to be described. It is a sort of mental growth with them; at every instant a bud shoots forth, and on this another and still another; each producing, increasing, blooming of itself, so that after a few moments we find first a green plant crop up, then a thicket, then a forest. A character appears to them, then an action, then a landscape, then a succession of actions, characters, landscapes, producing, completing, arranging themselves by instinctive development, as when in a dream we behold a train of figures which, without any outward compulsion, display and group themselves before our eyes. This fount of living and changing forms is inexhaustible in Spenser; he is always imaging; it is his specialty. He has but to close his eyes, and apparitions arise; they abound in him, crowd, overflow; in vain he pours them forth; they continually float up, more copious and more dense. Many times, following the inexhaustible stream, I have thought of the vapours which rise incessantly from the sea, ascend, sparkle, commingle their golden and snowy scrolls, while underneath them new mists arise, and others again beneath, and the splendid procession never grows dim or ceases.

But what distinguishes him from all others is the mode of his imagination. Generally with a poet his mind ferments vehemently and by fits and starts; his ideas gather, jostle each other, suddenly appear in masses and heaps, and burst forth in sharp, piercing, concentrative words; it seems that they need these sudden accumulations to imitate the unity and life-like energy of the objects which they reproduce; at least almost all the poets of that time, Shakspeare at their head, act thus. Spenser remains calm in the fervour of invention. The visions which would be fever to another, leave him at peace. They come and unfold themselves before him, easily, entire, uninterrupted, without starts. He is epic, that is, a narrator, not a singer like an ode-writer, nor a mimic like a play-writer. No modern is more like Homer. Like Homer and the great epic-writers, he only presents consecutive and noble, almost classical images, so nearly ideas, that the mind seizes them unaided and unawares. Like Homer, he is always simple and clear: he makes no leaps, he omits no argument, he robs no word of its primitive and ordinary meaning, he preserves the natural sequence of ideas. Like Homer again, he is redundant, ingenuous, even childish. He says everything, he puts down reflections which we have made beforehand; he repeats without limit his grand ornamental epithets. We can see that he beholds objects in a beautiful uniform light, with infinite detail; that he wishes to show all this detail, never fearing to see his happy dream change or disappear; that he traces its outline with a regular movement, never hurrying or slackening. He is even a little prolix, too unmindful of the public, too ready to lose himself and dream about the things he beholds. His thought expands in vast repeated comparisons, like those of the old Ionic poet. If a wounded giant falls, he finds him

> As an aged tree,
> High growing on the top of rocky clift,
> Whose hart-strings with keene steele nigh
> 　hewen be,
> The mightie trunck halfe rent with ragged rift,
> Doth roll adowne the rocks, and fall with
> 　fearefull drift.
>
> Or as a castle, reared high and round,
> By subtile engins and malitious slight
> Is undermined from the lowest ground,
> And her foundation forst, and feebled quight,
> At last downe falles; and with her heaped
> 　hight
> Her hastie ruine does more heavie make,
> And yields it selfe unto the victours might:
> Such was this Gyaunt's fall, that seemd to
> 　shake
> The stedfast globe of earth, as it for feare did
> 　quake.[6]

He develops all the ideas which he handles. All his phrases become periods. Instead of compressing, he expands. To bear this ample thought and its accompanying train, he requires a long stanza, ever renewed, long alternate verses, reiterated rhymes, whose uniformity and fulness recall the majestic sounds which undulate eternally through the woods and the fields. To unfold these epic faculties, and to display them in the sublime region where his soul is naturally borne, he requires an ideal stage, situated beyond the bounds of reality, with personages who could hardly exist, and in a world which could never be.

He made many miscellaneous attempts in sonnets, elegies, pastorals, hymns of love, little sparkling word pictures;[7] they were but essays, incapable for the most part of supporting his genius. Yet already his magnificent imagination appeared in them; gods, men, landscapes, the world which he sets in motion is a thousand miles from that in which we live. His ***Shepherd's Calendar***[8] is a thought-inspiring and tender pastoral, full of delicate loves, noble sorrows, lofty ideas, where no voice is heard but of thinkers and poets. His ***Visions of Petrarch and Du Bellay*** are admirable dreams, in which palaces, temples of gold, splendid landscapes, sparkling rivers, marvellous birds, appear in close succession as in an Oriental fairy-tale. If he sings a "***Prothalamion,***" he sees two beautiful swans, white as snow, who come softly swimming down amidst the songs of nymphs and vermeil roses, while the transparent water kisses their silken feathers, and murmurs with joy:

> There, in a meadow, by the river's side.
> A flocke of Nymphes I chaunced to espy,
> All lovely daughters of the Flood thereby,
> With goodly greenish locks, all loose untyde,
> As each had bene a bryde;
> And each one had a little wicker basket,
> Made of fine twigs, entrayled curiously,
> In which they gathered flowers to fill their
> 　flasket,
> And with fine fingers cropt full feateously
> The tender stalkes on hye.
> Of every sort, which in that meadow grew,
> They gathered some; the violet, pallid blew,
> The little dazie, that at evening closes,
> The virgin lillie, and the primrose trew,
> With store of vermeil roses,
> 　To deck their bridegroomes posies
> 　Against the brydale-day, which was not
> 　　long:
> Sweet Themmes! runne softly, till I end my
> 　song.
> With that I saw two Swannes of goodly
> 　hewe
> Come softly swimming downe along the lee;
> Two fairer birds I yet did never see;
> The snow, which doth the top of Pindus
> 　strew,
> Did never whiter shew . . .
> So purely white they were,

That even the gentle stream, the which them
    bare,
Seem'd foule to them, and bad his billowes
    spare
To wet their silken feathers, least they might
Soyle their fayre plumes with water not so
    fayre,
And marre their beauties bright,
That shone as heavens light,
Against their brydale day, which was not
    long:
Sweet Themmes! runne softly, till I end my
    song![9]

If he bewails the death of Sidney, Sidney becomes a
shepherd; he is slain like Adonis; around him gather
weeping nymphs:

The gods, which all things see, this same
    beheld,
And, pittying this paire of lovers trew,
Transformed them there lying on the field,
Into one flowre that is both red and blew:
It first growes red, and then to blew doth
    fade,
Like Astrophel, which thereinto was made.

And in the midst thereof a star appeares,
As fairly formd as any star in skyes:
Resembling Stella in her freshest yeares,
Forth darting beames of beautie from her eyes;
And all the day it standeth full of deow,
Which is the teares, that from her eyes did
    flow.[10]

His most genuine sentiments become thus fairy-like.
Magic is the mould of his mind, and impresses its
shape on all that he imagines or thinks. Involuntarily
he robs objects of their ordinary form. If he looks at a
landscape, after an instant he sees it quite differently.
He carries it, unconsciously, into an enchanted land;
the azure heaven sparkles like a canopy of diamonds,
meadows are clothed with flowers, a biped population
flutters in the balmy air, palaces of jasper shine among
the trees, radiant ladies appear on carved balconies
above galleries of emerald. This unconscious toil of
mind is like the slow crystallisations of nature. A moist
twig is cast into the bottom of a mine, and is brought
out again a hoop of diamonds.

At last he finds a subject which suits him, the greatest
joy permitted to an artist. He removes his epic, from
the common ground which, in the hands of Homer and
Dante, gave expression to a living creed, and depicted
national heroes. He leads us to the summit of fairyland, soaring above history, on that extreme verge
where objects vanish and pure idealism begins: "I have
undertaken a work," he says, "to represent all the moral
vertues, assigning to every vertue a knight to be the
patron and defender of the same; in whose actions and
feats of armes and chivalry the operations of that vertue, whereof he is the protector, are to be expressed,
and the vices and unruly appetites that oppose themselves against the same, to be beaten downe and overcome,"[11] In fact, he gives us an allegory as the foundation of his poem, not that he dreams of becoming a
wit, a preacher of moralities, a propounder of riddles.
He does not subordinate image to idea; he is a seer,
not a philosopher. They are living men and actions
which he sets in motion; only from time to time, in his
poem, enchanted palaces, a whole train of splendid
visions trembles and divides like a mist, enabling us to
catch a glimpse of the thought which raised and arranged it. When in his Garden of Adonis we see the
countless forms of all living things arranged in due
order, in close compass, awaiting life, we conceive
with him the birth of universal love, the ceaseless fertility of the great mother, the mysterious swarm of
creatures which rise in succession from her "wide
wombe of the world." When we see his Knight of the
Cross combating with a horrible woman-serpent in
defence of his beloved lady Una, we dimly remember
that, if we search beyond these two figures, we shall
find behind one, Truth, behind the other, Falsehood.
We perceive that his characters are not flesh and blood,
and that all these brilliant phantoms are phantoms, and
nothing more. We take pleasure in their brilliancy,
without believing in their substantiality; we are interested in their doings, without troubling ourselves about
their misfortunes. We know that their tears and cries
are not real. Our emotion is purified and raised. We do
not fall into gross illusion; we have that gentle feeling
of knowing ourselves to be dreaming. We, like him,
are a thousand leagues from actual life, beyond the
pangs of painful pity, unmixed terror, violent and bitter hatred. We entertain only refined sentiments, partly
formed, arrested at the very moment they were about
to affect us with too sharp a stroke. They slightly touch
us, and we find ourselves happy in being extricated
from a belief which was beginning to be oppressive.

What world could furnish materials to so elevated a
fancy? One only, that of chivalry; for none is so far
from the actual. Alone and independent in his castle,
freed from all the ties which society, family, toil, usually impose on the actions of men, the feudal hero had
attempted every kind of adventure, but yet he had done
less than he imagined; the boldness of his deeds had
been exceeded by the madness of his dreams. For want
of useful employment and an accepted rule, his brain
had laboured on an unreasoning and impossible track,
and the urgency of his wearisomeness had increased
beyond measure his craving for excitement. Under this
stimulus his poetry had become a world of imagery.
Insensibly strange conceptions had grown and multiplied in his brains, one over the other, like ivy woven
round a tree, and the original trunk had disappeared
beneath their rank growth and their obstruction. The

delicate fancies of the old Welsh poetry, the grand ruins of the German epics, the marvellous splendours of the conquered East, all the recollections which four centuries of adventure had scattered among the minds of men, had become gathered into one great dream; and giants, dwarfs, monsters, the whole medley of imaginary creatures, of superhuman exploits and splendid follies, were grouped around a unique conception, exalted and sublime love, like courtiers prostrated at the feet of their king. It was an ample and buoyant subject-matter, from which the great artists of the age, Ariosto, Tasso, Cervantes, Rabelais, had hewn their poems. But they belonged too completely to their own time, to admit of their belonging to one which had passed.[12] They created a chivalry afresh, but it was not genuine. The ingenious Ariosto, an ironical epicurean, delights his gaze with it, and grows merry over it, like a man of pleasure, a sceptic who rejoices doubly in his pleasure, because it is sweet, and because it is forbidden. By his side poor Tasso, inspired by a fanatical, revived, factitious Catholicism, amid the tinsel of an old school of poetry, works on the same subject, in sickly fashion, with great effort and scant success. Cervantes, himself a knight, albeit he loves chivalry for its nobleness, perceives its folly, and crushes it to the ground, with heavy blows, in the mishaps of the wayside inns. More coarsely, more openly, Rabelais, a rude commoner, drowns it with a burst of laughter, in his merriment and nastiness. Spenser alone takes it seriously and naturally. He is on the level of so much nobleness, dignity, reverie. He is not yet settled and shut in by that species of exact common sense which was to found and cramp the whole modern civilisation. In his heart he inhabits the poetic and shadowy land from which men were daily drawing further and further away. He is enamoured of it, even to its very language; he revives the old words, the expressions of the middle-age, the style of Chaucer, especially in the *Shepherd's Calendar*. He enters straightway upon the strangest dreams of the old story-tellers, without astonishment, like a man who has still stranger dreams of his own. Enchanted castles, monsters and giants, duels in the woods, wandering ladies, all spring up under his hands, the mediæval fancy with the mediæval generosity; and it is just because this world is unreal that it so suits his humour.

Is there in chivalry sufficient to furnish him with matter? That is but one world, and he has another. Beyond the valiant men, the glorified images of moral virtues, he has the gods, finished models of sensible beauty; beyond Christian chivalry he has the pagan Olympus; beyond the idea of heroic will which can only be satisfied by adventures and danger, there exists calm energy, which, by its own impulse, is in harmony with actual existence. For such a poet one ideal is not enough; beside the beauty of effort he places the beauty of happiness; he couples them, not deliberately as a philosopher, nor with the design of a

scholar like Goethe, but because they are both lovely; and here and there, amid armour and passages of arms, he distributes satyrs, nymphs, Diana, Venus, like Greek statues amid the turrets and lofty trees of an English park. There is nothing forced in the union; the ideal epic, like a superior heaven, receives and harmonises the two worlds; a beautiful pagan dream carries on a beautiful dream of chivalry; the link consists in the fact that they are both beautiful. At this elevation the poet has ceased to observe the differences of races and civilisations. He can introduce into his picture whatever he will; his only reason is, "That suited;" and there could be no better. Under the glossy-leaved oaks, by the old trunk so deeply rooted in the ground, he can see two knights cleaving each other, and the next instant a company of Fauns who came there to dance. The beams of light which have poured down upon the velvet moss, the green turf of an English forest, can reveal the dishevelled locks and white shoulders of nymphs. Do we not see it in Rubens? And what signify discrepancies in the happy and sublime illusion of fancy? Are there more discrepancies? Who perceives them, who feels them? Who does not feel, on the contrary, that to speak the truth, there is but one world, that of Plato and the poets; that actual phenomena are but outlines—mutilated, incomplete and blurred outlines—wretched abortions scattered here and there on Time's track, like fragments of clay, half moulded, then cast aside, lying in an artist's studio; that, after all, invisible forces and ideas, which for ever renew the actual existences, attain their fulfilment only in imaginary existences; and that the poet, in order to express nature in its entirety, is obliged to embrace in his sympathy all the ideal forms by which nature reveals itself? This is the greatness of his work; he has succeeded in seizing beauty in its fulness, because he cared for nothing but beauty.

The reader will feel that it is impossible to give in full the plot of such a poem. In fact, there are six poems, each of a dozen cantos, in which the action is ever diverging and converging again, becoming confused and starting again; and all the imaginings of antiquity and of the middle-age are, I believe, combined in it. The knight "pricks along the plaine," among the trees, and at a crossing of the paths meets other knights with whom he engages in combat; suddenly from within a cave appears a monster, half woman and half serpent, surrounded by a hideous offspring; further on a giant, with three bodies; then a dragon, great as a hill, with sharp talons and vast wings. For three days he fights him, and twice overthrown, he comes to himself only by aid of "a gracious ointment." After that there are savage tribes to be conquered, castles surrounded by flames to be taken. Meanwhile ladies are wandering in the midst of forests, on white palfreys, exposed to the assaults of miscreants, now guarded by a lion which follows them, now delivered by a band of satyrs who adore them. Magicians work manifold charms; palaces display their festivities; tilt-yards provide endless tour-naments; sea-gods, nymphs, fairies, kings, intermingle in these feasts, surprises, dangers.

You will say it is a phantasmagoria. What matter, if we see it? And we do see it, for Spenser does. His sincerity communicates itself to us. He is so much at home in this world, that we end by finding ourselves at home in it too. He shows no appearance of astonish-ment at astonishing events; he comes upon them so naturally, that he makes them natural; he defeats the miscreants, as if he had done nothing else all his life. Venus, Diana, and the old deities, dwell at his gate and enter his threshold without his taking any heed of them. His serenity becomes ours. We grow credulous and happy by contagion, and to the same extent as he. How could it be otherwise? Is it possible to refuse credence to a man who paints things for us with such accurate details and in such lively colours? Here with a dash of his pen he describes a forest for you; and are you not instantly in it with him? Beech trees with their silvery stems, "loftie trees iclad with sommers pride, did spred so broad, that heavens light did hide;" rays of light tremble on the bark and shine on the ground, on the reddening ferns and low bushes, which, sudden-ly smitten with the luminous track, glisten and glim-mer. Footsteps are scarcely heard on the thick beds of heaped leaves; and at distant intervals, on the tall herb-age, drops of dew are sparkling. Yet the sound of a horn reaches us through the foliage; how sweetly yet cheerfully it falls on the ear, amidst this vast silence! It resounds more loudly; the clatter of a hunt draws near; "eft through the thicke they heard one rudely rush;" a nymph approaches, the most chaste and beau-tiful in the world. Spenser sees her; nay more, he kneels before her:

> Her face so faire, as flesh it seemed not,
> But hevenly pourtraict of bright angels hew,
> Cleare as the skye, withouten blame or blot,
> Through goodly mixture of complexions dew;
> And in her cheekes the vermeill red did shew
> Like roses in a bed of lillies shed,
>   The which ambrosiall odours from them
>   threw,
> And gazers sence with double pleasure fed,
> Hable to heale the sicke and to revive the
>   ded.
>
> In her faire eyes two living lamps did flame,
> Kindled above at th' Hevenly Makers light,
> And darted fyrie beames out of the same;
> So passing persant, and so wondrous bright,
> That quite bereav'd the rash beholders sight:
> In them the blinded god his lustfull fyre
> To kindle oft assayd, but had no might;
> For, with dredd maiestie and awfull yre,
> She broke his wanton darts, and quenched
>   bace desyre.

> Her yvorie forhead, full of bountie brave,
> Like a broad table did itselfe dispred,
> For Love his loftie triumphes to engrave,
> And write the battailes of his great godhed:
> All good and honour might therein be red;
> For there their dwelling was. And, when she
>   spake,
> Sweete wordes, like dropping honny, she did
>   shed;
> And 'twixt the perles and rubins softly brake
> A silver sound, that heavenly musicke seemd
>   to make.
>
> Upon her eyelids many Graces sate,
> Under the shadow of her even browes,
> Working belgardes and amorous retrate;
> And everie one her with a grace endowes,
> And everie one with meekenesse to her
>   bowes:
> So glorious mirrhour of celestiall grace,
> And soveraine moniment of mortall vowes,
> How shall frayle pen descrive her heavenly
>   face,
> For feare, through want of skill, her beauty to
>   disgrace!
>
> So faire, and thousand thousand times more
>   faire,
> She seemd, when she presented was to sight;
> And was yclad, for heat of scorching aire,
> All in a silken Camus lilly whight,
> Purfled upon with many a folded plight,
> Which all above besprinckled was throughout
> With golden aygulets, that glistred bright,
> Like twinckling starres; and all the skirt about
> Was hemd with golden fringe.
>
> Below her ham her weed did somewhat
>   trayne,
> And her streight legs most bravely were
>   embayld
> In gilden buskins of costly cordwáyne,
> All bard with golden bendes, which were
>   entayld
> With curious antickes, and full fayre aumayld:
> Before, they fastned were under her knee
> In a rich iewell, and therein entrayld
> The ends of all the knots, that none might see
> How they within their fuldings close
>   enwrapped bee.
>
> Like two faire marble pillours they were
>   seene,
> Which doe the temple of the gods support,
> Whom all the people decke with girlands
>   greene,
> And honour in their festivall resort;
> Those same with stately grace and princely
>   port

She taught to tread, when she herselfe would
    grace;
But with the woody nymphes when she did
    play,
Or when the flying libbard she did chace,
She could them nimbly move, and after fly
    apace.

And in her hand a sharpe bore-speare she
    held,
And at her backe a bow and quiver gay,
Stuft with steel-headed dartes wherewith she
    queld
The salvage beastes in her victorious play,
Knit with a golden bauldricke which forelay
Athwart her snowy brest, and did divide
Her daintie paps; which, like young fruit in
    May,
Now little gan to swell, and being tide
Through her thin weed their places only
    signifide.

Her yellow lockes, crisped like golden wyre,
About her shoulders weren loosely shed,
And, when the winde emongst them did
    inspyre,
They waved like a penon wyde dispred
And low behinde her backe were scattered:
And, whether art it were or heedlesse hap,
As through the flouring forrest rash she fled,
In her rude heares sweet flowres themselves
    did lap,
And flourishing fresh leaves and blossomes
    did enwrap.[13]

The daintie rose, the daughter of her morne,
More deare than life she tendered, whose
    flowre
The girlond of her honour did adorne;
Ne suffered she the middayes scorching
    powre.
Ne the sharp northerne wind thereon to
    showre;
But lapped up her silken leaves most chayre,
Whenso the froward skye began to lowre;
But, soone as calmed was the cristall ayre,
She did it fayre dispred, and let to florish
    fayre.[14]

He is on his knees before her, I repeat, as a child on
Corpus Christi day, among flowers and perfumes, transported with admiration, so that he sees a heavenly light
in her eyes, and angel's tints on her cheeks, even
impressing into her service Christian angels and pagan
graces to adorn and wait upon her; it is love which
brings such visions before him;

Sweet love, that doth his golden wings embay
In blessed nectar and pure pleasures well.

Whence this perfect beauty, this modest and charming
dawn, in which he assembles all the brightness, all the
sweetness, all the virgin graces of the full morning?
What mother begat her, what marvellous birth brought
to light such a wonder of grace and purity? One day,
in a sparkling, solitary fountain, where the sunbeams
shone, Chrysogone was bathing with roses and violets.

It was upon a sommers shinie day,
When Titan faire his beamës did display,
In a fresh fountaine, far from all mens vew,
She bath'd her brest the boyling heat t' allay;
She bath'd with roses red and violets blew,
And all the sweetest flowers that in the forrest
    grew.
Till faint through yrkesome wearines adowne
Upon the grassy ground herselfe she layd
To sleepe, the whiles a gentle slombring
    swowne
Upon her fell all naked bare displayd.[15]

The beams played upon her body, and "fructified" her.
The months rolled on. Troubled and ashamed, she went
into the "wildernesse," and sat down, "every sence
with sorrow sore opprest." Meanwhile Venus, searching for her boy Cupid, who had mutinied and fled
from her, "wandered in the world." She had sought
him in courts, cities, cottages, promising "kisses sweet,
and sweeter things, unto the man that of him tydings
to her brings."

Shortly unto the wastefull woods she came,
Whereas she found the goddesse (Diana) with
    her crew,
After late chace of their embrewed game,
Sitting beside a fountaine in a rew;
Some of them washing with the liquid dew
From off their dainty limbs the dusty sweat
And soyle, which did deforme their lively
    hew;
Others lay shaded from the scorching heat
The rest upon her person gave attendance
    great.
She, having hong upon a bough on high
Her bow and painted quiver, had unlaste
Her silver buskins from her nimble thigh,
And her lanck loynes ungirt, and brests
    unbraste,
After her heat the breathing cold to taste;
Her golden lockes, that late in tresses bright
Embreaded were for hindring of her haste,
Now loose about her shoulders hong undight,
And were with sweet Ambrosia all
    besprinckled light.[16]

Diana, surprised thus, repulses Venus, "and gan to
smile, in scorne of her vaine playnt," swearing that if
she should catch Cupid, she would clip his wanton
wings. Then she took pity on the afflicted goddess,

and set herself with her to look for the fugitive. They came to the "shady covert" where Chrysogone, in her sleep, had given birth "unawares" to two lovely girls, "as faire as springing day." Diana took one, and made her the purest of all virgins. Venus carried off the other to the Garden of Adonis, "the first seminary of all things, that are borne to live and dye;" where Psyche, the bride of Love, disports herself; where Pleasure, their daughter, wantons with the Graces; where Adonis, "lapped in flowres and pretious spycery," "liveth in eternal bliss," and came back to life through the breath of immortal Love. She brought her up as her daughter, selected her to be the most faithful of loves, and after long trials, gave her hand to the good knight Sir Scudamore.

That is the kind of thing we meet with in the wondrous forest. Are you ill at ease there, and do you wish to leave it because it is wondrous? At every bend in the alley, at every change of the light, a stanza, a word, reveals a landscape or an apparition. It is morning, the white dawn gleams faintly through the trees; bluish vapours veil the horizon, and vanish in the smiling air; the springs tremble and murmur faintly amongst the mosses, and on high the poplar leaves begin to stir and flutter like the wings of butterflies. A knight alights from his horse, a valiant knight, who has unhorsed many a Saracen, and experienced many an adventure. He unlaces his helmet, and on a sudden you perceive the cheeks of a young girl;

> Which doft, her golden lockes, that were
>   upbound
> Still in a knot, unto her heeles downe traced,
> And like a silken veile in compasse round
> About her backe and all her bodie wound;
> Like as the shining skie in summers night,
> What time the dayes with scorching heat
>   abound,
> Is creasted all with lines of firie light,
> That it prodigious seemes in common peoples
>   sight.[17]

It is Britomart, a virgin and a heroine, like Clorinda or Marfisa,[18] but how much more ideal! The deep sentiment of nature, the sincerity of reverie, the ever-flowing fertility of inspiration, the German seriousness, reanimate in this poem classical or chivalrous conceptions, even when they are the oldest or the most trite. The train of splendours and of scenery never ends. Desolate promontories, cleft with gaping chasms; thunder-stricken and blackened masses of rocks, against which the hoarse breakers dash; palaces sparkling with gold, wherein ladies, beauteous as angels, reclining carelessly on purple cushions, listen with sweet smiles to the harmony of music played by unseen hands; lofty silent walks, where avenues of oaks spread their motionless shadows over clusters of virgin violets, and turf which never mortal foot has trod;—to all these

beauties of art and nature he adds the marvels of mythology, and describes them with as much of love and sincerity as a painter of the Renaissance or an ancient poet. Here approach on chariots of shell, Cymoënt and her nymphs:

> A teme of dolphins raunged in aray
> Drew the smooth charett of sad Cymoënt;
> They were all taught by Triton to obay
> To the long raynes at her commaundëment:
> As swifte as swallowes on the waves they
>   went,
> That their brode flaggy finnes no fome did
>   reare,
> Ne bubling rowndell they behinde them sent;
> The rest, of other fishes drawen weare;
> Which with their finny oars the swelling sea
>   did sheare.[19]

Nothing, again, can be sweeter or calmer than the description of the palace of Morpheus:

> He, making speedy way through spersed ayre,
> And through the world of waters wide and
>   deepe,
> To Morpheus house doth hastily repaire.
> Amid the bowels of the earth full steepe,
> And low, where dawning day doth never
>   peepe
> His dwelling is; there Tethys his wet bed
> Doth ever wash, and Cynthia still doth steepe
> In silver deaw his ever-drouping hed,
> Whiles sad Night over him her mantle black
>   doth spred.
> And, more to lulle him in his slumber soft,
> A trickling streame from high rock tumbling
>   downe
> And ever-drizzling raine upon the loft,
> Mixt with a murmuring winde, much like the
>   sowne
> Of swarming bees, did cast him in a swowne.
> No other noyse, nor peoples troublous cryes,
> As still are wont t' annoy the walled towne,
> Might there be heard: but careless Quiet lyes,
> Wrapt in eternall silence farre from enimyes.[20]

Observe also in a corner of this forest, a band of satyrs dancing under the green leaves. They come leaping like wanton kids, as gay as birds of joyous spring. The fair Hellenore, whom they have chosen for "May-lady," "daunst lively" also, laughing, and "with girlonds all bespredd." The wood re-echoes the sound of their "merry pypes." "Their horned feet the greene gras wore." "All day they daunced with great lustyhedd," with sudden motions and alluring looks, while about them their flock feed on "the brouzes" at their pleasure.[21] In every book we see strange processions pass by, allegorical and picturesque shows, like those which were then displayed at the courts of princes; now a masquerade of Cupid, now of the Rivers, now of the Months, now of the Vices. Imagination was never more prodigal or inventive. Proud Lucifera advances in a chariot "adorned all with gold and girlonds gay," beaming like the dawn, surrounded by a crowd of courtiers whom she dazzles with her glory and splendour: "six unequall beasts" draw her along, and each of these is ridden by a Vice. Idleness "upon a slouthfull asse . . . in habit blacke . . . like to an holy monck," sick for very laziness, lets his heavy head droop, and holds in his hand a breviary which he does not read; gluttony, on "a filthie swyne," crawls by in his deformity, "his belly . . . upblowne with luxury, and eke with fatnesse swollen were his eyne; and like a crane his necke was long and fyne," drest in vine-leaves, through which one can see his body eaten by ulcers, and vomiting along the road the wine and flesh with which he is glutted. Avarice seated between "two iron coffers," "upon a camell loaden all with gold," is handling a heap of coin, with thread-bare coat, hollow cheeks, and feet stiff with gout. Envy "upon a ravenous wolfe still did chaw between his cankred teeth a venemous tode, that all the poison ran about his chaw," and his discoloured garment "ypainted full of eies," conceals a snake wound about his body. Wrath, covered with a torn and bloody robe, comes riding on a lion, brandishing about his head "a burning brond," his eyes sparkling, his face pale as ashes, grasping in his feverish hand the haft of his dagger. The strange and terrible procession passes on, led by the solemn harmony of the stanzas; and the grand music of oft repeated rhymes sustains the imagination in this fantastic world, which with its mingled horrors and splendours, has just been opened to its flight.

Yet all this is little. However much mythology and chivalry can supply, they do not suffice for the needs of this poetical fancy. Spenser's characteristic is the vastness and overflow of his picturesque invention. Like Rubens, whatever he creates is beyond the region of all traditions, but complete in all parts, and expresses distinct ideas. As with Rubens, his allegory swells its proportions beyond all rule, and withdraws fancy from all law, except in so far as it is necessary to harmonise forms and colours. For, if ordinary minds receive from allegory a certain weight which oppresses them, lofty imaginations receive from it wings which carry them aloft. Freed by it from the common conditions of life, they can dare all things, beyond imitation, apart from probability, with no other guides but their inborn energy and their shadowy instincts. For three days Sir Guyon is led by the cursed spirit, the tempter Mammon, in the subterranean realm, across wonderful gardens, trees laden with golden fruits, glittering palaces, and a confusion of all worldly treasures. They have descended into the bowels of the earth, and pass through caverns, unknown abysses, silent depths. "An ugly Feend . . . with monstrous stalke behind him stept," without Guyon's knowledge, ready to devour him on

the least show of covetousness. The brilliancy of the gold lights up hideous figures, and the beaming metal shines with a beauty more seductive in the gloom of the infernal prison

> That Houses forme within was rude and
>   strong,
> Lyke an huge cave hewne out of rocky clifte,
> From whose rough vaut the ragged breaches
>   hong
> Embost with massy gold of glorious guifte,
> And with rich metall loaded every rifte,
> That heavy ruine they did seeme to threatt;
> And over them Arachne high did lifte
> Her cunning web, and spred her subtile nett,
> Enwrapped in fowle smoke and clouds more
>   black than iett.

> Both roofe, and floore, and walls, were all of
>   gold,
> But overgrowne with dust and old decay,
> And hid in darknes, that none could behold
> The hew thereof; for vew of cherefull day
> Did never in that House itselfe display,
> But a faint shadow of uncertein light;
> Such as a lamp, whose life does fade away;
> Or as the moone, cloathed with clowdy night,
> Does show to him that walkes in feare and
>   sad affright.

> In all that rowme was nothing to be seene
> But huge great yron chests and coffers strong,
> All bard with double bends, that none could
>   weene
> Them to enforce by violence or wrong;
> On every side they placed were along.
> But all the grownd with sculs was scattered
> And dead mens bones, which round about
>   were flong;
> Whose lives, it seemed, whilome there were
>   shed,
> And their vile carcases now left unburied. . . .

> Thence, forward he him ledd and shortly
>   brought
> Unto another rowme, whose dore forthright
> To him did open as it had beene taught:
> Therein an hundred raunges weren pight,
> And hundred fournaces all burning bright;
> By every fournace many Feends did byde,
> Deformed creatures, horrible in sight;
> And every Feend his busie paines applyde
> To melt the golden metall, ready to be tryde.

> One with great bellowes gathered filling ayre,
> And with forst wind the fewell did inflame;
> Another did the dying bronds repayre
> With yron tongs, and sprinckled ofte the same
> With liquid waves, fiers Vulcans rage to tame,

Who, maystring them, renewd his former heat:
Some scumd the drosse that from the metall
   came;
Some stird the molten owre with ladles great:
And every one did swincke, and every one
   did sweat . . .

He brought him, through a darksom narrow
   strayt,
To a broad gate all built of beaten gold:
The gate was open; but therein did wayt
A sturdie Villein, stryding stiffe and bold,
As if the Highest God defy he would:
In his right hand an yron club he held,
But he himselfe was all of golden mould,
Yet had both life and sence, and well could
   weld
That cursed weapon, when his cruell foes he
   queld . . .

He brought him in. The rowme was large and
   wyde,
As it some gyeld or solemne temple weare;
Many great golden pillours did upbeare
The massy roofe, and riches huge sustayne;
And every pillour decked was full deare
With crownes, and diademes, and titles vaine,
Which mortall princes wore whiles they on
   earth did rayne.

A route of people there assembled were,
Of every sort and nation under skye,
Which with great uprore preaced to draw nere
To th' upper part, where was advaunced hye
A stately siege of soveraine maiestye;
And thereon satt a Woman gorgeous gay,
And richly cladd in robes of royaltye,
That never earthly prince in such aray
His glory did enhaunce, and pompous pryde
   display . . .

There, as in glistring glory she did sitt,
She held a great gold chaine ylincked well,
Whose upper end to highest heven was knitt,
And lower part did reach to lowest hell.[22]

No artist's dream matches these visions: the glow of the furnaces beneath the vaults of the cavern, the lights flickering over the crowded figures, the throne, and the strange glitter of the gold shining in every direction through the darkness. The allegory assumes gigantic proportions. When the object is to show temperance struggling with temptations, Spenser deems it necessary to mass all the temptations together. He is treating of a general virtue; and as such a virtue is capable of every sort of resistance, he requires from it every sort of resistance alike;—after the test of gold, that of pleasure. Thus the grandest and the most exquisite spectacles follow and are contrasted with each other, and all are supernatural; the graceful and the terrible are side by side,—the happy gardens close by with the cursed subterranean cavern.

No gate, but like one, being goodly dight
With bowes and braunches, which did broad
   dilate
Their clasping armes in wanton wreathings
   intricate:
So fashioned a porch with rare device,
Archt over head with an embracing vine,
Whose bounches hanging downe seemed to
   entice
All passers-by to taste their lushious wine,
And did themselves into their hands incline,
As freely offering to be gathered;
Some deepe empurpled as the hyacine,
Some as the rubine laughing sweetely red,
Some like faire emeraudes, not yet well
   ripened. . . .

And in the midst of all a fountaine stood,
Of richest substance that on earth might bee,
So pure and shiny that the silver flood
Through every channell running one might
   see;
Most goodly it with curious ymageree
Was over-wrought, and shapes of naked
   boyes,
Of which some seemed with lively iollitee
To fly about, playing their wanton toyes,
Whylest others did themselves embay in liquid
   ioyes.

And over all of purest gold was spred
A trayle of yvie in his native hew;
For the rich metall was so coloured,
That wight, who did not well avis'd it vew,
Would surely deeme it to bee yvie trew;
Low his lascivious armes adown did creepe,
That themselves dipping in the silver dew
Their fleecy flowres they fearfully did steepe,
Which drops of christall seemd for wantones
   to weep.

Infinit streames continually did well
Out of this fountaine, sweet and faire to see,
The which into an ample laver fell,
And shortly grew to so great quantitie,
That like a little lake it seemd to bee;
Whose depth exceeded not three cubits hight,
That through the waves one might the bottom
   see,
All pav'd beneath with jaspar shining bright,
That seemd the fountaine in that sea did sayle
   upright. . . .

The ioyous birdes, shrouded in chearefull
   shade,

Their notes unto the voice attempred sweet;
Th' angelicall soft trembling voyces made
To th' instruments divine respondence meet;
The silver-sounding instruments did meet
With the base murmur of the waters fall;
The waters fall with difference discreet,
Now soft, now loud, unto the wind did call;
The gentle warbling wind low answered to all.

    . . .

Upon a bed of roses she was layd,
As faint through heat, or dight to pleasant sin:
And was arayd, or rather disarayd,
All in a vele of silke and silver thin,
That hid no with her alabaster skin,
But rather shewd more white, if more might
    bee:
More subtile web Arachne cannot spin;
Nor the fine nets, which oft we woven see
Of scorched deaw, do not in th' ayre more
    lightly flee.

Her snowy brest was bare to ready spoyle
Of hungry eies, which n' ote therewith be
    fild;
And yet, through languour of her late sweet
    toyle,
Few drops, more cleare then nectar, forth
    distild,
That like pure orient perles adowne it trild;
And her faire eyes, sweet smyling in delight,
Moystened their fierie beames, with which she
    thrild
Fraile harts, yet quenched not, like starry
    lights
Which sparckling on the silent waves, does
    seeme more bright.[23]

Do we find here nothing but fairy land? Yes; here are finished pictures true and complete, composed with a painter's feeling, with choice of tints and outlines; our eyes are delighted by them. This reclining Acrasia has the pose of a goddess, or of one of Titian's courtesans. An Italian artist might copy these gardens, these flowing waters, these sculptured loves, those wreaths of creeping ivy thick with glossy leaves and fleecy flowers. Just before, in the infernal depths, the lights, with their long streaming rays, were fine, half-smothered by the darkness; the lofty throne in the vast hall, between the pillars, in the midst of a swarming multitude, connected all the forms around it by drawing all looks towards one centre. The poet, here and throughout, is a colourist and an architect. However fantastic his world may be, it is not factitious; if it does not exist, it might have been; indeed, it should have been; it is the fault of circumstances if they do not so group themselves as to bring it to pass; taken by itself, it possesses that internal harmony by which a real thing, even a still higher harmony, exists, inasmuch as, without any re-

gard to real things, it is altogether, and in its least detail, constructed with a view to beauty. Art has made its appearance: this is the great characteristic of the age, which distinguishes the ***Faërie Queene*** from all similar tales heaped up by the middle-age. Incoherent, mutilated, they lie like rubbish, or rough-hewn stones, which the weak hands of the trouvères could not build into a monument. At last the poets and artists appear, and with them the conception of beauty, to wit, the idea of general effect. They understand proportions, relations, contrasts; they compose. In their hands the blurred vague sketch becomes defined, complete, separate; it assumes colour—is made a picture. Every object thus conceived and imaged acquires a definite existence as soon as it assumes a true form; centuries after, it will be acknowledged and admired, and men will be touched by it; and more, they will be touched by its author; for, besides the object which he paints, the poet paints himself. His ruling idea is stamped upon the work which it produces and controls. Spenser is superior to his subject, comprehends it fully, frames it with a view to its end, in order to impress upon it the proper mark of his soul and his genius. Each story is modulated with respect to another, and all with respect to a certain effect which is being worked out. Thus a beauty issues from this harmony,—the beauty in the poet's heart,—which his whole work strives to express; a noble and yet a cheerful beauty, made up of moral elevation and sensuous seductions, English in sentiment, Italian in externals, chivalric in subject, modern in its perfection, representing a unique and wonderful epoch, the appearance of paganism in a Christian race, and the worship of form by an imagination of the North.

Notes

[1] It is very doubtful whether Spenser was so poor as he is generally believed to have been.—TR.

[2] "He died for want of bread, in King Street." Ben Jonson, quoted by Drummond.

[3] *Hymns of Love and Beauty; of heavenly Love and Beauty.*

[4] *A Hymne in Honour of Beautie, l. 92-105.*

[5] *A Hymne in Honour of Love, l. 176-182.*

[6] *The Faërie Queene,* i. c. 8, st. 22, 23.

[7] *The Shepherd's Calendar, Amoretti, Sonnets, Prothalamion, Epithalamion, Muiopotmos, Virgil's Gnat, The Ruines of Time, The Teares of the Muses,* etc.

[8] Published in 1589; dedicated to Philip Sidney.

[9] *Prothalamion, l. 19-54.*

[10] *Astrophel, l.* 181-192.

[11] Words attributed to him by Lodowick Bryskett, *Discourse of Civil Life,* ed. 1606, p. 26.

[12] Ariosto, 1474-1533. Tasso, 1544-1595. Cervantes, 1547-1616. Rabelais, 1483-1553.

[13] *The Faërie Queene,* ii. c. 3, st. 22-30.

[14] *Ibid.* iii. c. 5, st. 51.

[15] *The Faërie Queene,* iii. c. 6, st. 6 and 7.

[16] *The Faërie Queene,* iii. c. 6, st. 17 and 18.

[17] *The Faërie Queene,* iv. c. 1, st. 13.

[18] Clorinda, the heroine of the infidel army in Tasso's epic poem *Jerusalem Delivered;* Marfisa, an Indian Queen, who figures in Ariosto's *Orlando Furioso,* and also in Boyardo's *Orlando Innamorato.*—TR.

[19] *The Faërie Queene,* iii. c. 4, st. 33.

[20] *The Faërie Queene,* i. c. 1, st. 39 and 41.

[21] *Ibid.* iii. c. 10, st. 43-45.

[22] *The Faërie Queene,* ii. c. 7, st. 28-46.

[23] *The Faërie Queene,* ii. c. 12, st. 53-78.

J. W. Mackail (essay date 1909)

SOURCE: "'Spenser,'" in *The Springs of Helicon: A Study in the Progress of English Poetry from Chaucer to Milton,* Longmans, Green, and Co., 1909, pp. 71-134.

[*In the following excerpt from his study of major English Renaissance poets, Mackail discusses Spenser's work with a focus on poetic influences and techniques.*]

I

The Middle Ages died hard; and nowhere harder than in this island of the West, which was already marked among other nations by two specific qualities—a tenacious conservatism, and an instinct for adapting rather than replacing old institutions, for making changes and even revolutions under accustomed names and inherited forms. The coming of the Renaissance into England was strange, troubled, irregular. In some ways one might say it never came at all, or came in so imperfect a shape, with such transformed features, that it seems to demand another name. This was so over the whole field of civilisation, in religion and politics as well as in art. But in poetry the process of change was especially intricate: the threads of influence, the lines of growth, are complex and not easy to disentangle.

The fifteenth century was emphatically, not only in this country but throughout Europe, not an age of great poetry. In England the Chaucerians continued, with ever-dwindling inspiration, with growing loss of imaginative hold on life and power of interpreting it, the tradition created and fixed by Chaucer himself. Beyond the Chaucerians we have the mystery plays, the ballads, a small supply of scattered lyrics: a heap of confused scraps, among which the vital process most visible is rather the decay which precedes germination than germination itself. The earlier Italian Renaissance had in poetry been succeeded by a long period of stagnation. Petrarch and Boccaccio died in 1374 and 1375; for a full century afterwards there is no Italian poet of the first or second rank, no outstanding mark in the progress of poetry. The *quattrocentisti* are the painters. In literature it was the age not of the poets but of the scholars. Just at the end of the fifteenth century comes Boiardo's *Orlando.* Boiardo died in 1494, the year of the French invasion of Italy. In France there had been the same lull and pause; François Villon is there the chief poet of a century which was in the main occupied with other things than poetry.

Early in the sixteenth century there was a great revival of poetry in Italy, and, a little later, in France, under an impulse partly native, partly communicated from Italy. The impact of this movement reached England just at a time when, even apart from it, there were signs of a poetic revival. The joy of life had come back to letters; and the joy of letters once more flooded over life. When the head of the English Petrarch fell on the scaffold in 1547, the new movement had been fully launched on its course.

In the age which followed—Spenser's age, though it was too various and too splendid in its poetical progress and achievement to be described adequately as the age of Spenser—we may then trace and mark at least four intertwined motive forces or impulses; the native, the classical, the French, and the Italian. The interaction of these impulses was in the highest degree complex and subtle. We need not be too curious in attempting to assign to each a separate and proper force; still less can we assign to any one such exclusive preponderance as would allow us to regard the others as relatively unimportant. But we shall never properly appreciate Spenser and Spenser's age unless we realise vividly in him, and in it, the presence of all four in mutual interaction.

First then—and it is proper to place it first, because the poetry of every country must be considered as what it is, a function of the national life—we see in the

English poetry of this age an authentic revival of the native lyrical impulse. In this, English poetry holds of none and borrows of none. It is apart from scholarship, apart from any effect of foreign models, apart from the Renaissance itself, regarded as a European movement which overflowed into England. The English lyric poetry of the sixteenth century is as self-originating, as independent of external influences, as the Greek lyric poetry of the seventh and sixth centuries before Christ. Secondly, we have the classical impulse; the effect on poetry of the revival of learning in the previous generation, that golden age of the scholars, of Greece rediscovered and Rome revitalised; and, together with this, the revived and enlarged appreciation of the earlier Italian classics, of Petrarch and to a less extent of Dante. Thirdly, we have the continuous impulse of the immense and splendid body of contemporary Italian poetry, right through the sixteenth century, from Sannazaro and Ariosto at its beginning to Guarini and Tasso towards its end. This impulse came in part directly; in part as transmitted through the French Renaissance, and thus inextricably interwoven with the fourth and last influence, that of France. The French Pléiade, just in the middle of the century, had an immediate and long-continued effect on the development of poetry in England which can scarcely be over-estimated. Spenser's own earlier poetry is modelled more immediately and obviously on that of Clément Marot than on the Italian poets from whom Marot drew; and the French influence continued to grow more and more important in English poetry for upwards of a century, through the successive stages of its history—in Du Bellay and Ronsard, in Du Bartas, in Corneille and the classicists. But, as had been the case already in the age of Chaucer, while the influence of French form and structure was more immediate, more extensive, and more patent, we must look beyond these for the deeper inspiration. The progress of poetry (that I may quote Gray's brief and pregnant words) was from Greece to Italy, and from Italy to England.

All these influences, native, classical, French Renaissance, and Italian, mingle and accumulate in Spenser. It is thus—as well as from his own genius and from the imposing mass and brilliance of his production— that he is the central figure in the English poetry of the sixteenth century.

With Spenser we are at the full centre of the English Renaissance. For all his Chaucerianism, he is, as Chaucer in his time had been, a modern of the moderns. The change in the sky from evening to morning had passed a generation earlier. Surrey and Wyatt, slender as is the volume of their work, had quietly made ancient literature of the whole of earlier English poetry. They changed an epoch, or at least unmistakeably marked its change. Gawain Douglas's translation of Virgil and Surrey's are only thirty years apart in time: but they belong to two different worlds. The change

was just consummated when Spenser was born. Six years later, the Elizabethan age began. Six years more bring us to the birth of Shakespeare.

Thus in Spenser we see the full tide of the Renaissance surging up through many channels round the stranded ship of English poetry, floating her, and bearing her off by confused currents upon a new and adventurous voyage. That age, like our own, went almost mad over education; and Spenser represents not only the enlarged outlook and heightened ambitions of the new world, but also its rich scholarship. He went to Cambridge at seventeen, and studied there for seven years; it was an education almost as full and elaborate as Milton's or Virgil's. There he lived among a circle of ardent scholars, and received that bent towards classicism, as classicism was then understood, which is one of the main threads of influence that run through the whole of his poetry.

That classicism of the sixteenth century was a very mixed and intricate thing. On one side, following the great Italian humanists, it plunged deeply into Plato and the Platonic school. On another, Ovid was its master, and it sought to reinstate the brilliance, the dexterity, the accomplishment, which the Græco-Roman civilisation had reached before it fell into decay. On yet another, it read largely and deeply in ancient history, to gain knowledge of the past which might be applied to actual life, and to recover what it described in a compendious phrase as the wisdom of the ancients. On literature it had an influence for both good and evil. The fatal tendency of classicism is to see life through books, and to take it at second hand. Its natural instinct is to copy, and in doing so, to copy the inferior classics, who are more copiable, and then to go on copying itself. Its scholarship tends towards pedantry; its poets tend to become rhetoricians. The influence of Ovid colours the whole mass of Elizabethan poetry; that of Seneca greatly hampered the growth of the English drama. Bembo and Politian were ranked as masters alongside of Virgil. "The tragedies of Buchanan do justly bring forth a divine admiration," says Sidney in his *Apology for Poetry*. Bembo himself was urgent on Ariosto to write Latin poetry only, as bringing greater fame and more assured permanence. There was a similar delusion among the circle of scholars with whom Spenser lived and studied at Cambridge. They held one or both of two positions. Latin was the common international language of educated Europe, and therefore all poetry that should make a universal appeal must be written in Latin; or at least, the Latin poets were the classics, and therefore any English poetry which meant to take rank as classical must be written as nearly as possible in the Latin manner. If only the former of these doctrines had been held, no great harm would have been done. The native instinct for poetry might have been trusted to take care of itself. But it was different with the latter. A serious and what might have been a disastrous attempt was made to guide the stream of poetry into artificial channels; to copy the conventions of Latin poetry; even to transplant its metrical forms, as those of Greece had been transplanted into Latin poetry itself.

But this is a sort of thing that cannot be done in the same language twice; and in English poetry it had already been done once. The conquest and almost complete submergence of the native English metrical forms, under the influence of the first Renaissance and the decisive effect of Chaucer's genius, had fixed the lines of English poetry once for all. In his furnace the two metals had run into an alloy which was finer, harder, and more ductile than either of its two constituents. Something of loss there had been, but a greater gain. The Chaucerian metal became the basis of a standard currency, capable indeed of modification, enrichment, refinement, but in its main substance national and permanent. It was fine enough to be run into the most delicate moulds, flexible enough to meet, age after age, the ever-shifting and moving requirements of poetry. If Spenser had at any time been in danger of being carried away by the new ideas, he was saved from this by two things; his own admiration and almost worship of Chaucer on the one hand, and, on the other hand, the education which had made him familiar not only with the Latin and with some of the Greek classics, but with the consummate achievements already made by French and Italian poets in their own languages in the age just preceding his own, and those still being made by their successors. The goal of his poetical ambition lay clear before him; it was to be the English Ariosto, the English Ronsard; perhaps to be even more, but this was denied to him, the English Virgil.

When Spenser left Cambridge in 1576, he was the chief figure among a closely associated circle of poets and scholars which may remind us in many ways of the circle of Virgil during the years previous to the appearance of the Eclogues. They were full of the enthusiasm of youth. In other European countries the poetry of the late Renaissance was at its greatest visible splendour; it had reached the full maturity which is recognised afterwards—not at the time—as presaging the decline. The *Lusiads* had appeared in 1572; the *Aminta* in 1573; the *Sepmaine* followed in 1579; and the *Gierusalemme Liberata* in 1581. English poetry was still on its full curve of ascent. It felt itself at the beginning of a new age.

Just then Spenser, returning to London after two years of further study and practice in the north of England, made that acquaintance with Philip Sidney which disengaged the movement of English poetry in its complete force. The new Virgil had found his Gallus. Sidney was two years younger than Spenser, but he was one of those in whom natural precocity has been stimulated yet further by circumstance and education. The

eldest son of the Lord President of Wales, he had been marked out from birth for great things, and his education had been, even for that age, elaborate almost beyond example. He came to Oxford at thirteen. Four years there were followed by three more spent in travelling all over the Continent, making the Grand Tour on a scale and with advantages which sent him back with a European reputation and conversant with the whole civilised life of Europe. He returned to England a finished soldier, courtier, patriot, and poet. When he met Spenser he was only four-and-twenty; but he had already been English ambassador to the Emperor, and was already hailed in the ecstatic language of that age as the Messiah of poetry. His death at thirty-two was said to have plunged all England into mourning: both during his life and afterwards he was idolised by almost every one who had known him. Not himself by the amount or quality of his poetry rising into the rank of the great poets, "having slipt into the title of a poet," as he says of himself, he yet still impresses us, as he impressed them, with a sense of poetical distinction and even genius. Not only so, but he had a native critical faculty which was developed by study, by wide and varied reading, and by acquaintance with the whole movement of contemporary culture, into an instrument of exquisite fineness, to which his serious Puritan temper lent a yet keener edge. Of the function of poetry he says, in a few simple words that are startling in their clear insight and exactness, that it is "to make the too much loved earth more lovely."

On Spenser at all events (as through Spenser on the whole subsequent course of English poetry) the influence of Sidney was momentous. Its first result was the publication, in the year after they became acquainted, of the ***Shepherds Calendar***. This was the manifesto of the new poetry. It was dedicated to Sidney as Virgil's Eclogues were to Gallus; and like them, it not only placed its author at the head of contemporary poets, but was the symbol and keynote of a new world in poetry.

Its importance in this respect was at once recognised by the world, as it had been by Spenser himself and by the whole circle to which he belonged. Perhaps no work in poetry has ever been launched on its course more elaborately, with such an armament of defence, explanation, and apology. The twelve poems of which it consists were embedded in a mass of prefaces, introductions, and commentaries. How far these were the work of E. K. (if E. K. be a real person, Edward Kirke or another), how far of Spenser himself, or of others, is not clear: what is certain is that they represent the views and enthusiasm of the whole school, and that in speaking of Spenser as they do, under the title of "our new poet," they meant to enforce, with all the emphasis in their power, their confidence that this was the new poetry. The curious verses, and these are Spenser's own, attached as an *envoi* to the end of the volume, while for form's sake they disclaim rivalry with the great poets of an earlier age, Chaucer and Langland, yet make the claim formally and expressly for the new poetry that it shall outwear time and continue till the world's dissolution. The claim was really made not for these twelve poems, but for the new poetry, for the English poetry of the Elizabethan age. It was a great claim; and it was fully justified.

Of the twelve eclogues themselves there is no particular occasion to speak here in detail. They are a strange, almost chaotic, mixture of styles and manners, ranging in metre from the elaborate artificiality of the sestine in the eighth to the jigging couplets of the second and fifth, and in subject from the exquisite pastoral lyric of the fourth to the ecclesiastical polemics of the ninth. All, and more than all, of the adverse criticism that may be made against Virgil's Eclogues may be made against these. Of them, as of their Virgilian prototypes, it may be said, "They have all the vices and weaknesses of imitative poetry. Nor are these failings redeemed by any brilliant finish of workmanship. The execution is uncertain, hesitating, sometimes extraordinarily feeble. Even the versification is curiously unequal and imperfect." Yet of these Spenserian eclogues also one may go on to say, as of Virgil's, that granted all this, it does not touch the specific charm of which these poems first disclosed the secret. The **Shepherds Calendar** has no distinct style, but it has the germination of many. It is full of metrical device and experiment. It contains, in the tenth eclogue, preludings of large-scale work in chivalrous romance. Finally, here and there, and especially in the first and twelfth, which are really a single poem cut into two in order to open and close the collection, may be distinctly heard the new note that is personal to Spenser, his unmatched fluency of melody.

From the moment of the appearance of this volume Spenser became not only the leading representative of the new poetry, but the recognised head of living English poets. This position he retained until his death. In the twenty years between, the mass of his production was enormous. The three volumes of 1590, 1591, and 1596 contain between forty and fifty thousand lines. Much more, according both to probability and to direct evidence, was written by him, and either suppressed or lost. The **Faerie Queene** alone, as we possess it, extends to close on thirty-five thousand lines; and we have little more than half of it as it was planned. An allegorical romance of seventy thousand lines in length is a thing that imagination almost boggles at—or would do so at least in any age less adventurous, less confident, and less profuse than that of the matured Renaissance.

Throughout the whole sphere of life, in its crimes and virtues, in its attempts and achievements, that age was possessed by a spirit of excess, an intoxication of great-

ness. It set itself deliberately to outdo all that had hitherto been done. It built and voyaged and discovered and conquered colossally. In our own National Gallery, where it is one of the splendours of the great Venetian Room, is a portrait, by the Brescian painter Moretto, of Count Martinengo-Cesaresco, killed young in the French wars of religion. He is richly dressed in silk and furs, a gilded sword-hilt showing from under the heavy cloak. On a table by him are an antique lamp and some coins. His elbow rests on a pile of silken cushions, and his head leans, with a sort of intensity of languor, on his open palm. The face is that of one in the full prime of life and of great physical strength; very handsome, heavy and yet tremulously sensitive, the large eyes gazing at something unseen, and seeming to dream of vastness. On his bonnet is a golden plaque, with three words of Greek inscribed on it, . . . "Oh, I desire too much." Who the Giulia was whom he desired is among the things that have gone to oblivion; but the longing which the portrait has immortalised is not for one woman, were she like Beatrice or Helen, but for the whole world. These ambiguous words are a cloudy symbol; and that picture is a portrait of the spirit of the Renaissance.

As regards poetry in particular, that age ran to length, to extravagance, to redundance. This is true of almost all the Elizabethan poetry except in what is perhaps its finest flower, its lyrics; and even in these, taken collectively and not singly, the same quality is found in their superabundant profusion. The tradition of endlessness in poems was indeed not new; it was an inheritance from the Middle Ages. The romances of the thirteenth and fourteenth centuries handed on the quality of exorbitant length to the romantic epics of the sixteenth. But the new age bettered the example, and in this one point unhappily learned no lesson from its classical models. With regard to no time are the lines addressed by Tennyson to the ancient poets more appropriate:

> You should be jubilant that you flourished
>   here
> Before the love of letters, overdone,
> Had swampt the sacred poets with themselves.

The *Roman de la Rose* is often quoted as an instance of the mediæval extravagance. But its twenty-two thousand lines are a modest figure compared with the thirty-five thousand of the *Orlando Innamorato* and the forty thousand of the *Orlando Furioso*. The earlier Italian Renaissance, with its slenderer resources and its purer taste, had kept within the bounds of the ancient precedent. The *Divina Commedia* is shorter than the *Iliad;* the *Teseide* is the same length as the *Aeneid*. Spenser in the **Faerie Queene** proposed to himself to outdo Ariosto, as much as Ariosto had outdone all his predecessors. For this intention of his we have express evidence. Harvey, who from his narrow classical prejudices, as well as from his severer taste, disliked the whole scheme of the poem, and would have recalled poetry from the extravagances of chivalrous romance to a more antique or more modern concentration, wrote to Spenser in 1580 in these words: "The *Orlando Furioso* you will needs seem to emulate and hope to overgo, as you flatly professed yourself in one of your last letters." But apart from any particular ambition to produce a larger poem than had hitherto been known, Spenser possessed the terrible Elizabethan fluency to a degree beyond all his contemporaries. Under the stimulus of his example, reinforcing the instinct for profusion which is the note of the whole period, this torrent of poetic fluency poured on until the language sank exhausted under it. Then, and not till then, the inevitable and wholesome reaction came towards precision and succinctness. That reaction was powerfully aided by the strenuous scholarship of the seventeenth century, and by the impression made throughout the whole republic of letters by the French classical school. Moderation, sobriety, clarity became the aim of poets; and limits were set to the length as well as to the scope of poems which the general sense of later times has accepted as proper. The *Paradise Lost* reverts to the scale of the *Aeneid*. Even in the nineteenth century the most fluent and melodious of modern English poets kept, by instinct or judgment, within the same limits. The *Life and Death of Jason* and the *Story of Sigurd the Volsung* are, for all their copiousness and even diffuseness, each a little shorter than Milton's epic.

Yet Spenser's instinct, like that of all great artists as regards their own art, was in the main sound; for it is the mass and volume of his poetry, not less than its lavish and intricate beauty, that gives him his place and importance among the poets. He has been a vast quarry and playground for generation after generation of poets: like the Precious Strand in his own poem, a land

> Bestrowed all with rich array
> Of pearls and precious stones of great assay,
> And all the gravel mixed with golden ore.

He is the most inexhaustible and, in a way, the most various of the English poets. All his successors have loved, admired, plundered, imitated him; Milton and Pope, Wordsworth and Keats, a hundred others; not one but has dug in that gravel and brought away golden ore from it for his own use. In him they found that "enormous bliss" which Milton, in a phrase of daring felicity, ascribes to his Earthly Paradise:

> A wilderness with thicket overgrown
> Grotesque and wild: and overhead upgrew
> Insuperable height of loftiest shade,
> Cedar and pine and fir and branching palm,
> A silvan scene, and as the ranks ascend
> Shade above shade, a woody theatre

> Of stateliest view. Yet higher than their tops
> The verdurous wall of Paradise upsprung,
> And higher than that wall a circling row
> Of goodliest trees loaden with fairest fruit,
> Blossoms and fruits at once of golden hue,
> Appeared, with gay enamell'd colours mixt
> On which the sun more glad impressed his beams
> Than in fair evening cloud, or humid bow
> When God hath showered the earth: so lovely seemed
> That landscape.

Over and over again, as one plunges through the depths of that wilderness—

> A wilderness of sweets, for nature here
> Wantoned as in her prime and played at will
> Her virgin fancies—

one comes, scarcely with surprise, on phrases and passages that might be those of our greatest poets in their most superb and characteristic manner. It is impossible here, though it would be fascinating, to pursue this into detail; but two or three instances will show what I mean.

> Scarcely had Phœbus in the glooming East
> Yet harnessed his fiery-footed team:

that is Shakespeare, the Shakespeare of *Romeo and Juliet*.

> And taking usury of time forepast
> Fit for such ladies and such lovely knights:

that is Shakespeare again, the Shakespeare of the Sonnets.

> Many an Angel's voice
> Singing before the eternal Majesty
> In their trinal triplicities on high:

that is the younger voice of Milton.

> And ever and anon the rosy red
> Flasht thro' her face:

one might fancy that the unmistakeable note and accent of Tennyson.

This immense poetic flexibility, this amazing profusion and variety in style as well as in language—for in his vocabulary, too, Spenser is copious beyond the common copiousness of the Elizabethans—is a poetical quality of rare value; it is not of the essence, and does not imply the quality, of a supreme poet. As poetry produces its greatest effects through few and simple words, so some of the greatest poets have been scrupulously frugal in their language, and their style has been simple to austerity. Higher than the verdurous wall of Paradise, higher than the encircling fruit-laden trees, is the secret hill-top where the Muse sits among her chosen, and gives them, as Milton says, large prospect into the nether empire.

> As some rich tropic mountain, that infolds
>   All change, from flats of scattered palms
> Sloping thro' five great zones of climate,
>   holds
>   His head in snows and calms.

The image of perfection which art condenses out of the flying vapours of the world may be only blurred and dispersed by copiousness of invention and splendour of ornament: so hard is it for a rich man to enter into the kingdom.

To compare one great artist with another is often futile, and not seldom misleading; but such comparison may be more suggestive, and is less dangerous, when there can be no question of setting the two against one another. So far as there can be any analogy between arts so wholly different as those of poetry and history, Spenser might be called the English Livy. In both you have the same fluency and melodiousness, the same power of handling language on an immense scale with unexhausted elasticity. Both deliberately set themselves to outdo, in scale and volume, what had hitherto been done in a special field of literature, and succeeded in achieving their purpose. Both chose a subject-matter of great intricacy, involving many tedious passages and much repetition; neither ever tires of repeating himself, or seems to lose interest in what he is doing. Doubt has been expressed whether, if the *Faerie Queene* had been completed, any reader would ever have got to the end of it; the same apprehension may be, and indeed has been, hinted at as regards the one hundred and seven lost books of the *Historiae ab Urbe Condita*. Both authors were possessed by the greatness of a floating and imperfectly grasped ideal; Rome to Livy, chivalry to Spenser, mean all that is noble and glorious, but their power of hard thought is not great, and they are often found draping in their stately and musical rhetoric not only commonplaces, but absurdities. Innovators and conquerors in the field of letters, they were at the same time impassioned though not profound or accurate lovers and students of the earlier and purer national literature. They gave a new copiousness, a new range and flexibility to their language; but to the eyes of scholars and critics they often made wild work of it. The Patavinity which was reproached in Livy has its analogy in Spenser, whose use of the Chaucerian language and idiom is extraordinarily erratic, and whose archaism, while, according to the testimony of Fuller, it impaired his popularity and even diminished his sales, is so inaccurate as to fill scientific students of language with a feeling little short of

horror. Both he and Livy were borne on through their immense task not merely by fluency and enthusiasm, but by a love of commonplace moralising which was inexhaustible, and by an almost complete absence of humour. Livy never felt that his story was flat; Spenser never felt that his romanticism was absurd. No one who had the gift of laughter, who felt the comedy of life, could have gone gravely on through the third book of the *Faerie Queene*. Over and over again it moves a smile in the reader, but never once in the writer. In this book, it is true, there occur the only two passages in the whole poem which it is possible to regard as intentionally humorous. There is something like a flicker of amusement in the description of Britomartis and her nurse at church in the second canto; but such humour as there is in the stanza is more probably unconscious:—

> Early the morrow next, before that day
> His joyous face did to the world reveal,
> They both uprose and took their ready way
> Unto the Church, their prayers to appeal
> With great devotion, and with little zeal:
> For the fair Damsel from the holy herse
> Her love-sick heart to other thoughts did steal;
> And that old Dame said many an idle verse
> Out of her daughter's heart fond fancies to
>   reverse.

One can fancy with what an exquisite blending of fun and tenderness Chaucer would have treated the scene. The other passage is where the Squire of Dames, in the seventh canto, tells the story of the three women who had repelled his advances. In it Spenser *apprend d'être fif* with rather calamitous results. The story itself is a traditional *fabliau,* a piece of ponderous mediæval wit. It is incorporated rather than assimilated by Spenser: its proper place is in the *Moyen de Parvenir,* not in the *Faerie Queene,* where it is strikingly out of tone with its surroundings. "Thereat full heartily laughed Satyrane," we are told: he may have done so, but probably no reader of the poem has ever felt inclined to follow his example.

So too, with his feeling about the past and his attitude towards his own age. Following the common fashion of his period, which was indeed more or less the common fashion of human nature, he is perpetually, even to weariness, insisting on the degeneracy of modern times, on the vices of civilisation, the decay of chivalry, the treachery and ingratitude of courts. "O goodly usage of these antique times, in which the sword was servant unto right:" this is a theme on which he is perpetually embroidering, much as Orlando (not Ariosto's Orlando, Shakespeare's) eulogises "the constant service of the antique world, when service sweat for duty, not for meed." He is fond of thinking of his romantic imaginary world, "this delightful land of faerie," as he truly calls it, as though it were some golden age that had actually existed in the past, when

> Antique age, yet in the infancy
> Of time, did live then like an innocent.

He was not only a romantic dreamer and student, but a man of large and disappointed ambitions. In a famous passage in his *Mother Hubberd's Tale* he draws, with mordant truth, and in swift brilliant couplets worthy of Pope himself, the wretchedness of a courtier's life:

> So pitiful a thing is suitor's state!
> Most miserable man, whom wicked fate
> Hath brought to court, to sue for had-ywist,
> That few have found, and many one hath
>   missed!
> Full little knowest thou that hast not tried
> What hell it is in suing long to bide:
> To lose good days that might be better spent,
> To waste long nights in pensive discontent,
> To speed to-day, to be put back to-morrow,
> To feed on hope, to pine with fear and
>   sorrow,
> To have thy prince's grace, yet want her
>   peers',
> To have thy asking, yet wait many years,
> To fret thy soul with crosses and with cares,
> To eat thy heart through comfortless despairs,
> To fawn, to crouch, to wait, to ride, to run,
> To spend, to give, to want, to be undone.

His *View of the Present State of Ireland* shows him on this side of his nature, the keen, hard, not over-scrupulous Puritan politician. In the prologue to the fifth book of the *Faerie Queene* he sets forth a sort of philosophy of history, in which the gorgeous language and versification give an imposing semblance of coherence to what is in effect a combination of the romantic cry, that glory and loveliness have passed away, with an ecstatic eulogy of Tudor absolutism. The Platonic doctrine of the Great Year is there used with extraordinary effect to enforce the progressive degeneracy of the world; but he does not, like Virgil in the fourth Eclogue, regard the vast cycle as nearing its close, and a new golden age in prospect; the movement is still on its downward arc: and poetry itself is the anodyne rather than the vital function of life. It is just this want of touch between art and life that prevents Spenser, with all his poetical gift and accomplishment, from taking a place in the first rank of poets. "This," he says himself in another of these prologues into which he put his deepest thought, or what he took for thought,

> Of some the abundance of an idle brain
> Will judged be, and painted forgery:

and such indeed is the matured judgment of posterity. But abundance has never been more inexhaustible, or forgery more magnificently painted. Like his own magic crystal devised by Merlin,

> It round and hollow-shaped was
> Like to the world itself, and seemed a world
>   of glass.

Into that crystal we may still plunge our eyes with ever renewed fascination.

The Platonism which is expressly set forth in many passages like that which I have cited, and in whole poems like the Hymns to Heavenly Love and Heavenly Beauty, was the side of Greek literature which appealed most strongly to the Renaissance. It satisfied, and fed to a greater intensity, their sense of vastness, their intoxication with language, their longing to transcend all limits. It is the only side of Greece which had a visible influence on Spenser himself. He was, according to contemporary testimony which may be taken for what it is worth, "perfect in the Greek tongue"; an accomplished scholar, that is to say, according to the standard of what was in England not an age of high or severe scholarship. But the distinctively Greek quality is wholly absent from his poetry; he is, in that sense of the terms, a romantic and not a classic. This is patent as regards the whole tone and colour of his poetry; and even for traces of any influence on him from Homer, from the Greek lyrists, or from the Attic tragedians we may search through him in vain. The only specific translations or adaptations from the Greek that are to be noted throughout the *Faerie Queene* are from Græco-Roman epigrams in the Anthology, and these he very likely knew only in Latin versions. Among the Greek poets proper, he seems scarcely to have gone back beyond Theocritus. The Greek clarity, the Greek purity, were alien from his luxurious romantic temperament. This is not said in disparagement; for he too had heard the Muses singing, though not on the mountain or in seven-gated Thebes; and we can hardly wish him to have been other than he was.

A great deal of well-meant nonsense has been talked about Spenser's purity, in the other sense of that ambiguous word. He was a poet of high if rather vague and sentimental idealisms. The scope of the *Faerie Queene* is expressly stated by him to be the fashioning twelve moral virtues. But its end, he says, in words which are more significant, is to fashion a gentleman. There is a profound difference between a gentleman and a saint; and the gentleman of that age, in Tennyson's phrase, hovered between war and wantonness; he inherited the corruption of the age of chivalry as well as the rich sensuousness of the Renaissance. It has been a fashion to extol Spenser at the expense of Ariosto. But the lightheartedness, the gay inconsequence, of the Italian poet is combined with a natural goodness quite as great as that underlying Spenser's rather heavy and forced morality. Ariosto had no consciousness of a mission, beyond that of producing an endless stream of melodious and brilliant poetry. He belongs to a time before the Renaissance had sickened of its own Palace of Art; he accepted life in a large way, he saw all the humour and beauty and brightness of it. The beauty of goodness always appeals to him. His Bradamante is as pure as Britomartis, and ten times more loveable. He has no sentimental illusions about his world of knights and ladies; but he frankly thinks it a very good and beautiful world. The *gran bontà de' cavalieri antichi* is a thing about which he is quite in earnest. It is not without significance that his greatest enthusiasm is for Vittoria Colonna; a very different kind of patroness and heroine from Queen Elizabeth. He certainly makes no parade of morals. But with one or two exceptions, there is hardly anything in the *Orlando Furioso* that is not suitable to be read aloud, even according to the taste of the present day; the same cannot be said of the *Faerie Queene*. And when Spenser lapses into sensuousness, it is with a certain clumsiness from which Ariosto was saved, not by a higher ideal, but by a more refined and educated taste. In Spenser, as in so much English art—as in so much English work beyond the sphere of art—there is a trace left of the insular grossness, a strain of something a little forced and exaggerated. He is hardly of the centre.

But the centre had for the time been lost. An iron age had displaced the golden time of Raphael and Ariosto and Erasmus. The brave attempt of Humanism to breathe fresh life into the Middle Ages, and carry the old world alive and unbroken into the new age, had been made and had failed. The religious wars broke out before the middle of the sixteenth century. Thenceforth the whole of life became one vast field of battle between the revolutionary Reformation and the Catholic reaction. These bitter enemies had one, and but one, disastrous feature in common, a fanatical hatred of great and humane art. In Italy the sunset of the Renaissance lingered; but the shadow of the Catholic reaction is already visible in Tasso's romantic epic. In England the revolution which, in the historian's striking words, laid its foundations in the murder of the English Erasmus, and set up its gates in the blood of the English Petrarch, left a long heritage of sombre restlessness, of doubt and gloom. It has often been remarked as strange, even as unaccountable, that throughout the earlier years of the Elizabethan age there is an all but universal cry that poetry is dead or dying, that barbarism and ignorance have flooded in. The *Tears of the Muses,* published by Spenser in 1591, and written not long before, is one prolonged complaint of this.

> Heaps of huge words uphoarded hideously
> With horrid sound though having little sense,

are all, he says, that is left of the palace of poetry. The truth was that, in her secular movement, poetry was breaking up and transforming herself. A new generation was already at the doors, one which was in turn to sweep up and put away the Renaissance, as the Renaissance had swept up and put away the Middle Ages.

It was not only at the doors, but within them. Night's candles were burnt out, and jocund day stood tiptoe on the misty mountain tops. The world was moving at a prodigious speed, and poetry had to quit her ancient seats, to whirl and follow the sun. The year 1591 is remarkable in letters, not only for the *Tears of the Muses* volume, but for another work in which there is a satirical allusion to the *Tears of the Muses*. That work was the *Midsummer Night's Dream*. Of the life of Nicholas Bottom (who has been called, not without some colour of reason, the hero of that play) we unhappily know as little as we do of the lives of Autolycus' aunts. But if he did not marry till middle life, his son might very well have handled a pike at Naseby.

Thus Spenser, like so many other great poets, represents the late splendour of a descending and fast disappearing tradition. The realm in which he was so great an innovator, so wide an explorer and conqueror, was even before his death passing into other hands. Much of his work has faded away and become obsolete; but his great argosy came into harbour. He lives effectively in a few sonnets, in one superb ode, and in the *Faerie Queene*.

The *Epithalamion,* in Johnson's stately phrase of compliment, "it were vain to blame, and useless to praise." For sustained beauty of execution, for melodiousness in which the most melodious of English poets excels even his own standard, for richness of ornament that stops just short of excess, and does not either blur the outline or clog the movement, it easily takes the first place, not only among Spenser's own lyrics, but among all English odes. The mechanism of the verse is a marvel of delicate intricacy. The twenty-three long undulating stanzas into which it is divided by the recurrent but perpetually varying refrain are all based on the same general rhythmical scheme of subdivision, but with variations of internal structure devised with extreme skill to prevent monotony, to give the play and freedom of a live organism. It is possible to read the poem, even to be familiar with it, and not to recognise until after more minute inspection that the normal nineteen-line stanza is varied with three other forms of stanza, two of eighteen and one of seventeen lines, and that the arrangement of the rhymes has further delicate variations. The Ode was Spenser's latest lyric, written after his hand had for years been occupied on the large decorative canvas of the allegorical epic. It was written for a personal occasion:

Take these lines, look lovingly and nearly,
Lines I write the first time and the last time.
He who works in fresco steals a hair-brush,
Makes a strange art of an art familiar,
Fills his lady's missal-marge with flowerets.

From it he returned to his main work, to the *Faerie Queene;* and to his main work we may now turn. Edward Phillips, nearly a century afterwards, speaks of it as "being for great invention and poetic height judged little inferior, if not equal, to the chief of the ancient Greeks and Latins, or the modern Italians." What Phillips said or thought would itself be of little importance; but there is reason to believe that the judgment he speaks of is that of Milton.

II

In reading the *Faerie Queene,* as in reading all poetry, we cannot appreciate it duly without the study and the effort requisite to let us place ourselves more or less at the poet's point of view, to let us understand, or not wholly misunderstand, what he meant by poetry and what poetry meant to him. But we cannot appreciate it, in its essential quality as poetry, at all, unless we approach it with an unclouded mind, and disengage ourselves from commentaries and theories. The child's vision must, if it were possible, be combined with the scholar's understanding. This is a hard saying, but the thing itself is hard. The course lies straight and narrow between the rock and the whirlpool. Appreciation only comes of study; study too often dims and sophisticates appreciation. The attempt to be made here must be not to lose ourselves either in a mist of theories, or in a quicksand of facts; but to disengage, as far as may be, the poetical quality of the poem in form and substance; to estimate, as far as may be, the degree to which it actually condenses, from the flying vapour of language and life, an image of perfection. For while the value of a poem is manifold, its value as poetry is just this.

Spenser has left us in no doubt as to what he meant by poetry and what he meant to do in his great poem. It is a subject on which he is never tired of discoursing. He recurs to it over and over again, both in his elaborate prefaces and introductions, and more incidentally in many passages of the *Faerie Queene* itself. The loose construction and leisurely movement of the poem give him full opportunity for personal digressions and passages of homiletic or imaginative exposition. In these expositions of his doctrine and practice there is the same melodious fluency which is the primary quality of his poetry itself; the same fecundity of illustration and ornament, the same lofty if somewhat vague and inconsequent idealism. The image of perfection which he set himself to embody was, in his own words, that of a noble person fashioned in virtuous and gentle discipline. It was life at its utmost height and richness.

Before it lay the whole pageant of the world, the kingdom and the power and the glory of it. "In that Faery Queen," he says, in words which for him are unusually precise, "I mean glory." This word of glory is the keynote of the whole Renaissance; the glory of discovery, of conquest, of possession, of mastery. The achievement of this glory was "virtue"; the virtue of the statesman, the ruler, and the soldier, enlarged by liberal studies and bathed in the splendours of romance. The twelve moral virtues, to the glorification of which the twelve books of the *Faerie Queene* were to be devoted, were all summed up in the crowning virtue of magnificence; and this "magnificence" is almost the same thing as "courtesy," courtiership, the conduct of life by the masters of the world, lords over the five senses and the visible earth. Such glory was transitory, like this world itself; but it was the nearest approach which this world gave to immortality.

The vehicle chosen by Spenser to set forth his vision of the world's glory was that of the chivalrous romance. The *Faerie Queene* is not an epic; both in its author's genius and in its own purpose it is alien from the epic tension and concentration. He speaks of following Homer and Virgil; but this is because the *Iliad* and the *Aeneid* were read by him, and affected him, as romances. The romantic epic, as it had been lately attempted by Tasso, was a hybrid product, destined to be sterile. Spenser does not seem himself to notice any distinction of kind between Tasso and Ariosto. But his own poem is a still more complex hybridisation; it is the spirit of Tasso working on the method of Ariosto. The *Faerie Queene* has not, and was not meant to have, the epic unity, the epic structural and organic composition. It has no story, or if it has, the story has neither beginning nor end, and does not really matter. It has no dramatic life, no tragical interplay of human will and passion. It has no hero, for its hero is an abstraction, or rather a shifting series of abstractions. It is a romance wrapped in the imperial robes of the epic, but lacking her sceptre and crown. It is a pageant and allegory of life, while the epic is the imaginative embodiment of life itself.

All poetry is an allegory, in the sense that it embodies, in concrete symbols, a meaning larger and nobler than that which its literal words convey. In this sense, the amount of allegory in a poem depends not so much on the poet as on the reader. Homer and Virgil were allegorised, both in ancient and in modern times, to such an extent that their true outlines were lost, their true quality as poetry obscured, though it was still instinctively felt. But in Spenser the allegory is throughout conscious and purposed; it is of the structure and essence of the poem. In his prefatory letter prefixed to the *Faerie Queene,* he describes it in set terms as a continued allegory; and this is the case. But his specific use of allegory, and with it the specific quality of the poem, was determined by the fact that, with immense imagination and endless fertility of invention and language, he had neither the narrative nor the dramatic gift. He has little power—one might say he has little wish—of telling a story or realising a situation. The *Pilgrim's Progress* is an allegory more expressly and closely than the **Faerie Queene**. But Bunyan's narrative gift is so certain, his dramatic instinct is so fine, that the allegorical abstractions with which he purports to be dealing take flesh and blood on them almost without his will, and become real human beings. There are no real human beings in the **Faerie Queene**.

The amount of allegory in it of course varies very much, as does its quality and complexity. In its large lines the poem is an allegorising of abstractions, of virtues or vices, of physical or mental functions, of philosophical or theological ideas, even of political situations. Each book allegorises one of the virtues. Many of the episodes are elaborate and detailed allegories on their own account: such as the long and tedious description of the human body as the Castle of Alma in the ninth canto of the second book, or the siege of that same castle at the wards of the five senses in the eleventh canto. Others follow the mediæval manner more closely. An impersonation like Lady Praise-Desire in the House of Temperance, with the poplar-branch in her hand, or the description of the entrance to the temple of Venus, with its porters Doubt and Delay, and its gate of Good Desert guarded by the giant Danger, might come straight from the *Romaunt of the Rose,* and belongs to a tradition which never had been very happy, and from which Chaucer himself had long ago decisively broken away. This is hardly allegory at all; still less so are those parts of the poem which deal with contemporary history after the fashion of the *roman à clef.* It is in these that the poetry is at its lowest temperature; they are not so much poetry as versified politics. Much of the fifth book is of this kind. The trial of Duessa before Mercilla is mere pamphleteering. All that is needed to convert it into a political tract is to replace the names; to speak plainly of Mary and Elizabeth instead of calling them Duessa and Mercilla, and to substitute for the names of Care and Zeal those of Cecil and Walsingham. In the three cantos which follow, even this slight veil is dropped, because it was not really worth while keeping it up. Belgium, Spain, Henry of Bourbon, are introduced openly under their own names. The poetic imagination ebbs away, leaving only a sort of bleached rhetorical framework. Even the language becomes little removed from that of prose. Except for a few inversions of order brought about by the necessities of rhyme, there is stanza after stanza that has nothing, either in imagination or in style, to distinguish it from the florid heavy prose of that period. It is Spenser become mechanical, the Spenserian manner become a trick. How nobly he recovered himself later, those will not need to be reminded who have followed the poem to the end—or

not to the end, for there is none, but to the point where it was broken off by the poet's death.

There is a natural tendency in the human mind to confuse imagination with imagery. The difference between them is that between creation on the one hand and invention on the other, and it is vital. Spenser thought (so far as he did think) in images. His inventiveness, his faculty for pouring forth an endless stream of imagery, is unsurpassed, just as is his faculty for conveying this imagery in unfailingly fluent and melodious language. He is a complete master of decorative art, so far as this very fertility and fluency do not, as we may think, lead him to make his decoration too intricate, to overload his ornament. But while all art is decoration, it is not in its merely decorative quality that art can be great art, can fully realise its function. To do this, it must rise from invention to creation. Its imagery must be transmuted by imagination; it must not only adorn, but interpret and, in a sense, make life.

If Spenser is not, in the full sense of the term, one of the first order of poets, it is because, while he does possess this higher gift of creative and interpretative imagination, he possesses it intermittently, capriciously, and imperfectly. The **Faerie Queene** does not move. It lives, but hardly with full life. It is not that his poetry does not represent the actual world. No poetry does. It is that it does not create a world more real than the actual world. It drifts, at the suggestion of complex influences, through a sea of dreams. It fluctuates between moral allegory and unmoralised romance, now swerving into passages of crude realism, and again soaring to ideal heights of imagination. But the poet's genius is so great, his resources are so vast, and his handling of them so easy and adroit, that he absorbs the reader into his own dream. His fabric rises into the air like an exhalation; as the gleaming pageant floats and passes before us, we are hardly conscious, any more than we are conscious in actual dreaming, of its inconsequence and unsubstantiality. Scenes melt into one another; nothing is surprising. It is all iridescent, magnified, wrapped and floating in a luminous mist.

In the last canto of the last completed book of the **Faerie Queene,** Spenser himself makes a claim for the poem which is of a different nature. The image of the epic, with its high imaginative tension and concentrated creative energy, hung before him as a poetic ideal; but it became in his hands, like his ideal figures and scenes, something filmy, elusive, and unsubstantial. In this passage he lays claim to unity and purpose in his long train of romantic imagery; and does so, very characteristically, by means of a new piece of romantic imagery of just the same texture as the rest.

> Like as a ship, that through the ocean wide
> Directs her course unto one certain coast,
> Is met of many a counter wind and tide

With which her winged speed is let and crost,
And she herself in stormy surges tost,
Yet, making many a board and many a bay,
Still winneth way, ne hath her compass lost;
Right so it fares with me in this long way
Whose course is often stayed, yet never is
    astray.

Right so it does nothing of the sort. Even had he lived to catch up all the interlaced or floating threads of the poem, and to bring them out to a conclusion, it would not have made any material difference. We are not in the least interested in the progress of the action in the *Faerie Queene;* or rather, there is no progress of the action for us to be interested in. It is difficult to remember, as we read it, whom we are reading about, or how they came there. They drop out and reappear capriciously; we are pleased to meet them, we half think we have seen them before, and it does not matter when they are gone. They move among one another, weaving intricate and lovely patterns, and as the pattern still flows out of the loom, "his web, reeled off, curls and goes out like steam." Into these chambers of imagery the breath of fresh outer air hardly enters; it would blow the whole fabric away.

This enchanted atmosphere, this luminous mist of romantic feeling and glittering imagery, pervades the whole poem. But it varies from point to point, like some actual vapour that collects or clears, lifts or drops, under light variable airs.

Far off they saw the silver-misty morn,
Rolling her smoke about the royal mount,
That rose between the forest and the field.
At times the summit of the high city flashed:
At times the spires and turrets half-way down
Pricked thro' the mist; at times the great gate
    shone
Only, that opened on the field below;
Anon, the whole fair city had disappeared.

Sometimes it condenses into a cloud through which we move heavily, and the figures loom indistinct and spectral. Sometimes a rift of sky blows open, and a corner of the landscape is seen in clear daylight. In these little clear islets we may find what is perhaps Spenser at his best, though not at his most characteristic: in those rare and pleasant simpler touches where the poetry becomes lucid and close to life, or in those passages, not rare, where it rises to some great nobleness of expression, some great elevation of sentiment. Spenser's Chaucerianism was no mere muddle of antiquarian pedantry; it was a real love and admiration, a poetical sympathy that makes him write now and then, for a few lines together, with the freshness and charm of Chaucer. If I may venture to put it so, he sometimes drops into poetry. When he has almost wearied us with Britomartis, he suddenly writes of her thus:

One day, whenas she long had sought for ease
In every place, and every place thought best,
Yet found no place that could her liking
    please,
She to a window came that opened west,
Towards which coast her love his way
    addrest:
There, looking forth, she in her heart did find
Many vain fancies working her unrest,
And sent her winged thoughts more swift than
    wind
To bear unto her love the message of her
    mind.

It is like cool water. The same clear simplicity comes with the same lovely effect in many single lines. Calepine, when he is recovered of his wounds, goes out, as Palamon or Arcite might go, "to take the air and hear the thrushes' song." "What Maygame hath misfortune made of you?" the Amazon asks Artegall when she finds him in prison, touched by surprise to forget all her rhetoric. In the beautiful pastoral incident which fills several cantos of the sixth book, Spenser reverts not only to the free romantic manner of the *Arcadia,* but to a simpler, fresher style and language than that to which he had wrought himself when he planned to make his poem not only a romance but an epic and an allegory of life.

One day, as they all three together went
To the green wood to gather strawberries—

how unlike this is to the highly-charged, slowly-wheeling, rich verse that we think of as Spenserian!

    It is old and plain:
The spinsters and the knitters in the sun
Do use to chant it: it is silly sooth
And dallies with the innocence of love
Like the old age.

Of course he cannot keep it up; the traditions of high romance must be observed; and the first thing that happens in the wood is that a tiger comes out of it, "with fell claws full of fierce gormandise, and greedy mouth wide-gaping like hell-gate." The hero, who has "no weapon but his shepherd's hook to serve the vengeance of his wrathful will," at once fells the tiger to the earth with it, and before the formidable beast can recover, hews off its head—whether with the shepherd's hook or not, the chivalrous spirit of romance does not pause to inquire.

And just as Spenser's genuine love and admiration of Chaucer combine with the instinctive resurgence in him, as in all the poetry of his age, of the native lyrical impulse, to make him write now and then with Chaucerian freshness and simplicity, so his genuine love and admiration of the classics make the *Faerie Queene* in many passages rise to an almost classic height. In the flowing loosely-woven texture of the poem there are many lines and stanzas, and even whole passages, which stand out from the rest in virtue of a concentration, a precision, a dignity which are the qualities of the classics. It would be tedious to develop this point by large illustration; and in any case the search and the selection must be made by each reader for himself; and the search is delightful, even apart from the added delight of recognition or discovery. It would be easy to collect and dwell upon many single lines that have this quality of exalted beauty, lines like the famous

> Glistering in arms and battailous array;

or

> Wasting the strength of her immortal age;

or

> Spreading pavilions for the birds to bower.

It is curious to notice how all these lines, though they were not chosen in order to bring out the point, but simply for their own sake, are participial; they convey an image incidentally in the course of the main movement of the passages in which they are set. This is true of the poem generally. It is like the English architecture of the same period, still Gothic in main substance and structure, but enriched by classic detail. Its classicism is decorative, not constructional. This is the case likewise with the longer passages or whole stanzas which reach, or suggest, the classic manner.

> Both roof and floor and walls were all of
>   gold,
> But overgrown with dust and old decay,
> And hid in darkness, that none could behold
> The hue thereof; for view of cheerful day
> Did never in that house itself display,
> But a faint shadow of uncertain light:
> Such as a lamp whose life does fade away,
> Or as the moon, clothed with cloudy night,
> Does shew to him that walks in fear and sad
>   affright.

That is the classical manner; not that of the great classics, it is true; . . . it is a diluted secondary classicism more like that of Apollonius or Statius. But the stanza is only one out of three in which the House of Riches is described; the other two, which precede and follow it, are in the loaded intricate manner which is normal to Spenser, and which is in direct antithesis to the classical. Nor would it be possible, even if the poet had wished to do so, to adapt the classical manner to the imaginative substance of the poem (if substance it might be called that substance had none), which is that

of a vast pageant moving through a dream.

This pageant-like or dream-like quality makes the *Faerie Queene* approximate to a masque or interlaced series of masques rather than to an epic. There is no difference of plane between the figures and the ornament; for the figures are the ornament; "You shamefast are, but shamefastness itself is she," says Alma to Guyon; she might equally well have put it the other way. The episodes nearly always break off in the middle, or rather, do not so much break off as melt away. It is singular how many of the cantos end on this note of vanishing:

> Eftsoons he fled away and might nowhere be
>   seen—

or

> The while false Archimage and Atin fled
>   apace—

or

> And from Prince Arthur fled with wings of
>   idle fear—

or most strikingly, and with most studied and splendid effect, in the wonderful line which closes the Mutability cantos,

> And Nature's self did vanish, whither no man
>   wist.

It is a piece of deliberate art with Spenser that he hardly ever finishes a story. He does finish the story of Cambell and Canace in the fourth book, and makes a sad bungle of it. The variations in the texture of the poem are given, the stages in its movement are marked, chiefly by points at which the continuous pageantry, like a stream spreading into pools, expands, rather than concentrates, into set pageants of unusual elaboration and magnificence. The Masque of Cupid, at the end of the third book, is the best known of these, as it is perhaps the greatest. Almost as well known is the pageant of the Months in the seventh book. Of the same type, though with a difference of subject and treatment, is the chronicle of the kings of Britain, a sort of masque of British history, towards the end of the second book, and the marriage procession of the rivers towards the end of the fourth. To the ninth, tenth, and eleventh cantos of the sixth book, which stand quite by themselves, some further reference will be made.

So much it is indispensable to keep in view with regard to the quality and substance of the *Faerie Queene* as poetry. We may now go on to consider with a fuller appreciation the metrical vehicle which Spenser chose for it, the famous Spenserian stanza. It is one of the four great English metrical forms for poetry written on a large scale; and it is rightly and indissolubly connected with the name of Spenser; for he both introduced it and perfected it. No one of the other three metres is called after the name of a single poet. Chaucer invented (or to all intents and purposes invented) two of them, the rhyme-royal and the heroic couplet. The former of the two he also carried to perfection. But for various reasons, it has not been so continuously and habitually used by later poets as the other three; and to call it the Chaucerian verse would do injustice to Chaucer's other and greater invention: for though Chaucer's crowning masterpiece is in the former metre, the larger part of his mature work, and that by which he is most universally known, is in the latter. The heroic couplet itself was used by Chaucer with consummate skill, and established by him as a standard form of English verse. But it afterwards underwent great changes and developments. It cannot be associated exclusively with any poet's name, but it is perhaps associated most closely in common usage with a later age and with the shape it took in the hands of Dryden and Pope. The last of the four dominant forms of English verse, the unrhymed decasyllable, has also passed through many phases and received new qualities from more than one great poet. But the Spenserian verse was not only created and established by Spenser, but left by him in its final form. It has never gone out of use. It was written freely through both the seventeenth and the eighteenth centuries. In the great renascence of English poetry a hundred years ago it occupied a leading position. Shelley, Byron, Scott, Keats, all used it largely. None of them gave it any new quality: and it still remains exactly what Spenser left it.

Technically the Spenserian stanza consists of the interlaced double quatrain (what metrical treatises call the eight-line ballad-stave) which was introduced into England by Chaucer, with the addition of a twelve-syllabled ninth line rhyming with the eighth. But this addition completely changes its character; it gives it a new rhythm and a new balance, and one totally unlike that of any form of verse previously used. Spenser's stanza is, in the full sense of the words, a fresh creation. Careful scrutiny may indeed pick out, here and there in the earlier part of the *Faerie Queene,* a stanza in which the ninth line comes as a sort of afterthought, and the other eight preserve something of the ballad-stave cadence; but these are few, and only recognisable when one looks for them. Normally and habitually the ninth line is felt coming through the whole stanza, which implies it and converges upon it.

Spenser was no doubt led to the invention of his stanza by the desire to find an English form of verse which should be the equivalent, and a little more than the equivalent, of the Italian rhymed octave. From Boc-

caccio to Tasso, the *ottava rima* had reigned undisputed in Italy as the vehicle for the heroic romance and for the regular epic. It was one admirably suited to the genius and structure of the Italian language. But it did not accommodate itself well to English, nor to French, in which the English metricists sought their models. Chaucer instinctively passed by the metre of Boccaccio; Spenser, as instinctively, passed by the metre of Ariosto and Tasso. Chaucer syncopated the octave stanza into the rhyme-royal, Spenser expanded it into the Spenserian. In both cases the effect was to produce a vehicle that was more romantic and complex; that fell short possibly of the serenity and balance of the Italian octave, but gained in richness and harmony. The long swaying rhythms of the new stanza were exactly suited to a style like Spenser's, loaded with ornament and almost stationary in movement. It allowed him full amplitude; it held, it even invited and reinforced, the quality of boundlessness in his genius, the immense superflux of language and fancy. It is worth noting that the rhyme-royal where Spenser uses it, in the four *Hymns,* gives something of the effect of a curtailed Spenserian; it has not the authentic cadence. But these poems were written after he had invented and begun to use his proper medium.

Like most metrical forms, the Spenserian stanza has its excellences and its defects. For poetry which consists of a stream of pageants it is exactly suited. It is no less apt as a vehicle of imaginative reflection, for thought translating itself in images. It lends itself to rich effects produced by accumulated touches. When, as it often does, it swells up to the very end; or when, to produce a different effect, it slowly ebbs off; or when, as is equally characteristic with Spenser, it slides forward with equable rhythms till near the end, and then, in the eighth and ninth lines, rises into a great crescendo and storm of sound, it is little short of miraculous. To embark on quotations is a formidable matter, but just one instance of each kind of effect may be given. An instance of the first, almost too well known, but still endlessly delightful to repeat, is from the description of the Garden of Acrasia (II. xii. 71):

> The joyous birds, shrouded in cheerful shade,
> Their notes unto the voice attempered sweet:
> The angelical soft trembling voices made
> To the instruments divine respondence meet:
> The silver-sounding instruments did meet
> With the base murmur of the water's fall:
> The water's fall, with difference discreet,
> Now soft, now loud, unto the wind did call:
> The gentle warbling wind low answered to all.

As an instance of the second may be taken a stanza of equal beauty and celebrity, the famous invocation to Chaucer (IV. ii. 34), with its singular likeness, in phrasing and rhythm as well as in substance, to those exquisite verses of William Morris which come as the *envoi* to the *Earthly Paradise:*

> Then pardon, O most sacred happy spirit,
> That I thy labours lost may thus revive
> And steal from thee the meed of thy due merit
> That none durst ever whilst thou wast alive:
> And being dead, in vain yet many strive;
> Ne dare I like; but thro' infusion sweet
> Of thine own spirit which doth in me survive
> I follow here the footing of thy feet
> That with thy meaning so I may the rather
>   meet.

For an instance, finally, of the third kind, we may go to one of the innumerable combats between a knight and two Paynims—mostly in common form and a little tedious, but in this case lifted to a new splendour by the blaze and crash of the final line (II. viii. 37):

> Horribly then he gan to rage and rail
> Cursing his gods and himself damning deep.
> But when his brother saw the red blood rail
> Adown so fast, and all his armour steep,
> For very fellness loud he gan to weep,
> And said: Caitiff, curse on thy cruel hand
> That twice hath sped; yet shall it not thee
>   keep
> From the third brunt of this my fatal brand:
> Lo! where the dreadful Death behind thy back
>   doth stand.

Such are some, and only some, of the effects of which the stanza is capable. On the other hand, it often drags and becomes languid. The last line sometimes seems pure surplusage; sometimes one may say the same of more than the last line. The thought, and even the imagery, become exhausted before the end of the stanza is reached. Spenser's fluency is unfailing; but there are many places where the fluency becomes mere verbosity, many where the stanza seems stuffed out with anything that comes first to hand. It is this that lies at the root of Spenser's strange lapses into bald prose. He recovers from them swiftly, but there they are: in single lines like

> Though otherwise it did him little harm;

or

> Then very doubtful was the war's event;

or

> But the rude porter, that no manners had;

and even more markedly in some longer passages that are mere untransmuted lumps from the debased prose romances of the period, such as,

> But turn we now back to that lady free
> Whom late we left riding upon an ass;

or the amazing account of her adventures given by Priscilla to Calidore in the second canto of Book VI. It fills eight stanzas, and is all as bad as can be; I will only give one gem out of the heap:

> Then, as it were to avenge his wrath on me,
> When forward we should fare he flat refused
> To take me up (as this young man did see)
> But forced to trot on foot, and foul misused,
> Punching me with the butt-end of his spear.

Doll Tearsheet might talk so: did talk so in fact, the very next year, in the squalid but powerful scene where she makes her last appearance on Shakespeare's stage.

Finally, as a vehicle for narrative poetry, the Spenserian verse is inherently faulty, because it lacks speed. Its movement is not progressive; it is like that of spreading and interlacing circles. Spenser was no doubt naturally without that rare quality, the narrative gift; but he deliberately (and very likely rightly) chose a metrical form for the **Faerie Queene** which emphasised this deficiency. The same thing is true of the stanza as used by other poets. Compare Keats's two masterpieces; how heavy, how struggling, is the narrative movement in the *Eve of St. Agnes* when set beside the swift, clear brightness of *Lamia!* or compare the endless circumvolutions of Shelley in the *Revolt of Islam* with the sense of life and movement in the *Witch of Atlas.* Even Byron, the swiftest of English poets, becomes slow and almost languid in *Childe Harold.* In his *Don Juan,* where rapidity was essential, he abandoned the Spenserian verse, and boldly launched into the Italian rhymed octave, though he did not succeed in naturalising it, and *Don Juan* remains a long metrical *tour de force.* And if we take Byron where he is swiftest and most himself—the Byron of the *Giaour*—the difference is almost incredible.

> The foremost Tartar's in the gap
> Conspicuous by his yellow cap—

it is safe to say that Spenser, or any one writing in the Spenserian manner, would have spent a whole stanza in getting over the ground that this fierce swift couplet covers in a single stride. Byron himself could hardly have done otherwise; for so essentially is the Spenserian stanza Spenser's creation, that it cannot be written at all except in a manner nearly akin to his.

This perilous fluency, this unbounded melodiousness, is at once Spenser's strength and his weakness as an artist. It displeased the classicists of his own time. His friend Harvey honestly disliked the **Faerie Queene,** and said so roundly to Spenser himself. "Hobgoblin running away with the garland from Apollo" he calls it, in a phrase which one can hardly fancy Spenser would either forgive or forget. He sets the whole thing down, rather petulantly, to some foolish ambition in Spenser to outdo Ariosto on his own lines. Harvey's opinions on poetry were not those of a poet, and are perhaps not of special value. But in this instance he expresses the feeling not merely of classicist pedantry, but of classical judgment. Every one knows that we have only half of the *Faerie Queene* as planned; that it was to have extended to twelve books, and something like sixty thousand or seventy thousand lines. What is not so widely known, or at least so clearly remembered, is that these twelve books were only the first part of a still more gigantic scheme. If that scheme had been carried out, we should have had a poem, or a mass of poetry, of something more like one hundred and fifty thousand lines. This would substantially exceed even the sixty thousand couplets into which the *Shah Nameh,* through successive accretions, became swollen in the hands of Firdausi and his pupils or continuators. It would have been a poem which, in Lord Cockburn's celebrated phrase, would have exhausted Time and encroached on Eternity.

But towards the end of the sixth book of the *Faerie Queene* we become conscious of a great and significant change of tone. It occurs subtly and silently, like dawn overspreading the sky. But it means that the spirit of the poet, and of his art, has changed. The Renaissance is tiring of itself; poetry is returning to life: and with the same movement life is returning to poetry.

The note of change comes with the reversion to pastoral at the opening of the ninth canto.

> Now turn again my team, thou jolly swain,
> Back to the furrow which I lately left.

The note here is very different from that of the elaborate high-flown introductions to which we have been accustomed hitherto. The immediate reference is merely to his customary process of taking up the dropped thread of his romance. But it suggests more: it suggests a return to the furrow in another sense, a return to the pleasant villages and farms, to the opener air, from the enchanted atmosphere, heavy and luminous, of courtly romance.

> A soft air fans the cloud apart; there comes
> A glimpse of that dark world where I was
>   born.

The *Faerie Queene* becomes a *Winter's Tale* in the beautiful episode which follows. The

> shepherd grooms
> Playing on pipes and carolling apace,
> The whiles their beasts there in the budded
>   brooms

> Beside them fed, and nipt the tender blooms,

are those of the *Shepherds Calendar* back again, but softened, etherealised, lit by romance. Pastorella, the one figure in the whole of the *Faerie Queene* who is all but human, reminds one of Shakespeare's Perdita. Like Perdita she needs must turn in the story into a king's daughter lost and hidden among shepherds; such was the tradition of romance, that might not lightly be broken. But, king's daughter or not, she brings with her the breath and beauty of common life. The vanity of ambition is a theme on which throughout the poem Spenser has been perpetually discoursing; but here, for the first time, it brings with it the vanity of courtliness, the evanescence of the Renaissance ideal. Melibœus the shepherd, Pastorella's reputed father, has been a courtier himself in his youth, has sold himself for hire and spent his youth in vain; now, in one of Spenser's most exquisite stanzas, he tells how he has gone back to sweet peace, and "this lovely quiet life which I inherit here." His sermon on content and simplicity is Spenser speaking in his own voice, sincerely, without either self-consciousness or strain. Pastorella-Perdita "had ever learned to love the lowly things." With the reversion towards simplicity is mingled a strain of grave religion. It is not only that "happy peace" and "the perfect pleasures" grow in common life, and all the rest is but a "painted shadow of false bliss": it is that the whole gorgeous fabric of romantic chivalry is a lure, "set to entrap unwary fools in their eternal bales." And so, when the shepherds are "met to make their sports and merry glee, as they are wont in fair sunshiny weather," we are reminded not only of the *Winter's Tale* but of the *Pilgrim's Progress.* "If a man was to come here in the summer time, and if he also delighted himself in the sight of his eyes, he might see that that would be delightful to him. Some have wished that the next way to their Father's house were here, that they might be troubled no more with either hills or mountains to go over; but the way is the way, and there's an end."

This new land is as yet but dimly seen: it is coloured and half concealed by the iridescent vapour. While still among the shepherds, Calidore strays back into fairyland, to the Acidalian hill where he sees the Graces dancing, not to the lyre of Apollo, but to the pipe of Colin Clout. But when he moves towards them, they all vanish out of his sight, "and are clean gone, which way he never knew," and Colin Clout is left piping on the hillside alone. The candles of the mediæval world are burned out; but the eyes of those who issue from the brilliantly lit palace are still dazzled and cannot see things clearly. In the uncertain light, that pleasant simple countryside seems one in which tigers attack strawberry-gatherers, and are decapitated with sheephooks. "Exit pursued by a bear," is the famous stage-direction at the end of the first part of the *Winter's Tale:* sixteen years pass, and then "enter Autolycus, singing."

So Spenser pulls himself back, at the opening doorway into daylight and the new world. Calidore's life among the shepherds was making him unmindful of his vow and of the queen's commands. He leaves Pastorella-Perdita and goes on the quest of the Blatant Beast. We are back in the full current of allegorical romance. But the spell, once snapped, cannot be quite rewoven; the poem flutters for a little on a broken wing, and stops.

It stops, or the poet's death stopped it. The story of the last three months of his life is one of confused horror. Fire and sword of an Irish rising; his home sacked and burned, and his newborn child perishing in the flames; a wretched winter-flight to England; a stony welcome there, a month or two of misery and illness, and death "for lack of bread" they said, if it be not incredible: such was the tragic end. Twelve years later was published the magnificent fragment, "two *Cantos of Mutability,* which, both for form and matter, appear to be the parcel of some following book of the *Faerie Queene*, under the legend of Constancy." They may be conjectured to have been written in the last year of his life, and perhaps with some premonition of its approaching end. They renew the earlier splendours of the poem, but with a deeper and graver music. In single lines and phrases there is an organ-tone that can scarcely be matched elsewhere in Spenser; and the Titaness, proud and fair,

> Being of stature tall as any there
> Of all the Gods, and beautiful of face
> As any of the Goddesses in place,

stands out among the swaying tapestry-figures of Spenser's pageantries like some colossal sculpture of Michelangelo's. He lapses into his old decorative manner in the episode of Arlo-hill; in the simile of the cat in the dairy (the forty-seventh stanza of the first of the two cantos) it almost looks as if he were parodying himself. But from that he rises again to the great speech of Mutability; to the summoning and appearing before the throne of Nature of the procession of the Seasons and the Months, Day and Night, the Hours, Life and Death; and to the final doom pronounced by Nature, which sums up, in a few majestic words, the whole system and government of the Universe. Then Nature herself vanishes: the lights go out; silence falls; and through the silence comes one last echo and cadence of sound, a prayer to be granted the Eternal Peace.

Thus Spenser, in the old Northern phrase, "changed his life," and was laid beside Chaucer in the Abbey Church at Westminster. His life, his vision of poetry as a pageant of life, his conception of poetry as a function of life, were splendid and transitory. They ceased; while life, and with it poetry, moved on.

William Nelson (essay date 1963)

SOURCE: "That True Glorious Type," in *The Poetry of Edmund Spenser: A Study*, Columbia University Press, 1963, pp. 116-46.

[*In the following excerpt from a study of Spenser's poetry, Nelson analyzes Spenser's use of allegorical types to convey his meaning. He focuses on Spenser's use of Queen Elizabeth as "that true glorious type" of gentleness and nobility.*]

In the strange and various forest of **The Faerie Queene** many lose their way and succumb at last to the monster Error or, worse still, to exasperation and boredom. Omens for the journey are particularly unpropitious if the traveler enters upon it guided by the Aristotelian dictum that plot is the "first principle, and, as it were, the soul" of an epic poem, for here it will lead him only into a morass. He is better off if he comes armed, like the Red Cross Knight, with faith, faith in the book itself and in the guiding signs within it. By faith in the book I mean a disposition to believe that whatever the history of its composition may have been, the poem as it was presented to Queen Elizabeth is neither an incoherent and improbable tale worth reading only for the charm of its quaint and delicious passages nor a farrago of bits and pieces hastily thrown together to make a volume but, like Spenser's other poems, a carefully considered composition in which theme, rather than fable, is the central structural element. And by faith in its signs, I mean the belief that Spenser's announcements of his intention, both in the text itself and in the letter addressed to Sir Walter Ralegh which was appended to the first edition, are designed to give "great light to the Reader" rather than to mislead him. It would hardly be necessary to make these affirmations were it not for the number of interpreters of **The Faerie Queene** who begin by denying them. Of course, the reader may conclude (as I do not) that the only order in **The Faerie Queene** is of the kind imposed by the stargazer upon the scattered lights of the sky, and that the poet's professions of purpose, like those of many a Renaissance author, are no more than a formal bow to the critical dogma of his time. The proof lies in the poem.

The first lines of **The Faerie Queene** are themselves a sign to the reader, though their meaning is hidden in an obscurity not of Spenser's making. Had he begun with the words "I sing of arms and the man" no reader could doubt that he wished his poem to be recognized as of the genre of the *Aeneid*. But in Spenser's edition of Vergil's poem, as in all Renaissance editions, the opening words were not "Arma virumque cano" but the following verses, probably Vergilian indeed but rejected by Vergil's first editor, Varius:

> Ille ego qui quondam gracili modulatus avena
> Carmen, et egressus silvis, vicina coegi

Ut quamvis avido parerent arva colono
Gratum opus agricolis: at nunc horrentia
    Martis
Arma virumque cano . . .

The beginning of **The Faerie Queene** is an unmistakable allusion to these lines:

Lo I the man, whose Muse whilome did
    maske,
    As time her taught in lowly Shepheards
    weeds,
    Am now enforst a far unfitter taske,
    For trumpets sterne to chaunge mine Oaten
    reeds

The poet so announces that his principal model is
Vergil's *Aeneid*.

If Spenser's text of the poem he wished to imitate
differs from our own, his understanding of its intention
and method differs even more radically. Since he was
a man of independence and originality it would be
risky to assume that he accepted without question the
standard textbook interpretations of Vergil current in
his time. Nevertheless, a comparison of his letter to
Ralegh with a typical Renaissance introduction to the
Aeneid helps to make clear what he meant by beginning as he did. Among the many sixteenth-century
editions of Vergil's poems a considerable number are
substantial folio volumes in which the text is surrounded
by a sea of commentary. Commonly, such editions
include the annotations of various scholars, the work
of the late classical grammarians Servius and Donatus
and of Renaissance humanists. Of the later commentaries that of Jodocus Badius Ascensius, otherwise Josse
Bade van Assche, famous Flemish scholar and publisher, is surely one of the most frequently reprinted.[1]

After explaining the form of the title of Vergil's poem,
Badius announces its purpose as "simul et iucunda et
idonea dicere vitae." This is the second line of that
distich of Horace's *Ars poetica* which Ben Jonson translates:

Poets would either profit or delight
Or mixing sweet and fit, teach life the right.[2]

The poet, Badius declares, undertook the task of teaching "life the right" because he knew that there could
be nothing more useful to a commonwealth than to be
led by a prince who was clement, prudent, brave, temperate, and endowed with the other virtues. He therefore depicted such a prince in the *Aeneid,* prophesying
that he would be imitated by Augustus, just as Xenophon had portrayed a Cyrus, not exactly as he was, but
as he should have been ("ut Xenophon de Cyro fecisse
perhibetur, non semper qualis fuit, sed qualem fuisse
decuit perscribens"). By this means he suggested to

Augustus both the necessity of imitating the ancestor
to whom he traced his origin, a man whom he described as most pious, just, brave, temperate, etc., and
the disgrace that he would incur if he degenerated from
the honorable customs and virtues of his forebears.
Besides this general intention which he shares with all
good writers, Badius explains, Vergil had a number of
particular ones ("speciales atque peculiares"). He
wished to crown his poetic career with a work in the
grand manner, as he had begun it in his youth with the
humble pastoral and progressed in his maturity to the
middle style of the *Georgics*. And since he had equaled
Theocritus in his eclogues and Hesiod in his *Georgics*
he desired in his great work to equal that prince of
poets and fountain of ingenuity, Homer. Indeed he
overwent Homer ("illi praestare demonstrat"). What
the Greek poet needed the forty-eight books of his
Odyssey and *Iliad* to express, Vergil said in twelve.
For Homer had described the contemplative life in the
person of Ulysses and the active life in his account of
the Trojan war, while Vergil combined them both in
one, treating of the former (which he signified by the
word *virum* in "arma virumque cano") in his first six
books and of the latter (*arma*) in the last six books.
Besides considering other "special" intentions of the
Aeneid, Badius summarizes the events of its story in
chronological or historical order, pointing out as he
does so that poetical narration follows a very different
sequence.[3]

Some verbal correspondences between this essay and
Spenser's letter are worth noting. Like Badius, Spenser distinguishes between his general intention and "particular purposes or by-accidents." His choice of a historical fiction to embody his meaning he defends as
"most plausible and pleasing," and since the word *plausible* must here have its old meaning of "deserving of
approval," the expression translates Horace's "iucunda
et idonea."[4] And like Badius Spenser cites the precedent of Xenophon who "in the person of Cyrus and the
Persians fashioned a governement such as might best
be." But phrases of this kind are so much the common
currency of Renaissance criticism that they demonstrate
rather Spenser's familiarity with the tradition than his
use of Badius as a "source."

It is in terms of matter and emphasis that Spenser's
letter shows itself to be modeled after the kind of introductory essay that is found in sixteenth-century
editions of the *Aeneid*. As Vergil's intention is said to
be the portrayal of a virtuous prince, so Spenser begins
by asserting his purpose "to fashion a gentleman or
noble person in vertuous and gentle discipline." For
the fabulous Aeneas Spenser offers Arthur "before he
was king." Arthur cannot serve as a figure for Elizabeth, as Aeneas for Augustus, but Spenser explains
that she is "shadowed" in Arthur's beloved Gloriana
and in Belphoebe. If Vergil's method is justified by an
appeal to the precedents of Homer and Xenophon,

Spenser relies for authority upon those two writers, upon Vergil himself, and upon Ariosto and Tasso. Badius' division of the subject of the nature of the hero-prince into the branches designated by *virum* and *arma* is paralleled by Spenser's partition into *ethice* and *politice*. The list of virtues ascribed to Aeneas is like the list of virtues combined in Arthur and represented separately by the twelve subsidiary heroes; the one catalogue begins with "pius," the other with "Holinesse." And Spenser's letter ends with a summary of the events of his story told, not according to "the Methode of a Poet historical," but in the manner of a historiographer who "discourseth of affayres orderly as they were donne, accounting as well the times as the actions."

For his linking of Ariosto and Tasso with Homer, Vergil, and Xenophon as writers on the theme of the virtuous hero, Spenser had ample authority in contemporary comment on their poems. The editions in which he must have read the Italian poets were supplied with introductions resembling that of Badius to the *Aeneid*. Tasso himself provided explanatory prefaces to his *Rinaldo* and his *Gerusalemme Liberata,* and his essay on the latter, like the letter to Ralegh, repeats the accepted dogma concerning the division of the great subject:

> Of the life of the Contemplative Man, the Comedy of Dantes and the Odysses, are (as it were) in every part thereof a Figure: but the civil Life is seen to be shadowed throughout the Iliads, and Aeneids also, although in this there be rather set out a mixture of Action and Contemplation.[5]

There has been much argument as to whether Tasso's moralizations of his poems reflect his original intention or a more or less grudging concession to the pressures of counter-Reformation critical theory, but the question is irrelevant to the present purpose. Like Tasso's poems, the *Orlando Furioso* came to Spenser's hands as a work in this didactic tradition. Few readers today will believe that Ariosto's purpose was to portray a prince like Aeneas or Cyrus. But there are a number of plainly moralistic episodes in the *Orlando,* fully equipped with appropriately named allegorical personages, and the problem of extracting a useful meaning from the rest of the poem was easily within the capacity of the critics of the time. Sixteenth-century editors of the *Orlando* regularly discovered in it a portrait of the heroic leader, and one of them, Orazio Toscanella, compiler of *Belleze del Furioso di M. Lodovico Ariosto* (1574), describes Ariosto's method in just the way that Spenser describes his own. Ariosto, he says,

> placed several virtues in several individuals, one virtue in one character and another in another character, in order to fashion out of all the characters

a well-rounded and perfect man. A well-rounded and perfect man is one adorned with all the virtues.[6]

Spenser calls this well-roundedness "magnificence . . . which vertue . . . (according to Aristotle and the rest) . . . is the perfection of all the rest, and conteineth in it them all."

By Spenser's own account, then, the intention of *The Faerie Queene* is "to fashion a gentleman or noble person," and this he confirms by announcing in the prologue to his poem that its "argument" is "that true glorious type" of Queen Elizabeth, the type of gentleness and nobility. The word "fashion" in his statement of purpose is open to misconstruction. It may be taken to mean that Spenser proposed to show how experience and training make a truly virtuous man out of one who is only potentially virtuous. But in the present case, Spenser's use of "fashion" echoes a long-established tradition which shows that he must intend by it not "educate" or "train" but "represent," "delineate." Cicero's *De oratore* introduces its subject with the statement "we have to picture to ourselves in our discourse (*fingendus est nobis oratione nostra*) an orator from whom every blemish has been taken away."[7] Castiglione makes Sir Frederic propose that one of the company "take it in hand to shape in wordes (*formare con parole*) a good Courtier," and the author declares his intention to "fashion such a Courtier as the Prince that shall be worthie to have him in his service, although his state be but small, may notwithstanding be called a mighty Lord."[8] It is in this acceptation that the *Oxford English Dictionary* understands "fashioning" as it appears on the title page of Spenser's poem: "*The Faerie Queene.* Disposed into twelve bookes, Fashioning XII. Morall vertues." And in the sentence immediately preceding that in which "to fashion a gentleman" occurs, Spenser explains that the purpose of his letter is "to discover unto you the general intention and meaning, which . . . I have fashioned." Furthermore, Spenser goes on to explain that in fulfillment of his design he has labored "to pourtraict in Arthure, before he was king, the image of a brave knight, perfected in the twelve private morall vertues." He does not say that he has shown Arthur in the process of achieving that perfection. Of course, since the "fashion" of a man includes that which determines his character, training and experience enter into it to the extent that one believes them to be effective agents. But Spenser announces here, not that he has written the story of an education, but that, like Badius' Vergil and Toscanella's Ariosto, he has described a man who combines in himself the chivalric and the moral disciplines, a virtuous gentleman. And when he exclaims at the beginning of the last canto of the Legend of Temperaunce,

> Now gins this goodly frame of Temperance
> Fairely to rise

he is saying that he has portrayed the virtue itself, not the growth of that virtue in its champion.

It is difficult for most modern readers to disabuse themselves of the idea that character development must be an essential feature of any extended narrative that pretends to be more than merely an entertainment. Stories in which the growth of the hero is a principal motif are of course not uncommon in medieval and Renaissance literature: *Parzifal* is a notable instance, and the progressive lightening and illumination of Dante's soul is obviously important to the structure of the *Commedia*. The humanist Christophoro Landino reads the *Aeneid* as an ascent of the hero from the fleshly concerns of Troy to the purity of the contemplative life symbolized by the conquest of Latium.[9] But although the question of the role of character in an epic poem was endlessly discussed by Renaissance critics, no writer on the subject with whose work I am familiar recommends the growth or education of the hero as a subject for the narrative poet. Indeed, the Aristotelian principle of consistency ("The fourth point [with respect to character] is consistency: for though the subject of the imitation, who suggested the type, be inconsistent, still he must be consistently inconsistent"[10]) and the Horatian emphasis on decorum were read as prescribing stability of character, so that one Italian critic says flatly, "The poet, once he has undertaken to imitate somebody, keeps him always and everywhere exactly the same as he was when first introduced."[11] Tasso's Godfrey is typical, I think, of the kind of heroic figure envisaged by Renaissance criticism. His victory is achieved, not through the perfecting of his nature, but through the overcoming of obstacles which prevent that nature from exercising its proper functions. These are the victories won by Spenser's gentle knights.

A gentleman or nobleman is distinguished from Everyman by the fact that he bears both a private and a public character. Spenser's use of the words *ethice* and *politice* to describe the study of these two aspects of the gentle nature suggests a reference to Aristotle's *Ethics* and *Politics,* linked treatises the first of which concerns the good man, the second the state in which men are made good. In describing the *Odyssey* and Tasso's *Rinaldo* as concerned with the former, the *Iliad* and the *Gerusalemme* with the latter, and the *Aeneid* and the *Orlando Furioso* with both, Spenser accepts the conclusions of the criticism of his time. His own work is to deal with "ethics," as portrayed in Arthur before he became king, "which if I finde to be well accepted, I may be perhaps encoraged, to frame the other part of polliticke vertues in his person, after that hee came to be king."[12]

The division between the "ethical" and "political" realms needs to be understood as precisely as possible, particularly because Spenser is often accused of abandoning it in the later books. What he has to say about Queen Elizabeth and the role she plays in the poem helps to clarify the matter. After identifying Gloriana as "glory" in his general intention but "the most excellent and glorious person of our soveraine the Queene" in his particular, Spenser continues: "For considering she beareth two persons, the one of a most royall Queene or Empresse, the other of a most vertuous and beautifull Lady, this latter part in some places I doe express in Belphoebe." The poet's language indicates a familiarity with the famous legal doctrine of "the king's two bodies," a doctrine which a recent student describes as "a distinctive feature of English political thought in the age of Elizabeth and the early Stuarts."[13] The doctrine is carefully set forth in connection with a much-discussed case of the fourth year of Elizabeth. The decision was agreed upon by all of the crown lawyers and reported by the great Elizabethan jurist Edmund Plowden ("'The case is altered,' quoth Plowden"):

> For the King has in him two Bodies, *viz.,* a Body natural, and a Body politic. His Body natural (if it be considered in itself) is a Body mortal, subject to all Infirmities that come by Nature or Accident, to the Imbecility of Infancy or old Age, and to the like Defects that happen to the natural Bodies of other People. But his Body politic is a Body that cannot be seen or handled, consisting of Policy and Government, and constituted for the Direction of the People, and the Management of the public weal, and this Body is utterly void of Infancy, and old Age, and other natural Defects and Imbecilities, which the Body natural is subject to, and for this Cause, what the King does in his Body politic, cannot be invalidated or frustrated by any Disability in his natural Body.[14]

The bodies are joined in somewhat the same way as the membership of a corporation and the corporation itself, or as humanity and divinity in Christ.

Spenser's Gloriana was evidently intended to represent this union and so the necessary connection between *The Faerie Queene* and that second "polliticke" poem. Often it required great legal subtlety to distinguish between the king natural and the king politic. But Spenser's understanding of the difference appears most clearly, I think, where it has been most often challenged. In the Legend of Justice, Queen Mercilla sits surrounded by the emblems of her regality as presiding officer at the trial of Duessa. But when the court, the body of which she is the head, arrives at its verdict, she does not pronounce it. She does not let "due vengeance" light upon the culprit but

> rather let in stead thereof to fall
> Few perling drops from her faire lampes of light;
> The which she covering with her purple pall
> Would have the passion hid, and up arose withall.

(v.ix.50)

The passion and tears, inevitable and praiseworthy in a virtuous queen natural, are nevertheless the sign of an "imbecility" to which the queen politic, by definition, cannot be subject.[15]

The theme of the noble man as "body natural" having been determined, Spenser then chose the "historicall fiction" of Arthur as the most suitable means by which to express it. So, at least, he describes the process. It has been argued most ingeniously that in fact he did not begin in this way at all, that the moral intention came late and was superimposed upon what was originally a romantic narrative.[16] In the absence of unambiguous independent testimony—and it is absent—such an argument cannot be decisive. It may be that in 1589 Spenser himself would not have been able to say whether it was a dream of Britomart or a determination to benefit the commonwealth that led to the composition of his poem. But the question in any case is not directly pertinent to an attempt to understand the meaning of **The Faerie Queene,** a poem which we read, not as it evolved in the mind of its author, but as it was dedicated to Queen Elizabeth and published in 1590 and 1596.

The choice of Arthur as hero was dictated by a number of considerations, among them those which Spenser mentions: he was "most fitte for the excellency of his person, being made famous by many mens former workes, and also furthest from the daunger of envy, and suspition of present time." Certainly the myth so sedulously fostered by Henry VII that Arthur was of the line of British kings whom the Tudors claimed as their ancestors and a descendant of Vergil's Aeneas also played a part in his election. Spenser recalls the story by deriving the family of Elizabeth from his own fictions, Artegall and Britomart, and so eventually from Aeneas' grandson, Brutus. That the poet placed any credence in the tale of the ancient Trojan ancestry of the Tudors or in the reliability of Geoffrey of Monmouth as a historian is at least doubtful. In a passage in *A Vewe of the Present State of Irelande*[17] he laughs at the vanity of Englishmen who believe that Brutus was the founder of Britain, and Sidney similarly refuses to take the story seriously.[18] But Spenser was not striving for historical accuracy in **The Faerie Queene,** and for his poetic purpose the myth of the Tudor descent from Troy, used with deliberate vagueness, provided him with a useful parallel to Vergil's link between Aeneas and Augustus.[19]

It is Arthur "before he was king" who is to provide the historical fiction for the delineation of the "private morall vertues." Since the tradition told Spenser very little about Arthur before the beginning of his reign he was free to invent what actions he liked. How he would have adapted the more fully documented story of Arthur the king to an exposition of

the politic virtues it is impossible to guess; perhaps he never formulated the plan except in the most general terms. It was this *Iliad* to complement Spenser's *Odyssey,* a poem about Arthur as defender and lawgiver of the commonwealth, that Milton intended to write, I think. The scattered references to his proposed "Arthuriad" suggest a matter of battling armies and national crises, the kind of matter that finds no place in Spenser's poem about Arthur as a private man. Milton, it is believed, gave up the idea of an "Arthuriad" because of his doubts as to the historicity of the accounts of ancient Britain. If so, he belonged to that considerable Renaissance school that held that a true poem must be true in its fable as well as in its meaning. Spenser did not.

The Faerie Queene does not pretend to be an account of events that actually took place. We are now so accustomed to the convention of serious fiction that it requires an effort to recapture the attitude that demanded of a writer that he account to the world for his telling of a story palpably false. The argument of Sidney's *Apology for Poetry* in fact turns upon such a justification: a poem is not a lie, he says, both because the reader is not invited to accept it as history and because it is tied to "the general reason of things" if not to "the particuler truth of things."[20] It is this "general reason of things" that Spenser claims to be expressing when he describes his work as "a continued allegory or darke conceit."

In recent years a number of brilliant studies have thrown much light on the use of allegory in the Middle Ages, and that use was surely a powerful influence upon later allegorists. But what may be said of the method of the *Divine Comedy,* the *Romance of the Rose,* and *Piers Plowman* does not necessarily apply to **The Faerie Queene.** Spenser claims as his models not those poems but the *Aeneid,* the *Orlando,* and the *Gerusalemme.* Whatever *allegory* may have meant in medieval usage, it had both a particular and a general acceptation in the Renaissance, the particular defined in terms of its nature, the general in terms of its function. The former sense, that given in textbooks of rhetoric from classical times onward, makes allegory a species of metaphor, "a Trope of a sentence, or forme of speech which expresseth one thing in words and another in sense." It is distinguished in its class by the fact that its literal elements and the meanings they signify are multiple rather than single: "In a Metaphore there is a translation of one word onely, in an Allegorie of many, and for that cause an Allegorie is called a continued Metaphore."[21] The examples of this figure of speech given by the rhetoricians are derived indifferently from prose and poetry, the Bible and secular letters. One writer offers as a typical instance the following line from Vergil's eclogues:

Stop up your streames (my lads) the medes
  have drunk ther fill

explaining it thus:

> As much to say, leave of now, yee have talked of
> the matter inough: for the shepheards guise in many
> places is by opening certaine sluces to water their
> pastures, so as when they are wet inough they shut
> them againe: this application is full Allegoricke.[22]

Spenser's familiarity with this sense of "allegory" is
obvious both from his application to the word of the
standard epithet "continued" and from his frequent use
of such extended metaphors in the poem. Amoret with
her heart laid open and bleeding is a figure of speech
for a woman tormented in spirit; Orgoglio deflated like
an empty bladder tells us that pride is merely puffed
up; Arthur's dream of Gloriana is a metaphorical statement of the noble vision of glorious achievement. These
are "allegories" within the definition of the rhetoricians and there are many like them in **The Faerie
Queene**. In Spenser's practice they are often presented
dramatically or pictorially, a technique resembling that
of medieval allegory and of the allegorical pageants,
paintings, and "emblems" of the Renaissance. But
Spenser says that his poem is an allegory, not merely
that there are allegories in it.

It is the functional significance of the word which is
uppermost in Spenser's mind. Tasso's explanation of
his *Gerusalemme Liberata* provides the gloss:

> Heroical Poetry (as a living Creature, wherein two
> Natures are conjoyned) is compounded of Imitation
> and Allegory: with the one she allureth unto her the
> Minds and Ears of Men, and marvellously delighteth
> them; with the other, either in Vertue or Knowledge,
> she instructeth them. And as the Heroically written
> Imitation of an Other, is nothing else but the Pattern
> and Image of Humane Action: so the Allegory of
> an Heroical Poem is none other than the Glass and
> Figure of Humane Life. But Imitation regardeth the
> Actions of Man subjected to the outward Senses,
> and about them being principally employed, seeketh
> to represent them with effectual and expressive
> Phrases, such as lively set before our Corporal Eyes
> the things represented: It doth not consider the
> Customs, Affections, or Discourses of the Mind, as
> they be inward, but only as they come forth thence,
> and being manifested in Words, in Deeds, or Working,
> do accompany the Action. On the other side, Allegory
> respecteth the Passions, the Opinions and Customs,
> not only as they do appear, but principally in their
> being hidden and inward; and more obscurely doth
> express them with Notes (as a Man may say) mystical,
> such as only the Understanders of the Nature of things
> can fully comprehend.[23]

Beyond the vague statement that it is difficult to understand and is expressed by obscure "notes"—a "dark

conceit" in Spenser's phrase—Tasso is not concerned
with the method of allegory. What is salient for him is
its purpose, instruction in virtue and knowledge and
investigation of the inward as well as the outward motions of man, the presentation of "the Glass and Figure
of Humane Life." Sir John Harington's "Briefe and
Summarie Allegorie of Orlando Furioso" shows how
such a definition is applied.[24] The "two principall heads
and common places" of the *Orlando* he takes to be
love and arms. Under the former he expounds the
meaning of Rogero's adventures with Alcina, the temptation of pleasure, and Logestilla, or virtue. These
episodes are "allegories" in method. But Harington also
declares that "the whole booke is full of examples of
men and women, that in this matter of love, have been
notable in one kinde or other." His exposition of the
theme of arms begins with "the example of two mightie Emperours, one of which directeth all his counsels
by wisdom, learning, and Religion; But the other being
rash, and unexperienced, ruined himselfe and his countrie." These are exemplary fictions, metaphoric only in
the sense that their characters are types representative
of many individuals, but they find place in the "generall Allegorie of the whole worke" because they
contribute to its didactic purpose. Renaissance allegorical explanations of the *Aeneid* similarly depend indifferently upon the elucidation of "continued" metaphors
and the lessons to be learned from the example of the
characters of the story. Spenser himself makes no sharp
division between allegory and fictional example: although at one point he describes his work as "clowdily
enwrapped in Allegoricall devises," at another he declares the method of the *Cyropaedia* to be doctrine "by
ensample" and adds, "So have I laboured to doe in the
person of Arthure."

Spenser's method is in fact best disclosed by his practice. The episode of Malbecco, Hellenore, and Paridell,
the principal subject of the ninth and tenth cantos of
the Legend of Chastitie, serves as a convenient illustration, for while its intention is unmistakable, the
rhetorical techniques employed in its telling are mar-
velously varied and complex. The tale begins as a
fabliau of the hoariest type, a comedy involving the
miserly, jealous husband, his pretty, wanton wife, and
the polished seducer. Such situations are sometimes
called "realistic," yet the names of the characters at
once give the story a meaning beyond the particular:
"Malbecco" is from the Italian *becco* which means both
"cuckold" and "he-goat"; "Hellenore" and "Paridell"
are intended to suggest the types of Helen and Paris of
Troy. Malbecco's passions for his money and his wife
are presented in parallel so that one becomes a figure
for the other: he is not properly entitled either to the
gold or to the girl, he makes no use of either, he keeps
both locked up and fears constantly for their loss. His
blindness in one eye serves as a metaphor for the
watchful blindness of jealousy, for although he keeps
up a sleepless, self-tormenting vigil he is unable to see

what goes on at his side, the seduction of Hellenore by Paridell. That affair is described realistically: Paridell "sent close messages of love to her at will"; metaphorically: "She sent at him one firie dart, whose hed / Empoisned was with privy lust, and gealous dred"; and symbolically: "[she] in her lap did shed her idle draught, / Shewing desire her inward flame to slake." That inward flame leads to the fire set by Hellenore to cover her escape, a fire compared with the conflagration which consumed Troy, Helen and Hellenore, wantons both, joying in wanton destruction. Now the realm of realism is left quite behind, for Hellenore, having been abandoned by the rake Paridell, finds refuge as the common mistress of a band of satyrs, half-goats who herd goats, her sexual passion satisfied at last. And when Malbecco tries to rescue her from her happy predicament, the goats butt him with their horns—give him the "horn" for which he was named at his christening. Finally, consumed by the "long anguish and self-murdring thought" of his jealous nature he is changed into a strange creature with crooked claws dwelling in a cave overhung by a tremendous cliff

> which ever and anon
> Threates with huge ruine him to fall upon,
> That he dare never sleepe, but that one eye
> Still ope he keepes for that occasion
>
> (III.X.58)

There he lives forever, so deformed "that he has quight / Forgot he was a man, and Gealosie is hight."[25]

This is not a story in the ordinary sense of the word, for the movement is inward, not onward. The transformations of Malbecco and Hellenore are not really transformations at all but revelations of their essence. The poet's purpose has been to lay bare the sterile, destructive, and dehumanizing power of the passions of greed, jealousy, and lust, and to this end he has made use of every means at his command, exemplary tale, myth, metaphor extended and simple, simile, symbol, and direct statement. As narrative, the episode is self-contained, for neither Malbecco nor Hellenore appears earlier or again, but the ideas which it expresses are presented in parallel and contrast, echoed, analyzed, developed, and refined throughout the Legend of Chastitie. To distinguish among the rhetorical tools by which this is accomplished is a task which would require the sharpest of definitions and infinite subtlety in applying them, for the poetical stream flows unbroken from one into another. Fortunately, it is not a task that need be undertaken here, for it offers little help in understanding the poem. Rather, the theme of discourse suggests itself through its repeated statement in a variety of forms, and once manifested reciprocally illuminates the "dark conceits" by which it is expressed.

The models for his method which Spenser acknowledges in the letter to Ralegh include only classical and Renaissance works. He is also indebted, though I think not as profoundly, to specifically medieval traditions. The influence of the morality drama is particularly evident in the Legend of Holinesse. Since the subject of many of these plays is human salvation, their protagonists meet obstacles similar to those which hinder the Red Cross Knight, and like that Knight they must be saved by God's mercy. The central characters of the later moralities—for their popularity persisted well into the sixteenth century—tend to be one or another kind of human rather than Mankind in general, and John Skelton's *Magnificence* presents a prince, or magnificent man, as its hero. The trials of Magnificence parallel those of St. George. The vicious influences playing upon him are disguised as virtuous ones, just as Duessa poses as Fidessa and Archimago as the Red Cross Knight. As a result of his delusion he falls into the clutches of Despair and is about to commit suicide when Good Hope snatches away his dagger and he is regenerated by Redress, Sad Circumspection, and Perseverance. The influence of the long tradition of medieval allegorical poetry on *The Faerie Queene* is also clear. Spenser owes to it such devices as the gardens of love, the pageant of the sins, the arms of the Red Cross Knight, the masque of Cupid, and the Blatant Beast. An analogue to the Beast occurs in a late example of such poetry, Stephen Hawes's *Pastime of Pleasure,*[26] a poem which is strikingly similar to *The Faerie Queene* in general conception, for Graunde Amour, like the Red Cross Knight, is clad in the armor described by St. Paul,[27] and his passion for La Belle Pucelle is as much a metaphor for the noble man's hunger for glory as Arthur's love for Gloriana. Indeed, the idea of a quest for a high goal as the central motive is common to medieval story of many kinds, from saints' lives to chivalric adventures. And since a heroic quest is central to the *Aeneid* also, Spenser found it appropriate to his Vergilian treatment of the matter of Arthur.

But the goal is not Prince Arthur's guide, as the hope of a new Troy is for Aeneas and the conquest of Jerusalem for Tasso's Godfrey. The narrative structure of *The Faerie Queene* is, in fact, almost frivolously weak. Having fallen in love with the Faerie Queene in a dream, like Sir Thopas in Chaucer's burlesque tale, Arthur thereafter wanders in and out of the poem, rescuing the unfortunate, contending with villains, and chasing the beautiful Florimell. Only a parenthetical observation that he wished his beloved were as fair as Florimell reminds the reader that his romantic attachment persists. The chivalric quests of the titular heroes of the successive books can be taken no more seriously. St. George sets out to kill the dragon besieging the castle of Una's parents and that is all we hear of his interest in the matter until the very end of his legend. In the second book, Guyon's task is to destroy Acrasia's Bower, but he is otherwise occupied for most of his career. Britomart is absent from much of her Legend of Chastitie and she learns of Amoret's imprisonment and undertakes to rescue her only in the eleventh canto. The story of Cambel and Triamond is merely an episode in the Legend of Friendship. Neither the rescue of Irena nor the hunt for the Blatant Beast dominates the action of the last two books, and there is no sign of a champion or of a quest in the fragmentary seventh. There are, to be sure, hundreds of stories in Spenser's poem, many of them brilliantly told, but *The Faerie Queene* is not, in any significant sense, a story. If plot is soul, the poem cannot escape damnation.

Nor does *The Faerie Queene* become coherent if the reader seeks for a continuing moral tale of which the literal one is a metaphor. In the first episode of the first book, the Red Cross Knight enters the Wandering Wood and conquers monstrous Error. When he leaves the Wood does he leave Error behind him and thereafter walk in the way of Truth? In fact, he, like all men, spends his mortal life in the Wood battling with the monster. Has he done with despair when he escapes from Despair? Even in his final struggle with the Old Dragon he wishes he were dead. Seduced by Will and Grief, he abandons Una, his true faith. If he is therefore faith-less he is nevertheless able to conquer Sans Foy, or faithlessness. Then he enters Lucifera's House of Pride in company with the figure of Falsehood, Duessa. In this state he fights with Sans Joy and is at the point of defeat when his "quickning faith" rescues him and turns the tide. This happens in Canto v, yet St. George is not reunited with his Faith until the end of Canto viii. By the dwarf's help he escapes from that House of Pride only to be caught in the arms of Duessa by the giant of pride, Orgoglio. Those commentators who read the Legend of Holinesse as a Christian's progress make a difference between Lucifera and the giant; I cannot find it in the text. To be sure, the carcasses behind Lucifera's palace are those guilty ones who have been destroyed by the sin of pride while the bodies on the floor of Orgoglio's castle are the innocents and martyrs who have been destroyed by the sinfulness of the proud. Lucifera, usurping queen of man's soul, is attended by the mortal sins of which she is chief and source; Orgoglio, usurping tyrant of the world, by a seven-headed monster whose tail reaches to the house of the heavenly gods. These are inward and outward aspects of the same sin, that sin of pretended glory which is false at its foundation, as the House of Pride is built on a hill of sand and the great Orgoglio is brought down by a blow at the leg. A recent student of *The Faerie Queene* analyzes the Legend of Holinesse into ten "acts,"[28] but if the episodes are properly so described the whole is scarcely a neatly constructed play.

Confusion also besets the reader who follows the characters of *The Faerie Queene* in the hope of extracting from their adventures an orderly lesson in morality. In the course of Florimell's desperate flight from her various pursuers she escapes from a horrid spotted beast by leaping into the boat of a poor old fisherman. As she does so she loses her golden girdle. Since in later books we learn that this girdle will not stay bound about ladies who are unchaste we may be led to conclude that Florimell has now lost her maidenhead. One commentator[29] accepts this logic and finds confirmation for it in "the apparently innocent line that she was driven to great distress 'and taught the carefull Mariner to play' (III.viii.20)" although the grammar of the passage in question makes it quite clear that Fortune, who drove Florimell to distress, taught her to play the troubled mariner, not that Florimell taught the fisherman erotic games. Surely, the unhappy girl is here made to lose her girdle only in order that Satyrane may have it to bind the spotted beast, for when the fisherman attacks her she cries to heaven, and not in vain:

> See how the heavens, of voluntary grace
> And soveraine favour towards chastity,
> Doe succour send to her distressed cace:
> So much high God doth innocence embrace
>
> (III.viii.29)

Even if God is deluded about Florimell's chastity, it seems unlikely that the poet is also. Yet later in the same canto he exclaims in her praise, "Most vertuous virgin!" The fallacy of reading Spenser's allegory rigidly becomes patent when it is observed that the Snowy Florimell, who is not enough of a virgin to wear the girdle in the fourth book (v.19-20), has somehow become able to bind it about her waist by the time of her trial in the fifth (iii.24).

Reading the Florimell story as a continued narrative leads to the suggestion that she is a kind of Proserpina, that her imprisonment beneath the sea by Proteus and her eventual betrothal to Marinell constitute a retelling of the vegetation myth.[30] Indeed, her flowery name, the icicles on Proteus' beard, and the effect of the warmth of her presence on the moribund Marinell seem to support such a reading. But if this is what Spenser intended by the story taken as a whole, he was perverse enough to addle his readers unmercifully by making the duration of Florimell's bondage not six months but seven.

If Spenser had thought that the greatness of his poem rested upon its fable and its characters, I presume that he would have been careful to make them coherent and consistent. Yet when he came to write the letter to Ralegh he described the beginning of Sir Guyon's quest in a manner directly contradicted by the text he was introducing. He brings Amoret to the point of reunion with her long lost Scudamour only to forget all about her and allow her to drop out of sight. In the space of twenty stanzas "lewd Claribell" unaccountably becomes "good Sir Claribell" (IV.ix.20, 40). Britomart's traveling companion is now called the Red Cross Knight and now Sir Guyon; it does not seem to matter to the author who he is. However Spenser came to make the errors in the first place they apparently did not bring themselves to his attention when he revised. Spenser was no hasty publisher of his works, and he must have read his manuscript through thoroughly before permitting it to assume the immortality of print. What escaped his notice must have been those matters to which he paid little attention.

Sometimes, in fact, Spenser sees fit to introduce a note of burlesque into his narration of even the most heroic and pathetic actions. This should not surprise us, for the combination of jest and earnest is a firm and ancient rhetorical tradition.[31] Spenser uses humor occasionally only, for in general he strives to maintain the mood of "beautifull old rime, / In praise of Ladies dead, and lovely Knights." But its presence, though often overlooked, should warn us not to read his stories too solemnly. The beautiful and virtuous Serena has been captured by fierce cannibals. After consultation, they decide

> to let her
> Sleepe out her fill, without encomberment:
> For sleepe they sayd would make her battill[a]
> better.
>
> (VI.viii.38)

And when she is saved by her beloved Calepine she cannot say a word because she is in "so unwomanly a mood." The unhappy wife of Sir Bruin adopts a child rescued from the jaws of a bear, taking it as "her owne by liverey and seisin"[b] (VI.iv.37). The heroine Britomart meets an Amazon in mortal battle:

> The Trumpets sound, and they together run
>   With greedy rage, and with their faulchins
>   smot;
> Ne either sought the others strokes to shun,
> But through great fury both their skill
>   forgot,
> And practicke use in armes: ne spared not
> Their dainty parts, which nature had created
> So faire and tender, without staine or spot,
> For other uses
>
> (V.vii.29)

Britomart tilts with Scudamour, and

> entertained him in so rude a wise
> That to the ground she smote both horse and
>   man;
> Whence neither greatly hasted to arise,
> But on their common harmes together did
>   devise.
>
> (IV.vi.10)

After Artegall has laid low the immense giant Grantorto at the climax of the fifth book, "He lightly reft his head, to ease him of his paine" (xii.23). Lines of this kind are common enough to qualify the tone of the poem.

Sometimes it is difficult to tell whether Spenser is being intentionally witty or unintentionally absurd, for he does not signal his reader as Ariosto and Chaucer do. No one doubts that Chaucer is mocking a literary convention when he says, in his account of the battle between Palamon and Arcite, "Up to the ancle foghte they in hir blood." But when Spenser tells of the wound inflicted on the Old Dragon by the Knight of the Red Cross,

> Forth flowed fresh
> A gushing river of blacke goarie blood,
> That drowned all the land, whereon he stood;
> The streame thereof would drive a water mill
>
> (I.xi.22)

he is thought to be straining so hard for effect that he falls into nonsense.

Perhaps he is guilty here, though he is so sophisticated a writer that one must suspect the judgment. But it cannot be argued that Spenser's hydraulic metaphor must be taken seriously because the inner meaning of the battle between St. George and the Dragon is deeply in earnest. Such an argument depends upon the critical assumption that in proper poetry the story and its significance must both tend to the same effect. If the assumption is valid—and I am not sure that it is—then Spenser's method is often quite improper. In terms of the narrative, Guyon's faint when he emerges from the Cave of Mammon can arouse only sympathy for his plight—he has been without food and water for three days and the fresh air is too much for him. But the meaning of this swoon is that Guyon is a wicked man, undeserving of his rescue by the freely given grace of God. A monster that vomits up a collection of books and papers is merely ridiculous; as a symbol of the kind of error into which man's blindness leads him she is no laughing matter. There is, to be sure, a point of contact between the mood of these tales and what they signify, for if human weakness is sinful it is also pathetic, and if human error is damnable it is also grotesque. The story may so serve to inflect its underlying meaning in much the same way as a shadow influences the perception of the object which produces it. But one does not confuse shadow and object.

One kind of inconsistency in Spenser's narrative which is sometimes ascribed to changes in his plans and to shifting literary influences upon him is, I think, an essential part of his grand design, although it has not previously been recognized as such. It is apparent and it has often been remarked that the style of ***The Faerie***

Queene is not uniform throughout: the Legend of Holinesse is the life of a saint, an *imitatio Christi;* the Legend of Chastitie is notably in Ariosto's manner; the Legend of Courtesie has the character of pastoral romance. If this is inconsistency, it is of the kind the reader should be led to expect from a consideration of Spenser's practice in his other poems. In *The Shepheardes Calender* he evidently strives for the greatest possible range of meter, mood, and manner. The four episodes of *Mother Hubberds Tale* are bound together by a common theme, yet each is handled differently. And the letter to Ralegh makes clear the poet's desire to avoid monotony in *The Faerie Queene:* "But of the xii. other virtues, I make xii. other knights the patrones, for the more variety of the history."

The varying styles of the successive books of *The Faerie Queene* serve a purpose of greater weight than the avoidance of monotony. The "patrons" of those books are indeed different from each other and engage in different kinds of action. This is so, I believe, because Spenser intended his readers to recognize in them reflections of particular literary models in just the same way as they recognized in the first half of the *Aeneid* an imitation of the *Odyssey* and in the latter half an imitation of the *Iliad*. The Legend of St. George echoes the saint's life in *The Golden Legend*. Sir Guyon is a hero of classical epic, like Aeneas and Odysseus. Britomart and Florimell inevitably recall Ariosto's Bradamante and Angelica. The titular story of Cambel and Triamond in the Legend of Friendship is based on Chaucer's unfinished *Squire's Tale,* and reminiscences of that story and the one told by the Knight recur frequently throughout the book. Artegall is compared directly with Hercules, Bacchus, and Osiris, the mythical founders of civilization. The adventures of Sir Calidore are of the type found in the Greek romances and imitated by Sidney in the *Arcadia*. The fragmentary Cantos of Mutabilitie clearly imitate Ovid's *Metamorphoses*. In the following chapters I shall suggest why Spenser may have thought these models suitable to the subjects which he wished to treat. It was surely in his character as a poet not only to seek the greatest variety possible in the general form of the epic poem as he understood it but also to display his technical virtuosity by imitating within the compass of a single work a great range of the literary models available to him and to his contemporaries.

This hunger for complexity, for binding into one the multiple and for revealing the multiple in the one, shows itself in almost every aspect of Spenser's technique. The stanza which he invented for the poem is itself such a various unit. Its closest relatives are the Italian ottava rima (*abababcc*), rhyme royal (*ababbcc*), and the stanza used by Chaucer in the *Monk's Tale* (*ababbcbc*). In the first two forms the final couplet rhymes independently of the rest; the *Monk's Tale* stanza lacks a clear-cut conclusion. By adding an alexandrine rhyming with *c* to this last verse pattern, Spenser introduces metrical variety and at the same time supplies an ending which is linked to rather than separated from the remainder. Stanza is joined to stanza by frequent echoes in the first line of one of the sound or thought of the last line preceding it, and analogous links tie together canto with canto and book with book. To the amalgamation in his stanza of Italian and English forms Spenser adds a Vergilian touch by occasionally leaving a verse unfinished in the manner of the *Aeneid*.

The invention of the names of the characters of *The Faerie Queene* betrays a similar habit of mind. They are designedly derived from different languages: Pyrochles is Greek, Munera Latin, Alma Italian (and also both Latin and Hebrew), Sans Foy French, the first half of Ruddymane English. Many of the names are portmanteaus into which Spenser has stuffed a multiplicity of meanings. "Britomart," for example, reminded his Elizabethan readers of Ariosto's heroine Bradamante as well as of Britomartis, the chaste daughter of Carme whom ancient myth identified with Diana,[32] while at the same time the etymology "martial Briton" must have been inescapable, for Boccaccio calls Britomartis "Britona, Martis filia."[33]

The key ideas of his moral teaching are expressed by as many different symbols as the poet can imagine: the power which binds the disparate or antagonistic is represented by the figure of Concord flanked by Love and Hate; by the hermaphrodite Venus and the snake about her legs whose head and tail are joined together; by the lady Cambina, her team of angry lions, her Aesculapian rod, and her cup of nepenthe. These reciprocal processes of unification and multiplication reflect a conception of the universe which makes it all one, yet unimaginably rich.

There is a plenitude of story in *The Faerie Queene,* martial, amatory, and domestic; myth, fairy tale, chivalric adventure, and anecdote. Some of these tales Spenser invents himself; others he borrows from biblical, classical, medieval, and contemporary sources. He has no sense of impropriety in setting together the true and the fabulous, the familiar and the heroic, the Christian and the pagan. Rather, he seems to seek occasion to do so, either "for the more variety of the history" or to demonstrate the universality of the theme he is expounding. What he borrows he makes his own, without the slightest respect for the integrity or the intention of the original. His ruthless use of Vergil's story of Dido and Aeneas serves as an example. The words spoken by Aeneas when he meets his mother on the Carthaginian shore are put into the mouth of the buffoon Trompart, while the portrait of Venus is made over into a portrait of the Diana-like Belphoebe. Aeneas' account of his past experiences at dinner with Dido inspires Guyon's table conversation with Medina. Dido's alternate name, Elissa, is given to Medina's mo-rose sister. Dido's dying speech is echoed by the sui-cide Amavia, and as Iris shears a lock of hair from the one so Guyon does from the other. Again, elements of the legendary story of St. George are used in several ways in Book I, but the incident of George's binding the dragon with a girdle and leading it about as a tame thing is transferred to Sir Satyrane in Book III. Chaucer's *Squire's Tale* provides the basis for the story of Cambel and Triamond; the episode in which a lovesick bird is restored to its fickle mate "By mediacion of Cambalus" suggests the reconciling of Timias and Belphoebe by mediation of a lovesick bird.

Sometimes Spenser seems almost perverse in the way he turns his borrowed matter upside down. The pathetic interchange between the heroine of Chastity, Britomart, and her nurse Glauce is taken almost verbatim from that between Ciris, or Scylla, daughter of the king of Megara, and her nurse Carme in a poem attributed to Vergil. This is the Carme whose daughter Britomartis once fled from the embraces of Minos into some fishermen's nets at the seashore, like Florimell in Spenser's tale. Ciris, maddened by love for the same Minos who is now besieging Megara, rapes from her father's head the crimson lock which protects the city, and so brings destruction upon her home, her kindred, and herself. She is as bad a girl as Spenser's Britomart is a good one, a symbol of lust as Britomart is of chastity. Arthur's miraculous shield is another instance of imitation by reversal. It was originally the property of Atalanta, in the *Orlando Furioso*. Sir John Harington explains its principal significance:

> In the shield, whose light amazed the lookers on, and made them fall down astonied, may be Allegorically meant the great pompes of the world, that make shining shewes in the bleared eyes of vaine people, and blind them, and make them to admire and fall downe before them . . . either else may be meant the flaring beauties of some gorgeous women that astonish the eyes of weake minded men.[34]

But in Spenser's version this trumpery shield becomes the divine power that destroys illusion:

> all that was not such, as seemd in sight,
> Before that shield did fade, and suddeine fall.
> (I.vii.35)

That which hides the truth Spenser turns into that which reveals it.

This reshaping and reworking of borrowed material is neither random nor perverse. Behind it lies the constant determination to make story the servant of intention. The process can be seen clearly in the different coloring given to parcels of a continuous narrative when it is used to express different ideas. The history of

Britain from its beginnings in the judgment of Paris and the fall of Troy is told in three installments, in Arthur's book of *Briton moniments* in Book II and in Merlin's prophecy to Britomart and Paridell's account of his ancestry in Book III. Arthur reads his book in the House of Alma, the house which is well governed because each division of it obeys its mistress. The theme of this part of the history of Britain suits the house in which it is read, for it

> of this lands first conquest did devize,
> And old division into Regiments,
> Till it reduced was to one mans governments.
> (II.ix.59)

Merlin's contribution to the history is a glorious prophecy which interprets and justifies the pain of the lovesick Britomart:

> For so must all things excellent begin,
> And eke enrooted deepe must be that Tree,
> Whose big embodied braunches shall not lin,[c]
> Till they to heavens hight forth stretched bee.
> For from thy wombe a famous Progenie
> Shall spring, out of the auncient Troian blood,
> Which shall revive the sleeping memorie
> Of those same antique Peres the heavens brood,
> Which Greeke and Asian rivers stained with their blood.
> (III.iii.22)

When it is revived by the false lover Paridell, however, that sleeping memory becomes an exemplum of the sterile consequence of the lust of his ancestor Paris:

> Troy, that art now nought, but an idle name,
> And in thine ashes buried low dost lie,
> Though whilome far much greater then thy fame,
> Before that angry Gods, and cruell skye
> Upon thee heapt a direfull destinie,
> What boots it boast thy glorious descent,
> And fetch from heaven thy great Genealogie,
> Sith all thy worthy prayses being blent,[d]
> Their of-spring hath embaste,[e] and later glory shent.
> (III.ix.33)

Urged by Britomart, Paridell remembers that the Trojan line did not altogether die out, for Aeneas, son of "Venus faire," after long suffering married the daughter of old Latinus:

> Wedlock contract in bloud, and eke in blood
> Accomplished, that many deare complaind:

The rivall slaine, the victour through the
flood
Escaped hardly, hardly praisd his wedlock
good.

(III.ix.42)

Not Paridell but Britomart celebrates the glory of Rome, the second Troy, and prophesies the rise of that third Troy, Britain,

That in all glory and great enterprise,
Both first and second Troy shall dare to
equalise.

(III.ix.44)

In the context of Prince Arthur, the history demonstrates the necessity of rule; in that of Britomart, the creativeness of love; in that of Paridell, the destructiveness of lust.

Within **The Faerie Queene,** the unit is the book or legend. It is made up of episodes and "allegories" invented to illuminate its theme. Typically, a book begins with an encounter between new characters and those of its predecessor, there is a climax or shift of emphasis approximately at midpoint, and the end is marked by some great action. Apart from these loose formal characteristics, however, the constituent elements are not sequential in their arrangement; they are truly episodic, obeying no law of progress or development. Rather, they are so placed as to produce effects of variety and contrast. They are tied not to each other but to the principal subject of discourse, and to this they contribute analytically or comprehensively, directly or by analogy, by affirmation or denial.

In Spenser's poem, intention is the soul, while the stories, characters, symbols, figures of speech, the ring of the verse itself constitute the body:

of the soule the bodie forme doth take:
For soule is forme, and doth the bodie make.
(HB, 132-33)

Only from the made body can the form be inferred, however, and this is the kind of inference that Spenser expects of his readers. One may take hold of the meaning of a book almost anywhere in it, for it is everywhere there. I have entitled the chapter dealing with the Legend of Holinesse "The Cup and the Serpent," the symbol which Fidelia holds, but it might as well have been called "Mount Sinai and the Mount of Olives," "Sans Joy and the Promise," "Hope in Anguish," "The Burning Armor," "Una and the Veil," or "The Tree and the Living Well." Each of these in its own way and with its own inflection is a figure for the paradox of life and death which I take to be central to the book. What that paradox means and how it may be resolved Spenser never says directly. I think it was the

nature of his mind rather than the fear of losing his audience that kept him from delivering his discipline "plainly in way of precepts." He could no more state his abstract theme apart from its expression in this world than a painter could draw the idea of a chair. The result is the richness of **The Faerie Queene.**

Notes

ᵃ battill: become fat and fleshy, as cattle do.

ᵇ by liverey and seisin: legal language for the delivery of property into the corporal possession of a person.

ᶜ lin: cease.

ᵈ blent: hidden from sight.

ᵉ embaste: debased.

1 I have used the edition entitled *P. Virgilii Maronis Opera cum Servii, Donati, et Ascensii commentariis* (Venice, 1542) (cited hereafter as *Virgilii Opera*). Badius' preface to the *Aeneid* is at fols. 101v-102r. On the subject of Vergil's influence on Spenser see Merritt Y. Hughes, *Virgil and Spenser* (Berkeley, 1929).

2 More properly, the line may be rendered: "Or to speak words at once pleasing and useful to life." But Jonson's version suggests the way in which Renaissance writers understood Horace.

3 "Et hic est ordo rerum gestarum, aut quae pro gestis a poeta recitantur, verum alius longe ordo a poeta observatur."

4 Cooper's *Thesaurus,* the standard Latin-English dictionary of Spenser's time, translates *plausibilis:* "Receyved with joye and clappynge of the handes: acceptable: pleasaunte: plausible."

5 *Godfrey of Bulloigne,* tr. Edward Fairfax (first printed 1600; London, 1687), Sig. A 2 (r).

6 Quoted and translated by D. L. Aguzzi, "Allegory in the Heroic Poetry of the Renaissance" (unpublished dissertation, Columbia University, 1959), p. 208. The passage is also cited by Susannah Jane McMurphy, *Spenser's Use of Ariosto for Allegory* (University of Washington Publications, Language and Literature, Vol. II, 1924), p. 15. G. P. Pigna, in *I romanzi* (1554), ascribes a similar method rather to the romance than to the epic: "The romances readily devote themselves to several deeds of several men, but . . . they concern especially one man who should be celebrated over all the others. And thus they agree with the epic in taking a single person, but not so in taking a single action, for they take as many of them as seem to be sufficient. The number is 'sufficient' when they have put the

heroes in all those honorable actions which are sought in a perfect knight" (Bernard Weinberg, *A History of Literary Criticism in the Italian Renaissance* [Chicago, 1961], I, 445-46).

[7] 1.xxvi.118, tr. E. W. Sutton (Loeb Classical Library, London, 1948). Compare also Cicero's *Orator,* ii.7: "Atque ego in summo oratore fingendo talem informabo qualis fortasse nemo fuit."

[8] Everyman's Library edition of Hoby's translation, pp. 16, 29.

[9] Christophoro Landino, *Camaldulenses disputationes* (Strasbourg, 1508), Books III and IV.

[10] *Poetics,* xv.4 (tr. S. H. Butcher).

[11] Dionigi Altanagi, *Ragionamento de la eccelentia et perfettione de la historia* (1559), quoted by Weinberg, *History of Literary Criticism,* I, 458.

[12] By the time Spenser came to write the *Amoretti* he may have decided to follow Vergil's example in making ethics the subject of the first six books of his poem and politics the subject of the last six. So he seems to say in Sonnet LXXX when he promises to attempt "that second worke" after resting from his labor on "those six books" he had already written.

[13] Ernst H. Kantorowicz, *The King's Two Bodies, a Study in Medieval Political Theology* (Princeton, 1957), p. 42.

[14] Quoted *ibid.,* p. 7.

[15] When Mercilla is at last forced by "strong constraint" to doom Duessa she suffers "more then needfull naturall remorse" (V.X.4).

[16] The case is forcefully presented by J. W. Bennett, *The Evolution of "The Faerie Queene"* (Chicago, 1942; reprinted New York, 1960).

[17] *Works,* IX, 82.

[18] See T. D. Kendrick, *British Antiquity* (London, 1950), pp. 128 ff.

[19] Compare the attitude of Ronsard with respect to his story of Francus as he expresses it in the 1587 preface to the *Françiade,* cited by I. Silver, *Ronsard and the Hellenistic Renaissance in France* (St. Louis, 1961), pp. 145-46.

[20] *Elizabethan Critical Essays,* ed. G. Gregory Smith (Oxford, 1904), I, 164.

[21] Henry Peacham, *The Garden of Eloquence* (1593),

facsimile reproduction (Gainesville, Fla., Scholars' Facsimiles and Reprints, 1954), p. 25.

[22] George Puttenham, *The Arte of English Poesie* (first printed 1589), ed. G. D. Willcock and A. Walker (Cambridge, 1936), p. 187.

[23] *Godfrey of Bulloigne,* Sig. A I (r-v).

[24] *Orlando Furioso in English Heroicall Verse* (first printed 1591; London, 1634), pp. 405 ff. Susannah McMurphy (*Spenser's Use of Ariosto,* p. 15) notes that what commentators on the *Orlando Furioso* mean by allegory "is often merely the moral lesson that may be derived from the incidents. The characters are not embodied virtues and vices, neither are their actions symbolic of spiritual experiences; they are often only men and women who offer examples of virtue and vice, prudence or folly, from which the observer may derive profit."

[25] It has not been remarked, I think, that the transformation of Malbecco is imitated from that of Daedalion in Ovid's *Metamorphoses,* XI, ll. 338-45:

> Effugit ergo omnes, veloxque cupidine leti
> Vertice Parnasi potitur. miseratus Apollo,
> Cum se Daedalion saxo misisset ab alto,
> Fecit avem et subitis pendentem sustulit alis,
> Oraque adunca dedit, curvos dedit unguibus
>   hamos,
> Virtutem antiquam, maiores corpore vires.
> Et nunc accipiter, nulli satis aequus, in omnes
> Saevit aves, aliisque dolens fit causa dolendi.

I have previously noted (*Modern Language Notes,* LXVIII [1953], 226-29) that Spenser drew suggestions for the Malbecco story from *George Gascoigne's Adventures of Master F. J.,* and despite the strictures of Waldo McNeir ("Ariosto's Sospetto, Gascoigne's Suspicion, and Spenser's Malbecco," in *Festschrift für Walther Fischer* [Heidelberg, 1959]) the conclusion still seems to me valid.

[26] *The Pastime of Pleasure* (1509), ed. W. E. Mead (London, for the Early English Text Society, O.S. No. 173, 1928), pp. 192 ff. The name of Hawes's monster is "malice prevy."

[27] *Ibid.,* pp. 129-30.

[28] A. C. Hamilton, *The Structure of Allegory in 'The Faerie Queene'* (Oxford, 1961), pp. 59 ff. For the view that the Legend of Holinesse is not a continued allegorical narrative but is organized in terms of "concepts" according to "the arrangement of Christian doctrines customary in Renaissance theological treatises and confessionals" see Virgil K. Whitaker, "The Theological Structure of the *Faerie Queene,* Book I," in

That Soveraine Light: Essays in Honor of Edmund Spenser, 1552-1952 (Baltimore, 1952).

[29] Hamilton, *Structure of Allegory,* pp. 150-52.

[30] Northrop Frye, "The Structure of Imagery in '*The Faerie Queene,*'" *University of Toronto Quarterly,* XXX (1961), 123.

[31] See the excursus entitled "Jest in Earnest in Medieval Literature" in E. R. Curtius, *European Literature and the Latin Middle Ages,* tr. W. R. Trask (New York, 1953), pp. 417-35. On the subject of Spenser's use of humor see also W. B. C. Watkins, *Shakespeare and Spenser* (Princeton, 1950; reprinted Cambridge, Mass., 1961), Note I, and R. O. Evans, "Spenserian Humor: *Faerie Queene* III and IV," *Neuphilologische Mitteilungen,* LX (1959), 288-99.

[32] See the pseudo-Vergilian *Ciris,* ll. 294 ff.

[33] See H. G. Lotspeich, *Classical Mythology in the Poetry of Edmund Spenser* (Princeton, 1932), p. 43. Henry Lyte in a curious book entitled *The Light of Britayne* (1588, reprinted "at the Public Press of Richard and Arthur Taylor," 1814) identifies Britomartis with "Diana of Calydonia sylva" and with Queen Elizabeth, "The bright Britona of Britayne."

[34] *Orlando Furioso in English Heroicall Verse,* p. 15.

Thomas H. Cain (essay date 1978)

SOURCE: "1590: The Poem to the Poem," in *Praise in "The Faerie Queene,"* University of Nebraska Press, 1978, pp. 37-57.

[*In the following excerpt from a study of praise in Spenser's* Faerie Queene, *Cain presents the poem as a tribute to Queen Elizabeth.*]

The Muse of "The Faerie Queene"

Ariosto invokes no muse in the *Orlando* (although the third canto invokes Apollo). But stanzas 2-4 of Spenser's proem invoke the Virgin Muse, Cupid, and the deified queen. Their insistent structural logic appears from the first words of each stanza: "Helpe then, O holy Virgin"; "And thou most dreaded impe"; "And with them eke, O Goddesse." This triple invocation facilitates encomium, for it greatly expands the idea of the poet's inadequacy, suggests the strategy of the hymn, and implies that the subject is three times greater than any attempted before. The muse invoked in stanza 2 particularly fits the encomiastic intention.

> Helpe then, O holy Virgin chiefe of nine,
>   Thy weaker Novice to performe thy will,

Lay forth out of thine everlasting scryne
The antique rolles, which there lye hidden still,
Of Faerie knights and fairest Tanaquill,
    Whom that most noble Briton Prince so long
Sought through the world, and suffered so much ill,
    That I must rue his undeserved wrong:
O helpe thou my weake wit, and sharpen my dull tong.

Whether the muse invoked as "holy Virgin chiefe of nine" is Clio, muse of history, or Calliope, muse of epic, depends on whether one considers *The Faerie Queene* history or epic. On this basis F. M. Padelford argued for Calliope and Josephine Waters Bennett for Clio. H. G. Lotspeich admitted possible ambiguity but felt "fairly certain that Clio was intended." But D. T. Starnes's evidence from sixteenth-century dictionaries such as those of the Stephanus family shows that Spenser's muse is Calliope. He argues effectively that Spenser's contemporaries clearly recognized the poem as heroic; that invocation of the epic muse is hence natural; and that Renaissance lexicographers knew Calliope as "'praestantissima,' the most excellent of the Muses"Chence Spenser's "chiefe of nine."[13] Starnes's argument is convincing. But no writer on Spenser's muse has noticed that he particularly associates the epic muse Calliope with encomium.

The confusion between Clio and Calliope arises from misinterpretation of Spenser's use of "historicall" in the Letter to Raleigh, and from the similar attributes of Clio and Calliope in *The Teares of the Muses*. When in the Letter Spenser speaks of the "historicall fiction" of his poem, he means heroic narrative and not history in our sense, as he makes clear by claiming to "have followed all the antique Poets historicall" and their successors, and then naming the epicists Homer, Virgil, Ariosto, and Tasso. Spenser also distinguishes between the chronological method of the historian and the artificial method of the heroic poet: "For the Methode of a Poet historicall is not such, as of an Historiographer. For an Historiographer discourseth of affayres orderly as they were donne, accounting as well the times as the actions, but a Poet thrusteth into the middest, even where it most concerneth him, and there recoursing to the things forepaste, and divining of thinges to come, maketh a pleasing Analysis of all."[14] The idea is a commonplace among sixteenth-century Italian literary theorists: that history's natural, chronological, *ab ovo* order distinguishes it from heroic poetry's artificial, plotted, in medias res order.[15] By claiming to begin in medias res, Spenser declares that *The Faerie Queene* is not history as the historiographer would write it but a historical fiction proper to the epic poet. His muse should thus be Calliope.

In *The Teares of the Muses* (1591), Clio and Calliope have similar functions and attributes. Both claim to immortalize men's deeds through the articulation of praise; both have the trumpet as their proper symbolic instrument; both focus on celebration of "auncestrie" (*genus*); and both use epideictic terms to voice the familiar humanist complaint of the neglect of poets and scholars, Clio speaking of blame and Calliope of praise. But only Calliope fuses the ideas of praise and epic, as when she speaks of great men "Whose living praises in heroick style, / It is my chief profession to compyle" (431-32). The phrase "living praises in heroick style" adapts "Carmina Calliope libris heroica mandat" ("Calliope commits heroic songs to writing?) from *De inventis musarum*, in Spenser's time considered Virgilian and hence of great authority.[16] These mnemonic verses list the Muses' names and functions in an order Spenser follows in *The Teares*. By adapting Calliope's line to construe "Carmina" as "praises," Spenser deliberately makes Calliope the muse of encomiastic epic—exactly the kind of poem he announces in the first stanza of his proem. For, in spite of qualities common to Clio and Calliope in *The Teares,* only Calliope claims "heroick style." (In *De inventis* as in *The Teares* Clio is in no way associated with epic.) Hence, the muse invoked in stanza 2 of the proem is Calliope.

Spenser's references to Calliope in *Aprill* (100) and *June* (57) show his awareness of the tradition which acknowledges her as supreme muse and muse of encomium. Both references foreshadow *The Faerie Queene*. But because Spenser twice invokes Clio in that poem it is important to understand her interaction with Calliope. In general, the muse in charge remains Calliope unless Spenser announces a shift to Clio for material arranged in the *ab ovo* manner proper to the historiographer.

The first invocation of Clio prefaces Merlin's account of "My glorious Soveraines goodly auncestrie" (III. iii. 4). This chronicle-history proceeds "by dew degrees" from Britomart to Elizabeth, realizing the encomiastic topos *genus* while exactly following what Spenser describes as the historiographer's method. But the reiterated imperative "Begin, O Clio" makes it clear that another muse has heretofore been in charge. This invocation denotes a temporary shift in encomiastic method—from heroic praise to historiographical praise—without implying any change in the poem's generic status as encomiastic epic. Significantly, Spenser embeds this excursus into chronicle-history in that section of *The Faerie Queene* (i.e. III.i-iii) which is most unmistakably organized by the heroic principle in medias res.

That Calliope is in charge of the larger poem is apparent from the Arlo digression in *Mutabilitie* where Spenser again invokes Clio to tell how an Irish *locus amoenus* "Was made the most unpleasant, and most

ill. / Meane while, O Clio, lend Calliope thy quill" (VII. vi. 37). While the syntactical ambiguity makes it unclear who is lending a quill to whom, the context removes all ambivalence. Spenser explicitly tells how Arlo declined from "Whylome" (ii. 38) down "to this day" (vi. 55)—i.e. the historiographer's arrangement. So the muse of *The Faerie Queene* is Calliope, who here defers to Clio for a pseudohistorical digression. There can be no doubt that it is Calliope whom Spenser reinvokes at the end of the digression as "thou greater Muse" (vii. I), the muse traditionally "praestantissima," "chiefe of nine," and hence greater than Clio.

Spenser's precedent here may be Statius, whose *Thebiad* invokes both Clio and Calliope. In the *Aeneid,* however, Virgil invokes Calliope once (9. 525), Erato once (7. 37), but elsewhere simply a muse or muses (1. 8, 7. 641, 10. 163). Similarly, Spenser twice invokes an unnamed muse (I. xi. 7; IV. xi. 9) but Calliope is presupposed. These multiple invocations work tactically to make his poem resemble the *Aeneid,* just as Tasso's make *Gerusalemme liberata* fit his concept of neoclassical epic. At the same time, when we recall the single invocation in *Orlando furioso*—Apollo solicited to facilitate praise of the Este dynastyCthen Spenser's reinvocations appear as part of the stratagem insinuating the superiority of *The Faerie Queene* as encomium.

Elizabeth Virgo-Venus as Muse

As well as Calliope, the poet also invokes the subject of praise, the queen herself—explicitly in stanza 4 and implicitly by figure in the invocations of Calliope (st. 2) and Cupid (st. 3). In fact, the three invocations proceed calculatedly from implication to revelation.

The liturgical language of invocation in stanza 2— "Helpe then, O holy Virgin chiefe of nine, / Thy weaker Novice to perform thy will"—indicates the device of transferring the Virgin's epithets to the Virgin Queen. In fact, Spenser places the invocation to parallel Tasso's in the corresponding second stanza of the *Gerusalemme:*

> O Musa, tu che di caduchi allori
> non circondi la fronte in Elicona,
> ma su nel cielo infra i beati cori
> hai di stelle immortali aurea corona
>
> [O heavenly muse, that not with fading bays
>   Deckest thy brow by th'Heliconian spring,
> But sittest, crown'd with stars' immortal rays,
>   In heaven where legions of bright angels
>   sing]
>   [Fairfax's trans.]

The attributes of heavenly choirs and crown of stars indicate that Tasso's muse is not, as some editors suggest, Urania (inescapably one of the Heliconian nine), nor a hypothetical "Christian muse," but specifically the Virgin Mary in her state of assumption. The fifteenth-century *Speculum humanae salvationis* explains that the attributes of the Virgin of the Assumption are those of the Woman Clothed with the Sun in the Apocalypse, who conquers the dragon and ascends to heaven; the half-moon beneath her feet symbolizes the transitory things of this world (Tasso's "fading bays") and her crown of stars is the twelve apostles.[17] Spenser adapts Tasso's Virgin muse to the cult of the Virgin Queen by a matching invocation. The adaptation implies that the poet who announces himself as Virgil and overgoes Ariosto means as well to overgo Tasso. As a stratagem of propaganda the invocation asserts the superiority of the poet of the Protestant Virgo to the chief poet of the Counter Reformation.

In this light, the epithet "chiefe of nine" becomes ambiguous: as well as chief among nine, Calliope as leader of the Muses, it can also mean as chief over nine, the Virgin Queen herself as tenth muse. One recalls the woodcut of Eliza presiding over the Muses in *Aprill,* just as in its text she adds a fourth to the three Graces. In deliberate contrast to Tasso's Virgin who stands aloof from the Muses, her brows never crowned with Helicon's fading laurels, Spenser's "holy Virgin, chiefe of nine" makes all the ancient poetic forces extensions of her power to inspire. The paradox of the Virgin Queen with the Muses in her train who is simultaneously Calliope, the muse who praises the queen, is of a piece with the *Aprill* paradox where Eliza both creates and receives her own praise.[18]

Encomium of Elizabeth was a political act. In his adversion to Tasso's invocation, Spenser develops an image of the Virgin Muse's "everlasting scryne" (Latin *scrinium,* chest or coffer) that is both political and encomiastic. For when he asks her to "Lay forth out of thine everlasting scryne / The antique rolles, which there lye hidden still" containing the ancient matters of Faery and Britain, he catches at the canonical formula used to epitomize the papal claim to absolute authority, in particular over the emperor: *in scrinio pectoris omnia* ("all things are in the chest of his breast"). This formula was well-known in sixteenth-century polemic. In his *Delle Allusioni, imprese, et emblemi sopra la vita di Gregorio XIII libri VI,* an emblem book praising the great pope who presided over the mission to England, Principio Fabricii depicts a winged dragon (Gregory's personal device) with books falling from a cavity in its breast (i.e. *scrinium pectoris*. . .). But Elizabeth's religious settlement depended on the Henrician Act of Supremacy and its assertion of the supremacy in England of monarch over pope. Its defenders advert sardonically to the *in scrinio* tag in their polemics, the official Anglican apologist John Jewel, for instance, scorning the notion "that all law and right is locked up in the treasury of the Pope's breast."[19]

Spenser's appropriation of the formula is also polemical and asserts the Virgin Queen's authority against the pope's. To make her *scrinium* "everlasting" is to dismiss the papal claim as innovative. In fact, this is the first instance in the poem of the antipapalism that colors Books I and V. It is important to remember, however, that the formula is also part of the invocation of the Virgin Queen as muse where the poet appears as a "Novice" just beginning to study antiquities of Faery and Britain that have always existed in her everlasting *scrinium.* (In the chronicle materials in II. x and III. iii Elizabeth is both temporal goal and simultaneously present from the beginning and so indeed contains all of British-Faery history inside herself.) By implicitly twisting the formula into *in scrinio pectoris poesis,* Spenser makes it cooperate in the by now familiar paradox of the Faery Queen creating **The Faerie Queene**.

A similar paradox pervades the invocation of Cupid in the proem's third stanza, where Elizabeth again is subliminally present.

> And thou most dreaded impe of highest Ioue,
>   Faire Venus sonne, that with thy cruell dart
>   At that good knight so cunningly didst rove,
>   That glorious fire it kindled in his hart,
>   Lay now thy deadly Heben bow apart,
>   And with thy mother milde come to mine ayde:
>   Come both, and with you bring triumphant Mart,
>   In loues and gentle jollities arrayd,
> After his murdrous spoiles and bloudy rage allayd.

While Cupid impels the hero toward Gloriana, he is also the erotic force emanating from her. In fact, Spenser does not call him Eros or Cupid but "Faire Venus sonne." Together the two invocations of stanzas 2 and 3 express the Virgo-Venus paradox well-suited to the Virgin Queen who controlled great courtiers like Leicester and Hatton with amatory manipulations; who made marriage negotiations the successful instrument of a foreign policy designed to prevent alliance of the Catholic powers France and Spain; and who, even more, was a Virgin Queen mystically married (in the words of a broadsheet of 1571) to "My dear lover England."[20]

By uniting "triumphant Mart" with Venus "*After* his murdrous spoiles and bloudy rage allayd," Spenser may have incorporated into stanza 3 a timely allusion to the victory over the Armada. The national euphoria that followed the victory naturally found expression in increased adulation of Elizabeth: for instance, on 24 November 1588 she entered London formally in a triumph; and her Accession Day (17 November) became a major annual festival.[21] In a national poem in her praise an allegory of the Armada's defeat would be encomiastically invaluable. It would be particularly apt in Book I, because the English, with an eye to propaganda as well as piety, carefully attributed their delivery to a clearly Protestant God: "God breathed and they were scattered" was the motto of one of Elizabeth's Armada medals.[22] But the sixteen months between the victory and Ponsonby's entry of ***The Faerie Queene*** in the Stationers' Register on 1 December 1598 would scarcely have given Spenser time to redesign Book I so as to include such an episode. He could easily introduce an Armada allusion into the proem, however, without disturbing the poem's structure, as he may have done with the image of triumphant Mars led by Venus and Cupid. If so, the invocation of stanza 3 presents an anti-Spanish Venus, served by Mars, to complement the antipapal Virgin of stanza 2.[23]

In stanzas 2 and 3 we see Spenser managing his words to gain a secondary set of meanings that insinuate a sense of Elizabeth's immanence and anticipate an encomiastic technique in the poem at large. For, besides representing the queen through fictive *genus* and protagonists who befigure her by *res gestae* and *comparatio,* Spenser also often maneuvers otherwise apparently incidental details into connotative positions where they give off momentary reflections of the queen and imply that she is the principle informing the world as well as the poem.

Stanza 4: An Orphic Hymn

> And with them eke, O Goddesse heavenly
>   bright,
>   Mirrour of grace and Majestie divine,
>   Great Lady of the greatest Isle, whose light
>   Like Phoebus lampe throughout the world
>   doth shine,
>   Shed thy faire beames into my feeble eyne,
>   And raise my thoughts too humble and too
>   vile,
>   To thinke of that true glorious type of thine,
>   The argument of mine afflicted stile:
> The which to heare, vouchsafe, O dearest dred
>   a-while.

The last stanza of the proem follows the two-part structure of the hymns attributed in the Renaissance to Orpheus: praise by accumulated epithets, then petition, to which Spenser adds in the alexandrine a *votum,* or gesture of offering. There are three such epithets. The first, "O Goddesse heavenly bright," practices the strange veneration of Elizabeth as quasi-divine. The cult was not merely poetic. Roy Strong has pointed out that the queen's image was held to be genuinely sacral and mysteriously expressive of the monarch herself, even by Anglican apologists who otherwise rejected images as Romish superstition; and that people of all classes wore her image on medals and cameos for its beneficent effects.[24] The first epithet not only express-

es the cult of *diva Elizabetha* but, through "heavenly bright," also especially associates her with Astraea stellified as Virgo (under which sign, almost too appropriately, Elizabeth was born) and with the Venus Coelestis of the Neoplatonists.

The three epithets progress from the deified to the more nearly human. The second, "Mirrour of grace and Majestie divine," establishes the divine empress's proper relation to God: she makes visible his two main attributes of grace and majesty (analogous to the more usual mercy and justice). The mirror image occurs in all three proems of 1590. The second and third declare that the poem provides mirrors of the queen's realm and person. But in the first, she is the mirror—a mediatrix who communicates the divine ineffability to human perception. This Christ-like role expresses the Protestant cult of Elizabeth as national savior.

The third epithet brings us from goddess and mirror to localized national "Lady": "Great Lady of the greatest Isle, whose light / Like Phoebus lampe throughout the world doth shine." Here, Spenser appropriates the motto of Philip II's impresa *Iam illustrabit omnia* ("Now he will illumine all things"); which depicted Apollo driving his sun-chariot over land and sea,[25] and so asserts that Philip's claim to world domination and championship of the true faith properly belong to Elizabeth. The allusion is apt as a post-Armada gesture, transparently promoting anti-Hispanic imperial ambitions, and turning the outdoing topos to propaganda.

Together these three epithets form a triad typical of Renaissance Neoplatonism, in which the middle term serves to mediate between the two otherwise potentially opposed terms. Here, Elizabeth contains all three elements of the triad in herself. While apotheosis as goddess allies her with God, her intermediate function as a mirror allows her divinity to become visible in the human queen of a real isle. Because she mirrors God's attributes of grace and majesty, to see her is, in some sense, to perceive God himself.[26] That Elizabeth bridges the potentially opposed realms of heaven and earth is an idealistic conception essential to Spenser's encomium as presented in 1590. By defining a real monarch, it avoids the traditional Augustinian dualism between the Cities of God and This World that would set heaven and England at odds and that would place a low valuation on human achievement in the service of the state. In fact, Spenser's poem of 1590 implies as enthusiastic an estimate of human capability at its best as can be found in Renaissance humanism. Because Elizabeth is a goddess, Gloriana's knights can pursue their quests in this world, secure in the knowledge that the good they achieve in her service will be recognized in heaven. And the poet can sing her praise, knowing that it will be in harmony with the angels' hymns. Thus, the triad whereby Elizabeth unites heaven and earth must necessarily begin the first overt piece of her encomium in *The Faerie Queene.*

The hymn of stanza 4 balances on its fifth line—"Shed thy faire beames into my feeble eyne"—which, like the stanza, is in one half devoted to the queen, in the other to the poet. This line marks the typical division of an Orphic hymn into praise and petition. In the stanza's second half, the poet petitions the goddess for inspiration to "raise my thoughts too humble and too vile, / To thinke of that true glorious type of thine." The inability topos is prominent here, and the adjectives applied to the poet—"humble," "vile," "afflicted"—have their Latin senses of physical lowness. But the extremes of exaltation and abasement and the idea of a humble poet who may be raised to behold a celestial mirror recapitulate Piers's vision of Colin's ascent in *October.* The parallel reminds us that the poet's self-abasement effects advertisement. Indeed, the last two lines bring the paradox into the open, the eighth with its "argument of my afflicted style" still bespeaking inability and the passive poet's dependence on inspiration from the potentially creative goddess if the poem is to come into existence, while the alexandrine— "The which to heare, vouchsafe, O dearest dred a- while"—presents the poem as fait accompli and the poet as active creator, with the queen now the passive receptor. Because the queen is a goddess the poem is made possible, but the articulation of her true glorious type depends on the hymnic powers of the English Orpheus.

Epic as Hymn

As an Orphic hymn, the fourth stanza implies that the epic it prefaces is also in some sense a hymn. Indeed, at the beginning of Book I the poet confirms his identification with the hymnist Orpheus by a judiciously placed tree catalog. A. C. Hamilton has suggested that "contemporary readers would have responded" to this catalog "as an imitation by which the poet reveals his kinship with Orpheus who first moved trees with his song."[27] The main poets to make the tree catalog conventional are in fact precisely those antecedent to Colin in the *Calender:* Chaucer, from whose tree catalog in the *Parliament of Fowls* (176- 82) Spenser borrows details; Virgil, in *Eclogues* 8. 61-68; and, most important, Orpheus himself, whose song Ovid describes as convoking a mixed grove of trees and making them dance (*Met.* 10. 90-104). As a result, the catalog appears as a signature of the poet who fulfills Orpheus's hymnic role. Prominent in the list of trees is "the Laurell, meed of mightie Conquerours / And Poets sage" (1. 9). Its epithets not only hint at an equivalence of heroes and poet as figures in the poem, but also pointedly imply that Spenser expects official recognition as national epicist; "meed" inevitably suggests pecuniary as well as honorific reward.

By making an Orphic hymn its immediate preface, Spenser imputes a hymnic cast to *The Faerie Queene,* its "argument" said to be the goddess's true glorious type. The imputation finds raison d'être in Renaissance literary theory, where the hymn was affirmed the oldest kind of poem and, in accordance with the principle of decorum, often declared the highest: gods supersede princes. The revival of the literary hymn by Pius II, Pontano, Marullo, Vida, Scaliger, Ronsard, and Spenser in *Fowre Hymnes* is in part a humanist response to the Homeric, Orphic, and Callimachan hymns and in part an effort to provide modern examples to fill a gap at the apex of the hierarchy of kinds.[28] But when the Virgilian career-model made epic the highest ambition of Renaissance poets, the theoretical supremacy of the hymn was rather awkward. In his *Poetices* (1. 3), for instance, Scaliger acknowledges this supremacy, but he repeatedly proclaims the *Aeneid* the greatest of poems. Similarly, Sidney agrees that the hymnic poets were "chiefe both in antiquitie and excellencie," yet asserts that among the genres "the Heroicall . . . is not onely a kinde, but the best and most accomplished kinde of Poetry."[29]

But the epideictic view of literature avoids the inconsistency by emphasizing that hymn and epic are similar: the fact that the Callimachan and longer Homeric hymns were mainly laudatory narratives of the god's deeds made them appear as divine equivalents to the epic conceived of as encomiastic biography of a hero. Puttenham, whose theory of literature is clearly epideictic, properly distinguishes hymn and epic according to decorum as highest and second-highest kinds but then somewhat blurs divine and princely matters by making them "all high subjects, and therefore are delivered over to the Poets Hymnick & historicall who be occupied either in divine laudes, or in heroicall reports." And he straddles the genres by using heroic terms to describe "all your Hymnes & Encomia of Pindarus & Callimachus, not very histories but a maner of historicall reportes."[30] If we note that the Orphic and shorter Homeric hymns apostrophize the god (usually by a series of epithets or attributes) and close with a prayer and that the Callimachan and longer Homeric hymns augment these two features with a long narrative, we begin to see that there is a spectrum of hymnic genres, moving from the paeanic Orphic hymn to the longer narrative hymn to the hymnic or encomiastically conceived epic. Because of the veneration of the *Aeneid,* the literary hymn, in spite of its position in theory, was in practical terms simply not credible as supreme genre and the epic was. But the epideictic theorist's approximation of hymn and epic bridges the impasse by allowing epic to take on a hymnic function (at least abstractly) and so assert its de facto supremacy without undue threat to the hierarchic scheme of the genres.

At this point, it is worth turning back to the first alexandrine of *The Faerie Queene:* "Fierce warres and faithfull loves shall moralize my song." The syntax here seems perverse: one expects the line should say that "fierce wars and faithful loves are moralized in my song"—that is, allegorized heroic and erotic narratives make up the poem. But Spenser instead insinuates that "my song" has priority over both narrative and allegory, that epic is subordinate to *carmen*. If we read "song" as meaning hymn or encomium, we can see that, given the theoretical concept of hymnic epic, Spenser has designed the line to say that his poem is essentially a hymn and secondarily an allegorical epic. And, in fact, a little less than a year after **The Faerie Queene** appeared, he describes it as a set of hymns to Eliza who "hath praises in all plenteousnesse" showered on her by "Colin her owne Shepherd. / That her with heavenly hymnes doth deifie" (**Daphnaida**, 227-30).

Thus, if we see in **The Faerie Queene** only an allegorized romantic epic, we resist Spenser's assertion that it is encomium. In the epideictic categorization of genres, the epic is by nature encomiastic. What Spenser's first proem tells us is that, in his epic, encomium takes precedence over events. It will be easier to see how the episodes of the poem are encomiastic if we realize that when Spenser associates his epic with Virgil's he assumes that the *Aeneid* is a panegyrical biography (the Fulgentian view, explained in chapter 1); that each of Aeneas's acts bespeaks his praiseworthy mastery of one of the virtues proper to a hero; and that praise of Aeneas implies praise of his supposed descendant, Augustus. Similarly, in **The Faerie Queene** each successful episode in a knight's quest redounds to Gloriana's praise, and each unsuccessful episode falls short of contributing to that praise, though it cannot detract from it. Thus, Elizabeth, through her fictional "true glorious type," not only originates the quests and receives their achievement as a sacrifice to her glory, so that the quests are ultimately hers; but she is also the criterion by which each knight's degree of success or failure is measured. For the demigoddesses who preside over the ideal forms of each virtue (like Caelia and Alma) are types of Elizabeth, as Spenser eventually tells us.[31] The knights' goals are consequently identical with the queen herself, just as the goal of the quest that coordinates the others, Arthur's, is the Faery Queen. Hence, her panegyrical biography is made up of their efforts to achieve the virtues which she embodies and which she inspires. Thus, in a broad sense, each book of the poem can be considered an act of encomium—one of the "heavenly hymns" that "deifie" her.

But there are also passages, episodes, and especially figures in **The Faerie Queene** that express Elizabeth's praise in more specific ways. Spenser draws our attention to several of these in the proems to Books II and III. An investigation of some of these notably encomiastic features in the poem of 1590 is the subject of the next three chapters.

Notes

. . .[13] The arguments of Padelford and Bennett are summarized in *Variorum F.Q.,* I: app. 9. Lotspeich, *Classical Mythology in Spenser's Poetry* (Princeton: Princeton University Press, 1932), pp. 84-85. Starnes, "Spenser and the Muses," *TSLL,* 22 (1942): 31-58. Patrick Spurgeon, "Spenser's Muses," *Renaissance Papers* 1968, ed. G. W. Williams, Southeastern Renaissance Conference (Columbia, S.C., 1969), pp. 15-23, argues that both muses are involved.

[14] This follows Boccaccio on the same subject almost verbatim: "For poets are not like historians, who begin their account at some convenient beginning and describe events in the unbroken order of their occurrence to the end . . . But poets, by a far nobler device, begin their proposed narrative in the midst of the events, or sometimes even near the end; and thus they find excuse for telling preceding events which seem to have been omitted." *Genealogiae* 14. 13; trans. Charles G. Osgood, *Boccaccio on Poetry* (Princeton: Princeton University Press, 1930), pp. 67-68. Boccaccio notes the tradition describing Lucan's *Pharsalia* as versified history rather than epic because of its chronological organization. Among the numerous anomalies of the Letter to Raleigh in relation to the poem it purports to describe is that whatever sense we may have of in medias res organization in *F.Q.* I and II is stimulated by the Letter and not the poem. Curiously, the Letter makes nothing of the unmistakable in medias res order of the first three cantos of Book III which mirror the device exactly as it appears in its locus classicus, *Aeneid* 1-3.

[15] See Weinberg, *Literary Criticism,* pp. 41-42, 724.

[16] In his April and November glosses E. K. accepts *De inventis* as Virgil's, although Robert Stephanus had correctly attributed them to Ausonius. Starnes, "Spenser and the Muses," p. 40.

[17] Louis Réau, *Iconographie de l'art chrétien,* 2 vols. (Paris: Presses universitaires de France, 1955-59), vol. 2, pt. 2, p. 617. Tasso's invocation alludes to Petrarch's famous canzone to the Virgin (*Rime,* 366) where the Woman Clothed with the Sun is clearly one of her types: "Vergine bella, che di sol vestita, / coronata di stelle." Strong, *Portraits,* p. 42, points out that the veneration of Elizabeth after her death as "Saint Elizabeth" and as the second Virgin in heaven uses the image of the queen as "a portent in the skies, arrayed in the attributes of the Virgin as the Woman of the Apocalypse."

[18] The difference between the two poets in these parallel passages points toward a broader contrast between their epics: Spenser's patriotism leads him to daring

forms of the Christian-humanist synthesis; Tasso, alert to Tridentine strictures, is wary of heterodoxy. He seems to have altered his initial invocation at least three times: see Robert M. Durling, *The Figure of the Poet in Renaissance Epic* (Cambridge, Mass.: Harvard University Press, 1965,), pp. 195-96.

[19] *Delle allusioni* (Rome, 1588), 3. 4. 2 (p. 176). Jewel, *An Apology of the Church of England,* ed. J. E. Booty, Folger Documents of Tudor and Stuart Civilization (Ithaca: Cornell University Press, 1963), p. 41; and ibid., Introduction, p. xv, for Alexander Nowell's use of the formula. I am grateful to Barbara Bernhart for drawing my attention to this formula and Fabricii's use of it.

[20] Quoted by Jenkins, *Elizabeth,* p. 158, and by Wilson, *England's Eliza,* p. 4.

[21] Roy C. Strong, "The Accession Day of Queen Elizabeth I," *JWCI,* 21 (1958): 92-93 and n. 48.

[22] Garrett Mattingly, *The Armada* (Boston: Houghton Mifflin, 1962), p. 390.

[23] Cf. the curious reinvocation at I. xi. 5-7 that *plays down* Redcrosse's fight with the dragon in favor of some later "worke . . . of endlesse prayse" that will depict the war "Twixt that great faery Queene and Paynim king." This seems to be another allusion to the Armada.

[24] Strong, *Portraits,* pp. 39-40. This phenomenon in the Middle Ages is the subject of Ernst H. Kantorowicz, *The King's Two Bodies: A Study in Medieval Political Theology* (Princeton: Princeton University Press, 1957).

[25] On the impresa and its relevance to Book V, see Aptekar, *Icons of Justice,* pp. 82-83, and René Graziani, "Philip II's *Impresa* and Spenser's Souldan," *JWCI,* 27 (1964): 322-24.

[26] On triads in Spenser, see Alastair Fowler, "Emanations of Glory: Neoplatonic Order in Spenser's *Faerie Queene,*" in Judith M. Kennedy and James A. Reither, eds., *A Theatre for Spenserians* (Toronto: University of Toronto Press, 1973), pp. 53-82. On intermediaries in the triad, the Renaissance locus classicus is Ficino's *Commentary on the Symposium,* 6. 1-6. The only complete translation is *Commentaire sur le Banquet de Platon,* trans. Raymond Marcel (Paris: Société d'Edition "Les Belles Lettres," 1956).

[27] "Spenser and the Common Reader," *ELH,* 35 (1968): 618.

[28] On the genre in the Renaissance, see Philip Rollinson, "The Renaissance of the Literary Hymn," *Renais-* *sance Papers* 1969, ed, G. W. Williams, Southeastern Renaissance Conference (Columbia, S.C., 1970), pp. 11-20. On elements of royal praise in *Fowre Hymnes,* see Elliott M. Hill, "Flattery in Spenser's *Fowre Hymnes,*" *WVUPP,* 15 (1966): 22-35. Also, but more obliquely, Jon A. Quitslund, "Spenser's Image of Sapience," *SRen,* 16 (1969): 181-213; and Sears Jayne, "Attending to Genre: Spenser's *Hymnes,*" a paper read at the 1971 Modern Language Association meeting and summarized in *SpN,* 3 (1972), no. I, pp. 5-6.

[29] *Prose Works,* 3:9-10, 25.

[30] *Arte,* 3. 6; 1. 19; ed. Willcock and Walker, pp. 152, 41.

[31] See *F.Q.* VI. x. 28 where Colin apologizes to Gloriana for omitting her from the central role in the vision of ideal courtesy. The apology indicates the presence of a royal type in each core canto in the preceding books.

Helena Shire (essay date 1978)

SOURCE: "Poetic Background,"in *A Preface to Spenser,* Longman Group, Ltd., 1978, p. 88-130.

[*In the following excerpt from a study of Spenser's background and work, Shire introduces the literary and poetic context for Spenser's writing.*]

> The poet's eye in a fine frenzy rolling
> Doth glance from heaven to earth, from earth
>   to heaven
> And as imagination bodies forth
> The forms of things unknown, the poet's pen
> Turns them to shapes and gives to airy
>   nothing
> A local habitation and a name.
>
>   Shakespeare, *A Midsummer Night's Dream*

A new poetry for Elizabeth's England

Certain regions of belief and attitude in Elizabethan times have been explored because they differed from ours today and acquaintance with them would help us to draw near to Spenser's poetry. We are now confronted with that poetryCagain different in so many ways from ours today. We must find out how it works. We need to discern what the poet believed himself to be doing, what he aimed to achieve and by what means, and the reasons why he did so. In this project two things are difficult. First, there are voices enough from the sixteenth century of poet and of theorist, foreign or native, to inform us on those matters, but the terms they use are unfamiliar coinage to our minds or, worse, they are oldfashioned and misleading as to the values they represent. Then there are certain important issues wherein poet and writer about poetry were *at that time* so completely agreed that these issues are not mentioned, far less debated.

The well-known verses quoted above come from Duke Theseus, a notable sceptic as to poetry or enchantment; but his words show what was taken for granted about the process of imaginative composition, though he speaks to discountenance it. A poet was inspired: his vision could be seen as a coming and going between earth and heaven, whence proceeded forms that shaped and ordered his purpose and matter, thus rendering the 'ideal' accessible in earthly terms. Certainly a general agreement existed on the nature of poetry and the special status of the poet. It was the fruit of more than a century of discussion and experiment, development and achievement, since the revival of learning had brought the poetry and philosophy of antiquity powerfully into the current of new thought and writing in western Europe, and since poetry in 'the sweet now style' had arisen in Italy, blossomed with Petrarch and spread to France with the work of du Bellay and Ronsard, to take firm root in England with the writing of Philip Sidney. At this point Spenser enters the story.

With this new poetry in the Renaissance style 'the theory and practice . . . form such a coherent unity that any poem written in what is called the Italianate tradition is a concrete embodiment of the theory that lies behind it, and even a slight working knowledge of this can add unsuspected dimensions to the poetry'. To begin then with the theory, and in the simplest terms possible. The view of the universe and of the nature of reality in which a poet was operating was still the hierarchical cosmos, in which the universal and the particular were bound together in a complex system of correspondences. If earth is a microcosmos, everything on earth is an earthly, finite, imperfect, perishable version of its ideal, perfect archetype existing in heaven. If the archetype is the true, the real, the ideal, then man should concern himself with that rather than with the imperfect manifestations he is in contact with in his everyday life. For if he comes to understand the real, the essential, he will understand fully and evaluate justly the imperfect manifestations of 'actual' experience.

A poet is a 'seer'—one who perceives the true, the real; his aim in his poetry is to express what he has perceived and convey it to those who hear or read his poems. The experience of hearing or reading the poems means for the receiver access to the true, the real, via the poet's vision—a process that brings the reader enlightenment. Poetry is didactic, not in the sense of finger-wagging precept but in that the poem well understood widens and deepens human experience. The

effect to which contemporary readers of Spenser's poetry testify is, again and again, a 'fulness of joy', 'As who therein can ever joy their fill', or

> but let one dwell upon them [the works] and he shall feel a strange fullness and roundness in all he saith. . . . The most generous wines tickle the palate least but they are no sooner in the stomach but by their warmth and strength there, they discover what they are.

In the reading of poetry the enlarging of scope in perception and knowledge, the enriching of consciousness brings joy, or pleasure or delight. All three words are used and are sometimes interchangeable. When 'pleasure' is used, the argument recognizes the sensuous appeal of the verse medium—delectable pictures, rhythm, harmony proportion, sweet sound—and the fact that such appeal may make a moral lesson palatable, as with a 'medicine of cherries'. But 'delight' was intended also to convey that moment of excitement and achievement with which one nowadays exclaims 'I *see*'. It registers the moment of shared vision, of discovery of correspondence revealed by the poet, of access to the 'truth', of contact with the real.

That poetry should give 'profit and delight' was confirmed in classical theory; Horace had said it in his *Art of Poetry*. When the use of poetry to man was called in question this was apt to be the reply. And so the function of poetry came to be defined as the discovery of truth (uncovering or revealing of the real, the ideal) and the giving of profit and delight. The function of poetry was extended farther along the line of discovery and imparting of truth to an inculcating of fresh insights spiritual, moral or (as we should say) psychological. Poetry had for centuries been regarded as a kind of rhetoric, belonging, that is, to the art of persuasion. Poetry in discovering the true, the real, should display virtues in their true brave colours and expose vices in their essential hatefulness, and so win men to love virtue and wish to cleave to it and hate, avoid and cast out vice. Poetry presented a picture of true kingship or heroism or loyalty, or the very essence of envy or malice; but it could go farther. By bodying forth the virtue to be attained only with effort, the easy and alluring vice, the evil seeming good, the moral dilemma, it could so involve the receiving mind that a mental act of choice and of will took place. 'Poetry' says George Puttenham 'inveigleth the judgement of man, and carrieth his opinion this way and that' (*The Arte of English Poesie,* I, iv, p. 8). For instance, as we follow with our reason the argument between Despair and Redcrosse (see pp. 146-9) we, not being weary and spent as the Knight is, perceive the dangerous traps and will him to avoid them and to prevail. We have undergone the moral discipline of resisting despair through participating in the knight's adventure, reading the allegory from the inside.

A poet is also a maker. He was called so in earlier English and the Greek word *poesis* means 'making'. As he belongs to the microcosm and was himself created in God's image, his act of making is a repetition in little, an imitation, of God's great act of creation. It follows that what he makes will of necessity be created on the model of the ordered universe: of its very nature it should have order, harmony, proportion, hierarchy. Every aspect of it should be in keeping. Every contributory part of it should be 'in place', as everything has its appointed place in a sacral universe. Every part should have a vital relationship with other parts and with the whole. A poem thus conceived and executed had *decorum*. A poet observed decorum when he manifested the sense of what belongs to what, of what is fitting in context.

Decorum as a concept operates over the whole range of poetic theory and practice. As hierarchy was manifest in the cosmos and manifest in the pattern of man's living on earth from monarch downwards rank on rank, there belonged to each level a mode of converse that conveyed the part they played in the whole: royal, heroic, courtly, scholarly . . . and so down to rustic and simple. So in poetry a treating of kings or heroes should be done in high and splendid terms, courtly matters should be couched in the speech of courts, and at the other end of the scale country matters and rustic manners should use simple, rough words and even rustic, regional turns of speech. The writing of a poem, then, is not only a matter of perceiving a vista of truth, reality, the ideal, and of communicating the perception but also of rendering it in the form, style and language that will best express it and present it to best advantage. (Clothes must fit perfectly and should be chosen to meet the occasion.) Hierarchy and rank in the universe made it natural that there should be different ranks in creative writing. Here the example of classical literature helped with its developed system of 'kinds'. Epic and tragedy are noble—to them a high style belongs. Pastoral treats of country matters and allows a satiric vein, so its style is low, simple and rough; being simple it was held to be well suited for a poet's first flight. A 'mean' or middle style of writing best suits the elegiac complaint and many varieties of poetry of love.

'Decorum' in large means literary 'kind' chosen according to the poet's purpose and subject-matter. In small it governs the choice of single words in their sentence or line of verse. An adjective is chosen not primarily in order to extend by an individual added detail the scope of the noun it qualifies; far less is it chosen to evince the author's powers of observation; it belongs to the whole stanza, indeed to the whole poem. For instance in **Prothalamion** stanza 3. . . the waters are bidden not to wet the silken feathers' of the two swans who are most fair and white and pure. 'Silken' is precise and vivid as conveying delicacy and vulner-

able finery and as reflecting on plumage of swans; but it is also there as the first hint of the major metaphor of the poem, for the swans will later be revealed as human brides on their way by river-barge to their betrothal ceremony. The silk belongs to the bridal gowns to come. Epithets that did not 'work' in this energetic way were condemned by Ronsard as lazy, *oisifs*.

Decorum is a much-embracing virtue of Spenser's poetry. In **The Shepheardes Calender** the new poet is praised in the introductory Epistle for

> his complaints of love so lovely, his discourses of pleasure so pleasantly, his pastorall rudenesse, his moral wiseness, his dewe observing of Decorum everywhere, in personages, in seasons, in matter, in speach, and generally in al seemly simplicitie of handeling his matter and framing his words.

As to 'framing his words' we have seen it in the example of 'silken' above. The word is *in place*. Being in place and energetically contributing to the whole, it helps bind part to part and part to whole. So decorum is a dynamic principle in making a poem. And for the reader the perception of decorum at work is an experience both artistic and moral. 'What is in place' for renaissance poetry will not separate from the greater issue in the ordered universe—where 'nothing is there by chance'.

Imitation of Nature. From the idea of poet as maker, we recall, derived the concept of imaginative composition fashioned on the model of the created universe. Such a process of creative composition went by the name of *imitation of nature*. Nature is divinely ordered, not formless but the source of form. The famous lines from Shakespeare given above express this process. The poet, inspired with vision from heaven, casts his eye up to heaven for form with which to express it; 'things unknown' in Theseus' phrase, are the ideal, the real, the true; the poet's pen then embodies them in earthly terms. The 'shaping spirit of imagination' derives from celestial pattern the order, harmony and proportion with which it endows its artefact, the poem.

How did an 'imitation of nature' show itself as successfully achieved, in a poem? In a total coherence. Metaphor, simile or personification that enters the poem must contribute to its value as an artistic construction; those of the 'April ode'. . .will serve as example. If number or set is introduced in any way into the substance or ordering of the poem it will be meaningful. (The concept of 'completeness' could not enter into a poem through a treatment of *three* of the four elements). In so contributing to the whole of the poem either in content or in form, imagery, set or number take part in conveying the 'truth', which is the poem's purpose.

The use of poetic imagery, then, is not primarily decorative, though it may make for beauty, variety and enrichment of the whole effect. (Nor is it there because revelatory of the personal experience or subconscious trains of association in the mind of the poet.) But it is chosen and used of set purpose to direct the receiving mind to the *value* of what is being expressed. Again and again in *The Faerie Queene* an epithet, a simile or metaphor delivers the tacit message '*Think* what values are entailed!' The use of the epithet 'golden' in Book II, in the name of Guyon's horse Brigador (Bridle of Gold) and in many other places, directs the mind to the golden mean of temperance, a vital expression of the Book's Legend. The character in an adventure may be oblivious for the moment, or plain mistaken, as to what he is confronted with; but the reader can receive the poet's message if he is 'wary and wise'. The mythological simile that ends the description of Belphoebe/Gloriana is a good example of energetic poetic imagery: it 'dilates' the meaning, carrying it into new regions, enriching by the parallel and at the same time aiding the precise delineation of the poet's intention.

'Imitation of the model' had a further meaning, deriving from the first somewhat in this fashion: if poetry is an imitation of nature and excellent poets of antiquity had imitated nature excellently well, poets of the present age could learn how it was done from study of their poems. Such examples in Latin or Greek became intermediary models, as it were. Examples of excellence in description, in debate, in depiction of character through speech, in celebration of the ruler were studied, translated, analysed, discussed and reproduced in modern languages and used as models in fresh composition. The Gloss in *The Shepheardes Calender* draws attention to many points where the new poet has learned from makers of classical antiquity, or from earlier French or English poetry. The scale of the model used ranges from a turn of phrase, a figure of rhetoric, an inset fable or song, to the whole eclogue for 'September' as imitated from Mantuan and 'December' from Marot. If we remember that the aim of such imitation was to 'learn how to do it well' and the outcome was an enormous widening and enriching of the scope of English poetry, we will not misjudge it. The mind receiving the poetry, if not lettered in Latin, French or Greek, enjoyed what it otherwise would not have reached: both the matter and something of the manner. The reader who knew the original had a pleasure like that of one listening to variations on a theme in music, the delighted recognition of points made in the implied parallel.

A poet learned his art through imitation of a model. Once master of his craft he could by a similar gesture pit his skill against that of a fellow poet in literary contest, as shepherd poets did in a singing match. Spenser calls this 'overgoing'. He set out to 'overgo'

Ariosto in certain parts of *The Faerie Queene*—indeed in the passage studied from Book II in the critical analyses. . . . He overgoes the French poet Marot in the lament for Dido, 'some mayden of greate bloud' in *The Shepheardes Calender*. Marot had written an elegy in pastoral mode for the Queen Mother of France, recently dead: 'De Madame Loyse de Savoye, mère du Roy'. In a single-standing eclogue of two shepherds Colin and Thenot, Colin the poet is requested to sing a mourning song in honour of the royal lady; he complies in a piece of 'ten times ten verses' (200 lines) and is then thanked and praised. The verse pattern is uniform throughout, continuous quatrains interlinked by rhyme, *abab, bcbc* and so on. Colin expresses the sense of loss felt for the well-loved royal lady and nature mourns in sympathy assuming mourning colours. Then the mood changes and he bids his verses cease to plain, for she is in the Elysian fields of the blessed. It is a beautiful and elegant poem in a mode that was perhaps 'old-fashioned' to poets of Spenser's day.

Spenser takes the theme, the persons of the shepherds and the verse form, and devises afresh an elegy for the unknown 'Dido'. He 'dilates' the theme by making it part of a greater coherence, his *Calender*. It now belongs to the season of dying in nature, to November. The lament is now *in place* in cosmic rhythm, and under the deadly archer Sagittarius, as the wood-cut shows. He distinguishes the lament from the speeches of Thenot and Colin by giving it a distinctive stanza. The stanza has a refrain element that marks by a change in its wording the change in mood from sorrow to joy: 'O heavie herse . . . O carefull verse' becomes 'O happy herse . . . O ioyfull verse'. The meaning is now articulate in the form. The whole is well trussed up togetherCin the phrase of the 'Epistle' that precedes *The Calender*. And form and meaning are at one in the reiterated refrain word 'herse'.

This is an excellent example of Spenser's 'wittinesse in devising, his pithinesse in uttering', again to quote the Epistle. This Renaissance pun is worth expounding. A modern reader knows 'hearse' and 'rehearse' but probably does not connect them; in fact 'rehearsal' probably *sounds* as if it were connected with hearing, 'a hearing of music in practice'. But all these words are in fact derived from the French word for harrow: to rehearse is to go over the ground again in preparation. From 'herse' as harrow the word came to designate the funeral bier which it resembled, and so to mean 'funeral ceremony' in Spenser's day. For him too the *sound* of the word embraced 'hearing' as well as recital. All these senses are made to reverberate in his poem as 'herse' echoes 'verse' throughout the elegy, voicing the quick of the poem's meaning.

> But now sike happy cheere is turnd to heavie chaunce
> Such pleasaunce now displast by dolors dint:

All Musick sleepes, where death doth leade
  the daunce
And shepherds wonted solace is extinct.
The blue in black, the greene in gray is tinct.
  The gaudie girlonds deck her grave,
The faded flowers her corse embrave
  O heauie herse
Morne nowe my Muse, now morne with teares
  besprint
  O carefull verse.

Spenser's ideas on the poet and on poetry were to have
been expounded in his 'The English Poet', a work
mentioned in *The Calender* as ready for print, but never
published. Into the October Eclogue, however, he has
poured as much as he could of his beliefs and intuition
on this matter, his learning and his faith in his vocation: why the poet should be honoured by great men,
the poet as seer and maker wielding extraordinary
powers, the poet's inspiration, and his art bordering on
that of magic.

The theme of poetry and inspiration belongs to October, month of the wine harvest in the old tradition of
'works and days', for 'Bacchus fruite is frend to Phoebus wise'. It belongs under Scorpio, sign of intellect
and genius. The woodcut shows in the background a
'Florentine academy' with gentlemen grouped in discussion. From them advances into the shepherd scene
a pastoral poet, bearing crook and pan-pipes and
crowned with leaves—Bacchus' ivy or laurel for acclaim? The new Renaissance poetry is honoured in
The Calender, its potentialities explored, its nature exemplified and expounded; and it is portrayed enjoying
its due place in the cosmic scheme.

Pastoral and allegory

Allegory is metaphor sustained and explored. In pastoral the metaphor is of the shepherd living in a shepherd-land, who is everyman in his realm and in Christendom. By the same token in Spenser's heroic poem
the metaphor is of the knight of chivalric virtue who is
'on his way' of endeavour in Faerieland, committed to
be champion of a virtue and ready to challenge powers
that oppose it, whether in the world or within himself.

In his pastoral poetry—*The Calender, Colin Clout* or
Book VI of *The Faerie Queene*—Spenser shows that
he is deeply versed in the long tradition of poetic pastoral, from the Greeks through Vergil and Mantuan to
Skelton or Marot. The nature of that pastoral tradition
and Spenser's contribution to it has been wisely expounded by Professor Kermode in his volume *English
Pastoral Poetry*. It will serve our purpose here rather
to show how Spenser went to the root of the shepherd
metaphor as understood by plain people and how he
then did something completely new in making his first
pastoral a *Calender* of shepherds.

The metaphor of the shepherd in earlier pastoral had
established a relation of shepherd-land to actual life:
action there was 'ideal' in that it was human action
reduced to simpler terms and 'removed' from more
sophisticated civilization, which nonetheless it cast light
on. In that 'ideal' landscape could be presented the
essentials of the human lot.

In poetic pastoral certain patterns of activity, certain
roles and themes, had become favourites: the good
shepherd and the bad, the young and the old, at work
with their flocks, the singing and piping of the shepherd in his hours of pastime and his simple joys and
sorrows in love, a country commonwealth at peace
with praise of the ruler. The relationship of shepherd-
land to sophisticated society was rendered specifically
in one of the themes: the shepherd's journey, from
countryside to town and back again, with a telling of
what he had learned.

The metaphor of the pastoral shepherd was familiar to
every schoolboy who learned Latin, as the eclogues of
Mantuan, Latin poet of fifteenth-century Italy, were an
elementary textbook in common use. These were imitations of Vergil's eclogues and they made, more pro-
nouncedly that he had done, satiric comment on contemporary society. In Tudor England classical eclogues
had been printed in translation and eclogues had been
composed in English in imitation, for instance by
Barclay. 'Eclogues' means 'select pieces' and such
eclogues were separate poems, 'episodes of shepherd
life' rendered in dialogue, sometimes with narrative
introduction and conclusion, presented alone or in a
series.

Pastoral was regarded as the easiest and least ambitious of poetic kinds, 'in which a young poet could
fittingly take his first flight'. The style was simple,
'low', even harsh where satire had hard things to say.
Spenser in his first poetic endeavour aptly chose pastoral. But he took the pastoral of poetic tradition into
a region it had not known. His pastoral work was to be
Renaissance poetry in its fullest power. First, as to 'the
part and the whole'. Spenser says in his preface that
'eclogues' does not mean 'select pieces'; the Greek
word means 'goat-songs'. His book of verses will be
no miscellany. His pastoral volume is a whole, a cycle
not a series, with each part related to each other part
in parallel and contrast, the sequence providing a pleasing variety of pieces moral, recreative or satirical; what
is more, each single eclogue is now related to each
other and to the whole through cosmic perspective.

Number comes into it. Vergil's eclogues had been ten,
a good round number such as Romans liked. Spenser
makes his eclogues twelve, 'proportionable to the
twelve moneths', as his title announces. He has taken
the pastoral's programme of scenes in shepherd-land
that showed man's works and pastimes at various sea-

sons and has related that work and pastime to the great medieval scheme of 'the labours of the months'. The activity or topic of each eclogue is related to its seasonable time in the solar cycle of the year, the course of the months in character under their zodiac signs, and there is tacit reference to the year of the Church. Thus poetic 'truth', in the sense of how any phenomenon belonged to the sacral universe, is perceived, and imitation of nature is achieved for pastoral in a new way. In this new dimension decorum is observed throughout, both in form and content.

Secondly, Spenser enriched and extended the pastoral genre by combining it with another. (*Combinatio* was a skill of the rhetorician.) He laid Vergil's eclogues beside another very different book, but one also treating of the shepherd as everyman. This was 'an old book', familiar to men of Renaissance Europe in print in many languages, in English *The Kalendar and compost of Shepherds, Le compost et kalendrier des bons bergiers*. It was as we saw, a handbook for everyman 'the shepherd', bringing together all he needed to know for his physical moral and spiritual wellbeing. It gave a régime of diet for the season, a tree of the virtues and vices (with penalties), the main sacraments and prayers of the Church; it taught him to find his way by the stars and showed in diagrams how his body was constituted and conditioned by celestial powers of planet or zodiac sign. It was illustrated by many woodcuts which included pages giving the character of each month, its labours or pastimes, its zodiac sign and its religious festivals. . . .

Thirdly, Spenser, learning from earlier theological writing in French on the 'shepherd' theme, now explored the metaphor of the shepherd in terms of the sacral universe. (In a way he was providing a Christian gloss for Vergil's pastoral, as Renaissance scholars did for a classical text.) The shepherd of traditional pastoral poetry was everyman; but scripture showed 'the shepherd' as a far richer metaphor. The shepherd was Christ himself in his own words of parable, the good shepherd, keeper of the Christian flock. His antetype in the Old Testament was Abel, a good shepherd as Spenser points outCand his forerunner was David, shepherd-boy who became king, ancestor on earth of Christ, singer of 'the Psalms'. God in the twenty-third psalm led the human soul as a shepherd by quiet waters, as is seen in the picture for the December eclogue. Shepherd as *episcopus* was the bishop of the Christian Church, who carried a crook as emblem of his office. At several points the two uses of the metaphor confirmed one another. The pastoral shepherd sang of love, David of love of God. By thinking in parallel God could be figured as Pan, God of shepherds all. As the head of the Christian Church on earth was, in England since Henry VIII's reign, the monarch, Eliza is Queen of shepherds all; her pastoral genealogy shows her as daughter of Pan and Syrinx.

Exploration of the metaphor of the shepherd enriched the character of shepherd-land. The shepherd's journey in 'September' shows an eclogue of Mantuan done in reverse; Diggon Davie has journeyed not to the city or court but to a wilder land far in the west where 'all is of misery' and his curious dialect, echoing Celtic-English, brings news which can only be from Ireland. The May eclogue in a fable extends the view to Scotland—the court a goat-pen and the kid the boy king seduced by a wily Catholic. Universals of pastoral are linked by hint or name-conceit to particular living instances. The friend is Hobbinol/Harvey, critic of the poet-shepherd's singing. Two bishop-shepherds suggest the Bishop of Rochester (Roffy) and Grindal (Algrind). And Spenser (of the Merchant Taylors' School) is, aptly, Colin Clout: *'Colin'* had been the French poet Marot's pastoral name for himself and Colin Clout was that of the English poet Skelton under King Henry VIII. (Spenser's devising draws all these into one name-idea.) Historical pertinence gave particular examples of the general 'truth', as it was to do in **The Faerie Queene**. The delight of the reader in following the poet's invention was spiced with an element of 'delicious you-know-who'. The poet-shepherd emerges as chief among shepherd rôles. And Colin Clout we shall hear sing again in a later pastoral eclogue, play again in the apt Book of **The Faerie Queene**.

Spenser's reader, opening the pages of this work by an unknown poet, would see eclogues like Vergil's but with a title and pictures that strongly recalled those of the familiar handbook (indeed the month pictures were designed, like those in that volume, on the pattern of a Book of Hours). His imagination was challenged to relate the metaphor of the shepherd in one and in the other, to discern wherein lay the aptness of each woodcut to its eclogue's meaning. As in a Book of Hours the scene might be located by a significant building in the background. And the matter and manner of the shepherds' discourse would be deepened by its timing in season on earth and in the heavens.

For instance January, cold and wet under Aquarius the Water-carrier, shows the shepherd Colin Clout in a wintry landscape tending a dejected flock by a sheepcote. On the horizon is a strange group of buildingsCthe Coliseum for Rome, the bridge at Avignon for Petrarch, the twin towers of Rochester Cathedral, and a church; thus Colin is 'placed' as young Spenser, secretary at Rochester, pastoral poet of Christendom in a poetic tradition of Vergil, Mantuan and Petrarch. In the foreground lie his shepherd's bagpipes, broken. Colin's discourse is a plaint of love's pain and dejection in tune with the barren wintry season with its icy tears; unloved by Rosalind he has broken his pipe. And the 'broken pipe' glances by metaphor at the Circumcision, the feast of the Christian year with which January opens, when Christ suffered his first pain on earth for love of mankind. . . .The eclogues for April and May are treated in the critical analysis of the 'April ode'.

The book was, moreover, a calendar that took the particular year 1579 and reflected life in the realm and Christendom in that year, showing issues and personalities of import in it. The year was the twenty-first of Elizabeth's reign, in number a 'turning-point' of life, as Petrarch expounded. The calendar was itself a focus of interest and anxiety at the time, as we have seen. Spenser made this one of poetry, the particular thus achieving universality. He endowed this year of his sovereign's reign with 'durance perpetual'.

> Loe I have made a Calender for every yeare
> That steele in strength and time in durance
>   shall outweare
> And if I marked well the starres revolution
> It shall continewe till the world's dissolution.

In the great gesture of Renaissance creative writing, poetry should be seen to conquer time, in terms of time's own instrument. It was a project brilliant in conception and of dazzling ambition. Spenser the poet by it established himself as an accomplished Renaissance poet in English; but as a young man green in judgment he o'erreached himself in vaulting ambition, and 'fell on the other'. The **Calender** indeed bodied forth the year 1579 in its essence, showing its place in the pattern of history unfolding; but the poet as 'seer' had seen more and spoken more 'truly' than certain great ones could tolerate.

One final feature of **The Shepheardes Calender** was remarkable. Each Eclogue had a Gloss, as scholarly texts did. Here unusual or difficult words were explained, figures of rhetoric noted, classical references explained and any use of literary 'model' noted. That is to say the new poetic work was presented as for serious study. But a teasing note can be detected here and there. The maker of the Gloss is one 'E. K.', who may be Spenser's friend Edward Kirke but is as likely to stand for Edmundus Kalendarius—Spenser the **Calender**-maker. This is a clever young man's production. For instance some of the woodcuts feature bird flight and in the Gloss augury by bird flight is recommended as worth a young man's study! No one has cracked the code here, but something momentous in the events of the year 1579 may be registered. The Renaissance poet's delight in the arcane, that was to lead Spenser to use Egyptian symbol in Britomart's dream in his heroic poem, is already here. In his first work Spenser's poetry may indeed be 'perceived of the leaste, understoode of the mooste, but judged only by the learned'.

Judith H. Anderson (essay date 1982)

SOURCE: "In liuing colours and right hew: The Queen

of Spenser's Central Books," in *Critical Essays on Edmund Spenser*, edited by Mihoko Suzuki, Prentice Hall International, 1982, pp. 168-82.

[In the following essay, Anderson analyzes the significance of the complex and often critical portrait of Queen Elizabeth in books III and IV of The Faerie Queene.]

Even in the 1590 *Faerie Queene,* Spenser's reverence for Queen Elizabeth is accompanied by a cautionary awareness of the temptations and dangers of queenly power and by a complementary awareness of the cost—the denial or exclusion of human possibilitiesCan ennobling Idea exacts of its bearer. The one is evident in the House of Pride and Cave of Mammon, and the other in the treatment of Belphoebe. The attainments of Una, the "goodly maiden Queene," are threatened demonically by their perversion in Lucifera, the "mayden Queene" of Pride, and parodied again in Book II by the verbally reiterative image of Philotime.[1] Belphoebe, beautiful, inspiring, and goddesslike, is momentarily locked in comic encounter with Braggadocchio in Book II, an encounter which, though it leaves the worth of her ideal essentially untarnished, resembles another famous encounter between honor and instinct: between Hotspur's extravagant idealism, his "easy leap, / To pluck bright honor from the pale-fac'd moon," and Falstaff's unenlightened but earthy sense: "Can honor set to a leg?"[2] Specifically aligned with Queen Elizabeth in the Letter to Ralegh and in the proem to Book III, the chaste Belphoebe is in human terms both an aspiration and an extreme, paradoxically both more and less nearly complete than ordinary mortals.

In the 1596 *Faerie Queene,* while still persuaded of the value of the queenly ideal, Spenser is more disillusioned—or at least less illusioned—with the real Queen and her court. In the notorious proem to Book IV, he complains openly of misconceived criticisms of *The Faerie Queene* emanating from Elizabeth's court and goes so far as to summon help from Eros for "that sacred Saint my soueraigne Queene." He urges *Venus dearling doue,* a benign Cupid, to "Sprinckle" the Queen's "heart, and haughtie courage soften, / That she may hearke to loue, and read this lesson often." Thus introduced by hope for improvement in queenly attitudes and by implied criticism of her present ones, Books IV to VI are bedeviled by recurrent images of revilement and public infamy: Ate, Slander, Malfont, Envy, Detraction, the Blatant Beast. Most of these glance at the Queen, the Queen's court, or events impossible to dissociate from the Queen without transforming her into a mythic ideal isolated from historyCat best a hope or an unrealized promise but no longer, by any stretch of the epic imagination, a present reality. In the proem to Book VI—the beginning of *The Faerie Queene*'s end—this is the route Spenser attempts, but with a trail of hesitation, bitterness, and painful reassessment still fresh behind him.

Despite recognition of the poet's cautionary awareness in Books I to III and despite his more open disappointment in Books IV to VI, we have been reluctant to admit their persistence and strength, especially as they touch the Queen. We rightly note the danger to a mere poet of criticizing his sovereign and the real power the cult of the Virgin Queen exerted over men's imaginations. Nothing in this paper denies these realities, but my argument considers them large designs in the poem's fabric rather than its whole cloth.

Reluctance to see the extent to which Spenser criticizes the Queen does him a particular disservice in Books III and IV. Here it obscures the relation of ideal or antique image to the present age, a relation of which the Queen is the measure throughout the poem, and thus it obscures the developing relation of Faerie to history and of fiction to life. Still more serious, to my mind, this reluctance leads us to pretend that the poet did not really mean certain lines or hear certain verbal ambiguities and, in short, was not fully sensitive to his own words or alert to their surrounding contexts.[3] My present undertaking is to examine several passages in Books III and IV that involve verbal cruxes, the Queen, and the relation of present age to antique image. These passages indicate that Spenser's depiction of the Queen's bright image is more complexly shaded in Book III than is generally acknowledged and is in Book IV more critical, perhaps shockingly so. In Book IV, something of the nightmare image of the slanderous Beast who bites "without regard of person or of time" at the end of Book VI is already present and implicates the Queen.

I

In the proem to Book III, the poet observes a distinction between present and past and between truth and Faerie image that is absent from the proems to Books I and II, and without them, its significance could easily pass unnoticed. In the first of these proems, the living Queen, "Great Lady of the greatest Isle," is a "Mirrour of grace and Maiestie diuine," and the poem is a reflection, in effect itself a mirror, of "that true glorious type" of the Queen. In the proem to Book II, despite poetic play about the location of Faerie, the Queen is the living reflection of the "antique Image," and so the poem, or Faerie image, is a "faire mirrhour" of her "face" and "realmes." The first two proems present one continuous, unbroken reflection: the Queen reflects Divinity; like the Queen herself, the poem reflects the glorious origins, person, and reign of the living Queen.

Referring to the Queen's face, realms, and ancestry, the final stanza of Proem II offers an apology for the antique Faerie image that is in fact a confident justification of it:

> The which O pardon me thus to enfold
> In couert vele, and wrap in shadowes light,
> That feeble eyes your glory may behold,
> Which else could not endure those beames bright,
> But would be dazled with exceeding light.

The dazzling brightness of the living Queen is enfolded in shadow to enlighten feeble eyes, enabling them to behold true glory. This veil reveals a single truth instead of obscuring it, and these shadows, unlike those in the second three books, do not splinter truth or transform its character. They do not make true glory truly fictive.

In the proem to Book III, the poem continues to be the Queen's mirror, and although she is now invited to view herself "In mirrours more then one"—that is, in Gloriana or in Belphoebe—both glasses are essentially virtuous and can be seen primarily as an outfolding of the good Queen rather than as a dispersion of her unity. But as I have noted elsewhere, in this proem the present embodiment also begins to vie with the antique image, living Queen with Antiquity, and, indeed, to challenge it.[4] Uneasy nuances (not quite tensions) cluster around the word "living." In order to perceive the fairest virtue, chastity in this case, one "Need but behold the pourtraict of her [the Queen's] hart, / If pourtrayed it might be by any liuing art." The poet continues, "But liuing art may not least part expresse, / Nor life-resembling pencill it can paint . . . Ne Poets wit, that passeth Painter farre." Then comes a plea for pardon that recalls the one in the second proem:

> But O dred Soueraine
> Thus farre forth pardon, sith that choicest wit
> Cannot your glorious pourtraict figure plaine
> That I in coloured showes may shadow it,
> And antique praises vnto present persons fit.

More opaque than the "shadowes light" of Proem II, these shadows testify to the poet's "want of words" and wit more than they serve the purpose of revelation. The poem here becomes a slightly compromised "coloured show" that can only shadow the Queen's "glorious pourtraict" and tailor antique praises to present persons, a "fit" that sounds neither so natural nor so close as the continuity of bright reflections in Proems I and II. The poem becomes the glass through which the living sovereign's true portrait is somewhat obscurely seen.

The difference in tone and emphasis between Proems II and III might, I suppose, be attributed to an unusually severe onset of the modesty topos or, that failing, to one of Spenser's regrettable catnaps, this time right on the threshold of Book III. But if these dismissals of particular significance were adequate, the lines that directly follow Spenser's apology for "coloured showes" and "antique praises" would positively resonate with his shameful snoring. They refer to the depiction of Queen Elizabeth in Sir Walter Ralegh's *Cynthia:* "But if in liuing colours, and right hew, / Your selfe you couet to see pictured, / Who can it doe more liuely, or more trew . . . ?" When Spenser thus sets the "liuing colours" and "right hew" of his sovereign, Queen Elizabeth, against his own "colourd showes" and "antique praises," he introduces into the poem a far-reaching distinction between life and antiquity, historical present and mythic past, current truth and Faerie image. Spenser himself glosses and simultaneously reinforces the startling phrases "liuing colours" and "right hew" two lines later: *living* colors are "liuely" or lifelike, and the *right* hue is true-to-life or, more simply, "trew."

Referring a true and lively picture of the Queen to Ralegh's *Cynthia,* Spenser is unlikely to have meant a picture that is merely realistic or unembellished by art. Ralegh's fragmentary *Ocean to Cynthia,* much of which relates to Ralegh's imprisonment in 1592, a disgrace subsequent to publication of Book III, is the best indication of *Cynthia*'s nature we have, and while Ralegh's voice in it is distinct, individual, and passionate, such highly artificial modes as the Petrarchan ("Such heat in Ize, such fier in frost") and the pastoral ("Vnfolde thy flockes and leue them to the feilds") are also much in evidence.[5] The nostalgic—indeed, the bereaved—employment of pastoral in *Ocean to Cynthia* suggests that the Shepherd of the Ocean's earlier versions of *Cynthia,* written in less desperate straits, might have been more conventional than less so.[6] When Spenser writes of the living colors and right hue of *Cynthia,* he implies a portrayal that is less hieratic and allegorical but more contemporary and personal than his own. Such a portrayal as Ralegh's might be less universal and more ephemeral, but it belongs more truly to time.

Spenser's reference to Ralegh certainly does not discredit the Faerie image but does limit its authority unless that image itself can be expanded to embrace life more closely. The third proem provides a particularly apt introduction to a book in which time and eternity or present age and ideal image are not so smoothly continuous. Nothing quite like the "heauenly noise / Heard sound through all the Pallace pleasantly" at the betrothal of Una—a noise like the voices of angels "Singing before th'eternall maiesty, / In their trinall triplicities on hye"—reverberates through Book III, and no one quite like the brilliantly winged angel who succors Guyon materializes to rescue its heroes. In fact, the closest we get to an angel in this book is Timias' illusion that Belphoebe is one when he wakens from his swoon to find her ministering to his wounds: "Mercy deare Lord . . . what grace is this," he asks, "To send thine Angell from her bowre of blis, / To comfort me in my distressed plight?" (v. 35). And even he adds on second thought, "Angell, or Goddesse do I call thee

right?" thereby echoing Virgil's famous lines from Aeneas' meeting with Venus in the guise of Diana's maiden and avouching his perception that this angelic illusion originates in a more worldly pantheon than Una's "trinall triplicities."[7]

A blushing Belphoebe disclaims the angelic or godly status Timias imputes to her and declares herself simply a maid and "mortall wight" (36). Unfortunately her declaration is exactly what Timias might have longed, but should never have been allowed, to hear, for he falls irrevocably and irremediably in love with her. Belphoebe not only denies him a reciprocal love but also fails to comprehend or even to recognize the nature of his response to her. More than once the poet criticizes her failure as a "Madnesse" that saves "a part, and lose(s) the whole" (43, cf. 42).

While Timias languishes in love's torments, Belphoebe spares no pains to ease him, but still not comprehending his malady, "that sweet Cordiall, which can restore / A loue-sick hart, she did to him enuy," or refuse to give. Few readers or rereaders of these lines are prepared for those that follow, in which "that sweet Cordiall . . . that soueraigne salue" is suddenly transformed to "That dainty Rose, the daughter of her Morne," whose flower, lapped in "her silken leaues" she shelters from midday sun and northern wind: "But soone as calmed was the Christall aire, / She did it faire dispred, and let to florish faire" (51). As Donald Cheney has suggested, precise equivalents for these lines do not exist. "For her," he adds, "the rose is a rose, not a euphemism."[8]

But surely not just a rose, either. Belphoebe's dainty blossom soon opens into a flower strongly redolent of myth: "Eternall God," we learn, "In Paradize whilome did plant this flowre" and thence fetched it to implant in "earthly flesh." Soon we recognize the flower as the ur-rose that flourishes "In gentle Ladies brest, and bounteous race / Of woman kind" and "beareth fruit of honour and all chast desire" (52). A truly marvelous hybrid, this is none other than the *rosa moralis universalis.* It is hardly surprising that one of Spenser's eighteenth-century editors compared the rose to Milton's "Immortal Amarant" in the third book of *Paradise Lost,* "a flow'r which once / In Paradise, fast by the Tree of Life, / Began to bloom."[9]

In Belphoebe's transformation from uncomprehending nurse to vestal votaress of the rose, to antique origin and a fructifying virtue undifferentiated by time, person, or place, Timias is forgotten. Her specific relation to him will not align with the general moral statement into which it is transformed. Honor and chaste desire, the fruit of the flower, are indeed virtuous, but Timias' love is honorable in Book III, and his desire, if not virginal, is decent and pure and, in these senses, chaste. The general moral statement not only transcends the particular case but wholly misses it. Timias is one person these antique praises of the flower do not fit, and when we consider that Belphoebe's use of tobacco (v. 32) to heal Timias' wounds signals an obvious allusion to Ralegh, we might also think one "present person."

Having glorified the rose, the poet appears in no hurry to return from antique ideal to the person of Belphoebe. He directly addresses the "Faire ympes of beautie" and urges them to emulate their origin by adorning their garlands with "this faire flowre . . . Of chastity and vertue virginall." These "ympes" (shoots, scions) of beauty are preeminently the "Ladies in the Court," to judge both from the poet's present address and its resemblance to the final dedicatory sonnet of *The Faerie Queen*.[10] Timias aside, the poet opts for the general application of the antique ideal to his present world of readers. But with the poet's final promise that the flower will not only embellish the ladies' beauty but also crown them "with heauenly coronall, / Such as the Angels weare before Gods tribunall," we might feel for a moment that we have somehow traveled beyond even Timias' first flush of illusion to a still simpler, purer, less earthly vision (53).

The poet's address to the ladies continues in the next stanza, where he now commends to their attention not the beatifying rose, upon which he has spent the myth-making of the previous stanzas, but Belphoebe herself as true exemplar of its virtue. In effect he returns the rose, but now in its glorified form, to her person. Of particular note in the present stanza are the initial occurrences of the word "faire" and the phrases "none liuing" and "ensample dead," curious phrases whether taken alone, together, or with the "liuing colours and right hew" of the third proem:

> To youre faire selues a faire ensample frame,
> Of this faire virgin, this *Belphoebe* faire,
> To whom in perfect loue, and spotlesse fame
> Of chastitie, none liuing may compaire:
> Ne poysnous Enuy iustly can empaire
> The prayse of her fresh flowring Maidenhead;
> For thy she standeth on the highest staire
> Of th'honorable stage of womanhead,
> That Ladies all may follow her ensample dead.

The repetition of "faire" is insistent, even anxiously so, but it enforces a link between present persons and Belphoebe. This link, if only a matter of rhetoric and fair appearance, suggests a series of steps from the ladies' "faire selues," surely many of whom were bound to marry; to a generalized "ensample" of purity, to its more exclusive, or higher, form, virginity; and finally to the individual fulfillment of virginity in fair Belphoebe herself, who is found on the "highest staire . . . of womanhead."[11] The poet's conception of a series

of steps—that is, a "staire"—becomes additionally significant once we have looked closely at the other verbal oddities in the stanza.[12]

The first of these, the phrase "none liuing," presumably means "none of you ladies" or "no one living," since the poet here addresses his present audience, "youre faire selues," and compares them to Belphoebe, the exemplar of ideal chastity, to which "none liuing" has yet attained. Alternatively, if we take the word "liuing" to be applicable to Belphoebe, the phrase could mean "no other living lady" except Belphoebe herself. This is the meaning of a remarkably similar claim about chaste Florimell earlier in the same canto where her dwarf declares of her, "Liues none this day, that may with her compare / In stedfast chastitie" (v. 8).[13] But there are also significant differences between a claim made by a distraught dwarf within the narrative context of Faerie and one made by the poet himself and addressed to an audience outside the poem. We readily see that the loyal dwarf speaks loosely or hyperbolically. He really means no *other* living lady in all the realm of Faerie is chaster than Florimell or simply that she is the chastest lady imaginable. The word "liuing," however, is not so readily defused in relation to Belphoebe, who mirrors the chastity of the living Queen, especially when it occurs in a direct address to the poet's living audience. If in this context we were to consider Belphoebe "liuing," then she seems actually to become the Queen, a development at variance with statements in the proem to Book III and downright embarrassing when we reach "her ensample dead" in the alexandrine of this stanza. Such a radical dissolution of the fictional character of Belphoebe is entirely unexpected and would probably be largely wasted or, worse, misunderstood.

The natural reading of the phrase "none liuing" is, as suggested, the obvious one, "no one living" or simply "no living lady." While this reading does not refer specifically or directly to the Queen, it increases the distance between Belphoebe as a mythic ideal and any living referent, including the Queen, and thus the distance between antiquity and present age. The increased distance reflects the strains between ideal exemplar and human response in the story of Belphoebe and Timias and helps to bring their story to an appropriate conclusion in 1590.

But if the obvious reading of "none liuing" is also the right one, it is designed to give us another, longer pause for thought when we reread the alexandrine that succeeds it: Belphoebe "standeth on the highest staire . . . of womanhead, / That Ladies all may follow her ensample dead." If Belphoebe is a mythic ideal who has moved farther away from a living referent, what has she to do with death? First she seems to be mythic in this stanza and now to belong to history. The obvious reading of "none liuing" and the alexandrine clearly do not as yet accord.

The phrase "ensample dead," when glossed at all, is taken to be an ellipsis of the clause "when she is dead,"[14] and it can be referred to the occurrence of a parallel construction in Merlin's prophecy to Britomart of the child or "Image" Artegall will leave with her when he is dead (III.iii.29):

> With thee yet shall he leaue for memory
> Of his late puissaunce, his Image dead,
> That liuing him in all actiuity
> To thee shall represent.

But the phrase "ensample dead" could just as well mean "her dead, or lifeless, example." At first glance, before we are startled into reassessment, this is exactly what it seems to mean, and if this were in fact all it meant, it would serve as a chilling comment on the ideal Belphoebe embodies and, although at a distinctly greater remove than before, on that of the Queen as well. This alternative meaning of "ensample dead" also finds a relevant parallel in an alexandrine of Book III. It occurs when the witch creates false Florimell, that parody of coldly sterile, lifeless Petrarchism: "and in the stead / Of life, she put a Spright to rule the carkasse dead" (viii.7). Death is this carcass' present condition (dead carcass), not its future one (when dead).

The occurrence in a single stanza of two verbal cruxes as immediately and obviously related as life ("none liuing") and death ("ensample dead") is unlikely to be adventitious. The reading "dead example"—the more obvious reading of "ensample dead"—accords better with the more obvious reading of "none liuing," since it does not require, as does the alternative "when she is dead," an abrupt and irrational shift from mythic to historical reference and, to put it bluntly, from an ageless Belphoebe to an aging Elizabeth. There is no way for us to cancel the obvious reading of "ensample dead," but perhaps we need not stop with its dispiriting message. In the context of Timias' highly Petrarchan adoration and idealization of Belphoebe, the alternative reading, "ensample [when she is] dead," need not refer to death as an exclusively physical event. It can also be taken in a way that makes sense of the mythic Belphoebe's connection with death and offers the positive reflection on her ideal that balances, though it cannot wholly offset, the negative one.

In its Petrarchan context, the reading "when she is dead" points to the resolution of the conflict between body and spirit that comes with the lady's physical death and spiritual transcendence. The phrase "ensample dead" therefore implies the ideal, the life-in-death, that the deadly carcass, the death-in-life, of false Florimell parodies. This reading of the phrase balances the cold reality of human loss—death, denial, lifeless

example—with high praise of Belphoebe and of the Queen whose chastity, if only dimly, she still mirrors. At the same time, it continues Belphoebe's movement away from an earthly reality and suggests the only possible solution of Timias' dilemma—and seemingly the destined conclusion of Ralegh's—to be the symbolic or actual transfiguration of Belphoebe into pure spirit.[15]

Looking back at the same stanza with our Petrarchan reading in mind, we might be struck anew by the phrases "perfect loue" and "spotlesse fame." It suddenly makes more sense that "none liuing" should be perfect or spotless in Book III, where the possibility of a living Una has receded like a setting sun, and that the "highest staire . . . of womanhead" should be reached with the lady's transformation through death into spirit. Presumably this is also the "staire" on which worthy emulators of the true rose are crowned "with heauenly coronall . . . before Gods tribunall."

It is even tempting to see a relation between the Petrarchan praise of fair Belphoebe in Book III and the first of Ralegh's commendatory sonnets to accompany *The Faerie Queene:*

> Me thought I saw the graue, where *Laura* lay
> Within that Temple, where the vestall flame
> Was wont to burne, and passing by that way,
> To see that buried dust of liuing fame,
> Whose tombe faire loue, and fairer vertue
>   kept,
> All suddenly I saw the Faery Queene:
> At whose approach the soule of *Petrarke*
>   wept,
> And from thenceforth those graces were not
>   seene.
> For they this Queene attended, in whose steed
> Obliuion laid him downe on *Lauras* herse.

But there is also a significant distance between this vision of Laura's living successor and Spenser's fully idealized Belphoebe, whose rose opens fully only in death. Perhaps because farther removed from it personally, Spenser saw more clearly the temporal, human cost—to Belphoebe and Timias both—of the fully realized Petrarchan vision. By the writing of Book III, he certainly knew that in time Laura's tomb could only be replaced by another's "ensample dead."[16]

II

When Belphoebe is last seen in Book III, response to her is poised between timeless and temporal truth, rather than being torn apart by their conflict. In Book IV, Belphoebe's next and also her last appearance, this duality of response to her remains, but with a difference. Her estrangement from Timias intersects with his relation to Amoret, Belphoebe's twin sister; and

Belphoebe's reconciliation with Timias clashes conspicuously with the abandonment and slander of Amoret. With Timias' reconciliation and Amoret's revilement, duality of judgment and of truth can no longer be contained in a single phrase or image or even in a single character or event. Belphoebe herself—or what she was in Book III, an ideal maintaining some relation to worldly reality—is fractured. The alternatives of love and loss, of timeless and temporal truth, are no longer grasped together, no longer simultaneous and complementary dimensions of awareness, as they were in the phrase "ensample dead." They have become sharply distinct and are in danger of becoming mutually exclusive. The distance between ideal image and present age, antique praises and living colors, is widening rapidly.

The story of Belphoebe and Timias is inseparable from the last stages of Amoret's story in Book IV. Wounded and then tended by Timias, Amoret becomes the unwitting cause of Belphoebe's estrangement from him. She is part of their story, and when she is simply abandoned by them in the middle of it, she becomes, both narratively and morally, a loose end waiting to be woven into the larger design. Amoret's ties with the story of Belphoebe and Timias are also symbolic and thematic. The ruby that helps to bring Belphoebe back to Timias is "Shap'd like a heart, yet bleeding of the wound, / And with a little golden chaine about it bound" (viii.6). A jeweler's replica of Amoret's heart in the Masque of Cupid, this lapidarian heart that Belphoebe once gave Timias alludes to Amoret's real one, suggesting contrast with, as well as resemblance to, it. The twin birth of Belphoebe and Amoret, the complementary maids of Diana and Venus, provides a richly allegorical backdrop to their aborted reunion, and although Amoret is much more complexly human than an abstract conception of Love or Amor, the latter is one kind of meaning she carries when she is wounded, then abandoned, and later reviled. The most provocative imitation of Amoret's thematic congruence with Belphoebe comes when the poet interrupts his narrative during Slander's revilement of Amoret to recall an Edenic age when the "glorious flowre" of beauty flourished, a time when " . . . antique age yet in the infancie / Of time, did liue then like an innocent, / In simple truth and blamelesse chastitie" (IV.viii.30). Antiquity, ideal image, mythic flower, even chastityCthe poet associates them all now with Amoret or, more accurately, with her revilement.

In addition to the connections between the stories of Amoret and of Belphoebe and Timias sketched above, there are pointed contrasts. The reconciliation of Belphoebe and Timias is extremely artificial, effected through the agency of a sympathetic turtle dove and a lapidary's heart and totally removed from temporal reality. When he is reconciled, Timias' condition anticipates Melibee's self-enclosed vulnerability: he is

"Fearlesse of fortunes chaunge or enuies dread, / And eke all mindlesse of his owne deare Lord" (viii.18). Still more noticeable, even while the estrangement of Belphoebe from Timias alludes unmistakably to Ralegh's fall from queenly favor, their reconciliation in Book IV conflicts with the real state of Ralegh's affairs in 1596.[17] After Ralegh's secret marriage to Elizabeth Throckmorton, one of the Queen's maids of honor, and the consequent imprisonment of them both in 1592, he was, although released fairly quickly from prison, not in fact reconciled to the Queen until 1597. His wife, left to languish in prison longer than he, never returned to favor with the Queen. In the reconciliation of Timias and Belphoebe, artificial thus means twice unreal—unreal at once in manner and in reference.

The abandonment of Amoret contrasts sharply with the artifice of reconciliation. When Arthur finds her in the forest, she is "almost dead and desperate," ingloriously wounded and unromantically in need. In his effort to shelter Amoret (and her less vulnerable companion, Aemylia), Arthur unwittingly takes her to the House of Slander, a foul old woman "stuft with rancour and despight / Vp to the throat" (24). Once they are within her house, an indignant and somewhat bitter poet intrudes at length in the narrative to connect Slander to the present age ("Sith now of dayes") and to oppose this age to the ideal or antique image. Slander's railings therefore have a general historicity or timeliness pointedly attributed to them for which Amoret's own adventures—apart from the topicality of her relation to Timias' estrangement from Belphoebe—fail to account. In short, what befalls Amoret in the two cantos she shares with Belphoebe and Timias looks very much like the other half of their story, the half muted in Belphoebe's withdrawal from Timias and suppressed in her return to him. What befalls Amoret unfolds the "inburning wrath" of Belphoebe (viii.17) and gives tongue to the revilement and infamy that Ralegh's secret marriage incurred.

Writing presumably in 1592 from the Tower, Ralegh contrasted the Queen's formerly gracious favor to him with his present state:

> Thos streames seeme standinge puddells
>   which, before,
> Wee saw our bewties in, so weare they cleere.
> Bellphebes course is now obserude no more,
> That faire resemblance weareth out of date.
> Our Ocean seas are but tempestius waves
> And all things base that blessed wear of late.
>   [ll. 269-74]

If we remember Spenser's final vision of Belphoebe in 1590, with its series of "faire" steps from living audience to the highest ideal, these words from *Ocean to Cynthia* have an added edge. But even without this refinement, they afford a commentary on the distance we have seen opening between living Queen and ideal image, in this case, Belphoebe: as the imprisoned Ralegh again observes of this distance, "A Queen shee was to mee, no more Belphebe, / A Lion then, no more a milke white Dove" (ll. 327-28). The extreme artificiality of the reconciliation of Belphoebe and Timias in Book IV bears a similar testimony. As the distance widens, as an ideal Belphoebe becomes further detached from living reference, other kinds of references to the present age build up and push intrusively into Faerie. Their violence and their ugliness, unparalleled by the more controlled images of evil in Books I, II, and even III, do not just threaten the Faerie vision but actually violate it.

The old hag who reviles Amoret, her companion, and her would-be rescuer is nothing short of hideous, as extreme in her violent ugliness as conciliatory dove and ruby-heart are in their artificiality. The poet seems almost unable to put a stop to his description of her. "A foule and loathly creature" with "filthy lockes," she sits in her house "Gnawing her nayles for felnesse and for yre, / And there out sucking venime to her parts entyre" (23-24). The description continues for another two stanzas with a reiterative emphasis and expansiveness that partial quotation hardly conveys. She abuses all goodness, frames causeless crimes, steals away good names. Nothing can be done so well "aliue"—that is, in life—without her depriving it of "due praise." As the poet continues, castigating the verbal poison Slander spues forth from her hellish inner parts, she becomes an unmistakable precursor first of Detraction and then of that poet's nightmare, the Blatant Beast, "For like the strings of Aspes, that kill with smart, / Her spightfull words did pricke, and wound the inner part."[18]

"Such was that Hag," the poet concludes, "vnmeet to host such guests, / Whom greatest Princes court would welcome fayne" (27). Then, just before the poet in his own voice breaks into the narrative for five stanzas to decry the distance between antique age and present corruption, he praises the patience of Slander's "guests," who endure every insult she can offer, "And vnto rest themselues all onely lent, / Regardlesse of that queane so base and vilde, / To be vniustly blamd, and bitterly reuilde" (IV.viii.28). *Quean,* meaning "harlot," "hussy," or in Spenser's case, "hag," is not the same word as *queen,* and it should be obvious from the poet's virulent description of Slander that she is not an image of the Virgin Queen.[19] But the word "queane" in this context is not disposed of so easily, nor is the possibility that for one awful moment the image of the bitter old woman glances at the living Queen.

Philologists have been reluctant to recognize the likelihood of the homonymic pun on *quean/queen* in Renaissance English that exists in modern English. Kök-eritz notes that contemporary philological evidence proves the possibility of such a pun in colloquial speech but doubts that polite speakers would have found the pun readily accessible. Dobson likewise notes the distinction in pronunciation of the two vowels in educated southern speech but allows for vulgar or dialectical variations in which the pun would exist.[20] The pun is therefore possible but unlikely or inappropriate in a polite context, an argument that might, indeed, recommend it on grounds of aesthetic decorum—not to say political prudence—for the impassioned description of an impolite hag. The historical imagination is hard pressed to picture a courtier who would be likely to explain such a pun to the Queen or even willing to admit recognition of its presence.

Admitting the pun in Spenser's use of *quean,* we might regard it as one of the many signs in Book IV that the poem is becoming more private and personal, but we can do so without having to argue that the pun or at the very least the possibility of wordplay would not have been recognized by a number of Spenser's readers. Wordplay on the combination *quean/queen* has a long history, in part because of its alliterative potential, as, for example, in Langland's lines, "At churche in the charnel cheorles aren vuel to knowe, / Other a knyght fro a knaue, other a queyne fro a queene."[21] In passing, I should also note that in an age of printing like the Renaissance the spelling of *quean*—"queen" and "queyn" in Thynne's Chaucer—was a visual invitation to wordplay, which philology would be inclined to discount.[22] Whatever its causes, the pun on *quean/ queen* almost certainly exists in Shakespeare's *Antony and Cleopatra* when Enobarbus quips that Apollodorus has carried "A certaine Queene to *Caesar* in a Matris" (II.vi.72).[23] The same pun also occurs in Middleton's *A Trick to Catch the Old One* when Witt-Good disclaims youth's follies, including "sinful Riotts, / Queanes Evills, Doctors diets" (V.ii.185-86). The evils of queans are venereal, but highly qualified readers agree that the pun on *quean/queen* and the consequent play on *king's evil* (scrofula) is present here.[24] Contemporary dramatic use of a pun argues its accessibility to auditors, and a play on diseases dependent on the pun urges this fact.

To my mind, the most illuminating information about Spenser's calling Slander a "queane" is that this is his sole use of the word. Occasion, Duessa, Impatience, Impotence, the witch who creates false Florimell—not a one of these hags wears this common Renaissance label, and we might almost suppose that Spenser was deliberately avoiding it. That he should suddenly have used the word "queane" accidentally or innocently in a context inseparable from Belphoebe, Timias, and the relation of Faerie ideal to present age defies credibility, and does so much more, in view of Spenser's verbal sensitivity, than does the possibility that he alludes momentarily to the Queen.

As with Belphoebe's rose in Book III, there are now no precise or steady equivalents for the figures gathered in Slander's House: Amoret does not equal Elizabeth Throckmorton, Arthur does not equal Ralegh, Aemylia does not equal anybody, and Slander certainly does not equal the Queen.[25] In the moments and ways I have suggested, however, what happens to Amoret reflects on one level the scandal, wrath, and disgrace Ralegh's marriage unleashed, and briefly the poet holds up to his sovereign the kind of distorted reflection found in a hideous cartoon. The figures of Lucifera, Philotime, and false Florimell bear witness that such a distorted image—such parody—is not entirely alien to the poet's techniques in earlier books, but it recurs here with a difference. Lucifera is not a missing side of Una or of the Queen but a denial of what they truly are. Where she is a possible threat, Slander is a present reality.[26] Complex yet still balanced and grasped together in Book III, contrasting violently and centrifugally in Book IV, opposite words, opposite meanings, and opposite realities figure crucially in the troubled process of reassessing the relation of the Faerie vision to the living Queen.

Notes

[1] *The Faerie Queene* I.xxi.8, 23; iv.8, II.vii.44-45. All Spenserian references are to *Works: A Variorum Edition,* ed. Edwin A. Greenlaw et al., 11 vols. (Baltimore: Johns Hopkins University Press, 1932-57), cited hereafter as *Var.*

[2] *Henry IV* I.iii.201-02, V.i.131, ed. Herschel Baker, in *The Riverside Shakespeare* (Boston: Houghton Mifflin, 1974).

[3] Long since, in an illuminating and liberating article, Louis Martz showed that Spenser was not unaware of comic nuances in his sonnets: "The *Amoretti*: 'Most Goodly Temperature,'" in *Form and Convention in the Poetry of Edmund Spenser,* ed. William Nelson (New York: Columbia University Press, 1961), pp. 146-68. We continue to make progress regarding the poet's control of his meaning elsewhere, but slowly sometimes.

[4] This paragraph borrows from my "What comes after Chaucer's *BUT:* Adversative Constructions in Spenser," in *Acts of Interpretation: The Text in Its Context,* ed. Mary J. Carruthers and Elizabeth D. Kirk (Norman Okla.: Pilgrim Books, 1982), n. 6.

[5] "The 11th: and last booke of the Ocean to Scinthia," ll. 69, 497 ff., cf. 29-30, *The Poems of Sir Walter Ralegh,* ed. Agnes M. C. Latham (London: Routledge & Kegan Paul, 1951). All references to *Ocean to Cynthia* are to this edition. On the dating of *Cynthia,* see Latham's introduction, pp. Xxxvi-xl; and Stephen J. Greenblatt, *Sir Walter Ralegh: The Renaissance Man*

and His Roles (New Haven: Yale University Press, 1973), pp. 12-13.

[6] In "Colin Clovts Come Home Againe," Spenser calls Ralegh "shepheard of the Ocean" (l. 66); see also ll. 164, 174-75 in connection with the dating of *Cynthia.* On possible earlier versions of *Cynthia,* see Agnes M. C. Latham, ed., *Sir Walter Raleigh: Selected Prose and Poetry* (London: Athlone Press, 1965), p. 25, and on the style of *Cynthia,* pp. 210-11. Greenblatt's discussion of *Cynthia* is invaluable (pp. 77-98); his remarks on pastoral are especially pertinent (pp. 80, 84-85).

[7] See *Var.,* 3:245-46 (xxvii ff.), but also 3:247 (xxxv). The Virgilian text is available in *Var.,* 2:219 (xxxii.6-xxxiii.4): "O—quam te memorem, virgo? Namque haud tibi vultus / Mortalis, nec vox hominem sonat; O, dea, certe." Given Spenser's earlier association of this passage with Belphoebe (II.iii.33), its bearing on Timias' lines is unmistakable.

[8] *Spenser's Image of Nature: Wild Man and Shepherd in "The Faerie Queene"* (New Haven: Yale University Press, 1966), p. 102.

[9] *Var.,* 3:248 (lii). The reference is to Ralph Church's edition, 1758.

[10] *Var.,* 3:198. The full title of the final sonnet is "To all the gratious and beautifull Ladies in the Court."

[11] Cf. *Faerie Queene* III.v.53: "Of chastity and vertue virginall." Chastity and virginity are not identical in this line.

[12] *OED,* s.v. *Stair sb,* 1: "An ascending series . . . of steps"; 2: "One of a succession of steps"; 2d. *fig:* "A step of degree in a (metaphorical) ascent or in a scale of dignity"; 2e: "A high position."

[13] A. C. Hamilton, ed., *The Faerie Queene* (London: Longman, 1977), p. 354, aligns this claim about Florimell with that about Belphoebe.

[14] Hamilton, ed., *The Faerie Queene,* p. 354. Hamilton's sensitivity to the need of a gloss is notable.

[15] Cf. Louis Adrian Montrose's highly provocative analysis of Petrarchan sublimation in "'The perfecte paterne of a Poete': The Poetics of Courtship in *The Shepheardes Calender,*" *TSLL* 21 (1979), 34-67, esp. p. 54 (November Eclogue: Dido/Elissa).

[16] In *Mirror and Veil: The Historical Dimension of Spenser's "Faerie Queene"* (Chapel Hill: University of North Carolina Press, 1977), pp. 113-14, Michael O'Connell rightly locates a "sense of paradox" in the final stanza of III.v, the result especially of the word

"Nathlesse." Although I do not agree with all of O'Connell's views on p. 114, this sense of paradox follows naturally from my own reading of the penultimate stanza ("ensample dead") and fittingly concludes the canto.

[17] See O'Connell, *Mirror and Veil,* p. 116; and A. L. Rowse, *Ralegh and the Throckmortons* (London: Macmillan, 1962), pp. 164, 204-06.

[18] Cf. *Faerie Queene* V.xii.36, VI.vi.1.

[19] *OED,* s.v. *Quean,* 1; s.v. *Queen* (etymology): *quean* and *queen* have an ablaut-relationship. Thomas P. Roche, Jr., ed., *The Faerie Queene* (Harmondsworth, Middlesex: Penguin, 1978), p. 1176, glosses *quean* as *hag.* This meaning seems obvious from several examples in the *OED* and is the most appropriate one for Spenser's context.

[20] Helge Kökeritz, *Shakespeare's Pronunciation* (New Haven: Yale University Press, 1960), p. 88; E. J. Dobson, *English Pronunciation 1500-1700* (Oxford: Oxford University Press, Clarendon Press, 1968), 2:640, 612, n. 2.

[21] *The Vision of William concerning Piers the Plowman in Three Parallel Texts,* ed. Walter W. Skeat (London: Oxford University Press, 1886), C.IX.45-46 (my punctuation). For a concise discussion of Langland's "punning" on quean/queen and its basis in Old English, see Mary Carruthers, *The Search for St. Truth: A Study of Meaning in "Piers Plowman"* (Evanston: Northwestern University Press, 1973), pp. 60-61, n. 19. Carruthers discusses a second instance of wordplay in Langland's line "*bere* nis no quen queyn*tere bat* quyk is o lyue" (A.II.14: George Kane, ed.).

[22] Chaucer, *Works 1532,* supplemented by material from the editions of 1542, 1561, 1598, and 1602 (London: Scolar Press, 1969), fol. 104, verso, Manciples Prologue, l. 34; fol. 165, verso, column a, l. 19.

[23] From the Norton facsimile of the First Folio.

[24] Quotation from Middleton is from Charles Barber's edition (Berkeley: University of California Press, 1968); Barber considers the play on *king's evil* "doubtless." For the same view, see James T. Henke, *Renaissance Dramatic Bawdy (Exclusive of Shakespeare): An Annotated Glossary and Critical Essays, Jacobean Drama Studies,* 39 (Salzburg: Institut für Englische und Literatur Universität Salzburg, 1974), 2:249.

[25] On the presence of Aemylia and other levels of meaning in IV.viii, see my "Whatever Happened to Amoret? The Poet's Role in Book IV of *The Faerie Queene,*" *Criticism* 13 (1971), 180-200, esp. 181-85.

[26] Near the end of the poet's praise of antiquity and denunciation of the present, he first appears to compliment the Queen but does not in fact do so. Instead he speaks with an evasive ambiguity that is to become increasingly characteristic of his compliments to her and, it would appear, of his disillusionment with her. In xxxii.8, "her glorious flowre" is beauty's (l. 1). In xxxiii.5, the word "her," while ambiguous, logically refers to beauty's glorious flower in l. 6 (chastity, to judge from Book III); from this flower proceed the "drops" or dew or nectar of virtue. The near, but failed, reference of the pronouns in these stanzas to the living Queen is further testimony of the distance between her and the ideal image.

Nicholas Canny (essay date 1983)

SOURCE: "Edmund Spenser and the Development of an Anglo-Irish Identity," in *The Yearbook of English Studies: Colonial Imperial Themes,* Special Number, Vol. 13, 1983, pp. 1-19.

[*In the following essay Canny argues for the value of Spenser's* View of the Present State of Ireland *as a contribution to the political theory of colonization and the history of Ireland.*]

Spenser's *View of the Present State of Ireland,* composed in 1596, has long been accepted as a fundamental contribution to the theory of colonization, but it has not been adequately appreciated as a political text because commentators have at once exaggerated and diminished its originality.[1] The exaggeration has happened because scholars have contended that Spenser's opinions were altogether more advanced than those held by any of his contemporaries in Ireland, and the diminution has resulted from the attribution of these advanced opinions to the influence of Machiavelli, Montaigne, Bodin, and, most recently, of Calvin.[2] It is argued in this paper that neither exaggeration nor diminution is warranted; both tendencies can be accounted for by the application of that approach to intellectual history whereby the scholar who proceeds from the assumption that all ideas can be traced to a fundamental thinker sets himself the task of identifying the influence exerted by one of these great progenitors upon his chosen author. This method has frequently been challenged, and the most convincing alternative approach to the study of intellectual history has been well demonstrated in Quentin Skinner's *Foundations of Modern Political Thought.*[3] Here Skinner proceeds from the assumption that all political theorists are acquainted with a broad range of ideas, and that it is the force of circumstances which compels each author to select from those available to him that body of ideas which provides him with a sense of purpose and direction. Thus, as Skinner sees it, the intellectual historian should continue the effort to trace influences, but should also seek to relate each text to the context in which it was produced, with a view to explaining the author's process of selection.[4]

When Spenser's *View* is analysed in this fashion it immediately becomes evident that it was a tract designed to serve the interests of those engaged upon the conquest and colonization of Ireland at the end of the sixteenth century, and that the advanced opinion to be found there can be explained by the peculiar, not to say precarious, circumstances in which these individuals found themselves. Furthermore it becomes evident that the ideas expressed there were the product of a conscious process of selection and rejection by the author, and a glance at the letters and political texts composed by Spenser's English contemporaries in Ireland shows that they resorted to similar ideas in response to the challenges that confronted them. This last observation deprives Spenser of any claims to uniqueness, but his is still the most elegant and coherent expression of that particular set of ideas which those engaged upon the conquest of Ireland found particularly useful during the final decades of the sixteenth century. But, as will be argued, these ideas were considered relevant not only by Spenser and his contemporaries but by successive generations of English settlers in Ireland, at least until the end of the seventeenth century. These had resort to Spenser's ideas (and they even referred to and imitated his *View*) with such frequency that we can accept the ideas enunciated by him as having provided them with an identity and sense of moral purpose which sustained them throughout the travails of the seventeenth century.

When placed under scrutiny it appears that Spenser's *View* comprises three separate but related sections. The central section (pp. 37-95), devoted to describing the barbaric condition of the Gaelic Irish, has little by way of description that was not to be found in literally scores of compositions by English or Old English authors from the time of Giraldus Cambrensis forward. In delineating a series of stages of social development, and in situating the Irish (with their supposed progenitors the Scythians) at the least developed stage, Spenser was advancing a notion that had become a commonplace among those engaged upon the conquest of Ireland for the previous thirty years.[5] Of more recent adoption among English settlers in Ireland was the contention that most of the Old English population had degenerated from their original placing of about midway on the scale of social development to a position so lowly as to allow the conclusion that 'the chiefest abuses which are now in that realm are grown from the English, and the English that were are now much more lawless and licentious than the very wild Irish' (*View*, p. 63, and see p. 151).

In making this assertion Spenser was clearly attempting the denigration of that element of the population of Ireland which had most influence with the queen and her government in England. That he should seek to do so is consistent with his concern in the first section of the book to discredit the policy favoured by the Old English for the reform of their Gaelic neighbours. But while dismissing the Old English as unfit to undertake any work of reform, Spenser also declared as hopeless the reform strategy they favoured, because it failed to take cognizance of the cardinal assumption around which the *View* was organized: that man's social condition is determined by his environment (p. 68, and see pp. 151-53). To seek the uplift of a socially backward or a degenerate population without first destroying those environmental factors which imprisoned it in its backwardness was, in Spenser's opinion, a futile exercise, and was more likely to occasion revolt than to promote social accommodation (pp. 94-95).

Lest any should miss the drift of his argument, Spenser devoted the lengthy first section of his work (pp. 1-37) to demonstrating the specific shortcomings of the Old English reform strategy, and he returned repeatedly to these points throughout his discourse. By sponsoring the regnal act of 1541 and by encouraging the government to engage in compacts with Gaelic chieftains, the Old English members of that parliament had 'instead of so great and meritorious a service as they boast they performed to the king in bringing all the Irish to acknowledge him for their liege, [done] great hurt unto his title and [had] left a perpetual gall in the mind of that people' (p.9). This dramatic rejection of developments in which the Old English took pride, and which a recent historian has elevated to the plane of a constitutional revolution,[6] was justified by Spenser's assertion that Henry VIII had inherited from his predecessor clear title to all of Ireland by the right of conquest, and that the recognition of this fact had made the Irish population 'bound to his obedience'. Now that this reality had been cast in doubt by the act of kingship, and now that the government had sought to win by persuasion the allegiance of the Gaelic chiefs, it was being suggested to them that they were bound to the English crown 'but with terms' where previously they recognized that 'their lives, their lands, and their liberties were in his free power to appoint what tenures, what laws, what conditions he would over them, against which there could be no rightful resistance; or if there were, he might when he would establish them with a stronger hand' (pp. 9-10).

The extension of the English common law to the entire population of Ireland which followed upon the events of 1541 had, in Spenser's opinion, inflicted a further hurt upon the king's interests because it enabled those who bore no respect for the common law to exploit its safeguards to serve their own advantage. Several instances of how such exploitation could occur were cited by Spenser, and almost all of these related to trial by jury. This system, which could operate successfully in

England, was totally unsuited to Irish conditions where people considered themselves bound in conscience more by the will of their lord than by their oaths. Under such circumstances, Spenser averred, the Irish had no scruples over presenting false evidence or returning unfair verdicts when this served their own or their master's ends. As a consequence, Spenser claimed, grave injustice was being inflicted alike upon the crown and upon English settlers in Ireland, and these examples supported Spenser's more sweeping contentions that each system of law was appropriate only for that society which produced it, and that injustice would invariably result from any attempt to transfer law from one society to another 'according to the simple rule of right' (pp. 10-11, 21-31).

Having thus disposed of the Old English reform strategy, and having dismissed the Old English as potential reformers, the way was clear for Spenser in the third section of his work (pp. 91-170) to advance his own proposals. Like the Old English, Spenser stressed that the Irish were amenable to reform, but having rejected the notion that the English common law might be applied to them to achieve their regeneration he set himself to describe how it was possible 'to apply the people and fit them to the laws' (pp. 141-42).

The programme outlined by Spenser involved the pursuit of five sequential processes before the Irish population would attain a level of social development sufficiently advanced to enable them to derive benefit from the English commom law, the application of which would thereafter prevent them from relapsing to their former condition. The first process, lasting for about eighteen months, was the military one, whereby the English government would provide a force of 10,000 foot and 1,000 horse which would move against the principal seats of rebellion in the country (p. 98). It was recommended that the rebel leaders should be given an opportunity to submit, but that no quarter should be given in the event of their rejecting this overture for unconditional surrender. Those remaining in arms would be those who would 'never be made dutiful and obedient, nor brought to labour or civil conversation', and Spenser had no scruple about recommending the summary execution of those who were so addicted to 'a licentious life' that there was 'no hope of their amendment or recovery'. Having said this, he expressed himself satisfied that the amount of blood-letting would be negligible, and he predicted, on the basis of his experience in Munster, that far more people would die as a consequence of the famine which would result from the persistence of the rebel leaders with a hopeless struggle. Spenser considered this the most unfortunate aspect of his programme, and he was clearly moved to pity by the terrible scenes of starvation which he had witnessed during the previous war in Munster, and which he graphically described (p. 104).

But in describing this episode Spenser defended the actions of Lord Grey de Wilton, who had been accused by his enemies of being 'a bloody man' who regarded the lives of the queen's Irish subjects 'no more than dogs'. During that war, Spenser professed, 'there perished not many by the sword', and even then it was 'the necessity of that present state of things [which] enforced him to that violence'. Since the greatest loss of life among the Irish had been effected 'by the extremity of famine, which they themselves had wrought', Spenser found little difficulty in citing Grey's military endeavours as an example of the campaign that he envisaged for all of Ireland (pp. 104-06).

In doing so, however, Spenser indicated how the beneficial consequences of Grey's actions had been defeated because the queen had hearkened to those who criticized his actions, with the result that

> the noble lord eftsoons was blamed, the wretched people pitied and new counsels plotted in which it was concluded that a general pardon should be sent over to all that would accept of it; upon which all former purposes were blanked, the governor at a bay, and not only all that great and long charge which she had before been at quite lost and cancelled, but also all that hope of good which was even at the door put back and clean frustrate. (p. 106)

Thus, as Spenser saw it, there was no point in the government undertaking the war against the crown's rebels in Ireland unless there was a firm determination to proceed to the second process, which involved placing the subdued country under military control and introducing English settlers to the confiscated lands of the erstwhile rebels (pp. 125-29).

The purpose behind the second process was to substitute a new focus of power and authority for the lords whose tyrannical rule was held responsible for corrupting the environment in which the Irish population lived. Existing septs and kinship groups were to be dissolved, and the Irish population was to be resettled on seignories, or in towns to be situated close to the proposed fortifications. There they were to be intermingled with English settlers who would instruct them in the ways of civil living and acquaint them with manufacturing skills and advanced agricultural methods. In this way an apparently military arrangement could become a first step towards the erection of 'that perfect establishment and new commonwealth' (p. 121) which Spenser envisaged for Ireland.

Once organized within this new framework, Spenser recommended that each Irishman should be sworn to the crown, and become a pledge for the loyalty of his neighbours. All would be obliged to pay a composition rent to the crown, which would meet the cost of maintaining soldiers in the country, and each province should be subject to a president and council who would have responsibility for the maintenance of civil order. The people, organized in hundreds, would be required to 'assemble themselves once every year with their pledges, and to present themselves before the justices of the peace which shall be thereunto appointed to be surveyed and numbered'. The purpose of these annual surveys was to detect any defectors from the new dispensation, and to ensure that every individual would have a surname peculiar to himself, as well as 'a certain trade of life'. By thus promoting individualism and self-sufficiency, and by insisting that English people be intermingled with the Irish population, it was hoped that the Irishman would 'not only not depend upon the head of [his] sept as now they do but also [would] in short time learn quite to forget his Irish nation'. This, it was believed, would bring the Irish to identify with their English superiors, thus effecting 'an union of manners and conformity of minds, to bring them to be one people'.[7]

Idleness was to be prohibited within this new arrangement, and those who had hitherto led an idle life, or who had concentrated on pastoral farming, were to devote themselves to intensive farming or be cut off by martial law. This stage of the reform process would thus open the way for the proper development and exploitation of Ireland's natural resources, and it was required that the first generation of Irishmen born into this new condition would be instructed at school

> in grammar and in the principles of sciences . . . whereby they will in short time grow up to that civil conversation that both the children will loathe the former rudeness in which they were bred, and also their parents will, even by the ensample of their young children, perceive the foulness of their own brutish behaviour compared to theirs, for learning hath that wonderful power of itself that it can soften and temper the most stern and savage nature.[8]

Once this stage had been attained the way was open for the missionary endeavour if 'some discreet ministers of their countrymen' who 'by their mild persuasions and instructions as also by their sober life and conversation, may draw them first to understand and afterwards to embrace the doctrine of their salvation' (p. 161). Finally it was conceded that upon the successful completion of this missionary endeavour the Irish population would have been sufficiently advanced to appreciate and derive full benefit from the operation of the English common law.

The novelty of the proposals being advanced by Spenser becomes apparent when we compare them with the issues that concerned political theorists in contemporary England. Like Spenser, they considered reform to

be a worthy objective of government, but their principal concern in advocating reform was to uphold the status quo by forestalling social dislocation.[9] Spenser on the other hand was dismissing the social order that he had witnessed in Ireland as unacceptable, and was providing a formula for its overthrow and for the erection of a new social order to replace it. In doing so Spenser was recommending innovation as a desirable end, and he cited necessity as a justifiable pretext for employing questionable means to the attainment of that end. This strictly secular approach, which bears striking resemblance to Machiavellian thought, was provided with a humane appearance by Spenser's insistence that the employment of the sword as an instrument of reform was altogether less destructive of human life than its alternative, the halter.[10] Spenser also reiterated his claim that his objective was an essentially humanistic one, and his juxtaposing the barbarism of Ireland with the civility of England suggested that it was also a Christian objective. By thus focusing attention on the desirability of the ends which were held in prospect, he hoped to divert attention from any doubts that might be fostered over his citing necessity as a justification for action. Then, for the benefit of those whose faintheartedness derived from concern over the costs involved, Spenser laid emphasis on the material benefits which would accrue to England, no less than to Ireland, from the implementation of his programme.

The advanced character of the ideas enunciated by Spenser will be evident from this analysis, but it will now be shown that these ideas were commonplace among Spenser's English contemporaries in Ireland and that it was the circumstances in which they found themselves which forced them to adopt ideas which, initially at least, they did not find particularly congenial.

Almost every English-born author writing of Ireland during the 1580s and 1590s was insistent upon the development of a clearly-defined radical programme of reform which would involve the erection of a completely new commonwealth upon firm foundations. Most, like Spenser, had resort to surgical or horticultural metaphors, but one original spirit likened Ireland to an old cloak which had been patched and mended so frequently that it would bear with no further repair and required replacement.[11] This insistence upon novelty implied a rejection of the conciliatory measures favoured by the Old English in Ireland, but many writers went beyond implications to launch an open attack upon the Old English and to question their very civility. These were most vulnerable to attack on account of their lack of enthusiasm for the established church, but Barnaby Rich, who had been berating the Old English for this ever since the 1560s, was (and saw himself to be) an isolated figure among the New English in Ireland.[12] Then suddenly, in the 1580s, accusations such as Rich had always been associated with became a standard ingredient in the letters and tracts of the New English. The most strident critic of the Old English, against whom Barnaby Rich sounds moderate and tolerant, was Andrew Trollope, who composed two lengthy tracts on Ireland during the late 1580s.[13] In the first of these he proved himself the most negative critic of the Gaelic Irish population, and his lurid description of their barbarism led him to the conclusion that they were not 'thrifty and civil or human creatures, but heathen or rather savage and brute beasts' (f. 97ʳ). When launching on this description Trollope excluded, in conventional fashion, the residents of 'the walled towns' from his blanket condemnation of the Irish, but their exclusion was ignored as he proceeded, as when he remarked of the Old English that 'when they might get opportunity [they] spared not the committing of any kind of treason or mischief and manifested themselves to burning hatred and malice against all the English nation'. Support for this charge was provided by reference to an onslaught made by a mob in Waterford ('one of the civilest towns in Ireland') upon the wife of Sir William Drury, and to the popular expectation in Dublin that 'the throats of all the English nation had been cut at one instant' (ff. 98ᵛ-99ʳ).

Incidents such as these were sufficient to satisfy Trollope that the outward appearance of civility presented by the Old English lawyers was no more than a veneer to cloak their evil intent. Those who attended service were declared hypocrites, and those Old English officials who partook of communion, and even Old English bishops, were found inadequate because some of their relatives were notorious Catholics. The advances made by the Counter-Reformation among the Old English justified Trollope's remark (to Burghley, f. 204ʳ) that he would 'undertake sooner reform of religion [of] a country among the wild Irish than the English Pale', and he cited 'the chronicles and common experience' as proof that there had never been 'Irish man in authority which upon trial had proved a true subject'. This meant in effect, claimed Trollope (to Walsingham, ff. 99ᵛ-100ᵛ), that Ireland would never be reformed until 'true English hearts [would] rule there', and he called for the summary dismissal of 'all Irish councillors, Irish judges, and all Irish officers' as the first step towards reform.

But as well as dismissing the Old English strategy for reform and denouncing the Old English as would-be reformers, the New English had come increasingly to insist on their right to step outside the law when seeking to implement their programme. Richard Beacon, who had served with Spenser as an official on the provincial council of Munster, devoted an entire pamphlet, entitled *Solon His Follie* (Oxford, 1594), to the defence of Sir Richard Bingham, who had acknowledged that when serving as president of Connacht he had ignored legal niceties to prosecute those whom he suspected of plotting insurrection against the state. In

Beacon's allegorical account of this episode, Bingham in Connacht was likened to a Roman general who was forced by necessity to take summary action against the rebellious Gauls who, if given time, would have been able to achieve his overthrow.

The defence of Bingham became as important as the defence of Lord Grey de Wilton to the New English in Ireland, and the fact that one John Merbury, a captain who had served under Bingham in Connacht, could advance rationalizations similar to those of Spenser and Beacon is one measure of the popularity these views enjoyed even among the less well educated of the New English. Merbury was concerned with proving 'it necessary to make war in Connacht', and he justified Bingham in taking the offensive because war was the means 'to have that province, and her realm of Ireland replenished with people'. 'Rigour', averred Merbury, 'hath his time in all governments', and its employment in the particular circumstances was justified because the number who would suffer was 'so small in respect of the multitude of the rest that in good policies and in the use of many old commonwealths the lives of so few have been thought well given for the preservation of so many'. Realizing, however, that this secular argument would provoke moral objections, Merbury posed the rhetorical question if it was 'against Christian policy for the safety of all the rest to punish by justice and utterly to root out a few inveterate tyrants ravening robbers and violent murderers of mankind?'. The question required no answer for Merbury, but by way of consolation for those whose consciences were not yet put at rest he protested that:

> If the customs they pretend can stand with any law divine, natural or civil, if they can convey unto themselves any title of inheritance by succession lawful, or by good purchase to those lands they claim, I say God forbid they should be taken from them; yea I say more if they can present in good reason and not as rebels . . . of fresh memory it might be thought wrong to take such their living from them. But on the otherside if they whom they have dispossessed by meer wrong make continual claim, have the help of the law on their side, by good means repossess their own, yield their duty to God first and to her Majesty their prince and country next. Wherefore then I say hath God ordained her Majesty prince over them, but to defend them and maintain them in their right against the destroyer?

Thus, as Merbury saw it, the government was required by moral not less than pragmatic considerations to dispense with due legal process whenever circumstances dictated that this best served its purpose. 'These carrion crows devour the seed, these weeds choke the corn: why should they not be killed and weeded out in time?'[14] While Merbury recognized that conflict could occur, between the moral code by which officers of the crown should always be bound and the secular expedients that seemed to provide a solution to their difficulties, others did not admit of this possibility. Some even went so far as to suggest that no tension would exist as long as men were guided by reason in choosing their ends. Sir John Perrott, who served as lord deputy of Ireland in 1584-88, remarked that when discussing secular expedients 'a man should set aside God, who in government admitteth no policy that is besides, much less directly against, His will', but he then proceeded to demonstrate that when argued 'with good reason' the policy that would emerge would be in full conformity with Christian principles.[15]

Besides his concern to dovetail the new English reform programme with Christian morality, Perrott, again like Spenser and his contemporaries, drew attention to the material benefits that would derive from the implementation of the programme and cited these as evidence of its godly purpose. Lest men think that his call for 'severe correction' be considered 'a more cruel sentence' than he intended, Perrott emphasized that it was far from his purpose 'to desire any expiration, but rather that all might be saved that were good for the country to be saved'. While stressing the humane considerations that dictated restraint, Perrott also conceded that moderation was essential because 'otherwise there would be such a vacuity of ground there (as it is already too great) that your realm of England though it be most populous . . . were not able to spare people to replenish the wastes'. Developing this point Perrott asserted that

> scarce the fourth foot of Ireland [was] at this hour manured; and of that scarce the fourth penny profit made that the soil would yield, if through a reformation the husbandman might have a safe and peaceable use both of it and his cattle. And yet I say nothing of mines, and a number of other hidden commodities that a civil reformed government would bring with it. (sig. A⁴, B³)

Thus, as Perrott saw it, nothing should be permitted to stand in the way of reformation because the existing condition of Ireland was 'neither godly, nor honourable', whereas 'a reformation will breed competent wealth, and competent wealth containeth men in a liking obedience where desperate beggary runneth headlong to rebellion' (sig. D²).

Much the same point was developed by Andrew Trollope (to Walsingham f. 98) and, as was noted, this utilitarian rationalization also characterized Spenser's text. But while it is possible to demonstrate that several of Spenser's ideas enjoyed common currency among his contemporaries in Ireland, the most convincing evidence that Spenser's *View* was a representative statement is the striking similarity between his argument and that developed in the treatise *Croftus*,

Sive de Hibernia composed by Sir William Herbert, a close neighbour and fellow planter with Edmund Spenser in Munster.[16] Insufficiency and degeneracy of the earlier English settlers in Ireland was thought by Herbert to be principally responsible for the barbaric condition of Ireland, and, like Spenser, he advocated a thorough conquest followed by plantation as the only means to achieve a regeneration of Irish society. Herbert also identified various stages in the process of uplift, and he differed from Spenser only in advancing the missionary endeavour by two stages. This was possible in Herbert's scheme because he recognized the possibility of training missionaries to preach in the Irish language and of translating the Bible and religious discourses into Irish. In recommending this course of action, and in giving it practical demonstration on his Munster estate, Herbert made it quite clear (pp. 54-55) that he was merely exploiting the Irish language as an instrument to hasten the Irish population to a level of civility equal to that of the English, at which point they would abandon their native language in favour of that of the conqueror.

These few example serve to sustain the point that Spenser's opinions were quite typical of those engaged upon the conquest of Ireland, and also make it clear that the *View* can no longer be regarded as the quick response of one individual to the overthrow by Irish rebels of the recently-established English settlement in Munster. The elegance of the discourse suggests that Spenser's *View* was composed only after long cognition, and the coincidence of opinion between himself and his contemporaries in Ireland suggests that Spenser engaged in discussion with his fellow planters and officials before he committed himself to paper. The outbreak of rebellion in Munster in 1594-95 may have added a new urgency to the composition and may explain its appearance in 1596, but we can safely assume that Spenser's *View*, like Herbert's *Croftus*, would have been written even without the overthrow of his plantation in Munster: a suggestion that becomes all the more plausible when it is recognized that it was the civil Old English of the Pale, rather than the rebellious population of Munster, who were isolated by Spenser for particular criticism. In seeking for the context in which the *View* was produced we must look therefore beyond the outbreak of rebellion in 1594 to seek for a general breakdown of relations between the more articulate members of the Old English community and the New English settlers in Ireland.

Tension between these two elements had been evident since at least the middle decade of the sixteenth century, and the Palesmen had repeatedly displayed their ability to exert influence over the queen and bring her to recall a lord deputy whose policies did not meet with their approval. Such endeavours had naturally produced friction between the Pale community and the English followers of the particular lord deputy, but did not have lasting effects, and successive governors were forced willy-nilly to combine whatever policy they favoured for Ireland with some variant upon the surrender and regrant strategy that had become an *idée fixe* with Old English reformers. This did much to win the acquiescence of political spokesmen from the Pale with continued rule from England; the alienation of the Palesmen from English rule was also avoided because most administrative and judicial posts in Dublin were held by people of Irish birth and because some English-born officials identified closely with the interests and ideas of the Pale community. This last development was facilitated by the conformity of most prominent Irish-born officials with the established church, and whatever their differences over policy, Old and New English were united by their mutual contempt for the Gaelic inhabitants of the island. Interest rather than principle explains the occasional breakdown in relations between the Pale community and their succession of governors that usually occurred when the governor's call for financial support from the Pale towards the maintenance of the army exceeded the communal perception of what was just and equitable.

This tense but highly predictable relationship between government and community suddenly gave way in 1579 to a collapse which resulted in the alienation of the Pale community from all English-born servitors in the country. Events of the following years exacerbated an already difficult situation, and by the mid 1580s it was acknowledged by both sides that mutual trust and understanding would never again be restored. Each side stove for the total victory which could only result from the destruction of the other, and it was against this background and in this atmosphere of mutual recrimination that Spenser's *View* and the other discourses that have been discussed were produced.

Religious considerations (the increasing attachment of English servitors to a more stridently Protestant position, and the gradual penetration of Counter-Reformation ideas within the Pale) contributed to the polarization between government and community, but of far greater consequence was the chain of events that followed upon the outbreak of the second Desmond rebellion in 1579. Gerald Fitzgerald, the fourteenth earl of Desmond, had long resented what he regarded as the intrusion upon his authority that resulted from the introduction of a provincial presidency in Munster, but he had studiously held back from the brink, and the government had made some tactful compromises to retain his allegiance. But official concern with compromise was abandoned once the earl's cousin, James Fitzmaurice Fitzgerald, returned from the continent backed by a Papally appointed force, and once the earl's brother, John of Desmond, symbolized his rejection of English rule by the murder of Captain Henry Davells. Here was evidence, protested the English-born officials in Dublin, of a general revolt of the Irish population against English rule, and their case for a general conspiracy spearheaded by the Pope was substantiated by the outbreak in July 1580 of a second religiously-inspired revolt, this time within the Pale itself and led by James Eustace, Viscount Baltinglass.[17] No opportunity should be lost, it was averred, to make an example of those of English descent who had so flagrantly made manifest their disobedience to the crown, and the government pressed home its advantage to track down and prosecute all who had engaged in the Munster rebellion.[18]

The ruthlessness with which the Earl of Desmond and his followers were pursued and the plans that were outlined for the future reorganization of Munster left the entire Old English community in disarray: first because the clear distinction that had previously been maintained in the treatment accorded Gaelic and Old English lords was now being suspended; and secondly because the implementation of the proposed plantation in Munster threatened to strengthen the position of the New English in Ireland, thus enabling them to challenge the dominant position hitherto enjoyed by the Old English in parliament and government. Thus, as the Old English saw it, their very survival as a privileged élite depended upon their ability to frustrate the intentions of the New English, and the only means that they could see to achieving this was to seek to discredit all New English servitors in the eyes of the queen. The severe measures taken by Arthur Lord Grey de Wilton in the suppression of the rebellions in both Munster and the Pale provided the Old English with an ideal subject on which to base their allegations, and they pressed also for an official investigation of the conduct of Sir Richard Bingham as president in Connacht.[19] The essential point being made was that no conspiracy existed, but that the Old English lords (who were well disposed towards the crown) were being goaded into rebellion by the harsh, ill-advised, and frequently illegal actions of English officials and soldiers whose only concern was self-advancement. This argument, and the investigations that produced evidence to substantiate it, were pursued with such persistence that the New English were thrown back on the defensive, and literature such as we have been considering was that produced in defence of their actions and ambitions.

The discussion of the context in which Spenser's *View* and other such works were produced will explain why the Old English were isolated for particular attack. But since the Old English had taken the initiative, the New English authors were forced to defend themselves in the terms that had been selected by their opponents, and the extent to which the terms of the exchange were set by the Old English will become evident from a study of a letter composed in 1581 by Sir Nicholas White, an Irish-born barrister who served as Master of the Rolls during the late sixteenth century. Borrowing the medical metaphors so beloved by the New English, White contended that his long service in Ireland had taught him 'by experience what things the stomach of that body can and cannot digest'. The reform of the Gaelic Irish was, he admitted, an intractable problem that called for severe measures, and his purpose in writing was to persuade the queen that the 'violent and warlike government' which might be appropriate for the Gaelic Irish should not be extended to the Old English population. The policy being pursued by the queen's officers in Ireland would, he averred, 'exhaust her Majesty's treasure, waste her revenue, depopulate the Pale, weaken her [Old] English nobility, that have been and may be made the security of this state, leave the wild Irish to their desires that be the peril thereof, and consume with misery of the wars her soldiers which she sendeth hither'. Of these possible consequences, the most serious in White's eyes was that of losing the traditional allegiance of the Old English nobility, and he emphasized 'what a strong garrison without pay the seed of English blood hath made to her crown since their first planting, which are easier reformed than supplanted and more to be esteemed for the priority of their tenures than others that seek by posteriority to go before'.[20]

The others being referred to by White were the New English servitors, and as well as providing details of their corruption and insensitivity, White questioned the motives that underlay their military policy. Those who advised the queen 'to spare for no cost to translate this kingdom of the new' were likened by White to 'artisans that persuade owners of ancient houses to pull them down for altering of fashion wherein they seek more their own setting a work than to do the owners' profit'. As White warmed to his theme he contrasted himself, a native of Ireland who through years of service had proved his concern for his country, with the New English 'malcontents' who would 'seek to better [their] state by change', and he concluded with the aphorism that 'innovations hath been in all ages accounted dangerous, and the busiest men that way be not the profitablest ministers'. By thus accusing the New English of being innovators, White was in effect identifying them with the political philosophy of Machiavelli which he knew to be repugnant to the queen and her advisers in England. The queen should, he claimed, avoid committing the government of Ireland 'to such as cannot govern themselves', lest it lose her the loyalty of her subjects; she should avoid 'the rooting out of ancient nobility' lest it alter the situation whereby she was 'of all her nobility feared for love, and not loved for fear'; she should avoid the appointment of 'judges that be bloody' lest their severe judgements 'work things of dangerous effects'; and he warned that the queen should above all avoid extending 'the uttermost of her correction' to those who were wanting in duty lest 'it may so happen that, thinking all law were ended, there might arise other men' more

difficult to control. In other words, while advocating the merits of 'a temperate and peaceable government', White was hoping, by drawing attention to the chaos that would result from innovation, to deflect the queen from the policy being recommended to her by her officials in Ireland.

That Nicholas White was not alone in implying that the New English were being guided by the godless Machiavelli is evident from William Herbert's curt denial of the charge of 'being Italianated', stating that there was 'nothing more swerving from [his] conscience and course of life'.[21] But deny what they would, the New English could not conceal the fact that innovation was their ambition and necessity their guiding principle, which explains their need to argue that a policy of innovation was dictated and justified by the moral imperatives of the particular situation. Then, as if by way of consolation to those who were not fully satisfied, the New English laid stress on the material benefits that would derive from their chosen course of action, and they looked forward to the day when the Irish population, once relieved from the tyranny of their lords, would recognise the good that was being placed before them and would thus come to embrace English culture and civility.

The New English were, as we have seen, forced to resort to these rationalizations in order to vindicate themselves in the eyes of the government in England, but it is also probable that the various arguments served to sustain those who engaged in the more gruesome aspects of the Elizabethan conquest. That the ideas of Spenser and his contemporaries did provide the New English with a sense of moral purpose is also suggested by the continued popularity of these ideas throughout the seventeenth century. John Davies, who had witnessed the completion of the conquest and was responsible both for arranging a plantation in Ulster and for extending English common law into the hitherto rebellious provinces, adhered rigidly to the ideas of Spenser when outlining his *Discovery of the True Causes why Ireland was Never Entirely Subdued* until the commencement of the reign of James I. Davies chose a historical framework for his work, and explained the failure of all previous attempts to bring Ireland to subjection by reference to the failure of successive monarchs to recognize the parallel between good husbandry and good government:

> For the husbandman must first break the land before it be made capable of good seed: and when it is thoroughly broken and manured, if he do not forthwith cast good seed into it, it will grow wild again, and bear nothing but weeds. So a barbarous country must be first broken by a war before it will be capable of good government; and when it is fully subdued and conquered, if it be not well planted and governed after the conquest, it will eftsoons return to the former barbarism.

The first to recognize the parallel, claimed Davies, was Queen Elizabeth, who duly broke the country by war and who thus made it possible for him, as the attorney general of King James I, to set about planting and governing the country. There was no doubt in his mind that the plans laid by himself for a mixed plantation of settler and native in the province of Ulster would produce a more prosperous and harmonious outcome than any previous effort at colonization in Ireland. But since Davies, like Spenser, believed 'the principal mark and effect of a perfect conquest' to be the extension of 'laws to a conquered people', he took special satisfaction from the eagerness with which the Irish population availed themselves of the benefit of English common law. Even then, Davies realized that he operated in a period of transition and that it would continue to be necessary for law to 'make her progress and circuit about the realm, under the protection of the sword (as *Virgo* the figure of Justice is by *Leo* in the *Zodiac*) until the people have perfectly learned the lesson of obedience and the conquest be established in the hearts of all men'. Judging from the evidence of improvement that he witnessed about him, Davies did not think it long before this would be accomplished, and he looked forward eagerly to 'the next generation' who would 'in tongue and heart, and every way else become English; so as there [would] be no difference or distinction but the Irish sea between us'.[22]

Belying the optimism of Davies was, however, his suspicion of closely-knit kinship groups the members of which would 'assemble and conspire, and rise in multitudes against the crown', and would 'even now, in the time of peace', hinder 'an indifferent trial . . . between the king and the subject, or between party and party, by reason of this general kindred and consanguinity' (pp. 172-73). This, we will recall, was seen by Spenser as the principal obstacle in the way of reform in Ireland, and Davies's acknowledgement that Irish kinship groups were still dominant in particular areas was an admission on his part that Spenser's prescription for reform had not been adhered to in every detail.

This was so obvious to one of Davies's contemporaries that he donned the mantle of Spenser under the pseudonym 'E.S.' and presented King James with *A Survey of the Present Estate of Ireland, Anno 1615*. The purpose of the author's survey was to measure the extent to which Spenser's advice had been followed, and he concluded, on the basis of his knowledge of conditions in Munster, that the conquest had not been fully implemented and that the educative and missionary aspect of the programme had been totally neglected. This meant that the indigenous lords still enjoyed excessive authority over the population and were able to provide support and patronage to seminary priests who, in turn, were taking it upon themselves to adjudicate upon disputes between the king's subjects. The extension of common law, the advancement of English

to displace Irish as the dominant language of the country, and the progress of the reformation in Ireland were all thought to be hindered by these impediments to reform. Even more disastrous, in the opinion of E.S., was the decay of the recently-established plantation in Munster because the settlers, having been situated in an environment which was still corrupt, had succumbed to that corruption in the same way that all previous English settlers in Ireland had done. If anything was to survive of the Munster plantation it was essential, claimed E.S., that the settlers be strictly segregated from the natives until such time as those had been freed from the tyranny of their lords and had been exposed to the full thrust of the projected effort towards education and reform. Failing that, claimed E.S., there was nothing in prospect but a relapse of Ireland to its former barbarism:

> Every Irish lord in this country doth hold it for a principal maxim to keep his tenants and vassals in ignorance, not suffering a schoolmaster to come amongst them, nor suffer them to learn to speak English, because they shall neither understand God, the King, nor his laws, but repair always to their lord who is the man that they say under God knows and can do all things, and their prayer is God, our Lady and my Lord such a one help me, and their ordinary oath is by their lord's hand.[23]

This criticism was quite close to that offered previously by Edmund Spenser and his contemporaries, and it was also commonplace among English settlers in Ireland who were almost driven to despair by the crown's reluctance to have them push the conquest of Ireland to its conclusion. The continued popularity and relevance of Spenser to planters in Ireland explains why Spenser's *View,* which had previously circulated in manuscript, was finally published in Dublin in 1633, and we can assume that it provided wonderful consolation to the New English planters when they struggled with Thomas Wentworth (afterwards Earl of Strafford) to retain political and social control over the country of their adoption.[24]

But while all the New English planters in Ireland felt threatened by the survival of knots of kinship within the Irish lordships, they did not all agree with E.S. that they should stand aloof from the Irish population who lived within those parts of the country which had been brought under effective planter control. Native cultivators of the soil were seen to be essential to the economical survival of the planters, who could justify retaining them in their midst by claiming that they were being reformed by the example of civil living presented to them by the settler population. This concern to justify a departure from the strict letter of Spenser's prescription goes some way towards explaining the attention devoted by the principal planters to the promotion of manufacturing centres and advanced agriculture on their estates: all of which they described as works of charity. Their success in attracting many Irish to participate in these endeavours satisfied them that they had been correct not only in choosing, with Spenser, the sword instead of the halter, but in choosing to accelerate the reform stage of Spenser's programme and to permit mixed plantation within their own spheres of influence even before the desired conquest had been implemented throughout the country as a whole.[25]

The confidence and optimism of the planters was particularly evident in their strong attachment to place, and in their assumption of the description 'Irishman' at a time when the long established Catholic settlers of Norman descent had, for political reasons, taken to describing themselves as Old English. But the confidence and complacency which had previously characterized planter society in Ireland suddenly gave way to fear and suspicion with the unexpected outburst of rebellion in 1641. The planters more than ever protested their attachment to the localities that had been recently developed and improved by themselves, and they took credit for having been 'the introducers of all good things to Ireland'. But the description 'Irish', which they had previously inclined towards, was now utterly rejected as something contemptible, and they proclaimed themselves British Protestants who had been set upon by the Irish 'barbarians', who had both declined the hand of friendship that had been extended towards them and had, by their mindless destruction, 'endeavoured quite to extinguish the memory of [the planters] and of all the civility and good things by them introduced amongst all that wild nation'.[26]

In this atmosphere of hate and revenge it was to be expected that Spenser's preference for the sword over the halter would be reversed, and the call now was for execution and for an abandonment of any effort to reform a people who, by their actions, had shown themselves unworthy of commiseration. Many of the English who came in Cromwell's army to suppress the revolt were of this same opinion, and one of their number, Captain Richard Lawrence, advocated a rigid policy of apartheid in a pamphlet entitled *The Interest of England in the Irish Transplantation Stated* (Dublin, 1655).[27] By this time, however, the initial shock of the rebellion had been absorbed and wiser counsels were beginning to prevail even in England, where one brave spirit recommended that 'he that desire to advance the plantation of Ireland can hardly find better hints than are in Mr. Ed. Spenser his *View of the State of Ireland*, published almost three score years ago, 1596'.[28] But by then this advice was hardly necessary for those who had been previously involved with Ireland, because they recognized that a strict policy of segregation would spell economic disaster for themselves. This explains why Vincent Gookin, a Munster planter and prominent political figure among the New

English, rushed immediately to contradict the contentions made by Lawrence. Mixed plantation was, protested Gookin, a sound method of settlement once political dominance had been achieved over the Irish, because the planters might then 'safely taste the good of the Irish without fearing the ill'.[29]

What Gookin had to say was in strict conformity with Spenser's thinking, and it is significant that the next author writing anonymously (from the planter's perspective) on the subject of reform of the Irish should adopt a title, *The Present State of Ireland, Together with some Remarks upon the Ancient State Thereof* (London, 1673), which was reminiscent of Spenser's discourse. The efforts at settlement previous to 1641 had, however laudable, suffered from one major defect in that they had been attempted before the conquest of the country had been fully implemented. The planters in Ireland had failed, according to this anonymous writer, to 'translate the ancient inhabitants to other dwellings', and by leaving them undisturbed in their traditional places of habitation had 'left the old inhabitants to shift for themselves, who being strong in body and daily increasing in number . . . would undoubtedly be ready, when any occasion offered itself, to disturb our quiet'. The occasion had come in 1641, but the author was satisfied that this had provided the planters with an opportunity to rectify the previous deficiency by implementing a total conquest of the country. Thus, as he saw the situation in 1673, 'the eternal peace of Ireland which was so solidly discoursed of and stoutly fought for in Queen Elizabeth's time; and very far proceeded in by King James I, had been absolutely perfected . . . according to all human appearance by the last settlement of Ireland confirmed by his gracious Majesty King Charles the Second' (pp. 59, 74).

Because the conquest had been fully implemented, the author of *The Present State of Ireland* believed there was 'no need to fear as formerly' since the 'numerous habitations in most parts of the kingdom' would 'draw the Irish from their wonted barbarism', while the English would 'no longer lapse to barbarism through intermarriage' (p. 74). By thus laying stress on the environmental transformation that had occurred, this author was placing himself in the direct tradition of Spenser, whose ideas now served to provide planters in Ireland with a sense of mission, and of identity. The development of yet another rebellion at the end of the seventeenth century occasioned some planters to regret that they had not resorted to the halter in preference to the sword, but optimism was restored with the suppression of that rebellion, and the Protestant ascendancy of the eighteenth century symbolized their confidence in the future by promoting manufacturing on their estates and by creating artificial towns and villages.[30] In practice these did little to achieve the uplift of the native population, which would have been evidenced in the final analysis by their identification with the established church, but the effort did much to satisfy the Protestant population that they had a positive role in Ireland and that, with Spenser (*View*, p. 2), they believed 'nothing so hard but that through wisdom may be mastered and subdued, since the poet says that the wise man shall rule even over the stars, much more over the earth'.

Notes

[1] *A View of the Present State of Ireland,* edited by W. L. Renwick (Oxford, 1970), is referred to hereafter as *View*, with page references in the text.

[2] See *View*, pp. 188-90; Brendan Bradshaw, 'Sword, Word and Strategy in the Reformation in Ireland', *Historical Journal,* 21 (1978), 475-502, and 'The Elizabethans and the Irish: A Muddled Model', *Studies,* 70 (1981), 233-44.

[3] Two volumes (Cambridge, 1978).

[4] See *Foundations,* I, x-xv, and 'Meaning and Understanding in the History of Ideas', *History and Theory,* 8 (1969), 3-53.

[5] See Nicholas Canny, *The Elizabethan Conquest of Ireland: A Pattern Established, 1565-76* (Brighton, 1976), pp. 116-36.

[6] Brendan Bradshaw, *The Irish Constitutional Revolution of the Sixteenth Century* (Cambridge, 1979).

[7] *View,* pp. 140-56 (pp. 153, 156).

[8] *View,* pp. 156-59. (p. 159).

[9] See G. R. Elton, *Reform and Renewal: Thomas Cromwell and the Common Weal* (Cambridge, 1973); Felix Raab, *The English Face of Machiavelli* (London, 1964).

[10] See Skinner, *Foundations,* 1, 128-38; Felix Gilbert, *Machiavelli and Guicciardini* (Princeton, 1965); J. G. A. Pocock, *The Machiavellian Moment* (Princeton, 1975), especially pp. 156-82; *View,* p. 95.

[11] See, for an example of the more common treatment, the anonymous 'Discourse for the Government of Ireland' (P.R.O., S.P. 63/87/81, f. 28).

[12] See, 'Book of Barnaby Rich on the Reformation in Ireland', 1589 (P.R.O., S.P. 63/144/35, ff. 104-13); Rich to Burghley, 20 May 1591 (P.R.O., S.P. 63/158/12, ff. 21-23).

[13] Andrew Trollope to Walsingham, 12 September 1585 (P.R.O., S.P. 63/85/39, ff. 96ᵛ-102ʳ); Trollope to Burghley, 26 October 1587 (P.R.O., S.P. 63/131/64, ff. 200ᵛ-204ʳ).

[14] Captain John Merbury on Revolt in Connacht, 27 September 1589 (P.R.O., S.P. 63/146/57, ff. 177-79).

[15] E.C.S., *The Government of Ireland under Sir John Perrott, 1584-8* (London, 1626), sig. D¹-D².

[16] Edited by W. E. Buckley (London, 1887).

[17] See *A New History of Ireland,* edited by T. W. Moody, F. X. Martin, and F. J. Byrne, Volume III, *Early Modern Ireland 1534-1691* (Oxford, 1976), pp. 105-15, 107.

[18] For the government's determination in this respect see Geoffrey Fenton to Burghley, 6 December 1583 (P.R.O., S.P. 63/106/4).

[19] On Connacht during this period see Bernadette Cunningham, 'Political and Social Change in the Lordships of Clanricard and Thomond, 1569-1641' (M.A. thesis, University College, Galway, 1979).

[20] Nicholas White to Burghley, 23 December 1581 (P.R.O., S.P. 63/87/55, ff. 151ʳ-52ᵛ).

[21] Sir William Herbert to Sir Valentine Browne, 1 January 158/9 (P.R.O., S.P. 63/140/14).

[22] *A Discovery of the True Causes why Ireland was Never Entirely Subdued, and Brought under Obedience of the Crown of England, until the Beginning of His Majestie's Happy Reign* (London, 1612), pp. 4-5, 100, 74, 272.

[23] *A Survey of the present Estate of Ireland, Anno 1615, Addressed to His Most Excellent Majesty James the First . . . by His Most Humble Subject E:S* (San Marino, California, Huntington Library, EL. 1746), ff. 10ʳ-15ᵛ. This vellum-bound tract was obviously the work of an individual who had been engaged upon the plantation effort in Munster.

[24] For the New English struggle with Wentworth see H. F. Kearney, *Strafford in Ireland, 1633-41* (Manchester, 1961).

[25] This point is developed in Nicholas Canny, *The Upstart Earl: A Study of the Social and Mental World of Richard Boyle, First Earl of Cork, 1566-1643* (Cambridge, 1982), see especially pp. 19-40, 124-38.

[26] Gerard Boate, *Ireland's Natural History* (London, 1652), pp. 89, 114. Although composed by two Dutch scientists, Arnold and Gerard Boate, who accompanied Cromwell's army to Ireland, the ideas expressed there can be accepted as those of the New English because the authors 'discussed the matter with several gentlemen who had been to Ireland, especially Sir William Parsons and Sir Richard Parsons'.

27 The author recommended that the English in Ireland settle apart even from those Irish 'late deemed converts to the Protestant religion' (p. 18).

28 This is a statement from the paper *Perfect Diurnall*, No. 130, 7 June 1652, p. 1928. I am grateful to my colleague Dr Tadgh Foley for this reference.

29 *The Author and Case of Transplanting . . . Vindicated* (London, 1655), pp. 40-41.

30 See L. M. Cullen, *The Emergence of Modern Ireland, 1600-1900* (London, 1981), especially pp. 39-60. It will be clear that the present author disagrees fundamentally on this point with Brendan Bradshaw, who has written that Ireland emerged from the seventeenth century 'with an apartheid constitution in law and in practice, religion providing the criterion for discrimination. The protestant ascendancy had acquired a strong incentive to leave Ireland for the greater part Catholic' ('Sword, Word and Strategy', p. 502).

Robin Headlam Wells (essay date 1983)

SOURCE: "To Sound Her Praises: Introduction," in *Spenser's Faerie Queene and the Cult of Elizabeth*, Barnes & Noble Books, 1983, pp. 1-28.

[*In the following excerpt from a study of* The Faerie Queene *in relation to the cult of Elizabeth, Wells analyzes Spenser's use of allegory to honor Queen Elizabeth.*]

1. The Poetry of Praise

> Great wrong I doe, I can it not deny,
>   to that most sacred Empresse my dear dred,
>   not finishing her Queene of faery,
>   that mote enlarge her liuing prayses dead.
>   (*Amoretti*, XXXIII)[1]

Spenser had completed six books of **The Faerie Queene** when he published the **Amoretti** in 1595. The apologetic tone of sonnet no. 33 suggests that he probably knew that his original plans for a poem consisting of twelve books devoted to the 'priuate morall vertues', to be followed by another twelve devoted to the 'politicke vertues',[2] would never be realized. But more important than what this sonnet tells us of Spenser's state of mind is what it says concerning the purpose of his epic. As a poetic tribute to Elizabeth, **The Faerie Queene** was intended to 'enlarge her prayses'.

Renaissance criticism, following a tradition going back at least as far as Plato, accorded a special status to the poetry of praise.[3] Puttenham, in his defence of the dignity of poetry, claims that, second only to poetry written in praise of the immortal gods, is that which

honours 'the worthy gests of noble Princes.'[4] However humble his own position might be, the poet could lay claim to a unique office, since he alone was able to offer the glory of immortality through verse. As Spenser himself remarks in a sonnet addressed to the Earl of Northumberland:

> The sacred Muses haue made alwaies clame
> To be the Nourses of nobility,
> And Registres of euerlasting fame.[5]

In the Renaissance it was believed that the highest poetic kind was the epic, and most critics were agreed that the function of epic was essentially epideictic, that is, to display the virtues of some great man as a pattern for emulation.[6] The poem which was universally held to be the supreme example of its genre was the *Aeneid*. Donatus, writing in the fourth century, claimed that 'If anyone wants to measure Virgil's genius, his morality, the nature of his speech, his knowledge, character, and skill in rhetoric, he must first learn whom he undertakes to praise in his poem.'[7] This view of the *Aeneid* is repeated in Fulgentius's *De Contentia Virgiliana* (c. sixth century), a work which has been described as 'the most characteristic monument we possess of Virgil's celebrity during the times of Christian barbarism'.[8] Although Fulgentius's commentary turns the *Aeneid* into something akin to a medieval allegory of Everyman in which epic combats are seen as psychomachia, the underlying conception of the poem as 'panegyrical biography'[9] is one which formed the basis of most Renaissance interpretations of Virgil. As late as 1715 it was argued that

> the whole *Aeneis* of Virgil may be said to be an allegory, if we consider Aeneas as representing Augustus Caesar and his conducting the remains of his countrymen from the ruins of Troy to a new settlement in Italy as emblematical of Augustus' modelling a new government out of the ruins of the aristocracy and establishing the Romans, after the confusion of the civil war, in a peaceable and flourishing condition.[10]

Such a view of the *Aeneid* is also substantially Spenser's. Indeed it has been claimed that 'Of all sixteenth-century epics, none better illustrates the continuity of the Fulgentius tradition than Edmund Spenser's **Faerie Queene**.'[11] That Spenser himself wished **The Faerie Queene** to be identified with this tradition is apparent from the way he deliberately modelled his own poetic career on Virgil's example. Already in the 'October' eclogue of **The Shepheardes Calender** we find him alluding to the passage in the third book of the *Georgics* (10-30) where Virgil speaks of the heroic poem he intends to write in honour of Augustus. To Piers's suggestion that he turn from lesser matters and honour 'fayre Elisa' by singing 'of bloody Mars, of wars, of giusts', Cuddie replies that he has indeed heard of how 'Romish Tityrus'

> left his Oaten reede,
> Whereon he earst had taught his flocks to
> feede,
> And laboured lands to yield the timely eare,
> And eft did sing of warres and deadly drede,
> So as the Heauens did quake his verse to
> here.
>
> ('October', 56-60)

If Spenser's choice of the pastoral mode for his apprentice work is clearly based on Virgil's example, it is well known also that he closely identified the epic poem he was anticipating in these lines with the *Aeneid*.[12]

To describe *The Faerie Queene* as a poem of praise belonging to a long tradition of epideictic poetry is not, of course, to say anything new. Many critics have asserted what Spenser himself tells us in his letter to Ralegh, namely that *The Faerie Queene* was designed as a glorification of Elizabeth and the British nation.[13] However, although Cain is right in saying that 'Spenser's great poem exists to praise Elizabeth',[14] this does not mean that it is merely an elaborate vehicle for flattery. The purpose of epideictic poetry is essentially moral. The special nature of the responsibilities assumed by the panegyrist is perhaps best explained by Erasmus writing in 1504:

> Those who believe panegyrics are nothing but flattery seem to be unaware of the purpose and aim of the extremely far-sighted men who invented this kind of composition, which consists in presenting princes with a pattern of goodness, in such a way as to reform bad rulers, improve the good, educate the boorish, reprove the erring, arouse the indolent, and cause even the hopelessly vicious to feel some inward stirrings of shame.[15]

In proclaiming the moral function of praise Erasmus is rehearsing a commonplace of classical and Renaissance poetics;[16] he is also anticipating the treatise which he presented to his own patron twelve years later on the occasion of his appointment as counsellor to Charles V (then Archduke of Burgundy). As a *speculum principis, The Education of a Christian Prince* belongs to an ancient tradition of hortatory treatises on the subject of kingship.[17] Although Erasmus characterizes his book as a work of praise,[18] his object is an ethical one. Underlying his portrait of the Christian ruler are two principles which are also fundamental to the conception of *The Faerie Queene* as a mirror for Elizabeth: first, that the prince, as God's deputy on earth, is to be seen as performing a function in the hierarchy of the state analogous to that performed by God in the universal order of things (pp. 158-9), and, second, that

upon the moral character of the prince depends the well-being of the state (p. 157). By defining the characteristics of the ideal prince and comparing these with an image of the corrupt ruler, Erasmus is in effect creating a pattern of Christian conduct to which all men should aspire. Informing the whole book is the humanist belief in the moral value of learning. As Spenser says in *The Teares of the Muses,*

> By knowledge wee do learne our selues to
> knowe,
> And what to man, and what to God wee owe.
>
> From hence wee mount aloft vnto the skie,
> And looke into the Christall firmament . . .
>
> (503-6)

The Faerie Queene does not offer the reader a scheme of practical education; nevertheless, as a moral poem which undertakes to instruct the reader in the nature of virtue, it testifies to the belief—central to Erasmus's thought, and indeed to the humanist movement as a whole—that knowledge brings us nearer to God. As one recent critic has said, the various books of the poem trace 'a sequence displaying the dignity of man, a progression of learning for the reader'.[19]

In so far as he is presenting his reader with an image of princely magnificence in the figure of Arthur, Spenser may be seen to be writing within a clearly defined tradition of treatises on kingship. But when he announces his intention of fashioning 'a gentleman or noble person in vertuous and gentle discipline',[20] it is the courtesy book rather than the prince's mirror with which his poem may best be compared.[21] Many scholars have written on Spenser's debt to the courtesy tradition and to Castiglione in particular.[22] Whereas the *speculum* concerns itself with the virtues of the ideal prince and offers advice on the art of government, the courtesy book is less specialized in its subject matter and deals with the education and accomplishments of noblemen and courtiers. In their most elementary form Renaissance courtesy books were little more than manuals of self-improvement. However, the more serious writers of the period are unanimous in their insistence that the courtier's accomplishments are worth nothing if they are not devoted to the cause of realizing what Sir Thomas Elyot terms the 'iuste publike weale'.[23] Castiglione's claim that the courtier must employ his accomplishments as a means of gaining the goodwill and favour of his prince and that he should use the influence he wins in this way to supply the prince with virtuous counsel,[24] is a favourite maxim among Renaissance humanists.

The close similarities between the *speculum principis* and the courtesy book are illustrated in the work of Castiglione's most celebrated English imitator.[25] Addressed to Henry VIII, *The Boke Named the Gover-*

nour is both a manual on the art of government which offers its dedicatee a portrait of the ideal ruler, and at the same time a handbook of education for the sons of English gentlemen. Of the vast number of pedagogic treaties which appeared in the sixteenth century, Elyot's book is arguably the most important so far as Spenser is concerned. Indeed it has been claimed that *The Governour* and **The Faerie Queene** 'have almost identical aims'.[26] Although this is an exaggeration, it is true that Spenser, like Elyot, does combine elements of the *speculum principis* with certain features of the courtesy book. That Spenser saw these two functions of his poem as aspects of a single meaning is clear from his statement in the letter to Ralegh of his intentions regarding the character of Prince Arthur. As Virgil had combined features of Homer's Agamemnon and his Ulysses in the single figure of Aeneas, says Spenser, so Arthur is to be seen as a composite figure representing 'a good gouernour and a vertuous man'.[27]

Spenser's general intention may be summed up, then, as being to praise Elizabeth by presenting her with a portrait of the ideal ruler—a portrait which she would recognize as her own, but which would at the same time serve as a pattern of conduct for her courtiers. Summarized in this way **The Faerie Queene** sounds not unlike a versification of *The Governour*. What this account does not recognize is the political dimension of Spenser's poem. In addition to its pedagogic aspect, **The Faerie Queene** is a national epic whose purpose is to celebrate Queen Elizabeth as the predestined ruler of an elect nation. In this respect it has more in common with the *Aeneid* than with *The Governour*. In celebrating a national ideal Spenser, like Virgil, employs one of the favourite *topoi* of the epideictic poet and constructs a genealogy—part mythical and part historical—in which he traces his prince's ancestry to its supposedly divine origins. Since it is sometimes claimed that the Elizabethans were quite uncritical in their appetite for literature dealing with the mythical history of their country . . . , it is important to consider the status of Spenser's genealogical material, particularly with regard to his use of typology as a means of proclaiming the predestinate nature of Elizabeth's rule.

2. Allegory and Typology

In one of the commendatory verses annexed to **The Faerie Queene** (chosen, no doubt, for the aptness of its sentiments rather than its poetic merit) explicit comparison is made between Spenser and Virgil:

> Graue Muses march in triumph and with
>   prayses,
> Our Goddesse here hath giuen you leaue to
>   land:
> And biddes this rare dispenser of your graces
> Bow downe his brow vnto her sacred hand.
> Desertes findes dew in that most princely
>   doome,
> In whose sweete brest are all the Muses
>   bredde:
> So did that great *Augustus* erst in Roome
> With leaues of fame adorne his Poets hedde.
> Faire be the guerdon of your *Faery Queene,*
> Euen of the fairest that the world hath seene.[28]

Although Spenser never won the royal patronage which the author of these verses anticipates, his poem has much in common with Virgil's. Indeed the similarities between the *Aeneid* and **The Faerie Queene** would have appeared far more striking to the Renaissance reader than they do to us. The modern student, familiar with the idea that **The Faerie Queene** has a number of different levels of meaning, might possibly be surprised to be told that the *Aeneid* had a similar fourfold significance. But in the Middle Ages and the Renaissance it was commonly accepted that, in addition to its literal significance, Virgil's narrative embodied certain moral and political meanings. Boccaccio, for example, tells us that 'concealed within the veil' ('sub velamento latet poetico') of the story of Aeneas's abandonment of Dido are three ulterior purposes: first, to offer a universal moral truth concerning the need to subdue the destructive passions; second, to glorify Augustus by praising Aeneas's steadfast devotion to his political destiny; and third to celebrate the martial successes of the Roman people in terms of the events which prefigured these triumphs.[29]

Boccaccio's interpretation of Virgil is clearly based on the analogy of contemporary scriptural exegesis. But although he speaks of the poet's fourfold purpose, his method cannot properly be compared with that of a true allegorist like Aquinas. For, of the three levels of meaning which Boccaccio finds in addition to the literal significance of Virgil's narrative, it is only the first which is, strictly speaking, allegorical (in this case, tropological); the latter two are typological. The distinction is important. Where moral allegory is usually timeless and characteristically involves the use of signs—more or less arbitrary in themselves—to point to moral or spiritual truths which have a universal applicability, typology reveals a pattern in the course of history by establishing connections between events or persons which have a historical reality.[30] For Boccaccio there was no more need to explain the difference between allegory and typology than there was for Spenser, writing some 300 years later. However, such a way of reading literature belongs essentially to a premodern culture; and the twentieth-century critic must spell out distinctions which would have been self-evident to Boccaccio's and Spenser's readers.

The literary use of typology is familiar enough to students of medieval drama.[31] However, unlike the medieval writer, who is dramatizing events which—so far as he is concerned—have a historical reality, Spenser creates an imaginary world. In establishing parallels between the fictional characters who inhabit this world and the real historical person whom they prefigure, Spenser is attributing a providential significance to contemporary events in much the same way that the New Testament writer sees in the past a series of figures prognosticating Christ. But the analogy is not a true one. Where the New Testament writer concerns himself only with historical realities, Spenser creates characters which are, for the most part, purely fictional. This mingling of the fictional and the real presents critical problems of a very different nature from those associated with the miracle play. Because these problems have received scant critical attention and because, as a consequence, there is some confusion about what we mean when we speak of typology in *The Faerie Queene,*[32] it is necessary to rehearse a subject whose general principles are by now well established.[33]

As an exegetical method typology originates in St Paul and other New Testament writers who interpreted certain events and persons in the Old Testament as . . . prefigurations of Christ; as a method of composition, however, typology antedates the Christian era. Medieval and Renaissance commentators on the *Aeneid* were fully aware, as we have seen, of the way Virgil links events widely separated in time in order to show that they form steps in an historical progression culminating in the reign of Augustus.[34] If the patterns of recurrence and prefiguration we find in the *Aeneid* bear similarities to those in the Bible, this is because they are the product of a similar view of history. Typology is essentially the product of a theory of history which sees events not simply as sequence, but as significant elements of a divine plan. Such a providential view of history is not, of course, unique to Christendom.

In praising his sovereign, Spenser, like Virgil, used typology to suggest that her reign had been anticipated or foreshadowed by events in the ancient past. Whether Virgil intended the allegorical meanings his medieval commentators found in the *Aeneid* we shall probably never know; with Spenser we are on surer ground. We know that, in addition to its historical aspect, *The Faerie Queene* is a 'continued Allegory, or darke conceit' designed to illustrate a humanist ideal of moral conduct. This mixing of allegory and typology is one of the characteristic features of the poem. On the one hand there are purely allegorical characters such as Furor, or Malbecco, who clearly have no typological significance; on the other hand there are characters like Belphoebe, whose significance is primarily typological and who tell us very little about the nature of the virtue which they supposedly represent. Between these two extremes are those characters such as Mercilla or Britomart who are both 'historical' types foreshadowing their antitype, Queen Elizabeth, and also allegorical symbols of the virtues which form the subjects of the books in which they appear.

We must be clear, however, exactly what is implied by describing a character like Britomart as a type of Queen Elizabeth. *The Faerie Queene* is a poem which makes extensive use of prophecy and historical parallelism. But these do not in themselves necessarily involve typology. For example, in the final stanza of the proem to Book V Spenser invokes his muse:

> Dread Souerayne Goddesse, that doest highest sit
>   In seate of iudgement, in th'Almighties stead,
>   And with magnificke might and wondrous wit
>   Doest to thy people righteous doome aread,
>   That furthest Nations filles with awfull dread,
>   Pardon the boldnesse of thy basest thrall,
>   That dare discourse of so diuine a read,
>   As thy great iustice praysed ouer all:
> The instrument whereof loe here thy *Artegall.*

The terms in which Spenser addresses his 'Souerayne Goddesse' make it impossible to say whether he is speaking to Astraea or Queen Elizabeth. In fact, of course, he is doing both. Behind the familiar Elizabethan identification of the Queen with the goddess of justice lies the prophetic annunciation of Virgil's fourth Eclogue: 'iam redit et Virgo, redeunt Saturnia regna'. It was to these famous words that chroniclers like Richard Nicols were alluding when they hailed Elizabeth's reign as a return to the golden age:

> No sooner did this Empires royall crowne
> Begirt the temples of her princelie hed;
> But that *Ioue*-borne *Astraea* straight came downe
> From highest heauen againe, to which in dread
> Of earths unpietie before shee fled:
> Well did shee know, *Elizaes* happie reigne
> Would then renew the golden age againe.[35]

But if Spenser, like so many of his contemporaries, is suggesting that Elizabeth represents the fulfilment of Virgilian prophecy, that she is indeed Astraea *rediviva,* this does not mean that the relationship is typological. For an antitype is not a reincarnation of the type by which it has been anticipated, but a fulfilment of its hidden meaning. In a truly typological relationship type and antitype always retain their separate identities. It would be improper, therefore, to describe as typological that form of prophetic recurrence which is in fact a recapitulation, though, as we shall see, prophecy does not exclude typology.

It may help to clarify the unique relationship between type and antitype if we consider another form of reiterative relationship in *The Faerie Queene* which is, nevertheless, not typological. When Paridell abducts Malbecco's wife Hellenore (III, x, 1 ff.) in a crude re-enactment of the tale he had been telling Britomart the previous evening (III, ix, 33-7), we scarcely need to be told by the narrator that his lover is 'a second *Hellene*' (13), or that the firing of Malbecco's castle recalls the sack of Troy (12). But although Paridell and Hellenore are clearly linked both by name and temperament with their notorious forbears, they are not their antitypes. In no sense can they be said to reveal the true signifi-cance of the past. Paridell the seducer and Hellenore the faithless wife are human stereotypes who tell us no more about their originals than Paris and Helen tell us about them. The relationship is simply analogical. By investing this allegory of concupiscence, infidelity and jealousy with historical echoes, Spenser is doing no more than reminding his reader that human nature is the same in all ages, and that what was capable of bringing about chaos in the past is still capable of doing so now.

Paridell, Hellenore and Malbecco are personifications of the moral evils against which Britomart is pledged to fight; as the champion of fidelity she is the allegor-ical antithesis of everything they represent. But when Spenser describes this 'Magnificke Virgin' (V, vii, 21) in terms which evoke her illustrious descendant, Queen Elizabeth, he is writing not as an allegorist, but as a typologist. For it is only in the distant future when another 'royall virgin'—celebrated, like Britomart, for her chastity—shall come to rule a divided world, that the true meaning of Britomart's 'perillous emprize' will be revealed (III, iii, 48-9). Although her reign has been prophesied by Merlin, Elizabeth is not a reincarnation of Britomart, but a fulfilment of the divine historical plan foreshadowed in the deeds of her heroic ances-tress.

It would be wrong to suggest that *The Faerie Queene* cannot be understood without making these distinc-tions. Nevertheless, they are ones which Spenser's contemporaries regarded as significant,[36] and some awareness of them may sharpen our understanding of the kind of poem *The Faerie Queene* is. If Spenser treats characters like Britomart, now as types of Eliz-abeth, now as allegorical symbols, we may reasonably assume that this is not because he was as confused as a good many of his twentieth-century readers are about the difference between typology and allegory, but be-cause such a technique was to some extent dictated by his 'whole intention' in writing *The Faerie Queene*. As an epideictic poet he is attempting both to define an abstract ideal of 'vertuous and gentle discipline' as a pattern for emulation, and also to praise Queen Eliz-abeth as predestined ruler of a chosen people. To ac-complish this latter purpose Spenser made use of two quite separate typological traditions: a classical tradi-tion and a Christian tradition. The body of classical legend which forms part of the mythical background

of *The Faerie Queene* is well known and need not detain us long; the Christian material, though familiar to Spenserians in principle, is deployed in a more extensive and systematic fashion than is generally rec-ognized. In the remaining sections of this introduction I shall try to show how Spenser combines this heter-ogeneous material to reveal the providential nature of Elizabeth's reign.

3. The Myth of Troy

Although she is referred to only through the medium of prophecy, and then not by her own name, Queen Elizabeth nevertheless dominates *The Faerie Queene* in much the same way that Augustus's presence can be felt throughout the *Aeneid,* in spite of the fact that he never actually appears in the poem. As protagonists *in absentia* Augustus and Elizabeth have much in com-mon: each is portrayed as the instrument of a provi-dential purpose, a peace-bringer descended from the gods, who is at the same time a dispenser of ruthless justice. To enforce the parallel Spenser begins *The Faerie Queene* with a direct allusion to the *Aeneid.*[37] But undue emphasis should not be given to this initial echoing of Virgil, for in the poem as a whole there is little explicit verbal parallelism. Although certain inci-dents, such as Duessa's journey to the underworld in Book I, canto v, for example, are loosely based on passages in the *Aeneid,* these parallels are not always of thematic significance, and in form the poem owes more to Ariosto and Tasso than it does to Virgil.

Spenser does, however, link his poem with the *Aeneid* in a more radical way. Just as Virgil, by connecting Roman history with its legendary past, had shown Augustus to be the instrument of a providential plan, so Spenser employs ancient myth to glorify Queen Elizabeth. It is, moreover, the same myth which Virgil had used to claim divine ancestry for Augustus, that Spenser uses in *The Faerie Queene*. In Book III, can-to iii, Britomart visits the cave of Merlin where it is revealed that from her

> a famous Progenie
> Shall spring, out of the auncient *Troian*
>   blood,
>   Which shall reuiue the *sleeping* memorie
> Of those same antique Peres the heauens
>   brood,
> Which *Greeke* and *Asian* riuers stained with
>   their blood.
>
>   (III, iii, 22)

The passage is a direct imitation of the third canto of the *Orlando Furioso* where Bradamante similarly learns of her Trojan ancestry and is told by Merlin of the glorious deeds of her descendants. Spenser, like Arios-to, is deliberately inviting comparison between his poem and the *Aeneid*. Later, in Book III, canto ix, we discover that Britomart, herself an ancestor of Elizabeth, is 'lineally extract' from Brutus, great-grandson of Aeneas and founder of Troynovaunt, or London. Elizabeth is thus shown to be, like Augustus, a direct descendant of the gods through Aeneas, and her reign to be the fulfilment of a divine plan.

As it is told in **The Faerie Queene** the Troy story is a complex one, for instead of presenting its events in chronological order, Spenser divides his narrative into four main parts. The first part of the story dealing with the flight of Aeneas from Troy and the founding by Ascanius of a new Troy in Alba Longa, is told by Paridell to Britomart in Malbecco's castle (III, ix, 40-3). When Britomart mentions the building of a third Troy by descendants of Aeneas, Paridell recalls the details, which he had until then forgotten, of Brutus's accidental parricide, his years of self-imposed exile and his eventual conquest of Albion. For the second part of the story, dealing with Brutus's descendants, we have to turn back to Book II, canto x, where Prince Arthur reads a chronicle of British kings from Brutus to his own father Uther Pendragon. The continuation of this chronicle, beginning with Arthur's grandson and tracing the descent as far as Cadwallader, last of the British kings, is related in the form of a prophecy by Merlin in Book III, canto iii. With the coming of the Saxons and the death of Cadwallader the succession of British kings is finally broken. But Merlin prophesies that in due time the British line will be restored, that the country will be united, and that a royal virgin will reign in glorious peace. This final part of the story, dealing with the Tudor dynasty, is then retold in Book III, canto x, in the form of a history of Faeryland.

Spenser's reason for presenting the story in such a disjointed form was principally chronological: since the action of **The Faerie Queene** is presumed to have taken place before Arthur's accession, all later events would necessarily have to take the form of prophecy. Such, however, was the popularity in Elizabethan England of the Trojan myth that Spenser could afford to distort his narrative without risk of losing his readers.[38] This popularity is not difficult to account for. By tracing his nation's ancestry to ancient Troy, the chronicler was able to show that his people were not barbarians, but had been marked out by providence for a special purpose. Since national pride is a commodity of no great rarity, it is not surprising to find that in medieval Western Europe the Trojan myth was 'everybody's game';[39] as early as the seventh century, Frankish legend had spoken of a Trojan national ancestry, while closer to Spenser's own time we find Ariosto employing the same myth in his glorification of the House of Este.

In England the Trojan myth owed its currency to Geoffrey of Monmouth. Drawing on fragmentary literary sources and orally transmitted material, Geoffrey created in his *Historia Regum Britanniae* (c. 1135) a masterpiece of imaginative literature which dominated antiquarian thought for centuries to come: 'within fifteen years of its publication not to have read it was a matter of reproach; it became a respected text-book of the Middle Ages; it was incorporated in chronicle after chronicle; it was turned into poetry; it swept away opposition with the ruthless force of a great epic . . .'[40] Geoffrey's chronicle of ancient British kings from Brutus to Cadwallader became the most important single source not only for medieval chronicles, but also for apologists of the Tudor right to accession. Of especial significance was Geoffrey's portrayal of Brutus as a man marked out by divine prophecy as the founder of a universal empire. When Brutus petitions the gods to reveal his destiny he is told to seek an island beyond France where giants once lived but which is now uninhabited. There he would find a land fit for his descendants, where another Troy would be built and kings would be born to whom the whole world would bow.[41]

The idea of the British nation as one destined for worldwide sovereignty reappears in popular Tudor literature. Among the stories added by John Higgins to the *Mirror for Magistrates,* for example, is the *Tale of Albanact* (one of Brutus's three sons), in which, following Geoffrey, the poet relates how Diana appeared to Brutus in a dream prophesying that he would establish a new kingdom in an island beyond France where he would build 'an other stately Troye':

> Here of thy progenye and stocke, shall mighty
> kinges descende:
> And vnto them as subiecte, all the worlde
> shall bowe and bende.[42]

Such a myth had its obvious political uses. It was revived by Henry VII on his accession as a way of justifying his claim to the throne. Hall records how, claiming to be able to trace his ancestry back to Cadwallader, Henry encouraged the idea that he represented a fulfilment of the ancient prophecy that a British king would return to rule the land.[43] The myth was revived for similar reasons during Elizabeth's reign and became a familiar feature of the patriotic minor literature which flourished in the 1580s and 1590s.[44] Chronicles from Geoffrey onwards had kept the Trojan myth alive, and it now found expression in pageants, narrative poems and plays celebrating the glory of England's Queen and tracing her ancestry back to Brutus.

When we speak of the popularity of the Trojan myth in Elizabethan England we must be clear that no historiographer worthy of the title ever accorded it the status of historical fact.[45] It was antiquarians such as Leland and Churchyard and poets such as Baldwin, Peele, Warner, Nicols and of course Spenser himself who popularised the myth. In doing so they were continuing a medieval chronicle tradition in which moral utility was the writer's chief concern. Unlike the historiographer, the poet was considered to be free to adapt his historical material to suit his moral purpose. One of the most memorable passages in Sidney's *Defence of Poetry* deals with precisely this distinction. Where the historiographer is bound to record only 'what men have done' the poet,

> Disdaining to be tied to any such subjection, lifted up with the vigour of his own invention, doth grow in effect another nature, in making things either better than nature bringeth forth, or, quite anew, forms such as never were in nature, as the Heroes, Demigods, Cyclops, Chimeras, Furies, and such like: so as he goeth hand in hand with nature, not enclosed within the narrow warrant of her gifts, but freely ranging only within the zodiac of his own wit.[46]

The poet imitates not an imperfect sensible world, but an ideal world. It is by 'feigning notable images' of virtue or vice that he is able to 'lead and draw us to as high a perfection, as our degenerate souls, made worse by their clayey lodgings, can be capable of'. It would be naive, Sidney tells us, to suppose that there ever existed so perfect a prince as Xenophon's Cyrus or so excellent a man as Virgil's Aeneas. Yet by taking the idealized heroes of mythology and literature as models of our own conduct we encourage the growth of the virtues they embody.[47]

When Spenser incorporated the Trojan myth in *The Faerie Queene* he did not wish to suggest that the British were in a literal sense descended from Troy; indeed elsewhere he speaks with scorn of those 'vaine *Englishmen*' who claimed that Brutus 'first conquered and inhabited this Land, it being . . . impossible to proove, that there was ever any such *Brutus of England* . . .'.[48] The relationship is typological: in showing that the events of Elizabeth's reign have been foreshadowed by events in the ancient world Spenser is suggesting that they are to be seen as part of a divine historical plan. Though the Troy story is dealt with only in Books II and III of *The Faerie Queene,* it forms an essential part of the mythico-historical background of the whole poem. Rightly to understand the historic significance that Spenser attributed to Elizabeth we must see her, like Virgil's Augustus, as a descendant of the gods, born to bring peace to a divided world.

4. Marian Iconography

Virgil's praise of Augustus in terms of the legendary ancestor by whom he is shown to have been prefigured provided a typological model for Renaissance epideictic poets. The fact that Virgil was a pagan writer did not matter. A long tradition of interpreting the enigmatic fourth Eclogue as unconscious Christian prophecy[49] offered justification for regarding the empire foretold by Anchises (*Aeneid,* VI, 756 ff.) as preparatory for the coming of Christ, while, conversely, the birth of Christ was spoken of as heralding the return of the golden age.[50] In this way Virgilian myth was assimilated to a Christian view of world history. Thus when Spenser gives his reader the sequel to the Troy story in Books II and III of *The Faerie Queene* and traces, in the form of prophecy, its future events as far as Elizabeth's England he is in effect extending the Christian providential view of history back into the ancient world and forward into the present. What the Trojan myth could not suggest, however, was Elizabeth's specifically Protestant destiny. To convey the idea that the British were in a particular religious sense a 'chosen and peculier people'[51] Spenser drew on a popular tradition of biblical typology.

In tracing Britomart's descent from 'auncient Troian blood' (III, iii, 22), Spenser links his heroine with a familiar body of classical legend. But when he describes her genealogical tree as a

> worthy stock, from which the branches sprong,
> That in late yeares so faire a blossome bare,
> As thee, O Queene, the matter of my song.
>
> (III, iv, 3)

it is to a Christian typological tradition that he is alluding. The prophetic blossoming tree whose branches stretch to heaven's height (III, iii, 22) echoes the familiar image of the *Virga Iesse* in Isaiah, XI. Owing, perhaps, to the verbal similarity of *virga* (rod) and *virgo* (virgin), the Tree of Jesse came to be identified in the Middle Ages as a type of the Virgin Mary.[52] Indeed so habitual in medieval and Renaissance iconography was this interpretation of Isaiah, that to employ such a familiar image in a sixteenth-century poem was to guarantee the evocation of Marian associations. Since Britomart is herself a type of Queen Elizabeth this means that Spenser is establishing a typological connection between Elizabeth and the Virgin Mary.

It may at first seem strange to find an Elizabethan poet drawing parallels between his prince and the Catholic Queen of Heaven, more particularly since the Reformed Church of which she was Supreme Governor had been zealous to abolish what it saw as the idolatrous, Romish and hence unpatriotic veneration and invocation of the saints, especially that of the Virgin Mary. However, Spenser was not alone in making this comparison. Secularized versions of the Tree of Jesse are not uncommon in Elizabethan patriotic literature. In *The Misfortunes of Arthur* the ghost of Gorlois addresses the queen as

That vertuous *Virgo* borne for *Brytaines*
blisse:
That piereless braunch of *Brute*: that sweete
remaine
Of *Priam's* state: that hope of springing *Troy*:
Which time to come, and many ages hence
Shall of all warres compound eternall peace.[53]

Virgilian and Christian traditions are here combined to express the idea of Elizabeth's role as predestined inaugurator of a new golden age of 'Religion, ease and health'.

The most explicit identification of Elizabeth with the Virgin of the Tree of Jesse is the illustration on the title page of Stow's *Annals* where the traditional iconography of the *Virga Iesse* has been adapted to a Tudor genealogy with Queen Elizabeth as the royal flower 'enraced', like the Blessed Virgin, in 'stocke of earthly flesh' (*FQ, III, v, 52*).[54]

That identification of the Queen with the Virgin Mary was a central feature of the cult of Elizabeth is well known.[55] What is not widely understood is the way in which Spenser systematically exploits this typology in his characterization of most of the important regal female figures in **The Faerie Queene**. A review of the more important aspects of the cult of the Virgin Mary and the ascription to Elizabeth of Marian attributes will serve to show how perfectly suited this material was to Spenser's purpose.

From the time of the early Church Fathers Mary was revered in her own person as Mother of God,[56] and in symbol as the Church in its true faith.[57] By the end of the Middle Ages the cult of her person had grown to enormous proportions, emphasizing her quasi-divine powers and privileges as predestined Queen of heaven and hell,[58] co-redeeming vanquisher of death and the devil,[59] mystical bride of Christ,[60] miraculous protectress, and merciful intercessor for all mankind, both in this world and at the Day of Judgement.[61] Her feast days were highly popular, not least the day of her Nativity and the day of her Assumption into heaven. It was from these special powers, privileges and devotions that the Virgin Mary was firmly divested by the Church reformers in their zeal to return to the orthodoxy of the primitive Church.

The abolition of such deep-rooted beliefs could hardly be accomplished without leaving an emotional and intellectual gap in the life of Christendom. As Wilson has remarked, 'Human devotion changes more slowly than its objects shift. From 1558 to 1603 the virgin queen of England was the object of a love not dissimilar in quality from that which for centuries had warmed English hearts that looked to the virgin Queen of Heaven for all grace.'[62] However, it is important to realize that the adaptation of Marian imagery to the

praise of Elizabeth was rare until the mid-1570s,[63] and that when it did become current its purpose was more than sentimental or merely metaphoric. Rather it is to be seen as a later extension of the very earliest attempts to identify Elizabeth as a predestined champion of the Protestant cause; as such it had a precise historical and apocalyptic function.

As soon as Elizabeth acceded to the throne she was greeted as a godly prince providentially appointed to deliver a chosen people from Antichrist. 'Let us daily call to God with lifted up hearts and hands for her preservation and long life', wrote John Aylmer in 1559 in reply to Knox's *Monstrous Regiment of Women*, 'that she may many years carry the sword of our defence, and therewith cut off the head of that Hydra, the Antichrist of Rome, in such sort that it may never grow again in this realm of England.'[64] With the publication of Jewel's *Apology of the Church of England* in 1562 and of the English version of Foxe's *Acts and Monuments* in the following year, the predestinate nature of the role the new queen was to play—already firmly implanted in the popular mind through civic pageantry[65]—received the confirmation of a seemingly overwhelming weight of historical evidence. As Haller has shown, the great achievement of the *Acts and Monuments* was to demonstrate that 'by all the signs to be found in scripture and history the will of God was about to be fulfilled in England by a prince perfect in her obedience to her vocation . . .'[66]

What was not apparent in the early years of Elizabeth's reign was the apocalyptic significance of her virginity. Quite apart from the consideration that to be ruled by a woman ran counter to natural law, there was much pressure on her to marry for the sake of ensuring the succession.[67] But the longer Elizabeth reigned, miraculously impregnable to Catholic plots and presumptive husbands, the greater was the tendency for Protestant Elizabethans to see the adulation of their Virgin Queen as a precise and proper substitute for the cult of the Virgin Mary. '*Vivat ELIZA!* for an *Ave MARI!*' sings Dowland,[68] while Dekker (born c. 1570) declares that his own generation 'never shouted any other *Aue* than her name . . .'[69] As her reign wore on the pious hopes expressed in the allegorical pageantry of the accession-day festivities were naturally transformed into confident tributes to Elizabeth's godly statesmanship. By the 1580s it was a common belief that 'the whole course of hir Maiesties life is myraculous'.[70] November 17 was fervently kept as a day of patriotic rejoicing, 'in the forme of an Holy-day',[71] to celebrate the date of 'saint' Elizabeth's accession to the throne. Another day of celebration which gave particular offence to English Catholics was Elizabeth's birthday, for September 7 was also the feast of the Nativity of the Blessed Virgin Mary. Thomas Holland, in a sermon for 17 November 1599, adverts to the complaint that Protestants contemptuously ignored the

Virgin's nativity and 'insteede thereof, most solemnly doe celebrate the birth-day of Q. Elizabeth', even to the extent that in St Paul's Cathedral

> That Antiphone or Himne that was accustomably in the end of the service song by the Quier in the honor of the blessed Virgin, is now converted (as it is reported by common fame) to the laude and honor of Queene Elizabeth, thereby to sounde her praises.[72]

The transference to Elizabeth of certain deep-rooted devotional habits no doubt filled an important emotional gap in the lives of her subjects. But it would be misleading to suggest that the reasons for this phenomenon were purely intuitive: the celebration, in the later years of her reign, of Elizabeth as a post-figuration of the Virgin Mary is an important but neglected ramification of the nationalistic propaganda whose essential features had been definitively established in the *Acts and Monuments*. From the first year of her reign, some time before Marian comparisons had begun to be made, Elizabeth was likened to the biblical Deborah who saved God's chosen race from the idolatrous heathen.[73] But later in her reign, in the mid-1570s, other Old Testament analogies became popular. From that time onwards Elizabeth is frequently likened to Judith and Esther,[74] both of whom were formerly types of the Virgin Mary in her conquest of the Devil;[75] she is compared with the Queen of Sheba[76] (another type of Mary), whose homage to Solomon symbolized the faith and worship of the true Church;[77] she is seen as a daughter of King David, a virgin begotten of the Lord and espoused to God's only son to rule over Sion;[78] her people are a second Israel,[79] her country a second Canaan, the promised land flowing with milk and honey.[80]

The motive behind these comparisons is not sentimental but political. In drawing parallels between his Queen and certain Old Testament figures who are themselves types of the Virgin Mary, the panegyrist is implying that Elizabeth's royal virginity signifies the fulfilment of God's special will for his chosen people. Though the promise contained in these Old Testament figures was fulfilled in the Blessed Virgin, her life does not represent a consummation of the historical process of which it forms a part. For the antitype itself contains the promise of a future event and looks forward to the end of time and the establishment of God's kingdom on earth.[81] As a post-figuration of the Virgin Mary, Elizabeth performs a crucial role in this millenial plan. For if Mary is, above all, a type of the Church, then Elizabeth's triumph over popery could be seen as the defeat of Antichrist prophesied in the Apocalypse, and the institution over which she presided as indubitably the one true Church.[82]

It is not surprising, therefore, that the coincidence of Elizabeth's own nativity with Mary's should have been regarded as more than a happy accident of fate. To the Protestant Elizabethan it seemed to be a divine omen, whose full import—that the entire reign of the Virgin Queen and her Anglican Church had been authorized, miraculously sustained and sanctified by divine providence—was indisputably confirmed by the date of Elizabeth's death, 24 March 1603. The fact that 'This Maiden Queen Elizabeth came into this world the Eve of the Nativity of the blessed Virgin Mary; and died on the Eve of the Annunciation of the Virgin Mary'[83] was a clear sign of predestination. Dekker wrote:

> Shee came in with the falle of the leafe, and went away in the Spring: her life (which was dedicated to Virginitie,) both beginning & closing vp a miraculous Mayden circle: for she was borne vpon a Lady Eue, and died vpon a Lady Eue.[84]

When Elizabeth was addressed as queen of heaven and hell,[85] vanquisher of death and the devil,[86] mystical bride of Christ,[87] miraculous protectress and merciful intercessor,[88] few educated Elizabethans would have failed to recognize the apocalyptic significance of such appellations: it was as if she had, by providential design, attained a symbolic kinship with the Virgin Mary, and so, without any impropriety, could be venerated by Protestant patriots in the terms and images reserved for the honour of the Queen of Heaven.

Nowhere is the belief that the resemblances between Elizabeth and Mary were the coherent revelations of a divine purpose clearer than in the English and Latin verses composed in commemoration of Elizabeth's death. Here we find not only quasi-Marian litanies of her titles and epithets, but also the most direct and explicit comparisons between the two women. 'Do you wish to know the reason why it was on the Eve of Lady Day that the holy Eliza ascended into heaven?' asked the anonymous author of one Latin elegy. His answer was simple:

> being on the point of death she chose that day for herself because in their lives these two were as one. Mary was a Virgin, she, Elizabeth, was also; Mary was blessed; Beta was blessed among the race of women. Mary's heir was a prince, Elizabeth was the heir of a prince. Mary bore God in her womb, but Elizabeth bore God in her heart. Although in all other respects they are like twins, it is in this latter respect alone that they are not of equal rank.[89]

For an Elizabethan poet undertaking to vindicate his prince's claim to be the restorer of the one true Church the tradition of veneration which culminates in these memorial verses provided a vehicle of praise which was uniquely suited to his purpose. If Elizabeth's sex created serious problems for an epideictic poet writing in the heroic mode, at the same time it made available to him a form of praise which no poet had been able to use before. The reason why Spenser's use of these techniques has, on the whole, gone unnoticed is probably the fact that he often combines Marian and classical imagery in describing the same character. Belphoebe in Book II and Cynthia in the 'Mutabilitie' fragment are the most notable examples of this fusion of the Christian with the pagan. However, it is important that we distinguish between the purely metaphoric significance of the latter—the stock in trade of the epideictic poet—and the typological significance of the former. When Spenser compares Elizabeth with a classical goddess like Cynthia he is writing figuratively: he wishes to persuade us that Elizabeth possesses those virtues of which Cynthia is a personification. But when he uses Marian imagery to describe the same character he is implying that the relationship between Elizabeth and the Virgin Mary is not just an imaginary one, but a kinship of character and of providential function between two historical figures. The resemblances between them—too complete to be explained as mere coincidence—appeared to confirm the fact that Elizabeth was no ordinary ruler, but indeed a 'Prince of peace from heauen blest' (*FQ*, IV, proem, 4).

Marian typology thus complements the Trojan myth; together they form the background of a poem which can, in the fullest sense of the term, be described as a work of Christian humanism. Allusion to these two bodies of mythico-historical matter is by no means continuous throughout *The Faerie Queene*: as Virgil allows his reader occasionally to catch, as it were, a glimpse of Augustus, without his ever appearing in the *Aeneid* in person, so Spenser reminds his reader, at certain dramatic moments in the narrative, that the events which he is witnessing have a significance beyond their literal, or indeed their allegorical meaning— a significance which can only be perceived in its entirety within the context of a Christian humanist view of world history.

In addressing his poem to Queen Elizabeth and telling her that she may trace her own 'great auncestry' in its 'antique Image' (II, proem, 4), Spenser set himself a twofold task—a task which is perhaps best summed up by Erasmus when he claims that the purpose of the epideictic writer is to present his prince with an image of virtue, both as a pattern for emulation and as a warning against the dereliction of his sacred responsibility. The virtues which form the subjects of the six completed books of *The Faerie Queene* are to be understood, then, not simply as facets of a Renaissance ideal of human conduct, but as attributes of Queen Elizabeth. . . .

LIST OF ABBREVIATIONS

BJRL Bulletin of the John Rylands Library

ELH Journal of English Literary History

ES English Studies

JMRS Journal of Medieval and Renaissance Studies

JWCI Journal of the Warburg and Courtauld Institutes

MLR Modern Language Review

PMLA Publications of the Modern Language Association of America

Notes

[1] All quotations from Spenser are from *The Poetical Works of Edmund Spenser,* edited by J. C. Smith and E. de Selincourt, one vol. edn (Oxford, 1924).

[2] Letter to Ralegh, Smith and de Selincourt, p. 407.

[3] The best modern account of the theory of praise in Renaissance literature is O. B. Hardison, Jr., *The Enduring Monument: A Study of the Idea of Praise in Renaissance Literary Theory and Practice* (Westport, Conn., 1962). See also Theodore Burgess, *Epideictic Literature* (Chicago, 1902); A. Leigh De Neef, 'Epideictic Rhetoric and the Renaissance Lyric', *JMRS,* 3 (1973), 203-31; Barbara Kiefer Lewalski, *Donne's 'Anniversaries' and the Poetry of Praise: The Creation of a Symbolic Mode* (Princeton, 1973), pp. 15-41; James D. Garrison, *Dryden and the Tradition of Panegyric* (Berkeley, Los Angeles and London, 1975), pp. 1-82; Thomas H. Cain, *Praise in 'The Faerie Queene'* (Lincoln, Nebr., 1978), pp. 1-10; John W. O'Malley, *Praise and Blame in Renaissance Rome: Rhetoric, Doctrine, and Reform in the Sacred Orators of the Papal Court, c. 1450-1521* (Durham, N.C., 1979), pp. 36-76; Richard S. Peterson, *Imitation and Praise in the Poems of Ben Jonson* (New Haven, Conn. and London, 1981), pp. 1-43.

[4] George Puttenham, *The Arte of English Poesie,* edited by Gladys Doidge Willcock and Alice Walker (Cambridge, 1936), p. 24.

[5] Smith and de Selincourt, p. 411.

[6] Epideictic poetry. . . means literally poetry of display. On the analogy of epideictic oratory it normally signifies poetry of praise. (Epideictic oratory is one of the three classical divisions of rhetoric; see Aristotle, *Rhetoric,* I, iii, 3; [Cicero?] *Rhetorica ad Herennium,* I, ii, 2; Cicero, *De Inventione,* I, v, 7; *De Oratore,* I, xxxi, 141; Quintilian, *Institutio Oratore,* III, iv; Menander Rhetor, I, i, 1-14.)

[7] *Donati interpretationes Virgilianae,* quoted by Hardison, p. 33 (Hardison's translation). Servius (c. fourth-fifth century) likewise claimed that Virgil's intention was 'to imitate Homer and to praise Augustus in terms

of his ancestors' (Introduction to *P. Vergilii Carmina Commentarii,* quoted by D. L. Drew, *The Allegory of the 'Aeneid'* (Oxford, 1927), p. 98 (my translation)). On Servius as an interpreter of Virgil, see also Michael O'Connell, *Mirror and Veil: The Historical Dimension of Spenser's 'Faerie Queene'* (Chapel Hill, N.C., 1977), pp. 25-31. As O'Connell writes: 'Servius held a position of unique authority and honor in sixteenth-century editions of Vergil. Indeed his commentary was practically inescapable by Renaissance readers of Vergil . . .' (pp. 25-6).

[8] Domenico Comparetti, *Vergil in the Middle Ages,* translated by E. F. M. Benecke (London, 1895), p. 108.

[9] Hardison, p. 78.

[10] John Hughes, 'An Essay on Allegorical Poetry' (1715) rpt. in *Edmund Spenser: A Critical Anthology,* edited by Paul J. Alpers (Harmondsworth, 1969), p. 82. Cf. Dryden: 'Virgil . . . designed to form a perfect prince, and would insinuate that Augustus, whom he calls Aeneas in his poem, was truly such . . .', 'Dedication of the Aeneis', *Essays of John Dryden,* edited by W. P. Ker, 2 vols (New York, 1961), II, 179.

[11] Hardison, p. 80.

[12] Many scholars have written on Spenser's debt to Virgil. See in particular Merritt Y. Hughes, *Virgil and Spenser* (New York, 1929); Wm. Stanford Webb, 'Vergil in Spenser's Epic Theory', *ELH,* 4 (1937), 62-84; Josephine Waters Bennett, *The Evolution of 'The Faerie Queene'* (New York, 1942), pp. 6 ff.; William Nelson, *The Poetry of Edmund Spenser* (New York and London, 1963), pp. 117 ff.; O'Connell, pp. 23-30.

[13] 'In that Faery Queene I meane glory in my generall intention, but in my particular I conceiue the most excellent and glorious person of our soueraine the Queene, and her kingdome in Faery land' (Letter to Ralegh, Smith and de Selincourt, p. 407). See Edwin Greenlaw, *Studies in Spenser's Historical Allegory,* Johns Hopkins Monographs in Literary History, II (Baltimore, 1932); Frances Yates, 'Queen Elizabeth as Astraea', *JWCI,* 10 (1947), 27-82; Hardison, pp. 80-4; Frank Kermode, 'The Faerie Queene, I and V', *BJRL,* 47 (1964), rpt. in *Shakespeare, Spenser, Donne: Renaissance Essays* (London, 1971), p. 40; Cain, *Praise in 'The Faerie Queene',* passim.

[14] *Praise in 'The Faerie Queene',* p. 1.

[15] Letter to Jean Desmarez, *The Correspondence of Erasmus,* translated by R. A. B. Mynors and D. F. S. Thomson, 2 vols. (Toronto, 1975), II, 81.

[16] See Hardison, pp. 27-42.

[17] For discussions of the *speculum principis* tradition see John E. Mason, *Gentlefolk in the Making: Studies in the History of English Courtesy Literature and Related Topics from 1531-1774* (Philadelphia, 1935), pp. 10-11; Lester K. Born, introduction to a translated edition of Erasmus's *Education of a Christian Prince,* Columbia University Records of Civilisation, XXVII (New York, 1936), pp. 44-130.

[18] Dedicatory Epistle to *The Education of a Christian Prince,* edited by Born, pp. 135-6.

[19] Helena Shire, *A Preface to Spenser* (London, 1978), p. 84.

[20] Letter to Ralegh, Smith and de Selincourt, p. 407.

[21] The standard works on the Renaissance courtesy book are Ruth Kelso, *The Doctrine of the English Gentleman in the Sixteenth Century,* University of Illinois Studies in Language and Literature, XIV (Urbana, Ill., 1929) and Mason, *Gentlefolk in the Making.*

[22] See in particular Mohinimohan Bhattacherje, *Studies in Spenser* (Calcutta, 1929) extract rpt. in *The Works of Edmund Spenser,* Variorum edition, edited by Edwin Greenlaw, Charles Grosvenor Osgood, Frederick Morgan Padelford and Ray Heffner, 10 vols (Baltimore, 1932-49), Books VI and VII, 328-33; H. S. V. Jones, *A Spenser Handbook* (New York, 1930), pp. 287-92; A. C. Judson, 'Spenser's Theory of Courtesy', *PMLA,* 47 (1932), 122-36; Fritz Caspari, *Humanism and the Social Order in Tudor England* (Chicago, 1954), pp. 176-80.

[23] 'Proheme' to *The Boke Named the Governor* (1531), edited by Foster Watson, Everyman edition (London, 1907), p. xxxi. For further discussion of this point see Robin Headlam Wells, 'Spenser and the Courtesy Tradition: Form and Meaning in the Sixth Book of *The Faerie Queene',* *ES,* 58 (1977), 226-8.

[24] *The Book of the Courtier,* translated by Sir Thomas Hoby, Everyman edition (1928; rpt. London, 1966), pp. 260-1.

[25] On Elyot's debt to Castiglione and the differences as well as similarities between *The Courtier* and *The Governour* see John M. Major, *Sir Thomas Elyot and Renaissance Humanism* (Lincoln, Nebr., 1964), pp. 61-76.

[26] Caspari, p. 183.

[27] Smith and de Selincourt, p. 407.

[28] Smith and de Selincourt, p. 409.

[29] *Genealogie Deorum Gentilium Libri,* edited by

Vincenzo Romano, *Opere,* 7 vols (Bari, 1928-51), VII, 721-3. On Boccaccio's influence in Renaissance England see Charles G. Osgood (ed.), *Boccaccio on Poetry: Being the Preface and the Fourteenth and Fifteenth Books of Boccaccio's 'Genealogie Deorum Gentilium'* (1930; rpt. Indianapolis, 1956), p. xliv.

[30] It was the arbitrary nature of much medieval interpretation of the Bible which led to the condemnation of this form of hermeneutics by Reformation exegetes. For the Protestant seeking the one true sense of Scripture, allegorists of the school of Philo were held in deep suspicion because they dealt with arcana. The typologist, on the other hand, sought only to reveal an aspect of the literal meaning of sacred texts. (See Lewalski, pp. 150-6. See also Philip Rollinson, *Classical Theories of Allegory and Christian Culture* (Pittsburg and Brighton, 1981), pp. 29-86.)

[31] See V. A. Kolve, *The Play Called Corpus Christi* (London, 1966), pp. 63 ff.

[32] In one of the fullest of the rare discussions of typology in *The Faerie Queene* Angus Fletcher consistently and wrongly equates typology not only with prophecy, but with parody and literary parallelism of the most general kind (*The Prophetic Moment: An Essay on Spenser* (Chicago, 1971), pp. 57-132). To say that 'Insofar as Book II seems grossly analogous to Book I it has always been read in a typological way . . .' (p. 84) or that the names of the rivers attending the marriage of the Thames and the Medway in Book IV 'Come from the matrix of Ovidian typology' (p. 96) does more to obscure the meaning of typology than to clarify it.

[33] The most scholarly modern discussion of typology is still Erich Auerbach's 'Figura' in *Scenes from the Drama of European Literature* (New York, 1959), pp. 11-76. See also Auerbach, *Mimesis: The Representation of Reality in Western Literature* (1946; rpt. New York, 1953), pp. 13-14; 42-3; 64-6; Austin Farrer, 'Typology', *The Expository Times,* 67 (1956), 228-31; K. J. Woollcombe, 'The Biblical Origins and Patristic Development of Typology' in *Essays on Typology,* edited by G. W. H. Lampe and K. J. Woollcombe (London, 1957), pp. 39-75; Jean Danielou S. J., *From Shadows to Reality: Studies in the Biblical Typology of the Fathers,* translated by Dom Wulstan Hibberd (London, 1960), pp. 1-7 and passim; Thomas M. Davis, 'The Tradition of Puritan Typology', *Early American Literature,* 5 (1970), 1-50, rpt. in *Typology and Early American Literature,* edited by Sacvan Bercovitch (Amherst, Mass., 1972), pp. 11-45; John MacQueen, *Allegory* (London, 1970), pp. 18-23; Karlfried Froehlich, '"Always to keep to the Literal Sense in Holy Scripture Means to kill One's Soul": The State of Biblical Hermeneutics at

the Beginning of the Fifteenth Century' in *Literary Uses of Typology from the Late Middle Ages to the Present,* edited by Earl Miner (Princeton, 1977), pp. 20-48; Mason I. Lowance, Jr., *The Language of Canaan: Metaphor and Symbol in New England from the Puritans to the Transcendentalists* (Cambridge, Mass. and London, 1980), pp. 13-27.

In recent years there have appeared some outstanding studies of typology in literature. See in particular A. C. Charity, *Events and their Afterlife: The Dialectics of Christian Typology in the Bible and Dante* (Cambridge, 1966); Stephen Manning, 'Scriptural Exegesis and the Literary Critic', *Early American Literature,* 5 (1970), 51-73 rpt. in Bercovitch, pp. 47-66; Lewalski, *Donne's 'Anniversaries',* pp. 149-58; Robert Hollander, 'Typology and Secular Literature: Some Medieval Problems and Examples' in Miner, pp. 3-19; Steven N. Zwicker, 'Politics and Panegyric: The Figural Mode from Marvell to Pope' in Miner, pp. 115-46.

[34] The first modern critic to draw attention to this aspect of the *Aeneid* is Drew, *The Allegory of the 'Aeneid',* p. 4. See also Hollander, 'Typology and Secular Literature', p. 6.

[35] Richard Nicols, *Englands Eliza: or The Victoriovs and Trivmphant Reigne of that Virgin Empresse of Sacred Memorie, ELIZABETH . . .* printed in *A Mirovr for Magistrates,* edited by John Higgins (London, 1610), p. 784.

[36] See Lewalski, pp. 150-8.

[37] Spenser's edition, like all Renaissance editions of the *Aeneid,* began, as Nelson reminds us (p. 117), not with the words 'Arma virumque cano . . .' but:

> Ille ego qui quondam gracili modulatus avena
> Carmen, et egressus silvis, vicina coegi
> Ut quamvis avido parerent arva colono
> Gratum opus agricolis: at nunc horrentia
>   Martis
> Arma virumque cano . . .

[38] For discussions of the Trojan myth from a literary point of view see A. E. Parsons, 'The Trojan Legend in England', *MLR,* 24 (1929), 253-64, 394-408 and Greenlaw, *Studies in Spenser's Historical Allegory,* pp. 1-58. T. D. Kenrick (*British Antiquity* (London, 1950), passim), and F. J. Levy (*Tudor Historical Thought* (San Marino, 1967), pp. 65-6) consider the myth from the points of view of the Tudor antiquarian and historian respectively.

[39] Kenrick, p. 3.

[40] Kenrick, p. 7.

41

> Brute sub occasu solistrans gallica regna.
> Insula in occeano est habitata gigantibus olim.
> Nunc deserta quidem gentibus apta tuis.
> Illa tibi fietque tuis locus aptus aeuum.
> Hec erit & natis attera troia tuis.
> Hie de prole tua reges nascentur & ipsis.
> Totius terrae subditus orbis erit.

(*The* Historia Regum Britanniae *of Geoffrey of Monmouth,* edited by Acton Griscom (London, 1929), p. 239.)

42 *Parts Added to The Mirror for Magistrates,* edited by Lily B. Campbell (Cambridge, 1946), p. 55.

43 *The Union of the Two Noble and Illustre Famelies of Lancastre & Yorke, Beeyng, Long in Continual Discension for the Crowne of this Noble Realme, with all the Actes Done in Bothe the Tymes of the Princes* . . . (1548; rpt. London, 1809), p. 423.

44 The myth was also revived on James I's accession. See Charles Bowie Millican, *Spenser and The Table Round,* Harvard Studies in Comparative Literature, VIII (Cambridge, Mass., 1932), pp. 127-41 and Glynne Wickham, *Shakespeare's Dramatic Heritage* (London, 1969), pp. 250-8.

45 See Appendix, 'Polydore Vergil and English Historiography'.

46 *A Defence of Poetry, Miscellaneous Prose of Sir Philip Sidney,* edited by Katherine Duncan-Jones and Jan Van Dorsten (Oxford, 1973), p. 78.

47 Sidney, p. 79.

48 *A View of the Present State of Ireland, Variorum Spenser, The Prose Works* (1949), edited by Rudolf Gottfried, p. 82.

49 See Comparetti, *Vergil in the Middle Ages,* pp. 99-101; Yates, 'Queen Elizabeth as Astraea', pp. 32-3; Marina Warner, *Alone of All Her Sex: The Myth and the Cult of the Virgin Mary* (London, 1976), pp. 264-5.

50 Lydgate, for example, writes, 'Sythe [Christ] is borne with so fayre a face, / The golden worlde makying to retourne, / The worlde of pece, the kyngdome of Satourne . . .' (*Life of Our Lady,* edited by Joseph A. Lauritis, Ralph A. Klinefelter and Vernon F. Gallagher, Duquesne Studies in Philosophy, II (Pittsburg, 1961), p. 533).

51 John Lyly, *Euphues' Glass for Europe, The Complete Works of John Lyly,* edited by R. Warwick Bond, 3 vols (Oxford, 1902), II, 205.

52 See Arthur Watson, *The Early Iconography of the Tree of Jesse* (Oxford, 1934). In medieval Marian literature the Virgin Mary is sometimes compared, as empress, with the most illustrious pagan rulers of the ancient world and her royal lineage with theirs. See, for example, *The Myroure of oure Ladye,* edited by John Henry Blunt, Early English Text Society (London, 1873), pp. 216, 258-9; John Lydgate, *Life of Our Lady,* pp. 252-3. In constructing a mythical genealogy for Queen Elizabeth, Spenser conflates the pagan with the Christian.

53 Quoted by Elkin Calhoun Wilson, *England's Eliza,* Harvard Studies in English, XX (1939; rpt. London, 1966), p. 103. Elizabeth is similarly described as a 'matchlesse flower' springing from 'the Royall Garden of a King' in Bacon's prophecy from Greene's *Friar Bacon and Friar Bungay* (see Wilson, pp. 103-4).

54 The same illustration is used in the 1580 edition of the *Annals,* entitled *The Chronicles of England.*

55 See Yates, 'Queen Elizabeth as Astraea', pp. 74-5; John Buxton, *Elizabethan Taste* (London, 1963), p. 50; Jean Wilson, *Entertainments for Elizabeth I* (Woodbridge, 1980), pp. 21-2.

56 See the *New Catholic Encyclopaedia* (Washington, D.C., 1967) under 'Mother of God'.

57 See Warner, pp. 104-5.

58 See Émile Mâle, *Religious Art in France: XIII Century,* translated by Dora Nussey (London, 1913), p. 235.

59 See Mirella Levi D'Ancona, *The Iconography of the Immaculate Conception in the Middles Ages and Early Renaissance,* Monographs on Archaeology and Fine Arts sponsored by the Archaeological Institute of America and the College Art Association of America, VII (New York, 1957), pp. 20-8, 32-3 and Rosemary Woolf, *The English Religious Lyric in the Middle Ages* (Oxford, 1968), pp. 121-3.

60 See Warner, pp. 121-33, 247. The imagery is drawn from the Canticles and the Apocalypse, XXI, 2.

61 See D'Ancona, pp. 34-5; Mâle, pp. 23-66; Woolf, pp. 123-4.

62 Wilson, *England's Eliza,* p. 215. Much of the illustrative material contained in the following paragraphs is taken from Wilson's invaluable compilation of Elizabethan panegyric. Although Wilson discusses the Elizabethan habit of comparing the Queen with the Virgin Mary in a chapter somewhat obliquely entitled 'Diana', many Marian analogies are to be found in oth-

er chapters, often in a form whose significance was apparently not recognised by him.

[63] See Wilson, passim.

[64] *An Harborowe for faithfull and true subjectes* (1559), quoted by William Haller, *Foxe's Book of Martyrs and the Elect Nation* (London, 1963), p. 88.

[65] At the royal entry of 1558 Elizabeth was represented as Deborah, judge and restorer of Israel, 'sent / From Heaven, a long comfort to us thy subjectes all'. See *The Progresses and Public Processions of Queen Elizabeth,* edited by John Nichols, 3 vols (1788-1805; rpt. London, 1823), I, 56.

[66] Haller, p. 225.

[67] See J. E. Neale, *Queen Elizabeth* (London, 1934), Chs. V, XV.

[68] *The Second Book of Airs* (1600) (quoted by Wilson, p. 206).

[69] Thomas Dekker, *The Wonderfull Yeare* (1603) (quoted by Wilson, p. 393).

[70] Henri Estienne, *The Stage of Popish toyes* (1581) (quoted by Wilson, p. 225). Cf. also Thomas Bentley, *The monument of matrones,* 'The first Chapter of the HEAST', reproduced by Wilson in a plate facing p. 220: God has 'miraculouslie deliuered [Elizabeth] out of so manie & so great dangers . . .' In her ageless virginity, too, she is 'Heauens miracle' (*Histriomastix* (c. 1589), quoted by Wilson, p. 109). For the Virgin Mary's agelessness see Warner, p. 95.

[71] Thomas Holland, *A sermon preached at Pauls in London* (1599) (quoted by Wilson, p. 223, n. 100).

[72] Quoted by Wilson, pp. 221-2.

[73] See above, note 65.

[74] Cf. Thomas Deloney, *The ouerthrow of proud Holofernes, and the triumph of vertuous Queene Iudith* (1588): 'How often hath our Iudith sau'd, / and kept vs from decay: / Gainst Holofernes, Deuill and Pope . . .' (quoted by Wilson, p. 44). For other examples of Elizabeth as Judith see Wilson, pp. 36, 81, 185, 372, 380. As with Judith, analogies between Elizabeth and Esther, who preserved her people against the plots of Haman, were especially popular after the defeat of the Armada. For examples see Wilson, pp. 81, 101 n. 27, 185, 376, 380.

[75] See Woolf, p. 285.

[76] Thomas Holland's sermon for 17 November 1599 compares Elizabeth (*'Regia Virgo'*) with the Queen of Sheba (see Wilson, p. 223, n. 100).

[77] See Mâle, p. 157.

[78] In Thomas Bentley's *The Monument of matrones* God addresses Elizabeth in the following words: 'Elizabeth, thou Virgin mine, the KINGS Daughter, and fairest among women; most full of beautie and maiestie: attend a litle to my Heast, and marke what I shall say. Thou art my Daughter in deede, this daie haue I begotten thee, and espoused thee to thy king CHRIST, my Sonne; crowned thee with my gifts, and appointed thee QVEENE, to reigne vpon my holie mount Zion' (reproduced by Wilson in a plate facing p. 220).

[79] In *The monument of matrones* God declares to Elizabeth: '[I have] annointed thee with holie oile, to be the Queene, the Mother, and the Nursse of my people in Israel . . .' (Wilson, plate facing p. 220). Lyly speaks of England as 'a new *Israel*' in *Euphues' Glass for Europe,* p. 205.

[80] See the poems extracted by Wilson, pp. 376, 387.

[81] Isabel Rivers is misleading when she writes: 'the antitype once and for all fulfils the type and the meaning hidden in it' (*Classical and Christian Ideas in English Renaissance Poetry* (London, 1979), p. 149). As Auerbach argues, both type and antitype 'have something provisional and incomplete about them; they point to one another and both point to something in the future, something still to come, which will be the actual, real, and definitive event' ('Figura', p. 58).

[82] Interpretations of the Apocalypse as an allegorical prophecy of the struggle between the English Protestants and their persecutors were common in the sixteenth century. . . .

[83] Memorial inscription in Westminster Abbey cited by Buxton, p. 51. Buxton notes that the 'Lady Chapels which their grandfathers had built on to the east end of English churches were now replaced by . . . secular shrines for their devotion to the Queen' (p. 50).

[84] *The Wonderfull Yeare* (quoted by Wilson, pp. 220-1).

[85] In Dekker's *Old Fortunatus* (1599) it is claimed of Eliza that 'heau'n and hell her power obey' (quoted by Wilson, p. 116).

[86] In *Idea the Shepheards Garland* (1593) Drayton depicts Elizabeth as the Marian composite of the Second Eve, trampling the serpent of Eden under her heel (Genesis, III, 15), and the woman of the

Apocalypse threatened by the beast or dragon with seven heads (Revelation, XII, 3-4) when he writes 'And thy large empyre stretch her armes from east unto the west, / And thou under thy feet mayst tread, that foule seven-headed beast' (quoted by Wilson, p. 146). The seven-headed beast is to be interpreted in regular Protestant fashion as the papacy. See, for example Bale's *Image of Both Churches.* In his paraphrase of Revelation, XII, 3 Bale writes, 'this is the very papacy here in Europe, which is the general antichrist of all the whole world almost' (*Select Works of John Bale,* edited by Henry Christmas, Parker Society Reprints (Cambridge, 1849), p. 407). On the traditional conflation of Genesis, III, 15 with Revelation, XII, 3-4 see Warner, pp. 244-6.

[87] See above, note 78.

[88] In a ballad of 1584 celebrating her triumph over Catholic plots, Elizabeth, the 'pearle of princes' and 'renowned virgin queen' is represented as a protector of her loyal followers from the rod of God's vengeance for sin (see Wilson, pp. 32-4). On the Virgin Mary as protecting intercessor see Louis Réau, *Iconographie De L'Art Chrétien,* 6 vols. (Paris, 1955-9), III (1957), 116-17.

[89]

> Scire cupis causam pridie cur, sacra, diei
> *Virginis,* ad superas scandit *Elisa* domus?
> Disce brevi: moritura diem sibi legerat istum,
> Caetera quod paribus, par sit vtrisq; dies.
> Virgo *Maria* fuit, fuit illa: beata *Maria,*
> Inter foemineum *Beta* beata genus.
> Haeres *huic* princeps fuit, *altera* principis
> 　haeres,
> *Haec* vtero gessit, corde sed *illa* Deum.
> Caetera cum similes, cum caetera poeme
> 　gemellae,
> Hoc vno parilem non habuere statum . . .

(Lines from an anthology of Latin funeral verses published by Oxford University in 1603 (quoted by Wilson, p. 382).)

Maureen Quilligan (essay date 1987)

SOURCE: "The Comedy of Female Authority in *The Faerie Queene,*" in *English Literary Renaissance,* Vol. 17, No. 2, Spring, 1987, pp. 156-71.

[*In the following essay, Quilligan analyzes the allegorical representation of female power and authority in* The Faerie Queene.]

Basing his argument on Anthony Munday's recasting

of an Italian play acted before Queen Elizabeth in 1585, Albert Baugh reasoned some time ago that "it would seem the Queen's taste was for the braggadocchio of Captain Crackstone, who adds malapropism to his other absurdities of the miles gloriosus."[1] Baugh's shrewd guess not only shows how Spenser's coinages have entered the language, but also supports the notion that Spenser's decision to present Belphoebe on her first appearance in *The Faerie Queene* in the company of Braggadocchio and Trompart may owe something to his sense of what the Queen might herself have found amusing. If she liked to laugh at braggadocio captains—a taste further exhibited by her affection for Falstaff—the conspicuously irrelevant scene of Book II, canto iii may have been a subtle hint that Spenser deliberately aimed to please by shadowing his dread sovereign's chastity and womanly beauty in the figure of Belphoebe.[2]

Readers' responses are generically central to allegory, and the response of Elizabeth, Spenser's first reader and the imperial dedicatrix of the entire epic, is more central than most.[3] We know that Elizabeth's regime was very careful about pictorial representations of her physical person—and that if she disliked what an author published about her marriage program, for example, she could have his hand cut off (as she did of the too-aptly named John Stubbs).[4] Spenser had to tread very delicately in his portrayal of Belphoebe, having named her as explicitly as he does, one of the "mirrors more than one" in which Elizabeth could "chuse" "her selfe to see" (III, Proem, 5). We of course never see the other mirror in which Elizabeth's rule, as opposed to her chastity, is "fashioned"—and it is significant that the closest we come to Gloriana's presence in the text in Arthur's dream is also a moment, when viewed intertextually, that is interestingly occluded by comic elements. As a replay of Chaucer's Tale of Sir Topas, Arthur's dream of "The Faerie Queene" is wildly disjunct in its high, heroic, and romantic seriousness from the banal, bumping prolixity of the pilgrim Chaucer's first effort at a story in *The Canterbury Tales;* justly, Harry Baily remarks, the "drasty rhyming is not worth a tord!" Spenser's apparent deafness to Chaucer's wonderful joke on himself is, however, most interesting for the way Chaucer's Sir Topas prepares for another bumbling knight's comic interaction with a noble exemplar of the faerie queene in Spenser's text. Having rewritten Chaucer's comedy out of Arthur's dream in Book I, Spenser uses it to frame his first direct representation of Elizabeth's female authority in the character of Belphoebe in Book II. There is something funny going on in Spenser's representations of Elizabeth in *The Faerie Queene* and it may be useful to question what the prevalence of comedy says about Spenser's attitudes toward Elizabeth's gynocratic rule.[5]

The scene with Braggadocchio is not only one of the most comic moments in the epic, it has—if I am correct in my assumption of further generic background—a cultural connection to the Renaissance problem of female authority, if authority is thought to name in part that power by which a female might speak in public. Braggadocchio and Trompart are characters whose names suggest that if they are not taken directly from, then at least they are coherent with, the masks of the Captain and his wily servant in the Italian *commedia dell'arte*. While it has proved impossible for scholars to trace the specifics of the presence of *commedia dell'arte* companies in England, they were known to have played there during the last decades of the century and caused much comment, especially about the presence of women in their troupes. E. K. Chambers and K. M. Lea both guess that a group of players who performed for the court at Windsor in 1574 were "probably those who provoked" Thomas Norton's objections against the "unchaste, shamelesse & unnaturall tomblings of the Italion Woemen."[6] Englishmen who traveled abroad had, perhaps not surprisingly, a more cosmopolitan approach to professional women actresses, but they also register cultural shock at public female performance: thus Thomas Coryat reports his visit to a Venetian theater:

> Here I observed certain things that I never saw before. For I saw women acte, a thing that I never saw before, though I have heard that it hath sometimes been used in London, & they performed it with as good a grace, action, gesture & whatsoever convenient for a Player, as ever I saw any masculine actor. Also their noble and famous Cortezans came to this comedy, but so disguised that a man cannot perceive them.[7]

Coryat's observation indicates quite neatly, I think, the distinct if subtle boundary between public and private realms that organized for an Elizabethan Englishman a woman's proper place in society. Here it is disorganized by the surprising public self presentation of the professional Italian actress, and the equally odd private appearance in the audience of the "famous Cortezans" or already public women.[8] Another English traveler to Florence, Fynes Moryson, also specifically noted the skill of Italian actresses in speaking extempore:

> . . . in Florence they have a house where all yeere long a comedy was played by professed players once in the weeke . . . , and the partes of wemen were played by wemen, and the cheefe actours had not their partes fully penned, but speak much extempory or upon agreement between themselves, espetially the wemen, whose speeches were full of wantonnes, though not grosse baudry. . . . And one Lucinia a woman player, was so liked of the Florentines, as when shee dyed they made her a monument with an Epitaphe.[9]

If, as I would like to suggest, Spenser is specifically signalling his readers to think of a *commedia dell'arte*

generic framework for his scene with Braggadocchio and Belphoebe, he is also marking the scene as a moment where the cultural line is drawn between a woman's licit private sphere and a culturally suspect public arena. This signalling is done for the most part by a humor more grossly physical than we find anywhere else in the epic. As in Norton's objection to the Italian women's "tombling," the physical action of the mime-like movement of the *commedia* was, from an English perspective, all the more striking because performed by women. The action in canto iii, Book II is quickened to a slapstick pace not only by Braggadocchio's terrified fall from his horse and his diving into a bush, but by the earlier set-up of Braggadocchio's and Tromapart's fear at having seen Archimago flap away to get Arthur's sword:

> He stayd not for more bidding, but away
>   Was suddein vanished out of his sight:
>   The Northerne wind his wings did broad
>   display
> At his command, and reared him vp light
> From off the earth to take his aerie flight.
>   They lookt about, but no where could espie
> Tract of his foot: then dead through great
>   affright
>   They both nigh were, and each bad other
>   flie:
> Both fled attonce, ne euer backe returned eie.
>
> (II. iii.19)[10]

The Magician was a legitimate mask in and of itself in the *commedia dell'arte,* and one Archimago distinctly and comically wears. We not only see Archimago transform himself into a winged creature in the presence of Braggadocchio and Trompart, we see him transformed into a comic figure, tricked by the transparent swagger of Braggadocchio's bluster.

In a tradition later made much of by Shakespeare, the *commedia dell'arte* often functioned in its improvisational methods to produce laughs by the juxtaposition of dialects—in Italy the braggart Captain usually spoke Spanish, for instance—and much of the humor as well as verbal wit of the action derived from the literal idiocy of the characters: they often simply misunderstood each other. Similarly, the usually acute Archimago takes Braggadocchio at face value, and the conversation between Belphoebe and Braggadocchio is a virtual set piece of verbal misunderstandings. Their mutual misprision is prepared for, however, by the physical comedy of Belphoebe's mistaking Braggadocchio's rustlings in the underbrush for her stricken deer so that she "gan a deadly shaft aduauance," only to be stopped by Trompart. The pure slapstick peaks when Braggadocchio makes his appearance on hands and knees, crawling out of the bush into which he had dived at the sound of Belphoebe's approach:

with that he crauld out of his nest,
 Forth creeping on his caitiue hands and
 thies,
 And standing stoutly vp, his loftie crest
Did fiercly shake, and rowze, as comming late
 from rest.

(II.iii.35)

The stanza-long simile that compares Braggadocchio to a "fearefull fowle" who has hidden herself from a hawk reverses gender in a comedic way that is neatly matched by Belphoebe's answer to Braggadocchio's question about who she is:

But what art thou, ô ladie, which doest range
 In this wilde forrest, where no pleasure is,
 And doest not it for ioyous court exchaunge
 Emongst thine equall peres, where happie
 blis
 And all delight does raigne, much more then
 this? . . .

The wood is fit for beasts, the court is fit for
 thee.

(II.iii.39)

For her part, Belphoebe does not answer why she, a *lady,* dwells in the woods but instead discourses on why anyone—a man, say—would wish to avoid the court.

Who so in pompe of proud estate (quoth she)
 Does swim, and bathe himselfe in courtly
 blis,
 Does waste his dayes in darke obscuritee,
 And in obliuion euer buried is: . . .

Abroad in armes, at home in studious kind
Who seekes with painfull toile, shall honor
 soonest find.

(II.iii.40)

Such a dialogue about abstractions like "honor" and the moral problems of life at court could have been heard in the *commedia dell'arte;* but Belphoebe's problem in answering why *she* is in the woods has to do with the constraints imposed by a different genre altogether—the genre of narrative allegory. As in the *commedia,* however, the generic problem has to do with the question of appropriate gender: may a female *act?* In narrative allegory, figures of authority are traditionally feminine. One thinks of Lady Philosophy, Lady Nature, Lady Holy Church, Reason (in *Roman de la Rose*)—the list could go on.

The reason for this tradition is essentially grammatical. To take a specifically significant example, the particular noun *auctor, auctoris,* or "author" in Latin is, like the people it has traditionally designated, masculine; then, in order to turn this noun into an abstract general,

the class and gender need to be transformed. The word for "authority" itself is, in Latin, *auctoritas, auctoritatis,* noun feminine. Because of the generic linguistic interests of allegory, with its parades of personifications and its need to animate nouns, we are given landscapes filled with important female speakers. The striking resistance of medieval literary figures of authority to take on masculine gender is neatly displayed in the controversy Jean Gerson and Christine de Pizan carried on in the so-called "Querelle de la Rose"; in a debate of no small interest to students of the reception of the *Roman de la Rose,* of allegory, and of the history of feminist polemic, Christine had objected to Jean de Meun's obscene language and misogyny. Gerson, a distinguished medieval humanist, had supported Christine's position, in the process creating a male-gendered figure of authority, Theological Eloquence, to argue his points in the case. In Gerson's text this personification takes masculine pronouns. However, in Christine's text and in the texts of other parties to the debate, the grammar follows the gender of Latin *eloquentia,* noun feminine.[11]

In her function as a figure of authority in Spenser's text, Belphoebe, like Boethius' Lady Philosophy for instance, begins a brief disquisition on "honor"—"In woods, in waues, in warres *she* wonts to dwell / And will be found with perill and with paine, / Ne can the man, that moulds in idle cell, / Vnto her happy mansion attaine" (II.iii.41 [my italics]). Belphoebe is not only out in the woods to win honor, she is in some sense herself honor, not only because of her gender, which insists she be taken allegorically as a figure of *auctoritas,* but also because she historically represents Elizabeth, the cultural source of honors in Spenser's society. (This designation Spenser makes clear when he gives her Timias as a lover; *time* = honor.) There is, however, another counter-pressure in the narrative that compels us to see Belphoebe as herself a protagonist, freely ranging about the landscape, capable of experiencing her own history in the text. The potential fissure that begins to open between these twin forces is solved by Braggadocchio's comic blindness to the problem: before Spenser's presentation of Belphoebe as both a protagonist in a chivalric narrative and also an allegorical figure of authority can entirely split apart, Braggadocchio makes his move, thereby interrupting her disquisition on the evils of life at court.

In Princes court, The rest she would haue
 said,
 But that the foolish man, fild with delight
 Of her sweet words, that all his sence
 dismaid,
 And with her wondrous beautie rauisht
 quight,
 Gan burne in filthy lust, and leaping light,
 Thought in his bastard armes her to
 embrace.

(II.iii.42)

Braggadocchio's lewd action is completely out of keeping with the way allegorical authorities are traditionally treated. One cannot imagine even the libidinous lover of the *Roman de la Rose* making a grab at Lady Raison, much less Chaucer's erotically defunct narrator in the *Parlement of Foules* making a pass at Lady Nature. Braggadocchio's lunge stops the discourse cold and reassigns Belphoebe her role as a character of romance. Had Belphoebe's authoritative critique become fuller, Spenser would have been in the precarious predicament of having the named representation of Elizabeth roundly criticize the sloth and decadence of Elizabeth's own court. (With a similar comic abruptness in Book III, Spenser evades direct reference to the succession problem by having Merlin fall into his fainting fit before finishing hs prognostications.) Here, easily outmaneuvering Braggadocchio, Belphoebe menaces him with her javelin, turns on her heels, and flees—not to re-enter the poem for another fourteen cantos.

Harry Berger, Jr., has pointed to the problem Belphoebe's conspicuously irrelevant position poses in an interpretation of the third canto: "Consciously [Belphoebe] bespeaks honor, rejects love and passion; unconsciously she is an object of sexual no less than divine and royal devotion."[12] Another way of drawing the distinction that does not require us to posit a novelistic psyche for Belphoebe is to notice the generic conflict. Females in allegory may be figures of authority because they have the appropriate gender for moral or immoral abstractions; they usually counsel, or seduce, the male protagonist whose adventures carry the process of "fashioning." To make a female an actor in an allegory is to complicate an already complicated set of gender distinctions in an already complicated genre of narrative. As Berger comments, "There is a shade of the sinister about" Belphoebe because she "mysteriously combines . . . two different women," essentially Diana, an innocent unselfaware goddess, and Penthesilea, a self-conscious female warrior (p. 140). The relationship between Diana and Penthesilea becomes equally if not more problematic in Book V, as we shall see; what seems immediately interesting about Berger's heroic struggles to make sense of Belphoebe's troublesomely sinister appearance in the midst of comedy in Book II, is to note the contrast she embodies, between a speaking subject and a desired object. The subject/object split in the representation of a female character may become a problem for any male author, but it is potentially more troubling for an allegorist who works in a genre that already assigns a great deal of authority to female characters. Spenser's problem in the character of Belphoebe is further compounded, of course, by the historically anomalous political authority held by a female in his culture, especially because Spenser is attempting to represent in his narrative that figure's

femaleness (her chastity) as opposed to her political sovereignty.[13]

Spenser's solution to the problem of shadowing Elizabeth is to bring in the clowns. In comedy, the male cultural response to the doubled erotic and political power of a female may legitimately include laughter. His specific signalling of the *commedia dell'arte* in the character of Braggadocchio implicitly indicates the already achieved transgression of usual cultural limits that was inherent in Elizabeth's female rulership: her presence as a female, capable of acting in public, continues to remain a shock to the patriarchal system; it is constantly in need of recuperation through the ideological functioning of what we call Elizabethan literature.[14]

Spenser approaches the same generic and cultural problems in his presentation of Britomart, exemplar of chastity and also the narrative protagonist of Book III. He answers the problem not only by having her cross-dressed, but by surrounding her with comedy. Again Spenser makes the humor absolutely explicit. When laughter explodes in this narrative, it is Merlin, "brusting forth in laughter" at Glauce's lame lies, but the whole scene between Glauce and Britomart is in itself also wonderfully comic, not only in Britomart's exaggerated petrarchist sufferings but also when the old nurse in her useless spells chants to her charge, "Come daughter come, come; spit vpon my face, / Spit thrise vpon me, thrise vpon me spit; / Th'uneuen number for this business is most fit" (III.ii.50). (Indeed, Glauce's bustling ability to get the plot of Book III going after Merlin's magico-prophetic ineffectiveness may also recall the plot-business of the zanies in the *commedia*, but I do not at all wish to press the point.) Earlier in Book III, the virtual bedroom farce between Britomart and Malecasta (although it ends with Gardante's wounding of the heroine) is another case in point. Spenser gives us in this episode a mockery of female fear of sexual violation that he elsewhere treats seriously.

Britomart and Belphoebe are, of course, not always comic. However, the double authority granted to these two females, both as actors in the narrative and representations of the same authoritative abstraction (chastity), grants them too much cultural power. Autonomous subjects as well as erotically desirable objects, their sexual allure is first presented in comic scenes, where the inappropriateness of sexually desiring them is represented in both cases by a character whose lust is comically ineffectual (Braggadocchio and Malecasta).

Spenser makes Belphoebe's desirability very explicit in the blazon he inserts into the comic interlude of canto iii of Book II. The blazon itself, being the most conspicuously irrelevant part of the canto, is beautifully analyzed by Berger (pp. 120-49). Feminist criticism has recently taught us to see in the genre of blazon, however, a subversive movement against female erotic power as well as a celebration of it. Nancy J. Vickers has argued most persuasively that the piecemeal anatomy of female beauty in conventional Petrarchan blazon not only praises each individual body part but also enacts a dismemberment of the female corpus so celebrated.[15] In Spenser's blazon Belphoebe has a conspicuous "ham," and the folk festival that bedecks the pillars that are like her legs has a hint of the carnivalesque, a comic cultural moment that allows for many reversals of hierarchy, including those of gender. In these ways, the blazon so conspicuously arresting the forward movement of the narrative, while it presents Belphoebe's beauty as a hieratic vision of female perfection, is qualified by its comic context. To use Vickers' understanding of the blazon—that Diana so described is Diana dismembered—is to see how Spenser's blazon functions as a further movement against Diana/Belphoebe's (and Elizabeth's) power to dismember those mortal males who would look upon her; such a display therefore reinforces the qualification of female power by exposing the female body to an anatomizing gaze.

The epic simile that rightly troubled Berger compares Belphoebe to the divine Diana as well as to the mortal Penthesilea. And Diana, of course, as the goddess of chastity (and mentor of Belphoebe) has a peculiar power throughout Spenser's epic. Significantly, she, too, often appears in comic contexts. In Book III, for example, we see Venus invade her realm in a grand trespass on her territory (though not a dangerous one, as it would have been, tradition teaches us, had a mortal male done the same). Spenser's comedic treatment of the Actaeon myth (for Venus comes upon Diana at her bath) reverses the tragic tone of his precursor text, just as his serious treatment of Chaucer's joke in Arthur's dream of the Faerie Queene turns comedy to heroics. It is not so much that Spenser presents the Diana-Venus episode with overt humor, as that, by suppressing mention of Actaeon, he conspicuously rewrites tragedy out of the famous moment by removing the potential for sexual violation. Diana, having hung up her bow and quiver on a tree bough, is bathing in a fountain:

> And her lancke loynes vngirt, and breasts
>   vnbraste,
> After her heat the breathing cold to taste;
> Her golden lockes, that late in tresses bright
> Embreaded were for hindring of her haste,
> Now loose about her shoulders hong
>   vndight,
> And were with sweet Ambrosia all besprinkled
>   light.

> Soon as she Venus saw behind her backe,
> She was asham'd to be so loose surprized,
> And woxe half wroth against her damzels
>   slacke,
> That had not her thereof before auized,
> But suffred her so carelessly disguized
> Be ouertaken.

> (III.vi.18-19)

Venus is out hunting not for stags but for her wayward son Cupid; eyeing Diana's nymphs with great and comic care, she notes that he could easily have hidden himself among them (III.vi.23).

> For he is faire and fresh in face and guize,
> As any Nymph (let not it be enuyde.)
> So saying euery Nymph full narrowly she
>   eyde.

> (III.vi.23)

Later, of course, in the Mutabilitie Cantos, and in another comic rewriting of the Actaeon myth, Spenser treats Diana herself to an epic simile that compares her to a housewife, busy with her dairy, while silly Faunus is compared to a beast who had kicked over all the creaming pans (VII.vi.48). Unlike Venus, who may without danger interrupt Diana at her bath, Faunus, having arranged with the pliable Molanna the same Actaeon-like transgression, makes a mistake: he laughs out loud.

> There Faunus saw that pleased much his eye,
> And made his hart to tickle in his brest,
> That for great ioy of some-what he did spy,
> He could him not containe in silent rest;
> But breaking forth in laughter, loud profest
> His foolish thought. A foolish Faune indeed,
> That couldst not hold thy selfe so hidden
>   blest,
> But wouldest needs thine owne conceit
>   areed.
> Babblers vnworthy been of so diuine a meed.

> (VII.vi.46)

This laughter at female nakedness has its part in the larger comedic vision played out in the Mutabilitie Cantos—where Spenser, no babbler, keeps silent about the anatomy of another powerful female figure of authority, Dame Nature. The second rewrite of the Actaeon story, in this setting, insists more forcefully than the Venus episode that the power of Diana can be contained. Though some of her nymphs suggest gelding Faunus, his punishment is neither castration, nor a displaced version of it, such as being transformed into a stag and hunted to death by dogs. Faunus is merely draped with a redundant deer's skin and chased by the nymphs in a humorous parody of the murderous rout of Actaeon. The story, however, does end in a tragedy of sorts, for Ireland, if not for Faunus. Spenser reveals that Ireland is itself dismembered. Diana's curse on the spot where Faunus glimpsed her "somewhat" leaves Ireland prey to wolves and thieves so that they "all those Woods deface" (VII.vi.55). The real Diana whose neglect has "defaced" Ireland, is, of course, Elizabeth herself.

The goddess Diana has the authority to cause a tragedy no matter how comically she is presented in the poem, no matter how mocked her power to dismember may be. If Diana can threaten in Book III to clip Cupid's wanton wings "that he no more shall fly" (III.vi.24), and must be mollified by the sweet flattery of Venus; if Diana can comedically harass an unmetamorphosed Faunus, these comic representations indicate very real power. It should not be forgotten that what is shadowed here is the ability to cause not only metamorphic wounds, as in Belphoebe's wounding of Timias, or Britomart's unhorsing of Guyon, but also real ones. Stubbs and his awfully apt name may leap to mind. The power an absolute sovereign has is a capital authority. She may not only cut off hands, but also heads.

In the blazon in canto iii of Book II, Belphoebe is also compared to an Amazon queen as well as to Diana. An Amazon appears again in the poem in the guise of Radigund in Book V (a book in which Braggadocchio has a further set of scenes). Radigund defeats Artegall (the hero who almost manages to save Ireland before being called back to Gloriana's court) and dresses him in women's weeds (which males are not loath to do themselves for the purposes of dramatic representation). In that attire, he toils at women's work until saved by his lady-love, the now not-so-comic Britomart. Artegall succumbs to Radigund in a very specific manner, one which is echoed and repeated in other parts of the text, as if to call attention to its significant presentation of a particular female body part—the head:

> He to her lept with deadly dreadfull looke,
> And her sunshynie helmet soone vnlaced,
> Thinking at once both head and helmet to
>   haue raced.
>
> But when as he discouered had her face,
> He saw his sences straunge astonishment. . .
>
> At sight thereof his cruell minded hart
> Empierced was with pittiful regard
>
> (V.v.11-13)

In almost all its details an exact replica of Artegall's first encounter with Britomart, this scene also echoes an earlier battle between Artegall and Radigund which contains some bizarre rhyming wit and which Spenser

may have intended to be comic: Radigund has Sir Terpin at her mercy, but she is pausing much like a she-bear standing over "the carkasse of some beast too weak," when Artegall attacks her:

> Whom when as Artegall in that distresse
>   By chaunce beheld, he left the bloudy
>   slaughter,
> In which he swam, and ranne to his
>   redresse.
> There her assayling fiercely fresh, he raught
>   her
> Such an huge stroke, that it of sence
>   distraught her:
> And had she not it warded warily,
> It had depriu'd her mother of a daughter.
>
> (V.iv.41)

Such distinctively "feminine" rhymes are unusual in *The Faerie Queene,* especially so in the major rhyme of the stanza, repeated four times (at lines 2, 4, 5, and 7). With the "feminine" stress of the internal rhyme between "mother" and "daughter" of line 7, Spenser is obviously signalling the gender of the rhyme scheme, here exaggerated to the point of humor. Though the comedy of rhyming "daughter" with "slaughter" is grisly enough, it works to defuse the power Radigund here displays. Spenser is having the same kind of fun, I suspect, that Sidney has when he analyzes the differences between Italian, French, and English and their various possibilities for rhyme.

> Lastly, even the very ryme it selfe, the Italian cannot put in the last silable, by the French named the Masculine ryme, but still in the next to last, which the French call the Female; or the next before that, which the Italians term *Sdrucciola.* The example of the former is, *Buono, Suono,* of the *Sdrucciola, Femina, Semina.* The French, of the other side, hath both the Male, as *Bon, Son,* and the Female, as *Plaise, Taise.* But the *Sdrucciola* hee hath not: where the English hath all three, as *Due, True, Father, Rather, Motion, Potion*; with much more which might be sayde, but that I find already, the triflingnes of this discourse, is too much enlarged.[16]

Sidney is intrigued by the gendered French labels for the different kinds of rhymes, and provides in his examples a witty commentary on appropriate cultural roles for the different genders. Good / sound is male in French; the "sliding" rhyme in Italian is woman / seed; the feminine rhyme in French turns out to be please / silence. Patriarchy writes the English examples as well: Due, True, Father, Rather (as if what one might think of rather than a father is motion / potion).

In like manner, Spenser doubtless expected his readers to sense the wittiness of the rhymes on daughter / slaughter, and to have the comedy of the bizarre music call attention to the transgression of gender roles in Radigund's Amazon kingdom, a transgression deserving the text's violent laughter. When violence makes its appearance in this narrative, it is, of course, another female that deprives Radigund's mother of her daughter—and there is no obvious comedy involved. That it is an Amazonian *head* which goes rolling when Britomart vanquishes Radigund, rather than, as in Homer an arm, or as in Vergil, an unspecified limb, or another body part, is significant for the interest the episode specifically has in female sovereignty.[17]

> She her so rudely on the helmet smit,
>   That it empierced to the very braine,
> And her proud person low prostrated on the
>   plaine.
>
> Where being layd, the wrothfull Britonesse
>   Stayd not, till she came to her selfe againe,
>   But in revenge both of her loues distresse,
>   And her late vile reproch, though vaunted
>   vaine,
>   And also of her wound, which sore did
>   paine,
>   She with one stroke both head and helmet
>   cleft.
>
>   (V.vii.33-34)

In a book notable for the dismemberments Talus wreaks on the unruly inhabitants of faerieland, this capital punishment for the usurping female ruler silently testifies to the same cultural discomfort that lies hidden behind the "Etc." in Elizabeth's title on the epic's dedication page. She may quite legitimately be "Defender of the Faith," a title she inherited from her father. But she may not quite so easily be styled "Head of the Church" as he had named himself. (The first parliament decided upon the more abstract "governor" and we read the "Etc." everywhere.)[18] A female head to a male body politic poses the problem of monstrosity Knox trumpeted so impoliticly months before Elizabeth ascended the throne, and she was continually forced to remind her Parliaments, in exactly those terms, of her authority: "I will deal therein for your safety, and offer it to you as your Prince and head without request; for it is monstrous that the feet should direct the head."[19]

When Britomart goes to rescue Artegall from his dungeon, where his punishment is not only to wear women's garments, but to sew clothes (for wages, no less), Britomart's single remark does not so much make a joke as drain a festival of its comedy: she says to the cross-dressed Artegall, "What May-game hath misfortune made of you?" Maid Marian in May

games, as Natalie Zemon Davis points out, was often a disguised male: "when it came to the Morris Dance with Robin, the Hobby Horse, the dragon, and the rest, the Marian was a man."[20] Such comic and festive cross-dressing, anthropologically speaking, promotes fecundity as well as the momentary loosening of hierarchical order necessary in a rigid social structure. Yet, as Davis concludes in her study of the gender reversals of festival occasions, "The holiday role of the woman-on-top confirmed subjection throughout society, but it also promoted resistance to it." That Spenser is concerned with the real political facts of the powerful cultural misrule at work in his own society is manifest in the Britomart/Radigund episode. In reinstating masculine rule over Radigund's Amazon empire, Britomart reinstitutes a governing structure that obtains everywhere but in England under Elizabeth. The May-game comedy is a personal tragedy for Artegall. Its disorder is only righted when Britomart reasserts a hierarchy that uniquely does not hold in Spenser's own culture. Female authority here is not funny, because it is real.

Belphoebe, Braggadocchio, and Spenser's blazon may go on feeling conspicuously irrelevant to the program of temperance a rather humorless Guyon pursues in Book II, but the comedy of that moment cues the representation of female authority Spenser stages throughout the epic he titled **The Faerie Queene**. If he seems to have risked a lot, we must remember that the strain of humor he used may have been already authorized by Elizabeth. What she may have found funny about a Falstaff, enhorned and mocked by a society of women, may have been different from what the male political nation found comic in Braggadocchio or Faunus. But we all know what a relief it is to laugh at our terrors. If Queen Elizabeth could laugh at the kind of fears that became all too real with the braggadocio of an Essex, Spenser's readers could laugh at the power that was real enough, finally, to cut off the Earl's head.

Notes

[1] *A Literary History of English,* ed. Albert C. Baugh, (New York, 1948), p. 450.

[2] A tradition dateable by John Dennis' 1702 dedication to his reworking of *The Merry Wives of Windsor* as *The Comical Gallant* has it that Shakespeare's play "was written at [Queen Elizabeth's] command, and by her direction, and she was so eager to see it acted that she commanded it to be finished in fourteen days; and was afterward, as tradition tells us, very well pleased at the representation." Cited in G. B. Harrison, *Shakespeare: The Complete Works* (New York, 1948), p. 937.

[3] Jonathan Goldberg, *Endlesse Worke: Spenser and the Structures of Discourse* (Baltimore, Md., 1981), ch. 3; see also Maureen Quilligan, *Milton's Spenser: The Politics of Reading* (Ithaca, N.Y., 1983), ch. 4.

[4] See Roy Strong, *Portraits of Queen Elizabeth I* (Oxford, 1963); for discussion of the debacle of Stubbs' punishment, see Wallace T. MacCaffrey, *Queen Elizabeth and the Making of Policy, 1572-1588* (Princeton, N.J., 1981), pp. 256-62.

[5] That Spenser chose to present Gloriana through a serious rewrite of Chaucer's most self-deprecatingly comic tale in *The Canterbury Tales* should perhaps alert us to the other problem of "authority" Spenser confronts in writing his epic, not only Elizabeth's as sovereign political power, but Chaucer's as most influential English precursor. The two, at least at their first appearance in Book I of *The Faerie Queene,* seem to be closely connected. For a discussion of Book II of *The Faerie Queene,* arguing its fundamental support of the complicated ideologies of the Elizabethan regime, and to which the present argument is offered as a partial qualification, see Stephen Greenblatt, *Renaissance Self-Fashioning: from More to Shakespeare* (Chicago, 1980), ch. 4.

[6] K. M. Lea, *Italian Popular Comedy: A Study in the Commedia dell'Arte, 1560-1620 with Special Reference to the English Stage* (1934; rpt. New York, 1962), p. 354.

[7] Lea, p. 345.

[8] On the public/private dichotomy see Joan Kelly, "Did Women Have a Renaissance?" in *Becoming Visible: Women in European History,* ed. Renate Bridenthal and Claudia Koonz (Boston, 1977), pp. 139-64; for a discussion of the culturally transgressive rhetoric at the center of the "public" courtezan's role in Italy, see Ann R. Jones, "City Women and Their Audiences," in *Rewriting the Renaissance: The Discourses of Sexual Difference in Early Modern Europe,* ed. Margaret W. Ferguson, Maureen Quilligan, and Nancy J. Vickers (Chicago, 1986), pp. 299-316.

[9] Cited Lea, p. 343.

[10] Citations of *The Faerie Queene* are *The Poetical Works of Edmund Spenser,* eds. J. C. Smith and E. De Selincourt, (1912; rpt. London, 1960).

[11] Christine, for her part, has some witty play with the figure of Raison in the *Livre de la Cité des Dames;* her Lady Raison explains to Christine as interlocutor that all those who wrote against women in the past did so without her authority, i.e., misogyny is irrational. It is a superficially gentle but pro-foundly subversive joke. That Spenser may have known *The Boke of the Cyte of Ladyes* in Brian Anslay's translation (1521) is a distinct possibility (rpt. *Distaves and Dames: Renaissance Treatises for and about Women,* ed. Diane Bornstein (New York, 1978). For the documents in the "querelle," see *La Querelle de la Rose: Letters and Documents,* ed. Joseph L. Baird and John R. Kane (Chapel Hill, N.C., 1978). The *Cite* is available in French only in manuscript, and in "The 'Livre *de la Cité des Dames,'*: A Critical Edition," ed. Maureen Curnow, (Ph.D. Diss. Vanderbilt, 1975). For the modern English translation, see *The Book of the City of Ladies,* trans. Earl Jeffrey Richards, (New York, 1982).

[12] Harry Berger, Jr., *The Allegorical Temper: Vision and Reality in Book II of Spenser's Faerie Queene* (1957; rpt. Hamden, Conn., 1967), p. 140.

[13] Elizabeth's authority was absolutist and therefore differed radically from the power of any queen reigning in England after the Constitutional changes of 1688.

[14] Louis Montrose argues for the close interplay between sexual and monarchal politics in "*A Midsummer Night's Dream* and the Shaping Fantasies of Elizabethan Culture: Gender, Power, Form," in *Rewriting the Renaissance,* pp. 65-87: "the woman to whom *all* Elizabethan men were vulnerable was Queen Elizabeth herself. Within legal and fiscal limits, she held the power of life and death over every Englishman, the power to advance or frustrate the worldly desires of all her subjects" (p. 77).

[15] Nancy J. Vickers, "Diana Described: Scattered Woman and Scattered Rhyme," *Critical Inquiry* 8 (1981), 265-79.

[16] Sir Philip Sidney, *An Apologie for Poetrie* in *Criticism,* ed. Mark Schorer, Josephine Miles, and Gordon MacKenzie (New York, 1948), p. 430.

[17] This significant head may also pinpoint Spenser's rewriting of another female authority. In Christine de Pisan's *Book of the City of Ladies,* Penthesilea meets her death by a blow to the brain: "they smashed through all her armor and struck off a large quarter of her helmet. Pyrrhus was there, and seeing her bare head with its blond hair, dealt her such a great blow that he split open her head and brain. So died the brave Penthesilea, a terrible loss to the Trojans and a profound sorrow for all her land which went into deep mourning, and rightly so, for afterward a woman of her caliber never again ruled over the Amazons" (Richards, trans., p. 51). Spenser may be rewriting Christine when he gives Artegall a very different response to shearing off Britomart's helmet:

The wicked stroke vpon her helmet chaunst,
   And with the force, which in it selfe it bore,
   Her ventayle shard away, and thence forth
      glaunst
   A down in vaine, ne harm'd her any more.
   With that her angels face, vnseene afore,
   Like to the ruddie morne appeard in sight . . .

And round about the same, her yellow heare
   Hauing through stirring loosd their wonted
      band,
   Like to a golden border did appeare, . . .

And as his hand hevp againe did reare,
   Thinking to worke on her his vtmost
      wracke,
   His powrelesse arme benumbd with secret
      feare
   From his reuengefull purpose shronke
      abacke. . . .

And he himselfe long gazing thereupon,
   At last fell humbly down vpon his knee,
   And of his wonder made religion.
                                   (IV.vi.19-22)

[18] Norman L. Jones, *Faith by Statute: Parliament and the Settlement of Religion, 1559* (London, 1982): "The opposition by all parties to the idea of a female head of the church must have been an important factor in the Queen's decision to seek the governorship" (p.130). The debate in Parliament reflected a far milder version of Knox's statement: "And no less monstrous is the bodie of that common welth, where a woman beareth empire. For either doth it lack a lawfull heade (as in very deed it doth) or els there is an idol exalted in the place of a true head," *The First Blast of the Trumpet Against the Monstrous Regiment of Women,* ed. Edward Arber (London, 1878), p. 27.

[19] Neville Williams, *Elizabeth I, Queen of England* (London, 1971), p. 139.

[20] Natalie Zemon Davis, *Society and Culture in Early Modern France,* ch. 5, "Women on Top," (Stanford, Cal., 1965), p. 151.

FURTHER READING

Biography

Waller, Gary. *Edmund Spenser: A Literary Life.* New York: Macmillan, 1994, 211 p.
   Biographical study of Spenser, with an emphasis on the professional and social contexts which shaped his writing.

Criticism

Alpers, Paul J. *The Poetry of "The Faerie Queene."* Columbia, Mo.: University of Missouri Press, 1982, 415 p.
   An introductory analysis of *The Faerie Queene.*

Bednarz, James P. "Ralegh in Spenser's Historical Allegory." *Spenser Studies* IV (1983): 49-70.
   Analysis of the allegorical representation of the relationship between Spenser's friend Raleigh and Queen Elizabeth in *The Faerie Queene.*

Berger, Harry, Jr., ed. *Spenser: A Collection of Critical Essays.* Englewood Cliffs, N.J.: Prentice-Hall, 1968, 182 p.
   Collection of ten seminal essays on Spenser divided into two sections: the minor poems and *The Faerie Queene.*

Colie, Rosalie L. *Paradoxia Epidemica: The Renaissance Tradition of Paradox.* Princeton: Princeton University Press, 1966, 553 p.
   Discusses Spenser's use of allegory in *The Faerie Queene* and argues for a less tidy scheme than has traditionally been suggested.

Cook, Patrick J. *Milton, Spenser, and the Epic Tradition.* Aldershot: Scolar Press, 1996, 201 p.
   Comparative study of the epic, from the classical tradition to Milton, with an emphasis on Spenser and Milton.

Curran, John E., Jr. "Spenser and the Historical Revolution: Briton Moniments and the Problem of Roman Britain." *Clio* 25, No. 3 (Spring 1996): 273-92.
   Argues that Spenser understood the profound changes historiography was undergoing in the sixteenth century and reflected this knowledge in the "Briton Moniments" section of *The Faerie Queene.*

Durling, Robert M. *The Figure of the Poet in Renaissance Epic.* Cambridge, Mass.: Harvard University Press, 1965, 280 p.
   A survey study of Renaissance representations of the poet, beginning with ancient and medieval influences and culminating with Spenser.

Frushell, Richard C., ed. *Contemporary Thought on Edmund Spenser.* Carbondale, Ill.: Southern Illinois University Press, 1975, 240 p.
   A collection of essays focusing on twentieth-century criticism of Spenser's work. Includes a bibliography of criticism from 1900 to 1970.

Giamatti, A. Bartlett. *The Earthly Paradise and the Renaissance Epic.* Princeton: Princeton University Press, 1966, 374 p.
   Chapter on Spenser discusses the influence of earlier epic on Spenser's treatment of earthly paradise and the ways in which the poet uses, deviates from, and

molds the ideas he found there to suit his artistic purposes.

———. "A Prince and Her Poet." In *The Yale Review* 73, No. 3 (April. 1984): 321-37.

Discusses Elizabeth, Spenser, his poem to her, and the politics of the Elizabethan court.

Goldberg, Jonathan. *Endlesse Worke: Spenser and the Structures of Discourse.* Baltimore: The Johns Hopkins University Press, 1981, 177 p.

Discusses the idea of artistic (and emotional) closure as it pertains to Spenser's style.

Hamilton, A.C. *The Structure of Allegory in "The Faerie Queene."* Oxford: The Clarendon Press, 1961, 227 p.

Overview of the allegorical structures of Spenser's poem.

Helgerson, Richard. "The New Poet Presents Himself." In *Self-Crowned Laureates*, pp. 55-101. Berkeley: University of California Press, 1983.

Analyzes Spenser's reputation and his attitudes toward his career as represented in his poetry.

Henniger, S.K. Jr. *Sidney and Spenser: The Poet as Maker.* University Park: The Pennsylvania State University Press, 1989, 646 p.

Argues that Spenser and Sidney led a transformation in narrative strategies that marked a return to the Aristotelian idea of imitation as the purpose of poetry.

Lewis, C. S. *Spenser's Images of Life.* Cambridge: Cambridge University Press, 1967, 143 p.

Readable study of the iconography of *The Faerie Queene* with an emphasis on the historical and cultural contexts for Spenser's imagery.

Maccaffrey, Isabel G. *Spenser's Allegory: The Anatomy of Imagination.* Princeton: Princeton University Press, 1976, 445 p.

Orderly assessment of *The Faerie Queene* which argues that Spenser's thematic purpose was to explore ways of knowing available to human beings and to define the possibilities of moral action.

Nelson, William, ed. *Form and Convention in the Poetry of Edmund Spenser: Selected Papers from the English Institute.* New York: Columbia University Press, 1961, 188 p.

Collection of six critical essays on Spenser, including several on the "Epithalamion" and the "Prothalamion."

Radcliffe, David Hill. *Edmund Spenser: A Reception History.* Columbia, S.C.: Camden House, 1996, 239 p.

A survey and analysis of Spenserian criticism from his own time to the present day.

Roche, Thomas P., Jr. *The Kindly Flame: A Study of the Third and Fourth Books of Spenser's "The Faerie Queene."* Princeton: Princeton University Press, 1964, 220 p.

Detailed readings explaining the third and fourth books of Spenser's epic, which are often held to be exceedingly complex or incoherent. Argues that the more complex structure of those books is required to exemplify the virtues of chastity and friendship.

Schleiner, Louise. *Cultural Semiotics, Spenser, and the Captive Woman.* Bethlehem, Penn.: Lehigh University Press, 1995, 278 p.

Draws on the work of Frederic Jameson and A.-J. Greimas for a semiotic analysis of the conflicts between classes and factions in Spenser's poetry. The emphasis is on relations between male and female.

Steadman, John M. *Moral Fiction in Milton and Spenser.* Columbia, Mo.: University of Missouri Press, 1995, 200 p.

A comparative study of the epics of Spenser and Milton, focusing on the relationship between moral vision and the poet's persona and poetic structures used in each.

Suzuki, Mihoko, ed. *Critical Essays on Edmund Spenser.* New York: G. K. Hall & Co., 1996, 282 p.

Collection of recent critical essays bringing innovative theoretical approaches to Spenser. Focuses on *The Faerie Queene* and *The Shepheardes Calender*.

Watkins, John. *The Specter of Dido: Spenser and Virgilian Epic.* New Haven: Yale University Press, 1995, 208 p.

Studies Spenser's use of Virgilian conventions in *The Faerie Queene,* focusing on portrayals of seductive women.

Welsford, Enid. *Spenser, Fowre Hymns, Epithalamion: A Study of Edmund Spenser's Doctrine of Love.* Oxford: Basil Blackwell, 1967, 215 p.

Introduction and analysis to the theme of love in Spenser's love poems, with historical context and reprints of the poems.

Williams, Kathleen. *Spenser's World of Glass: A Reading of "The Faerie Queene."* Berkeley: University of California Press, 1966, 241 p.

Overview analysis of *The Faerie Queene* with detailed examination of important passages and critical themes.

Woodhouse, A. S. P. *The Poet and His Faith: Religion and Poetry in England from Spenser to Eliot and Auden.* Chicago: University of Chicago Press, 1965, 304 p.

Survey of the influence of religious beliefs on the work of English poets, with a chapter on Spenser and Elizabethan England.

Additional coverage of Spenser's life and career is contained in the following source published by Gale Research: *Literature Criticism from 1400 to 1800,* **Vol. 5.**

Literature
Criticism from
1400 to 1800

Cumulative Indexes

How to Use This Index

The main references

Calvino, Italo
1923-1985.....CLC 5, 8, 11, 22, 33, 39,
73; SSC 3

list all author entries in the following Gale Literary Criticism series:

BLC = *Black Literature Criticism*
CLC = *Contemporary Literary Criticism*
CLR = *Children's Literature Review*
CMLC = *Classical and Medieval Literature Criticism*
DA = *DISCovering Authors*
DC = *Drama Criticism*
HLC = *Hispanic Literature Criticism*
LC = *Literature Criticism from 1400 to 1800*
NCLC = *Nineteenth-Century Literature Criticism*
PC = *Poetry Criticism*
SSC = *Short Story Criticism*
TCLC = *Twentieth-Century Literary Criticism*
WLC = *World Literature Criticism, 1500 to the Present*

The cross-references

See also CANR 23; CA 85-88;
obituary CA 116

list all author entries in the following Gale biographical and literary sources:

AAYA = *Authors & Artists for Young Adults*
AITN = *Authors in the News*
BEST = *Bestsellers*
BW = *Black Writers*
CA = *Contemporary Authors*
CAAS = *Contemporary Authors Autobiography Series*
CABS = *Contemporary Authors Bibliographical Series*
CANR = *Contemporary Authors New Revision Series*
CAP = *Contemporary Authors Permanent Series*
CDALB = *Concise Dictionary of American Literary Biography*
CDBLB = *Concise Dictionary of British Literary Biography*
DLB = *Dictionary of Literary Biography*
DLBD = *Dictionary of Literary Biography Documentary Series*
DLBY = *Dictionary of Literary Biography Yearbook*
HW = *Hispanic Writers*
JRDA = *Junior DISCovering Authors*
MAICYA = *Major Authors and Illustrators for Children and Young Adults*
MTCW = *Major 20th-Century Writers*
NNAL = *Native North American Literature*
SAAS = *Something about the Author Autobiography Series*
SATA = *Something about the Author*
YABC = *Yesterday's Authors of Books for Children*

Literary Criticism Series
Cumulative Author Index

Abasiyanik, Sait Faik 1906-1954
See Sait Faik
See also CA 123

Abbey, Edward 1927-1989 ...... CLC 36, 59
See also CA 45-48; 128; CANR 2, 41

Abbott, Lee K(ittredge) 1947- ...... CLC 48
See also CA 124; CANR 51; DLB 130

Abe, Kobo
1924-1993 .... CLC 8, 22, 53, 81;
DAM NOV
See also CA 65-68; 140; CANR 24; MTCW

Abelard, Peter c. 1079-c. 1142 ... CMLC 11
See also DLB 115

Abell, Kjeld 1901-1961 .... CLC 15
See also CA 111

Abish, Walter 1931- .... CLC 22
See also CA 101; CANR 37; DLB 130

Abrahams, Peter (Henry) 1919- ..... CLC 4
See also BW 1; CA 57-60; CANR 26;
DLB 117; MTCW

Abrams, M(eyer) H(oward) 1912- ... CLC 24
See also CA 57-60; CANR 13, 33; DLB 67

Abse, Dannie
1923- ... CLC 7, 29; DAB; DAM POET
See also CA 53-56; CAAS 1; CANR 4, 46;
DLB 27

Achebe, (Albert) Chinua(lumogu)
1930- ..... CLC 1, 3, 5, 7, 11, 26, 51, 75;
BLC; DA; DAB; DAC; DAM MST,
MULT, NOV; WLC
See also AAYA 15; BW 2; CA 1-4R;
CANR 6, 26, 47; CLR 20; DLB 117;
MAICYA; MTCW; SATA 40;
SATA-Brief 38

Acker, Kathy 1948- .... CLC 45
See also CA 117; 122; CANR 55

Ackroyd, Peter 1949- .... CLC 34, 52
See also CA 123; 127; CANR 51; DLB 155;
INT 127

Acorn, Milton 1923- .... CLC 15; DAC
See also CA 103; DLB 53; INT 103

Adamov, Arthur
1908-1970 .... CLC 4, 25; DAM DRAM
See also CA 17-18; 25-28R; CAP 2; MTCW

Adams, Alice (Boyd)
1926- .... CLC 6, 13, 46; SSC 24
See also CA 81-84; CANR 26, 53;
DLBY 86; INT CANR-26; MTCW

Adams, Andy 1859-1935 .... TCLC 56
See also 1

Adams, Douglas (Noel)
1952- .... CLC 27, 60; DAM POP
See also AAYA 4; BEST 89:3; CA 106;
CANR 34; DLBY 83; JRDA

Adams, Francis 1862-1893 ...... NCLC 33

Adams, Henry (Brooks)
1838-1918 ..... TCLC 4, 52; DA; DAB;
DAC; DAM MST
See also CA 104; 133; DLB 12, 47

Adams, Richard (George)
1920- .... CLC 4, 5, 18; DAM NOV
See also AAYA 16; AITN 1, 2; CA 49-52;
CANR 3, 35; CLR 20; JRDA; MAICYA;
MTCW; SATA 7, 69

Adamson, Joy(-Friederike Victoria)
1910-1980 .... CLC 17
See also CA 69-72; 93-96; CANR 22;
MTCW; SATA 11; SATA-Obit 22

Adcock, Fleur 1934- .... CLC 41
See also CA 25-28R; CAAS 23; CANR 11,
34; DLB 40

Addams, Charles (Samuel)
1912-1988 .... CLC 30
See also CA 61-64; 126; CANR 12

Addison, Joseph 1672-1719 .... LC 18
See also CDBLB 1660-1789; DLB 101

Adler, Alfred (F.) 1870-1937 ...... TCLC 61
See also CA 119

Adler, C(arole) S(chwerdtfeger)
1932- .... CLC 35
See also AAYA 4; CA 89-92; CANR 19,
40; JRDA; MAICYA; SAAS 15;
SATA 26, 63

Adler, Renata 1938- .... CLC 8, 31
See also CA 49-52; CANR 5, 22, 52;
MTCW

Ady, Endre 1877-1919 .... TCLC 11
See also CA 107

Aeschylus
525B.C.-456B.C. .... CMLC 11; DA;
DAB; DAC; DAM DRAM, MST
See also DLB 176; YABC

Afton, Effie
See Harper, Frances Ellen Watkins

Agapida, Fray Antonio
See Irving, Washington

Agee, James (Rufus)
1909-1955 .... TCLC 1, 19; DAM NOV
See also AITN 1; CA 108; 148;
CDALB 1941-1968; DLB 2, 26, 152

Aghill, Gordon
See Silverberg, Robert

Agnon, S(hmuel) Y(osef Halevi)
1888-1970 .... CLC 4, 8, 14
See also CA 17-18; 25-28R; CAP 2; MTCW

Agrippa von Nettesheim, Henry Cornelius
1486-1535 .... LC 27

Aherne, Owen
See Cassill, R(onald) V(erlin)

Ai 1947- .... CLC 4, 14, 69
See also CA 85-88; CAAS 13; DLB 120

Aickman, Robert (Fordyce)
1914-1981 .... CLC 57
See also CA 5-8R; CANR 3

Aiken, Conrad (Potter)
1889-1973 .... CLC 1, 3, 5, 10, 52;
DAM NOV, POET; SSC 9
See also CA 5-8R; 45-48; CANR 4;
CDALB 1929-1941; DLB 9, 45, 102;
MTCW; SATA 3, 30

Aiken, Joan (Delano) 1924- .... CLC 35
See also AAYA 1; CA 9-12R; CANR 4, 23,
34; CLR 1, 19; DLB 161; JRDA;
MAICYA; MTCW; SAAS 1; SATA 2,
30, 73

Ainsworth, William Harrison
1805-1882 .... NCLC 13
See also DLB 21; SATA 24

Aitmatov, Chingiz (Torekulovich)
1928- .... CLC 71
See also CA 103; CANR 38; MTCW;
SATA 56

Akers, Floyd
See Baum, L(yman) Frank

Akhmadulina, Bella Akhatovna
1937- .... CLC 53; DAM POET
See also CA 65-68

Akhmatova, Anna
1888-1966 .... CLC 11, 25, 64;
DAM POET; PC 2
See also CA 19-20; 25-28R; CANR 35;
CAP 1; MTCW

Aksakov, Sergei Timofeyvich
1791-1859 .... NCLC 2

Aksenov, Vassily
See Aksyonov, Vassily (Pavlovich)

Aksyonov, Vassily (Pavlovich)
1932- .... CLC 22, 37, 101
See also CA 53-56; CANR 12, 48

Akutagawa, Ryunosuke
1892-1927 .... TCLC 16
See also CA 117; 154

Alain 1868-1951 .... TCLC 41

Alain-Fournier .... TCLC 6
See also Fournier, Henri Alban
See also DLB 65

Alarcon, Pedro Antonio de
1833-1891 .... NCLC 1

Alas (y Urena), Leopoldo (Enrique Garcia)
1852-1901 .... TCLC 29
See also CA 113; 131; HW

Albee, Edward (Franklin III)
1928- ...CLC 1, 2, 3, 5, 9, 11, 13, 25,
53, 86; DA; DAB; DAC; DAM DRAM,
MST; WLC
See also AITN 1; CA 5-8R; CABS 3;
CANR 8, 54; CDALB 1941-1968; DLB 7;
INT CANR-8; MTCW

Anderson, Robert (Woodruff)
1917- .... **CLC 23; DAM DRAM**
See also AITN 1; CA 21-24R; CANR 32;
DLB 7

Anderson, Sherwood
1876-1941 .... **TCLC 1, 10, 24; DA;
DAB; DAC; DAM MST, NOV; SSC 1;
WLC**
See also CA 104; 121; CDALB 1917-1929;
DLB 4, 9, 86; DLBD 1; MTCW

Andier, Pierre
See Desnos, Robert

Andouard
See Giraudoux, (Hippolyte) Jean

Andrade, Carlos Drummond de ...... **CLC 18**
See also Drummond de Andrade, Carlos

Andrade, Mario de 1893-1945 ..... **TCLC 43**

Andreae, Johann V(alentin)
1586-1654 .... **LC 32**
See also DLB 164

Andreas-Salome, Lou 1861-1937 ... **TCLC 56**
See also DLB 66

Andrewes, Lancelot 1555-1626 .... **LC 5**
See also DLB 151, 172

Andrews, Cicily Fairfield
See West, Rebecca

Andrews, Elton V.
See Pohl, Frederik

Andreyev, Leonid (Nikolaevich)
1871-1919 .... **TCLC 3**
See also CA 104

Andric, Ivo 1892-1975 .... **CLC 8**
See also CA 81-84; 57-60; CANR 43;
DLB 147; MTCW

Angelique, Pierre
See Bataille, Georges

Angell, Roger 1920- .... **CLC 26**
See also CA 57-60; CANR 13, 44; DLB 171

Angelou, Maya
1928- .... **CLC 12, 35, 64, 77; BLC; DA;
DAB; DAC; DAM MST, MULT, POET,
POP**
See also AAYA 7, 20; BW 2; CA 65-68;
CANR 19, 42; DLB 38; MTCW;
SATA 49; YABC

Annensky, Innokenty (Fyodorovich)
1856-1909 .... **TCLC 14**
See also CA 110; 155

Annunzio, Gabriele d'
See D'Annunzio, Gabriele

Anon, Charles Robert
See Pessoa, Fernando (Antonio Nogueira)

Anouilh, Jean (Marie Lucien Pierre)
1910-1987 ...... **CLC 1, 3, 8, 13, 40, 50;
DAM DRAM**
See also CA 17-20R; 123; CANR 32;
MTCW

Anthony, Florence
See Ai

Anthony, John
See Ciardi, John (Anthony)

Anthony, Peter
See Shaffer, Anthony (Joshua); Shaffer,
Peter (Levin)

Anthony, Piers 1934- .. **CLC 35; DAM POP**
See also AAYA 11; CA 21-24R; CANR 28,
56; DLB 8; MTCW; SAAS 22; SATA 84

Antoine, Marc
See Proust, (Valentin-Louis-George-Eugene-)
Marcel

Antoninus, Brother
See Everson, William (Oliver)

Antonioni, Michelangelo 1912- ..... **CLC 20**
See also CA 73-76; CANR 45

Antschel, Paul 1920-1970
See Celan, Paul
See also CA 85-88; CANR 33; MTCW

Anwar, Chairil 1922-1949 .... **TCLC 22**
See also CA 121

Apollinaire, Guillaume
1880-1918 .... **TCLC 3, 8, 51;
DAM POET; PC 7**
See also Kostrowitzki, Wilhelm Apollinaris
de
See also CA 152

Appelfeld, Aharon 1932- .... **CLC 23, 47**
See also CA 112; 133

Apple, Max (Isaac) 1941- .... **CLC 9, 33**
See also CA 81-84; CANR 19, 54; DLB 130

Appleman, Philip (Dean) 1926- ..... **CLC 51**
See also CA 13-16R; CAAS 18; CANR 6,
29, 56

Appleton, Lawrence
See Lovecraft, H(oward) P(hillips)

Apteryx
See Eliot, T(homas) S(tearns)

Apuleius, (Lucius Madaurensis)
125(?)-175(?) .... **CMLC 1**

Aquin, Hubert 1929-1977 .... **CLC 15**
See also CA 105; DLB 53

Aragon, Louis
1897-1982 ..... **CLC 3, 22; DAM NOV,
POET**
See also CA 69-72; 108; CANR 28;
DLB 72; MTCW

Arany, Janos 1817-1882 .... **NCLC 34**

Arbuthnot, John 1667-1735 .... **LC 1**
See also DLB 101

Archer, Herbert Winslow
See Mencken, H(enry) L(ouis)

Archer, Jeffrey (Howard)
1940- .... **CLC 28; DAM POP**
See also AAYA 16; BEST 89:3; CA 77-80;
CANR 22, 52; INT CANR-22

Archer, Jules 1915- .... **CLC 12**
See also CA 9-12R; CANR 6; SAAS 5;
SATA 4, 85

Archer, Lee
See Ellison, Harlan (Jay)

Arden, John
1930- ..... **CLC 6, 13, 15; DAM DRAM**
See also CA 13-16R; CAAS 4; CANR 31;
DLB 13; MTCW

Arenas, Reinaldo
1943-1990 ...... **CLC 41; DAM MULT;
HLC**
See also CA 124; 128; 133; DLB 145; HW

Arendt, Hannah 1906-1975 ..... **CLC 66, 98**
See also CA 17-20R; 61-64; CANR 26;
MTCW

Aretino, Pietro 1492-1556 .... **LC 12**

Arghezi, Tudor .... **CLC 80**
See also Theodorescu, Ion N.

Arguedas, Jose Maria
1911-1969 .... **CLC 10, 18**
See also CA 89-92; DLB 113; HW

Argueta, Manlio 1936- .... **CLC 31**
See also CA 131; DLB 145; HW

Ariosto, Ludovico 1474-1533 .... **LC 6**

Aristides
See Epstein, Joseph

Aristophanes
450B.C.-385B.C. .... **CMLC 4; DA;
DAB; DAC; DAM DRAM, MST; DC 2**
See also DLB 176; YABC

Arlt, Roberto (Godofredo Christophersen)
1900-1942 ..... **TCLC 29; DAM MULT;
HLC**
See also CA 123; 131; HW

Armah, Ayi Kwei
1939- .... **CLC 5, 33; BLC;
DAM MULT, POET**
See also BW 1; CA 61-64; CANR 21;
DLB 117; MTCW

Armatrading, Joan 1950- .... **CLC 17**
See also CA 114

Arnette, Robert
See Silverberg, Robert

**Arnim, Achim von (Ludwig Joachim von
Arnim)** 1781-1831 .... **NCLC 5**
See also DLB 90

Arnim, Bettina von 1785-1859 .... **NCLC 38**
See also DLB 90

Arnold, Matthew
1822-1888 ..... **NCLC 6, 29; DA; DAB;
DAC; DAM MST, POET; PC 5; WLC**
See also CDBLB 1832-1890; DLB 32, 57

Arnold, Thomas 1795-1842 ...... **NCLC 18**
See also DLB 55

Arnow, Harriette (Louisa) Simpson
1908-1986 .... **CLC 2, 7, 18**
See also CA 9-12R; 118; CANR 14; DLB 6;
MTCW; SATA 42; SATA-Obit 47

Arp, Hans
See Arp, Jean

Arp, Jean 1887-1966 .... **CLC 5**
See also CA 81-84; 25-28R; CANR 42

Arrabal
See Arrabal, Fernando

Arrabal, Fernando 1932- ... **CLC 2, 9, 18, 58**
See also CA 9-12R; CANR 15

Arrick, Fran .... **CLC 30**
See also Gaberman, Judie Angell

Artaud, Antonin (Marie Joseph)
1896-1948 ... **TCLC 3, 36; DAM DRAM**
See also CA 104; 149

Arthur, Ruth M(abel) 1905-1979 .... **CLC 12**
See also CA 9-12R; 85-88; CANR 4;
SATA 7, 26

Artsybashev, Mikhail (Petrovich)
1878-1927 .... **TCLC 31**

Bailey, Paul 1937- . . . . CLC 45
See also CA 21-24R; CANR 16; DLB 14

Baillie, Joanna 1762-1851 . . . . NCLC 2
See also DLB 93

Bainbridge, Beryl (Margaret)
1933- . . . . CLC 4, 5, 8, 10, 14, 18, 22, 62;
DAM NOV
See also CA 21-24R; CANR 24, 55;
DLB 14; MTCW

Baker, Elliott 1922- . . . . CLC 8
See also CA 45-48; CANR 2

Baker, Jean H. . . . . TCLC 3, 10
See also Russell, George William

Baker, Nicholson
1957- . . . . CLC 61; DAM POP
See also CA 135

Baker, Ray Stannard 1870-1946 . . . TCLC 47
See also CA 118

Baker, Russell (Wayne) 1925- . . . . . . CLC 31
See also BEST 89:4; CA 57-60; CANR 11,
41; MTCW

Bakhtin, M.
See Bakhtin, Mikhail Mikhailovich

Bakhtin, M. M.
See Bakhtin, Mikhail Mikhailovich

Bakhtin, Mikhail
See Bakhtin, Mikhail Mikhailovich

Bakhtin, Mikhail Mikhailovich
1895-1975 . . . . CLC 83
See also CA 128; 113

Bakshi, Ralph 1938(?)- . . . . CLC 26
See also CA 112; 138

Bakunin, Mikhail (Alexandrovich)
1814-1876 . . . . NCLC 25, 58

Baldwin, James (Arthur)
1924-1987 . . . . . . CLC 1, 2, 3, 4, 5, 8, 13,
15, 17, 42, 50, 67, 90; BLC; DA; DAB;
DAC; DAM MST, MULT, NOV, POP;
DC 1; SSC 10; WLC
See also AAYA 4; BW 1; CA 1-4R; 124;
CABS 1; CANR 3, 24;
CDALB 1941-1968; DLB 2, 7, 33;
DLBY 87; MTCW; SATA 9;
SATA-Obit 54

Ballard, J(ames) G(raham)
1930- . . . . CLC 3, 6, 14, 36; DAM NOV,
POP; SSC 1
See also AAYA 3; CA 5-8R; CANR 15, 39;
DLB 14; MTCW; SATA 93

Balmont, Konstantin (Dmitriyevich)
1867-1943 . . . . TCLC 11
See also CA 109; 155

Balzac, Honore de
1799-1850 . . . . NCLC 5, 35, 53; DA;
DAB; DAC; DAM MST, NOV; SSC 5;
WLC
See also DLB 119

Bambara, Toni Cade
1939-1995 . . . . . . CLC 19, 88; BLC; DA;
DAC; DAM MST, MULT
See also AAYA 5; BW 2; CA 29-32R; 150;
CANR 24, 49; DLB 38; MTCW; YABC

Bamdad, A.
See Shamlu, Ahmad

Banat, D. R.
See Bradbury, Ray (Douglas)

Bancroft, Laura
See Baum, L(yman) Frank

Banim, John 1798-1842 . . . . NCLC 13
See also DLB 116, 158, 159

Banim, Michael 1796-1874 . . . . . . NCLC 13
See also DLB 158, 159

Banjo, The
See Paterson, A(ndrew) B(arton)

Banks, Iain
See Banks, Iain M(enzies)

Banks, Iain M(enzies) 1954- . . . . CLC 34
See also CA 123; 128; INT 128

Banks, Lynne Reid . . . . CLC 23
See also Reid Banks, Lynne
See also AAYA 6

Banks, Russell 1940- . . . . CLC 37, 72
See also CA 65-68; CAAS 15; CANR 19,
52; DLB 130

Banville, John 1945- . . . . CLC 46
See also CA 117; 128; DLB 14; INT 128

Banville, Theodore (Faullain) de
1832-1891 . . . . NCLC 9

Baraka, Amiri
1934- . . . . CLC 1, 2, 3, 5, 10, 14, 33;
BLC; DA; DAC; DAM MST, MULT,
POET, POP; DC 6; PC 4
See also Jones, LeRoi
See also BW 2; CA 21-24R; CABS 3;
CANR 27, 38; CDALB 1941-1968;
DLB 5, 7, 16, 38; DLBD 8; MTCW;
YABC

Barbauld, Anna Laetitia
1743-1825 . . . . NCLC 50
See also DLB 107, 109, 142, 158

Barbellion, W. N. P. . . . . TCLC 24
See also Cummings, Bruce F(rederick)

Barbera, Jack (Vincent) 1945- . . . . . . CLC 44
See also CA 110; CANR 45

Barbey d'Aurevilly, Jules Amedee
1808-1889 . . . . NCLC 1; SSC 17
See also DLB 119

Barbusse, Henri 1873-1935 . . . . TCLC 5
See also CA 105; 154; DLB 65

Barclay, Bill
See Moorcock, Michael (John)

Barclay, William Ewert
See Moorcock, Michael (John)

Barea, Arturo 1897-1957 . . . . TCLC 14
See also CA 111

Barfoot, Joan 1946- . . . . CLC 18
See also CA 105

Baring, Maurice 1874-1945 . . . . TCLC 8
See also CA 105; DLB 34

Barker, Clive 1952- . . . CLC 52; DAM POP
See also AAYA 10; BEST 90:3; CA 121;
129; INT 129; MTCW

Barker, George Granville
1913-1991 . . . . . CLC 8, 48; DAM POET
See also CA 9-12R; 135; CANR 7, 38;
DLB 20; MTCW

Barker, Harley Granville
See Granville-Barker, Harley
See also DLB 10

Barker, Howard 1946- . . . . CLC 37
See also CA 102; DLB 13

Barker, Pat(ricia) 1943- . . . . CLC 32, 94
See also CA 117; 122; CANR 50; INT 122

Barlow, Joel 1754-1812 . . . . NCLC 23
See also DLB 37

Barnard, Mary (Ethel) 1909- . . . . CLC 48
See also CA 21-22; CAP 2

Barnes, Djuna
1892-1982 . . . CLC 3, 4, 8, 11, 29; SSC 3
See also CA 9-12R; 107; CANR 16, 55;
DLB 4, 9, 45; MTCW

Barnes, Julian (Patrick)
1946- . . . . CLC 42; DAB
See also CA 102; CANR 19, 54; DLBY 93

Barnes, Peter 1931- . . . . CLC 5, 56
See also CA 65-68; CAAS 12; CANR 33,
34; DLB 13; MTCW

Baroja (y Nessi), Pio
1872-1956 . . . . TCLC 8; HLC
See also CA 104

Baron, David
See Pinter, Harold

Baron Corvo
See Rolfe, Frederick (William Serafino
Austin Lewis Mary)

Barondess, Sue K(aufman)
1926-1977 . . . . CLC 8
See also Kaufman, Sue
See also CA 1-4R; 69-72; CANR 1

Baron de Teive
See Pessoa, Fernando (Antonio Nogueira)

Barres, Maurice 1862-1923 . . . . . . TCLC 47
See also DLB 123

Barreto, Afonso Henrique de Lima
See Lima Barreto, Afonso Henrique de

Barrett, (Roger) Syd 1946- . . . . CLC 35

Barrett, William (Christopher)
1913-1992 . . . . CLC 27
See also CA 13-16R; 139; CANR 11;
INT CANR-11

Barrie, J(ames) M(atthew)
1860-1937 . . . . TCLC 2; DAB;
DAM DRAM
See also CA 104; 136; CDBLB 1890-1914;
CLR 16; DLB 10, 141, 156; MAICYA; 1

Barrington, Michael
See Moorcock, Michael (John)

Barrol, Grady
See Bograd, Larry

Barry, Mike
See Malzberg, Barry N(athaniel)

Barry, Philip 1896-1949 . . . . TCLC 11
See also CA 109; DLB 7

Bart, Andre Schwarz
See Schwarz-Bart, Andre

Barth, John (Simmons)
1930- . . . . . . CLC 1, 2, 3, 5, 7, 9, 10, 14,
27, 51, 89; DAM NOV; SSC 10
See also AITN 1, 2; CA 1-4R; CABS 1;
CANR 5, 23, 49; DLB 2; MTCW

Belloc, (Joseph) Hilaire (Pierre Sebastien
    Rene Swanton)
    1870-1953 . . . **TCLC 7, 18; DAM POET**
    See also CA 106; 152; DLB 19, 100, 141,
    174; 1

Belloc, Joseph Peter Rene Hilaire
    See Belloc, (Joseph) Hilaire (Pierre Sebastien
    Rene Swanton)

Belloc, Joseph Pierre Hilaire
    See Belloc, (Joseph) Hilaire (Pierre Sebastien
    Rene Swanton)

Belloc, M. A.
    See Lowndes, Marie Adelaide (Belloc)

Bellow, Saul
    1915- . . . . . . **CLC 1, 2, 3, 6, 8, 10, 13, 15,
        25, 33, 34, 63, 79; DA; DAB; DAC;
        DAM MST, NOV, POP; SSC 14; WLC**
    See also AITN 2; BEST 89:3; CA 5-8R;
    CABS 1; CANR 29, 53;
    CDALB 1941-1968; DLB 2, 28; DLBD 3;
    DLBY 82; MTCW

Belser, Reimond Karel Maria de 1929-
    See Ruyslinck, Ward
    See also CA 152

Bely, Andrey . . . . **TCLC 7; PC 11**
    See also Bugayev, Boris Nikolayevich

Benary, Margot
    See Benary-Isbert, Margot

Benary-Isbert, Margot 1889-1979 . . . **CLC 12**
    See also CA 5-8R; 89-92; CANR 4;
    CLR 12; MAICYA; SATA 2;
    SATA-Obit 21

Benavente (y Martinez), Jacinto
    1866-1954 . . . . . **TCLC 3; DAM DRAM,
        MULT**
    See also CA 106; 131; HW; MTCW

Benchley, Peter (Bradford)
    1940- . . . . . **CLC 4, 8; DAM NOV, POP**
    See also AAYA 14; AITN 2; CA 17-20R;
    CANR 12, 35; MTCW; SATA 3, 89

Benchley, Robert (Charles)
    1889-1945 . . . . **TCLC 1, 55**
    See also CA 105; 153; DLB 11

Benda, Julien 1867-1956 . . . . **TCLC 60**
    See also CA 120; 154

Benedict, Ruth (Fulton)
    1887-1948 . . . . **TCLC 60**
    See also CA 158

Benedikt, Michael 1935- . . . . **CLC 4, 14**
    See also CA 13-16R; CANR 7; DLB 5

Benet, Juan 1927- . . . . **CLC 28**
    See also CA 143

Benet, Stephen Vincent
    1898-1943 . . . . . . **TCLC 7; DAM POET;
        SSC 10**
    See also CA 104; 152; DLB 4, 48, 102; 1

Benet, William Rose
    1886-1950 . . . . . **TCLC 28; DAM POET**
    See also CA 118; 152; DLB 45

Benford, Gregory (Albert) 1941- . . . . **CLC 52**
    See also CA 69-72; CAAS 27; CANR 12,
    24, 49; DLBY 82

Bengtsson, Frans (Gunnar)
    1894-1954 . . . . **TCLC 48**

Benjamin, David
    See Slavitt, David R(ytman)

Benjamin, Lois
    See Gould, Lois

Benjamin, Walter 1892-1940 . . . . . **TCLC 39**

Benn, Gottfried 1886-1956 . . . . **TCLC 3**
    See also CA 106; 153; DLB 56

Bennett, Alan
    1934- . . . **CLC 45, 77; DAB; DAM MST**
    See also CA 103; CANR 35, 55; MTCW

Bennett, (Enoch) Arnold
    1867-1931 . . . . **TCLC 5, 20**
    See also CA 106; 155; CDBLB 1890-1914;
    DLB 10, 34, 98, 135

Bennett, Elizabeth
    See Mitchell, Margaret (Munnerlyn)

Bennett, George Harold 1930-
    See Bennett, Hal
    See also BW 1; CA 97-100

Bennett, Hal . . . . **CLC 5**
    See also Bennett, George Harold
    See also DLB 33

Bennett, Jay 1912- . . . . **CLC 35**
    See also AAYA 10; CA 69-72; CANR 11,
    42; JRDA; SAAS 4; SATA 41, 87;
    SATA-Brief 27

Bennett, Louise (Simone)
    1919- . . . . . **CLC 28; BLC; DAM MULT**
    See also BW 2; CA 151; DLB 117

Benson, E(dward) F(rederic)
    1867-1940 . . . . **TCLC 27**
    See also CA 114; 157; DLB 135, 153

Benson, Jackson J. 1930- . . . . **CLC 34**
    See also CA 25-28R; DLB 111

Benson, Sally 1900-1972 . . . . **CLC 17**
    See also CA 19-20; 37-40R; CAP 1;
    SATA 1, 35; SATA-Obit 27

Benson, Stella 1892-1933 . . . . **TCLC 17**
    See also CA 117; 155; DLB 36, 162

Bentham, Jeremy 1748-1832 . . . . . **NCLC 38**
    See also DLB 107, 158

Bentley, E(dmund) C(lerihew)
    1875-1956 . . . . **TCLC 12**
    See also CA 108; DLB 70

Bentley, Eric (Russell) 1916- . . . . . . **CLC 24**
    See also CA 5-8R; CANR 6; INT CANR-6

Beranger, Pierre Jean de
    1780-1857 . . . . **NCLC 34**

Berdyaev, Nicolas
    See Berdyaev, Nikolai (Aleksandrovich)

Berdyaev, Nikolai (Aleksandrovich)
    1874-1948 . . . . **TCLC 67**
    See also CA 120; 157

Berdyayev, Nikolai (Aleksandrovich)
    See Berdyaev, Nikolai (Aleksandrovich)

Berendt, John (Lawrence) 1939- . . . . **CLC 86**
    See also CA 146

Berger, Colonel
    See Malraux, (Georges-)Andre

Berger, John (Peter) 1926- . . . . . . **CLC 2, 19**
    See also CA 81-84; CANR 51; DLB 14

Berger, Melvin H. 1927- . . . . **CLC 12**
    See also CA 5-8R; CANR 4; CLR 32;
    SAAS 2; SATA 5, 88

Berger, Thomas (Louis)
    1924- . . . . **CLC 3, 5, 8, 11, 18, 38;
        DAM NOV**
    See also CA 1-4R; CANR 5, 28, 51; DLB 2;
    DLBY 80; INT CANR-28; MTCW

Bergman, (Ernst) Ingmar
    1918- . . . . **CLC 16, 72**
    See also CA 81-84; CANR 33

Bergson, Henri 1859-1941 . . . . **TCLC 32**

Bergstein, Eleanor 1938- . . . . **CLC 4**
    See also CA 53-56; CANR 5

Berkoff, Steven 1937- . . . . **CLC 56**
    See also CA 104

Bermant, Chaim (Icyk) 1929- . . . . . . **CLC 40**
    See also CA 57-60; CANR 6, 31, 57

Bern, Victoria
    See Fisher, M(ary) F(rances) K(ennedy)

Bernanos, (Paul Louis) Georges
    1888-1948 . . . . **TCLC 3**
    See also CA 104; 130; DLB 72

Bernard, April 1956- . . . . **CLC 59**
    See also CA 131

Berne, Victoria
    See Fisher, M(ary) F(rances) K(ennedy)

Bernhard, Thomas
    1931-1989 . . . . **CLC 3, 32, 61**
    See also CA 85-88; 127; CANR 32, 57;
    DLB 85, 124; MTCW

Berriault, Gina 1926- . . . . **CLC 54**
    See also CA 116; 129; DLB 130

Berrigan, Daniel 1921- . . . . **CLC 4**
    See also CA 33-36R; CAAS 1; CANR 11,
    43; DLB 5

Berrigan, Edmund Joseph Michael, Jr.
    1934-1983
    See Berrigan, Ted
    See also CA 61-64; 110; CANR 14

Berrigan, Ted . . . . **CLC 37**
    See also Berrigan, Edmund Joseph Michael,
    Jr.
    See also DLB 5, 169

Berry, Charles Edward Anderson 1931-
    See Berry, Chuck
    See also CA 115

Berry, Chuck . . . . **CLC 17**
    See also Berry, Charles Edward Anderson

Berry, Jonas
    See Ashbery, John (Lawrence)

Berry, Wendell (Erdman)
    1934- . . . . **CLC 4, 6, 8, 27, 46;
        DAM POET**
    See also AITN 1; CA 73-76; CANR 50;
    DLB 5, 6

Berryman, John
    1914-1972 . . . . . . **CLC 1, 2, 3, 4, 6, 8, 10,
        13, 25, 62; DAM POET**
    See also CA 13-16; 33-36R; CABS 2;
    CANR 35; CAP 1; CDALB 1941-1968;
    DLB 48; MTCW

Bertolucci, Bernardo 1940- . . . . **CLC 16**
    See also CA 106

Bertrand, Aloysius 1807-1841 . . . . **NCLC 31**

Bertran de Born c. 1140-1215 . . . . . **CMLC 5**

Besant, Annie (Wood) 1847-1933 . . . **TCLC 9**
    See also CA 105

Bessie, Alvah 1904-1985. . . . . **CLC 23**
See also CA 5-8R; 116; CANR 2; DLB 26

Bethlen, T. D.
See Silverberg, Robert

Beti, Mongo. . . . **CLC 27; BLC; DAM MULT**
See also Biyidi, Alexandre

Betjeman, John
1906-1984 . . . . **CLC 2, 6, 10, 34, 43;**
DAB; DAM MST, POET
See also CA 9-12R; 112; CANR 33, 56;
CDBLB 1945-1960; DLB 20; DLBY 84;
MTCW

Bettelheim, Bruno 1903-1990 . . . . . . **CLC 79**
See also CA 81-84; 131; CANR 23; MTCW

Betti, Ugo 1892-1953 . . . . **TCLC 5**
See also CA 104; 155

Betts, Doris (Waugh) 1932-. . . . **CLC 3, 6, 28**
See also CA 13-16R; CANR 9; DLBY 82;
INT CANR-9

Bevan, Alistair
See Roberts, Keith (John Kingston)

Bialik, Chaim Nachman
1873-1934 . . . . **TCLC 25**

Bickerstaff, Isaac
See Swift, Jonathan

Bidart, Frank 1939- . . . . **CLC 33**
See also CA 140

Bienek, Horst 1930-. . . . . **CLC 7, 11**
See also CA 73-76; DLB 75

Bierce, Ambrose (Gwinett)
1842-1914(?) . . . . **TCLC 1, 7, 44; DA;**
DAC; DAM MST; SSC 9; WLC
See also CA 104; 139; CDALB 1865-1917;
DLB 11, 12, 23, 71, 74

Biggers, Earl Derr 1884-1933 . . . . . **TCLC 65**
See also CA 108; 153

Billings, Josh
See Shaw, Henry Wheeler

Billington, (Lady) Rachel (Mary)
1942- . . . . **CLC 43**
See also AITN 2; CA 33-36R; CANR 44

Binyon, T(imothy) J(ohn) 1936- . . . . **CLC 34**
See also CA 111; CANR 28

Bioy Casares, Adolfo
1914-. . . . . **CLC 4, 8, 13, 88;**
DAM MULT; HLC; SSC 17
See also CA 29-32R; CANR 19, 43;
DLB 113; HW; MTCW

Bird, Cordwainer
See Ellison, Harlan (Jay)

Bird, Robert Montgomery
1806-1854 . . . . **NCLC 1**

Birney, (Alfred) Earle
1904- . . . . **CLC 1, 4, 6, 11; DAC;**
DAM MST, POET
See also CA 1-4R; CANR 5, 20; DLB 88;
MTCW

Bishop, Elizabeth
1911-1979 . . . . . . **CLC 1, 4, 9, 13, 15, 32;**
DA; DAC; DAM MST, POET; PC 3
See also CA 5-8R; 89-92; CABS 2;
CANR 26; CDALB 1968-1988; DLB 5,
169; MTCW; SATA-Obit 24

Bishop, John 1935-. . . . . **CLC 10**
See also CA 105

Bissett, Bill 1939-. . . . . **CLC 18; PC 14**
See also CA 69-72; CAAS 19; CANR 15;
DLB 53; MTCW

Bitov, Andrei (Georgievich) 1937-. . . **CLC 57**
See also CA 142

Biyidi, Alexandre 1932-
See Beti, Mongo
See also BW 1; CA 114; 124; MTCW

Bjarme, Brynjolf
See Ibsen, Henrik (Johan)

Bjornson, Bjornstjerne (Martinius)
1832-1910 . . . . **TCLC 7, 37**
See also CA 104

Black, Robert
See Holdstock, Robert P.

Blackburn, Paul 1926-1971 . . . . . . **CLC 9, 43**
See also CA 81-84; 33-36R; CANR 34;
DLB 16; DLBY 81

Black Elk
1863-1950 . . . . . **TCLC 33; DAM MULT**
See also CA 144; NNAL

Black Hobart
See Sanders, (James) Ed(ward)

Blacklin, Malcolm
See Chambers, Aidan

Blackmore, R(ichard) D(oddridge)
1825-1900 . . . . **TCLC 27**
See also CA 120; DLB 18

Blackmur, R(ichard) P(almer)
1904-1965 . . . . **CLC 2, 24**
See also CA 11-12; 25-28R; CAP 1; DLB 63

Black Tarantula
See Acker, Kathy

Blackwood, Algernon (Henry)
1869-1951 . . . . **TCLC 5**
See also CA 105; 150; DLB 153, 156, 178

Blackwood, Caroline
1931-1996 . . . . **CLC 6, 9, 100**
See also CA 85-88; 151; CANR 32;
DLB 14; MTCW

Blade, Alexander
See Hamilton, Edmond; Silverberg, Robert

Blaga, Lucian 1895-1961 . . . . **CLC 75**

Blair, Eric (Arthur) 1903-1950
See Orwell, George
See also CA 104; 132; DA; DAB; DAC;
DAM MST, NOV; MTCW; SATA 29

Blais, Marie-Claire
1939- . . . . **CLC 2, 4, 6, 13, 22; DAC;**
DAM MST
See also CA 21-24R; CAAS 4; CANR 38;
DLB 53; MTCW

Blaise, Clark 1940-. . . . . **CLC 29**
See also AITN 2; CA 53-56; CAAS 3;
CANR 5; DLB 53

Blake, Nicholas
See Day Lewis, C(ecil)
See also DLB 77

Blake, William
1757-1827 . . . . **NCLC 13, 37, 57; DA;**
DAB; DAC; DAM MST, POET; PC 12;
WLC
See also CDBLB 1789-1832; DLB 93, 163;
MAICYA; SATA 30

Blake, William J(ames) 1894-1969 . . . **PC 12**
See also CA 5-8R; 25-28R

Blasco Ibanez, Vicente
1867-1928 . . . . . . **TCLC 12; DAM NOV**
See also CA 110; 131; HW; MTCW

Blatty, William Peter
1928- . . . . **CLC 2; DAM POP**
See also CA 5-8R; CANR 9

Bleeck, Oliver
See Thomas, Ross (Elmore)

Blessing, Lee 1949-. . . . . **CLC 54**

Blish, James (Benjamin)
1921-1975 . . . . **CLC 14**
See also CA 1-4R; 57-60; CANR 3; DLB 8;
MTCW; SATA 66

Bliss, Reginald
See Wells, H(erbert) G(eorge)

Blixen, Karen (Christentze Dinesen)
1885-1962
See Dinesen, Isak
See also CA 25-28; CANR 22, 50; CAP 2;
MTCW; SATA 44

Bloch, Robert (Albert) 1917-1994. . . **CLC 33**
See also CA 5-8R; 146; CAAS 20; CANR 5;
DLB 44; INT CANR-5; SATA 12;
SATA-Obit 82

Blok, Alexander (Alexandrovich)
1880-1921 . . . . **TCLC 5**
See also CA 104

Blom, Jan
See Breytenbach, Breyten

Bloom, Harold 1930-. . . . . **CLC 24**
See also CA 13-16R; CANR 39; DLB 67

Bloomfield, Aurelius
See Bourne, Randolph S(illiman)

Blount, Roy (Alton), Jr. 1941- . . . . . **CLC 38**
See also CA 53-56; CANR 10, 28;
INT CANR-28; MTCW

Bloy, Leon 1846-1917. . . . . **TCLC 22**
See also CA 121; DLB 123

Blume, Judy (Sussman)
1938- . . . **CLC 12, 30; DAM NOV, POP**
See also AAYA 3; CA 29-32R; CANR 13,
37; CLR 2, 15; DLB 52; JRDA;
MAICYA; MTCW; SATA 2, 31, 79

Blunden, Edmund (Charles)
1896-1974 . . . . **CLC 2, 56**
See also CA 17-18; 45-48; CANR 54;
CAP 2; DLB 20, 100, 155; MTCW

Bly, Robert (Elwood)
1926- . . . . **CLC 1, 2, 5, 10, 15, 38;**
DAM POET
See also CA 5-8R; CANR 41; DLB 5;
MTCW

Boas, Franz 1858-1942. . . . . **TCLC 56**
See also CA 115

Bobette
See Simenon, Georges (Jacques Christian)

Boccaccio, Giovanni
1313-1375 . . . . **CMLC 13; SSC 10**

Bochco, Steven 1943-. . . . . **CLC 35**
See also AAYA 11; CA 124; 138

Bodenheim, Maxwell 1892-1954 . . . **TCLC 44**
See also CA 110; DLB 9, 45

Bodker, Cecil 1927- . . . . **CLC 21**
See also CA 73-76; CANR 13, 44; CLR 23;
MAICYA; SATA 14

Boell, Heinrich (Theodor)
1917-1985 . . . . **CLC 2, 3, 6, 9, 11, 15, 27,**
32, 72; DA; DAB; DAC; DAM MST,
NOV; SSC 23; WLC
See also CA 21-24R; 116; CANR 24;
DLB 69; DLBY 85; MTCW

Boerne, Alfred
See Doeblin, Alfred

Boethius 480(?)-524(?) . . . . **CMLC 15**
See also DLB 115

Bogan, Louise
1897-1970 . . . . **CLC 4, 39, 46, 93;**
DAM POET; PC 12
See also CA 73-76; 25-28R; CANR 33;
DLB 45, 169; MTCW

Bogarde, Dirk . . . . **CLC 19**
See also Van Den Bogarde, Derek Jules
Gaspard Ulric Niven
See also DLB 14

Bogosian, Eric 1953- . . . . **CLC 45**
See also CA 138

Bograd, Larry 1953- . . . . **CLC 35**
See also CA 93-96; CANR 57; SAAS 21;
SATA 33, 89

Boiardo, Matteo Maria 1441-1494 . . . . **LC 6**

Boileau-Despreaux, Nicolas
1636-1711 . . . . **LC 3**

Bojer, Johan 1872-1959 . . . . **TCLC 64**

Boland, Eavan (Aisling)
1944- . . . . **CLC 40, 67; DAM POET**
See also CA 143; DLB 40

Bolt, Lee
See Faust, Frederick (Schiller)

Bolt, Robert (Oxton)
1924-1995 . . . . . . **CLC 14; DAM DRAM**
See also CA 17-20R; 147; CANR 35;
DLB 13; MTCW

Bombet, Louis-Alexandre-Cesar
See Stendhal

Bomkauf
See Kaufman, Bob (Garnell)

Bonaventura . . . . **NCLC 35**
See also DLB 90

Bond, Edward
1934- . . . **CLC 4, 6, 13, 23; DAM DRAM**
See also CA 25-28R; CANR 38; DLB 13;
MTCW

Bonham, Frank 1914-1989 . . . . **CLC 12**
See also AAYA 1; CA 9-12R; CANR 4, 36;
JRDA; MAICYA; SAAS 3; SATA 1, 49;
SATA-Obit 62

Bonnefoy, Yves
1923- . . . . . . **CLC 9, 15, 58; DAM MST,**
POET
See also CA 85-88; CANR 33; MTCW

Bontemps, Arna(ud Wendell)
1902-1973 . . . . **CLC 1, 18; BLC;**
DAM MULT, NOV, POET
See also BW 1; CA 1-4R; 41-44R; CANR 4,
35; CLR 6; DLB 48, 51; JRDA;
MAICYA; MTCW; SATA 2, 44;
SATA-Obit 24

Booth, Martin 1944- . . . . **CLC 13**
See also CA 93-96; CAAS 2

Booth, Philip 1925- . . . . **CLC 23**
See also CA 5-8R; CANR 5; DLBY 82

Booth, Wayne C(layson) 1921- . . . . . **CLC 24**
See also CA 1-4R; CAAS 5; CANR 3, 43;
DLB 67

Borchert, Wolfgang 1921-1947 . . . . . **TCLC 5**
See also CA 104; DLB 69, 124

Borel, Petrus 1809-1859 . . . . **NCLC 41**

Borges, Jorge Luis
1899-1986 . . . **CLC 1, 2, 3, 4, 6, 8, 9, 10,**
13, 19, 44, 48, 83; DA; DAB; DAC;
DAM MST, MULT; HLC; SSC 4; WLC
See also AAYA 19; CA 21-24R; CANR 19,
33; DLB 113; DLBY 86; HW; MTCW

Borowski, Tadeusz 1922-1951 . . . . . . **TCLC 9**
See also CA 106; 154

Borrow, George (Henry)
1803-1881 . . . . **NCLC 9**
See also DLB 21, 55, 166

Bosman, Herman Charles
1905-1951 . . . . **TCLC 49**

Bosschere, Jean de 1878(?)-1953 . . . **TCLC 19**
See also CA 115

Boswell, James
1740-1795 . . . . . . **LC 4; DA; DAB; DAC;**
DAM MST; WLC
See also CDBLB 1660-1789; DLB 104, 142

Bottoms, David 1949- . . . . **CLC 53**
See also CA 105; CANR 22; DLB 120;
DLBY 83

Boucicault, Dion 1820-1890 . . . . . . **NCLC 41**

Boucolon, Maryse 1937(?)-
See Conde, Maryse
See also CA 110; CANR 30, 53

Bourget, Paul (Charles Joseph)
1852-1935 . . . . **TCLC 12**
See also CA 107; DLB 123

Bourjaily, Vance (Nye) 1922- . . . . **CLC 8, 62**
See also CA 1-4R; CAAS 1; CANR 2;
DLB 2, 143

Bourne, Randolph S(illiman)
1886-1918 . . . . **TCLC 16**
See also CA 117; 155; DLB 63

Bova, Ben(jamin William) 1932- . . . . **CLC 45**
See also AAYA 16; CA 5-8R; CAAS 18;
CANR 11, 56; CLR 3; DLBY 81;
INT CANR-11; MAICYA; MTCW;
SATA 6, 68

Bowen, Elizabeth (Dorothea Cole)
1899-1973 . . . . . . **CLC 1, 3, 6, 11, 15, 22;**
DAM NOV; SSC 3
See also CA 17-18; 41-44R; CANR 35;
CAP 2; CDBLB 1945-1960; DLB 15, 162;
MTCW

Bowering, George 1935- . . . . **CLC 15, 47**
See also CA 21-24R; CAAS 16; CANR 10;
DLB 53

Bowering, Marilyn R(uthe) 1949- . . . **CLC 32**
See also CA 101; CANR 49

Bowers, Edgar 1924- . . . . **CLC 9**
See also CA 5-8R; CANR 24; DLB 5

Bowie, David . . . . **CLC 17**
See also Jones, David Robert

Bowles, Jane (Sydney)
1917-1973 . . . . **CLC 3, 68**
See also CA 19-20; 41-44R; CAP 2

Bowles, Paul (Frederick)
1910- . . . . **CLC 1, 2, 19, 53; SSC 3**
See also CA 1-4R; CAAS 1; CANR 1, 19,
50; DLB 5, 6; MTCW

Box, Edgar
See Vidal, Gore

Boyd, Nancy
See Millay, Edna St. Vincent

Boyd, William 1952- . . . . **CLC 28, 53, 70**
See also CA 114; 120; CANR 51

Boyle, Kay
1902-1992 . . . . . **CLC 1, 5, 19, 58; SSC 5**
See also CA 13-16R; 140; CAAS 1;
CANR 29; DLB 4, 9, 48, 86; DLBY 93;
MTCW

Boyle, Mark
See Kienzle, William X(avier)

Boyle, Patrick 1905-1982 . . . . **CLC 19**
See also CA 127

Boyle, T. C. 1948-
See Boyle, T(homas) Coraghessan

Boyle, T(homas) Coraghessan
1948- . . . . . **CLC 36, 55, 90; DAM POP;**
SSC 16
See also BEST 90:4; CA 120; CANR 44;
DLBY 86

Boz
See Dickens, Charles (John Huffam)

Brackenridge, Hugh Henry
1748-1816 . . . . **NCLC 7**
See also DLB 11, 37

Bradbury, Edward P.
See Moorcock, Michael (John)

Bradbury, Malcolm (Stanley)
1932- . . . . **CLC 32, 61; DAM NOV**
See also CA 1-4R; CANR 1, 33; DLB 14;
MTCW

Bradbury, Ray (Douglas)
1920- . . . . . **CLC 1, 3, 10, 15, 42, 98; DA;**
DAB; DAC; DAM MST, NOV, POP;
WLC
See also AAYA 15; AITN 1, 2; CA 1-4R;
CANR 2, 30; CDALB 1968-1988; DLB 2,
8; INT CANR-30; MTCW; SATA 11, 64

Bradford, Gamaliel 1863-1932 . . . . . **TCLC 36**
See also DLB 17

Bradley, David (Henry, Jr.)
1950- . . . . . . **CLC 23; BLC; DAM MULT**
See also BW 1; CA 104; CANR 26; DLB 33

Bradley, John Ed(mund, Jr.)
1958- . . . . **CLC 55**
See also CA 139

Bradley, Marion Zimmer
1930- . . . . **CLC 30; DAM POP**
See also AAYA 9; CA 57-60; CAAS 10;
CANR 7, 31, 51; DLB 8; MTCW;
SATA 90

Bradstreet, Anne
1612(?)-1672 . . . . . . **LC 4, 30; DA; DAC;**
DAM MST, POET; PC 10
See also CDALB 1640-1865; DLB 24

Brady, Joan 1939- . . . . **CLC 86**
See also CA 141

Brother Antoninus
  See Everson, William (Oliver)

Broughton, T(homas) Alan 1936- . . . **CLC 19**
  See also CA 45-48; CANR 2, 23, 48

Broumas, Olga 1949- . . . . **CLC 10, 73**
  See also CA 85-88; CANR 20

Brown, Alan 1951- . . . . **CLC 99**

Brown, Charles Brockden
  1771-1810 . . . . **NCLC 22**
  See also CDALB 1640-1865; DLB 37, 59, 73

Brown, Christy 1932-1981 . . . . **CLC 63**
  See also CA 105; 104; DLB 14

Brown, Claude
  1937- . . . . . **CLC 30; BLC; DAM MULT**
  See also AAYA 7; BW 1; CA 73-76

Brown, Dee (Alexander)
  1908- . . . . **CLC 18, 47; DAM POP**
  See also CA 13-16R; CAAS 6; CANR 11,
  45; DLBY 80; MTCW; SATA 5

Brown, George
  See Wertmueller, Lina

Brown, George Douglas
  1869-1902 . . . . **TCLC 28**

Brown, George Mackay
  1921-1996 . . . . **CLC 5, 48, 100**
  See also CA 21-24R; 151; CAAS 6;
  CANR 12, 37; DLB 14, 27, 139; MTCW;
  SATA 35

Brown, (William) Larry 1951- . . . . . . **CLC 73**
  See also CA 130; 134; INT 133

Brown, Moses
  See Barrett, William (Christopher)

Brown, Rita Mae
  1944- . . . . . **CLC 18, 43, 79; DAM NOV,
                                         POP**
  See also CA 45-48; CANR 2, 11, 35;
  INT CANR-11; MTCW

Brown, Roderick (Langmere) Haig-
  See Haig-Brown, Roderick (Langmere)

Brown, Rosellen 1939- . . . . **CLC 32**
  See also CA 77-80; CAAS 10; CANR 14, 44

Brown, Sterling Allen
  1901-1989 . . . . **CLC 1, 23, 59; BLC;
                                    DAM MULT, POET**
  See also BW 1; CA 85-88; 127; CANR 26;
  DLB 48, 51, 63; MTCW

Brown, Will
  See Ainsworth, William Harrison

Brown, William Wells
  1813-1884 . . . . **NCLC 2; BLC;
                                       DAM MULT; DC 1**
  See also DLB 3, 50

Browne, (Clyde) Jackson 1948(?)- . . . **CLC 21**
  See also CA 120

Browning, Elizabeth Barrett
  1806-1861 . . . . **NCLC 1, 16, 61; DA;
     DAB; DAC; DAM MST, POET; PC 6;
                                             WLC**
  See also CDBLB 1832-1890; DLB 32

Browning, Robert
  1812-1889 . . . . **NCLC 19; DA; DAB;
             DAC; DAM MST, POET; PC 2**
  See also CDBLB 1832-1890; DLB 32, 163;
  YABC; 1

Browning, Tod 1882-1962 . . . . **CLC 16**
  See also CA 141; 117

Brownson, Orestes (Augustus)
  1803-1876 . . . . **NCLC 50**

Bruccoli, Matthew J(oseph) 1931- . . **CLC 34**
  See also CA 9-12R; CANR 7; DLB 103

Bruce, Lenny . . . . **CLC 21**
  See also Schneider, Leonard Alfred

Bruin, John
  See Brutus, Dennis

Brulard, Henri
  See Stendhal

Brulls, Christian
  See Simenon, Georges (Jacques Christian)

Brunner, John (Kilian Houston)
  1934-1995 . . . . . **CLC 8, 10; DAM POP**
  See also CA 1-4R; 149; CAAS 8; CANR 2,
  37; MTCW

Bruno, Giordano 1548-1600 . . . . **LC 27**

Brutus, Dennis
  1924- . . . . . **CLC 43; BLC; DAM MULT,
                                               POET**
  See also BW 2; CA 49-52; CAAS 14;
  CANR 2, 27, 42; DLB 117

Bryan, C(ourtlandt) D(ixon) B(arnes)
  1936- . . . . **CLC 29**
  See also CA 73-76; CANR 13;
  INT CANR-13

Bryan, Michael
  See Moore, Brian

Bryant, William Cullen
  1794-1878 . . . . . **NCLC 6, 46; DA; DAB;
               DAC; DAM MST, POET**
  See also CDALB 1640-1865; DLB 3, 43, 59

Bryusov, Valery Yakovlevich
  1873-1924 . . . . **TCLC 10**
  See also CA 107; 155

Buchan, John
  1875-1940 . . . . **TCLC 41; DAB;
                                         DAM POP**
  See also CA 108; 145; DLB 34, 70, 156; 2

Buchanan, George 1506-1582 . . . . **LC 4**

Buchheim, Lothar-Guenther 1918- . . . **CLC 6**
  See also CA 85-88

Buchner, (Karl) Georg
  1813-1837 . . . . **NCLC 26**

Buchwald, Art(hur) 1925- . . . . **CLC 33**
  See also AITN 1; CA 5-8R; CANR 21;
  MTCW; SATA 10

Buck, Pearl S(ydenstricker)
  1892-1973 . . . . **CLC 7, 11, 18; DA; DAB;
                         DAC; DAM MST, NOV**
  See also AITN 1; CA 1-4R; 41-44R;
  CANR 1, 34; DLB 9, 102; MTCW;
  SATA 1, 25

Buckler, Ernest
  1908-1984 . . **CLC 13; DAC; DAM MST**
  See also CA 11-12; 114; CAP 1; DLB 68;
  SATA 47

Buckley, Vincent (Thomas)
  1925-1988 . . . . **CLC 57**
  See also CA 101

Buckley, William F(rank), Jr.
  1925- . . . . **CLC 7, 18, 37; DAM POP**
  See also AITN 1; CA 1-4R; CANR 1, 24,
  53; DLB 137; DLBY 80; INT CANR-24;
  MTCW

Buechner, (Carl) Frederick
  1926- . . . . . . **CLC 2, 4, 6, 9; DAM NOV**
  See also CA 13-16R; CANR 11, 39;
  DLBY 80; INT CANR-11; MTCW

Buell, John (Edward) 1927- . . . . **CLC 10**
  See also CA 1-4R; DLB 53

Buero Vallejo, Antonio 1916- . . . **CLC 15, 46**
  See also CA 106; CANR 24, 49; HW;
  MTCW

Bufalino, Gesualdo 1920(?)- . . . . **CLC 74**

Bugayev, Boris Nikolayevich 1880-1934
  See Bely, Andrey
  See also CA 104

Bukowski, Charles
  1920-1994 . . . . **CLC 2, 5, 9, 41, 82;
                           DAM NOV, POET; PC 18**
  See also CA 17-20R; 144; CANR 40;
  DLB 5, 130, 169; MTCW

Bulgakov, Mikhail (Afanas'evich)
  1891-1940 . . . . **TCLC 2, 16;
                      DAM DRAM, NOV; SSC 18**
  See also CA 105; 152

Bulgya, Alexander Alexandrovich
  1901-1956 . . . . **TCLC 53**
  See also Fadeyev, Alexander
  See also CA 117

Bullins, Ed
  1935- . . . . **CLC 1, 5, 7; BLC;
                    DAM DRAM, MULT; DC 6**
  See also BW 2; CA 49-52; CAAS 16;
  CANR 24, 46; DLB 7, 38; MTCW

Bulwer-Lytton, Edward (George Earle Lytton)
  1803-1873 . . . . **NCLC 1, 45**
  See also DLB 21

Bunin, Ivan Alexeyevich
  1870-1953 . . . . **TCLC 6; SSC 5**
  See also CA 104

Bunting, Basil
  1900-1985 . . . . **CLC 10, 39, 47;
                                         DAM POET**
  See also CA 53-56; 115; CANR 7; DLB 20

Bunuel, Luis
  1900-1983 . . . . **CLC 16, 80;
                                   DAM MULT; HLC**
  See also CA 101; 110; CANR 32; HW

Bunyan, John
  1628-1688 . . . . . . **LC 4; DA; DAB; DAC;
                              DAM MST; WLC**
  See also CDBLB 1660-1789; DLB 39

Burckhardt, Jacob (Christoph)
  1818-1897 . . . . **NCLC 49**

Burford, Eleanor
  See Hibbert, Eleanor Alice Burford

Burgess, Anthony
  . **CLC 1, 2, 4, 5, 8, 10, 13, 15, 22, 40, 62,
                              81, 94; DAB**
  See also Wilson, John (Anthony) Burgess
  See also AITN 1; CDBLB 1960 to Present;
  DLB 14

Burke, Edmund
1729(?)-1797 . . . . . **LC 7, 36; DA; DAB;**
DAC; DAM MST; WLC
See also DLB 104

Burke, Kenneth (Duva)
1897-1993 . . . . **CLC 2, 24**
See also CA 5-8R; 143; CANR 39; DLB 45,
63; MTCW

Burke, Leda
See Garnett, David

Burke, Ralph
See Silverberg, Robert

Burke, Thomas 1886-1945 . . . . **TCLC 63**
See also CA 113; 155

Burney, Fanny 1752-1840 . . . . **NCLC 12, 54**
See also DLB 39

Burns, Robert 1759-1796 . . . . **PC 6**
See also CDBLB 1789-1832; DA; DAB;
DAC; DAM MST, POET; DLB 109;
WLC

Burns, Tex
See L'Amour, Louis (Dearborn)

Burnshaw, Stanley 1906- . . . . . **CLC 3, 13, 44**
See also CA 9-12R; DLB 48

Burr, Anne 1937- . . . . **CLC 6**
See also CA 25-28R

Burroughs, Edgar Rice
1875-1950 . . . . **TCLC 2, 32; DAM NOV**
See also AAYA 11; CA 104; 132; DLB 8;
MTCW; SATA 41

Burroughs, William S(eward)
1914- . . . . . . **CLC 1, 2, 5, 15, 22, 42, 75;**
DA; DAB; DAC; DAM MST, NOV,
POP; WLC
See also AITN 2; CA 9-12R; CANR 20, 52;
DLB 2, 8, 16, 152; DLBY 81; MTCW

Burton, Richard F. 1821-1890 . . . . **NCLC 42**
See also DLB 55

Busch, Frederick 1941- . . . **CLC 7, 10, 18, 47**
See also CA 33-36R; CAAS 1; CANR 45;
DLB 6

Bush, Ronald 1946- . . . . **CLC 34**
See also CA 136

Bustos, F(rancisco)
See Borges, Jorge Luis

Bustos Domecq, H(onorio)
See Bioy Casares, Adolfo; Borges, Jorge
Luis

Butler, Octavia E(stelle)
1947- . . . . . **CLC 38; DAM MULT, POP**
See also AAYA 18; BW 2; CA 73-76;
CANR 12, 24, 38; DLB 33; MTCW;
SATA 84

Butler, Robert Olen (Jr.)
1945- . . . . **CLC 81; DAM POP**
See also CA 112; DLB 173; INT 112

Butler, Samuel 1612-1680 . . . . **LC 16**
See also DLB 101, 126

Butler, Samuel
1835-1902 . . . . . . **TCLC 1, 33; DA; DAB;**
DAC; DAM MST, NOV; WLC
See also CA 143; CDBLB 1890-1914;
DLB 18, 57, 174

Butler, Walter C.
See Faust, Frederick (Schiller)

Butor, Michel (Marie Francois)
1926- . . . . **CLC 1, 3, 8, 11, 15**
See also CA 9-12R; CANR 33; DLB 83;
MTCW

Buzo, Alexander (John) 1944- . . . . . . **CLC 61**
See also CA 97-100; CANR 17, 39

Buzzati, Dino 1906-1972 . . . . **CLC 36**
See also CA 33-36R; DLB 177

Byars, Betsy (Cromer) 1928- . . . . **CLC 35**
See also AAYA 19; CA 33-36R; CANR 18,
36, 57; CLR 1, 16; DLB 52;
INT CANR-18; JRDA; MAICYA;
MTCW; SAAS 1; SATA 4, 46, 80

Byatt, A(ntonia) S(usan Drabble)
1936- . . . **CLC 19, 65; DAM NOV, POP**
See also CA 13-16R; CANR 13, 33, 50;
DLB 14; MTCW

Byrne, David 1952- . . . . **CLC 26**
See also CA 127

Byrne, John Keyes 1926-
See Leonard, Hugh
See also CA 102; INT 102

Byron, George Gordon (Noel)
1788-1824 . . . . . **NCLC 2, 12; DA; DAB;**
DAC; DAM MST, POET; PC 16; WLC
See also CDBLB 1789-1832; DLB 96, 110

Byron, Robert 1905-1941 . . . . **TCLC 67**

C. 3. 3.
See Wilde, Oscar (Fingal O'Flahertie Wills)

Caballero, Fernan 1796-1877 . . . . . **NCLC 10**

Cabell, Branch
See Cabell, James Branch

Cabell, James Branch 1879-1958 . . . **TCLC 6**
See also CA 105; 152; DLB 9, 78

Cable, George Washington
1844-1925 . . . . **TCLC 4; SSC 4**
See also CA 104; 155; DLB 12, 74;
DLBD 13

Cabral de Melo Neto, Joao
1920- . . . . **CLC 76; DAM MULT**
See also CA 151

Cabrera Infante, G(uillermo)
1929- . . . . . **CLC 5, 25, 45; DAM MULT;**
HLC
See also CA 85-88; CANR 29; DLB 113;
HW; MTCW

Cade, Toni
See Bambara, Toni Cade

Cadmus and Harmonia
See Buchan, John

Caedmon fl. 658-680 . . . . **CMLC 7**
See also DLB 146

Caeiro, Alberto
See Pessoa, Fernando (Antonio Nogueira)

Cage, John (Milton, Jr.) 1912- . . . . . **CLC 41**
See also CA 13-16R; CANR 9;
INT CANR-9

Cahan, Abraham 1860-1951 . . . . **TCLC 71**
See also CA 108; 154; DLB 9, 25, 28

Cain, G.
See Cabrera Infante, G(uillermo)

Cain, Guillermo
See Cabrera Infante, G(uillermo)

Cain, James M(allahan)
1892-1977 . . . . **CLC 3, 11, 28**
See also AITN 1; CA 17-20R; 73-76;
CANR 8, 34; MTCW

Caine, Mark
See Raphael, Frederic (Michael)

Calasso, Roberto 1941- . . . . **CLC 81**
See also CA 143

Calderon de la Barca, Pedro
1600-1681 . . . . **LC 23; DC 3**

Caldwell, Erskine (Preston)
1903-1987 . . . . **CLC 1, 8, 14, 50, 60;**
DAM NOV; SSC 19
See also AITN 1; CA 1-4R; 121; CAAS 1;
CANR 2, 33; DLB 9, 86; MTCW

Caldwell, (Janet Miriam) Taylor (Holland)
1900-1985 . . . . **CLC 2, 28, 39;**
DAM NOV, POP
See also CA 5-8R; 116; CANR 5

Calhoun, John Caldwell
1782-1850 . . . . **NCLC 15**
See also DLB 3

Calisher, Hortense
1911- . . . . . **CLC 2, 4, 8, 38; DAM NOV;**
SSC 15
See also CA 1-4R; CANR 1, 22; DLB 2;
INT CANR-22; MTCW

Callaghan, Morley Edward
1903-1990 . . . . . **CLC 3, 14, 41, 65; DAC;**
DAM MST
See also CA 9-12R; 132; CANR 33;
DLB 68; MTCW

Callimachus
c. 305B.C.-c. 240B.C. . . . . **CMLC 18**
See also DLB 176

Calvin, John 1509-1564 . . . . **LC 37**

Calvino, Italo
1923-1985 . . . . . **CLC 5, 8, 11, 22, 33, 39,**
73; DAM NOV; SSC 3
See also CA 85-88; 116; CANR 23; MTCW

Cameron, Carey 1952- . . . . **CLC 59**
See also CA 135

Cameron, Peter 1959- . . . . **CLC 44**
See also CA 125; CANR 50

Campana, Dino 1885-1932 . . . . **TCLC 20**
See also CA 117; DLB 114

Campanella, Tommaso 1568-1639 . . . . **LC 32**

Campbell, John W(ood, Jr.)
1910-1971 . . . . **CLC 32**
See also CA 21-22; 29-32R; CANR 34;
CAP 2; DLB 8; MTCW

Campbell, Joseph 1904-1987 . . . . . . **CLC 69**
See also AAYA 3; BEST 89:2; CA 1-4R;
124; CANR 3, 28; MTCW

Campbell, Maria 1940- . . . . . . **CLC 85; DAC**
See also CA 102; CANR 54; NNAL

Campbell, (John) Ramsey
1946- . . . . **CLC 42; SSC 19**
See also CA 57-60; CANR 7; INT CANR-7

Campbell, (Ignatius) Roy (Dunnachie)
1901-1957 . . . . **TCLC 5**
See also CA 104; 155; DLB 20

Campbell, Thomas 1777-1844 . . . . **NCLC 19**
See also DLB 93; 144

Campbell, Wilfred . . . . **TCLC 9**
See also Campbell, William

Campbell, William   1858(?)-1918
See Campbell, Wilfred
See also CA 106; DLB 92

Campion, Jane . . . . **CLC 95**
See also CA 138

Campos, Alvaro de
See Pessoa, Fernando (Antonio Nogueira)

Camus, Albert
    1913-1960 . . . . **CLC 1, 2, 4, 9, 11, 14, 32,
    63, 69; DA; DAB; DAC; DAM DRAM,
    MST, NOV; DC 2; SSC 9; WLC**
See also CA 89-92; DLB 72; MTCW

Canby, Vincent   1924- . . . . **CLC 13**
See also CA 81-84

Cancale
See Desnos, Robert

Canetti, Elias
    1905-1994 . . . . **CLC 3, 14, 25, 75, 86**
See also CA 21-24R; 146; CANR 23;
    DLB 85, 124; MTCW

Canin, Ethan   1960- . . . . **CLC 55**
See also CA 131; 135

Cannon, Curt
See Hunter, Evan

Cape, Judith
See Page, P(atricia) K(athleen)

Capek, Karel
    1890-1938 . . . . . . **TCLC 6, 37; DA; DAB;
    DAC; DAM DRAM, MST, NOV; DC 1;
    WLC**
See also CA 104; 140

Capote, Truman
    1924-1984 . . . . . . **CLC 1, 3, 8, 13, 19, 34,
    38, 58; DA; DAB; DAC; DAM MST,
    NOV, POP; SSC 2; WLC**
See also CA 5-8R; 113; CANR 18;
    CDALB 1941-1968; DLB 2; DLBY 80,
    84; MTCW; SATA 91

Capra, Frank   1897-1991 . . . . **CLC 16**
See also CA 61-64; 135

Caputo, Philip   1941- . . . . **CLC 32**
See also CA 73-76; CANR 40

Card, Orson Scott
    1951- . . . . . . **CLC 44, 47, 50; DAM POP**
See also AAYA 11; CA 102; CANR 27, 47;
    INT CANR-27; MTCW; SATA 83

Cardenal, Ernesto
    1925- . . . . **CLC 31; DAM MULT,
    POET; HLC**
See also CA 49-52; CANR 2, 32; HW;
    MTCW

Cardozo, Benjamin N(athan)
    1870-1938 . . . . **TCLC 65**
See also CA 117

Carducci, Giosue   1835-1907 . . . . . . **TCLC 32**

Carew, Thomas   1595(?)-1640 . . . . **LC 13**
See also DLB 126

Carey, Ernestine Gilbreth   1908- . . . . **CLC 17**
See also CA 5-8R; SATA 2

Carey, Peter   1943- . . . . **CLC 40, 55, 96**
See also CA 123; 127; CANR 53; INT 127;
    MTCW; SATA 94

Carleton, William   1794-1869 . . . . . . **NCLC 3**
See also DLB 159

Carlisle, Henry (Coffin)   1926- . . . . . **CLC 33**
See also CA 13-16R; CANR 15

Carlsen, Chris
See Holdstock, Robert P.

Carlson, Ron(ald F.)   1947- . . . . **CLC 54**
See also CA 105; CANR 27

Carlyle, Thomas
    1795-1881 . . . . **NCLC 22; DA; DAB;
    DAC; DAM MST**
See also CDBLB 1789-1832; DLB 55; 144

Carman, (William) Bliss
    1861-1929 . . . . **TCLC 7; DAC**
See also CA 104; 152; DLB 92

Carnegie, Dale   1888-1955 . . . . **TCLC 53**

Carossa, Hans   1878-1956 . . . . **TCLC 48**
See also DLB 66

Carpenter, Don(ald Richard)
    1931-1995 . . . . **CLC 41**
See also CA 45-48; 149; CANR 1

Carpentier (y Valmont), Alejo
    1904-1980 . . . . **CLC 8, 11, 38;
    DAM MULT; HLC**
See also CA 65-68; 97-100; CANR 11;
    DLB 113; HW

Carr, Caleb   1955(?)- . . . . **CLC 86**
See also CA 147

Carr, Emily   1871-1945 . . . . **TCLC 32**
See also DLB 68

Carr, John Dickson   1906-1977 . . . . . . **CLC 3**
See also CA 49-52; 69-72; CANR 3, 33;
    MTCW

Carr, Philippa
See Hibbert, Eleanor Alice Burford

Carr, Virginia Spencer   1929- . . . . **CLC 34**
See also CA 61-64; DLB 111

Carrere, Emmanuel   1957- . . . . **CLC 89**

Carrier, Roch
    1937- . . . **CLC 13, 78; DAC; DAM MST**
See also CA 130; DLB 53

Carroll, James P.   1943(?)- . . . . **CLC 38**
See also CA 81-84

Carroll, Jim   1951- . . . . **CLC 35**
See also AAYA 17; CA 45-48; CANR 42

Carroll, Lewis . . . . **NCLC 2, 53; PC 18; WLC**
See also Dodgson, Charles Lutwidge
See also CDBLB 1832-1890; CLR 2, 18;
    DLB 18, 163, 178; JRDA

Carroll, Paul Vincent   1900-1968 . . . . **CLC 10**
See also CA 9-12R; 25-28R; DLB 10

Carruth, Hayden
    1921- . . . . . . **CLC 4, 7, 10, 18, 84; PC 10**
See also CA 9-12R; CANR 4, 38; DLB 5,
    165; INT CANR-4; MTCW; SATA 47

Carson, Rachel Louise
    1907-1964 . . . . **CLC 71; DAM POP**
See also CA 77-80; CANR 35; MTCW;
    SATA 23

Carter, Angela (Olive)
    1940-1992 . . . . . . **CLC 5, 41, 76; SSC 13**
See also CA 53-56; 136; CANR 12, 36;
    DLB 14; MTCW; SATA 66;
    SATA-Obit 70

Carter, Nick
See Smith, Martin Cruz

Carver, Raymond
    1938-1988 . . . . **CLC 22, 36, 53, 55;
    DAM NOV; SSC 8**
See also CA 33-36R; 126; CANR 17, 34;
    DLB 130; DLBY 84, 88; MTCW

Cary, Elizabeth, Lady Falkland
    1585-1639 . . . . **LC 30**

Cary, (Arthur) Joyce (Lunel)
    1888-1957 . . . . **TCLC 1, 29**
See also CA 104; CDBLB 1914-1945;
    DLB 15, 100

Casanova de Seingalt, Giovanni Jacopo
    1725-1798 . . . . **LC 13**

Casares, Adolfo Bioy
See Bioy Casares, Adolfo

Casely-Hayford, J(oseph) E(phraim)
    1866-1930 . . . . **TCLC 24; BLC;
    DAM MULT**
See also BW 2; CA 123; 152

Casey, John (Dudley)   1939- . . . . **CLC 59**
See also BEST 90:2; CA 69-72; CANR 23

Casey, Michael   1947- . . . . **CLC 2**
See also CA 65-68; DLB 5

Casey, Patrick
See Thurman, Wallace (Henry)

Casey, Warren (Peter)   1935-1988 . . . **CLC 12**
See also CA 101; 127; INT 101

Casona, Alejandro . . . . **CLC 49**
See also Alvarez, Alejandro Rodriguez

Cassavetes, John   1929-1989 . . . . **CLC 20**
See also CA 85-88; 127

Cassian, Nina   1924- . . . . **PC 17**

Cassill, R(onald) V(erlin)   1919- . . . **CLC 4, 23**
See also CA 9-12R; CAAS 1; CANR 7, 45;
    DLB 6

Cassirer, Ernst   1874-1945 . . . . **TCLC 61**
See also CA 157

Cassity, (Allen) Turner   1929- . . . . **CLC 6, 42**
See also CA 17-20R; CAAS 8; CANR 11;
    DLB 105

Castaneda, Carlos   1931(?)- . . . . **CLC 12**
See also CA 25-28R; CANR 32; HW;
    MTCW

Castedo, Elena   1937- . . . . **CLC 65**
See also CA 132

Castedo-Ellerman, Elena
See Castedo, Elena

Castellanos, Rosario
    1925-1974 . . . . . . **CLC 66; DAM MULT;
    HLC**
See also CA 131; 53-56; CANR 58;
    DLB 113; HW

Castelvetro, Lodovico   1505-1571 . . . . . **LC 12**

Castiglione, Baldassare   1478-1529 . . . **LC 12**

Castle, Robert
See Hamilton, Edmond

Castro, Guillen de   1569-1631 . . . . **LC 19**

Castro, Rosalia de
    1837-1885 . . . . . . **NCLC 3; DAM MULT**

Cather, Willa
See Cather, Willa Sibert

Chernyshevsky, Nikolay Gavrilovich
1828-1889 .... **NCLC 1**

Cherry, Carolyn Janice 1942-
See Cherryh, C. J.
See also CA 65-68; CANR 10

Cherryh, C. J. .... **CLC 35**
See also Cherry, Carolyn Janice
See also DLBY 80; SATA 93

Chesnutt, Charles W(addell)
1858-1932 .... **TCLC 5, 39; BLC;**
DAM MULT; SSC 7
See also BW 1; CA 106; 125; DLB 12, 50,
78; MTCW

Chester, Alfred 1929(?)-1971....... **CLC 49**
See also CA 33-36R; DLB 130

Chesterton, G(ilbert) K(eith)
1874-1936 .... **TCLC 1, 6, 64;**
DAM NOV, POET; SSC 1
See also CA 104; 132; CDBLB 1914-1945;
DLB 10, 19, 34, 70, 98, 149, 178; MTCW;
SATA 27

Chiang Pin-chin 1904-1986
See Ding Ling
See also CA 118

Ch'ien Chung-shu 1910- .... **CLC 22**
See also CA 130; MTCW

Child, L. Maria
See Child, Lydia Maria

Child, Lydia Maria 1802-1880 .... **NCLC 6**
See also DLB 1, 74; SATA 67

Child, Mrs.
See Child, Lydia Maria

Child, Philip 1898-1978 .... **CLC 19, 68**
See also CA 13-14; CAP 1; SATA 47

Childers, (Robert) Erskine
1870-1922 .... **TCLC 65**
See also CA 113; 153; DLB 70

Childress, Alice
1920-1994 .... **CLC 12, 15, 86, 96; BLC;**
DAM DRAM, MULT, NOV; DC 4
See also AAYA 8; BW 2; CA 45-48; 146;
CANR 3, 27, 50; CLR 14; DLB 7, 38;
JRDA; MAICYA; MTCW; SATA 7, 48,
81

Chin, Frank (Chew, Jr.) 1940-........ **DC 7**
See also CA 33-36R; DAM MULT

Chislett, (Margaret) Anne 1943- .... **CLC 34**
See also CA 151

Chitty, Thomas Willes 1926-....... **CLC 11**
See also Hinde, Thomas
See also CA 5-8R

Chivers, Thomas Holley
1809-1858 .... **NCLC 49**
See also DLB 3

Chomette, Rene Lucien 1898-1981
See Clair, Rene
See also CA 103

Chopin, Kate
.... **TCLC 5, 14; DA; DAB; SSC 8**
See also Chopin, Katherine
See also CDALB 1865-1917; DLB 12, 78;
YABC

Chopin, Katherine 1851-1904
See Chopin, Kate
See also CA 104; 122; DAC; DAM MST,
NOV

Chretien de Troyes
c. 12th cent. - .... **CMLC 10**

Christie
See Ichikawa, Kon

Christie, Agatha (Mary Clarissa)
1890-1976 ...... **CLC 1, 6, 8, 12, 39, 48;**
DAB; DAC; DAM NOV
See also AAYA 9; AITN 1, 2; CA 17-20R;
61-64; CANR 10, 37; CDBLB 1914-1945;
DLB 13, 77; MTCW; SATA 36

Christie, (Ann) Philippa
See Pearce, Philippa
See also CA 5-8R; CANR 4

Christine de Pizan 1365(?)-1431(?) .... **LC 9**

Chubb, Elmer
See Masters, Edgar Lee

Chulkov, Mikhail Dmitrievich
1743-1792 .... **LC 2**
See also DLB 150

Churchill, Caryl 1938- ... **CLC 31, 55; DC 5**
See also CA 102; CANR 22, 46; DLB 13;
MTCW

Churchill, Charles 1731-1764........ **LC 3**
See also DLB 109

Chute, Carolyn 1947- .... **CLC 39**
See also CA 123

Ciardi, John (Anthony)
1916-1986 .... **CLC 10, 40, 44;**
DAM POET
See also CA 5-8R; 118; CAAS 2; CANR 5,
33; CLR 19; DLB 5; DLBY 86;
INT CANR-5; MAICYA; MTCW;
SATA 1, 65; SATA-Obit 46

Cicero, Marcus Tullius
106B.C.-43B.C. .... **CMLC 3**

Cimino, Michael 1943-............. **CLC 16**
See also CA 105

Cioran, E(mil) M. 1911-1995....... **CLC 64**
See also CA 25-28R; 149

Cisneros, Sandra
1954- ..... **CLC 69; DAM MULT; HLC**
See also AAYA 9; CA 131; DLB 122, 152;
HW

Cixous, Helene 1937-............. **CLC 92**
See also CA 126; CANR 55; DLB 83;
MTCW

Clair, Rene.................... **CLC 20**
See also Chomette, Rene Lucien

Clampitt, Amy 1920-1994 ... **CLC 32; PC 19**
See also CA 110; 146; CANR 29; DLB 105

Clancy, Thomas L., Jr. 1947-
See Clancy, Tom
See also CA 125; 131; INT 131; MTCW

Clancy, Tom..... **CLC 45; DAM NOV, POP**
See also Clancy, Thomas L., Jr.
See also AAYA 9; BEST 89:1, 90:1

Clare, John
1793-1864 .... **NCLC 9; DAB;**
DAM POET
See also DLB 55, 96

Clarin
See Alas (y Urena), Leopoldo (Enrique
Garcia)

Clark, Al C.
See Goines, Donald

Clark, (Robert) Brian 1932-........ **CLC 29**
See also CA 41-44R

Clark, Curt
See Westlake, Donald E(dwin)

Clark, Eleanor 1913-1996 .... **CLC 5, 19**
See also CA 9-12R; 151; CANR 41; DLB 6

Clark, J. P.
See Clark, John Pepper
See also DLB 117

Clark, John Pepper
1935- .... **CLC 38; BLC; DAM DRAM,**
MULT; DC 5
See also Clark, J. P.
See also BW 1; CA 65-68; CANR 16

Clark, M. R.
See Clark, Mavis Thorpe

Clark, Mavis Thorpe 1909- .... **CLC 12**
See also CA 57-60; CANR 8, 37; CLR 30;
MAICYA; SAAS 5; SATA 8, 74

Clark, Walter Van Tilburg
1909-1971 .... **CLC 28**
See also CA 9-12R; 33-36R; DLB 9;
SATA 8

Clarke, Arthur C(harles)
1917- .... **CLC 1, 4, 13, 18, 35;**
DAM POP; SSC 3
See also AAYA 4; CA 1-4R; CANR 2, 28,
55; JRDA; MAICYA; MTCW; SATA 13,
70

Clarke, Austin
1896-1974 ...... **CLC 6, 9; DAM POET**
See also CA 29-32; 49-52; CAP 2; DLB 10,
20

Clarke, Austin C(hesterfield)
1934- .... **CLC 8, 53; BLC; DAC;**
DAM MULT
See also BW 1; CA 25-28R; CAAS 16;
CANR 14, 32; DLB 53, 125

Clarke, Gillian 1937- .... **CLC 61**
See also CA 106; DLB 40

Clarke, Marcus (Andrew Hislop)
1846-1881 .... **NCLC 19**

Clarke, Shirley 1925-............. **CLC 16**

Clash, The
See Headon, (Nicky) Topper; Jones, Mick;
Simonon, Paul; Strummer, Joe

Claudel, Paul (Louis Charles Marie)
1868-1955 .... **TCLC 2, 10**
See also CA 104

Clavell, James (duMaresq)
1925-1994 .... **CLC 6, 25, 87;**
DAM NOV, POP
See also CA 25-28R; 146; CANR 26, 48;
MTCW

Cleaver, (Leroy) Eldridge
1935- ..... **CLC 30; BLC; DAM MULT**
See also BW 1; CA 21-24R; CANR 16

Cleese, John (Marwood) 1939- ..... **CLC 21**
See also Monty Python
See also CA 112; 116; CANR 35; MTCW

Cleishbotham, Jebediah
See Scott, Walter

Cleland, John 1710-1789 .... **LC 2**
See also DLB 39

Clemens, Samuel Langhorne 1835-1910
    See Twain, Mark
    See also CA 104; 135; CDALB 1865-1917;
    DA; DAB; DAC; DAM MST, NOV;
    DLB 11, 12, 23, 64, 74; JRDA;
    MAICYA; 2

Cleophil
    See Congreve, William

Clerihew, E.
    See Bentley, E(dmund) C(lerihew)

Clerk, N. W.
    See Lewis, C(live) S(taples)

Cliff, Jimmy.....................CLC 21
    See also Chambers, James

Clifton, (Thelma) Lucille
    1936-.............CLC 19, 66; BLC;
                DAM MULT, POET; PC 17
    See also BW 2; CA 49-52; CANR 2, 24, 42;
    CLR 5; DLB 5, 41; MAICYA; MTCW;
    SATA 20, 69

Clinton, Dirk
    See Silverberg, Robert

Clough, Arthur Hugh 1819-1861.. NCLC 27
    See also DLB 32

Clutha, Janet Paterson Frame 1924-
    See Frame, Janet
    See also CA 1-4R; CANR 2, 36; MTCW

Clyne, Terence
    See Blatty, William Peter

Cobalt, Martin
    See Mayne, William (James Carter)

Cobbett, William 1763-1835 ..... NCLC 49
    See also DLB 43, 107, 158

Coburn, D(onald) L(ee) 1938-......CLC 10
    See also CA 89-92

Cocteau, Jean (Maurice Eugene Clement)
    1889-1963 .... CLC 1, 8, 15, 16, 43; DA;
    DAB; DAC; DAM DRAM, MST, NOV;
                                        WLC
    See also CA 25-28; CANR 40; CAP 2;
    DLB 65; MTCW

Codrescu, Andrei
    1946-..........CLC 46; DAM POET
    See also CA 33-36R; CAAS 19; CANR 13,
    34, 53

Coe, Max
    See Bourne, Randolph S(illiman)

Coe, Tucker
    See Westlake, Donald E(dwin)

Coetzee, J(ohn) M(ichael)
    1940-......CLC 23, 33, 66; DAM NOV
    See also CA 77-80; CANR 41, 54; MTCW

Coffey, Brian
    See Koontz, Dean R(ay)

Cohan, George M. 1878-1942 ..... TCLC 60
    See also CA 157

Cohen, Arthur A(llen)
    1928-1986 ....CLC 7, 31
    See also CA 1-4R; 120; CANR 1, 17, 42;
    DLB 28

Cohen, Leonard (Norman)
    1934-.... CLC 3, 38; DAC; DAM MST
    See also CA 21-24R; CANR 14; DLB 53;
    MTCW

Cohen, Matt 1942-..........CLC 19; DAC
    See also CA 61-64; CAAS 18; CANR 40;
    DLB 53

Cohen-Solal, Annie 19(?)-..........CLC 50

Colegate, Isabel 1931-.............CLC 36
    See also CA 17-20R; CANR 8, 22; DLB 14;
    INT CANR-22; MTCW

Coleman, Emmett
    See Reed, Ishmael

Coleridge, Samuel Taylor
    1772-1834 ..... NCLC 9, 54; DA; DAB;
    DAC; DAM MST, POET; PC 11; WLC
    See also CDBLB 1789-1832; DLB 93, 107

Coleridge, Sara 1802-1852...... NCLC 31

Coles, Don 1928- ....CLC 46
    See also CA 115; CANR 38

Colette, (Sidonie-Gabrielle)
    1873-1954 ....TCLC 1, 5, 16;
                    DAM NOV; SSC 10
    See also CA 104; 131; DLB 65; MTCW

Collett, (Jacobine) Camilla (Wergeland)
    1813-1895 .... NCLC 22

Collier, Christopher 1930-.........CLC 30
    See also AAYA 13; CA 33-36R; CANR 13,
    33; JRDA; MAICYA; SATA 16, 70

Collier, James L(incoln)
    1928-............CLC 30; DAM POP
    See also AAYA 13; CA 9-12R; CANR 4,
    33; CLR 3; JRDA; MAICYA; SAAS 21;
    SATA 8, 70

Collier, Jeremy 1650-1726..........LC 6

Collier, John 1901-1980...........SSC 19
    See also CA 65-68; 97-100; CANR 10;
    DLB 77

Collingwood, R(obin) G(eorge)
    1889(?)-1943 .... TCLC 67
    See also CA 117; 155

Collins, Hunt
    See Hunter, Evan

Collins, Linda 1931-..............CLC 44
    See also CA 125

Collins, (William) Wilkie
    1824-1889 .... NCLC 1, 18
    See also CDBLB 1832-1890; DLB 18, 70,
    159

Collins, William
    1721-1759 .... LC 4; DAM POET
    See also DLB 109

Collodi, Carlo 1826-1890........ NCLC 54
    See also Lorenzini, Carlo
    See also CLR 5

Colman, George
    See Glassco, John

Colt, Winchester Remington
    See Hubbard, L(afayette) Ron(ald)

Colter, Cyrus 1910- ....CLC 58
    See also BW 1; CA 65-68; CANR 10;
    DLB 33

Colton, James
    See Hansen, Joseph

Colum, Padraic 1881-1972........CLC 28
    See also CA 73-76; 33-36R; CANR 35;
    CLR 36; MAICYA; MTCW; SATA 15

Colvin, James
    See Moorcock, Michael (John)

Colwin, Laurie (E.)
    1944-1992.........CLC 5, 13, 23, 84
    See also CA 89-92; 139; CANR 20, 46;
    DLBY 80; MTCW

Comfort, Alex(ander)
    1920-.............CLC 7; DAM POP
    See also CA 1-4R; CANR 1, 45

Comfort, Montgomery
    See Campbell, (John) Ramsey

Compton-Burnett, I(vy)
    1884(?)-1969 ......CLC 1, 3, 10, 15, 34;
                                DAM NOV
    See also CA 1-4R; 25-28R; CANR 4;
    DLB 36; MTCW

Comstock, Anthony 1844-1915 .... TCLC 13
    See also CA 110

Comte, Auguste 1798-1857....... NCLC 54

Conan Doyle, Arthur
    See Doyle, Arthur Conan

Conde, Maryse
    1937-.......CLC 52, 92; DAM MULT
    See also Boucolon, Maryse
    See also BW 2

Condillac, Etienne Bonnot de
    1714-1780 .... LC 26

Condon, Richard (Thomas)
    1915-1996 .....CLC 4, 6, 8, 10, 45, 100;
                                DAM NOV
    See also BEST 90:3; CA 1-4R; 151;
    CAAS 1; CANR 2, 23; INT CANR-23;
    MTCW

Confucius
    551B.C.-479B.C........CMLC 19; DA;
                DAB; DAC; DAM MST
    See also YABC

Congreve, William
    1670-1729 ....LC 5, 21; DA; DAB;
    DAC; DAM DRAM, MST, POET;
                                DC 2; WLC
    See also CDBLB 1660-1789; DLB 39, 84

Connell, Evan S(helby), Jr.
    1924-.......CLC 4, 6, 45; DAM NOV
    See also AAYA 7; CA 1-4R; CAAS 2;
    CANR 2, 39; DLB 2; DLBY 81; MTCW

Connelly, Marc(us Cook)
    1890-1980 ....CLC 7
    See also CA 85-88; 102; CANR 30; DLB 7;
    DLBY 80; SATA-Obit 25

Connor, Ralph .... TCLC 31
    See also Gordon, Charles William
    See also DLB 92

Conrad, Joseph
    1857-1924 .... TCLC 1, 6, 13, 25, 43, 57;
    DA; DAB; DAC; DAM MST, NOV;
                            SSC 9; WLC
    See also CA 104; 131; CDBLB 1890-1914;
    DLB 10, 34, 98, 156; MTCW; SATA 27

Conrad, Robert Arnold
    See Hart, Moss

Conroy, Donald Pat(rick)
    1945-... CLC 30, 74; DAM NOV, POP
    See also AAYA 8; AITN 1; CA 85-88;
    CANR 24, 53; DLB 6; MTCW

Constant (de Rebecque), (Henri) Benjamin
      1767-1830 .... **NCLC 6**
   See also DLB 119

Conybeare, Charles Augustus
   See Eliot, T(homas) S(tearns)

Cook, Michael 1933- .... **CLC 58**
   See also CA 93-96; DLB 53

Cook, Robin 1940- .... **CLC 14; DAM POP**
   See also BEST 90:2; CA 108; 111;
      CANR 41; INT 111

Cook, Roy
   See Silverberg, Robert

Cooke, Elizabeth 1948- .... **CLC 55**
   See also CA 129

Cooke, John Esten 1830-1886..... **NCLC 5**
   See also DLB 3

Cooke, John Estes
   See Baum, L(yman) Frank

Cooke, M. E.
   See Creasey, John

Cooke, Margaret
   See Creasey, John

Cook-Lynn, Elizabeth
      1930- .... **CLC 93; DAM MULT**
   See also CA 133; DLB 175; NNAL

Cooney, Ray .... **CLC 62**

Cooper, Douglas 1960- .... **CLC 86**

Cooper, Henry St. John
   See Creasey, John

Cooper, J(oan) California
      .... **CLC 56; DAM MULT**
   See also AAYA 12; BW 1; CA 125;
      CANR 55

Cooper, James Fenimore
      1789-1851 .... **NCLC 1, 27, 54**
   See also CDALB 1640-1865; DLB 3;
      SATA 19

Coover, Robert (Lowell)
      1932- .... **CLC 3, 7, 15, 32, 46, 87;**
                     DAM NOV; SSC 15
   See also CA 45-48; CANR 3, 37, 58;
      DLB 2; DLBY 81; MTCW

Copeland, Stewart (Armstrong)
      1952- .... **CLC 26**

Coppard, A(lfred) E(dgar)
      1878-1957 .... **TCLC 5; SSC 21**
   See also CA 114; DLB 162; 1

Coppee, Francois 1842-1908 ...... **TCLC 25**

Coppola, Francis Ford 1939- ...... **CLC 16**
   See also CA 77-80; CANR 40; DLB 44

Corbiere, Tristan 1845-1875 ..... **NCLC 43**

Corcoran, Barbara 1911- .... **CLC 17**
   See also AAYA 14; CA 21-24R; CAAS 2;
      CANR 11, 28, 48; DLB 52; JRDA;
      SAAS 20; SATA 3, 77

Cordelier, Maurice
   See Giraudoux, (Hippolyte) Jean

Corelli, Marie 1855-1924........ **TCLC 51**
   See also Mackay, Mary
   See also DLB 34, 156

Corman, Cid...................... **CLC 9**
   See also Corman, Sidney
   See also CAAS 2; DLB 5

Corman, Sidney 1924-
   See Corman, Cid
   See also CA 85-88; CANR 44; DAM POET

Cormier, Robert (Edmund)
      1925- .... **CLC 12, 30; DA; DAB; DAC;**
                     DAM MST, NOV
   See also AAYA 3, 19; CA 1-4R; CANR 5,
      23; CDALB 1968-1988; CLR 12; DLB 52;
      INT CANR-23; JRDA; MAICYA;
      MTCW; SATA 10, 45, 83

Corn, Alfred (DeWitt III) 1943- .... **CLC 33**
   See also CA 104; CAAS 25; CANR 44;
      DLB 120; DLBY 80

Corneille, Pierre
      1606-1684 .... **LC 28; DAB; DAM MST**

Cornwell, David (John Moore)
      1931- .... **CLC 9, 15; DAM POP**
   See also le Carre, John
   See also CA 5-8R; CANR 13, 33; MTCW

Corso, (Nunzio) Gregory 1930-... **CLC 1, 11**
   See also CA 5-8R; CANR 41; DLB 5, 16;
      MTCW

Cortazar, Julio
      1914-1984 ...... **CLC 2, 3, 5, 10, 13, 15,**
                     33, 34, 92; DAM MULT, NOV; HLC;
                     SSC 7
   See also CA 21-24R; CANR 12, 32;
      DLB 113; HW; MTCW

CORTES, HERNAN 1484-1547..... **LC 31**

Corwin, Cecil
   See Kornbluth, C(yril) M.

Cosic, Dobrica 1921- .... **CLC 14**
   See also CA 122; 138

Costain, Thomas B(ertram)
      1885-1965 .... **CLC 30**
   See also CA 5-8R; 25-28R; DLB 9

Costantini, Humberto
      1924(?)-1987 .... **CLC 49**
   See also CA 131; 122; HW

Costello, Elvis 1955-............. **CLC 21**

Cotes, Cecil V.
   See Duncan, Sara Jeannette

Cotter, Joseph Seamon Sr.
      1861-1949 .... **TCLC 28; BLC;**
                     DAM MULT
   See also BW 1; CA 124; DLB 50

Couch, Arthur Thomas Quiller
   See Quiller-Couch, Arthur Thomas

Coulton, James
   See Hansen, Joseph

Couperus, Louis (Marie Anne)
      1863-1923 .... **TCLC 15**
   See also CA 115

Coupland, Douglas
      1961- .... **CLC 85; DAC; DAM POP**
   See also CA 142; CANR 57

Court, Wesli
   See Turco, Lewis (Putnam)

Courtenay, Bryce 1933-........... **CLC 59**
   See also CA 138

Courtney, Robert
   See Ellison, Harlan (Jay)

Cousteau, Jacques-Yves 1910-...... **CLC 30**
   See also CA 65-68; CANR 15; MTCW;
      SATA 38

Coward, Noel (Peirce)
      1899-1973 .... **CLC 1, 9, 29, 51;**
                     DAM DRAM
   See also AITN 1; CA 17-18; 41-44R;
      CANR 35; CAP 2; CDBLB 1914-1945;
      DLB 10; MTCW

Cowley, Malcolm 1898-1989 .... **CLC 39**
   See also CA 5-8R; 128; CANR 3, 55;
      DLB 4, 48; DLBY 81, 89; MTCW

Cowper, William
      1731-1800 ...... **NCLC 8; DAM POET**
   See also DLB 104, 109

Cox, William Trevor
      1928- .... **CLC 9, 14, 71; DAM NOV**
   See also Trevor, William
   See also CA 9-12R; CANR 4, 37, 55;
      DLB 14; INT CANR-37; MTCW

Coyne, P. J.
   See Masters, Hilary

Cozzens, James Gould
      1903-1978 .... **CLC 1, 4, 11, 92**
   See also CA 9-12R; 81-84; CANR 19;
      CDALB 1941-1968; DLB 9; DLBD 2;
      DLBY 84; MTCW

Crabbe, George 1754-1832...... **NCLC 26**
   See also DLB 93

Craddock, Charles Egbert
   See Murfree, Mary Noailles

Craig, A. A.
   See Anderson, Poul (William)

Craik, Dinah Maria (Mulock)
      1826-1887 .... **NCLC 38**
   See also DLB 35, 163; MAICYA; SATA 34

Cram, Ralph Adams 1863-1942.... **TCLC 45**

Crane, (Harold) Hart
      1899-1932 .... **TCLC 2, 5; DA; DAB;**
                     DAC; DAM MST, POET; PC 3; WLC
   See also CA 104; 127; CDALB 1917-1929;
      DLB 4, 48; MTCW

Crane, R(onald) S(almon)
      1886-1967 .... **CLC 27**
   See also CA 85-88; DLB 63

Crane, Stephen (Townley)
      1871-1900 ...... **TCLC 11, 17, 32; DA;**
                     DAB; DAC; DAM MST, NOV, POET;
                     SSC 7; WLC
   See also AAYA 21; CA 109; 140;
      CDALB 1865-1917; DLB 12, 54, 78; 2

Crase, Douglas 1944- .... **CLC 58**
   See also CA 106

Crashaw, Richard 1612(?)-1649...... **LC 24**
   See also DLB 126

Craven, Margaret
      1901-1980 .... **CLC 17; DAC**
   See also CA 103

Crawford, F(rancis) Marion
      1854-1909 .... **TCLC 10**
   See also CA 107; DLB 71

Crawford, Isabella Valancy
      1850-1887 .... **NCLC 12**
   See also DLB 92

Crayon, Geoffrey
   See Irving, Washington

Creasey, John 1908-1973.......... **CLC 11**
   See also CA 5-8R; 41-44R; CANR 8;
      DLB 77; MTCW

Crebillon, Claude Prosper Jolyot de (fils)
1707-1777 . . . . **LC 28**

Credo
See Creasey, John

Creeley, Robert (White)
1926- . . . . . **CLC 1, 2, 4, 8, 11, 15, 36, 78;**
DAM POET
See also CA 1-4R; CAAS 10; CANR 23, 43;
DLB 5, 16, 169; MTCW

Crews, Harry (Eugene)
1935- . . . . **CLC 6, 23, 49**
See also AITN 1; CA 25-28R; CANR 20,
57; DLB 6, 143; MTCW

Crichton, (John) Michael
1942- . . . . **CLC 2, 6, 54, 90; DAM NOV,**
POP
See also AAYA 10; AITN 2; CA 25-28R;
CANR 13, 40, 54; DLBY 81;
INT CANR-13; JRDA; MTCW; SATA 9,
88

Crispin, Edmund . . . . **CLC 22**
See also Montgomery, (Robert) Bruce
See also DLB 87

Cristofer, Michael
1945(?)- . . . . **CLC 28; DAM DRAM**
See also CA 110; 152; DLB 7

Croce, Benedetto 1866-1952 . . . . . . **TCLC 37**
See also CA 120; 155

Crockett, David 1786-1836 . . . . **NCLC 8**
See also DLB 3, 11

Crockett, Davy
See Crockett, David

Crofts, Freeman Wills
1879-1957 . . . . **TCLC 55**
See also CA 115; DLB 77

Croker, John Wilson 1780-1857 . . **NCLC 10**
See also DLB 110

Crommelynck, Fernand 1885-1970 . . **CLC 75**
See also CA 89-92

Cronin, A(rchibald) J(oseph)
1896-1981 . . . . **CLC 32**
See also CA 1-4R; 102; CANR 5; SATA 47;
SATA-Obit 25

Cross, Amanda
See Heilbrun, Carolyn G(old)

Crothers, Rachel 1878(?)-1958 . . . . . **TCLC 19**
See also CA 113; DLB 7

Croves, Hal
See Traven, B.

Crow Dog, Mary (Ellen) (?)- . . . . **CLC 93**
See also Brave Bird, Mary
See also CA 154

Crowfield, Christopher
See Stowe, Harriet (Elizabeth) Beecher

Crowley, Aleister . . . . **TCLC 7**
See also Crowley, Edward Alexander

Crowley, Edward Alexander 1875-1947
See Crowley, Aleister
See also CA 104

Crowley, John 1942- . . . . **CLC 57**
See also CA 61-64; CANR 43; DLBY 82;
SATA 65

Crud
See Crumb, R(obert)

Crumarums
See Crumb, R(obert)

Crumb, R(obert) 1943- . . . . **CLC 17**
See also CA 106

Crumbum
See Crumb, R(obert)

Crumski
See Crumb, R(obert)

Crum the Bum
See Crumb, R(obert)

Crunk
See Crumb, R(obert)

Crustt
See Crumb, R(obert)

Cryer, Gretchen (Kiger) 1935- . . . . . . **CLC 21**
See also CA 114; 123

Csath, Geza 1887-1919 . . . . **TCLC 13**
See also CA 111

Cudlip, David 1933- . . . . **CLC 34**

Cullen, Countee
1903-1946 . . . . . . **TCLC 4, 37; BLC; DA;**
DAC; DAM MST, MULT, POET
See also BW 1; CA 108; 124;
CDALB 1917-1929; DLB 4, 48, 51;
MTCW; SATA 18; YABC

Cum, R.
See Crumb, R(obert)

Cummings, Bruce F(rederick) 1889-1919
See Barbellion, W. N. P.
See also CA 123

Cummings, E(dward) E(stlin)
1894-1962 . . . . . . **CLC 1, 3, 8, 12, 15, 68;**
DA; DAB; DAC; DAM MST, POET;
PC 5; WLC 2
See also CA 73-76; CANR 31;
CDALB 1929-1941; DLB 4, 48; MTCW

Cunha, Euclides (Rodrigues Pimenta) da
1866-1909 . . . . **TCLC 24**
See also CA 123

Cunningham, E. V.
See Fast, Howard (Melvin)

Cunningham, J(ames) V(incent)
1911-1985 . . . . **CLC 3, 31**
See also CA 1-4R; 115; CANR 1; DLB 5

Cunningham, Julia (Woolfolk)
1916- . . . . **CLC 12**
See also CA 9-12R; CANR 4, 19, 36;
JRDA; MAICYA; SAAS 2; SATA 1, 26

Cunningham, Michael 1952- . . . . **CLC 34**
See also CA 136

Cunninghame Graham, R(obert) B(ontine)
1852-1936 . . . . **TCLC 19**
See also Graham, R(obert) B(ontine)
Cunninghame
See also CA 119; DLB 98

Currie, Ellen 19(?)- . . . . **CLC 44**

Curtin, Philip
See Lowndes, Marie Adelaide (Belloc)

Curtis, Price
See Ellison, Harlan (Jay)

Cutrate, Joe
See Spiegelman, Art

Czaczkes, Shmuel Yosef
See Agnon, S(hmuel) Y(osef Halevi)

Dabrowska, Maria (Szumska)
1889-1965 . . . . **CLC 15**
See also CA 106

Dabydeen, David 1955- . . . . **CLC 34**
See also BW 1; CA 125; CANR 56

Dacey, Philip 1939- . . . . **CLC 51**
See also CA 37-40R; CAAS 17; CANR 14,
32; DLB 105

Dagerman, Stig (Halvard)
1923-1954 . . . . **TCLC 17**
See also CA 117; 155

Dahl, Roald
1916-1990 . . . . . . **CLC 1, 6, 18, 79; DAB;**
DAC; DAM MST, NOV, POP
See also AAYA 15; CA 1-4R; 133;
CANR 6, 32, 37; CLR 1, 7, 41; DLB 139;
JRDA; MAICYA; MTCW; SATA 1, 26,
73; SATA-Obit 65

Dahlberg, Edward 1900-1977 . . . **CLC 1, 7, 14**
See also CA 9-12R; 69-72; CANR 31;
DLB 48; MTCW

Dale, Colin . . . . **TCLC 18**
See also Lawrence, T(homas) E(dward)

Dale, George E.
See Asimov, Isaac

Daly, Elizabeth 1878-1967 . . . . **CLC 52**
See also CA 23-24; 25-28R; CAP 2

Daly, Maureen 1921- . . . . **CLC 17**
See also AAYA 5; CANR 37; JRDA;
MAICYA; SAAS 1; SATA 2

Damas, Leon-Gontran 1912-1978 . . . **CLC 84**
See also BW 1; CA 125; 73-76

Dana, Richard Henry Sr.
1787-1879 . . . . **NCLC 53**

Daniel, Samuel 1562(?)-1619 . . . . **LC 24**
See also DLB 62

Daniels, Brett
See Adler, Renata

Dannay, Frederic
1905-1982 . . . . **CLC 11; DAM POP**
See also Queen, Ellery
See also CA 1-4R; 107; CANR 1, 39;
DLB 137; MTCW

D'Annunzio, Gabriele
1863-1938 . . . . **TCLC 6, 40**
See also CA 104; 155

Danois, N. le
See Gourmont, Remy (-Marie-Charles) de

d'Antibes, Germain
See Simenon, Georges (Jacques Christian)

Danticat, Edwidge 1969- . . . . **CLC 94**
See also CA 152

Danvers, Dennis 1947- . . . . **CLC 70**

Danziger, Paula 1944- . . . . **CLC 21**
See also AAYA 4; CA 112; 115; CANR 37;
CLR 20; JRDA; MAICYA; SATA 36,
63; SATA-Brief 30

Da Ponte, Lorenzo 1749-1838 . . . . **NCLC 50**

Dario, Ruben
1867-1916 . . . . . **TCLC 4; DAM MULT;**
HLC; PC 15
See also CA 131; HW; MTCW

Darley, George 1795-1846 . . . . **NCLC 2**
See also DLB 96

Darwin, Charles 1809-1882 . . . . . . **NCLC 57**
See also DLB 57, 166

Daryush, Elizabeth 1887-1977. . . . **CLC 6, 19**
See also CA 49-52; CANR 3; DLB 20

Dashwood, Edmee Elizabeth Monica de la Pasture 1890-1943
See Delafield, E. M.
See also CA 119; 154

Daudet, (Louis Marie) Alphonse
1840-1897 . . . . **NCLC 1**
See also DLB 123

Daumal, Rene 1908-1944 . . . . **TCLC 14**
See also CA 114

Davenport, Guy (Mattison, Jr.)
1927- . . . . **CLC 6, 14, 38; SSC 16**
See also CA 33-36R; CANR 23; DLB 130

Davidson, Avram 1923-
See Queen, Ellery
See also CA 101; CANR 26; DLB 8

Davidson, Donald (Grady)
1893-1968 . . . . **CLC 2, 13, 19**
See also CA 5-8R; 25-28R; CANR 4;
DLB 45

Davidson, Hugh
See Hamilton, Edmond

Davidson, John 1857-1909 . . . . **TCLC 24**
See also CA 118; DLB 19

Davidson, Sara 1943- . . . . **CLC 9**
See also CA 81-84; CANR 44

Davie, Donald (Alfred)
1922-1995 . . . . **CLC 5, 8, 10, 31**
See also CA 1-4R; 149; CAAS 3; CANR 1,
44; DLB 27; MTCW

Davies, Ray(mond Douglas) 1944- . . **CLC 21**
See also CA 116; 146

Davies, Rhys 1903-1978 . . . . **CLC 23**
See also CA 9-12R; 81-84; CANR 4;
DLB 139

Davies, (William) Robertson
1913-1995 . . . . . **CLC 2, 7, 13, 25, 42, 75,**
91; DA; DAB; DAC; DAM MST, NOV,
POP; WLC
See also BEST 89:2; CA 33-36R; 150;
CANR 17, 42; DLB 68; INT CANR-17;
MTCW

Davies, W(illiam) H(enry)
1871-1940 . . . . **TCLC 5**
See also CA 104; DLB 19, 174

Davies, Walter C.
See Kornbluth, C(yril) M.

Davis, Angela (Yvonne)
1944- . . . . **CLC 77; DAM MULT**
See also BW 2; CA 57-60; CANR 10

Davis, B. Lynch
See Bioy Casares, Adolfo; Borges, Jorge
Luis

Davis, Gordon
See Hunt, E(verette) Howard, (Jr.)

Davis, Harold Lenoir 1896-1960 . . . . **CLC 49**
See also CA 89-92; DLB 9

Davis, Rebecca (Blaine) Harding
1831-1910 . . . . **TCLC 6**
See also CA 104; DLB 74

Davis, Richard Harding
1864-1916 . . . . **TCLC 24**
See also CA 114; DLB 12, 23, 78, 79;
DLBD 13

Davison, Frank Dalby 1893-1970 . . . **CLC 15**
See also CA 116

Davison, Lawrence H.
See Lawrence, D(avid) H(erbert Richards)

Davison, Peter (Hubert) 1928- . . . . . **CLC 28**
See also CA 9-12R; CAAS 4; CANR 3, 43;
DLB 5

Davys, Mary 1674-1732 . . . . **LC 1**
See also DLB 39

Dawson, Fielding 1930- . . . . **CLC 6**
See also CA 85-88; DLB 130

Dawson, Peter
See Faust, Frederick (Schiller)

Day, Clarence (Shepard, Jr.)
1874-1935 . . . . **TCLC 25**
See also CA 108; DLB 11

Day, Thomas 1748-1789 . . . . **LC 1**
See also DLB 39; 1

Day Lewis, C(ecil)
1904-1972 . . . . **CLC 1, 6, 10;**
DAM POET; PC 11
See also Blake, Nicholas
See also CA 13-16; 33-36R; CANR 34;
CAP 1; DLB 15, 20; MTCW

Dazai, Osamu . . . . **TCLC 11**
See also Tsushima, Shuji

de Andrade, Carlos Drummond
See Drummond de Andrade, Carlos

Deane, Norman
See Creasey, John

de Beauvoir, Simone (Lucie Ernestine Marie Bertrand)
See Beauvoir, Simone (Lucie Ernestine
Marie Bertrand) de

de Brissac, Malcolm
See Dickinson, Peter (Malcolm)

de Chardin, Pierre Teilhard
See Teilhard de Chardin, (Marie Joseph)
Pierre

Dee, John 1527-1608 . . . . **LC 20**

Deer, Sandra 1940- . . . . **CLC 45**

De Ferrari, Gabriella 1941- . . . . **CLC 65**
See also CA 146

Defoe, Daniel
1660(?)-1731 . . . . **LC 1; DA; DAB; DAC;**
DAM MST, NOV; WLC
See also CDBLB 1660-1789; DLB 39, 95,
101; JRDA; MAICYA; SATA 22

de Gourmont, Remy(-Marie-Charles)
See Gourmont, Remy (-Marie-Charles) de

de Hartog, Jan 1914- . . . . **CLC 19**
See also CA 1-4R; CANR 1

de Hostos, E. M.
See Hostos (y Bonilla), Eugenio Maria de

de Hostos, Eugenio M.
See Hostos (y Bonilla), Eugenio Maria de

Deighton, Len . . . . **CLC 4, 7, 22, 46**
See also Deighton, Leonard Cyril
See also AAYA 6; BEST 89:2;
CDBLB 1960 to Present; DLB 87

Deighton, Leonard Cyril 1929-
See Deighton, Len
See also CA 9-12R; CANR 19, 33;
DAM NOV, POP; MTCW

Dekker, Thomas
1572(?)-1632 . . . . . **LC 22; DAM DRAM**
See also CDBLB Before 1660; DLB 62, 172

Delafield, E. M. 1890-1943 . . . . **TCLC 61**
See also Dashwood, Edmee Elizabeth
Monica de la Pasture
See also DLB 34

de la Mare, Walter (John)
1873-1956 . . . . **TCLC 4, 53; DAB; DAC;**
DAM MST, POET; SSC 14; WLC
See also CDBLB 1914-1945; CLR 23;
DLB 162; SATA 16

Delaney, Franey
See O'Hara, John (Henry)

Delaney, Shelagh
1939- . . . . **CLC 29; DAM DRAM**
See also CA 17-20R; CANR 30;
CDBLB 1960 to Present; DLB 13;
MTCW

Delany, Mary (Granville Pendarves)
1700-1788 . . . . **LC 12**

Delany, Samuel R(ay, Jr.)
1942- . . . . **CLC 8, 14, 38; BLC;**
DAM MULT
See also BW 2; CA 81-84; CANR 27, 43;
DLB 8, 33; MTCW

De La Ramee, (Marie) Louise 1839-1908
See Ouida
See also SATA 20

de la Roche, Mazo 1879-1961 . . . . . . **CLC 14**
See also CA 85-88; CANR 30; DLB 68;
SATA 64

Delbanco, Nicholas (Franklin)
1942- . . . . **CLC 6, 13**
See also CA 17-20R; CAAS 2; CANR 29,
55; DLB 6

del Castillo, Michel 1933- . . . . **CLC 38**
See also CA 109

Deledda, Grazia (Cosima)
1875(?)-1936 . . . . **TCLC 23**
See also CA 123

Delibes, Miguel . . . . **CLC 8, 18**
See also Delibes Setien, Miguel

Delibes Setien, Miguel 1920-
See Delibes, Miguel
See also CA 45-48; CANR 1, 32; HW;
MTCW

DeLillo, Don
1936- . . . . . **CLC 8, 10, 13, 27, 39, 54, 76;**
DAM NOV, POP
See also BEST 89:1; CA 81-84; CANR 21;
DLB 6, 173; MTCW

de Lisser, H. G.
See De Lisser, H(erbert) G(eorge)
See also DLB 117

De Lisser, H(erbert) G(eorge)
1878-1944 . . . . **TCLC 12**
See also de Lisser, H. G.
See also BW 2; CA 109; 152

Dixon, Paige
See Corcoran, Barbara

Dixon, Stephen 1936-..... **CLC 52; SSC 16**
See also CA 89-92; CANR 17, 40, 54;
DLB 130

Dobell, Sydney Thompson
1824-1874 .... **NCLC 43**
See also DLB 32

Doblin, Alfred .... **TCLC 13**
See also Doeblin, Alfred

Dobrolyubov, Nikolai Alexandrovich
1836-1861 .... **NCLC 5**

Dobyns, Stephen 1941-........... **CLC 37**
See also CA 45-48; CANR 2, 18

Doctorow, E(dgar) L(aurence)
1931- ..... **CLC 6, 11, 15, 18, 37, 44, 65;**
DAM NOV, POP
See also AITN 2; BEST 89:3; CA 45-48;
CANR 2, 33, 51; CDALB 1968-1988;
DLB 2, 28, 173; DLBY 80; MTCW

Dodgson, Charles Lutwidge 1832-1898
See Carroll, Lewis
See also CLR 2; DA; DAB; DAC;
DAM MST, NOV, POET; MAICYA; 2

Dodson, Owen (Vincent)
1914-1983 .... **CLC 79; BLC;**
DAM MULT
See also BW 1; CA 65-68; 110; CANR 24;
DLB 76

Doeblin, Alfred 1878-1957....... **TCLC 13**
See also Doblin, Alfred
See also CA 110; 141; DLB 66

Doerr, Harriet 1910- .... **CLC 34**
See also CA 117; 122; CANR 47; INT 122

Domecq, H(onorio) Bustos
See Bioy Casares, Adolfo; Borges, Jorge
Luis

Domini, Rey
See Lorde, Audre (Geraldine)

Dominique
See Proust, (Valentin-Louis-George-Eugene-)
Marcel

Don, A
See Stephen, Leslie

Donaldson, Stephen R.
1947- .... **CLC 46; DAM POP**
See also CA 89-92; CANR 13, 55;
INT CANR-13

Donleavy, J(ames) P(atrick)
1926- .... **CLC 1, 4, 6, 10, 45**
See also AITN 2; CA 9-12R; CANR 24, 49;
DLB 6, 173; INT CANR-24; MTCW

Donne, John
1572-1631 .... **LC 10, 24; DA; DAB;**
DAC; DAM MST, POET; PC 1
See also CDBLB Before 1660; DLB 121,
151

Donnell, David 1939(?)-........... **CLC 34**

Donoghue, P. S.
See Hunt, E(verette) Howard, (Jr.)

Donoso (Yanez), Jose
1924-1996 .... **CLC 4, 8, 11, 32, 99;**
DAM MULT; HLC
See also CA 81-84; 155; CANR 32;
DLB 113; HW; MTCW

Donovan, John 1928-1992 .... **CLC 35**
See also AAYA 20; CA 97-100; 137;
CLR 3; MAICYA; SATA 72;
SATA-Brief 29

Don Roberto
See Cunninghame Graham, R(obert)
B(ontine)

Doolittle, Hilda
1886-1961 ..... **CLC 3, 8, 14, 31, 34, 73;**
DA; DAC; DAM MST, POET; PC 5;
WLC
See also H. D.
See also CA 97-100; CANR 35; DLB 4, 45;
MTCW

Dorfman, Ariel
1942- .... **CLC 48, 77; DAM MULT;**
HLC
See also CA 124; 130; HW; INT 130

Dorn, Edward (Merton) 1929-... **CLC 10, 18**
See also CA 93-96; CANR 42; DLB 5;
INT 93-96

Dorsan, Luc
See Simenon, Georges (Jacques Christian)

Dorsange, Jean
See Simenon, Georges (Jacques Christian)

Dos Passos, John (Roderigo)
1896-1970 ...... **CLC 1, 4, 8, 11, 15, 25,**
34, 82; DA; DAB; DAC; DAM MST,
NOV; WLC
See also CA 1-4R; 29-32R; CANR 3;
CDALB 1929-1941; DLB 4, 9; DLBD 1;
DLBY 96; MTCW

Dossage, Jean
See Simenon, Georges (Jacques Christian)

Dostoevsky, Fedor Mikhailovich
1821-1881 ...... **NCLC 2, 7, 21, 33, 43;**
DA; DAB; DAC; DAM MST, NOV;
SSC 2; WLC

Doughty, Charles M(ontagu)
1843-1926 .... **TCLC 27**
See also CA 115; DLB 19, 57, 174

Douglas, Ellen .... **CLC 73**
See also Haxton, Josephine Ayres;
Williamson, Ellen Douglas

Douglas, Gavin 1475(?)-1522....... **LC 20**

Douglas, Keith 1920-1944 .... **TCLC 40**
See also DLB 27

Douglas, Leonard
See Bradbury, Ray (Douglas)

Douglas, Michael
See Crichton, (John) Michael

Douglas, Norman 1868-1952 ..... **TCLC 68**

Douglass, Frederick
1817(?)-1895 .... **NCLC 7, 55; BLC; DA;**
DAC; DAM MST, MULT; WLC
See also CDALB 1640-1865; DLB 1, 43, 50,
79; SATA 29

Dourado, (Waldomiro Freitas) Autran
1926- .... **CLC 23, 60**
See also CA 25-28R; CANR 34

Dourado, Waldomiro Autran
See Dourado, (Waldomiro Freitas) Autran

Dove, Rita (Frances)
1952- .... **CLC 50, 81; DAM MULT,**
POET; PC 6
See also BW 2; CA 109; CAAS 19;
CANR 27, 42; DLB 120

Dowell, Coleman 1925-1985....... **CLC 60**
See also CA 25-28R; 117; CANR 10;
DLB 130

Dowson, Ernest (Christopher)
1867-1900 .... **TCLC 4**
See also CA 105; 150; DLB 19, 135

Doyle, A. Conan
See Doyle, Arthur Conan

Doyle, Arthur Conan
1859-1930 .... **TCLC 7; DA; DAB;**
DAC; DAM MST, NOV; SSC 12; WLC
See also AAYA 14; CA 104; 122;
CDBLB 1890-1914; DLB 18, 70, 156, 178;
MTCW; SATA 24

Doyle, Conan
See Doyle, Arthur Conan

Doyle, John
See Graves, Robert (von Ranke)

Doyle, Roddy 1958(?)-............ **CLC 81**
See also AAYA 14; CA 143

Doyle, Sir A. Conan
See Doyle, Arthur Conan

Doyle, Sir Arthur Conan
See Doyle, Arthur Conan

Dr. A
See Asimov, Isaac; Silverstein, Alvin

Drabble, Margaret
1939- .... **CLC 2, 3, 5, 8, 10, 22, 53;**
DAB; DAC; DAM MST, NOV, POP
See also CA 13-16R; CANR 18, 35;
CDBLB 1960 to Present; DLB 14, 155;
MTCW; SATA 48

Drapier, M. B.
See Swift, Jonathan

Drayham, James
See Mencken, H(enry) L(ouis)

Drayton, Michael 1563-1631........ **LC 8**

Dreadstone, Carl
See Campbell, (John) Ramsey

Dreiser, Theodore (Herman Albert)
1871-1945 ..... **TCLC 10, 18, 35; DA;**
DAC; DAM MST, NOV; WLC
See also CA 106; 132; CDALB 1865-1917;
DLB 9, 12, 102, 137; DLBD 1; MTCW

Drexler, Rosalyn 1926- .... **CLC 2, 6**
See also CA 81-84

Dreyer, Carl Theodor 1889-1968.... **CLC 16**
See also CA 116

Drieu la Rochelle, Pierre(-Eugene)
1893-1945 .... **TCLC 21**
See also CA 117; DLB 72

Drinkwater, John 1882-1937 ..... **TCLC 57**
See also CA 109; 149; DLB 10, 19, 149

Drop Shot
See Cable, George Washington

Droste-Hulshoff, Annette Freiin von
1797-1848 .... **NCLC 3**
See also DLB 133

Drummond, Walter
See Silverberg, Robert

Drummond, William Henry
1854-1907 . . . . TCLC 25
See also DLB 92

Drummond de Andrade, Carlos
1902-1987 . . . . CLC 18
See also Andrade, Carlos Drummond de
See also CA 132; 123

Drury, Allen (Stuart) 1918- . . . . CLC 37
See also CA 57-60; CANR 18, 52;
INT CANR-18

Dryden, John
1631-1700 . . . . LC 3, 21; DA; DAB;
DAC; DAM DRAM, MST, POET;
DC 3; WLC
See also CDBLB 1660-1789; DLB 80, 101,
131

Duberman, Martin 1930- . . . . CLC 8
See also CA 1-4R; CANR 2

Dubie, Norman (Evans) 1945- . . . . . . CLC 36
See also CA 69-72; CANR 12; DLB 120

Du Bois, W(illiam) E(dward) B(urghardt)
1868-1963 . . . . CLC 1, 2, 13, 64, 96;
BLC; DA; DAC; DAM MST, MULT,
NOV; WLC
See also BW 1; CA 85-88; CANR 34;
CDALB 1865-1917; DLB 47, 50, 91;
MTCW; SATA 42

Dubus, Andre
1936- . . . . CLC 13, 36, 97; SSC 15
See also CA 21-24R; CANR 17; DLB 130;
INT CANR-17

Duca Minimo
See D'Annunzio, Gabriele

Ducharme, Rejean 1941- . . . . CLC 74
See also DLB 60

Duclos, Charles Pinot 1704-1772 . . . . . LC 1

Dudek, Louis 1918- . . . . CLC 11, 19
See also CA 45-48; CAAS 14; CANR 1;
DLB 88

Duerrenmatt, Friedrich
1921-1990 . . . . . . CLC 1, 4, 8, 11, 15, 43;
DAM DRAM
See also CA 17-20R; CANR 33; DLB 69,
124; MTCW

Duffy, Bruce (?)- . . . . CLC 50

Duffy, Maureen 1933- . . . . CLC 37
See also CA 25-28R; CANR 33; DLB 14;
MTCW

Dugan, Alan 1923- . . . . CLC 2, 6
See also CA 81-84; DLB 5

du Gard, Roger Martin
See Martin du Gard, Roger

Duhamel, Georges 1884-1966 . . . . CLC 8
See also CA 81-84; 25-28R; CANR 35;
DLB 65; MTCW

Dujardin, Edouard (Emile Louis)
1861-1949 . . . . TCLC 13
See also CA 109; DLB 123

Dulles, John Foster 1888-1959 . . . . TCLC 72
See also CA 115; 149

Dumas, Alexandre (Davy de la Pailleterie)
1802-1870 . . . . NCLC 11; DA; DAB;
DAC; DAM MST, NOV; WLC
See also DLB 119; SATA 18

Dumas, Alexandre
1824-1895 . . . . NCLC 9; DC 1

Dumas, Claudine
See Malzberg, Barry N(athaniel)

Dumas, Henry L. 1934-1968 . . . . . CLC 6, 62
See also BW 1; CA 85-88; DLB 41

du Maurier, Daphne
1907-1989 . . . . CLC 6, 11, 59; DAB;
DAC; DAM MST, POP; SSC 18
See also CA 5-8R; 128; CANR 6, 55;
MTCW; SATA 27; SATA-Obit 60

Dunbar, Paul Laurence
1872-1906 . . . . . . TCLC 2, 12; BLC; DA;
DAC; DAM MST, MULT, POET; PC 5;
SSC 8; WLC
See also BW 1; CA 104; 124;
CDALB 1865-1917; DLB 50, 54, 78;
SATA 34

Dunbar, William 1460(?)-1530(?) . . . . LC 20
See also DLB 132, 146

Duncan, Dora Angela
See Duncan, Isadora

Duncan, Isadora 1877(?)-1927 . . . . . TCLC 68
See also CA 118; 149

Duncan, Lois 1934- . . . . CLC 26
See also AAYA 4; CA 1-4R; CANR 2, 23,
36; CLR 29; JRDA; MAICYA; SAAS 2;
SATA 1, 36, 75

Duncan, Robert (Edward)
1919-1988 . . . . CLC 1, 2, 4, 7, 15, 41, 55;
DAM POET; PC 2
See also CA 9-12R; 124; CANR 28; DLB 5,
16; MTCW

Duncan, Sara Jeannette
1861-1922 . . . . TCLC 60
See also CA 157; DLB 92

Dunlap, William 1766-1839 . . . . NCLC 2
See also DLB 30, 37, 59

Dunn, Douglas (Eaglesham)
1942- . . . . CLC 6, 40
See also CA 45-48; CANR 2, 33; DLB 40;
MTCW

Dunn, Katherine (Karen) 1945- . . . . . CLC 71
See also CA 33-36R

Dunn, Stephen 1939- . . . . CLC 36
See also CA 33-36R; CANR 12, 48, 53;
DLB 105

Dunne, Finley Peter 1867-1936 . . . . TCLC 28
See also CA 108; DLB 11, 23

Dunne, John Gregory 1932- . . . . CLC 28
See also CA 25-28R; CANR 14, 50;
DLBY 80

Dunsany, Edward John Moreton Drax
Plunkett 1878-1957
See Dunsany, Lord
See also CA 104; 148; DLB 10

Dunsany, Lord . . . . TCLC 2, 59
See also Dunsany, Edward John Moreton
Drax Plunkett
See also DLB 77, 153, 156

du Perry, Jean
See Simenon, Georges (Jacques Christian)

Durang, Christopher (Ferdinand)
1949- . . . . CLC 27, 38
See also CA 105; CANR 50

Duras, Marguerite
1914-1996 . . . . . CLC 3, 6, 11, 20, 34, 40,
68, 100
See also CA 25-28R; 151; CANR 50;
DLB 83; MTCW

Durban, (Rosa) Pam 1947- . . . . CLC 39
See also CA 123

Durcan, Paul
1944- . . . . CLC 43, 70; DAM POET
See also CA 134

Durkheim, Emile 1858-1917 . . . . . . TCLC 55

Durrell, Lawrence (George)
1912-1990 . . . . CLC 1, 4, 6, 8, 13, 27, 41;
DAM NOV
See also CA 9-12R; 132; CANR 40;
CDBLB 1945-1960; DLB 15, 27;
DLBY 90; MTCW

Durrenmatt, Friedrich
See Duerrenmatt, Friedrich

Dutt, Toru 1856-1877 . . . . NCLC 29

Dwight, Timothy 1752-1817 . . . . . . NCLC 13
See also DLB 37

Dworkin, Andrea 1946- . . . . CLC 43
See also CA 77-80; CAAS 21; CANR 16,
39; INT CANR-16; MTCW

Dwyer, Deanna
See Koontz, Dean R(ay)

Dwyer, K. R.
See Koontz, Dean R(ay)

Dylan, Bob 1941- . . . . . . CLC 3, 4, 6, 12, 77
See also CA 41-44R; DLB 16

Eagleton, Terence (Francis) 1943-
See Eagleton, Terry
See also CA 57-60; CANR 7, 23; MTCW

Eagleton, Terry . . . . CLC 63
See also Eagleton, Terence (Francis)

Early, Jack
See Scoppettone, Sandra

East, Michael
See West, Morris L(anglo)

Eastaway, Edward
See Thomas, (Philip) Edward

Eastlake, William (Derry)
1917-1997 . . . . CLC 8
See also CA 5-8R; 158; CAAS 1; CANR 5;
DLB 6; INT CANR-5

Eastman, Charles A(lexander)
1858-1939 . . . . . TCLC 55; DAM MULT
See also DLB 175; NNAL; 1

Eberhart, Richard (Ghormley)
1904- . . CLC 3, 11, 19, 56; DAM POET
See also CA 1-4R; CANR 2;
CDALB 1941-1968; DLB 48; MTCW

Eberstadt, Fernanda 1960- . . . . CLC 39
See also CA 136

Echegaray (y Eizaguirre), Jose (Maria Waldo)
1832-1916 . . . . TCLC 4
See also CA 104; CANR 32; HW; MTCW

Echeverria, (Jose) Esteban (Antonino)
1805-1851 . . . . NCLC 18

Echo
See Proust, (Valentin-Louis-George-Eugene-)
Marcel

Eckert, Allan W. 1931- . . . . **CLC 17**
See also AAYA 18; CA 13-16R; CANR 14,
45; INT CANR-14; SAAS 21; SATA 29,
91; SATA-Brief 27

Eckhart, Meister 1260(?)-1328(?) . . **CMLC 9**
See also DLB 115

Eckmar, F. R.
See de Hartog, Jan

Eco, Umberto
1932- . . . **CLC 28, 60; DAM NOV, POP**
See also BEST 90:1; CA 77-80; CANR 12,
33, 55; MTCW

Eddison, E(ric) R(ucker)
1882-1945 . . . . **TCLC 15**
See also CA 109; 156

Eddy, Mary (Morse) Baker
1821-1910 . . . . **TCLC 71**
See also CA 113

Edel, (Joseph) Leon 1907- . . . . . . **CLC 29, 34**
See also CA 1-4R; CANR 1, 22; DLB 103;
INT CANR-22

Eden, Emily 1797-1869 . . . . **NCLC 10**

Edgar, David
1948- . . . . **CLC 42; DAM DRAM**
See also CA 57-60; CANR 12; DLB 13;
MTCW

Edgerton, Clyde (Carlyle) 1944- . . . . **CLC 39**
See also AAYA 17; CA 118; 134; INT 134

Edgeworth, Maria 1768-1849 . . . **NCLC 1, 51**
See also DLB 116, 159, 163; SATA 21

Edmonds, Paul
See Kuttner, Henry

Edmonds, Walter D(umaux) 1903- . . **CLC 35**
See also CA 5-8R; CANR 2; DLB 9;
MAICYA; SAAS 4; SATA 1, 27

Edmondson, Wallace
See Ellison, Harlan (Jay)

Edson, Russell . . . . **CLC 13**
See also CA 33-36R

Edwards, Bronwen Elizabeth
See Rose, Wendy

Edwards, G(erald) B(asil)
1899-1976 . . . . **CLC 25**
See also CA 110

Edwards, Gus 1939- . . . . **CLC 43**
See also CA 108; INT 108

Edwards, Jonathan
1703-1758 . . . . **LC 7; DA; DAC;**
DAM MST
See also DLB 24

Efron, Marina Ivanovna Tsvetaeva
See Tsvetaeva (Efron), Marina (Ivanovna)

Ehle, John (Marsden, Jr.) 1925- . . . . **CLC 27**
See also CA 9-12R

Ehrenbourg, Ilya (Grigoryevich)
See Ehrenburg, Ilya (Grigoryevich)

Ehrenburg, Ilya (Grigoryevich)
1891-1967 . . . . **CLC 18, 34, 62**
See also CA 102; 25-28R

Ehrenburg, Ilyo (Grigoryevich)
See Ehrenburg, Ilya (Grigoryevich)

Eich, Guenter 1907-1972 . . . . **CLC 15**
See also CA 111; 93-96; DLB 69, 124

Eichendorff, Joseph Freiherr von
1788-1857 . . . . **NCLC 8**
See also DLB 90

Eigner, Larry . . . . **CLC 9**
See also Eigner, Laurence (Joel)
See also CAAS 23; DLB 5

Eigner, Laurence (Joel) 1927-1996
See Eigner, Larry
See also CA 9-12R; 151; CANR 6

Einstein, Albert 1879-1955 . . . . **TCLC 65**
See also CA 121; 133; MTCW

Eiseley, Loren Corey 1907-1977 . . . . . **CLC 7**
See also AAYA 5; CA 1-4R; 73-76;
CANR 6

Eisenstadt, Jill 1963- . . . . **CLC 50**
See also CA 140

Eisenstein, Sergei (Mikhailovich)
1898-1948 . . . . **TCLC 57**
See also CA 114; 149

Eisner, Simon
See Kornbluth, C(yril) M.

Ekeloef, (Bengt) Gunnar
1907-1968 . . . . **CLC 27; DAM POET**
See also CA 123; 25-28R

Ekelof, (Bengt) Gunnar
See Ekeloef, (Bengt) Gunnar

Ekwensi, C. O. D.
See Ekwensi, Cyprian (Odiatu Duaka)

Ekwensi, Cyprian (Odiatu Duaka)
1921- . . . . . . **CLC 4; BLC; DAM MULT**
See also BW 2; CA 29-32R; CANR 18, 42;
DLB 117; MTCW; SATA 66

Elaine . . . . **TCLC 18**
See also Leverson, Ada

El Crummo
See Crumb, R(obert)

Elia
See Lamb, Charles

Eliade, Mircea 1907-1986 . . . . **CLC 19**
See also CA 65-68; 119; CANR 30; MTCW

Eliot, A. D.
See Jewett, (Theodora) Sarah Orne

Eliot, Alice
See Jewett, (Theodora) Sarah Orne

Eliot, Dan
See Silverberg, Robert

Eliot, George
1819-1880 . . . . . **NCLC 4, 13, 23, 41, 49;**
DA; DAB; DAC; DAM MST, NOV;
WLC
See also CDBLB 1832-1890; DLB 21, 35, 55

Eliot, John 1604-1690 . . . . **LC 5**
See also DLB 24

Eliot, T(homas) S(tearns)
1888-1965 . . . . . **CLC 1, 2, 3, 6, 9, 10, 13,**
15, 24, 34, 41, 55, 57; DA; DAB; DAC;
DAM DRAM, MST, POET; PC 5;
WLC 2
See also CA 5-8R; 25-28R; CANR 41;
CDALB 1929-1941; DLB 7, 10, 45, 63;
DLBY 88; MTCW

Elizabeth 1866-1941 . . . . **TCLC 41**

Elkin, Stanley L(awrence)
1930-1995 . . . . . . **CLC 4, 6, 9, 14, 27, 51,**
91; DAM NOV, POP; SSC 12
See also CA 9-12R; 148; CANR 8, 46;
DLB 2, 28; DLBY 80; INT CANR-8;
MTCW

Elledge, Scott . . . . **CLC 34**

Elliot, Don
See Silverberg, Robert

Elliott, Don
See Silverberg, Robert

Elliott, George P(aul) 1918-1980 . . . . . **CLC 2**
See also CA 1-4R; 97-100; CANR 2

Elliott, Janice 1931- . . . . **CLC 47**
See also CA 13-16R; CANR 8, 29; DLB 14

Elliott, Sumner Locke 1917-1991 . . . **CLC 38**
See also CA 5-8R; 134; CANR 2, 21

Elliott, William
See Bradbury, Ray (Douglas)

Ellis, A. E. . . . . **CLC 7**

Ellis, Alice Thomas . . . . **CLC 40**
See also Haycraft, Anna

Ellis, Bret Easton
1964- . . . . **CLC 39, 71; DAM POP**
See also AAYA 2; CA 118; 123; CANR 51;
INT 123

Ellis, (Henry) Havelock
1859-1939 . . . . **TCLC 14**
See also CA 109

Ellis, Landon
See Ellison, Harlan (Jay)

Ellis, Trey 1962- . . . . **CLC 55**
See also CA 146

Ellison, Harlan (Jay)
1934- . . . . . . **CLC 1, 13, 42; DAM POP;**
SSC 14
See also CA 5-8R; CANR 5, 46; DLB 8;
INT CANR-5; MTCW

Ellison, Ralph (Waldo)
1914-1994 . . . . **CLC 1, 3, 11, 54, 86;**
BLC; DA; DAB; DAC; DAM MST,
MULT, NOV; SSC 26; WLC
See also AAYA 19; BW 1; CA 9-12R; 145;
CANR 24, 53; CDALB 1941-1968;
DLB 2, 76; DLBY 94; MTCW

Ellmann, Lucy (Elizabeth) 1956- . . . . **CLC 61**
See also CA 128

Ellmann, Richard (David)
1918-1987 . . . . **CLC 50**
See also BEST 89:2; CA 1-4R; 122;
CANR 2, 28; DLB 103; DLBY 87;
MTCW

Elman, Richard 1934- . . . . **CLC 19**
See also CA 17-20R; CAAS 3; CANR 47

Elron
See Hubbard, L(afayette) Ron(ald)

Eluard, Paul . . . . **TCLC 7, 41**
See also Grindel, Eugene

Elyot, Sir Thomas 1490(?)-1546 . . . . . **LC 11**

Elytis, Odysseus
1911-1996 . . . . **CLC 15, 49, 100;**
DAM POET
See also CA 102; 151; MTCW

Farley, Walter (Lorimer)
1915-1989 . . . . CLC 17
See also CA 17-20R; CANR 8, 29; DLB 22;
JRDA; MAICYA; SATA 2, 43

Farmer, Philip Jose 1918- . . . . CLC 1, 19
See also CA 1-4R; CANR 4, 35; DLB 8;
MTCW; SATA 93

Farquhar, George
1677-1707 . . . . LC 21; DAM DRAM
See also DLB 84

Farrell, J(ames) G(ordon)
1935-1979 . . . . CLC 6
See also CA 73-76; 89-92; CANR 36;
DLB 14; MTCW

Farrell, James T(homas)
1904-1979 . . . . CLC 1, 4, 8, 11, 66
See also CA 5-8R; 89-92; CANR 9; DLB 4,
9, 86; DLBD 2; MTCW

Farren, Richard J.
See Betjeman, John

Farren, Richard M.
See Betjeman, John

Fassbinder, Rainer Werner
1946-1982 . . . . CLC 20
See also CA 93-96; 106; CANR 31

Fast, Howard (Melvin)
1914- . . . . CLC 23; DAM NOV
See also AAYA 16; CA 1-4R; CAAS 18;
CANR 1, 33, 54; DLB 9; INT CANR-33;
SATA 7

Faulcon, Robert
See Holdstock, Robert P.

Faulkner, William (Cuthbert)
1897-1962 . . . . . CLC 1, 3, 6, 8, 9, 11, 14,
18, 28, 52, 68; DA; DAB; DAC;
DAM MST, NOV; SSC 1; WLC
See also AAYA 7; CA 81-84; CANR 33;
CDALB 1929-1941; DLB 9, 11, 44, 102;
DLBD 2; DLBY 86; MTCW

Fauset, Jessie Redmon
1884(?)-1961 . . . . CLC 19, 54; BLC;
DAM MULT
See also BW 1; CA 109; DLB 51

Faust, Frederick (Schiller)
1892-1944(?) . . . . . TCLC 49; DAM POP
See also CA 108; 152

Faust, Irvin 1924- . . . . CLC 8
See also CA 33-36R; CANR 28; DLB 2, 28;
DLBY 80

Fawkes, Guy
See Benchley, Robert (Charles)

Fearing, Kenneth (Flexner)
1902-1961 . . . . CLC 51
See also CA 93-96; DLB 9

Fecamps, Elise
See Creasey, John

Federman, Raymond 1928- . . . . . . CLC 6, 47
See also CA 17-20R; CAAS 8; CANR 10,
43; DLBY 80

Federspiel, J(uerg) F. 1931- . . . . CLC 42
See also CA 146

Feiffer, Jules (Ralph)
1929- . . . . . . CLC 2, 8, 64; DAM DRAM
See also AAYA 3; CA 17-20R; CANR 30;
DLB 7, 44; INT CANR-30; MTCW;
SATA 8, 61

Feige, Hermann Albert Otto Maximilian
See Traven, B.

Feinberg, David B. 1956-1994 . . . . . CLC 59
See also CA 135; 147

Feinstein, Elaine 1930- . . . . CLC 36
See also CA 69-72; CAAS 1; CANR 31;
DLB 14, 40; MTCW

Feldman, Irving (Mordecai) 1928- . . . . CLC 7
See also CA 1-4R; CANR 1; DLB 169

Felix-Tchicaya, Gerald
See Tchicaya, Gerald Felix

Fellini, Federico 1920-1993 . . . . . CLC 16, 85
See also CA 65-68; 143; CANR 33

Felsen, Henry Gregor 1916- . . . . CLC 17
See also CA 1-4R; CANR 1; SAAS 2;
SATA 1

Fenton, James Martin 1949- . . . . CLC 32
See also CA 102; DLB 40

Ferber, Edna 1887-1968 . . . . CLC 18, 93
See also AITN 1; CA 5-8R; 25-28R; DLB 9,
28, 86; MTCW; SATA 7

Ferguson, Helen
See Kavan, Anna

Ferguson, Samuel 1810-1886 . . . . . NCLC 33
See also DLB 32

Fergusson, Robert 1750-1774 . . . . LC 29
See also DLB 109

Ferling, Lawrence
See Ferlinghetti, Lawrence (Monsanto)

Ferlinghetti, Lawrence (Monsanto)
1919(?)- . . . . CLC 2, 6, 10, 27;
DAM POET; PC 1
See also CA 5-8R; CANR 3, 41;
CDALB 1941-1968; DLB 5, 16; MTCW

Fernandez, Vicente Garcia Huidobro
See Huidobro Fernandez, Vicente Garcia

Ferrer, Gabriel (Francisco Victor) Miro
See Miro (Ferrer), Gabriel (Francisco
Victor)

Ferrier, Susan (Edmonstone)
1782-1854 . . . . NCLC 8
See also DLB 116

Ferrigno, Robert 1948(?)- . . . . CLC 65
See also CA 140

Ferron, Jacques 1921-1985 . . . CLC 94; DAC
See also CA 117; 129; DLB 60

Feuchtwanger, Lion 1884-1958 . . . . . TCLC 3
See also CA 104; DLB 66

Feuillet, Octave 1821-1890 . . . . . . NCLC 45

Feydeau, Georges (Leon Jules Marie)
1862-1921 . . . . . TCLC 22; DAM DRAM
See also CA 113; 152

Fichte, Johann Gottlieb
1762-1814 . . . . NCLC 62
See also DLB 90

Ficino, Marsilio 1433-1499 . . . . LC 12

Fiedeler, Hans
See Doeblin, Alfred

Fiedler, Leslie A(aron)
1917- . . . . CLC 4, 13, 24
See also CA 9-12R; CANR 7; DLB 28, 67;
MTCW

Field, Andrew 1938- . . . . CLC 44
See also CA 97-100; CANR 25

Field, Eugene 1850-1895 . . . . NCLC 3
See also DLB 23, 42, 140; DLBD 13;
MAICYA; SATA 16

Field, Gans T.
See Wellman, Manly Wade

Field, Michael . . . . TCLC 43

Field, Peter
See Hobson, Laura Z(ametkin)

Fielding, Henry
1707-1754 . . . . . . LC 1; DA; DAB; DAC;
DAM DRAM, MST, NOV; WLC
See also CDBLB 1660-1789; DLB 39, 84,
101

Fielding, Sarah 1710-1768 . . . . LC 1
See also DLB 39

Fierstein, Harvey (Forbes)
1954- . . . . . CLC 33; DAM DRAM, POP
See also CA 123; 129

Figes, Eva 1932- . . . . CLC 31
See also CA 53-56; CANR 4, 44; DLB 14

Finch, Robert (Duer Claydon)
1900- . . . . CLC 18
See also CA 57-60; CANR 9, 24, 49;
DLB 88

Findley, Timothy
1930- . . . . . . CLC 27; DAC; DAM MST
See also CA 25-28R; CANR 12, 42;
DLB 53

Fink, William
See Mencken, H(enry) L(ouis)

Firbank, Louis 1942-
See Reed, Lou
See also CA 117

Firbank, (Arthur Annesley) Ronald
1886-1926 . . . . TCLC 1
See also CA 104; DLB 36

Fisher, M(ary) F(rances) K(ennedy)
1908-1992 . . . . CLC 76, 87
See also CA 77-80; 138; CANR 44

Fisher, Roy 1930- . . . . CLC 25
See also CA 81-84; CAAS 10; CANR 16;
DLB 40

Fisher, Rudolph
1897-1934 . . . . TCLC 11; BLC;
DAM MULT; SSC 25
See also BW 1; CA 107; 124; DLB 51, 102

Fisher, Vardis (Alvero) 1895-1968 . . . . CLC 7
See also CA 5-8R; 25-28R; DLB 9

Fiske, Tarleton
See Bloch, Robert (Albert)

Fitch, Clarke
See Sinclair, Upton (Beall)

Fitch, John IV
See Cormier, Robert (Edmund)

Fitzgerald, Captain Hugh
See Baum, L(yman) Frank

FitzGerald, Edward 1809-1883 . . . . NCLC 9
See also DLB 32

Fitzgerald, F(rancis) Scott (Key)
1896-1940 . . . . TCLC 1, 6, 14, 28, 55;
DA; DAB; DAC; DAM MST, NOV;
SSC 6; WLC
See also AITN 1; CA 110; 123;
CDALB 1917-1929; DLB 4, 9, 86;
DLBD 1; DLBY 81, 96; MTCW

Fraser, George MacDonald 1925-.... **CLC 7**
See also CA 45-48; CANR 2, 48

Fraser, Sylvia 1935-.............. **CLC 64**
See also CA 45-48; CANR 1, 16

Frayn, Michael
1933- .... **CLC 3, 7, 31, 47;**
DAM DRAM, NOV
See also CA 5-8R; CANR 30; DLB 13, 14;
MTCW

Fraze, Candida (Merrill) 1945-..... **CLC 50**
See also CA 126

Frazer, J(ames) G(eorge)
1854-1941 .... **TCLC 32**
See also CA 118

Frazer, Robert Caine
See Creasey, John

Frazer, Sir James George
See Frazer, J(ames) G(eorge)

Frazier, Ian 1951-................ **CLC 46**
See also CA 130; CANR 54

Frederic, Harold 1856-1898...... **NCLC 10**
See also DLB 12, 23; DLBD 13

Frederick, John
See Faust, Frederick (Schiller)

Frederick the Great 1712-1786...... **LC 14**

Fredro, Aleksander 1793-1876..... **NCLC 8**

Freeling, Nicolas 1927-........... **CLC 38**
See also CA 49-52; CAAS 12; CANR 1, 17,
50; DLB 87

Freeman, Douglas Southall
1886-1953 .... **TCLC 11**
See also CA 109; DLB 17

Freeman, Judith 1946-............ **CLC 55**
See also CA 148

Freeman, Mary Eleanor Wilkins
1852-1930 .... **TCLC 9; SSC 1**
See also CA 106; DLB 12, 78

Freeman, R(ichard) Austin
1862-1943 .... **TCLC 21**
See also CA 113; DLB 70

French, Albert 1943- .... **CLC 86**

French, Marilyn
1929-................ **CLC 10, 18, 60;**
DAM DRAM, NOV, POP
See also CA 69-72; CANR 3, 31;
INT CANR-31; MTCW

French, Paul
See Asimov, Isaac

Freneau, Philip Morin 1752-1832.. **NCLC 1**
See also DLB 37, 43

Freud, Sigmund 1856-1939 .... **TCLC 52**
See also CA 115; 133; MTCW

Friedan, Betty (Naomi) 1921-...... **CLC 74**
See also CA 65-68; CANR 18, 45; MTCW

Friedlander, Saul 1932-........... **CLC 90**
See also CA 117; 130

Friedman, B(ernard) H(arper)
1926-...................... **CLC 7**
See also CA 1-4R; CANR 3, 48

Friedman, Bruce Jay 1930-.... **CLC 3, 5, 56**
See also CA 9-12R; CANR 25, 52; DLB 2,
28; INT CANR-25

Friel, Brian 1929-............ **CLC 5, 42, 59**
See also CA 21-24R; CANR 33; DLB 13;
MTCW

Friis-Baastad, Babbis Ellinor
1921-1970 .... **CLC 12**
See also CA 17-20R; 134; SATA 7

Frisch, Max (Rudolf)
1911-1991 ..... **CLC 3, 9, 14, 18, 32, 44;**
DAM DRAM, NOV
See also CA 85-88; 134; CANR 32;
DLB 69, 124; MTCW

Fromentin, Eugene (Samuel Auguste)
1820-1876 .... **NCLC 10**
See also DLB 123

Frost, Frederick
See Faust, Frederick (Schiller)

Frost, Robert (Lee)
1874-1963 .... **CLC 1, 3, 4, 9, 10, 13, 15,**
26, 34, 44; DA; DAB; DAC; DAM MST,
POET; PC 1; WLC
See also AAYA 21; CA 89-92; CANR 33;
CDALB 1917-1929; DLB 54; DLBD 7;
MTCW; SATA 14

Froude, James Anthony
1818-1894 .... **NCLC 43**
See also DLB 18, 57, 144

Froy, Herald
See Waterhouse, Keith (Spencer)

Fry, Christopher
1907- ..... **CLC 2, 10, 14; DAM DRAM**
See also CA 17-20R; CAAS 23; CANR 9,
30; DLB 13; MTCW; SATA 66

Frye, (Herman) Northrop
1912-1991 .... **CLC 24, 70**
See also CA 5-8R; 133; CANR 8, 37;
DLB 67, 68; MTCW

Fuchs, Daniel 1909-1993 .... **CLC 8, 22**
See also CA 81-84; 142; CAAS 5;
CANR 40; DLB 9, 26, 28; DLBY 93

Fuchs, Daniel 1934-.............. **CLC 34**
See also CA 37-40R; CANR 14, 48

Fuentes, Carlos
1928- ...... **CLC 3, 8, 10, 13, 22, 41, 60;**
DA; DAB; DAC; DAM MST, MULT,
NOV; HLC; SSC 24; WLC
See also AAYA 4; AITN 2; CA 69-72;
CANR 10, 32; DLB 113; HW; MTCW

Fuentes, Gregorio Lopez y
See Lopez y Fuentes, Gregorio

Fugard, (Harold) Athol
1932- .... **CLC 5, 9, 14, 25, 40, 80;**
DAM DRAM; DC 3
See also AAYA 17; CA 85-88; CANR 32,
54; MTCW

Fugard, Sheila 1932- .... **CLC 48**
See also CA 125

Fuller, Charles (H., Jr.)
1939- .... **CLC 25; BLC; DAM DRAM,**
MULT; DC 1
See also BW 2; CA 108; 112; DLB 38;
INT 112; MTCW

Fuller, John (Leopold) 1937-....... **CLC 62**
See also CA 21-24R; CANR 9, 44; DLB 40

Fuller, Margaret .... **NCLC 5, 50**
See also Ossoli, Sarah Margaret (Fuller
marchesa d')

Fuller, Roy (Broadbent)
1912-1991 .... **CLC 4, 28**
See also CA 5-8R; 135; CAAS 10;
CANR 53; DLB 15, 20; SATA 87

Fulton, Alice 1952-.............. **CLC 52**
See also CA 116; CANR 57

Furphy, Joseph 1843-1912....... **TCLC 25**

Fussell, Paul 1924-.............. **CLC 74**
See also BEST 90:1; CA 17-20R; CANR 8,
21, 35; INT CANR-21; MTCW

Futabatei, Shimei 1864-1909..... **TCLC 44**
See also DLB 180

Futrelle, Jacques 1875-1912 ...... **TCLC 19**
See also CA 113; 155

Gaboriau, Emile 1835-1873...... **NCLC 14**

Gadda, Carlo Emilio 1893-1973 .... **CLC 11**
See also CA 89-92; DLB 177

Gaddis, William
1922-..... **CLC 1, 3, 6, 8, 10, 19, 43, 86**
See also CA 17-20R; CANR 21, 48; DLB 2;
MTCW

Gage, Walter
See Inge, William (Motter)

Gaines, Ernest J(ames)
1933- .... **CLC 3, 11, 18, 86; BLC;**
DAM MULT
See also AAYA 18; AITN 1; BW 2;
CA 9-12R; CANR 6, 24, 42;
CDALB 1968-1988; DLB 2, 33, 152;
DLBY 80; MTCW; SATA 86

Gaitskill, Mary 1954-............. **CLC 69**
See also CA 128

Galdos, Benito Perez
See Perez Galdos, Benito

Gale, Zona
1874-1938 ...... **TCLC 7; DAM DRAM**
See also CA 105; 153; DLB 9, 78

Galeano, Eduardo (Hughes) 1940-... **CLC 72**
See also CA 29-32R; CANR 13, 32; HW

Galiano, Juan Valera y Alcala
See Valera y Alcala-Galiano, Juan

Gallagher, Tess
1943- .. **CLC 18, 63; DAM POET; PC 9**
See also CA 106; DLB 120

Gallant, Mavis
1922- .... **CLC 7, 18, 38; DAC;**
DAM MST; SSC 5
See also CA 69-72; CANR 29; DLB 53;
MTCW

Gallant, Roy A(rthur) 1924- .... **CLC 17**
See also CA 5-8R; CANR 4, 29, 54;
CLR 30; MAICYA; SATA 4, 68

Gallico, Paul (William) 1897-1976 ... **CLC 2**
See also AITN 1; CA 5-8R; 69-72;
CANR 23; DLB 9, 171; MAICYA;
SATA 13

Gallo, Max Louis 1932-........... **CLC 95**
See also CA 85-88

Gallois, Lucien
See Desnos, Robert

Gallup, Ralph
See Whitemore, Hugh (John)

Galsworthy, John
1867-1933 ...... **TCLC 1, 45; DA; DAB;
DAC; DAM DRAM, MST, NOV;
SSC 22; WLC 2**
See also CA 104; 141; CDBLB 1890-1914;
DLB 10, 34, 98, 162

Galt, John 1779-1839........... **NCLC 1**
See also DLB 99, 116, 159

Galvin, James 1951-.............. **CLC 38**
See also CA 108; CANR 26

Gamboa, Federico 1864-1939..... **TCLC 36**

Gandhi, M. K.
See Gandhi, Mohandas Karamchand

Gandhi, Mahatma
See Gandhi, Mohandas Karamchand

Gandhi, Mohandas Karamchand
1869-1948 ..... **TCLC 59; DAM MULT**
See also CA 121; 132; MTCW

Gann, Ernest Kellogg 1910-1991.... **CLC 23**
See also AITN 1; CA 1-4R; 136; CANR 1

Garcia, Cristina 1958-............ **CLC 76**
See also CA 141

Garcia Lorca, Federico
1898-1936 ... **TCLC 1, 7, 49; DA; DAB;
DAC; DAM DRAM, MST, MULT,
POET; DC 2; HLC; PC 3; WLC**
See also CA 104; 131; DLB 108; HW;
MTCW

Garcia Marquez, Gabriel (Jose)
1928- .... **CLC 2, 3, 8, 10, 15, 27, 47, 55,
68; DA; DAB; DAC; DAM MST,
MULT, NOV, POP; HLC; SSC 8; WLC**
See also AAYA 3; BEST 89:1, 90:4;
CA 33-36R; CANR 10, 28, 50; DLB 113;
HW; MTCW

Gard, Janice
See Latham, Jean Lee

Gard, Roger Martin du
See Martin du Gard, Roger

Gardam, Jane 1928-.............. **CLC 43**
See also CA 49-52; CANR 2, 18, 33, 54;
CLR 12; DLB 14, 161; MAICYA;
MTCW; SAAS 9; SATA 39, 76;
SATA-Brief 28

Gardner, Herb(ert) 1934-......... **CLC 44**
See also CA 149

Gardner, John (Champlin), Jr.
1933-1982 ..... **CLC 2, 3, 5, 7, 8, 10, 18,
28, 34; DAM NOV, POP; SSC 7**
See also AITN 1; CA 65-68; 107;
CANR 33; DLB 2; DLBY 82; MTCW;
SATA 40; SATA-Obit 31

Gardner, John (Edmund)
1926- .... **CLC 30; DAM POP**
See also CA 103; CANR 15; MTCW

Gardner, Miriam
See Bradley, Marion Zimmer

Gardner, Noel
See Kuttner, Henry

Gardons, S. S.
See Snodgrass, W(illiam) D(e Witt)

Garfield, Leon 1921-1996......... **CLC 12**
See also AAYA 8; CA 17-20R; 152;
CANR 38, 41; CLR 21; DLB 161; JRDA;
MAICYA; SATA 1, 32, 76;
SATA-Obit 90

Garland, (Hannibal) Hamlin
1860-1940 .... **TCLC 3; SSC 18**
See also CA 104; DLB 12, 71, 78

Garneau, (Hector de) Saint-Denys
1912-1943 .... **TCLC 13**
See also CA 111; DLB 88

Garner, Alan
1934- .... **CLC 17; DAB; DAM POP**
See also AAYA 18; CA 73-76; CANR 15;
CLR 20; DLB 161; MAICYA; MTCW;
SATA 18, 69

Garner, Hugh 1913-1979 .... **CLC 13**
See also CA 69-72; CANR 31; DLB 68

Garnett, David 1892-1981 .... **CLC 3**
See also CA 5-8R; 103; CANR 17; DLB 34

Garos, Stephanie
See Katz, Steve

Garrett, George (Palmer)
1929- .... **CLC 3, 11, 51**
See also CA 1-4R; CAAS 5; CANR 1, 42;
DLB 2, 5, 130, 152; DLBY 83

Garrick, David
1717-1779 .... **LC 15; DAM DRAM**
See also DLB 84

Garrigue, Jean 1914-1972 .... **CLC 2, 8**
See also CA 5-8R; 37-40R; CANR 20

Garrison, Frederick
See Sinclair, Upton (Beall)

Garth, Will
See Hamilton, Edmond; Kuttner, Henry

Garvey, Marcus (Moziah, Jr.)
1887-1940 .... **TCLC 41; BLC;
DAM MULT**
See also BW 1; CA 120; 124

Gary, Romain .... **CLC 25**
See also Kacew, Romain
See also DLB 83

Gascar, Pierre .... **CLC 11**
See also Fournier, Pierre

Gascoyne, David (Emery) 1916- .... **CLC 45**
See also CA 65-68; CANR 10, 28, 54;
DLB 20; MTCW

Gaskell, Elizabeth Cleghorn
1810-1865 .... **NCLC 5; DAB;
DAM MST; SSC 25**
See also CDBLB 1832-1890; DLB 21, 144,
159

Gass, William H(oward)
1924- ... **CLC 1, 2, 8, 11, 15, 39; SSC 12**
See also CA 17-20R; CANR 30; DLB 2;
MTCW

Gasset, Jose Ortega y
See Ortega y Gasset, Jose

Gates, Henry Louis, Jr.
1950- .... **CLC 65; DAM MULT**
See also BW 2; CA 109; CANR 25, 53;
DLB 67

Gautier, Theophile
1811-1872 .... **NCLC 1, 59;
DAM POET; PC 18; SSC 20**
See also DLB 119

Gawsworth, John
See Bates, H(erbert) E(rnest)

Gay, Oliver
See Gogarty, Oliver St. John

Gaye, Marvin (Penze) 1939-1984 ... **CLC 26**
See also CA 112

Gebler, Carlo (Ernest) 1954-....... **CLC 39**
See also CA 119; 133

Gee, Maggie (Mary) 1948-........ **CLC 57**
See also CA 130

Gee, Maurice (Gough) 1931-....... **CLC 29**
See also CA 97-100; SATA 46

Gelbart, Larry (Simon) 1923- ... **CLC 21, 61**
See also CA 73-76; CANR 45

Gelber, Jack 1932-........ **CLC 1, 6, 14, 79**
See also CA 1-4R; CANR 2; DLB 7

Gellhorn, Martha (Ellis) 1908-.. **CLC 14, 60**
See also CA 77-80; CANR 44; DLBY 82

Genet, Jean
1910-1986 ...... **CLC 1, 2, 5, 10, 14, 44,
46; DAM DRAM**
See also CA 13-16R; CANR 18; DLB 72;
DLBY 86; MTCW

Gent, Peter 1942-................. **CLC 29**
See also AITN 1; CA 89-92; DLBY 82

Gentlewoman in New England, A
See Bradstreet, Anne

Gentlewoman in Those Parts, A
See Bradstreet, Anne

George, Jean Craighead 1919-...... **CLC 35**
See also AAYA 8; CA 5-8R; CANR 25;
CLR 1; DLB 52; JRDA; MAICYA;
SATA 2, 68

George, Stefan (Anton)
1868-1933 .... **TCLC 2, 14**
See also CA 104

Georges, Georges Martin
See Simenon, Georges (Jacques Christian)

Gerhardi, William Alexander
See Gerhardie, William Alexander

Gerhardie, William Alexander
1895-1977 .... **CLC 5**
See also CA 25-28R; 73-76; CANR 18;
DLB 36

Gerstler, Amy 1956-............. **CLC 70**
See also CA 146

Gertler, T. .... **CLC 34**
See also CA 116; 121; INT 121

gfgg........................ **CLC XvXzc**

Ghalib........................ **NCLC 39**
See also Ghalib, Hsadullah Khan

Ghalib, Hsadullah Khan 1797-1869
See Ghalib
See also DAM POET

Ghelderode, Michel de
1898-1962 .... **CLC 6, 11; DAM DRAM**
See also CA 85-88; CANR 40

Ghiselin, Brewster 1903-......... **CLC 23**
See also CA 13-16R; CAAS 10; CANR 13

Ghose, Zulfikar 1935-............ **CLC 42**
See also CA 65-68

Ghosh, Amitav 1956-............. **CLC 44**
See also CA 147

Giacosa, Giuseppe 1847-1906 ...... **TCLC 7**
See also CA 104

Gibb, Lee
See Waterhouse, Keith (Spencer)

Gibbon, Lewis Grassic . . . . TCLC 4
See also Mitchell, James Leslie

Gibbons, Kaye
1960- . . . . CLC 50, 88; DAM POP
See also CA 151

Gibran, Kahlil
1883-1931 . . . . TCLC 1, 9; DAM POET,
POP; PC 9
See also CA 104; 150

Gibran, Khalil
See Gibran, Kahlil

Gibson, William
1914- . . . . CLC 23; DA; DAB; DAC;
DAM DRAM, MST
See also CA 9-12R; CANR 9, 42; DLB 7;
SATA 66

Gibson, William (Ford)
1948- . . . . CLC 39, 63; DAM POP
See also AAYA 12; CA 126; 133; CANR 52

Gide, Andre (Paul Guillaume)
1869-1951 . . . . TCLC 5, 12, 36; DA;
DAB; DAC; DAM MST, NOV; SSC 13;
WLC
See also CA 104; 124; DLB 65; MTCW

Gifford, Barry (Colby) 1946- . . . . CLC 34
See also CA 65-68; CANR 9, 30, 40

Gilbert, W(illiam) S(chwenck)
1836-1911 . . . . . TCLC 3; DAM DRAM,
POET
See also CA 104; SATA 36

Gilbreth, Frank B., Jr. 1911- . . . . . . CLC 17
See also CA 9-12R; SATA 2

Gilchrist, Ellen
1935- . . . . CLC 34, 48; DAM POP;
SSC 14
See also CA 113; 116; CANR 41; DLB 130;
MTCW

Giles, Molly 1942- . . . . CLC 39
See also CA 126

Gill, Patrick
See Creasey, John

Gilliam, Terry (Vance) 1940- . . . . CLC 21
See also Monty Python
See also AAYA 19; CA 108; 113;
CANR 35; INT 113

Gillian, Jerry
See Gilliam, Terry (Vance)

Gilliatt, Penelope (Ann Douglass)
1932-1993 . . . . CLC 2, 10, 13, 53
See also AITN 2; CA 13-16R; 141;
CANR 49; DLB 14

Gilman, Charlotte (Anna) Perkins (Stetson)
1860-1935 . . . . TCLC 9, 37; SSC 13
See also CA 106; 150

Gilmour, David 1949- . . . . CLC 35
See also CA 138, 147

Gilpin, William 1724-1804 . . . . . . NCLC 30

Gilray, J. D.
See Mencken, H(enry) L(ouis)

Gilroy, Frank D(aniel) 1925- . . . . CLC 2
See also CA 81-84; CANR 32; DLB 7

Gilstrap, John 1957(?)- . . . . CLC 99

Ginsberg, Allen (Irwin)
1926-1997 . . . . . CLC 1, 2, 3, 4, 6, 13, 36,
69; DA; DAB; DAC; DAM MST, POET;
PC 4; WLC 3
See also AITN 1; CA 1-4R; 157; CANR 2,
41; CDALB 1941-1968; DLB 5, 16, 169;
MTCW

Ginzburg, Natalia
1916-1991 . . . . CLC 5, 11, 54, 70
See also CA 85-88; 135; CANR 33;
DLB 177; MTCW

Giono, Jean 1895-1970 . . . . CLC 4, 11
See also CA 45-48; 29-32R; CANR 2, 35;
DLB 72; MTCW

Giovanni, Nikki
1943- . . . . . . CLC 2, 4, 19, 64; BLC; DA;
DAB; DAC; DAM MST, MULT, POET;
PC 19
See also AITN 1; BW 2; CA 29-32R;
CAAS 6; CANR 18, 41; CLR 6; DLB 5,
41; INT CANR-18; MAICYA; MTCW;
SATA 24; YABC

Giovene, Andrea 1904- . . . . CLC 7
See also CA 85-88

Gippius, Zinaida (Nikolayevna) 1869-1945
See Hippius, Zinaida
See also CA 106

Giraudoux, (Hippolyte) Jean
1882-1944 . . . . TCLC 2, 7; DAM DRAM
See also CA 104; DLB 65

Gironella, Jose Maria 1917- . . . . CLC 11
See also CA 101

Gissing, George (Robert)
1857-1903 . . . . TCLC 3, 24, 47
See also CA 105; DLB 18, 135

Giurlani, Aldo
See Palazzeschi, Aldo

Gladkov, Fyodor (Vasilyevich)
1883-1958 . . . . TCLC 27

Glanville, Brian (Lester) 1931- . . . . . . CLC 6
See also CA 5-8R; CAAS 9; CANR 3;
DLB 15, 139; SATA 42

Glasgow, Ellen (Anderson Gholson)
1873(?)-1945 . . . . TCLC 2, 7
See also CA 104; DLB 9, 12

Glaspell, Susan 1882(?)-1948 . . . . . . TCLC 55
See also CA 110; 154; DLB 7, 9, 78; 2

Glassco, John 1909-1981 . . . . CLC 9
See also CA 13-16R; 102; CANR 15;
DLB 68

Glasscock, Amnesia
See Steinbeck, John (Ernst)

Glasser, Ronald J. 1940(?)- . . . . CLC 37

Glassman, Joyce
See Johnson, Joyce

Glendinning, Victoria 1937- . . . . CLC 50
See also CA 120; 127; DLB 155

Glissant, Edouard
1928- . . . . CLC 10, 68; DAM MULT
See also CA 153

Gloag, Julian 1930- . . . . CLC 40
See also AITN 1; CA 65-68; CANR 10

Glowacki, Aleksander
See Prus, Boleslaw

Gluck, Louise (Elisabeth)
1943- . . . . CLC 7, 22, 44, 81;
DAM POET; PC 16
See also CA 33-36R; CANR 40; DLB 5

Glyn, Elinor 1864-1943 . . . . TCLC 72
See also DLB 153

Gobineau, Joseph Arthur (Comte) de
1816-1882 . . . . NCLC 17
See also DLB 123

Godard, Jean-Luc 1930- . . . . CLC 20
See also CA 93-96

Godden, (Margaret) Rumer 1907- . . . CLC 53
See also AAYA 6; CA 5-8R; CANR 4, 27,
36, 55; CLR 20; DLB 161; MAICYA;
SAAS 12; SATA 3, 36

Godoy Alcayaga, Lucila 1889-1957
See Mistral, Gabriela
See also BW 2; CA 104; 131; DAM MULT;
HW; MTCW

Godwin, Gail (Kathleen)
1937- . . . . CLC 5, 8, 22, 31, 69;
DAM POP
See also CA 29-32R; CANR 15, 43; DLB 6;
INT CANR-15; MTCW

Godwin, William 1756-1836 . . . . . . NCLC 14
See also CDBLB 1789-1832; DLB 39, 104,
142, 158, 163

Goebbels, Josef
See Goebbels, (Paul) Joseph

Goebbels, (Paul) Joseph
1897-1945 . . . . TCLC 68
See also CA 115; 148

Goebbels, Joseph Paul
See Goebbels, (Paul) Joseph

Goethe, Johann Wolfgang von
1749-1832 . . . . NCLC 4, 22, 34; DA;
DAB; DAC; DAM DRAM, MST,
POET; PC 5; WLC 3
See also DLB 94

Gogarty, Oliver St. John
1878-1957 . . . . TCLC 15
See also CA 109; 150; DLB 15, 19

Gogol, Nikolai (Vasilyevich)
1809-1852 . . . . NCLC 5, 15, 31; DA;
DAB; DAC; DAM DRAM, MST; DC 1;
SSC 4; WLC
See also

Goines, Donald
1937(?)-1974 . . . . CLC 80; BLC;
DAM MULT, POP
See also AITN 1; BW 1; CA 124; 114;
DLB 33

Gold, Herbert 1924- . . . . CLC 4, 7, 14, 42
See also CA 9-12R; CANR 17, 45; DLB 2;
DLBY 81

Goldbarth, Albert 1948- . . . . CLC 5, 38
See also CA 53-56; CANR 6, 40; DLB 120

Goldberg, Anatol 1910-1982 . . . . CLC 34
See also CA 131; 117

Goldemberg, Isaac 1945- . . . . CLC 52
See also CA 69-72; CAAS 12; CANR 11,
32; HW

Gray, Simon (James Holliday)
1936- .... **CLC 9, 14, 36**
See also AITN 1; CA 21-24R; CAAS 3;
CANR 32; DLB 13; MTCW

Gray, Spalding
1941- ...... **CLC 49; DAM POP; DC 7**
See also CA 128

Gray, Thomas
1716-1771 ...... **LC 4; DA; DAB; DAC;**
DAM MST; PC 2; WLC
See also CDBLB 1660-1789; DLB 109

Grayson, David
See Baker, Ray Stannard

Grayson, Richard (A.) 1951- .... **CLC 38**
See also CA 85-88; CANR 14, 31, 57

Greeley, Andrew M(oran)
1928- .... **CLC 28; DAM POP**
See also CA 5-8R; CAAS 7; CANR 7, 43;
MTCW

Green, Anna Katharine
1846-1935 .... **TCLC 63**
See also CA 112

Green, Brian
See Card, Orson Scott

Green, Hannah .... **CLC 3**
See also CA 73-76

Green, Hannah
See Greenberg, Joanne (Goldenberg)

Green, Henry 1905-1973 ..... **CLC 2, 13, 97**
See also Yorke, Henry Vincent
See also DLB 15

Green, Julian (Hartridge) 1900-
See Green, Julien
See also CA 21-24R; CANR 33; DLB 4, 72;
MTCW

Green, Julien .... **CLC 3, 11, 77**
See also Green, Julian (Hartridge)

Green, Paul (Eliot)
1894-1981 ...... **CLC 25; DAM DRAM**
See also AITN 1; CA 5-8R; 103; CANR 3;
DLB 7, 9; DLBY 81

Greenberg, Ivan 1908-1973
See Rahv, Philip
See also CA 85-88

Greenberg, Joanne (Goldenberg)
1932- .... **CLC 7, 30**
See also AAYA 12; CA 5-8R; CANR 14,
32; SATA 25

Greenberg, Richard 1959(?)- .... **CLC 57**
See also CA 138

Greene, Bette 1934- .... **CLC 30**
See also AAYA 7; CA 53-56; CANR 4;
CLR 2; JRDA; MAICYA; SAAS 16;
SATA 8

Greene, Gael .... **CLC 8**
See also CA 13-16R; CANR 10

Greene, Graham
1904-1991 .... **CLC 1, 3, 6, 9, 14, 18, 27,**
37, 70, 72; DA; DAB; DAC; DAM MST,
NOV; WLC
See also AITN 2; CA 13-16R; 133;
CANR 35; CDBLB 1945-1960; DLB 13,
15, 77, 100, 162; DLBY 91; MTCW;
SATA 20

Greer, Richard
See Silverberg, Robert

Gregor, Arthur 1923- .... **CLC 9**
See also CA 25-28R; CAAS 10; CANR 11;
SATA 36

Gregor, Lee
See Pohl, Frederik

Gregory, Isabella Augusta (Persse)
1852-1932 .... **TCLC 1**
See also CA 104; DLB 10

Gregory, J. Dennis
See Williams, John A(lfred)

Grendon, Stephen
See Derleth, August (William)

Grenville, Kate 1950- .... **CLC 61**
See also CA 118; CANR 53

Grenville, Pelham
See Wodehouse, P(elham) G(renville)

Greve, Felix Paul (Berthold Friedrich)
1879-1948
See Grove, Frederick Philip
See also CA 104; 141; DAC; DAM MST

Grey, Zane
1872-1939 .... **TCLC 6; DAM POP**
See also CA 104; 132; DLB 9; MTCW

Grieg, (Johan) Nordahl (Brun)
1902-1943 .... **TCLC 10**
See also CA 107

Grieve, C(hristopher) M(urray)
1892-1978 .... **CLC 11, 19; DAM POET**
See also MacDiarmid, Hugh; Pteleon
See also CA 5-8R; 85-88; CANR 33;
MTCW

Griffin, Gerald 1803-1840 .... **NCLC 7**
See also DLB 159

Griffin, John Howard 1920-1980.... **CLC 68**
See also AITN 1; CA 1-4R; 101; CANR 2

Griffin, Peter 1942- .... **CLC 39**
See also CA 136

Griffith, D(avid Lewelyn) W(ark)
1875(?)-1948 .... **TCLC 68**
See also CA 119; 150

Griffith, Lawrence
See Griffith, D(avid Lewelyn) W(ark)

Griffiths, Trevor 1935- .... **CLC 13, 52**
See also CA 97-100; CANR 45; DLB 13

Grigson, Geoffrey (Edward Harvey)
1905-1985 .... **CLC 7, 39**
See also CA 25-28R; 118; CANR 20, 33;
DLB 27; MTCW

Grillparzer, Franz 1791-1872...... **NCLC 1**
See also DLB 133

Grimble, Reverend Charles James
See Eliot, T(homas) S(tearns)

Grimke, Charlotte L(ottie) Forten
1837(?)-1914
See Forten, Charlotte L.
See also BW 1; CA 117; 124; DAM MULT,
POET

Grimm, Jacob Ludwig Karl
1785-1863 .... **NCLC 3**
See also DLB 90; MAICYA; SATA 22

Grimm, Wilhelm Karl 1786-1859 .. **NCLC 3**
See also DLB 90; MAICYA; SATA 22

Grimmelshausen, Johann Jakob Christoffel
von 1621-1676 .... **LC 6**
See also DLB 168

Grindel, Eugene 1895-1952
See Eluard, Paul
See also CA 104

Grisham, John 1955- .. **CLC 84; DAM POP**
See also AAYA 14; CA 138; CANR 47

Grossman, David 1954- .... **CLC 67**
See also CA 138

Grossman, Vasily (Semenovich)
1905-1964 .... **CLC 41**
See also CA 124; 130; MTCW

Grove, Frederick Philip .... **TCLC 4**
See also Greve, Felix Paul (Berthold
Friedrich)
See also DLB 92

Grubb
See Crumb, R(obert)

Grumbach, Doris (Isaac)
1918- .... **CLC 13, 22, 64**
See also CA 5-8R; CAAS 2; CANR 9, 42;
INT CANR-9

Grundtvig, Nicolai Frederik Severin
1783-1872 .... **NCLC 1**

Grunge
See Crumb, R(obert)

Grunwald, Lisa 1959- .... **CLC 44**
See also CA 120

Guare, John
1938- .... **CLC 8, 14, 29, 67;**
DAM DRAM
See also CA 73-76; CANR 21; DLB 7;
MTCW

Gudjonsson, Halldor Kiljan 1902-
See Laxness, Halldor
See also CA 103

Guenter, Erich
See Eich, Guenter

Guest, Barbara 1920- .... **CLC 34**
See also CA 25-28R; CANR 11, 44; DLB 5

Guest, Judith (Ann)
1936- .... **CLC 8, 30; DAM NOV, POP**
See also AAYA 7; CA 77-80; CANR 15;
INT CANR-15; MTCW

Guevara, Che .... **CLC 87; HLC**
See also Guevara (Serna), Ernesto

Guevara (Serna), Ernesto 1928-1967
See Guevara, Che
See also CA 127; 111; CANR 56;
DAM MULT; HW

Guild, Nicholas M. 1944- .... **CLC 33**
See also CA 93-96

Guillemin, Jacques
See Sartre, Jean-Paul

Guillen, Jorge
1893-1984 ...... **CLC 11; DAM MULT,**
POET
See also CA 89-92; 112; DLB 108; HW

Guillen, Nicolas (Cristobal)
1902-1989 .... **CLC 48, 79; BLC;**
DAM MST, MULT, POET; HLC
See also BW 2; CA 116; 125; 129; HW

Guillevic, (Eugene) 1907- .... **CLC 33**
See also CA 93-96

Guillois
See Desnos, Robert

Hansberry, Lorraine (Vivian)
1930-1965 . . . . . . **CLC 17, 62; BLC; DA; DAB; DAC; DAM DRAM, MST, MULT; DC 2**
See also BW 1; CA 109; 25-28R; CABS 3; CANR 58; CDALB 1941-1968; DLB 7, 38; MTCW

Hansen, Joseph 1923- . . . . **CLC 38**
See also CA 29-32R; CAAS 17; CANR 16, 44; INT CANR-16

Hansen, Martin A. 1909-1955 . . . . . **TCLC 32**

Hanson, Kenneth O(stlin) 1922- . . . . **CLC 13**
See also CA 53-56; CANR 7

Hardwick, Elizabeth
1916- . . . . **CLC 13; DAM NOV**
See also CA 5-8R; CANR 3, 32; DLB 6; MTCW

Hardy, Thomas
1840-1928 . . . . . . **TCLC 4, 10, 18, 32, 48, 53, 72; DA; DAB; DAC; DAM MST, NOV, POET; PC 8; SSC 2; WLC**
See also CA 104; 123; CDBLB 1890-1914; DLB 18, 19, 135; MTCW

Hare, David 1947- . . . . **CLC 29, 58**
See also CA 97-100; CANR 39; DLB 13; MTCW

Harford, Henry
See Hudson, W(illiam) H(enry)

Hargrave, Leonie
See Disch, Thomas M(ichael)

Harjo, Joy 1951- . . . **CLC 83; DAM MULT**
See also CA 114; CANR 35; DLB 120, 175; NNAL

Harlan, Louis R(udolph) 1922- . . . . . **CLC 34**
See also CA 21-24R; CANR 25, 55

Harling, Robert 1951(?)- . . . . **CLC 53**
See also CA 147

Harmon, William (Ruth) 1938- . . . . . **CLC 38**
See also CA 33-36R; CANR 14, 32, 35; SATA 65

Harper, F. E. W.
See Harper, Frances Ellen Watkins

Harper, Frances E. W.
See Harper, Frances Ellen Watkins

Harper, Frances E. Watkins
See Harper, Frances Ellen Watkins

Harper, Frances Ellen
See Harper, Frances Ellen Watkins

Harper, Frances Ellen Watkins
1825-1911 . . . . **TCLC 14; BLC; DAM MULT, POET**
See also BW 1; CA 111; 125; DLB 50

Harper, Michael S(teven) 1938- . . **CLC 7, 22**
See also BW 1; CA 33-36R; CANR 24; DLB 41

Harper, Mrs. F. E. W.
See Harper, Frances Ellen Watkins

Harris, Christie (Lucy) Irwin
1907- . . . . **CLC 12**
See also CA 5-8R; CANR 6; DLB 88; JRDA; MAICYA; SAAS 10; SATA 6, 74

Harris, Frank 1856-1931 . . . . **TCLC 24**
See also CA 109; 150; DLB 156

Harris, George Washington
1814-1869 . . . . **NCLC 23**
See also DLB 3, 11

Harris, Joel Chandler
1848-1908 . . . . **TCLC 2; SSC 19**
See also CA 104; 137; DLB 11, 23, 42, 78, 91; MAICYA; 1

Harris, John (Wyndham Parkes Lucas)
Beynon 1903-1969
See Wyndham, John
See also CA 102; 89-92

Harris, MacDonald . . . . **CLC 9**
See also Heiney, Donald (William)

Harris, Mark 1922- . . . . **CLC 19**
See also CA 5-8R; CAAS 3; CANR 2, 55; DLB 2; DLBY 80

Harris, (Theodore) Wilson 1921- . . . . **CLC 25**
See also BW 2; CA 65-68; CAAS 16; CANR 11, 27; DLB 117; MTCW

Harrison, Elizabeth Cavanna 1909-
See Cavanna, Betty
See also CA 9-12R; CANR 6, 27

Harrison, Harry (Max) 1925- . . . . . . **CLC 42**
See also CA 1-4R; CANR 5, 21; DLB 8; SATA 4

Harrison, James (Thomas)
1937- . . . . . . **CLC 6, 14, 33, 66; SSC 19**
See also CA 13-16R; CANR 8, 51; DLBY 82; INT CANR-8

Harrison, Jim
See Harrison, James (Thomas)

Harrison, Kathryn 1961- . . . . **CLC 70**
See also CA 144

Harrison, Tony 1937- . . . . **CLC 43**
See also CA 65-68; CANR 44; DLB 40; MTCW

Harriss, Will(ard Irvin) 1922- . . . . . . **CLC 34**
See also CA 111

Harson, Sley
See Ellison, Harlan (Jay)

Hart, Ellis
See Ellison, Harlan (Jay)

Hart, Josephine
1942(?)- . . . . **CLC 70; DAM POP**
See also CA 138

Hart, Moss
1904-1961 . . . . . . **CLC 66; DAM DRAM**
See also CA 109; 89-92; DLB 7

Harte, (Francis) Bret(t)
1836(?)-1902 . . . . **TCLC 1, 25; DA; DAC; DAM MST; SSC 8; WLC**
See also CA 104; 140; CDALB 1865-1917; DLB 12, 64, 74, 79; SATA 26

Hartley, L(eslie) P(oles)
1895-1972 . . . . **CLC 2, 22**
See also CA 45-48; 37-40R; CANR 33; DLB 15, 139; MTCW

Hartman, Geoffrey H. 1929- . . . . **CLC 27**
See also CA 117; 125; DLB 67

Hartmann von Aue
c. 1160-c. 1205 . . . . **CMLC 15**
See also DLB 138

Hartmann von Aue 1170-1210 . . . . **CMLC 15**

Haruf, Kent 1943- . . . . **CLC 34**
See also CA 149

Harwood, Ronald
1934- . . . . **CLC 32; DAM DRAM, MST**
See also CA 1-4R; CANR 4, 55; DLB 13

Hasek, Jaroslav (Matej Frantisek)
1883-1923 . . . . **TCLC 4**
See also CA 104; 129; MTCW

Hass, Robert
1941- . . . . **CLC 18, 39, 99; PC 16**
See also CA 111; CANR 30, 50; DLB 105; SATA 94

Hastings, Hudson
See Kuttner, Henry

Hastings, Selina . . . . **CLC 44**

Hathorne, John 1641-1717 . . . . **LC 38**

Hatteras, Amelia
See Mencken, H(enry) L(ouis)

Hatteras, Owen . . . . **TCLC 18**
See also Mencken, H(enry) L(ouis); Nathan, George Jean

Hauptmann, Gerhart (Johann Robert)
1862-1946 . . . . . . **TCLC 4; DAM DRAM**
See also CA 104; 153; DLB 66, 118

Havel, Vaclav
1936- . . . . **CLC 25, 58, 65; DAM DRAM; DC 6**
See also CA 104; CANR 36; MTCW

Haviaras, Stratis . . . . **CLC 33**
See also Chaviaras, Strates

Hawes, Stephen 1475(?)-1523(?) . . . . . **LC 17**

Hawkes, John (Clendennin Burne, Jr.)
1925- . . . . . . **CLC 1, 2, 3, 4, 7, 9, 14, 15, 27, 49**
See also CA 1-4R; CANR 2, 47; DLB 2, 7; DLBY 80; MTCW

Hawking, S. W.
See Hawking, Stephen W(illiam)

Hawking, Stephen W(illiam)
1942- . . . . **CLC 63**
See also AAYA 13; BEST 89:1; CA 126; 129; CANR 48

Hawthorne, Julian 1846-1934 . . . . . **TCLC 25**

Hawthorne, Nathaniel
1804-1864 . . . . . . **NCLC 39; DA; DAB; DAC; DAM MST, NOV; SSC 3; WLC**
See also AAYA 18; CDALB 1640-1865; DLB 1, 74; 2

Haxton, Josephine Ayres 1921-
See Douglas, Ellen
See also CA 115; CANR 41

Hayaseca y Eizaguirre, Jorge
See Echegaray (y Eizaguirre), Jose (Maria Waldo)

Hayashi Fumiko 1904-1951 . . . . . . **TCLC 27**
See also DLB 180

Haycraft, Anna
See Ellis, Alice Thomas
See also CA 122

Hayden, Robert E(arl)
1913-1980 . . . . . . **CLC 5, 9, 14, 37; BLC; DA; DAC; DAM MST, MULT, POET; PC 6**
See also BW 1; CA 69-72; 97-100; CABS 2; CANR 24; CDALB 1941-1968; DLB 5, 76; MTCW; SATA 19; SATA-Obit 26

Hayford, J(oseph) E(phraim) Casely
See Casely-Hayford, J(oseph) E(phraim)

Hayman, Ronald 1932-............ **CLC 44**
See also CA 25-28R; CANR 18, 50;
DLB 155

Haywood, Eliza (Fowler)
1693(?)-1756 .... **LC 1**

Hazlitt, William 1778-1830 ...... **NCLC 29**
See also DLB 110, 158

Hazzard, Shirley 1931- .... **CLC 18**
See also CA 9-12R; CANR 4; DLBY 82;
MTCW

Head, Bessie
1937-1986 .... **CLC 25, 67; BLC;**
DAM MULT
See also BW 2; CA 29-32R; 119; CANR 25;
DLB 117; MTCW

Headon, (Nicky) Topper 1956(?)- ... **CLC 30**

Heaney, Seamus (Justin)
1939- ...... **CLC 5, 7, 14, 25, 37, 74, 91;**
DAB; DAM POET; PC 18
See also CA 85-88; CANR 25, 48;
CDBLB 1960 to Present; DLB 40;
DLBY 95; MTCW; YABC

Hearn, (Patricio) Lafcadio (Tessima Carlos)
1850-1904 .... **TCLC 9**
See also CA 105; DLB 12, 78

Hearne, Vicki 1946- .... **CLC 56**
See also CA 139

Hearon, Shelby 1931-............ **CLC 63**
See also AITN 2; CA 25-28R; CANR 18,
48

Heat-Moon, William Least .... **CLC 29**
See also Trogdon, William (Lewis)
See also AAYA 9

Hebbel, Friedrich
1813-1863 .... **NCLC 43; DAM DRAM**
See also DLB 129

Hebert, Anne
1916- .... **CLC 4, 13, 29; DAC;**
DAM MST, POET
See also CA 85-88; DLB 68; MTCW

Hecht, Anthony (Evan)
1923- ...... **CLC 8, 13, 19; DAM POET**
See also CA 9-12R; CANR 6; DLB 5, 169

Hecht, Ben 1894-1964 .... **CLC 8**
See also CA 85-88; DLB 7, 9, 25, 26, 28, 86

Hedayat, Sadeq 1903-1951........ **TCLC 21**
See also CA 120

Hegel, Georg Wilhelm Friedrich
1770-1831 .... **NCLC 46**
See also DLB 90

Heidegger, Martin 1889-1976 ...... **CLC 24**
See also CA 81-84; 65-68; CANR 34;
MTCW

Heidenstam, (Carl Gustaf) Verner von
1859-1940 .... **TCLC 5**
See also CA 104

Heifner, Jack 1946- .... **CLC 11**
See also CA 105; CANR 47

Heijermans, Herman 1864-1924 ... **TCLC 24**
See also CA 123

Heilbrun, Carolyn G(old) 1926-..... **CLC 25**
See also CA 45-48; CANR 1, 28, 58

Heine, Heinrich 1797-1856 .... **NCLC 4, 54**
See also DLB 90

Heinemann, Larry (Curtiss) 1944- .. **CLC 50**
See also CA 110; CAAS 21; CANR 31;
DLBD 9; INT CANR-31

Heiney, Donald (William) 1921-1993
See Harris, MacDonald
See also CA 1-4R; 142; CANR 3, 58

Heinlein, Robert A(nson)
1907-1988 ...... **CLC 1, 3, 8, 14, 26, 55;**
DAM POP
See also AAYA 17; CA 1-4R; 125;
CANR 1, 20, 53; DLB 8; JRDA;
MAICYA; MTCW; SATA 9, 69;
SATA-Obit 56

Helforth, John
See Doolittle, Hilda

Hellenhofferu, Vojtech Kapristian z
See Hasek, Jaroslav (Matej Frantisek)

Heller, Joseph
1923- .... **CLC 1, 3, 5, 8, 11, 36, 63; DA;**
DAB; DAC; DAM MST, NOV, POP;
WLC
See also AITN 1; CA 5-8R; CABS 1;
CANR 8, 42; DLB 2, 28; DLBY 80;
INT CANR-8; MTCW

Hellman, Lillian (Florence)
1906-1984 ...... **CLC 2, 4, 8, 14, 18, 34,**
44, 52; DAM DRAM; DC 1
See also AITN 1, 2; CA 13-16R; 112;
CANR 33; DLB 7; DLBY 84; MTCW

Helprin, Mark
1947- .... **CLC 7, 10, 22, 32;**
DAM NOV, POP
See also CA 81-84; CANR 47; DLBY 85;
MTCW

Helvetius, Claude-Adrien
1715-1771 .... **LC 26**

Helyar, Jane Penelope Josephine 1933-
See Poole, Josephine
See also CA 21-24R; CANR 10, 26;
SATA 82

Hemans, Felicia 1793-1835 ...... **NCLC 29**
See also DLB 96

Hemingway, Ernest (Miller)
1899-1961 .... **CLC 1, 3, 6, 8, 10, 13, 19,**
30, 34, 39, 41, 44, 50, 61, 80; DA;
DAC; DAM MST, NOV; SSC 25; WLC
See also AAYA 19; CA 77-80; CANR 34;
CDALB 1917-1929; DLB 4, 9, 102;
DLBD 1; DLBY 81, 87, 96; MTCW

Hempel, Amy 1951-.............. **CLC 39**
See also CA 118; 137

Henderson, F. C.
See Mencken, H(enry) L(ouis)

Henderson, Sylvia
See Ashton-Warner, Sylvia (Constance)

Henley, Beth .... **CLC 23; DC 6**
See also Henley, Elizabeth Becker
See also CABS 3; DLBY 86

Henley, Elizabeth Becker 1952-
See Henley, Beth
See also CA 107; CANR 32; DAM DRAM,
MST; MTCW

Henley, William Ernest
1849-1903 .... **TCLC 8**
See also CA 105; DLB 19

Hennissart, Martha
See Lathen, Emma
See also CA 85-88

Henry, O......... **TCLC 1, 19; SSC 5; WLC**
See also Porter, William Sydney

Henry, Patrick 1736-1799 .... **LC 25**

Henryson, Robert 1430(?)-1506(?).... **LC 20**
See also DLB 146

Henry VIII 1491-1547 .... **LC 10**

Henschke, Alfred
See Klabund

Hentoff, Nat(han Irving) 1925- ..... **CLC 26**
See also AAYA 4; CA 1-4R; CAAS 6;
CANR 5, 25; CLR 1; INT CANR-25;
JRDA; MAICYA; SATA 42, 69;
SATA-Brief 27

Heppenstall, (John) Rayner
1911-1981 .... **CLC 10**
See also CA 1-4R; 103; CANR 29

Heraclitus
c. 540B.C.-c. 450B.C......... **CMLC 22**
See also DLB 176

Herbert, Frank (Patrick)
1920-1986 ...... **CLC 12, 23, 35, 44, 85;**
DAM POP
See also AAYA 21; CA 53-56; 118;
CANR 5, 43; DLB 8; INT CANR-5;
MTCW; SATA 9, 37; SATA-Obit 47

Herbert, George
1593-1633 .... **LC 24; DAB;**
DAM POET; PC 4
See also CDBLB Before 1660; DLB 126

Herbert, Zbigniew
1924- .... **CLC 9, 43; DAM POET**
See also CA 89-92; CANR 36; MTCW

Herbst, Josephine (Frey)
1897-1969 .... **CLC 34**
See also CA 5-8R; 25-28R; DLB 9

Hergesheimer, Joseph
1880-1954 .... **TCLC 11**
See also CA 109; DLB 102, 9

Herlihy, James Leo 1927-1993 ...... **CLC 6**
See also CA 1-4R; 143; CANR 2

Hermogenes fl. c. 175- .... **CMLC 6**

Hernandez, Jose 1834-1886 ...... **NCLC 17**

Herodotus c. 484B.C.-429B.C..... **CMLC 17**
See also DLB 176

Herrick, Robert
1591-1674 ..... **LC 13; DA; DAB; DAC;**
DAM MST, POP; PC 9
See also DLB 126

Herring, Guilles
See Somerville, Edith

Herriot, James
1916-1995 .... **CLC 12; DAM POP**
See also Wight, James Alfred
See also AAYA 1; CA 148; CANR 40;
SATA 86

Herrmann, Dorothy 1941-......... **CLC 44**
See also CA 107

Herrmann, Taffy
See Herrmann, Dorothy

Hersey, John (Richard)
1914-1993 .... **CLC 1, 2, 7, 9, 40, 81, 97;**
DAM POP
See also CA 17-20R; 140; CANR 33;
DLB 6; MTCW; SATA 25;
SATA-Obit 76

Herzen, Aleksandr Ivanovich
1812-1870 .... **NCLC 10, 61**

Herzl, Theodor 1860-1904 .... **TCLC 36**

Herzog, Werner 1942- .... **CLC 16**
See also CA 89-92

Hesiod c. 8th cent. B.C.- .... **CMLC 5**
See also DLB 176

Hesse, Hermann
1877-1962 .... **CLC 1, 2, 3, 6, 11, 17, 25,**
69; DA; DAB; DAC; DAM MST, NOV;
SSC 9; WLC
See also CA 17-18; CAP 2; DLB 66;
MTCW; SATA 50

Hewes, Cady
See De Voto, Bernard (Augustine)

Heyen, William 1940- .... **CLC 13, 18**
See also CA 33-36R; CAAS 9; DLB 5

Heyerdahl, Thor 1914- .... **CLC 26**
See also CA 5-8R; CANR 5, 22; MTCW;
SATA 2, 52

Heym, Georg (Theodor Franz Arthur)
1887-1912 .... **TCLC 9**
See also CA 106

Heym, Stefan 1913- .... **CLC 41**
See also CA 9-12R; CANR 4; DLB 69

Heyse, Paul (Johann Ludwig von)
1830-1914 .... **TCLC 8**
See also CA 104; DLB 129

Heyward, (Edwin) DuBose
1885-1940 .... **TCLC 59**
See also CA 108; 157; DLB 7, 9, 45;
SATA 21

Hibbert, Eleanor Alice Burford
1906-1993 .... **CLC 7; DAM POP**
See also BEST 90:4; CA 17-20R; 140;
CANR 9, 28; SATA 2; SATA-Obit 74

Hichens, Robert S. 1864-1950 ..... **TCLC 64**
See also DLB 153

Higgins, George V(incent)
1939- .... **CLC 4, 7, 10, 18**
See also CA 77-80; CAAS 5; CANR 17, 51;
DLB 2; DLBY 81; INT CANR-17;
MTCW

Higginson, Thomas Wentworth
1823-1911 .... **TCLC 36**
See also DLB 1, 64

Highet, Helen
See MacInnes, Helen (Clark)

Highsmith, (Mary) Patricia
1921-1995 .... **CLC 2, 4, 14, 42;**
DAM NOV, POP
See also CA 1-4R; 147; CANR 1, 20, 48;
MTCW

Highwater, Jamake (Mamake)
1942(?)- .... **CLC 12**
See also AAYA 7; CA 65-68; CAAS 7;
CANR 10, 34; CLR 17; DLB 52;
DLBY 85; JRDA; MAICYA; SATA 32,
69; SATA-Brief 30

Highway, Tomson
1951- ..... **CLC 92; DAC; DAM MULT**
See also CA 151; NNAL

Higuchi, Ichiyo 1872-1896 ...... **NCLC 49**

Hijuelos, Oscar
1951- .... **CLC 65; DAM MULT, POP;**
HLC
See also BEST 90:1; CA 123; CANR 50;
DLB 145; HW

Hikmet, Nazim 1902(?)-1963 ...... **CLC 40**
See also CA 141; 93-96

Hildegard von Bingen
1098-1179 .... **CMLC 20**
See also DLB 148

Hildesheimer, Wolfgang
1916-1991 .... **CLC 49**
See also CA 101; 135; DLB 69, 124

Hill, Geoffrey (William)
1932- ... **CLC 5, 8, 18, 45; DAM POET**
See also CA 81-84; CANR 21;
CDBLB 1960 to Present; DLB 40;
MTCW

Hill, George Roy 1921- .... **CLC 26**
See also CA 110; 122

Hill, John
See Koontz, Dean R(ay)

Hill, Susan (Elizabeth)
1942- .. **CLC 4; DAB; DAM MST, NOV**
See also CA 33-36R; CANR 29; DLB 14,
139; MTCW

Hillerman, Tony
1925- .... **CLC 62; DAM POP**
See also AAYA 6; BEST 89:1; CA 29-32R;
CANR 21, 42; SATA 6

Hillesum, Etty 1914-1943 .... **TCLC 49**
See also CA 137

Hilliard, Noel (Harvey) 1929- ...... **CLC 15**
See also CA 9-12R; CANR 7

Hillis, Rick 1956- .... **CLC 66**
See also CA 134

Hilton, James 1900-1954 .... **TCLC 21**
See also CA 108; DLB 34, 77; SATA 34

Himes, Chester (Bomar)
1909-1984 .... **CLC 2, 4, 7, 18, 58; BLC;**
DAM MULT
See also BW 2; CA 25-28R; 114; CANR 22;
DLB 2, 76, 143; MTCW

Hinde, Thomas .... **CLC 6, 11**
See also Chitty, Thomas Willes

Hindin, Nathan
See Bloch, Robert (Albert)

Hine, (William) Daryl 1936- .... **CLC 15**
See also CA 1-4R; CAAS 15; CANR 1, 20;
DLB 60

Hinkson, Katharine Tynan
See Tynan, Katharine

Hinton, S(usan) E(loise)
1950- .... **CLC 30; DA; DAB; DAC;**
DAM MST, NOV
See also AAYA 2; CA 81-84; CANR 32;
CLR 3, 23; JRDA; MAICYA; MTCW;
SATA 19, 58

Hippius, Zinaida .... **TCLC 9**
See also Gippius, Zinaida (Nikolayevna)

Hiraoka, Kimitake 1925-1970
See Mishima, Yukio
See also CA 97-100; 29-32R; DAM DRAM;
MTCW

Hirsch, E(ric) D(onald), Jr. 1928- ... **CLC 79**
See also CA 25-28R; CANR 27, 51;
DLB 67; INT CANR-27; MTCW

Hirsch, Edward 1950- .... **CLC 31, 50**
See also CA 104; CANR 20, 42; DLB 120

Hitchcock, Alfred (Joseph)
1899-1980 .... **CLC 16**
See also CA 97-100; SATA 27;
SATA-Obit 24

Hitler, Adolf 1889-1945 .... **TCLC 53**
See also CA 117; 147

Hoagland, Edward 1932- .... **CLC 28**
See also CA 1-4R; CANR 2, 31, 57; DLB 6;
SATA 51

Hoban, Russell (Conwell)
1925- .... **CLC 7, 25; DAM NOV**
See also CA 5-8R; CANR 23, 37; CLR 3;
DLB 52; MAICYA; MTCW; SATA 1,
40, 78

Hobbes, Thomas 1588-1679 .... **LC 36**
See also DLB 151

Hobbs, Perry
See Blackmur, R(ichard) P(almer)

Hobson, Laura Z(ametkin)
1900-1986 .... **CLC 7, 25**
See also CA 17-20R; 118; CANR 55;
DLB 28; SATA 52

Hochhuth, Rolf
1931- ..... **CLC 4, 11, 18; DAM DRAM**
See also CA 5-8R; CANR 33; DLB 124;
MTCW

Hochman, Sandra 1936- .... **CLC 3, 8**
See also CA 5-8R; DLB 5

Hochwaelder, Fritz
1911-1986 ...... **CLC 36; DAM DRAM**
See also CA 29-32R; 120; CANR 42;
MTCW

Hochwalder, Fritz
See Hochwaelder, Fritz

Hocking, Mary (Eunice) 1921- ..... **CLC 13**
See also CA 101; CANR 18, 40

Hodgins, Jack 1938- .... **CLC 23**
See also CA 93-96; DLB 60

Hodgson, William Hope
1877(?)-1918 .... **TCLC 13**
See also CA 111; DLB 70, 153, 156, 178

Hoeg, Peter 1957- .... **CLC 95**
See also CA 151

Hoffman, Alice
1952- .... **CLC 51; DAM NOV**
See also CA 77-80; CANR 34; MTCW

Hoffman, Daniel (Gerard)
1923- .... **CLC 6, 13, 23**
See also CA 1-4R; CANR 4; DLB 5

Hoffman, Stanley 1944- .... **CLC 5**
See also CA 77-80

Hoffman, William M(oses) 1939- ... **CLC 40**
See also CA 57-60; CANR 11

Hoffmann, E(rnst) T(heodor) A(madeus)
1776-1822 .... **NCLC 2; SSC 13**
See also DLB 90; SATA 27

Hofmann, Gert 1931-............ **CLC 54**
See also CA 128

Hofmannsthal, Hugo von
1874-1929 .... **TCLC 11; DAM DRAM;
DC 4**
See also CA 106; 153; DLB 81, 118

Hogan, Linda
1947- .... **CLC 73; DAM MULT**
See also CA 120; CANR 45; DLB 175;
NNAL

Hogarth, Charles
See Creasey, John

Hogarth, Emmett
See Polonsky, Abraham (Lincoln)

Hogg, James 1770-1835 .... **NCLC 4**
See also DLB 93, 116, 159

Holbach, Paul Henri Thiry Baron
1723-1789 .... **LC 14**

Holberg, Ludvig 1684-1754 .... **LC 6**

Holden, Ursula 1921-............ **CLC 18**
See also CA 101; CAAS 8; CANR 22

Holderlin, (Johann Christian) Friedrich
1770-1843 .... **NCLC 16; PC 4**

Holdstock, Robert
See Holdstock, Robert P.

Holdstock, Robert P. 1948-........ **CLC 39**
See also CA 131

Holland, Isabelle 1920- .... **CLC 21**
See also AAYA 11; CA 21-24R; CANR 10,
25, 47; JRDA; MAICYA; SATA 8, 70

Holland, Marcus
See Caldwell, (Janet Miriam) Taylor
(Holland)

Hollander, John 1929-...... **CLC 2, 5, 8, 14**
See also CA 1-4R; CANR 1, 52; DLB 5;
SATA 13

Hollander, Paul
See Silverberg, Robert

Holleran, Andrew 1943(?)-........ **CLC 38**
See also CA 144

Hollinghurst, Alan 1954-....... **CLC 55, 91**
See also CA 114

Hollis, Jim
See Summers, Hollis (Spurgeon, Jr.)

Holly, Buddy 1936-1959 .... **TCLC 65**

Holmes, John
See Souster, (Holmes) Raymond

Holmes, John Clellon 1926-1988.... **CLC 56**
See also CA 9-12R; 125; CANR 4; DLB 16

Holmes, Oliver Wendell
1809-1894 .... **NCLC 14**
See also CDALB 1640-1865; DLB 1;
SATA 34

Holmes, Raymond
See Souster, (Holmes) Raymond

Holt, Victoria
See Hibbert, Eleanor Alice Burford

Holub, Miroslav 1923-............ **CLC 4**
See also CA 21-24R; CANR 10

Homer
c. 8th cent. B.C.-..... **CMLC 1, 16; DA;
DAB; DAC; DAM MST, POET**
See also DLB 176; YABC

Honig, Edwin 1919-............. **CLC 33**
See also CA 5-8R; CAAS 8; CANR 4, 45;
DLB 5

Hood, Hugh (John Blagdon)
1928-.................... **CLC 15, 28**
See also CA 49-52; CAAS 17; CANR 1, 33;
DLB 53

Hood, Thomas 1799-1845........ **NCLC 16**
See also DLB 96

Hooker, (Peter) Jeremy 1941-...... **CLC 43**
See also CA 77-80; CANR 22; DLB 40

hooks, bell .... **CLC 94**
See also Watkins, Gloria

Hope, A(lec) D(erwent) 1907- .... **CLC 3, 51**
See also CA 21-24R; CANR 33; MTCW

Hope, Brian
See Creasey, John

Hope, Christopher (David Tully)
1944- .... **CLC 52**
See also CA 106; CANR 47; SATA 62

Hopkins, Gerard Manley
1844-1889 .... **NCLC 17; DA; DAB;
DAC; DAM MST, POET; PC 15; WLC**
See also CDBLB 1890-1914; DLB 35, 57

Hopkins, John (Richard) 1931-...... **CLC 4**
See also CA 85-88

Hopkins, Pauline Elizabeth
1859-1930 .... **TCLC 28; BLC;
DAM MULT**
See also BW 2; CA 141; DLB 50

Hopkinson, Francis 1737-1791 ...... **LC 25**
See also DLB 31

Hopley-Woolrich, Cornell George 1903-1968
See Woolrich, Cornell
See also CA 13-14; CANR 58; CAP 1

Horatio
See Proust, (Valentin-Louis-George-Eugene-)
Marcel

Horgan, Paul (George Vincent O'Shaughnessy)
1903-1995 ...... **CLC 9, 53; DAM NOV**
See also CA 13-16R; 147; CANR 9, 35;
DLB 102; DLBY 85; INT CANR-9;
MTCW; SATA 13; SATA-Obit 84

Horn, Peter
See Kuttner, Henry

Hornem, Horace Esq.
See Byron, George Gordon (Noel)

**Horney, Karen (Clementine Theodore
Danielsen)** 1885-1952....... **TCLC 71**
See also CA 114

Hornung, E(rnest) W(illiam)
1866-1921 .... **TCLC 59**
See also CA 108; DLB 70

Horovitz, Israel (Arthur)
1939- .... **CLC 56; DAM DRAM**
See also CA 33-36R; CANR 46; DLB 7

Horvath, Odon von
See Horvath, Oedoen von
See also DLB 85, 124

Horvath, Oedoen von 1901-1938... **TCLC 45**
See also Horvath, Odon von
See also CA 118

Horwitz, Julius 1920-1986........ **CLC 14**
See also CA 9-12R; 119; CANR 12

Hospital, Janette Turner 1942-..... **CLC 42**
See also CA 108; CANR 48

Hostos, E. M. de
See Hostos (y Bonilla), Eugenio Maria de

Hostos, Eugenio M. de
See Hostos (y Bonilla), Eugenio Maria de

Hostos, Eugenio Maria
See Hostos (y Bonilla), Eugenio Maria de

Hostos (y Bonilla), Eugenio Maria de
1839-1903 .... **TCLC 24**
See also CA 123; 131; HW

Houdini
See Lovecraft, H(oward) P(hillips)

Hougan, Carolyn 1943- .... **CLC 34**
See also CA 139

Household, Geoffrey (Edward West)
1900-1988 .... **CLC 11**
See also CA 77-80; 126; CANR 58;
DLB 87; SATA 14; SATA-Obit 59

Housman, A(lfred) E(dward)
1859-1936 ...... **TCLC 1, 10; DA; DAB;
DAC; DAM MST, POET; PC 2**
See also CA 104; 125; DLB 19; MTCW;
YABC

Housman, Laurence 1865-1959 ..... **TCLC 7**
See also CA 106; 155; DLB 10; SATA 25

Howard, Elizabeth Jane 1923- ... **CLC 7, 29**
See also CA 5-8R; CANR 8

Howard, Maureen 1930- ..... **CLC 5, 14, 46**
See also CA 53-56; CANR 31; DLBY 83;
INT CANR-31; MTCW

Howard, Richard 1929- ...... **CLC 7, 10, 47**
See also AITN 1; CA 85-88; CANR 25;
DLB 5; INT CANR-25

Howard, Robert E(rvin)
1906-1936 .... **TCLC 8**
See also CA 105; 157

Howard, Warren F.
See Pohl, Frederik

Howe, Fanny 1940- .... **CLC 47**
See also CA 117; CAAS 27; SATA-Brief 52

Howe, Irving 1920-1993.......... **CLC 85**
See also CA 9-12R; 141; CANR 21, 50;
DLB 67; MTCW

Howe, Julia Ward 1819-1910 ..... **TCLC 21**
See also CA 117; DLB 1

Howe, Susan 1937-............... **CLC 72**
See also DLB 120

Howe, Tina 1937-................ **CLC 48**
See also CA 109

Howell, James 1594(?)-1666 .... **LC 13**
See also DLB 151

Howells, W. D.
See Howells, William Dean

Howells, William D.
See Howells, William Dean

Howells, William Dean
1837-1920 .... **TCLC 7, 17, 41**
See also CA 104; 134; CDALB 1865-1917;
DLB 12, 64, 74, 79

Howes, Barbara 1914-1996 .... **CLC 15**
See also CA 9-12R; 151; CAAS 3;
CANR 53; SATA 5

Hrabal, Bohumil 1914-1997..... **CLC 13, 67**
See also CA 106; 156; CAAS 12; CANR 57

Hsun, Lu
See Lu Hsun

Hubbard, L(afayette) Ron(ald)
1911-1986 .... **CLC 43; DAM POP**
See also CA 77-80; 118; CANR 52

Huch, Ricarda (Octavia)
1864-1947 .... **TCLC 13**
See also CA 111; DLB 66

Huddle, David 1942- .... **CLC 49**
See also CA 57-60; CAAS 20; DLB 130

Hudson, Jeffrey
See Crichton, (John) Michael

Hudson, W(illiam) H(enry)
1841-1922 .... **TCLC 29**
See also CA 115; DLB 98, 153, 174;
SATA 35

Hueffer, Ford Madox
See Ford, Ford Madox

Hughart, Barry 1934-............. **CLC 39**
See also CA 137

Hughes, Colin
See Creasey, John

Hughes, David (John) 1930- .... **CLC 48**
See also CA 116; 129; DLB 14

Hughes, Edward James
See Hughes, Ted
See also DAM MST, POET

Hughes, (James) Langston
1902-1967 ..... **CLC 1, 5, 10, 15, 35, 44;**
BLC; DA; DAB; DAC; DAM DRAM,
MST, MULT, POET; DC 3; PC 1;
SSC 6; WLC
See also AAYA 12; BW 1; CA 1-4R;
25-28R; CANR 1, 34; CDALB 1929-1941;
CLR 17; DLB 4, 7, 48, 51, 86; JRDA;
MAICYA; MTCW; SATA 4, 33

Hughes, Richard (Arthur Warren)
1900-1976 ...... **CLC 1, 11; DAM NOV**
See also CA 5-8R; 65-68; CANR 4;
DLB 15, 161; MTCW; SATA 8;
SATA-Obit 25

Hughes, Ted
1930- .... **CLC 2, 4, 9, 14, 37; DAB;**
DAC; PC 7
See also Hughes, Edward James
See also CA 1-4R; CANR 1, 33; CLR 3;
DLB 40, 161; MAICYA; MTCW;
SATA 49; SATA-Brief 27

Hugo, Richard F(ranklin)
1923-1982 .... **CLC 6, 18, 32;**
DAM POET
See also CA 49-52; 108; CANR 3; DLB 5

Hugo, Victor (Marie)
1802-1885 .... **NCLC 3, 10, 21; DA;**
DAB; DAC; DAM DRAM, MST, NOV,
POET; PC 17; WLC
See also DLB 119; SATA 47

Huidobro, Vicente
See Huidobro Fernandez, Vicente Garcia

Huidobro Fernandez, Vicente Garcia
1893-1948 .... **TCLC 31**
See also CA 131; HW

Hulme, Keri 1947-............... **CLC 39**
See also CA 125; INT 125

Hulme, T(homas) E(rnest)
1883-1917 .... **TCLC 21**
See also CA 117; DLB 19

Hume, David 1711-1776............. **LC 7**
See also DLB 104

Humphrey, William 1924-......... **CLC 45**
See also CA 77-80; DLB 6

Humphreys, Emyr Owen 1919-..... **CLC 47**
See also CA 5-8R; CANR 3, 24; DLB 15

Humphreys, Josephine 1945-.... **CLC 34, 57**
See also CA 121; 127; INT 127

Huneker, James Gibbons
1857-1921 .... **TCLC 65**
See also DLB 71

Hungerford, Pixie
See Brinsmead, H(esba) F(ay)

Hunt, E(verette) Howard, (Jr.)
1918-....................... **CLC 3**
See also AITN 1; CA 45-48; CANR 2, 47

Hunt, Kyle
See Creasey, John

Hunt, (James Henry) Leigh
1784-1859 ...... **NCLC 1; DAM POET**

Hunt, Marsha 1946-............. **CLC 70**
See also BW 2; CA 143

Hunt, Violet 1866-1942 .... **TCLC 53**
See also DLB 162

Hunter, E. Waldo
See Sturgeon, Theodore (Hamilton)

Hunter, Evan
1926- .... **CLC 11, 31; DAM POP**
See also CA 5-8R; CANR 5, 38; DLBY 82;
INT CANR-5; MTCW; SATA 25

Hunter, Kristin (Eggleston) 1931-... **CLC 35**
See also AITN 1; BW 1; CA 13-16R;
CANR 13; CLR 3; DLB 33;
INT CANR-13; MAICYA; SAAS 10;
SATA 12

Hunter, Mollie 1922-............. **CLC 21**
See also McIlwraith, Maureen Mollie
Hunter
See also AAYA 13; CANR 37; CLR 25;
DLB 161; JRDA; MAICYA; SAAS 7;
SATA 54

Hunter, Robert (?)-1734............. **LC 7**

Hurston, Zora Neale
1903-1960 .... **CLC 7, 30, 61; BLC; DA;**
DAC; DAM MST, MULT, NOV; SSC 4
See also AAYA 15; BW 1; CA 85-88;
DLB 51, 86; MTCW; YABC

Huston, John (Marcellus)
1906-1987 .... **CLC 20**
See also CA 73-76; 123; CANR 34; DLB 26

Hustvedt, Siri 1955-............. **CLC 76**
See also CA 137

Hutten, Ulrich von 1488-1523....... **LC 16**
See also DLB 179

Huxley, Aldous (Leonard)
1894-1963 ..... **CLC 1, 3, 4, 5, 8, 11, 18,**
35, 79; DA; DAB; DAC; DAM MST,
NOV; WLC
See also AAYA 11; CA 85-88; CANR 44;
CDBLB 1914-1945; DLB 36, 100, 162;
MTCW; SATA 63

Huysmans, Charles Marie Georges
1848-1907
See Huysmans, Joris-Karl
See also CA 104

Huysmans, Joris-Karl.......... **TCLC 7, 69**
See also Huysmans, Charles Marie Georges
See also DLB 123

Hwang, David Henry
1957- .... **CLC 55; DAM DRAM; DC 4**
See also CA 127; 132; INT 132

Hyde, Anthony 1946-............. **CLC 42**
See also CA 136

Hyde, Margaret O(ldroyd) 1917- ... **CLC 21**
See also CA 1-4R; CANR 1, 36; CLR 23;
JRDA; MAICYA; SAAS 8; SATA 1, 42,
76

Hynes, James 1956(?)-............ **CLC 65**

Ian, Janis 1951- .... **CLC 21**
See also CA 105

Ibanez, Vicente Blasco
See Blasco Ibanez, Vicente

Ibarguengoitia, Jorge 1928-1983.... **CLC 37**
See also CA 124; 113; HW

Ibsen, Henrik (Johan)
1828-1906 ...... **TCLC 2, 8, 16, 37, 52;**
DA; DAB; DAC; DAM DRAM, MST;
DC 2; WLC
See also CA 104; 141

Ibuse Masuji 1898-1993.......... **CLC 22**
See also CA 127; 141; DLB 180

Ichikawa, Kon 1915-............. **CLC 20**
See also CA 121

Idle, Eric 1943-.................. **CLC 21**
See also Monty Python
See also CA 116; CANR 35

Ignatow, David 1914-...... **CLC 4, 7, 14, 40**
See also CA 9-12R; CAAS 3; CANR 31, 57;
DLB 5

Ihimaera, Witi 1944- .... **CLC 46**
See also CA 77-80

Ilf, Ilya...................... **TCLC 21**
See also Fainzilberg, Ilya Arnoldovich

Illyes, Gyula 1902-1983............. **PC 16**
See also CA 114; 109

Immermann, Karl (Lebrecht)
1796-1840 .... **NCLC 4, 49**
See also DLB 133

Inchbald, Elizabeth 1753-1821 ... **NCLC 62**
See also DLB 39, 89

Inclan, Ramon (Maria) del Valle
See Valle-Inclan, Ramon (Maria) del

Infante, G(uillermo) Cabrera
See Cabrera Infante, G(uillermo)

Ingalls, Rachel (Holmes) 1940-..... **CLC 42**
See also CA 123; 127

Ingamells, Rex 1913-1955 .... **TCLC 35**

Inge, William (Motter)
1913-1973 .. **CLC 1, 8, 19; DAM DRAM**
See also CA 9-12R; CDALB 1941-1968;
DLB 7; MTCW

Ingelow, Jean 1820-1897 .... **NCLC 39**
See also DLB 35, 163; SATA 33

Ingram, Willis J.
See Harris, Mark

Innaurato, Albert (F.) 1948(?)- . . **CLC 21, 60**
See also CA 115; 122; INT 122

Innes, Michael
See Stewart, J(ohn) I(nnes) M(ackintosh)

Ionesco, Eugene
1909-1994 . . . . **CLC 1, 4, 6, 9, 11, 15, 41, 86; DA; DAB; DAC; DAM DRAM, MST; WLC**
See also CA 9-12R; 144; CANR 55; MTCW; SATA 7; SATA-Obit 79

Iqbal, Muhammad 1873-1938 . . . . . **TCLC 28**

Ireland, Patrick
See O'Doherty, Brian

Iron, Ralph
See Schreiner, Olive (Emilie Albertina)

Irving, John (Winslow)
1942- . . . . . **CLC 13, 23, 38; DAM NOV, POP**
See also AAYA 8; BEST 89:3; CA 25-28R; CANR 28; DLB 6; DLBY 82; MTCW

Irving, Washington
1783-1859 . . . . . **NCLC 2, 19; DA; DAB; DAM MST; SSC 2; WLC**
See also CDALB 1640-1865; DLB 3, 11, 30, 59, 73, 74; 2

Irwin, P. K.
See Page, P(atricia) K(athleen)

Isaacs, Susan 1943- . . . **CLC 32; DAM POP**
See also BEST 89:1; CA 89-92; CANR 20, 41; INT CANR-20; MTCW

Isherwood, Christopher (William Bradshaw)
1904-1986 . . . . **CLC 1, 9, 11, 14, 44; DAM DRAM, NOV**
See also CA 13-16R; 117; CANR 35; DLB 15; DLBY 86; MTCW

Ishiguro, Kazuo
1954- . . . . . . **CLC 27, 56, 59; DAM NOV**
See also BEST 90:2; CA 120; CANR 49; MTCW

Ishikawa, Hakuhin
See Ishikawa, Takuboku

Ishikawa, Takuboku
1886(?)-1912 . . . . **TCLC 15; DAM POET; PC 10**
See also CA 113; 153

Iskander, Fazil 1929- . . . . **CLC 47**
See also CA 102

Isler, Alan (David) 1934- . . . . **CLC 91**
See also CA 156

Ivan IV 1530-1584 . . . . **LC 17**

Ivanov, Vyacheslav Ivanovich
1866-1949 . . . . **TCLC 33**
See also CA 122

Ivask, Ivar Vidrik 1927-1992 . . . . . . **CLC 14**
See also CA 37-40R; 139; CANR 24

Ives, Morgan
See Bradley, Marion Zimmer

J. R. S.
See Gogarty, Oliver St. John

Jabran, Kahlil
See Gibran, Kahlil

Jabran, Khalil
See Gibran, Kahlil

Jackson, Daniel
See Wingrove, David (John)

Jackson, Jesse 1908-1983 . . . . **CLC 12**
See also BW 1; CA 25-28R; 109; CANR 27; CLR 28; MAICYA; SATA 2, 29; SATA-Obit 48

Jackson, Laura (Riding) 1901-1991
See Riding, Laura
See also CA 65-68; 135; CANR 28; DLB 48

Jackson, Sam
See Trumbo, Dalton

Jackson, Sara
See Wingrove, David (John)

Jackson, Shirley
1919-1965 . . . . **CLC 11, 60, 87; DA; DAC; DAM MST; SSC 9; WLC**
See also AAYA 9; CA 1-4R; 25-28R; CANR 4, 52; CDALB 1941-1968; DLB 6; SATA 2

Jacob, (Cyprien-)Max 1876-1944 . . . **TCLC 6**
See also CA 104

Jacobs, Jim 1942- . . . . **CLC 12**
See also CA 97-100; INT 97-100

Jacobs, W(illiam) W(ymark)
1863-1943 . . . . **TCLC 22**
See also CA 121; DLB 135

Jacobsen, Jens Peter 1847-1885 . . **NCLC 34**

Jacobsen, Josephine 1908- . . . . **CLC 48**
See also CA 33-36R; CAAS 18; CANR 23, 48

Jacobson, Dan 1929- . . . . **CLC 4, 14**
See also CA 1-4R; CANR 2, 25; DLB 14; MTCW

Jacqueline
See Carpentier (y Valmont), Alejo

Jagger, Mick 1944- . . . . **CLC 17**

Jakes, John (William)
1932- . . . . **CLC 29; DAM NOV, POP**
See also BEST 89:4; CA 57-60; CANR 10, 43; DLBY 83; INT CANR-10; MTCW; SATA 62

James, Andrew
See Kirkup, James

James, C(yril) L(ionel) R(obert)
1901-1989 . . . . **CLC 33**
See also BW 2; CA 117; 125; 128; DLB 125; MTCW

James, Daniel (Lewis) 1911-1988
See Santiago, Danny
See also CA 125

James, Dynely
See Mayne, William (James Carter)

James, Henry Sr. 1811-1882 . . . . . **NCLC 53**

James, Henry
1843-1916 . . . . . . **TCLC 2, 11, 24, 40, 47, 64; DA; DAB; DAC; DAM MST, NOV; SSC 8; WLC**
See also CA 104; 132; CDALB 1865-1917; DLB 12, 71, 74; DLBD 13; MTCW

James, M. R.
See James, Montague (Rhodes)
See also DLB 156

James, Montague (Rhodes)
1862-1936 . . . . **TCLC 6; SSC 16**
See also CA 104

James, P. D. . . . . **CLC 18, 46**
See also White, Phyllis Dorothy James
See also BEST 90:2; CDBLB 1960 to Present; DLB 87

James, Philip
See Moorcock, Michael (John)

James, William 1842-1910 . . . . . **TCLC 15, 32**
See also CA 109

James I 1394-1437 . . . . **LC 20**

Jameson, Anna 1794-1860 . . . . **NCLC 43**
See also DLB 99, 166

Jami, Nur al-Din 'Abd al-Rahman
1414-1492 . . . . **LC 9**

Jandl, Ernst 1925- . . . . **CLC 34**

Janowitz, Tama
1957- . . . . **CLC 43; DAM POP**
See also CA 106; CANR 52

Japrisot, Sebastien 1931- . . . . **CLC 90**

Jarrell, Randall
1914-1965 . . . . **CLC 1, 2, 6, 9, 13, 49; DAM POET**
See also CA 5-8R; 25-28R; CABS 2; CANR 6, 34; CDALB 1941-1968; CLR 6; DLB 48, 52; MAICYA; MTCW; SATA 7

Jarry, Alfred
1873-1907 . . . . **TCLC 2, 14; DAM DRAM; SSC 20**
See also CA 104; 153

Jarvis, E. K.
See Bloch, Robert (Albert); Ellison, Harlan (Jay); Silverberg, Robert

Jeake, Samuel, Jr.
See Aiken, Conrad (Potter)

Jean Paul 1763-1825 . . . . **NCLC 7**

Jefferies, (John) Richard
1848-1887 . . . . **NCLC 47**
See also DLB 98, 141; SATA 16

Jeffers, (John) Robinson
1887-1962 . . . . **CLC 2, 3, 11, 15, 54; DA; DAC; DAM MST, POET; PC 17; WLC**
See also CA 85-88; CANR 35; CDALB 1917-1929; DLB 45; MTCW

Jefferson, Janet
See Mencken, H(enry) L(ouis)

Jefferson, Thomas 1743-1826 . . . . **NCLC 11**
See also CDALB 1640-1865; DLB 31

Jeffrey, Francis 1773-1850 . . . . **NCLC 33**
See also DLB 107

Jelakowitch, Ivan
See Heijermans, Herman

Jellicoe, (Patricia) Ann 1927- . . . . . . **CLC 27**
See also CA 85-88; DLB 13

Jen, Gish . . . . **CLC 70**
See also Jen, Lillian

Jen, Lillian 1956(?)-
See Jen, Gish
See also CA 135

Jenkins, (John) Robin 1912- . . . . **CLC 52**
See also CA 1-4R; CANR 1; DLB 14

Jennings, Elizabeth (Joan)
1926- . . . . **CLC 5, 14**
See also CA 61-64; CAAS 5; CANR 8, 39; DLB 27; MTCW; SATA 66

Jennings, Waylon 1937- . . . . **CLC 21**

Jensen, Johannes V. 1873-1950.... **TCLC 41**

Jensen, Laura (Linnea) 1948- ...... **CLC 37**
See also CA 103

Jerome, Jerome K(lapka)
1859-1927 ..../.... **TCLC 23**
See also CA 119; DLB 10, 34, 135

Jerrold, Douglas William
1803-1857 .... **NCLC 2**
See also DLB 158, 159

Jewett, (Theodora) Sarah Orne
1849-1909 .... **TCLC 1, 22; SSC 6**
See also CA 108; 127; DLB 12, 74;
SATA 15

Jewsbury, Geraldine (Endsor)
1812-1880 .... **NCLC 22**
See also DLB 21

Jhabvala, Ruth Prawer
1927- .... **CLC 4, 8, 29, 94; DAB;
DAM NOV**
See also CA 1-4R; CANR 2, 29, 51;
DLB 139; INT CANR-29; MTCW

Jibran, Kahlil
See Gibran, Kahlil

Jibran, Khalil
See Gibran, Kahlil

Jiles, Paulette 1943-.......... **CLC 13, 58**
See also CA 101

Jimenez (Mantecon), Juan Ramon
1881-1958 ..... **TCLC 4; DAM MULT,
POET; HLC; PC 7**
See also CA 104; 131; DLB 134; HW;
MTCW

Jimenez, Ramon
See Jimenez (Mantecon), Juan Ramon

Jimenez Mantecon, Juan
See Jimenez (Mantecon), Juan Ramon

Joel, Billy .... **CLC 26**
See also Joel, William Martin

Joel, William Martin 1949-
See Joel, Billy
See also CA 108

John of the Cross, St. 1542-1591 .... **LC 18**

Johnson, B(ryan) S(tanley William)
1933-1973 .... **CLC 6, 9**
See also CA 9-12R; 53-56; CANR 9;
DLB 14, 40

Johnson, Benj. F. of Boo
See Riley, James Whitcomb

Johnson, Benjamin F. of Boo
See Riley, James Whitcomb

Johnson, Charles (Richard)
1948- .... **CLC 7, 51, 65; BLC;
DAM MULT**
See also BW 2; CA 116; CAAS 18;
CANR 42; DLB 33

Johnson, Denis 1949-............ **CLC 52**
See also CA 117; 121; DLB 120

Johnson, Diane 1934-........ **CLC 5, 13, 48**
See also CA 41-44R; CANR 17, 40;
DLBY 80; INT CANR-17; MTCW

Johnson, Eyvind (Olof Verner)
1900-1976 .... **CLC 14**
See also CA 73-76; 69-72; CANR 34

Johnson, J. R.
See James, C(yril) L(ionel) R(obert)

Johnson, James Weldon
1871-1938 .... **TCLC 3, 19; BLC;
DAM MULT, POET**
See also BW 1; CA 104; 125;
CDALB 1917-1929; CLR 32; DLB 51;
MTCW; SATA 31

Johnson, Joyce 1935-............ **CLC 58**
See also CA 125; 129

Johnson, Lionel (Pigot)
1867-1902 .... **TCLC 19**
See also CA 117; DLB 19

Johnson, Mel
See Malzberg, Barry N(athaniel)

Johnson, Pamela Hansford
1912-1981 .... **CLC 1, 7, 27**
See also CA 1-4R; 104; CANR 2, 28;
DLB 15; MTCW

Johnson, Robert 1911(?)-1938..... **TCLC 69**

Johnson, Samuel
1709-1784 ..... **LC 15; DA; DAB; DAC;
DAM MST; WLC**
See also CDBLB 1660-1789; DLB 39, 95,
104, 142

Johnson, Uwe
1934-1984 .... **CLC 5, 10, 15, 40**
See also CA 1-4R; 112; CANR 1, 39;
DLB 75; MTCW

Johnston, George (Benson) 1913- ... **CLC 51**
See also CA 1-4R; CANR 5, 20; DLB 88

Johnston, Jennifer 1930-.......... **CLC 7**
See also CA 85-88; DLB 14

Jolley, (Monica) Elizabeth
1923- .... **CLC 46; SSC 19**
See also CA 127; CAAS 13

Jones, Arthur Llewellyn 1863-1947
See Machen, Arthur
See also CA 104

Jones, D(ouglas) G(ordon) 1929-.... **CLC 10**
See also CA 29-32R; CANR 13; DLB 53

Jones, David (Michael)
1895-1974 .... **CLC 2, 4, 7, 13, 42**
See also CA 9-12R; 53-56; CANR 28;
CDBLB 1945-1960; DLB 20, 100; MTCW

Jones, David Robert 1947-
See Bowie, David
See also CA 103

Jones, Diana Wynne 1934- .... **CLC 26**
See also AAYA 12; CA 49-52; CANR 4,
26, 56; CLR 23; DLB 161; JRDA;
MAICYA; SAAS 7; SATA 9, 70

Jones, Edward P. 1950-.......... **CLC 76**
See also BW 2; CA 142

Jones, Gayl
1949- .... **CLC 6, 9; BLC; DAM MULT**
See also BW 2; CA 77-80; CANR 27;
DLB 33; MTCW

Jones, James 1921-1977.... **CLC 1, 3, 10, 39**
See also AITN 1, 2; CA 1-4R; 69-72;
CANR 6; DLB 2, 143; MTCW

Jones, John J.
See Lovecraft, H(oward) P(hillips)

Jones, LeRoi .... **CLC 1, 2, 3, 5, 10, 14**
See also Baraka, Amiri

Jones, Louis B. .... **CLC 65**
See also CA 141

Jones, Madison (Percy, Jr.) 1925- ... **CLC 4**
See also CA 13-16R; CAAS 11; CANR 7,
54; DLB 152

Jones, Mervyn 1922-.......... **CLC 10, 52**
See also CA 45-48; CAAS 5; CANR 1;
MTCW

Jones, Mick 1956(?)- .... **CLC 30**

Jones, Nettie (Pearl) 1941-........ **CLC 34**
See also BW 2; CA 137; CAAS 20

Jones, Preston 1936-1979 .... **CLC 10**
See also CA 73-76; 89-92; DLB 7

Jones, Robert F(rancis) 1934-....... **CLC 7**
See also CA 49-52; CANR 2

Jones, Rod 1953- .... **CLC 50**
See also CA 128

Jones, Terence Graham Parry
1942- .... **CLC 21**
See also Jones, Terry; Monty Python
See also CA 112; 116; CANR 35; INT 116

Jones, Terry
See Jones, Terence Graham Parry
See also SATA 67; SATA-Brief 51

Jones, Thom 1945(?)-............. **CLC 81**
See also CA 157

Jong, Erica
1942- .... **CLC 4, 6, 8, 18, 83;
DAM NOV, POP**
See also AITN 1; BEST 90:2; CA 73-76;
CANR 26, 52; DLB 2, 5, 28, 152;
INT CANR-26; MTCW

Jonson, Ben(jamin)
1572(?)-1637 ...... **LC 6, 33; DA; DAB;
DAC; DAM DRAM, MST, POET;
DC 4; PC 17; WLC**
See also CDBLB Before 1660; DLB 62, 121

Jordan, June
1936- ..... **CLC 5, 11, 23; DAM MULT,
POET**
See also AAYA 2; BW 2; CA 33-36R;
CANR 25; CLR 10; DLB 38; MAICYA;
MTCW; SATA 4

Jordan, Pat(rick M.) 1941-........ **CLC 37**
See also CA 33-36R

Jorgensen, Ivar
See Ellison, Harlan (Jay)

Jorgenson, Ivar
See Silverberg, Robert

Josephus, Flavius c. 37-100...... **CMLC 13**

Josipovici, Gabriel 1940-........ **CLC 6, 43**
See also CA 37-40R; CAAS 8; CANR 47;
DLB 14

Joubert, Joseph 1754-1824 .... **NCLC 9**

Jouve, Pierre Jean 1887-1976...... **CLC 47**
See also CA 65-68

Joyce, James (Augustine Aloysius)
1882-1941 .... **TCLC 3, 8, 16, 35, 52;
DA; DAB; DAC; DAM MST, NOV,
POET; SSC 26; WLC**
See also CA 104; 126; CDBLB 1914-1945;
DLB 10, 19, 36, 162; MTCW

Jozsef, Attila 1905-1937......... **TCLC 22**
See also CA 116

Juana Ines de la Cruz 1651(?)-1695 ... **LC 5**

Judd, Cyril
See Kornbluth, C(yril) M.; Pohl, Frederik

Julian of Norwich 1342(?)-1416(?) .... **LC 6**
See also DLB 146

Juniper, Alex
See Hospital, Janette Turner

Junius
See Luxemburg, Rosa

Just, Ward (Swift) 1935- .... **CLC 4, 27**
See also CA 25-28R; CANR 32;
INT CANR-32

Justice, Donald (Rodney)
1925- .... **CLC 6, 19; DAM POET**
See also CA 5-8R; CANR 26, 54;
DLBY 83; INT CANR-26

Juvenal c. 55-c. 127 .... **CMLC 8**

Juvenis
See Bourne, Randolph S(illiman)

Kacew, Romain 1914-1980
See Gary, Romain
See also CA 108; 102

Kadare, Ismail 1936- .... **CLC 52**

Kadohata, Cynthia .... **CLC 59**
See also CA 140

Kafka, Franz
1883-1924 .... **TCLC 2, 6, 13, 29, 47, 53;**
DA; DAB; DAC; DAM MST, NOV;
SSC 5; WLC
See also CA 105; 126; DLB 81; MTCW

Kahanovitsch, Pinkhes
See Der Nister

Kahn, Roger 1927- .... **CLC 30**
See also CA 25-28R; CANR 44; DLB 171;
SATA 37

Kain, Saul
See Sassoon, Siegfried (Lorraine)

Kaiser, Georg 1878-1945 .... **TCLC 9**
See also CA 106; DLB 124

Kaletski, Alexander 1946- .... **CLC 39**
See also CA 118; 143

Kalidasa fl. c. 400- .... **CMLC 9**

Kallman, Chester (Simon)
1921-1975 .... **CLC 2**
See also CA 45-48; 53-56; CANR 3

Kaminsky, Melvin 1926-
See Brooks, Mel
See also CA 65-68; CANR 16

Kaminsky, Stuart M(elvin) 1934- ... **CLC 59**
See also CA 73-76; CANR 29, 53

Kane, Francis
See Robbins, Harold

Kane, Paul
See Simon, Paul (Frederick)

Kane, Wilson
See Bloch, Robert (Albert)

Kanin, Garson 1912- .... **CLC 22**
See also AITN 1; CA 5-8R; CANR 7;
DLB 7

Kaniuk, Yoram 1930- .... **CLC 19**
See also CA 134

Kant, Immanuel 1724-1804 ...... **NCLC 27**
See also DLB 94

Kantor, MacKinlay 1904-1977 ...... **CLC 7**
See also CA 61-64; 73-76; DLB 9, 102

Kaplan, David Michael 1946- ...... **CLC 50**

Kaplan, James 1951- .... **CLC 59**
See also CA 135

Karageorge, Michael
See Anderson, Poul (William)

Karamzin, Nikolai Mikhailovich
1766-1826 .... **NCLC 3**
See also DLB 150

Karapanou, Margarita 1946- ...... **CLC 13**
See also CA 101

Karinthy, Frigyes 1887-1938 ..... **TCLC 47**

Karl, Frederick R(obert) 1927- ..... **CLC 34**
See also CA 5-8R; CANR 3, 44

Kastel, Warren
See Silverberg, Robert

Kataev, Evgeny Petrovich 1903-1942
See Petrov, Evgeny
See also CA 120

Kataphusin
See Ruskin, John

Katz, Steve 1935- .... **CLC 47**
See also CA 25-28R; CAAS 14; CANR 12;
DLBY 83

Kauffman, Janet 1945- .... **CLC 42**
See also CA 117; CANR 43; DLBY 86

Kaufman, Bob (Garnell)
1925-1986 .... **CLC 49**
See also BW 1; CA 41-44R; 118; CANR 22;
DLB 16, 41

Kaufman, George S.
1889-1961 ...... **CLC 38; DAM DRAM**
See also CA 108; 93-96; DLB 7; INT 108

Kaufman, Sue .... **CLC 3, 8**
See also Barondess, Sue K(aufman)

Kavafis, Konstantinos Petrou 1863-1933
See Cavafy, C(onstantine) P(eter)
See also CA 104

Kavan, Anna 1901-1968 ...... **CLC 5, 13, 82**
See also CA 5-8R; CANR 6, 57; MTCW

Kavanagh, Dan
See Barnes, Julian (Patrick)

Kavanagh, Patrick (Joseph)
1904-1967 .... **CLC 22**
See also CA 123; 25-28R; DLB 15, 20;
MTCW

Kawabata, Yasunari
1899-1972 .... **CLC 2, 5, 9, 18;**
DAM MULT; SSC 17
See also CA 93-96; 33-36R; DLB 180

Kaye, M(ary) M(argaret) 1909- ..... **CLC 28**
See also CA 89-92; CANR 24; MTCW;
SATA 62

Kaye, Mollie
See Kaye, M(ary) M(argaret)

Kaye-Smith, Sheila 1887-1956 ..... **TCLC 20**
See also CA 118; DLB 36

Kaymor, Patrice Maguilene
See Senghor, Leopold Sedar

Kazan, Elia 1909- .... **CLC 6, 16, 63**
See also CA 21-24R; CANR 32

Kazantzakis, Nikos
1883(?)-1957 .... **TCLC 2, 5, 33**
See also CA 105; 132; MTCW

Kazin, Alfred 1915- .... **CLC 34, 38**
See also CA 1-4R; CAAS 7; CANR 1, 45;
DLB 67

Keane, Mary Nesta (Skrine) 1904-1996
See Keane, Molly
See also CA 108; 114; 151

Keane, Molly .... **CLC 31**
See also Keane, Mary Nesta (Skrine)
See also INT 114

Keates, Jonathan 19(?)- .... **CLC 34**

Keaton, Buster 1895-1966 .... **CLC 20**

Keats, John
1795-1821 .... **NCLC 8; DA; DAB;**
DAC; DAM MST, POET; PC 1; WLC
See also CDBLB 1789-1832; DLB 96, 110

Keene, Donald 1922- .... **CLC 34**
See also CA 1-4R; CANR 5

Keillor, Garrison .... **CLC 40**
See also Keillor, Gary (Edward)
See also AAYA 2; BEST 89:3; DLBY 87;
SATA 58

Keillor, Gary (Edward) 1942-
See Keillor, Garrison
See also CA 111; 117; CANR 36;
DAM POP; MTCW

Keith, Michael
See Hubbard, L(afayette) Ron(ald)

Keller, Gottfried
1819-1890 .... **NCLC 2; SSC 26**
See also DLB 129

Kellerman, Jonathan
1949- .... **CLC 44; DAM POP**
See also BEST 90:1; CA 106; CANR 29, 51;
INT CANR-29

Kelley, William Melvin 1937- ...... **CLC 22**
See also BW 1; CA 77-80; CANR 27;
DLB 33

Kellogg, Marjorie 1922- .... **CLC 2**
See also CA 81-84

Kellow, Kathleen
See Hibbert, Eleanor Alice Burford

Kelly, M(ilton) T(erry) 1947- .... **CLC 55**
See also CA 97-100; CAAS 22; CANR 19,
43

Kelman, James 1946- .... **CLC 58, 86**
See also CA 148

Kemal, Yashar 1923- .... **CLC 14, 29**
See also CA 89-92; CANR 44

Kemble, Fanny 1809-1893 .... **NCLC 18**
See also DLB 32

Kemelman, Harry 1908-1996 .... **CLC 2**
See also AITN 1; CA 9-12R; 155; CANR 6;
DLB 28

Kempe, Margery 1373(?)-1440(?) ..... **LC 6**
See also DLB 146

Kempis, Thomas a 1380-1471 .... **LC 11**

Kendall, Henry 1839-1882 .... **NCLC 12**

Keneally, Thomas (Michael)
1935- ...... **CLC 5, 8, 10, 14, 19, 27, 43;**
DAM NOV
See also CA 85-88; CANR 10, 50; MTCW

Kennedy, Adrienne (Lita)
1931- ..... **CLC 66; BLC; DAM MULT;**
DC 5
See also BW 2; CA 103; CAAS 20; CABS 3;
CANR 26, 53; DLB 38

Kennedy, John Pendleton
1795-1870 .... **NCLC 2**
See also DLB 3

Kennedy, Joseph Charles 1929-
See Kennedy, X. J.
See also CA 1-4R; CANR 4, 30, 40;
SATA 14, 86

Kennedy, William
1928- ... **CLC 6, 28, 34, 53; DAM NOV**
See also AAYA 1; CA 85-88; CANR 14,
31; DLB 143; DLBY 85; INT CANR-31;
MTCW; SATA 57

Kennedy, X. J. .... **CLC 8, 42**
See Kennedy, Joseph Charles
See also CAAS 9; CLR 27; DLB 5;
SAAS 22

Kenny, Maurice (Francis)
1929- .... **CLC 87; DAM MULT**
See also CA 144; CAAS 22; DLB 175;
NNAL

Kent, Kelvin
See Kuttner, Henry

Kenton, Maxwell
See Southern, Terry

Kenyon, Robert O.
See Kuttner, Henry

Kerouac, Jack ..... **CLC 1, 2, 3, 5, 14, 29, 61**
See also Kerouac, Jean-Louis Lebris de
See also CDALB 1941-1968; DLB 2, 16;
DLBD 3; DLBY 95

Kerouac, Jean-Louis Lebris de 1922-1969
See Kerouac, Jack
See also AITN 1; CA 5-8R; 25-28R;
CANR 26, 54; DA; DAB; DAC;
DAM MST, NOV, POET, POP; MTCW;
WLC

Kerr, Jean 1923- .... **CLC 22**
See also CA 5-8R; CANR 7; INT CANR-7

Kerr, M. E. .... **CLC 12, 35**
See also Meaker, Marijane (Agnes)
See also AAYA 2; CLR 29; SAAS 1

Kerr, Robert .... **CLC 55**

Kerrigan, (Thomas) Anthony
1918- .... **CLC 4, 6**
See also CA 49-52; CAAS 11; CANR 4

Kerry, Lois
See Duncan, Lois

Kesey, Ken (Elton)
1935- ..... **CLC 1, 3, 6, 11, 46, 64; DA;**
DAB; DAC; DAM MST, NOV, POP;
WLC
See also CA 1-4R; CANR 22, 38;
CDALB 1968-1988; DLB 2, 16; MTCW;
SATA 66

Kesselring, Joseph (Otto)
1902-1967 ..... **CLC 45; DAM DRAM,**
MST
See also CA 150

Kessler, Jascha (Frederick) 1929- .... **CLC 4**
See also CA 17-20R; CANR 8, 48

Kettelkamp, Larry (Dale) 1933- .... **CLC 12**
See also CA 29-32R; CANR 16; SAAS 3;
SATA 2

Key, Ellen 1849-1926 .... **TCLC 65**

Keyber, Conny
See Fielding, Henry

Keyes, Daniel
1927- .... **CLC 80; DA; DAC;**
DAM MST, NOV
See also CA 17-20R; CANR 10, 26, 54;
SATA 37

Keynes, John Maynard
1883-1946 .... **TCLC 64**
See also CA 114; DLBD 10

Khanshendel, Chiron
See Rose, Wendy

Khayyam, Omar
1048-1131 .... **CMLC 11; DAM POET;**
PC 8

Kherdian, David 1931- .... **CLC 6, 9**
See also CA 21-24R; CAAS 2; CANR 39;
CLR 24; JRDA; MAICYA; SATA 16, 74

Khlebnikov, Velimir .... **TCLC 20**
See also Khlebnikov, Viktor Vladimirovich

Khlebnikov, Viktor Vladimirovich 1885-1922
See Khlebnikov, Velimir
See also CA 117

Khodasevich, Vladislav (Felitsianovich)
1886-1939 .... **TCLC 15**
See also CA 115

Kielland, Alexander Lange
1849-1906 .... **TCLC 5**
See also CA 104

Kiely, Benedict 1919- .... **CLC 23, 43**
See also CA 1-4R; CANR 2; DLB 15

Kienzle, William X(avier)
1928- .... **CLC 25; DAM POP**
See also CA 93-96; CAAS 1; CANR 9, 31;
INT CANR-31; MTCW

Kierkegaard, Soren 1813-1855.... **NCLC 34**

Killens, John Oliver 1916-1987..... **CLC 10**
See also BW 2; CA 77-80; 123; CAAS 2;
CANR 26; DLB 33

Killigrew, Anne 1660-1685.......... **LC 4**
See also DLB 131

Kim
See Simenon, Georges (Jacques Christian)

Kincaid, Jamaica
1949- .... **CLC 43, 68; BLC;**
DAM MULT, NOV
See also AAYA 13; BW 2; CA 125;
CANR 47; DLB 157

King, Francis (Henry)
1923- .... **CLC 8, 53; DAM NOV**
See also CA 1-4R; CANR 1, 33; DLB 15,
139; MTCW

King, Martin Luther, Jr.
1929-1968 .... **CLC 83; BLC; DA; DAB;**
DAC; DAM MST, MULT
See also BW 2; CA 25-28; CANR 27, 44;
CAP 2; MTCW; SATA 14; YABC

King, Stephen (Edwin)
1947- .... **CLC 12, 26, 37, 61;**
DAM NOV, POP; SSC 17
See also AAYA 1, 17; BEST 90:1;
CA 61-64; CANR 1, 30, 52; DLB 143;
DLBY 80; JRDA; MTCW; SATA 9, 55

King, Steve
See King, Stephen (Edwin)

King, Thomas
1943- ..... **CLC 89; DAC; DAM MULT**
See also CA 144; DLB 175; NNAL

Kingman, Lee..................... **CLC 17**
See also Natti, (Mary) Lee
See also SAAS 3; SATA 1, 67

Kingsley, Charles 1819-1875 ..... **NCLC 35**
See also DLB 21, 32, 163; 2

Kingsley, Sidney 1906-1995........ **CLC 44**
See also CA 85-88; 147; DLB 7

Kingsolver, Barbara
1955- .... **CLC 55, 81; DAM POP**
See also AAYA 15; CA 129; 134; INT 134

Kingston, Maxine (Ting Ting) Hong
1940- .... **CLC 12, 19, 58; DAM MULT,**
NOV
See also AAYA 8; CA 69-72; CANR 13,
38; DLB 173; DLBY 80; INT CANR-13;
MTCW; SATA 53; YABC

Kinnell, Galway
1927- .... **CLC 1, 2, 3, 5, 13, 29**
See also CA 9-12R; CANR 10, 34; DLB 5;
DLBY 87; INT CANR-34; MTCW

Kinsella, Thomas 1928- .... **CLC 4, 19**
See also CA 17-20R; CANR 15; DLB 27;
MTCW

Kinsella, W(illiam) P(atrick)
1935- .... **CLC 27, 43; DAC;**
DAM NOV, POP
See also AAYA 7; CA 97-100; CAAS 7;
CANR 21, 35; INT CANR-21; MTCW

Kipling, (Joseph) Rudyard
1865-1936 ...... **TCLC 8, 17; DA; DAB;**
DAC; DAM MST, POET; PC 3; SSC 5;
WLC
See also CA 105; 120; CANR 33;
CDBLB 1890-1914; CLR 39; DLB 19, 34,
141, 156; MAICYA; MTCW; 2

Kirkup, James 1918- .... **CLC 1**
See also CA 1-4R; CAAS 4; CANR 2;
DLB 27; SATA 12

Kirkwood, James 1930(?)-1989 ...... **CLC 9**
See also AITN 2; CA 1-4R; 128; CANR 6,
40

Kirshner, Sidney
See Kingsley, Sidney

Kis, Danilo 1935-1989 .... **CLC 57**
See also CA 109; 118; 129; MTCW

Kivi, Aleksis 1834-1872 .... **NCLC 30**

Kizer, Carolyn (Ashley)
1925- ..... **CLC 15, 39, 80; DAM POET**
See also CA 65-68; CAAS 5; CANR 24;
DLB 5, 169

Klabund 1890-1928.............. **TCLC 44**
See also DLB 66

Klappert, Peter 1942-............. **CLC 57**
See also CA 33-36R; DLB 5

Klein, A(braham) M(oses)
1909-1972 . . . . **CLC 19; DAB; DAC;**
DAM MST
See also CA 101; 37-40R; DLB 68

Klein, Norma 1938-1989 . . . . **CLC 30**
See also AAYA 2; CA 41-44R; 128;
CANR 15, 37; CLR 2, 19;
INT CANR-15; JRDA; MAICYA;
SAAS 1; SATA 7, 57

Klein, T(heodore) E(ibon) D(onald)
1947- . . . . **CLC 34**
See also CA 119; CANR 44

Kleist, Heinrich von
1777-1811 . . . . **NCLC 2, 37;**
DAM DRAM; SSC 22
See also DLB 90

Klima, Ivan 1931- . . . . . **CLC 56; DAM NOV**
See also CA 25-28R; CANR 17, 50

Klimentov, Andrei Platonovich 1899-1951
See Platonov, Andrei
See also CA 108

Klinger, Friedrich Maximilian von
1752-1831 . . . . **NCLC 1**
See also DLB 94

Klopstock, Friedrich Gottlieb
1724-1803 . . . . **NCLC 11**
See also DLB 97

Knapp, Caroline 1959- . . . . **CLC 99**
See also CA 154

Knebel, Fletcher 1911-1993 . . . . **CLC 14**
See also AITN 1; CA 1-4R; 140; CAAS 3;
CANR 1, 36; SATA 36; SATA-Obit 75

Knickerbocker, Diedrich
See Irving, Washington

Knight, Etheridge
1931-1991 . . . . **CLC 40; BLC;**
DAM POET; PC 14
See also BW 1; CA 21-24R; 133; CANR 23;
DLB 41

Knight, Sarah Kemble 1666-1727 . . . . . **LC 7**
See also DLB 24

Knister, Raymond 1899-1932 . . . . . . **TCLC 56**
See also DLB 68

Knowles, John
1926- . . . . . . **CLC 1, 4, 10, 26; DA; DAC;**
DAM MST, NOV
See also AAYA 10; CA 17-20R; CANR 40;
CDALB 1968-1988; DLB 6; MTCW;
SATA 8, 89

Knox, Calvin M.
See Silverberg, Robert

Knox, John c. 1505-1572 . . . . **LC 37**
See also DLB 132

Knye, Cassandra
See Disch, Thomas M(ichael)

Koch, C(hristopher) J(ohn) 1932- . . . **CLC 42**
See also CA 127

Koch, Christopher
See Koch, C(hristopher) J(ohn)

Koch, Kenneth
1925- . . . . **CLC 5, 8, 44; DAM POET**
See also CA 1-4R; CANR 6, 36, 57; DLB 5;
INT CANR-36; SATA 65

Kochanowski, Jan 1530-1584 . . . . **LC 10**

Kock, Charles Paul de
1794-1871 . . . . **NCLC 16**

Koda Shigeyuki 1867-1947
See Rohan, Koda
See also CA 121

Koestler, Arthur
1905-1983 . . . . **CLC 1, 3, 6, 8, 15, 33**
See also CA 1-4R; 109; CANR 1, 33;
CDBLB 1945-1960; DLBY 83; MTCW

Kogawa, Joy Nozomi
1935- . . . . . . **CLC 78; DAC; DAM MST,**
MULT
See also CA 101; CANR 19

Kohout, Pavel 1928- . . . . **CLC 13**
See also CA 45-48; CANR 3

Koizumi, Yakumo
See Hearn, (Patricio) Lafcadio (Tessima
Carlos)

Kolmar, Gertrud 1894-1943 . . . . . . **TCLC 40**

Komunyakaa, Yusef 1947- . . . . . . **CLC 86, 94**
See also CA 147; DLB 120

Konrad, George
See Konrad, Gyoergy

Konrad, Gyoergy 1933- . . . . . . **CLC 4, 10, 73**
See also CA 85-88

Konwicki, Tadeusz 1926- . . . . . **CLC 8, 28, 54**
See also CA 101; CAAS 9; CANR 39;
MTCW

Koontz, Dean R(ay)
1945- . . . . . . **CLC 78; DAM NOV, POP**
See also AAYA 9; BEST 89:3, 90:2;
CA 108; CANR 19, 36, 52; MTCW;
SATA 92

Kopit, Arthur (Lee)
1937- . . . . . **CLC 1, 18, 33; DAM DRAM**
See also AITN 1; CA 81-84; CABS 3;
DLB 7; MTCW

Kops, Bernard 1926- . . . . **CLC 4**
See also CA 5-8R; DLB 13

Kornbluth, C(yril) M. 1923-1958 . . . . **TCLC 8**
See also CA 105; DLB 8

Korolenko, V. G.
See Korolenko, Vladimir Galaktionovich

Korolenko, Vladimir
See Korolenko, Vladimir Galaktionovich

Korolenko, Vladimir G.
See Korolenko, Vladimir Galaktionovich

Korolenko, Vladimir Galaktionovich
1853-1921 . . . . **TCLC 22**
See also CA 121

Korzybski, Alfred (Habdank Skarbek)
1879-1950 . . . . **TCLC 61**
See also CA 123

Kosinski, Jerzy (Nikodem)
1933-1991 . . . . **CLC 1, 2, 3, 6, 10, 15, 53,**
70; DAM NOV
See also CA 17-20R; 134; CANR 9, 46;
DLB 2; DLBY 82; MTCW

Kostelanetz, Richard (Cory) 1940- . . **CLC 28**
See also CA 13-16R; CAAS 8; CANR 38

Kostrowitzki, Wilhelm Apollinaris de
1880-1918
See Apollinaire, Guillaume
See also CA 104

Kotlowitz, Robert 1924- . . . . **CLC 4**
See also CA 33-36R; CANR 36

Kotzebue, August (Friedrich Ferdinand) von
1761-1819 . . . . **NCLC 25**
See also DLB 94

Kotzwinkle, William 1938- . . . **CLC 5, 14, 35**
See also CA 45-48; CANR 3, 44; CLR 6;
DLB 173; MAICYA; SATA 24, 70

Kowna, Stancy
See Szymborska, Wislawa

Kozol, Jonathan 1936- . . . . **CLC 17**
See also CA 61-64; CANR 16, 45

Kozoll, Michael 1940(?)- . . . . **CLC 35**

Kramer, Kathryn 19(?)- . . . . **CLC 34**

Kramer, Larry 1935- . . **CLC 42; DAM POP**
See also CA 124; 126

Krasicki, Ignacy 1735-1801 . . . . **NCLC 8**

Krasinski, Zygmunt 1812-1859 . . . . **NCLC 4**

Kraus, Karl 1874-1936 . . . . **TCLC 5**
See also CA 104; DLB 118

Kreve (Mickevicius), Vincas
1882-1954 . . . . **TCLC 27**

Kristeva, Julia 1941- . . . . **CLC 77**
See also CA 154

Kristofferson, Kris 1936- . . . . **CLC 26**
See also CA 104

Krizanc, John 1956- . . . . **CLC 57**

Krleza, Miroslav 1893-1981 . . . . **CLC 8**
See also CA 97-100; 105; CANR 50;
DLB 147

Kroetsch, Robert
1927- . . . . **CLC 5, 23, 57; DAC;**
DAM POET
See also CA 17-20R; CANR 8, 38; DLB 53;
MTCW

Kroetz, Franz
See Kroetz, Franz Xaver

Kroetz, Franz Xaver 1946- . . . . **CLC 41**
See also CA 130

Kroker, Arthur 1945- . . . . **CLC 77**

Kropotkin, Peter (Aleksieevich)
1842-1921 . . . . **TCLC 36**
See also CA 119

Krotkov, Yuri 1917- . . . . **CLC 19**
See also CA 102

Krumb
See Crumb, R(obert)

Krumgold, Joseph (Quincy)
1908-1980 . . . . **CLC 12**
See also CA 9-12R; 101; CANR 7;
MAICYA; SATA 1, 48; SATA-Obit 23

Krumwitz
See Crumb, R(obert)

Krutch, Joseph Wood 1893-1970 . . . . **CLC 24**
See also CA 1-4R; 25-28R; CANR 4;
DLB 63

Krutzch, Gus
See Eliot, T(homas) S(tearns)

Krylov, Ivan Andreevich
1768(?)-1844 . . . . **NCLC 1**
See also DLB 150

Kubin, Alfred (Leopold Isidor)
1877-1959 . . . . **TCLC 23**
See also CA 112; 149; DLB 81

Kubrick, Stanley 1928- . . . . **CLC 16**
See also CA 81-84; CANR 33; DLB 26

Kumin, Maxine (Winokur)
1925- . . . . . **CLC 5, 13, 28; DAM POET;
PC 15**
See also AITN 2; CA 1-4R; CAAS 8;
CANR 1, 21; DLB 5; MTCW; SATA 12

Kundera, Milan
1929- . . . . **CLC 4, 9, 19, 32, 68;
DAM NOV; SSC 24**
See also AAYA 2; CA 85-88; CANR 19,
52; MTCW

Kunene, Mazisi (Raymond) 1930- . . . **CLC 85**
See also BW 1; CA 125; DLB 117

Kunitz, Stanley (Jasspon)
1905- . . . . **CLC 6, 11, 14; PC 19**
See also CA 41-44R; CANR 26, 57;
DLB 48; INT CANR-26; MTCW

Kunze, Reiner 1933- . . . . **CLC 10**
See also CA 93-96; DLB 75

Kuprin, Aleksandr Ivanovich
1870-1938 . . . . **TCLC 5**
See also CA 104

Kureishi, Hanif 1954(?)- . . . . **CLC 64**
See also CA 139

Kurosawa, Akira
1910- . . . . **CLC 16; DAM MULT**
See also AAYA 11; CA 101; CANR 46

Kushner, Tony
1957(?)- . . . . **CLC 81; DAM DRAM**
See also CA 144

Kuttner, Henry 1915-1958 . . . . **TCLC 10**
See also Vance, Jack
See also CA 107; 157; DLB 8

Kuzma, Greg 1944- . . . . **CLC 7**
See also CA 33-36R

Kuzmin, Mikhail 1872(?)-1936 . . . . **TCLC 40**

Kyd, Thomas
1558-1594 . . . . . . **LC 22; DAM DRAM;
DC 3**
See also DLB 62

Kyprianos, Iossif
See Samarakis, Antonis

La Bruyere, Jean de 1645-1696 . . . . . . **LC 17**

Lacan, Jacques (Marie Emile)
1901-1981 . . . . **CLC 75**
See also CA 121; 104

**Laclos, Pierre Ambroise Francois Choderlos
de** 1741-1803 . . . . **NCLC 4**

Lacolere, Francois
See Aragon, Louis

La Colere, Francois
See Aragon, Louis

La Deshabilleuse
See Simenon, Georges (Jacques Christian)

Lady Gregory
See Gregory, Isabella Augusta (Persse)

Lady of Quality, A
See Bagnold, Enid

**La Fayette, Marie (Madelaine Pioche de la
Vergne Comtes** 1634-1693 . . . . . . **LC 2**

Lafayette, Rene
See Hubbard, L(afayette) Ron(ald)

Laforgue, Jules
1860-1887 . . . . **NCLC 5, 53; PC 14;
SSC 20**

Lagerkvist, Paer (Fabian)
1891-1974 . . . . **CLC 7, 10, 13, 54;
DAM DRAM, NOV**
See also Lagerkvist, Par
See also CA 85-88; 49-52; MTCW

Lagerkvist, Par . . . . **SSC 12**
See also Lagerkvist, Paer (Fabian)

Lagerloef, Selma (Ottiliana Lovisa)
1858-1940 . . . . **TCLC 4, 36**
See also Lagerlof, Selma (Ottiliana Lovisa)
See also CA 108; SATA 15

Lagerlof, Selma (Ottiliana Lovisa)
See Lagerloef, Selma (Ottiliana Lovisa)
See also CLR 7; SATA 15

La Guma, (Justin) Alex(ander)
1925-1985 . . . . **CLC 19; DAM NOV**
See also BW 1; CA 49-52; 118; CANR 25;
DLB 117; MTCW

Laidlaw, A. K.
See Grieve, C(hristopher) M(urray)

Lainez, Manuel Mujica
See Mujica Lainez, Manuel
See also HW

Laing, R(onald) D(avid)
1927-1989 . . . . **CLC 95**
See also CA 107; 129; CANR 34; MTCW

Lamartine, Alphonse (Marie Louis Prat) de
1790-1869 . . . . . **NCLC 11; DAM POET;
PC 16**

Lamb, Charles
1775-1834 . . . . **NCLC 10; DA; DAB;
DAC; DAM MST; WLC**
See also CDBLB 1789-1832; DLB 93, 107,
163; SATA 17

Lamb, Lady Caroline 1785-1828 . . **NCLC 38**
See also DLB 116

Lamming, George (William)
1927- . . . . **CLC 2, 4, 66; BLC;
DAM MULT**
See also BW 2; CA 85-88; CANR 26;
DLB 125; MTCW

L'Amour, Louis (Dearborn)
1908-1988 . . . . **CLC 25, 55; DAM NOV,
POP**
See also AAYA 16; AITN 2; BEST 89:2;
CA 1-4R; 125; CANR 3, 25, 40;
DLBY 80; MTCW

Lampedusa, Giuseppe (Tomasi) di
1896-1957 . . . . **TCLC 13**
See also Tomasi di Lampedusa, Giuseppe
See also DLB 177

Lampman, Archibald 1861-1899 . . **NCLC 25**
See also DLB 92

Lancaster, Bruce 1896-1963 . . . . **CLC 36**
See also CA 9-10; CAP 1; SATA 9

Lanchester, John . . . . **CLC 99**

Landau, Mark Alexandrovich
See Aldanov, Mark (Alexandrovich)

Landau-Aldanov, Mark Alexandrovich
See Aldanov, Mark (Alexandrovich)

Landis, Jerry
See Simon, Paul (Frederick)

Landis, John 1950- . . . . **CLC 26**
See also CA 112; 122

Landolfi, Tommaso 1908-1979 . . . **CLC 11, 49**
See also CA 127; 117; DLB 177

Landon, Letitia Elizabeth
1802-1838 . . . . **NCLC 15**
See also DLB 96

Landor, Walter Savage
1775-1864 . . . . **NCLC 14**
See also DLB 93, 107

Landwirth, Heinz 1927-
See Lind, Jakov
See also CA 9-12R; CANR 7

Lane, Patrick
1939- . . . . **CLC 25; DAM POET**
See also CA 97-100; CANR 54; DLB 53;
INT 97-100

Lang, Andrew 1844-1912 . . . . **TCLC 16**
See also CA 114; 137; DLB 98, 141;
MAICYA; SATA 16

Lang, Fritz 1890-1976 . . . . **CLC 20**
See also CA 77-80; 69-72; CANR 30

Lange, John
See Crichton, (John) Michael

Langer, Elinor 1939- . . . . **CLC 34**
See also CA 121

Langland, William
1330(?)-1400(?) . . . . . . **LC 19; DA; DAB;
DAC; DAM MST, POET**
See also DLB 146

Langstaff, Launcelot
See Irving, Washington

Lanier, Sidney
1842-1881 . . . . . . **NCLC 6; DAM POET**
See also DLB 64; DLBD 13; MAICYA;
SATA 18

Lanyer, Aemilia 1569-1645 . . . . . . **LC 10, 30**
See also DLB 121

Lao Tzu . . . . **CMLC 7**

Lapine, James (Elliot) 1949- . . . . **CLC 39**
See also CA 123; 130; CANR 54; INT 130

Larbaud, Valery (Nicolas)
1881-1957 . . . . **TCLC 9**
See also CA 106; 152

Lardner, Ring
See Lardner, Ring(gold) W(ilmer)

Lardner, Ring W., Jr.
See Lardner, Ring(gold) W(ilmer)

Lardner, Ring(gold) W(ilmer)
1885-1933 . . . . **TCLC 2, 14**
See also CA 104; 131; CDALB 1917-1929;
DLB 11, 25, 86; MTCW

Laredo, Betty
See Codrescu, Andrei

Larkin, Maia
See Wojciechowska, Maia (Teresa)

Larkin, Philip (Arthur)
1922-1985 . . . . **CLC 3, 5, 8, 9, 13, 18, 33,
39, 64; DAB; DAM MST, POET**
See also CA 5-8R; 117; CANR 24;
CDBLB 1960 to Present; DLB 27;
MTCW

Author Index

Lord Houghton
See Milnes, Richard Monckton

Lord Jeffrey
See Jeffrey, Francis

Lorenzini, Carlo 1826-1890
See Collodi, Carlo
See also MAICYA; SATA 29

Lorenzo, Heberto Padilla
See Padilla (Lorenzo), Heberto

Loris
See Hofmannsthal, Hugo von

Loti, Pierre . . . . **TCLC 11**
See also Viaud, (Louis Marie) Julien
See also DLB 123

Louie, David Wong 1954- . . . . **CLC 70**
See also CA 139

Louis, Father M.
See Merton, Thomas

Lovecraft, H(oward) P(hillips)
1890-1937 . . . . **TCLC 4, 22; DAM POP;
SSC 3**
See also AAYA 14; CA 104; 133; MTCW

Lovelace, Earl 1935- . . . . **CLC 51**
See also BW 2; CA 77-80; CANR 41;
DLB 125; MTCW

Lovelace, Richard 1618-1657 . . . . **LC 24**
See also DLB 131

Lowell, Amy
1874-1925 . . . . **TCLC 1, 8; DAM POET;
PC 13**
See also CA 104; 151; DLB 54, 140

Lowell, James Russell 1819-1891 . . **NCLC 2**
See also CDALB 1640-1865; DLB 1, 11, 64,
79

Lowell, Robert (Traill Spence, Jr.)
1917-1977 . . . **CLC 1, 2, 3, 4, 5, 8, 9, 11,
15, 37; DA; DAB; DAC; DAM MST,
NOV; PC 3; WLC**
See also CA 9-12R; 73-76; CABS 2;
CANR 26; DLB 5, 169; MTCW

Lowndes, Marie Adelaide (Belloc)
1868-1947 . . . . **TCLC 12**
See also CA 107; DLB 70

Lowry, (Clarence) Malcolm
1909-1957 . . . . **TCLC 6, 40**
See also CA 105; 131; CDBLB 1945-1960;
DLB 15; MTCW

Lowry, Mina Gertrude 1882-1966
See Loy, Mina
See also CA 113

Loxsmith, John
See Brunner, John (Kilian Houston)

Loy, Mina . . . . **CLC 28; DAM POET; PC 16**
See also Lowry, Mina Gertrude
See also DLB 4, 54

Loyson-Bridet
See Schwob, (Mayer Andre) Marcel

Lucas, Craig 1951- . . . . **CLC 64**
See also CA 137

Lucas, George 1944- . . . . **CLC 16**
See also AAYA 1; CA 77-80; CANR 30;
SATA 56

Lucas, Hans
See Godard, Jean-Luc

Lucas, Victoria
See Plath, Sylvia

Ludlam, Charles 1943-1987 . . . . . **CLC 46, 50**
See also CA 85-88; 122

Ludlum, Robert
1927- . . . **CLC 22, 43; DAM NOV, POP**
See also AAYA 10; BEST 89:1, 90:3;
CA 33-36R; CANR 25, 41; DLBY 82;
MTCW

Ludwig, Ken . . . . **CLC 60**

Ludwig, Otto 1813-1865 . . . . **NCLC 4**
See also DLB 129

Lugones, Leopoldo 1874-1938 . . . . . **TCLC 15**
See also CA 116; 131; HW

Lu Hsun 1881-1936 . . . . . . **TCLC 3; SSC 20**
See also Shu-Jen, Chou

Lukacs, George . . . . **CLC 24**
See also Lukacs, Gyorgy (Szegeny von)

Lukacs, Gyorgy (Szegeny von) 1885-1971
See Lukacs, George
See also CA 101; 29-32R

Luke, Peter (Ambrose Cyprian)
1919-1995 . . . . **CLC 38**
See also CA 81-84; 147; DLB 13

Lunar, Dennis
See Mungo, Raymond

Lurie, Alison 1926- . . . . **CLC 4, 5, 18, 39**
See also CA 1-4R; CANR 2, 17, 50; DLB 2;
MTCW; SATA 46

Lustig, Arnost 1926- . . . . **CLC 56**
See also AAYA 3; CA 69-72; CANR 47;
SATA 56

Luther, Martin 1483-1546 . . . . **LC 9, 37**
See also DLB 179

Luxemburg, Rosa 1870(?)-1919 . . . . **TCLC 63**
See also CA 118

Luzi, Mario 1914- . . . . **CLC 13**
See also CA 61-64; CANR 9; DLB 128

Lyly, John 1554(?)-1606 . . . . **DC 7**
See also DAM DRAM; DLB 62, 167

L'Ymagier
See Gourmont, Remy (-Marie-Charles) de

Lynch, B. Suarez
See Bioy Casares, Adolfo; Borges, Jorge
Luis

Lynch, David (K.) 1946- . . . . **CLC 66**
See also CA 124; 129

Lynch, James
See Andreyev, Leonid (Nikolaevich)

Lynch Davis, B.
See Bioy Casares, Adolfo; Borges, Jorge
Luis

Lyndsay, Sir David 1490-1555 . . . . . . **LC 20**

Lynn, Kenneth S(chuyler) 1923- . . . . **CLC 50**
See also CA 1-4R; CANR 3, 27

Lynx
See West, Rebecca

Lyons, Marcus
See Blish, James (Benjamin)

Lyre, Pinchbeck
See Sassoon, Siegfried (Lorraine)

Lytle, Andrew (Nelson) 1902-1995 . . **CLC 22**
See also CA 9-12R; 150; DLB 6; DLBY 95

Lyttelton, George 1709-1773 . . . . **LC 10**

Maas, Peter 1929- . . . . **CLC 29**
See also CA 93-96; INT 93-96

Macaulay, Rose 1881-1958 . . . . . **TCLC 7, 44**
See also CA 104; DLB 36

Macaulay, Thomas Babington
1800-1859 . . . . **NCLC 42**
See also CDBLB 1832-1890; DLB 32, 55

MacBeth, George (Mann)
1932-1992 . . . . **CLC 2, 5, 9**
See also CA 25-28R; 136; DLB 40; MTCW;
SATA 4; SATA-Obit 70

MacCaig, Norman (Alexander)
1910- . . . . . **CLC 36; DAB; DAM POET**
See also CA 9-12R; CANR 3, 34; DLB 27

MacCarthy, (Sir Charles Otto) Desmond
1877-1952 . . . . **TCLC 36**

MacDiarmid, Hugh
. . . . **CLC 2, 4, 11, 19, 63; PC 9**
See also Grieve, C(hristopher) M(urray)
See also CDBLB 1945-1960; DLB 20

MacDonald, Anson
See Heinlein, Robert A(nson)

Macdonald, Cynthia 1928- . . . . . . **CLC 13, 19**
See also CA 49-52; CANR 4, 44; DLB 105

MacDonald, George 1824-1905 . . . . . **TCLC 9**
See also CA 106; 137; DLB 18, 163, 178;
MAICYA; SATA 33

Macdonald, John
See Millar, Kenneth

MacDonald, John D(ann)
1916-1986 . . . . **CLC 3, 27, 44;
DAM NOV, POP**
See also CA 1-4R; 121; CANR 1, 19;
DLB 8; DLBY 86; MTCW

Macdonald, John Ross
See Millar, Kenneth

Macdonald, Ross . . . . . **CLC 1, 2, 3, 14, 34, 41**
See also Millar, Kenneth
See also DLBD 6

MacDougal, John
See Blish, James (Benjamin)

MacEwen, Gwendolyn (Margaret)
1941-1987 . . . . **CLC 13, 55**
See also CA 9-12R; 124; CANR 7, 22;
DLB 53; SATA 50; SATA-Obit 55

Macha, Karel Hynek 1810-1846 . . **NCLC 46**

Machado (y Ruiz), Antonio
1875-1939 . . . . **TCLC 3**
See also CA 104; DLB 108

Machado de Assis, Joaquim Maria
1839-1908 . . . . . **TCLC 10; BLC; SSC 24**
See also CA 107; 153

Machen, Arthur . . . . **TCLC 4; SSC 20**
See also Jones, Arthur Llewellyn
See also DLB 36, 156, 178

Machiavelli, Niccolo
1469-1527 . . . . **LC 8, 36; DA; DAB;
DAC; DAM MST**
See also YABC

MacInnes, Colin 1914-1976 . . . . . . **CLC 4, 23**
See also CA 69-72; 65-68; CANR 21;
DLB 14; MTCW

MacInnes, Helen (Clark)
1907-1985 ..... **CLC 27, 39; DAM POP**
See also CA 1-4R; 117; CANR 1, 28, 58;
DLB 87; MTCW; SATA 22;
SATA-Obit 44

Mackay, Mary 1855-1924
See Corelli, Marie
See also CA 118

Mackenzie, Compton (Edward Montague)
1883-1972 .... **CLC 18**
See also CA 21-22; 37-40R; CAP 2;
DLB 34, 100

Mackenzie, Henry 1745-1831 .... **NCLC 41**
See also DLB 39

Mackintosh, Elizabeth 1896(?)-1952
See Tey, Josephine
See also CA 110

MacLaren, James
See Grieve, C(hristopher) M(urray)

Mac Laverty, Bernard 1942- .... **CLC 31**
See also CA 116; 118; CANR 43; INT 118

MacLean, Alistair (Stuart)
1922-1987 .... **CLC 3, 13, 50, 63;**
DAM POP
See also CA 57-60; 121; CANR 28; MTCW;
SATA 23; SATA-Obit 50

Maclean, Norman (Fitzroy)
1902-1990 .... **CLC 78; DAM POP;**
SSC 13
See also CA 102; 132; CANR 49

MacLeish, Archibald
1892-1982 .... **CLC 3, 8, 14, 68;**
DAM POET
See also CA 9-12R; 106; CANR 33; DLB 4,
7, 45; DLBY 82; MTCW

MacLennan, (John) Hugh
1907-1990 .... **CLC 2, 14, 92; DAC;**
DAM MST
See also CA 5-8R; 142; CANR 33; DLB 68;
MTCW

MacLeod, Alistair
1936- ...... **CLC 56; DAC; DAM MST**
See also CA 123; DLB 60

MacNeice, (Frederick) Louis
1907-1963 ...... **CLC 1, 4, 10, 53; DAB;**
DAM POET
See also CA 85-88; DLB 10, 20; MTCW

MacNeill, Dand
See Fraser, George MacDonald

Macpherson, James 1736-1796 ...... **LC 29**
See also DLB 109

Macpherson, (Jean) Jay 1931- ...... **CLC 14**
See also CA 5-8R; DLB 53

MacShane, Frank 1927- .... **CLC 39**
See also CA 9-12R; CANR 3, 33; DLB 111

Macumber, Mari
See Sandoz, Mari(e Susette)

Madach, Imre 1823-1864 .... **NCLC 19**

Madden, (Jerry) David 1933- .... **CLC 5, 15**
See also CA 1-4R; CAAS 3; CANR 4, 45;
DLB 6; MTCW

Maddern, Al(an)
See Ellison, Harlan (Jay)

Madhubuti, Haki R.
1942- .... **CLC 6, 73; BLC;**
DAM MULT, POET; PC 5
See also Lee, Don L.
See also BW 2; CA 73-76; CANR 24, 51;
DLB 5, 41; DLBD 8

Maepenn, Hugh
See Kuttner, Henry

Maepenn, K. H.
See Kuttner, Henry

Maeterlinck, Maurice
1862-1949 ...... **TCLC 3; DAM DRAM**
See also CA 104; 136; SATA 66

Maginn, William 1794-1842....... **NCLC 8**
See also DLB 110, 159

Mahapatra, Jayanta
1928- .... **CLC 33; DAM MULT**
See also CA 73-76; CAAS 9; CANR 15, 33

Mahfouz, Naguib (Abdel Aziz Al-Sabilgi)
1911(?)-
See Mahfuz, Najib
See also BEST 89:2; CA 128; CANR 55;
DAM NOV; MTCW

Mahfuz, Najib .... **CLC 52, 55**
See also Mahfouz, Naguib (Abdel Aziz
Al-Sabilgi)
See also DLBY 88

Mahon, Derek 1941- .... **CLC 27**
See also CA 113; 128; DLB 40

Mailer, Norman
1923- ...... **CLC 1, 2, 3, 4, 5, 8, 11, 14,**
28, 39, 74; DA; DAB; DAC; DAM MST,
NOV, POP
See also AITN 2; CA 9-12R; CABS 1;
CANR 28; CDALB 1968-1988; DLB 2,
16, 28; DLBD 3; DLBY 80, 83; MTCW

Maillet, Antonine 1929- ...... **CLC 54; DAC**
See also CA 115; 120; CANR 46; DLB 60;
INT 120

Mais, Roger 1905-1955 .... **TCLC 8**
See also BW 1; CA 105; 124; DLB 125;
MTCW

Maistre, Joseph de 1753-1821 .... **NCLC 37**

Maitland, Frederic 1850-1906 ..... **TCLC 65**

Maitland, Sara (Louise) 1950- ...... **CLC 49**
See also CA 69-72; CANR 13

Major, Clarence
1936- .... **CLC 3, 19, 48; BLC;**
DAM MULT
See also BW 2; CA 21-24R; CAAS 6;
CANR 13, 25, 53; DLB 33

Major, Kevin (Gerald)
1949- .... **CLC 26; DAC**
See also AAYA 16; CA 97-100; CANR 21,
38; CLR 11; DLB 60; INT CANR-21;
JRDA; MAICYA; SATA 32, 82

Maki, James
See Ozu, Yasujiro

Malabaila, Damiano
See Levi, Primo

Malamud, Bernard
1914-1986 ...... **CLC 1, 2, 3, 5, 8, 9, 11,**
18, 27, 44, 78, 85; DA; DAB; DAC;
DAM MST, NOV, POP; SSC 15; WLC
See also AAYA 16; CA 5-8R; 118; CABS 1;
CANR 28; CDALB 1941-1968; DLB 2,
28, 152; DLBY 80, 86; MTCW

Malaparte, Curzio 1898-1957 ..... **TCLC 52**

Malcolm, Dan
See Silverberg, Robert

Malcolm X .... **CLC 82; BLC**
See also Little, Malcolm
See also YABC

Malherbe, Francois de 1555-1628..... **LC 5**

Mallarme, Stephane
1842-1898 .... **NCLC 4, 41;**
DAM POET; PC 4

Mallet-Joris, Francoise 1930- ...... **CLC 11**
See also CA 65-68; CANR 17; DLB 83

Malley, Ern
See McAuley, James Phillip

Mallowan, Agatha Christie
See Christie, Agatha (Mary Clarissa)

Maloff, Saul 1922- .... **CLC 5**
See also CA 33-36R

Malone, Louis
See MacNeice, (Frederick) Louis

Malone, Michael (Christopher)
1942- .... **CLC 43**
See also CA 77-80; CANR 14, 32, 57

Malory, (Sir) Thomas
1410(?)-1471(?) ...... **LC 11; DA; DAB;**
DAC; DAM MST
See also CDBLB Before 1660; DLB 146;
SATA 59; SATA-Brief 33; YABC

Malouf, (George Joseph) David
1934- .... **CLC 28, 86**
See also CA 124; CANR 50

Malraux, (Georges-)Andre
1901-1976 ...... **CLC 1, 4, 9, 13, 15, 57;**
DAM NOV
See also CA 21-22; 69-72; CANR 34, 58;
CAP 2; DLB 72; MTCW

Malzberg, Barry N(athaniel) 1939-... **CLC 7**
See also CA 61-64; CAAS 4; CANR 16;
DLB 8

Mamet, David (Alan)
1947- .... **CLC 9, 15, 34, 46, 91;**
DAM DRAM; DC 4
See also AAYA 3; CA 81-84; CABS 3;
CANR 15, 41; DLB 7; MTCW

Mamoulian, Rouben (Zachary)
1897-1987 .... **CLC 16**
See also CA 25-28R; 124

Mandelstam, Osip (Emilievich)
1891(?)-1938(?) ...... **TCLC 2, 6; PC 14**
See also CA 104; 150

Mander, (Mary) Jane 1877-1949... **TCLC 31**

Mandeville, John fl. 1350- .... **CMLC 19**
See also DLB 146

Mandiargues, Andre Pieyre de .... **CLC 41**
See also Pieyre de Mandiargues, Andre
See also DLB 83

Mandrake, Ethel Belle
See Thurman, Wallace (Henry)

Mangan, James Clarence
1803-1849 .... **NCLC 27**

Maniere, J.-E.
See Giraudoux, (Hippolyte) Jean

Manley, (Mary) Delariviere
1672(?)-1724 .... **LC 1**
See also DLB 39, 80

Mann, Abel
See Creasey, John

Mann, Emily 1952-................. **DC 7**
See also CA 130; CANR 55

Mann, (Luiz) Heinrich 1871-1950... **TCLC 9**
See also CA 106; DLB 66

Mann, (Paul) Thomas
1875-1955 .... **TCLC 2, 8, 14, 21, 35, 44,
60; DA; DAB; DAC; DAM MST, NOV;
SSC 5; WLC**
See also CA 104; 128; DLB 66; MTCW

Mannheim, Karl 1893-1947 ...... **TCLC 65**

Manning, David
See Faust, Frederick (Schiller)

Manning, Frederic 1887(?)-1935 ... **TCLC 25**
See also CA 124

Manning, Olivia 1915-1980 ...... **CLC 5, 19**
See also CA 5-8R; 101; CANR 29; MTCW

Mano, D. Keith 1942- .... **CLC 2, 10**
See also CA 25-28R; CAAS 6; CANR 26,
57; DLB 6

Mansfield, Katherine
.. **TCLC 2, 8, 39; DAB; SSC 9, 23; WLC**
See also Beauchamp, Kathleen Mansfield
See also DLB 162

Manso, Peter 1940- .... **CLC 39**
See also CA 29-32R; CANR 44

Mantecon, Juan Jimenez
See Jimenez (Mantecon), Juan Ramon

Manton, Peter
See Creasey, John

Man Without a Spleen, A
See Chekhov, Anton (Pavlovich)

Manzoni, Alessandro 1785-1873 .. **NCLC 29**

Mapu, Abraham (ben Jekutiel)
1808-1867 .... **NCLC 18**

Mara, Sally
See Queneau, Raymond

Marat, Jean Paul 1743-1793 .... **LC 10**

Marcel, Gabriel Honore
1889-1973 .... **CLC 15**
See also CA 102; 45-48; MTCW

Marchbanks, Samuel
See Davies, (William) Robertson

Marchi, Giacomo
See Bassani, Giorgio

Margulies, Donald............... **CLC 76**

Marie de France c. 12th cent. -.... **CMLC 8**

Marie de l'Incarnation 1599-1672.... **LC 10**

Marier, Captain Victor
See Griffith, D(avid Lewelyn) W(ark)

Mariner, Scott
See Pohl, Frederik

Marinetti, Filippo Tommaso
1876-1944 .... **TCLC 10**
See also CA 107; DLB 114

Marivaux, Pierre Carlet de Chamblain de
1688-1763 .... **LC 4; DC 7**

Markandaya, Kamala .... **CLC 8, 38**
See also Taylor, Kamala (Purnaiya)

Markfield, Wallace 1926-.......... **CLC 8**
See also CA 69-72; CAAS 3; DLB 2, 28

Markham, Edwin 1852-1940 ..... **TCLC 47**
See also DLB 54

Markham, Robert
See Amis, Kingsley (William)

Marks, J
See Highwater, Jamake (Mamake)

Marks-Highwater, J
See Highwater, Jamake (Mamake)

Markson, David M(errill) 1927- .... **CLC 67**
See also CA 49-52; CANR 1

Marley, Bob.................... **CLC 17**
See also Marley, Robert Nesta

Marley, Robert Nesta 1945-1981
See Marley, Bob
See also CA 107; 103

Marlowe, Christopher
1564-1593 ..... **LC 22; DA; DAB; DAC;
DAM DRAM, MST; DC 1; WLC**
See also CDBLB Before 1660; DLB 62

Marlowe, Stephen 1928-
See Queen, Ellery
See also CA 13-16R; CANR 6, 55

Marmontel, Jean-Francois
1723-1799 .... **LC 2**

Marquand, John P(hillips)
1893-1960 .... **CLC 2, 10**
See also CA 85-88; DLB 9, 102

Marques, Rene
1919-1979 ...... **CLC 96; DAM MULT;
HLC**
See also CA 97-100; 85-88; DLB 113; HW

Marquez, Gabriel (Jose) Garcia
See Garcia Marquez, Gabriel (Jose)

Marquis, Don(ald Robert Perry)
1878-1937 .... **TCLC 7**
See also CA 104; DLB 11, 25

Marric, J. J.
See Creasey, John

Marrow, Bernard
See Moore, Brian

Marryat, Frederick 1792-1848 .... **NCLC 3**
See also DLB 21, 163

Marsden, James
See Creasey, John

Marsh, (Edith) Ngaio
1899-1982 ...... **CLC 7, 53; DAM POP**
See also CA 9-12R; CANR 6, 58; DLB 77;
MTCW

Marshall, Garry 1934-........... **CLC 17**
See also AAYA 3; CA 111; SATA 60

Marshall, Paule
1929- .... **CLC 27, 72; BLC;
DAM MULT; SSC 3**
See also BW 2; CA 77-80; CANR 25;
DLB 157; MTCW

Marsten, Richard
See Hunter, Evan

Marston, John
1576-1634 .... **LC 33; DAM DRAM**
See also DLB 58, 172

Martha, Henry
See Harris, Mark

Martial c. 40-c. 104 .... **PC 10**

Martin, Ken
See Hubbard, L(afayette) Ron(ald)

Martin, Richard
See Creasey, John

Martin, Steve 1945-............. **CLC 30**
See also CA 97-100; CANR 30; MTCW

Martin, Valerie 1948-............. **CLC 89**
See also BEST 90:2; CA 85-88; CANR 49

Martin, Violet Florence
1862-1915 .... **TCLC 51**

Martin, Webber
See Silverberg, Robert

Martindale, Patrick Victor
See White, Patrick (Victor Martindale)

Martin du Gard, Roger
1881-1958 .... **TCLC 24**
See also CA 118; DLB 65

Martineau, Harriet 1802-1876.... **NCLC 26**
See also DLB 21, 55, 159, 163, 166; 2

Martines, Julia
See O'Faolain, Julia

Martinez, Enrique Gonzalez
See Gonzalez Martinez, Enrique

Martinez, Jacinto Benavente y
See Benavente (y Martinez), Jacinto

Martinez Ruiz, Jose 1873-1967
See Azorin; Ruiz, Jose Martinez
See also CA 93-96; HW

Martinez Sierra, Gregorio
1881-1947 .... **TCLC 6**
See also CA 115

Martinez Sierra, Maria (de la O'LeJarraga)
1874-1974 .... **TCLC 6**
See also CA 115

Martinsen, Martin
See Follett, Ken(neth Martin)

Martinson, Harry (Edmund)
1904-1978 .... **CLC 14**
See also CA 77-80; CANR 34

Marut, Ret
See Traven, B.

Marut, Robert
See Traven, B.

Marvell, Andrew
1621-1678 ...... **LC 4; DA; DAB; DAC;
DAM MST, POET; PC 10; WLC**
See also CDBLB 1660-1789; DLB 131

Marx, Karl (Heinrich)
1818-1883 .... **NCLC 17**
See also DLB 129

Masaoka Shiki.................. **TCLC 18**
See also Masaoka Tsunenori

Masaoka Tsunenori 1867-1902
See Masaoka Shiki
See also CA 117

Masefield, John (Edward)
1878-1967 .... **CLC 11, 47; DAM POET**
See also CA 19-20; 25-28R; CANR 33;
CAP 2; CDBLB 1890-1914; DLB 10, 19,
153, 160; MTCW; SATA 19

Maso, Carole 19(?)- .... **CLC 44**

Mason, Bobbie Ann
1940- .... **CLC 28, 43, 82; SSC 4**
See also AAYA 5; CA 53-56; CANR 11,
31, 58; DLB 173; DLBY 87;
INT CANR-31; MTCW

Mason, Ernst
See Pohl, Frederik

Mason, Lee W.
See Malzberg, Barry N(athaniel)

Mason, Nick 1945-.............. **CLC 35**

Mason, Tally
See Derleth, August (William)

Mass, William
See Gibson, William

Masters, Edgar Lee
1868-1950 ...... **TCLC 2, 25; DA; DAC;
DAM MST, POET; PC 1**
See also CA 104; 133; CDALB 1865-1917;
DLB 54; MTCW; YABC

Masters, Hilary 1928- .... **CLC 48**
See also CA 25-28R; CANR 13, 47

Mastrosimone, William 19(?)-...... **CLC 36**

Mathe, Albert
See Camus, Albert

Mather, Cotton 1663-1728.......... **LC 38**
See also CDALB 1640-1865; DLB 24, 30,
140

Mather, Increase 1639-1723 .... **LC 38**
See also DLB 24

Matheson, Richard Burton 1926- ... **CLC 37**
See also CA 97-100; DLB 8, 44; INT 97-100

Mathews, Harry 1930-......... **CLC 6, 52**
See also CA 21-24R; CAAS 6; CANR 18,
40

Mathews, John Joseph
1894-1979 ...... **CLC 84; DAM MULT**
See also CA 19-20; 142; CANR 45; CAP 2;
DLB 175; NNAL

Mathias, Roland (Glyn) 1915-...... **CLC 45**
See also CA 97-100; CANR 19, 41; DLB 27

Matsuo Basho 1644-1694............ **PC 3**
See also DAM POET

Mattheson, Rodney
See Creasey, John

Matthews, Greg 1949- .... **CLC 45**
See also CA 135

Matthews, William 1942-......... **CLC 40**
See also CA 29-32R; CAAS 18; CANR 12,
57; DLB 5

Matthias, John (Edward) 1941-...... **CLC 9**
See also CA 33-36R; CANR 56

Matthiessen, Peter
1927- .... **CLC 5, 7, 11, 32, 64;
DAM NOV**
See also AAYA 6; BEST 90:4; CA 9-12R;
CANR 21, 50; DLB 6, 173; MTCW;
SATA 27

Maturin, Charles Robert
1780(?)-1824 .... **NCLC 6**
See also DLB 178

Matute (Ausejo), Ana Maria
1925- .... **CLC 11**
See also CA 89-92; MTCW

Maugham, W. S.
See Maugham, W(illiam) Somerset

Maugham, W(illiam) Somerset
1874-1965 ...... **CLC 1, 11, 15, 67, 93;
DA; DAB; DAC; DAM DRAM, MST,
NOV; SSC 8; WLC**
See also CA 5-8R; 25-28R; CANR 40;
CDBLB 1914-1945; DLB 10, 36, 77, 100,
162; MTCW; SATA 54

Maugham, William Somerset
See Maugham, W(illiam) Somerset

Maupassant, (Henri Rene Albert) Guy de
1850-1893 ..... **NCLC 1, 42; DA; DAB;
DAC; DAM MST; SSC 1; WLC**
See also DLB 123

Maupin, Armistead
1944- .... **CLC 95; DAM POP**
See also CA 125; 130; CANR 58; INT 130

Maurhut, Richard
See Traven, B.

Mauriac, Claude 1914-1996........ **CLC 9**
See also CA 89-92; 152; DLB 83

Mauriac, Francois (Charles)
1885-1970 .... **CLC 4, 9, 56; SSC 24**
See also CA 25-28; CAP 2; DLB 65;
MTCW

Mavor, Osborne Henry 1888-1951
See Bridie, James
See also CA 104

Maxwell, William (Keepers, Jr.)
1908- .... **CLC 19**
See also CA 93-96; CANR 54; DLBY 80;
INT 93-96

May, Elaine 1932- .... **CLC 16**
See also CA 124; 142; DLB 44

Mayakovski, Vladimir (Vladimirovich)
1893-1930 .... **TCLC 4, 18**
See also CA 104; 158

Mayhew, Henry 1812-1887 ...... **NCLC 31**
See also DLB 18, 55

Mayle, Peter 1939(?)-............. **CLC 89**
See also CA 139

Maynard, Joyce 1953-............ **CLC 23**
See also CA 111; 129

Mayne, William (James Carter)
1928- .... **CLC 12**
See also AAYA 20; CA 9-12R; CANR 37;
CLR 25; JRDA; MAICYA; SAAS 11;
SATA 6, 68

Mayo, Jim
See L'Amour, Louis (Dearborn)

Maysles, Albert 1926- .... **CLC 16**
See also CA 29-32R

Maysles, David 1932-............ **CLC 16**

Mazer, Norma Fox 1931- .... **CLC 26**
See also AAYA 5; CA 69-72; CANR 12,
32; CLR 23; JRDA; MAICYA; SAAS 1;
SATA 24, 67

Mazzini, Guiseppe 1805-1872 .... **NCLC 34**

McAuley, James Phillip
1917-1976 .... **CLC 45**
See also CA 97-100

McBain, Ed
See Hunter, Evan

McBrien, William Augustine
1930- .... **CLC 44**
See also CA 107

McCaffrey, Anne (Inez)
1926- ...... **CLC 17; DAM NOV, POP**
See also AAYA 6; AITN 2; BEST 89:2;
CA 25-28R; CANR 15, 35, 55; DLB 8;
JRDA; MAICYA; MTCW; SAAS 11;
SATA 8, 70

McCall, Nathan 1955(?)- .... **CLC 86**
See also CA 146

McCann, Arthur
See Campbell, John W(ood, Jr.)

McCann, Edson
See Pohl, Frederik

McCarthy, Charles, Jr. 1933-
See McCarthy, Cormac
See also CANR 42; DAM POP

McCarthy, Cormac
1933- .... **CLC 4, 57, 59, 101**
See also McCarthy, Charles, Jr.
See also DLB 6, 143

McCarthy, Mary (Therese)
1912-1989 ...... **CLC 1, 3, 5, 14, 24, 39,
59; SSC 24**
See also CA 5-8R; 129; CANR 16, 50;
DLB 2; DLBY 81; INT CANR-16;
MTCW

McCartney, (James) Paul
1942- .... **CLC 12, 35**
See also CA 146

McCauley, Stephen (D.) 1955- ..... **CLC 50**
See also CA 141

McClure, Michael (Thomas)
1932- .... **CLC 6, 10**
See also CA 21-24R; CANR 17, 46;
DLB 16

McCorkle, Jill (Collins) 1958-...... **CLC 51**
See also CA 121; DLBY 87

McCourt, James 1941-............. **CLC 5**
See also CA 57-60

McCoy, Horace (Stanley)
1897-1955 .... **TCLC 28**
See also CA 108; 155; DLB 9

McCrae, John 1872-1918........ **TCLC 12**
See also CA 109; DLB 92

McCreigh, James
See Pohl, Frederik

McCullers, (Lula) Carson (Smith)
1917-1967 .... **CLC 1, 4, 10, 12, 48, 100;
DA; DAB; DAC; DAM MST, NOV;
SSC 9, 24; WLC**
See also AAYA 21; CA 5-8R; 25-28R;
CABS 1, 3; CANR 18;
CDALB 1941-1968; DLB 2, 7, 173;
MTCW; SATA 27

McCulloch, John Tyler
See Burroughs, Edgar Rice

McCullough, Colleen
1938(?)- .... **CLC 27; DAM NOV, POP**
See also CA 81-84; CANR 17, 46; MTCW

McDermott, Alice 1953- . . . . **CLC 90**
See also CA 109; CANR 40

McElroy, Joseph 1930- . . . . **CLC 5, 47**
See also CA 17-20R

McEwan, Ian (Russell)
1948- . . . . **CLC 13, 66; DAM NOV**
See also BEST 90:4; CA 61-64; CANR 14,
41; DLB 14; MTCW

McFadden, David 1940- . . . . **CLC 48**
See also CA 104; DLB 60; INT 104

McFarland, Dennis 1950- . . . . **CLC 65**

McGahern, John
1934- . . . . **CLC 5, 9, 48; SSC 17**
See also CA 17-20R; CANR 29; DLB 14;
MTCW

McGinley, Patrick (Anthony)
1937- . . . . **CLC 41**
See also CA 120; 127; CANR 56; INT 127

McGinley, Phyllis 1905-1978 . . . . . . **CLC 14**
See also CA 9-12R; 77-80; CANR 19;
DLB 11, 48; SATA 2, 44; SATA-Obit 24

McGinniss, Joe 1942- . . . . **CLC 32**
See also AITN 2; BEST 89:2; CA 25-28R;
CANR 26; INT CANR-26

McGivern, Maureen Daly
See Daly, Maureen

McGrath, Patrick 1950- . . . . **CLC 55**
See also CA 136

McGrath, Thomas (Matthew)
1916-1990 . . . . **CLC 28, 59; DAM POET**
See also CA 9-12R; 132; CANR 6, 33;
MTCW; SATA 41; SATA-Obit 66

McGuane, Thomas (Francis III)
1939- . . . . **CLC 3, 7, 18, 45**
See also AITN 2; CA 49-52; CANR 5, 24,
49; DLB 2; DLBY 80; INT CANR-24;
MTCW

McGuckian, Medbh
1950- . . . . **CLC 48; DAM POET**
See also CA 143; DLB 40

McHale, Tom 1942(?)-1982 . . . . . . **CLC 3, 5**
See also AITN 1; CA 77-80; 106

McIlvanney, William 1936- . . . . **CLC 42**
See also CA 25-28R; DLB 14

McIlwraith, Maureen Mollie Hunter
See Hunter, Mollie
See also SATA 2

McInerney, Jay
1955- . . . . **CLC 34; DAM POP**
See also AAYA 18; CA 116; 123;
CANR 45; INT 123

McIntyre, Vonda N(eel) 1948- . . . . . **CLC 18**
See also CA 81-84; CANR 17, 34; MTCW

McKay, Claude
. . . . **TCLC 7, 41; BLC; DAB; PC 2**
See also McKay, Festus Claudius
See also DLB 4, 45, 51, 117

McKay, Festus Claudius 1889-1948
See McKay, Claude
See also BW 1; CA 104; 124; DA; DAC;
DAM MST, MULT, NOV, POET;
MTCW; WLC

McKuen, Rod 1933- . . . . **CLC 1, 3**
See also AITN 1; CA 41-44R; CANR 40

McLoughlin, R. B.
See Mencken, H(enry) L(ouis)

McLuhan, (Herbert) Marshall
1911-1980 . . . . **CLC 37, 83**
See also CA 9-12R; 102; CANR 12, 34;
DLB 88; INT CANR-12; MTCW

McMillan, Terry (L.)
1951- . . . . . . **CLC 50, 61; DAM MULT,
NOV, POP**
See also AAYA 21; BW 2; CA 140

McMurtry, Larry (Jeff)
1936- . . . . **CLC 2, 3, 7, 11, 27, 44;
DAM NOV, POP**
See also AAYA 15; AITN 2; BEST 89:2;
CA 5-8R; CANR 19, 43;
CDALB 1968-1988; DLB 2, 143;
DLBY 80, 87; MTCW

McNally, T. M. 1961- . . . . **CLC 82**

McNally, Terrence
1939- . . . **CLC 4, 7, 41, 91; DAM DRAM**
See also CA 45-48; CANR 2, 56; DLB 7

McNamer, Deirdre 1950- . . . . **CLC 70**

McNeile, Herman Cyril 1888-1937
See Sapper
See also DLB 77

McNickle, (William) D'Arcy
1904-1977 . . . . . . **CLC 89; DAM MULT**
See also CA 9-12R; 85-88; CANR 5, 45;
DLB 175; NNAL; SATA-Obit 22

McPhee, John (Angus) 1931- . . . . . . **CLC 36**
See also BEST 90:1; CA 65-68; CANR 20,
46; MTCW

McPherson, James Alan
1943- . . . . **CLC 19, 77**
See also BW 1; CA 25-28R; CAAS 17;
CANR 24; DLB 38; MTCW

McPherson, William (Alexander)
1933- . . . . **CLC 34**
See also CA 69-72; CANR 28;
INT CANR-28

Mead, Margaret 1901-1978 . . . . **CLC 37**
See also AITN 1; CA 1-4R; 81-84;
CANR 4; MTCW; SATA-Obit 20

Meaker, Marijane (Agnes) 1927-
See Kerr, M. E.
See also CA 107; CANR 37; INT 107;
JRDA; MAICYA; MTCW; SATA 20, 61

Medoff, Mark (Howard)
1940- . . . . **CLC 6, 23; DAM DRAM**
See also AITN 1; CA 53-56; CANR 5;
DLB 7; INT CANR-5

Medvedev, P. N.
See Bakhtin, Mikhail Mikhailovich

Meged, Aharon
See Megged, Aharon

Meged, Aron
See Megged, Aharon

Megged, Aharon 1920- . . . . **CLC 9**
See also CA 49-52; CAAS 13; CANR 1

Mehta, Ved (Parkash) 1934- . . . . **CLC 37**
See also CA 1-4R; CANR 2, 23; MTCW

Melanter
See Blackmore, R(ichard) D(oddridge)

Melikow, Loris
See Hofmannsthal, Hugo von

Melmoth, Sebastian
See Wilde, Oscar (Fingal O'Flahertie Wills)

Meltzer, Milton 1915- . . . . **CLC 26**
See also AAYA 8; CA 13-16R; CANR 38;
CLR 13; DLB 61; JRDA; MAICYA;
SAAS 1; SATA 1, 50, 80

Melville, Herman
1819-1891 . . . . . **NCLC 3, 12, 29, 45, 49;
DA; DAB; DAC; DAM MST, NOV;
SSC 1, 17; WLC**
See also CDALB 1640-1865; DLB 3, 74;
SATA 59

Menander
c. 342B.C.-c. 292B.C. . . . . **CMLC 9;
DAM DRAM; DC 3**
See also DLB 176

Mencken, H(enry) L(ouis)
1880-1956 . . . . **TCLC 13**
See also CA 105; 125; CDALB 1917-1929;
DLB 11, 29, 63, 137; MTCW

Mendelsohn, Jane 1965(?)- . . . . **CLC 99**
See also CA 154

Mercer, David
1928-1980 . . . . **CLC 5; DAM DRAM**
See also CA 9-12R; 102; CANR 23;
DLB 13; MTCW

Merchant, Paul
See Ellison, Harlan (Jay)

Meredith, George
1828-1909 . . **TCLC 17, 43; DAM POET**
See also CA 117; 153; CDBLB 1832-1890;
DLB 18, 35, 57, 159

Meredith, William (Morris)
1919- . . **CLC 4, 13, 22, 55; DAM POET**
See also CA 9-12R; CAAS 14; CANR 6, 40;
DLB 5

Merezhkovsky, Dmitry Sergeyevich
1865-1941 . . . . **TCLC 29**

Merimee, Prosper
1803-1870 . . . . **NCLC 6; SSC 7**
See also DLB 119

Merkin, Daphne 1954- . . . . **CLC 44**
See also CA 123

Merlin, Arthur
See Blish, James (Benjamin)

Merrill, James (Ingram)
1926-1995 . . . . **CLC 2, 3, 6, 8, 13, 18, 34,
91; DAM POET**
See also CA 13-16R; 147; CANR 10, 49;
DLB 5, 165; DLBY 85; INT CANR-10;
MTCW

Merriman, Alex
See Silverberg, Robert

Merritt, E. B.
See Waddington, Miriam

Merton, Thomas
1915-1968 . . **CLC 1, 3, 11, 34, 83; PC 10**
See also CA 5-8R; 25-28R; CANR 22, 53;
DLB 48; DLBY 81; MTCW

Merwin, W(illiam) S(tanley)
1927- . . . . . . **CLC 1, 2, 3, 5, 8, 13, 18, 45,
88; DAM POET**
See also CA 13-16R; CANR 15, 51; DLB 5,
169; INT CANR-15; MTCW

Metcalf, John 1938- . . . . **CLC 37**
See also CA 113; DLB 60

Mohr, Nicholasa
    1935- ..... **CLC 12; DAM MULT; HLC**
    See also AAYA 8; CA 49-52; CANR 1, 32;
    CLR 22; DLB 145; HW; JRDA; SAAS 8;
    SATA 8

Mojtabai, A(nn) G(race)
    1938- .... **CLC 5, 9, 15, 29**
    See also CA 85-88

Moliere
    1622-1673 ..... **LC 28; DA; DAB; DAC;**
    DAM DRAM, MST; WLC

Molin, Charles
    See Mayne, William (James Carter)

Molnar, Ferenc
    1878-1952 ..... **TCLC 20; DAM DRAM**
    See also CA 109; 153

Momaday, N(avarre) Scott
    1934- ..... **CLC 2, 19, 85, 95; DA; DAB;**
    DAC; DAM MST, MULT, NOV, POP
    See also AAYA 11; CA 25-28R; CANR 14,
    34; DLB 143, 175; INT CANR-14;
    MTCW; NNAL; SATA 48;
    SATA-Brief 30; YABC

Monette, Paul 1945-1995......... **CLC 82**
    See also CA 139; 147

Monroe, Harriet 1860-1936...... **TCLC 12**
    See also CA 109; DLB 54, 91

Monroe, Lyle
    See Heinlein, Robert A(nson)

Montagu, Elizabeth 1917-........ **NCLC 7**
    See also CA 9-12R

Montagu, Mary (Pierrepont) Wortley
    1689-1762 .... **LC 9; PC 16**
    See also DLB 95, 101

Montagu, W. H.
    See Coleridge, Samuel Taylor

Montague, John (Patrick)
    1929- .... **CLC 13, 46**
    See also CA 9-12R; CANR 9; DLB 40;
    MTCW

Montaigne, Michel (Eyquem) de
    1533-1592 ...... **LC 8; DA; DAB; DAC;**
    DAM MST; WLC

Montale, Eugenio
    1896-1981 .... **CLC 7, 9, 18; PC 13**
    See also CA 17-20R; 104; CANR 30;
    DLB 114; MTCW

Montesquieu, Charles-Louis de Secondat
    1689-1755 .... **LC 7**

Montgomery, (Robert) Bruce 1921-1978
    See Crispin, Edmund
    See also CA 104

Montgomery, L(ucy) M(aud)
    1874-1942 .... **TCLC 51; DAC;**
    DAM MST
    See also AAYA 12; CA 108; 137; CLR 8;
    DLB 92; DLBD 14; JRDA; MAICYA; 1

Montgomery, Marion H., Jr. 1925- .. **CLC 7**
    See also AITN 1; CA 1-4R; CANR 3, 48;
    DLB 6

Montgomery, Max
    See Davenport, Guy (Mattison, Jr.)

Montherlant, Henry (Milon) de
    1896-1972 .... **CLC 8, 19; DAM DRAM**
    See also CA 85-88; 37-40R; DLB 72;
    MTCW

Monty Python
    See Chapman, Graham; Cleese, John
    (Marwood); Gilliam, Terry (Vance); Idle,
    Eric; Jones, Terence Graham Parry; Palin,
    Michael (Edward)
    See also AAYA 7

Moodie, Susanna (Strickland)
    1803-1885 .... **NCLC 14**
    See also DLB 99

Mooney, Edward 1951-
    See Mooney, Ted
    See also CA 130

Mooney, Ted .... **CLC 25**
    See also Mooney, Edward

Moorcock, Michael (John)
    1939- .... **CLC 5, 27, 58**
    See also CA 45-48; CAAS 5; CANR 2, 17,
    38; DLB 14; MTCW; SATA 93

Moore, Brian
    1921- ...... **CLC 1, 3, 5, 7, 8, 19, 32, 90;**
    DAB; DAC; DAM MST
    See also CA 1-4R; CANR 1, 25, 42; MTCW

Moore, Edward
    See Muir, Edwin

Moore, George Augustus
    1852-1933 .... **TCLC 7; SSC 19**
    See also CA 104; DLB 10, 18, 57, 135

Moore, Lorrie .... **CLC 39, 45, 68**
    See also Moore, Marie Lorena

Moore, Marianne (Craig)
    1887-1972 .... **CLC 1, 2, 4, 8, 10, 13, 19,**
    47; DA; DAB; DAC; DAM MST, POET;
    PC 4
    See also CA 1-4R; 33-36R; CANR 3;
    CDALB 1929-1941; DLB 45; DLBD 7;
    MTCW; SATA 20; YABC

Moore, Marie Lorena 1957-
    See Moore, Lorrie
    See also CA 116; CANR 39

Moore, Thomas 1779-1852....... **NCLC 6**
    See also DLB 96, 144

Morand, Paul 1888-1976 .. **CLC 41; SSC 22**
    See also CA 69-72; DLB 65

Morante, Elsa 1918-1985........ **CLC 8, 47**
    See also CA 85-88; 117; CANR 35;
    DLB 177; MTCW

Moravia, Alberto
    1907-1990 .... **CLC 2, 7, 11, 27, 46;**
    SSC 26
    See also Pincherle, Alberto
    See also DLB 177

More, Hannah 1745-1833 .... **NCLC 27**
    See also DLB 107, 109, 116, 158

More, Henry 1614-1687............. **LC 9**
    See also DLB 126

More, Sir Thomas 1478-1535 .... **LC 10, 32**

Moreas, Jean.................... **TCLC 18**
    See also Papadiamantopoulos, Johannes

Morgan, Berry 1919- .... **CLC 6**
    See also CA 49-52; DLB 6

Morgan, Claire
    See Highsmith, (Mary) Patricia

Morgan, Edwin (George) 1920-..... **CLC 31**
    See also CA 5-8R; CANR 3, 43; DLB 27

Morgan, (George) Frederick
    1922- .... **CLC 23**
    See also CA 17-20R; CANR 21

Morgan, Harriet
    See Mencken, H(enry) L(ouis)

Morgan, Jane
    See Cooper, James Fenimore

Morgan, Janet 1945- .... **CLC 39**
    See also CA 65-68

Morgan, Lady 1776(?)-1859...... **NCLC 29**
    See also DLB 116, 158

Morgan, Robin 1941-.............. **CLC 2**
    See also CA 69-72; CANR 29; MTCW;
    SATA 80

Morgan, Scott
    See Kuttner, Henry

Morgan, Seth 1949(?)-1990 .... **CLC 65**
    See also CA 132

Morgenstern, Christian
    1871-1914 .... **TCLC 8**
    See also CA 105

Morgenstern, S.
    See Goldman, William (W.)

Moricz, Zsigmond 1879-1942 ..... **TCLC 33**

Morike, Eduard (Friedrich)
    1804-1875 .... **NCLC 10**
    See also DLB 133

Mori Ogai .... **TCLC 14**
    See also Mori Rintaro

Mori Rintaro 1862-1922
    See Mori Ogai
    See also CA 110

Moritz, Karl Philipp 1756-1793 ...... **LC 2**
    See also DLB 94

Morland, Peter Henry
    See Faust, Frederick (Schiller)

Morren, Theophil
    See Hofmannsthal, Hugo von

Morris, Bill 1952-................ **CLC 76**

Morris, Julian
    See West, Morris L(anglo)

Morris, Steveland Judkins 1950(?)-
    See Wonder, Stevie
    See also CA 111

Morris, William 1834-1896 .... **NCLC 4**
    See also CDBLB 1832-1890; DLB 18, 35,
    57, 156, 178

Morris, Wright 1910-... **CLC 1, 3, 7, 18, 37**
    See also CA 9-12R; CANR 21; DLB 2;
    DLBY 81; MTCW

Morrison, Arthur 1863-1945 ...... **TCLC 72**
    See also CA 120; 157; DLB 70, 135

Morrison, Chloe Anthony Wofford
    See Morrison, Toni

Morrison, James Douglas 1943-1971
    See Morrison, Jim
    See also CA 73-76; CANR 40

Morrison, Jim .... **CLC 17**
    See also Morrison, James Douglas

Nakos, Lilika 1899(?)- . . . . **CLC 29**

Narayan, R(asipuram) K(rishnaswami)
 1906- . . . . . . **CLC 7, 28, 47; DAM NOV;**
SSC 25
See also CA 81-84; CANR 33; MTCW;
SATA 62

Nash, (Fredric) Ogden
 1902-1971 . . . . **CLC 23; DAM POET**
See also CA 13-14; 29-32R; CANR 34;
CAP 1; DLB 11; MAICYA; MTCW;
SATA 2, 46

Nathan, Daniel
See Dannay, Frederic

Nathan, George Jean 1882-1958 . . . **TCLC 18**
See also Hatteras, Owen
See also CA 114; DLB 137

Natsume, Kinnosuke 1867-1916
See Natsume, Soseki
See also CA 104

Natsume, Soseki 1867-1916 . . . . . **TCLC 2, 10**
See also Natsume, Kinnosuke
See also DLB 180

Natti, (Mary) Lee 1919-
See Kingman, Lee
See also CA 5-8R; CANR 2

Naylor, Gloria
 1950- . . . . . **CLC 28, 52; BLC; DA; DAC;**
DAM MST, MULT, NOV, POP
See also AAYA 6; BW 2; CA 107;
CANR 27, 51; DLB 173; MTCW; YABC

Neihardt, John Gneisenau
 1881-1973 . . . . **CLC 32**
See also CA 13-14; CAP 1; DLB 9, 54

Nekrasov, Nikolai Alekseevich
 1821-1878 . . . . **NCLC 11**

Nelligan, Emile 1879-1941 . . . . **TCLC 14**
See also CA 114; DLB 92

Nelson, Willie 1933- . . . . **CLC 17**
See also CA 107

Nemerov, Howard (Stanley)
 1920-1991 . . . . **CLC 2, 6, 9, 36;**
DAM POET
See also CA 1-4R; 134; CABS 2; CANR 1,
27, 53; DLB 5, 6; DLBY 83;
INT CANR-27; MTCW

Neruda, Pablo
 1904-1973 . . . . . **CLC 1, 2, 5, 7, 9, 28, 62;**
DA; DAB; DAC; DAM MST, MULT,
POET; HLC; PC 4; WLC
See also CA 19-20; 45-48; CAP 2; HW;
MTCW

Nerval, Gerard de
 1808-1855 . . . . . **NCLC 1; PC 13; SSC 18**

Nervo, (Jose) Amado (Ruiz de)
 1870-1919 . . . . **TCLC 11**
See also CA 109; 131; HW

Nessi, Pio Baroja y
See Baroja (y Nessi), Pio

Nestroy, Johann 1801-1862 . . . . . . **NCLC 42**
See also DLB 133

Netterville, Luke
See O'Grady, Standish (James)

Neufeld, John (Arthur) 1938- . . . . . . **CLC 17**
See also AAYA 11; CA 25-28R; CANR 11,
37, 56; MAICYA; SAAS 3; SATA 6, 81

Neville, Emily Cheney 1919- . . . . . . **CLC 12**
See also CA 5-8R; CANR 3, 37; JRDA;
MAICYA; SAAS 2; SATA 1

Newbound, Bernard Slade 1930-
See Slade, Bernard
See also CA 81-84; CANR 49;
DAM DRAM

Newby, P(ercy) H(oward)
 1918- . . . . **CLC 2, 13; DAM NOV**
See also CA 5-8R; CANR 32; DLB 15;
MTCW

Newlove, Donald 1928- . . . . **CLC 6**
See also CA 29-32R; CANR 25

Newlove, John (Herbert) 1938- . . . . . **CLC 14**
See also CA 21-24R; CANR 9, 25

Newman, Charles 1938- . . . . **CLC 2, 8**
See also CA 21-24R

Newman, Edwin (Harold) 1919- . . . . **CLC 14**
See also AITN 1; CA 69-72; CANR 5

Newman, John Henry
 1801-1890 . . . . **NCLC 38**
See also DLB 18, 32, 55

Newton, Suzanne 1936- . . . . **CLC 35**
See also CA 41-44R; CANR 14; JRDA;
SATA 5, 77

Nexo, Martin Andersen
 1869-1954 . . . . **TCLC 43**

Nezval, Vitezslav 1900-1958 . . . . . . **TCLC 44**
See also CA 123

Ng, Fae Myenne 1957(?)- . . . . **CLC 81**
See also CA 146

Ngema, Mbongeni 1955- . . . . **CLC 57**
See also BW 2; CA 143

Ngugi, James T(hiong'o) . . . . **CLC 3, 7, 13**
See also Ngugi wa Thiong'o

Ngugi wa Thiong'o
 1938- . . . . . **CLC 36; BLC; DAM MULT,**
NOV
See also Ngugi, James T(hiong'o)
See also BW 2; CA 81-84; CANR 27, 58;
DLB 125; MTCW

Nichol, B(arrie) P(hillip)
 1944-1988 . . . . **CLC 18**
See also CA 53-56; DLB 53; SATA 66

Nichols, John (Treadwell) 1940- . . . . **CLC 38**
See also CA 9-12R; CAAS 2; CANR 6;
DLBY 82

Nichols, Leigh
See Koontz, Dean R(ay)

Nichols, Peter (Richard)
 1927- . . . . **CLC 5, 36, 65**
See also CA 104; CANR 33; DLB 13;
MTCW

Nicolas, F. R. E.
See Freeling, Nicolas

Niedecker, Lorine
 1903-1970 . . . . **CLC 10, 42; DAM POET**
See also CA 25-28; CAP 2; DLB 48

Nietzsche, Friedrich (Wilhelm)
 1844-1900 . . . . **TCLC 10, 18, 55**
See also CA 107; 121; DLB 129

Nievo, Ippolito 1831-1861 . . . . **NCLC 22**

Nightingale, Anne Redmon 1943-
See Redmon, Anne
See also CA 103

Nik. T. O.
See Annensky, Innokenty (Fyodorovich)

Nin, Anais
 1903-1977 . . . . . . **CLC 1, 4, 8, 11, 14, 60;**
DAM NOV, POP; SSC 10
See also AITN 2; CA 13-16R; 69-72;
CANR 22, 53; DLB 2, 4, 152; MTCW

Nishiwaki, Junzaburo 1894-1982 . . . . **PC 15**
See also CA 107

Nissenson, Hugh 1933- . . . . **CLC 4, 9**
See also CA 17-20R; CANR 27; DLB 28

Niven, Larry . . . . **CLC 8**
See also Niven, Laurence Van Cott
See also DLB 8

Niven, Laurence Van Cott 1938-
See Niven, Larry
See also CA 21-24R; CAAS 12; CANR 14,
44; DAM POP; MTCW

Nixon, Agnes Eckhardt 1927- . . . . . . **CLC 21**
See also CA 110

Nizan, Paul 1905-1940 . . . . **TCLC 40**
See also DLB 72

Nkosi, Lewis
 1936- . . . . . **CLC 45; BLC; DAM MULT**
See also BW 1; CA 65-68; CANR 27;
DLB 157

Nodier, (Jean) Charles (Emmanuel)
 1780-1844 . . . . **NCLC 19**
See also DLB 119

Nolan, Christopher 1965- . . . . **CLC 58**
See also CA 111

Noon, Jeff 1957- . . . . **CLC 91**
See also CA 148

Norden, Charles
See Durrell, Lawrence (George)

Nordhoff, Charles (Bernard)
 1887-1947 . . . . **TCLC 23**
See also CA 108; DLB 9; SATA 23

Norfolk, Lawrence 1963- . . . . **CLC 76**
See also CA 144

Norman, Marsha
 1947- . . . . **CLC 28; DAM DRAM**
See also CA 105; CABS 3; CANR 41;
DLBY 84

Norris, Benjamin Franklin, Jr.
 1870-1902 . . . . **TCLC 24**
See also Norris, Frank
See also CA 110

Norris, Frank
See Norris, Benjamin Franklin, Jr.
See also CDALB 1865-1917; DLB 12, 71

Norris, Leslie 1921- . . . . **CLC 14**
See also CA 11-12; CANR 14; CAP 1;
DLB 27

North, Andrew
See Norton, Andre

North, Anthony
See Koontz, Dean R(ay)

North, Captain George
See Stevenson, Robert Louis (Balfour)

North, Milou
See Erdrich, Louise

Northrup, B. A.
See Hubbard, L(afayette) Ron(ald)

Oneal, Elizabeth 1934-
   See Oneal, Zibby
   See also CA 106; CANR 28; MAICYA;
     SATA 30, 82

Oneal, Zibby . . . . **CLC 30**
   See also Oneal, Elizabeth
   See also AAYA 5; CLR 13; JRDA

O'Neill, Eugene (Gladstone)
   1888-1953 . . . . . . **TCLC 1, 6, 27, 49; DA;**
     DAB; DAC; DAM DRAM, MST; WLC
   See also AITN 1; CA 110; 132;
     CDALB 1929-1941; DLB 7; MTCW

Onetti, Juan Carlos
   1909-1994 . . . . **CLC 7, 10; DAM MULT,**
     NOV; SSC 23
   See also CA 85-88; 145; CANR 32;
     DLB 113; HW; MTCW

O Nuallain, Brian 1911-1966
   See O'Brien, Flann
   See also CA 21-22; 25-28R; CAP 2

Oppen, George 1908-1984 . . . . **CLC 7, 13, 34**
   See also CA 13-16R; 113; CANR 8; DLB 5,
     165

Oppenheim, E(dward) Phillips
   1866-1946 . . . . **TCLC 45**
   See also CA 111; DLB 70

Origen c. 185-c. 254 . . . . **CMLC 19**

Orlovitz, Gil 1918-1973 . . . . **CLC 22**
   See also CA 77-80; 45-48; DLB 2, 5

Orris
   See Ingelow, Jean

Ortega y Gasset, Jose
   1883-1955 . . . . . **TCLC 9; DAM MULT;**
     HLC
   See also CA 106; 130; HW; MTCW

Ortese, Anna Maria 1914- . . . . **CLC 89**
   See also DLB 177

Ortiz, Simon J(oseph)
   1941- . . . . **CLC 45; DAM MULT,**
     POET; PC 17
   See also CA 134; DLB 120, 175; NNAL

Orton, Joe . . . . **CLC 4, 13, 43; DC 3**
   See also Orton, John Kingsley
   See also CDBLB 1960 to Present; DLB 13

Orton, John Kingsley 1933-1967
   See Orton, Joe
   See also CA 85-88; CANR 35;
     DAM DRAM; MTCW

Orwell, George
   . . . . . **TCLC 2, 6, 15, 31, 51; DAB; WLC**
   See also Blair, Eric (Arthur)
   See also CDBLB 1945-1960; DLB 15, 98

Osborne, David
   See Silverberg, Robert

Osborne, George
   See Silverberg, Robert

Osborne, John (James)
   1929-1994 . . . . . **CLC 1, 2, 5, 11, 45; DA;**
     DAB; DAC; DAM DRAM, MST; WLC
   See also CA 13-16R; 147; CANR 21, 56;
     CDBLB 1945-1960; DLB 13; MTCW

Osborne, Lawrence 1958- . . . . **CLC 50**

Oshima, Nagisa 1932- . . . . **CLC 20**
   See also CA 116; 121

Oskison, John Milton
   1874-1947 . . . . . **TCLC 35; DAM MULT**
   See also CA 144; DLB 175; NNAL

Ossoli, Sarah Margaret (Fuller marchesa d')
   1810-1850
   See Fuller, Margaret
   See also SATA 25

Ostrovsky, Alexander
   1823-1886 . . . . **NCLC 30, 57**

Otero, Blas de 1916-1979 . . . . **CLC 11**
   See also CA 89-92; DLB 134

Otto, Whitney 1955- . . . . **CLC 70**
   See also CA 140

Ouida . . . . **TCLC 43**
   See also De La Ramee, (Marie) Louise
   See also DLB 18, 156

Ousmane, Sembene 1923- . . . . **CLC 66; BLC**
   See also BW 1; CA 117; 125; MTCW

Ovid
   43B.C.-18(?) . . . **CMLC 7; DAM POET;**
     PC 2

Owen, Hugh
   See Faust, Frederick (Schiller)

Owen, Wilfred (Edward Salter)
   1893-1918 . . . . . . **TCLC 5, 27; DA; DAB;**
     DAC; DAM MST, POET; PC 19; WLC
   See also CA 104; 141; CDBLB 1914-1945;
     DLB 20

Owens, Rochelle 1936- . . . . **CLC 8**
   See also CA 17-20R; CAAS 2; CANR 39

Oz, Amos
   1939- . . . . **CLC 5, 8, 11, 27, 33, 54;**
     DAM NOV
   See also CA 53-56; CANR 27, 47; MTCW

Ozick, Cynthia
   1928- . . . . **CLC 3, 7, 28, 62; DAM NOV,**
     POP; SSC 15
   See also BEST 90:1; CA 17-20R; CANR 23,
     58; DLB 28, 152; DLBY 82;
     INT CANR-23; MTCW

Ozu, Yasujiro 1903-1963 . . . . **CLC 16**
   See also CA 112

Pacheco, C.
   See Pessoa, Fernando (Antonio Nogueira)

Pa Chin . . . . **CLC 18**
   See also Li Fei-kan

Pack, Robert 1929- . . . . **CLC 13**
   See also CA 1-4R; CANR 3, 44; DLB 5

Padgett, Lewis
   See Kuttner, Henry

Padilla (Lorenzo), Heberto 1932- . . . **CLC 38**
   See also AITN 1; CA 123; 131; HW

Page, Jimmy 1944- . . . . **CLC 12**

Page, Louise 1955- . . . . **CLC 40**
   See also CA 140

Page, P(atricia) K(athleen)
   1916- . . . . **CLC 7, 18; DAC; DAM MST;**
     PC 12
   See also CA 53-56; CANR 4, 22; DLB 68;
     MTCW

Page, Thomas Nelson 1853-1922 . . . . **SSC 23**
   See also CA 118; DLB 12, 78; DLBD 13

Paget, Violet 1856-1935
   See Lee, Vernon
   See also CA 104

Paget-Lowe, Henry
   See Lovecraft, H(oward) P(hillips)

Paglia, Camille (Anna) 1947- . . . . **CLC 68**
   See also CA 140

Paige, Richard
   See Koontz, Dean R(ay)

Paine, Thomas 1737-1809 . . . . **NCLC 62**
   See also CDALB 1640-1865; DLB 31, 43,
     73, 158

Pakenham, Antonia
   See Fraser, (Lady) Antonia (Pakenham)

Palamas, Kostes 1859-1943 . . . . **TCLC 5**
   See also CA 105

Palazzeschi, Aldo 1885-1974 . . . . **CLC 11**
   See also CA 89-92; 53-56; DLB 114

Paley, Grace
   1922- . . . . **CLC 4, 6, 37; DAM POP;**
     SSC 8
   See also CA 25-28R; CANR 13, 46;
     DLB 28; INT CANR-13; MTCW

Palin, Michael (Edward) 1943- . . . . . **CLC 21**
   See also Monty Python
   See also CA 107; CANR 35; SATA 67

Palliser, Charles 1947- . . . . **CLC 65**
   See also CA 136

Palma, Ricardo 1833-1919 . . . . **TCLC 29**

Pancake, Breece Dexter 1952-1979
   See Pancake, Breece D'J
   See also CA 123; 109

Pancake, Breece D'J . . . . **CLC 29**
   See also Pancake, Breece Dexter
   See also DLB 130

Panko, Rudy
   See Gogol, Nikolai (Vasilyevich)

Papadiamantis, Alexandros
   1851-1911 . . . . **TCLC 29**

Papadiamantopoulos, Johannes 1856-1910
   See Moreas, Jean
   See also CA 117

Papini, Giovanni 1881-1956 . . . . **TCLC 22**
   See also CA 121

Paracelsus 1493-1541 . . . . **LC 14**
   See also DLB 179

Parasol, Peter
   See Stevens, Wallace

Pareto, Vilfredo 1848-1923 . . . . **TCLC 69**

Parfenie, Maria
   See Codrescu, Andrei

Parini, Jay (Lee) 1948- . . . . **CLC 54**
   See also CA 97-100; CAAS 16; CANR 32

Park, Jordan
   See Kornbluth, C(yril) M.; Pohl, Frederik

Parker, Bert
   See Ellison, Harlan (Jay)

Parker, Dorothy (Rothschild)
   1893-1967 . . . . **CLC 15, 68;**
     DAM POET; SSC 2
   See also CA 19-20; 25-28R; CAP 2;
     DLB 11, 45, 86; MTCW

Parker, Robert B(rown)
   1932- . . . . . . **CLC 27; DAM NOV, POP**
   See also BEST 89:4; CA 49-52; CANR 1,
     26, 52; INT CANR-26; MTCW

Parkin, Frank 1940-.............. **CLC 43**
See also CA 147

Parkman, Francis, Jr.
1823-1893 .... **NCLC 12**
See also DLB 1, 30

Parks, Gordon (Alexander Buchanan)
1912- ... **CLC 1, 16; BLC; DAM MULT**
See also AITN 2; BW 2; CA 41-44R;
CANR 26; DLB 33; SATA 8

Parmenides
c. 515B.C.-c. 450B.C........ **CMLC 22**
See also DLB 176

Parnell, Thomas 1679-1718.......... **LC 3**
See also DLB 94

Parra, Nicanor
1914- ...... **CLC 2; DAM MULT; HLC**
See also CA 85-88; CANR 32; HW; MTCW

Parrish, Mary Frances
See Fisher, M(ary) F(rances) K(ennedy)

Parson
See Coleridge, Samuel Taylor

Parson Lot
See Kingsley, Charles

Partridge, Anthony
See Oppenheim, E(dward) Phillips

Pascal, Blaise 1623-1662........... **LC 35**

Pascoli, Giovanni 1855-1912 ..... **TCLC 45**

Pasolini, Pier Paolo
1922-1975 .... **CLC 20, 37; PC 17**
See also CA 93-96; 61-64; DLB 128, 177;
MTCW

Pasquini
See Silone, Ignazio

Pastan, Linda (Olenik)
1932- .... **CLC 27; DAM POET**
See also CA 61-64; CANR 18, 40; DLB 5

Pasternak, Boris (Leonidovich)
1890-1960 ...... **CLC 7, 10, 18, 63; DA;**
DAB; DAC; DAM MST, NOV, POET;
PC 6; WLC
See also CA 127; 116; MTCW

Patchen, Kenneth
1911-1972 ... **CLC 1, 2, 18; DAM POET**
See also CA 1-4R; 33-36R; CANR 3, 35;
DLB 16, 48; MTCW

Pater, Walter (Horatio)
1839-1894 .... **NCLC 7**
See also CDBLB 1832-1890; DLB 57, 156

Paterson, A(ndrew) B(arton)
1864-1941 .... **TCLC 32**
See also CA 155

Paterson, Katherine (Womeldorf)
1932- .... **CLC 12, 30**
See also AAYA 1; CA 21-24R; CANR 28;
CLR 7; DLB 52; JRDA; MAICYA;
MTCW; SATA 13, 53, 92

Patmore, Coventry Kersey Dighton
1823-1896 .... **NCLC 9**
See also DLB 35, 98

Paton, Alan (Stewart)
1903-1988 ...... **CLC 4, 10, 25, 55; DA;**
DAB; DAC; DAM MST, NOV; WLC
See also CA 13-16; 125; CANR 22; CAP 1;
MTCW; SATA 11; SATA-Obit 56

Paton Walsh, Gillian 1937-
See Walsh, Jill Paton
See also CANR 38; JRDA; MAICYA;
SAAS 3; SATA 4, 72

Paulding, James Kirke 1778-1860.. **NCLC 2**
See also DLB 3, 59, 74

Paulin, Thomas Neilson 1949-
See Paulin, Tom
See also CA 123; 128

Paulin, Tom..................... **CLC 37**
See also Paulin, Thomas Neilson
See also DLB 40

Paustovsky, Konstantin (Georgievich)
1892-1968 .... **CLC 40**
See also CA 93-96; 25-28R

Pavese, Cesare
1908-1950 ..... **TCLC 3; PC 13; SSC 19**
See also CA 104; DLB 128, 177

Pavic, Milorad 1929-............. **CLC 60**
See also CA 136

Payne, Alan
See Jakes, John (William)

Paz, Gil
See Lugones, Leopoldo

Paz, Octavio
1914- .... **CLC 3, 4, 6, 10, 19, 51, 65;**
DA; DAB; DAC; DAM MST, MULT,
POET; HLC; PC 1; WLC
See also CA 73-76; CANR 32; DLBY 90;
HW; MTCW

p'Bitek, Okot
1931-1982 .... **CLC 96; BLC;**
DAM MULT
See also BW 2; CA 124; 107; DLB 125;
MTCW

Peacock, Molly 1947-............. **CLC 60**
See also CA 103; CAAS 21; CANR 52;
DLB 120

Peacock, Thomas Love
1785-1866 .... **NCLC 22**
See also DLB 96, 116

Peake, Mervyn 1911-1968....... **CLC 7, 54**
See also CA 5-8R; 25-28R; CANR 3;
DLB 15, 160; MTCW; SATA 23

Pearce, Philippa .... **CLC 21**
See also Christie, (Ann) Philippa
See also CLR 9; DLB 161; MAICYA;
SATA 1, 67

Pearl, Eric
See Elman, Richard

Pearson, T(homas) R(eid) 1956- .... **CLC 39**
See also CA 120; 130; INT 130

Peck, Dale 1967- .... **CLC 81**
See also CA 146

Peck, John 1941-................. **CLC 3**
See also CA 49-52; CANR 3

Peck, Richard (Wayne) 1934-...... **CLC 21**
See also AAYA 1; CA 85-88; CANR 19,
38; CLR 15; INT CANR-19; JRDA;
MAICYA; SAAS 2; SATA 18, 55

Peck, Robert Newton
1928- .. **CLC 17; DA; DAC; DAM MST**
See also AAYA 3; CA 81-84; CANR 31;
CLR 45; JRDA; MAICYA; SAAS 1;
SATA 21, 62

Peckinpah, (David) Sam(uel)
1925-1984 .... **CLC 20**
See also CA 109; 114

Pedersen, Knut 1859-1952
See Hamsun, Knut
See also CA 104; 119; MTCW

Peeslake, Gaffer
See Durrell, Lawrence (George)

Peguy, Charles Pierre
1873-1914 .... **TCLC 10**
See also CA 107

Pena, Ramon del Valle y
See Valle-Inclan, Ramon (Maria) del

Pendennis, Arthur Esquir
See Thackeray, William Makepeace

Penn, William 1644-1718.......... **LC 25**
See also DLB 24

Pepys, Samuel
1633-1703 ..... **LC 11; DA; DAB; DAC;**
DAM MST; WLC
See also CDBLB 1660-1789; DLB 101

Percy, Walker
1916-1990 .... **CLC 2, 3, 6, 8, 14, 18, 47,**
65; DAM NOV, POP
See also CA 1-4R; 131; CANR 1, 23;
DLB 2; DLBY 80, 90; MTCW

Perec, Georges 1936-1982 .... **CLC 56**
See also CA 141; DLB 83

Pereda (y Sanchez de Porrua), Jose Maria de
1833-1906 .... **TCLC 16**
See also CA 117

Pereda y Porrua, Jose Maria de
See Pereda (y Sanchez de Porrua), Jose
Maria de

Peregoy, George Weems
See Mencken, H(enry) L(ouis)

Perelman, S(idney) J(oseph)
1904-1979 ...... **CLC 3, 5, 9, 15, 23, 44,**
49; DAM DRAM
See also AITN 1, 2; CA 73-76; 89-92;
CANR 18; DLB 11, 44; MTCW

Peret, Benjamin 1899-1959 .... **TCLC 20**
See also CA 117

Peretz, Isaac Loeb
1851(?)-1915 .... **TCLC 16; SSC 26**
See also CA 109

Peretz, Yitzkhok Leibush
See Peretz, Isaac Loeb

Perez Galdos, Benito 1843-1920 ... **TCLC 27**
See also CA 125; 153; HW

Perrault, Charles 1628-1703 .... **LC 2**
See also MAICYA; SATA 25

Perry, Brighton
See Sherwood, Robert E(mmet)

Perse, St.-John .... **CLC 4, 11, 46**
See also Leger, (Marie-Rene Auguste) Alexis
Saint-Leger

Perutz, Leo 1882-1957.......... **TCLC 60**
See also DLB 81

Peseenz, Tulio F.
See Lopez y Fuentes, Gregorio

Pesetsky, Bette 1932-............. **CLC 28**
See also CA 133; DLB 130

Peshkov, Alexei Maximovich 1868-1936
See Gorky, Maxim
See also CA 105; 141; DA; DAC;
DAM DRAM, MST, NOV

Pessoa, Fernando (Antonio Nogueira)
1888-1935 . . . . **TCLC 27; HLC**
See also CA 125

Peterkin, Julia Mood 1880-1961. . . . **CLC 31**
See also CA 102; DLB 9

Peters, Joan K(aren) 1945- . . . . **CLC 39**
See also CA 158

Peters, Robert L(ouis) 1924- . . . . **CLC 7**
See also CA 13-16R; CAAS 8; DLB 105

Petofi, Sandor 1823-1849 . . . . **NCLC 21**

Petrakis, Harry Mark 1923- . . . . **CLC 3**
See also CA 9-12R; CANR 4, 30

Petrarch
1304-1374 . . . . **CMLC 20; DAM POET;**
PC 8

Petrov, Evgeny . . . . **TCLC 21**
See also Kataev, Evgeny Petrovich

Petry, Ann (Lane) 1908-1997. . . **CLC 1, 7, 18**
See also BW 1; CA 5-8R; 157; CAAS 6;
CANR 4, 46; CLR 12; DLB 76; JRDA;
MAICYA; MTCW; SATA 5;
SATA-Obit 94

Petursson, Halligrimur 1614-1674 . . . . **LC 8**

Philips, Katherine 1632-1664. . . . . . . **LC 30**
See also DLB 131

Philipson, Morris H. 1926- . . . . **CLC 53**
See also CA 1-4R; CANR 4

Phillips, Caryl
1958- . . . . **CLC 96; DAM MULT**
See also BW 2; CA 141; DLB 157

Phillips, David Graham
1867-1911 . . . . **TCLC 44**
See also CA 108; DLB 9, 12

Phillips, Jack
See Sandburg, Carl (August)

Phillips, Jayne Anne
1952- . . . . **CLC 15, 33; SSC 16**
See also CA 101; CANR 24, 50; DLBY 80;
INT CANR-24; MTCW

Phillips, Richard
See Dick, Philip K(indred)

Phillips, Robert (Schaeffer) 1938-. . . **CLC 28**
See also CA 17-20R; CAAS 13; CANR 8;
DLB 105

Phillips, Ward
See Lovecraft, H(oward) P(hillips)

Piccolo, Lucio 1901-1969. . . . . **CLC 13**
See also CA 97-100; DLB 114

Pickthall, Marjorie L(owry) C(hristie)
1883-1922 . . . . **TCLC 21**
See also CA 107; DLB 92

Pico della Mirandola, Giovanni
1463-1494 . . . . **LC 15**

Piercy, Marge
1936- . . . . **CLC 3, 6, 14, 18, 27, 62**
See also CA 21-24R; CAAS 1; CANR 13,
43; DLB 120; MTCW

Piers, Robert
See Anthony, Piers

Pieyre de Mandiargues, Andre 1909-1991
See Mandiargues, Andre Pieyre de
See also CA 103; 136; CANR 22

Pilnyak, Boris . . . . **TCLC 23**
See also Vogau, Boris Andreyevich

Pincherle, Alberto
1907-1990 . . . . . **CLC 11, 18; DAM NOV**
See also Moravia, Alberto
See also CA 25-28R; 132; CANR 33;
MTCW

Pinckney, Darryl 1953- . . . . **CLC 76**
See also BW 2; CA 143

Pindar 518B.C.-446B.C.. . . . **CMLC 12; PC 19**
See also DLB 176

Pineda, Cecile 1942- . . . . **CLC 39**
See also CA 118

Pinero, Arthur Wing
1855-1934 . . . . . **TCLC 32; DAM DRAM**
See also CA 110; 153; DLB 10

Pinero, Miguel (Antonio Gomez)
1946-1988 . . . . **CLC 4, 55**
See also CA 61-64; 125; CANR 29; HW

Pinget, Robert 1919- . . . . **CLC 7, 13, 37**
See also CA 85-88; DLB 83

Pink Floyd
See Barrett, (Roger) Syd; Gilmour, David;
Mason, Nick; Waters, Roger; Wright,
Rick

Pinkney, Edward 1802-1828 . . . . . **NCLC 31**

Pinkwater, Daniel Manus 1941- . . . . **CLC 35**
See also Pinkwater, Manus
See also AAYA 1; CA 29-32R; CANR 12,
38; CLR 4; JRDA; MAICYA; SAAS 3;
SATA 46, 76

Pinkwater, Manus
See Pinkwater, Daniel Manus
See also SATA 8

Pinsky, Robert
1940- . . **CLC 9, 19, 38, 94; DAM POET**
See also CA 29-32R; CAAS 4; CANR 58;
DLBY 82

Pinta, Harold
See Pinter, Harold

Pinter, Harold
1930- . . . . . **CLC 1, 3, 6, 9, 11, 15, 27, 58,**
73; DA; DAB; DAC; DAM DRAM,
MST; WLC
See also CA 5-8R; CANR 33; CDBLB 1960
to Present; DLB 13; MTCW

Piozzi, Hester Lynch (Thrale)
1741-1821 . . . . **NCLC 57**
See also DLB 104, 142

Pirandello, Luigi
1867-1936 . . . . . . **TCLC 4, 29; DA; DAB;**
DAC; DAM DRAM, MST; DC 5;
SSC 22; WLC
See also CA 104; 153

Pirsig, Robert M(aynard)
1928- . . . . **CLC 4, 6, 73; DAM POP**
See also CA 53-56; CANR 42; MTCW;
SATA 39

Pisarev, Dmitry Ivanovich
1840-1868 . . . . **NCLC 25**

Pix, Mary (Griffith) 1666-1709 . . . . . . **LC 8**
See also DLB 80

Pixerecourt, Guilbert de
1773-1844 . . . . **NCLC 39**

Plaatje, Sol(omon) T(shekisho)
1876-1932 . . . . **TCLC 71**
See also BW 2; CA 141

Plaidy, Jean
See Hibbert, Eleanor Alice Burford

Planche, James Robinson
1796-1880 . . . . **NCLC 42**

Plant, Robert 1948- . . . . **CLC 12**

Plante, David (Robert)
1940- . . . . **CLC 7, 23, 38; DAM NOV**
See also CA 37-40R; CANR 12, 36, 58;
DLBY 83; INT CANR-12; MTCW

Plath, Sylvia
1932-1963 . . . . . **CLC 1, 2, 3, 5, 9, 11, 14,**
17, 50, 51, 62; DA; DAB; DAC;
DAM MST, POET; PC 1; WLC
See also AAYA 13; CA 19-20; CANR 34;
CAP 2; CDALB 1941-1968; DLB 5, 6,
152; MTCW

Plato
428(?)B.C.-348(?)B.C.. . . . . **CMLC 8; DA;**
DAB; DAC; DAM MST
See also DLB 176; YABC

Platonov, Andrei . . . . **TCLC 14**
See also Klimentov, Andrei Platonovich

Platt, Kin 1911- . . . . **CLC 26**
See also AAYA 11; CA 17-20R; CANR 11;
JRDA; SAAS 17; SATA 21, 86

Plautus c. 251B.C.-184B.C.. . . . . **DC 6**

Plick et Plock
See Simenon, Georges (Jacques Christian)

Plimpton, George (Ames) 1927-. . . . . **CLC 36**
See also AITN 1; CA 21-24R; CANR 32;
MTCW; SATA 10

Plomer, William Charles Franklin
1903-1973 . . . . **CLC 4, 8**
See also CA 21-22; CANR 34; CAP 2;
DLB 20, 162; MTCW; SATA 24

Plowman, Piers
See Kavanagh, Patrick (Joseph)

Plum, J.
See Wodehouse, P(elham) G(renville)

Plumly, Stanley (Ross) 1939- . . . . . . **CLC 33**
See also CA 108; 110; DLB 5; INT 110

Plumpe, Friedrich Wilhelm
1888-1931 . . . . **TCLC 53**
See also CA 112

Poe, Edgar Allan
1809-1849 . . . . **NCLC 1, 16, 55; DA;**
DAB; DAC; DAM MST, POET; PC 1;
SSC 1, 22; WLC
See also AAYA 14; CDALB 1640-1865;
DLB 3, 59, 73, 74; SATA 23

Poet of Titchfield Street, The
See Pound, Ezra (Weston Loomis)

Pohl, Frederik 1919- . . . . . **CLC 18; SSC 25**
See also CA 61-64; CAAS 1; CANR 11, 37;
DLB 8; INT CANR-11; MTCW;
SATA 24

Poirier, Louis 1910-
See Gracq, Julien
See also CA 122; 126

Pteleon
See Grieve, C(hristopher) M(urray)
See also DAM POET

Puckett, Lute
See Masters, Edgar Lee

Puig, Manuel
1932-1990 . . . . **CLC 3, 5, 10, 28, 65;**
DAM MULT; HLC
See also CA 45-48; CANR 2, 32; DLB 113;
HW; MTCW

Purdy, Al(fred Wellington)
1918- . . . . **CLC 3, 6, 14, 50; DAC;**
DAM MST, POET
See also CA 81-84; CAAS 17; CANR 42;
DLB 88

Purdy, James (Amos)
1923- . . . . **CLC 2, 4, 10, 28, 52**
See also CA 33-36R; CAAS 1; CANR 19,
51; DLB 2; INT CANR-19; MTCW

Pure, Simon
See Swinnerton, Frank Arthur

Pushkin, Alexander (Sergeyevich)
1799-1837 . . . . . **NCLC 3, 27; DA; DAB;**
DAC; DAM DRAM, MST, POET;
PC 10; WLC
See also SATA 61

P'u Sung-ling 1640-1715 . . . . **LC 3**

Putnam, Arthur Lee
See Alger, Horatio, Jr.

Puzo, Mario
1920- . . . . . **CLC 1, 2, 6, 36; DAM NOV,**
POP
See also CA 65-68; CANR 4, 42; DLB 6;
MTCW

Pygge, Edward
See Barnes, Julian (Patrick)

Pym, Barbara (Mary Crampton)
1913-1980 . . . . **CLC 13, 19, 37**
See also CA 13-14; 97-100; CANR 13, 34;
CAP 1; DLB 14; DLBY 87; MTCW

Pynchon, Thomas (Ruggles, Jr.)
1937- . . . . . **CLC 2, 3, 6, 9, 11, 18, 33, 62,**
72; DA; DAB; DAC; DAM MST, NOV,
POP; SSC 14; WLC
See also BEST 90:2; CA 17-20R; CANR 22,
46; DLB 2, 173; MTCW

Pythagoras
c. 570B.C.-c. 500B.C. . . . . **CMLC 22**
See also DLB 176

Qian Zhongshu
See Ch'ien Chung-shu

Qroll
See Dagerman, Stig (Halvard)

Quarrington, Paul (Lewis) 1953-. . . . **CLC 65**
See also CA 129

Quasimodo, Salvatore 1901-1968 . . . **CLC 10**
See also CA 13-16; 25-28R; CAP 1;
DLB 114; MTCW

Quay, Stephen 1947- . . . . **CLC 95**

Quay, The Brothers
See Quay, Stephen; Quay, Timothy

Quay, Timothy 1947-. . . . . **CLC 95**

Queen, Ellery. . . . . **CLC 3, 11**
See also Dannay, Frederic; Davidson,
Avram; Lee, Manfred B(ennington);
Marlowe, Stephen; Sturgeon, Theodore
(Hamilton); Vance, John Holbrook

Queen, Ellery, Jr.
See Dannay, Frederic; Lee, Manfred
B(ennington)

Queneau, Raymond
1903-1976 . . . . **CLC 2, 5, 10, 42**
See also CA 77-80; 69-72; CANR 32;
DLB 72; MTCW

Quevedo, Francisco de 1580-1645. . . . **LC 23**

Quiller-Couch, Arthur Thomas
1863-1944 . . . . **TCLC 53**
See also CA 118; DLB 135, 153

Quin, Ann (Marie) 1936-1973 . . . . . . **CLC 6**
See also CA 9-12R; 45-48; DLB 14

Quinn, Martin
See Smith, Martin Cruz

Quinn, Peter 1947-. . . . . **CLC 91**

Quinn, Simon
See Smith, Martin Cruz

Quiroga, Horacio (Sylvestre)
1878-1937 . . . . . **TCLC 20; DAM MULT;**
HLC
See also CA 117; 131; HW; MTCW

Quoirez, Francoise 1935-. . . . . **CLC 9**
See also Sagan, Francoise
See also CA 49-52; CANR 6, 39; MTCW

Raabe, Wilhelm 1831-1910 . . . . **TCLC 45**
See also DLB 129

Rabe, David (William)
1940- . . . . . . **CLC 4, 8, 33; DAM DRAM**
See also CA 85-88; CABS 3; DLB 7

Rabelais, Francois
1483-1553 . . . . . . **LC 5; DA; DAB; DAC;**
DAM MST; WLC

Rabinovitch, Sholem 1859-1916
See Aleichem, Sholom
See also CA 104

Rachilde 1860-1953 . . . . **TCLC 67**
See also DLB 123

Racine, Jean
1639-1699 . . . . **LC 28; DAB; DAM MST**

Radcliffe, Ann (Ward)
1764-1823 . . . . **NCLC 6, 55**
See also DLB 39, 178

Radiguet, Raymond 1903-1923 . . . . **TCLC 29**
See also DLB 65

Radnoti, Miklos 1909-1944 . . . . **TCLC 16**
See also CA 118

Rado, James 1939-. . . . . **CLC 17**
See also CA 105

Radvanyi, Netty 1900-1983
See Seghers, Anna
See also CA 85-88; 110

Rae, Ben
See Griffiths, Trevor

Raeburn, John (Hay) 1941-. . . . . . . **CLC 34**
See also CA 57-60

Ragni, Gerome 1942-1991 . . . . **CLC 17**
See also CA 105; 134

Rahv, Philip 1908-1973 . . . . **CLC 24**
See also Greenberg, Ivan
See also DLB 137

Raine, Craig 1944-. . . . . **CLC 32**
See also CA 108; CANR 29, 51; DLB 40

Raine, Kathleen (Jessie) 1908- . . . **CLC 7, 45**
See also CA 85-88; CANR 46; DLB 20;
MTCW

Rainis, Janis 1865-1929 . . . . **TCLC 29**

Rakosi, Carl. . . . . **CLC 47**
See also Rawley, Callman
See also CAAS 5

Raleigh, Richard
See Lovecraft, H(oward) P(hillips)

Raleigh, Sir Walter
1554(?)-1618 . . . . **LC 31, 39**
See also CDBLB Before 1660; DLB 172

Rallentando, H. P.
See Sayers, Dorothy L(eigh)

Ramal, Walter
See de la Mare, Walter (John)

Ramon, Juan
See Jimenez (Mantecon), Juan Ramon

Ramos, Graciliano 1892-1953 . . . . . **TCLC 32**

Rampersad, Arnold 1941-. . . . . **CLC 44**
See also BW 2; CA 127; 133; DLB 111;
INT 133

Rampling, Anne
See Rice, Anne

Ramsay, Allan 1684(?)-1758 . . . . **LC 29**
See also DLB 95

Ramuz, Charles-Ferdinand
1878-1947 . . . . **TCLC 33**

Rand, Ayn
1905-1982 . . . . . . **CLC 3, 30, 44, 79; DA;**
DAC; DAM MST, NOV, POP; WLC
See also AAYA 10; CA 13-16R; 105;
CANR 27; MTCW

Randall, Dudley (Felker)
1914- . . . . . . **CLC 1; BLC; DAM MULT**
See also BW 1; CA 25-28R; CANR 23;
DLB 41

Randall, Robert
See Silverberg, Robert

Ranger, Ken
See Creasey, John

Ransom, John Crowe
1888-1974 . . . . **CLC 2, 4, 5, 11, 24;**
DAM POET
See also CA 5-8R; 49-52; CANR 6, 34;
DLB 45, 63; MTCW

Rao, Raja 1909- . . . **CLC 25, 56; DAM NOV**
See also CA 73-76; CANR 51; MTCW

Raphael, Frederic (Michael)
1931-. . . . . **CLC 2, 14**
See also CA 1-4R; CANR 1; DLB 14

Ratcliffe, James P.
See Mencken, H(enry) L(ouis)

Rathbone, Julian 1935- . . . . **CLC 41**
See also CA 101; CANR 34

Rattigan, Terence (Mervyn)
1911-1977 . . . . **CLC 7; DAM DRAM**
See also CA 85-88; 73-76;
CDBLB 1945-1960; DLB 13; MTCW

Richardson, John
1796-1852 . . . . NCLC 55; DAC
See also DLB 99

Richardson, Samuel
1689-1761 . . . . . . LC 1; DA; DAB; DAC;
DAM MST, NOV; WLC
See also CDBLB 1660-1789; DLB 39

Richler, Mordecai
1931- . . . . CLC 3, 5, 9, 13, 18, 46, 70;
DAC; DAM MST, NOV
See also AITN 1; CA 65-68; CANR 31;
CLR 17; DLB 53; MAICYA; MTCW;
SATA 44; SATA-Brief 27

Richter, Conrad (Michael)
1890-1968 . . . . CLC 30
See also AAYA 21; CA 5-8R; 25-28R;
CANR 23; DLB 9; MTCW; SATA 3

Ricostranza, Tom
See Ellis, Trey

Riddell, J. H. 1832-1906 . . . . TCLC 40

Riding, Laura . . . . CLC 3, 7
See also Jackson, Laura (Riding)

Riefenstahl, Berta Helene Amalia 1902-
See Riefenstahl, Leni
See also CA 108

Riefenstahl, Leni . . . . CLC 16
See also Riefenstahl, Berta Helene Amalia

Riffe, Ernest
See Bergman, (Ernst) Ingmar

Riggs, (Rolla) Lynn
1899-1954 . . . . . TCLC 56; DAM MULT
See also CA 144; DLB 175; NNAL

Riley, James Whitcomb
1849-1916 . . . . . . TCLC 51; DAM POET
See also CA 118; 137; MAICYA; SATA 17

Riley, Tex
See Creasey, John

Rilke, Rainer Maria
1875-1926 . . . . TCLC 1, 6, 19;
DAM POET; PC 2
See also CA 104; 132; DLB 81; MTCW

Rimbaud, (Jean Nicolas) Arthur
1854-1891 . . . . . NCLC 4, 35; DA; DAB;
DAC; DAM MST, POET; PC 3; WLC

Rinehart, Mary Roberts
1876-1958 . . . . TCLC 52
See also CA 108

Ringmaster, The
See Mencken, H(enry) L(ouis)

Ringwood, Gwen(dolyn Margaret) Pharis
1910-1984 . . . . CLC 48
See also CA 148; 112; DLB 88

Rio, Michel 19(?)- . . . . CLC 43

Ritsos, Giannes
See Ritsos, Yannis

Ritsos, Yannis 1909-1990 . . . . . CLC 6, 13, 31
See also CA 77-80; 133; CANR 39; MTCW

Ritter, Erika 1948(?)- . . . . CLC 52

Rivera, Jose Eustasio 1889-1928 . . . TCLC 35
See also HW

Rivers, Conrad Kent 1933-1968 . . . . . . CLC 1
See also BW 1; CA 85-88; DLB 41

Rivers, Elfrida
See Bradley, Marion Zimmer

Riverside, John
See Heinlein, Robert A(nson)

Rizal, Jose 1861-1896 . . . . NCLC 27

Roa Bastos, Augusto (Antonio)
1917- . . . . CLC 45; DAM MULT; HLC
See also CA 131; DLB 113; HW

Robbe-Grillet, Alain
1922- . . . . . . CLC 1, 2, 4, 6, 8, 10, 14, 43
See also CA 9-12R; CANR 33; DLB 83;
MTCW

Robbins, Harold
1916- . . . . CLC 5; DAM NOV
See also CA 73-76; CANR 26, 54; MTCW

Robbins, Thomas Eugene 1936-
See Robbins, Tom
See also CA 81-84; CANR 29; DAM NOV,
POP; MTCW

Robbins, Tom . . . . CLC 9, 32, 64
See also Robbins, Thomas Eugene
See also BEST 90:3; DLBY 80

Robbins, Trina 1938- . . . . CLC 21
See also CA 128

Roberts, Charles G(eorge) D(ouglas)
1860-1943 . . . . TCLC 8
See also CA 105; CLR 33; DLB 92;
SATA 88; SATA-Brief 29

Roberts, Elizabeth Madox
1886-1941 . . . . TCLC 68
See also CA 111; DLB 9, 54, 102;
SATA 33; SATA-Brief 27

Roberts, Kate 1891-1985 . . . . CLC 15
See also CA 107; 116

Roberts, Keith (John Kingston)
1935- . . . . CLC 14
See also CA 25-28R; CANR 46

Roberts, Kenneth (Lewis)
1885-1957 . . . . TCLC 23
See also CA 109; DLB 9

Roberts, Michele (B.) 1949- . . . . CLC 48
See also CA 115; CANR 58

Robertson, Ellis
See Ellison, Harlan (Jay); Silverberg, Robert

Robertson, Thomas William
1829-1871 . . . . NCLC 35; DAM DRAM

Robeson, Kenneth
See Dent, Lester

Robinson, Edwin Arlington
1869-1935 . . . . TCLC 5; DA; DAC;
DAM MST, POET; PC 1
See also CA 104; 133; CDALB 1865-1917;
DLB 54; MTCW

Robinson, Henry Crabb
1775-1867 . . . . NCLC 15
See also DLB 107

Robinson, Jill 1936- . . . . CLC 10
See also CA 102; INT 102

Robinson, Kim Stanley 1952- . . . . . . CLC 34
See also CA 126

Robinson, Lloyd
See Silverberg, Robert

Robinson, Marilynne 1944- . . . . CLC 25
See also CA 116

Robinson, Smokey . . . . CLC 21
See also Robinson, William, Jr.

Robinson, William, Jr. 1940-
See Robinson, Smokey
See also CA 116

Robison, Mary 1949- . . . . CLC 42, 98
See also CA 113; 116; DLB 130; INT 116

Rod, Edouard 1857-1910 . . . . TCLC 52

Roddenberry, Eugene Wesley 1921-1991
See Roddenberry, Gene
See also CA 110; 135; CANR 37; SATA 45;
SATA-Obit 69

Roddenberry, Gene . . . . CLC 17
See also Roddenberry, Eugene Wesley
See also AAYA 5; SATA-Obit 69

Rodgers, Mary 1931- . . . . CLC 12
See also CA 49-52; CANR 8, 55; CLR 20;
INT CANR-8; JRDA; MAICYA;
SATA 8

Rodgers, W(illiam) R(obert)
1909-1969 . . . . CLC 7
See also CA 85-88; DLB 20

Rodman, Eric
See Silverberg, Robert

Rodman, Howard 1920(?)-1985 . . . . . CLC 65
See also CA 118

Rodman, Maia
See Wojciechowska, Maia (Teresa)

Rodriguez, Claudio 1934- . . . . CLC 10
See also DLB 134

Roelvaag, O(le) E(dvart)
1876-1931 . . . . TCLC 17
See also CA 117; DLB 9

Roethke, Theodore (Huebner)
1908-1963 . . . . . . CLC 1, 3, 8, 11, 19, 46,
101; DAM POET; PC 15
See also CA 81-84; CABS 2;
CDALB 1941-1968; DLB 5; MTCW

Rogers, Thomas Hunton 1927- . . . . . CLC 57
See also CA 89-92; INT 89-92

Rogers, Will(iam Penn Adair)
1879-1935 . . . TCLC 8, 71; DAM MULT
See also CA 105; 144; DLB 11; NNAL

Rogin, Gilbert 1929- . . . . CLC 18
See also CA 65-68; CANR 15

Rohan, Koda . . . . TCLC 22
See also Koda Shigeyuki

Rohmer, Eric . . . . CLC 16
See also Scherer, Jean-Marie Maurice

Rohmer, Sax . . . . TCLC 28
See also Ward, Arthur Henry Sarsfield
See also DLB 70

Roiphe, Anne (Richardson)
1935- . . . . CLC 3, 9
See also CA 89-92; CANR 45; DLBY 80;
INT 89-92

Rojas, Fernando de 1465-1541 . . . . . . LC 23

**Rolfe, Frederick (William Serafino Austin
Lewis Mary)** 1860-1913 . . . . . . TCLC 12
See also CA 107; DLB 34, 156

Rolland, Romain 1866-1944 . . . . TCLC 23
See also CA 118; DLB 65

Rolle, Richard c. 1300-c. 1349 . . . CMLC 21
See also DLB 146

Rolvaag, O(le) E(dvart)
See Roelvaag, O(le) E(dvart)

Romain Arnaud, Saint
See Aragon, Louis

Romains, Jules 1885-1972 . . . . CLC 7
See also CA 85-88; CANR 34; DLB 65;
MTCW

Romero, Jose Ruben 1890-1952 . . . TCLC 14
See also CA 114; 131; HW

Ronsard, Pierre de
1524-1585 . . . . LC 6; PC 11

Rooke, Leon
1934- . . . . CLC 25, 34; DAM POP
See also CA 25-28R; CANR 23, 53

Roosevelt, Theodore 1858-1919 . . . . TCLC 69
See also CA 115; DLB 47

Roper, William 1498-1578 . . . . LC 10

Roquelaure, A. N.
See Rice, Anne

Rosa, Joao Guimaraes 1908-1967 . . . CLC 23
See also CA 89-92; DLB 113

Rose, Wendy
1948- . . . . CLC 85; DAM MULT; PC 13
See also CA 53-56; CANR 5, 51; DLB 175;
NNAL; SATA 12

Rosen, Richard (Dean) 1949- . . . . CLC 39
See also CA 77-80; INT CANR-30

Rosenberg, Isaac 1890-1918 . . . . . . TCLC 12
See also CA 107; DLB 20

Rosenblatt, Joe . . . . CLC 15
See also Rosenblatt, Joseph

Rosenblatt, Joseph 1933-
See Rosenblatt, Joe
See also CA 89-92; INT 89-92

Rosenfeld, Samuel 1896-1963
See Tzara, Tristan
See also CA 89-92

Rosenstock, Sami
See Tzara, Tristan

Rosenstock, Samuel
See Tzara, Tristan

Rosenthal, M(acha) L(ouis)
1917-1996 . . . . CLC 28
See also CA 1-4R; 152; CAAS 6; CANR 4,
51; DLB 5; SATA 59

Ross, Barnaby
See Dannay, Frederic

Ross, Bernard L.
See Follett, Ken(neth Martin)

Ross, J. H.
See Lawrence, T(homas) E(dward)

Ross, Martin
See Martin, Violet Florence
See also DLB 135

Ross, (James) Sinclair
1908- . . . . . . CLC 13; DAC; DAM MST;
SSC 24
See also CA 73-76; DLB 88

Rossetti, Christina (Georgina)
1830-1894 . . . . . NCLC 2, 50; DA; DAB;
DAC; DAM MST, POET; PC 7; WLC
See also DLB 35, 163; MAICYA; SATA 20

Rossetti, Dante Gabriel
1828-1882 . . . . NCLC 4; DA; DAB;
DAC; DAM MST, POET; WLC
See also CDBLB 1832-1890; DLB 35

Rossner, Judith (Perelman)
1935- . . . . CLC 6, 9, 29
See also AITN 2; BEST 90:3; CA 17-20R;
CANR 18, 51; DLB 6; INT CANR-18;
MTCW

Rostand, Edmond (Eugene Alexis)
1868-1918 . . . . . . TCLC 6, 37; DA; DAB;
DAC; DAM DRAM, MST
See also CA 104; 126; MTCW

Roth, Henry 1906-1995 . . . . CLC 2, 6, 11
See also CA 11-12; 149; CANR 38; CAP 1;
DLB 28; MTCW

Roth, Joseph 1894-1939 . . . . TCLC 33
See also DLB 85

Roth, Philip (Milton)
1933- . . . . . . CLC 1, 2, 3, 4, 6, 9, 15, 22,
31, 47, 66, 86; DA; DAB; DAC;
DAM MST, NOV, POP; SSC 26; WLC
See also BEST 90:3; CA 1-4R; CANR 1, 22,
36, 55; CDALB 1968-1988; DLB 2, 28,
173; DLBY 82; MTCW

Rothenberg, Jerome 1931- . . . . CLC 6, 57
See also CA 45-48; CANR 1; DLB 5

Roumain, Jacques (Jean Baptiste)
1907-1944 . . . . TCLC 19; BLC;
DAM MULT
See also BW 1; CA 117; 125

Rourke, Constance (Mayfield)
1885-1941 . . . . TCLC 12
See also CA 107; 1

Rousseau, Jean-Baptiste 1671-1741 . . . LC 9

Rousseau, Jean-Jacques
1712-1778 . . . . LC 14, 36; DA; DAB;
DAC; DAM MST; WLC

Roussel, Raymond 1877-1933 . . . . . TCLC 20
See also CA 117

Rovit, Earl (Herbert) 1927- . . . . CLC 7
See also CA 5-8R; CANR 12

Rowe, Nicholas 1674-1718 . . . . LC 8
See also DLB 84

Rowley, Ames Dorrance
See Lovecraft, H(oward) P(hillips)

Rowson, Susanna Haswell
1762(?)-1824 . . . . NCLC 5
See also DLB 37

Roy, Gabrielle
1909-1983 . . . . CLC 10, 14; DAB; DAC;
DAM MST
See also CA 53-56; 110; CANR 5; DLB 68;
MTCW

Rozewicz, Tadeusz
1921- . . . . CLC 9, 23; DAM POET
See also CA 108; CANR 36; MTCW

Ruark, Gibbons 1941- . . . . CLC 3
See also CA 33-36R; CAAS 23; CANR 14,
31, 57; DLB 120

Rubens, Bernice (Ruth) 1923- . . . CLC 19, 31
See also CA 25-28R; CANR 33; DLB 14;
MTCW

Rubin, Harold
See Robbins, Harold

Rudkin, (James) David 1936- . . . . . . CLC 14
See also CA 89-92; DLB 13

Rudnik, Raphael 1933- . . . . CLC 7
See also CA 29-32R

Ruffian, M.
See Hasek, Jaroslav (Matej Frantisek)

Ruiz, Jose Martinez . . . . CLC 11
See also Martinez Ruiz, Jose

Rukeyser, Muriel
1913-1980 . . . . CLC 6, 10, 15, 27;
DAM POET; PC 12
See also CA 5-8R; 93-96; CANR 26;
DLB 48; MTCW; SATA-Obit 22

Rule, Jane (Vance) 1931- . . . . CLC 27
See also CA 25-28R; CAAS 18; CANR 12;
DLB 60

Rulfo, Juan
1918-1986 . . . . CLC 8, 80; DAM MULT;
HLC; SSC 25
See also CA 85-88; 118; CANR 26;
DLB 113; HW; MTCW

Rumi, Jalal al-Din 1297-1373 . . . . CMLC 20

Runeberg, Johan 1804-1877 . . . . . . NCLC 41

Runyon, (Alfred) Damon
1884(?)-1946 . . . . TCLC 10
See also CA 107; DLB 11, 86, 171

Rush, Norman 1933- . . . . CLC 44
See also CA 121; 126; INT 126

Rushdie, (Ahmed) Salman
1947- . . . . CLC 23, 31, 55, 100; DAB;
DAC; DAM MST, NOV, POP
See also BEST 89:3; CA 108; 111;
CANR 33, 56; INT 111; MTCW; YABC

Rushforth, Peter (Scott) 1945- . . . . . CLC 19
See also CA 101

Ruskin, John 1819-1900 . . . . TCLC 63
See also CA 114; 129; CDBLB 1832-1890;
DLB 55, 163; SATA 24

Russ, Joanna 1937- . . . . CLC 15
See also CA 25-28R; CANR 11, 31; DLB 8;
MTCW

Russell, George William 1867-1935
See Baker, Jean H.
See also CA 104; 153; CDBLB 1890-1914;
DAM POET

Russell, (Henry) Ken(neth Alfred)
1927- . . . . CLC 16
See also CA 105

Russell, Willy 1947- . . . . CLC 60

Rutherford, Mark . . . . TCLC 25
See also White, William Hale
See also DLB 18

Ruyslinck, Ward 1929- . . . . CLC 14
See also Belser, Reimond Karel Maria de

Ryan, Cornelius (John) 1920-1974 . . . CLC 7
See also CA 69-72; 53-56; CANR 38

Ryan, Michael 1946- . . . . CLC 65
See also CA 49-52; DLBY 82

Ryan, Tim
See Dent, Lester

Rybakov, Anatoli (Naumovich)
1911- . . . . CLC 23, 53
See also CA 126; 135; SATA 79

Ryder, Jonathan
See Ludlum, Robert

Ryga, George
1932-1987 . . CLC 14; DAC; DAM MST
See also CA 101; 124; CANR 43; DLB 60

S. S.
See Sassoon, Siegfried (Lorraine)

Saba, Umberto 1883-1957 .... **TCLC 33**
See also CA 144; DLB 114

Sabatini, Rafael 1875-1950 ...... **TCLC 47**

Sabato, Ernesto (R.)
1911- .... **CLC 10, 23; DAM MULT;**
HLC
See also CA 97-100; CANR 32; DLB 145;
HW; MTCW

Sacastru, Martin
See Bioy Casares, Adolfo

Sacher-Masoch, Leopold von
1836(?)-1895 .... **NCLC 31**

Sachs, Marilyn (Stickle) 1927- ..... **CLC 35**
See also AAYA 2; CA 17-20R; CANR 13,
47; CLR 2; JRDA; MAICYA; SAAS 2;
SATA 3, 68

Sachs, Nelly 1891-1970 .... **CLC 14, 98**
See also CA 17-18; 25-28R; CAP 2

Sackler, Howard (Oliver)
1929-1982 .... **CLC 14**
See also CA 61-64; 108; CANR 30; DLB 7

Sacks, Oliver (Wolf) 1933- .... **CLC 67**
See also CA 53-56; CANR 28, 50;
INT CANR-28; MTCW

Sade, Donatien Alphonse Francois Comte
1740-1814 .... **NCLC 47**

Sadoff, Ira 1945-.................. **CLC 9**
See also CA 53-56; CANR 5, 21; DLB 120

Saetone
See Camus, Albert

Safire, William 1929-............. **CLC 10**
See also CA 17-20R; CANR 31, 54

Sagan, Carl (Edward) 1934-1996.... **CLC 30**
See also AAYA 2; CA 25-28R; 155;
CANR 11, 36; MTCW; SATA 58;
SATA-Obit 94

Sagan, Francoise .... **CLC 3, 6, 9, 17, 36**
See also Quoirez, Francoise
See also DLB 83

Sahgal, Nayantara (Pandit) 1927-... **CLC 41**
See also CA 9-12R; CANR 11

Saint, H(arry) F. 1941- .... **CLC 50**
See also CA 127

St. Aubin de Teran, Lisa 1953-
See Teran, Lisa St. Aubin de
See also CA 118; 126; INT 126

Sainte-Beuve, Charles Augustin
1804-1869 .... **NCLC 5**

Saint-Exupery, Antoine (Jean Baptiste Marie
Roger) de
1900-1944 .... **TCLC 2, 56; DAM NOV;**
WLC
See also CA 108; 132; CLR 10; DLB 72;
MAICYA; MTCW; SATA 20

St. John, David
See Hunt, E(verette) Howard, (Jr.)

Saint-John Perse
See Leger, (Marie-Rene Auguste) Alexis
Saint-Leger

Saintsbury, George (Edward Bateman)
1845-1933 .... **TCLC 31**
See also DLB 57, 149

Sait Faik .... **TCLC 23**
See also Abasiyanik, Sait Faik

Saki .... **TCLC 3; SSC 12**
See also Munro, H(ector) H(ugh)

Sala, George Augustus .... **NCLC 46**

Salama, Hannu 1936-............. **CLC 18**

Salamanca, J(ack) R(ichard)
1922- .... **CLC 4, 15**
See also CA 25-28R

Sale, J. Kirkpatrick
See Sale, Kirkpatrick

Sale, Kirkpatrick 1937-........... **CLC 68**
See also CA 13-16R; CANR 10

Salinas, Luis Omar
1937- ..... **CLC 90; DAM MULT; HLC**
See also CA 131; DLB 82; HW

Salinas (y Serrano), Pedro
1891(?)-1951 .... **TCLC 17**
See also CA 117; DLB 134

Salinger, J(erome) D(avid)
1919- ...... **CLC 1, 3, 8, 12, 55, 56; DA;**
DAB; DAC; DAM MST, NOV, POP;
SSC 2; WLC
See also AAYA 2; CA 5-8R; CANR 39;
CDALB 1941-1968; CLR 18; DLB 2, 102,
173; MAICYA; MTCW; SATA 67

Salisbury, John
See Caute, David

Salter, James 1925- .... **CLC 7, 52, 59**
See also CA 73-76; DLB 130

Saltus, Edgar (Everton)
1855-1921 .... **TCLC 8**
See also CA 105

Saltykov, Mikhail Evgrafovich
1826-1889 .... **NCLC 16**

Samarakis, Antonis 1919- .... **CLC 5**
See also CA 25-28R; CAAS 16; CANR 36

Sanchez, Florencio 1875-1910..... **TCLC 37**
See also CA 153; HW

Sanchez, Luis Rafael 1936-........ **CLC 23**
See also CA 128; DLB 145; HW

Sanchez, Sonia
1934- ...... **CLC 5; BLC; DAM MULT;**
PC 9
See also BW 2; CA 33-36R; CANR 24, 49;
CLR 18; DLB 41; DLBD 8; MAICYA;
MTCW; SATA 22

Sand, George
1804-1876 .... **NCLC 2, 42, 57; DA;**
DAB; DAC; DAM MST, NOV; WLC
See also DLB 119

Sandburg, Carl (August)
1878-1967 .... **CLC 1, 4, 10, 15, 35; DA;**
DAB; DAC; DAM MST, POET; PC 2;
WLC
See also CA 5-8R; 25-28R; CANR 35;
CDALB 1865-1917; DLB 17, 54;
MAICYA; MTCW; SATA 8

Sandburg, Charles
See Sandburg, Carl (August)

Sandburg, Charles A.
See Sandburg, Carl (August)

Sanders, (James) Ed(ward) 1939- ... **CLC 53**
See also CA 13-16R; CAAS 21; CANR 13,
44; DLB 16

Sanders, Lawrence
1920- .... **CLC 41; DAM POP**
See also BEST 89:4; CA 81-84; CANR 33;
MTCW

Sanders, Noah
See Blount, Roy (Alton), Jr.

Sanders, Winston P.
See Anderson, Poul (William)

Sandoz, Mari(e Susette)
1896-1966 .... **CLC 28**
See also CA 1-4R; 25-28R; CANR 17;
DLB 9; MTCW; SATA 5

Saner, Reg(inald Anthony) 1931- .... **CLC 9**
See also CA 65-68

Sannazaro, Jacopo 1456(?)-1530...... **LC 8**

Sansom, William
1912-1976 ...... **CLC 2, 6; DAM NOV;**
SSC 21
See also CA 5-8R; 65-68; CANR 42;
DLB 139; MTCW

Santayana, George 1863-1952..... **TCLC 40**
See also CA 115; DLB 54, 71; DLBD 13

Santiago, Danny .... **CLC 33**
See also James, Daniel (Lewis)
See also DLB 122

Santmyer, Helen Hoover
1895-1986 .... **CLC 33**
See also CA 1-4R; 118; CANR 15, 33;
DLBY 84; MTCW

Santoka, Taneda 1882-1940...... **TCLC 72**

Santos, Bienvenido N(uqui)
1911-1996 ...... **CLC 22; DAM MULT**
See also CA 101; 151; CANR 19, 46

Sapper .... **TCLC 44**
See also McNeile, Herman Cyril

Sapphire 1950- .... **CLC 99**

Sappho
fl. 6th cent. B.C.- .... **CMLC 3;**
DAM POET; PC 5
See also DLB 176

Sarduy, Severo 1937-1993 .... **CLC 6, 97**
See also CA 89-92; 142; CANR 58;
DLB 113; HW

Sargeson, Frank 1903-1982 .... **CLC 31**
See also CA 25-28R; 106; CANR 38

Sarmiento, Felix Ruben Garcia
See Dario, Ruben

Saroyan, William
1908-1981 ..... **CLC 1, 8, 10, 29, 34, 56;**
DA; DAB; DAC; DAM DRAM, MST,
NOV; SSC 21; WLC
See also CA 5-8R; 103; CANR 30; DLB 7,
9, 86; DLBY 81; MTCW; SATA 23;
SATA-Obit 24

Sarraute, Nathalie
1900- .... **CLC 1, 2, 4, 8, 10, 31, 80**
See also CA 9-12R; CANR 23; DLB 83;
MTCW

Sarton, (Eleanor) May
1912-1995 .... **CLC 4, 14, 49, 91;**
DAM POET
See also CA 1-4R; 149; CANR 1, 34, 55;
DLB 48; DLBY 81; INT CANR-34;
MTCW; SATA 36; SATA-Obit 86

Sartre, Jean-Paul
1905-1980 . . . . **CLC 1, 4, 7, 9, 13, 18, 24, 44, 50, 52; DA; DAB; DAC; DAM DRAM, MST, NOV; DC 3; WLC**
See also CA 9-12R; 97-100; CANR 21; DLB 72; MTCW

Sassoon, Siegfried (Lorraine)
1886-1967 . . . . **CLC 36; DAB; DAM MST, NOV, POET; PC 12**
See also CA 104; 25-28R; CANR 36; DLB 20; MTCW

Satterfield, Charles
See Pohl, Frederik

Saul, John (W. III)
1942- . . . . . . **CLC 46; DAM NOV, POP**
See also AAYA 10; BEST 90:4; CA 81-84; CANR 16, 40

Saunders, Caleb
See Heinlein, Robert A(nson)

Saura (Atares), Carlos   1932- . . . . **CLC 20**
See also CA 114; 131; HW

Sauser-Hall, Frederic   1887-1961 . . . . **CLC 18**
See also Cendrars, Blaise
See also CA 102; 93-96; CANR 36; MTCW

Saussure, Ferdinand de
1857-1913 . . . . **TCLC 49**

Savage, Catharine
See Brosman, Catharine Savage

Savage, Thomas   1915- . . . . **CLC 40**
See also CA 126; 132; CAAS 15; INT 132

Savan, Glenn   19(?)- . . . . **CLC 50**

Sayers, Dorothy L(eigh)
1893-1957 . . . . . **TCLC 2, 15; DAM POP**
See also CA 104; 119; CDBLB 1914-1945; DLB 10, 36, 77, 100; MTCW

Sayers, Valerie   1952- . . . . **CLC 50**
See also CA 134

Sayles, John (Thomas)
1950- . . . . **CLC 7, 10, 14**
See also CA 57-60; CANR 41; DLB 44

Scammell, Michael   1935- . . . . **CLC 34**
See also CA 156

Scannell, Vernon   1922- . . . . **CLC 49**
See also CA 5-8R; CANR 8, 24, 57; DLB 27; SATA 59

Scarlett, Susan
See Streatfeild, (Mary) Noel

Schaeffer, Susan Fromberg
1941- . . . . **CLC 6, 11, 22**
See also CA 49-52; CANR 18; DLB 28; MTCW; SATA 22

Schary, Jill
See Robinson, Jill

Schell, Jonathan   1943- . . . . **CLC 35**
See also CA 73-76; CANR 12

Schelling, Friedrich Wilhelm Joseph von
1775-1854 . . . . **NCLC 30**
See also DLB 90

Schendel, Arthur van   1874-1946 . . . **TCLC 56**

Scherer, Jean-Marie Maurice   1920-
See Rohmer, Eric
See also CA 110

Schevill, James (Erwin)   1920- . . . . **CLC 7**
See also CA 5-8R; CAAS 12

Schiller, Friedrich
1759-1805 . . . . **NCLC 39; DAM DRAM**
See also DLB 94

Schisgal, Murray (Joseph)   1926- . . . . . **CLC 6**
See also CA 21-24R; CANR 48

Schlee, Ann   1934- . . . . **CLC 35**
See also CA 101; CANR 29; SATA 44; SATA-Brief 36

Schlegel, August Wilhelm von
1767-1845 . . . . **NCLC 15**
See also DLB 94

Schlegel, Friedrich   1772-1829 . . . . **NCLC 45**
See also DLB 90

Schlegel, Johann Elias (von)
1719(?)-1749 . . . . **LC 5**

Schlesinger, Arthur M(eier), Jr.
1917- . . . . **CLC 84**
See also AITN 1; CA 1-4R; CANR 1, 28, 58; DLB 17; INT CANR-28; MTCW; SATA 61

Schmidt, Arno (Otto)   1914-1979 . . . . **CLC 56**
See also CA 128; 109; DLB 69

Schmitz, Aron Hector   1861-1928
See Svevo, Italo
See also CA 104; 122; MTCW

Schnackenberg, Gjertrud   1953- . . . . . **CLC 40**
See also CA 116; DLB 120

Schneider, Leonard Alfred   1925-1966
See Bruce, Lenny
See also CA 89-92

Schnitzler, Arthur
1862-1931 . . . . **TCLC 4; SSC 15**
See also CA 104; DLB 81, 118

Schopenhauer, Arthur
1788-1860 . . . . **NCLC 51**
See also DLB 90

Schor, Sandra (M.)   1932(?)-1990 . . . **CLC 65**
See also CA 132

Schorer, Mark   1908-1977 . . . . **CLC 9**
See also CA 5-8R; 73-76; CANR 7; DLB 103

Schrader, Paul (Joseph)   1946- . . . . . . **CLC 26**
See also CA 37-40R; CANR 41; DLB 44

Schreiner, Olive (Emilie Albertina)
1855-1920 . . . . **TCLC 9**
See also CA 105; DLB 18, 156

Schulberg, Budd (Wilson)
1914- . . . . **CLC 7, 48**
See also CA 25-28R; CANR 19; DLB 6, 26, 28; DLBY 81

Schulz, Bruno
1892-1942 . . . . **TCLC 5, 51; SSC 13**
See also CA 115; 123

Schulz, Charles M(onroe)   1922- . . . . **CLC 12**
See also CA 9-12R; CANR 6; INT CANR-6; SATA 10

Schumacher, E(rnst) F(riedrich)
1911-1977 . . . . **CLC 80**
See also CA 81-84; 73-76; CANR 34

Schuyler, James Marcus
1923-1991 . . . . . **CLC 5, 23; DAM POET**
See also CA 101; 134; DLB 5, 169; INT 101

Schwartz, Delmore (David)
1913-1966 . . . **CLC 2, 4, 10, 45, 87; PC 8**
See also CA 17-18; 25-28R; CANR 35; CAP 2; DLB 28, 48; MTCW

Schwartz, Ernst
See Ozu, Yasujiro

Schwartz, John Burnham   1965- . . . . **CLC 59**
See also CA 132

Schwartz, Lynne Sharon   1939- . . . . . **CLC 31**
See also CA 103; CANR 44

Schwartz, Muriel A.
See Eliot, T(homas) S(tearns)

Schwarz-Bart, Andre   1928- . . . . **CLC 2, 4**
See also CA 89-92

Schwarz-Bart, Simone   1938- . . . . **CLC 7**
See also BW 2; CA 97-100

Schwob, (Mayer Andre) Marcel
1867-1905 . . . . **TCLC 20**
See also CA 117; DLB 123

Sciascia, Leonardo
1921-1989 . . . . **CLC 8, 9, 41**
See also CA 85-88; 130; CANR 35; DLB 177; MTCW

Scoppettone, Sandra   1936- . . . . **CLC 26**
See also AAYA 11; CA 5-8R; CANR 41; SATA 9, 92

Scorsese, Martin   1942- . . . . **CLC 20, 89**
See also CA 110; 114; CANR 46

Scotland, Jay
See Jakes, John (William)

Scott, Duncan Campbell
1862-1947 . . . . **TCLC 6; DAC**
See also CA 104; 153; DLB 92

Scott, Evelyn   1893-1963 . . . . **CLC 43**
See also CA 104; 112; DLB 9, 48

Scott, F(rancis) R(eginald)
1899-1985 . . . . **CLC 22**
See also CA 101; 114; DLB 88; INT 101

Scott, Frank
See Scott, F(rancis) R(eginald)

Scott, Joanna   1960- . . . . **CLC 50**
See also CA 126; CANR 53

Scott, Paul (Mark)   1920-1978 . . . . **CLC 9, 60**
See also CA 81-84; 77-80; CANR 33; DLB 14; MTCW

Scott, Walter
1771-1832 . . . . **NCLC 15; DA; DAB; DAC; DAM MST, NOV, POET; PC 13; WLC**
See also CDBLB 1789-1832; DLB 93, 107, 116, 144, 159; 2

Scribe, (Augustin) Eugene
1791-1861 . . . . **NCLC 16; DAM DRAM; DC 5**

Scrum, R.
See Crumb, R(obert)

Scudery, Madeleine de   1607-1701 . . . . . **LC 2**

Scum
See Crumb, R(obert)

Scumbag, Little Bobby
See Crumb, R(obert)

Seabrook, John
See Hubbard, L(afayette) Ron(ald)

Sealy, I. Allan   1951- . . . . **CLC 55**

Search, Alexander
See Pessoa, Fernando (Antonio Nogueira)

Sebastian, Lee
See Silverberg, Robert

Sebastian Owl
See Thompson, Hunter S(tockton)

Sebestyen, Ouida 1924- . . . . **CLC 30**
See also AAYA 8; CA 107; CANR 40;
CLR 17; JRDA; MAICYA; SAAS 10;
SATA 39

Secundus, H. Scriblerus
See Fielding, Henry

Sedges, John
See Buck, Pearl S(ydenstricker)

Sedgwick, Catharine Maria
1789-1867 . . . . **NCLC 19**
See also DLB 1, 74

Seelye, John 1931- . . . . **CLC 7**

Seferiades, Giorgos Stylianou 1900-1971
See Seferis, George
See also CA 5-8R; 33-36R; CANR 5, 36;
MTCW

Seferis, George . . . . **CLC 5, 11**
See also Seferiades, Giorgos Stylianou

Segal, Erich (Wolf)
1937- . . . . **CLC 3, 10; DAM POP**
See also BEST 89:1; CA 25-28R; CANR 20,
36; DLBY 86; INT CANR-20; MTCW

Seger, Bob 1945- . . . . **CLC 35**

Seghers, Anna . . . . **CLC 7**
See also Radvanyi, Netty
See also DLB 69

Seidel, Frederick (Lewis) 1936- . . . . . **CLC 18**
See also CA 13-16R; CANR 8; DLBY 84

Seifert, Jaroslav
1901-1986 . . . . **CLC 34, 44, 93**
See also CA 127; MTCW

Sei Shonagon c. 966-1017(?) . . . . . . **CMLC 6**

Selby, Hubert, Jr.
1928- . . . . **CLC 1, 2, 4, 8; SSC 20**
See also CA 13-16R; CANR 33; DLB 2

Selzer, Richard 1928- . . . . **CLC 74**
See also CA 65-68; CANR 14

Sembene, Ousmane
See Ousmane, Sembene

Senancour, Etienne Pivert de
1770-1846 . . . . **NCLC 16**
See also DLB 119

Sender, Ramon (Jose)
1902-1982 . . **CLC 8; DAM MULT; HLC**
See also CA 5-8R; 105; CANR 8; HW;
MTCW

Seneca, Lucius Annaeus
4B.C.-65 . . . . . . **CMLC 6; DAM DRAM;
DC 5**

Senghor, Leopold Sedar
1906- . . . . . **CLC 54; BLC; DAM MULT,
POET**
See also BW 2; CA 116; 125; CANR 47;
MTCW

Serling, (Edward) Rod(man)
1924-1975 . . . . **CLC 30**
See also AAYA 14; AITN 1; CA 65-68;
57-60; DLB 26

Serna, Ramon Gomez de la
See Gomez de la Serna, Ramon

Serpieres
See Guillevic, (Eugene)

Service, Robert
See Service, Robert W(illiam)
See also DAB; DLB 92

Service, Robert W(illiam)
1874(?)-1958 . . . . . . **TCLC 15; DA; DAC;
DAM MST, POET; WLC**
See also Service, Robert
See also CA 115; 140; SATA 20

Seth, Vikram
1952- . . . . **CLC 43, 90; DAM MULT**
See also CA 121; 127; CANR 50; DLB 120;
INT 127

Seton, Cynthia Propper
1926-1982 . . . . **CLC 27**
See also CA 5-8R; 108; CANR 7

Seton, Ernest (Evan) Thompson
1860-1946 . . . . **TCLC 31**
See also CA 109; DLB 92; DLBD 13;
JRDA; SATA 18

Seton-Thompson, Ernest
See Seton, Ernest (Evan) Thompson

Settle, Mary Lee 1918- . . . . **CLC 19, 61**
See also CA 89-92; CAAS 1; CANR 44;
DLB 6; INT 89-92

Seuphor, Michel
See Arp, Jean

**Sevigne, Marie (de Rabutin-Chantal) Marquise
de** 1626-1696 . . . . **LC 11**

Sewall, Samuel 1652-1730 . . . . **LC 38**
See also DLB 24

Sexton, Anne (Harvey)
1928-1974 . . . . **CLC 2, 4, 6, 8, 10, 15, 53;
DA; DAB; DAC; DAM MST, POET;
PC 2; WLC**
See also CA 1-4R; 53-56; CABS 2;
CANR 3, 36; CDALB 1941-1968; DLB 5,
169; MTCW; SATA 10

Shaara, Michael (Joseph, Jr.)
1929-1988 . . . . **CLC 15; DAM POP**
See also AITN 1; CA 102; 125; CANR 52;
DLBY 83

Shackleton, C. C.
See Aldiss, Brian W(ilson)

Shacochis, Bob . . . . **CLC 39**
See also Shacochis, Robert G.

Shacochis, Robert G. 1951-
See Shacochis, Bob
See also CA 119; 124; INT 124

Shaffer, Anthony (Joshua)
1926- . . . . **CLC 19; DAM DRAM**
See also CA 110; 116; DLB 13

Shaffer, Peter (Levin)
1926- . . . . . . **CLC 5, 14, 18, 37, 60; DAB;
DAM DRAM, MST; DC 7**
See also CA 25-28R; CANR 25, 47;
CDBLB 1960 to Present; DLB 13;
MTCW

Shakey, Bernard
See Young, Neil

Shalamov, Varlam (Tikhonovich)
1907(?)-1982 . . . . **CLC 18**
See also CA 129; 105

Shamlu, Ahmad 1925- . . . . **CLC 10**

Shammas, Anton 1951- . . . . **CLC 55**

Shange, Ntozake
1948- . . . . **CLC 8, 25, 38, 74; BLC;
DAM DRAM, MULT; DC 3**
See also AAYA 9; BW 2; CA 85-88;
CABS 3; CANR 27, 48; DLB 38; MTCW

Shanley, John Patrick 1950- . . . . **CLC 75**
See also CA 128; 133

Shapcott, Thomas W(illiam) 1935- . . **CLC 38**
See also CA 69-72; CANR 49

Shapiro, Jane . . . . **CLC 76**

Shapiro, Karl (Jay) 1913- . . **CLC 4, 8, 15, 53**
See also CA 1-4R; CAAS 6; CANR 1, 36;
DLB 48; MTCW

Sharp, William 1855-1905 . . . . **TCLC 39**
See also DLB 156

Sharpe, Thomas Ridley 1928-
See Sharpe, Tom
See also CA 114; 122; INT 122

Sharpe, Tom . . . . **CLC 36**
See also Sharpe, Thomas Ridley
See also DLB 14

Shaw, Bernard . . . . **TCLC 45**
See also Shaw, George Bernard
See also BW 1

Shaw, G. Bernard
See Shaw, George Bernard

Shaw, George Bernard
1856-1950 . . . **TCLC 3, 9, 21; DA; DAB;
DAC; DAM DRAM, MST; WLC**
See also Shaw, Bernard
See also CA 104; 128; CDBLB 1914-1945;
DLB 10, 57; MTCW

Shaw, Henry Wheeler
1818-1885 . . . . **NCLC 15**
See also DLB 11

Shaw, Irwin
1913-1984 . . . . **CLC 7, 23, 34;
DAM DRAM, POP**
See also AITN 1; CA 13-16R; 112;
CANR 21; CDALB 1941-1968; DLB 6,
102; DLBY 84; MTCW

Shaw, Robert 1927-1978 . . . . **CLC 5**
See also AITN 1; CA 1-4R; 81-84;
CANR 4; DLB 13, 14

Shaw, T. E.
See Lawrence, T(homas) E(dward)

Shawn, Wallace 1943- . . . . **CLC 41**
See also CA 112

Shea, Lisa 1953- . . . . **CLC 86**
See also CA 147

Sheed, Wilfrid (John Joseph)
1930- . . . . **CLC 2, 4, 10, 53**
See also CA 65-68; CANR 30; DLB 6;
MTCW

Sheldon, Alice Hastings Bradley
1915(?)-1987
See Tiptree, James, Jr.
See also CA 108; 122; CANR 34; INT 108;
MTCW

Sheldon, John
See Bloch, Robert (Albert)

Simpson, N(orman) F(rederick)
1919- .... **CLC 29**
See also CA 13-16R; DLB 13

Sinclair, Andrew (Annandale)
1935- .... **CLC 2, 14**
See also CA 9-12R; CAAS 5; CANR 14, 38;
DLB 14; MTCW

Sinclair, Emil
See Hesse, Hermann

Sinclair, Iain 1943-.............. **CLC 76**
See also CA 132

Sinclair, Iain MacGregor
See Sinclair, Iain

Sinclair, Irene
See Griffith, D(avid Lewelyn) W(ark)

Sinclair, Mary Amelia St. Clair 1865(?)-1946
See Sinclair, May
See also CA 104

Sinclair, May................... **TCLC 3, 11**
See also Sinclair, Mary Amelia St. Clair
See also DLB 36, 135

Sinclair, Roy
See Griffith, D(avid Lewelyn) W(ark)

Sinclair, Upton (Beall)
1878-1968 ...... **CLC 1, 11, 15, 63; DA;
DAB; DAC; DAM MST, NOV; WLC**
See also CA 5-8R; 25-28R; CANR 7;
CDALB 1929-1941; DLB 9;
INT CANR-7; MTCW; SATA 9

Singer, Isaac
See Singer, Isaac Bashevis

Singer, Isaac Bashevis
1904-1991 .... **CLC 1, 3, 6, 9, 11, 15, 23,
38, 69; DA; DAB; DAC; DAM MST,
NOV; SSC 3; WLC**
See also AITN 1, 2; CA 1-4R; 134;
CANR 1, 39; CDALB 1941-1968; CLR 1;
DLB 6, 28, 52; DLBY 91; JRDA;
MAICYA; MTCW; SATA 3, 27;
SATA-Obit 68

Singer, Israel Joshua 1893-1944 ... **TCLC 33**

Singh, Khushwant 1915-.......... **CLC 11**
See also CA 9-12R; CAAS 9; CANR 6

Sinjohn, John
See Galsworthy, John

Sinyavsky, Andrei (Donatevich)
1925- .... **CLC 8**
See also CA 85-88

Sirin, V.
See Nabokov, Vladimir (Vladimirovich)

Sissman, L(ouis) E(dward)
1928-1976 .... **CLC 9, 18**
See also CA 21-24R; 65-68; CANR 13;
DLB 5

Sisson, C(harles) H(ubert) 1914-..... **CLC 8**
See also CA 1-4R; CAAS 3; CANR 3, 48;
DLB 27

Sitwell, Dame Edith
1887-1964 .... **CLC 2, 9, 67;
DAM POET; PC 3**
See also CA 9-12R; CANR 35;
CDBLB 1945-1960; DLB 20; MTCW

Sjoewall, Maj 1935-.............. **CLC 7**
See also CA 65-68

Sjowall, Maj
See Sjoewall, Maj

Skelton, Robin 1925- .... **CLC 13**
See also AITN 2; CA 5-8R; CAAS 5;
CANR 28; DLB 27, 53

Skolimowski, Jerzy 1938- .... **CLC 20**
See also CA 128

Skram, Amalie (Bertha)
1847-1905 .... **TCLC 25**

Skvorecky, Josef (Vaclav)
1924- .... **CLC 15, 39, 69; DAC;
DAM NOV**
See also CA 61-64; CAAS 1; CANR 10, 34;
MTCW

Slade, Bernard................ **CLC 11, 46**
See also Newbound, Bernard Slade
See also CAAS 9; DLB 53

Slaughter, Carolyn 1946-......... **CLC 56**
See also CA 85-88

Slaughter, Frank G(ill) 1908- ...... **CLC 29**
See also AITN 2; CA 5-8R; CANR 5;
INT CANR-5

Slavitt, David R(ytman) 1935-.... **CLC 5, 14**
See also CA 21-24R; CAAS 3; CANR 41;
DLB 5, 6

Slesinger, Tess 1905-1945 .... **TCLC 10**
See also CA 107; DLB 102

Slessor, Kenneth 1901-1971....... **CLC 14**
See also CA 102; 89-92

Slowacki, Juliusz 1809-1849 ..... **NCLC 15**

Smart, Christopher
1722-1771 ... **LC 3; DAM POET; PC 13**
See also DLB 109

Smart, Elizabeth 1913-1986........ **CLC 54**
See also CA 81-84; 118; DLB 88

Smiley, Jane (Graves)
1949- .... **CLC 53, 76; DAM POP**
See also CA 104; CANR 30, 50;
INT CANR-30

Smith, A(rthur) J(ames) M(arshall)
1902-1980 ....**CLC 15; DAC**
See also CA 1-4R; 102; CANR 4; DLB 88

Smith, Adam 1723-1790........... **LC 36**
See also DLB 104

Smith, Alexander 1829-1867 ..... **NCLC 59**
See also DLB 32, 55

Smith, Anna Deavere 1950-........ **CLC 86**
See also CA 133

Smith, Betty (Wehner) 1896-1972... **CLC 19**
See also CA 5-8R; 33-36R; DLBY 82;
SATA 6

Smith, Charlotte (Turner)
1749-1806 .... **NCLC 23**
See also DLB 39, 109

Smith, Clark Ashton 1893-1961 .... **CLC 43**
See also CA 143

Smith, Dave................. **CLC 22, 42**
See also Smith, David (Jeddie)
See also CAAS 7; DLB 5

Smith, David (Jeddie) 1942-
See Smith, Dave
See also CA 49-52; CANR 1; DAM POET

Smith, Florence Margaret 1902-1971
See Smith, Stevie
See also CA 17-18; 29-32R; CANR 35;
CAP 2; DAM POET; MTCW

Smith, Iain Crichton 1928- .... **CLC 64**
See also CA 21-24R; DLB 40, 139

Smith, John 1580(?)-1631 .... **LC 9**

Smith, Johnston
See Crane, Stephen (Townley)

Smith, Joseph, Jr. 1805-1844 .... **NCLC 53**

Smith, Lee 1944-.............. **CLC 25, 73**
See also CA 114; 119; CANR 46; DLB 143;
DLBY 83; INT 119

Smith, Martin
See Smith, Martin Cruz

Smith, Martin Cruz
1942- ..... **CLC 25; DAM MULT, POP**
See also BEST 89:4; CA 85-88; CANR 6,
23, 43; INT CANR-23; NNAL

Smith, Mary-Ann Tirone 1944-..... **CLC 39**
See also CA 118; 136

Smith, Patti 1946- .... **CLC 12**
See also CA 93-96

Smith, Pauline (Urmson)
1882-1959 .... **TCLC 25**

Smith, Rosamond
See Oates, Joyce Carol

Smith, Sheila Kaye
See Kaye-Smith, Sheila

Smith, Stevie .... **CLC 3, 8, 25, 44; PC 12**
See also Smith, Florence Margaret
See also DLB 20

Smith, Wilbur (Addison) 1933-..... **CLC 33**
See also CA 13-16R; CANR 7, 46; MTCW

Smith, William Jay 1918- .... **CLC 6**
See also CA 5-8R; CANR 44; DLB 5;
MAICYA; SAAS 22; SATA 2, 68

Smith, Woodrow Wilson
See Kuttner, Henry

Smolenskin, Peretz 1842-1885.... **NCLC 30**

Smollett, Tobias (George) 1721-1771 .. **LC 2**
See also CDBLB 1660-1789; DLB 39, 104

Snodgrass, W(illiam) D(e Witt)
1926- .... **CLC 2, 6, 10, 18, 68;
DAM POET**
See also CA 1-4R; CANR 6, 36; DLB 5;
MTCW

Snow, C(harles) P(ercy)
1905-1980 .... **CLC 1, 4, 6, 9, 13, 19;
DAM NOV**
See also CA 5-8R; 101; CANR 28;
CDBLB 1945-1960; DLB 15, 77; MTCW

Snow, Frances Compton
See Adams, Henry (Brooks)

Snyder, Gary (Sherman)
1930- .. **CLC 1, 2, 5, 9, 32; DAM POET**
See also CA 17-20R; CANR 30; DLB 5, 16,
165

Snyder, Zilpha Keatley 1927-...... **CLC 17**
See also AAYA 15; CA 9-12R; CANR 38;
CLR 31; JRDA; MAICYA; SAAS 2;
SATA 1, 28, 75

Soares, Bernardo
See Pessoa, Fernando (Antonio Nogueira)

Stapledon, (William) Olaf
1886-1950 . . . . **TCLC 22**
See also CA 111; DLB 15

Starbuck, George (Edwin)
1931-1996 . . . . **CLC 53; DAM POET**
See also CA 21-24R; 153; CANR 23

Stark, Richard
See Westlake, Donald E(dwin)

Staunton, Schuyler
See Baum, L(yman) Frank

Stead, Christina (Ellen)
1902-1983 . . . . **CLC 2, 5, 8, 32, 80**
See also CA 13-16R; 109; CANR 33, 40;
MTCW

Stead, William Thomas
1849-1912 . . . . **TCLC 48**

Steele, Richard   1672-1729 . . . . **LC 18**
See also CDBLB 1660-1789; DLB 84, 101

Steele, Timothy (Reid)   1948- . . . . **CLC 45**
See also CA 93-96; CANR 16, 50; DLB 120

Steffens, (Joseph) Lincoln
1866-1936 . . . . **TCLC 20**
See also CA 117

Stegner, Wallace (Earle)
1909-1993 . . . **CLC 9, 49, 81; DAM NOV**
See also AITN 1; BEST 90:3; CA 1-4R;
141; CAAS 9; CANR 1, 21, 46; DLB 9;
DLBY 93; MTCW

Stein, Gertrude
1874-1946 . . . . . . **TCLC 1, 6, 28, 48; DA;
DAB; DAC; DAM MST, NOV, POET;
PC 18; WLC**
See also CA 104; 132; CDALB 1917-1929;
DLB 4, 54, 86; MTCW

Steinbeck, John (Ernst)
1902-1968 . . . . . . **CLC 1, 5, 9, 13, 21, 34,
45, 75; DA; DAB; DAC; DAM DRAM,
MST, NOV; SSC 11; WLC**
See also AAYA 12; CA 1-4R; 25-28R;
CANR 1, 35; CDALB 1929-1941; DLB 7,
9; DLBD 2; MTCW; SATA 9

Steinem, Gloria   1934- . . . . **CLC 63**
See also CA 53-56; CANR 28, 51; MTCW

Steiner, George
1929- . . . . **CLC 24; DAM NOV**
See also CA 73-76; CANR 31; DLB 67;
MTCW; SATA 62

Steiner, K. Leslie
See Delany, Samuel R(ay, Jr.)

Steiner, Rudolf   1861-1925 . . . . **TCLC 13**
See also CA 107

Stendhal
1783-1842 . . . . **NCLC 23, 46; DA; DAB;
DAC; DAM MST, NOV; WLC**
See also DLB 119

Stephen, Leslie   1832-1904 . . . . **TCLC 23**
See also CA 123; DLB 57, 144

Stephen, Sir Leslie
See Stephen, Leslie

Stephen, Virginia
See Woolf, (Adeline) Virginia

Stephens, James   1882(?)-1950 . . . . . . **TCLC 4**
See also CA 104; DLB 19, 153, 162

Stephens, Reed
See Donaldson, Stephen R.

Steptoe, Lydia
See Barnes, Djuna

Sterchi, Beat   1949- . . . . **CLC 65**

Sterling, Brett
See Bradbury, Ray (Douglas); Hamilton,
Edmond

Sterling, Bruce   1954- . . . . **CLC 72**
See also CA 119; CANR 44

Sterling, George   1869-1926 . . . . **TCLC 20**
See also CA 117; DLB 54

Stern, Gerald   1925- . . . . **CLC 40, 100**
See also CA 81-84; CANR 28; DLB 105

Stern, Richard (Gustave)   1928- . . . **CLC 4, 39**
See also CA 1-4R; CANR 1, 25, 52;
DLBY 87; INT CANR-25

Sternberg, Josef von   1894-1969 . . . . . **CLC 20**
See also CA 81-84

Sterne, Laurence
1713-1768 . . . . . . **LC 2; DA; DAB; DAC;
DAM MST, NOV; WLC**
See also CDBLB 1660-1789; DLB 39

Sternheim, (William Adolf) Carl
1878-1942 . . . . **TCLC 8**
See also CA 105; DLB 56, 118

Stevens, Mark   1951- . . . . **CLC 34**
See also CA 122

Stevens, Wallace
1879-1955 . . . . **TCLC 3, 12, 45; DA;
DAB; DAC; DAM MST, POET; PC 6;
WLC**
See also CA 104; 124; CDALB 1929-1941;
DLB 54; MTCW

Stevenson, Anne (Katharine)
1933- . . . . **CLC 7, 33**
See also CA 17-20R; CAAS 9; CANR 9, 33;
DLB 40; MTCW

Stevenson, Robert Louis (Balfour)
1850-1894 . . . . . **NCLC 5, 14; DA; DAB;
DAC; DAM MST, NOV; SSC 11; WLC**
See also CDBLB 1890-1914; CLR 10, 11;
DLB 18, 57, 141, 156, 174; DLBD 13;
JRDA; MAICYA; 2

Stewart, J(ohn) I(nnes) M(ackintosh)
1906-1994 . . . . **CLC 7, 14, 32**
See also CA 85-88; 147; CAAS 3;
CANR 47; MTCW

Stewart, Mary (Florence Elinor)
1916- . . . . **CLC 7, 35; DAB**
See also CA 1-4R; CANR 1; SATA 12

Stewart, Mary Rainbow
See Stewart, Mary (Florence Elinor)

Stifle, June
See Campbell, Maria

Stifter, Adalbert   1805-1868 . . . . . . **NCLC 41**
See also DLB 133

Still, James   1906- . . . . **CLC 49**
See also CA 65-68; CAAS 17; CANR 10,
26; DLB 9; SATA 29

Sting
See Sumner, Gordon Matthew

Stirling, Arthur
See Sinclair, Upton (Beall)

Stitt, Milan   1941- . . . . **CLC 29**
See also CA 69-72

Stockton, Francis Richard   1834-1902
See Stockton, Frank R.
See also CA 108; 137; MAICYA; SATA 44

Stockton, Frank R. . . . . **TCLC 47**
See also Stockton, Francis Richard
See also DLB 42, 74; DLBD 13;
SATA-Brief 32

Stoddard, Charles
See Kuttner, Henry

Stoker, Abraham   1847-1912
See Stoker, Bram
See also CA 105; DA; DAC; DAM MST,
NOV; SATA 29

Stoker, Bram
1847-1912 . . . . **TCLC 8; DAB; WLC**
See also Stoker, Abraham
See also CA 150; CDBLB 1890-1914;
DLB 36, 70, 178

Stolz, Mary (Slattery)   1920- . . . . **CLC 12**
See also AAYA 8; AITN 1; CA 5-8R;
CANR 13, 41; JRDA; MAICYA;
SAAS 3; SATA 10, 71

Stone, Irving
1903-1989 . . . . **CLC 7; DAM POP**
See also AITN 1; CA 1-4R; 129; CAAS 3;
CANR 1, 23; INT CANR-23; MTCW;
SATA 3; SATA-Obit 64

Stone, Oliver (William)   1946- . . . . . . **CLC 73**
See also AAYA 15; CA 110; CANR 55

Stone, Robert (Anthony)
1937- . . . . **CLC 5, 23, 42**
See also CA 85-88; CANR 23; DLB 152;
INT CANR-23; MTCW

Stone, Zachary
See Follett, Ken(neth Martin)

Stoppard, Tom
1937- . . . . . . **CLC 1, 3, 4, 5, 8, 15, 29, 34,
63, 91; DA; DAB; DAC; DAM DRAM,
MST; DC 6; WLC**
See also CA 81-84; CANR 39;
CDBLB 1960 to Present; DLB 13;
DLBY 85; MTCW

Storey, David (Malcolm)
1933- . . . . . . **CLC 2, 4, 5, 8; DAM DRAM**
See also CA 81-84; CANR 36; DLB 13, 14;
MTCW

Storm, Hyemeyohsts
1935- . . . . **CLC 3; DAM MULT**
See also CA 81-84; CANR 45; NNAL

Storm, (Hans) Theodor (Woldsen)
1817-1888 . . . . **NCLC 1**

Storni, Alfonsina
1892-1938 . . . . . **TCLC 5; DAM MULT;
HLC**
See also CA 104; 131; HW

Stoughton, William   1631-1701 . . . . . . **LC 38**
See also DLB 24

Stout, Rex (Todhunter)   1886-1975 . . . **CLC 3**
See also AITN 2; CA 61-64

Stow, (Julian) Randolph   1935- . . **CLC 23, 48**
See also CA 13-16R; CANR 33; MTCW

Stowe, Harriet (Elizabeth) Beecher
1811-1896 . . . . . **NCLC 3, 50; DA; DAB;
DAC; DAM MST, NOV; WLC**
See also CDALB 1865-1917; DLB 1, 12, 42,
74; JRDA; MAICYA; 1

Tallent, Elizabeth (Ann) 1954- ..... **CLC 45**
See also CA 117; DLB 130

Tally, Ted 1952- .... **CLC 42**
See also CA 120; 124; INT 124

Tamayo y Baus, Manuel
1829-1898 .... **NCLC 1**

Tammsaare, A(nton) H(ansen)
1878-1940 .... **TCLC 27**

Tam'si, Tchicaya U
See Tchicaya, Gerald Felix

Tan, Amy (Ruth)
1952- .... **CLC 59; DAM MULT, NOV,
POP**
See also AAYA 9; BEST 89:3; CA 136;
CANR 54; DLB 173; SATA 75

Tandem, Felix
See Spitteler, Carl (Friedrich Georg)

Tanizaki, Jun'ichiro
1886-1965 ...... **CLC 8, 14, 28; SSC 21**
See also CA 93-96; 25-28R; DLB 180

Tanner, William
See Amis, Kingsley (William)

Tao Lao
See Storni, Alfonsina

Tarassoff, Lev
See Troyat, Henri

Tarbell, Ida M(inerva)
1857-1944 .... **TCLC 40**
See also CA 122; DLB 47

Tarkington, (Newton) Booth
1869-1946 .... **TCLC 9**
See also CA 110; 143; DLB 9, 102;
SATA 17

Tarkovsky, Andrei (Arsenyevich)
1932-1986 .... **CLC 75**
See also CA 127

Tartt, Donna 1964(?)- .... **CLC 76**
See also CA 142

Tasso, Torquato 1544-1595 .... **LC 5**

Tate, (John Orley) Allen
1899-1979 .... **CLC 2, 4, 6, 9, 11, 14, 24**
See also CA 5-8R; 85-88; CANR 32;
DLB 4, 45, 63; MTCW

Tate, Ellalice
See Hibbert, Eleanor Alice Burford

Tate, James (Vincent) 1943- ... **CLC 2, 6, 25**
See also CA 21-24R; CANR 29, 57; DLB 5,
169

Tavel, Ronald 1940- .... **CLC 6**
See also CA 21-24R; CANR 33

Taylor, C(ecil) P(hilip) 1929-1981... **CLC 27**
See also CA 25-28R; 105; CANR 47

Taylor, Edward
1642(?)-1729 .... **LC 11; DA; DAB;
DAC; DAM MST, POET**
See also DLB 24

Taylor, Eleanor Ross 1920- .... **CLC 5**
See also CA 81-84

Taylor, Elizabeth 1912-1975 ... **CLC 2, 4, 29**
See also CA 13-16R; CANR 9; DLB 139;
MTCW; SATA 13

Taylor, Henry (Splawn) 1942- ...... **CLC 44**
See also CA 33-36R; CAAS 7; CANR 31;
DLB 5

Taylor, Kamala (Purnaiya) 1924-
See Markandaya, Kamala
See also CA 77-80

Taylor, Mildred D. .... **CLC 21**
See also AAYA 10; BW 1; CA 85-88;
CANR 25; CLR 9; DLB 52; JRDA;
MAICYA; SAAS 5; SATA 15, 70

Taylor, Peter (Hillsman)
1917-1994 ..... **CLC 1, 4, 18, 37, 44, 50,
71; SSC 10**
See also CA 13-16R; 147; CANR 9, 50;
DLBY 81, 94; INT CANR-9; MTCW

Taylor, Robert Lewis 1912- .... **CLC 14**
See also CA 1-4R; CANR 3; SATA 10

Tchekhov, Anton
See Chekhov, Anton (Pavlovich)

Tchicaya, Gerald Felix
1931-1988 .... **CLC 101**
See also CA 129; 125

Tchicaya U Tam'si
See Tchicaya, Gerald Felix

Teasdale, Sara 1884-1933 .... **TCLC 4**
See also CA 104; DLB 45; SATA 32

Tegner, Esaias 1782-1846 .... **NCLC 2**

Teilhard de Chardin, (Marie Joseph) Pierre
1881-1955 .... **TCLC 9**
See also CA 105

Temple, Ann
See Mortimer, Penelope (Ruth)

Tennant, Emma (Christina)
1937- .... **CLC 13, 52**
See also CA 65-68; CAAS 9; CANR 10, 38;
DLB 14

Tenneshaw, S. M.
See Silverberg, Robert

Tennyson, Alfred
1809-1892 .... **NCLC 30; DA; DAB;
DAC; DAM MST, POET; PC 6; WLC**
See also CDBLB 1832-1890; DLB 32

Teran, Lisa St. Aubin de .... **CLC 36**
See also St. Aubin de Teran, Lisa

Terence
195(?)B.C.-159B.C. ..... **CMLC 14; DC 7**

Teresa de Jesus, St. 1515-1582 ...... **LC 18**

Terkel, Louis 1912-
See Terkel, Studs
See also CA 57-60; CANR 18, 45; MTCW

Terkel, Studs .... **CLC 38**
See also Terkel, Louis
See also AITN 1

Terry, C. V.
See Slaughter, Frank G(ill)

Terry, Megan 1932- .... **CLC 19**
See also CA 77-80; CABS 3; CANR 43;
DLB 7

Tertz, Abram
See Sinyavsky, Andrei (Donatevich)

Tesich, Steve 1943(?)-1996 ...... **CLC 40, 69**
See also CA 105; 152; DLBY 83

Teternikov, Fyodor Kuzmich 1863-1927
See Sologub, Fyodor
See also CA 104

Tevis, Walter 1928-1984 .... **CLC 42**
See also CA 113

Tey, Josephine .... **TCLC 14**
See also Mackintosh, Elizabeth
See also DLB 77

Thackeray, William Makepeace
1811-1863 .... **NCLC 5, 14, 22, 43; DA;
DAB; DAC; DAM MST, NOV; WLC**
See also CDBLB 1832-1890; DLB 21, 55,
159, 163; SATA 23

Thakura, Ravindranatha
See Tagore, Rabindranath

Tharoor, Shashi 1956- .... **CLC 70**
See also CA 141

Thelwell, Michael Miles 1939- ..... **CLC 22**
See also BW 2; CA 101

Theobald, Lewis, Jr.
See Lovecraft, H(oward) P(hillips)

Theodorescu, Ion N. 1880-1967
See Arghezi, Tudor
See also CA 116

Theriault, Yves
1915-1983 .. **CLC 79; DAC; DAM MST**
See also CA 102; DLB 88

Theroux, Alexander (Louis)
1939- .... **CLC 2, 25**
See also CA 85-88; CANR 20

Theroux, Paul (Edward)
1941- .... **CLC 5, 8, 11, 15, 28, 46;
DAM POP**
See also BEST 89:4; CA 33-36R; CANR 20,
45; DLB 2; MTCW; SATA 44

Thesen, Sharon 1946- .... **CLC 56**

Thevenin, Denis
See Duhamel, Georges

Thibault, Jacques Anatole Francois
1844-1924
See France, Anatole
See also CA 106; 127; DAM NOV; MTCW

Thiele, Colin (Milton) 1920- .... **CLC 17**
See also CA 29-32R; CANR 12, 28, 53;
CLR 27; MAICYA; SAAS 2; SATA 14,
72

Thomas, Audrey (Callahan)
1935- .... **CLC 7, 13, 37; SSC 20**
See also AITN 2; CA 21-24R; CAAS 19;
CANR 36, 58; DLB 60; MTCW

Thomas, D(onald) M(ichael)
1935- .... **CLC 13, 22, 31**
See also CA 61-64; CAAS 11; CANR 17,
45; CDBLB 1960 to Present; DLB 40;
INT CANR-17; MTCW

Thomas, Dylan (Marlais)
1914-1953 ... **TCLC 1, 8, 45; DA; DAB;
DAC; DAM DRAM, MST, POET;
PC 2; SSC 3; WLC**
See also CA 104; 120; CDBLB 1945-1960;
DLB 13, 20, 139; MTCW; SATA 60

Thomas, (Philip) Edward
1878-1917 ...... **TCLC 10; DAM POET**
See also CA 106; 153; DLB 19

Thomas, Joyce Carol 1938- .... **CLC 35**
See also AAYA 12; BW 2; CA 113; 116;
CANR 48; CLR 19; DLB 33; INT 116;
JRDA; MAICYA; MTCW; SAAS 7;
SATA 40, 78

Thomas, Lewis 1913-1993 .... **CLC 35**
See also CA 85-88; 143; CANR 38; MTCW

Trevor, William
1928- . . . . . **CLC 7, 9, 14, 25, 71; SSC 21**
See also Cox, William Trevor
See also DLB 14, 139

Trifonov, Yuri (Valentinovich)
1925-1981 . . . . **CLC 45**
See also CA 126; 103; MTCW

Trilling, Lionel 1905-1975 . . . . **CLC 9, 11, 24**
See also CA 9-12R; 61-64; CANR 10;
DLB 28, 63; INT CANR-10; MTCW

Trimball, W. H.
See Mencken, H(enry) L(ouis)

Tristan
See Gomez de la Serna, Ramon

Tristram
See Housman, A(lfred) E(dward)

Trogdon, William (Lewis) 1939-
See Heat-Moon, William Least
See also CA 115; 119; CANR 47; INT 119

Trollope, Anthony
1815-1882 . . . . . **NCLC 6, 33; DA; DAB;**
DAC; DAM MST, NOV; WLC
See also CDBLB 1832-1890; DLB 21, 57,
159; SATA 22

Trollope, Frances 1779-1863 . . . . . **NCLC 30**
See also DLB 21, 166

Trotsky, Leon 1879-1940 . . . . **TCLC 22**
See also CA 118

Trotter (Cockburn), Catharine
1679-1749 . . . . **LC 8**
See also DLB 84

Trout, Kilgore
See Farmer, Philip Jose

Trow, George W. S. 1943- . . . . **CLC 52**
See also CA 126

Troyat, Henri 1911- . . . . **CLC 23**
See also CA 45-48; CANR 2, 33; MTCW

Trudeau, G(arretson) B(eekman) 1948-
See Trudeau, Garry B.
See also CA 81-84; CANR 31; SATA 35

Trudeau, Garry B. . . . . **CLC 12**
See also Trudeau, G(arretson) B(eekman)
See also AAYA 10; AITN 2

Truffaut, Francois 1932-1984 . . . **CLC 20, 101**
See also CA 81-84; 113; CANR 34

Trumbo, Dalton 1905-1976 . . . . **CLC 19**
See also CA 21-24R; 69-72; CANR 10;
DLB 26

Trumbull, John 1750-1831 . . . . **NCLC 30**
See also DLB 31

Trundlett, Helen B.
See Eliot, T(homas) S(tearns)

Tryon, Thomas
1926-1991 . . . . . . **CLC 3, 11; DAM POP**
See also AITN 1; CA 29-32R; 135;
CANR 32; MTCW

Tryon, Tom
See Tryon, Thomas

Ts'ao Hsueh-ch'in 1715(?)-1763 . . . . . . **LC 1**

Tsushima, Shuji 1909-1948
See Dazai, Osamu
See also CA 107

Tsvetaeva (Efron), Marina (Ivanovna)
1892-1941 . . . . **TCLC 7, 35; PC 14**
See also CA 104; 128; MTCW

Tuck, Lily 1938- . . . . **CLC 70**
See also CA 139

Tu Fu 712-770 . . . . **PC 9**
See also DAM MULT

Tunis, John R(oberts) 1889-1975 . . . **CLC 12**
See also CA 61-64; DLB 22, 171; JRDA;
MAICYA; SATA 37; SATA-Brief 30

Tuohy, Frank . . . . **CLC 37**
See also Tuohy, John Francis
See also DLB 14, 139

Tuohy, John Francis 1925-
See Tuohy, Frank
See also CA 5-8R; CANR 3, 47

Turco, Lewis (Putnam) 1934- . . . **CLC 11, 63**
See also CA 13-16R; CAAS 22; CANR 24,
51; DLBY 84

Turgenev, Ivan
1818-1883 . . . . **NCLC 21; DA; DAB;**
DAC; DAM MST, NOV; DC 7; SSC 7;
WLC

Turgot, Anne-Robert-Jacques
1727-1781 . . . . **LC 26**

Turner, Frederick 1943- . . . . **CLC 48**
See also CA 73-76; CAAS 10; CANR 12,
30, 56; DLB 40

Tutu, Desmond M(pilo)
1931- . . . . . **CLC 80; BLC; DAM MULT**
See also BW 1; CA 125

Tutuola, Amos
1920- . . . . **CLC 5, 14, 29; BLC;**
DAM MULT
See also BW 2; CA 9-12R; CANR 27;
DLB 125; MTCW

Twain, Mark
. . . . **TCLC 6, 12, 19, 36, 48, 59; SSC 26;**
WLC
See also Clemens, Samuel Langhorne
See also AAYA 20; DLB 11, 12, 23, 64, 74

Tyler, Anne
1941- . . . . **CLC 7, 11, 18, 28, 44, 59;**
DAM NOV, POP
See also AAYA 18; BEST 89:1; CA 9-12R;
CANR 11, 33, 53; DLB 6, 143; DLBY 82;
MTCW; SATA 7, 90

Tyler, Royall 1757-1826 . . . . **NCLC 3**
See also DLB 37

Tynan, Katharine 1861-1931 . . . . **TCLC 3**
See also CA 104; DLB 153

Tyutchev, Fyodor 1803-1873 . . . . . **NCLC 34**

Tzara, Tristan
1896-1963 . . . . . . **CLC 47; DAM POET**
See also Rosenfeld, Samuel; Rosenstock,
Sami; Rosenstock, Samuel
See also CA 153

Uhry, Alfred
1936- . . . . . **CLC 55; DAM DRAM, POP**
See also CA 127; 133; INT 133

Ulf, Haerved
See Strindberg, (Johan) August

Ulf, Harved
See Strindberg, (Johan) August

Ulibarri, Sabine R(eyes)
1919- . . . . **CLC 83; DAM MULT**
See also CA 131; DLB 82; HW

Unamuno (y Jugo), Miguel de
1864-1936 . . . **TCLC 2, 9; DAM MULT,**
NOV; HLC; SSC 11
See also CA 104; 131; DLB 108; HW;
MTCW

Undercliffe, Errol
See Campbell, (John) Ramsey

Underwood, Miles
See Glassco, John

Undset, Sigrid
1882-1949 . . . . **TCLC 3; DA; DAB;**
DAC; DAM MST, NOV; WLC
See also CA 104; 129; MTCW

Ungaretti, Giuseppe
1888-1970 . . . . **CLC 7, 11, 15**
See also CA 19-20; 25-28R; CAP 2;
DLB 114

Unger, Douglas 1952- . . . . **CLC 34**
See also CA 130

Unsworth, Barry (Forster) 1930- . . . . **CLC 76**
See also CA 25-28R; CANR 30, 54

Updike, John (Hoyer)
1932- . . . . . . **CLC 1, 2, 3, 5, 7, 9, 13, 15,**
23, 34, 43, 70; DA; DAB; DAC;
DAM MST, NOV, POET, POP;
SSC 13; WLC
See also CA 1-4R; CABS 1; CANR 4, 33,
51; CDALB 1968-1988; DLB 2, 5, 143;
DLBD 3; DLBY 80, 82; MTCW

Upshaw, Margaret Mitchell
See Mitchell, Margaret (Munnerlyn)

Upton, Mark
See Sanders, Lawrence

Urdang, Constance (Henriette)
1922- . . . . **CLC 47**
See also CA 21-24R; CANR 9, 24

Uriel, Henry
See Faust, Frederick (Schiller)

Uris, Leon (Marcus)
1924- . . . . **CLC 7, 32; DAM NOV, POP**
See also AITN 1, 2; BEST 89:2; CA 1-4R;
CANR 1, 40; MTCW; SATA 49

Urmuz
See Codrescu, Andrei

Urquhart, Jane 1949- . . . . **CLC 90; DAC**
See also CA 113; CANR 32

Ustinov, Peter (Alexander) 1921- . . . . **CLC 1**
See also AITN 1; CA 13-16R; CANR 25,
51; DLB 13

U Tam'si, Gerald Felix Tchicaya
See Tchicaya, Gerald Felix

U Tam'si, Tchicaya
See Tchicaya, Gerald Felix

Vaculik, Ludvik 1926- . . . . **CLC 7**
See also CA 53-56

Vaihinger, Hans 1852-1933 . . . . **TCLC 71**
See also CA 116

Valdez, Luis (Miguel)
1940- . . . . . **CLC 84; DAM MULT; HLC**
See also CA 101; CANR 32; DLB 122; HW

Voinovich, Vladimir (Nikolaevich)
1932- .... **CLC 10, 49**
See also CA 81-84; CAAS 12; CANR 33;
MTCW

Vollmann, William T.
1959- ...... **CLC 89; DAM NOV, POP**
See also CA 134

Voloshinov, V. N.
See Bakhtin, Mikhail Mikhailovich

Voltaire
1694-1778 ..... **LC 14; DA; DAB; DAC;
DAM DRAM, MST; SSC 12; WLC**

von Daeniken, Erich 1935- .... **CLC 30**
See also AITN 1; CA 37-40R; CANR 17,
44

von Daniken, Erich
See von Daeniken, Erich

von Heidenstam, (Carl Gustaf) Verner
See Heidenstam, (Carl Gustaf) Verner von

von Heyse, Paul (Johann Ludwig)
See Heyse, Paul (Johann Ludwig von)

von Hofmannsthal, Hugo
See Hofmannsthal, Hugo von

von Horvath, Odon
See Horvath, Oedoen von

von Horvath, Oedoen
See Horvath, Oedoen von

von Liliencron, (Friedrich Adolf Axel) Detlev
See Liliencron, (Friedrich Adolf Axel)
Detlev von

Vonnegut, Kurt, Jr.
1922- ...... **CLC 1, 2, 3, 4, 5, 8, 12, 22,
40, 60; DA; DAB; DAC; DAM MST,
NOV, POP; SSC 8; WLC**
See also AAYA 6; AITN 1; BEST 90:4;
CA 1-4R; CANR 1, 25, 49;
CDALB 1968-1988; DLB 2, 8, 152;
DLBD 3; DLBY 80; MTCW

Von Rachen, Kurt
See Hubbard, L(afayette) Ron(ald)

von Rezzori (d'Arezzo), Gregor
See Rezzori (d'Arezzo), Gregor von

von Sternberg, Josef
See Sternberg, Josef von

Vorster, Gordon 1924- .... **CLC 34**
See also CA 133

Vosce, Trudie
See Ozick, Cynthia

Voznesensky, Andrei (Andreievich)
1933- ...... **CLC 1, 15, 57; DAM POET**
See also CA 89-92; CANR 37; MTCW

Waddington, Miriam 1917- .... **CLC 28**
See also CA 21-24R; CANR 12, 30;
DLB 68

Wagman, Fredrica 1937- .... **CLC 7**
See also CA 97-100; INT 97-100

Wagner, Richard 1813-1883........ **NCLC 9**
See also DLB 129

Wagner-Martin, Linda 1936-........ **CLC 50**

Wagoner, David (Russell)
1926- .... **CLC 3, 5, 15**
See also CA 1-4R; CAAS 3; CANR 2;
DLB 5; SATA 14

Wah, Fred(erick James) 1939-...... **CLC 44**
See also CA 107; 141; DLB 60

Wahloo, Per 1926-1975 .... **CLC 7**
See also CA 61-64

Wahloo, Peter
See Wahloo, Per

Wain, John (Barrington)
1925-1994 .... **CLC 2, 11, 15, 46**
See also CA 5-8R; 145; CAAS 4; CANR 23,
54; CDBLB 1960 to Present; DLB 15, 27,
139, 155; MTCW

Wajda, Andrzej 1926-............. **CLC 16**
See also CA 102

Wakefield, Dan 1932-............. **CLC 7**
See also CA 21-24R; CAAS 7

Wakoski, Diane
1937- .... **CLC 2, 4, 7, 9, 11, 40;
DAM POET; PC 15**
See also CA 13-16R; CAAS 1; CANR 9;
DLB 5; INT CANR-9

Wakoski-Sherbell, Diane
See Wakoski, Diane

Walcott, Derek (Alton)
1930- .... **CLC 2, 4, 9, 14, 25, 42, 67, 76;
BLC; DAB; DAC; DAM MST, MULT,
POET; DC 7**
See also BW 2; CA 89-92; CANR 26, 47;
DLB 117; DLBY 81; MTCW

Waldman, Anne 1945- .... **CLC 7**
See also CA 37-40R; CAAS 17; CANR 34;
DLB 16

Waldo, E. Hunter
See Sturgeon, Theodore (Hamilton)

Waldo, Edward Hamilton
See Sturgeon, Theodore (Hamilton)

Walker, Alice (Malsenior)
1944- .... **CLC 5, 6, 9, 19, 27, 46, 58;
BLC; DA; DAB; DAC; DAM MST,
MULT, NOV, POET, POP; SSC 5**
See also AAYA 3; BEST 89:4; BW 2;
CA 37-40R; CANR 9, 27, 49;
CDALB 1968-1988; DLB 6, 33, 143;
INT CANR-27; MTCW; SATA 31;
YABC

Walker, David Harry 1911-1992.... **CLC 14**
See also CA 1-4R; 137; CANR 1; SATA 8;
SATA-Obit 71

Walker, Edward Joseph 1934-
See Walker, Ted
See also CA 21-24R; CANR 12, 28, 53

Walker, George F.
1947- .... **CLC 44, 61; DAB; DAC;
DAM MST**
See also CA 103; CANR 21, 43; DLB 60

Walker, Joseph A.
1935- .... **CLC 19; DAM DRAM, MST**
See also BW 1; CA 89-92; CANR 26;
DLB 38

Walker, Margaret (Abigail)
1915- .... **CLC 1, 6; BLC; DAM MULT**
See also BW 2; CA 73-76; CANR 26, 54;
DLB 76, 152; MTCW

Walker, Ted.................... **CLC 13**
See also Walker, Edward Joseph
See also DLB 40

Wallace, David Foster 1962-....... **CLC 50**
See also CA 132

Wallace, Dexter
See Masters, Edgar Lee

Wallace, (Richard Horatio) Edgar
1875-1932 .... **TCLC 57**
See also CA 115; DLB 70

Wallace, Irving
1916-1990 ..... **CLC 7, 13; DAM NOV,
POP**
See also AITN 1; CA 1-4R; 132; CAAS 1;
CANR 1, 27; INT CANR-27; MTCW

Wallant, Edward Lewis
1926-1962 .... **CLC 5, 10**
See also CA 1-4R; CANR 22; DLB 2, 28,
143; MTCW

Walley, Byron
See Card, Orson Scott

Walpole, Horace 1717-1797......... **LC 2**
See also DLB 39, 104

Walpole, Hugh (Seymour)
1884-1941 .... **TCLC 5**
See also CA 104; DLB 34

Walser, Martin 1927-............. **CLC 27**
See also CA 57-60; CANR 8, 46; DLB 75,
124

Walser, Robert
1878-1956 .... **TCLC 18; SSC 20**
See also CA 118; DLB 66

Walsh, Jill Paton.................. **CLC 35**
See also Paton Walsh, Gillian
See also AAYA 11; CLR 2; DLB 161;
SAAS 3

Walter, Villiam Christian
See Andersen, Hans Christian

Wambaugh, Joseph (Aloysius, Jr.)
1937- .... **CLC 3, 18; DAM NOV, POP**
See also AITN 1; BEST 89:3; CA 33-36R;
CANR 42; DLB 6; DLBY 83; MTCW

Wang Wei 699(?)-761(?)........... **PC 18**

Ward, Arthur Henry Sarsfield 1883-1959
See Rohmer, Sax
See also CA 108

Ward, Douglas Turner 1930-....... **CLC 19**
See also BW 1; CA 81-84; CANR 27;
DLB 7, 38

Ward, Mary Augusta
See Ward, Mrs. Humphry

Ward, Mrs. Humphry
1851-1920 .... **TCLC 55**
See also DLB 18

Ward, Peter
See Faust, Frederick (Schiller)

Warhol, Andy 1928(?)-1987........ **CLC 20**
See also AAYA 12; BEST 89:4; CA 89-92;
121; CANR 34

Warner, Francis (Robert le Plastrier)
1937- .... **CLC 14**
See also CA 53-56; CANR 11

Warner, Marina 1946-............ **CLC 59**
See also CA 65-68; CANR 21, 55

Warner, Rex (Ernest) 1905-1986.... **CLC 45**
See also CA 89-92; 119; DLB 15

Wentworth, Robert
  See Hamilton, Edmond

Werfel, Franz (V.) 1890-1945 ...... **TCLC 8**
  See also CA 104; DLB 81, 124

Wergeland, Henrik Arnold
  1808-1845 .... **NCLC 5**

Wersba, Barbara 1932-............. **CLC 30**
  See also AAYA 2; CA 29-32R; CANR 16,
  38; CLR 3; DLB 52; JRDA; MAICYA;
  SAAS 2; SATA 1, 58

Wertmueller, Lina 1928- .... **CLC 16**
  See also CA 97-100; CANR 39

Wescott, Glenway 1901-1987....... **CLC 13**
  See also CA 13-16R; 121; CANR 23;
  DLB 4, 9, 102

Wesker, Arnold
  1932- .... **CLC 3, 5, 42; DAB;**
                              DAM DRAM
  See also CA 1-4R; CAAS 7; CANR 1, 33;
  CDBLB 1960 to Present; DLB 13;
  MTCW

Wesley, Richard (Errol) 1945-....... **CLC 7**
  See also BW 1; CA 57-60; CANR 27;
  DLB 38

Wessel, Johan Herman 1742-1785 .... **LC 7**

West, Anthony (Panther)
  1914-1987 .... **CLC 50**
  See also CA 45-48; 124; CANR 3, 19;
  DLB 15

West, C. P.
  See Wodehouse, P(elham) G(renville)

West, (Mary) Jessamyn
  1902-1984 .... **CLC 7, 17**
  See also CA 9-12R; 112; CANR 27; DLB 6;
  DLBY 84; MTCW; SATA-Obit 37

West, Morris L(anglo) 1916-..... **CLC 6, 33**
  See also CA 5-8R; CANR 24, 49; MTCW

West, Nathanael
  1903-1940 ..... **TCLC 1, 14, 44; SSC 16**
  See also CA 104; 125; CDALB 1929-1941;
  DLB 4, 9, 28; MTCW

West, Owen
  See Koontz, Dean R(ay)

West, Paul 1930- .... **CLC 7, 14, 96**
  See also CA 13-16R; CAAS 7; CANR 22,
  53; DLB 14; INT CANR-22

West, Rebecca 1892-1983 .. **CLC 7, 9, 31, 50**
  See also CA 5-8R; 109; CANR 19; DLB 36;
  DLBY 83; MTCW

Westall, Robert (Atkinson)
  1929-1993 .... **CLC 17**
  See also AAYA 12; CA 69-72; 141;
  CANR 18; CLR 13; JRDA; MAICYA;
  SAAS 2; SATA 23, 69; SATA-Obit 75

Westlake, Donald E(dwin)
  1933- .... **CLC 7, 33; DAM POP**
  See also CA 17-20R; CAAS 13; CANR 16,
  44; INT CANR-16

Westmacott, Mary
  See Christie, Agatha (Mary Clarissa)

Weston, Allen
  See Norton, Andre

Wetcheek, J. L.
  See Feuchtwanger, Lion

Wetering, Janwillem van de
  See van de Wetering, Janwillem

Wetherell, Elizabeth
  See Warner, Susan (Bogert)

Whale, James 1889-1957 .... **TCLC 63**

Whalen, Philip 1923-............ **CLC 6, 29**
  See also CA 9-12R; CANR 5, 39; DLB 16

Wharton, Edith (Newbold Jones)
  1862-1937 ...... **TCLC 3, 9, 27, 53; DA;**
        DAB; DAC; DAM MST, NOV; SSC 6;
                                  WLC
  See also CA 104; 132; CDALB 1865-1917;
  DLB 4, 9, 12, 78; DLBD 13; MTCW

Wharton, James
  See Mencken, H(enry) L(ouis)

Wharton, William (a pseudonym)
  .... **CLC 18, 37**
  See also CA 93-96; DLBY 80; INT 93-96

Wheatley (Peters), Phillis
  1754(?)-1784 .... **LC 3; BLC; DA; DAC;**
        DAM MST, MULT, POET; PC 3; WLC
  See also CDALB 1640-1865; DLB 31, 50

Wheelock, John Hall 1886-1978.... **CLC 14**
  See also CA 13-16R; 77-80; CANR 14;
  DLB 45

White, E(lwyn) B(rooks)
  1899-1985 .. **CLC 10, 34, 39; DAM POP**
  See also AITN 2; CA 13-16R; 116;
  CANR 16, 37; CLR 1, 21; DLB 11, 22;
  MAICYA; MTCW; SATA 2, 29;
  SATA-Obit 44

White, Edmund (Valentine III)
  1940- .... **CLC 27; DAM POP**
  See also AAYA 7; CA 45-48; CANR 3, 19,
  36; MTCW

White, Patrick (Victor Martindale)
  1912-1990 .. **CLC 3, 4, 5, 7, 9, 18, 65, 69**
  See also CA 81-84; 132; CANR 43; MTCW

White, Phyllis Dorothy James 1920-
  See James, P. D.
  See also CA 21-24R; CANR 17, 43;
  DAM POP; MTCW

White, T(erence) H(anbury)
  1906-1964 .... **CLC 30**
  See also CA 73-76; CANR 37; DLB 160;
  JRDA; MAICYA; SATA 12

White, Terence de Vere
  1912-1994 .... **CLC 49**
  See also CA 49-52; 145; CANR 3

White, Walter F(rancis)
  1893-1955 .... **TCLC 15**
  See also White, Walter
  See also BW 1; CA 115; 124; DLB 51

White, William Hale 1831-1913
  See Rutherford, Mark
  See also CA 121

Whitehead, E(dward) A(nthony)
  1933- .... **CLC 5**
  See also CA 65-68; CANR 58

Whitemore, Hugh (John) 1936-..... **CLC 37**
  See also CA 132; INT 132

Whitman, Sarah Helen (Power)
  1803-1878 .... **NCLC 19**
  See also DLB 1

Whitman, Walt(er)
  1819-1892 ..... **NCLC 4, 31; DA; DAB;**
        DAC; DAM MST, POET; PC 3; WLC
  See also CDALB 1640-1865; DLB 3, 64;
  SATA 20

Whitney, Phyllis A(yame)
  1903- .... **CLC 42; DAM POP**
  See also AITN 2; BEST 90:3; CA 1-4R;
  CANR 3, 25, 38; JRDA; MAICYA;
  SATA 1, 30

Whittemore, (Edward) Reed (Jr.)
  1919- .... **CLC 4**
  See also CA 9-12R; CAAS 8; CANR 4;
  DLB 5

Whittier, John Greenleaf
  1807-1892 .... **NCLC 8, 59**
  See also DLB 1

Whittlebot, Hernia
  See Coward, Noel (Peirce)

Wicker, Thomas Grey 1926-
  See Wicker, Tom
  See also CA 65-68; CANR 21, 46

Wicker, Tom .... **CLC 7**
  See also Wicker, Thomas Grey

Wideman, John Edgar
  1941- .... **CLC 5, 34, 36, 67; BLC;**
                                DAM MULT
  See also BW 2; CA 85-88; CANR 14, 42;
  DLB 33, 143

Wiebe, Rudy (Henry)
  1934- .... **CLC 6, 11, 14; DAC;**
                                  DAM MST
  See also CA 37-40R; CANR 42; DLB 60

Wieland, Christoph Martin
  1733-1813 .... **NCLC 17**
  See also DLB 97

Wiene, Robert 1881-1938........ **TCLC 56**

Wieners, John 1934-.............. **CLC 7**
  See also CA 13-16R; DLB 16

Wiesel, Elie(zer)
  1928- ...... **CLC 3, 5, 11, 37; DA; DAB;**
        DAC; DAM MST, NOV
  See also AAYA 7; AITN 1; CA 5-8R;
  CAAS 4; CANR 8, 40; DLB 83;
  DLBY 87; INT CANR-8; MTCW;
  SATA 56; YABC

Wiggins, Marianne 1947-.......... **CLC 57**
  See also BEST 89:3; CA 130

Wight, James Alfred 1916-
  See Herriot, James
  See also CA 77-80; SATA 55;
  SATA-Brief 44

Wilbur, Richard (Purdy)
  1921- ... **CLC 3, 6, 9, 14, 53; DA; DAB;**
        DAC; DAM MST, POET
  See also CA 1-4R; CABS 2; CANR 2, 29;
  DLB 5, 169; INT CANR-29; MTCW;
  SATA 9

Wild, Peter 1940-................ **CLC 14**
  See also CA 37-40R; DLB 5

Wilde, Oscar (Fingal O'Flahertie Wills)
  1854(?)-1900 .... **TCLC 1, 8, 23, 41; DA;**
        DAB; DAC; DAM DRAM, MST, NOV;
                              SSC 11; WLC
  See also CA 104; 119; CDBLB 1890-1914;
  DLB 10, 19, 34, 57, 141, 156; SATA 24

Woiwode, L.
See Woiwode, Larry (Alfred)

Woiwode, Larry (Alfred)   1941-... **CLC 6, 10**
See also CA 73-76; CANR 16; DLB 6;
INT CANR-16

Wojciechowska, Maia (Teresa)
1927- .... **CLC 26**
See also AAYA 8; CA 9-12R; CANR 4, 41;
CLR 1; JRDA; MAICYA; SAAS 1;
SATA 1, 28, 83

Wolf, Christa   1929- .... **CLC 14, 29, 58**
See also CA 85-88; CANR 45; DLB 75;
MTCW

Wolfe, Gene (Rodman)
1931- .... **CLC 25; DAM POP**
See also CA 57-60; CAAS 9; CANR 6, 32;
DLB 8

Wolfe, George C.   1954- .... **CLC 49**
See also CA 149

Wolfe, Thomas (Clayton)
1900-1938 ..... **TCLC 4, 13, 29, 61; DA;**
DAB; DAC; DAM MST, NOV; WLC
See also CA 104; 132; CDALB 1929-1941;
DLB 9, 102; DLBD 2; DLBY 85; MTCW

Wolfe, Thomas Kennerly, Jr.   1931-
See Wolfe, Tom
See also CA 13-16R; CANR 9, 33;
DAM POP; INT CANR-9; MTCW

Wolfe, Tom .... **CLC 1, 2, 9, 15, 35, 51**
See also Wolfe, Thomas Kennerly, Jr.
See also AAYA 8; AITN 2; BEST 89:1;
DLB 152

Wolff, Geoffrey (Ansell)   1937- ..... **CLC 41**
See also CA 29-32R; CANR 29, 43

Wolff, Sonia
See Levitin, Sonia (Wolff)

Wolff, Tobias (Jonathan Ansell)
1945- .... **CLC 39, 64**
See also AAYA 16; BEST 90:2; CA 114;
117; CAAS 22; CANR 54; DLB 130;
INT 117

Wolfram von Eschenbach
c. 1170-c. 1220 .... **CMLC 5**
See also DLB 138

Wolitzer, Hilma   1930- .... **CLC 17**
See also CA 65-68; CANR 18, 40;
INT CANR-18; SATA 31

Wollstonecraft, Mary   1759-1797...... **LC 5**
See also CDBLB 1789-1832; DLB 39, 104,
158

Wonder, Stevie .... **CLC 12**
See also Morris, Steveland Judkins

Wong, Jade Snow   1922-........... **CLC 17**
See also CA 109

Woodcott, Keith
See Brunner, John (Kilian Houston)

Woodruff, Robert W.
See Mencken, H(enry) L(ouis)

Woolf, (Adeline) Virginia
1882-1941 ...... **TCLC 1, 5, 20, 43, 56;**
DA; DAB; DAC; DAM MST, NOV;
SSC 7; WLC
See also CA 104; 130; CDBLB 1914-1945;
DLB 36, 100, 162; DLBD 10; MTCW

Woollcott, Alexander (Humphreys)
1887-1943 .... **TCLC 5**
See also CA 105; DLB 29

Woolrich, Cornell   1903-1968...... **CLC 77**
See also Hopley-Woolrich, Cornell George

Wordsworth, Dorothy
1771-1855 .... **NCLC 25**
See also DLB 107

Wordsworth, William
1770-1850 .... **NCLC 12, 38; DA; DAB;**
DAC; DAM MST, POET; PC 4; WLC
See also CDBLB 1789-1832; DLB 93, 107

Wouk, Herman
1915- .. **CLC 1, 9, 38; DAM NOV, POP**
See also CA 5-8R; CANR 6, 33; DLBY 82;
INT CANR-6; MTCW

Wright, Charles (Penzel, Jr.)
1935- .... **CLC 6, 13, 28**
See also CA 29-32R; CAAS 7; CANR 23,
36; DLB 165; DLBY 82; MTCW

Wright, Charles Stevenson
1932- .... **CLC 49; BLC 3;**
DAM MULT, POET
See also BW 1; CA 9-12R; CANR 26;
DLB 33

Wright, Jack R.
See Harris, Mark

Wright, James (Arlington)
1927-1980 .... **CLC 3, 5, 10, 28;**
DAM POET
See also AITN 2; CA 49-52; 97-100;
CANR 4, 34; DLB 5, 169; MTCW

Wright, Judith (Arandell)
1915- .... **CLC 11, 53; PC 14**
See also CA 13-16R; CANR 31; MTCW;
SATA 14

Wright, L(aurali) R.   1939-........ **CLC 44**
See also CA 138

Wright, Richard (Nathaniel)
1908-1960 .... **CLC 1, 3, 4, 9, 14, 21, 48,**
74; BLC; DA; DAB; DAC; DAM MST,
MULT, NOV; SSC 2; WLC
See also AAYA 5; BW 1; CA 108;
CDALB 1929-1941; DLB 76, 102;
DLBD 2; MTCW

Wright, Richard B(ruce)   1937- ...... **CLC 6**
See also CA 85-88; DLB 53

Wright, Rick   1945-............... **CLC 35**

Wright, Rowland
See Wells, Carolyn

Wright, Stephen Caldwell   1946- .... **CLC 33**
See also BW 2

Wright, Willard Huntington   1888-1939
See Van Dine, S. S.
See also CA 115

Wright, William   1930-............ **CLC 44**
See also CA 53-56; CANR 7, 23

Wroth, LadyMary   1587-1653(?) ..... **LC 30**
See also DLB 121

Wu Ch'eng-en   1500(?)-1582(?)........ **LC 7**

Wu Ching-tzu   1701-1754 .... **LC 2**

Wurlitzer, Rudolph   1938(?)- ... **CLC 2, 4, 15**
See also CA 85-88; DLB 173

Wycherley, William
1641-1715 ..... **LC 8, 21; DAM DRAM**
See also CDBLB 1660-1789; DLB 80

Wylie, Elinor (Morton Hoyt)
1885-1928 .... **TCLC 8**
See also CA 105; DLB 9, 45

Wylie, Philip (Gordon)   1902-1971... **CLC 43**
See also CA 21-22; 33-36R; CAP 2; DLB 9

Wyndham, John.................... **CLC 19**
See also Harris, John (Wyndham Parkes
Lucas) Beynon

Wyss, Johann David Von
1743-1818 .... **NCLC 10**
See also JRDA; MAICYA; SATA 29;
SATA-Brief 27

Xenophon
c. 430B.C.-c. 354B.C......... **CMLC 17**
See also DLB 176

Yakumo Koizumi
See Hearn, (Patricio) Lafcadio (Tessima
Carlos)

Yanez, Jose Donoso
See Donoso (Yanez), Jose

Yanovsky, Basile S.
See Yanovsky, V(assily) S(emenovich)

Yanovsky, V(assily) S(emenovich)
1906-1989 .... **CLC 2, 18**
See also CA 97-100; 129

Yates, Richard   1926-1992 ..... **CLC 7, 8, 23**
See also CA 5-8R; 139; CANR 10, 43;
DLB 2; DLBY 81, 92; INT CANR-10

Yeats, W. B.
See Yeats, William Butler

Yeats, William Butler
1865-1939 ..... **TCLC 1, 11, 18, 31; DA;**
DAB; DAC; DAM DRAM, MST,
POET; WLC
See also CA 104; 127; CANR 45;
CDBLB 1890-1914; DLB 10, 19, 98, 156;
MTCW

Yehoshua, A(braham) B.
1936- .... **CLC 13, 31**
See also CA 33-36R; CANR 43

Yep, Laurence Michael   1948-...... **CLC 35**
See also AAYA 5; CA 49-52; CANR 1, 46;
CLR 3, 17; DLB 52; JRDA; MAICYA;
SATA 7, 69

Yerby, Frank G(arvin)
1916-1991 .... **CLC 1, 7, 22; BLC;**
DAM MULT
See also BW 1; CA 9-12R; 136; CANR 16,
52; DLB 76; INT CANR-16; MTCW

Yesenin, Sergei Alexandrovich
See Esenin, Sergei (Alexandrovich)

Yevtushenko, Yevgeny (Alexandrovich)
1933- .... **CLC 1, 3, 13, 26, 51;**
DAM POET
See also CA 81-84; CANR 33, 54; MTCW

Yezierska, Anzia   1885(?)-1970 ..... **CLC 46**
See also CA 126; 89-92; DLB 28; MTCW

Yglesias, Helen   1915-........... **CLC 7, 22**
See also CA 37-40R; CAAS 20; CANR 15;
INT CANR-15; MTCW

Yokomitsu Riichi   1898-1947 ...... **TCLC 47**

Yonge, Charlotte (Mary)
1823-1901 . . . . **TCLC 48**
See also CA 109; DLB 18, 163; SATA 17

York, Jeremy
See Creasey, John

York, Simon
See Heinlein, Robert A(nson)

Yorke, Henry Vincent 1905-1974 . . . **CLC 13**
See also Green, Henry
See also CA 85-88; 49-52

Yosano Akiko 1878-1942 . . **TCLC 59; PC 11**

Yoshimoto, Banana . . . . **CLC 84**
See also Yoshimoto, Mahoko

Yoshimoto, Mahoko 1964-
See Yoshimoto, Banana
See also CA 144

Young, Al(bert James)
1939- . . . . . **CLC 19; BLC; DAM MULT**
See also BW 2; CA 29-32R; CANR 26;
DLB 33

Young, Andrew (John) 1885-1971 . . . . **CLC 5**
See also CA 5-8R; CANR 7, 29

Young, Collier
See Bloch, Robert (Albert)

Young, Edward 1683-1765 . . . . **LC 3**
See also DLB 95

Young, Marguerite (Vivian)
1909-1995 . . . . **CLC 82**
See also CA 13-16; 150; CAP 1

Young, Neil 1945- . . . . **CLC 17**
See also CA 110

Young Bear, Ray A.
1950- . . . . **CLC 94; DAM MULT**
See also CA 146; DLB 175; NNAL

Yourcenar, Marguerite
1903-1987 . . . . **CLC 19, 38, 50, 87;
DAM NOV**
See also CA 69-72; CANR 23; DLB 72;
DLBY 88; MTCW

Yurick, Sol 1925- . . . . **CLC 6**
See also CA 13-16R; CANR 25

Zabolotskii, Nikolai Alekseevich
1903-1958 . . . . **TCLC 52**
See also CA 116

Zamiatin, Yevgenii
See Zamyatin, Evgeny Ivanovich

Zamora, Bernice (B. Ortiz)
1938- . . . . . **CLC 89; DAM MULT; HLC**
See also CA 151; DLB 82; HW

Zamyatin, Evgeny Ivanovich
1884-1937 . . . . **TCLC 8, 37**
See also CA 105

Zangwill, Israel 1864-1926 . . . . **TCLC 16**
See also CA 109; DLB 10, 135

Zappa, Francis Vincent, Jr. 1940-1993
See Zappa, Frank
See also CA 108; 143; CANR 57

Zappa, Frank . . . . **CLC 17**
See also Zappa, Francis Vincent, Jr.

Zaturenska, Marya 1902-1982 . . . . **CLC 6, 11**
See also CA 13-16R; 105; CANR 22

Zeami 1363-1443 . . . . **DC 7**

Zelazny, Roger (Joseph)
1937-1995 . . . . **CLC 21**
See also AAYA 7; CA 21-24R; 148;
CANR 26; DLB 8; MTCW; SATA 57;
SATA-Brief 39

Zhdanov, Andrei A(lexandrovich)
1896-1948 . . . . **TCLC 18**
See also CA 117

Zhukovsky, Vasily 1783-1852 . . . . **NCLC 35**

Ziegenhagen, Eric . . . . **CLC 55**

Zimmer, Jill Schary
See Robinson, Jill

Zimmerman, Robert
See Dylan, Bob

Zindel, Paul
1936- . . . . . **CLC 6, 26; DA; DAB; DAC;
DAM DRAM, MST, NOV; DC 5**
See also AAYA 2; CA 73-76; CANR 31;
CLR 3, 45; DLB 7, 52; JRDA; MAICYA;
MTCW; SATA 16, 58

Zinov'Ev, A. A.
See Zinoviev, Alexander (Aleksandrovich)

Zinoviev, Alexander (Aleksandrovich)
1922- . . . . **CLC 19**
See also CA 116; 133; CAAS 10

Zoilus
See Lovecraft, H(oward) P(hillips)

Zola, Emile (Edouard Charles Antoine)
1840-1902 . . . . . . **TCLC 1, 6, 21, 41; DA;
DAB; DAC; DAM MST, NOV; WLC**
See also CA 104; 138; DLB 123

Zoline, Pamela 1941- . . . . **CLC 62**

Zorrilla y Moral, Jose 1817-1893 . . **NCLC 6**

Zoshchenko, Mikhail (Mikhailovich)
1895-1958 . . . . **TCLC 15; SSC 15**
See also CA 115

Zuckmayer, Carl 1896-1977 . . . . **CLC 18**
See also CA 69-72; DLB 56, 124

Zuk, Georges
See Skelton, Robin

Zukofsky, Louis
1904-1978 . . . . **CLC 1, 2, 4, 7, 11, 18;
DAM POET; PC 11**
See also CA 9-12R; 77-80; CANR 39;
DLB 5, 165; MTCW

Zweig, Paul 1935-1984 . . . . **CLC 34, 42**
See also CA 85-88; 113

Zweig, Stefan 1881-1942 . . . . **TCLC 17**
See also CA 112; DLB 81, 118

Zwingli, Huldreich 1484-1531 . . . . . . **LC 37**
See also DLB 179

Literary Criticism Series
Cumulative Topic Index

This index lists all topic entries in Gale's *Classical and Medieval Literature Criticism, Contemporary Literary Criticism, Literature Criticism from 1400 to 1800, Nineteenth-Century Literature Criticism,* and *Twentieth-Century Literary Criticism.*

Topic Index

Topic Index

Topic Index

LC Cumulative Nationality Index

AFGHAN
Babur **18**

AMERICAN
Bradstreet, Anne **4, 30**
Edwards, Jonathan **7**
Eliot, John **5**
Franklin, Benjamin **25**
Hathorne, John **38**
Hopkinson, Francis **25**
Knight, Sarah Kemble **7**
Mather, Cotton **38**
Mather, Increase **38**
Munford, Robert **5**
Penn, William **25**
Sewall, Samuel **38**
Stoughton, William **38**
Taylor, Edward **11**
Washington, George **25**
Wheatley (Peters), Phillis **3**
Winthrop, John **31**

BENINESE
Equiano, Olaudah **16**

CANADIAN
Marie de l'Incarnation **10**

CHINESE
Lo Kuan-chung **12**
P'u Sung-ling **3**
Ts'ao Hsueh-ch'in **1**
Wu Ch'eng-en **7**
Wu Ching-tzu **2**

DANISH
Holberg, Ludvig **6**
Wessel, Johan Herman **7**

DUTCH
Erasmus, Desiderius **16**
Lipsius, Justus **16**
Spinoza, Benedictus de **9**

ENGLISH
Addison, Joseph **18**
Andrewes, Lancelot **5**
Arbuthnot, John **1**
Aubin, Penelope **9**
Bacon, Francis **18, 32**
Beaumont, Francis **33**
Behn, Aphra **1, 30**
Boswell, James **4**
Bradstreet, Anne **4, 30**
Brooke, Frances **6**
Bunyan, John **4**
Burke, Edmund **7, 36**
Butler, Samuel **16**
Carew, Thomas **13**
Cary, Elizabeth, Lady Falkland **30**
Cavendish, Margaret Lucas **30**
Caxton, William , **17**
Chapman, George **22**
Charles I **13**
Chatterton, Thomas **3**
Chaucer, Geoffrey **17**
Churchill, Charles **3**
Cleland, John **2**
Collier, Jeremy **6**
Collins, William **4**
Congreve, William **5, 21**
Crashaw, Richard **24**
Daniel, Samuel **24**
Davys, Mary **1**
Day, Thomas **1**
Dee, John **20**
Defoe, Daniel **1**

Dekker, Thomas **22**
Delany, Mary (Granville Pendarves) **12**
Dennis, John **11**
Devenant, William **13**
Donne, John **10, 24**
Drayton, Michael **8**
Dryden, John **3, 21**
Elyot, Sir Thomas **11**
Equiano, Olaudah **16**
Fanshawe, Ann **11**
Farquhar, George **21**
Fielding, Henry **1**
Fielding, Sarah **1**
Fletcher, John **33**
Foxe, John **14**
Garrick, David **15**
Gray, Thomas **4**
Hakluyt, Richard **31**
Hawes, Stephen **17**
Haywood, Eliza (Fowler) **1**
Henry VIII **10**
Herbert, George **24**
Herrick, Robert **13**
Hobbes, Thomas **36**
Howell, James **13**
Hunter, Robert **7**
Johnson, Samuel **15**
Jonson, Ben(jamin) **6, 33**
Julian of Norwich **6**
Kempe, Margery **6**
Killigrew, Anne **4**
Kyd, Thomas **22**
Langland, William **19**
Lanyer, Aemilia **10, 30**
Lilly, William **27**
Locke, John **7**
Lovelace, Richard **24**
Lyttelton, George **10**

LC Cumulative Title Index

"The 21th: and last booke of the Ocean to
Scinthia" (Raleigh) **31**:265, 271-80, 282-4,
286-8
"The 23rd Psalme" (Herbert) **24**:274-75
XCVI Sermons (Andrewes) **5**:19, 22-5, 28, 33,
41
"A Chaulieu" (Rousseau) **9**:344
"A Chretophle de Choiseul" (Ronsard) **6**:433
"A Courtin" (Rousseau) **9**:343-44
"A de Lannoy" (Rousseau) **9**:345
"A Denyse sorciere" (Ronsard) **6**:430
"A Gui Peccate Prieur de Sougé" (Ronsard)
6:437
"A Guillaume Des Autels" (Ronsard) **6**:433
"A Janne impitoyable" (Ronsard) **6**:419
"A Jean de Morel" (Ronsard) **6**:433
"A la fontaine Bellerie" (Ronsard) **6**:419, 430
"A la paix" (Rousseau) **9**:344
"A la reine sur sa bien-venüe en France"
(Malherbe)
  See "Ode à Marie de Médicis, sur sa
  Bienvenue en France"
"A la reyne mère sur les heureux succez de sa
régence" (Malherbe)
  See "Ode pour la Reine Mère du Roy
  pendant sa Régence"
"A l'ambassadeur de Venise" (Rousseau) **9**:344
"A l'empereur, après la conclusion de la
quadruple alliance" (Rousseau) **9**:344
"A l'impératrice Amélie" (Rousseau) **9**:343
"A M. de Grimani" (Rousseau) **9**:340
A une veuve"
"A une veuve" (Rousseau) **9**:340, 344
"A Zinzindorf" (Rousseau)
  See "Ode au comte de Sinzendorff"
"Aaron" (Herbert) **24**:237

"Abbatis Eurditae" (Erasmus) **16**:128
"Abbot and the Learned Lady" (Erasmus)
16:123, 142, 193
L'abbrégé de l'art poétique françois (Ronsard)
6:406, 419, 427
L'A.B.C. (Voltaire) **14**:405
Abdelazer; or, The Moor's Revenge (Behn)
1:28, 33, 39; **30**:67, 70-1, 77, 81
Abecedarium Naturae (Bacon) **18**:187
"Abel's blood" (Vaughan) **27**:300, 377-79
*Der abenteuerliche Simplicissimus, Teutsch,
das hist: Die Beschreibun dess Lebens eines
seltzamen Vaganten, gennant Melchio
Sternfels von Fuchsheim* (Grimmelshausen)
6:235-48, 252
*Der abentheuerliche, wunderbare und
unerhörte Ritter Hopffen-sack* (Beer) **5**:54-
5
Abhandlung von der Nachahmung (Schlegel)
5:274, 282-83
*Abhandlung von der Unähnlichkeit in der
Nachahmung* (Schlegel) **5**:274
Abode of Spring (Jami)
  See *Baháristán*
"Abra; or, The Georgian Sultana" (Collins)
4:210
Abraham and Isaac (Chester)
  See *Abraham, Lot, and Melchysedeck*
Abraham and Isaac (N-Town) **34**:181, 208
Abraham and Isaac (Towneley) **34**:251, 267,
288-9, 325
Abraham and Isaac (York)
  See *Abraham's Sacrifice*
Abraham, Lot, and Melchysedeck (Chester)
34:92, 107-8, 111, 126-7, 131, 139
Abraham's Sacrifice (York) **34**:332, 364, 386-7

Abrege de la vie de Jesus Christ (Pascal)
35:365
*Abridgements of the History of Rome and
England* (Goldsmith) **2**:71
Abridgment of English History (Burke)
  See *An Essay towards an Abridgement of
  the English History*
Absalom and Achitophel (Dryden) **3**:180,
185, 187, 189-92, 199, 201, 205, 213,
216-22, 225, 228, 231, 234, 240-43, 246;
21:51, 53-7, 64-5, 86-7, 90-1, 94, 101-03,
111-13
Absalom's Hair (Calderon de la Barca)
  See *Los cabellos de Absalón*
Absalom's Locks (Calderon de la Barca) **23**:64
"Absolute Retreat" (Finch)
  See "The Petition for an Absolute Retreat"
Acajou et Zirphile (Duclos) **1**:185, 187
An Accidence; or, The Path-Way to Experience
(Smith) **9**:381-82
*The Accomplish'd Rake; or, Modern Fine
Gentleman* (Davys) **1**:99-100
*An Account of a Battel between the Ancient
and Modern Books in St. James's Library*
(Swift)
  See *A Tale of a Tub, Written for the Universal
  Improvement of Mankind, to Which is
  Added an Account of a Battel between
  the Ancient and Modern Books in St.
  James's Library*
*An Account of Corsica, The Journal of a Tour
to that Island; and the Memoirs of Pascal
Paoli* (Boswell) **4**:16, 25, 31, 33, 60, 71,
77-8
"An Account of the English Poets" (Addison)
18:6, 16, 38-9, 41, 61

Title Index

Title Index

Title Index

Title Index

Title Index

Title Index

Title Index

Title Index

Title Index

Title Index

Title Index

Title Index

Title Index

ISBN 0-7876-1248-0

9 780787 612481

90000